# International Encyclopedia of the SOCIAL SCIENCES

DAVID L. SILLS EDITOR

VOLUME 8

The Macmillan Company & The Free Press

# International
# Encyclopedia of the
# SOCIAL
# SCIENCES

# I

[ C O N T I N U E D ]

## INTERNATIONAL MONETARY ECONOMICS

*For an integration of international monetary economics with the theory of international trade, see* International trade, *article on* Theory.

## I
### BALANCE OF PAYMENTS

From the earliest times trade has involved discrepancies in values exchanged, settled in credit or money, and these discrepancies constitute the origin of the concept of "balance of payments." The generic meaning of the term today is the excess of receipts over payments of *any* economic entity, although the concept was initially applied to, and received its greatest elaboration in, the theory of international trade. The term itself entered the English economic literature during the mercantilist period, eventually replacing "overplus," "remayne," "overvalue," "balance of accounts," "balance of remittance," and "grand balance of payments" (Viner 1937, pp. 1, 13, 14).

In its original usage a "balance of payments" meant an "excess of payments over receipts" and under the gold standard this excess meant a gold outflow. But the term soon acquired the neutral meaning of the "state of the balance of international accounts," whether negative or positive. Thus, one speaks of a "balance of payments problem" whether gold is flowing in or out, and the term "balance of payments theory" is used to cover the entire subject, not just that aspect of it pertaining to an excess of payments.

The mercantilists used the adjectives "favorable" and "unfavorable" to identify, respectively, inflows and outflows of gold, but these terms were rejected during the classical reaction to mercantilism on the grounds that goods, not gold, constituted true wealth and that there was nothing intrinsically favorable about an export of goods in exchange for gold. Alternative terms like "active" and "passive" and "positive" and "negative" came into temporary favor, but they proved equally unsatisfactory; there is nothing "passive" about a gold outflow, for example. The terms in favor today are "surplus" and "deficit," and their identification with accounting practice renders them free of any important ambiguity.

The balance sheet of international accounts, or "accounting balance of payments," is a statement recording transactions between residents (or citizens) of a given country and the rest of the world. Transactions are either *debit items*, which arise from *purchases*, or *credit items*, which arise from *sales*. Sales of goods, of claims, and of gold and foreign exchange are credit items, and purchases of goods, of claims, and of gold and foreign exchange are debit items.

All transactions (sales or purchases) have a dual character—a sale of something implies a purchase of something else. When a good is sold for money the ownership of the good and the ownership of money change hands in opposite directions, the ratio between the two payments being the money price of the good. It follows that the value of the goods payment equals the value of the money payment, so that the sum of debit items arising from purchases is equal to the sum of credit items arising from sales.

The identity between debits and credits is preserved even when transactions include gifts, reparations payments, and other unrequited transfers. In the balance of payments accounts an unrequited transfer to foreign residents is recorded as a debit, and the means by which the transfer is financed (a sale of goods, of claims, or of gold or foreign exchange itself) is recorded as a credit. Thus, the accounting balance of payments is a tautology, and therefore it has no economic (market) significance. Its significance lies rather in its role as the basis on which accounts are organized and as the starting point from which balance of payments analysis proceeds.

The accounting balance of payments records both regular transactions *and* transactions made to settle any gap between regular purchases and sales (U.S. Congress 1965). The problem in constructing a useful *operational* definition of the balance of payments is thus the problem of separating "regular" transactions from "settling" transactions, a distinction best suited to the purpose of balance of payments analysis.

The balance of payments, if operationally defined in this way, can be regarded as an "error signal" announcing the need for a change in economic policy, a signal of actual or potential threat to the existing exchange system. Since exchange rates are typically "pegged" to some international asset at a fixed price (usually with a small margin between buying and selling rates), the authorities must maintain stocks of the international asset, and the balance of payments ought to reflect present or future threats to the size of those stocks. It is this feature of the present exchange-rate system that suggests a definition of the balance of payments as *the change in international reserves*, thus converting the burden of finding an operational definition of the balance of payments into the problem of determining which assets are to be counted as international reserves.

Of the assets to be counted among reserves the most important—in the sense that it is the most immediately useful—is the one to which the currency is pegged. To a country whose currency is pegged to gold the most important reserve is gold; to a country whose currency is pegged to the U.S. dollar the most important reserve is the U.S. dollar; and so on for countries whose currencies are pegged to the pound sterling, the French franc, or some minor international currency.

Most countries also hold (what they regard as) reserves in assets that are close substitutes for the asset to which they peg their currencies. The United States (as of 1966) pegs the dollar to gold and holds the bulk of its reserves in gold; the United Kingdom, however, pegs the pound sterling to the dollar yet holds the bulk of its reserves in gold. Other countries hold gold, dollars, and sterling in varying proportions that reflect not their immediate exchange stabilization needs but the asset preferences of the monetary authorities in charge of the reserves (Kenen 1963). Since gold, dollars, and sterling are all acceptable reserve assets, substitutable for one another at a fixed price (within small margins), a central bank can diversify its portfolio of assets beyond that immediately needed for working balances.

There is a third category of assets, the changes in which are (and should be) incorporated into the balance of payments. In 1946, when operations of the International Monetary Fund (IMF) began, each member country deposited with the IMF a subscription, of which 25 per cent was paid in gold and 75 per cent in its own currency; on the basis of this subscription that country can "draw" (that is, borrow) other convertible currencies, depositing in exchange additional quantities of its own currency. In other words, when a country draws from the IMF it sells its own currency to the IMF and acquires in exchange a foreign (convertible) currency that it "needs," and when a country repays a drawing on the IMF it "repurchases" its own currency, paying for it with a convertible foreign currency. Drawings from the IMF constitute a credit item in the balance of payments, and repurchases constitute a debit item, since drawings represent a receipt of foreign exchange and repurchases a payment. To these transactions a country must add the transactions of other member countries in its currency when they draw or repurchase, and the net sum of all such transactions in the time during which the balance of payments is measured is called the change in the Net Fund Position (the Net Fund Position is the difference between the subscription or quota and IMF holdings of the domestic currency). Since changes in the Net Fund Position affect a country's liquidity in the sense that they alter the country's capacity to defend its exchange system, those changes should be counted in an operational definition of the country's balance of payments, along with changes in gold and in holdings of convertible currencies.

Before analyzing the implications of this definition in a global context, it is necessary to clear up a source of some confusion among nonspecialists about the "time dimensions" of the balance of payments.

The balance of payments—the change in reserves over time—is a *flow per unit of time*. But items recorded in the balance of payments accounts (like the national income accounts) represent the accumulated flow over a *specified period of time*. The balance of payments of a country over, say, a year is the integral of the flow during the year and thus is a stock.

Suppose reserves, $R$, fluctuate between time $t = t_0$ and time $t = t_1$ according to the equation $R = R(t)$. Then the balance of payments equation, $B(t) \equiv dR/dt \equiv R'(t)$, reflects the slope of the function $R(t)$; conversely, $R(t)$ reflects the integral of $B(t)$ over past history. If the time from $t_0$ to $t_1$ is, say, a year, then $\bar{B}$, the balance of payments over the year, is

$$\bar{B} = \int_{t_0}^{t_1} B(t)\, dt,$$

where $\bar{B} \equiv \Delta R \equiv R_{t_1} - R_{t_0}$. The stocks of reserves at given periods of time are therefore related to the balance of payments by equations like

$$R_{t_1} = R_{t_0} + \int_{t_0}^{t_1} B(t)\, dt.$$

Analogous concepts apply to every entry in the balance of payments accounts. Thus, if $C(t)$ represents the net balance of payments (surplus) on *capital* account at time $t$, then $D_{t_1}$, the accumulated net debtor position of a country at time $t_1$, is

$$D_{t_1} = D_{t_0} + \int_{t_0}^{t_1} C(t)\, dt,$$

where $D_{t_0}$ represents the initial debtor position at time $t = t_0$.

**International consistency of definitions.** Analytical precision requires that balance of payments definitions be internationally consistent. To develop the analysis in a global context, then, we divide a country's accounting balance of payments into regular and settling transactions. Thus, if $B_i$ denotes the balance of regular transactions of country $i$ and $B_i'$ the balance of settling transactions, we have a balance of payments identity, true for each of $n$ countries in the world:

(1) $$B_i + B_i' \equiv 0.$$

Since $B_i'$ represents the *net exports* of the settling items (balance of payments deficit), $B_i' < 0$ implies *increasing* international reserves. Specifically, $B_i' + dR_i/dt \equiv 0$, where $R_i$ is the level of reserves in country $i$ and

(2) $$B_i \equiv \frac{dR_i}{dt}.$$

For all countries,

(3) $$\sum_{i=1}^{n} B_i \equiv \sum_{i=1}^{n} \frac{dR_i}{dt} \equiv \frac{dR}{dt}$$

(where $R$ represents world reserves), and unless both sides of the identity equal zero it appears that the global balance of regular transactions, $\sum_{i=1}^{n} B_i$, can be other than zero!

The apparent paradox is, of course, easily dismissed. The balance of the payments of the world as a whole *is* identically zero; this identity has become known as Cournot's law because of the extensive use Cournot made of the proposition. Cournot's law, however, does not imply that the balance of payments of the world *excluding the transactions of the monetary authorities* ($B_i'$) is necessarily zero. The inequality $dR/dt > 0$ simply means that the monetary authorities are acquiring, collectively, reserve assets from the private sector, whereas $dR/dt < 0$ means they are losing reserve assets to the private sector.

Assume, for example, that central banks peg their currencies to gold and hold no other reserve assets, as is the case under (one version of) the gold standard, and start with the accounting identity (1) above. The settling transactions, $B_i'$, are central bank net trade in gold (net purchases if positive, net sales if negative) with private markets. If we now separate the net balance of trade in gold from $B_i$, the balance of regular transactions, we have the relation

(4) $$B_i = B_i^* + B_i^g,$$

and equation (1) becomes

(5) $$B_i^* + B_i^g + B_i' \equiv 0,$$

where $B_i^g$ denotes net exports of gold from the private sector and $B_i^*$ includes everything else in $B_i$. Then, since $B_i' \equiv -dR_i/dt$, we can rewrite (5) as

(6) $$B_i^* + B_i^g \equiv \frac{dR_i}{dt}.$$

For all countries,

(7) $$\sum B_i^* + \sum B_i^g \equiv \sum \frac{dR_i}{dt},$$

where the summations extend over all countries. But $B_i^*$ represents the net exports of (nongold) commodities in the world as a whole and must be zero, and so of course

(8) $$\sum B_i^g \equiv \sum \frac{dR_i}{dt}.$$

The net private exports of gold in the world as a whole equals the sum of the gold purchases of the monetary authorities (Høst-Madsen 1962).

When gold production exceeds the disappearance of gold for use as hoards, in industry, and in the arts, world monetary reserves increase, and when gold production falls short of total private uses, world monetary reserves decrease. In other words, there is an excess of surpluses over deficits, or an excess of deficits over surpluses, in the world as a whole, depending on whether gold production exceeds, or falls short of, new private purchases of gold.

A similar analysis can be developed for the key currency system. Assume that countries hold reserves not only in gold but also in the national currency of a particular country—for example, the United States—designated country 1, and proceed as before by dividing the balance of payments accounts of the typical country into regular and settling transactions ($B_i + B_i' \equiv 0$).

A distinction must now be made between the reserve center (country 1) and the rest of the world. For the other countries, $2, \cdots, n$, the settling transactions are composed of sales of both gold and dollars, whereas the settling transactions of the reserve center will be gold sales alone or gold sales plus an increase in the dollar assets held by foreign countries, depending on whether a *net* or *gross* concept of reserves for the reserve center is used.

Denote the gold assets of country $i$ by $G_i$ and its dollar assets by $C_{1i}$. Then the balance of payments of the $n$ countries can be defined as follows, using a *net* concept of reserves for the reserve center.

$$(9) \quad \begin{aligned} B_1 &\equiv \frac{dG_1}{dt} - \frac{dL_1}{dt} \\ B_2 &\equiv \frac{dG_2}{dt} + \frac{dC_{12}}{dt} \\ &\vdots \qquad \vdots \qquad \vdots \\ B_n &\equiv \frac{dG_n}{dt} + \frac{dC_{1n}}{dt}, \end{aligned}$$

where $L_1$, the liabilities of the reserve center to the rest of the world, is identically equal to $\sum_{i=2}^{n} C_{1i}$, since the "dollar liabilities" of the United States (country 1) are the same as the dollar assets of the rest of the world.

Under this (net) concept of the first country's balance of payments, the excess of surpluses over deficits in the world as a whole is the same as under the gold standard, since

$$(10) \quad \begin{aligned} \sum_{i=1}^{n} B_i &\equiv \sum_{i=1}^{n} \frac{dG_i}{dt} + \sum_{i=2}^{n} \frac{dC_{1i}}{dt} - \frac{dL_1}{dt} \\ &\equiv \sum_{i=1}^{n} \frac{dG_i}{dt}. \end{aligned}$$

But had we used a gross concept of the reserves of the key currency center, the balance of payments of country 1 would instead have been simply written $B_1 \equiv dG_1/dt$ with $dL_1/dt$ incorporated (with a positive sign) in $B_1$ as a capital movement. In that case the excess of surpluses over deficits in the world as a whole would have been

$$(11) \quad \sum_{i=1}^{n} \frac{dG_i}{dt} + \sum_{i=2}^{n} \frac{dC_{1i}}{dt} \equiv \sum_{i=1}^{n} \frac{dG_i}{dt} + \frac{dL_1}{dt},$$

that is, the increase in world monetary gold holdings plus the increase in monetary liabilities of the reserve center.

What consideration should lead us to prefer the use of a net to a gross concept of reserves, or vice versa? This is a controversial question. If one country were the sole creator of international monetary reserves (assuming monetary gold is constant), and if its currency were universally acceptable for the payment of international debts, it would be fulfilling the role, for all practical purposes, of an "international bank," and to regard its balance of payments as zero would be consistent with the concept of the balance of payments as an error signal.

At the present time there is no international legal tender and therefore no legal justification for treating one country's deficit as being any different from any other country's deficit, even though in practice the U.S. dollar and the British pound closely approximate true international reserve media. In a formal sense, then, it may be better to adopt the net concept of reserves of the key currency country and thus treat an increase in key currency liabilities to foreign monetary authorities as a deficit of the key country. Adopting that convention means modifying the concept of the balance of payments as an error signal and thus qualifying the extent to which a deficit in the balance of payments requires a change in policy or is a threat to the existing exchange system. The net definition preserves symmetry, but at the cost of the usefulness of the balance of payments as an error signal. Instead of regarding a zero balance as a target of policy, the reserve center must try to generate a deficit acceptable both to itself and to the rest of the world, so as to permit an appropriate growth of foreign holdings of its currency and reserves.

Let us now complete the system by allowing for an arbitrary number of reserve currencies (as under a multiple-currency system) and also IMF transactions. Let $C_{ij}$ be the holdings of the currency of country $i$ by the monetary authorities in country $j$; $L_i$, the outstanding short-term liabilities of country $i$ to monetary authorities in the rest of the world; $G_i$, the monetary gold holdings of country $i$; and $F_i$, the Net Fund Position of country $i$ defined as country $i$'s quota less IMF holdings of country $i$'s currency.

Then the balance of payments equation can be comprehensively represented by the following equations:

(12)

$$B_1 = \frac{dG_1}{dt} + \frac{dF_1}{dt} - \frac{dL_1}{dt} + \frac{dC_{21}}{dt} + \cdots + \frac{dC_{n1}}{dt}$$

$$B_2 = \frac{dG_2}{dt} + \frac{dF_2}{dt} + \frac{dC_{12}}{dt} - \frac{dL_2}{dt} + \cdots + \frac{dC_{n2}}{dt}$$

$$\vdots \qquad \vdots \qquad \vdots \qquad \vdots \qquad \vdots \qquad \vdots$$

$$B_n = \frac{dG_n}{dt} + \frac{dF_n}{dt} + \frac{dC_{1n}}{dt} + \frac{dC_{2n}}{dt} + \cdots - \frac{dL_n}{dt}.$$

The excess of surpluses over deficits still equals the increase in monetary gold reserves in this system, since

$$\sum_{i=1}^{n} \frac{dL_i}{dt} \equiv \sum_{i=1}^{n} \sum_{j=1}^{n} \frac{dC_{ij}}{dt}$$

and

$$\sum_{j=1}^{n} \frac{dF_j}{dt} \equiv 0.$$

The latter identity follows from the definition of a change in the Net Fund Position of a country, every increase in IMF holdings of one currency implying a decrease in its holdings of another currency.

**Approaches to analysis.** The balance of payments is related to other aspects of the economic system because it describes the transactions of all the residents of the country with the rest of the world. These connections have given rise to three approaches to balance of payments analysis that can be compared most simply by assuming at first that there are no capital movements (this means that the balance of trade and the balance of payments are the same).

The "elasticity approach" works directly (Robinson 1937) on the balance of payments equation,

(13) $$B = X - M,$$

where $X$ is the value of exports and $M$ is the value of imports. By differentiating (13) with respect to an exogenous parameter (say, the exchange rate), a criterion can be established which shows the effects of a change in the parameter on the balance of trade, assuming that export and import prices adjust to equate the demand and supply of exports and imports. In the literature the usual method of

analysis has been to assume that exports depend on the price of exports and imports on the price of imports (an inadequate vestige of partial equilibrium analysis) and then to translate these relations into elasticities.

A second method, the "absorption approach," makes use of the fact that, from national income accounting,

(14) $$B = Y - E,$$

where $Y$ is income and $E$ is domestic expenditure (Meade 1951), or "absorption" (Alexander 1952). This equation directs attention to the fact that the balance of trade can be improved by a policy change, such as a devaluation, only if income is increased by more than expenditure.

A third approach, which may be called the "monetary approach," stresses the fact that the balance of payments implies a change in the foreign reserves of the monetary authorities (the central bank) and that the central bank's total assets, which can be divided into "foreign assets" (reserves) and other assets (for example, government bonds), must equal its monetary liabilities. Thus, the increase in reserves ($R$), which equals (in the case of no capital movements) the balance of trade, must be equal to the difference between central bank credit creation and new central bank money. When the banking system is taken as a whole, and interbank transactions are canceled, this means that

(15) $$B = H - C,$$

where $H$ is hoarding (additional domestic money holdings) by the public and $C$ is credit creation by the banking system as a whole. This approach, which is valid even when there are capital movements, directs attention to the fact that the balance of payments cannot be improved unless credit creation is less than hoarding (Johnson 1958).

It is not meaningful to question the validity of the three approaches. The terms can be defined so that they are all correct and assert identical propositions, even if capital movements are included. Suppose, for example, that all variables are defined as ex post, realized entities. Then from national income accounting we have $Y \equiv E + B$; from banking accounts we have $H \equiv C + R$; and from the balance of payments accounts we have $R \equiv B - T$, where $T$ represents net capital exports. It follows, then, that $R \equiv B - T \equiv Y - E - T \equiv H - C$.

The identity of the three approaches, when they are properly interpreted, does not mean that each approach is not in itself useful. The fact that an improvement in the balance of payments must imply an increase in $Y - E - T$, an increase in $R$, and an increase in $H - C$ provides additional checks on the logic of balance of payment policies.

**Anatomy of disequilibrium.**   Recognition of the alternative categories that lead to the three approaches to the balance of payments serves as a useful introduction to policies of *adjustment* of the balance of payments and to the extent to which adjustment is discretionary or automatic. As we have seen, the three approaches are the same if the categories are defined *ex post*—that is, as *realized* variables. However, differences in the approaches become apparent when we conceive of the categories as *ex ante*—that is, as representative of *intentions*.

Let us define three concepts where the variables are now conceived of in the ex ante sense:

$$L \equiv Y - E - T,$$

which we may identify with the excess flow demand for money in the economy;

$$F \equiv T - B,$$

which we may identify with the excess flow demand for foreign exchange; and

$$X \equiv E + B - Y,$$

which is the excess demand for domestic goods, and let us assume that ex post and ex ante balance of payments are identical. These three identities, which are interdependent since the arguments on the right sum to zero, can be used for anatomizing disequilibrium situations and thus for providing a guide to economic policy.

To do so we must introduce explicit functional relations expressing how $X$, $F$, and $L$ are "determined." We may, for example, express these categories as functions of, say, the price level of domestic goods ($P$), the exchange rate ($\pi$), and the money supply ($M$). Then we would have three equations in three unknowns:

(16)
$$\begin{aligned} X(P, \pi, M) &= 0 \\ F(P, \pi, M) &= 0 \\ L(P, \pi, M) &= 0. \end{aligned}$$

But these equations would not be sufficient to give us a determinate system, since the equations are not independent; that is, if excess flow demand for money is zero and excess flow demand for foreign exchange is zero, then excess demand for domestic goods must be zero. We have one degree of freedom and can thus fix arbitrarily any one of $M$, $\pi$, or $P$. If we fix $M$ we have a flexible-exchange, flexible-price system with a constant money supply; if we fix $P$ we have a flexible-exchange system with domestic price level stabilization and a constant money supply; and if we fix $\pi$ we have a fixed-exchange system with a variable money supply.

As an example we may suppose that the exchange rate, $\pi$, is fixed. Then graphs of the equations, drawn under plausible assumptions, intersect at a common point (see Figure 1).

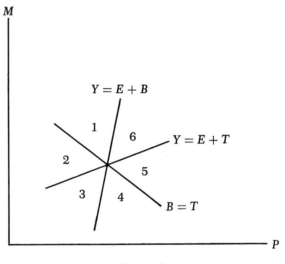

*Figure 1*

Each of the numbered sectors in Figure 1 corresponds to a particular set of equilibrium conditions. Thus, in sector 1, $X > 0$, $F > 0$, and $L < 0$; in sector 2, $X > 0$, $F < 0$, and $L < 0$; and so on for each of the sectors.

From this information and from knowledge of the position of disequilibrium, it is usually possible to determine the directions in which the variables ($M$ and $P$ in this case) must move in order to restore equilibrium. In other words, *by investigating the nature—the anatomy—of the disequilibrium we can find the location of the equilibrium point.*

This analytical approach has many applications. In the context of the preceding discussion we may hold another variable—say, $M$—constant and measure on the axes fluctuations in $P$ and $\pi$. Or we may analyze quite different foreign trade systems using interest rates, real income, or money income as variables. But the principles of analysis remain the same, and the subject is ideally suited to dynamic analysis, since any disequilibrium situation implies monetary, price level, exchange rate, or income adjustments tending to restore equilibrium.

*The exchange market.*   Balance of payments adjustment should be explained in the context of present institutional arrangements. Exchange rates are pegged through central bank (or treasury) intervention in the exchange market at "support points." When the domestic demand for foreign exchange sufficiently exceeds the supply, the price rises until it reaches the upper support point at which the central bank sells reserves from its own stock in exchange for its own currency; similarly, when the supply of foreign exchange sufficiently exceeds demand the price falls until it reaches the lower support point at which the central bank intervenes by purchasing foreign exchange to prevent further appreciation of the domestic currency. (Intervention may also take place between the support points.)

The mechanism is illustrated in Figure 2, in which the demand and supply of dollars in exchange for German marks is plotted. To simplify, dollars are taken to represent all foreign exchange, and the market is taken to encompass all transactions, including those in connected forward markets (Machlup 1939–1940).

The $DD$ curve plots the demand curve for dollars on the part of German residents as a function of the price of dollars, on the assumption that the mark prices of German goods and the dollar prices of foreign goods are constant. The area under the curve at any given price represents the sum of marks that German residents will pay for the quantity of dollars represented on the abscissa; in this sense the demand for dollars by German residents simultaneously represents the supply of marks offered by German residents in exchange for dollars.

The curve $SS$ represents the supply of dollars offered by the rest of the world in exchange for

marks at given exchange rates, again on the assumption that the mark prices of German goods and the dollar prices of goods in the rest of the world are constant. The curve $SS$ simultaneously represents the supply of dollars and the demand for marks, the latter being indicated by the area described at any price–quantity relationship on the supply schedule.

The free market price would be $P_0$, determined by the intersection of $SS$ and $DD$, at which the quantity $Q_0$ of dollars would be exchanged for $P_0Q_0$ of marks. It is assumed that the initial price $P_0$ is within the support points, which are taken to be $\frac{3}{4}$ of one per cent below and above the "par value," which is DM 4.00 per dollar in accordance with the IMF "par value" prevailing in 1966.

Suppose now that in the rest of the world there is a spontaneous increase in the demand for German goods. This implies an increase in the supply of dollars, at any given price, so that $SS$ shifts to the right—to, say, $S'S'$. Such a shift in a free market would mean that the price of the dollar would fall below the (lower dollar and upper mark) support point of DM 3.97 per dollar. But the free market adjustment would be prevented by the German central bank which would step into the market at the rate DM 3.97 per dollar (or perhaps even sooner) to prevent the appreciation of the mark beyond the set limits.

Specifically, at the rate DM 3.97 = \$1 there will be an excess supply of dollars equal to the horizontal distance on the graph between $DD$ and $S'S'$ at that rate, an amount equal to $Q_1Q_2$ dollars; this means an excess demand for marks equal to the shaded area on the graph. To stabilize the rate at DM 3.97 the German central bank will buy up $Q_1Q_2$ of dollars and supply to the market the area $ABQ_2Q_1$ of marks; the former (distance) represents Germany's balance of payments surplus expressed in dollars and the latter (area) Germany's surplus measured in marks.

The process of stabilization just considered automatically produces equilibrating forces tending to correct the disequilibrium. The German central bank is taking up the excess supply of dollars on the market, and (barring the creation of additional dollars in the rest of the world) this must eventually reduce spending in the part of the world using dollars, thereby shifting the supply curve $S'S'$ to the left as prices in the rest of the world fall (or interest rates rise). Similarly, the additional supplies of marks created by the German central bank must eventually shift $DD$ to the right as German prices (the prices of German goods) rise (or interest rates

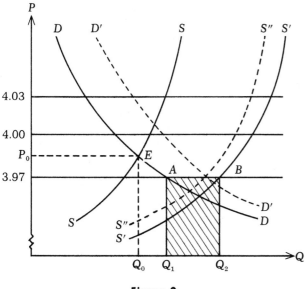

**Figure 2**

fall). After price levels or interest rates have adjusted, a new equilibrium would be established at the dollar support point indicated by the intersection of $D'D'$ and $S''S''$.

This automatic adjustment process may, however, be resisted by the monetary authorities. The practice of "sterilizing" the monetary effects of foreign exchange (or gold) purchases and sales has become widespread as countries look for means of adjusting the balance of payments other than that implicit in price level (or interest rate) adjustments. Central banks may prefer to delay adjustment for a time by allowing reserves to be built up or depleted.

**Adjustment and the "world price level."** The preceding analysis is applicable to a single small economy facing the rest of the world; *small* countries have to correct balance of payments disequilibria by their own individual actions. But in the context of the world economy, balance in $n-1$ countries implies balance in the $n$th country, so there is an extra degree of freedom. The problem of what country, if any, is to be spared the adoption of corrective policies, how adjustment should be divided between countries, and to what use the extra degree of freedom might be put can be termed the "redundancy problem" or the "degree of freedom problem," but equally correctly it might be called the "international standard problem," for its solution involves the establishment of an international standard and consideration of the question of the world price level.

One use to which the extra degree of freedom might be put is for the main key currency country to stabilize its domestic price level, ignoring the balance of payments constraint, and to leave balance of payments adjustment to the other countries; the larger the key currency country the more closely this policy approaches a policy of world price stability. An alternative is to make price level adjustments inversely proportional to the size of the country. As we shall see, this would in a rough way correspond to the analogue of a common currency and would under certain assumptions exactly correspond to the policies necessary to achieve world price stability.

The problem may be seen clearly in the context of either a flexible-exchange rate arrangement (Sohmen 1961) or a pure gold standard system; as a by-product the stability of these systems will also be investigated. Consider first the case in which the authorities express their exchange rates in terms of an abstract unit of account, such as the "1944 gold dollar" (which is the IMF unit of account), and adjust their exchange rates when their

balances are in disequilibrium according to the equations

$$(17) \qquad \frac{d\pi_i}{dt} = \alpha_i B_i(\pi_1, \cdots, \pi_n), \qquad i = 1, \cdots, n,$$

where $B_i$ is the balance of payments (surplus) of the $i$th country, $\pi_i$ the price of its currency expressed in terms of the IMF unit of account, and $\alpha_i$ a constant determined by policy. We know that

$$(18a) \qquad \sum_{i=1}^{n} B_i \equiv 0,$$

so

$$(18b) \qquad \sum_{i=1}^{n} \frac{1}{\alpha_i} \frac{d\pi_i}{dt} \equiv 0.$$

From this, by integration over time,

$$(19) \qquad \sum_{i=1}^{n} \frac{1}{\alpha_i} \pi_i = \text{a constant}.$$

The "absolute" level of exchange rates, weighted by the constants $1/\alpha_i$, is fixed. What does this mean?

The balance of payments equations are homogeneous of degree zero (that is, increasing all exchange rates by a factor $k$ will leave each country's balance of payments unchanged), and this seems to imply that absolute prices are indeterminate. From a static viewpoint this is correct, since the doubling of exchange rates that are expressed in abstract units of account is a mere accounting change that cannot affect real balances of payments. But the dynamic system explicitly rules out such a doubling; if some exchange rates are rising others must be falling, and this fact preserves the level of absolute prices for the countries involved. If, for example, there are two countries, the dynamic adjustment is restrained along the line

$$(1/\alpha_1)P_1 + (1/\alpha_2)P_2 = \text{a constant}$$

by Cournot's law that the sum of all balances of payments is zero.

The meaning of the restraint is that by the appropriate choice of speeds of adjustment for the various countries (that is, a choice of the $\alpha_i$) weights can be given to the exchange rates of the various countries to preserve a specified absolute exchange rate "level." If, for example, world monetary authorities stabilized a weighted average of exchange rates, where the weights reflect the size of countries, the $\alpha_i$ would be large for small countries and small for large countries.

The adjustment mechanism under the gold standard, as under the preceding synthetic exchange rate system, was more or less automatic in the sense that central banks were expected to re-act to gold outflows and inflows by more restrictive and less restrictive monetary policies, respectively, which would in turn react upon price and wage levels, lowering them in the deficit countries and raising them in the surplus countries. These price changes, in turn, were expected to shift expenditure from surplus to deficit countries, thus reducing and eventually eliminating the disequilibrium. Recent studies suggest that the element of discretion under the gold standard was greater than has hitherto been supposed, but the theory is correct in its broad outline even if its practice has been somewhat oversimplified.

To understand the formal mechanism of adjustment under the gold standard system it is helpful to translate a simplified model of that system into mathematical terms. Let $B_i$ represent the balance of payments surplus or gold outflow of the $i$th country expressed in terms of gold, and let $P_i$ represent the gold price of the goods produced in country $i$. The balances of payments can then be written as functions of the prices of home-produced goods in each country in the system, so that

$$(20) \qquad \frac{dG_i}{dt} = B_i(P_1, P_2, \cdots, P_n),$$

where $G_i$ is the gold stock of the $i$th country and $dG_i/dt$ its change over time. The authorities of each country were expected to keep that country's gold stock at a given proportion of its money supply, so that

$$(21) \qquad G_i = r_i M_i,$$

where $r_i$ is the ratio of gold reserves to the money stock $(M_i)$ in the $i$th country. This relationship can be adjusted to take account of gold coins in circulation or lags in the response of banks to excess reserves, but this is an unnecessary complication for our present purposes.

There was a further relationship connecting the money stock to the price level in each country according to the quantity theory of money, which, in one of its versions, can be written

$$(22) \qquad M_i V_i = P_i O_i,$$

where $O_i$ is total production in the $i$th country and $V_i$ is the income velocity of money. To simplify drastically we shall assume that both $O_i$ and $V_i$ are constant. [See MONEY, article on QUANTITY THEORY.]

Equations (21) and (22) complete the system, for by differentiating them we get

$$(23) \qquad \frac{dG_i}{dt} = r_i \frac{dM_i}{dt},$$

$$(24) \qquad V_i \frac{dM_i}{dt} = O_i \frac{dP_i}{dt};$$

hence,

$$(25) \qquad \frac{dG_i}{dt} = r_i \frac{O_i}{V_i} \frac{dP_i}{dt}.$$

Substituting from (25) into (20) then gives

$$(26) \qquad r_i \frac{O_i}{V_i} \frac{dP_i}{dt} = B_i(P_1, \cdots, P_n)$$

or

$$(27) \qquad \frac{1}{P_i} \frac{dP_i}{dt} = \frac{V_i}{r_i P_i O_i} B_i(P_1, \cdots, P_n).$$

The presence of the national income term $(P_i O_i)$ in equation (27) indicates that the larger is the size of the country the smaller will be the percentage change over time in the domestic price level in relation to any given balance of payments surplus, and this leads to the theorem that given $V_i$ and $r_i$, the time rate of adjustment of the price levels to disequilibria in the balance of payments *will be inversely proportional* to the size of the country (Mundell 1965, pp. 16–19). More generally, if we use $\beta_i$ to represent the balance of payments of the $i$th country expressed as a proportion of its national income we have

$$(28) \qquad \frac{1}{P_i} \frac{dP_i}{dt} = \frac{V_i}{r_i} \beta_i,$$

which shows that the percentage adjustment in the price level is directly proportional to the payments disequilibrium expressed as a fraction of income.

This formula relates the adjustment of the price level to balance of payments disequilibria, but it would not be correct to identify this with the "speed of correction" of the balance of payments unless the percentage adjustment in prices and in the balance of payments were identical. The speed of correction is identified with the term $K_i$ in the equation

$$(29) \qquad \frac{dB_i}{dt} = K_i B_i(P_1, \cdots, P_n),$$

where $K_i$ is, for simplicity, taken to be a constant. What will determine the magnitude of $K_i$?

To investigate the meaning of $K_i$ assume, for the moment, that every other price level except that of the adjustment country is constant. Then

$$(30) \qquad \frac{dB_i}{dt} = \frac{\partial B_i}{\partial P_i} \frac{dP_i}{dt} \equiv b_{ii} \frac{dP_i}{dt},$$

where $b_{ii}$ expresses the change in the $i$th country's balance of payments when the price level rises. Substituting into (30) for $dP_i/dt$ from (26) then gives

$$(31) \qquad \frac{dB_i}{dt} = \frac{V_i}{r_i} \frac{b_{ii}}{O_i} B_i.$$

It follows then from (29) that

$$(32) \qquad K_i = \frac{V_i}{r_i} \frac{b_{ii}}{O_i}.$$

The expression $b_{ii}/O_i$ is a dimensionless ratio, since $b_{ii}$ is an elasticity factor weighted by a quantity; specifically, $b_{ii}$ is proportional to the "elasticity of the balance of payments." Hence, the speed of correction can be written

$$(33) \qquad K_i = \frac{V_i}{r_i} \epsilon_i \sigma_i,$$

where $\epsilon_i$ is the elasticity factor and $\sigma_i$ is the share of exports in domestic output. (Note that $K_i$ is a pure number per unit of time identical in dimension to income velocity $V_i$.)

Until now we have assumed that only one country's price level is adjusting. If we relax this assumption the formula for the speed of correction must be modified. Specifically, instead of (30) we must write

$$(34) \qquad \frac{dB_i}{dt} = \sum_{j=1}^{n} b_{ij} \frac{dP_j}{dt}$$

to allow for simultaneous price adjustments in all countries. Substituting for $dP_j/dt$ from equation (26) as before, we get

$$(35) \qquad \frac{dB_i}{dt} = \sum_{j=1}^{n} b_{ij} \frac{V_j}{r_j O_j} B_j,$$

and we cannot find a unique rate of correction without considering the entire system of equations.

The world price level under the gold standard system is determined by the monetary gold stock. Summing over the equations (see (21) and (22)),

$$(36) \qquad G_i = r_i M_i = r_i \frac{O_i}{V_i} P_i,$$

we get

$$(37) \qquad G = \sum_{i=1}^{n} r_i \frac{O_i}{V_i} P_i.$$

But what determines changes in the monetary gold stock?

Central bank acquisition of gold is a residual demand: official reserves rise or fall according to whether there is an excess private supply or demand. Excess private demand is the difference between consumption-plus-hoarding and production-plus-dishoarding and will depend upon the general price and cost levels in each country. (Excess demand tends to rise with national price levels both because demand increases, via substitution effects, and because supply decreases as costs rise and profits in gold mining fall.) It follows,

then, that the system of differential equations expressing the gold standard mechanism can be written as follows:

$$(38) \qquad \begin{aligned} -\frac{dG}{dt} &= B_0(P_1, \cdots, P_n) \\ r_i \frac{O_i}{V_i} \frac{dP_i}{dt} &= B_i(P_1, \cdots, P_n), \quad i = 1, \cdots, n, \end{aligned}$$

where $B_0$ is the excess flow demand for gold outside central banks. Since $\sum_{i=0}^{n} B_i \equiv 0$, it follows that

$$(39) \qquad \sum_{i=1}^{n} \frac{r_i O_i}{V_i} \frac{dP_i}{dt} = -B_0(P_1, \cdots, P_n),$$

which indicates that changes in the world price level are determined by private demand and supply conditions for gold.

To investigate the stability of the gold standard system it is convenient to make explicit the forms of the functional relationships

$$(40) \qquad B_i = B_i(P_1, \cdots, P_n)$$

by expanding them in a Taylor series about their equilibrium values and omitting all but the linear terms. We then have the system

$$(41) \qquad \frac{dP_i}{dt} = \alpha_i \sum_{j=1}^{n} b_{ij}(P_j - P_j^0), \qquad i = 1, \cdots, n,$$

where $\alpha_i = V_i/r_i O_i$ and $P_j^0$ is the equilibrium price level in country $j$. The system (41) has a solution of the form

$$(42) \qquad P_i = P_i^0 + \sum_{j=1}^{n} A_{ij} e^{\lambda_j t},$$

where the $\lambda$'s are the roots of the $n$th-order characteristic equation

$$(43) \qquad |\alpha_i b_{ij} - \delta_{ij} \lambda| = 0.$$

For stability, $P_i$ must approach $P_i^0$ as $t$ approaches $\infty$, which means that every $\lambda_j$ must have negative real parts.

For arbitrary values of the $b_{ij}$, of course, nothing can be asserted about stability. But under the assumption that an increase in the price level worsens that country's balance of payments and improves the balance of payments of every other country, progress can be made. In that case it is known that the system is stable if and only if the principal minors of the matrix of the system oscillate in sign as follows:

$$(44) \qquad \begin{aligned} b_{ii} &< 0; \\ \begin{vmatrix} b_{ii} & b_{ij} \\ b_{ji} & b_{jj} \end{vmatrix} &> 0; \\ \begin{vmatrix} b_{ii} & b_{ij} & b_{ik} \\ b_{ji} & b_{jj} & b_{jk} \\ b_{ki} & b_{kj} & b_{kk} \end{vmatrix} &< 0; \qquad \text{etc.} \end{aligned}$$

For these conditions (the so-called "Hicks conditions") to be satisfied the column or row sums must be negative (or at least not positive). Now let us write $-b_{0j} \equiv \sum_{j=1}^{n} b_{ij}$ for the column sums and $-b_{i0} \equiv \sum_{i=1}^{n} b_{ij}$ for the row sums and inquire into the meaning of $b_{i0}$ and $b_{0j}$.

We know that $\sum B_i \equiv dG/dt$, the increase in the monetary gold stock, and this provides the clue to the interpretation of the row and column sums. From the preceding section we know that the increase in the monetary gold stock is the difference between current private supply of and demand for gold and that the excess demand for gold depends on the prices. Assuming this relationship to be linear in the prices, the system can be written as follows:

$$(45) \quad \begin{aligned} -\frac{dG}{dt} &= b_{01}(P_1 - P_1^0) + \cdots + b_{0n}(P_n - P_n^0) \\ \frac{1}{\alpha_i}\frac{dP_i}{dt} &= b_{i1}(P_1 - P_1^0) + \cdots + b_{in}(P_n - P_n^0), \\ & \qquad\qquad\qquad\qquad i = 1, \cdots, n. \end{aligned}$$

The column sums of the coefficients on the right are zero, so that $\sum_{i=1}^{n} b_{ij} \equiv -b_{0j}$. On the assumption that each $b_{0j} > 0$ (that is, that an increase in the price level in the jth country causes an excess demand for gold) every column sum in the original matrix is negative, and from stability proofs in other branches of theory we can conclude that the gold standard system is stable.

ROBERT A. MUNDELL

### BIBLIOGRAPHY

ALEXANDER, SIDNEY S. 1952 Effects of a Devaluation on a Trade Balance. International Monetary Fund, *Staff Papers* 2:263–278.

HØST-MADSEN, POUL 1962 Asymmetries Between Balance of Payments Surpluses and Deficits. International Monetary Fund, *Staff Papers* 9:182–199.

JOHNSON, HARRY G. 1958 *International Trade and Economic Growth: Studies in Pure Theory.* Cambridge, Mass.: Harvard Univ. Press; London: Allen & Unwin. → See especially Chapter 5, "Towards a General Theory of the Balance of Payments."

KENEN, PETER B. 1963 *Reserve-asset Preferences of Central Banks and Stability of the Gold Exchange Standard.* Princeton Studies in International Finance, No. 10. Princeton Univ., Department of Economics, International Finance Section.

MACHLUP, FRITZ (1939–1940) 1963 The Theory of Foreign Exchanges. Pages 104–158 in American Economic Association, *Readings in the Theory of International Trade.* Homewood, Ill.: Irwin.

MEADE, JAMES E. (1951) 1952 *The Balance of Payments.* Rev. ed. Oxford Univ. Press.

MUNDELL, ROBERT A. 1965 *The International Monetary System: Conflict and Reform.* Montreal: Private Planning Association of Canada, Canadian Trade Committee.

ROBINSON, JOAN (1937) 1963 The Foreign Exchanges. Pages 83–103 in American Economic Association, *Readings in the Theory of International Trade.* Homewood, Ill.: Irwin.

SOHMEN, EGON 1961 *Flexible Exchange Rates: Theory and Controversy.* Univ. of Chicago Press.

U.S. CONGRESS, JOINT ECONOMIC COMMITTEE 1965 *Balance of Payments Statistics of the United States: Report of the Subcommittee on Economic Statistics.* Washington: Government Printing Office.

VINER, JACOB 1937 *Studies in the Theory of International Trade.* New York: Harper.

## II
### EXCHANGE RATES

The national currencies of different countries are bought and sold against each other on the foreign-exchange markets. *Exchange rates* are the prices of one currency in terms of another (e.g., the price of one pound sterling on a particular day may be $2.801). There are a variety of forms in which a currency may be offered on the foreign-exchange markets. Unless otherwise specified, the term "exchange rate" (to be quite exact, the *spot* rate of exchange) applies to the rate for sight deposits. Bank notes and coins sell at different rates that reflect their higher handling costs. The *forward-exchange market* is yet another type of market for national currencies. On this market, claims to future delivery of a currency are transacted.

Although foreign-exchange markets in different countries may be widely separated geographically, *arbitrage* (simultaneous purchase and sale of a currency at different locations) guarantees that the exchange rates between any pair of currencies in different markets hardly differ from each other [see SPECULATION, HEDGING, AND ARBITRAGE]. Only the existence of exchange controls (a term used for all forms of government licensing of foreign-exchange transactions; see section 4 below) may prevent arbitrage from performing this function.

A currency is said to have appreciated if its price in terms of other currencies has risen. Depreciation indicates a movement in the opposite direction. The term "devaluation" is generally reserved for the downward adjustment of a currency under the system of adjustably-pegged exchange rates (see section 3).

## 1. Demand and supply of foreign exchange

Most transactions in foreign exchange arise in connection with international trade. Unilateral transfers (private gifts, governmental grants-in-aid, or reparations) constitute another component of the demand and supply of foreign exchange. Capital movements (acquisitions of assets in one country by the residents of another) are a third source. Finally, there are transactions of the monetary authorities for the purpose of limiting the movement of exchange rates.

A widely held view is that the dominant factors determining the equilibrium values of exchange rates at any time are the price levels in different countries. An acceptable version of this *purchasing power parity theory* (an expression coined by Gustav Cassel) of the foreign exchanges cannot claim that exchange rates always move exactly in proportion to the relative movements of certain aggregate price indices. No single price index for an economy can serve as an exact indicator of the relative "purchasing power" of a currency, and not all commodities and services whose prices enter into any one of the customary price indices can be traded internationally. In addition, sustained changes in capital movements may clearly affect the long-run equilibrium values of exchange rates even without changes of commodity prices. The relative competitiveness of the industries of different countries on the world markets, indicated primarily by the prices they charge, is nevertheless a factor of crucial importance for the rating of national currencies on the exchange markets. For *given* levels of capital transfers and the prices of all other commodities, a rise in the price of any commodity that can be traded internationally will tend to cause depreciation of the currency in question. The legitimacy of a purchasing power parity theory in this limited sense cannot be denied.

The issue of whether or not changes in price levels should be regarded as the principal cause of disturbances in the foreign-exchange markets has frequently been the source of controversy. The first extensively documented debate of this kind was the "bullion controversy" during the time of the Napoleonic wars. After the suspension of specie payments by the Bank of England in 1797, the pound sterling had on several occasions depreciated noticeably on the foreign-exchange markets. The "bullionists," headed by David Ricardo, attributed the decline to the fact that, in their view, prices in Great Britain were too high (Ricardo 1810). The "anti-bullionists," on the other hand, pointed to the heavy load of financial transfers to Britain's allies on the Continent as the basic cause. The dispute can be simply resolved by saying that the pound had depreciated because, with the increased level of capital movements to other countries, prices of actual and potential export goods were too high to make possible a sufficient export surplus at the previous exchange rate. The same issues have been debated, and opinions have divided on exactly the same lines, in connection with the balance of payments difficulties of the United States in the late 1950s and the 1960s.

During the German hyperinflation in the early 1920s, an extreme version of the anti-bullionist argument was used to deny the claim that domestic inflation was the cause of the rapid depreciation of the reichsmark. According to this view, currency depreciation in the wake of capital flight was, on the contrary, the original source of domestic inflation. As prices rose, expansion of the money supply by the Reichsbank only served to satisfy the growing need for cash to finance the rapidly increasing money value of transactions. The proponents of this school of thought overlooked the fact that capital flight would not have occurred in the first place if domestic policy had been less conducive to inflation.

Equilibrium exchange rates may be affected by changes in consumer preferences, techniques of production, the level of business activity, or by governmental policies that lead to changes in world demand for the exports of different countries. Central banks can affect the levels of exchange rates by changing interest rates and thereby influencing international capital flows or by direct purchases and sales on the foreign-exchange markets. Finally, governments may exercise an influence on the private demand for foreign exchange, and hence on equilibrium exchange rates, by the imposition of exchange controls (see section 4).

Although attention usually centers on the effects of all these forces on the *spot* markets of foreign exchange, it should be recognized that they exercise their influence on *forward* markets as well. An importer who has to make a payment in foreign currency three months hence, for example, may relieve himself of the speculative risk involved by purchasing the required amount of this currency forward. Failure to do so makes him a foreign-exchange speculator.

Coverage on the forward-exchange market is not, on the other hand, a form of insurance, in which other market participants would necessarily have to assume, against payment of an insurance premium, the exchange risk of which commercial traders relieve themselves. In the absence of official intervention the bulk of forward exchange demanded by importers in a given country will, as a rule, be supplied by exporters who face an exchange risk of the opposite type. Even if disequilibrium between commercial offers and demands for forward exchange develops, there is no need for speculators to enter. If the pressure of excess demand or supply of forward exchange were to lead to an appreciable change of the forward rate in question, arbitrage would develop between this and other forward markets as well as between it and the spot market ("covered interest arbitrage"). To arrive at an equilibrium, these capital movements have to establish a difference between spot and forward rates that is approximately equal to the difference between the earnings from investments in fixed-interest securities of the relevant maturity in the two countries involved (for details, see Sohmen 1961, chapter 4).

## 2. Effects of exchange-rate changes

Let us assume that the rating of a currency on the exchange markets falls as a result of autonomous capital movements or of deliberate government action. The effects of depreciation on the physical quantities of exports and imports are practically certain. If the foreign prices of a country's exports were to remain unchanged (a condition that would be approximately satisfied if the country produced only a negligible part of the total world supply of its export commodities), their prices per unit in terms of domestic currency will rise in the exact proportion of depreciation. If, at the opposite extreme, *domestic* prices were to remain constant, the unit prices of exports in terms of *foreign* currencies must fall in proportion to the depreciation. In the real world, depreciation will usually lead to an intermediate result. The implied movement of domestic and foreign prices of exports will tend to encourage increased production as well as an increase in the quantities demanded abroad. The effect of depreciation on the physical quantities of imports will be the exact opposite: they will tend to fall.

With both unit values and quantities of exports rising, depreciation must necessarily increase the value of exports in terms of domestic currency. This is not, however, assured for the value of exports in terms of foreign currencies. The percentage fall in their foreign prices may, on the average, be greater than the percentage increase of the quantities sold. The value of exports in terms of foreign currencies would then be lower after depreciation. By similar reasoning it can be seen that depreciation always lowers the value of a country's imports in terms of foreign currencies, whereas the effect on their value in domestic currency is uncertain. The combined effect of depreciation on the *balance of trade* (the value of exports minus the value of imports) depends on the elasticities of supply and demand of all exportable and importable goods and services as well as on the value of the trade balance before depreciation (Robinson 1937; Vanek 1962, chapter 5).

In a simple theoretical model with only two commodities, infinite supply elasticities, and an initial trade balance of zero, the criterion for an improvement of the balance of trade after depreciation reduces to the condition that the sum of the demand elasticities of imports and exports must exceed unity.

There have been frequent attempts to estimate the values of the demand elasticities of internationally traded commodities in order to find out whether or not these elasticities are high enough to assure with reasonable certainty that currency depreciation will lead to an improvement of a country's balance of trade (see the survey by Cheng 1959). The difficulties associated with the attempt to estimate demand elasticities are so formidable, however, that the significance of these findings is rather doubtful (Orcutt 1950).

A corollary of the proposition that currency depreciation may fail to improve the foreign balance if demand elasticities are too low is that the foreign-exchange market is unstable under these conditions. It cannot be concluded, however, that a system of flexible exchange rates would then be unable to function. In the real world, perverse reactions will, if they occur at all, be confined to a limited range of exchange-rate values. Freely fluctuating rates must always come to rest in a region where the condition that depreciation improves the trade balance is fulfilled (cf. Sohmen 1961, chapter 1).

It should be emphasized that one can meaningfully discuss the role of price elasticities of internationally traded commodities only if it is assumed that the monetary authorities succeed in keeping the general price level reasonably stable. The possibility that the values of demand elasticities may be too low for stability is not to be confused with the possibility that general inflation may thwart the expected effect of depreciation.

Some authors have questioned the relevance of the "elasticity approach" to balance of payments problems, on the grounds that measures affecting the level at which resources are being used by the domestic economy (the level of "absorption"), for example, fiscal and monetary policies, will always be vastly more important for a country's balance of payments than the effects of changes in relative prices brought about by exchange-rate movements. From the simple identity, $X - M \equiv Y - A$, which states that the excess of exports ($X$) over imports ($M$) will always have to equal the excess of a country's real output ($Y$) over its real expenditure or absorption ($A$), it is easily deduced that any increase in the value of the left-hand side implies a corresponding increase in the expression on the right. Especially under conditions of full employment, depreciation will, in the view of protagonists of the "absorption approach," be totally ineffective unless it is accompanied by policies designed to reduce real domestic expenditure (Alexander 1952). This school tends to neglect the possibility of improvements in the efficiency of resource allocation that may occur as a result of the restoration of equilibrium in the foreign-exchange markets and the subsequent removal of artificial barriers to trade and capital movements. Such improvements may raise the level of output sufficiently to allow for an increase of exports relative to imports, even with constant domestic expenditure (Machlup 1955).

The discussion of elasticities in international trade concentrates on the reactions to adjustments of exchange rates to a new (and thereafter constant) level. The role of expectations concerning future exchange-rate movements will also be significant, as long as governments are not committed to keeping exchange rates immutably stable for all eternity. Expectations are particularly important in the case of capital movements. Any change in exchange rates has a decisive influence on the profitability of existing fixed-interest investments. The willingness to undertake capital transfers will therefore depend crucially on expected future changes of exchange rates [see SPECULATION, HEDGING, AND ARBITRAGE].

## 3. Alternative monetary systems

**Common currency.** A common currency provides an extreme example of rigidly and unalterably fixed exchange rates between the monetary units of the member regions. The existence of a common monetary unit enforces identical monetary policies in every region as a consequence of the fact that exchange rates between regional currency units can never deviate from their ratios of 1:1.

**Pegged exchange rates and gold standards.** A system of pegged exchange rates between different national currencies can be brought about by official interventions on the foreign-exchange markets. As a rule, currencies are not held at one single rate that would be immutable over time. Instead, a *parity* is established between any pair of currencies around which exchange rates can move within prescribed limits. Historically, the classic example of such a system was the *gold standard*. Currency parities were automatically established by central banks fulfilling an obligation to buy and sell unlimited quantities of gold at a fixed price in terms of their national currencies. Gold arbitrage limited the movements of exchange rates within the "gold points," determined by the costs of shipping gold from one country to another. As soon as an ex-

change rate tended to move beyond these limits, it became profitable to buy gold from one central bank and sell it to another. Since a sustained gold outflow threatened to exhaust their reserves, central banks losing gold were forced to raise interest rates. A sufficient rise of interest rates relative to those abroad had the usual consequence of inducing an inflow of capital, reversing a tendency toward depreciation and bringing the gold outflow to a halt. Over the longer run, monetary contraction also tends to restrain domestic demand, to lower domestic prices relative to those abroad, and thus to favor exports and reduce imports.

During the era of the historic gold standard, many central banks began to feel that the holding of gold was a rather unrewarding practice. By holding deposits with foreign banks in countries practicing the gold standard or by holding short-term government obligations of such countries, they could earn interest on their assets while feeling certain that they nevertheless had immediate access to gold whenever required. This system, known as the *gold-exchange standard*, became particularly widespread during the 1920s. Its viability was always threatened, however, by the possibility that too many holders of monetary assets denominated in gold-standard currencies might simultaneously present their claims for conversion into gold, for the central banks of the gold-standard countries would always hold gold amounting to only a fraction of the total claims against them.

No country is now practicing the gold standard, properly speaking, in the sense that its currency would be redeemable into gold for the general public. The United States has, however, entered an obligation to honor all demands of the monetary authorities of other countries for conversion of their dollar claims into gold for "legitimate monetary purposes." The exact meaning of this qualification has never been specified.

**The "adjustable peg" and the IMF.** A basic feature of the systems described so far was the constancy of currency parities. The present system, as incorporated in the *Articles of Agreement* (1944) of the International Monetary Fund (IMF), differs from them in that parities (around which exchange rates are allowed to fluctuate up to 1 per cent of parity on either side) may be altered in case of a "fundamental disequilibrium" (art. IV, 5). As originally envisaged, parity adjustments under this arrangement (commonly described as the system of the "adjustable peg") were to be carried out after consultation with the IMF, and only with its approval if the change exceeded 10 per cent of the initial par value. The impossibility of providing an operationally meaningful definition of a "fundamental disequilibrium," and the obvious danger of snowballing speculation whenever the intention of carrying out a parity adjustment becomes known to a wider circle, have made this provision in the *Articles of Agreement* a dead letter. Inevitably, parity adjustments are always prepared in the greatest secrecy and usually without prior consultation with the IMF.

**Flexible exchange rates.** In a system of flexible exchange rates, central banks do not intervene on the exchange markets with the purpose of restricting exchange-rate movements within narrow limits. Such a system is generally held to be compatible with minor purchases and sales of foreign exchange to iron out small fluctuations, as long as these interventions do not go against a basic trend. An active use of monetary policy to prevent undesirably wide fluctuations of exchange rates is, of course, perfectly compatible with a system of flexible rates. Since there is no obligation, however, to subject monetary policy exclusively to the goal of avoiding a depletion of foreign-exchange reserves at constant currency parities, it may be used more freely for other objectives, such as full employment or price-level stability.

## 4. Exchange controls

Currency conversion may be subject to various kinds of restrictions. The most severe form of exchange controls would be one under which a special permission is required for every single transaction on the foreign-exchange markets. There may, on the other hand, be a general permission for certain types of transactions (e.g., all those related to commercial trade), while others may require individual licensing. The IMF *Articles of Agreement* (art. VIII, 2) require member countries to guarantee currency convertibility for commercial payments but not necessarily for capital movements. Apart from exchange controls, properly speaking, other measures of limiting the demand for foreign exchange, such as tariffs, quotas, and special taxes on the purchase of foreign assets, have been used for the purpose of balance of payments adjustments. Exchange restrictions may differentiate between residents and nonresidents of a country in the relative freedom granted each group to carry out foreign-exchange transactions. The restoration of convertibility for nonresidents by most countries of western Europe at the end of 1958 was one of the most important postwar steps toward full currency convertibility.

The most common reason for introducing exchange controls is the threat of exhaustion of a country's gold and foreign-exchange reserves if its government is committed to supporting exchange rates at levels at which there is a sustained excess demand for foreign exchange. Convertibility has, however, been interfered with on some occasions in order to check a persistent excess *supply* of foreign exchange. Switzerland and West Germany, for example, have during the 1960s used a ban on interest payments on bank deposits of nonresidents to reduce an excessive capital inflow. A system of flexible rates, being defined as one in which the central bank is not committed to intervening on the exchange markets, is intrinsically more compatible with full convertibility than a system of pegged rates.

The existence of exchange controls makes possible the division of the foreign-exchange market into separate compartments with different exchange rates. Such systems of multiple exchange rates were in use in some countries during the 1930s and became particularly widespread after World War II. They may take the form of having one exchange rate for commercial transactions and a different one (perhaps a flexible rate) for capital movements. There may also be differences between the exchange rates applied to exports and to imports of different commodities.

Bilateral clearing agreements may require approximate balancing of the trade flows between two countries. The foreign-exchange proceeds from the exports to the partner country will then generally not be convertible into other currencies. This practice leads, among other things, to implied cross rates of exchange between different currencies that will generally be at variance with each other. Considerable efficiency losses may result for the countries concerned, not only from administrative waste but also as a result of the distortion of the price structure brought about by arrangements of this kind.

## 5. Fixed versus flexible exchange rates

One of the most basic issues in comparing alternative monetary systems centers on the relative advantages of *fixed* versus *flexible* exchange rates. It is somewhat misleading to state the alternatives in this simple manner. The word "fixed" suggests stability, whereas "flexible" carries a connotation of instability. The absence of official interventions on the foreign-exchange markets does not imply that exchange rates would necessarily have to be unstable. Sufficiently flexible monetary policy can always assure as high a degree of stability of exchange rates as may be desired. The system incorporated in the *Articles of Agreement* of the IMF, on the other hand, does not guarantee permanent stability of exchange rates. It is therefore illegitimate to claim for this system the advantages of a common currency area, in which the constancy of "exchange rates" is assured by a unified monetary policy.

The disadvantage of relatively greater exchange-rate instability, if it should indeed occur under flexible rates as a consequence of inadequate monetary and other policies of certain governments, has to be weighed against the restrictions of trade and payments to which governments frequently see themselves forced by balance of payments difficulties associated with a system of pegged rates (see 4 above). Apart from this danger, the possibility that certain governments may from time to time be forced to apply monetary policies conflicting with the goals of full employment or price stability has been pointed out as the most objectionable feature of pegged rates. It was primarily this feature that brought about the demise of the gold-exchange standard during the great depression of the 1930s. Apart from the fact that there is greater leeway for monetary policy to pursue domestic objectives if exchange rates are flexible, given changes in interest rates also have a substantially more powerful effect on domestic employment under flexible exchange rates. This is a consequence of the fact that capital movements induced by interest-rate changes do not, as under fixed rates, operate primarily on the foreign-exchange reserves of the central bank but immediately induce changes of the balance on current account. The capital outflow encouraged by a lowering of domestic interest rates, for example, brings about currency depreciation, which in turn induces an increase of exports and a reduction of imports. This change results in an immediate rise of effective demand and hence of employment. The opposite follows in the case of an attempt to combat an inflationary boom by monetary contraction (Sohmen 1961, chapters 2, 4; Mundell 1963).

EGON SOHMEN

[*See also* INTERNATIONAL TRADE; *and* INTERNATIONAL TRADE CONTROLS.]

### BIBLIOGRAPHY

ALEXANDER, SIDNEY S. 1952 Effects of a Devaluation on a Trade Balance. International Monetary Fund, *Staff Papers* 2:263–278.

CHENG, HANG SHENG 1959 Statistical Estimates of Elasticities and Propensities in International Trade: A Survey of Published Studies. International Monetary Fund, *Staff Papers* 7:107–158.

FRIEDMAN, MILTON 1953 *Essays in Positive Economics.* Univ. of Chicago Press. → See especially pages 157–203, "The Case for Flexible Exchange Rates."

HABERLER, GOTTFRIED (1933) 1936 *The Theory of International Trade, With Its Applications to Commercial Policy.* London: Hodge. → First published in German.

INTERNATIONAL MONETARY FUND 1944 *Articles of Agreement, International Monetary Fund, United Nations Monetary and Financial Conference, Bretton Woods, N.H., July 1 to 22, 1944.* Washington: The Fund.

JOHNSON, HARRY G. 1958 *International Trade and Economic Growth: Studies in Pure Theory.* London: Allen & Unwin; Cambridge, Mass.: Harvard Univ. Press.

KEYNES, JOHN MAYNARD (1930) 1958–1960 *A Treatise on Money.* 2 vols. London: Macmillan. → Volume 1: *The Pure Theory of Money.* Volume 2: *The Applied Theory of Money.*

MACHLUP, FRITZ (1939–1940) 1963 The Theory of Foreign Exchanges. Pages 104–158 in American Economic Association, *Readings in the Theory of International Trade.* Homewood, Ill.: Irwin.

MACHLUP, FRITZ 1955 Relative Prices and Aggregate Spending in the Analysis of Devaluation. *American Economic Review* 45:255–278.

MUNDELL, ROBERT A. 1963 Capital Mobility and Stabilization Policy Under Fixed and Flexible Exchange Rates. *Canadian Journal of Economics and Political Science* 29:475–485.

ORCUTT, GUY H. 1950 Measurement of Price Elasticities in International Trade. *Review of Economics and Statistics* 32:117–132.

RICARDO, DAVID (1810) 1951 The High Price of Bullion. Pages 47–127 in David Ricardo, *Works and Correspondence.* Volume 3: *Pamphlets and Papers, 1809–1811.* Edited by Piero Sraffa. Cambridge Univ. Press.

ROBINSON, JOAN (1937) 1963 The Foreign Exchanges. Pages 83–103 in American Economic Association, *Readings in the Theory of International Trade.* Homewood, Ill.: Irwin.

SOHMEN, EGON 1961 *Flexible Exchange Rates: Theory and Controversy.* Univ. of Chicago Press.

VANEK, JAROSLAV 1962 *International Trade: Theory and Economic Policy.* Homewood, Ill.: Irwin.

## III
### INTERNATIONAL MONETARY ORGANIZATION

International transactions under a system of fixed exchange rates give rise to surpluses and deficits in the balance of payments of transacting countries, as the two preceding articles have pointed out. These surpluses and deficits must be settled. This article discusses the mechanisms for international settlements—both arrangements that evolved more or less spontaneously, such as the international gold standard, and formal organizations, such as the International Monetary Fund.

### The gold standard

**The classical gold standard.** The universal use of silver, or silver and gold, for the coinage of money created a fixed tie between the currencies of the principal trading countries and established, in effect, an international monetary system. In the seventeenth and eighteenth centuries silver and gold coin were regarded as providing a national currency, and although some silver coins had a wide international circulation, this did not alter the essentially national character of the monetary system. The present international monetary system may be said to have begun in 1816 when England based its monetary system on the gold sovereign and limited the legal tender of silver coins. The primacy of gold emerged in the nineteenth century with the growth of world trade, in which England played a major role as exporter and importer and as shipper and entrepôt dealer. Sterling became the currency in which much of the world's trade was conducted, and drafts in virtually all currencies could be bought and sold for sterling. Nevertheless, until the 1870s silver remained one of the two standard money metals. In the next thirty years, however, bimetallism was abandoned nearly everywhere. The shift from bimetallism was justified as necessary to make the national monetary systems conform to the international monetary system based on gold.

Under the classical gold standard each country defined its monetary unit as a specific quantity of gold and undertook the free coinage of gold in this monetary unit or a convenient multiple of it. This established a mint parity for each currency in terms of other gold standard currencies. Foreign exchange rates could vary from the mint parity only within narrow limits created by the cost of shipping gold from one center to another. Prior to World War I, the dollar exchange rate for sterling, for example, could not ordinarily be higher or lower than $4.8665, the mint parity, plus or minus about two cents per pound sterling, which is the cost of shipping gold between New York and London.

In the late nineteenth century gold coins formed an important part of the money in circulation. The value of all other forms of money was maintained by requiring their redemption in gold coin, which necessitated a close but indirect tie between the stock of gold and the money supply. This tie was reinforced in all gold standard countries by national legislation requiring gold reserves against bank notes, and sometimes against deposits held with the central bank.

Because of the considerable amount of coined gold in circulation and the high ratio of gold reserves to the money supply, domestic money was virtually equivalent to foreign exchange. An inflow or outflow of gold acted quickly to increase or decrease the domestic money supply. The maintenance of the gold value of the currency became the primary objective of economic policy. Central

banking techniques, such as a flexible bank rate, were devised to assure a prompt response of the monetary system to the balance of payments and to avoid or minimize gold movements, particularly the outflow of gold.

The classical gold standard came to an end with World War I. Even before this, innovations were introduced, consciously or unconsciously, that loosened the tie between national monetary systems and gold. Since 1941 there have been many major changes in the gold standard, so that the present international monetary system is basically different from the gold standard from which it gradually evolved.

**Redemption and convertibility.** The classical gold standard, in which gold coins circulated widely, was not well adapted to the needs of highly developed industrial countries. With the growth of banking, the circulation of gold coins became small relative to the use of bank notes and bank deposits. The tie between gold coins and other forms of money was retained by requiring the redemption of bank notes in gold and by requiring central banks to maintain a gold reserve against their note issue. Redemption was an essential part of the mechanism by which exchange and bullion dealers kept exchange rates within the range established by mint parities and the cost of shipping gold.

The use of gold coin as money was virtually brought to an end by World War I. In all belligerent countries, gold coins were withdrawn from circulation and gold reserves were concentrated in the central banks. When the United Kingdom restored the gold standard in 1925, it adopted the gold bullion standard. The national currency was made redeemable in gold bars of 400 ounces (about $8,270 at the parity of 1925). Thus, gold was readily available for gold and exchange arbitrage but not for circulation.

In the United States, redemption of currency into gold coin was maintained until 1933. During the great depression, a considerable amount of gold coin and gold certificates went into hoards. After the dollar became *de facto* depreciated, Congress abrogated the gold clause in contracts and made all obligations payable in legal tender—that is, in any form of currency or coin. The Gold Reserve Act of 1934 established a new gold standard for the United States at $35 a fine ounce, with gold used only for international settlements. Gold could no longer be coined, and private holding of gold coin by U.S. residents was forbidden, a prohibition extended in 1961 to the holding of gold abroad.

Under the classical gold standard, governments did not ordinarily intervene in the exchange market. The foreign exchange value of currencies was maintained by foreign exchange and bullion dealers through gold and exchange arbitrage. In the 1930s, when currencies were no longer firmly tied to gold, most countries began intervening in the exchange market to keep exchange rates within a desired range.

The concept of the redemption or convertibility of money into gold is now entirely different from that of the classical gold standard. No country undertakes the domestic redemption of money into gold, although in some countries private holding of gold is permitted and gold may be acquired in private transactions. But all of the leading countries do maintain the convertibility of their currencies into foreign exchange, at least for nonresidents, through the exchange market.

**Gold and international monetary reserves.** International monetary reserves under the classical gold standard consisted largely of the gold coin in circulation (in the United States, also gold certificates) and the gold reserves held by the monetary authorities as backing for the currency and other central bank obligations. Although most of the gold reserves were legally committed to backing the currency, the reserve requirements could be suspended in time of crisis. In addition to required reserves, the monetary authorities usually held some free gold so that an outflow of gold did not necessarily compel an immediate contraction of the money supply. In some instances, countries held foreign exchange reserves in addition to gold reserves.

While bankers and exchange dealers were developing the practice of holding sterling in order to carry on their exchange business, some governments were evolving the gold exchange standard by pegging their currencies to gold standard currencies. This form of the gold standard was devised to maintain stable exchange rates when direct redemption of the currency in gold was not feasible or when creating exchange by shipping gold would have involved long delay and high costs.

The wide use of the gold exchange standard grew out of World War I. As an interim step in restoring the gold standard, some continental European countries pegged the exchange rate to gold standard currencies—at first the dollar and later sterling—by drawing on or building up balances of dollars and sterling. At the end of 1928, the foreign exchange reserves held by all countries are estimated to have constituted one-fourth of all monetary reserves. The great depression and the devaluation of virtually all currencies entailed considerable loss (as measured in terms of the gold equivalent) from the holding of foreign exchange reserves.

Since 1939 there has been an enormous increase in the holding of foreign exchange as monetary reserves. The United Kingdom financed much of its overseas wartime expenditures through the sale of sterling for national currencies. At the end of 1950, after sterling had been devalued, these holdings amounted to nearly $10,000 million. Since then, the gross sterling liabilities have increased very little.

Foreign official holdings of U.S. dollars increased moderately during the war but were soon drawn down. At the end of 1949 they amounted to only $2,900 million. When foreign countries rebuilt their reserves, a major part was in the form of dollars. From 1950 to 1957, inclusive, the increase in official dollar holdings was over $5,000 million. From 1958 to September 1966, when U.S. payments were in persistent deficit, a larger proportion of the settlements was in gold, although official dollar holdings increased by about $4,800 million.

At the end of September 1966, the gold reserves of all countries outside the communist bloc amounted to $41,000 million and their total foreign exchange reserves were $23,500 million. In addition, $21,000 million of gold and currencies was held by the International Monetary Fund as a common reserve for all its members, and it had general arrangements to borrow up to $6,000 million from ten of its members (the Group of Ten).

**Modification of the gold standard.** No aspect of the gold standard reveals more clearly the change in its nature than the attitude toward gold parities. The maintenance of the historic parity of the currency in terms of gold was long regarded as a matter of national honor. After specie payments had been suspended for 20 years, England adopted the gold standard in 1816 and resumed the redemption of Bank of England notes in 1821, despite the deflation that this entailed. During the Civil War, the premium on gold in terms of greenbacks rose as high as 150 per cent in the United States. Nevertheless, a deflation was undertaken that made it possible to resume specie payments in 1878.

The concern to maintain historic gold parities ended with World War I, and the great depression. The war brought inflation, and the currencies of all belligerents depreciated, except the dollar. While France and Italy stabilized the exchange value of their currencies and adopted new gold parities during the 1920s, the United Kingdom undertook a prolonged deflation to restore the prewar parity of sterling. In Germany, where the mark had been destroyed in the hyperinflation, a new currency was established at the end of 1924 at the old parity with gold.

War is the great destroyer of the gold standard. The need to finance war expenditures results in an expansion of the currency and in inflation. The wartime expansion of money and credit exhausts the money-creating power of gold standard countries. Since gold production is adversely affected by the higher level of costs, the growth of the gold base for the monetary system is much reduced after a war. This explains the widespread fears of a gold shortage in the 1920s.

The uneven wartime inflation also generates centers of deflation after the war. The countries that attempt to restore the historic parities of their currencies must undertake a deflation that reduces their imports and puts pressure on international prices, particularly of basic commodities. The countries that stabilize at a depreciated exchange rate may set the value of their currencies too low because the new parity is based on an exchange rate that reflects a capital outflow that is brought to an end when the currency is stabilized. Thus, the countries with the newly established parities tend to have a payments surplus and to draw reserves from the deficit countries. These errors were fortunately avoided after World War II, for reasons that will be discussed below.

During the great depression the international gold standard collapsed, and from 1933 to 1937 countries followed a policy of extreme nationalism. Currencies were devalued competitively, tariffs were raised and other restrictions on trade were intensified, and exchange controls and multiple currency devices were introduced. Because currency depreciation was generally associated with monetary expansion, the domestic effects of devaluations were favorable. On the other hand, they intensified the depression in the gold-bloc countries—France, the Netherlands, Belgium, and Switzerland.

Currency devaluations began early in the depression. In September 1931 sterling was depreciated by about 30 per cent. On January 31, 1934, the dollar was formally devalued by 41 per cent and, in 1935 and 1936, the currencies of the gold-bloc countries were devalued. The gold standard, so laboriously restored from 1925 to 1930, was abandoned by every great trading country by 1936. The great depression swept away not only the newly established parities but also the historic gold parity of the dollar, sterling, the Netherlands guilder, and the Swiss franc. It was not until the link between gold and currencies was severed that the depres-

sion could be brought to an end and a slow recovery begun.

Under the classical gold standard, as we have seen, the maintenance of the gold value of the currency was the primary, if not the sole, objective of economic policy. In the past generation, the objectives of policy have been broadened to encompass the economy as a whole. In the United States, the Employment Act of 1946 states that the objectives of economic policy are to promote maximum employment, production, and purchasing power, within the framework of monetary stability. Other countries have formally or tacitly adopted similar objectives.

### Formal international organizations

**Bank for International Settlements.** The only enduring international financial institution created in the interwar period is the Bank for International Settlements (BIS). The concept of a politically independent bank which would be the focal point for international financial cooperation gained great support during the 1920s. By a convention signed at The Hague in January 1930, when the Young Plan on German reparations was adopted, the Swiss government undertook to grant a charter to the BIS. The moratorium on war debts and reparations payments sharply limited this phase of its work. In the crisis of 1931, however, the BIS took an active role in the emergency credits provided by governments and central banks. At the end of March 1966, the resources of the BIS amounted to nearly $2,600 million. It frequently participates in credits granted by central banks to deal with pressures in the exchange market. In recent years, the BIS has acted as agent for the European Payments Union, the European Steel and Coal Community, and the European Monetary Fund. The BIS is the center for frequent meetings of governors of central banks. Its research and statistical work is of a very high order.

**The International Monetary Fund.** The lessons of World War I were well remembered in the formulation of international financial policy during and after World War II, and the monetary problems of the postwar period were not left to improvisation. Instead, the United States and the United Kingdom prepared independent plans for international monetary cooperation. These plans are best known under the names of their principal authors—the White Plan and the Keynes Plan. Other plans were proposed by Canada and France.

The Keynes Plan proposed the creation of an International Clearing Union (ICU) based on an international unit, the bancor, with a value fixed (but not unalterably) in terms of gold. The bancor was to be accepted as the equivalent of gold by member countries in the settlement of international balances. Central banks of member countries would keep accounts with the ICU. The ICU would not have subscribed capital; instead, countries were to be given overdraft facilities up to a prescribed quota based on their international trade. Countries with a surplus in international payments would accumulate credit balances; those with a deficit would build up debit balances. Moderate interest charges would be levied on both debit and credit balances. As the ICU would be a closed payments system, with bancor holdings not convertible, the debits and credits would necessarily be equal and there could be no question of the adequacy of its resources for meeting the reserve credit requirements of its members within the quota limits. The members of the ICU would agree among themselves on the initial par values of their currencies in terms of bancor, which could be changed thereafter only with the permission of the ICU. Under certain conditions of persistent deficit, the ICU could request a member to devalue its currency and could require it to repay part of its indebtedness out of its gold and foreign exchange reserves. In general, the ICU was not to concern itself with the domestic economic policies of its members.

The White Plan proposed the creation of an International Stabilization Fund (ISF) to maintain orderly exchange arrangements. Each member country would have to agree on a par value of its currency defined in terms of an international monetary unit (unitas) equivalent to $10 in gold. Changes in parities could be made only after consultation and with the approval of the ISF. Members would not be permitted to impose exchange controls without the approval of the ISF and would be obligated to remove existing exchange controls. To provide the ISF with resources, members would be assigned quotas and would subscribe gold and their own currencies to the amount of these quotas. Members could purchase foreign exchange from the ISF with their own currencies—up to one-fourth of their quotas annually, with maximum net credits not to exceed 100 per cent of their quotas. Drawings in larger amount could be made only with special approval after waiver of the quota limits. Members would have to repay drawings in gold and convertible foreign exchange when their reserves increased.

The ISF would have been given wide powers under the White Plan. Members acquiring currencies in settlement of international payments could sell them to the ISF either for their own currencies or for foreign exchange. Thus, the ISF would have assured the convertibility of any currency acquired by a member in settlement of a balance-of-payments surplus. As the reserve credits of the ISF were to be given in specific currencies, the operations contemplated could exhaust its holdings of the currency of a country with a large and persistent surplus. The plan, therefore, provided that if it appeared that a currency would become scarce, the ISF would issue a report to the surplus country with recommendations designed to restore the ISF's holdings of the scarce currency.

The principal differences between the two plans may be summarized as follows. The ISF would have had wide powers of intervention through international financial operations undertaken on its own initiative. The ICU would have been a passive institution, providing reserve credit facilities only on the initiative of its members. The ISF contemplated the use of the exchange market for settling international balances; the ICU contemplated the clearing of such balances through its accounts. The ICU would not itself have held gold or currencies, and the role of gold in international payments would have been circumscribed. The ISF would have had its own resources of gold and currencies subscribed by members, and gold was to have a significant role as reserves and in international settlements. Finally, under the ICU the responsibility for restoring international equilibrium would be shared by debtor and creditor countries, while under the ISF it would have fallen primarily on debtor countries. The reserve credit facilities would have been far larger under the ICU and would have been available on more generous terms.

After two years of preliminary discussion, President Roosevelt invited 44 countries to the Monetary and Financial Conference at Bretton Woods, New Hampshire, which met July 1–22, 1944. The report of the commission on the International Monetary Fund (IMF) provides an authoritative history of the negotiations from the first publication of the tentative proposals to the Final Act adopted at Bretton Woods (Rasminsky 1948). The IMF followed in form the proposal of the United States, but included many details from the British and Canadian proposals.

The International Bank for Reconstruction and Development (the World Bank) was also established at Bretton Woods to make loans for long-term reconstruction and development with funds borrowed in private capital markets. The greater part of the capital of the institution, subscribed by member countries, was a guarantee fund to be called on to meet losses and defaults. While the

World Bank retained the basic principles of the U.S. plan, a number of important safeguarding provisions were added. [*See* FOREIGN AID, *article on* ECONOMIC ASPECTS.]

**Operations of the IMF.** The IMF was organized in 1946 and began exchange operations in 1947. Its first task was to establish initial par values for the currencies of its members, which were usually based on the exchange rates that prevailed after the war. The Articles of Agreement of the IMF require all countries to establish the parity of their currencies in terms of gold and to maintain exchange rates within one per cent of parity. This obligation can be met by intervening in the exchange market to keep currencies within the prescribed range or by undertaking to buy and sell gold freely in settlement of international transactions. The United States is the only country that has accepted the obligation of buying and selling gold freely under this provision of the Fund Agreement.

The IMF was aware that changes in parity would become necessary. Initial par values were designed to enable countries to maintain exports until their productive capacity had been restored or until a recession halted the expansion of world trade. By 1949, coincident with a U.S. recession, a major readjustment of parities had become necessary, and the devaluations were approved promptly in September 1949. In fact, it has never been difficult for IMF members to change their parities. To September 1966, the IMF has approved about forty major exchange-rate adjustments. In some instances, the IMF has urged members to establish more realistic parities, and it has accepted fluctuating exchange rates where they were necessary to avoid restrictions on trade.

An important objective of the IMF is to eliminate foreign exchange restrictions and to maintain the convertibility of currencies. During the postwar transitional period, members were permitted to retain and modify wartime exchange restrictions and, when necessary, to impose new exchange restrictions temporarily with the approval of the IMF.

The convertibility of currencies in connection with current international transactions was required by the Fund Agreement after the transition period. Under this provision, balances of a member's currency held by central banks of other members must be converted by the member either in the currency of the country requesting the conversion or in gold. In practice, the obligation is fulfilled when countries support their currencies in the exchange market, without exchange control, using monetary reserves or the resources of the Fund for this purpose. Beginning in 1950, the IMF began an annual examination of restrictions in effect and consulted with members on their further retention. The great trading countries gradually relaxed and removed their exchange restrictions, but it was not until February 1961 that all of them had made their currencies convertible. As of September 1966, 27 of the 104 members of the IMF, including all of the large industrial countries, had accepted the obligation of convertibility.

The IMF periodically reviews the economic and financial position of its members and advises them on their policies. Such review is an essential part of a proposal by a member to change the parity of its currency or to draw on the resources of the IMF outside quota limits. The staff of the IMF must, therefore, maintain a continuous review of the economic situation of all member countries. From time to time, members request the IMF to study specific problems and to prepare programs for monetary reform. These studies have been very useful, although members have occasionally experienced political difficulty in implementing the recommendations. The IMF also has a comprehensive training program for technicians of member countries. The research work of the IMF staff has been outstanding. The IMF is an indispensable source of statistical information, and its publications are noted for careful analytical work.

A major purpose of the IMF is to provide resources with which members can meet balance-of-payments deficits while taking corrective measures. The need for resources for this purpose has grown steadily. The original quotas assigned at Bretton Woods (which measure the gold and currencies subscribed to the IMF) amounted to $8,800 million. Since the Soviet Union did not accept membership, other countries delayed taking up membership, and China never paid its subscription, the IMF began operations with less than $7,000 million of resources. The addition of new members, the upward adjustment of individual quotas, and two general increases in quotas brought the resources of the IMF to about $21,000 million by 1966.

For various reasons, drawings on the IMF in the first ten years (1947 to 1956) amounted to less than $2,000 million. From 1957 to 1966, however, drawings amounted to nearly $11,000 million. As these data indicate, the IMF has become the world's major source of reserve credit. For this reason, members must have assurance that they can use their quotas in time of need. Under present policies, countries have virtually complete assurance that they can draw on the resources of the

IMF to the extent that they have provided net resources (gold tranche drawings) to the IMF. They have the benefit of the doubt on drawings in the first credit tranche (25 per cent of the quota). As a member's drawings become larger relative to its quota, it must meet more exacting tests to assure that its policies will be conducive to the restoration of its balance of payments. In recent years, the IMF has shown flexibility in devising methods that give its members greater assurance on drawings. Under appropriate circumstances, the IMF will make stand-by arrangements under which a country can draw an agreed amount. The IMF has also established a policy of providing compensatory credits for countries whose exports have declined temporarily. Such credits are available with somewhat greater ease than ordinary quota drawings.

The resources of the IMF are a revolving fund for use by all members. If drawings were not repaid at an appropriate time, the IMF would become illiquid and could not provide needed reserve credit. Under the Articles of Agreement, drawings must be repaid when a country's reserve position has improved rather than at a fixed date, although the IMF may require repayment of drawings that have been outstanding for an excessive period of time. The IMF now generally requires countries to repay drawings in three years, with an outside limit of five years. Repayments of drawing on the IMF amounted to $7,700 million as of September 1966. The IMF makes a moderate transactions charge for drawings, and levies continuous use-charges (interest) on net credit extended to its members.

The IMF seeks to promote exchange stability, to maintain orderly exchange arrangements among members, and to avoid competitive exchange depreciation. Nevertheless, a country is not expected to deflate its economy in order to restore its balance of payments; it may instead propose a change in the par value of its currency. The Fund Agreement states that the primary objectives of economic policy are to facilitate the expansion and balanced growth of international trade, and to contribute thereby to the promotion and maintenance of high levels of employment and real income and to the development of the productive resources of all members. This is by no means inconsistent with exchange stability, assuming the revision of parities when necessary.

**Regional monetary arrangements.** The European Payments Union (EPU), the most important of the regional arrangements for international monetary cooperation, was established in July 1950 to facilitate multilateral settlements among the European countries that participated in the Marshall Plan. Originally, any participating country with a surplus in its bilateral payments arrangements with another participating country could offset this surplus against a deficit with other participating countries. Beginning in July 1956, multilateral settlements were made through the exchange market, with the central banks of the surplus countries acquiring the currencies of other members and presenting them for monthly settlement. The settlement provisions for cumulative surplus and deficit positions were gradually strengthened. The EPU was liquidated in December 1958 when most of the participating countries made their currencies convertible among themselves.

The European Fund (EF), a part of the European Monetary Agreement, was established on liquidation of the EPU. Its 16 members include all the countries of western and southern Europe that were in the EPU, and Spain, which was not. The EF provides its members with short-term credits, not exceeding two years, to meet temporary overall balance-of-payments difficulties. Through March 1966, there were 25 drawings totaling $315 million, of which $195 million was repaid.

In 1963, the Council for Mutual Economic Assistance (COMECON) agreed to establish an International Bank for Economic Cooperation (IBEC) to facilitate multilateral clearing within the Soviet bloc. The capital of IBEC is 300 million transferable rubles ($330 million at the parity of exchange), of which the Soviet Union subscribed 116 million rubles. The eight members of IBEC include all of the European countries in the Soviet bloc and Mongolia. Operations were begun on January 1, 1964. IBEC may grant credits to the monetary authorities of the COMECON countries for settlement needs within the system, seasonal credits to offset fluctuations in export receipts, promotion credits to increase trade within the bloc, balance-of-payments loans to finance deficits, and loans for multinational construction projects. IBEC may also accept deposits from member countries in transferable rubles, in gold, and in fully convertible Western currencies. While IBEC has undertaken considerable clearing operations and has extended short-term credits, the persistent imbalance in the payments among participating countries has led Poland (a payments surplus country) to propose that settlement be made in convertible currencies to enable participating countries to finance their deficits with the West. The financing of trade between the Soviet bloc and the West has become an important function of IBEC.

In 1952, seven central banks founded the Center

for Latin American Studies (CEMLA), which now has 20 members—17 in Latin America, plus Jamaica, the Philippines, and Surinam—as well as a number of collaborating members. At present, the functions of CEMLA are limited to discussions, training programs, research, and publications.

## International monetary reform

**Changes before 1966.** The International Monetary Fund (IMF), as formulated at Bretton Woods, reflected the conditions that its founders foresaw in the early postwar period. Because the IMF was not intended to finance relief, reconstruction, and development, its resources were expected to be adequate for a period in which the United States would be in surplus and during which drawings of members would be tightly controlled.

International payments problems have become far different from those that confronted the IMF immediately after the war. World trade and investment have increased enormously. The pattern of world payments has shifted from a large surplus in the United States and a deficit in Europe to a large deficit in the United States and a surplus in Europe. The IMF has had to adapt its policies to the new situation. This has involved three major steps: giving members greater assurance of access to IMF resources, increasing the quotas of members, and strengthening the liquidity of the IMF. Policies on drawings were gradually liberalized. A general increase in quotas by 50 per cent was made in 1959–1960 and by another 25 per cent in 1966. But these quota increases could not of themselves increase the liquidity of the IMF sufficiently to give members assurance of being able to make drawings within their quota limits.

Because the IMF provides resources to its members in specific currencies, it must have enough of the currencies of the surplus countries to cover an adequate proportion of the undrawn quotas of members that may have deficits. So long as the United States was a surplus country, the IMF was well supplied with currencies on which its members could draw, particularly with its conservative policy on drawings. After the United States became a deficit country in 1958, net drawings on the IMF in dollars would have meant that the United States was financing the payments of other deficit countries. If the IMF was to be the means through which surplus countries financed the deficit countries, it had to increase its holdings of the currencies of the surplus countries of continental Europe. This could not be done merely through a general increase in quotas, as the larger holdings of the surplus currencies would be matched proportionately by the larger drawing rights of deficit countries. A reasonable differential increase in the quotas of the continental European countries would have strengthened the liquidity of the IMF, but not sufficiently.

The IMF's need for the currencies of the surplus countries was greatly increased by the restoration of currency convertibility in Europe, the easier movement of short-term funds between the major financial centers, and the growth of foreign holdings of U.S. dollars. An economic or political crisis anywhere in the world could touch off a large-scale flight from the dollar and from sterling that would require resources far greater than those of the IMF. To avoid a breakdown of the international payments system in a crisis, the IMF needed access to massive credits from all potential surplus countries. At the annual meeting of the IMF in 1961, the United States took the initiative in discussions designed to assure the IMF supplementary resources in time of need. An agreement—General Arrangements to Borrow (GAB)—was reached by ten countries (International Monetary Fund 1962, pp. 234–245) to provide $6,000 million of their currencies to the IMF under specified conditions if needed to forestall or cope with an impairment of the international monetary system. By September 1966, the IMF had borrowed nearly $1,000 million under GAB.

With the convertibility of European currencies, the freer movement of short-term funds among the major financial centers made it desirable for the United States to undertake forward and spot exchange transactions to offset exchange rate movements which could disrupt the exchange market and result in a drain on U.S. gold reserves. The policy of intervention in the exchange market, which had been common prior to the war, was resumed in 1961. To facilitate these exchange operations, the Federal Reserve entered into reciprocal currency arrangements (swaps) with the Group of Ten, Austria, Switzerland, and the Bank for International Settlements under which they agreed to provide their currencies against dollars and the Federal Reserve undertook to provide dollars against their currencies. At the end of September 1966, the reciprocal currency arrangements provided for aggregate U.S. swaps of $4,500 million (see Federal Reserve Bank of New York).

The United States has drawn on the IMF to meet its own needs and to facilitate the use of dollars in repayments to the IMF. Dollar-holding countries repaying drawings on the IMF must do so in gold or in the convertible currency of a member country whose currency is held by the IMF in an amount less than 75 per cent of that member's quota. Until 1958, virtually all drawings and repayments in currency were in dollars. After the United States made drawings on the IMF to meet part of its own payments deficit, IMF holdings of dollars exceeded 75 per cent of the quota, and dollars could no longer be used for repayments. To enable dollar-holding countries to repay the IMF, the United States has drawn European currencies and Canadian dollars, which are eligible for repayments to the IMF, and has exchanged these currencies for dollars. Such drawings and repayments do not affect IMF holdings of eligible currencies and are therefore regarded as technical drawings. They do increase IMF holdings of dollars and reduce its holdings of the currencies of the repaying countries.

Because the currencies of members of the IMF are defined in terms of gold, and gold is used for the settlement of international balances, confidence in currencies requires assurance that the official price of gold in monetary transactions, $35 an ounce, will be maintained. Private trading in gold is common in the Far East, the Middle East, and in some European countries. The price of gold in these markets reflects speculative attitudes toward local currencies as well as the persistent demand for gold for hoarding. The London gold market, which had been closed at the beginning of the war, was reopened in 1954. This is a dollar market, as buyers must acquire the sterling for gold purchases with dollars. Gold supplies for this market come mainly from South Africa and the Soviet Union. In October 1960, the price of gold in the London market rose to more than $40 an ounce. Such a rise in the price of gold could seriously impair confidence in the major currencies and undermine the international payments system. For this reason, the central banks of eight countries agreed to share the responsibility for maintaining an orderly gold market in London, supplying gold when demand exceeds supply and absorbing gold when supply exceeds demand. The share of the United States in this arrangement (the London gold pool) is 50 per cent. The pool has succeeded in avoiding excessive fluctuations in the price of gold. This has held down speculation, although it has facilitated the accumulation of gold in hoards.

**Providing for the growth of reserves.** International monetary reserves consist of gold; dollars, sterling, and other foreign exchange; and net creditor claims (the gold tranche) on the IMF, which have some of the characteristics of reserves. The world monetary system is basically the gold exchange standard, supplemented and strengthened by the IMF. The gold exchange standard has been subject to periodic criticism and re-examination since the 1920s. The attitude of most countries toward it has been ambivalent. On the one hand, it is regarded as necessary to provide reserves for a growing world economy in which the increase of monetary gold is inadequate. On the other hand, it is criticized as limiting the self-corrective features of the automatic gold standard and imparting an inflationary bias to the world economy. In particular, it is said that because reserve centers can finance a substantial part of their payments deficits through the accumulation of their currencies by foreign monetary authorities, they can delay corrective measures to restore their payments position. While the gold exchange standard has worked well in the postwar period, it involves risks that could seriously weaken the international monetary system.

The gold exchange standard is not a reliable method of providing monetary reserves. The monetary reserves of all countries outside the communist bloc have increased from $13,000 million in 1928 to about $70,000 million in 1966, of which over $6,000 million is in net creditor claims (gold tranche) on the IMF. This growth of reserves, although adequate for the period as a whole, has been the result of fortuitous conditions that cannot recur. The general devaluation of currencies from 1931 to 1937 increased the dollar price of gold by 70 per cent. Because of this, gold reserves rose from about $10,000 million in 1928 to over $25,000 million in 1937. Without the revaluation of gold, the gold reserves of $41,000 million in 1966 would have been worth only $24,000 million, even if the same volume of gold had gone into monetary reserves. From 1939 to 1945, monetary reserves in sterling increased by about £3 billion U.K. as the United Kingdom paid for much of its overseas military expenditures in sterling. Finally, from 1950 to 1966, monetary reserves in dollars increased by about $10,000 million as foreign monetary authorities accumulated dollars in settlement of U.S. payments deficits. The growth of foreign exchange reserves cannot continue at such a rate. There has been no increase in monetary reserves in sterling since 1951, and the world cannot be expected to absorb dollars in monetary reserves on the scale of recent years.

The U.S. payments deficit was the principal source of the increase in monetary reserves from 1958 to 1966. The gold reserves of all countries outside the communist bloc increased by about $4,000 million in this period, while foreign exchange reserves increased by about $6,000 million, mainly in dollars. Once the U.S. payments position is restored, there will be little or no increase in monetary reserves in the form of foreign exchange.

The increase of monetary reserves will then have to come almost wholly from newly mined gold and from gold sales of the Soviet Union not absorbed by industrial uses or by private hoards. From 1960 to 1966, the increase in gold reserves, including those of the IMF, has averaged about $500 million a year—slightly more than one per cent of total gold reserves and about three-fourths of one per cent of total monetary reserves. The reserve needs of the world cannot be met out of increments of monetary gold and should not be met by much larger accumulations of foreign exchange.

The growth of foreign exchange reserves has sharply changed the composition of the world's monetary reserves. In 1937, gold constituted 91 per cent of total monetary reserves of all countries outside the communist bloc. In 1949, gold constituted 76 per cent of total monetary reserves, excluding net creditor claims on the IMF (gold tranche). In 1966, gold constituted 64 per cent of the total of such monetary reserves. Since gold is the only ultimate reserve asset and since foreign exchange holdings are convertible into gold, the steady growth in foreign exchange reserves relative to gold exposes the world to the danger of a monetary crisis if there should be a flight from dollars and sterling into gold. It is essential to have a more rational system of providing for the growth of monetary reserves and to reduce the present sensitivity of the world economy to gold as the ultimate reserve asset.

Robert Triffin has proposed (1960) that the reserve system be reformed by changing the IMF into a world central bank. The present net positions of members of the IMF would be converted into deposits for creditor countries and loans for debtor countries. Members would be required to hold part of their reserves as deposits at the IMF, denominated in an international currency unit. These deposits could be made from existing holdings of dollars and sterling. No further reserves would be created in foreign exchange, and present reserves in the form of dollars and sterling would gradually be liquidated. The future growth of reserves would take place through loans and investments of the IMF. As it would be very difficult to maintain a large revolving portfolio of short-term loans, primary reliance for the growth of reserves would have to be placed on investments, much as the Federal Reserve increases bank reserves through the purchase of U.S. government securities. Maxwell Stamp, formerly an adviser to the Bank of England, has proposed that the investments of the IMF be in bonds of the World Bank or other development agencies, thus linking the creation of reserves with the financing of development (Stamp et al. 1965).

Another proposal for providing monetary reserves suggests the creation of a new reserve asset, the Reserve Unit, backed by the currencies of the leading countries and having a guaranteed value in gold (Bernstein 1963). Each participating country would deposit an agreed amount of its own currency with the IMF, which would act as trustee, and would receive in return a corresponding amount of Reserve Units. The participation of each country would be based on its quota in the IMF, perhaps supplemented by its commitment under GAB. In order to assure the acceptability of the Reserve Units, the participants would initially be limited to a group of ten or fifteen countries whose currencies have unquestioned standing in world finance. Other countries would become participants in the issue of Reserve Units as the acceptability of their currencies for backing the new reserve asset is established. To enable all countries to share equitably in the creation of reserves, the participating countries would provide the IMF with their own currencies for use in its operations, in the same proportion to the issue of Reserve Units that the quotas of the nonparticipating countries bear to the total quotas of the IMF. The issue of Reserve Units could be at a rate that would assure an adequate but not excessive increase in aggregate monetary reserves. Reserve Units could be used either alone or with gold and dollars in the settlement of international balances. Variant forms of the Reserve Unit plan have been proposed by Robert V. Roosa, former Under Secretary of the U.S. Treasury for Monetary Affairs (1965), and by a committee of experts of the United Nations (United Nations Conference . . . 1965). The report of this committee (the UNCTAD proposal) envisaged the participation of all members of the IMF in the issuance of Reserve Units and the use of the principal currencies backing the Reserve Units for financing development.

Another method of providing for the growth of reserves would be to increase the resources of the IMF and to give members assured access to these resources through special drawing rights, which could qualify as reserves. Whatever method of creating reserves is adopted, it is essential to strengthen the IMF in order to enable it to perform its functions as the central institution for international monetary cooperation and the principal agency concerned with international monetary reserves. If the issue of Reserve Units is to have a truly international basis some means must be found for placing the administration and management of the system in the IMF, with all its members sharing directly or indirectly in the new reserves that are created.

**Coordination of national monetary policies.** International monetary cooperation includes the provision of credits, the setting of monetary standards, and the coordination of national monetary policies. Central banks of the leading countries have always been generous in providing short-term credits to one another to meet temporary needs in a period of crisis. With the establishment of the IMF these financial needs have been met systematically on a relatively large scale and under more liberal repayment provisions.

While countries have generally been in agreement on what constituted appropriate international monetary standards, these were not codified and made into an international obligation until the establishment of the IMF. Standards for international behavior on exchange rates, on exchange control, and on currency convertibility are part of the statutes of the IMF. Despite the difficulty in securing complete conformity with these standards, they have been very helpful in maintaining an orderly international monetary system.

Much the most difficult aspect of international monetary cooperation is the coordination of national monetary policies. The maintenance of a balanced pattern of international payments is a responsibility of both deficit and surplus countries. Obviously, it is of great importance that the measures taken by the large industrial countries should be harmonious and that they should be conducive to monetary stability. These countries have accepted the principle that their policies should be subject to multilateral surveillance. The Organization for Economic Cooperation and Development, which includes all of the large industrial countries except the Soviet bloc, undertakes a regular review of the economic situation and the economic policies of the participating countries. In time, these discussions may lead to an accepted code of responsibilities for deficit and for surplus countries in restoring and maintaining a balanced pattern of international payments.

EDWARD M. BERNSTEIN

### BIBLIOGRAPHY

AUBOIN, ROGER 1955 *The Bank for International Settlements, 1930–1955.* Princeton Univ., Department of Economics and Sociology, International Finance Section.

BAGEHOT, WALTER (1873) 1927 *Lombard Street: A Description of the Money Market.* New ed. Edited by Hartley Withers. London: Murray. → A paperback edition was published in 1962 by Irwin.

BERNSTEIN, EDWARD M. 1963 A Practical Program for International Monetary Reserves. Model, Roland & Co., *Quarterly Review* [1963] Fourth Quarter: 1–8.

BLOOMFIELD, ARTHUR I. 1959 *Monetary Policy Under the International Gold Standard, 1880–1914.* New York: Federal Reserve Bank.

BROWN, WILLIAM A. JR. 1940 *The International Gold Standard Reinterpreted, 1914–1939.* 2 vols. New York: National Bureau of Economic Research.

CASSEL, GUSTAV 1922 *Money and Foreign Exchange After 1914.* New York: Macmillan.

FEDERAL RESERVE BANK OF NEW YORK *Monthly Review of Credit and Business Conditions.* → See especially the September 1966 issue, which includes "Treasury and Federal Reserve Foreign Exchange Operations," by Charles Coombs.

GILBERT, MILTON 1966 *Problems of the International Monetary System.* Princeton Univ., Department of Economics, International Finance Section.

GROUP OF TEN 1965 *Report of the Study Group on the Creation of Reserve Assets.* Washington: Government Printing Office.

GROUP OF TEN 1966 *Communiqué of Ministers and Governors and Report of Deputies.* The Hague: Ministers and Governors of the Group of Ten Countries. → The ministerial meeting of the Group of Ten (Belgium, Canada, France, Germany, Italy, Japan, the Netherlands, Sweden, the United Kingdom, and the United States) was held July 25–26, 1966, in The Hague.

HANSEN, ALVIN H. 1965 *The Dollar and the International Monetary System.* New York: McGraw-Hill.

HARROD, ROY 1965 *Reforming the World's Money.* New York: McGraw-Hill.

*International Monetary Arrangements: The Problem of Choice; Report on the Deliberations of an International Study Group of 32 Economists,* by Fritz Machlup et al. 1964 Princeton Univ., Department of Economics, International Finance Section.

INTERNATIONAL MONETARY FUND 1962 *Annual Report.* Washington: The Fund. → See also the other annual reports and especially Chapter 2 of the 1966 volume.

KEYNES, JOHN MAYNARD 1933 *The Means to Prosperity.* New York: Harcourt.

LEAGUE OF NATIONS 1932 *Report of the Gold Delegation of the Financial Committee.* Geneva: The League.

NATIONAL INDUSTRIAL CONFERENCE BOARD 1966 *Gold and World Monetary Problems.* New York: Macmillan.

RASMINSKY, LOUIS 1948 Report on the International Monetary Fund. Volume 1, pages 864–913 in United Nations Monetary and Financial Conference, Bretton Woods, New Hampshire, 1944, *Proceedings and Documents.* Washington: Government Printing Office.

ROOSA, ROBERT V. 1965 *Monetary Reform for the World Economy.* New York: Harper.

RUSSELL, HENRY B. 1898 *International Monetary Conferences.* New York: Harper.

STAMP, MAXWELL; TRIFFIN, ROBERT; and BERNSTEIN, EDWARD M. 1965 The Reform of the International Monetary System. *Moorgate and Wall Street* [1965], Summer.

TRIFFIN, ROBERT (1960) 1961 *Gold and the Dollar Crisis: The Future of Convertibility.* Rev. ed. New Haven: Yale Univ. Press.

UNITED NATIONS CONFERENCE ON TRADE AND DEVELOPMENT, GENEVA, *1964* 1965 *International Monetary Issues and the Developing Countries: Report of the Group of Experts.* New York: United Nations.

U.S. TREASURY DEPARTMENT 1948 Preliminary Draft Outline of a Proposal for an International Stabilization Fund of the United and Associated Nations. Volume 2, pages 1597–1615 in United Nations Monetary and Financial Conference, Bretton Woods,

New Hampshire, 1944, *Proceedings and Documents*. Washington: Government Printing Office. → See also the texts of a proposal for an International Clearing Union (United Kingdom) and for an International Exchange Union (Canada) in Volume 2, pages 1548–1573 and pages 1575–1596.

WILLIS, HENRY P. 1901 *A History of the Latin Monetary Union: A Study of International Monetary Action.* Univ. of Chicago Press.

## IV
### PRIVATE INTERNATIONAL CAPITAL MOVEMENTS

Private international capital movements are transactions that create or transfer financial claims between the residents of different countries. The participants are banks, individuals, and corporations. The claims are common stock, bonds, money-market instruments, deeds to real property, promissory notes, and bank deposits.

A capital-exporting country is one that obtains new claims on foreigners larger than its new liabilities; its citizens use current savings to acquire foreign assets, not just for domestic capital formation. A capital-importing country is one that incurs new liabilities larger than its new foreign claims; it draws on foreign savings to supplement its own. A creditor country is one whose total foreign claims exceed its total foreign debts. A debtor country is one whose total foreign debts exceed its total foreign claims. The United States is a net creditor and an exporter of private capital. It was also a net creditor in the 1930s but was importing capital rather than exporting it: its total foreign claims were larger than its foreign debts, but it was repatriating its past investments. The United States was a net debtor before 1914 but exported capital between 1896 and 1914; it was repaying its past foreign borrowings.

## Components

Most governments classify capital movements by maturity, separating "long-term" and "short-term" foreign claims. But this method of classification does not reveal very much about investors' motives. Stocks and bonds (long-term claims) may be bought to make quick gains, while three-month commercial loans (short-term claims) may resemble long-term credit because they are renewed repeatedly. Furthermore, long-term bonds may be bought near redemption, to serve as close substitutes for money-market paper.

The following method of classification, using U.S. data for purposes of illustration, may be more illuminating.

**Direct investments.** Direct investments are international transactions between related enter-

### Table 1 — U.S. private capital exports, 1962 (millions of dollars)

| | | |
|---|---:|---:|
| Total private foreign investment | | 4,475 |
| Direct investment (including reinvestment) | | 2,759 |
| Purchases of long-term foreign securities (net) | | 961 |
| Purchases of new foreign issues | 1,076 | |
| Purchases of outstanding issues (net) | 55 | |
| *Less* redemptions of foreign issues | − 170 | |
| Other long-term lending and investment (net) | | 248 |
| Short-term investment (net) | | 507 |
| In short-term dollar claims (net) | 487 | |
| In short-term foreign-currency claims (net) | 20 | |

*Sources: Based on data in U.S. Department of Commerce 1963a and 1963b.*

prises—"parent" companies and their foreign affiliates. Direct investment starts when a firm creates a new foreign affiliate or buys a controlling interest in an established foreign firm. Direct investment continues as the parent buys more stock in its affiliate, reinvests its profits, or makes loans to its affiliate. The affiliate may be separately incorporated under foreign law (a subsidiary), or a simple extension of its parent (a branch). It may compete with its parent, making the same product for sale abroad, or may complement its parent, producing components or raw materials. In some cases, several firms may share a foreign affiliate; the Iraq Petroleum Company is jointly owned by British, Dutch, French, and American companies. In other cases, one firm may exercise control; this arrangement dominates in manufacturing and the service trades.

In recent years direct investment has accounted for over half of private American foreign investment (see Table 1), and for three-fifths of total U.S. private foreign claims (see Table 2).

### Table 2 — U.S. private foreign assets, 1962 (millions of dollars)

| | | |
|---|---:|---:|
| Total private foreign assets | | 59,810 |
| Direct investments | | 37,145 |
| Mining and smelting | 3,183 | |
| Petroleum | 12,661 | |
| Manufacturing | 13,212 | |
| Public utilities, trade, and other | 8,089 | |
| Other long-term claims | | 15,431 |
| Foreign dollar bonds | 6,373 | |
| Other foreign securities | 5,429 | |
| Bank loans and other long-term claims | 3,629 | |
| Short-term claims | | 7,234 |
| Bank loans and acceptance credits* | 3,877 | |
| Supplier credits and other dollar claims* | 2,445 | |
| Foreign currency claims | 912 | |

* Division estimated.

*Sources: Based on data in U.S. Department of Commerce 1963b; and [U.S.] Board of Governors of the Federal Reserve System 1963.*

**Portfolio investments.** Transactions in stocks, bonds, and money-market instruments, involving independent firms or individuals, are classified as portfolio investments. Bank deposits should also be included here, being close substitutes for short-term securities. New issues of foreign securities are the chief component of American portfolio investment, but purchases of "seasoned" securities are also large (see Table 1). Most foreign bonds sold in New York are denominated in U.S. dollars, but American investors have also bought securities valued in other currencies, such as Canadian and European stocks and bonds and British treasury bills.

Transactions in government securities lie on the edge of private portfolio investment. Most statisticians treat capital as "private" if the lender is an individual, bank, or corporation. They treat capital as "public" if the lender is a government or intergovernmental institution. Thus American purchases of World Bank bonds are treated as private capital, while World Bank loans to private enterprise are treated as public capital. The dollar bank deposits of foreign governments are likewise treated as public capital, even though the debtor is a private institution.

**Bank loans and supplier credits.** Major banks have always made short-term loans to foreigners. Recently, however, commercial banks have also made long-term loans, some of them for five years or more. Supplier credit is also familiar to foreign trade and finance, and may be growing in volume and duration.

Bank lending differs from portfolio investment because the lender cannot ordinarily sell his claims prior to maturity. In one important case, moreover, the lender does not even transfer cash to the foreign borrower: When a British bank supplies "acceptance credit," it endorses a foreigner's promise to pay. The bank thereby enables a British exporter to sell his goods for cash—to sell off a foreigner's promissory note. The buyer of the foreign bill puts up the cash but has recourse to the bank that has endorsed the foreign note. London was the chief source of bank loans and acceptance credit prior to World War II, but New York has outdistanced London in the last few years. At the end of 1962, U.S. bank loans and acceptance credits totaled $3,900 million (see Table 2).

Major manufacturers also finance foreign sales without recourse to banks. They provide supplier credits that range to several months or years. Short-term supplier credits are quite common; they arise whenever an exporter delivers goods before taking payment. But other supplier credits are longer and more formal, with scheduled repayments. Data on supplier credits are very scarce; few countries collect any statistics on the business claims and debts of foreigners. But these credits may be large and are most surely volatile. Several writers have described huge "leads and lags" in international payments—variations in cash flows relative to trade flows, resulting from changes in total supplier credit.

## Magnitude

Private investment has played a major role in the evolution of the world economy. In the nineteenth century, it opened up the vast interior of the United States and other regions for new settlement. It aided economic reconstruction after World War I, then made a larger contribution to the international financial collapse of the 1930s. Private investment grew large again in the 1950s, propelling the economic integration of the Atlantic economy and aiding development at the periphery. But the source, destination, and composition of private capital were different in each period.

**Before World War II.** Britain was the world's largest foreign investor in the nineteenth century. By 1914, her overseas assets totaled $18,000 million (see Table 3). France and Germany also supplied capital, but on a smaller scale.

### Table 3 — Value of major foreign investments, 1913–1914 (millions of dollars)

| Investments by: | | Investments in: | |
|---|---|---|---|
| United Kingdom | 18,000 | Europe | 12,000 |
| France | 9,000 | North America | 10,500 |
| Germany | 5,800 | Latin America | 8,500 |
| United States | 3,500 | Asia | 6,000 |
| Other countries | 7,700 | Other countries | 7,000 |
| Total | 44,000 | Total | 44,000 |

Source: Adapted from North 1962, p. 24.

British claims included important direct investments, but most British assets were foreign bonds. Britain made large loans to foreign governments, then made larger loans to private enterprise. In the third quarter of the nineteenth century "financing governments *per se* appeared less attractive than financing productive enterprises. Railroads were the great favorite, and European capital was often coupled with European emigrants, entrepreneurs, and engineering talent in the construction of overseas railroads" (North 1962, p. 15).

Some European capital went to the tropics—to the less developed countries of our own day. But these investments were quite small compared to those in the newly settled temperate-zone areas and were less successful in fostering development (Nurkse 1961, p. 136).

**The interwar period.**    Britain continued to export capital in the 1920s but was overtaken by the United States. The United States began to repay its own debts after 1896 and became a net creditor during World War I, when the Allied Powers sold off most of their dollar assets to buy war materiel.

Although U.S. direct investment was quite large, U.S. foreign lending was still larger. In 1924–1928, $5,700 million of foreign securities were issued in New York. Germany sold a full $1,100 million; Canada and Latin America accounted for $2,300 million. After 1928, the United States ceased exporting capital (see Table 4). Repayments on old loans overtook new lending, and European funds sought safe haven in the United States. In fact, every major supplier of capital became a net importer in 1930–1938; the debtor countries were hard pressed to meet their obligations and many were compelled to default on interest and principal.

**Table 4 — Foreign investment in the interwar period[a]
(millions of dollars)**

|  | 1921–1929 | 1930–1938 |
|---|---|---|
| *Net capital exports:* | | |
| United States | 5,990 | −4,964 |
| United Kingdom | 3,425 | −893 |
| France (to overseas territories) | 3,037 | −94 |
| Other countries[b] | 1,044 | −402 |
|  | *Direct* | *Portfolio* |
| *Value of foreign investments, 1929:* | | |
| United States | 7,500 | 7,100 |
| United Kingdom | 7,900 | 8,900 |

a. Measured by the balance on current account and gold movements; includes public capital.
b. Switzerland, Sweden, and the Netherlands.

Source: Based on data in United Nations 1949.

**The postwar period.**    The United States has made huge foreign investments since World War II. This time, however, direct investment has been larger than new lending; yet U.S. purchases of new foreign securities have grown enormously since 1958. The market for foreign bonds has finally revived, and some observers look for "financial integration" by way of New York (Kindleberger 1963).

Other countries also made new foreign investments in the late 1950s. The creation of the European Common Market inspired large capital movements within western Europe, especially direct investment. In addition, western Europe has supplied impressive sums to the less developed countries (see Table 5). Yet European lenders are still hampered by controls. Although most major currencies are "convertible," many European governments still restrict capital transfers by their own citizens. Very few countries grant free access to their capital markets, and most countries regulate commercial-bank lending to foreigners.

**Table 5 — Flow of long-term capital to the less developed countries, 1961 (millions of dollars)**

|  | United States | Other countries* | Total |
|---|---|---|---|
| Public grants and credits | 3,486 | 2,639 | 6,125 |
| Private capital | 1,218 | 1,957 | 3,175 |
| Direct investment | 970 | 1,186 | 2,156 |
| Other lending | 250 | 661 | 911 |
| Flow through international agencies | − 2 | 110 | 108 |

* Western Europe, Canada, and Japan.

Source: Based on data in Organization for Economic Cooperation and Development 1963.

## Private capital movements and economic welfare

Foreign investment redistributes world savings, allowing more rapid capital formation in countries that borrow and less rapid capital formation in countries that lend. Foreign investment reallocates resources, changing the pattern of output and trade. But economists have been slow to stress these effects; for many years, they treated foreign trade and foreign investment as though there were no connection between them. As Caves puts it:

Classical international trade theory lived apart from the general theory of domestic production and exchange solely because of its assumption that factors of production are immobile among nations. Thus it paradoxically ignored the relations between the international movements of goods and factors, or at best dealt with them in asides about "colonial trade," in the century of the greatest international factor movements of modern times.    (1960, p. 121)

**The classical analysis.**    Although economic theory did not connect trade and investment, it used very similar methods and models to explain both of them. In each case, it sought to assess the impact on world output and income. Thus, the case for free trade evolved from a demonstration that free trade would permit specialization, allowing every country to make the best use of its resources. With pure competition everywhere, the return to capital (the interest rate) would equal the "marginal product" of capital—the contribution of the last dollar of capital to local output and income. If, then, one country had higher interest rates and attracted foreign funds, global output would be increased; capital would have moved to the country where it had the highest productivity and could increase output most.

This theory of capital movements was indifferent to the distribution of income between countries. Yet the allocation of world savings that maximized world output would not necessarily be the "best" for the capital-exporting country. The capital-exporting country would maximize its *own* income by investing less abroad and more at home than required to achieve maximum world income (Jasay 1960). But the classical theory of capital movements, like classical trade theory, was "cosmopolitan"; it barely explored this sort of conflict.

**The factor-endowments analysis.** The analyses of foreign trade and foreign investment were not fully integrated until economic theory had connected foreign trade to the international distribution of capital, labor, and natural resources. This approach to trade theory argues that specialization and trade result from perceptible differences in national endowments. Countries that are short of capital will import capital-intensive goods; countries that are short of labor will import labor-intensive goods. A capital shortage will be reflected in the return on capital (the interest rate), and capital-intensive products will be relatively costly. A country with a capital shortage will therefore import capital-intensive products and will export other goods. Hence, trade will substitute for capital movements, relieving capital scarcity where it is most severe and reducing interest rate disparities. Conversely, international capital movements will alter foreign trade because they will make endowments more similar and will level interest rate differences.

But carried to its logical conclusion, modern theory reaches an anomalous conclusion: If there is pure competition and free trade, there will not be any foreign investment. In the models most often used to analyze foreign trade, free trade will *equalize* all factor prices, including interest rates, removing the motive for capital movements. In consequence, the theory of capital movements has become an austere catalogue of reasons for predicting imperfect factor-price equalization (see for example, Meade 1955, part 3). Capital movements will occur only when there are trade barriers or when certain standard assumptions are violated.

Trade theory has another puzzling implication: Mundell has shown that trade barriers could evoke capital that would be completely destructive of trade (Caves 1960, p. 124). If private capital will move to obliterate differences in interest rates, the smallest trade barrier will become prohibitive. Tariffs or transport costs will alter relative interest

rates, causing capital to flow. The capital transfer will not cease until it has brought interest rates back to equality. When this has happened, however, costs of production will also be equalized, and there can be no more trade.

The factor-endowments approach to trade theory can be reformulated to forecast trade *and* investment. The necessary modification was suggested some years ago (Iversen 1935, p. 26). Trade theories usually calculate the interest rate from the rental income on capital goods (machinery, etc.). They should instead perceive that every factor of production embodies some capital and that all factor payments include some interest. This same point is also stressed by recent writers on investment in humans. [*See* CAPITAL, HUMAN.] If this more general concept of capital were used, trade theory would no longer forecast equal interest rates under free trade and would not preclude capital movements (Kenen 1965).

**The taxation of foreign-source income.** If private investment is to foster an efficient international allocation of capital, it must fulfill the classical injunction, transferring capital from countries where its productivity is low to countries where its productivity is high. In actual fact, however, investors respond to the after-tax return on capital, not to the pretax return, which reflects productivity. Hence, substantial differences in national tax rates will distort the international allocation of capital.

Differences in tax rates are quite large and are sometimes reinforced by differences in definitions of income (U.S. Congress 1962, part 1, p. 179), although tax treaties and national tax policies offset or overlay some of the differences. Many governments have entered into bilateral tax treaties that forestall the "double taxation" of foreign-source income. Under these treaties, each government forgoes its right to tax income earned in the other, or allows its own citizens a tax credit for their payments to the other. The United States goes much further, granting a tax credit for all income taxes paid to other governments in respect to income earned abroad.

Yet the U.S. tax system is not completely neutral. American corporations do not pay U.S. taxes on income from subsidiaries until they receive that income in dividends. Hence, they can defer their U.S. taxes by reinvesting income earned abroad. Even if it were completely neutral, moreover, it might still be imperfect. When two tax systems differ only in their rates, tax credits impose "export neutrality" on investors in the high-tax country (Musgrave 1960, pp. 84–85). They face the same total tax bill whether they invest at home or abroad. Yet export neutrality does not ensure efficient allocation if companies can shift their taxes onto their customers by charging higher prices. In this case, "import neutrality" would be needed to achieve an efficient allocation of capital. On this principle, all firms producing for a single market would be taxed at the same rate, no matter where their owners lived. Unfortunately, one cannot secure both kinds of neutrality unless all tax rates are the same.

Although many countries seek export neutrality in their taxation of foreign-source income, several have departed from this principle to stimulate private investment in the less developed countries. The United States has considered a special tax credit for U.S. firms investing in Latin America and other low-income areas. Other governments give similar concessions.

## Private capital movements and financial policy

There are two ways to finance an export of capital—with compensating movements of public capital, including gold and foreign-exchange reserves, or with compensating movements of goods and services. As government financing is necessarily limited, a continuing capital outflow must be offset by an increased net transfer of goods or services.

**The transfer problem.** Few international financial problems have had more study than those involved in transferring capital by changing the flow of trade. Ricardo, Thornton, Cairnes, and other early writers give complete descriptions of the "transfer problem." Later economists reviewed the same issues in the debate on reparations after World War I (Iversen 1935, chapter 5). But modern transfer theory differs from its antecedents because it employs the new tools furnished by macroeconomic analysis. It concludes that capital movements will induce some trade changes but warns that these may not suffice to offset the entire transfer of capital (Meade 1951, pp. 88–94). A financial transfer from one country to another will depress aggregate expenditure in the capital-exporting country and will augment aggregate expenditure in the capital-importing country. These changes in spending will decrease the imports and increase the exports of the capital-exporting country. But the change in its trade balance may not be as large as the capital flow. In this case, public policy must impose secondary changes in total spending or must allow exchange rate changes.

Transfer analysis can also be used to study repatriation. Had this been done in the 1920s, the international financial crisis of the 1930s might

not have been so severe. Because few borrowers looked to the problems of repayment, too few were ready to service all their debts when foreign lending came to an end. Similar problems exist today. Many of the less developed countries may be too heavily burdened by foreign debt (Avramovic & Gulhati 1960). But the new transfer problem differs from its predecessors because direct investment has been relatively large and this type of investment need not be repaid on a fixed schedule. Furthermore, direct-investment income tends to rise and fall along with the host country's total foreign earnings. When, therefore, earnings are high and dividends have to be paid, foreign-exchange receipts may also be high, allowing easy transfer.

**Direct investment and overseas production.** But standard transfer analysis ignores a host of major problems connected with direct investment. The output of direct-investment affiliates may compete with exports by the parent company and may re-enter the parent's home market. Hence, direct investment can generate complex payments problems and can cause major changes in the structure of employment. American companies already manufacture more abroad than they export from the United States, and their output has been growing very fast. Furthermore, direct-investment enterprises can account for a substantial share of output and employment in the host country (Dunning 1958, chapter 2).

**Interest rates and capital movements.** The recent increases of portfolio investment and of U.S. short-term lending have given rise to new research on the influence of interest rates. One comprehensive study (Bell 1962) assigned them a small role. But other studies (U.S. Congress 1963, pp. 153–208) take a rather different view. They contend that some flows are quite interest-sensitive, responding to the key rates in New York, London, and the "Eurodollar" market.

If interest rates are this influential, governments may be compelled to regard monetary policy as an international financial instrument and forgo its application to domestic aims. [See MONETARY POLICY.] They may sometimes be able to control capital exports by intervening in the foreign-exchange market; by altering the costs of "forward" foreign-exchange transactions, they can offset interest rate differences (Einzig 1961, chapters 32, 44–46). But many governments balk at systematic intervention, fearing that they would invite speculative flows. Furthermore, many capital transfers do not involve forward transactions and would not be halted by changes in the cost of forward cover (U.S. Congress 1963, pp. 156–158).

**Exchange rates and capital movements.** Speculative capital flows were very large in the 1920s and have reappeared in the postwar period. They can take many forms, ranging from "leads and lags" in commercial payments on through outright purchases of foreign securities. At one time, most economists held that speculation would be destabilizing. They favored fixed exchange rates to discourage speculation. As Nurkse put it:

Anticipatory purchases of foreign exchange tend to produce or at any rate to hasten the anticipated fall in the exchange value of the national currency, and the actual fall may set up or strengthen expectations in a further fall. The dangers of such cumulative and self-aggravating movements under a regime of freely fluctuating exchanges are clearly demonstrated by the French experience of 1922–26. Exchange rates in such circumstances are bound to become highly unstable, and the influence of psychological factors may at times be overwhelming. (League of Nations 1944, p. 118)

But some economists take the opposite view—that fixed exchange rates are more likely to induce destabilizing speculation. Under fixed exchange rates, speculators can assault a weak currency too easily because they are not penalized for error. If they are proved wrong, they can reverse their positions at very little cost. With flexible exchange rates, by contrast, errors could be very expensive. Speculators might be compelled to buy a currency at a higher price than the one at which they sold it. Critics of the present system also argue that exchange-rate changes would be self-limiting if the exchange rate were free to fluctuate (Meade 1951, chapter 17). As the price of a currency falls, it becomes a bargain and speculators will begin to buy it, halting the price decline. But this argument implies that speculators use some notion of "normality" to judge exchange-rate variations. In the absence of strong views as to the "normal" rate, speculation could still be destabilizing.

PETER B. KENEN

### BIBLIOGRAPHY

AVRAMOVIC, DRAGOSLAV; and GULHATI, RAVI 1960 *Debt Servicing Problems of Low Income Countries, 1956–1958.* Baltimore: Johns Hopkins Press; Oxford Univ. Press.

BELL, PHILIP W. 1962 Private Capital Movements and the U.S. Balance-of-Payments Position. Pages 395–481 in U.S. Congress, Joint Economic Committee, *Factors Affecting the U.S. Balance of Payments.* 87th Congress, 2d Session. Washington: Government Printing Office.

BLOOMFIELD, ARTHUR I. 1963 *Short-term Capital Movements Under the Pre-1914 Gold Standard.* Princeton Studies in International Finance, No. 11. Princeton Univ. Press.

CAVES, RICHARD E. 1960 *Trade and Economic Structure: Models and Methods.* Harvard Economic Studies, Vol. 115. Cambridge, Mass.: Harvard Univ. Press.

DOMAR, EVSEY D. 1950 The Effects of Foreign Investment on the Balance of Payments. *American Economic Review* 40:805–826.

DUNNING, JOHN H. 1958 *American Investment in British Manufacturing Industry.* New York: Essential Books; London: Allen & Unwin.

EINZIG, PAUL 1961 *A Dynamic Theory of Forward Exchange.* New York: St. Martins; London: Macmillan.

IVERSEN, CARL (1935) 1936 *Aspects of the Theory of International Capital Movements.* 2d ed. Oxford Univ. Press.

JASAY, A. E. 1960 The Social Choice Between Home and Overseas Investment. *Economic Journal* 70:105–113.

KENEN, PETER B. 1965 Nature, Capital and Trade. *Journal of Political Economy* 73:437–460.

KINDLEBERGER, CHARLES P. 1963 European Economic Integration and the Development of a Single Financial Center for Long-term Capital. *Weltwirtschaftliches Archiv* 90:189–210. → Contains summaries in French and German.

LEAGUE OF NATIONS, SECRETARIAT, FINANCIAL SECTION AND ECONOMIC INTELLIGENCE SERVICE 1944 *International Currency Experience: Lessons of the Inter-war Period,* by Ragnar Nurkse. Geneva: League of Nations.

MEADE, JAMES EDWARD 1951 *The Theory of International Economic Policy.* Volume 1: Balance of Payments. Oxford Univ. Press.

MEADE, JAMES EDWARD 1955 *The Theory of International Economic Policy.* Volume 2: Trade and Welfare. Oxford Univ. Press.

MIKESELL, RAYMOND F. (editor) 1962 *U.S. Private and Government Investment Abroad.* Eugene: Univ. of Oregon.

MUSGRAVE, RICHARD A. 1960 Criteria for Foreign Tax Credit. Pages 83–93 in Tax Institute of America, *Taxation and Operations Abroad.* A symposium conducted by the Institute, Dec. 3–4, 1959. Princeton, N.J.: The Institute.

NORTH, DOUGLASS C. 1962 International Capital Movements in Historical Perspective. Pages 10–43 in Raymond F. Mikesell (editor), *U.S. Private and Government Investment Abroad.* Eugene: Univ. of Oregon.

NURKSE, RAGNAR 1961 *Equilibrium and Growth in the World Economy: Economic Essays.* Edited by Gottfried Haberler and Robert M. Stern. Harvard Economic Studies, Vol. 118. Cambridge, Mass.: Harvard Univ. Press.

OHLIN, BERTIL (1933) 1957 *Interregional and International Trade.* Harvard Economic Studies, Vol. 39. Cambridge, Mass.: Harvard Univ. Press.

ORGANIZATION FOR ECONOMIC COOPERATION AND DEVELOPMENT 1963 *The Flow of Financial Resources to Developing Countries in 1961.* Paris: The Organization.

PENROSE, EDITH T. 1956 Foreign Investment and the Growth of the Firm. *Economic Journal* 66:220–235.

SAMUELSON, PAUL A. 1952 The Transfer Problem and Transport Costs: The Terms of Trade When Impediments Are Absent. *Economic Journal* 62:278–304.

UNITED NATIONS, SECRETARIAT 1949 *International Capital Movements During the Inter-war Period.* New York: United Nations. → Also published in French.

[U.S.] BOARD OF GOVERNORS OF THE FEDERAL RESERVE SYSTEM 1963 Consolidated Statement of Condition of All Federal Reserve Banks. *Federal Reserve Bulletin* [1963]:1266–1267.

U.S. CONGRESS, JOINT ECONOMIC COMMITTEE 1963 *Hearings: The United States Balance of Payments.* Part 1: Current Problems and Policies. 88th Congress, 1st Session. Washington: Government Printing Office.

U.S. CONGRESS, SENATE FINANCE COMMITTEE 1962 *Revenue Act of 1962: Hearings.* 87th Congress, 2d Session. Washington: Government Printing Office.

U.S. DEPARTMENT OF COMMERCE, OFFICE OF BUSINESS ECONOMICS 1963a The Balance of International Payments During the First Quarter, 1963. *Survey of Current Business* [1963], June: 17–26.

U.S. DEPARTMENT OF COMMERCE, OFFICE OF BUSINESS ECONOMICS 1963b U.S. International Investments. *Survey of Current Business* [1963], August: 19–22.

# INTERNATIONAL ORGANIZATION

## I
### THE PROCESS AND THE INSTITUTIONS

International organization is the process by which states establish and develop formal, continuing institutional structures for the conduct of certain aspects of their relationships with each other. It represents a reaction to the extreme decentralization of the traditional system of international relations and an effort by statesmen to adapt the mechanics of that system to the requirements posed by the constantly increasing complexity of the interdependence of states. Particular international organizations may be regarded as manifestations of the organizing process on the international level.

### The history of international organization

The process of international organization had its origins in the nineteenth century, largely in Europe. Innovations associated with the rise of industrialism and the introduction of new methods of transport and communication stimulated the creation of special-purpose agencies, usually called public international unions, designed to facilitate the collaboration of governments in dealing with economic, social, and technical problems. Notable among these were the International Telegraphic Union (1865) and the Universal Postal Union (1874), which survived to become specialized agencies of the United Nations system (the former under the title International Telecommunication Union) after World War II. In the political field,

an effort to institutionalize the dominant role of the great powers of Europe was undertaken at the Congress of Vienna in 1815. While the resultant Concert of Europe did not assume the character of a standing political organization, the same pattern functioned until World War I as the framework for a system of occasional great-power conferences which lent some substance to the idea that the European family of states constituted an organized entity. This concept was broadened by the Hague Conferences of 1899 and 1907, which admitted small states as well as great powers, and extra-European as well as European states, to participation in collective political deliberations. Near the end of the nineteenth century, the establishment of the Pan American Union and the initiation of a series of inter-American conferences reinforced the Monroe Doctrine and Simón Bolívar's pronouncements by giving institutional expression to the idea that the states of the Western Hemisphere constituted a distinct subgroup within the larger multistate system.

These nineteenth-century beginnings provided, in large measure, the basis for the phenomenal development of international organization since World War I. Certain distinctions which emerged during this period—between political and non-political agencies, between the status of great powers and that of small states, between regional and geographically undefined organizations—were to prove significant in the later course of international organization. Basic patterns of institutional structure and procedure were evolved. The trend toward broadening the conception of international organization to include entities beyond the confines of the European state system was initiated. Most importantly, the dual motivations of international institution building—(a) the urge to promote coordinated responses by states to the problems of peaceful intercourse in an era of growing economic, social, and technical interdependence, and (b) the recognition of the necessity for moderating conflict in the political and military spheres—became operative in this period.

The establishment of the League of Nations and its affiliate, the International Labour Organisation, at the end of World War I represented the first attempt to combine into one general organization the disparate elements of organizational development which had emerged during the previous century. The League was the first general international organization in several senses: (a) it pulled together the threads of the great-power council, the general conference of statesmen, and the technically oriented international bureau; (*b*) it was a multipurpose organization, although its primary focus was on the political and security problems of war and peace; and (*c*) it was, in principle, a world-wide institution, even though it retained much of the nineteenth-century emphasis upon the centrality of Europe in international affairs.

After World War II, the League was superseded by the United Nations, a general organization which derived its major features from the nineteenth-century heritage and the lessons of experience, both positive and negative, provided by the League. The United Nations was conceived as the central component of a varied and decentralized system of international institutions that would include both autonomous specialized agencies, following the pattern first set by the public international unions, and such regional organizations as existed or might be created by limited groups of states. The organizational design formulated in the United Nations Charter called for the active coordination of the work of the specialized agencies by the central institution, primarily through the agency of its Economic and Social Council, and the utilization and control of regional agencies, largely through the Security Council.

In actuality, the organizational system of the post-World War II era has involved the operation of approximately a dozen specialized agencies, many of them newly created, coordinated with varying degrees of effectiveness by the United Nations. The post-1945 system has also involved the proliferation of regional organizations of every sort, most of them functioning quite independently, without any genuine tie to the central organization. The term "United Nations system" may, therefore, properly be used to refer to the United Nations and the specialized agencies, but it does not embrace the considerable number of regional organizations which have developed independently.

The total network of international institutions also comprises more than one hundred intergovernmental agencies outside the scope of the United Nations system, dealing with a vast range of problems and providing a variety of mechanisms for the conduct of relations among states. These are supplemented by approximately 1,500 nongovernmental organizations which promote international consultation and activity in specialized fields at the unofficial level (*Yearbook of International Organizations* 1962–1963).

### The conceptual basis

The conception of international relations underlying international organization is frequently described as idealistic, in the sense that it minimizes the element of conflict and emphasizes the potentialities of harmony and cooperation in the relationships of states. International organizations are characterized, by supporters and critics alike, as arrangements for cooperation among states. Most accurately, international organization can be said to rest upon a dualistic conception of international relations, one which acknowledges both conflictual and cooperative relationships as basic features of the multistate system. In principle, international organization represents an attempt to minimize conflict and maximize collaboration among participating states, treating conflict as an evil to be controlled and cooperation as a good to be promoted. In these terms, international organization both denies the inevitability of war and other manifestations of hostility among nations and expresses a commitment to the harmonization of international relations.

In fact, a more sophisticated analysis of international organization reveals a much more complex approach to the conflictual and cooperative aspects of international affairs than that described above. Some international agencies are primarily concerned with problems of conflict, while others emphasize the promotion of collaboration: within the United Nations, for instance, the Security Council is illustrative of the former type and the Economic and Social Council of the latter. Moreover, conflicting interests of states intrude upon programs of cooperation, making it necessary for cooperation-oriented agencies to deal with problems of conflict, and the common interests of states provide the means by which conflict-oriented agencies undertake to cope with tendencies toward international disorder. Thus, the North Atlantic Treaty Organization is a regional agency inspired by the East–West conflict after World War II, but it relies upon cooperation among its members to enable it to meet the dangers posed by that conflict. Similarly, the concept of collective security envisages cooperative action by most members of a general international organization as the essential means for deterring or defeating aggression.

It is significant that both the League of Nations and the United Nations were established in the aftermath of major world wars and were conceived primarily as means for preventing the recurrence of such catastrophic struggles; the Charter of the United Nations begins with the expression of determination "to save succeeding generations from the scourge of war, which twice in our lifetime has brought untold sorrow to mankind." General international organization in the twentieth century is a reaction to the grim reality of violent conflict among states and a response to the danger of future conflict. In the United Nations system, preoccupation with the conflictual aspect of international relations is so great that the official ideology requires the formal justification of virtually every cooperative project, however useful it may promise to be in itself, in terms of its putative contribution to the avoidance of war. Article 55 of the United Nations Charter calls for collaborative activity in the economic, social, health, cultural, educational, and human rights fields, "with a view to the creation of conditions of stability and well-being which are necessary for peaceful and friendly relations among nations. . . ." Article 76 lists as the first objective of the United Nations trusteeship system the furtherance of international peace and security Moreover, the functional theory of international organization, which explicitly stresses the development of agencies devoted to cooperative solution of problems in the economic and social realm, is ultimately concerned with the issue of political and military struggle; functionalism treats the promotion of welfare as an indirect approach to the prevention of warfare [see INTERNATIONAL INTEGRATION, *article on* FUNCTIONALISM AND FUNCTIONAL INTEGRATION]. On the whole, international organization has reflected greater concern with the probability of conflict than with the possibility of cooperation.

In the final analysis, governmental leaders of member states impose their conceptions of international relations upon international organization and determine the ends toward which and the means by which international agencies operate. While international institutions tend to some limited degree to develop corporate viewpoints and purposes, usually through professional staff members who identify themselves with the organizations which they serve, these institutions are essentially instruments of their member states. Hence, international organization reflects the variety of viewpoints and purposes which prevails among governments. In the United Nations, a fundamental issue is whether the world organization should serve primarily as a battlefield or a peace conference, an arena for conflict or a chamber for the settlement of disputes. Some statesmen are primarily interested in the waging of political battles and others concentrate more on the mitigation of conflict. Moreover, some leaders give priority to the stimulation of effective international cooperation and treat the organization as a workshop for economic and social collaboration rather than as an agency concerned with conflict. Whether the United Nations emphasizes the conflictual or the cooperative aspects of international relations is determined less by the formal statement of the organization's nature and purpose contained in its charter than by the day-to-day outcome of the political process of the organization, in which members vie with each other for control over the utilization of its mechanism. International organization does not introduce a distinctive conception of international relations but gives expression to whatever viewpoints may be dominant in the international political arena.

This analysis indicates that international organization is essentially a process of developing a new structural and procedural framework for the interplay of national governments within the context of the multistate system. It represents an attempt by statesmen to improve the operation of that system by enhancing the institutional equipment available for the conduct of relations among states and by promoting the general acceptance of standards of state behavior compatible with the minimum requirements of an orderly system. Insofar as international organization represents a reformist movement within the multistate system, it expresses the awareness of national leaders that international order is requisite to the promotion and protection of the most basic interests of their states. The quest for order through international organization does not involve repudiation of national interests or subordination of national interests to an overriding internationalism, but at most it involves the redefinition of national interests in conformity with the demands of increasing interdependence and the commitment of statesmen to the pursuit of those interests within the revised framework provided by international organization. It should occasion no surprise that governments undertake to use international agencies as instruments of their national policies. Such agencies are created and maintained by governments for instrumental purposes, and their usefulness depends upon the disposition of statesmen to resort to them for the promotion of values deemed compatible with national interests. International organization reflects the view that world order is not more important *than* national interests, but that it is important *to* national interests [see SYSTEMS ANALYSIS, *article on* INTERNATIONAL SYSTEMS].

## The character of international organization

**Internationalism.** In keeping with this emphasis upon the national values of member states, international organizations have generally functioned as loose associations, heavily dependent upon the voluntary acceptance by states of the obligations of membership, upon the development of consensus among governments as to programs and policies, and upon techniques of persuasion and political influence rather than command and coercion. In limited areas, international agencies have been endowed with legislative authority and enforcement procedures, but their capacity to function is based essentially upon processes of political accommodation. Usefulness to states, not power over states, is the secret of such strength as an international institution may acquire or possess.

The symbol of the dependence of international organization upon the will of states is the *veto*— the formally acknowledged competence of a state to frustrate majority decision and block action deemed incompatible with its interests. This constitutional capacity has been progressively relinquished by states, in favor of decision making by simpler or qualified majorities. In the United Nations, this trend has reached the point of confining the veto power to the Security Council, within which only the five major powers holding permanent seats are authorized to veto certain decisions of a nonprocedural character. Even this limited veto power has been eroded in practice, so that its negative effect upon majority will is seldom definitive. Despite this apparent diminution of the veto in international institutions, individual states—particularly the major powers—retain a basic capacity, grounded in political reality more than in constitutional documents, to inhibit the effective functioning of international agencies. If the concept of the veto is broadened beyond the negative vote to include all available manifestations of nonsupport and opposition, it becomes clear that all international agencies, regardless of their constitutional provisions, are ultimately dependent upon the capacity to promote substantial consensus among their members. Indeed, the veto rule is, in positive terms, the rule of unanimity; the latter suggests the fundamentally consensual character of international institutions.

While international organization has sometimes been criticized as involving too radical and idealistic a transformation of international relations, the tendency since World War II has been to compare it unfavorably with a hypothetical world government. Noting the limited capabilities of international agencies for controlling the behavior of states, advocates of world government have insisted that nothing short of the replacement of the multistate system by a global federation, involving the creation of a central institution endowed with authoritative and coercive powers comparable to those of national governments, will suffice to prevent catastrophic war. This point of view has gained widespread acceptance, with the result that the observation that "the United Nations is not, of course, a world government" has become a standard introduction to discussions of the inadequacy of international organization. Critical evaluation of international institutions has tended to measure them against the standard of governmental institutions and to attribute significant value to them only to the degree that they conform to that standard.

**Supranationalism.** From the point of view of approaching world government, the high point in the evolution of international organization since World War II is the development of the European Community, which began with the creation of the European Coal and Steel Community by France, West Germany, Italy, Belgium, the Netherlands, and Luxembourg, and subsequently expanded its functional scope with the establishment of the European Economic Community and the European Atomic Energy Community by the same group of states. Certain features of these institutions, including the conferment of significant policy-making and executive authority upon commissions composed of members acting independently of their governments on behalf of the community as a whole, and the capacity of community organs to deal directly and authoritatively with individuals and business enterprises within member states, have led to their characterization as supranational agencies.

The concept of supranationalism has not been precisely defined, but it is clearly intended to designate governmentlike qualities. Supranational institutions are regarded as falling between the poles of federal government and international organization and are defined in terms of their approximation of the former and their deviation from the latter. The adoption of this new designation for the institutions of the European Community suggests a difference in kind from conventional international organizations. The crucial differentiation implied in the concept of supranationalism concerns the relationship between a supranational agency and the governments of member states. In contrast to an international organization, a supranational body is thought to be superior to its member states and relatively independent of their consent and support in its operations. Supranationalism, in short, symbolizes the proposition that certain international organizations have achieved substantial emancipation from the control of national governments and acquired an autonomous role in international affairs [*see* INTERNATIONAL INTEGRATION, *article on* GLOBAL INTEGRATION].

The institutions of the European Community have developed remarkable innovations in international organization, and they show promise of leading toward the development of a full-fledged federal arrangement among their member states. Nevertheless, it appears that the quality of supranationalism is not so meaningful in practice as it is impressive in theory. The achievements of the Community have depended upon the successful development of consensus among the governments of member states, not upon the evasion of the necessity for such consensus; the effectiveness of the institutions has rested not upon the elimination of the veto in theory but upon the achievement of unanimity in practice. The evidence provided by the European experience does not suggest that supranationalism offers international institutions a realistic escape from their dependence upon governments. It does indicate that, under appropriate circumstances, the innovations associated with supranationalism may facilitate the development and implementation of the willingness of governments to move ahead in ambitious programs of common action [see INTERNATIONAL INTEGRATION, article on REGIONAL INTEGRATION].

For better or for worse, the development of the United Nations system has not pointed toward the evolution of a global federal system or even toward the quasi-federalism of supranational institutions. The expanding membership of the organization has testified to the proliferation of new states and to the increasing dominance within the United Nations of the view that it should be a universal institution which mirrors the complex realities of the multistate system. This expansion of the organization has completed the process of eliminating the European parochialism of international institutions, making formal acknowledgment of the global character of the international system. The rise to primacy within the United Nations of the General Assembly, the organ in which all member states enjoy equality of formal status and voting capacity, is in part attributable to the fact that this body comprises an unprecedentedly comprehensive collection of spokesmen for the units of the multistate system.

Far from undermining the position of national states as the primary actors on the international scene, international organization since World War II has in fact served to strengthen their position by enhancing their viability and effectiveness. States newly formed from colonial empires have been particularly reliant upon membership in the United Nations to provide symbolic confirmation of their emergence to independent status and to give them a political base for promoting the causes which they deem most essential to the consolidation of their position: the definitive elimination of the colonial system, the concentration of international agencies upon the provision of technical and developmental aid to the economically underdeveloped countries, and the prevention of major war. By providing postindependence assistance of various kinds, a diplomatic training ground, and the institutional context within which new states may individually and collectively bring their influence to bear upon international affairs, the United Nations and its specialized agencies have contributed to the working of the multistate system in the difficult period of the drastic alteration of its dimensions and the intensification of its heterogeneity.

## The prevention of war

The multistate system has undergone radical change since World War II, not only in the sense that decolonization has effected the quantitative and qualitative transformation of its membership but also in the sense that a series of revolutions in the technology of military power, combined with a fundamental political and ideological cleavage between the states best equipped to exploit the new technology, has radically altered the problem of security and given new urgency to the prevention of military conflict. Under these circumstances, the crucial test of international organization has to do with its relevance to the task of preventing the destruction of the multistate system.

**Collective security.** Prior to the era of general international organization, the modern state system relied upon the autonomous manipulation of power relationships by its independent units, both singly and in competitive alliances, for the achievement of the stability of the system and the security of its members. This arrangement, known as the balance-of-power system, was not subjected to attempts at significant revision until the formation of the League of Nations. The Hague Conferences of 1899 and 1907 introduced plans for disarmament agreements and institutionalized procedures for pacific settlement of disputes as alternative approaches to peace and security. The founders of the League gave institutional meaning to these approaches by incorporating them in the basic covenant of the new organization. As their major contribution to the restructuring of international relations, they added the concept of collective security [see COLLECTIVE SECURITY]. In practice, however, members of the League were reluctant to accept the obligations and risks which an operative system of collective security implied for them.

Except for a half-hearted and abortive attempt to invoke the scheme in order to frustrate Italian aggression against Ethiopia in 1935, they virtually discarded this approach to the problems of war and peace.

Despite the failure of the League to translate the concept of collective security into a working system, the ideal of establishing such a system caught hold. When statesmen and scholars contemplated the problem of launching a new organizational enterprise after World War II, they appeared almost to take it for granted that a world organization should adopt collective security as the central approach to the maintenance of international peace. The Charter of the United Nations, as formulated at the San Francisco Conference in 1945, endorsed the principle of collective security but repudiated its general applicability by giving the major powers the constitutional power to veto the actions of the Security Council. The formulators of the charter, in fact, rejected the notion that this approach to the ordering of international relations was relevant to the critical problems of war and peace that might arise after World War II. The issue of the feasibility of effectuating collective security against the opposition of a great power has been reopened from time to time, but political realism has prevailed, and instead of expanding the coverage of the coercive system envisaged in the charter, members of the United Nations have in practice abandoned all efforts to establish that system. It is thoroughly in keeping with the history of attitudes toward collective security that the United Nations should have endorsed the principle in general terms, denied the possibility of its application in the most crucial cases, shifted toward the position that the restriction upon its implementation should be lifted, and finally discarded any meaningful commitment to give effect to the concept.

**Defensive alliances.** In the period since World War II, the struggle between the massive blocs led by the Soviet Union and the United States, commonly designated as the cold war, has stimulated the use of international organizations for purposes quite different from that of implementing collective security. The primary response to the threat of war resulting from the aggressive policy of a great power has been the adaptation of the forms and procedures of international organization to serve the purposes of defensive alliances. The North Atlantic Treaty Organization (NATO) is the prime example of the combining of a conventional alliance with the institutional devices developed by the modern process of international organization. The formation of NATO in reaction to the expansionist tendencies of the Soviet Union represented, in fact,

the following of the advice implicitly tendered in the United Nations Charter to states confronted with the danger of aggression by a great power; the charter's renunciation of the intent or expectation that the United Nations should provide security in such a situation is followed, in article 51, by acknowledgment of the propriety of arrangements for collective self-defense. Insofar as international agencies have a realistic role to play in deterring or defeating military ventures by major powers, it is evident that this role devolves upon regional or selective-membership agencies, composed of states perceiving a common threat to their security and resolved to combine their strength in support of a common defensive policy—not upon general organizations such as the United Nations [see ALLIANCES].

**Preventive diplomacy.** While the pragmatic division of labor among international institutions assigns the basic function of military defense to agencies of the NATO variety and not to a global organization attempting to effectuate the principle of collective security, this assignment leaves a significant group of functions to the United Nations. From its beginning, this organization has provided a political forum and a setting for diplomacy —public and private, formal and informal—and has exhibited flexibility in the provision of mechanisms and procedures for assisting states to reach agreed settlements of disputes. An essentially new function, albeit an outgrowth of the organization's development of instrumentalities for pacific settlement, emerged in 1956 with the creation of the United Nations Emergency Force (UNEF) and, more definitively, in 1960 with the launching of the United Nations Operation in the Congo (ONUC). This function was given the title "preventive diplomacy" by Secretary-General Dag Hammarskjöld. It deserves to be noted as the major innovation produced by the United Nations in the realm of approaches to the maintenance of peace through the functioning of international agencies. Preventive diplomacy represents the organization's tentative answer to the question of what major function in the political and security realm it may be able to substitute for the unattainable ideal of providing collective security.

Preventive diplomacy, developed pragmatically in response to the Middle Eastern crisis of 1956 and the Congo crisis of 1960, was ably articulated in theoretical terms by Secretary-General Hammarskjöld (Hammarskjöld 1960). It involves the intervention of the United Nations in areas of conflict outside of, or peripheral to, the cold war struggle, for the purpose of forestalling the competitive intrusion of the rival power blocs into those areas. As in the cases of UNEF and ONUC, this intervention is carried out by military forces placed at the disposal of and under the direction of the organization by states other than the great powers, and, so far as possible, disassociated from the rival blocs. The mission of the forces, which are dispatched to the scene with the consent of the parties most directly involved, is not to combat an aggressor but to stabilize the local situation so as to prevent the area's becoming a new zone of cold war competition. A basic requirement of this kind of operation is the consent of the major powers, who, recognizing a common interest in the avoidance of a military showdown, are confident that the United Nations will not favor any one of them in its conduct of the operation. This requirement suggests the fundamental limitations of preventive diplomacy. It is a function which can be carried out by international organization on behalf of competitive great powers only to the extent that political and other circumstances make it acceptable to those powers. Preventive diplomacy is a modest concept in that it assigns international organization only the role of assisting rival powers in the avoidance of unwanted confrontations, not that of exercising coercive control over disturbers of the international peace. Nevertheless, it represents the most significant role presently available to general international organization in the stabilization of an international situation dominated by great-power struggles [see DIPLOMACY].

## Operationalism and politics

The espousal by the United Nations of the function of preventive diplomacy was only one aspect of a general trend toward the expansion of the operational responsibilities and capabilities of international institutions. The development of the United Nations and its specialized agencies has taken these institutions beyond the minimal function of providing facilities for multilateral diplomatic interchange, to the actual administration of programs and execution of operations in both the economic and the political realms. Many of these programs have been initiated in response to the demand for international assistance to underdeveloped countries in their quest for economic advance. This expansion of the executive function and capacity, in the case of the United Nations in particular, has accompanied the evolution of the secretary-generalship into a post of leadership and policy direction. The status of the secretary-general as a kind of chief executive of the organization has been achieved as the product of a steady evolution, but the precariousness of this result is indicated by the opposition which it has sporadically evoked.

These developments have given rise to controversy over the issue of the political direction and control of the programs sponsored and administered by international agencies. States are not realistically divisible into those which support and those which oppose international organization or those which accept and those which reject the principle of expanding the executive capacity of international agencies. The policies of states with respect to international institutions are dependent upon conceptions of national interests and expectations as to whether or not the activities of those institutions will be compatible with and conducive to the protection and promotion of national interests. In short, states are actually divisible into those which have and those which lack confidence that they and their political allies can exercise effective control over the functioning of particular international agencies or the operation of given programs. No state is committed to the support or the rejection of international operations as a matter of principle, without regard to the nature of their policy direction and control. In the final analysis, member states support or oppose specific international activities in proportion to their success or failure in influencing the nature of the policy which these activities serve.

The struggle of states for control over the policy and activities of the organization has been particularly intense in the United Nations. Such issues as the admission of new members, the integrity of the veto power, the expansion of the realm of competence of the General Assembly, and the financing and general policy direction of the Congo operation have illustrated this point. There has also been a trend toward the organization of member states into distinct blocs and the development of shifting patterns of alignment of states and groups of states in the debates and votes of the General Assembly.

All these developments indicate the emergence of a distinctive and significant political process within the United Nations. This phenomenon is disturbing to idealists who have looked to international organization for the abolition of international politics and the establishment of the rule of law in all its purity on a global scale. From a more realistic point of view, it suggests the coming of age of international organization; the intensity of the political contest is a measure of the significance attached to the institution.

## The study of international organization

The development of the politics of international organization as a part of the larger sphere of international politics has been paralleled by the evolution of a political emphasis in the scholarly study of international organization. In its earliest phases, this study was generally characterized by a legal emphasis which was frequently accompanied by a strong value commitment to the amelioration of international politics. Scholarship in this field was largely a quest for structural and legal reforms applicable to the international system. Since World War II, specialists in international organization have tended to be less dominated by aversion to international politics, less oriented toward legal analysis, and more cognizant of the political aspects of the interplay of states within the framework of international agencies. Numerous studies have been made of the policies and attitudes of particular states toward and within the United Nations and other international institutions, and pioneer research has been undertaken on the development of bloc affiliations, voting patterns, and other aspects of the political processes within international agencies.

Research of this type has been largely focused on the United Nations and the regional institutions of western Europe, leaving a need for systematic political analysis of other institutions, global and regional, in order to develop an understanding of the full range of the international organizational system. As researchers provide analyses of the political processes within and the political impacts of an increasing number of international agencies, it may become possible to develop the field of comparative international organization as an area of study which may contribute to an understanding of international politics in the broadest sense.

Trends in international organization research since World War II suggest the possibility that the study of international institutions, of the foreign policies of particular states, and of the international political system as a whole may be integrated in a way conducive to the more sophisticated analysis of the general nature of the interaction of states in a multistate context which is itself undergoing fundamental transformations.

INIS L. CLAUDE, JR.

[See also INTERNATIONAL INTEGRATION; INTERNATIONAL LAW; INTERNATIONAL POLITICS; TRUSTEESHIP. *Guides to other relevant material may be found under* INTERNATIONAL RELATIONS; WAR.]

### BIBLIOGRAPHY

ALKER, HAYWARD R.; and RUSSETT, B. M. 1965 *World Politics in the General Assembly.* Yale Studies in Political Science, No. 15. New Haven: Yale Univ. Press.

ASHER, ROBERT E. et al. 1957 *The United Nations and Promotion of the General Welfare.* Washington: Brookings Institution.

BLOOMFIELD, LINCOLN P. 1960 *The United Nations and U.S. Foreign Policy.* Boston: Little.

CLARK, GRENVILLE; and SOHN, LOUIS B. (1958) 1960 *World Peace Through World Law.* 2d ed., rev. Cambridge, Mass.: Harvard Univ. Press.

CLAUDE, INIS L. (1956) 1964 *Swords Into Plowshares.* 3d ed. New York: Random House.

DALLIN, ALEXANDER 1962 *The Soviet Union at the United Nations.* New York: Praeger.

*Everyman's United Nations.* (1948) 1963 New York: United Nations Office of Public Information.

GOODRICH, LELAND M.; and SIMONS, ANNE P. 1955 *The United Nations and the Maintenance of International Peace and Security.* Washington: Brookings Institution.

HAAS, ERNST B. 1958 *The Uniting of Europe: Political, Social, and Economic Forces, 1950–1957.* Stanford Univ. Press.

HAAS, ERNST B. 1964 *Beyond the Nation-state: Functionalism and International Organization.* Stanford Univ. Press.

HAMMARSKJÖLD, DAG 1960 Introduction. In United Nations, Secretary-General, *Annual Report . . .* New York: United Nations.

HOVET, THOMAS (1958) 1960 *Bloc Politics in the United Nations.* Cambridge, Mass.: Harvard Univ. Press.

*International Organization.* → Published since 1947 by the World Peace Foundation.

MANGONE, GERARD J. 1954 *A Short History of International Organization.* New York: McGraw-Hill.

MITRANY, DAVID (1943) 1946 *A Working Peace System.* 4th ed. London: National Peace Council.

NICHOLAS, HERBERT G. (1959) 1962 *The United Nations as a Political Institution.* 2d ed. Oxford Univ. Press.

PADELFORD, NORMAN J.; and GOODRICH, LELAND M. (editors) 1965 *The United Nations in the Balance: Accomplishments and Prospects.* New York: Praeger.

PHELAN, EDWARD J. (1936) 1949 *Yes and Albert Thomas.* New York: Columbia Univ. Press.

POLITICAL AND ECONOMIC PLANNING 1959 *European Organisations.* London: Allen & Unwin.

RUSSELL, RUTH B.; and MUTHER, JEANNETTE E. 1958 *A History of the United Nations Charter.* Washington: Brookings Institution.

SCHWEBEL, STEPHEN M. 1952 *The Secretary-General of the United Nations: His Political Powers and Practice.* Cambridge, Mass.: Harvard Univ. Press.

*United Nations Monthly Chronicle.* → Successor to *United Nations Review.*

UNITED NATIONS *Yearbook.* → Published since 1946/1947.

WALTERS, FRANCIS P. (1952) 1960 *A History of the League of Nations.* London: Oxford Univ. Press.

*Yearbook of International Organizations.* 9th ed. 1962–1963 Brussels: Union of International Associations.

ZIMMERN, ALFRED E. 1936 *The League of Nations and the Rule of Law: 1918–1935.* London: Macmillan.

## II

## ADMINISTRATION

International administration embraces the performance of tasks by the staffs of agencies established by and responsible to a number of national governments. It consists of a body of practices and procedures in part virtually identical with those of public administration at the national level, in part presenting characteristics peculiar to cross-cultural relations. Not a distinct discipline, international administration as a field of study has drawn variously from the materials and techniques of domestic public administration, international law and organization, diplomacy, and comparative politics.

## Historical development

International administration is of comparatively recent origin. Its emergence stems partly from the commissions set up in Europe during the nineteenth century to regulate the use of international rivers, such as the Rhine (in 1804), the Danube (in 1856), and, later, others, and partly from various technical bureaus known as public administrative unions, established for informational and coordinative purposes in such areas as postal and telegraph services, patents, copyrights, and public health, from the 1870s onward. Typically, the pattern of these small, functional agencies included a general conference or assembly, a supervisory board or council, and a permanent office, staffed either by personnel on loan from the host government or by direct multinational recruitment. The headquarters of these organizations were all located in Europe, chiefly at Geneva, Berne, and Paris. The only extra-European example, prior to the present century, was the Pan American Union (PAU), created in 1890 in Washington and then known as the Commercial Bureau of the American Republics.

International administration received a major impetus with the establishment in 1920 of the League of Nations and its affiliate, the International Labour Organisation (ILO). The year-round work of the League, as a multipurpose organization with important political functions, was handled by a central secretariat at Geneva—an organ whose personnel reached about 700 at its peak, in the early 1930s. Within its more circumscribed sphere, the ILO developed an office staff of about 600. All told, the administrative bureaucracies of pre-World War II international agencies, including the PAU and various independent technical bureaus, probably did not exceed 1,500 established posts at any given time.

World War II and its aftermath were marked by a striking proliferation of intergovernmental instrumentalities, notably the United Nations (UN) and such related functional agencies as the Food and Agriculture Organization (FAO), the United Nations Educational, Scientific and Cultural Organization (UNESCO), the World Health Organization (WHO), the International Civil Aviation Organization (ICAO), the International Bank for Reconstruction and Development (IBRD), and the International Monetary Fund (IMF). Concurrently, in 1946 the League of Nations was liquidated, and its assets and certain of its legal responsibilities were transferred to the UN; the ILO survived, under expanded constitutional terms of reference adopted in 1944.

In addition to the foregoing *global* agencies, a substantial number of new organizations at the *regional* level came into being in the noncommunist world during the 1940s and 1950s—all with an administrative apparatus of one sort or another. In the collective-defense field these regional institutions include the North Atlantic Treaty Organization (NATO), the Central Treaty Organization (CENTO) in the Middle East, and the Southeast Asia Treaty Organization (SEATO), with headquarters at Bangkok. In western Europe a significant movement toward international "integration," which began shortly after the close of World War II, led to the creation of (1) the Organization for European Economic Cooperation (OEEC), succeeded in 1960 by the Organization for Economic Cooperation and Development (OECD), with the addition of the United States, Canada, and a little later, Japan, as members; (2) the Council of Europe at Strasbourg; and (3) the so-called European communities, consisting of the Coal and Steel Community (ECSC), the European Economic Community (EEC)—popularly known as the Common Market, and the European Atomic Energy Community (EURATOM). These three communities, in contrast to the previously typical pattern of international organization, are characterized by a limited *supra*nationalism, with authority to control certain aspects of the economic and technical policies of the six member nations (France, West Germany, Italy, Belgium, Netherlands, and Luxembourg—constituting what is often called "Little Europe"), thus giving rise to unprecedented forms of administrative action at the international level.

**Dimensions in the 1960s.**    The functional sweep of international administration in the 1960s, while still restricted in comparison with that of major national bureaucracies, had acquired dimensions far wider than those before World War II. This expansion can be shown quantitatively by comparing personnel and budgets. For the UN family of agencies, in the fiscal year 1962/1963 the aggregate number of persons on the payroll approximated 20,000 (not counting the uniformed personnel of the "peace-keeping" forces then maintained by the UN in the Middle East and the Congo). This is roughly fifteen times the number employed by the League and ILO a generation earlier. In addition, some 11,000 civilians were employed by the leading regional agencies, distributed as follows: NATO, 2,250; OECD, 1,200; the three European communities, 6,830; PAU, 750. In budgetary terms, the high point of aggregate League and ILO annual expenditure was only about $13 million, whereas the UN system in 1963 spent nearly $500 million. (This sum covers not only "regular" budget activities but various special voluntary programs and the cost of maintaining peace-keeping units in the field.)

Another significant difference between international administration today and prior to World War II resides in the far greater geographical dispersion of the former's activities. A generation ago nearly all the employees of the League, the ILO, and the PAU were stationed at the central headquarters of their respective organizations; today at least half of the 20,000 civilians working for the UN family of organizations are on field assignments of varying duration, some of them staffing a network of field offices and others participating in field projects of the "technical assistance" variety —virtually throughout the world, except for the Soviet bloc and Communist China. For the two major technical cooperation programs operated by the UN system, over 4,000 experts were engaged in field undertakings during the year 1963. (Because of the nonavailability of detailed data, the present account does not deal with the kind of "international" administration involved in such special relationships as exist between the Soviet Union and its eastern European "satellites.")

### Functions of international bureaucracies

The combined staffs of present-day international agencies may be said to constitute a "microcosm" of the *world* community in the making or of the *regional* communities now emerging. The functions performed by these bureaucracies fall broadly into two categories: housekeeping and substantive.

The main *housekeeping* functions are the processing of personnel and budget actions, the handling of procurement, accounts, and audit, and in particular the management of international meetings (preparation of agenda and supporting documentation, physical arrangements, recording and reporting, etc.). These actions are not intrinsically different from similar actions within a national bureaucracy save in two respects—the necessity of interlinguistic communication and the utilization of funds in different national currencies. Translators, interpreters, and language editors play an indispensable part in the life of an international secretariat; nearly one-fourth of the UN staff in

New York, for example, consists of personnel serving as "groundkeepers" for meetings and as processors of records and reports.

The *substantive* roles of international officials, in roughly ascending order of discretionary action, include the following: (1) the gathering and dissemination of information—the clearinghouse function; (2) the conduct of research; (3) the registration of treaties (UN and PAU only); (4) the planning, formulation, and coordination of operational programs; (5) the implementation of such programs in the field; (6) the staffing and management of field missions in the domain of peace keeping and peaceful settlement, including truce supervision and border-policing arrangements; (7) assistance in negotiating group decisions and agreements among governments; and finally, upon occasion, (8) the assumption of responsibility for mediating diplomatic controversies. To this list should be added, in the case of the supranational European communities, the exercise of authority to impose fines, orders, or taxes on governments and industrial firms and, for NATO, the conduct of military staff and planning operations and the handling of various logistical and communications problems.

Increasingly, especially in the major agencies, the present-day activity of international bureaucracies tends to range far beyond the traditional "ministerial" duties characteristic of earlier organizations. This enlarged role derives partly from a liberal interpretation of the provisions of constituent instruments (as in the European communities, NATO, and to some extent the UN) and partly from the explicit or tacit delegation of discretionary authority to administrative heads when there seems no other way of moving from diplomatic deadlock to effective crisis action (as, notably, in the UN during recent years), or where, by the very nature of the situation, continuous executive action is required for an indefinite period of time (as, for example, with UN operations in the Congo).

Even so, it should be noted that, except to some extent in the new European communities, international civil servants are obliged to operate in a consensual environment. In contrast to the officials of national governments, they lack powers of coercion and there is no judicial or police authority to sanction their decisions. Whatever impact they manage to make depends essentially on their skill in negotiation, persuasion, the provision of advice, and the contriving of generally acceptable solutions to problems. They do not directly administer public services, nor in any *juristic* sense do they deal directly with individuals or private groups inside member countries, although, in the context of multilateral technical assistance, international experts do develop close, informal relations with local people, thereby circumventing the legal barriers of "domestic jurisdiction."

## Special problems

International administration is confronted with a number of special problems that exist either not at all or only in minor degree within national administrations.

**Manpower.** The first and possibly the most important of these problems is concerned with the selection and status of staff. Staff recruitment is complicated by the necessity of observing the principle of wide geographic distribution, which, particularly in world-wide organizations, may conflict in practice with the criteria of "competence and efficiency." The existence of low educational standards, along with an acute shortage of specialized personnel, in most of the developing countries makes it difficult for them to provide suitably equipped candidates for posts in agency secretariats. The result, according to many observers, is an unavoidable lowering of performance standards at the international level, since all countries, for prestige and other reasons, insist on having their staff "quotas." (To date the quota distribution for the UN Secretariat has been based on national budgetary contributions, but a strong movement has recently got under way to have this changed to allow more weight to the population factor.) The seriousness of the problem may in time be alleviated through the development by the UN of adequate in-service training programs, along with the improvement of trained manpower resources in the less advanced countries.

A second special feature of personnel management evoking difficulties relates to the process of evaluating individual candidates with widely different cultural backgrounds. In this connection performance tests may be, and are, effectively utilized to recruit such categories of personnel as clerks, stenographers, accountants, junior statisticians, translators, interpreters, and editors; but for persons expected to perform general intellectual work, reliable "culture-free" tests do not yet appear to be available: non-Westerners are probably not testable by adaptations of tests standardized on Western populations, "because so little is known about the thought patterns and mental processes of individuals from other cultures" (Torre 1963, p. 88). There are still numerous geographical areas where the "objective" type of examination is relatively unknown. When the results of the essay type have to be translated from one language into another, it may turn out to be more a test of the examiner than of the candidate. Nor has the interview technique been used very imaginatively, untrained interviewers, for the most part, being resorted to because of the substantial costs of maintaining round-the-world teams of skilled personnel technicians. Research is urgently needed on the kinds of personal qualities that are essential for successful adaptation to cross-cultural work situations and on practicable methods of discovering such qualities at the recruitment stage.

A further problem is how to achieve, in multinational staffs exposed to a nationalistic environment, the independence, impartiality, and loyalty that ideally should characterize their behavior. This problem has been dramatically pointed up by the Communist claim (voiced by Khrushchev in the 1960 UN General Assembly) that there can be no "neutral men"—in the ideological sense. International civil servants are legally forbidden to seek or receive instructions from their governments or other external authorities, but this does not prevent them from having to deal with extraneous political pressures of one kind or another. There is no simple solution to this problem. Suffice it to say that the vast majority of UN employees clearly are loyal and dedicated civil servants. To protect them against unfair or arbitrary employment treatment provoked by outside pressures, there have been established independent administrative tribunals, to which they have the right of appeal under certain conditions (Friedmann & Fatouros 1957).

**Organization.** A second set of problems arises from the loose, decentralized organizational pattern of the UN system. In effect, the UN proper and the so-called specialized agencies are tied together only on a kind of partnership basis, through voluntary interagency agreements and a network of more or less informal interstaff working arrangements. Since the functional boundaries of the different agencies lack precision and to some extent actually overlap, it has become necessary to devise methods and procedures with a view to an orderly coordination of their activity. This is an extremely involved and never-ending process, for which there is no absolute parallel in national government organization.

Another difficulty deriving from organizational pluralism is that the action directives, not infrequently vague or ambiguous, that flow from the congeries of representative organs (assemblies, councils, commissions, boards) within the UN sometimes put administrative officials in situations where available human and budgetary resources are inadequate to implement properly the melange of "legislative" mandates given to hard-pressed staffs. Efforts to mitigate such predicaments by fuller advance consultation and program planning by intergovernmental organs have thus far been only moderately effective.

To a lesser extent, similar organizational problems appear to confront the recently established European communities in their relations with one another, e.g., the Common Market in its relations with the Coal and Steel Community. Here, however, the trend seems to be toward a progressive consolidation of the organs and services of these communities into what may eventually emerge as a unified economic and possibly political framework for Little Europe.

**Communication.** A third category of significant differentials between international and national administration concerns communication. Not only does the physical space factor play a more important role internationally than within the context of national bureaucracies (excepting world-wide national foreign-service establishments), but the psychological barriers to effective communication in staff work situations are much greater, both at headquarters and in field relationships. Communication difficulties originate in part from the multilingual composition of staff groups, especially when it is necessary for staff members to employ a language not their own in involved negotiations or in the drafting of complex documents reflecting group decisions. Over and beyond the language factor, semantic misunderstandings may often lead to confusion.

Inherent in this context is the need for adjustment of the divergent traditions, procedures, and concepts of administration with which incoming personnel may be identified. Illustrations of such differences include methods of handling correspondence, the role of the "front office," the relation of budgetary and personnel to substantive (program) units, the career status of employees, the use of informal task forces as an administrative device, and the attitude of male employees toward female supervisors. There is some reason for believing that different nationality groups have differing capacities to make such adjustments at the international level. Accordingly, an important aspect of the task of administrative leadership is to devise experimentally ways of recognizing cultural differences in work assignments and procedures. Tendencies toward national "cliquishness" call for the conscious development of positive incentives to teamwork on the part of management. In certain international secretariats, staff morale and operat-

ing standards have been stimulated by such policies; in others, where the top leadership has failed to enlist the unstinted effort of the rank and file, an indifferent, unimaginative kind of performance has often resulted.

### Current research and future needs

The literature relating to international administration has tended, to date, to be historical, legalistic, or broadly descriptive in character. Much of the writing on the subject has been incidental to a primary concern in either international law or organization. Since the epoch of the League of Nations, a limited number of treatises by former practitioners (e.g., Lie 1954; Loveday 1956; Ranshofen-Wertheimer 1945) have appeared. These works present in more or less organized fashion reflections on the authors' professional experiences and in certain cases provide insightful evaluations of past practices. There has been only one significant attempt by a trained participant–observer to "capture and record" the process of decision making inside an organization (Ascher 1951). Scholarly general surveys of the evolution of individual international agencies (e.g., Laves & Thomson 1957) have appeared in recent years, but their treatment of administration is typically limited to a single chapter or to scattered cursory comments.

A new development within the past decade has been the emergence of a few studies of international administration "in depth" (Berkov 1957; Glick 1957; Sharp 1961), dealing with headquarters–field relationships in the conduct of operational programs and attempting to draw conclusions on how to adjust centrifugal and centripetal forces within such programs. In addition to documentary analysis, the authors of these studies have utilized interviewing and observation techniques both at headquarters and in the field.

The totality of empirical research directly focused on international administration remains decidedly spotty and largely noncumulative. Individual studies have tended to be carried out without regard for the findings of other studies, if only because of the glaring subject-matter gaps in what is still the pioneer stage of systematic research in this field. No special models for empirical verification may yet be said to have been produced. Indeed, it is a fair question whether international administration should be studied with a view to its acquiring a discipline of its own, apart from public administration in general or from international organization. As noted earlier, the field is marked by a number of significant differences from the study of national administration, but are these differences of kind or merely of degree? On this point there is considerable divergence of opinion.

**Need for comparative research.** Probably the most fruitful approach to the systematic exploration of international administrative behavior would be to design a series of studies for the purpose of evaluating the impact of one or more factors peculiar to administration at the international level—by comparing agencies, processes, or case situations. From such inquiries it should become possible to discover the conditions under which recurring patterns of behavior may be anticipated. Stated differently, the patient pursuit of the comparative method should provide findings from which empirical theories of international administration that are not culture-bound might emerge.

The subject-matter areas for such research are legion, so marked has been the neglect of the field by scholars. By way of illustration, a number of such areas are listed below, under three broad headings: personnel, organization and procedure, and substantive roles of international bureaucracies.

The area of *personnel* would include studies of (1) samples of staff recruitment in cognate agencies in terms of social origins, educational backgrounds, motivation of applicants, and subsequent levels of performance; (2) the impact of "geographic distribution" on communication, standards of performance, staff morale, etc., in a technical agency, such as the Universal Postal Union, as compared with an essentially political organization, such as the UN; (3) the role of "informal" staff groupings in the communication process of related agencies; (4) the role perceptions held by professional personnel in an intergovernmental as compared with a supranational organization (e.g., the ILO and the ECSC; (5) the impact of differing styles of administrative leadership on staff morale in cognate agencies (e.g., the ILO and WHO), or in the same agency over time (e.g., the UN under Lie and then under Hammarskjöld).

*Organization and procedure* studies would involve evaluations of (1) the use of informal committee and working-party techniques as devices for adjusting differing concepts and patterns of administration in similar agencies; (2) the roles of differently structured "front offices" in the international administration of cognate agencies; (3) the effectiveness of agency field-reporting systems in relation to form, frequency, and routing of reports and utilization of reports as feedback; (4) the headquarters–field communications process in similar agencies, in order to discover, by means of the intensive examination of procedures and case situations, the causes of and remedies for misun-

derstandings, blockages, and crossed lines; (5) the regional structures of related UN agencies, with the object of determining whether there is any significant correlation between the degree of decentralization and program effectiveness in different culture areas; (6) the economic and social program-coordinative devices evolved by the UN family of organizations since their establishment; (7) the overhead costs of field-program conduct in UN agencies in relation to program size, geographic spread, and degree of devolution of program execution to field units.

The last general area of study, that of the *substantive roles of international bureaucracies*, would concern itself with (1) methods of attaining policy consensus in the secretariat of an intergovernmental agency, such as the OECD, in comparison with a partially supranational body, such as the EEC; (2) case studies of substantive decision making relating to different types of situations in the same agency and the same type of situation in similar agencies; (3) comparative studies of project programming for technical assistance, as illustrated by the World Bank, the UN Expanded Program of Technical Assistance, and the UN Special Fund; (4) sample studies of the impact of UN field-program operations on local community attitudes toward the UN system and on related policies of the recipient governments; (5) analyses of the kinds of influence exerted by professional staffs on an agency's substantive policies (e.g., program formulation, the resolution of crises, etc.) in relation to the functional character of the agency and the degree of consensus in its policy-control organs; (6) inquiries designed to determine the conditions of *constructive* policy role-playing by the bureaucracies of different types of organizations.

For the most part the suggestions listed above represent areas or problems concerning which there is at present little systematic knowledge. In order to explore some of them meaningfully, political scientists and public administration experts would most likely need to enlist the collaboration of psychiatrists, social psychologists, and other experts in group dynamics. In certain cases (e.g., the impact of international programs on grass-roots attitudes in non-Western countries) the cultural anthropologist might provide useful insights.

For maximum objectivity, much of the behavioral research in the field of international administration should be conducted under multinational auspices. Otherwise there will always lurk the danger of cultural bias. This possibility, to be sure, is much more real in regard to the culturally heterogeneous *global* agencies, where East and West,

North and South all meet, than in the more homo-geneous *regional* institutions in the Western hemi-sphere or in the North Atlantic community. There are, of course, certain practical difficulties in mak-ing arrangements for multinational research teams, particularly in view of the relatively backward state of the social sciences in most non-Western coun-tries.

A second condition for the effective investigation of the kinds of problems outlined above is the close cooperation of officials with the outside research scholar or team. Since most senior officials tend to be very busy, it is important that the investigators not let themselves become minor nuisances to harassed practitioners. In addition, the outside in-vestigators must give satisfactory assurances that the anonymity of their informants will be carefully respected. But these conditions are not insuperable obstacles; ordinarily they can be met, with the exercise of patience and discretion.

**The outlook**

Indications are not lacking that international administration will continue to proliferate in the foreseeable future. Its dimensions give promise of expanding, both at the global and the regional level. If and as the United Nations further develops its peace-keeping activities, not only may it become desirable to attach a military-planning unit to its headquarters (where a military adviser to the sec-retary-general was recently installed), thereby call-ing for personnel conversant with military technol-ogy, but the realization of any concrete plan for international arms control would require admini-strative arrangements of some kind for inspection purposes, as well as, possibly, the creation of a permanent international peace force. The staffing of such arrangements would bring the engineer and the scientist more directly into the world's bureaucratic apparatus than ever before.

Concurrently or perhaps sooner, the projection of international cooperation into the realm of outer space presumably will add to the substantive role of certain categories of UN personnel, who will not only aid in the formulation of legal regulations to govern the peaceful use of outer space but also handle inspection and monitoring operations.

A third possibility is that the scope of multilateral economic and social programs will further expand over the coming years. The establishment of a UN-sponsored capital-assistance program is by no means out of the question, either in conjunction with the present Special Fund, or else through a separate arrangement. In this domain, also, the lending roles of the existing world financial insti-tutions (the International Bank for Reconstruction and Development, the International Finance Corpo-ration, the International Development Association) bid fair to grow, while the International Monetary Fund may be called upon to elaborate and admin-ister a new and stronger type of world monetary mechanism.

Globally, the development of the foregoing func-tional activities will scarcely add up to any sort of world government. Regardless of whether such a goal should be deemed by the West to be politically desirable, its likelihood would appear to be too remote to affect the basic patterns of international cooperation in the near future. But even under a world state, while administration would become either "unitary" or "federal" in the legal sense, it would still remain multicultural in composition. The complexities of behavioral relations now con-fronting international agencies would by no means disappear. The interflow of personnel, hierarchi-cally as well as laterally, through governmental administrations might well increase, but there would still remain serious problems of intercultural adjustment.

Regionally, a wide spread of international insti-tutions would seem to be in the offing. Signs already discernible in all the major areas—Europe, the Middle East, Asia, Africa, and Latin America —suggest such an evolution. The contours of some of these new arrangements are now only barely visible, and it is impossible to predict just how the over-all regional picture will look by, say, the 1980s. In any event, the picture is not likely to be a tidy one: the institutional gamut will probably run from a congeries of loose, limited-purpose groupings (such as the Organization of African Unity, in-augurated in 1963) through free-trade associations and customs unions to more strongly knit supra-nationalistic organizations. Should any consider-able devolution of control from Moscow take place within the present Soviet orbit, it is not inconceiv-able that some sort of "confederal" institutionalized relationship might replace the existing Communist-party control apparatus.

As international administration grows in variety and in depth, there is cause for hope that the re-sources of the social sciences may become steadily more adequate to the task of analyzing and illumi-nating its key problems, as well as providing valu-able operational prescriptions to policy makers.

WALTER R. SHARP

[*See also* ADMINISTRATION; BUREAUCRACY; CIVIL SERV-ICE; DIPLOMACY; LOYALTY. *Other relevant material may be found in* PUBLIC ADMINISTRATION.]

### BIBLIOGRAPHY

ASCHER, CHARLES S.  1951  *Program-making in UNESCO, 1946–1951: A Study in the Processes of International Administration*. Chicago: Public Administration Service.

ASHER, ROBERT E. et al.  1957  *The United Nations and Promotion of the General Welfare*. Washington: Brookings Institution. → An authoritative, scholarly analysis of policy and administration.

BAILEY, SYDNEY D.  (1962) 1964  *The Secretariat of the United Nations*. 2d ed., rev. New York: Carnegie Endowment for International Peace. → Chief emphasis is on the political aspects of the Secretariat's operation.

BERKOV, ROBERT  1957  *The World Health Organization: A Study in Decentralized International Administration*. Geneva: Droz.

FRIEDMANN, WOLFGANG G.; and FATOUROS, A. A.  1957  The United Nations Administrative Tribunal. *International Organization* 11:13–29.

GLICK, PHILIP M.  1957  *The Administration of Technical Assistance: Growth in the Americas*. Univ. of Chicago Press. → An excellent comparison of United States and United Nations programs.

HAAS, ERNST B.  1964  *Beyond the Nation-state: Functionalism and International Organization*. Stanford Univ. Press.

HILL, MARTIN  (1945) 1946  *The Economic and Financial Organization of the League of Nations: A Survey of Twenty-five Years' Experience*. Washington: Carnegie Endowment for International Peace. → A brief, sympathetic description by a former League official.

HILL, NORMAN L.  1931  *International Administration*. New York: McGraw-Hill. → The first general textbook; legalistic in approach.

*International Organization*. → Published since 1947 by the World Peace Foundation. Contains informative articles on current developments, as well as selected bibliographies.

LAVES, WALTER H. C.; and THOMSON, CHARLES A.  1957  *UNESCO: Purpose, Progress, Prospects*. Bloomington: Indiana Univ. Press. → The most comprehensive treatment of UNESCO in English.

LIE, TRYGVE  1954  *In the Cause of Peace: Seven Years With the United Nations*. New York: Macmillan. → A moderately revealing memoir by the first secretary-general of the United Nations.

LINDBERG, LEON  1965  Decision Making and Integration in the European Community. *International Organization* 19:56–81.

LOVEDAY, ALEXANDER  1956  *Reflections on International Administration*. Oxford: Clarendon Press. → Based on many years' experience as a senior League of Nations official.

RANSHOFEN-WERTHEIMER, EGON F.  1945  *The International Secretariat: A Great Experiment in International Administration*. Washington: Carnegie Endowment for International Peace. → The definitive treatment of the League of Nations Secretariat by a former staff member.

SAYRE, FRANCIS B.  1919  *Experiments in International Administration*. New York and London: Harper. → Case studies of selected early international agencies.

SCHENKMAN, JACOB  1955  *International Civil Aviation Organization*. Geneva: Droz. → Valuable for its chapter on the regional organization of the ICAO.

SCHWEBEL, STEPHEN M.  1952  *The Secretary-General of the United Nations: His Political Powers and Practice*. Cambridge, Mass.: Harvard Univ. Press. → A critical analysis of the evolution of the United Nations secretary-generalship during the term of Trygve Lie.

SEWELL, JAMES P.  1966  *Functionalism and World Politics: A Study Based on United Nations Programs Financing Economic Development*. Princeton Univ. Press. → Compares the operational impact of the IBRD, IFC, IDA, and the UN Special Fund in a "functionalist" context.

SHARP, WALTER R.  1958  The Study of International Administration. *World Politics* 11:103–117. → Includes suggestions for research.

SHARP, WALTER R.  1961  *Field Administration in the United Nations System: The Conduct of International Economic and Social Programs*. New York: Praeger.

TORRE, MOTTRAM (editor)  1963  *The Selection of Personnel for International Service*. Geneva and New York: World Federation for Mental Health.

YOUNG, TIEN-CHENG  1958  *International Civil Service: Principles and Problems*. Brussels: International Institute of Administrative Sciences.

## III
### FINANCING

There are many hundreds of international organizations more or less active at the present time. Some of these are governmental organizations, composed exclusively of state members; some are private and have no states among their members; many are mixed, with both states and private organizations or individuals as members. The financing patterns and practices of these organizations are quite diverse, regardless of the nature of their membership. However, except for the very few organizations that either provide specific services for which fees are collected—such as the registration of trademarks—or subsist on the earnings of capital—as does the International Bank—almost all the associations have one overshadowing financial problem in common: how to collect assessments or pledges in the absence of effective sanctions. In the best of circumstances collecting a bill without effective enforcement measures is difficult. It is much more difficult to collect a bill for expenses incurred in pursuit of organizational policies to which some members are actively opposed, a frequent occurrence in international organizations. Both these difficulties occur with some acuteness in the United Nations and the specialized agencies. This article will, therefore, concentrate on the financing of the fifteen governmental organizations that make up the United Nations complex.

### Methods of financing

Even in a spectrum limited to the United Nations organizations, the financing picture is almost incredibly complicated. It is possible to distinguish at least eight varieties of program and budget operations of the United Nations organizations that pose entirely different financing problems: (1) regular budgets financed through assessments upon members according to agreed contribution formulas; (2) emergency operations financed through assessments upon members according to the agreed formulas; (3) recurrent operations financed by special arrangements concerning contributions with members who are primary parties at interest; (4) recurrent operations financed by voluntary contributions of members; (5) recurrent operations financed by voluntary contributions from members, nonmembers, and private individuals; (6) *ad hoc* operations of variable duration financed from voluntary contributions; (7) regular budgets financed through organizational earnings; (8) investment budgets financed through the use of capital or the sale of organizational or organizationally guaranteed securities.

**Assessments.** The "regular" budgets of the United Nations organizations financed by assessments are eleven in number. Their total value in 1963, as reported by the Advisory Committee on Administrative and Budgetary Questions, was about $189 million. The largest was that of the United Nations itself, $87 million; the smallest was the Intergovernmental Maritime Consultative Organization, $421,000. These budgets are prepared by the responsible executive officers or authorities of the several organizations and adopted by their legislative bodies. The budgets are subject to review of their program and expenditure proposals by the Advisory Committee on Administrative and Budgetary Questions, which, in accordance with the UN Charter, reports to the General Assembly through Committee V; the views of the General Assembly on the budgets are communicated to the organizations and to the member states. Although without binding effect, these views are very influential in the councils of the specialized agencies. The contributions formulas utilized by the organizations tend generally to follow that of the United Nations itself, which is based upon comparative ability of each member to pay, as measured by its gross national product, with certain adjustments and modifications. However, some of the organizations introduce other factors especially related to their purposes. The International Civil Aviation Organization, for example, weights its contribution formula 75 per cent on ability to pay and 25 per cent on the relative volume of the ton-kilometers of international air transport flown by air lines of the member states, as an index of the interest in and importance of civil aviation among the contracting governments. Although payment is slow, virtually all the assessments for the regular budgets are eventually collected. The United Nations, for example, normally collects about 80 per cent of the annual assessment by the end of the year for which it is levied, about 95 per cent of the assessment by the closing months of the following year, and about 99 per cent by the end of the second year.

The most dramatic examples of emergency financing are provided by the United Nations Emergency Force established after the Suez incident in 1956 and the United Nations operation in the Congo, which began in 1960. In 1956 the United States offered to contribute $10 million toward the cost of the emergency force if other countries would contribute an equal amount—that is, to increase its share under the formula from 33⅓ per cent to 50 per cent, of a total assessment of $20 million. This offer was accepted by the General Assembly and established the assessment formula whereby the General Assembly spread costs of the emergency force over 1957, 1958, and 1959. In 1960 the assessment formula was changed to relieve the members least able to pay, while several of the richer members waived drawbacks to which they were entitled by reason of special services or commodities supplied the emergency force. All of the Iron Curtain countries ignored the assessments; Yugoslavia was the only communist state to support the undertaking. As a result of the refusal of the Iron Curtain countries to pay, and the delinquency of others, total arrears and defaults amounted to about one-third of total assessments. The Congo operation was of a different magnitude. In 1960 the General Assembly spread $48.5 million on the basis of the 1960 formula. In 1962 it spread $100 million for the Congo operation, against an estimated cost of $135 million, as "expenses of the Organization," without reference to its levying authority under article 17 of the charter, nor did it define the levy as a "binding legal obligation." The ambiguity of the resolution led to the advisory opinion by the World Court, on July 20, 1962, upholding the levy as a legal obligation binding on the members. The default of the communist bloc, France, South Africa, and others, and the arrearages of many of the smaller states, led to the UN bond issue of $200 million in 1962. The financing of emergency operations remains one of the largest and most perilous of the unresolved issues confronting the United Nations.

Perhaps the clearest illustration of the financing of special benefit operations by an international agency is the joint-support program operated by the International Civil Aviation Organization (ICAO). For example, 18 nations cooperate, under the supervision of ICAO, in maintaining radio and weather stations in the northern Atlantic. The 9 floating ocean stations are supplied with ships by 7 of the contracting states, and 11 others, whose aircraft fly northern Atlantic routes, make cash contributions. Each contribution is individually negotiated, but its value in money or kind is generally proportionate to the contributor's use of the northern Atlantic air lanes.

**Voluntary contributions.** The Expanded Program of Technical Assistance, inaugurated in 1950, and the Special Fund, launched in 1959, provide the best examples of international "voluntary" programs financed from contributions of members. The Expanded Program of Technical Assistance began with $20 million, contributed by 54 members; its annual budget in 1963 was more than $45 million, subscribed by about 100 governments. The Special Fund finances actual preparatory and pre-investment costs for major economic and social development projects; its annual expenditures on such operations have reached $60 million.

The United Nations Children's Fund (UNICEF) is not only the oldest program financed by members, nonmembers, and private individuals but is perhaps the most successful international philanthropic undertaking in history. It started in 1947 with $15 million, contributed by the United States government. By 1963 its annual budget from governments, including nonmembers of the UN, was more than $23 million, and an additional $8 million was realized from private contributions and the sale of UNICEF greeting cards. The International Refugee Program, which began as a purely intergovernmental organization, has likewise secured important resources in recent years from private sources.

The United Nations Korean Relief Agency (UNKRA), which has been liquidated, the United Nations Relief and Works Agency for Palestine Refugees in the Near East (UNRWA), and the United Nations Development Fund for the Congo provide examples of *ad hoc* operations financed from voluntary contributions. UNKRA began its work in 1951 with a budget of about $500,000. It reached the peak of its operations in the years 1953, 1954, and 1955, with expenditures of $58 million, $47 million, and $32 million respectively. From 1951 through 1960 it spent a total of $149 million contributed by 40 governments, of which 70 per cent was contributed by the United States and 20 per cent by the United Kingdom. UNRWA was established in 1949, following the partition of Palestine. By the end of 1962 it had spent about $434 million, of which about 70 per cent was supplied by the United States, while the United King-

dom, France, and Canada contributed an additional 25 per cent. The United Nations Fund for the Congo set a goal of $100 million for economic and social development in the new republic; by 1963 less than half this amount had been subscribed, of which the U.S. contribution was more than 75 per cent.

**Self-financing.** The administrative budgets of the International Bank for Reconstruction and Development, the International Monetary Fund, and the International Finance Corporation are examples of regular budgets financed through organizational earnings. These earnings are derived from interest and other charges on loans, advances, and investments made from capital subscribed by member states or surcharges on loans guaranteed by the bank. No recurrent assessments on members are involved in meeting these budgets.

The International Bank for Reconstruction and Development derives the funds for its investments from the use of capital subscribed by member states and from the sale of the securities of members with the bank's guarantee to public and private investors. The International Finance Corporation also participates in the financing of development enterprises through the use of capital funds and through the sale of paper representing a combination of equity and loan investment. The ability of these organizations to make loans and investments is a function of their own liquidity, of the availability of funds in the private money markets, and, most important, the prestige of the lending institutions.

### Political problems

Profound difficulties arise in fixing the levels of activity and financial support of international organizations. With respect to regular activities financed by agreed annual assessments, these difficulties arise from (a) the insistence of the United States on restricting its contribution to not more than one-third of the total assessment and (b) the probably very substantial underassessment of the Soviet Union and its satellites (in 1964 the U.S.S.R. paid 14.97 per cent of the regular UN budget, while the United States paid 32.02 per cent). These facts produce two consequences: first, since most of the other members have very limited possibilities of increasing their contributions, the activities of the organizations are held to a low level; second, to the extent that activities are expanded, a heavy burden is thrown upon the members least able to pay. Although the sanction of withdrawal of voting rights (which has never been invoked by the UN but has been used by some of the specialized agencies) is sufficient to secure eventual compliance, payment is slow and the burden upon working capital funds is heavy.

The crisis in UN finances, however, has actually been produced by emergency peace-keeping operations, for which many of its members accept no financial responsibility and to most of which the Soviet bloc, along with a varying but substantial group of associates, is actively opposed. Moreover, under the UN Charter the sanction procedures involving the suspension of voting privileges are facultative, not mandatory. The General Assembly is understandably reluctant to invoke sanctions against a major power. But until the problem of financing peace-keeping expenditures is satisfactorily resolved—and no solution other than enforceable assessments seems realistic—the United Nations will continue to teeter on the edge of bankruptcy.

The problem arising with respect to activities financed by voluntary contributions is likewise the low ceiling created by United States policy in limiting its percentage contribution, coupled with the outright refusal of the communist bloc to contribute at all. The UN's Expanded Program of Technical Assistance, therefore, continues to be a token operation in comparison with the national programs of the United States, the United Kingdom, France, the Colombo Plan nations, and the U.S.S.R.

The only types of international budgets that do not encounter continuing difficulties in obtaining support are those which finance activities with a definable cash-in-hand value for the participants, such as the ICAO northern Atlantic weather stations, or the administrative budgets financed from earnings on capital, such as those of the World Bank, International Monetary Fund, and International Finance Corporation. Although extensive attention has been given in academic circles to the development of independent revenue sources for activities without strong economic appeal—all the way from imposing a 3 per cent sales tax to giving Antarctica to the UN as a dowry—no viable proposals have so far materialized. Indeed, the idea of independent financing commands little support—and considerable outright opposition—in political circles of many nations. The prospect is that multilateral international cooperation will, as a consequence of financial limitations, continue to function at a low level of achievement. In view of developing political trends toward nonalignment and the resulting circumscription of bilateral cooperation, the outlook is for a steady decline in all international financial cooperation.

ROWLAND EGGER

[*See also* BUDGETING; POLITICAL FINANCING.]

BIBLIOGRAPHY

CLARK, GRENVILLE; and SOHN, LOUIS B. (1958) 1960 *World Peace Through World Law.* 2d ed., rev. Cambridge, Mass.: Harvard Univ. Press.

COMMISSION TO STUDY THE ORGANIZATION OF PEACE 1957 *Strengthening the United Nations.* New York: Harper.

GROSS, LEO 1963 Expenses of the United Nations for Peace-keeping Operations: The Advisory Opinion of the International Court of Justice. *International Organization* 17:1–35.

HOGG, JOHN FERGUSSON 1962 Peace-keeping Costs and Charter Obligations: Implications of the International Court of Justice Decision (July 20, 1962) on Certain Expenses of the United Nations. *Columbia Law Review* 62:1230–1263.

INTERNATIONAL COURT OF JUSTICE 1962 *Pleadings: Certain Expenses of the United Nations (Article 17, Paragraph 2 of the Charter)—Advisory Opinion of July 20, 1962.* The Hague: The Court.

LEAGUE OF NATIONS, SECRETARIAT, INFORMATION SECTION (1923) 1928 *The League of Nations: Financial Administration and Apportionment of Expenses,* by Sir Herbert Ames (financial director). Rev. ed. Geneva: The League.

NICHOLS, CALVIN J. 1961 *Financing the United Nations: Problems and Prospects.* Massachusetts Institute of Technology Center for International Studies, United Nations Project. Cambridge, Mass.: The Institute.

SINGER, J. DAVID 1961 *Financing International Organization: The United Nations Budget Process.* The Hague: Nijhoff.

STOESSINGER, JOHN G. 1961 Financing the United Nations. *International Conciliation* 535:1–72.

STOESSINGER, JOHN G. et al. 1964 *Financing the United Nations System.* Washington: Brookings Institution.

TAUBENFELD, HOWARD J. 1961 A Treaty for Antarctica. *International Conciliation* 531:245–322.

UNITED NATIONS GENERAL ASSEMBLY 1962a *Budget Estimates for the Financial Year 1963 and Information Annexes.* New York: United Nations.

UNITED NATIONS GENERAL ASSEMBLY, ADVISORY COMMITTEE ON ADMINISTRATIVE AND BUDGETARY QUESTIONS 1962b *Seventh Report to the General Assembly at Its Seventeenth Session.* New York: United Nations.

U.S. DEPT. OF STATE 1962 *Information on the Operations and Financing of the United Nations.* Committee on Foreign Relations, U.S. Senate; Committee on Foreign Affairs, U.S. House of Representatives. Washington: Government Printing Office.

# INTERNATIONAL POLITICS

*This article discusses the important institutions, processes, and problems in the relations among nations. For detailed information about related topics, see under* INTERNATIONAL RELATIONS.

Problems of war and peace and of conflict and cooperation among independent political entities have long fascinated statesmen and scholars—in ancient China and India, among the Greek city-states of the fifth century B.C., in Renaissance Italy, and in the Western state system, which in our own day has become a world system. Because the members of this Western state system have been nation-states, the study of political relations in a system of multiple sovereignties has come to be known as inter-*national* relations.

However, "the state" is a mere shorthand expression for a very complex set of relationships among the individuals of which it is composed. To understand the relations between states, one is therefore driven to the study of human behavior and of interpersonal relations both within and between states, since there is no sharp line separating domestic from world politics. Important insights for this study can be gained from many disciplines: history, economics, sociology, psychology, anthropology, geography, and law, as well as political science.

## The Western state system

The substance of international politics is conflict and its adjustment among groups of people who acknowledge no common supreme authority. While the Western state system has in the last three centuries been remarkably efficient in preserving the independence of nation-states and has been flexible enough to permit the progressive fulfillment of aspirations for national independence throughout the world, it has done so at the cost of intermittent war, including about a dozen general wars into which all, or almost all, of the great powers were eventually drawn. It is because this political process has so often involved war or the threat of war that its study has come to be thought important. Thus, however objective the treatment of the topics studied, there has been a strong normative element in their selection. The study of international relations has been developed by scholars who believe that the future is at most semideterminated and that scholarship can help men move toward a future of their own choice. In the atomic age this quest for a functional equivalent to large-scale war has been given a new urgency.

The vision of a better world, or at least one better organized than the world that floundered into the 1914–1918 war, was the inspiration of the generation of scholars in America and Britain who breathed life into the then new academic specialty. It was a vision dominated by the colossal spirit of Woodrow Wilson. Peace, he thought and preached, was within reach once the "war to end war" had been won. The essential elements in the Wilsonian program for achieving general and permanent peace included a world system of democratically organized states, international understanding, in-

ternational arbitration, disarmament, national self-determination, open diplomacy, mechanisms for peaceful change, and an alliance of all against any aggressor. A complete prescription for a better world has to do more, however, than list the conditions under which peace with justice would prevail. In a world political arena in which the governments of nation-states are the leading actors and the loyalties of men are primarily to their respective nation-states, it is not "the world," but men charged with promoting and maintaining the security and well-being of the inhabitants of particular nation-states, who make the decisions that shape the future. A second generation of scholars has put more emphasis on clarifying questions of national policy and on elaborating theoretical constructs than on making blueprints for a warless world. [*See* INTERNATIONAL RELATIONS.]

As the Western state system has become a world system, the necessity for the student of international relations to appreciate diversities and uniformities among states and cultures has become acute. The intensive development of studies of the non-Europeanized areas of the world after World War II and the concurrent emphasis on comparative politics are responses to these twin requirements. From the vast array of potentially relevant data, the international relations scholar has a staggeringly difficult task of selection and organization. From the historian, the geographer, and the area specialist particularly come the data for understanding the behavior of individual states. From the students of comparative politics, comparative social systems, and international law come the data for the discovery of behavioral regularities among classes of states and even of states in general. From the international systems theorists come the analytical models with specified "essential rules" to which concrete systems with their behavioral regularities may be compared. [*See* SYSTEMS ANALYSIS, *article on* INTERNATIONAL SYSTEMS.]

Both the Western state system as a whole and the behavior of its constituent units are constantly changing. Identifying the major transformations in the system is a central task for the scholar who wishes to chart the limits of choice open to the makers of public policy with specified value preferences.

Concurrent with the transformation of a state system of European origin into a world system have been other great transformations: unprecedented roles are being played by the United States and the Soviet Union, superpowers peripheral to Europe. From its west European area of origin the appeal of nationalism has spread outward to the Afro–

Asian world, and along with it demands for higher living standards and the dignity of participating in political life. Control of foreign relations in the advanced countries has become democratized; at the same time the tasks of the makers of foreign policy have become increasingly complex and difficult. While the bearers of the most advanced technology have in each era enjoyed dominant positions in the state system of that era, science and technology have suddenly emerged as important and semi-independent short-run variables in the equations of world politics. The old states of western Europe and those across the ocean that share European culture are drawing together in varying forms of association for economic and security purposes. New tasks have been posed for those responsible for military defense, especially for the policy makers in the superpowers. They must maintain a high level of peacetime defense mobilization, form peacetime alliances in which coalition military planning is extremely detailed, embark upon massive programs of foreign economic and military aid, and pursue a vigorous psychological strategy—with at least as much emphasis on deterring major war as on winning it. Ideological differences divide the most powerful groupings of states.

We shall discuss in turn the actors on the stage of world politics, the goals and claims of these actors, the bases of their power, and the methods and instrumentalities by which the power is applied in the pursuit of goals. Actors, goals, bases of influence, instrumentalities—these are all artificial constructs which have to be fitted together to produce an analytical model with some resemblance to the real world; but as long as they are recognized as abstractions useful for focusing on particular aspects of international relations, they should not mislead.

### The actors

**State actors.**    The modern nation-state began to emerge in the fifteenth century with the division of Europe into units whose monarchs recognized no superior authority.

*Sovereignty.*    The distinguishing characteristic for international relations became sovereignty, defined by Grotius as "that power whose acts are not subject to the control of another so that they may be made void by the act of any other human will." Nevertheless, the restraints of international law can be discerned even at this period: even when they felt no moral restraint, absolute monarchs usually found it convenient to observe certain rules of conduct in their relations with each other, rules that reflected their Christian and Roman heritage.

Thus, there was a "suborganized" state system, and not pure anarchy.

In domestic affairs the divine-right king gave way in the course of time, but not everywhere at the same rate, to constitutional government. As representatives of the ruled became the rulers in the nineteenth century, their governments became more and more amenable to the influence of organized sectors of the public. This development did not reduce the role of violence in interstate politics. In fact, as the monarch's business became the people's business, the nation in arms could wage war with a mobilization of its energies far more intensive than any divine-right king could have imagined. Relations between states became subject to irrational outbursts of feeling directed against foreigners and foreign governments suspected of hostile intentions to both people and state. [See SOVEREIGNTY.]

*Nationality and self-determination.*    In the nineteenth century the sovereign-state had become a nation-state. Its inhabitants were supposed to be united by a common nationality and separated from other nation-states by this characteristic. Efforts to define nationality in terms of common language, racial heritage, customs, religion, and so forth are insufficient to explain the existing patterns of loyalty to contemporary nation-states. A sense of nationality is subjective, and people belong to the nationality to which they feel they belong, for whatever reason. However, more often than not, states seem to have come into being before the nation that might have demanded their creation was formed. This is not to depreciate the power of feelings of national solidarity, for demands for national self-determination generated most of the bitter conflicts of the nineteenth and early twentieth centuries.

The doctrine of national self-determination, according to which all people of one nationality are entitled to dwell together in order to govern themselves in a state of their own—despite any or all economic, historical, or other obstacles—proved so strong a moving force that it continues in our own day in a modified form. Yet even in Europe the doctrine proved very difficult to apply. It provided no clear basis for defining the territorial limits of a particular nationality and made no adequate provision for the people of the marches. Furthermore, it offered no way to identify the "national" will. The earlier excesses committed in the name of nationalism, the promise of rising living standards implicit in the reduction of intra-European trade barriers, and the obsolescence of European-sized states as independently defensible units in a world of superpowers have since 1945 driven the peoples of western Europe to play down nationality as a unifying force against outsiders. It is ironic to find the same slogans used in the Afro–Asian world today, where circumstances are greatly at variance with those in Europe in the nineteenth century. Lacking the cohesion of older political communities, many of these newer units are led by men who play upon their followers' fear of outsiders. [See NATION.]

More and more, the life of the people has become identified with what the government does, even in the least socialistically inclined states. The prevalence of the welfare state suggests that individuals gain more than physical and psychological security in identifying themselves with their nation; they secure valuable material advantages as well. In the 1960s more than 125 entities are formally recognized as states. Yet hardly more than half of them exhibit the classical attributes of a viable sovereign state. While they all have a population and in most cases a clearly defined territorial base, many of them lack a "people." The government is often not in effective control within the country, and its authority is not always recognized outside the national territory. In many of the "fledgling" states, who is to govern is not yet clearly settled; instead of law and order there are constant outbreaks of rebellion. [See STATE.]

**Nonstate actors.**    States are not the sole significant actors in international relations. On the formal level must be added various kinds of organizations of states that governments have formed in order to increase their physical security or to achieve economic benefits (or even, in some cases, to satisfy their humanitarian impulses). There are a large number of functional international organizations and the almost universal United Nations. In addition, there are many regional "special-purpose" organizations. The institutions of the European communities can even to a minor degree act without the specific consent of each member state. Even military alliances may take the form of a regional international organization, the most highly developed being the North Atlantic Treaty Organization (NATO). Groups of states, whether or not formally organized, often act together as blocs for diplomatic purposes. [See INTERNATIONAL ORGANIZATION, *article on* THE PROCESS AND THE INSTITUTIONS.]

Another form of association that can on occasion affect the course of world politics is the transnational grouping, such as the World Federation of Trade Unions and its noncommunist rival, the International Confederation of Free Trade Unions. The thin line that can be drawn between "public" and "private" becomes even thinner as we move on to cosmopolitan religious groups, such as the Roman Catholic church, or ideological groups, such as the world-wide communist movement.

This does not mean that the state is withering away as the prime actor in international relations. Even in the most effective international organizations, the will of the individual states still dominates the decision-making process. Each individual born and raised in a Western or Westernized society has indelibly imprinted on him membership in some national grouping. No matter how cosmopolitan his outlook, he will identify himself, and others will identify him, by this imprint. This habit of identifying individuals by their national affiliation is so ingrained that a Western observer often assumes members of non-European societies will inevitably outgrow their communal or tribal loyalties and put loyalty to the nation first. There is in the Western world a strengthening of transnational bonds, but they remain less strong than the bonds of nationality. They are strong enough to support a limited amount of joint action in world affairs among states with common goals, exposed to common threats.

**National decision makers.**    Scholars have long related individuals to the behavior of the nation-state actors by describing group attitudes—subnational, national, transnational, and supranational. A post-World War II phenomenon has been an intensified study of the behavior of decision-making elites in the various states.

Who are the most influential decision makers in international relations? They are first of all those who control the levers of power within the national governments. Some few individuals—e.g., the president of the United States, the prime minister of the United Kingdom, the chancellor of the German Federal Republic—are important because of their official positions. Other individuals—e.g., Charles de Gaulle, Joseph Stalin, Mao Tse-tung, Jawaharlal Nehru, and Gamal Abdel Nasser—would also be named, whatever their titular position in the government.

Even the influence of such august individuals, however, depends on their positions of leadership in official or unofficial groups of political importance, whether it be the Central Committee of the Communist Party in the Soviet Union, the clique of colonels in the Egyptian army, the British Trade Union Congress, the French bureaucratic elite, the committees of the United States Senate and House of Representatives, the tribal organization of Katanga, or the leading stockholders of the Belgian Union Minière.

Political parties as such are not often important participants in the making of foreign policy, which in the noncommunist world is frequently carried on in a relatively "nonpartisan" fashion. As the division between domestic and foreign policy becomes less precise, this may change. Formerly, even in the most democratically organized governments, strong pressure groups rarely directed their attention to issues of significance in foreign policy, although sometimes their activities had important foreign policy consequences. Tariffs and immigration policy in the United States, for example, were long shaped by domestic pressure groups heedless of the impact of their demands on the country's foreign relations. Today all the traditional economic groupings—agricultural, industrial, commercial, financial, and labor—to say nothing of noneconomic organizations, such as patriotic societies and religious groups, have international as well as domestic concerns. Finally, one should note how slight is the influence of the unorganized "mass" of the people on critical foreign policy decisions. Even in times of great crisis, when they may be whipped into a fury against another people, or, as in some underdeveloped countries, mobilized into crowds for paid demonstrations against the leaders' foes, their influence in the making of foreign policy is minimal. If "the people" have little to do with the making of foreign policy, "world public opinion" and "the conscience of mankind," by which Woodrow Wilson set great store, have even less. However, leaders of one state may make extremely effective appeals to the leaders and "attentive publics" of states not directly involved in a given dispute; in this very different sense, "world public opinion" may be important. [See FOREIGN POLICY.]

## National goals and the power base

As the scholar's understanding of the influences playing on national governments becomes more sophisticated and he grows more aware of different types of states and state behavior, he becomes less satisfied with generalized explanations regarding the goals and demands of states. The characteristic protestations of every premier and foreign minister that his state seeks only peace and prosperity do little to illuminate the objectives of either states in general or the particular state to whom these unexceptional aspirations are at the moment being attributed. But conventional "national interest" or "power" explanations are hardly more helpful. In a crisis of national survival the national interest is clear enough, but this tells us little about what the national interest is between crises or what kind of threat to what values constitutes a crisis. Nor does the proposition that states always seek to maximize their power position teach much about either the prediction or control of state behavior. It is no doubt true that each government takes all the steps which seem appropriate to it to attain its policy objectives and in that sense is trying to maximize its power position. But power for what and at what cost? With what intensity and what constancy of purpose? And with what skill are available resources mobilized and deployed to achieve the specified purposes? "Power" is thus not seen as the overriding goal of state behavior, nor as the ultimate value of statesmen, but rather as "that which produces its intended effect" (Wright 1955, p. 559).

The foregoing propositions may not explain the behavior of states, but they do suggest that the goals of particular governments at particular times may be classified, hypotheses may be developed regarding these classifications, and patterns of common behavior may be traced.

A state's goals may be inconsistent or in conflict with each other. There are goals that will assure two states being in conflict with each other, goals that states can share, goals that though separate are compatible, and goals that can be achieved only through interstate cooperation. The greater the number of states in the system, the more complicated and crisscrossed will these goal relationships become, and the greater the likelihood that groups of states will band together for certain common purposes.

**National security.** The primary goal of most governments in our own state system in recent centuries has been "security," which always includes safeguards against immediate threats to the physical integrity of the national homeland; it often includes safeguards against indirect, long-run, and contingent threats, and against threats to a way of life as well as to territory. The comprehensiveness of the goal of security for any given state is determined by what its government would be willing, if necessary, to wage war for. Thus security, like power, turns out to be an instrumental rather than an ultimate goal. Unlike power, however, it is an instrumental goal whose satisfaction does not necessarily deny similar satisfaction to other states. [See NATIONAL SECURITY.]

The occasional "great disturbers"—like Louis XIV, Napoleon, and Hitler, whose objectives seemed to their contemporaries to go so far beyond the requirement of security as to threaten the independence of all the rest—provoked the formation of grand alliances against themselves and thus demonstrated the interest in security which the allies in each case shared.

Today this primary goal of security seems more elusive than ever before, even in an age when a large proportion of literate people believe that their survival depends upon the survival of the rest of the world. It did not take the advent of nuclear weapons to make this the most important problem to solve. Two world wars with conventional weapons had already taught many people that widespread violence could destroy for the victor as well as for the vanquished many of those values which the government had been expected to promote and protect.

This brings us to the question of means, for both in international and in domestic politics the way in which ultimate goals are pursued may turn out to be more significant than the goals themselves. Here we may visualize a continuum of means–ends relationships, at the further end of which stand such ultimate goals as freedom, welfare, and human dignity—and, if all else be denied, survival. In the context of interstate relations, "survival" means the preservation of the nation-state as the carrier and promoter of the common values that characterize its people's way of life. The goal of survival cannot rationally be promoted by means which sacrifice the values that give the survival of a state meaning to the men who make or influence its foreign policy decisions. Thus, even in the period of overwhelming American superiority in nuclear arms, the offensive or preventive use of such weapons was among the excluded means.

**Mobilized power and power potential.** Power, the means of influencing the behavior of others in a specific manner, unlike money in the bank, is not available to be drawn on for any purpose. One can speak of a state's power as adequate or inadequate only in relation to particular purposes at particular times and places against particular competitors. On the other hand, one can speak of power potential as being generally great or small. At a very low level of organization of material and human resources, potential elements of a state's power are equally available for the achievement of a wide variety of policy objectives. How these elements will be mobilized depends on the particular policies pursued.

The rise of modern Germany from its modest Brandenburg–Prussian beginnings to a position from which it could challenge the whole European order in two twentieth-century wars is a reminder that a slender resource base may be sufficient to pose a fearful threat to opponents with incomparably greater unmobilized resources. The Chinese People's Republic, like the Soviet Union under Stalin, has demonstrated how a ruthless sacrifice of other human values may enable a state with a resource base smaller than that of its major opponent to vault rapidly to heights of influence. Fi-

nally, the capacity of apparently weak new countries in the first stages of economic development to extract favors from both sides in a period of bipolar competition is a source of continuing wonder. Power potential and the satisfaction of particular foreign policy demands are evidently not closely related.

Although great resources do not assure great power, they are a prerequisite to it. The ships and specie of sixteenth-century and seventeenth-century Spain and the Netherlands made great-power status possible for these countries, but after the seventeenth century were not capable of keeping the countries within the circle of the great powers. In the age of coal and iron Austria–Hungary and Italy could be great powers only in name. Strategic air and missile power calls for a mobilization in peacetime of industrial and human resources in magnitudes previously unimagined. This would seem to exclude all but two of this era's more than one hundred sovereignties from being in the first rank in that particular form of power competition.

Apart from the very special case of capacity to wage, threaten, or deter thermonuclear war against a power with a similar capability, how can one relate the capability of particular states and groups of states to implement their policy objectives to their respective power potential, i.e., to the bases of influence ultimately available to them? And what basic factors enter into the calculation of a state's potential? Some of these factors may impose restraints that cannot be overcome. And some on examination reveal opportunities for a significant enhancement of capacity to achieve certain kinds of objectives. [See MILITARY POWER POTENTIAL.]

Historical and geographic factors belong in the first category, for history cannot be relived, and the shape of the continents and the location of mineral resources remain fixed. Under present technological conditions a country's capacity to transcend limitations imposed by a meager energy potential appears restricted.

The population ratios between competing countries change slowly but inexorably and are hardly likely to be affected by calculations made in a foreign policy context. However, the numbers of people with particular desired military, scientific, industrial, professional, or administrative skills are subject to significant manipulation within a single decade; at least between countries of fairly advanced technology and roughly comparable populations, this may be of great political significance.

The rapid changes caused by the accelerating pace of scientific and technological advance, and particularly by its impact on military technology, open up a whole new aspect of international relations. New discoveries in science and technology promise much for the developing countries, but the fact remains that the rich countries get both absolutely and relatively richer, while the poorer ones have trouble even holding their own.

States with a large gross national product and a high per capita income are likely to be among the most powerful. Yet the significance of these indices for a state's power position can be understood only if one also takes into account the distribution of wealth and employment, rates of taxation, voluntary saving and consumption, and the investment of what has not been immediately consumed in particular forms of enterprise. Today, education and scientific research, as well as defense industries and the armed services, are categories of public investment with middle-run and long-run significance for world politics. The various factors contributing to power potential are intertwined, and it is particularly difficult to disentangle the economic factor from the others.

Only when one pays attention to these additional factors can one explain how the Soviet Union, poor in relation to the United States in terms of both gross national product and per capita income, has come to be one of the two most powerful countries in the world. In the Chinese People's Republic the data about gross national product and per capita income are even less adequate as explanations of its expanded influence in the Asian theater of world politics.

The material elements in a state's power potential may or may not be effectively mobilized for promoting its claims in international politics. Less tangible factors, such as national morale and capacity to evoke help from abroad, may be of primary importance in contributing to the actual power of a state in a particular conflict situation.

## Modes of state action

**War and the threat of war.** A state has several methods of influencing others, each of which requires a different way of mobilizing the elements that make up its power potential. The means longest and most intensively studied is, of course, the threat and use of violence. Long before Clausewitz enunciated his famous aphorism, statesmen acted as if they understood that war was an extension of politics. In the atomic age, however, a rational policy maker recoils from ordering the use of violence on a scale that may escalate into a two-way thermonuclear exchange. Thus, the attention of both men of affairs and scholars has been turned to deterrence—how to inhibit an enemy from launching a thermonuclear attack. The "delicate balance of terror" of the late 1950s and 1960s has given a fresh stimulus to research into arms races; it has also invited investigation into a variety of forms of nonnuclear warfare, including the "unconventional" warfare with which the world became familiar in southeast Asia and Algeria. This delicate balance has called for new thinking about ways of adjusting peacetime military policy to diplomatic policy and to national security policy as a whole, and of relating all of these to the requirements of domestic policy. There is an unfamiliar terrain to be studied between total war and total peace, with limited-war and cold-war intermediate bands in a spectrum of violent and nonviolent forms of political competition. [*See* WAR.]

All-out war has never been a rational, all-purpose instrument for securing and promoting the goals of foreign policy; for only the most urgent and precious objectives are worth the sacrifice of so much blood and treasure. In two world wars the administrative skills, patriotic sentiments, and high productivity of modern industrial states made it possible to allocate such massive resources to war that the technical possibilities of destruction and killing outran every conceivable objective except that of meeting the threat posed by other states with similar capabilities. It is still more difficult, in the era of strategic air and missile power, to conceive of unlimited war as a rational method for settling any conflict of interest between states. Only as a deterrent or as a retaliatory capability to compel an opponent to accept the settlement of conflicts at a less destructive level of competition can such military capabilities be rationally related to the objectives of foreign policy.

**Diplomacy.** The capacity to wage war is often necessary to support another method used by states to influence other states: diplomacy. Its practice goes back to antiquity, although the first permanent missions maintained in foreign countries date in our state system only from the late fifteenth century. Ambassadors are sent to negotiate with other governments. Negotiation implies bargaining, a willingness to give as well as to take, and an assumption that the parties wish to conclude a mutually advantageous exchange.

Contemporary demands on diplomacy, however, pose a number of problems for Western countries. The usefulness of diplomacy is limited in relations with the communists, who, though they are not always averse to bargaining, are more likely to conduct their "diplomacy" for propaganda purposes than for the purpose of reaching an agreement. Western diplomats also find difficulty in negotiating with some of the less experienced representatives of new or underdeveloped countries. The new diplomats do not always appreciate the value of long-established rules and understandings basic to successful diplomacy, including the importance of proven good faith.

"Open diplomacy," advocated earlier in the twentieth century by some nonprofessionals, is now seen to be still another obstacle to the conduct of mutually useful negotiations; it is now understood that it is "secret alliances" rather than confidential negotiations that were the proper objects of obloquy. These problems are compounded by a new development: the increasing use of multilateral or conference diplomacy. It remains true that the diplomat must, as one participant observed, find a firm basis for agreement or disagreement, as the case may be. [See DIPLOMACY.]

**Psychological and economic strategies.**  While diplomats deal with governments, those responsible for psychological strategy, a comparatively new instrumentality of states, work upon the attitudes of influential people behind the governments and only indirectly upon the governments themselves. Psychological strategy, the deliberate and extensive use of which dates roughly from World War I, enjoyed great success in disintegrating the military effort of the Central Powers in that war. Since World War II it has been extensively used to counter the appeal of world communism; it has also been used by the noncommunist governments in support of many other policy objectives. Subversion of hostile governments is only one of its uses. It may be employed in friendly countries to broaden the base of support for cooperative action and in uncommitted countries to gain new support for current policy objectives. Psychological strategy cannot be conducted wholly on a verbal level. Only substantive deeds consistent with the strategy can make it believable. In this respect, psychological strategy is no different from other instruments of state action; none of them can be efficiently used in isolation. [See PSYCHOLOGICAL WARFARE.]

Governments have long directed their trade relations with other states into desired channels (or obstructed those relations to the desired extent by tariffs, quotas, embargoes, and other trade restrictions). They have, especially in recent decades, become skillful in manipulating their currencies. A third mode of economic action, foreign aid, is in its contemporary peacetime form relatively new. Its intensive use dates from World War II, although states with more specie than manpower to send to battle have in former times subsidized their war partners.

Using economic means for political ends, however, often conflicts with using economic means for economic ends. Embargoes, tariffs, and quotas have been used to weaken or intimidate opponents and to strengthen or attract friends at great cost to the state's own economic welfare. Even more clear was the conflict between the prescriptions of classical economic theory relating to the specialization and efficient division of labor and efforts to make the state self-sufficient for defense purposes. Between the more advanced countries today, especially among the six nations of the European Economic Community, these conflicts are beginning to be eliminated through organized cooperation to broaden markets and increase security as a by-product. Even here, however, old-fashioned patriotism, vested interest groups such as subsidized farmers, and efforts to enhance the political influence of one state over another prevent the selection of what would in any purely economic calculus be the most rational policy choices. [See ECONOMIC WARFARE.]

**International law and organization.**  International law and international organization may provide effective modes of action for promoting those values which states share and can pursue together. International law is not meant to be a "maid of all work" but a fine instrument for adjusting certain types of interstate conflict. It cannot aid in settling the major ideological conflicts of the twentieth century. Many of the non-Western countries that were formerly colonies view some of its precepts as more appropriate for supporting the interests of their former masters than those of the new states. Nevertheless, techniques of international legal analysis, especially among friendly states of western European civilization, yield mutually satisfactory solutions to a wide variety of interstate disputes. Even between states unfriendly toward each other, international legal standards may regulate state behavior because failure to conform to such standards would mean the loss of advantages gained from having others do the same. [See INTERNATIONAL LAW.]

International organizations have become instruments of state policy only in the nineteenth and twentieth centuries. At the time of the Congress of Vienna, 1815, provision was already made for multilateral regulation of European international waterways, but the creation of formal international organizations for the cooperative performance of specific functions dates generally from the mid-nineteenth century. In the 1960s the United States belongs to over four hundred international organizations. Most of these are special-purpose organizations. Some of the most important are affiliated with the United Nations (as many of them had been with the League of Nations), e.g., the Universal Postal Union, the World Health Organization. The League of Nations and the United Nations, however, were organized with broader aims in mind; they were to provide for pacific settlement of disputes and for what came to be called collective security. Intended to be world-wide in membership, by 1967 the United Nations contained over 120 members and had become particularly useful for the smaller, newer states, who were more able to compete on equal terms in this forum than through normal channels of diplomacy or on the field of battle. The superpowers have seldom overlooked any opportunity to use the United Nations to score propaganda points against each other. The United Nations is unsuited in its present form, and probably no suitable form could be devised, for settling serious conflicts between the major powers. [See INTERNATIONAL ORGANIZATION.]

The juridical equality inherent in the concept of the existing multiple-sovereignty system is, however, very imperfectly reflected in the real world of international politics. Thus, in an imperial relationship the metropolitan power exercises close control over colonies, which ordinarily lack juridical status in the system; or a solar power may exercise a looser control over its satellites, who do retain their juridical status of sovereignty. Only the remnants of the colonial relationship survive in the noncommunist world; the satellite relationship, however, remains important, particularly in the Soviet bloc. While colonies have everywhere been throwing off the shackles of empire, there remains in some cases a very amorphous relationship, typified by the (British) Commonwealth of Nations and more recently by the French Community. The Commonwealth is a form of equal association between the former mother country and the former colonies. It is a voluntary association at the end point in a peaceful process of devolution. Some other associations, such as NATO and the European Communities, register piecemeal efforts at integration. Fusion and fission among states are taking place simultaneously but at different rates in different places with respect to different activities.

## Power relations, peace, and stability

Independent sovereign states or groups of associated states, however equal their legal status, have widely varying political and military capabilities, as indeed is implied by the continuing use of such terms as "great powers," "the superpowers," "the first-ranking powers," "the major states," etc. Yet the system of interstate relations and the identity of its members demonstrate an impressive continuity. Once born, sovereign states have rarely in recent centuries lost their identity through war or conquest. To understand why the small and weak survive in a world of great powers and, latterly, superpowers, one must consider the set of power relations that has characterized our "suborganized" Western state system.

**Balance of power.** The balance of power may be thought of as inherent in any political process: the world political process at any moment registers the equilibrium established by the amount and direction of pressure that each participant is applying. It may be thought of as a policy pursued by a leading participant to make that equilibrium stable. Finally, one may think of it as an institution in our Western state system: given the norm and the expectation that no one state is to become so powerful as to be capable of overturning the system, states have tended to build armaments and to form alliances to meet a clearly identified threat before some point of no return has been passed. Furthermore, great states have been unwilling to see other great states become greater by absorbing small states that lay between them.

In its classical form the stability of the balance of power rested upon several powers and the willingness of at least some of them to intervene or even to change sides to prevent any of the others from gaining hegemony. The reduction in number of first-ranking states, the ideological struggle that legitimizes and intensifies the all but inevitable competition between the "big two," and a military technology that compels the first-ranking states to remain in an advanced state of readiness to fight each other make the quest for stability in our time unremitting and burdensome. The lively competition between the two sides in a bipolar world for the good will of the peoples and governments of the nonaligned states and the ingenuity exhibited by each side in bringing pressure to bear upon the other without quite provoking general war are evidence that even under the adverse conditions of the 1960s the balancing process still operates to give some measure of stability to the existing world order. [See BALANCE OF POWER.]

Meanwhile, the Chinese People's Republic is developing as a serious rival to the Soviet Union in the communist bloc, while the economic revival of western Europe and the economic integration of the "Europe of the Six" are leading some observers to forecast that a system of three or even four superpowers might ultimately emerge. Yet none can challenge the United States and the Soviet

Union for pre-eminence in the field of strategic air and missile power, and it is by no means clear that development in either Europe or China of this kind of destructive power on a scale commensurate with the available resources of either will contribute to the stability of the system or to the security of its members.

**Universal and regional security systems.** Universal and regional security arrangements have been variously viewed as substitutes for and refinements of the balance of power. Although a universal system of collective security fulfilling the hopes raised by the signing of the United Nations charter has not been realized, regional security systems have been established. In a universal system a potential "aggressor" would be deterred by the prospect of cooperative action of all the others in coming to the defense of the state that had been attacked and would be checked by the mobilization of preponderant power against the aggression. Among the reasons why such a promise could not be fulfilled are that no government would be willing to commit itself beforehand to action against an unspecified aggressor, no matter how threatening it might be; that no collective force could be established in advance of aggression to enforce a United Nations decision against an aggressor; and that the potential aggressor might well have allies that would make action against it far from a "police action," i.e., far from one-sided. Juridically, enforcement action against a great-power aggressor might not be war; but politically and militarily, it would be war. All of these problems were illustrated in the case of the June 1950 attack on South Korea, the United Nations response to which is the closest thing to collective security the world has yet seen. [See COLLECTIVE SECURITY.]

Regional security arrangements have been predicated on the existence of an identifiable potential aggressor who is not a party to the arrangement. The guarantee which each member gives that an attack upon one will be regarded as an attack upon all appears more reliable, since the signatory states by their formal commitment have given specific advance indication of the contingencies which they regard as directly threatening. Unlike most traditional alliance partners, participants in post-World War II regional arrangements have found it possible to build up a joint defense force in advance of a possible war. They have been able to cooperate in the making of strategic plans that are intended as much to deter as to defeat aggression. In NATO, coalition military planning and command arrangements and the peacetime deployment of forces in accordance with the plans are very far advanced.

Organization is what especially distinguishes these regional security arrangements from previous alliances. [See ALLIANCES.]

"World government" is not a pattern of relationships that can be realistically discussed. If such a development were to take place, it would not eliminate the political process, but the leading actors in the world political process would no longer be "states." However, the assumption that violence would disappear even under such a regime is highly questionable.

## The study of international politics

At the beginning of the twentieth century international law and diplomatic history provided accepted tools for the analysis of international politics. In rough chronological order of emergence, we may identify the following additional approaches to the study: international government, with special reference to the League of Nations; various kinds of "devil" theories—with munitions makers, capitalists, and imperialists variously cast as the "devils"; geopolitics; the "realist" school, stressing the "power drives" of men and states; psychological approaches, emphasizing tensions as causes of war; the behavior of decision-making elites and the shaping of their perspectives; the study of national security policy, with particular attention to military aspects; game and bargaining theories; systems theory and the analysis of transformations in concrete systems; and conflict resolution. Some of these approaches, such as the "devil" theories, are dated and leave no visible mark on contemporary thinking about international relations; but in general the effect of this succession of new approaches has been cumulative.

There is as yet no overarching theory of international politics, and there are few signs that such a theory will emerge in the foreseeable future. Those who are striving to find explanations for phenomena in this field are experimenting in so many different directions that no clear pattern of future development is yet discernible.

Theoretical speculation about international relations is largely confined to the United States, as the bibliography suggests. The names of E. H. Carr and Charles A. W. Manning in England and Raymond Aron in France are nevertheless evidence that there is no American monopoly of theory. The long separation between theories of domestic politics and the study of international relations may be ending, for the "web of politics" comprehends both the civil order and the relatively anarchic international society.

Normative theories generally can be left to the

political philosopher for study and "grand design" theories to the political activist. Nevertheless, even for the "empirical–scientific" theorist, the choice of subject for data collecting and theorizing cannot be separated from the investigator's value preferences. In the second half of the twentieth century, conflict between the "free world" and that of the communists, the problems posed by the underdeveloped countries, and the questions raised by current interest in the building of an Atlantic (or a European) community have absorbed the attention of many scholars—especially those in America and Britain who may believe that the direction in which world political affairs move can in some measure be a matter of conscious choice.

The student of international politics may be able to show that certain goals currently sought are not attainable, or only attainable at too great a cost, while other goals may turn out on analysis to be more easily realized than earlier imagined. Thus, the scholar can increase the efficiency of the decision maker's calculus, helping him both in the selection of economical means and in the clarification of competing goals.

WILLIAM T. R. FOX AND ANNETTE BAKER FOX

[See also FOREIGN POLICY; PEACE; WAR.]

### BIBLIOGRAPHY

ARON, RAYMOND (1962) 1967 *Peace and War: A Theory of International Relations.* Garden City, N.Y.: Doubleday. → First published as *Paix et guerre entre les nations.*

BOZEMAN, ADDA B. 1960 *Politics and Culture in International History.* Princeton Univ. Press.

CARR, EDWARD H. (1939) 1962 *The Twenty Years' Crisis, 1919–1939: An Introduction to the Study of International Relations.* 2d ed. New York: St. Martins.

CLAUDE, INIS L. JR. (1962) 1964 *Power and International Relations.* New York: Random House.

CORBETT, PERCY E. 1951 *Law and Society in the Relations of States.* New York: Harcourt.

DUNN, FREDERICK S. 1951 *War and the Minds of Men.* New York: Harper.

EMERSON, RUPERT 1960 *From Empire to Nation: The Rise to Self-assertion of Asian and African Peoples.* Cambridge, Mass.: Harvard Univ. Press. → A paperback edition was published in 1962 by Beacon.

FOX, WILLIAM T. R. (editor) 1959 *Theoretical Aspects of International Relations.* Univ. of Notre Dame Press.

HERZ, JOHN H. 1959 *International Politics in the Atomic Age.* New York: Columbia Univ. Press. → A paperback edition was published in 1962.

HINSLEY, FRANCIS H. 1963 *Power and the Pursuit of Peace: Theory and Practice in the History of Relations Between States.* Cambridge Univ. Press.

HOFFMANN, STANLEY (editor) 1960 *Contemporary Theory in International Relations.* Englewood Cliffs, N.J.: Prentice-Hall.

KAPLAN, MORTON A. 1957 *System and Process in International Politics.* New York: Wiley.

KNORR, KLAUS E.; and VERBA, SIDNEY (editors) 1961 *The International System: Theoretical Essays.* Princeton Univ. Press.

LASSWELL, HAROLD D. 1935 *World Politics and Personal Insecurity.* New York and London: McGraw-Hill. → A paperback edition was published in 1965 by the Free Press.

LISKA, GEORGE 1957 *International Equilibrium: A Theoretical Essay on the Politics and Organization of Security.* Cambridge, Mass.: Harvard Univ. Press.

MANNING, CHARLES A. W. 1962 *The Nature of International Society.* New York: Wiley.

MORGENTHAU, HANS J. (1948) 1966 *Politics Among Nations: The Struggle for Power and Peace.* 4th ed., rev. New York: Knopf.

RENOUVIN, PIERRE E. G.; and DUROSELLE, JEAN-BAPTISTE 1964 *Introduction à la histoire des relations internationales.* Paris: Colin.

ROSECRANCE, RICHARD N. 1963 *Action and Reaction in World Politics: International Systems in Perspective.* Boston: Little.

RUSSETT, BRUCE M. 1965 *Trends in World Politics.* New York: Macmillan.

RUSSETT, BRUCE M. et al. 1964 *World Handbook of Political and Social Indicators.* New Haven: Yale Univ. Press. → Hayward R. Alker, Jr., Karl W. Deutsch, and Harold D. Lasswell are co-authors.

SPROUT, HAROLD H.; and SPROUT, MARGARET 1962 *Foundations of International Politics.* Princeton, N.J.: Van Nostrand.

SPROUT, HAROLD; and SPROUT, MARGARET 1965 *The Ecological Perspective on Human Affairs, With Special Reference to International Politics.* Princeton Univ. Press.

SPYKMAN, NICHOLAS J. 1942 *America's Strategy in World Politics: The United States and the Balance of Power.* New York: Harcourt.

WALTZ, KENNETH N. 1959 *Man, the State and War: A Theoretical Analysis.* New York: Columbia Univ. Press.

WOLFERS, ARNOLD 1962 *Discord and Collaboration: Essays on International Politics.* Baltimore: Johns Hopkins Press.

WRIGHT, QUINCY 1955 *The Study of International Relations.* New York: Appleton.

# INTERNATIONAL RELATIONS

*The articles under this heading deal with international relations as a field of study. Major elements of international politics are covered in* FOREIGN POLICY; INTERNATIONAL INTEGRATION; INTERNATIONAL LAW; INTERNATIONAL MONETARY ECONOMICS; INTERNATIONAL ORGANIZATION; INTERNATIONAL POLITICS; INTERNATIONAL TRADE. *Methods for the study of international relations are discussed in* COMMUNICATION, POLITICAL; CONFLICT; GEOGRAPHY, *article on* POLITICAL GEOGRAPHY; POWER; SIMULATION, *article on* POLITICAL PROCESSES; SYSTEMS ANALYSIS, *article on* INTERNATIONAL SYSTEMS. *Major concepts and policies are analyzed in* ALLIANCES; BALANCE OF POWER; COLLECTIVE SECURITY; CONTAINMENT; CRISIS; DETERRENCE; DISARMAMENT; DISENGAGEMENT;

NATIONAL INTEREST; NATIONAL SECURITY; NEU-
TRALISM AND NONALIGNMENT; PEACE; POWER
TRANSITION; TRUSTEESHIP. *Instruments of inter-
national politics are dealt with in* DIPLOMACY;
FOREIGN AID; INTERNATIONAL CULTURAL COOPERA-
TION; NEGOTIATION; SANCTIONS, INTERNATIONAL;
TECHNICAL ASSISTANCE; WAR. *Other relevant ma-
terial may be found under* MILITARY.

I. THE FIELD                    *Chadwick F. Alger*
II. IDEOLOGICAL ASPECTS             *John H. Herz*
III. PSYCHOLOGICAL ASPECTS    *Herbert C. Kelman*

# I
## THE FIELD

International relations is a human activity in
which persons from more than one nation, individually and in groups, interact. International relations are carried on by face-to-face contact and
through more indirect communications. Usage of
the term "international relations" by scholars in the
field is not consistent. Some use "international relations" and "international politics" interchangeably,
but many prefer to reserve "international politics"
for relations between governments and use "international relations" as a more inclusive term.
They consider international politics and subjects
such as international economics, international communications, international law, international war,
and international organization to be subcategories
of international relations.

In more popular discourse "international relations" is often used to refer to phenomena about
nations that do not involve relations between them.
Sometimes the study of foreign nations and foreign
governments is called international relations, but
this broad usage is diminishing. The study of international relations includes certain aspects of nations
and their governments, particularly foreign-policy-
making activity. But the more restricted usage that
is evolving includes only those characteristics of
nations that have the greatest effect on interaction
between nations. Advancing knowledge is making
possible more explicit boundaries for the field as
research more clearly identifies which characteristics of nations cause the greatest variation in their
relations with each other.

## History

Although men have written about international
relations for thousands of years, only in this century has the field begun to have some of the
characteristics of an academic discipline. The publication of *World Politics* by Paul Reinsch in 1900
is often cited as an early landmark in this development. Before World War I, courses in the field

were confined largely to diplomatic history, international law, and international economics. The war
stimulated the development of courses in international organization, international relations, and
international politics. Often these courses were devoted (and some still are) to the study of current
events and to preaching about how the world ought
to be organized. By the outbreak of World War II
a reaction to these modes of study had developed.
E. H. Carr's *The Twenty Years' Crisis, 1919–1939*
(1939), which was highly critical of research and
teaching in the field, and F. Schuman's *International Politics* (1933) indicated the beginning of the
"realist" (also sometimes called empirical) emphasis in the study of international relations. This
trend included both an effort to overcome idealistic
bias in research and teaching and an aspiration
toward more systematic study. A precursor of
future systematic work was Quincy Wright's monumental study of war from 1500 to 1940, published
in 1942.

After World War II the realist position was stated
persuasively by Hans Morgenthau in a highly successful and very influential textbook, *Politics
Among Nations* (1948). Morgenthau emphasized
the importance of power in the attainment of national objectives. Arguing largely against those who
deprecated "power politics," Morgenthau asserted
that the struggle for power occurs in all social relations and that international politics is not excepted
from this general proposition. Morgenthau's book
brought on widespread debate between the "realists"
and the "idealists." Although Morgenthau had defined power as the "ability to influence the minds
and actions of men" exercised by political, psychological, and military means, there was a tendency for realists to emphasize the importance of
military power. Idealists, on the other hand, stressed
the importance of assuring that ideological ends
not be subverted through the pursuit of tangible
instruments of power.

To a considerable degree the realist–idealist debate subverted the initial contribution of the realist
school to the development of an empirical science
of international relations. For many, realism became a goal toward which they believed policy
makers should aspire, rather than an enterprise
devoted to the explanation of actual international behavior. But the realist emphasis has left
significant legacies. One is the section devoted to
the elements of national power that appears in
most international relations textbooks. Morgenthau
lists the following components of national power:
geography, natural resources, industrial capacity,
military preparedness, population, national char-

acter, national morale, quality of diplomacy, and quality of government. Some writers, Organski, for example, tend to treat national power as something that can be represented by a single measure, through combining measurements of its components (1958).

As power tended to become the central concept in the international relations literature, concern developed about the analytic effectiveness of subsuming so much under one concept. There was particular difficulty in accounting for occasions when smaller nations influenced the behavior of larger nations, thus revealing the limitations of a single measure of national power. The tendency for the concept to become a fad rather than a useful analytic tool was underlined when Denis Sullivan, in an analysis of international relations textbooks (1963), found 17 different usages. The fact that individual authors use the concept in a number of ways compounds the confusion. [*See* POWER; POWER TRANSITION.]

As a moderately cohesive discipline of international relations was developing in the first half of the twentieth century, rapid social, technological, and scientific changes that would make much of this effort obsolete were already under way. The number of independent nations has doubled since 1900, reaching some 135 in 1966. By 1964 the number of international organizations had increased to some 1,900 (not including international business enterprises). Approximately 180 of these organizations are intergovernmental. Communication and transportation developments greatly changed the character of international relations and stimulated regional economic integration. Nuclear weapons altered the role of violence as an instrument for carrying out international relations. These changes so dramatically transformed the character of the international system that even the vocabulary of international relations rapidly became obsolete.

The horror of Hiroshima and Nagasaki and contemplation of the next generation of nuclear weapons' greater killing capacity brought a dramatic extension of interest in international relations. As a result, men of virtually all academic disciplines began contributing to the study of international relations.

Scientific change has not only affected the study of international relations through the impact of technological change on the data of international relations but also directly affected analytic techniques. While the twentieth-century world was self-consciously pondering the significance of rapidly developing knowledge in the physical sciences,

changes of potentially equal importance were taking place in the social sciences. A new generation of international relations scholars, armed with the contributions of an increasingly rigorous social science and aided by new norms for interdisciplinary collaboration, began making significant progress toward the development of a science of international relations. (See, e.g., Sprout & Sprout 1962 and the successive issues of *World Politics*, founded in 1948.) The concepts and techniques employed in analyzing such topics as decision making, conflict, game theory, bargaining, communication, systems, geography, attitudes, etc., were applied to problems in international relations. Machine data processing and computers extended the range of manageable problems, and man–computer and all-computer simulations permitted for the first time controlled experimentation in international relations.

### The state of the field

**Decision making.** Advances in social science are facilitating the handling of some of the problems that for a long time have troubled international relations scholars. One such problem is discovering the links between the gross characteristics of nations, such as measures of national power, and the specific behavior of individuals acting for nations. While most contributors to the literature on national power would not deny that variation in the individuals and groups making foreign policy decisions sometimes has significant effects, they have not provided analytic tools for assessing these effects.

In 1954 Snyder, Bruck, and Sapin published an influential monograph, *Decision-making as an Approach to the Study of International Politics*, that provided an analytic scheme suggesting the relevance of work in various areas of political science, sociology, social psychology, communication theory, and organizational behavior to the study of international relations. Their approach conceives of the actions of nations as resulting from the way identifiable decision makers define the action situation. It postulates that national decision-making behavior takes place in a complex organizational setting and can be accounted for by interrelations of three clusters of variables: organizational roles and relations, communication and information, and motivation. Four years later Snyder and Paige (1958) applied the scheme to the United States decision to intervene militarily in Korea in June 1950. This effort stimulated some refinements in the analytic scheme and helped to develop hypotheses linking the variables.

The work on decision making enriched the literature of international relations by demonstrating the relevance of concepts from other areas of social science. However, the collection of data on variables describing a specific decisional group presents methodological difficulties of a different order from those encountered in "measuring national power." Documentary materials may not even reveal the membership of a decision-making group, requiring the decision-making researcher to move from the library to field work in governmental agencies in his quest for data. Thus, decision-making analysis has stimulated the application of the field-research techniques of social science to the study of international relations. Problems in gaining access to foreign policy decision makers, because of the secrecy that traditionally surrounds their activity, require the international relations researcher not only to borrow field-research techniques of other social sciences but also to adapt them and to develop his own. [See DECISION MAKING.]

**Systems analysis.**   In 1955 Charles McClelland urged the application of general systems analysis, developed by the biologist Ludwig von Bertalanffy, to the study of international relations. This followed applications in physics, physical chemistry, and the social sciences. Bertalanffy developed his general systems approach as a result of perceiving similarities in conceptual schemes developed in fields of knowledge commonly considered to be widely separated. McClelland asserted that the application of the concepts and hypotheses of general systems analysis to international relations provides insights beyond those generally afforded by more traditional international relations approaches. For example, he stated that a general systems approach leads inquiry away from a concern with the accumulation of power, that its emphasis is instead on adaptive action. McClelland also believes that a systems perspective draws attention to quiet processes of growth, adjustment, and adaptation, thus overcoming tendencies to give too much attention to spectacular international events as causal factors (1955).

Morton Kaplan (1957) used a radically different method of systems analysis developed by W. Ross Ashby. This approach employs closed and simple systems, rather than general ones, and does not imply either the probability or the improbability of gradual change. Kaplan constructed six possible international systems and specified the environmental circumstances under which each is likely to persist and those under which it is likely to be transformed into one of the other kinds of systems. Kaplan did not provide historical examples of all

of his systems, since it is his goal to develop an analytic perspective that can handle all possible kinds of international systems, not just those that have occurred already. In *Action and Reaction in World Politics* (1963) Rosecrance also cites Ashby as he applies systems analysis to an examination of nine international systems that existed after 1740. From these historical cases he generates nine models.

Theories generated by the application of systems analysis move the study of international relations closer to rigorous comparative study. They provide concepts that can be applied across diverse geographic regions and in numerous historical periods. The propositions embedded within the theories invite refinement or rejection, thus encouraging researchers to move beyond description and on to the development of explanatory theory. [See SYSTEMS ANALYSIS.]

**Integration.**   Some taking an international systems perspective have focused on international integration. The development of integration as a major focus of international relations research has been spurred by regional integration, particularly in Europe in the post-World War II period. International relations scholars have a variety of usages for the term "integration." It is frequently used to mean (1) a specified state of an international system—e.g., a system where nations expect to have no war with each other or where citizens feel a strong sense of community; and (2) a system with certain kinds of central governmental institutions. Common in much of the integration literature is self-conscious concern with development of theory applicable to all international systems, universal and regional, through the study of systems more limited in scope. There also is a wide interest in discerning both the necessary and sufficient conditions for certain kinds of international governmental authority and the processes whereby such authorities can be established.

Case studies have provided the raw material for important integration work, but in contrast to most earlier work in international relations, the cases have not been ends in themselves but tools for the generation of general theory. In a pioneering work Karl Deutsch and Richard Van Wagenen, both political scientists, and a team of historians (Deutsch et al. 1957) examined ten cases of successful and unsuccessful integration in the North Atlantic area, ranging from the formation of England in the Middle Ages to the breakup of the union between Ireland and the United Kingdom in 1921. From these case studies they generated a list of conditions necessary for both amalgamated and pluralistic security communities. This effort borrowed a great deal from communications research.

Ernst Haas has preferred to study integration through firsthand depth research of one international organization at a time, using the organizations as "whetstones" for sharpening theory. His work on the European Steel and Coal Community (1958) and the International Labour Organisation (1964) has given much attention to the process whereby integration in one governmental function "spills over" into another area. The theoretical framework developed by Etzioni (1965) is influenced importantly by his native discipline, sociology. He has worked primarily with secondary sources in applying this framework to the European Economic Community, the Nordic Council, efforts to unite Egypt and Syria, and to the attempted Federation of the West Indies.

While the styles and interests of these contributors to the study of international integration vary a great deal, their efforts to build explicitly on the work of each other, although yet limited, is characteristic of a growing trend among international relations scholars. As they become more interested in general theory and less concerned with the uniqueness of individual cases, the possibilities for cumulative and cooperative development of knowledge are increasing in the whole field of international relations.

The work on integration is affecting traditional perspectives of the role of international organizations in the control of international violence and in the development of world order. Work such as that of Deutsch and his colleagues (1957) on pluralistic security communities (i.e., international systems in which nations do not expect to war with each other) raises serious questions about the validity of the often repeated proposition that world order can come only after the establishment of a world government. Furthermore, their hypotheses about necessary conditions for amalgamated security communities (e.g., mutual predictability of behavior, mutual responsiveness, and mobility of persons in politically relevant strata) have encouraged scholars to supplement traditional concern for ideal constitutional forms believed necessary for world order with empirical research on the necessary and sufficient conditions for the existence of international governmental apparatus.

An earlier alternative to the more grandiose world government schemes had been provided by functionalism, whose best-known advocate was David Mitrany in the 1940s. The key element in functionalism is the belief that international conflict can be diminished by the establishment of international welfare agencies manned by experts who, it is presumed, would be devoted to the achieving of their tasks on the basis of expert criteria, rather than to the acquisition of power. The work on integration, particularly that of Haas, who explicitly builds on the thought of the functionalists, offers some support for and a critique of functionalist theory, particularly in the development of more sophisticated theory linking international welfare activity and national political organization. [*See* INTERNATIONAL INTEGRATION *and* INTERNATIONAL ORGANIZATION.]

**Simulation.** Perhaps controlled experimentation in international relations is the most vivid indicator of ferment generated by borrowing from other disciplines. Formerly limited to the study of individual behavior and the study of small groups, experimental techniques have now been extended to decision making in business organizations, community conflict, and international relations. Simulation of international relations has also developed out of military war games. This heritage is recognized by Lincoln Bloomfield and Norman Padelford (1959) and others, who use the term "political gaming" to refer to their simulation efforts.

Some simulations of international relations have used human subjects, under quasi-laboratory conditions, who act for nations that are replicas of either actual nations or nations designed by the experimenter. There are also machine simulations, in which computers are used to simulate both the mental processes of decision makers and the social processes of international relations. Some simulate a specific situation, such as a crisis, whereas others simulate international systems that represent years of real-world time.

Like experimentation in other realms, simulation of international relations permits the student to have more control than he has in the study of the real world. It also permits the study of problems for which data are not available, possibly because the world has not yet produced the situation being studied. For example, in 1960 Richard Brody and Michael Driver ran 16 simulations of a two-bloc "cold war" international system, identical except that each simulation had different decision makers. Each of the 16 simulations began with two nuclear powers and each experienced nuclear proliferation at an identical time (see Brody 1963). This experiment permitted investigation of widespread proliferation of nuclear weapons before it occurred in the real world.

The most sustained effort in international relations simulation was begun by Harold Guetzkow in 1958 (see Guetzkow et al. 1963). His Inter-

Nation Simulation is an operating model of prototypic, rather than actual, nations. The model has been utilized in the experimental runs of Brody, as well as others. A variety of techniques is being used to validate the evolving model, including participation of diplomats in the simulation. The Inter-Nation Simulation and modifications of it have been used in research and teaching by a number of institutions in the United States, Latin America, Europe, and the Far East. The rapid spread of simulation activity suggests that controlled experimentation and the construction of operating models have a permanent place in the methodology of international relations. [*See* SIMULATION.]

**Military strategy.** The advent of nuclear weapons has stimulated more-widespread attention to military strategy and diminished the gulf that had developed—for both scholars and policy-makers—between military and political factors in international relations. As the destructive power of nuclear weapons increased, intense concern developed over the risks of nuclear war, particularly over the possibility of accidental nuclear war and the escalation of limited conventional wars into nuclear war. [*See* LIMITED WAR *and* NUCLEAR WAR.] In response, political scientists, psychologists, and economists began applying a wide range of social science knowledge to problems of military strategy. Thomas C. Schelling, an economist, called attention to the mixture of mutual dependence and conflict in relations between international adversaries. In his *Strategy of Conflict* he saw "enlightening similarities between, say, maneuvering in limited war and jockeying in a traffic jam, between deterring the Russians and deterring one's own children, or between the modern balance of terror and the ancient institution of hostages" (1960, p. v).

Fear that nuclear-weapons delivery systems, ostensibly developed to deter aggressors, might cause war encouraged the development of a literature on deterrence that enriched international relations discourse [*see* DETERRENCE]. As military planners and scholars attempted to discern how weapons systems could offer a credible deterrent to aggressors and at the same time not cause the war they were intended to prevent, the interdependence of national weapons systems became more apparent. Scholars became concerned not only with actual military capability of nations but also with the perceptions decision makers have of this capability and their inferences about its future use. These perceptions were seen to be influenced importantly by communications systems linking decision makers in different nations. Research on deterrence stimulated the application of social psychology, communications theory, and game theory to military strategy problems.

As deterrence of national military action came to be treated as one of many efforts to influence by discouragement, some began to ask why strategic planning did not include efforts to influence by encouragement. Thomas Milburn (1959) is one who called attention to the findings of psychological research that indicate that reward for desired behavior is sometimes more efficacious than punishment for undesired behavior in influencing human conduct. This kind of thinking encouraged an integration of research on military policy and research on policy utilizing other means of influence. [*See* MILITARY POLICY; NATIONAL SECURITY; STRATEGY.]

**Disarmament.** The overwhelmingly destructive power of nuclear weapons brought renewed interest in disarmament and arms limitation. Similar concern had been manifested at the time of the Hague Peace Conference at the turn of the century and also in the late 1920s and early 1930s. But the complex military technology of the nuclear age encouraged greater participation of physical scientists in disarmament discussion. Their involvement was partially a result of the obligation they felt to help control the destructive power they had created. The pages of the *Bulletin of Atomic Scientists* provide evidence of increased participation of physicists in arms-control and disarmament research and discussion. Their contributions to the technology of nuclear-test detection and nuclear-armament inspection began the development of a technology of nuclear control.

Disarmament study in the nuclear age also came to be concerned more with research into the relationship between societies and the organizations for waging war that they create. Machines of war had come to consume such a high proportion of national product in some nations that the economic consequences of disarmament were studied. The realization that disarmament would not bring an end to conflict fostered consideration of alternatives to violence that could be used for waging conflict in a disarmed world (e.g., Millis et al. 1961). This line of inquiry gradually brought a subtle but profound evolution in the interests of some international relations scholars, from concern with the causes of war to study of the causes of peace. [*See* DISARMAMENT.]

**Peace research.** At the outbreak of World War II one of the pioneers in the scientific study of international relations, Lewis F. Richardson, asserted, "There are many anti-war societies, but they are concerned with propaganda, not research. There is a wide public interest in the subject provided it is expressed in bold rhetoric, but not if it is a quantitative scientific study involving statistics and mathematics. There is no appropriate learned society" (1960, p. 284).

In the 1960s Richardson's statement would be less true because of the development of the peace research movement. Aspiring to equal the rigor of the physical sciences in the study of the necessary and sufficient conditions for peace, the movement was started primarily by social scientists outside the traditional field of international relations, and physical scientists, also, have been prominently involved. Examples of the better-known products of the peace research movement are *Conflict and Defense* (1962), by Kenneth Boulding, an economist; *The Peace Race* (1961), by Seymour Melman, an industrial engineer; and *Strategy and Conscience* (1964), by Anatol Rapoport, a mathematical biologist.

The peace research movement set up conferences and associations separate from the meetings of established professional societies. Peace research organizations, in the form of both professional associations and research institutes, have been created in a number of nations, primarily in Europe and North America. These developments have taken place in nations in which social science is developed most highly. Within the peace research movement considerable effort has been devoted to the establishment of international collaboration in developing a science of international peace free from national bias. [*See* PEACE.]

**Limited perspective of research.** Although international relations research has focused primarily on recent intergovernmental relations of a few great powers, there are tendencies toward more-inclusive interest, partially because of increasing interest in the development of general theory. Work on current regional international systems has made possible modest efforts at comparative international relations. Historical resources also provide opportunity for comparison (e.g., Rosecrance 1963). In *Politics and Culture in International History* (1960) Adda Bozeman overcomes the customary preoccupation of international relations scholars with Europe and North America. In a work that is global in scope, she assesses historical experience in international relations up to A.D. 1500. Despite these efforts at comparative inquiry, the attention of international relations researchers is still focused largely on a limited number of current intergovernmental relations—those with a high degree of conflict.

International relations research and theorizing has also tended to neglect nongovernmental inter-

national relations. There is considerable justification for the neglect, because of the degree to which governments dominate international relations and often exercise great control over nongovernmental international relations. On the other hand, the efforts of governments to control and to influence nongovernmental international relations suggest that officials may consider them more important than do scholars. There are numerous cases in which business investment has had an important effect on international relations, for example, United States business investment in Latin America. As former colonies have achieved independence, the actual and perceived influence of business interests of former governing nations has had a vital effect on intergovernmental relations. Some important research has been done on nongovernmental international relations, for example, Pool's recent work (1965) on the effect of international travel on national and international images and research by Herbert Kelman (1963) on the reactions of participants in exchange programs. But nongovernmental international relations tend not to be incorporated into the more general theoretical work in the field.

Nongovernmental international organizations also have been neglected, although some seventeen hundred of the approximately nineteen hundred international organizations (excluding international businesses) are nongovernmental. Studies of European integration have indicated the importance of international labor and management organizations in European integration. There are numerous anecdotal accounts of the effects of church organizations and business corporations on intergovernmental relationships. But there has been no concerted effort to study the consequences of variation in the number or character of nongovernmental international organizations on intergovernmental relationships in specific international systems.

**Conceptual issues.** The neglect of nongovernmental relations is partially a result of the traditional presumption that nations are single actors. The tendency to reify nations is diminishing; many writers now assert that when they say that nations act, this is only a shorthand way of indicating that human beings act for nations. But it is still customary for scholars to study the activities of all actors for a specific nation as if they were those of a single actor and to treat instances of contradictory behavior of different actors, when they are recognized at all, as aberrations.

As more national government departments have become involved in international relations and as participation in international organizations has increased, the number of sites at which a nation's representatives simultaneously interact with their counterparts from other nations has greatly increased. The ability of foreign offices to control or even to coordinate foreign policy seems to be declining. [See FOREIGN POLICY.] Assuming that nations are single actors inhibits investigation of the effects on international relations of variation in the number, location, and roles of actors that a nation has in the international system. Such variation may importantly affect the capacity of nations to adjust to and control external change.

Acknowledging that nations have multiple actors in international relations leads one to ask whom individual actors represent. Wilson was recognized as the representative of the United States at the Paris Peace Conference, but whom did he actually represent? What portion of a nation's attention and resources can individual national actors or all of a nation's actors command? What portion of a nation's attention and resources are commanded by actors not involved in international relations? These questions lead to the conclusion that nations comprise a variety of international and domestic actors, both governmental and nongovernmental, all acting in the name of the nation. Because some of these actors are domestic, they are part of the environment of the international system. Treating them as environment inhibits the misleading tendency to subsume total populations, resources, and activities of all nations under the rubric of international relations simply because virtually all mankind lives within nations. It is clear that variation in this environment affects the capacity of international actors to adjust to and control changes in the international system.

## The future

The study of international relations will continue to be affected by the urgency of war and peace problems and by increasing belief that research can contribute to the understanding and solution of these problems. International relations research will in the near future be even more affected by the twentieth-century revolution in social science than it has been in the past. It is probable that a separate body of international relations theory will not be developed and that international relations will be a part of the broader theoretical framework of intergroup relations.

It is likely that aspects of international relations will be increasingly incorporated into the concerns of each of the social sciences. This development can be observed already, for example, in the pages of the *Journal of Conflict Resolution*, an interdisciplinary quarterly devoted to research related to war and peace. It can also be seen in the growing number of sessions devoted to international relations at the meetings of professional societies of the different social sciences. The various kinds of human behavior which scholars have traditionally classified as diplomacy will be dissected and studied as cases of negotiation, legislative behavior, representative behavior, political socialization, communication, organizational behavior, etc. [See DIPLOMACY *and* NEGOTIATION.] These developments will tend to inhibit the growth of a coherent discipline, but there will be pressures toward coherence as members of different disciplines collaborate. This tendency is manifest in a volume edited by Kelman, *International Behavior* (1965), with contributions by political scientists, psychologists, sociologists, and an anthropologist. It is also revealed in the founding of the multidisciplinary International Studies Association in 1959.

As the field of international relations is integrated into the main stream of social science, it may be expected that the generalizations that international relations scholars advance will be subjected to rigorous testing through systematic data collection. High-speed computers already have made possible significant efforts to marshal data on hundreds of national social, political, and economic attributes and to analyze their relationship to international relations (see Russett et al. 1964). *Quantitative International Politics* (Singer 1967) reveals the growing tendency of scholars to use rigorous social science techniques for gathering and analyzing data. Scholars will probably also increase their efforts to gather data through field-research techniques, as a supplement to documentary sources and statistics provided by governments and international agencies. (See, e.g., Alger 1965.)

Continued change in patterns of international relations will, of course, intensify the conceptual problems of the field. The number, size, and importance of intergovernmental organizations and nongovernmental organizations will grow. The increased importance in international activity of social units other than nations will require scholars to develop conceptual schemes and theories that take them into account. This development will be encouraged by the increasing participation of social scientists other than political scientists in international relations research. It will be stimulated also by the increasing interest of political scientists in the relationship between societal characteristics and governmental organization.

It is likely, therefore, that future prescriptions

for world order, in contrast to those of the past, will be concerned more with the development of nongovernmental international relations: What kind of international society is needed to support certain kinds of central institutions? Can an international society with certain attributes provide desired restraints on violence and offer mechanisms for peaceful change, perhaps without highly developed central institutions? Insight into these questions is likely to be provided by theories of social control generated by research on intergroup relations in a variety of settings. The pursuit of data to test these theories in international systems will require the international relations scholar to extend his vision to phenomena often neglected: tourism, student exchange, trade, cultural exchange, international nongovernmental organizations (business, religious, philanthropic, professional), international media, etc.

Diligent application of man's scientific skills and resources to the problems of international relations in the concluding decades of the twentieth century could increase man's capability for international construction to the point where it will more nearly approximate his highly developed ability for international destruction.

CHADWICK F. ALGER

### BIBLIOGRAPHY

ALGER, CHADWICK F. 1965 Personal Contact in Intergovernmental Organizations. Pages 521–547 in Herbert Kelman (editor), *International Behavior: A Social-psychological Analysis.* New York: Holt.

BLOOMFIELD, LINCOLN; and PADELFORD, NORMAN J. 1959 Three Experiments in Political Gaming. *American Political Science Review* 53:1105–1115.

BOULDING, KENNETH E. 1962 *Conflict and Defense: A General Theory.* A publication of the Center for Research in Conflict Resolution at the University of Michigan. New York: Harper.

BOZEMAN, ADDA B. 1960 *Politics and Culture in International History.* Princeton Univ. Press.

BRODY, RICHARD A. 1963 Some Systemic Effects of the Spread of Nuclear Weapons Technology: A Study Through Simulation of a Multi-nuclear Future. *Journal of Conflict Resolution* 7:663–753.

CARR, EDWARD H. (1939) 1962 *The Twenty Years' Crisis, 1919–1939: An Introduction to the Study of International Relations.* 2d ed. New York: St. Martins.

DEUTSCH, KARL W. et al. 1957 *Political Community and the North Atlantic Area: International Organization in the Light of Historical Experience.* Princeton Univ. Press.

ETZIONI, AMITAI 1965 *Political Unification: A Comparative Study of Leaders and Forces.* New York: Holt.

FOX, WILLIAM T. R. (editor) 1959 *Theoretical Aspects of International Relations.* Univ. of Notre Dame Press.

GUETZKOW, HAROLD et al. 1963 *Simulation in International Relations: Developments for Research and Teaching.* Englewood Cliffs, N.J.: Prentice-Hall.

HAAS, ERNST B. 1958 *The Uniting of Europe: Political, Social, and Economic Forces, 1950–1957.* Stanford Univ. Press.

HAAS, ERNST B. 1964 *Beyond the Nation-state: Functionalism and International Organization.* Stanford Univ. Press.

HOFFMANN, STANLEY (editor) 1960 *Contemporary Theory in International Relations.* Englewood Cliffs, N.J.: Prentice-Hall.

KAPLAN, MORTON A. 1957 *System and Process in International Politics.* New York: Wiley.

KELMAN, HERBERT C. 1963 The Reactions of Participants in a Foreign Specialists Seminar to Their American Experience. *Journal of Social Issues* 19, no. 3: 61–114.

KELMAN, HERBERT C. (editor) 1965 *International Behavior: A Social-psychological Analysis.* New York: Holt.

KNORR, KLAUS E.; and VERBA, SIDNEY (editors) 1961 *The International System: Theoretical Essays.* Princeton Univ. Press.

McCLELLAND, CHARLES A. (1955) 1961 Applications of General Systems Theory in International Relations. Pages 412–420 in James N. Rosenau (editor), *International Politics and Foreign Policy: A Reader in Research and Theory.* New York: Free Press. → First published in Volume 12 of *Main Currents in Modern Thought.*

MELMAN, SEYMOUR 1961 *The Peace Race.* New York: Ballantine.

MILBURN, THOMAS W. 1959 What Constitutes Effective Deterrence? *Journal of Conflict Resolution* 3:138–145.

MILLIS, WALTER et al. 1961 *A World Without War.* New York: Washington Square Press.

MITRANY, DAVID (1943) 1966 *A Working Peace System.* Chicago: Quadrangle. → The 1966 edition includes additional material dated 1948–1965.

MORGENTHAU, HANS J. (1948) 1966 *Politics Among Nations: The Struggle for Power and Peace.* 4th ed. New York: Knopf.

ORGANSKI, A. F. K. 1958 *World Politics.* New York: Knopf.

POOL, ITHIEL DE SOLA 1965 Effects of Cross-national Contact on National and International Images. Pages 106–129 in Herbert C. Kelman (editor), *International Behavior: A Social-psychological Analysis.* New York: Holt.

RAPOPORT, ANATOL 1964 *Strategy and Conscience.* New York: Harper.

REINSCH, PAUL S. (1900) 1918 *World Politics at the End of the Nineteenth Century as Influenced by the Oriental Situation.* London: Macmillan.

RICHARDSON, LEWIS F. 1960 *Arms and Insecurity: A Mathematical Study of the Causes and Origins of War.* Edited by Nicolas Rashevsky and Ernesto Trucco. Pittsburgh: Boxwood. → Published posthumously.

ROSECRANCE, RICHARD N. 1963 *Action and Reaction in World Politics: International Systems in Perspective.* Boston: Little.

ROSENAU, JAMES N. (editor) 1961 *International Politics and Foreign Policy: A Reader in Research and Theory.* New York: Free Press.

RUSSETT, BRUCE M. et al. 1964 *World Handbook of Political and Social Indicators.* New Haven: Yale Univ. Press.

SCHELLING, THOMAS C. 1960 *The Strategy of Conflict.* Cambridge, Mass.: Harvard Univ. Press.

SCHUMAN, FREDERICK L. (1933) 1958 *International Politics.* 6th ed. New York: McGraw-Hill.

SINGER, J. DAVID 1962 *Deterrence, Arms Control, and Disarmament.* Columbus: Ohio State Univ. Press.

SINGER, J. DAVID (editor) 1967 *Quantitative International Politics: Insights and Evidence.* International Yearbook of Political Behavior Research, Vol. 6. New York: Free Press.

SNYDER, GLENN H. 1961 *Deterrence and Defense: Toward a Theory of National Security.* Princeton Univ. Press.

SNYDER, RICHARD C. 1962 Some Recent Trends in International Relations Theory and Research. Pages 103–172 in Austin Ranney (editor), *Essays on the Behavioral Study of Politics.* Urbana: Univ. of Illinois Press.

SNYDER, RICHARD C.; BRUCK, H. W.; and SAPIN, BURTON 1954 *Decision-making as an Approach to the Study of International Politics.* Foreign Policy Analysis Series, Vol. 3. Princeton Univ., Organizational Behavior Section.

SNYDER, RICHARD C.; BRUCK, H. W.; and SAPIN, BURTON (editors) 1962 *Foreign Policy Decision Making: An Approach to the Study of International Politics.* New York: Free Press.

SNYDER, RICHARD C.; and PAIGE, GLENN D. 1958 The United States Decision to Resist Aggression in Korea: The Application of an Analytical Scheme. *Administrative Science Quarterly* 3:341–378.

SPROUT, HAROLD H.; and SPROUT, MARGARET 1962 *Foundations of International Politics.* Princeton, N.J.: Van Nostrand.

SULLIVAN, DENIS G. 1963 Towards an Inventory of Major Propositions Contained in Contemporary Textbooks in International Relations. Ph.D. dissertation, Northwestern Univ.

WOLFERS, ARNOLD 1962 *Discord and Collaboration: Essays on International Politics.* Baltimore: Johns Hopkins Press.

WRIGHT, QUINCY (1942) 1965 *A Study of War.* 2d ed. With a commentary on war since 1942. Univ. of Chicago Press.

WRIGHT, QUINCY 1955 *The Study of International Relations.* New York: Appleton.

## II

### IDEOLOGICAL ASPECTS

In order to understand the role of ideology in international affairs it is important to distinguish between ideologies in and "theories" of international relations. Ideology is the more or less coherent and consistent sum total of ideas and views on life and the world (belief system, doctrine, *Weltanschauung*) that guides the attitudes of actual or would-be power holders: leaders of political units, such as nation-states or city-states, or of major organizations or movements, such as churches or political parties. Theory, on the other hand, refers to the more or less systematic entirety of concepts and ideas about international relations held and developed by individuals (such as political philosophers). Yet the connection between theories and ideologies can be close. Leaders,

power holders, and movements are often influenced by theorists whose concepts and ideas (although frequently in modified, especially in vulgarized, form) become the basis of their doctrine. In these instances, ideology can be defined either as the Idea (in the Hegelian sense) that tries to obtain or succeeds in obtaining Power or, in pragmatic terms, as theory that has become effective through the medium of social movements or power groups.

Movements or power holders are related to the international environment in two major ways: either their ideas and attitudes concerning the structure and nature of the world and concerning their status in the world form part and parcel of their original ideology or they find themselves subsequently involved in world relations and thus compelled to take a stand. To illustrate from the history of religious movements: Christianity, at first "otherworldly" and without its own international ideology, subsequently developed one (the doctrine of *bellum justum*, etc.), whereas Islam, possessing one from the outset, became an expanding, crusading movement right away.

In regard to the specific character of international ideologies, we may distinguish between "world-revolutionary" ideologies and all others. Great political movements, in initial stages of success, often develop ideas and expectations of the complete and imminent transformation of the world, including the international environment. The ideologies of both the French and the Bolshevist revolutionaries had such chiliastic expectations during the early phase of their respective revolutions. When these expectations fail to materialize, the world-revolutionary ideology usually changes into an ideology more or less closely tied to the power requirements of the respective units.

Examples of both types of ideology, the world-revolutionary and the more pragmatic, will occur in the survey of historical development that follows. From the vast number of internationally relevant ideologies this survey will select significant ones in three different areas: that of religious movements and churches (Islam, Christianity), that of democratic movements and attitudes (pacific democracy, democratic nationalism, economic liberalism, and internationalism), and that of (in the Western sense) undemocratic or antidemocratic doctrines and movements (integral nationalism, imperialism, and communism).

### Historical development

A definition of ideology as a system of thoughts and beliefs that becomes *effective* in movements or power units implies a connection between ideology and "masses." We hardly speak of ideology in reference to the motivations of a ruler in the age of monarchical absolutism, even where he is motivated by certain theories (such as that of *raison d'état*) in his foreign policy. But we speak meaningfully of ideology where nationalism or socialist ideas imbue entire populations. Ideology thus seems to have emerged when, in an age of modernization and the spread of literacy, masses were being mobilized for the support of movements and policies—that is, in Europe, approximately with the French Revolution. Prior to the rise of the masses to political influence, publics were usually passive followers of elites, which, in turn, were little affected by ideology. However, where efforts are made to instill over-all ideas and attitudes even into passive publics, or where both elites and masses are equally imbued with ideas leading to action, we may also legitimately speak of ideology. Such, in premodern times, was often the function of religious movements.

Islam. A prime example of the tremendous effect ideology can have on world affairs is offered by Islam. In contrast to more otherworldly religions, Islam from the outset regarded its function as this-worldly, proselytizing, and crusading. Its aim was to spread its creed over the entire world. The world was ultimately to be ruled by one ruler, the imam, whose authority was at once secular and religious. Until this goal was reached, a ceaseless holy war of conquest (jihad) was to be the instrument of the universalization of religion as well as of the expansion of secular control.

This universalism and exclusivism gave the early expansion of Islam its explosive force. The jihad was a "just war" to transform the *Dār ul-Harb* (the world of war, outside Islam, inhabited by unbelievers) into the *Dār ul-Islām* (the world controlled by Islam); participation in it guaranteed the believer paradise. This ideology is the prototype of all doctrines of "universal causes," where the world has to be saved and mankind is divided into those saved and those damned. It cannot recognize, as Islam did not, the equal status or coexistence of other communities. Therefore, a state of war, not peace, was the normal relationship between Muslims and non-Muslims, and even when the initial expansion of Islam had reached its limits, only short intervals of nonwar (up to ten years) were permitted. Subsequently, during what the Western world came to call the Middle Ages, an uneasy coexistence was established among the two Islamic empires and the two Christian empires, complete with balances of power, negotiations, treaties, and even a good deal of mutual toleration.

Ideologically, however, nonrecognition of the *dar al-harb* continued to be a principle of Muslim doctrine [see ISLAM].

Christianity. Christianity, like Islam, aimed at converting all mankind to its creed. But its efforts were less concentrated in time and space, warlike expansion or attempts at expansion occurring only intermittently (for example, Charlemagne's conversion of the Saxons, the Crusades, some aspects of the expansion of European powers into the non-European world during the age of discoveries). This universalist and proselytizing ideology had a lesser impact for two reasons. One was that Christianity, like Hinduism, arose as an otherworldly creed, concerned with the "inner man" and the salvation of his soul rather than with establishing the millennium in this world. Thus, even after the Christianization of the Roman Empire, when an ideology of the political and spiritual unity of Christendom became established, the Christian polity was conceived as one of peace, even in its relation with the world at large, and war was considered justified on specific grounds only (*bellum justum*, for example, as defense against an inflicted injury). Under these categories, "wars against infidels," crusades "to recover the Holy Land," were at times found to be "just wars," but the idea of an incessant state of "holy war" with the non-Christian world remained alien to Christianity even at the height of its universalist phase. The second reason Christianity's universalism remained less potent, in ideology as well as in practice, was that Western Christendom split into secular and spiritual contenders for supremacy. Two universalist ideologies, that of the empire and that of the papacy, neutralized each other, the result being a decline in the universalist idea and in the universalist powers in favor of the rising territorial state.

There remained aftereffects of Christian ideology, the most lasting, perhaps, being its pacifist, "nonviolent" component. Although never fully accepted into the main churches, Christian pacifism remained an undercurrent in more or less esoteric sects and denominations through the Middle Ages and modern times, coming to the fore in nineteenth-century "peace movements" as well as in twentieth-century integral or nuclear pacifism (for example, the "unilateralists" in the British disarmament movement). Here it often merges with secular ideologies of similar nature and purpose [see CHRISTIANITY].

Pacific democracy. The modern European state, established on the ruins of medieval Christian universalism, did not at first develop an international ideology of its own. The idea of *civitas maxima,* of a common bond encompassing all mankind, paled before the interests and conflicts of "sovereign" powers, which, run by small elites of rulers and their aristocratic and bureaucratic aides, could afford to be unconcerned about the ideas and attitudes of people at large. The doctrine of *raison d'état,* according to which each unit should consider its specific "national interests" as guideposts for action, determined the policies of these rulers without the intervention of significant ideology, unless one discerns such an ideology in the attenuating idea that some European equilibrium, or balance of power, should be maintained in the chaos of power politics.

With the rise of the European middle classes, however, ideas concerning the role that the "people" should play in the affairs of their countries came to the fore. Democratic ideology, the claim of the people to be the ultimate power in a given unit, produced two ideologies of international affairs, that of democratic nationalism and that of pacific democracy.

The latter arose from a contrasting of democratic aims and ideals with what are thought to be the results of nondemocracy in foreign affairs. Nondemocratic systems and their policies are said to result in perpetual conflict and war, since their elites are interested in their own prestige, glory, and the aggrandizement of their domain, and not in the welfare of the people. The ideology of pacific democracy considers this the deepest cause of the ancient and tragic story of warring mankind. Once the people take over the control of their destiny, all this will change radically: the people at large can only suffer from war, their basic common interest being in peace, and thus universal peace will result from the spread of democratic government over the world. This antinomy of warlike authoritarianism and peace-loving democracy was announced by a spokesman of the first great modern republican revolution, Thomas Paine, was taken up by Jefferson, and can be followed through to Woodrow Wilson (World War I fought "to make the world safe for democracy" and, in this way, to end all wars); it is still an important part of Western democractic ideology [*see* PACIFISM].

**Democratic nationalism.** Early nationalism is closely related to democratic ideology. Indeed, it may be said to arise logically from democratic premises: exactly as under domestic democracy individuals become self-determining on a basis of equality, internationally, the groups in which individuals are said to congregate "naturally"—nationalities—assert the right to become self-deter-

mining, free, and equal nation-states. Accordingly, the right of each nationality to establish itself as an independent political unit is proclaimed as the decisive principle of a new world order. Past systems and policies, under which dynastic rulers disregarded ethnic groups, cut them up, shifted populations hither and thither regardless of their wishes, are said to have led to constant conflict and war. With the recognition of national self-determination and the rise of nationalities to statehood, international relations will be radically transformed. According to the ideologists of early nationalism (Herder, Fichte, Mazzini), nations organized ethnically will live in peace and harmony with one another because none need aspire to anything the others have. Such nations are endowed each with its peculiar traits ("souls," according to political romanticism); they blossom when free and not interfered with; they are diverse but not superior or inferior, equal in their right to cultural fulfillment. Early nationalism, in intent and ideology, thus is pacific, humanitarian, equalitarian, and adverse to national expansionism and domination.

In its subsequent development nationalism has been beset by two major problems; one is the tendency to develop into the opposite of its original ideology, namely, an exclusivist and aggressive "integral" nationalism (see below), the other concerns the difficulty of agreeing on a simple and unequivocal criterion of what constitutes a nationality group, or "nation." In particular, could the relatively clear-cut ethnic–cultural criteria of European nationality groups be applied to non-European populations? Or would racial, linguistic, religious, or other standards be controlling? With the rise of the "new countries" to independence, the problem has become of crucial importance. What defines an African nation? Is there an Arab nation? Or one of the Maghreb? Or a Malayan one? In this respect, no unequivocal ideology has as yet been developed by the leaders or populations of the new units. There is some tendency to substitute larger units for "nationalities." Thus, in Africa, some advocate that entire continents should form the basic international units of the future, whereas others want to unite on the basis of race (*négritude*), and still others (probably the majority) trust the development of an artificially established unit (based on colonial boundary lines) into genuine nationhood [*see* NATIONALISM].

In general, the nationalism of the new nations still partakes of the characteristics of democratic nationalism. Even where expressed in negative terms ("anti-imperialism," "anticolonialism"), its emphasis is on each nation's right to a separate national identity. Indeed, through its opposition to ideologies and policies of racial or similar superiority, it has made equalitarian nationalism into a truly universalist ideology. Of this and other adaptations to twentieth-century conditions, the foreign-policy ideology developed by Jawaharlal Nehru in India is an outstanding example.

Nehru believed that a peaceful world of diverse nations is attainable; indeed, it is necessary to attain it, because the new nature of weapons and war and the rising demands of all people for basic needs and services no longer admit of the old game of power politics. But two centuries of applied nationalism have also shown that the harmonious result expected by the earlier nationalist ideology will not materialize easily. Mutual fear drives even self-determining nations into conflict; fear feeds on fear. A radical change of attitudes is therefore demanded from leaders and people, in particular vis-à-vis one's opponent. Gandhi's principles of toleration and avoidance of violence here influence Indian ideology. It assumes that in most situations violence can be avoided by the application of the five principles of *Panchshila* (mutual respect for territory, nonaggression, noninterference in internal affairs, equality and mutual benefit, and peaceful coexistence). However redundant these principles are, they indicate the thrust of an ideology that insists on the desirability and feasibility of peaceful international relations even though it realistically recognizes the elements of conflict and strife. To cope with the latter, nonalignment is advisable for nations not desiring to be drawn into the competition between major powers and blocs; this will, so it is hoped, not only protect the "neutrals" but also contribute to the attenuation of conflicts and provide the world with conciliators [*see* NEUTRALISM AND NONALIGNMENT].

**Economic liberalism.**    In addition to pacific democracy and nationalism, there was in the nineteenth century the rise of a third ideology of international peace and harmony, that of economic liberalism. The Manchester school (Cobden, Bright) and other free traders advocated the liberalization of world economic relations not only for its economic benefits but also because they were convinced that only in this way could the political conflicts of nations be eliminated. Thus, like pacific democracy and nationalism, this ideology is characterized by its monocausal nature; one major factor (in this instance, economic nationalism or mercantilism) accounts for the ills of the past: power politics, conflicts, wars. Abolish the cause (in this instance, eliminate the barriers in the

path of free exchange of goods and free migration), and political boundaries will become less vital and people and nations the world over interested in peaceful relations rather than in conflict and aggrandizement.

In more recent times, policies of foreign aid and development have often been connected with similar expectations: through such policies the emerging "poor" nations and populations of the world will be enabled to trade on an equal basis with the developed industrial countries; this way the gap between the affluent "North" and the destitute "South" will be closed and the otherwise threatening conflict between the impoverished and the rich turned into a beneficial common war against poverty.

**Internationalism.**    Although a monocausal approach often leads to dogmatism and fanaticism (one has the key to the correct interpretation of world affairs; therefore, one insists that only this key be used to open the door to the world's improvement), in the course of the nineteenth century many strands of the three pacific ideologies outlined above managed to unite in what may be called the mildly internationalist ideology of virtually all the more progressive forces in the Western world: the labor movement in its various groupings, portions of the trading and industrial (business) elites, Christian and other churches, and the general humanitarian "peace movement." The aim of this ideology was, and still is, a world in which nation-states continue to be the primary units of international affairs; where, ideally, all are ruled democratically and all are nationally self-determining; and where they settle their disputes peacefully through mediation, arbitration, and the use of international law in a setting of growing contact and cooperation. The experience of two world wars added first the League of Nations and then the United Nations to the list of instruments for the maintenance or enforcement of the peace. The same experience has led other internationalists to advocate more fundamental changes in international relations. Regionalism seeks the federation or integration of the traditional nation-states into larger and more viable units on the pattern of the European integration movement, in order to overcome the increasing splintering of the world of the new countries into an ever larger number of nations still claiming "sovereign equality." Still more radically, world federalists and others advocate the more or less complete subordination of national sovereignties to a world government, above all for the protection of world order in a disarmed world.

This optimistic "world rule of law" approach,

especially in its more moderate version, has characterized much in the attitudes of American, British, and other nations toward international affairs over the last hundred years. But it has been disturbed time and again by the shattering violence of opposite forces and contrary ideologies.

**Integral nationalism and imperialism.** In the age of the masses, elements that were intent on domination and aggrandizement had to oppose ideologies of the peace and equality of nations with counterideologies of their own. It would no longer do merely to voice principles of power politics. People at large had to be convinced that what was done in their name was right. Thus, toward the end of the nineteenth century, there arose in the major Western countries ideologies that undertook to justify expansion, colonialism, and racism by asserting "natural" superiorities and inferiorities of nations or races and by proclaiming that one's own group (nation, race) was by nature the superior one and was therefore entitled to control, or at least to lead, others. This claim may be expressed in a doctrine of the "white man's burden" to raise the other races of mankind to his level of civilization or in a theory of the "manifest destiny" of the Anglo-Saxon variety of white man to control the North American continent. It may extol the role of the Japanese to shape the destiny of Asia or, in its most radical form, may proclaim an "Aryan" supremacy over the entire world.

The last was the ideology of Hitlerism, whose "social Darwinism" was probably the only genuine belief system that underpinned the policies of conquest and extermination carried on by the Nazi regime. Social Darwinism, the application (or, rather, misapplication) of Darwinian principles to international relations, sees mankind divided into racial groups, all, like animal species, engaged in ceaseless struggle for survival; victory shows who is fittest and deserves to dominate. This emphasis on strife and glorification of war and victory in war became the hallmark of the ideology of that "integral" nationalism into which the earlier equalitarian and humanitarian nationalism was transformed in many countries, most significantly, perhaps, in the ideology of Italian fascism, which proclaimed that peace is a "sheep's paradise" where nations decay, whereas war brings out the virile virtues [see FASCISM; NATIONAL SOCIALISM].

**Communism.** Of all recent ideologies, that of communism has, perhaps, had the most profound bearing on world affairs. Communist ideology goes back to Marx, although original Marxism had relatively little in the way of a theory of international relations, stating that all class societies produce wars, that wars represent conflicts, not of nations but of their ruling classes, in which the ruled are used for mere "cannon fodder," and that the classless society to be established through the solidarity and the world-wide struggle of the proletariat will do away with war, merging nations in socialist brotherhood.

This ideal, as an expectation, was shared by all inheritors of the Marxian doctrine. They split, however, over the question of how to attain it. Democratic socialism, by and large, came to share the tenets of moderate internationalism (see above); communism condemned this approach as "bourgeois illusion," substituting for it Lenin's doctrine of imperialism.

Lenin held that imperialism, the expansion of capitalist countries and interests all over the world, marks the final phase of the capitalist system. The conflicts imperialism produces derive from competition over markets, investment opportunities, sources of raw material, and cheap labor; they are, therefore, inherent in the system that thus, sooner or later, results in world-wide wars among the imperialist powers. These wars will afford the proletariat, allied with the exploited masses of the colonial and semicolonial world, a chance for world revolution and for the transformation of capitalism into socialism.

Lenin's theory, by way of self-fulfilling prophecy, became the ideology of victorious Bolshevism. But the Soviet rulers were soon confronted with a novel question: when, contrary to their initial world-revolutionary expectations, the revolution failed to sweep the world, the problem of the relation between the two worlds of "socialism" (communism) and "imperialism" became crucial. There was no doubt in their minds—as there is none today—that the conflict was irreconcilable, that it would become global, and that it would end in the world-wide victory of communism. But communist ideology has been wavering and unclear about the "strategy" to be used for the attainment of this goal.

Lenin had commented upon "inevitable collisions" between Soviets and encircling imperialists. Stalin harped variably on "peaceful coexistence" and the danger of "capitalist aggression." Toward the end of his rule, although he reiterated, in Leninist fashion, the inevitability of wars *among* imperialist powers, he was inclined to consider war between the two camps avoidable in view of the increased strength of the Soviet camp. Khrushchev, claiming that Soviet nuclear might could now deter imperialist countries not only from attacking communist ones but also from warring among themselves, pronounced Lenin's doctrine of the "inevitability" of war outdated by developments;

there is no "fatalistic inevitability"; peaceful co-existence now and eventual nonviolent transition from capitalism to socialism are possible and, since major war threatens the survival of all, preferable. Class struggle on the international plane will continue in the form of economic and ideological competition.

The Chinese communist leadership, on the other hand, while not adhering strictly to the thesis of the inevitability of war either, insists that imperialist aggression can be deterred only by firm, energetic policy. The Chinese claim that a "low risk" policy emphasizing peaceful coexistence merely threatens to encourage such aggression. On the issue of internal revolutions, especially in the "underdeveloped" world (colonial and similar wars of "liberation"), Mao Tse-tung's ideology stresses the necessity of violence and the responsibility of the communist camp to aid and assist revolutionary forces all over the world. Here, too, Soviet ideology asserts the possibility of peaceful transitions.

Hence, contrary to the dogmatism with which the ideological dispute appears to be carried on, the chief differences between the Chinese and Soviet leaders actually concern issues of strategy and tactics—in particular, the degree of militancy needed to pursue their ideological goals. Both sides agree on the need for the doctrinal unity of the camp. As often before in the history of ideology, inability to agree on who decides in case of doctrinal disunity has led to the actual split, with the Chinese rejecting the Soviet leadership's claim to ideological primacy [see COMMUNISM; MARXISM].

## The role of ideology

The foregoing has made clear the impact of ideology on world affairs. Especially in recent times, there are few issues not carried on in an ideological framework; observers—practitioners as well as theoreticians—have, therefore, focused their attention on the problem of cause and effect. Are ideologies major causes of events and policies or are they secondary phenomena, slogans explaining, justifying, or veiling that which "really" underlies events, namely, strategic, economic, and other interests of nations and power groups? Marxism, for example, which itself has given rise to one of history's most powerful ideologies, plays down ideology as the mere "superstructure" of economic and class interests. Similarly disparaging attitudes have been expressed by such dissimilar actors as Hitler, Nehru, and de Gaulle.

It is easy to discover interests behind ideology, and the "realistic" trend in recent theory of international politics, emphasizing power and national interest, may account for the prevalence of this interpretation. But it needs more study and refinement, for example, distinction between movements aspiring to power, where the impact of ideology seems often stronger than that of "interest" (accounting for the utopian elements in such movements), and groups in power, which are more often and more strongly swayed by interests.

Even there, however, policies are only rarely conducted in entirely unideological fashion. They proceed in an environment of ideas, if not ideologies, which shapes the outlook and action of leaders and/or people. All policy is affected by the way in which reality is perceived. There is usually no uniform perception; even the most realistic statesman sees the world through some "prism," if not in "blinkers," applying his own interpretative framework to foreign affairs. Thus communist leaders, however realistic and "cold-blooded" they may be in their approach to world affairs, see the world in terms of class conflict, divided into "aggressive" and "peace-loving" forces. Even supposing that Stalin at some point had come to free himself completely from ideological considerations, viewing the world in terms of power interests exclusively, he could not have helped communicating with party, people, and communists abroad through the concepts and in the parlance of communism. Ideology similarly has affected the present Sino–Soviet conflict, which, obvious underlying conflicts of interests notwithstanding, would otherwise hardly be carried on in its peculiar acrimonious fashion, pulling into its vortex communist countries and parties all over the world.

## Research problems

Although a good deal of attention is being paid to specific ideological problems (for example, the Sino–Soviet dispute), the general and fundamental study of the relation of ideology to interests and of ideology's impact on policy is undoubtedly on the agenda of needed analysis and research. In this connection, attention should be paid not only to the national interest—the overriding political interest of the whole nation—but also to economic, social, and other special interests of subgroups within a nation. Careful and detailed research into the relation of specific ideologies to specific class, group, or national interests at a given time and place would seem to be more fruitful than speculations about general "causal" connections between national interests and broad ideologies.

More specifically, the following research areas might be explored: the impact of international events on ideologies (for example, the rise of new centers of power, bipolarity giving way to multipolarity in the international system and the influence of this transformation on the major ideologies); the interplay of different ideologies (for example, communism and the nationalism of the emerging nations); the difference in degree of the impact of ideologies on foreign policy (for example, in totalitarian as contrasted with liberal–democratic regimes); the extent to which publics share in the ideologies of leaders and the ways in which leaders try to mobilize ideological support for foreign policies; the way in which ideology affects the leaders' assessment of national interests. Also, a typology of international ideologies might be undertaken.

Analysis of this sort could conceivably affect policies. Study of ideology enables one to understand other peoples' "blinkers" and eventually, perhaps, one's own. This way the West might come to understand communist policy as based, in part at least, on fears rather than inherent aggressiveness; and communist countries might better understand the preoccupations of the West, particularly in the light of the gradual "erosion" of ideology that some observers see in the communist world. A resulting "deideologization" of foreign policies might dampen their emotional, crusading character, reducing tensions to conflicts over interest, where compromise is easier to achieve than in ideological struggle. The realization of the danger in which nuclear weapons have placed all mankind might contribute to deideologization (as apparently it has done in recent Soviet policy), thereby furnishing one perspective of reality common to all. With the dusk of ideology we might eventually witness the dawn of a true theory and practice of peace.

JOHN H. HERZ

[See also COLONIALISM; IDEOLOGY; IMPERIALISM; REVOLUTION; SOCIAL MOVEMENTS.]

#### BIBLIOGRAPHY

BAINTON, ROLAND H. 1960 Christian Attitudes Toward War and Peace. Nashville: Abingdon.

BENTWICH, NORMAN D. (1933) 1959 The Religious Foundations of Internationalism: A Study in International Relations Through the Ages. 2d ed. London: Allen & Unwin.

BRZEZINSKI, ZBIGNIEW K. (1960) 1961 The Soviet Bloc: Unity and Conflict. Rev. ed. New York: Praeger.

BURIN, FREDERIC S. 1963 The Communist Doctrine of the Inevitability of War. American Political Science Review 57:334–354.

ELBE, JOACHIM VON 1939 The Evolution of the Concept of the Just War in International Law. American Journal of International Law 33:665–688.

GOODMAN, ELLIOT R. (1960) 1961 The Soviet Design for a World State. New York: Columbia Univ. Press.

HARVARD UNIVERSITY, CENTER FOR INTERNATIONAL AFFAIRS 1960 Ideology and Foreign Affairs. Senate Committee on Foreign Relations, United States Foreign Policy Study, No. 10. Washington: Government Printing Office.

HERSCH, JEANNE 1956 Idéologies et réalité: Essai d'orientation politique. Paris: Plon.

HERZ, JOHN H. 1951 Political Realism and Political Idealism: A Study in Theories and Realities. Univ. of Chicago Press.

KHADDURI, MAJID (1941) 1955 War and Peace in the Law of Islam. Baltimore: Johns Hopkins Press. → First published as The Law of War and Peace in Islam: A Study in Moslem International Law.

LANGE, CHRISTIAN L.; and SCHOU, AUGUST 1919–1963 Histoire de l'internationalisme. 3 vols. Nobel Institute Publications, Vols. 4, 7–8. Oslo (Norway): Aschehoug; New York: Putnam. → Vol. 1: Jusqu' à la paix de Westphalie. Vol. 2: De la paix de Westphalie jusqu' au Congrès de Vienne.

LOWENTHAL, RICHARD 1964 World Communism: The Disintegration of a Secular Faith. Oxford Univ. Press.

RANGE, WILLARD 1961 Jawaharlal Nehru's World View: A Theory of International Relations. Athens: Univ. of Georgia Press.

RUSSELL, FRANK M. 1936 Theories of International Relations. New York: Appleton.

SIGMUND, PAUL E. (editor) 1963 The Ideologies of the Developing Nations. New York: Praeger.

ZAGORIA, DONALD S. 1962 The Sino–Soviet Conflict, 1956–1961. Princeton Univ. Press.

## III
### PSYCHOLOGICAL ASPECTS

During the 1950s, a new and rather vigorous area of specialization emerged that might loosely be called the "social psychology of international relations." The exact boundaries of this emerging field are hard to define, and it necessarily spans several disciplines. It is characterized by the systematic use of social-psychological concepts and methods in the development of theory, research, and policy analyses in international relations.

The concern of psychologists with problems of international relations did not, by any means, originate in the 1950s. Research efforts in this general area go back at least to the early 1930s, when studies on attitudes toward war and related matters were initiated. During the following years came various studies on national stereotypes; on attitudes toward war, war prevention, nationalism, and international affairs; and on sources of aggressive attitudes (for reviews, see Klineberg 1950 and Pear 1950). The steady development of public opinion research during these years also led to an accumulation of data relevant to national images and attitudes toward foreign policy issues (for an integration of opinion data, see Almond 1950). In addition to these research efforts, there were various attempts to develop theories of war and peace in psychological terms, using either psychoanalytic frameworks (e.g., Glover 1946) or general psychological frameworks, particularly the theory of learning (e.g., May 1943). Finally, psychologists and social scientists in related disciplines addressed themselves to the psychological barriers to peace and determinants of tension and offered recommendations for tension reduction and international cooperation (e.g., Society . . . 1945).

Despite this activity, one certainly could not speak of an area of specialization in the social psychology of international relations. The total volume of research on these problems was exceedingly small and touched only indirectly on the actual interaction between nations or their nationals. There was hardly any research designed to examine the interactions between individuals representing different nationalities on either an official or an unofficial basis, or to trace the psychological processes involved in international politics. Even the work on images and attitudes was largely done in the context of general attitude research or personality research, rather than in the context of internation behavior and the foreign policy process.

It is not surprising, therefore, that much that was written by psychologists and psychiatrists on questions of war and peace tended to be at a level removed from the interaction between nations. It did not grow out of specialized study of the psychological aspects of international relations but, rather, involved the application to the international situation of psychological principles derived from other areas of work. Such applications are highly relevant insofar as they deal with general psychological assumptions that might influence international policy. An example of a relevant application of this kind is the conclusion that there is no support from psychological research for the assumption that war is inevitable because it is rooted in human nature (cf. Society . . . 1945, p. 455). It is also possible to apply psychological principles derived from work in other areas to certain specific problems in international relations—such as the effects of stress on decision-making processes. Any attempt, however, to conceptualize the causes of war and the conditions for peace that starts from individual psychology rather than from an analysis of the relations between nation-states is of questionable relevance.

One might, therefore, question the assumption made by some psychological writers that one can understand the causes of war by examining the determinants of aggressive behavior in individuals. It is true that the behavior of states ultimately consists of the behaviors of individuals, but state behavior is the aggregation of a variety of behaviors on the part of many individuals who represent different roles, interests, and degrees of influence on final decisions and contribute in very different ways to the complex social processes that eventuate in a final outcome such as war. One cannot, therefore, expect that the behavior of a nation will be a direct reflection of the motives of its citizens or even its leaders. Although war involves aggressive behavior on the part of many individuals, it is not necessarily at the service of aggressive motives. Leaders may engage in aggressive behavior for strategic reasons, for example, and the population at large for reasons of social conformity. Even where aggressive motives are involved in predisposing national leaders to precipitate war and segments of the population to support it enthusiastically, their role in the causation of war cannot be understood without an examination of the societal (and intersocietal) processes that are involved in the decision to engage in war and of the way in which different elements of the society enter into these processes.

The emphasis on personal aggression is the most obvious limitation of some of the conceptualizations of war and peace that use individual psychology as their point of departure. The problem, however, is of a more general nature. Even a more complex analysis which recognizes that a variety of motives play a part in individuals' preferences for war or willingness to accept it is not a proper starting point for the study of war. War is a societal and intersocietal action carried out in a national and international political context. What has to be explained is the way in which nations, given various societal and political conditions, arrive at various international policies, including war. Part of this explanation involves motivations and perceptions of different individuals (including "the public") who play various roles in the larger societal process. But only if we know where and how these individuals fit into the larger process, and under what constraints they operate, will we be able to provide a relevant psychological analysis. Thus, a psychological analysis can never be complete and self-contained and be offered as an alternative to other theories of war (such as economic or political theories). It can contribute to a general theory of international relations only when the points in the process at which it is applicable have been properly identified.

The tendency, particularly in some of the earlier psychological and psychoanalytic writings on war and peace, to focus on aggression and other motives of individuals, without taking the societal and political context into account, has caused some specialists in international relations to question the relevance of psychological contributions. There is no inherent reason, however, why psychological studies cannot start from an analysis of international relations at their own level, and they are increasingly doing so. Relevant systematic contributions of this kind are particularly likely to come from *social* psychology, which tends to view individual behavior in its societal and organizational context and to take deliberate account of the institutional processes that shape the behavior of individual actors and are in turn shaped by it.

## Major approaches

The shortcomings of earlier work have not been entirely overcome, but there has been a change of such proportions since the 1950s that one is justified in saying that the social-psychological study of international relations has reached a new stage in its development. In absolute terms, the amount of research on these problems is still very small, and little dependable evidence has been accumulated. But the volume of work has greatly increased in recent years, and there has been a concomitant growth in quality and sophistication. There are now a number of research centers and research programs focusing partly or entirely on social-psychological aspects of international relations. The earlier work on international attitudes and public opinion continues at a greater rate and with greater methodological refinement, and attempts to link it to the foreign policy process have increased. In addition, there have been numerous studies of cross-national contact and interaction. There have been various attempts to study international conflict and its resolution experimentally and thus to deal more directly with issues of foreign policy making. Many of the investigators are acutely aware of the problems of generalization that this kind of research entails, and they make serious attempts to explore the international situation to which they hope to generalize and the conditions that would permit such generalization. In recent theoretical formulations, there is a greater tendency to start with questions at the level of international conflict and the interaction between nations, and then to see where psychological concepts can contribute to answering these questions. This has meant a decline in global approaches to the psychology of war and peace, with greater attention to the psychological analysis of specific subproblems. Similarly, psychological contributions to policy questions have tended to be more specific and more directly related to concrete issues in foreign affairs.

In short, we seem to be in the initial phase of a newly emerging area of specialization—a social psychology of international relations that deals with the problems of interaction between nations and the individuals within them at their own level, rather than as extensions of individual psychology. This area must be seen in the context of a broader development: the emergence of the behavioral study of international relations, in which social-psychological concepts and methods play an integral part. It is neither possible nor desirable to draw sharp lines between a social-psychological approach and this larger field, which by its very nature is interdisciplinary—not only in the sense that it represents a collaboration of investigators based in different disciplines but also in the sense that its concepts and methods represent a genuine pooling of the resources of different disciplines. Thus, social-psychological approaches are used not only by psychologists and sociologists but also quite frequently by political scientists, sometimes by anthropologists, economists, and mathematicians, and occasionally by historians. To a very large extent, it is precisely because current psychological work on international relations is embedded in a larger interdisciplinary effort and has close ties with political science that it is qualitatively different from the work of earlier years.

In addition to its interdisciplinary character, there are two other features that distinguish the behavioral study of international relations. One is the use of a variety of methods—laboratory experiments, simulation studies, surveys, observational studies, content analyses of historical documents, organizational studies, and interviews with informants—and the readiness with which investigators alternate the methods and combine them. The other is the combination of a variety of purposes and the absence of sharp divisions between concern with theory building and concern with practical application, between an interest in developing a methodology and an interest in dealing with policy issues.

Social-psychological approaches to international relations are part of this developing field and contribute to it. The types of social-psychological contributions that have been made will be summarized in terms of four interrelated categories.

(1) **"International behavior" of individuals.** The study of the "international behavior" of individuals is concerned with the ways in which individuals relate themselves to their own nation and other nations, to the international system as

a whole, to problems of foreign policy, and to the broader issues of war and peace. It also includes the study of actual interactions between individuals across national boundaries. The relevance of research in this category to international politics varies greatly, depending, for example, on whether it focuses on attitudes and interactions of diplomats and national decision makers or on those of average citizens contemplating foreign policy questions or traveling abroad. In any event, research on "the human dimension in international relations" (Klineberg 1964) is of interest in its own right and represents the most obvious and most direct contribution of social psychology. The following types of research within this category have been conducted in the 1950s and 1960s.

(a) *Images or stereotypes of other nations.* Studies have been concerned with the cross-national comparison of national images, the development of such images in children, the sources of images in personal experiences, the effects of cross-national contacts on images, their relationship to the political alignments between the nations in question, and their effect on the perception of individual nationals. Personality dispositions to like or dislike foreign nations in general and the personal meanings that images of a particular nation may have for different individuals have also been explored. But there has been only little systematic effort so far to relate images to national and international events and, in particular, to explore in detail the way in which they are affected by and in turn affect the relations between nations. Another area requiring more research is the relationship between images of other nations and images of their nationals, which are obviously interdependent but not completely so. (For reviews and bibliographies, see Duijker & Frijda 1960; Kelman 1965, part I.)

(b) *Attitudes toward international affairs.* Recent studies in the United States and Canada have intensively questioned national samples on a whole range of foreign policy issues, thus supplementing data from opinion polls, which generally use only one or two structured questions on a given issue. Such studies make it possible to explore the relationships between different sets of attitudes and images, between general policy orientations and reactions to specific issues, and between attitudes and various demographic variables.

There have also been a number of studies, usually focusing on special samples (such as students or residents of a particular geographical area), assessing attitudes in response to a specific inter-national situation, such as the Cuban crisis in 1962, or in relation to a specific policy issue, such as civil defense. In such studies, it is possible to examine in greater detail the way that reactions to specific issues are linked to the more general attitudes of individuals and groups toward foreign affairs. General attitudes, particularly the readiness of individuals to adopt a belligerent stand in international relations, have also been examined in a number of studies and related to the social characteristics and personality dispositions of the respondents, as well as to their reactions to communications about international events.

Finally, there is research under way to develop scaling procedures for international attitudes, which would, among other things, permit periodic attitude measurement as one indicator of the state of the international system. One crucial line of research, which is just beginning to take shape, is the investigation of the dynamics of attitudes on international affairs, focusing on the psychological and social processes involved in the development of general orientations toward foreign policy issues within a society and the crystallization of reactions in specific cases. The direct application of research on communication and attitude change to the area of international attitudes is a related research need. (See Christiansen 1959; Paul & Laulicht 1963; Scott 1965; Janis & Smith 1965; Rosenberg 1965.)

(c) *National and international loyalties.* A key area for social-psychological research is the study of the relationship of the individual to the nation-state, which in turn defines his relationship to the international system. There have been some studies of psychological aspects of nationalism, and the research on ethnocentrism certainly has some relevance here. But very little has been done on the nature of the commitment of the individual to the nation-state, his definition of the rights and duties of the citizen, the kinds of satisfactions he derives from his relation to the state, and his conceptions of the position and purposes of the nation in the international system. What is needed here is research on national ideology as it is communicated by the national system and interpreted by individuals and groups; on the way this ideology develops; on the kinds of behaviors it calls forth under various conditions of arousal (including various national symbols); and on the implications of different kinds of national ideology for international cooperation, participation in international organizations, and the willingness to surrender sovereignty to international bodies. A closely related area of research is the study of the determinants of an internationalist ideology, and particularly of the conditions for the development of multiple loyalties. One type of research to which increasing attention is being paid is the study of special subgroups within the population, such as the extreme right or the peace movement, that have special definitions of the role of the national vis-à-vis the nation-state and of the nation vis-à-vis the international system. The developing nationalism in emerging nations, the problems of dual loyalty for employees of international organizations, and the ideological underpinnings for such supranational agencies as the European Economic Community are all problems to which social-psychological research will increasingly address itself. (See Deutsch 1960; Perry 1957; Katz 1965; Alger 1965.)

(d) *Cross-national contacts.* In recent years there have been numerous studies of cross-national contact, dealing with the processes of interaction between nationals of different countries, the problems of adjustment in a foreign culture, and the effects of personal contacts on images and attitudes. Most of the studies have dealt with foreign students in the United States, but there have also been studies of foreign students in European countries as well as studies of American students, scholars, businessmen, and Peace Corps volunteers traveling abroad. There has been an interest in various applied problems in this area, such as the evaluation of international exchange programs, the selection of personnel for overseas work, and the conduct of international conferences. It would be very useful to link research on cross-national contacts with research on national and international loyalties by studying interactions among representatives of different countries in more official contexts, including international and supranational organizations, and the effects of such interactions on their integration into an international network. (See Pool 1965; Mishler 1965; Alger 1965.)

(2) **Foreign policy and international politics.** Research on foreign policy and international politics refers to the behavior of nations or of decision makers acting for their nations. It is concerned with the determinants of policy and their effects on the national and international systems, and in particular with international conflict and its resolution. This research is by no means specifically social-psychological, but social-psychological concepts and methods can contribute to a multidisciplinary attack on these problems. The following types of research within this category have been conducted in recent years.

(a) *Public opinion.* Public opinion research has much relevance to the study of internation behavior, provided that deliberate attention is paid to the way in which public opinion (both in general and on specific kinds of issues) affects the formulation and conduct of foreign policy. This, in turn, requires an analysis of the broader assumptions and purposes which serve as the context for foreign policy and within which public opinion can therefore influence the probability of various choices, and an analysis of the roles played by different segments of the public in the policy process.

Studies on the distribution of attitudes toward foreign policy issues in the population at large can be useful insofar as they give an indication of general "moods" that decision makers are likely to share and to take into account (cf. Almond 1950). Public opinion studies become more directly relevant if, as is increasingly true, they focus in whole or in part on certain elite groups. Some recent studies examined in detail the sources of attitudes of special elite groups toward specific foreign policy issues and the way in which these attitudes feed into the decision-making process. In addition to opinion studies per se, there has also been some research on the way in which different segments of the public relate themselves to foreign policy issues: the distribution of information, interest, and activity relating to foreign affairs within the general population; the characteristics of those who constitute attentive publics and opinion leaders; and (to a lesser extent) the way in which opinions on foreign policy matters circulate within the public.

There is a need for more detailed research on the actual processes whereby public opinion affects foreign policy decisions. Social-psychological studies might explore the conditions that generate a particular mood in the public, determine the choices it perceives, and mobilize certain segments of it into various kinds of action; or they might focus on decision makers and explore their general conception of the role of public opinion in the policy process, how they assess the shape of public opinion in any given situation, and the impact it has on their decision behavior. (See Hero 1959; Paul & Laulicht 1963; Rosenberg 1965; Robinson & Snyder 1965.)

(b) *Individual actors.* A recent focus for conceptualization and research in internation behavior has been the behavior of the individual actors who participate in the formulation and execution of foreign policy. Particular emphasis has been placed on the intellectual and organizational processes—the definition of the situation, the problem-solving procedures, the exercise of leadership, and the flow of communication and influence—that come into play when responsible decision makers choose between alternative actions to be taken by the state (cf. Snyder et al. 1962). This line of research is often, although not necessarily, based on the assumption that the decision makers in any given situation *are* the state and that the study of the decision-making process is therefore the most direct way of studying state behavior. This assumption is particularly appropriate where research focuses on specific major decision cases, as in the extensive and detailed study of the United States decision to resist aggression in Korea (see Snyder & Paige 1958).

A somewhat different approach to the study of international decision making has been used by another group of researchers, who have developed detailed methods of content analysis in terms of a number of psychological dimensions (North et al. 1963). This approach has been applied, for example, to a reconstruction of the events culminating in the decision to go to war in 1914 (see Zinnes et al. 1961). The emphasis here is on the relationship of the perceptions and emotional reactions of key individual actors in different countries to policy outcomes, in contrast with the Snyder model, which stresses interactional and organizational variables. Both approaches generate hypotheses about the process and outcome of decision making under varying conditions. They have also been applied outside of the context of specific decisions, both in the study of the assumptions and perceptions of individual decision makers that underlie their policy orientations and in the study of the goals and decision processes that characterize organizational units with foreign policy responsibilities.

Research on individual actors in the foreign policy process, in addition to representing a way of operationalizing the behavior of states, may also be designed to explore some of the links in the chain that eventuates in certain state acts. Here the assumption is not that the individuals observed constitute the state for the purposes in question but that they are important participants in and contributors to state action. By the same token, such research need not focus on the key decision makers but could deal with diplomats and other officials who play a variety of roles in the total process. Thus, there has been some research on individual participants in the foreign policy

process both within national foreign policy organizations, like the U.S. Department of State, and within international organizations, like the UN. The research has concerned itself with the kinds of assumptions and role definitions that these individuals bring to their tasks, the kinds of actions and interactions in which they engage in the course of their work, and the ways in which these feed into the foreign policy process and, directly or indirectly, have an impact upon it. (See Robinson & Snyder 1965; Pruitt 1965; and Alger 1965.)

(*c*) *Processes of interaction.* A research area that has blossomed within the past few years is the experimental study of interaction between individuals or groups, with an eye to illuminating processes of conflict and bargaining, of competition and cooperation, in the international arena. The experiments attempt to create laboratory situations that are analogous to the international situation—not by reproducing the international situation exactly but by incorporating some of its crucial features—and that permit controlled observation of some of the interaction processes which also characterize the relations between nations.

Three types of experimental approaches can be distinguished. The first, exemplified by the Inter-Nation Simulation (Guetzkow et al. 1963), involves the ambitious attempt to create, in the laboratory, simulated nations with varying characteristics. The subjects do not behave as individuals, as in small-group experiments, but play the roles of decision makers representing their nations and responsive to their constituencies. Various foreign policy moves on the part of decision makers (such as armament–disarmament, trade, aid, or alliance) and various outcomes for the international system (such as tension level, international cooperation, and the outbreak of limited or nuclear war) can be observed. With the introduction of experimental interventions and variations into the natural flow of the process, laboratory simulations can provide tests of specific hypotheses about the effects of various strategies, military and political conditions, and states of the international system, as well as the effects of different values, as reflected in personal and cultural characteristics of the decision makers.

The second type of experimental study is more remote from the interaction between nations but tries to reproduce some of its distinctive features. It takes the form of relatively simple two-man games, so structured that mixed (cooperative and competitive) motives are brought into play. Choices of strategy in this type of conflict situation, processes of explicit and tacit bargaining, and outcomes for each party have been studied as a function of such independent variables as the nature of the pay-offs, the characteristics of the players, the definition of the situation, the opportunity for communication, and the availability of threats. The players in these games behave as individuals, but the kinds of choices they must make have some structural similarities to those with which national decision makers are confronted. Various procedures have been developed for extending experimental games of this sort so as to incorporate an ever-growing number of the characteristics of international conflict.

The third type of experimental study involves the investigation of intergroup conflict, its manifestations, and its resolution in deliberately devised laboratory or field situations. In these studies, subjects actually behave as members and representatives of their experimentally created groups engaged in intergroup conflict. Although these groups are at a different level from the nations to which one would hope to generalize (characterized, among other things, by face-to-face interaction both within and between groups), they may provide some insights into international relations. Similarly, naturalistic studies of intergroup conflict and conflict resolution at different levels, such as studies of industrial or racial conflict, can serve as sources of insight about international conflict, provided that they are supplemented with research directly at the international level, along the lines of some recent studies of international negotiation. (See "Game Theory . . ." 1962; Sawyer & Guetzkow 1965; Pruitt 1965.)

(3) **The development of theory and methodology.** Traditionally, the discipline of international relations has tended to place its emphasis on historical, descriptive, and normative approaches. In recent years, however, many scholars in the field have become increasingly oriented toward the formulation of general propositions about internation behavior, grounded in empirical observations. This has led to the development of theoretical models and to a general concern with the problem of theory construction in international relations and with the search for a suitable methodology. Social-psychological approaches (along with others based, for example, in economics or sociology) are contributing to this process. Thus, concepts of motivation, perception, trust and suspicion, definition of the situation, stress, communication, leadership, influence, norm formation, role prescription, group cohesiveness, and loyalty enter importantly into various general conceptualizations of the interaction between nations and foreign policy making. Typically, these conceptualizations focus on the behavior of individual actors and their interactions, and this gives investigators some leverage for analyzing state behavior as well as the international system itself and facilitates the translation of theoretical variables into operational terms and, hence, the empirical testing of propositions.

The use of social-psychological concepts, therefore, has gone hand in hand with the use of social-psychological methods, such as survey research, intensive interviewing, systematic observation, laboratory experiments, and content analysis in terms of psychological variables. There are many unresolved issues surrounding the role of social-psychological concepts and methods in international relations, such as the question of the proper unit of analysis in this area and the question of generalization from the laboratory to real life, but they do represent potentially useful tools at the present stage of theoretical and methodological development. (See Knorr & Verba 1961; Snyder et al. 1962; North et al. 1963; Guetzkow 1957; Hoffmann 1959; Schelling 1960; Whitaker 1961.)

(4) **The formulation of policy recommendations.** Psychologists and other behavioral scientists have taken an increasingly active part in the foreign policy process during recent years by bringing their specialized knowledge or analytic approach to bear on concrete policy issues (see, for example, Russell 1961). This has involved policy-oriented examinations of the psychological assumptions underlying cold war strategies, such as the doctrine of deterrence, or negotiation procedures; of the psychological mechanisms that reinforce cold war tensions by blocking adaptive responses or promoting perceptual distortions; and of the implications of various existing or proposed programs, such as civil defense or foreign aid. Moreover, psychologists have developed specific proposals for new approaches to international relations designed to promote disarmament, tension reduction, and international cooperation and based, at least in part, on psychological considerations, such as Osgood's proposal for graduated reciprocation in tension reduction (1962). Some attention has also been paid to the all-important problem of the psychological and social conditions on which the viability of a disarmed world depends.

The value of social-psychological contributions becomes greatly enhanced to the extent to which policy recommendations can be backed up by research specifically designed to explore their implications. Along these lines, recent efforts to put some of Osgood's propositions to the experimental test can serve as an example. Social-psychological research can also contribute to the policy process by obtaining data that are directly relevant to certain policy questions. For example, research is now being initiated to determine the degree to which public opinion would tolerate foreign policy innovations. Policy-oriented research, particularly in the area of international conflict, faces many barriers, but it is the foundation on which social-psychological contributions to the policy process must ultimately rest.

HERBERT C. KELMAN

[*See also* BRAINWASHING; CONFLICT; FOREIGN POLICY; INTERNATIONAL POLITICS; PROPAGANDA; PSYCHOLOGICAL WARFARE; PUBLIC OPINION.]

### BIBLIOGRAPHY

*The major periodical source for contributions summarized in this article is the* Journal of Conflict Resolution. *Another important source is the* Journal of Social Issues. *Many relevant papers are reprinted in* Rosenau 1961. *Detailed reviews of special research problems can be found in* Kelman 1965.

ALGER, CHADWICK F. 1965 Personal Contact in Intergovernmental Organizations. Pages 523–547 in Herbert C. Kelman (editor), *International Behavior: A Social-psychological Analaysis.* New York: Holt.

ALMOND, GABRIEL A. (1950) 1960 *The American People and Foreign Policy.* New York: Praeger.

CHRISTIANSEN, BJØRN 1959 *Attitudes Towards Foreign Affairs as a Function of Personality.* Oslo Univ. Press.

DEUTSCH, KARL W. (1960) 1961 Toward an Inventory of Basic Trends and Patterns in Comparative and International Politics. Pages 450–468 in James N. Rosenau (editor), *International Politics and Foreign Policy: A Reader in Research and Theory.* New York: Free Press.

DUIJKER, H. C. J.; and FRIJDA, N. H. 1960 *National Character and National Stereotypes.* A trend report prepared for the International Union of Scientific Psychology. Amsterdam: North-Holland Publishing Co.

Game Theory, Bargaining, and International Relations. 1962 *Journal of Conflict Resolution* 6, no. 1:1–99.

GLOVER, EDWARD 1946 *War, Sadism and Pacifism: Further Essays on Group Psychology and War.* London: Allen & Unwin.

GUETZKOW, HAROLD (1950) 1961 Long Range Research in International Relations. Pages 53–59 in James N. Rosenau (editor), *International Politics and Foreign Policy: A Reader in Research and Theory.* New York: Free Press. → First published in Volume 4 of the *American Perspective.*

GUETZKOW, HAROLD (1957) 1961 Isolation and Collaboration: A Partial Theory of International Relations. Pages 152–163 in James N. Rosenau (editor), *International Politics and Foreign Policy: A Reader in Research and Theory.* New York: Free Press. → First published in Volume 1 of the *Journal of Conflict Resolution.*

GUETZKOW, HAROLD et al. 1963 *Simulation in International Relations: Developments for Research and Teaching.* Englewood Cliffs, N.J.: Prentice-Hall.

HERO, ALFRED O. 1959 *Americans in World Affairs.* World Peace Foundation, Studies in Citizen Participation in International Relations, Vol. 1. Boston: The Foundation.

HOFFMANN, STANLEY H. (1959) 1961 International Relations: The Long Road to Theory. Pages 421–437 in James N. Rosenau (editor), *International Politics and Foreign Policy: A Reader in Research and Theory.* New York: Free Press. → First published in Volume 11 of *World Politics.*

JANIS, IRVING L.; and SMITH, M. BREWSTER 1965 Effects of Education and Persuasion on National and International Images. Pages 190–235 in Herbert C. Kelman (editor), *International Behavior: A Social-psychological Analysis.* New York: Holt.

KATZ, DANIEL 1965 Nationalism and Strategies of International Conflict Resolution. Pages 356–390 in Herbert C. Kelman (editor), *International Behavior: A Social-psychological Analysis.* New York: Holt.

KELMAN, HERBERT C. (editor) 1965 *International Behavior: A Social-psychological Analysis.* New York: Holt.

KLINEBERG, OTTO 1950 *Tensions Affecting International Understanding: A Survey of Research.* Social Science Research Council, Bulletin No. 62. New York: The Council.

KLINEBERG, OTTO 1964 *The Human Dimension in International Relations.* New York: Holt.

KNORR, KLAUS E.; and VERBA, SIDNEY (editors) 1961 *The International System: Theoretical Essays.* Princeton Univ. Press.

MAY, MARK A. 1943 *A Social Psychology of War and Peace.* Published for the Institute of Human Relations. New Haven: Yale Univ. Press; Oxford Univ. Press.

MISHLER, ANITA L. 1965 Personal Contact in International Exchanges. Pages 550–561 in Herbert C. Kelman (editor), *International Behavior: A Social-psychological Analysis.* New York: Holt.

NORTH, ROBERT C. et al. 1963 *Content Analysis: A Handbook With Applications for the Study of International Crisis.* Evanston, Ill.: Northwestern Univ. Press.

OSGOOD, CHARLES E. 1962 *An Alternative to War or Surrender.* Urbana: Univ. of Illinois Press.

PAUL, JOHN P.; and LAULICHT, JEROME 1963 *In Your Opinion: Leaders' and Voters' Attitudes on Defence and Disarmament.* Clarkson, Ontario: Canadian Peace Research Institute.

PEAR, TOM H. (editor) 1950 *Psychological Factors of Peace and War.* New York: Philosophical Library.

PERRY, STEWART E. (1957) 1961 Notes on the Role of the Nation: A Social Psychological Concept for the Study of International Relations. Pages 87–97 in James N. Rosenau (editor), *International Politics and Foreign Policy: A Reader in Research and Theory.* New York: Free Press. → First published in Volume 1 of the *Journal of Conflict Resolution.*

POOL, ITHIEL DE SOLA 1965 Effects of Cross-national Contact on National and International Images. Pages 106–129 in Herbert C. Kelman (editor), *International Behavior: A Social-psychological Analysis.* New York: Holt.

PRUITT, DEAN G. 1965 Definition of the Situation as a Determinant of International Action. Pages 393–432 in Herbert C. Kelman (editor), *International Behavior: A Social-psychological Analysis.* New York: Holt.

ROBINSON, JAMES A.; and SNYDER, RICHARD C. 1965 Decision-making in International Politics. Pages 435–

463 in Herbert C. Kelman (editor), *International Behavior: A Social-psychological Analysis.* New York: Holt.

ROSENAU, JAMES N. (editor) 1961 *International Politics and Foreign Policy: A Reader in Research and Theory.* New York: Free Press.

ROSENBERG, MILTON J. 1965 Images in Relation to the Policy Process: American Public Opinion on Cold-war Issues. Pages 278–334 in Herbert C. Kelman (editor), *International Behavior: A Social-psychological Analysis.* New York: Holt.

RUSSELL, ROGER W. (editor) 1961 Psychology and Policy in a Nuclear Age. *Journal of Social Issues* 17, no. 3:1–87.

SAWYER, JACK; and GUETZKOW, HAROLD 1965 Bargaining and Negotiation in International Relations. Pages 466–520 in Herbert C. Kelman (editor), *International Behavior: A Social-psychological Analysis.* New York: Holt.

SCHELLING, THOMAS C. (1960) 1961 The Retarded Science of International Strategy. Pages 178–185 in James N. Rosenau (editor), *International Politics and Foreign Policy: A Reader in Research and Theory.* New York: Free Press. → First published in Schelling's *The Strategy of Conflict.*

SCOTT, WILLIAM A. 1965 Psychological and Social Correlates of International Images. Pages 71–103 in Herbert C. Kelman (editor), *International Behavior: A Social-psychological Analysis.* New York: Holt.

SNYDER, RICHARD C.; and PAIGE, GLENN D. (1958) 1961 The United States Decision to Resist Aggression in Korea: The Application of an Analytical Scheme. Pages 193–208 in James N. Rosenau (editor), *International Politics and Foreign Policy: A Reader in Research and Theory.* New York: Free Press. → First published in Volume 3 of the *Administrative Science Quarterly.*

SNYDER, RICHARD C. et al. (editors) 1962 *Foreign Policy Decision-making: An Approach to the Study of International Politics.* New York: Free Press.

SOCIETY FOR THE PSYCHOLOGICAL STUDY OF SOCIAL ISSUES 1945 *Human Nature and Enduring Peace.* Third Yearbook of the Society. Edited by Gardner Murphy. Boston: Houghton Mifflin.

WHITAKER, URBAN G. JR. 1961 Actors, Ends, and Means: A Coarse-screen Macro-theory of International Relations. Pages 438–448 in James N. Rosenau (editor), *International Politics and Foreign Policy: A Reader in Research and Theory.* New York: Free Press.

ZINNES, DINA A.; NORTH, ROBERT C.; and KOCH, HOWARD E. 1961 Capability, Threat and the Outbreak of War. Pages 469–482 in James N. Rosenau (editor), *International Politics and Foreign Policy: A Reader in Research and Theory.* New York: Free Press.

## INTERNATIONAL SANCTIONS

*See* SANCTIONS, INTERNATIONAL.

## INTERNATIONAL SYSTEMS

*See under* SYSTEMS ANALYSIS.

## INTERNATIONAL TRADE

*The field of international economics covers both international financial transactions and international trade in commodities and services. The first article below provides an integrated theory of these two major aspects of the field. The remaining articles under this entry deal with the theory and patterns of international trade. For government regulation of international trade, see* INTERNATIONAL TRADE CONTROLS. *For further discussion of international financial transactions, see* INTERNATIONAL MONETARY ECONOMICS. *Other important aspects of international trade are discussed in* INTERNATIONAL INTEGRATION, *article on* ECONOMIC UNIONS, *and in the article on* COMMODITY AGREEMENTS, INTERNATIONAL. *Also relevant is* COMMUNISM, ECONOMIC ORGANIZATION OF, *article on* INTERNATIONAL TRADE.

| | |
|---|---|
| I. THEORY | *Harry G. Johnson* |
| II. MATHEMATICAL THEORY | *Lionel W. McKenzie* |
| III. TERMS OF TRADE | *M. C. Kemp* |
| IV. PATTERNS OF TRADE | *Michael Michaely* |

### I
### THEORY

The theory of international trade is that branch of economic theory concerned with trade between nations and, more broadly, with all aspects of the economic relations between nations. The concept of a nation in this context is somewhat ambiguous and a matter of degree rather than of kind, but not so much so as to cause serious difficulty. To the classical economists, the distinguishing characteristic of a nation was the combination of internal mobility and international immobility of factors of production, an approximation that is, if anything, more appropriate to the twentieth than to the nineteenth century and still dominates the theory of international trade. It has, of course, long been recognized that a theory constructed on these assumptions is equally applicable to trade between geographic regions, whether these are contained within a larger national unit or themselves contain several nations. The theory can also be extended to the analysis of economic relations of groups in the economy between which mobility is restricted or absent, such as skilled and unskilled workers or (a recent application) white and colored workers where color discrimination exists. [*See* DISCRIMINATION, ECONOMIC.]

A nation may alternatively be distinguished by its political sovereignty, which entails both a special concern for nationals, as distinct from foreigners, and the existence of policies of intervention in economic relations with other nations. Sovereignty also entails a distinctive national currency, whose quantity and value in terms of other national currencies are subject to national control.

This definition of the nation as the object of analysis has become increasingly relevant with the growth of nationalism and of governmental economic management and planning in the twentieth century; and these trends have evoked major changes in the approach, as well as the content, of international trade theory. Nevertheless, the economic and political definitions of a nation correspond sufficiently closely to each other and to economic reality for the scope of international trade theory to be reasonably clearly defined.

The theory of international trade is the application of general value theory and monetary theory to a special case in which the microeconomic decision units (households and firms) are grouped into subunits (countries or regions) of the macro-economy differentiated from one another in the way just described. This special case emphasizes certain problems and approaches that are usually given much less prominence in general economic theory.

In the first place, the units of analysis are too large in relation to the whole for the methods of Marshallian partial-equilibrium analysis to be safely applied. While these methods have proved illuminating in particular contexts, at least transitionally, a general equilibrium approach to international trade theory is demanded by the nature of the problems. Second, the interest of the analysis frequently lies in the economic welfare of a particular national unit or the distribution of economic welfare among the owners of the different factors of production at the disposal of a particular national unit, rather than in the global welfare of the world economy. Third, the existence of separate national currencies necessitates a special concern with the problems of monetary equilibrium and particularly with the dynamics of monetary adjustment.

Broadly speaking, the theory of international trade has been historically developed largely in response to national concern with particular problems of international economic policy. One consequence has been that although in its early stages the theory contributed much to general economics, in modern times it has progressed mainly by refining and elaborating analytical techniques originating in general economic theory; an important exception, however, is the recently originated "theory of second best," a generalization from customs union theory capable of wide application in other branches of economics. Another consequence is that much of the literature of the subject is *ad hoc* and unsystematized. For this reason, and

also because the analytical techniques employed are among the most complex in economic theory, there exists an unusually wide gulf between the theory as understood by specialists and the principles commonly advanced in popular debate and public policy formation or even employed by general economists writing on international economic problems. The modern "classics" (Haberler 1933; Ohlin 1933) are seriously out of date in both orientation and technique, while the only postwar work of comparable analytical quality and range (Meade 1951–1955) is forbiddingly abstract and taxonomic in style. Fortunately, however, a number of excellent recent surveys of the field or major sections of it, including extensive bibliographies, are available to guide the interested reader (Caves 1960; Mundell 1960a; Haberler 1954; Johnson 1962; Bhagwati 1964; Corden 1965).

The theory of international trade is customarily divided into two major branches: the "pure," or "real," theory of international trade equilibrium ("the theory of international values") and the "monetary" theory of balance-of-payments adjustment ("the theory of the mechanism of adjustment"). The former is concerned with the determination of relative prices and real incomes in international trade, abstracting from the intervention of money. The implicit assumption that whatever adjustments of money wage and price levels or exchange rates required to preserve international monetary equilibrium do actually take place is a potent source of difficulty and confusion in applying the theory to actual problems. International monetary theory, in its classical formulation, was concerned with the automatic mechanism by which international monetary equilibrium was attained or preserved under the gold standard and, subsequently, with the automatic mechanisms of adjustment under fixed and floating exchange rate systems. Since World War II, however, the development of independent national economic policies aimed at full employment, price stability, and economic growth, with the consequent appearance of the maintenance of balance-of-payments equilibrium as a policy problem, has led to the reformulation of the theory of adjustment as an explicit theory of balance-of-payments policy. The pure theory of international trade deals with problems very similar to those posed in location theory but differs from location theory in the level of abstraction practiced and in taking relatively little account of transport costs and economies of scale as determinants of the location of economic activities and the pattern of trade. The separation of the two is unfortunate, and their integration is a desirable objective of future development. [See SPATIAL ECONOMICS.]

## The pure theory of international trade

**Comparative advantage and gains from trade.** The central concern of the pure theory of international trade is to explain the causes of international trade and the determination of the equilibrium prices and quantities of traded goods and to analyze the effects of trade on economic welfare; that is, the theory is concerned with both positive and normative questions. The normative concern is particularly dominant in the theory of the effects of tariffs and other governmental interventions in international trade—a perennial problem that has acquired new interest in the modern world of planned economic development based on protected industrialization and deliberate import-substitution.

*The classical theory.* The classical economists developed the basic concepts of the theory in two steps: Ricardo contributed the theory of comparative costs, which explained both the cause and the mutual beneficiality of international trade by international differences in relative costs of production; and John Stuart Mill added the principle that the relative prices of the goods exchanged must be such that the quantities demanded in international trade are equal to the quantities supplied. The theory of comparative costs is most easily understood from Ricardo's example: in England a gallon of wine costs 120 and a yard of cloth 100 units of work, while in Portugal the costs are 80 and 90 units of work, respectively. England has an absolute cost disadvantage in both goods but a comparative advantage in cloth, since the production of a yard of cloth involves sacrificing production of $1\frac{1}{8}$ gallons of wine in Portugal but only $\frac{5}{6}$ of a gallon in England, these being the prices of cloth in terms of wine that would rule in the two countries if labor in each is perfectly mobile and prices accurately reflect labor costs. Ignoring transport costs, a price of cloth in terms of wine anywhere between $\frac{5}{6}$ and $1\frac{1}{8}$ would make it profitable for England to export cloth and import wine and for Portugal to export wine and import cloth. By so doing, each could obtain more of each of the goods with the same amount of work or consume the same amounts with less expenditure of labor. This example conveys the fundamental point that the beneficiality of international trade depends in no way on the absolute levels of economic efficiency or "stages of economic development" of the trading partners but only on differences in their relative costs of

production in the absence of trade. It has been reformulated here so as to bring out the essential point that what matters is differences in the alternative opportunity costs of commodities in the absence of trade. Ricardo's own formulation, with its assumption of a single factor of production producing goods at constant costs and its concept of a fundamental unit of real cost (hours of work), unnecessarily tied trade theory to the labor theory of value. The result of his successors' attempts to abandon the simple labor theory of value while retaining the real cost concept was an increasingly cumbersome theoretical structure, which was ultimately abandoned in favor of the opportunity cost approach. This, the modern approach, can incorporate theories of production of any desired degree of complexity and specifically allows alternative opportunity cost to vary with changes in the production pattern. However, as soon as more than one factor of production is introduced, the analysis of the effects of trade on economic welfare becomes more complex than in the classical system, and the demonstration of gain from trade requires considerably more conceptual sophistication.

*The modern theory.* The modern approach to the question of the gains from trade recognizes that the inauguration of trade or a change in the conditions of trade, such as that involved in the erection or removal of tariff barriers, will have differential effects on the welfare of individuals—either by changing the relative prices facing them as consumers (affecting differentially individuals with different tastes) or by changing the relative prices paid for the factors of production (affecting differentially the incomes of individuals who own the factors in different ratios). The evaluation of gain or loss therefore necessitates interpersonal welfare comparisons, which must be excluded as illegitimate. In their absence, welfare conclusions can only be derived *either* on the (unrealistic) assumption that a social judgment of the desirable distribution of real income exists and is implemented consistently *or* in terms of potential welfare, that is, in the sense that in one situation everyone could be made no worse off and some be made better off than they would be in the alternative situation, by means of appropriate compensations through transfers of income.

Ethical neutrality further requires that this result should be true for all possible distributions of economic welfare (real income) among individuals, not merely for the distribution that happens to prevail before or after a change of situation. This requirement is satisfied by any change that makes more of all commodities (including leisure) available to the economy or, in the limit, no less of any commodity, regardless of how the community allocates its consumption among commodities. In technical terms, such a change produces an outward shift of the transformation frontier—the relation embodying the alternative maximal combinations of commodities and leisure the economy can produce with its resources and available technology.

Provided that domestic economic organization is such that free competition would maximize welfare in the potential sense (which requires the absence of "external effects" of production or consumption by one firm or consumer on the efficiency or welfare of others, and the absence of taxes and other distortions preventing prices from corresponding to relative marginal costs), the inauguration of international trade by a closed economy is such a potential-welfare-increasing change. The availability of international relative prices different from the relative prices ruling in the closed economy enables the country to "produce" goods more cheaply by exporting other goods in exchange for them. The gains from trade so obtained derive conceptually from two sources: the gain from substituting lower-cost for higher-cost goods in consumption (the consumption effect of trade) and the gain from diverting resources from direct, higher-cost to indirect, lower-cost production of goods imported from the world market (the production effect, or specialization effect, of trade). It is to be noted that the gains from trade do not depend on specialization in production: the gain from the consumption effect would accrue even if resources were completely immobile between industries.

In the same potential welfare sense, it can be shown that free trade will maximize world income by equating the marginal values of commodities to all consumers and the marginal costs of production of goods by all producers. This does not, however, imply that in the absence of international compensations a free trade policy will always maximize a country's economic welfare. While trade is always superior to self-sufficiency, restricted trade may be superior to free trade. This will be so if the country has any monopoly or monopsony power in world markets that it can exploit by appropriate tariffs or other restrictions. The exploitation of such power is, indeed, a necessary condition for maximizing the country's welfare: the tariff rate or degree of restriction required is analyzed in the theory of the optimum tariff and of optimum tariff structures. Moreover,

a country may attain a higher level of welfare by following an optimum tariff policy, even if other countries retaliate, than it would under universal free trade. Thus, the case for free trade, frequently asserted with considerable dogmatism in the past, appears in contemporary international trade theory as an extremely qualified proposition, dependent on the maintenance of international monetary stability, on efficient representation of alternative social opportunity costs by money costs and prices in the domestic currency, on the social acceptability of the resulting distribution of income or the adoption of a social policy with regard to income distribution, and on the possible need for international income transfers. [See INTERNATIONAL TRADE CONTROLS, *article on* TARIFFS AND PROTECTIONISM.]

The gains from international trade are obviously dependent on the difference between the prices for exports in terms of imports established in international trade ("the commodity terms of trade") and the prices that would rule in a closed economy. The classical economists attempted to relate the distribution of the gains from trade to the precise point between the closed-economy comparative cost ratios at which the equilibrium international price ratio fell. Clearly, however, this is inadequate, and the gains for an individual country can only be measured in theory by the application of one or another version of the compensation principle—that is, by calculating the amount of resources that could be extracted from a country while leaving it no worse off than it would have been in the absence of trade or by calculating the amount of resources that it would have to be given in the absence of trade to make it as well off as it would be if allowed to trade. In practice, while this approach has been applied in specialist studies of the welfare cost of protection, economists have generally been content to analyze changes in countries' gains from trade by reference to changes in an index expressing one or another concept of the terms of trade [see INTERNATIONAL TRADE, *article on* TERMS OF TRADE]. Of the various terms-of-trade concepts that have been developed, the most defensible and reliable is the commodity terms of trade—the price of imports in terms of exports or its reciprocal. The loss or gain accruing to a country as a result of short-run changes originating externally can be measured to a first approximation by the change in the commodity terms of trade multiplied by the value of imports. But changes in the commodity terms of trade, especially in the longer run, may be the result of internal developments—changes in productivity or changes in taste. In this case, their implications for economic welfare cannot be readily interpreted except in the circular sense that real income would have been measurably different if the terms of trade had remained unchanged.

**The Heckscher–Ohlin model.** The classical theory of international trade explained trade by differences in the comparative productivity of labor. This approach has its modern followers, who have been surprisingly successful in explaining differences in the relative shares of different countries in world imports of different products by differences in their relative labor productivity in the relevant industries. The existence of the differences in comparative costs underlying international trade, however, was merely assumed and not explained by the theory. Contemporary international trade theory attempts the more fundamental task of explaining these differences by differences in the ratios in which countries are endowed with factors of production. The theory originated with Heckscher (American Economic Association 1949, chapter 13) but was significantly elaborated by Ohlin (1933); in its contemporary form it owes a great deal to analytical techniques and propositions contributed by Samuelson (1948 and elsewhere). As commonly expounded and applied, the theory employs a simple but elegant model of production and distribution in the national economy, usually referred to as the Heckscher–Ohlin model, although its mechanics are, as mentioned, largely the work of Samuelson. The Heckscher–Ohlin model assumes a perfectly competitive economy in which two commodities (call them X and Y) are produced by two factors of production (call them K and L), utilizing production functions characterized by constant returns to scale and diminishing marginal rate of substitution between the factors. The quantities of the factors available are assumed fixed, and the production functions are assumed to be such that at any given ratio of the price of K to the price of L, the production of X is K-intensive and the production of Y is L-intensive, in the sense that X employs a higher ratio of K to L than does Y. For the analysis of international trade the world is assumed to be composed of two such national economies, the production functions and factors are assumed to be identical in the two countries, and the tastes of consumers in the two countries are assumed to be similar, in the sense that, at the same commodity price ratio, they will consume the two goods in roughly the same ratios.

The production side of this model has two fundamental properties, from which an extensive and elegant set of theorems can be derived. These result from the assumption of constant returns to scale, which makes the ratios in which factors are employed in the two industries depend only on their relative prices; the assumption of the invariance of relative factor intensity, which links relative factor prices uniquely to relative commodity prices; and the assumption of fixed factor endowments, which links the production pattern uniquely to commodity or factor prices. Consider a particular factor price ratio: this will fix the ratios in which factors are used in the two industries. The factor use ratios in combination with the factor price ratio will fix the relative costs of production and price ratio of the commodities. The factor use ratios in combination with the endowment ratio will fix the ratios in which the commodities are produced, since their aggregate factor requirements must just absorb all of the available factor supplies.

*Stolper–Samuelson relationship.* Now consider a rise in the relative price of factor K. This will raise the relative price of commodity X, which uses relatively more K than does commodity Y. It will induce a substitution of L for K in both industries, raising the marginal product of K and lowering that of L in terms of both X and Y, so that owners of K will be unambiguously better off and of L worse off, regardless of their tastes for the two goods. The induced decrease in the ratio of K to L in both industries, in combination with the fixed factor endowments, will necessitate an increase in the production of X (the K-intensive commodity) and a reduction in the production of Y, if all factor supplies are to remain employed.

Thus, as long as the economy produces both goods, there is a unique relation between the commodity price ratio, the factor price ratio, the real incomes of factor owners, and the pattern of production. An increase in the relative price of a commodity increases the relative price of the factor used intensively in producing it, raises the real income of that factor and lowers the real income of the other factor, and increases output of that commodity at the expense of the other. This relationship is known as the Stolper–Samuelson relationship (American Economic Association 1949, chapter 15).

*Rybczynski theorem.* Alternatively, consider an increase in the quantity of one factor available to the economy, the commodity price ratio and therefore the factor price ratio and factor-intensities remaining constant. To absorb the increased quantity of the factor while paying it the same price, the economy must release a quantity of the other factor to work in combination with it. This can only be done by contracting the industry that uses the other factor intensively and expanding the industry that uses the augmented factor intensively, thereby freeing some of the other factor for re-employment with the additional supply of the augmented factor. Hence, at constant commodity prices, an increase in the quantity of a factor implies an increased output of the good that uses it intensively and a reduction in the output of the other good. This relationship is referred to as the Rybczynski theorem (1955).

*Samuelson factor price equalization theorem.* It follows from the Rybczynski theorem that the country with a relative abundance (high endowment ratio) of a particular factor would, at any given commodity price ratio, produce relatively more of the commodity that uses that factor intensively; and hence that, assuming similarity of tastes, the price of that good would be relatively lower than in the other country, in closed-economy equilibrium. In other words, relative factor abundance gives rise to comparative advantage. It follows from the Stolper–Samuelson relation and the assumed identity of factor prices and production functions that the equalization of commodity prices in the two countries that would result from free trade in the absence of transport costs would tend to equalize relative factor prices (and, therefore, absolute factor prices, given the identity of production functions), and would in fact exactly equalize factor prices if both countries produced both goods (i.e., were "incompletely specialized") in the free trade equilibrium. In this case trade would serve as a complete substitute for factor movements, and immobility of factors would not prevent the maximization of world income. This is the Samuelson factor price equalization theorem (1948). It will generalize beyond the two-factor two-commodity model, factor prices being equalized as long as the number of goods produced in each country is equal to the number of factors, although the restrictions required on the factor-intensities of the commodities are necessarily more complex. The theorem has sometimes been cited as evidence of the irrelevance of international trade theory to the real world, on the grounds that the theorem is inconsistent with the existence of great inequality of income per head. This criticism is invalid, since the theorem relates to factor prices and not per capita income (which depends on factor endowment); and the theorem should be interpreted, not as a prediction about the real world, but as a statement of the necessary conditions for factor price equalization. The nonfulfillment of these conditions in the real world accounts for the observed inequalities of factor prices.

*Effect of tariffs.* The Stolper–Samuelson relation clarifies the theory of tariffs by permitting unambiguous conclusions about the effects of tariffs on the real incomes of factors. In the normal case, in which the two trading countries' demands for each other's exports are elastic, a tariff will improve a country's terms of trade and raise the internal price of imports, thus shifting production toward import-substitutes and raising the real income of the factor used intensively in producing them. Whether the country as a whole loses or gains (in the potential-welfare sense) depends on whether the tariff is sufficiently higher than the optimum tariff for the gain on the terms of trade to be offset by the restriction of trade volume. There are two "exceptional" cases: if the country's own demand for imports is inelastic and if those who spend the tariff proceeds have a stronger marginal preference for imports than the average consumer, the demand for imports may increase and the terms of trade turn against the country; if the foreign country's demand for imports is inelastic and if domestic consumers have a stronger marginal preference for the export good than do foreigners, the terms of trade may improve so much that the internal price of imports falls and the income-distribution effects are opposite to those normally expected (Bhagwati & Johnson 1961).

*Effect of economic growth.* The Rybczynski theorem is the foundation of the theory of the effects of economic growth on trade: an increase in the available quantity of the factor used intensively in the export industry must increase production of export goods and reduce production of import-substitutes at the initial equilibrium terms of trade, thereby making the country more dependent on imports and tending to turn the terms of trade against it; and the converse. An extension of the logic of the theorem indicates the effect of technical change: technical change in an industry reduces its relative costs; to restore the cost ratio to equality with the initial terms of trade, the relative price of the factor used intensively in that industry must rise. This will reduce the use ratio of that factor in both industries, requiring an expansion of the technically improved industry and a contraction of the other to keep the factors fully employed. The exception is the case where the technical change is strongly saving of the factor used relatively unintensively in the improved industry (i.e., the change raises the intensity of use of the already intensively used factor sufficiently to offset the induced factor substitutions). Barring the exception and excluding the complications associated with the effects of the redistribution of income between the factors on the demands for the goods, it follows that technical change will make the country more dependent or less dependent on trade, and worsen or improve its terms of trade, according to whether the change occurs in the export or the import-competing industry (Johnson 1962, chapter 4; Meier 1963, chapters 2, 3).

*Effect of transfer.* A standard problem in international trade theory concerns the effects on the terms of trade of a continuing transfer from one country to another, such as reparations payments, foreign investment, or a balance-of-payments surplus; the point of the problem being that if the transfer worsens the terms of trade, it imposes a "secondary burden," additional to the transfer itself, on the country making the transfer. Since the transfer shifts purchasing power from one country to the other, the question is simply whether its effect is to increase or decrease world demand for the exports of the country making the transfer. The criterion for this can be expressed in various ways. The one most commonly used is whether the sum of the proportions of the transfer by which the demand for imports is changed in the two countries exceeds or falls short of unity. Classical theory and the "common sense" of many economists indicate a presumption that the effect will be a worsening of the terms of trade. Such a presumption can be established theoretically, however, only on the assumption of unit income elasticities of demand for goods and of the presence of tariffs or of transport costs on imports incurred in the exported good, both of which will bias a country's marginal expenditure toward its export good. This analysis is not altered by the introduction of nontraded goods, since there is no presumption that these are closer substitutes for exported than for imported goods (Johnson 1958, chapter 7).

*Evaluation of the model.* The Heckscher–Ohlin model appears to provide a sensible explanation of the causes of trade and, in the factor price equalization theorem, provides a powerful argument for the beneficiality of freedom of trade. Its simplicity, however, derives from two of its assumptions, whose crucial importance has been revealed by intensive exploration of the model. This critical examination was prompted, on the one hand, by incredulity concerning the factor price equalization theorem and, on the other, by Leontief's empirical finding, derived from his input–output tables, that contrary to expectation

United States exports are more labor-intensive and less capital-intensive than United States imports (1953). Leontief rationalized this result by hypothesizing that American labor is three times as productive as foreign labor.

Exploration of the model has demonstrated, first, that demand differences may counteract the influence of differing factor endowments on trade patterns; second, that unless the elasticities of substitution are the same in the two industries, the relative factor-intensities of industries will reverse themselves as relative factor prices change. (This possibility has been confirmed by empirical studies applying the constant-elasticity-of-substitution production function.) More generally, if elasticities of substitution are variable, relative factor-intensities may reverse more than once. Such reversibility means that a rising relative price of a factor will be associated alternatively with a rising and a falling price of the commodity that initially uses it intensively (the falling relative commodity price occurring after the factor-intensity reversal). It implies that even with similar tastes in the two countries, comparative advantage, as reflected in closed-economy equilibrium comparative-cost ratios, need not reflect relative factor abundance; and that, since more than one relative factor price may be associated with a given commodity price ratio, free trade with incomplete specialization in both countries does not necessarily imply factor price equalization and may indeed imply a greater divergence of relative factor prices than would exist in the absence of trade.

These two theoretical considerations—demand differences and factor-intensity reversal—have been advanced to reconcile Leontief's findings with the theory. A more plausible argument is that in confining his calculations to labor and capital only, Leontief ignored the influence of third factors of production, such as natural resources, labor skill, or managerial ability, so that his results are not a fair test of the Heckscher–Ohlin theory. It has also been argued that these results may be attributable to the influence of the American tariff (Travis 1964).

The Heckscher–Ohlin theory is obviously a plausible approach to the explanation of trade in products for which localized natural resources are important; but it is equally obviously not very helpful in explaining the composition of trade in industrial products, both intermediate and finished, between advanced industrial nations, which accounts for a major share of total international trade. Various theoretical approaches to this problem have been suggested, none of which possess the logical rigor and elegance of the Heckscher–Ohlin model. Kravis (1956) has pointed to the influence of "availability" (existence and elasticity of marginal supplies) on trade between advanced nations. Burenstam Linder (1961) hypothesized that industry develops to supply the home market, adapts its products to the income level of that market, and exports primarily to countries with similar income levels. Travis (1964) and Johnson (1965a) have called attention to the influence of tariff structures on patterns of international trade. Others have emphasized such elements in industrial competitiveness as economies of scale, technological superiority based on research and development expenditure, and the availability of skilled labor ("human capital"). Vernon (1966) has attempted to integrate a number of these factors into a dynamic "product cycle" theory of international trade and investment. It is evident that further progress on this problem will require a deeper understanding of the economics of industry, including location theory, and that trade theorists will have to concern themselves with two aspects of international economic relations that have so far been relatively neglected: the influence of monopolistic competition on location and trade, and the content and influence of protectionist policies.

**Protection and the theory of second best.** Protection has been a perennial policy issue since long before the origins of international trade theory, and international trade theorists in the main tradition of the subject have consistently been concerned with advocating freedom of trade and exposing the innumerable fallacies of protectionist thinking. Two arguments for tariffs have, however, traditionally been acknowledged as valid—the terms of trade ("optimum tariff") argument, and the infant industry argument, favoring temporary protection of industries capable eventually of establishing themselves in international competition. With respect to these arguments, international trade theorists have confined themselves to observing that protection is justified only if the empirical conditions posited are actually present and to arguing the superiority of a subsidy over a tariff in the infant industry case.

Contemporary interest in the economic development of the underdeveloped countries has revived both these arguments for protection—especially the infant industry argument, which has been broadened into an infant economy argument—and has added a new argument, the so-called Manoilesco argument (Corden 1965, pp. 60–61). This argument bases a case for industrial protec-

tion on the assertion that wages in the industrial sector of backward countries exceed the alternative opportunity cost of labor, either because labor in the industrial sector receives a wage differential over agricultural labor that is not justified by skill or cost-of-living differences or because in peasant agriculture labor receives a share of output equal to its average product and in excess of its marginal product, which may be zero.

*Customs unions.* Interest in the theory of tariffs has also been generated by the movement toward economic integration in Europe and by the associated problem of the economic effects of customs unions and free trade areas. (Both of these involve elimination of tariff barriers to trade between the members and the retention of tariffs against outsiders, but a customs union entails unification of the national tariffs in a common schedule, whereas in a free trade area the members retain tariff autonomy.) Such arrangements entail a simultaneous movement toward free trade (among the members) and protection (of members' producers in each other's markets). The problem is whether the net result is a gain or a loss of economic welfare for individual members, the union as a whole, outsiders, and the world as a whole. [See INTERNATIONAL INTEGRATION, *article on* ECONOMIC UNIONS.]

The theoretical techniques required for dealing with these problems were provided by Viner (1950) in the concepts of trade creation and trade diversion: a customs union increases welfare to the extent that it creates trade by diverting demand from higher-cost domestic to lower-cost partner products and decreases welfare to the extent that it diverts trade from lower-cost, foreign to higher-cost, partner products. (A fuller analysis of the effects on the separate countries concerned must also take account of terms-of-trade effects.) Viner's analysis employed a classical constant-cost model and considered only effects on the location of production, but it was readily generalized by others to take account of substitutions among goods in consumption and of varying production costs.

Following Viner, Meade (1951–1955, vol. 2) developed an elaborate analytical apparatus for analyzing the effects of tariff and other policy changes on welfare when these changes are introduced in an economy whose equilibrium is distorted by tariffs, taxes, and other factors preventing prices from corresponding to the social costs or values of goods. The essence of the technique is to attach welfare weights, reflecting the divergences of social from market costs or values, to the changes in economic quantities induced by the tariff change and to assess the total effect by the sum of the changes so weighted; the weights may include adjustments based on interpersonal comparisons of utility for different groups. The technique yields a number of propositions about the circumstances in which a customs union is likely or unlikely to increase economic welfare and also the proposition that preferential tariff reduction is more likely to be beneficial than complete free trade in such a union. Its main importance, however, is in providing a theory that is capable of quantitative application to practical problems.

*The theory of second best.* A customs union is, from the free trade point of view, a second-best arrangement; and the problems dealt with in Meade's analysis all involve choices among alternatives when the first-best, or welfare-maximizing, solution is ruled out by assumption. This is the nature of most policy problems in economics, in other areas as well as international trade, so that Meade's theoretical construction is of great general applicability. The findings of customs union theory and of other policy-oriented branches of economics have been synthesized by Lipsey and Lancaster in "The General Theory of Second Best" (1956). The central proposition of this theory is that when some constraint prevents the competitive system from achieving a welfare maximum, the achievement of the attainable second-best maximum will generally require a variety of other interventions in the competitive process. This is a principle of great importance, for it implies that "piecemeal" policies of seeking to establish perfect competition in particular sectors of the economy may decrease rather than increase welfare and that the welfare effects of particular governmental interventions can only be evaluated in the light of detailed knowledge of the other distortions from perfectly competitive conditions existing in the economy.

The theory of second best casts the traditional arguments for tariff protection in a new light. All such arguments except the optimum tariff argument are second-best arguments, in the sense that they recommend the introduction of a distortion in the competitive system to offset other distortions alleged or believed to exist (in the investment market, commodity markets, or factor markets). The implementation of such protectionist policies cannot, therefore, lead to a first-best welfare maximum; whether it leads toward or away from a second-best welfare maximum depends on the empirical circumstances and cannot be determined by a priori argument (Johnson 1965*b*). Despite the importance of the issue and the vast literature that has accumulated on tariffs and protectionism, there have been virtually no attempts to measure the effects of tariffs and test empirically the arguments advanced for protection.

Finally, it should be observed that the contemporary theory of tariffs, customs unions, and so forth, adopts as its standard of economic welfare the satisfactions enjoyed by individuals in their capacity as private consumers. It is this standard that sets the international trade theorist in perennial conflict with protectionists and national policy makers in general. If trade theorists were to consider seriously the values of the latter, which entail a less atomistic concept of social welfare, many of their policy conclusions would be radically altered; but they might be far more effective in persuading nations to follow more economically rational international economic policies [*see* INTERNATIONAL TRADE CONTROLS, *article on* TARIFFS AND PROTECTIONISM].

## The monetary theory of balance-of-payments adjustment

**The classical adjustment mechanism.** The pure theory of international trade assumes that money prices and costs will adjust passively to the real equilibrium of the international economy. The classical explanation of this adjustment was provided in Hume's price–specie flow mechanism, originated to demonstrate the fallacy of the mercantilist view that national policy should aim at augmenting a country's stock of gold by taking measures to ensure a permanent surplus on the balance of trade. According to the theory, the stock of international money (which was initially identified with gold and silver, whose total quantity was assumed fixed, although the theory was subsequently extended to incorporate deposit money and the intervention of central banks) would tend automatically to be so distributed among nations that each would have the quantity it demanded, consistent with international equilibrium. An increase in the quantity of money in a particular country would raise prices there, decreasing exports and increasing imports, bringing the exchange rate to the gold-export point and inducing an outflow of gold, which would cause domestic prices to fall and foreign prices to rise until equilibrium was restored with a generally higher level of world prices.

This account of the adjustment mechanism, which follows Hume and Viner (see Viner 1932, p. 265), is unsatisfactory in two respects. First, it fails to bring out clearly that it is the expenditure of unwanted cash balances that leads to the import surplus and the corresponding gold flow and that it is the adjustment of actual to desired cash balances, through the combination of international redistribution of money and reduction of its purchasing power by rising prices, that eventually restores equilibrium. Second, in deducing the movements of prices involved in the adjustment process from a mechanical application of the quantity theory of money to the separate national economies as if they were partially closed off from trade, it not only imposes an arbitrary causal sequence but greatly exaggerates the necessity of international money flows to the adjustment process. The strategic role in the adjustment mechanism assigned to international money flows as a result of naive quantity theorizing was inappropriately carried over from the analysis of adjustment to monetary disturbances to the analysis of adjustment to real disturbances in the predominant tradition of classical trade theory. In the work of Taussig and Viner it gave rise to spurious problems associated with the fact that observed flows of international reserves seemed much too small, relative to the magnitude of disturbances, to account for the preservation of international equilibrium.

The minority tradition, represented by Ricardo and Wheatley, argued that the adjustment to nonmonetary disturbances would occur automatically through relative price changes, without an intervening sequence of money flows and inflationary–deflationary price movements. This view was strengthened by the recognition, in analyses of the transfer problem, of the equilibrating effects on the balance of payments of the changes in demands for goods associated with the transfer of purchasing power.

The difference in viewpoint over the importance of monetary adjustments in the correction of real disturbances is represented in the modern literature in the debate between Keynes and Ohlin over the problem of German reparations after World War I (American Economic Association 1949, chapters 6, 7). From the vantage point of modern monetary theory, it is clear that monetary adjustments will be called into play by real disturbances only to the extent that the latter entail monetary disturbances also, as, for example, when a decrease in demand for a country's exports or a transfer reduces its real income and demand for cash balances and prompts a transitional excess of expenditure over income in the form of a balance-of-payments deficit. Thus—contrary to the authoritative judgment of Viner (1932, p. 206)—Bastable, Wicksell, and Ohlin appear to have been justified in denying any significant role in the adjustment of real disturbances to price-level movements induced by gold movements.

*Purchasing power parity.* The classical theory of the adjustment mechanism and of international monetary equilibrium logically implies the theory of purchasing power parity, developed by Gustav Cassel for the analysis of exchange-rate changes in the period of monetary disturbance that followed World War I (the connection is denied in Viner 1932, p. 206, but well documented in Haberler [1954] 1961, pp. 45–51). The theory was discredited, largely as a result of Viner's criticisms, in the interwar period but has been revived in connection with postwar exchange-rate problems—first concerning the European currencies in the "dollar-shortage period" and later the question of the overvaluation of the American dollar. The theory concerns the relationship between the equilibrium exchange rates among national currencies and their respective domestic purchasing powers (in a floating exchange-rate system) or between national equilibrium price levels and the exchange rates (in a fixed exchange-rate system).

The absolute version of the theory asserts that equilibrium exchange rates or price levels must be such that currencies exchange at purchasing power parity: if £1 will buy in England goods that would cost $2.80 in the United States, a free exchange market will establish a rate of $2.80 to £1; and if the British government fixes the rate at $2.80 to £1, the price level in England must be such that £1 will buy the same quantity of goods in England as $2.80 will buy in the United States. This version of the theory is either a truism—if attention is confined to internationally traded goods, and tariffs and transport costs are ignored—or demonstrably wrong, since the prices of nontraded goods relative to traded goods in the various countries will vary according to the relative efficiency of these countries in producing nontraded as compared with traded goods.

The relative version of the theory asserts that equilibrium exchange rates will change in proportion to changes in relative purchasing power, or equilibrium price levels in proportion to changes in official exchange rates. This version of the theory ignores the influence of changes in tariffs and transfers or in real demand and supply conditions, which will have differential effects on the trading positions of countries and on their relative price levels. Nevertheless, it is a reasonable approximation for the analysis of short-run monetary disturbances of the type with which Cassel was concerned and provides a rough guide for policymakers obliged to decide the magnitude of exchange-rate changes. As a matter of fact, the exchange rates of the major countries do not depart very far (typically less than 20 per cent) from purchasing power parity. Haberler ([1954] 1961, p. 51) has argued that this reflects high elasticities of demand and supply in international trade.

**The theory of balance-of-payments policy.** The problems of international monetary disequilibrium that have beset the world economy since the end of World War I have prompted a rapid development and elaboration of the theory of international monetary adjustment and have transformed that theory from a theory of automatic mechanisms to a theory concerned with policy alternatives open to governments. The monetary disorganization that immediately followed World War I not only produced the purchasing-power-parity theory but led to recognition of the possible conflict between internal stability and external stability inherent in the choice of either a fixed or a floating exchange rate and to analysis of the comparative merits of the two systems. The circumstances of the restoration and collapse of the gold standard also stimulated theorizing on the role of capital movements, especially short-term capital movements, in the process of international equilibration and as a source of disequilibrium.

These issues again became lively with the postwar restoration of the convertibility of the European currencies and the reversal of the "dollar shortage." With respect to these issues, international monetary economists divide into four positions, which can be identified closely with the influence of a dominating historical experience: advocacy of a return to the classical gold standard, associated with the post-World War I experience of inflationary monetary policies in Europe; advocacy of a floating exchange-rate system, associated with the 1930s experience of international deflation; support of the present dollar-based International Monetary Fund system, associated with practical experience in managing it; and advocacy of the establishment of a world central bank, associated with faith in the possibility of intelligent international monetary management combined with recognition of the defects of the present hybrid system.

The debate over the alternatives has for the most part covered familiar ground, but significant advances have been made in understanding of the theory of a floating rate system (Friedman 1953; Sohmen 1961) and of the problems raised in such a system by capital movements (Mundell 1963). Mundell (1961) and McKinnon (1963) have cast the issues in an illuminating new way by raising the analytical issue of the optimal size and properties of a currency area; and Kenen (1960) has contributed a theoretical analysis of the problems of an international monetary system in which the currency of one country is held as a reserve by the others, in substitution for international reserve money. [*See* INTERNATIONAL MONETARY ECONOMICS.]

*Elasticity and absorption approaches.* The chief new analytical developments of the interwar period were the application of Keynesian multiplier theory to the mechanism of international adjustment by Metzler (American Economic Association 1949, chapter 8) and Machlup (1943) and the elaboration of the criterion for exchange stability by Robinson (American Economic Association 1949, chapter 4) and others. Multiplier analysis showed that in normal cases (a positive marginal propensity to save in both countries) part but not all of the adjustment to an international disturbance would be effected automatically by induced variations in income and employment. The exchange stability criterion is a mathematical expression in terms of the elasticities of demands for and supplies of imports and exports, such that exchange depreciation would tend to improve the trade balance if the expression is positive; a sufficient condition for stability is that the sum of the elasticities of demand for imports of the two countries be greater than unity. The exchange stability criterion was interpreted, insufficiently critically, as also being the condition for devaluation to improve the balance of payments; in terms of the model employed, this is only true if Keynesian unemployment exists and the marginal propensities to save are positive. The same analysis also yielded a criterion for whether or not depreciation would tend to worsen or improve the terms of trade. While Robinson and others argued a presumption that devaluation would worsen the terms of trade, on the grounds that a country's exports are likely to be more specialized than its imports, this argument is not convincing.

The theory so constructed was limited to Keynesian conditions of general unemployment, involved a sharp separation between the theories of the effects of income variations and of price changes, and still adhered to the mechanisms of adjustment formulation of the theory. In the postwar situation of general inflation and full or overfull employment, concern with questions of overvaluation of currencies and the probable effectiveness of devaluation led to considerable skepticism about the relevance of the "elasticity approach" to devaluation and to doubts about the capacity of devaluation to improve the trade balance. This "elasticity pessimism" was reinforced by empirical studies that indicated low elasticities of international demand (the techniques used in these studies have since been shown to be biased toward underestimating the elasticities).

The elasticity approach was challenged by Alexander (1952), who produced an alternative in the "absorption approach." In this approach the balance of trade is expressed, not as the difference between export and import values, but as the difference between total output and the total absorption of goods (i.e., the difference between national income and national expenditure). Devaluation will improve the trade balance only to the extent that it reduces absorption relative to output. If there are unemployed resources and an increase in output would raise absorption by a smaller amount than itself, devaluation can improve the trade balance by raising the demand for output. Otherwise, devaluation can improve the trade balance only through its indirect effects in reducing demand—for example, by reducing the real stock of money through increasing domestic prices, by redistributing income toward those with a higher propensity to save, or by increasing the real burden of a progressive tax structure—and these effects may be unfavorable rather than favorable. Subsequently, a number of international trade theorists have presented syntheses or reconciliations of the elasticity and absorption approaches. This is not a difficult problem, once it is recognized that the elasticity approach is primarily concerned with the effects of relative price changes in abstraction from limitations on total output and that the absorption approach is primarily concerned with the effects of money price-level changes in a situation of fixed aggregate supply.

*Policy objectives approach.* In essence, the elasticity-versus-absorption issue derived from the separation of the analyses of income variation and price variation in the new developments of the 1930s and reflected the need to integrate the two aspects of the adjustment mechanism. The required integration has been provided in the theory of economic policy elaborated in general terms by Tinbergen (1952) and with specific reference to international trade by Meade (1951–1955, vol. 1), whose work was published about the same time as Alexander's alternative approach to devaluation theory. This theory starts from the proposition that a government in a modern state has certain policy objectives, and its basic theorem is that to achieve these objectives the government must command as many independent policy instruments as it has objectives, independence meaning that the instruments have different effects on the economy. In Meade's work the objectives are taken to be internal balance (full employment) and external balance (equilibrium in the balance of payments). The instruments are fiscal and monetary policy for controlling the aggregate level of demand by the economy; and the exchange rate, the internal price level, or tariffs or other trade restrictions, for controlling the division of the aggregate foreign and domestic demand between domestic and foreign goods. As Johnson (1958, chapter 6) has reformulated the theory, a country with these two objectives needs to use both expenditure-reducing (or expenditure-increasing) policies, to make the level of the country's aggregate demand match its full-employment level of output, and expenditure-switching policies, to assure that this aggregate demand falls on the country's own domestic output by making the foreign demand for its exports exactly balance its demand for imports.

Meade's work is flawed by a tendency to imply that a specific policy instrument can be associated with each objective; in general, policy instruments influence the attainment of both objectives and must be conceived as being used jointly to obtain the objectives jointly. Mundell (1960*b*) has subsequently shown, however, that when the dynamics of policy operations are considered, stability of equilibrium requires that each policy instrument be governed by changes in the variable on which it has the relatively largest effect.

Meade's work and much of the literature of the postwar decade assumed that exchange rates could be changed or trade controls imposed if necessary, an assumption that has become decreasingly descriptive of the international monetary environment. In Meade's framework a country that is committed to a fixed exchange rate, is averse to the use of controls, and is pursuing both internal and external stability appears to have one instrument too few. But this apparent dilemma is resolved, once a distinction is drawn between the current account (influenced by the level of income and employment) and the capital account (influenced by the level of interest rates) of the balance of payments and it is recognized that expansion by fiscal policy tends to raise, and expansion by monetary policy to lower, interest rates. A country suffering unemployment and a balance-of-payments deficit can therefore achieve its two objectives by appropriately combining fiscal expansion with monetary restriction (Mundell 1963). A third common policy objective, acceleration of economic growth, can be accommodated by designing fiscal stimuli to encourage saving and investment. These extensions of the Meade model, however, while valid for short-run analysis, abstract from the longer-run question of how national price levels are to be realigned so as to eliminate the need to rely on policy-induced international capital movements for the maintenance of international equilibrium. In actual fact this longer-run adjustment now depends on the inability of surplus countries to prevent inflation and of deficit countries to maintain full employment. Much work remains to be done on the dynamics of this system and also on criteria for optimizing the adjustment process.

HARRY G. JOHNSON

### BIBLIOGRAPHY

ALEXANDER, SIDNEY S. 1952 Effects of a Devaluation on a Trade Balance. International Monetary Fund, *Staff Papers* 2:263–278.

AMERICAN ECONOMIC ASSOCIATION 1949 *Readings in the Theory of International Trade.* Edited by Howard S. Ellis and Lloyd A. Metzler. Philadelphia: Blakiston.

BHAGWATI, JAGDISH 1964 The Pure Theory of International Trade: A Survey. *Economic Journal* 74:1–84.

BHAGWATI, JAGDISH; and JOHNSON, HARRY G. 1961 A Generalized Theory of the Effects of Tariffs on the Terms of Trade. *Oxford Economic Papers* New Series 13:225–253. → A synthesis of the previous literature on this question.

[BURENSTAM] LINDER, STAFFAN 1961 *An Essay on Trade and Transformation.* New York: Wiley. → A suggestive but nonrigorous attack on the Heckscher–Ohlin model.

CAVES, RICHARD E. 1960 *Trade and Economic Structure: Models and Methods.* Harvard Economic Studies, Vol. 115. Cambridge, Mass.: Harvard Univ. Press. → A critical discussion of the Heckscher–Ohlin and other models of trade and their empirical testing.

CORDEN, W. M. 1965 *Recent Developments in the Theory of International Trade.* Special Papers in International Economics, No. 7. Princeton Univ., International Finance Section.

FRIEDMAN, MILTON (1953) 1959 *Essays in Positive Economics.* Univ. of Chicago Press. → See especially pages 157–203, "The Case for Flexible Exchange Rates."

HABERLER, GOTTFRIED (1933) 1936 *The Theory of International Trade, With Its Applications to Commercial Policy.* London: Hodge. → First published in German.

HABERLER, GOTTFRIED (1954) 1961 *A Survey of International Trade Theory.* Rev. & enl. ed. Princeton Univ., International Finance Section. → First published as "Aussenhandel" in *Handwörterbuch der Sozialwissenschaften.*

JOHNSON, HARRY G. 1958 *International Trade and Economic Growth: Studies in Pure Theory.* Cambridge, Mass.: Harvard Univ. Press.

JOHNSON, HARRY G. 1962 *Money, Trade and Economic Growth: Survey Lectures in Economic Theory.* Cambridge, Mass.: Harvard Univ. Press; London: Allen & Unwin. → Presentations of comparative cost theory, balance-of-payments theory, customs union theory, and the theory of trade and growth.

JOHNSON, HARRY G. 1965a The Theory of Tariff Structure, With Special Reference to World Trade and Development. Pages 9–29 in Harry G. Johnson and Peter B. Kenen, *Trade and Development.* Geneva: Droz.

JOHNSON, HARRY G. 1965b Optimal Trade Integration in the Presence of Domestic Distortions. Pages 3–33 in *Trade, Growth, and the Balance of Payments: Essays in Honor of Gottfried Haberler,* by Robert E. Baldwin et al. Chicago: Rand McNally.

KENEN, PETER B. 1960 International Liquidity and the Balance of Payments of a Reserve-currency Country. *Quarterly Journal of Economics* 74:572–586.

KRAVIS, IRVING B. 1956 "Availability" and Other Influences on the Commodity Composition of Trade. *Journal of Political Economy* 64:143–155.

LEONTIEF, WASSILY 1953 Domestic Production and Foreign Trade: The American Capital Position Re-examined. American Philosophical Society, *Proceedings* 97:332–349.

LIPSEY, R. G.; and LANCASTER, KELVIN 1956 The General Theory of Second Best. *Review of Economic Studies* 24, no. 1:11–32.

MACHLUP, FRITZ 1943 *International Trade and the National Income Multiplier.* Philadelphia: Blakiston.

McKINNON, RONALD I. 1963 Optimum Currency Areas. *American Economic Review* 53:717–725.

MEADE, JAMES E. 1951–1955 *The Theory of International Economic Policy.* 2 vols. Oxford Univ. Press. → Volume 1: *Balance of Payments.* Volume 2: *Trade and Welfare.*

MEIER, GERALD M. 1963 *International Trade and Development.* New York: Harper. → Detailed exposition of the theory of trade and growth. Contains an excellent bibliographical essay.

MUNDELL, ROBERT A. 1960a The Pure Theory of International Trade. *American Economic Review* 50:67–110. → A geometrical and mathematical presentation.

MUNDELL, ROBERT A. 1960b The Monetary Dynamics of International Adjustment Under Fixed and Flexible Exchange Rates. *Quarterly Journal of Economics* 74:227–257.

MUNDELL, ROBERT A. 1961 A Theory of Optimum Currency Areas. *American Economic Review* 51:657–665.

MUNDELL, ROBERT A. 1963 Capital Mobility and Stabilization Policy Under Fixed and Flexible Exchange Rates. *Canadian Journal of Economics and Political Science* 29:475–485.

OHLIN, BERTIL (1933) 1957 *Interregional and International Trade.* Harvard Economic Studies, Vol. 39. Cambridge, Mass.: Harvard Univ. Press.

RYBCZYNSKI, T. M. 1955 Factor Endowment and Relative Commodity Prices. *Economica* New Series 22:336–341.

SAMUELSON, PAUL A. 1948 International Trade and the Equalisation of Factor Prices. *Economic Journal* 58:163–184.

SOHMEN, EGON 1961 *Flexible Exchange Rates: Theory and Controversy.* Univ. of Chicago Press.

TINBERGEN, JAN 1952 *On the Theory of Economic Policy.* Amsterdam: North-Holland Publishing.

TRAVIS, WILLIAM P. 1964 *The Theory of Trade and Protection.* Cambridge, Mass.: Harvard Univ. Press.

VERNON, RAYMOND 1966 International Investment and International Trade in the Product Cycle. *Quarterly Journal of Economics* 80:190–207.

VINER, JACOB 1932 International Trade: Theory. Volume 8, pages 200–208 in *Encyclopaedia of the Social Sciences*. New York: Macmillan.

VINER, JACOB 1937 *Studies in the Theory of International Trade*. New York: Harper. → A monumental scholarly review of classical and neoclassical theory, containing much original analysis.

VINER, JACOB 1950 *The Customs Union Issue*. Studies in the Administration of International Law and Organization, No. 10. New York: Carnegie Endowment for International Peace.

## II

### MATHEMATICAL THEORY

There are several reasons for applying mathematical techniques to the development of international trade theory. First, there are parts of the theory of international trade that are difficult to state without using mathematical notation. Second, many of the arguments are more efficiently conducted and more easily verified if mathematical derivations are used. Finally, mathematical formulas are needed even in the simpler parts of the theory to prepare for econometric studies of trade, since econometric studies involve estimation of parameters from mathematical relations appearing in the theory of international trade.

In this article certain parts of trade theory that depend most heavily on mathematics will be summarized. Usually these will be parts of the theory where the number of countries, the number of goods traded, and the number of factors of production are all allowed to exceed two. The fact is that much of the theory based on just two countries, two goods, and two factors of production is best developed with use of mathematical expressions and derivations (Kemp 1964), but the use of mathematics is not equally compelling in such cases.

The mathematical theory will be treated in five sections devoted to specialization in production, factor price equalization, comparative statics, Keynesian theory, and existence of equilibrium. The topics covered are the basic theoretical structures rather than applications or specialized developments. Except for price rigidities in the Keynesian theory, it will be assumed that the market structure in each country is perfectly competitive. Transportation costs are neglected, except in the case of factors of production, for which they are assumed to be prohibitively high.

### Specialization in production

An early subject of the classical theory of trade concerns the determinants of what a country produces and thus may export. The Ricardian theory of comparative advantage (Viner 1937, chapter 8) deals with this question, as do the Haberler theory of opportunity costs ([1933] 1936, chapter 10) and the Heckscher–Ohlin theory of comparative costs (Ohlin 1933, chapter 2). Ricardo assumed constant rates of transformation between the goods in a nation's output. This is equivalent to supposing that there is but one factor of production, say, labor. Let $a_{ij}$ be the amount of labor needed to produce one unit of the $i$th good in the $j$th country. Then if there are two countries and two goods, country 1 should produce good 1 if $a_{11}/a_{12} < a_{21}/a_{22}$. This is the law of comparative advantage, which states that country 1 should produce good 1 even though the absolute cost of producing either good may be higher in country 1. It identifies the only direction of specialization in production that is consistent with efficiency in this case. It is also the only direction of specialization consistent with competitive equilibrium in the absence of impediments to trade, such as tariffs or excise taxes.

A generalized constant-cost model was extensively used by Graham (1948). However, when the number of countries and goods exceeds two, the criterion for efficient specialization is rather more complicated. Note that the criterion for two countries and two goods in the example cited could equally well be written $a_{11}a_{22} < a_{12}a_{21}$. In this form the criterion can be generalized to the Graham model, which has constant rates of transformation in each country, with any number of goods and countries. Let a specialization be defined as a relation between countries and goods that relates each country with the goods that it produces. If a specialization relates each country with precisely one good, it is called an assignment. Let us say that a specialization is efficient if it is not possible to increase the output of one good without reducing that of another or increasing the use of labor in some country. Then a specialization is efficient if and only if every assignment is efficient that can be derived from it by confining each country to only one of the goods that it produces in the specialization.

Suppose there are $n$ countries and $m$ goods. There are $m^n$ distinct assignments, which may be grouped into classes $S_k$, where all assignments that allot the same number of countries to the $i$th good, for each $i$, belong to the same class. Let $\alpha_k(j) = i$ represent the assignment of the $j$th country to the $i$th good in an assignment scheme $\alpha_k \epsilon S_k$. Then the assignment $\bar{\alpha}_k$ is efficient if and only if the product $\prod_i a_{\bar{\alpha}_k(i),i}$ is less than or equal to $\prod_i a_{\alpha_k(i),i}$ for any $\alpha_k \epsilon S_k$ (Jones 1961a; McKenzie 1954a). It is easily seen that this condition is not implied by the condition that the classical comparative advantage formula hold between each pair of countries in the assignment.

A specialization $\bar{\alpha}_k$ is efficient if it is not possible to shift countries from their assignments in $\bar{\alpha}_k$ toward their assignments in some other $\alpha_k \epsilon S_k$ in a way that increases one output without sacrificing any other output. Let $\Delta y_{\bar{\alpha}_k(i)}$ be the decrease in output in the $i$th country of the good to which it is assigned in $\bar{\alpha}_k$, and let $\Delta y_{\alpha_k(i)}$ be the increase in output of the good to which it is assigned in $\alpha_k$ when a unit of labor is shifted from one line of production to the other. Then $\Delta y_{\alpha_k(i)}/\Delta y_{\bar{\alpha}_k(i)} = a_{\bar{\alpha}_k(i),i}/a_{\alpha_k(i),i}$. Since the same number of countries are assigned to each good in $S_k$, for any $i$ there must be a country shifting into the good with index $\bar{\alpha}_k(i)$; that is, for some $j$, $\alpha_k(j) = \bar{\alpha}_k(i)$. Then it is possible to shift appropriate amounts of labor so that $\Delta y_{\alpha_k(j)} = \Delta y_{\bar{\alpha}_k(i)}$, and the output of this good is constant. Now it is clear that $\prod_i (\Delta y_{\alpha_k(i)}/\Delta y_{\bar{\alpha}_k(i)})$ $= \prod_i (a_{\bar{\alpha}_k(i),i}/a_{\alpha_k(i),i})$, and by choice of the intermediate substitutions the first product may be reduced to $\Delta y_{\alpha_k(j)}/\Delta y_{\bar{\alpha}_k(i)}$ for some $i$ and $j$, where $\alpha_k(j) = \bar{\alpha}_k(i)$. Thus, an improvement is possible if and only if this ratio exceeds 1, or no improvement is possible if $\prod_i (a_{\bar{\alpha}_k(i),i}/a_{\alpha_k(i),i}) \leqslant 1$. This is the condition given above.

The application of these conditions for efficient specialization can be extended by replacing the labor input ratios in each country with rates of substitution between goods at a point on the production frontier. Then, in the absence of joint production or intermediate products, the foregoing criterion may be applied to determine the efficiency of a specialization for a given world output. The world output must be mentioned explicitly, since the absence of constant costs in each country means that a specialization that is efficient for one world output can be inefficient for another.

However, the generalized criterion of comparative advantage fails in the presence of intermediate products if they are traded or in the presence of joint products (McKenzie 1955a). It should be kept in mind that because of the nature of the problem of specialization, countries may be on the boundaries of their production frontiers. In the general case of competitive efficiency, where factor supplies may vary, intermediate products may be traded, joint products may appear, but where production functions are homogeneous of first degree and external economies of production are absent, there is no direct way to characterize an efficient specialization. There is, however, an indirect or dual characterization.

Let $\boldsymbol{y}^{jk}$ be the vector of inputs and outputs of goods for the $k$th production process in the $j$th country when that process is operated at a unit level. Inputs are measured by negative numbers and outputs by positive numbers. Let $\boldsymbol{x}^{jk}$ be the corresponding vector of inputs of the immobile factors. Let $\boldsymbol{p}$ be a price vector for goods and $\boldsymbol{w}^j$ a price vector for factors in the $j$th country. Let $t_{jk}$ be the level of the $k$th production process in the $j$th country. Let the world net output of goods be $\boldsymbol{y}$ and the input of factors in the $j$th country be $\boldsymbol{x}^j$. Let $I_j$ be an index set for the production processes available in the $j$th country. An efficient world output $(\boldsymbol{y}, \boldsymbol{x}^1, \cdots, \boldsymbol{x}^n)$ is achieved if it is not possible to increase the output of a desired good or reduce the input of a desired factor, without reducing the output of some other desired good or increasing the input of some other desired factor or exceeding the available supply of some factor. Then the input–output combination $(\boldsymbol{y}, \boldsymbol{x}^1, \cdots, \boldsymbol{x}^n)$ is efficient if

$$
(1) \quad
\begin{aligned}
\boldsymbol{y} &= \sum_j \sum_k t_{jk} \boldsymbol{y}^{jk}, \\
\boldsymbol{x}^j &= \sum_k t_{jk} \boldsymbol{x}^{jk}, && \text{for all } j, \\
\boldsymbol{p} \cdot \boldsymbol{y}^{jk} + \boldsymbol{w}^j \cdot \boldsymbol{x}^{jk} &\leqslant 0, && \text{for all } k \epsilon I_j, \\
\boldsymbol{p} \cdot \boldsymbol{y}^{jk} + \boldsymbol{w}^j \cdot \boldsymbol{x}^{jk} &= 0, && \text{if } t_{jk} > 0,
\end{aligned}
$$

for some $t_{jk} \geqslant 0$, where $p_i > 0$ if the $i$th good is desired and $w_i^j > 0$ if the $i$th factor is desired in the $j$th country (Koopmans 1951, p. 82). On the other hand, if the sets $I_j$ are finite, these conditions are also necessary for efficiency. If some of the $I_j$ are infinite, it may not be possible to achieve positive prices for all desired goods and factors.

The conditions (1) say that for goods and factors a set of prices exists that are positive for desired goods and factors and such that no production processes can earn positive profits and all processes actually used earn zero profits. Of course, this means that efficient specializations are precisely those that can appear in a competitive equilibrium, given appropriate demand conditions. The result is proved by observing that the convex set, $Y$, of possible world input–output combinations must be disjoint from the convex set of input–output combinations that contain more of desired goods or less of desired factors than $(\boldsymbol{y}, \boldsymbol{x}^1, \cdots, \boldsymbol{x}^n)$. Thus there is a separating hyperplane between these sets, $\boldsymbol{p} \cdot \tilde{\boldsymbol{y}} + \sum \boldsymbol{w}^j \cdot \tilde{\boldsymbol{x}}^j = 0$, with $Y$ in the negative half space. The $\boldsymbol{p}$ and $\boldsymbol{w}^j$ defining this hyperplane are the $\boldsymbol{p}$ and $\boldsymbol{w}^j$ of the relations (1).

The Heckscher–Ohlin theory of comparative costs determined by factor scarcities can be used to derive some results on partial specialization in production when technology is the same in all countries, i.e., when $I_j = I$ for all $j$. If tastes are the same in all countries, these statements also apply to trade. (This is discussed in the section "Comparative statics," below.)

### Factor price equalization

The theory of factor price equalization from trade is, in a sense, converse to the theory of specialization in production. It is the absence of specialization of countries to different goods in production that favors factor price equality. In order to produce circumstances in which factor price equality is likely, differences between production processes in different countries, which tend to lead them to specialize in different lines of production, are assumed to be absent. Also, specialization theory begins with the Ricardian model, in which there is one factor in each country, while the problem of factor price equalization does not arise until more than one factor is present in each country.

The proposition that when the same kinds of factors of production and the same production functions are present in each country free trade will lead to partial or even complete factor price equality was first defended by Heckscher. The model of trade to which the proposition was applied has come to be known as the Heckscher–Ohlin model. It was given precise mathematical form by Samuelson (1953), who is chiefly responsible for the modern development. This model explains trade and specialization in terms of differences in the relative endowments of factors of production of the trading countries. It provides in the two-countries, two-goods, two-factors case the most frequently used model of trade in modern theory.

The theory of complete equalization of factor prices is equivalently a theory of uniqueness of factor prices given goods prices and certain ancillary conditions. Equations (1) may serve as the basic model if $I_j$ is set equal to $I$ for all $j$. It is assumed that there exist free disposal processes for excess supplies of factors, so that $p \geq 0$ and $w^j \geq 0$ for all $j$. Then given $p$ and $w$, the processes that are available in any country in an equilibrium are those for which $p \cdot y^k + w \cdot x^k = 0$. Suppose $(p, \tilde{w})$ are another equilibrium price set, so that certain processes will be available at these prices. Also suppose that factor supplies in the $j$th country are constant and equal to $x^j$. Let $K_w$ be the convex polyhedral cone in the factor space spanned by the input vectors $x^k$ of processes available at $(p, w)$, including disposal processes for zero-priced factors. Suppose that the number of factors is $r$ and that $K_w$ is $r$-dimensional. By the use of the profit conditions it can be shown that $x \in$ interior $K_w$ implies $p \cdot y + w \cdot x = 0$ and $p \cdot y + \tilde{w} \cdot x < 0$, so that

$\Delta w \cdot x < 0$, whereas $\tilde{x} \in K_{\tilde{w}}$ implies by the same argument that $\Delta w \cdot \tilde{x} \geq 0$. Thus, the interior of $K_w$ is disjoint from $K_{\tilde{w}}$ and if $x^j$ lies in the interior of $K_w$ it does not lie in $K_{\tilde{w}}$. This means that at $(p, \tilde{w})$ factor supplies are not fully used or disposed of and therefore that the factor price vector $\tilde{w}$ is not consistent with the goods price vector $p$ and the factor supplies $x^j$. In other words, $p$ and $x^j$ uniquely imply $w$ in competitive equilibrium, and if $x^j$ lies in $K_w$ for all $j$, factor prices are necessarily equal in all countries when the goods prices are given by $p$. Let us refer to $K_w$ as the diversification cone of $w$, given $p$. Then, given $p$, it is necessary for factor price equalization between countries $j_1$ and $j_2$ that $x^{j_1}$ and $x^{j_2}$ lie in the same diversification cone $K_w$, and it is sufficient for equalization that they lie in the interior of the same $K_w$ (McKenzie 1955$b$).

A second result for equalization of factor prices refers not to factor supplies but rather to the set of processes that countries use in common. Let us suppose that the $k$th process has an output of one unit of the $k$th good and that each process is integrated so that intermediate products do not appear explicitly. Suppose also that the minimum cost process, given any $w > 0$, is unique. Let the index of the minimum cost process for the $i$th good be $k_i$. Then competitive equilibrum requires $p_i = w \cdot x^{k_i}$ for each good that is produced, where $x^{k_i}$ depends on the factor price vector $w$. The matrix $A = [x^{k_i}]$ is the Jacobian matrix of a transformation $G : w \to p$ ($G$ maps factor prices into goods prices).

Suppose the number of goods equals the number of factors, so that $A$ is square. Then if the principal minors of $A$ are positive for all $w > 0$, the inverse mapping $G^{-1} : p \to w$ is defined over the set of all $p$ such that $p = wA(w)$ for some $w > 0$ (Gale & Nikaidô 1965). Therefore, given that two countries produce $r$ goods in common and that factor prices are positive in both countries, factor price equalization is implied when the condition of positive principal minors is met by the factor input matrix for these $r$ goods. It should be noted that this theorem requires that the countries produce at least as many goods in common in the competitive equilibrium as there are factors. In addition, the choice of the order of columns in $A$ implies an association of a particular factor with each good.

A third result relates factor price equalization to the direction in which factor prices change when goods prices change. The strong version of the Stolper–Samuelson theorem (Stolper & Samuelson 1941) holds if goods can be associated with factors in such a way that if a good rises in price while the prices of other goods are constant, its associated factor rises in price and all other factors fall in price. Thus, the associated factor has a real income that is unambiguously higher. This result is applied to show that the owners of a certain factor may benefit from appropriate tariffs.

Since $\mathbf{p} = \mathbf{w}\mathbf{A}$, and $\mathbf{w}d\mathbf{A} = 0$ by cost minimization, it follows that $d\mathbf{p} = d\mathbf{w}\mathbf{A}$ and $d\mathbf{w} = d\mathbf{p}\mathbf{A}^{-1}$. Thus, the Stolper–Samuelson theorem implies that $\mathbf{A}^{-1}$ has the sign distribution over its elements of a Leontief matrix. Such a matrix has a positive inverse only if its principal minors are all positive. But this implies that $\mathbf{A}$ has positive principal minors as well, so the factor price equalization theorem holds. In other words, the strong Stolper–Samuelson theorem over an interval of factor prices implies the factor price equalization theorem over the same interval (Chipman 1964).

In this last result and also in the previous one an essential role is played by a one-to-one association of factors and goods. This suggests that a good, which is traded, is a proxy for a factor, which is not. Thus, the equating of goods prices through trade achieves an equality of factor prices because the factors are, as it were, traded indirectly. It is the positivity of the principal minors of $\mathbf{A}$ that establishes the necessary connection between the goods and the factors. In the two-factors, two-goods case, this is equivalent to the assumption that relative factor intensities differ and are not reversed, for $|\mathbf{A}| \neq 0$ implies $|\mathbf{A}| > 0$ for an appropriate order of the columns. In the general case, it is implied if $\mathbf{A}$ has a dominant diagonal, that is, $x_k^k > \sum_{i \neq k} x_i^k$ for each $k$ (after units of measurement are redefined, if necessary).

A condition that is equivalent to the strong Stolper–Samuelson theorem is that for each $k$ there exists a nonnegative linear combination of the inputs into the process other than the $k$th that has amounts equal to those of the $k$th process of all inputs other than the $k$th and a smaller amount of the $k$th input than the $k$th process. This may be deduced directly from $\mathbf{A}\mathbf{A}^{-1} = \mathbf{I}$ and the fact that $\mathbf{A}^{-1}$ is a Leontief-type matrix. Let $\mathbf{A}^{-1} = [\alpha_{ji}]$ and $\mathbf{A} = [x_i^j]$. Then $-\sum_{j \neq k} x_i^j \alpha_{jk} = x_i^k \alpha_{kk}$, for $i \neq k$. Dividing through by $\alpha_{kk}$ gives the required linear combination for the $k$th process (Uekawa 1966).

It should be remarked that these results are concerned with complete equalization. It would be very desirable to have comparable results on partial equalization in the presence of impediments.

## Comparative statics

The preceding sections have been concerned with price and production patterns that are consistent with efficiency in production or with competitive equilibrium. Comparative statics deals with the shift in the equilibrium prices and quantities that may be associated with a change in some parameter of the trading system, for example, the level of a tariff or the supply of a factor [see STATICS AND DYNAMICS IN ECONOMICS; see also Mundell 1960]. This is the traditional realm of the two-by-two-by-two theory, but the generalization to $n$ countries, $n$ goods, and $r$ factors can sometimes be made. In order to discuss the effects of parameter changes on the terms of trade, one special feature of the simpler model will be retained, namely, that each country has one of the $n$ goods as its only export. This is at the opposite pole from the Graham model, which emphasizes the possibility that countries may have export goods in common.

Let $p_i$ be the price of the $i$th country's good in terms of the first country's good. Choose units so that initial prices equal one. Assume that monetary policy maintains a constant price for the export good in each country. Then the balance of payments of the $i$th country, $b_i$, measured in terms of the first country's good or currency, is a function of the prices $p_2, \cdots, p_n$ and whatever parameter $\alpha$ is subject to shifting. That is, the equations $b_i(p_2, \cdots, p_n, \alpha) = 0$, for $i = 1, \cdots, n$, determine an equilibrium position. Let $b_{ij} = \partial b_i / \partial p_j$, $b_{i\alpha} = \partial b_i / \partial \alpha$, and $\mathbf{B} = [b_{ij}]$, $i, j = 2, \cdots, n$. Then, assuming $\mathbf{B}$ is nonsingular,

$$\sum_{j=2}^{n} b_{ij} \frac{dp_j}{d\alpha} = -b_{i\alpha}, \qquad i = 2, \cdots, n,$$

(2)    or

$$\left[ \frac{dp_j}{d\alpha} \right] = -\mathbf{B}^{-1}[b_{i\alpha}],$$

where $[b_{i\alpha}]$ is a one-column matrix.

The method of comparative statics is to derive information from some prior relationships concerning the $b_{i\alpha}$ and then to place restrictions on $\mathbf{B}$ that allow conclusions to be drawn about the $dp_j / d\alpha$ from (2). In the two-country case the assumption that the foreign exchange market is stable in terms of Walrasian dynamics implies $b_{22} < 0$. Then the sign of $dp_2 / d\alpha$ is seen to be the same as the sign of $b_{2\alpha}$; that is, if the change improves the balance of payments when prices are given, then in the new equilibrium the price of the currency will rise enough to return the balance to 0. However, Walrasian stability of the multiple market is too weak to give results in (2). A stronger assumption that will give results is that $b_{ij} > 0$ for $i \neq j$ (the assumption that all exports are gross substitutes). This assumption implies that the equilibrium exists and is unique. It also implies that the equilibrium is globally stable. Note that $-\boldsymbol{B}$ is a Leontief-type matrix. On the other hand, $\sum_{i=2}^{n} b_{ij} = -b_{1j} < 0$, since by Cournot's law $\sum_{i=1}^{n} b_i(\boldsymbol{p}) = 0$. Thus, $\boldsymbol{B}$ has a dominant diagonal, and all the elements of $-\boldsymbol{B}^{-1}$ are nonnegative or are positive if $\boldsymbol{B}$ is irreducible.

The assumption that all exports are gross substitutes gives results parallel to those resulting from the assumption of stability in the two-country case (for which the assumptions are equivalent). For example, if productivity rises in the first country and no goods are inferior, the rate at which the $i$th balance changes with constant prices is $b_{i\alpha} = m_{i1}$, where $\alpha$ is the level of output and income in country 1, and $m_{i1}$ is the first country's marginal propensity to import from the $i$th country. Then $dp_j/d\alpha = -\sum_{i\neq 1}\beta_{ji}m_{i1} > 0$, where $\boldsymbol{B}^{-1} = [\beta_{ji}]$, $i, j \neq 1$. Since the choice of *numéraire* is arbitrary, we can conclude that all exchanges move against the country where the improvement has occurred.

Similarly it can be shown that the imposition of a uniform ad valorem tariff whose proceeds are distributed to consumers at home raises the relative price of the exports of the country imposing the tariff (Johnson 1960). However, unilateral transfer payments from the first to the $j$th country have an ambiguous effect. In this case $dp_j/d\alpha = \sum_{i\neq 1}(m_{i1} - m_{ij})\beta_{ji}$, and the sign is not definite.

The balance of payments, $b_i$, may be interpreted as the net gain of foreign exchange reserves and gold by the $i$th country per unit of time. Assume that the movement of other capital funds is not affected by a change in exchange rates. Assume also that surplus stocks are accumulated only where goods are exported. Then the change in $b_i$ will equal the change in the balance of trade or in the value of the excess demand by other countries for the $i$th good less the value of the excess demand by the $i$th country for other goods. Let $e_k^i$ be the excess demand for the $k$th good by the $i$th country—that is, the difference between demand for use and current production. Then $b_{ij} = -e_j^i - \sum_{k\neq i}e_{kj}^i + \sum_{h\neq i}e_{ij}^h$, where $e_{kj}^i = \partial e_k^i/\partial p_j$. Assume that hoarding or dishoarding of currency does not occur or is offset by changes in the money supply. Then from the definition of $e_k^i$ and the assumption concerning the flow of capital funds, Walras' law will imply $-\sum_{k\neq i}e_{kj}^i = e_{ij}^i + e_j^i$. Thus, $b_{ij}$ also equals $\sum_{h=1}^{n}e_{ij}^h$, the rate of change in the total excess demand for the $i$th good. This means that the international economy is equivalent to a barter economy for the purpose of the comparative statics analysis.

In the case of two countries only one price is free and $\boldsymbol{B} = b_{22} = -e_2^2 - e_{12}^2 + e_{22}^1$. The Marshall–Lerner stability condition is $b_{ii} < 0$ or $1 + \eta_1 + \eta_2 < 0$, where $\eta_2 = e_{12}^2/e_2^2$ and $\eta_1 = -e_{22}^1/e_2^2$ are the elasticities of import demand. (A searching examination of the stability problem for the exchanges and the distinction between this problem and that of devaluation may be found in Jones 1961*b*.)

A second type of result in comparative statics is implied by the strong Stolper–Samuelson theorem. Consider the factor input matrix $\boldsymbol{A} = [\boldsymbol{x}^{jk}]$ of a set of integrated processes, each having a single good as output. Assume that $\boldsymbol{A}$ is square. The $\boldsymbol{x}^{jk}$ are functions of the factor prices $\boldsymbol{w}$. A set of relations dual to those of the Stolper–Samuelson theory is $\boldsymbol{x}^j = \boldsymbol{A}\boldsymbol{y}^j$, where $\boldsymbol{y}^j$ is the output vector for these goods for the $j$th country and $\boldsymbol{x}^j$ is the vector of factor inputs into this production.

Consider a nearby equilibrium in which all the goods continue to be produced. Let $x_i^j$ increase while all prices and other components of $\boldsymbol{x}^j$ are constant. Then $d\boldsymbol{y}^j = \boldsymbol{A}^{-1}\boldsymbol{\delta}_i$, where all components of $\boldsymbol{\delta}_i$ are zero except the $i$th, which is equal to $\delta > 0$. The strong Stolper–Samuelson theorem means that the elements of $\boldsymbol{A}^{-1}$ have the signs proper to a Leontief matrix. Thus, the output of the $i$th good must increase, and the output of all other goods must decrease. Moreover, the conditions for factor price equalization are satisfied, so it is sufficient for the goods prices to remain constant for factor prices, and thus $\boldsymbol{A}$, to remain constant also. This is a generalized Rybczynski theorem (1955). If units are chosen so that all the $w_i = 1$ and all the $p_i = 1$, $\boldsymbol{p}\boldsymbol{A}^{-1} = \boldsymbol{w}$ implies that $\boldsymbol{A}^{-1}$ has a dominant diagonal. Then in each row of $\boldsymbol{A}$ the diagonal element is largest. Thus, an increase in $y_i^j$, accompanied by a decrease in $y_k^j$ of equal value, will lead to an increase in demand for the $i$th factor.

The generalized Rybczynski theorem is relevant also to patterns of specialization in production. Suppose technology is the same in each country. In a country where the $i$th factor is plentiful compared with the $j$th, a large output of the $i$th good may be expected in comparison with the $j$th in the absence of trade. If factor price equality between countries holds, an exact statement can be made. The $\boldsymbol{A}$ matrix will be the same in all countries and, therefore, $\boldsymbol{A}^{-1}$ will also be the same. Suppose $\boldsymbol{A}^{-1}$ is a Leontief-type matrix, or, in other words, that the generalized Rybczynski theorem holds. Total world production of the goods involved will not be affected by the uneven distribution of factors (transport costs are neglected). But between any two countries the value of output of a set of goods in the first country, associated with relatively more plentiful factors, will bear a higher ratio to the value of the other goods than in the second country. This is a consequence of the fact that $\boldsymbol{p}^1 \cdot \Delta \boldsymbol{y}^1 = \boldsymbol{p}^1 \boldsymbol{A}_{11}^{-1} \Delta \boldsymbol{x}^1 + \boldsymbol{p}^1 \boldsymbol{A}_{12}^{-1} \Delta \boldsymbol{x}^2 > 0$ if $\Delta \boldsymbol{x}^1 > 0$, $\Delta \boldsymbol{x}^2 < 0$, where $\boldsymbol{A}^{-1}$ has been partitioned according to

$$\boldsymbol{A}^{-1} = \begin{bmatrix} \boldsymbol{A}_{11}^{-1} & \boldsymbol{A}_{12}^{-1} \\ \boldsymbol{A}_{21}^{-1} & \boldsymbol{A}_{22}^{-1} \end{bmatrix}$$

The $\Delta \boldsymbol{x}$ is derived by comparison with an appropriate factor supply vector intermediate between those of the two countries.

This is a generalized Heckscher–Ohlin theorem. It is independent of the presence of other outputs, whether or not they are traded; if other outputs are present, factor supplies are measured net of the quantities employed in the production of the other outputs. The directions of trade, under the assumption of identical tastes between countries, are complementary to the directions of specialization in production.

In addition to the strong Stolper–Samuelson theorem there is a weak theorem that is closer to the intent of the original theorem for the two-factor, two-good case. The weak Samuelson–Stolper theorem says that $n$ goods and $n$ factors may be paired in such a way that an increase in the price of the $i$th good will lead to a proportionately larger increase in the price of the $i$th factor. An intermediate theorem of this type also concludes that the $i$th factor price rises proportionately more than does any other factor price. Uekawa (1966) has found interesting conditions that imply each of these results. The conditions for the latter theorem are easily interpreted in economic terms. If units are chosen so that all initial prices equal one, the matrix $\boldsymbol{A}$ is a share matrix—that is, $x_i^j$ is the share of the $i$th factor in the product of the $j$th industry. Let $J$ and $\bar{J}$ be a partition of the numbers $(1, \cdots, n)$. Suppose that for any $j_1$ and $j_2 \in J$, $\sum_{i \in J} x_i^{j_1} > \sum_{i \in \bar{J}} x_i^{j_2}$. This means that the share of the factors in $J$ in the product of industry $j_1$ exceeds the share of the factors in $\bar{J}$ in the product of industry $j_2$. This is a generalized factor intensity condition that implies the intermediate Stolper–Samuelson result, when it holds for all partitions.

## The Keynesian theory

After Keynes introduced his theory of short-run equilibrium with underemployment of labor in the 1930s, applications of Keynesian theory to trade between countries suffering from underemployment were not slow to follow. The $n$-country theory, developed by Metzler (1950), gives a multisector generalization of the Keynesian income multiplier. Prices are assumed to be rigid, and thus the only behavioral parameters of the system are marginal propensities to spend increments of income. In the pure multiplier model these are marginal propensities to spend on the outputs of the various countries. In addition, there is autonomous spending for subsistence and investment. Let $a_i$ be the level of autonomous spending on the output of the $i$th country, $y_i$ be the level of income and output in the $i$th country, and $m_{ij}$ be the marginal propensity of country $j$ to purchase the output of country $i$. Then equilibrium is given by

$$y_i = \sum_j m_{ij} y_j + a_i, \qquad i = 1, \cdots, n,$$

(3)    or

$$\boldsymbol{y} = (\boldsymbol{I} - \boldsymbol{M})^{-1} \boldsymbol{a},$$

where $\boldsymbol{M} = [m_{ij}]$ is the matrix of marginal propensities to spend. If it is assumed that $m_{ij} \geqslant 0$, $\boldsymbol{I} - \boldsymbol{M}$ has the sign distribution of a Leontief-type matrix. If it is also assumed that $\sum_i m_{ij} < 1$, then each element of $(\boldsymbol{I} - \boldsymbol{M})^{-1}$ is greater than or equal to zero and all the multipliers are nonnegative.

Corresponding to (3), there is a dynamic Keynesian system that is written

$$(4) \qquad \boldsymbol{y}(t+1) = \boldsymbol{M} \boldsymbol{y}(t) + \boldsymbol{a}.$$

Here $\boldsymbol{y}(t)$ is the income and output of period $t$, which in part determines the income of period $t + 1$. This system is stable provided the characteristic roots of $\boldsymbol{I} - \boldsymbol{M}$ are less than 1 in absolute value. Therefore, stability is implied if $\sum_i m_{ij} < 1$ for each $j$, that is, if the total marginal propensity to spend in each country is less than 1. Indeed, if $\boldsymbol{M} \geqslant 0$, $(\boldsymbol{I} - \boldsymbol{M})^{-1} \geqslant 0$ is equivalent to stability (McKenzie 1960). Let $(\boldsymbol{I} - \boldsymbol{M})^{-1} = [\mu_{ij}]$. Since $\mu_{ii} > \mu_{ij}$, for $i \neq j$, when the system is stable, a shift of spending from home to foreign goods is always harmful to home employment (Johnson 1958, chapter 8). Thus, in the Keynesian system, the correspondence principle (Samuelson 1947, p. 284) does provide comparative static results. On the other hand, $\sum_i m_{ij} > 1$ for each $j$ implies that the system is definitely unstable. Then a small fluctuation of autonomous spending may be magnified into a large and continuing fluctuation of incomes.

The pure multiplier model (4) may be expanded to allow for investment that depends on changes in the level of output. The result is an $n$-country multiplier–accelerator model (Brown & Jones 1962). Let $c_{ij}$ be the investment in the $i$th country's output consequent on a unit increase in the $j$th country's output. Then the multiplier–accelerator model is

$$\boldsymbol{y}(t+1) = \boldsymbol{M}\boldsymbol{y}(t) + \boldsymbol{C}[\boldsymbol{y}(t+1) - \boldsymbol{y}(t)] + \boldsymbol{a},$$

(5)     or

$$\boldsymbol{y}(t+1)$$
$$= [\boldsymbol{I} - (\boldsymbol{I} - \boldsymbol{C})^{-1}(\boldsymbol{I} - \boldsymbol{M})]\boldsymbol{y}(t) + (\boldsymbol{I} - \boldsymbol{C})^{-1}\boldsymbol{a}.$$

In this system, $m_{ij}$ is interpreted to exclude investment spending, so $\sum_i m_{ij} < 1$ is a natural assumption. The equilibrium solutions of (4) and (5) are the same, that is, $\boldsymbol{y} = (\boldsymbol{I} - \boldsymbol{M})^{-1}\boldsymbol{a}$. However, the stability of (5) is not assured by the nonnegativity of $(\boldsymbol{I} - \boldsymbol{M})^{-1}$. Suppose that the domestic acceleration coefficients $c_{ii}$ are larger than 1. Then $\boldsymbol{F} = -(\boldsymbol{I} - \boldsymbol{M})^{-1}(\boldsymbol{I} - \boldsymbol{C})$ is a nonnegative matrix with a positive diagonal. Let $\lambda$ be the maximal positive root of $\boldsymbol{F}$. Then $\boldsymbol{I} + \boldsymbol{F}^{-1}$, which is the coefficient matrix of $\boldsymbol{y}(t)$, has a root $\rho = 1 + 1/\lambda$, and the system is unstable. Thus, stability of the Keynesian model is unlikely in the absence of restraints arising from the scarcity of money balances relative to income and output (Tsiang 1961). These stabilizing restraints are neglected in the multiplier–accelerator models based on rigid prices and interest rates.

Another adaptation of (5) is to introduce an autonomous spending vector, $\rho_j^t \boldsymbol{a}^j$, for the $j$th country, that is rising over time. Then the matrix replacing $\boldsymbol{I} - \boldsymbol{M}$ in the equilibrium solution of (5) is $\rho_j(\boldsymbol{I} - \boldsymbol{C}) + (\boldsymbol{C} - \boldsymbol{M})$. This matrix has the sign pattern of a Leontief-type matrix if $\rho_j(1 - c_{ii}) + c_{ii} - m_{ii} > 0$ for each $i$. It has a positive inverse if it has a dominant diagonal—that is, if $(\rho_j - 1)\sum_i c_{ik} < \rho_j - \sum_i m_{ik}$ for each $k$, that is, if saving in each country from the expanded income is more than adequate to support the investment spending of that country induced by the autonomous spending on its output. There will be a solution, $\rho_j^t \boldsymbol{y}^j$, corresponding to any country's autonomous spending, and the sum of these is a solution for the case in which autonomous spending is present in each country.

The dominant diagonal of $\rho_j(\boldsymbol{I} - \boldsymbol{C}) + (\boldsymbol{C} - \boldsymbol{M})$ means that $\rho_j < \rho$, where $\rho$ is the positive characteristic root of $\boldsymbol{I} + \boldsymbol{F}^{-1}$. Thus, the repercussions of autonomous spending in the case where a meaningful equilibrium solution exists for the largest $\rho_j$ will eventually be swamped by any spending component associated with $\rho$; $\rho$ is the warranted growth rate defined by Harrod (1948, p. 81). Moreover, expansion at these rates must encounter labor shortages unless population expansion and technical progress provide sufficiently high natural growth rates by Harrod's definition.

A final possibility is to set autonomous spending equal to zero and examine a solution associated with $\rho$. Since $\boldsymbol{F}$, on the assumption $c_{ii} > 1$, is a nonnegative matrix with a positive diagonal and $\lambda$ is its maximal positive root, there is an associated positive characteristic vector $\bar{\boldsymbol{y}}$; $\bar{\boldsymbol{y}}$ is also a characteristic vector of $\boldsymbol{I} + \boldsymbol{F}^{-1}$ for $\rho$. Then $\rho^t \bar{\boldsymbol{y}}$ will be a solution of (5) that is relatively stable, provided that $\rho$ is the maximal root of $\boldsymbol{I} + \boldsymbol{F}^{-1}$. However, this does not follow from the maximal property of $\lambda$. In any case, an indefinite continuation of the growth path would again depend on natural growth rates at least as large as $\rho$ in each country. Thus, the developments based on the Keynesian model must be regarded as transitory. Unless there is deliberate government intervention, shortages will arise that require price adjustments or that lead to unbearable levels of unemployment. (See Johnson 1958, chapter 5, for some two-country examples of Harrod models.)

It is possible to combine the simple Keynesian model with price effects on demand like those that were described in the section "Comparative statics," above. The resulting model may be used to study the effects of devaluation on the balances of payments in a world of partial employment. Suppose elasticities of supply are infinite—that is, because underemployed resources are present, marginal costs do not rise significantly with increasing output. Initial prices are set equal to one. Let $\bar{\boldsymbol{B}} = [\bar{b}_{ij}]$, where $i$ and $j$ run from 1 to $n$, and $\bar{b}_{ij} = -e_j^i - \sum_{k \neq i} d_{kj}^i + \sum_{h \neq i} d_{ij}^h$, where $d_k^i(\boldsymbol{p})$ is the compensated demand function for the $k$th good in the $i$th country and $d_{kj}^i = \partial d_k^i / \partial p_j$. Then $\bar{\boldsymbol{B}}\, d\boldsymbol{p}$ may be treated as a variation in autonomous spending (see Johnson 1958, chapter 7, for related analysis of the two-country case). The resulting variation of real income will be $d\bar{\boldsymbol{y}} = (\boldsymbol{I} - \boldsymbol{M})^{-1}\bar{\boldsymbol{B}}\, d\boldsymbol{p}$ in equilibrium, where $d\bar{y}_i$ is defined as $dy_i - e^i \cdot d\boldsymbol{p}$. The change in the $j$th balance is $db_j = (1 - \sum_i m_{ij})d\bar{y}_j$. This may be interpreted as the excess of the increase in real income over the increase in real spending in the $j$th country.

Let $\boldsymbol{S}$ be the diagonal matrix with diagonal elements $s_i = (1 - \sum_i m_{ij})$. Then $d\boldsymbol{b} = \boldsymbol{S}(\boldsymbol{I} - \boldsymbol{M})^{-1}\bar{\boldsymbol{B}}\, d\boldsymbol{p} = \boldsymbol{D}\, d\boldsymbol{p}$ gives the consequences for balances of a set $d\boldsymbol{p}$ of currency devaluations. Suppose countries devalue when they are losing exchange reserves and revalue when they are gaining reserves. Suppose $\boldsymbol{I} - \boldsymbol{M}$ has a dominant diagonal. Then $(\boldsymbol{I} - \boldsymbol{M})^{-1}$ is nonnegative, and the diagonal element is largest in each row. However, even if $-\bar{\boldsymbol{B}}$ should be a Leontief-type matrix, convergence of the devaluation process is not assured in general. On the other hand, in the case of two countries the adjustment equations reduce to the familiar form $db_1 = (s_1 s_2 / \Delta) \bar{b}_{11} dp_1$, where $\Delta = |\boldsymbol{I} - \boldsymbol{M}|$, and $db_1 / dp_1 < 0$ (Jones 1960). If the effect of the change in terms of trade on spending is neglected, $b_{11}$ replaces $\bar{b}_{11}$ in this formula. Moreover, the devaluation process will converge in the general case if $\boldsymbol{D}$ has positive elements off the diagonal (Takayama 1961). Since by Cournot's law the column sums of $\boldsymbol{D}$ equal 0, the principal minors of $-\boldsymbol{D}$ are then Leontief-type matrices.

## Existence of equilibrium

Whether a meaningful equilibrium exists for a world economy with flexible prices characterized by relations like (1) and (2) is a difficult question, and only recently has much light been shed on it (McKenzie 1954b; Nikaidô 1956). Consider relations (1), where the $I_j$ may be infinite sets and distinct from each other. This is the general production model for a competitive world economy with its associated profit conditions. It is sufficiently comprehensive to allow for transportation activities carrying goods between countries, as well as for the possibility that the resources of different countries have different qualities and the production processes may differ. The model must be completed by adding relations to determine demand for output. If the role of government is introduced and investment demand is included, these relations will be extremely complicated. Also, the supply of factors may be variable. However, if the structure of expectations is specified (and taken to be independent of the fluctuations of prices that occur as the market seeks its equilibrium), a model that is very broad in scope is obtained by adding to (1) the relations

$$(6) \quad \begin{aligned} \boldsymbol{y} &= \sum_j f_1^j(\boldsymbol{p}, \boldsymbol{w}^j), \\ \boldsymbol{x}^j &= f_2^j(\boldsymbol{p}, \boldsymbol{w}^j), \qquad j = 1, \cdots, n. \end{aligned}$$

The proof of existence depends critically on continuity properties of the demand functions. In order to isolate the aspects of world trade, the countries may be treated as single consumers on the demand side. Then continuity of each country's demand function will be a reasonable assumption for all $(\boldsymbol{p}, \boldsymbol{w}^j) \neq 0$ that satisfy the profit conditions of (1), provided that each country can provide its own subsistence and can produce each good. Assume that demand cannot be satiated for all goods at once within the set of possible world outputs. Then there is a price vector $(\boldsymbol{p}^*, \boldsymbol{w}^{*1}, \cdots, \boldsymbol{w}^{*n})$ and a world input–output vector $(\boldsymbol{y}^*, \boldsymbol{x}^{*1}, \cdots, \boldsymbol{x}^{*n})$ that satisfy (1) and (6) simultaneously. However, these are precisely the conditions for a competitive

equilibrium, since the first two conditions of (1) say that $(\boldsymbol{y}^*, \boldsymbol{x}^{*1}, \cdots, \boldsymbol{x}^{*n})$ is compatible with the technology available, the second two conditions say that no other choice of inputs and outputs that is compatible with the technology can increase profits for any production process when the price vector is $(\boldsymbol{p}^*, \boldsymbol{w}^{*1}, \cdots, \boldsymbol{w}^{*n})$, and conditions (6) say that when the price vector is $(\boldsymbol{p}^*, \boldsymbol{w}^{*1}, \cdots, \boldsymbol{w}^{*n})$ the quantities $(\boldsymbol{y}^*, \boldsymbol{x}^{*1}, \cdots, \boldsymbol{x}^{*n})$ are demanded. Thus, the technological constraints, the profit conditions, and the demand conditions are met, so a competitive equilibrium is realized.

Virtually all the conditions that lead to the existence of the competitive equilibrium can be relaxed to some degree—for example, the assumptions of free disposal and insatiability. The conclusion seems to be that under the usual assumptions of the competitive model—in particular, linear homogeneity of production functions and continuity of demand (derivable from convexity of preferences)—an equilibrium may be expected to exist. It should be noted that the model described includes the pure trading model, which starts from fixed initial stocks of goods, as a special case.

Of course, this does not establish the stability, optimality, or uniqueness of an equilibrium (Koopmans 1957). Stability of a full market process seems unlikely unless a price *tâtonnement* is stable. However, a stable *tâtonnement* has been found only under special assumptions—for example, the assumption that all goods are gross substitutes or that the weak axiom of revealed preference holds for market demand functions (Arrow et al. 1959). Uniqueness of the full equilibrium is also special in much the same way as stability.

On the other hand, the optimality of the equilibrium, in Pareto's sense, is easily proved on assumptions significantly weaker than those allowing a proof of existence. The profit conditions of (1) immediately imply that the value of the input–output combination is maximized over the set of all technically feasible combinations given the equilibrium prices. That is, $\boldsymbol{p}^* \cdot \boldsymbol{y}^* + \sum_j \boldsymbol{w}^{*j} \cdot \boldsymbol{x}^{*j} \geqslant \boldsymbol{p}^* \cdot \boldsymbol{y} + \sum_j \boldsymbol{w}^{*j} \cdot \boldsymbol{x}^j$ for any $(\boldsymbol{y}, \boldsymbol{x}^1, \cdots, \boldsymbol{x}^n)$ that is compatible with relations (1). But if no one is satiated, the fact that no one is made worse off by a change means that the value of each person's consumption has not fallen at equilibrium prices; if someone is better off, his consumption must be worth more at these prices. Thus, to make anyone better off and no one worse off requires that the value of the input–output combination should rise. That is, $(\boldsymbol{y}, \boldsymbol{x}^1, \cdots, \boldsymbol{x}^n)$ better than $(\boldsymbol{y}^*, \boldsymbol{x}^{*1}, \cdots, \boldsymbol{x}^{*n})$ requires $\boldsymbol{p}^* \cdot \boldsymbol{y} + \sum_j \boldsymbol{w}^{*j} \cdot \boldsymbol{x}^j > \boldsymbol{p}^* \cdot \boldsymbol{y}^* + \sum_j \boldsymbol{w}^{*j} \cdot \boldsymbol{x}^{*j}$. However, this is excluded by the profit conditions.

Pareto optimality carries the implication that specialization in production is efficient, which confirms a claim made in the section "Specialization in production." Of course, there is no reason why one country, by imposing tariffs or other restraints on trade, cannot improve its position at the expense of others. Also the assumptions that are needed for Pareto optimality do not allow for external economies or economies of scale. [*See* ECONOMIC EQUILIBRIUM.]

LIONEL W. McKENZIE

[*See also* SPATIAL ECONOMICS, *article on* THE GENERAL EQUILIBRIUM APPROACH.]

### BIBLIOGRAPHY

ARROW, KENNETH J.; BLOCK, HENRY D.; and HURWICZ, LEONID 1959 On the Stability of the Competitive Equilibrium, II. *Econometrica* 27:82–109.

BROWN, MURRAY; and JONES, RONALD W. 1962 Economic Growth and the Theory of International Income Flows. *Econometrica* 30:88–97.

CHIPMAN, JOHN S. 1964 Factor Price Equalization and the Stolper–Samuelson Theorem [Abstract]. *Econometrica* 32:682–683.

CHIPMAN, JOHN S. 1965–1966 Survey of the Theory of International Trade. *Econometrica* 33:477–519, 685–760; 34:18–76. → Part 1: The Classical Theory; Part 2: The Neo-classical Theory; Part 3: The Modern Theory. Emphasizes the mathematical approach and covers the theory of comparative advantage, factor price equalization, and existence of equilibrium. However, comparative statics and Keynesian theory are omitted.

GALE, DAVID; and NIKAIDÔ, HUKUKANE 1965 The Jacobian Matrix and Global Univalence of Mappings. *Mathematische Annalen* 159:81–93.

GRAHAM, FRANK D. 1948 *The Theory of International Values.* Princeton Univ. Press.

HABERLER, GOTTFRIED (1933) 1936 *The Theory of International Trade, With Its Applications to Commercial Policy.* London: Hodge. → First published in German.

HARROD, R. F. (1948) 1960 *Towards a Dynamic Economics: Some Recent Developments of Economic Theory and Their Application to Policy.* London: Macmillan; New York: St. Martins.

JOHNSON, HARRY G. 1958 *International Trade and Economic Growth: Studies in Pure Theory.* Cambridge, Mass.: Harvard Univ. Press.

JOHNSON, HARRY G. 1960 The Pure Theory of International Trade: Comment. *American Economic Review* 50:721–722.

JONES, RONALD W. 1960 Depreciation and the Dampening Effect of Income Changes. *Review of Economics and Statistics* 42:74–80.

JONES, RONALD W. 1961a Comparative Advantage and the Theory of Tariffs: A Multi-country, Multi-commodity Model. *Review of Economic Studies* 28:161–175.

JONES, RONALD W. 1961b Stability Conditions in International Trade: A General Equilibrium Analysis. *International Economic Review* 2:199–209.

KEMP, MURRAY C. 1964 *The Pure Theory of International Trade.* Englewood Cliffs, N.J.: Prentice-Hall.

KOOPMANS, TJALLING C. 1951 Analysis of Production as an Efficient Combination of Activities. Pages 33–97 in Cowles Commission for Research in Economics, *Activity Analysis of Production and Allocation.* Edited by Tjalling C. Koopmans. New York: Wiley.

KOOPMANS, TJALLING C. 1957 *Three Essays on the State of Economic Science.* New York: McGraw-Hill. → An exposition of the theory of existence and optimality of competitive equilibrium is found in Chapter 1.

McKENZIE, LIONEL W. 1954a Specialization and Efficiency in World Production. *Review of Economic Studies* 21, no. 3:165–180.

McKENZIE, LIONEL W. 1954b On Equilibrium in Graham's Model of World Trade and Other Competitive Systems. *Econometrica* 22:147–161.

McKENZIE, LIONEL W. 1955a Specialization in Production and the Production Possibility Locus. *Review of Economic Studies* 23, no. 1:56–64.

McKENZIE, LIONEL W. 1955b Equality of Factor Prices in World Trade. *Econometrica* 23:239–257.

McKENZIE, LIONEL W. 1960 Matrices With Dominant Diagonals and Economic Theory. Pages 47–62 in Stanford Symposium on Mathematical Methods in the Social Sciences, Stanford University, 1959, *Mathematical Methods in the Social Sciences, 1959: Proceedings.* Stanford Univ. Press.

METZLER, LLOYD A. 1950 A Multiple-region Theory of Income and Trade. *Econometrica* 18:329–354.

MOSAK, JACOB L. 1944 *General-equilibrium Theory in International Trade.* Bloomington, Ind.: Principia Press. → The first major contribution to *n*-country, *n*-good theory using the general equilibrium approach.

MUNDELL, ROBERT A. 1960 The Pure Theory of International Trade. *American Economic Review* 50:67–110. → A survey of comparative statics for trade between countries having full employment. The last section is devoted to the *n*-country case.

NIKAIDÔ, HUKUKANE 1956 On the Classical Multilateral Exchange Problem. *Metroeconomica* 8:135–145.

OHLIN, BERTIL G. (1933) 1957 *Interregional and International Trade.* Harvard Economic Studies, Vol. 39. Cambridge, Mass.: Harvard Univ. Press.

RYBCZYNSKI, T. M. 1955 Factor Endowment and Relative Commodity Prices. *Economica* New Series 22: 336–341.

SAMUELSON, PAUL A. (1947) 1958 *Foundations of Economic Analysis.* Harvard Economic Studies, Vol. 80. Cambridge, Mass.: Harvard Univ. Press.

SAMUELSON, PAUL A. 1953 Prices of Factors and Goods in General Equilibrium. *Review of Economic Studies* 21:1–20.

STOLPER, WOLFGANG F.; and SAMUELSON, PAUL A. (1941) 1949 Protection and Real Wages. Pages 333–357 in American Economic Association, *Readings in the Theory of International Trade.* Philadelphia: Blakiston.

TAKAYAMA, AKIRA 1961 Stability in the Balance of Payments: A Multi-country Approach. *Journal of Economic Behavior* 1:135–147.

TSIANG, S. C. 1961 The Role of Money in Trade-balance Stability: Synthesis of the Elasticity and Absorption Approaches. *American Economic Review* 51:912–936.

UEKAWA, YASUO 1966 A Study of Some Topics in Mathematical Economics. Unpublished Ph.D. dissertation, Univ. of Rochester.

VINER, JACOB 1937 *Studies in the Theory of International Trade.* New York: Harper.

## III
### TERMS OF TRADE

The terms of trade appears as an important variable in aggregative economic analyses of, for example, national or regional imports, exports, wage rates, and real product. It also serves as an indicator of changes in national welfare, in the extent to which a country benefits from foreign trade, and in the international division of trading gain. In view of the disparate roles that the concept has played, it is not surprising that several alternative definitions are current.

In most statistical calculations, however, and in nearly all public and professional discussion, it is the *commodity*, or *net barter*, terms of trade that is involved. The commodity terms of trade may be defined as an index or indicator of the average price of a country's commodity exports in terms of its commodity imports. Thus, if $P_X(t)$ is an index of the prices of a country's commodity exports during a specified period, $t$, or at a point in time, $t$, and if $P_M(t)$ is an index of the prices of the country's commodity imports, the commodity terms of trade may be expressed as $T_C(t) = 100[P_X(t)/P_M(t)]$.

Similar definitions may be applied to the trade of a geographical region within a single country (e.g., the Mezzogiorno, the Paris Basin), to the trade of industrial sectors (e.g., the United States farm sector), and to the external trade of political or economic groupings of countries (e.g., the British Commonwealth, the European Economic Community). The definition is sometimes extended to embrace services (e.g., transportation services, the services of funds lent or borrowed), yielding the terms of trade on *current account*. Note that the commodity terms of trade is not defined for a country that has no commodity imports or commodity exports; similarly, one can imagine conditions under which the terms of trade on current account is not defined. Needless to say, such conditions are likely to be observed only during the first months of new settlements.

Evidently there are as many measures of the commodity terms of trade as there are combinations of export and import price indices. Each combination has its own field of relevance. Most available indices, however, are of the Paasche type, with weights proportional to current quantities [*see* INDEX NUMBERS].

**Historical behavior.** In recent years professional research and debate have focused on the existence and direction of long-term trends and cyclical swings in the terms on which broad and heterogeneous groups of commodities, especially primary products (including agricultural, mineral, forest, and fisheries products) and products of secondary manufacture, have traded against each other. The terms on which equally broad and heterogeneous groups of countries, notably the so-called underdeveloped and developed countries, have traded with each other, has been of comparable interest.

With only a few long time-series available, it cannot be pretended that any of the issues has been finally settled. The following conclusions, however, seem to be fairly firmly established. Thus, it seems clear that there has been no long-term trend in the terms of trade between primary and manufactured goods (Atallah 1958; Ellsworth 1956; Haberler [1954] 1961, pp. 280–289; Kindleberger 1956, pp. 258–275). Earlier views to the contrary (United Nations 1949, p. 72) were based on an uncritical interpretation of a particular estimate of the commodity terms of trade of a single exporter of manufactured goods, the United Kingdom, for the particular period 1876 to 1938 (League of Nations 1945, p. 18). It is now recognized that the behavior of the United Kingdom's terms of trade during that period was not typical of the behavior of the terms of trade of industrial European countries; nor was it even in the pattern of its own earlier nineteenth-century behavior (Morgan 1959; Imlah 1958, pp. 94–98; Schlote [1938] 1952, pp. 76, 154–155). Moreover, the index used suffers from the common technical weakness of including freight charges in import prices while excluding them from export prices. Such an index would be reliable if the United Kingdom provided no shipping services whatever, either for exports or imports. In fact, of course, British ships carried a large proportion of the world's cargo, including the United Kingdom's own imports and exports. Further, freight rates were, on the whole, declining after 1875. Hence, considered as an estimator of the British commodity terms of trade (or, for that matter, of the British terms of trade on current account), the index suffered from an upward trend bias.

While the view that there has been a downward drift in the terms on which primary products exchange against secondary manufactures has been discredited, Kindleberger has produced evidence in support of the related hypothesis that in the long run the terms of trade has tended to move in favor of those countries that were developing most rapidly and against stagnant or slowly developing countries, regardless of the *stage* of development attained by the latter (1956, pp. 263–264). However, the evidence is admittedly unreliable, and the generalization allows for many exceptions.

One might, perhaps, expect greater success in detecting cyclical patterns in the terms of trade, for it is a well-known feature of business cycles that in general the money prices of primary goods (including coal and other minerals) fluctuate with greater relative amplitude than the prices of secondary manufactures. One therefore would expect that the terms of trade of primary exporting countries would move cyclically, rising during periods of business improvement and deteriorating during periods of recession, and that the terms of trade of industrial countries would move countercyclically. Even here, however, every generalization must be severely circumscribed. Thus, it has been found that only in the period between World War I and World War II was there a reliable and widespread association between the level of business activity and the commodity terms of trade of industrial countries. For the United Kingdom, before 1914 the association was more often reversed than not, for before 1914 coal, iron, and steel, the prices of which typically fall heavily in depression, bulked much more largely in the United Kingdom's exports. Even for France and Germany, before 1914 the association is unreliable. The position has been well summarized by Kindleberger:

Taking prewar, interwar, and postwar periods together, it is clear that there is no simple, hard and fast generality about the relations between the business cycle and the merchandise terms of trade. The normal pattern for an industrial country exists: The terms of trade deteriorate in prosperity and improve in depression. However, this pattern is honored in the breach as well as in the observance, and may take on a substantial or a trivial amplitude. The rule has more validity in short, sharp inventory cycles, perhaps, than in more extended periods of depression and prosperity, though this cannot be adequately tested; certainly it has had more validity since 1930 than before, when in no country of Europe did the normal pattern long prevail. But it cannot be claimed that the normal pattern is currently valid. The year 1953 . . . was one of peak world prosperity in which the terms of trade turned consistently in favor of all the countries of Industrial Europe, except Belgium and Sweden, which behaved in the Korean crisis more like primary-producing countries. Unless information is available about the nature and intensity of the cycle, the structure of the economy concerned, and the long-run demand and supply positions of a country's major exports and imports, it is difficult to predict with assurance the cyclical behaviour of its terms of trade. (1956, pp. 155–156)

**The terms of trade and welfare.** The commodity terms of trade often is accepted as an indicator of national welfare or of a single country's gain from trade or share in the world gain from trade. It is, however, a very unreliable indicator.

That the commodity terms of trade cannot faithfully serve all three purposes is illustrated by a simple though artificial example. Imagine that a virtually self-sufficient country suffers some catastrophe (e.g., an earthquake or widespread fire or drought) that leaves it totally dependent on foreign sources of several indispensable materials. Clearly, the commodity terms of trade will turn against the country at a time when both the national gain from trade and the country's share in the world gain from trade are increasing and national welfare is declining. In fact, the commodity terms of trade is an unreliable indicator of welfare, however defined. To see this, imagine that an export industry (possibly the transportation industry) benefits from a substantial cost-reducing improvement in technology. In those circumstances, it is quite possible for the commodity terms of trade to deteriorate but for national well-being and even the national gain from trade and the country's share in the world gain to improve. Alternatively, suppose that the technological advance takes the form of a greatly improved product, produced, possibly, at only a slightly enhanced cost. In this case, from the point of view of the country's trading partners, the deterioration of their commodity terms of trade will fail to indicate the increase in their welfare or the enhancement of their trading gain.

Recognition of the fallibility of the commodity terms of trade as an indicator of gain or welfare has resulted in the resurrection of the classical definition of the terms of trade and in the development of several new definitions.

The *single factoral* terms of trade is obtained from the commodity terms of trade by correcting the latter for changes in the productivity of the export industries. Thus, if $\pi_x(t)$ is an index of productivity in the export industries during period $t$ or at time $t$, and if $T_{SF}(t)$ stands for the single factoral terms of trade, we may write $T_{SF}(t) = \pi_x(t) \cdot T_C(t)$. The purpose of the adjustment is obvious: it allows for the possibility that a decline in the commodity terms of trade produced by greater efficiency in the export industries might yet be associated with an improvement in both total welfare and the gain from trade. But this is not the only type of disturbance imaginable; and even if attention is restricted to disturbances of this kind, the single factoral terms of trade is an imperfect welfare indicator. Without going into details, it is possible to conceive of a situation in which an improvement in productivity in the export industry gives rise to a more than proportionate decline in the commodity terms of trade but also to an increase in both total welfare and the gains from trade. A fortiori, the single factoral terms of trade cannot accurately reflect the degree in which welfare or gain has changed. Its chief weakness, perhaps, lies in its failure to make allowance for changes in the volume of trade. This weakness is quite independent of the theoretical and practical difficulties of choosing and calculating an appropriate index of productivity.

Three further definitions of the terms of trade, all designed to facilitate welfare comparisons of one kind or another, may be mentioned briefly.

The *double factoral* terms of trade is obtained from the commodity terms of trade by correcting the latter for productivity changes in both the domestic and the foreign-export industries. This is the classical definition, implicit in the writings of Torrens and Senior and given formal expression by Marshall (1923, pp. 157, 161–163, 330 ff.). If $T_{DF}(t)$ stands for the double factoral terms of trade during period $t$ or at the point of time $t$, and if $\pi_M(t)$ is an index of productivity in the foreign-export industries, we may write $T_{DF}(t) = [\pi_x(t)/\pi_M(t)] \cdot T_C(t)$. In effect, the double factoral terms of trade measures the terms on which *resources* are bartered. Thus, its chief purpose is to serve as an indicator of the international division of the world gain from trade. Even allowing that the latter concept can be satisfactorily defined, the measure is, however, unsatisfactory, partly because, like the commodity and single factoral terms of trade, it fails to allow for variations in the international division of the volume of world trade.

The *income* terms of trade, $T_I(t)$, is defined as an index of the quantity of imports that could be purchased with the proceeds of a country's commodity exports. It may be obtained from the commodity terms of trade by multiplying the latter by an index of the quantity of exports (*see* Dorrance 1948, p. 52; Viner 1937, p. 563; Imlah 1958, pp. 92–93, 112–113). Symbolically, $T_I(t) = 100[P_x(t) \cdot E(t)/P_M(t)] = T_C(t) \cdot E(t)$, where $E(t)$ is an index of the quantity of exports. Thus, in the special case in which, on balance, capital movements, transfers, and trade in services cancel out, the income terms of trade coincides with the "capacity to import." The definition is interesting in that allowance is made for the volume of trade; but as an indicator of changes in welfare or trade gains, it, also, is quite unreliable. For any change in export quantities and prices that leaves unchanged the value of exports will

also leave undisturbed the income terms of trade. But it is not a matter of indifference, from the viewpoint of welfare or trade gain, whether export prices increase or decrease. Clearly it is possible, by changing the above illustration only slightly, to obtain a strong case in which the change in the income terms of trade is in the direction opposite that of the changes in welfare and trading gain.

The *gross barter* terms of trade, introduced by Taussig (1927, pp. 113–114), is defined as the ratio of an index of the quantity of commodity imports to an index of commodity exports. Like the income terms of trade, the gross barter terms of trade allows for changes in the volume of trade. Taussig argued that the gross barter terms of trade provided a better indicator of the gain from trade than did the simple commodity terms of trade, because it allowed for unilateral transfers, such as immigrants' remittances and indemnity payments. But such payments rarely arise from trade. Further, a country's gross barter terms of trade would show increased gain whenever the country engaged in foreign borrowing. (Further possible definitions are discussed in Viner 1937, pp. 559–561.)

None of the suggested modifications of the commodity terms of trade can be accepted as a reliable indicator of changes in total welfare, in the gain from trade, or in the international division of gain. The reason is that changes in the terms of trade, however defined, are almost always associated with changes in other variables (e.g., employment, volume of imports and exports, wage rates) having independent welfare significance. And how these other variables correlate with the terms of trade depends on the nature and initial impact of the disturbing factor. Generally speaking, any improvement in the commodity terms of trade that stems from a disturbance of foreign origin will be associated with enhanced well-being in all three senses. (One must, however, recognize the possibility that adjustment to the disturbance may be slow and accompanied by severe local unemployment, the existence of which outweighs all other considerations.) Similarly, any deterioration of the terms of trade of foreign origin usually will be associated with a deterioration of welfare. When the change is of local origin, however, the welfare outcome cannot be inferred from the movement of the terms of trade alone. It is necessary to know, in addition, the nature of the disturbance. As we have seen, a deterioration of the commodity terms of trade arising from cost-reducing technological changes in the export industries may or may not be associated with an improvement in welfare or in the gain from trade. Similarly, whether the terms of trade correctly signal the welfare implications of an import or export duty depends on the initial tariff level and the extent of the change in duty. There is an optimal tariff level, beyond which further increases are harmful to the tariff-imposing country.

As a welfare indicator, the terms of trade has never been more than a proxy, or substitute, for the individual commodity flows. The seriousness of its limitations in this role is now widely understood. As a result, the terms of trade is being replaced at the center of the policy stage by the commodity flows themselves.

*The future course of the terms of trade.* There have always been economists who claimed to have detected fundamental features of the world economy that would inexorably force the terms of trade between primary and manufactured commodities to follow a long-term trend in one direction or the other. There is, on the one hand, a long-standing tradition, originating in the classical writings of Torrens, Ricardo, and Malthus, that the law of diminishing returns in primary industry and the historical tendency of technological advances to favor secondary manufactures combine in the long-run to outweigh all other influences and force the terms of trade to move against manufactured goods (Torrens 1821, pp. 96, 98, 288–289). On the other hand, there is an influential modern view according to which Engel's law (extended to cover all primary products) combines with the monopolistic practices of industrial enterprises to force the terms of trade to move against primary products (United Nations 1950, pp. 8–14; Haberler 1961, pp. 280–289).

History has so far withheld its favor from both groups of prophets. No doubt it will continue to do so.

M. C. KEMP

### BIBLIOGRAPHY

ALLEN, R. G. D.; and ELY, J. EDWARD (editors) 1953 *International Trade Statistics.* London: Chapman; New York: Wiley.

ATALLAH, M. K. 1958 *The Long-term Movement of the Terms of Trade Between Agricultural and Industrial Products.* Rotterdam: Netherlands Economic Institute, Division of Balanced International Growth.

DORRANCE, G. S. 1948 The Income Terms of Trade. *Review of Economic Studies* 16, no. 1:50–56.

ELLSWORTH, PAUL T. 1956 The Terms of Trade Between Primary Producing and Industrial Countries. *Inter-American Economic Affairs* 10:47–65.

HABERLER, GOTTFRIED (1954) 1961 *A Survey of International Trade Theory.* Rev. & enl. ed. Princeton Univ., International Finance Section. → First published as

"Aussenhandel" in *Handwörterbuch der Sozialwissenschaften.* See especially Chapter 4.

HABERLER, GOTTFRIED 1961 Terms of Trade and Economic Development. Pages 275–297 in International Economic Association, *Economic Development for Latin America: Proceedings of a Conference.* Edited by Howard S. Ellis and Henry C. Wallich. London: Macmillan.

IMLAH, ALBERT H. 1958 *Economic Elements in the Pax Britannica: Studies in British Foreign Trade in the Nineteenth Century.* Cambridge, Mass.: Harvard Univ. Press.

KINDLEBERGER, CHARLES P. 1956 *The Terms of Trade: A European Case Study.* Cambridge, Mass.: M.I.T. Press; New York: Wiley.

LEAGUE OF NATIONS, SECRETARIAT, FINANCIAL SECTION AND ECONOMIC INTELLIGENCE SERVICE 1945 *Industrialization and Foreign Trade.* Geneva: The League.

MARSHALL, ALFRED 1923 *Money, Credit and Commerce.* London: Macmillan.

MORGAN, THEODORE 1959 The Long-run Terms of Trade Between Agriculture and Manufacturing. *Economic Development and Cultural Change* 8:1–23.

SCHLOTE, WERNER (1938) 1952 *British Overseas Trade From 1700 to the 1930's.* Oxford: Blackwell. → First published as *Entwicklung und Strukturwandlungen des englischen Aussenhandels.*

TAUSSIG, FRANK W. 1927 *International Trade.* New York: Macmillan.

TORRENS, ROBERT 1821 *An Essay on the Production of Wealth, With an Appendix in Which the Principles of Political Economy Are Applied to the Actual Circumstances of This Country.* London: Longmans.

UNITED NATIONS, DEPARTMENT OF ECONOMIC AFFAIRS 1949 *Relative Prices of Exports and Imports of Underdeveloped Countries: A Study of Post-war Terms of Trade Between Under-developed and Industrialized Countries.* Lake Success, N.Y.: United Nations.

UNITED NATIONS, ECONOMIC COMMISSION FOR LATIN AMERICA 1950 *The Economic Development of Latin America and Its Principal Problems.* Lake Success, N.Y.: United Nations, Dept. of Economic Affairs.

VINER, JACOB 1937 *Studies in the Theory of International Trade.* New York: Harper.

## IV
### PATTERNS OF TRADE

International transactions consist mostly of the exchanges of goods among nations. About four-fifths of all transactions are in goods; the other fifth includes mainly transactions in services—primarily transportation—whereas the rest are net transfers on capital account. A familiar and for many purposes most convenient classification of the goods that are exchanged in world trade distinguishes, in the broadest possible manner, two classes: primary goods (foodstuffs and raw materials) and manufactured goods. The first class includes those goods in which manufacturing activity contributes relatively little to the value of the good and in which a dominant role is played by natural resources—the availability of a suitable soil, a favorable climate, a plentiful supply of water, or mineral deposits. On the other hand, in the second class, which may include finished as well as semifinished goods, a substantial share of the value embodied in the good is provided by manufacturing processes, carried out with the aid of the services of labor and of capital.

The share of each class in world trade had been quite stable over a long period—from the last quarter of the nineteenth century until the early 1950s primary goods had usually formed somewhat less than two-thirds of all international trade in goods, fluctuations in the share being confined mostly to the range of 60 to 65 per cent of the total. Thus, for instance, primary goods were about 65 per cent of world trade in 1881, 63 per cent in 1913, 60 per cent in 1938, and 64 per cent in 1950. In more recent years this share has declined to about only one-half of total trade. It is hard to tell yet whether this represents a permanent move to a lower level or even a continuous trend still in force, particularly since this decline is to some extent due to a movement of relative prices, adverse to primary goods, which is not necessarily a long-term phenomenon. The majority of world trade, or at least half of it, is thus induced by variations among countries in the availability of natural resources; while variations among countries in the availability of capital, of labor force in general, and of particular human skills are the main source of the other part of world trade.

Each of the two classes of goods is dominated by a few important commodities. Among primary goods, petroleum has in modern times occupied a most conspicuous place. Other important raw materials in world trade are cotton, wool, coal, wood, pulp, and nonferrous ores, whereas coffee, wheat, sugar, and oilseeds are the most important foodstuffs. Among manufactures, machinery is by far the heaviest item in world trade; it is followed, among the finished goods, by transportation vehicles—chiefly road vehicles, but also ships and aircraft. Among semifinished goods, iron and steel, copper, paper, cotton fabrics, and textile yarn are the most important internationally traded goods.

**Relation to development stages.** By and large, the less developed the country—in terms of the level of its per capita income—the higher the share of primary goods in its exports. There are, of course, exceptions to this rule, such as Australia and New Zealand, on the one hand—countries with high per capita income levels which export mainly primary goods; or, on the other hand, Japan—a country with a relatively low per capita income, at least until a few years ago, which has traditionally concentrated its exports in manufac-

tured goods. As a rule, too, although this rule is violated more often, the less developed the economy, the higher the share of manufactures in its imports. It does not follow, however, as is often implied, that most of world trade consists of transactions in which one country trades primary goods for another country's manufactures or in which one of the parties to the transaction is an advanced country while the other is an underdeveloped country. Underdeveloped countries, it is true, rarely export manufactured goods, and although they often import primary goods in considerable amounts (mainly foodstuffs but also some raw materials) their trade may indeed be characterized as, by and large, the export of primary goods for manufactured goods from advanced countries. But trade of high-income countries—which constitutes the majority of world trade—is substantially different: most of these both export and import primary goods as well as manufactures, and they buy their imports from other advanced countries as well as from underdeveloped countries. Even if goods were classified in more detail than just into the two categories of primary goods and manufactures, it would be found that the composition of exports of most highly developed countries is quite similar to the composition of their imports. An important exception is the United Kingdom, which, almost alone among the major trading nations, exports manufactures almost exclusively, whereas it imports mainly primary goods. Because of its conspicuous place in world trade, the extreme case of Britain has often tended to be regarded as the rule rather than as an exception. In fact, however, the exchange of primary goods for other primary goods and of manufactures for other manufactures outweighs considerably the exchange of primary goods for manufactures. Likewise, the majority of world trade consists of transactions among highly developed countries rather than between these and the underdeveloped areas.

**Concentration of trade.** Highly developed and underdeveloped countries differ not only in the commodity composition of their trade but also in its commodity concentration. Most underdeveloped economies export primarily one good or very few goods, whereas advanced economies diversify their exports among goods of which none occupies an overwhelming share of the country's total exports. This is explained by the nature of each country's economy. In the underdeveloped economy, capital and labor skills are lacking; it specializes in goods for which it is best accommodated by nature, and these are usually very few. The capital and skills at the disposal of the advanced economy, on the other hand, qualify it for the production of and specialization in a large variety of goods. This does not imply, however, that the export of each primary good is concentrated in one country or among a handful of countries while the export of each manufactured good is distributed over a large number of countries. On the contrary, the export of primary goods is at least as diversified among countries as the export of manufactures. Apparently, the natural endowments required for the production of most of the raw materials and foodstuffs exist in a fairly large number of countries—although these countries are often found in geographic proximity. Thus, for instance, foodstuffs like rice, coffee, and cocoa are each produced in a fairly large number of countries, most of which will be found in the same geographic region. At the same time, it seems that the capital, human skill, knowledge, and organization required for the production of manufactures are much more concentrated among nations than might be expected from the fact that these, unlike natural resources, are factors which could conceivably be developed anywhere. Moreover, a high degree of export specialization prevails among industrial countries, each concentrating most of its exports in a certain selection of manufactured products. This specialization may well be as much a result of accidental "historical" developments—such as the role played by individual firms—as of the availability of certain factors of production in their broader definition. It may also result from differences in the size of the economy; the export of manufactured goods, such as aircraft or ships, whose production may profitably be undertaken only in an economy of a substantial size, tends to be concentrated in a small number of countries.

Imports of underdeveloped countries also tend to concentrate in a few commodities—although the measure of concentration is much lower, and the difference between underdeveloped and highly developed countries much less conspicuous, than in the case of exports. The consumption and investment requirements of an underdeveloped economy are not only lower, per capita, in absolute amounts but also less varied than those of an advanced country. Hence, the former is limited to a smaller variety of goods not only in its domestic production but also in its imports from abroad.

**The place of Europe.** Throughout modern times, Europe has been the major participant in international trade. Its quantitative importance has gradually declined, however, over the last few generations, particularly during the first half of the present century. The share of Europe (both Continental

and non-Continental) in world exports, which was about 53 per cent in 1900–1913, dropped to close to 50 per cent in 1925–1938 and to about 38 per cent in 1948–1950 (excluding the exports of Soviet-bloc countries from both European and world exports). Part of the loss has been regained during the 1950s. Europe's share increased to about 40 per cent in 1955 and 45 per cent in 1960. Approximately 40 per cent of Europe's trade has normally been concluded within the region, the other 60 per cent being the trade of Europe with non-European countries. Thus, even at the low point of the early postwar years, over 60 per cent of world trade consisted of transactions in which either one of the participants in trade—the exporter or the importer—or both were European countries. During the interwar years this percentage was, of course, considerably higher—from 70 to 75 per cent; still earlier, in the period 1900–1913, it amounted to over 80 per cent. Thus, over most of the present century only some 20 to 30 per cent of world trade consisted of the exchange of goods between one non-European country and another.

A large portion of Europe's trade with the outside world has traditionally been conducted with dependent countries—that is, European colonies or territories otherwise politically associated with a European power. This holds true particularly for the United Kingdom, whose trade with its dependencies constituted, in the interwar period, over half the total trade of Europe with its dependent territories, but it characterizes also the trade of France and of the smaller colonial countries in Europe. Altogether, this trade amounted in the interwar period to roughly one-half of Europe's total trade with the outside world, and this share tended to increase during that period. This portion of Europe's transactions consisted almost entirely of the export of manufactures in exchange for the import of primary goods. The combined trade of Europe and of its dependencies amounted during the interwar period to some 70 per cent of world trade; some 75 to 80 per cent of the trade of this combined group was conducted within the group, leaving only a slight portion for trade with the rest of the world. It should be noted that the increased tendency of the large European nations to trade with their associated territories came not only at the expense of countries outside Europe but also of countries within Europe, and in particular of the larger ones. The trade of the three major European trading nations—the United Kingdom, Germany, and France—among themselves, and particularly the exchange among them of manufactures, tended to decline during the interwar years.

Europe's predominance in world trade, even in the postwar world, is outstanding not only in relation to the size of its population (about one-sixth of the world's) but also in relation to its income. In the late 1950s, Europe's share in the gross national product of the non-Soviet world amounted to some 27 per cent, while its share in world trade (exports and imports) came to about 47 per cent. In contrast, the United States, with close to 48 per cent of the world's gross national product, contributed only 16 per cent of world trade. The ratio of trade to income was, thus, over five times higher in Europe than in the United States. Part of this difference is explained, of course, by the fact that Europe is divided into many independent nations, whereas the United States is a single political entity, with trade among its various segments by definition not constituting international trade. But the contrast does not disappear when intra-European trade is excluded, leaving only Europe's trade with the outside world; this trade (some 60 per cent, to recall, of Europe's total international trade) still amounts to 27 per cent of world trade—roughly three times that of the United States, in relation to the respective incomes of the two regions. No such sharp contrast appears between Europe and the rest of the world (that is, non-European countries other than the United States); the latter's share in the world's gross national product amounted to approximately 25 per cent, while its share in world trade reached 38 per cent, about one-third of it being conducted within the "region." In relation to the size of its income, the trade of this region with the outside world appears to be of practically the same magnitude as Europe's trade. The non-Soviet world may thus be viewed as consisting of three major "regions": the United States, Europe, and the "rest of the world." Whereas the first is predominantly self-contained, the last two tend to specialize, each complementing the economy of the other.

The decline of Europe's weight in world trade during the first half of the century was not felt equally by all European nations. The chief losers were the United Kingdom—the largest trading nation in Europe (and, at the beginning of this century as well as during the two preceding centuries, in the world)—and France. The major gainers among non-European countries were the United States and Japan. The former overtook the United Kingdom as the largest trader during the interwar years, increasing its lead after World War II. In 1928, the U.S. share in world trade (exports and imports) was 14 per cent to the United Kingdom's 13 per cent; in 1950 the respective shares were 17 per cent and 12 per cent, and in 1960 16 per cent and 10 per cent.

**Relation of changes in commodity and geographic patterns.** To a large extent, changes in the geographic pattern of trade have been conditioned by transformations in the commodity pattern and particularly by radical changes in the weight of various manufactures. Throughout the present century, the share of capital goods in the trade of manufactures has tended to increase and that of consumer goods to diminish. In some instances, a shift is also observed from a "lower" to a "higher" stage of manufacturing, such as from trade in metals to trade in machinery. The most conspicuous increase is found in the trade in motor vehicles; at the end of the last century this trade was insignificant, but by the middle of the present century it amounted to about 12 per cent of the total trade in manufactures. Another group whose share increased considerably is machinery, in particular electrical machinery. The heaviest loss, on the other hand, was suffered by textiles and apparel: the share of this group dropped from over 40 per cent of the total trade in manufactures at the end of the last century to less than 20 per cent by 1950. This trend has apparently been associated with the process of industrialization in formerly less developed economies. Industrialization leads to an increased demand for capital goods, on the one hand, and to the establishment of domestic industries—textiles being the most important case—which, on the other hand, substitute local production of consumer goods for imports.

Naturally, traditional specialization in relatively expanding industries should be conducive to an increase in a country's share in world exports, while a country whose exports consist largely of relatively contracting goods may be expected to suffer from the changing commodity composition of world trade. The most important country in the former position is the United States, whose exports of manufactures have always included a particularly high share of relatively expanding goods. The outstanding case in contrast is the United Kingdom, whose exports at the beginning of the century consisted, in very large measure, of relatively contracting goods, particularly textiles. Observations of these two large trading countries have sometimes led to the conclusion that changes in the geographic pattern of exports have been entirely or mostly due to the changing commodity structure of trade. This conclusion is unwarranted in so extreme a form; it is not even accurate for these two specific instances, and particularly not for the United Kingdom, where the trends in commodity composition of world trade have been a minor factor in affecting the country's share in world exports. Moreover, some of the countries whose trade in manufactures has expanded most have specialized in relatively stable, or even relatively contracting, industries. The most glaring example is Japan, whose exports before World War II—and to a gradually declining extent, also after it—have consisted largely of textiles; another important instance is Canada. Altogether, the correlation of countries whose shares in world trade have expanded with countries which specialize in relatively expanding industries, and vice versa, is rather weak. Changes in the commodity structure of trade have not been the major determinant of changes in the geographic pattern; this is true particularly for the first quarter of the present century, while during the second quarter the commodity structure did indeed play an important role in a few instances. Among the other factors which helped to pull down Europe's share in world trade, the two world wars certainly loom large. Besides the direct damages inflicted by the wars, they have led to the breaking of some traditional ties of Europe with its customers. In normal situations, tradition tends to endure and to play an important role in determining the geographical pattern of world trade. Similarly, the wars have contributed to the tapering off of European investment in the outside world, a factor which is also partly responsible for the declining share of Europe in world trade.

To some extent, the high-income, industrialized countries have specialized not only in the export of certain manufactures but also in the import of certain primary goods. This characterizes particularly the United Kingdom and the United States. Thus, there are foodstuffs like meat, butter, and tea, in which the United Kingdom accounts for more than half of world imports; or raw materials, such as zinc, petroleum, and wool, of which Great Britain imports about one-third of the world total and in which the United States is a relatively unimportant customer. In other goods, such as silk, coffee, tin, and rubber, the reverse is true. The share of continental Europe, on the other hand, is more uniform; in most important primary goods, it amounts to some one-third to one-half of the total.

**Multilateral trade and trading regions.** International transactions may be bilateral, where two countries exchange goods (and services) between themselves, or multilateral, where one country exports its goods to another while receiving its imports from a third country. In effect, the large majority of the world's transactions in goods are of a bilateral nature. During both the interwar and the postwar periods, multilateral transactions constituted only about 20 to 25 per cent of international exchanges of goods. The share of multilateral transactions is particularly low in the Soviet-bloc countries, where it amounted, during the 1950s, to merely some 10–12 per cent of total trade. It is also relatively low—about 20 per cent of trade—in the United States and Canada, in dollar countries in Latin America, in the United Kingdom, and in continental western Europe. Nondollar countries in Latin America, the "overseas sterling area," and the "rest of the world" conduct a more multilateral trade: there the share of multilateral transactions amounted to some 35 per cent of these countries' foreign trade in the 1950s.

Countries with a relatively high share of multilateral trade are almost exclusively, with the important exception of Japan, underdeveloped economies that export primary goods alone and whose individual shares in world trade are small. The highly developed countries, exporting mainly manufactures, may potentially maintain bilateral trade relations with other developed countries as well as with the underdeveloped. When one underdeveloped economy, on the other hand, happens to buy large quantities of primary goods from another, it cannot usually offer in exchange goods which the partner country may require. Trade relations of underdeveloped countries among themselves are therefore less likely to be bilateral than either the trade of developed countries among themselves or the trade between developed and underdeveloped economies.

It should be noted that a large amount of intraregional trade, within a given region, does not imply that this trade tends to be multilateral. On the contrary, within the three major trade regions that are commonly distinguished in the postwar world—the dollar bloc, the sterling area, and continental western Europe—intraregional trade tends to be less multilateral than the trade of the member countries with the outside world. This is particularly true for the dollar bloc. Here, each of the small trading countries conducts most of its trade with the United States; this trade is highly bilateral, and the small export or import surplus that results serves to finance (or is financed by) deficits (or surpluses) not in the trade with other countries in the region but in the trade with countries outside it. In the sterling area, too, multilateral balancing is considerably less significant in the trade of the area's members among themselves than in their trade with nonmembers. Here, too, trade surpluses (deficits) with the central member of the region— the United Kingdom—serve more to offset deficits (surpluses) with nonmember than with member nations. In contrast to the dollar bloc, though, a large amount of multilateral trade that does not involve the region's center sometimes takes place in the sterling area. Countries in continental western Europe, too, conduct their transactions among themselves somewhat more bilaterally than their trade with the outside world. Here, geographical distance is apparently of considerable importance: a particularly high share of both exports and imports of each European country flows to and from countries in its immediate neighborhood.

During the interwar period, a regular world-wide pattern of regional multilateral settlements was discernible (League of Nations 1942, pp. 73–97). If the world, excluding a few countries, is divided into tropical countries, the United States, other regions of recent settlement in the temperate belts, continental Europe, and noncontinental Europe, each of these five regions had an export surplus with all the regions following it on the list and an import surplus with all the regions preceding it on the list (except for an export surplus in the trade of the last region with the first). Toward the end of the interwar period, however, this pattern became somewhat blurred. In the postwar era, although the geographical distribution of trade and of multilateral transactions has been rather stable over most of the period, no such clear-cut regional pattern has yet been established.

MICHAEL MICHAELY

[See also COMMUNISM, ECONOMIC ORGANIZATION OF, article on INTERNATIONAL TRADE.]

### BIBLIOGRAPHY

BALDWIN, ROBERT E. 1958 The Commodity Composition of Trade: Selected Industrial Countries, 1900–1954. *Review of Economics and Statistics* 40 (Supplement), no. 1, part 2:50–71.

BECKERMAN, W. 1956 Distance and the Pattern of Intra-European Trade. *Review of Economics and Statistics* 38:31–40.

CAIRNCROSS, A. K.; and FAALAND, J. 1952 Long-term Trends in Europe's Trade. *Economic Journal* 62: 25–34.

*Commodity Trade Statistics.* → Published since 1949 by the United Nations Statistical Office.

*Direction of International Trade.* → Published since 1950 by the United Nations Statistical Office.

HIRSCHMAN, ALBERT O. 1945 *National Power and the Structure of Foreign Trade.* Publications of the Bureau of Business and Economic Research, University of California. Berkeley and Los Angeles: Univ. of California Press.

LEAGUE OF NATIONS, SECRETARIAT, FINANCIAL SECTION AND ECONOMIC INTELLIGENCE SERVICE 1941 *Europe's Trade: A Study of the Trade of European Countries With Each Other and With the Rest of the World.* Geneva: The League.

LEAGUE OF NATIONS, SECRETARIAT, FINANCIAL SECTION AND ECONOMIC INTELLIGENCE SERVICE 1942 *The Network of World Trade.* Geneva: The League.

LEAGUE OF NATIONS, SECRETARIAT, FINANCIAL SECTION AND ECONOMIC INTELLIGENCE SERVICE 1945 *Industrialization and Foreign Trade.* Geneva: The League.

LEWIS, W. A. 1952 World Production, Prices and Trade, 1870–1960. *Manchester School of Economic and Social Studies* 20:105–138.

MAIZELS, ALFRED 1963 *Industrial Growth and World Trade: An Empirical Study of Trends.* Cambridge Univ. Press.

MICHAELY, MICHAEL 1962a *Concentration in International Trade.* Amsterdam: North-Holland Publishing.

MICHAELY, MICHAEL 1962b Multilateral Balancing in International Trade. *American Economic Review* 52: 685–702.

ROBINSON, AUSTIN 1954 The Changing Structure of the British Economy. *Economic Journal* 64:443–461.

SVENNILSON, INGVAR 1954 *Growth and Stagnation in the European Economy.* Geneva: United Nations, Economic Commission for Europe.

THORBECKE, ERIK 1960 *The Tendency Towards Regionalization in International Trade, 1928–1956.* The Hague: Nijhoff.

TYSZYNSKI, H. 1951 World Trade in Manufactured Commodities, 1899–1950. *Manchester School of Economic and Social Studies* 19:272–304.

WOOLLEY, HERBERT B. 1958 Transactions Between World Areas in 1951. *Review of Economics and Statistics* 40 (Supplement), no. 1, part 2:10–35.

*Yearbook of International Trade Statistics.* → Published since 1950 by the United Nations Statistical Office.

## INTERNATIONAL TRADE CONTROLS

| | | |
|---|---|---|
| I. | TARIFFS AND PROTECTIONISM | *W. M. Corden* |
| II. | EXPORT SUBSIDIES AND DUMPING | *Franz Gehrels* |
| III. | QUANTITATIVE RESTRICTIONS AND QUOTAS | *Jagdish Bhagwati* |
| IV. | TRADE AGREEMENTS | *Raymond F. Mikesell* |
| V. | STATE TRADING | *J. Carter Murphy* |

### I

### TARIFFS AND PROTECTIONISM

In international economic usage, *protection* usually refers to acts of government policy which protect an industry from foreign competition, thus enabling the industry to earn higher incomes than it otherwise would. It can also be interpreted more broadly to include all government policies which assist industries that are either competing with imports or are actual or potential exporters. The four main protective devices are subsidies to domestic producers, taxes on imports, quantitative restrictions on imports, and state trading. Taxes on imports are historically the principal device. These taxes are usually called tariffs or customs duties, though sometimes other terms, such as import surcharges or equalizing duties, are used. Tariffs may be classified by motive and by form. Since a tariff will normally produce customs revenue, protect domestic output, reduce consumption of the protected product, and reduce imports, in motive it may be a revenue tariff, a protective tariff, a tariff designed to reduce consumption of a product, or a tariff to improve the balance of payments. The principal distinction is between the first two motives—revenue and protection. In practice, motives and actual effects are usually mixed. Individual tariffs may be classified by form according to whether they are ad valorem (a percentage of the value of the unit), specific (a fixed sum for each unit), or a combination of the two, whether ad valorem percentages are fixed or variable with the price of the import, and whether the tariffs allow for exemptions—for example, of imports destined for re-export.

A tariff schedule is a complicated document consisting often of several thousand different items. Not only may there be a separate tariff rate for each item, but in addition a tariff schedule may have several columns, so that there is more than one duty for each item. Historically, most countries have had at least two columns in their tariff schedules, the distinction being usually between a conventional and a general column, the conventional tariff applying to some or all imports from countries with which a tariff agreement has been concluded and the general tariff to the remaining imports. Most trade agreements include the so-called most-favored-nation clause, which provides that (when countries A and B sign an agreement) country A will not discriminate in any tariff item against imports from country B. When countries are linked by a network of trade agreements, all containing such a clause of general application, a system of nondiscriminatory tariffs results. If a country is part of a preferential area a third column will state the preferential tariff applying to some or all of the imports from fellow members of the area, this tariff being normally less than the conventional tariff. If all trade between members of the preference area is free of duty, though each member still has its own tariff on imports from other sources, there is an extreme form of preference area, a free trade area. One step beyond the free trade area is the customs union. As in the free trade area, all trade between the members is free of duty and other trade restrictions, but in addition the members of a customs union have a common external tariff applying to all imports from outside the area. They are in fact a single unit for tariff purposes. [*See* INTERNATIONAL INTEGRATION, *article on* ECONOMIC UNIONS.]

**History of protectionism.** The history of commercial policies—that is, government policies affecting international trade—is difficult to sum up. Tariff schedules and other instruments of protectionism are complex, and there is no easy way of aggregating the individual elements. Moreover, movements· toward or away from protectionism in different parts of the world have not been synchronized and have had many different causes, some special to particular countries. From the tariff histories of the principal industrial countries there does not emerge a consistent causal relationship to explain why tariffs or quotas were imposed, raised, or reduced at certain times. Much prominence is usually given to the arguments of the advocates and the critics of protectionism, and to the interplay of tariff policy with class or regional divisions. It is not always clear to what extent the arguments provide actual explanations or mere rationalizations of the course of events.

One may also wonder how important specific books and economic theories have been in influencing the course of tariff history. Adam Smith's *Wealth of Nations* (1776), Hamilton's *Report on the Subject of Manufactures* (1791) and List's *National System of Political Economy* (1841) were influential works, the first providing the intellectual support for the British and Continental free-trade movement, and the latter two for protection of infant manufacturing industry in the United States and Germany, respectively. But the British free-trade movement did not get under way until 50 years after the publication of Smith's book, United States protectionism lagged 25 years behind Hamilton's *Report*, while the Zollverein (the German customs union which preceded the establishment in 1871 of the German Empire) had a very moderate tariff, and when Germany did become protectionist after 1880 it was agriculture much more than manufacturing industry that was protected. The influence of "scribblers" was perhaps less than many tariff historians suggest. The legitimization by J. S. Mill in his *Principles of Political Economy* (1848) of the infant industry argument for protection, while convincing to most English economists, did not have any noticeable effect on tariff history. More recently, the terms of trade argument for protection, in the form in which theoretical economists have given it so much prominence, has made no apparent impact on actual commercial policies.

Some generalizations which may serve as guidelines through the tariff histories of the major Western industrial nations are, however, possible. The first is that war often leads to increases in protection. War usually gives rise to additional revenue needs. The revenue duties which are imposed have an incidental protective effect; after the war, when the extra revenue need disappears, the tariff is maintained so as to safeguard the infant industries established under the shelter of the tariff. War leads to a boom in demand for a wide range of industrial goods; after the war, tariffs may be imposed to compensate for the fall in demand. War may cut a country off from imports and thus provide a form of natural infant protection; after the war, this protection is replaced by tariff protection to ensure survival of the infants. Finally, special measures may be taken in wartime to develop industries producing goods essential to the military effort or to the living standards of a nation cut off from outside supplies. After the war these industries are maintained, both to preserve employment and capital values and in awareness of the strategic argument for protection. The protectionist histories of Britain, France, the United States, and Australia all provide support for this generalization. The beginnings of American protectionism can be traced to the effects of the War of 1812 in protecting infant American industries from British competition. High protectionism in the United States originated in the Civil War. Industry in the North boomed in response to the war-generated demand and naturally created pressures for its survival after the war. More important, the federal government's revenue needs soared during the war, and the customs were its principal source of revenue (Taussig 1888). Yet when the revenue needs fell after the war, the tariff was not reduced.

Another generalization which sheds some light on tariff history is that depressions, whether of the general cyclical type or long-term depressions in prices of particular products, generally lead to increases in protection. Falling prices automatically increase the protective incidence of specific duties. More important, the principal motive for protection is defensive—to protect sectional income levels from decline—and it is natural that when demand for the products of a country's industries falls, commercial policy should try to reduce or exclude foreign competition. The revival of protectionism in France and Germany in the late nineteenth century can be explained principally by the depression of 1873–1879 and by the more prolonged fall in agricultural prices produced by the new supplies from Russia and the New World. A great increase in protection all over the world resulted from the depression of the early 1930s. In particular, Britain,

which had been completely free trade from 1860 to World War I and remained predominantly free trade during the 1920s, finally became protectionist in 1931.

The converse of these two generalizations is that peace and prosperity usually encourage movements toward free trade. Prosperity and economic growth reduce protectionist pressure. In prolonged prosperity, industries become less dependent on protection and are less likely to insist that a trade barrier be maintained as an insurance against intensified foreign competition in the future. Moreover, prosperity is usually associated with rising prices and thus with automatic decline of the protective incidence of specific duties. Nevertheless, these generalizations do not, of course, explain all changes in tariff policy; for example, they do not explain the very high Hawley–Smoot tariff of the United States, which, though enacted in 1930, was conceived and lobbied for in the prosperous 1920s.

At the risk of some oversimplification, the state of world commercial policies in the 1960s may be summarized as follows. The nonindustrial countries use tariffs primarily for revenue, not protection, purposes. Taxes on trade, whether import taxes, export taxes, or the profits from a multiple exchange rate system, are usually the largest source of government revenue. In the semi-industrial or recently industrialized countries—notably, Canada, Australia, India, Brazil, and Argentina—tariffs or other restrictions on imports are primarily protective in intention and are essential to the preservation of substantial manufacturing industries. The protective tariff rates are usually high, and quantitative controls sometimes prohibitive; yet over-all tariff levels appear moderate because imports which are noncompetitive with domestic production, in particular raw material imports, are usually admitted free of duty. It is in these countries that industrial protection is a major element of economic policy and a topic of debate. In the advanced countries it is agricultural protection which is most important; the rates of protection are often high, varying between countries and products. Many European countries operate complex schemes, involving quantitative restrictions and variable import levies. Industrial protection in the advanced countries is much less significant, and recent years have seen important moves toward the freeing of world trade that affect mainly the trade in manufactured goods between the advanced countries. On the whole, the industrial protection of the advanced counties bears most heavily on "cheap-labor" products, such as textiles from Japan and Hong Kong, in which the advanced countries have lost their comparative advantage. The tariff structures of the advanced countries, as of the semi-industrialized ones, display in general the characteristic of "tariff escalation": tariff rates rise with the degree of processing contained in a product, basic materials often paying no tariff at all. Finally, in the communist countries the concept of protection as generally understood cannot be said to have any real significance [see COMMUNISM, ECONOMIC ORGANIZATION OF, *article on* INTERNATIONAL TRADE].

**Theories of protection.** An elaborate structure of economic theory concerned with the gains and losses from protection has grown up alongside the actual ebb and flow of world protectionism—sometimes influencing actual policies, as in the free trade movement of nineteenth-century Britain, and sometimes being influenced by them. The construction of a rigorous case for free trade was one of the earliest contributions of modern economic theory, and the free trade versus protection issue has preoccupied economists of most countries since Adam Smith. Much of this theory has developed out of attempts to refute crude protectionist beliefs or the advocacy of interest groups. To a lesser extent it has given precision and set boundaries to popular arguments. Sometimes it has even produced essentially new propositions.

The method of approach of most economic theorists to the problem is simple. The foundation is the classical case for free trade, first developed by Adam Smith and David Ricardo. The latter originated, in *On the Principles of Political Economy and Taxation* (1817), the formal law of comparative costs upon which the free trade case is now based. This classical case has been modified by a whole series of "arguments for protection." While the extent of the modification must depend on the circumstances of each situation, so that, strictly, nothing can be said without specifying situations and relevant magnitudes, it is probably a fair summary to say that most economists regard the free trade case as only modified and not refuted by the various protectionist arguments.

*Employment.* A perennially popular argument is that protection preserves or increases employment in the protected industries. The free trader's usual answer is that while employment will certainly be diverted into the protected industries, employment will be less elsewhere; the effect is thus a reshuffling rather than an increase in aggregate employment, a reshuffling into less productive activities which causes a real income loss. Full employment can always be maintained by fiscal and monetary policy along Keynesian lines, together with exchange rate adjustment to maintain exter-

nal balance. The modern amendment to this free trade logic is that exchange rate adjustment may not be possible for one reason or another, and the internal cost level may be inflexible downward. One can imagine a situation of unemployment and external deficit which ideally calls for exchange devaluation to divert expenditure from foreign to domestic goods. In the absence of exchange rate adjustment, or of substitute protectionist devices, fiscal and monetary policy would have to be used to reduce expenditure so as to restore external balance, thus increasing unemployment instead of reducing it. This result can be avoided by tariffs, which would take the place of devaluation as a device to shift spending from foreign to domestic goods. In this sense tariffs can maintain full employment. But the issue of an *optimum* pattern of tariffs remains; while various sets of tariffs will raise employment, some will achieve a given employment increase at less cost or a greater welfare gain than others.

A slight variant of the basic employment argument is the "population-sustaining" argument popular in countries such as Canada and Australia, where population growth by immigration is an object of policy and where the inflow of migrants is responsive to employment opportunities. The assumption is made that export demand is expanding only very slowly. To maintain growing employment and external equilibrium it may then be necessary, if free trade is to be maintained, to associate the requisite monetary expansion with frequent exchange devaluations—the latter to prevent the growth of imports exceeding the slow growth of exports. But frequent devaluations may not be possible. One way out is to sacrifice the monetary expansion for the sake of external balance; but this would discourage immigration. The other way out is to sacrifice free trade—to steadily widen the scope of tariffs, or to raise tariffs, as a second-best alternative to frequent devaluation. An essentially similar argument applies in underdeveloped countries where the employment-seeking work force is growing rapidly through natural increase while export demand is growing more slowly.

*Income redistribution.* A second argument for protection is that it alters the distribution of internal real incomes in a desirable direction. Clearly protection will make the income earners in the protected industry better off, particularly if the service they supply or the capital equipment they own is quite specific to the industry. It is obvious that protection, while usually benefiting some, harms others, notably consumers of the protected products and competing users of labor and materials.

These conflicts of interest are at the core of the political activities surrounding tariff making. Opposition to protection in Britain and the United States in the early nineteenth century was founded at least as much on the sectional interests of manufacturers (in Britain) and cotton growers (in the United States) as on any abstract case for free trade. But for a long time the common economic teaching was that while a small section could gain from protection, a large section—such as the aggregate of wage earners—could not, since its gains as protected producers would be more than offset by its losses as consumers. But an interesting theoretical development (Stolper & Samuelson 1941) has shown that, given certain assumptions, a gain to a large group *can* result. Whether such a redistribution of real income represents a gain or loss in national welfare is a question within the province of welfare economics [*see* WELFARE ECONOMICS].

The "pauper-labor" argument, which was the protectionist's stand-by in the United States in the period of the high McKinley and Dingley tariffs of the 1890s and which crops up whenever protection for labor-intensive industries is sought, is a variant of the income distribution argument. Imports of labor-intensive goods do tend to reduce the demand for some types of labor and so lower the real wages of this labor. But it is also true that the gains to other sections of the community from free trade may be so great that the gainers could compensate the losers. Aggregate welfare would then perhaps be maximized by free trade combined with compensation. But if the institutions of the society do not in fact ensure that compensation takes place, who is to say whether there is a net social gain or loss from protection—whether one man's gain is greater than another man's loss? Popular statements of the "pauper-labor" argument, however, usually contain fallacious elements. Cheap labor does not necessarily mean low prices for given qualities of product, and low prices for some products do not mean low prices for all. If a country's labor is really so cheap or efficient that it can sell everything cheaper, then clearly appreciation of its currency is required, though, indeed, tariffs imposed on its products by other countries may be a second-best alternative.

*Infant industry.* The infant industry argument for protection is the oldest and most respectable of the protection arguments. It has undergone considerable refinement. The main distinction is between the argument based on falling costs, which represent economies internal to firms and the benefits of which are reaped by firms themselves, and the so-called external economies. Support for protection

on the grounds of internal economies—that a firm's costs will fall with increased scale of output or over time—can only be given with reservations or for special cases. For, if a firm will eventually recover its initial losses, why should it require a subsidy, either direct or indirect? Can it not cover these losses from borrowed funds—to be repaid when costs later fall? One can readily think of situations where this is not possible or just would not happen; and in these situations the argument based on internal economies may be valid. Economists have given more attention to the case for protection based on external economies and have refined and classified the possible types of external economies. Most interesting are the external economies that are generated with the over-all growth of a manufacturing sector—economies external to the individual firms making up the sector, although internal to the sector as a whole. These economies provide the main justification for a general policy of industrial protection in countries which are semi-industrialized or show potentialities for industrialization. The discussion about the virtues, or otherwise, of a policy of *balanced growth* is closely related. This concept hinges on the interdependence of industries, especially of the different industries making up a manufacturing economy, an interdependence through both demand and supply. Any individual firm or industry may not find it profitable to expand, but if all expand together, maintaining some appropriate relation, they will all turn out to be socially and perhaps even privately profitable (Nurkse 1953). Against this must be set the advantages of unbalanced growth, among them the economies of specialization and the benefits to be derived from trade. A lively controversy is here unresolved.

*Terms of trade.* A country which restricts its trade, either by import tariffs or by export taxes, is likely to improve its terms of trade as a result. Restriction of demand may lower the prices at which foreign suppliers provide imports, and restriction of supply may raise export prices. On balance the gains from the terms of trade improvement may outweigh the losses from the country's reduced use of the international division of labor. A country, in fact, can act as a monopsonist or a monopolist. This is the terms of trade argument for protection. The element of gain which a country derives is at the expense of its trading partners, whose terms of trade will decline. Much elaborate theory has been spun around this general proposition, and it has yielded the concept of the "optimum tariff"—optimum to one country and not the world. Account has been taken of the possibility that other countries will retaliate against an "optimum tariff." If so, the terms of trade improvement may disappear and all countries may finally be worse off; although it is at least possible that when both countries restrict trade optimally, each responding to the other's restriction, on balance one of them may still finally be better off than before the whole exercise began. The terms of trade argument in the form in which it appears in the theoretical literature has not been of much practical significance. But in the process of growth countries have sometimes chosen to develop import-competing rather than export industries for fear that their terms of trade would otherwise deteriorate, and industrial protectionism in primary-product exporting countries is rooted to some extent in a belief in the price-inelasticity of demand for their exports.

*Second-best policies.* In underdeveloped countries the average income in the industrial or the "Westernized" sector of the economy is usually higher than that in the agricultural sector. There are various possible reasons for this; and to some extent the discrepancy may be only in money income and not real income. But it has been argued recently that insofar as there is a discrepancy not only in average real incomes but also in *marginal* returns—that is, insofar as a transfer of labor from the agricultural to the industrial sector would raise aggregate real income—protection of the advanced sector to encourage this labor transfer may be justified. This argument for protection needs to be carefully qualified and is not accepted without reservations. But it is interesting as an argument which is more or less special to underdeveloped countries. It is really a particular case of what has lately been recognized as a much larger category, the *second-best* argument for protection (Meade 1955). This argument applies whenever there is some distortion or disequilibrium in the internal economy, so that prices do not correctly reflect marginal costs. One remedy would be to eliminate the distortion directly; another would be to compensate with internal subsidies and taxes. But the politically and administratively most convenient remedy is often to compensate the distortion through carefully chosen commercial policies, such as tariffs. This is a second-best remedy because in compensating indirectly for internal distortions it creates new distortions—for example, in consumption patterns.

In a sense all the arguments for tariffs so far discussed are second-best arguments, justified by the impracticability of the "first-best" policies. It can be held that the best policy to maintain full employment is to combine fiscal and monetary adjustment with exchange rate variations. Internal incomes are best redistributed by nontrade taxes (such as income taxes), which finance direct subsidies. Infant industry protection is best provided by direct subsidies which benefit infants irrespective of whether they are import-competing or potential exporters. And the income of one country can be raised at the expense of another by direct international aid, so avoiding the trade-restricting effect of the optimum tariff. Yet to subsume all these arguments into a single second-best argument is to ignore the distorting by-products and administrative costs of what appear on the surface to be first-best policies.

*Economic growth.* Is there a special argument for protection on the grounds that it facilitates or stimulates economic growth? While the growth of the protected industries will no doubt be stimulated, the question is whether the over-all growth of the economy would have been less under free trade. Part of the answer is in the infant industry argument for protection: infant protection can be summed up as the incurring of a current loss for the sake of a future gain; if the expected future gain is indeed realized, then growth will have been fostered, although the issue still remains whether the current costs of this growth justify the future benefits. Another part of the answer is in the employment, or demand-generating, argument for protection; the incentive to invest will be lower in an underemployed than a fully employed economy. If protection is really needed to maintain full employment it also stimulates growth. There remain two ways in which protection can raise or lower growth rates. First, it may redistribute internal incomes toward or away from sections with a relatively high propensity to save; for example, savings out of industrial profits are generally higher than out of peasant incomes or out of rents, so that industrial protection tends to foster savings. Second, protection may raise the inducement to invest by increasing some or all profits or by reducing the risk element in investment. Thus investment is usually more responsive to profit increases in some than in other industries, so that protection of particular industries at the expense of other industries may affect the over-all growth rate. Furthermore, protection may bring about an over-all redistribution of real income away from wages or rents and toward profits, and so stimulate investment. A particular case of these relationships is the role of high and secure profits in protected industries in attracting foreign capital inflow. In all these cases the returns from growth may or may not outweigh the costs of protection.

*Methods of protection.*  All these arguments for protection do not distinguish between the methods of protection. There exists a fairly simple body of subsidiary analysis to assist the choice between the main methods—subsidies, tariffs, and quantitative import restrictions. Economists have tended to prefer the methods in that order—to prefer subsidies to tariffs because they distort only the production pattern and not the consumption pattern, and because their "cost" is more clearly apparent; and to prefer both subsidies and tariffs to quantitative import restrictions because of a predisposition in favor of the price mechanism and because of the monopoly profits that may be reaped under a scheme of quantitative restriction by holders of licenses to import. But beyond general arguments for protection and the broad choice of method, economic theory has provided little help in the construction of protective systems. We have seen that tariff schedules are usually complicated documents and that tariffs may assume many forms. The complexities in the tariff systems of most countries result from the piecemeal way, usually in response to numerous sectional pressures, in which tariff systems are constructed and amended and from the mixture of motives at work. One aim is often to tailor a tariff precisely to the object in view—for example, to achieve the desired protective effect with the minimum rise in prices to consumers and thus with the minimum incidental revenue effect. It is the pursuit of this aim which leads tariff makers in some countries (for example, Australia) to make detailed comparisons of production costs between countries and to construct complex tariffs which are finely adjusted to the estimated cost differences for those products which they have resolved to protect. But economists have not subjected the details of tariff making and the logic behind tariff structures to the same thorough analysis as they have the welfare effects of protection as a whole.

**Measurement of protection.**  Increasing attention is being paid to the need to measure the magnitudes and effects about which economists generalize. The various exercises in measurement connected with tariffs may be classified as follows. First of all, specific tariff rates and nontariff protection must be converted into ad valorem equivalents if one tariff or protective device is to be comparable with another. A problem is to discover the typical or "average" price to which each specific tariff rate applies. In the case of nontariff devices, the object is to discover the net result—the excess of the price received by the producer over the price of potential imports, expressed as a percentage of the latter. The main difficulty here is similar—to establish the prices of potential imports in those cases where actual imports have either been completely excluded or are unrepresentative of free-trade imports. A second step is to relate tariff rates to value added domestically rather than to the gross value of domestic output (which includes imported materials) and to allow for tariffs on imported materials. Such calculations yield *effective* protective rates (Barber 1955). For example, an apparent tariff rate of 10 per cent on cotton yarn will represent effective protection of 20 per cent when half of the yarn value (before duty) is raw cotton content, which would pay no duty if imported in that state. If the tariff on raw cotton were also 10 per cent, then the apparent and effective protection for yarn would both be 10 per cent. Calculations of effective protective rates are needed to determine the true impact of a protective system on an economy but have only recently been made systematically. They require detailed knowledge of the materials content in protected industries.

A further step is to calculate averages of tariff levels. Since one must sometimes sum up complex tariff schedules if one is to generalize at all, averages of tariff levels have frequently been calculated, though not always with awareness of the methodological traps. These averages usually refer to apparent, not effective, rates. The simplest and commonest method is to relate customs revenue to the value of total imports. The result is an average weighted by the value of imports after tariffs have been imposed. The higher a tariff, the more imports will be excluded, so that this method underweights the high tariff items. Indeed, a particular tariff which is so high as to be prohibitive will not enter the index at all. To avoid this bias, "unweighted" averages—that is, arithmetic averages of tariff rates—are sometimes calculated. The result then depends on the method of tariff classification and really has no coherent meaning. Yet another method is to weight by the value of the domestic production of items to which tariff rates apply. A practical difficulty here is that tariff classifications usually do not coincide with classifications of production statistics. This method in a sense yields the average, not of all tariffs, but only of the protective tariffs. It might be regarded as yielding an overstatement since it does not allow for items where there is no tariff but where a protective tariff could have been imposed. Other methods are to weight by consumption (imports plus domestic production) after tariffs have been imposed, to weight by the value of world trade, or to weight by the value of exports from some leading supplying countries. These latter methods are all approximations to what is often regarded as the preferable weighting system, namely, weighting by what imports would have been in the absence of tariffs. In fact, no method is ideal, since an average tariff, however calculated, cannot be a measure of the welfare or other effects of the tariff structure. Indeed, since the dispersion of tariffs has welfare implications, the use of a single figure to represent a complex tariff system may tend to obscure important implications.

Yet a further step is to estimate the effects of tariffs on output and employment (Salant & Vaccara 1961). The primary and the secondary effects of tariff imposition must here be distinguished. The primary effect consists of the direct rise in output or employment, when cost and exchange rate levels are given and when possible multiplier repercussions of the rise in incomes due to the initial rise in output are disregarded. It includes not only the effect on output and employment in the protected industry itself but also in industries which supply materials and components to it. The secondary effect allows for further repercussions. One possibility is that over-all employment and external equilibrium are maintained by exchange appreciation or by a rise in internal cost levels associated with the tariff increase. These adjustments would somewhat reduce employment in the newly protected industries. The other possibility is that the primary employment effect is not offset by deliberate policies—whether of exchange adjustment, cost adjustment, or demand reduction by fiscal or monetary policies—and is instead allowed to set off a multiplier process. A secondary rise in employment or in prices must then be added to the primary increase in employment.

Recently economists have become interested in the measurement of the welfare effects of protection (Corden 1957). The methodological problems involved are considerable. What is welfare? What is the precise configuration of the alternative situation with which the protection situation is being compared? The "cost" of protection, presumably, is the excess of free-trade welfare over protection welfare. How are changes in the distribution of income due to protection to be incorporated in the welfare measure? The simplest approach is to assume full employment in both situations, hold the terms of trade constant, ignore income distribution effects, and assume that free trade represents an optimum in the neoclassical sense. The cost of protection then results from a distortion of production and a distortion of consumption, both of which can be approximately measured, provided the effects of

protection on the quantities produced and consumed are known or can be estimated.

An interesting approach is to measure what has been called the *cash cost* of protection, namely, the value of the production subsidy which would be needed to achieve a protective result equivalent to that of tariffs or other trade restrictions (Young 1957). This cash cost is the excess of the value of protected output over the value of duty-free equivalent imports (at the current exchange rate). It has been estimated for Canada and Australia. It states the cost of protection in the same form as the costs of other subsidizing activities of the government are stated. It is thus not a net social cost; rather it is a gross cost against which the various benefits of protection must be offset.

W. M. Corden

[*See also* International trade.]

### BIBLIOGRAPHY

#### CLASSICAL WORKS

Hamilton, Alexander (1791) 1893 Report on the Subject of Manufactures. Pages 1–107 in Frank W. Taussig (editor), *State Papers and Speeches on the Tariff.* Cambridge, Mass.: Harvard Univ. Press.

List, Friedrich (1841) 1928 *The National System of Political Economy.* London: Longmans. → First published in German.

Mill, John Stuart (1848) 1961 *Principles of Political Economy, With Some of Their Applications to Social Philosophy.* 7th ed. Edited by W. J. Ashley. New York: Kelley.

Ricardo, David (1817) 1951 *Works and Correspondence.* Volume 1: On the Principles of Political Economy and Taxation. Cambridge Univ. Press.

Smith, Adam (1776) 1950 *An Inquiry Into the Nature and Causes of the Wealth of Nations.* 6th ed. 2 vols. Edited, with introduction, notes, marginal summary, and enlarged index, by Edwin Cannan. London: Methuen.

#### THEORETICAL WORKS

Barber, Clarence L. 1955 The Canadian Tariff Policy. *Canadian Journal of Economics and Political Science* 21:513–530.

Bhagwati, Jagdish 1964 The Pure Theory of International Trade. *Economic Journal* 74:1–84.

Corden, W. M. 1957 The Calculation of the Cost of Protection. *Economic Record* 33:29–51.

Haberler, Gottfried (1933) 1936 *The Theory of International Trade, With Its Applications to Commercial Policy.* London: Hodge. → First published as *Der internationale Handel.*

Meade, James E. 1955 *The Theory of International Economic Policy.* Volume 2: Trade and Welfare. Oxford Univ. Press. → See also the *Mathematical Supplement.*

Myint, Hla 1963 Infant Industry Arguments for Assistance to Industries in the Setting of Dynamic Trade Theory. Pages 173–193 in Roy F. Harrod and Douglas C. Hague (editors), *International Trade Theory in a Developing World: Proceedings of a Conference Held by the International Economic Association.* London:

Macmillan; New York: St. Martins. → A discussion of Myint's paper appears on pages 462–471.

NURKSE, RAGNAR (1953) 1962 *Problems of Capital Formation in Underdeveloped Countries.* New York: Oxford Univ. Press.

STOLPER, WOLFGANG F.; and SAMUELSON, PAUL A. (1941) 1949 Protection and Real Wages. Pages 333–357 in American Economic Association, *Readings in the Theory of International Trade.* Philadelphia: Blakiston.

FACTUAL AND HISTORICAL WORKS

BENHAM, FREDERIC C. 1941 *Great Britain Under Protection.* New York: Macmillan.

HAIGHT, FRANK A. 1941 *A History of French Commercial Policies.* New York: Macmillan.

NATIONAL INSTITUTE OF ECONOMIC AND SOCIAL RESEARCH 1943 *Trade Regulations & Commercial Policy of the United Kingdom.* Cambridge Univ. Press.

SALANT, WALTER S.; and VACCARA, BEATRICE 1961 *Import Liberalization and Employment: The Effects of Unilateral Reductions in United States Import Barriers.* Washington: Brookings Institution.

TAUSSIG, FRANK W. (1888) 1931 *The Tariff History of the United States.* 8th ed. New York: Putnam.

WOYTINSKY, WLADIMIR S.; and WOYTINSKY, EMMA S. 1955 *World Commerce and Governments: Trends and Outlook.* New York: Twentieth Century Fund. → See especially Chapter 6 on "Tariffs, Trade Agreements and Trade Restrictions."

YOUNG, JOHN H. 1957 *Canadian Commercial Policy.* Ottawa: Royal Commission on Canada's Economic Prospects.

## II
### EXPORT SUBSIDIES AND DUMPING

Subsidies on exports are any payments, direct or indirect, to producers resulting in export prices that are below domestic prices. Used in this sense we can say that exports of a number of American farm commodities are subsidized. The same is true whenever an exported good is freed from domestic indirect taxes.

An export subsidy has much in common with an ordinary subsidy placed on the production of an exportable good. Both tend to increase the production of the good in question and to raise its volume of export, but the former generally reduces domestic consumption (unless there are important economies of scale), while the latter increases both exports and home consumption. [*See* SUBSIDIES.]

The related but more emotive and less precise term "dumping" gained currency some time before World War I. As defined by Viner (1923), dumping refers to any reduction of foreign price below domestic price where such difference is not due to actual differences in cost of selling, production, or transportation. A firm may sell the same good abroad at a lower price than at home because foreign competition is more intense or its market position is less well established. Such price behavior has been explained in terms of the discriminating

monopolist, who maximizes profit by adjusting markup in each market to the elasticity of demand. But there is no precise theory to describe the behavior of firms attempting to break into new markets, or to defend existing markets against aggressive newcomers. These price reductions may be hidden in quality differentials, spurious quantity discounts, or favorable credit terms. Governments may support lower prices for exports by means of special freight rates, tax rebates, direct subsidies, or even special treatment of business combinations entered into for foreign trade purposes.

### Official policies and business practices

**International agreements.** Governmental views on direct or indirect subsidies for exports are ambiguous. International economic agreements of the post-World War II period and the organizations based on them have taken positions against discriminatory business practices in international trade. The abortive Havana Charter for an international trade organization contained an explicit condemnation of such practices. Its successor, the General Agreement on Tariffs and Trade (GATT), took over many parts of the Havana Charter but omitted the section dealing with discriminatory business practices. However, a GATT committee of experts has condemned dumping practices and approved antidumping duties. Curiously, they did not regard tax exemptions for exports to be a dumping device. The treaties establishing the European Coal and Steel Community (ECSC) and the European Common Market also deal with discriminatory business practices, including dumping. The ECSC especially has made important progress in eliminating the discrimination in pricing and freight charges formerly so common in both coal and steel.

On the other hand many countries, including the United States in the Webb–Pomerene Act of 1918, have legislation exempting business from prosecution for concerted actions in foreign trade, which would otherwise fall under antitrust laws.

**Cartel practices.** The interwar period saw an increase of business agreements to divide markets, exchange patents, and regulate prices. Overcapacity in numerous industries, changed political boundaries, and confiscation all created a climate conducive to protective arrangements among business firms. Mason (1946) reported the existence of private cartel agreements in such technical products as chemicals, electrical products, pharmaceuticals, and optical glass. A second group of agreements, mainly private but with government participation and support, included cement, steel products, tin plate, cables, dyes, paper, linoleum, plate glass, and numerous other products. A third group, usually with government participation and sometimes exclusively governmentally regulated, included rubber, tin, oil, kapok, sulfur, asbestos, tea, cocoa, coffee, quebracho, quinine, nitrates, aluminum, copper, sugar, lumber, phosphates, potash, and wheat.

The effect of any such agreement on price stability and price uniformity depends, of course, on the nature of the agreement. In the case of the first two groups, cartel arrangements often divided markets and tampered with prices. Home market prices were sometimes higher and sometimes lower than export prices; internal prices in producing countries differed considerably from one another. Stocking and Watkins (1946) give the dramatic examples of aluminum, electric light bulbs, magnesium, and steel, where clear evidence of discriminatory pricing existed. On the other hand, agreements on primary commodities probably had beneficial effects in maintaining orderly markets. Without them, individual governments might well have had stronger reason to interfere with free markets than they already had [see CARTELS AND TRADE ASSOCIATIONS; COMMODITY AGREEMENTS, INTERNATIONAL].

**U.S. antidumping laws.** U.S. legislation against dumping began with the tariff act of 1890, which provided a countervailing duty against export bounties by other countries on sugar. There followed the antidumping acts of 1916 and 1921. The latter is still in effect and gives the secretary of the treasury administrative responsibility for determining cases of dumping and imposing countervailing duties. Both excise tax refunds and exchange controls have been taken as justification for countervailing duties. However, at present only some dozen commodities are in fact subjected to countervailing duties. The determination of injury to domestic producers (one prerequisite for a remedial duty) has since 1954 been delegated to the U.S. Tariff Commission. A difficult point in applying the law is determination of the "fair value" of a good suspected of being imported and sold below such price. For this purpose either foreign market price or estimated cost of production is used. The determination procedure at present requires an average of eight to nine months, during which time *all* goods of the category in question are prevented from entering the United States.

**U.S. agricultural policy and dumping.** The export-dumping aspect of U.S. agricultural policy merits special attention. Under the Agricultural Adjustment Act of 1935 a part of customs revenues was earmarked for agricultural programs, includ-

ing subsidies for the export of cotton and wheat. Since 1949 these subsidies have been used mainly for fruit. The subsidy is paid directly to the commercial exporters and covers the difference between domestic and export price. More important by far are the Commodity Credit Corporation (CCC) sales under the Agricultural Act of 1949 (section 407) and later acts. Export sales by the CCC, usually at less than "support" prices, have included cotton, wheat, corn, peanuts, butter, cheese, dried milk, grass and cover-crop seeds, and a number of oils. The CCC's price-support losses to the end of 1961 totaled $2,200 million (not including the dairy program). A large part of this loss has been suffered through its export program, since domestic sales are at support price plus 5 per cent. [*See* AGRICULTURE, *article on* PRICE AND INCOME POLICIES.]

## Economic evaluation

**Import and export subsidies.** Only in recent decades have economists appreciated that the long-run effects of export and import subsidies are substantially the same. If a payment is made to encourage imports, resources are ultimately shifted out of import-competing home industries and into either the domestic or the exporting sectors. It is, however, necessary to depreciate the currency-exchange rate or lower domestic prices relative to foreign prices, in order to bring this shift about while maintaining external balance. Ultimately the value of both exports and imports are then increased in the same proportion, and the terms of trade altered in the same degree against the subsidizing country.

The foregoing stands in sharp contrast to most official views on the subject. Generally, export subsidies have acquired a bad name and are considered a legitimate cause for retaliation against the offending country. On the other hand, most countries would welcome enthusiastically any subsidy on imports put on by one of its trading partners.

**Effects on world efficiency.** The economist generally advocates measures which increase world trade because these improve the division of labor between countries. Such a view, however, needs a good deal of qualification. Reducing tariffs in an across-the-board, nondiscriminatory fashion tends to shift production to places of lower cost and thus increases world output. Such shifts are worthwhile so long as any differences in cost exist (making the appropriate adjustment for cost of transportation). Subsidies are more difficult to evaluate because they exist side by side with tariffs and other restrictions on trade. If there were no other distortions of the market we would conclude that subsidies worsen the allocation of resources because they encourage production in higher-cost places. Pushing trade beyond the level reached by a free market actually reduces world output, but where restrictions on the international flow of the same goods exist, subsidizing their movement by the exporting country tends to cancel the effect of the restriction. On the other hand, if the restrictions were mainly on trade in manufactures and the subsidies were mainly on farm commodities, the latter would tend to worsen the misallocation of resources already present [see INTERNATIONAL TRADE CONTROLS, *article on* TARIFFS AND PROTECTIONISM].

An additional complication is introduced by the fact that manufacturers often sell at a monopolistic price on protected domestic markets and at a lower one on foreign markets. If the degree of monopoly is higher in the domestic sector in question than in the rest of the domestic economy, the effect is for home consumption to be less than it would be under competitive pricing. On the other hand, the low export price tends to bring total output of the industry back toward where it should be, i.e., nearer where it would be under competitive conditions. The misallocation then may be mainly on the consumption side: consumers are paying different prices and could all be made better off if exchange among them were allowed to the point where all face the same set of relative prices. The point of this example is that to eliminate export dumping without lowering the domestic price of the dumped good may not bring any improvement of resource allocation. It may well bring about a less efficient allocation of production and put the world on a lower production-possibility curve.

We should consider also the question whether exemption of exports from sales and excise taxes amounts to a subsidy. The U.S. Treasury believes that it does, while GATT has stated that it does not. If domestic indirect taxes were the same proportion of price for all goods sold at home (and we neglect the abstruse problem of different substitutabilities between goods and leisure), then clearly an exemption from tax destroys the proportionality between prices and marginal costs. But the complexity of tax systems, not to mention imperfections of the market, makes the assumption of proportionality between prices and marginal costs highly questionable. One can therefore sympathize with the view of the GATT experts because exemption for exports may in some cases improve allocation.

We should emphasize that the foregoing arguments are made from the point of view of world efficiency and not from the national welfare point of view. Less interference with trade generally means that the world gets onto a higher production-possibility curve, i.e., it can, for the same combination of goods demanded, produce more of everything with the same productive effort. Removing all tariffs and subsidies, even if gradually, means the possible elimination of some national industries, reduced incomes for some groups in a nation, and perhaps worsened terms of trade for certain nations. Others must, however, become better off, and subject to some qualifications, those who gain could, if required, compensate those who lose. But compensation is seldom carried out in practice, so that who are the beneficiaries and who are the losers from an improvement of trade becomes an important question. [See INTERNATIONAL TRADE, *article on* THEORY.]

**Development argument.** An interesting economic argument for subsidies on exports is based on the infant-industry idea. One can protect a budding but not yet competitive industry that has export potential either by artificially raising the prices of competing imports or by lowering, via subsidies, the prices of the potential export goods. If the domestic market is large, tariffs may have the advantage of providing revenues—and this is an important consideration for undeveloped countries—and they may, in addition, favorably affect the terms of trade. If the domestic market is small a subsidy on exports, financed perhaps by means of a duty on the import of the same goods, has the advantage of opening a wider market for the industry. This permits a scale of production great enough for any potential economies of scale to be realized. The subsidy may have the additional political advantage of being both visible and inconvenient to the finance ministry; it may thus be a degree easier to remove when it is no longer necessary to an industry's survival.

In the case of many undeveloped countries this argument is strengthened by the presence of unemployed reserves of labor. The limited supply of agricultural land makes their effective employment in farming impossible. The social opportunity-cost of employing such labor in a newly established industry, even when counting capital costs and all costs of transferring labor, is less than private cost, if not by the whole amount of direct labor cost. Thus, even if no economies of scale were expected, there is justification for artificially lowering private money costs of production to something approaching estimated social cost.

The development of particular industries generally leads to (and indeed requires) a good deal of social infrastructure—housing, streets, schools, railroads, port facilities, electric power, communications, water, waste disposal, and so forth. This same social capital, which is an initial barrier to industrial development, provides the base for broad advance on many industrial fronts. Once this stage is reached costs may well become competitive in a number of activities at once, and the gradual removal of subsidies would lead not to a return of labor to agriculture or to inactivity but to a shifting of resources among a number of alternative industrial and service activities [see CAPITAL, SOCIAL OVERHEAD].

**Need for foreign exchange.** An immediate reason for subsidies on exports may be a shortage of foreign exchange due to domestic inflation combined with a fixed exchange rate. The subsidy may take the form of permitting exporters to surrender their foreign-exchange earnings at a premium rate. The existence of such a premium over the official parity is not, however, sufficient evidence for the existence of a subsidy. For example, Indonesia has for several years allowed exporters to sell foreign-exchange proceeds at higher than the official rate but has levied at the same time a tax on the exporters' "profits" from the transaction. In effect, importers were paying a higher price in local currency for foreign exchange than exporters received. This transaction amounted not to a subsidy but to a tax on trade—it is immaterial whether it be regarded as a tax on exports or on imports, since the ultimate effect of either is to reduce foreign trade. If there had been a subsidy on trade, this fact would have been evidenced by exporters receiving a higher price for their foreign exchange than importers paid—with the treasury paying out the difference. In general, a good rule of thumb for determining whether a country is on balance taxing or subsidizing trade is to see whether its treasury is receiving in duties more than it pays in subsidies or the reverse. Complications are added, however, under exchange rationing with more-or-less pegged rates. In that case, trade restriction is reflected partly in importers' profits rather than in tariff receipts.

**Employment effects.** In the 1930s export dumping gained disrepute for a reason which has since receded into the background. Foreign-exchange difficulties and severe unemployment both increased the temptation for governments to increase exports by artificial means and heightened the damage to other countries in similar difficulties. What were called "beggar-my-neighbor" remedies included such devices as export subsidies, import restrictions, and currency devaluation. At a time when policies to cope with unemployment were not

mastered by most governments, the response to exchange difficulties was often to depress domestic activity further through tightening of credit and budgetary stringency. Countervailing restrictions on imports as a remedy for the external imbalance were common; in consequence the world found itself both with depressed employment and severely restricted trade.

The precise employment effects of export subsidies are difficult to trace in all detail. For the subsidizing country there is an initial expansion of activity in the exporting industries, with multiplier ramifications in the rest of the economy. In the importing countries there is a downward multiplier process to the extent that the additional imports displace home production, while in competing exporter countries there is a downward multiplier process through the displacement of exports. The impact on employment in the importing country may be small if the substitutability of imports for home-produced goods is slight and could even be favorable through the positive effect of improved terms of trade and real income.

In the postwar era, when unemployment has only occasionally been a problem, and then a manageable one, it has been balance-of-payments considerations and special domestic interests which have dominated government attitudes toward export dumping. There has, however, been one case, that of West Germany in the 1960s, where hyper-full employment and a rising price level have been used as arguments for measures to increase imports and *discourage* exports.

Despite the many domestic and international market imperfections that make prescription on a single issue so difficult, a few general things can perhaps be said. In conjunction with more vigorous antitrust policy in the United States, an entirely new antitrust climate in Europe, and a general tendency toward less restriction on trade, the elimination of dumping will generally improve the allocation of resources. But given the particular interests involved, especially in agriculture, and the difficulties of uncovering discrimination when it exists, progress will be slow. Finally, export subsidies may have a definite place in furthering the development of industry in underdeveloped countries and therefore are a valid exception to the policy of removing interferences with trade.

FRANZ GEHRELS

BIBLIOGRAPHY

[BURENSTAM] LINDER, STAFFAN 1961 *An Essay on Trade and Transformation.* New York: Wiley.

CONTRACTING PARTIES TO THE GENERAL AGREEMENT ON TARIFFS AND TRADE 1958 *Anti-dumping and Countervailing Duties.* Geneva: The Contracting Parties.

EHRENHAFT, PETER D. 1958 Protection Against International Price Discrimination: United States Countervailing and Antidumping Duties. *Columbia Law Review* 58:44–76.

LERNER, ABBA P. (1936) 1953 The Symmetry Between Import and Export Taxes. Pages 123–133 in Abba P. Lerner, *Essays in Economic Analysis.* London: Macmillan.

MASON, EDWARD S. 1946 *Controlling World Trade: Cartels and Commodity Agreements.* New York and London: McGraw-Hill.

MEADE, JAMES E. 1951–1955 *The Theory of International Economic Policy.* 2 vols. Oxford Univ. Press. → Volume 1: *Balance of Payments.* Volume 2: *Trade and Welfare.*

ROBINSON, JOAN 1949 Beggar-My-Neighbor Remedies for Unemployment. Pages 393–407 in American Economic Association, *Readings in the Theory of International Trade.* Philadelphia: Blakiston.

SAMUELSON, P. A. 1962 The Gains From International Trade Once Again. *Economic Journal* 72:820–829.

STOCKING, GEORGE W.; and WATKINS, MYRON W. 1946 *Cartels in Action: Case Studies in International Business Diplomacy.* New York: Twentieth Century Fund.

U.S. COMMISSION ON FOREIGN ECONOMIC POLICY 1954 *Report to the President and the Congress.* Washington: Government Printing Office. → Commonly known as the Randall Commission Report.

VINER, JACOB 1923 *Dumping: A Problem in International Trade.* Univ. of Chicago Press.

### III

#### QUANTITATIVE RESTRICTIONS AND QUOTAS

Quantitative restrictions represent one of several policy instruments for dealing with problems of international trade and payments. Other instruments include tariffs on exports and imports, variations in the exchange rate, and monetary and fiscal policies.

In principle, restrictions can be placed on both current and capital transactions between countries. The transfer of capital, for example, can be controlled; this is a typical example of restrictions on capital account. This article will, however, focus on quantitative restrictions on *commodity trade* entering a country's current international accounts.

Construed in this way, quantitative restrictions represent the method of controlling foreign trade through quantitative specification of permissible imports (or exports). Hence these restrictions differ from tariff duties, which aim to control imports (or exports) by operating directly on the *price* at which commodities are imported (or exported).

Quantitative trade restrictions are imposed, in practice, on both exports and imports. However, those on exports are relatively rare. Recent examples are the quotas on exports (e.g., of cotton textiles) that Japan has applied to avoid the opprobrium of dumping and the quotas on certain agricultural exports (e.g., of oilseeds) that India has used to preserve internal supplies.

Import restrictions are imposed in a large number of ways. Where government purchases are involved, imports may be restricted without the need for any explicit licensing procedure. With private-sector imports, however, an import licensing system becomes inevitable.

Import licenses can take several forms. They may be stated in terms of value or in terms of physical quantity. There may, in addition, be an explicit over-all *quota* defining the maximum amount of the commodity permitted to enter the country during a specified period. Alternatively, licenses may be issued that specify particular quantities to be imported, without any over-all quota for the commodity. Frequently, all commodities are nominally put under import control, but some are permitted in automatically and without limit under a so-called open general license—as in the United Kingdom and India recently. In such cases licensing is not at all restrictive.

Import restrictions can be uniformly levied on all imports, or they can be discriminatory. The discrimination can be between different supplying *countries.* Alternatively, it may be between different *commodities.* These distinctions sometimes overlap, as when the discrimination is between two commodities each of which is exported by a different country. Indeed the practice of assigning quotas (as also tariffs) by detailed commodity categories has been criticized as an underhand method of evading most-favored-nation and nondiscrimination obligations. Import restrictions also discriminate frequently by *currency areas,* rather than by individual countries per se.

Import licenses are allocated to domestic importers in various ways, depending on convenience of administration and the economic objectives sought. Two steps are involved in the allocative process. The first is the classification of imports into different categories. Second, procedures have to be devised for allocating the permissible imports within each category to the various claimants.

The classifications vary from country to country. Thus one typical classification, used in India, divides import licenses into "established importers" (EI), "actual users" (AU), and "capital goods" (CG). Imports of consumer goods and spare parts require EI licenses, allocated to traders. Raw materials are imported through AU licenses, allocated to producers using them in their factories. Capital goods are imported through CG licenses, allocated to investors with approved projects.

The procedures for the actual allocation to the claimants *within* each category vary widely again. EI licenses may be allotted on the basis of previous shares of the traders; AU licenses, on the basis of respective production capacities. Allocations on the basis of "first come, first served" have been practiced, as in the United Kingdom (Hemming et al. 1959). Import licenses for raw materials and other goods are sometimes linked to resulting exports, as in India and Pakistan recently. Allocation by auction has been suggested—on the grounds of economic efficiency and revenue collection (Bhagwati 1962).

**History and present use.** The use of quantitative trade restrictions in international trade dates back to early times. However, since the original motivation in regulating trade appears to have been the collection of *revenue*, tariff levies on imports and exports preceded the rise of quantitative restrictions. Tariffs came to be supplemented significantly by quantitative trade restrictions when the objective of regulating trade became that of *protecting* domestic industries and improving the balance of payments.

While the use of restrictions diminished between 1750 and 1850, it was revived after World War I and intensified thereafter. Since World War II, however, the General Agreement on Tariffs and Trade (GATT) has attempted to turn the tide. In this, GATT has benefited from the similar objectives of the International Monetary Fund (IMF) with respect to exchange restrictions. (See Tew 1960 for contrasts and parallels between IMF and GATT rules concerning restrictions.) However, GATT's progress toward reduced restrictions has been halting thus far.

There are several reasons for this, most of them recognized by the GATT regulations themselves. Thus, while GATT forbids the use of quantitative restrictions—in article XI—it also explicitly makes provisions, in articles XII and XVIII:B, for their use under certain circumstances. Balance-of-payments difficulties must be cited to invoke either article, and article XVIII:B is applicable only to very low income countries. In addition, under article XVIII:C, the underdeveloped countries have the possibility of using quantitative restrictions to assist developing industries. (Also important in the early postwar years was article XIV, which permitted the use of restrictions against "scarce-currency" countries and by members going through a "transitional period." Today its importance is negligible.)

Needless to say, these articles, especially XII and XVIII:B, have been used continually. Besides, advanced countries have continued to use restrictions to protect domestic agriculture, contrary to GATT obligations. Moreover, nonmember countries frequently resort to restrictions.

As of the early 1960s, then, the use of restrictions is still considerable. On the one hand, the advanced countries have agreed to renounce use of restrictions as a regular practice, resorting to them only occasionally to ease severe balance-of-payments strains and more frequently (but with increasing difficulty) to protect domestic agricultural production. On the other hand, the majority of underdeveloped countries, with tight external accounts accompanying their planned developments, have maintained comprehensive import-control regimes, and there seems to be no sign of a change in this situation in the foreseeable future.

## Economic effects

The economic effects of quantitative restrictions have been analyzed in two distinct ways. One approach works out the effects of restrictions assuming that the balance of payments is always somehow kept balanced. This is the so-called *real* analysis. It deals with the question of the equivalence of, and differences between, tariffs and quotas and is basically an extension of tariff analysis, in the "pure" theory of international trade, to quota restrictions.

The other approach is more important from the practical point of view: it attempts to analyze quantitative restrictions as a policy instrument for handling balance-of-payments difficulties. The typical questions here concern the effectiveness of restrictions in correcting external deficits, both absolutely and in relation to devaluation and deflation. The desirability of *discriminatory* restrictions, which are frowned upon by IMF and GATT, has also been debated.

**Real analysis.** The real analysis is nearly always presented for import tariffs and quotas but applies equally, *mutatis mutandis*, to export tariffs and quotas. The analysis demonstrates that ad valorem tariffs and quotas have important similarities and differences.

Traditionally, the question is investigated in the framework of a partial-equilibrium model of a perfectly competitive industry. An ad valorem tariff will, generally speaking, restrict imports and raise revenue. If the tariff is prohibitively high, it will raise no revenue; if it does not restrict imports at all, it will merely raise revenue. Moreover, it is easily shown that, corresponding to every tariff rate, there is a *quota* that will produce *equivalent* results for the following variables: (1) domestic production of the imported commodity; (2) domestic price;

(3) foreign price; (4) domestic consumption; and (5) the quantity of imports. Consistent with this basic equivalence, in the sense defined, there is a well-known difference: a tariff raises revenue, whereas an equivalent quota does not. The revenue accrues as "monopoly" profit to the quota holders. This difference is clearly of importance.

But the foregoing proposition of equivalence holds only under perfectly competitive conditions in the import industry and breaks down if monopoly elements are introduced. For example, with a monopoly in domestic production, an import quota could well lead to a continuation of the internal monopoly. On the other hand, a tariff would permit imports freely at the tariff-inclusive price and, if the foreign supply is perfectly elastic, the domestic monopolist would eventually find himself in a perfectly competitive situation. Tariffs and quotas could thus lead to radically different market structures, and therefore equivalence, of the type obtaining under perfectly competitive assumptions, would not necessarily hold.

These propositions can be inferred from the current literature (e.g., Kindleberger 1953). A more systematic analysis of the equivalence proposition has recently been made, under alternative assumptions with respect to the market structure and allowing monopoly elements to obtain both in domestic production and in quota-holding, which underlines the crucial dependence of the equivalence proposition on the assumption of universally perfect competition (Bhagwati 1965).

**Balance-of-payments analysis.** The efficacy of quantitative import restrictions in reducing international deficits can be considered either in itself or in contrast to the effectiveness of other instruments of policy.

*Quantitative restrictions per se.* The primary effect of restrictions on imports is to cut imports. But there are secondary effects. The domestic expenditure, diverted from imports, will flow elsewhere. All of it may then cut into exports, leaving the original payments deficit unchanged. Secondary effects must therefore be carefully investigated.

Whether the *net* outcome of the primary and secondary effects can be expected to be favorable, in a specific case, is determined with reference to a proposition that forms the core of the newly developed absorption theory (Alexander 1952; Meade 1951). The proposition asserts that a balance-of-payments deficit reflects an excess of domestic investment over savings and hence any reduction in this deficit requires a reduction in domestic investment and/or an increase in domestic savings.

Thus, unless import restrictions lead to reduced investment or increased domestic savings, they cannot improve the balance of payments, and the secondary effect must necessarily offset the primary improvement. There are various ways in which import quotas may affect domestic savings and investment.

Savings can be affected, for example, in the following ways. (1) The restricted import of a commodity may result in "forced saving": expenditure may be held off in the expectation of reduction in restrictions in the near future; or there may be no adequate immediate substitute in consumption; or there may be a temporary time lag in shifting to alternative consumption. These arguments are plausible for "temporary" increases in saving; in the long run, consumption may be expected to readjust itself to the preceding level. (2) Alternatively, import restrictions may cause a shift of income toward profits (accruing to quota-holders). If there is a higher propensity to save by profit-earners than by others, there will be a rise in savings. (3) Counter to this runs the argument that the "distortion" caused by interference with the pattern of consumption can bring about a fall in real savings (via the fall in real income). (4) Even if none of the preceding possibilities holds and there is diversion of the *entire* expenditure from (prevented) imports to exportables and nontraded goods, additional savings can nonetheless be generated. This may happen, for example, if the indirect tax rates on the exportables, etc., are higher on the average than on the imports, thereby generating higher tax revenue than previously. (5) Alternatively, if the expenditure is shifted to nontraded goods, raising their prices under full employment, but the mobility of factors between exportable and nontraded goods is low, the (secondary) restrictive effect on the supply of exports would be less than the (primary) restrictive effect on imports. The reduced deficit would be attributable then to the "forced savings" in the nontraded goods sector. (6) Assume, however, that there is Keynesian underemployment. In this case, a shift in expenditure toward exportables and nontraded goods will have a multiplier effect on incomes, and if the marginal propensity to save is positive, domestic savings will increase, improving the balance of payments by the same amount (ruling out further repercussions through multiplier effects abroad).

Similarly, import restrictions could affect investment. (1) If the deficit is caused by inventory accumulation, quotas on raw material imports can well lead to inventory decline, that is, to reduced investment. (2) Similarly, if capital-goods imports are necessary to domestic investment, restrictions on them could affect domestic fixed investment.

Where, however, no such increase in domestic savings and/or reduction in domestic investment is possible, import restrictions will have to be accompanied by deflation in order to engineer an improvement in the balance of payments under conditions of full employment. Deflation alone will cause unemployment while correcting a deficit. A combination of import restrictions and deflation, on the other hand, will generally bring about both internal and external equilibrium—both full employment and balance in the international accounts. This is only a special case of Tinbergen's principle that $n$ instruments are, in general, necessary to achieve $n$ targets.

Restrictions have been analyzed, however, not merely from the viewpoint of their efficacy in reducing external deficits. Two interesting *welfare* questions have also been posed.

One relates to the *optimum* combination of deflation and import restrictions when the objectives are to achieve an assigned improvement in the balance of payments and to maximize the real income of the country, subject to the preceding constraint (Hemming & Corden 1958). Note that here maximization of real income replaces the achievement of full employment as an objective. Since deflation can produce less income (through reduced employment) and restrictions (through "distortions" in allocation of expenditure among commodities) can offset the income gain from improved terms of trade where relevant, the equilibrium condition naturally involves the equation of these two losses at the margin.

The other welfare question has been posed with respect to the use of *discriminatory* restrictions and relates *not* to national welfare but to *world welfare*. Although both IMF (by discouraging *exchange* restrictions in current accounts) and GATT (through article XIV) have set themselves against the use of discriminatory restrictions, theoretical opinion has continued to question this attitude from the viewpoint of world welfare. The classic articles of Frisch (1947; 1948) and Fleming (1951) have argued for discrimination and other writers (e.g., Tew 1960) have supported this case. Fleming's is the most persuasive argument, although based on assumptions of cardinal utility and interpersonal comparisons of welfare, since he formulates his analysis so as to maximize world *real income*, whereas Frisch rests his analysis largely on the debatable objective of maximizing world *trade*.

*Restrictions versus devaluation.* Although restrictions can be contrasted, in principle, with numerous alternative policy instruments, customarily the contrast is made between them and devaluation as methods of improving the balance of payments (Alexander 1951; Hemming & Corden 1958; Johnson 1958, chapter 6).

When the deficit is generated by "temporary" factors—such as a decision to shift from cash to inventory accumulation, an essentially "stock" decision (Johnson 1958)—restrictions and similar measures are naturally preferable to devaluation. Thus, in the example of inventory accumulation, restrictions can be chosen in such a way as to act directly on inventories, whereas a devaluation would start reorienting the economy's production and consumption decisions toward an external surplus. This orientation would then have to be *reversed* when the temporary change was itself reversed. Restrictions thus can avoid the costs of the far-ranging changes that devaluation implies.

On the other hand, when the deficit is of a "fundamental" nature—arising from a decision to consume more out of given income, an essentially "flow" decision (Johnson 1958)—the relative desirability of import restrictions or devaluation is more controversial. Most analysts resolve the issue by resorting to the equivalence of restrictions and ad valorem tariffs. They cite the optimum tariff argument, which admits tariffs under national monopoly power in trade, and then conclude that devaluation is a superior method of reducing deficits if the country has *already* placed optimum restrictions on trade (Johnson 1958). This view, however, rests on restrictive assumptions—for example, that the equivalence of tariffs and restrictions is universally valid.

Yet other arguments may favor restrictions. Destabilizing speculation, for example, is cited as a reason why devaluation is inferior (Tew 1960): a devaluation may destroy confidence in the currency's stability. On the other hand, the imposition of restrictions also may make speculators expect that a devaluation is on its way, so that devaluation is not necessarily inferior on such grounds. A more persuasive argument is that when a country's currency is being used as an international currency—as are the dollar and the pound sterling—devaluation could imperil the continuation of the system.

Perhaps the chief advantage of restrictions in correcting "flow" deficits consists in the *speed* with which they can work vis-à-vis devaluation, a difference of great importance to a country with hard-pressed reserves. The difference is easily explained.

Restrictions immediately curtail imports, while the substitution (and/or multiplier) effects inevitably involve time lags and thus cut into this favorable effect only later. On the other hand, devaluation depends on substitution effects for its effectiveness and hence takes time to improve the balance of payments. No formal models have yet been developed to examine this difference (and this is a serious lacuna in the analytical literature), but it can hardly be doubted that, in practice, governments are keenly conscious of it in their occasional resort to restrictions.

JAGDISH BHAGWATI

### BIBLIOGRAPHY

ALEXANDER, SIDNEY S. 1951 Devaluation Versus Import Restrictions as an Instrument for Improving Foreign Trade Balance. International Monetary Fund, *Staff Papers* 1:379–396.

ALEXANDER, SIDNEY S. 1952 Effects of a Devaluation on a Trade Balance. International Monetary Fund, *Staff Papers* 2:263–278.

BHAGWATI, JAGDISH 1962 Indian Balance of Payments Policy and Exchange Auctions. *Oxford Economic Papers* New Series 14:51–68.

BHAGWATI, JAGDISH 1965 On the Equivalence of Tariffs and Quotas. Pages 53–67 in *Trade, Growth, and the Balance of Payments: Essays in Honor of Gottfried Haberler.* Edited by Richard E. Caves, Harry G. Johnson, and Peter B. Kenen. Amsterdam: North-Holland Publishing; Chicago: Rand McNally.

CONTRACTING PARTIES TO THE GENERAL AGREEMENT ON TARIFFS AND TRADE 1951 *The Use of Quantitative Import Restrictions to Safeguard Balances of Payments: Incorporating the Second Report on the Discriminatory Application of Import Restrictions.* Geneva: The Contracting Parties.

CONTRACTING PARTIES TO THE GENERAL AGREEMENT ON TARIFFS AND TRADE 1959 *Review of Import Restrictions Under Articles XII: 4(b) and XVIII: 12(b).* Geneva: The Contracting Parties.

CONTRACTING PARTIES TO THE GENERAL AGREEMENT ON TARIFFS AND TRADE 1964 *The Role of GATT in Relation to Trade and Development.* Geneva: The Contracting Parties.

CORDEN, W. M. 1958 The Control of Imports: A Case Study; the United Kingdom Import Restrictions of 1951–1952. *Manchester School of Economic and Social Studies* 26:181–221.

CORDEN, W. M. 1960 The Geometric Representation of Policies to Attain Internal and External Balance. *Review of Economic Studies* 28:1–22.

FLEMING, J. M. 1951 On Making the Best of Balance of Payments Restrictions on Imports. *Economic Journal* 61:48–71.

FRISCH, RAGNAR 1947 On the Need for Forecasting a Multilateral Balance of Payments. *American Economic Review* 37:535–551.

FRISCH, RAGNAR 1948 Outline of a System of Multicompensatory Trade. *Review of Economics and Statistics* 30:265–271.

HAUSER, HEINRICH 1939 *Control of International Trade.* London: Routledge.

HEMMING, M. F. W.; and CORDEN, W. M. 1958 Import Restriction as an Instrument of Balance-of-payments Policy. *Economic Journal* 48:483–510.

HEMMING, M. F. W.; MILES, C. M.; and RAY, G. F. 1959 A Statistical Summary of the Extent of Import Control in the United Kingdom Since the War. *Review of Economic Studies* 26:75–109.

JOHNSON, HARRY G. 1958 *International Trade and Economic Growth: Studies in Pure Theory.* Cambridge, Mass.: Harvard Univ. Press.

KINDLEBERGER, CHARLES P. (1953) 1963 *International Economics.* 3d ed., rev. Homewood, Ill.: Irwin.

MEADE, JAMES EDWARD 1951 *The Theory of International Economic Policy.* Volume 1: Balance of Payments. Oxford Univ. Press.

NURKSE, RAGNAR 1956 The Relation Between Home Investment and External Balance in the Light of British Experience: 1945–1955. *Review of Economics and Statistics* 38:121–154.

SARGENT, J. R. 1957 Stocks and Quantitative Restrictions. Oxford, University of, Institute of Statistics, *Bulletin* 19:57–61.

TEW, BRIAN 1960 The Use of Restrictions to Suppress External Deficits. *Manchester School of Economic and Social Studies* 28:243–262.

VINER, JACOB 1934 Tariff. Volume 14, pages 514–523 in *Encyclopaedia of the Social Sciences.* New York: Macmillan.

## IV
## TRADE AGREEMENTS

Trade agreements broadly refer to commercial treaties and agreements between countries that deal mainly with customs duties and other treatment accorded by each party to goods originating in the other. They may be distinguished from treaties of friendship, commerce, and navigation, which deal more generally with economic relations among nations—such as the treatment of foreign investments, the rights of foreign nationals, and foreign shipping. In recent years, the term "trade agreement" has been applied more specifically to accords between two or more governments that provide for *reciprocal* reductions in specific customs duties, along with an agreement on other measures and policies affecting imports. Trade agreements may be bilateral or multilateral. However, the reader should be cautioned that the term "bilateral trade agreement" is frequently used to denote import quota agreements, which usually provide for a bilateral balancing of trade by means of import and export quotas and which have to be renegotiated after a short interval.

While certain elements of the modern reciprocal trade or tariff agreements are to be found in commercial treaties negotiated during the eighteenth and nineteenth centuries, probably the most important counterpart to the modern trade agreements is the Cobden–Chevalier Treaty of 1860 between Britain and France. Under this treaty, which was in effect until 1880, France reduced all prohibitions against English goods and lowered tariffs to a 30 per cent level until 1864 and thereafter to 24 per cent. Britain, in turn, admitted all French goods duty-free, except for wines and spirits. This treaty, which contained a most-favored-nation clause, served as a basis for similar treaties negotiated by France with several other European countries.

The United States had a limited experience with reciprocal tariff agreements from 1890 to 1909 under the authority provided by the McKinley Tariff Act of 1890 and the Dingley Tariff Act of 1897. Under the 1890 act, the president was authorized to negotiate concessions from other countries in return for continued duty-free treatment of certain of their products and was given the right to impose duties on these products as a bargaining weapon. Under the act of 1897, the president was authorized to negotiate, without congressional approval, concessions in return for the application of specified minimum rates on a few products; in addition, the president was empowered for the first time to negotiate agreements for general reciprocal tariff reductions on a limited scale and subject to congressional approval. While a few executive agreements were negotiated under both the 1890 and the 1897 tariff acts, no agreements requiring the consent of Congress received the approval of the Senate. The Tariff Act of 1909 repealed all of the reciprocity provisions of the previous legislation, and from that time until the passage of the reciprocal trade agreements amendment (to the Hawley–Smoot Tariff Act of 1930) which became law in June 1934, U.S. tariffs were not negotiable.

**The bilateral approach.** The 1934 reciprocal trade agreements amendment deserves special consideration not only because it embodied principles and procedures which had been developed in agreements among countries over a span of a hundred years or more, but also because many of its provisions and principles were reflected in the General Agreement on Tariffs and Trade (GATT) negotiated in 1947, which has become the instrument for multilateral tariff negotiations among the major countries of the world outside the Sino–Soviet bloc.

The 1934 reciprocal trade agreements amendment granted authority to the president to enter into foreign trade agreements with foreign governments "whenever he finds as a fact that any existing duties or other import restrictions of the United States or any foreign country are unduly burdening and restricting the foreign trade of the United States. . . ." In doing so he is permitted to "proclaim

such modifications of existing duties and other import restrictions, such additional import restrictions, or such continuance, and for such minimum periods, of existing customs or excise treatment of any article covered by foreign trade agreements." This authority was limited in that "no proclamation shall be made increasing or decreasing by more than 50 per centum any existing rate of duty or transferring any article between the dutiable and the free lists." Thus, the president had the power to change tariffs, within limits, by executive agreement with other countries, based on the principle of reciprocity in tariff relations. These procedures and principles were well grounded in the history of commercial agreements among countries, including the United States.

The 1934 amendment also explicitly provides for *unconditional* most-favored-nation treatment, since it states that when duties or other restrictions are once proclaimed they "shall apply to articles of growth, produce or manufacture of all foreign countries." While the *conditional* form and interpretation of most-favored-nation treatment was employed by the United States during the nineteenth century and in the early twentieth century, the Tariff Act of 1922 adopted the principle of equal commercial treatment, and from that time U.S. commercial treaties employed the unconditional form. In fact, by 1933, of the 625 most-favored-nation clauses in treaties and agreements the world over, only 8 per cent were phrased in the conditional form. Nevertheless, the 1934 law did provide certain flexibility in the application of the most-favored-nation clause. For example, the president was empowered to suspend the application of tariff concessions to countries discriminating against American commerce. Moreover, the provisions of the Anti-Dumping Act of 1921, as well as the provision for levying countervailing duties offsetting subsidies to exports granted by other countries, were continued under the 1934 law.

The use of the unconditional most-favored-nation form, together with the principle of more or less equal reciprocal advantage which the United States and other nations sought to achieve through bilateral negotiations, had a serious shortcoming. Each country tended to offer its initial and largest possible concession with respect to any particular commodity to the "principal foreign supplier" of that commodity, since to offer a concession to a minor supplier would be "giving away" an incommensurately reciprocated concession to the more important suppliers. This practice constituted a major limitation on bilateral negotiations which was partially remedied by the multilateral negotiations under the General Agreement on Tariffs and Trade adopted in 1947.

Following the passage of the 1934 reciprocal trade agreements amendment, the United States had concluded agreements with 21 countries by January 1, 1940. These provided for reductions or binding of tariffs accounting for 60 per cent of U.S. trade, with concessions being granted on more than a thousand rates and being received on some sixteen hundred rates. In addition, there were some reciprocal tariff agreements among other countries to which the United States was not a party but from which the United States gained certain uncompensated benefits as a consequence of the almost universal application of the unconditional most-favored-nation principle. However, after 1934, commercial agreements among other countries increasingly took the form of trade quota and payments agreements, as the practice of controlling trade by means of import quotas and exchange controls became more common.

The typical bilateral tariff agreement entered into by the United States contained a number of provisions in addition to those pertaining to the schedules of tariffs on which concessions were made. These provisions dealt with customs formalities, discriminatory treatment of foreign products and business enterprises within the negotiating countries, the use of import quotas, exchange controls, and other commercial policy matters. Most of these provisions had been included in commercial treaties among nations for many years. Moreover, these nontariff provisions affecting trade in commodities were, with certain modifications, embodied in the General Agreement on Tariffs and Trade of 1947.

**The multilateral approach.** Only a handful of bilateral tariff agreements were negotiated during World War II and the early postwar period, but the creation of permanent machinery for multilateral tariff negotiations and of an international agreement embodying commercial policy commitments constituted an important part of the postwar planning by the United States and its allies. The groundwork for the establishment of such institutional arrangements was laid in the course of the Anglo–American financial and trade discussions held in the fall of 1945, in the course of which the U.S. government published a document entitled *Proposals for Expansion of World Trade and Employment* (U.S. Department of State 1945) and the U.S. Secretary of State recommended the calling of an international conference on trade and employment by the UN in 1946. The U.S. proposals were discussed with the British representatives prior to

their publication and were agreed to in principle by the British as a part of the Anglo–American Financial and Commercial Agreement of December 1945 (for text, see "Anglo–American Trade . . ." 1946).

Early in 1946 a resolution was adopted by the Economic and Social Council of the United Nations that established a preparatory committee to draft an agenda for an international conference on trade and employment. Sessions of the preparatory committee were held in London, New York, and Geneva during 1946 and 1947, and a draft charter for an international trade organization was drawn up in Geneva in August 1947.

Simultaneously with the work of the preparatory committee in Geneva during the spring and summer of 1947, 23 countries participated in tariff negotiations. The bargaining was conducted on a product-by-product basis between pairs of countries, the products being confined to those for which one of the parties was the other's chief supplier. However, the simultaneous staging of the bilateral negotiations made it possible to broaden the bargaining on particular product duties to include concessions to countries other than the chief supplier. Thus, for example, country A would make a larger cut in its tariff which affected the exports of B, C, and D, provided the latter three countries each made various concessions on products of interest to A. This, indeed, is the advantage of simultaneous bargaining, which, although initially taking place on a bilateral basis under the chief supplier principle, at a later stage involves compensatory concessions by other suppliers of a particular product. The tariff reductions and bindings of existing rates, achieved as a consequence of these negotiations, were incorporated by the 23 contracting parties into a single document, the General Agreement on Tariffs and Trade, completed on October 30, 1947.

In addition to the lists of tariff concessions negotiated, the GATT included a number of general provisions with respect to the treatment of trade. By and large these provisions paralleled the rules adopted by the preparatory committee in the draft charter for an international trade organization. In addition to the principle of unconditional most-favored-nation treatment to be accorded to all contracting parties (which accounted for three-quarters of the world's trade before World War II), the provisions covered methods of customs administration, internal taxes and regulations, quotas and exchange controls, and the operation of state trading enterprises.

Part II of the General Agreement on Tariffs and

Trade, which contained general provisions relating to trade practices, was expected to be superseded by the charter of the International Trade Organization (ITO), which was negotiated in its final form at the UN Conference on Trade and Employment held in Havana from November 1947 to March 1948. On the other hand, GATT was a distinct instrument, recognized and referred to in the ITO charter, since it contained the schedule of tariff concessions which were negotiated at Geneva and which were to be expanded and altered from time to time in the course of subsequent negotiating meetings of the contracting parties. Also, it was expected that additional countries would become contracting parties to the GATT, but the advantages of membership, which included a guarantee of most-favored-nation treatment by other contracting parties, would be accorded only if the prospective members made tariff concessions to an extent regarded as satisfactory by the original 23 countries. It was expected that the general provisions of the GATT and the ITO charter would be parallel insofar as they dealt with matters concerned with the treatment of trade, and, in fact, certain changes were made in the Geneva protocol of the GATT at the Havana conference to conform with the ITO charter. However, the ITO charter was broader than the GATT since it established a trade organization and a secretariat with a special relationship to the UN and also provided for activities in the field of intergovernmental commodity agreements, restrictive business practices, and other matters not dealt with in the GATT.

The ITO never came into being, largely as a consequence of the failure of the U.S. Congress to approve the bill authorizing the president to accept membership on the part of the United States. However, the United States is a contracting party to the GATT by virtue of the authority of the president to negotiate agreements under the reciprocal trade agreements amendment. Nevertheless, the U.S. Congress has never specifically authorized or officially recognized U.S. membership in the contracting parties to the GATT. The contracting parties to the GATT continued to hold both tariff negotiating sessions and sessions dealing with problems arising out of operation of the agreement and proposals for amendments to the agreement. While the GATT has had a small secretariat with headquarters in Geneva, it has been hampered by the lack of a formal organizational structure and permanent legal status as an international organization. An attempt to remedy this shortcoming was made in 1955 by an agreement among the contracting parties on the establishment of an Organization for Trade Cooperation (OTC). However, the OTC never came into being; an administration bill authorizing U.S. membership was not submitted to the U.S. Congress.

*Constraints and escape provisions.* During the postwar period the president's authority to negotiate trade agreements has been extended and amended a number of times—beginning with the Trade Agreements Extension Act of 1945, which authorized decreases in rates of duties applicable to particular classifications of U.S. imports by not more than 50 per cent of the rates in effect on January 1, 1945. The Trade Agreements Extension Acts of 1955 and 1958 provided for additional rate reductions, while the Trade Expansion Act of 1962 (which was a new act and not simply an amendment to the Tariff Act of 1930) not only gave the president substantially increased rate-reducing authority but also established new principles for tariff bargaining which were especially suited for multilateral negotiations within the framework of the GATT.

While the president's rate-reducing authority was being expanded during the period prior to the 1962 act, the various amendments introduced several constraints on the application of tariff reductions to particular commodities. One of these checks on the president's power, which first appeared in the 1948 amendment, was the "peril point" provision. This required that the Tariff Commission survey all commodities on which the president proposed to negotiate agreements and that it specify rates of duty below which a threat of serious injury to U.S. industry would exist. In the event that the president reduced a rate below the peril point, he was required to communicate to the Congress his reasons for doing so.

A further check on the president's power was the "escape clause" requirement under which tariff concessions already granted could be withdrawn if they led to an increase in the quantity of imports (either in absolute amount or relative to the domestic market) such as to cause or threaten serious injury to U.S. industry. Procedures for escape clause action have been changed from time to time by congressional acts, but the 1958 act directed the Tariff Commission to make escape clause investigations "upon the request of the President, upon resolution of either House of Congress, upon resolution of either the Committee on Finance of the Senate or the Committee on Ways and Means of the House of Representatives, upon its own motion, or upon application of any interested party. . . ." If the Tariff Commission made a positive finding of injury and recommended an adjustment of rates of duty or the imposition of quotas, the president could accept or disapprove the recommendation, but, in the latter event, it still became effective when adopted by a two-thirds vote in each house of Congress.

Article XIX of the GATT provides for the withdrawal of a tariff concession if, as a result of unforeseen developments, there is such an increase in imports as to cause or threaten serious injury to domestic producers. The countries whose exports are affected by the withdrawal have the right to counterwithdrawals of concessions which have been granted in favor of imports from the country invoking article XIX. Hence, a large number of escape clause actions under article XIX could destroy the whole framework of concessions negotiated by the contracting parties in the course of the bargaining sessions because of the interdependent nature of the negotiating procedures and concessions. Fortunately, only a small number of concessions have actually been withdrawn by the contracting parties under the escape clause procedure. On the other hand, the continual threat of withdrawal of tariff concessions granted by the United States has constituted a barrier to the development of markets by foreigners in the United States.

*Nontariff provisions.*    If trade agreements dealt only with tariff concessions they would leave the way open for the parties to the agreement to nullify or impair the effects of the concessions by such actions as the imposition of import quotas and internal excise taxes, use of exchange controls or multiple exchange rates, a change in the procedures for valuation of the imported commodity for customs purposes, or other types of restrictive action. More importantly, the purpose of trade agreements, whether they be bilateral, or multilateral as in the case of the GATT, is to establish certain rules of fair trading practice which go beyond a concern for trade in the commodities on which tariff negotiations have been conducted.

Thus the GATT, which embodies many of the provisions typically found in bilateral trade agreements negotiated by the United States and other countries before 1947, contains, among others, provisions with respect to: (1) the avoidance of the use of internal taxes and other regulations applied to imported products so as to afford protection to domestic production; (2) freedom of transit of goods destined for another country across the territory of a contracting party; (3) standard rules regulating the conditions for the use of anti-dumping and countervailing duties; (4) regulations regarding the valuation of goods for customs purposes; (5) regulations with respect to the use of marks of origin to avoid their use as a means of unduly restricting imports; (6) the conditions under which import restrictions may be instituted to safeguard the balance of payments; (7) regulations for applying the rule of nondiscrimination in the use of import quotas, including exceptions to the rule; (8) regulations with respect to the use of export subsidies; (9) regulations governing state trading enterprises; (10) more lenient rules governing the use of protective devices employed by less developed countries; (11) special exceptions permitting the withdrawal of concessions or other actions arising from serious injury or the necessity of action for protecting national security interests; and (12) the conditions under which exceptions to the rules on nondiscrimination are permitted for countries forming customs unions or free trade areas.

This list is by no means exhaustive and some of the provisions of GATT are quite complex, such as the balance of payments exceptions to the rules on the use of import quotas, which were designed to parallel the relevant provisions found in the articles of agreement of the International Monetary Fund. The provisions regarding the use of quotas and other nontariff restrictions on trade in agricultural commodities constitute a broad exception designed to permit restrictions on imports of commodities under domestic price support programs (see amended text of the GATT in Contracting Parties to the General Agreement on Tariffs and Trade 1961).

*Limitations of product-by-product approach.*    The series of GATT tariff negotiations succeeded in reducing tariff rates on thousands of items and undoubtedly made a significant contribution to the expansion of international trade. However, by the late 1950s it had become clear to nearly all students of tariff bargaining that the principle of tariff negotiations on the basis of reciprocal gains to be achieved in bargaining on a product-by-product basis placed severe limitations on the potential liberalization of trade.

In part, the reason lay in the fact that negotiations with respect to individual products, which in the case of the United States were subject to the restrictions of both the peril point and the escape clause provisions of the Trade Agreements Acts, focused attention on injury to the domestic producers of these products and therefore left little room for further bargaining on a no-serious-injury basis. Actually the determination of the restrictive impact of tariffs on particular items and the quantitative effect of given tariff reductions on imports is extremely difficult. It is impossible to devise means of predicting the effects of a tariff reduction over a period of, say, five to ten years because of long-run shifts in demand and supply conditions. For example, the impact of the U.S. tariff reductions on certain manufactures in the early postwar period was deemed to be small at the time but may have been significant in 1963 after a substantial growth in U.S. imports of most categories of manufactures. Likewise, the value of concessions received in terms of the impact on exports cannot be projected with any degree of accuracy, at least beyond the first couple of years. Trade patterns are in the main determined by forces far more powerful than those exerted by a few percentage point changes in tariff rates.

In addition, the creation of the European Economic Community (EEC) in 1959 and the expectation that the six original members would be expanded to include all or most of the countries of western Europe, along with the possibility of other such regional trading groups, presented the prospect of very large free trading areas which discriminated in most products against the rest of the world. The only way to modify or eliminate such discrimination would be through extensive, across-the-board tariff reductions toward zero.

The product-by-product approach to reciprocity in tariff bargaining may also be criticized on theoretical grounds since the ultimate gains for a country arise from a general lowering of world trade barriers and not from an attempt to match import concessions on specific products against equivalent concessions by other countries. Consumers in all countries gain from a lowering of tariffs while, given flexibility of resources, all producers should gain directly or indirectly from a broadening of international markets.

**Linear reductions.** In recognition of both the practical and theoretical limitations of product-by-product bargaining, even within the framework of multilateral negotiations, the Kennedy administration proposed new legislative authority which was embodied in the U.S. Trade Expansion Act of 1962. This act broadened the power of the president, not only to negotiate additional percentage cuts in existing rates but also to reduce rates on categories of commodities without regard to bilateral reciprocity. The act also gave authority to reduce to zero the duties on tropical agricultural or forestry products not produced in significant quantities in the United States and on which the EEC had made significant import concessions. This broader authority, together with a new approach to the problem of injury, set the stage for tariff bargaining on a basis of "linear," or across-the-board, percentage cuts on broad categories of commodities, of up to

50 per cent on nearly all commodities and even larger cuts for certain commodities. According to the 1962 act, a finding of injury on the part of the Tariff Commission may, if accepted by the president, result in a decision by the president to impose an import restriction or to invoke the adjustment assistance provisions of the act. Such adjustment assistance may take the form, in the case of firms, of technical, financial, or tax assistance, and in the case of workers, of supplementary unemployment compensation, retraining assistance, or relocation allowances. In addition, the 1962 act greatly modified the restrictions placed on the president arising from the peril point provisions of the 1958 and earlier acts. The president is still required to submit a proposed negotiating list to the Tariff Commission, but instead of the commission's being required to set specific tariff points below which injury is likely to result, the 1962 act provides that the commission may present an analysis of the strengths and weaknesses of the industries that might be affected by tariff action. There are only a few commodities that are exempt from negotiation by statute under the 1962 act, principally the handful of commodities which previously had been subject to escape clause action.

The movement toward negotiations for linear tariff reduction, a practice widely employed by countries in the process of forming customs unions or free trade areas, met with considerable difficulty in the course of the GATT preparatory discussions for the tariff negotiations beginning in May 1964. The U.S. proposed a common percentage cut (as much as 50 per cent in most cases) in the U.S. tariff schedules covering most commodities, in the EEC common tariffs, and in the tariff schedules of most other industrialized countries. The EEC members took the position that allowance should be made for disparities in tariff rates—that a 50 per cent cut in an ad valorem tariff rate of 30 per cent should not be regarded as equivalent to a 50 per cent cut in an ad valorem rate of 10 per cent. At the time of writing, an acceptable compromise formula, which would take into account substantial disparities in rates, has not been reached among the contracting parties to the GATT.

**Further problems.** There were other issues facing the contracting parties prior to the 1964 tariff negotiations in Geneva which may require a change in the previous principles and procedures in bargaining on tariffs and other trade restrictions. There was, first of all, the existence of the EEC itself, which was moving rapidly toward a complete customs union with a common external tariff wall and a common policy for many agricultural products. The maintenance of agricultural prices within the EEC by means of variable levies on imports has greatly complicated the problem of tariff negotiations on such products with countries outside the EEC. It seems likely that international commodity agreements involving import quotas will be necessary to guarantee a share in the common market to traditional exporters of grains and certain other temperate zone products. Also, the negotiation by the EEC of preferential agreements with former African territories of the EEC members has resulted in serious discrimination against the products of Latin American and Asiatic countries and of African countries which were former British territories. In addition, nearly all less developed countries have requested preferential treatment for their exports to the industrialized countries as a means of promoting their exports (see United Nations Conference on Trade and Development 1964). These developments have weakened the application of the traditional most-favored-nation principle.

Economists have traditionally argued in favor of the most-favored-nation principle as a means of maximizing the gains from trade and of achieving an optimum allocation of world resources. On the other hand, some economists have challenged the traditional argument against preferential tariff treatment on the grounds that preferential treatment may simply serve to correct other disparities in the market or enable less developed countries to achieve economies of scale by expanding output [see INTERNATIONAL TRADE CONTROLS, *article on* TARIFFS AND PROTECTIONISM]. James E. Meade (1955, pp. 110–111) has argued that, contrary to the traditional approach to customs unions and that which is embodied in the GATT, a partial reduction of duties on imports from regional trading partners is more likely to increase welfare than is a complete removal of restrictions on trade within the preference area.

*Unilateral reduction.* It has been suggested that tariff reducing negotiations might be eliminated entirely in favor of unilateral reductions by individual countries, since countries will gain from a reduction of import barriers whether or not there is a reciprocal reduction of barriers to their exports. There are several answers to this argument. Perhaps the most significant one is that a country with a very large trade should use its bargaining power as a means of getting other countries to reduce their trade barriers. There is also the political argument that, because of sectoral losses, a government cannot easily reduce its tariffs unilaterally without obtaining an offsetting concession from other coun-

tries—even though such a unilateral tariff reduction might increase a country's total welfare. Finally, the welfare gains from unilateral tariff reductions are not always easy to prove. If imports increase without an expansion of exports, some shift in resources must take place if balance of payments equilibrium is to be maintained. Currency devaluation may thus be necessary to maintain equilibrium. But devaluation may have an adverse impact on the country's terms of trade, whereas if equilibrium is maintained by a reduction in import barriers abroad, an adverse reaction on terms of trade need not occur. Also, the effects of devaluation on the volume and pattern of a country's trade —that is, whether the major impact is on increasing exports or reducing imports—cannot be accurately predicted, but presumably both imports and exports will be affected. Thus, when countries engage in unilateral tariff reductions the prospective increase in trade, after taking into account the effects of actions for maintaining the trade balance, must be measured against any possible adverse welfare effects resulting from changes in the terms of trade.

If all countries were convinced that a general liberalization of trade would redound to their benefit, directly or indirectly, then a gradual, multilateral reduction of barriers in accordance with some universal formula would clearly be the best approach. Unfortunately, such a mutually acceptable formula for effective trade liberalization has not, as yet, been developed.

RAYMOND F. MIKESELL

### BIBLIOGRAPHY

*Anglo–American Trade and Financial Negotiations.* 1946 [U.S.] Board of Governors of the Federal Reserve System, *Federal Reserve Bulletin* 32:14–19.

BILLINGS, ELDEN E. 1963a *The European Common Market: A Basic List of Recent References.* Washington: Library of Congress, Legislative Reference Service.

BILLINGS, ELDEN E. 1963b *The General Agreement on Tariffs and Trade (GATT): Selected References, 1952–1963.* Washington: Library of Congress, Legislative Reference Service.

BROWN, WILLIAM A. 1950 *The United States and the Restoration of World Trade: An Analysis and Appraisal of the ITO Charter and the General Agreement on Tariffs and Trade.* Washington: Brookings Institution.

CATUDAL, HONORÉ M. 1961 The General Agreement on Tariffs and Trade: An Article-by-article Analysis in Layman's Language. U.S. Department of State, *Bulletin* 44:1010–1020; 45:35–42.

CONTRACTING PARTIES TO THE GENERAL AGREEMENT ON TARIFFS AND TRADE 1961 *The General Agreement on Tariffs and Trade (Text as Amended).* U.S. Department of State, Publication No. 7182. Washington: Government Printing Office. → Originally signed in 1947.

CULBERTSON, W. S. 1931 *Commercial Treaties*. Volume 4, pages 24–31 in *Encyclopaedia of the Social Sciences*. New York: Macmillan.

CURZON, GERARD (1965) 1966 *Multilateral Commercial Diplomacy: The General Agreement on Tariffs and Trade and Its Impact on National Commercial Policies and Techniques*. New York: Praeger.

FICKER, HERMANN 1962 *Reciprocal Trade Agreements Act and Tariffs: A Bibliography*. Washington: Library of Congress, Legislative Reference Service.

HAWKINS, HARRY C. 1951 *Commercial Treaties and Agreements: Principles and Practice*. New York: Rinehart.

ISAACS, ASHER 1948 *International Trade Tariff and Commercial Policies*. Chicago: Irwin. → See especially pages 243–281, "The Present Tariff of the United States."

JOHNSON, H. G. 1967 *Economic Policies Toward Less Developed Countries*. Washington: Brookings Institution.

KELLY, WILLIAM B. (editor) 1963 *Studies in United States Commercial Policy*. Chapel Hill: Univ. of North Carolina Press.

MEADE, JAMES E. 1955 *The Theory of Customs Unions*. Amsterdam: North-Holland Publishing.

MIKESELL, RAYMOND F. 1952 *United States Economic Policy and International Relations*. New York: McGraw-Hill. → See especially Chapter 6, "United States Commercial Policy" and Chapter 7, "Postwar Developments in United States Commercial Policy."

NATIONAL PLANNING ASSOCIATION, INTERNATIONAL COMMITTEE 1962 *Foreign Trade and Foreign Policy: A Statement by the NPA International Committee and a Report by Howard S. Piquet*. Washington: The Association.

PATTERSON, GARDNER 1966 *Discrimination in International Trade; the Policy Issues: 1945–1965*. Princeton Univ. Press.

UNITED NATIONS CONFERENCE ON TRADE AND DEVELOPMENT, GENEVA, *1964* 1964 *Proceedings*. Volume 1: Final Act and Report. New York: United Nations.

UNITED NATIONS CONFERENCE ON TRADE AND EMPLOYMENT, HAVANA, *1947–1948* 1948 *Havana Charter for an International Trade Organization and Final Act and Related Documents*. U.S. Dept. of State, Publication No. 3117. Washington: Government Printing Office.

U.S. CONGRESS, SENATE, COMMITTEE ON COMMERCE 1961 *The United States and World Trade; Challenges and Opportunities: Final Report of the Committee on Commerce*. 87th Congress, 1st Session, Senate Report No. 446. Washington: Government Printing Office.

U.S. DEPARTMENT OF STATE 1945 *Proposals for Expansion of World Trade and Employment*. U.S. Dept. of State, Publication No. 2411. Washington: Government Printing Office.

WILCOX, CLAIR 1949 *A Charter for World Trade*. New York: Macmillan.

## V

### STATE TRADING

There is difficulty in defining state trading precisely. At one extreme are corporations wholly owned by the state, with import or export monopoly privileges for certain commodities, such as India's State Trading Corporation; at the other are licensing, tax, and subsidy arrangements, often exercised in connection with an official monopoly of foreign exchange, which, while leaving individual transactions completely to the initiative of private parties, nevertheless sensitively impose the objectives of the state on each foreign trade transaction. Somewhere between these extremes are trading corporations only partially owned by governmental bodies, marketing boards in which government and private representatives join in controlling the trade, and government bodies which, while effecting no foreign transactions themselves, constitute such important sources of supply or demand for their national markets that they in fact control foreign trade. Examples of the last type of arrangement are the marketing organizations in the Federal Republic of Germany which have been in recent times the sole legal domestic purchasers of privately imported foodstuffs. The Grain Equalization Board of Austria is in a similar position. And only one step removed from these agencies, in form of operation, is the Commodity Credit Corporation in the United States.

The line between official and private cartels is often an arbitrary one except, perhaps, for the potentialities for public control. Official export boards for Danish butter and bacon, for example, upon shedding their official status in 1950, promptly reorganized as private monopolies.

On the basis that usage distinguishes state trading from other forms of government commercial regulation, it is reasonable to say that an agency engaged in state trading (1) must be actually executing individual trade transactions with foreigners (including taking title to the goods at some point), or have decisive influence on individual transactions executed by others, and (2) must be governed by decisions actually or potentially dominated by government officials.

The definition includes purchases by the state for the execution of such traditional functions as the establishment of diplomatic representation and military forces. It may also encompass official transactions in gold and foreign currencies. [*For discussion of state trading among countries within the communist bloc, see* COMMUNISM, ECONOMIC ORGANIZATION OF, *article on* INTERNATIONAL TRADE.]

Extensive state trading in peacetime has developed only since 1930. It is partly a legacy of the depression of the 1930s and of World War II. It has since spread under the stimulus of trade offers by communist countries and as a result of planning for economic growth in less developed regions.

**Quantitative significance.** Assessment of the quantitative significance of state trading is hampered by the imprecision of the term and by data inadequacies. It is probable, however, that if the activities of the Commodity Credit Corporation of the United States, those of national marketing boards everywhere, and trade between the communist bloc and the rest of the world are included, the proportion of world trade in which buyer or seller was an agent of the state was as much as 15–20 per cent in 1964. For some countries, of course, the proportion is much higher. The United Nations Economic Commission for Asia and the Far East (1964, p. 7) estimated that 70–80 per cent of Burmese exports and 30–50 per cent of imports were handled by state agencies in the early 1960s. The percentage of state-traded imports in Ceylon was put at 25–30, in India 40–50, and in Pakistan 30–50. China (Taiwan) was said to state-trade 60–70 per cent of its exports and Indonesia 45 per cent. Most European countries engage in state trading to some degree, and in France the list of state-imported commodities in 1962 included grains and flour, alcohol, tobacco and tobacco manufactures, sugar, oil seeds, fruit, vegetable oil, certain dairy products, solid mineral fuels, petroleum and petroleum products, electric power, gas, newsprint, and matches.

Agricultural commodities bulk largest among state-traded commodities. Rice trade, for example, was conducted by the government in 8 of 16 exporting countries and 8 of 15 importing countries in 1962. At the same time wheat was sold through national marketing boards in two of the four largest exporting countries (Canada and Australia) and exported from the United States with the aid of the Commodity Credit Corporation. In Europe, bread grains or grains in general have been purchased for a number of years through state agencies in France, the Federal Republic of Germany, Italy, Norway, Finland, and Turkey.

Manufactured and semiprocessed goods also appear in state trading. A number of less developed countries import capital equipment through state-controlled organizations (e.g., India and the United Arab Republic). Government participation in production as well as international trade is common in petroleum and petroleum products. Drugs and pharmaceuticals are imported by state agencies in a number of countries, and in Norway fishing equipment is state-imported. Coal and solid fuels are government-controlled in France and the United Kingdom. Alcohol is frequently a government monopoly, as are tobacco and tobacco products.

Even some services are subject to state trading. Many governments offer export loans, or export credit guarantees, or other financial services; and international transportation services—rail, ship, and air—together with radio and wire communica-

tions, are frequently furnished by government corporations.

**History.** State trading in a narrow sense is a modern phenomenon in the West. Although in ancient times trade in the Mediterranean region usually was strictly regulated and in some cases officially suppressed, it seems to have been conducted by private merchants for their own account. While trade and politics were tightly knit in the Italian city-states at their zenith, as they were in the north European commercial leagues of cities of the Renaissance, the actual timing and terms of individual foreign transactions in both these circumstances were still the prerogative of the private trader. The overseas joint stock companies of seventeenth-century Europe, although not agencies of the state, held state-granted monopolies in the trade with specific regions and are perhaps the most direct antecedents of modern state trading institutions. In the Orient, state trading existed in the seventeenth century and is probably much older than that.

World War I introduced extensive twentieth-century state trading. In the United States, shipping and the railways were requisitioned. Allied governments organized official purchasing missions, and there was some official preclusive buying. In the decade following the war this "interventionism" was reduced, but the depression of the 1930s brought pressures to find outlets for exports and to minimize the foreign exchange cost of imports. A number of the present commodity marketing boards and importing authorities have their roots in this period. World War II brought a reestablishment of purchasing missions and corporations for preclusive buying. The United Kingdom's Ministry of Food favored bulk-purchase transactions and spawned a number of national marketing boards, such as those still functioning in Australia and New Zealand.

**Objectives.** The purposes which motivate the creation or maintenance of state trading agencies in the present are varied. The chief aim of some agencies is to effect trade with communist bloc countries. State trading by the governments of Cambodia, Vietnam, and China (Taiwan) has been at one time or another an arrangement for receiving and accounting for United States aid. In the Philippines and Indonesia, state importing of consumer goods is aimed partly at favoring nationals over foreigners in retail and wholesale trade. The United Arab Republic imports through public enterprises to ensure conformity of foreign trade with the national development plan and to protect against illicit capital exports in the form of commodities. Food products are widely imported through government monopolies to ensure "reasonable" supplies and prices. And state monopolies for alcohol and drugs aim in part at the protection of public health. The most common motivation for state trading, however, is the desire to improve the national terms of trade through the elimination of private competition for foreign supplies or markets. Marketing boards may have as further purposes the standardization of quality and the fostering of production. The objectives of state trading organizations are usually multiple and shift from time to time as government policies are reformulated.

**Organization.**   The marketing board, directed by producer representatives but subject to ministerial authority, is the common form of export monopoly in the British Commonwealth. Elsewhere, the semi-autonomous, limited liability, public corporation, which may or may not have the same legal status as private corporations, predominates. In countries with extensive state trading, a mixture of forms is likely to be found, including purchasing missions, marketing boards, wholly and partially owned government corporations, government departments, and committees. A given agency may receive regular financing through ministerial budgets, be privileged to borrow from the national treasury or on the open market with government guarantee, or be dependent upon its own resources. Typically the origin of an agency is *ad hoc* and is a construction from pre-existing organizational facilities. The legal immunities of state trading entities from taxes and from suit in the courts vary from country to country and are not well established in international law.

**Economic effects.**   A not uncommon pairing of state objectives is to improve the country's international terms of trade and to raise public revenue by taxing exports. Consider the effects of a monopoly exporter seeking to obtain the greatest difference between export receipts and domestic cost. Such a monopoly maximizes profit by limiting exports until the marginal cost of its domestic purchases equals the marginal revenue of its export sales. In such a case, foreign production tends to be stimulated and foreign consumption retarded, while in the home market production tends to be retarded and consumption stimulated. An import monopoly's effects are similar but opposite in direction in the foreign and domestic markets when it acts to maximize profits. Where an import monopoly fails to charge the maximum price obtainable for supplies made available to the domestic market, "shortages" will appear which may necessitate rationing. Similarly, when an export monopoly restricts its sales without depressing domestic

prices, production or marketing controls may be necessary.

Monopolies may pay a premium for imports or subsidize exports as a form of foreign aid, as a device to sustain production and employment, or as a device of economic warfare. The form in which the national cost of these acts is distributed depends upon the agency's domestic pricing policies and sources of financing.

An agency may hold inventories and use them to buffer disparities of demand and supply within a given price range. Or it may act as a stabilizing financial fund, minimizing domestic price movements. The latter policy, however, carried out without limitations on domestic production or consumption and without buffering inventory adjustments, retards purchases or sales abroad when these transactions are most advantageous and stimulates them when prices are disadvantageous. Monopolistic traders may discriminate in the terms offered in each transaction and may discriminate continuously between markets that cannot be joined.

When state monopolies as sellers deal with monopolistic buyers, or several state monopolies constitute a market, the probable terms of the resulting transactions cannot be specified on the basis of economic theory [*see* MONOPOLY]. Such powers as a selling monopoly has depend upon the extent to which local production, or the resources employed in production, can be otherwise utilized in case foreign sales are restricted; the extent to which the foreign buyer has capabilities for duplicating the product or dispensing with it in consumption; and the expansibility of production and contractability of consumption in third countries. A country in a strong bargaining position may exact concessions by cessation or threat of cessation of trade. Monopoly powers tend to weaken with exercise, however, as a result of substitution by oppressed parties.

The theoretical case against monopoly in economic analysis has been diluted since the 1950s by a sharper understanding of forms of imperfect competition, by criticism of the nature of the welfare optimum obtainable in competitive static equilibrium, and by interest in the process of economic growth. In particular, the "theory of the second best," according to which, when one of the conditions for an optimum is denied, the remaining conditions for that optimum are no longer necessarily desirable even when obtainable, undermines the attack on countervailing monopoly. State trading organizations, in some circumstances, may accelerate progress in less developed countries, although their contribution to this end is by no means axiomatic.

**International control.** International agreements calling for the reduction of tariffs, the elimination of quantitative trade restrictions, and application of the most-favored-nation principle have considerably less significance when applied to countries with national trade monopolies than when enforced as rules of behavior for governments where markets are competitive. Private enterprise countries have therefore sought, without great success, a formula which would exact from countries with state trading enterprises commitments equivalent in effect to pledges of nondiscriminatory import liberalization.

In bilateral treaties of the 1930s, two approaches predominated. One required the state-trading country to purchase specified values of goods per annum in the agreement-partner country in return for most-favored-nation tariff treatment. The other, sometimes used as a supplement to the first, bound the state-trading nation to follow "commercial and financial considerations."

The loose commitment to follow "commercial considerations" has been repeated in the General Agreement on Tariffs and Trade (GATT). The GATT agreement, furthermore, notes that it is "of importance" for member countries to negotiate reductions of trade obstacles and requires that import monopolies report their price markups (art. XVIII). Article II.4 strictly forbids an import monopoly to apply such markups "so as to afford protection on the average" in excess of that negotiated in the tariff schedules.

The pledges contained in the GATT to conduct state trading without discrimination or domestic market protection are not entirely satisfactory. Similarly, suitable treatment of the possibility of dumping by state agencies has not been found. Discrimination, or lack of it, in purchasing and selling policies is extremely difficult to prove. Furthermore, a state entity is following "commercial principles" when it purchases and sells where and when its bargaining power is greatest. And in wholly planned economies, domestic prices and exchange rates have uncertain meaning.

**Trends.** State trading currently waxes in less developed countries while waning in the more developed ones. Although support for agriculture in the industrialized countries shows little sign of abatement, the organizational forms are in transition. The liquidation of the United Kingdom Ministry of Food eliminated the largest state trading organ in western Europe, and the Common Agricultural Policy of the European Economic Com-

munity intends to substitute a system of import levies for national trading organizations. The end of the Argentine Trade Promotion Institute took from Latin America its largest state trader, but in Africa and Asia state trading is increasing. Unfortunately, state trading is infectious, each monopoly appearing to justify a countervailing one.

J. CARTER MURPHY

BIBLIOGRAPHY

CONTRACTING PARTIES TO THE GENERAL AGREEMENT ON TARIFFS AND TRADE 1964 *The Role of GATT in Relation to Trade and Development.* Geneva: The Contracting Parties.

GENERAL AGREEMENT ON TARIFFS AND TRADE 1963 State Trading Enterprises: Notifications Pursuant to Article XVII 4(*a*). L/1949/Add. 1–26. Unpublished documents. → The most adequate single source of current data, these are unpublished documents representing government responses to a GATT questionnaire. Resolutions of the Contracting Parties call upon governments to respond fully to the questionnaire every third year after 1963 and to give annual notification of state trading measures.

HAWKINS, HARRY C. 1951 *Commercial Treaties and Agreements: Principles and Practice.* New York: Rinehart.

State Trading. 1959 *Law and Contemporary Problems* 24:241–528. → The entire issue is devoted to state trading.

UNITED NATIONS, ECONOMIC COMMISSION FOR ASIA AND THE FAR EAST 1964 *State Trading in Countries of the ECAFE Region.* New York: United Nations. → A general analysis with country studies.

VINER, JACOB 1943 *Trade Relations Between Free-market and Controlled Economies.* Geneva: League of Nations.

# INTERNMENT AND CUSTODY

Most societies have institutionalized custodial arrangements. These involve restraining some persons from exercising various freedoms enjoyed by ordinary members of that society, particularly freedom of movement but also freedom of social intercourse or privacy and autonomy in the choice and scheduling of activities.

It is difficult to form a universal, absolute definition of terms such as internment, imprisonment, captivity, confinement, or custody, because almost all members of any social order are held captive, in some degree, to locales, groupings, and activities by various powerfully restraining moral forces and ultimate sanctions. While custody statuses are clearly apparent at their oppressive extremes, such as punitive solitary confinement, only marginal, nominal, and subjective discriminations delimit many such states from others that we are more inclined to label as segregation, isolation, ostracism, or vertical status differentiation.

Internment statuses can be defined by reference to the special definitions placed on some persons relative to others by an authority, a group consensus, or the observational standpoint taken by the student of the particular social scene, but they cannot be defined in absolute, objective terms. For example, an observer may be able to detect only marginal objective differences between the freedoms possessed by the soldiers in the barracks and those of the prisoners in the guardhouse, but the social and subjective significance of the status differences may be vast. The life conditions of prisoners exiled to Siberia under both tsars and Bolsheviks in many instances objectively differed not at all from those of free laborers in the same areas. Penitentiary trusties, prisoners of war, and high-status persons under house arrest frequently are unguarded. Individuals can commit themselves voluntarily to mental hospitals. By entering cloistered orders, persons may be subjecting themselves to closer confinement and more rigid prescription of their activities than inmates of some "maximum security" prisons. The degree of restriction, the nature and intensity of coercion, and the volitional element each provides only partial and relative bases for identifying the social nature of custodial statuses.

**Functional considerations.** Custodial arrangements may serve a variety of latent and manifest functions that require the isolation or special control of individuals. These functions include punishment; insulation of persons perceived as posing a threat of injury to the group or contamination of it; facilitating either material or social exploitation; psychological manipulation directed toward personality change; marking ritual transitions to other statuses; symbolic affirmation or display of the lost or degraded status of the captive; or simply provision of a limbo state for human beings to whom the controlling group can ascribe no other appropriate status. Imprisonment also may be a way station to execution.

From the evolutionary point of view, institutionalized custody becomes increasingly important as a mode for performing these functions as social and cultural organization becomes more complex. For example, slavery has tended to develop only in relatively complex agricultural societies; the hostage is not typical of primitive forms of warfare; political imprisonment is a phenomenon of the state; and the concentration camp is a nineteenth-century innovation. As social orders become large and complex, killing and avoidance of contact become less adequate as mechanisms appropriate to the increasing number of situations that require dealing with the deviant member of the in-group, the stranger-enemy, or the social "non-person"; converting humans into exploitable resources; reshaping the egos and social identifications of persons to fit transformed social arrangements; or removing from the general social arena those who do not fit.

Certain internment and custody institutions have been particularly problematic to modern civilization and consequently are the subjects of highly developed and specialized fields of inquiry: slavery, the penitentiary, and the mental institution. However, this article will be concerned primarily with other forms of internment and custody that are associated with warfare and political domination. Although these custody arrangements do not form a well-defined, traditional subject matter, such as that of slavery, prisons, and mental institutions, they have nevertheless been important subjects of attention in the development of social thought and science.

## The prisoner of war

The status of the war captive poses a problem that has played an important role in the development of nationalism, international law, and humanitarianism. It was not long ago that writers on the evolution of international law and custom regarding prisoners of war could view the past as a record of continually more enlightened and humane practices (Spaight 1911). Progress from barbarity to humanitarianism was the organizing principle of the typical pre-World War II discussion of war captives, such as that of Trimble (1934). He traced a development from ancient to recent times in which the prevalent procedures changed successively from extermination, to enslavement, to ransom, and finally to regularized exchange and parole practices. Through much of history, war prisoners were regarded very much as were other spoils of war—booty to be destroyed, sold, or exploited at the pleasure of the individual soldier or chieftain who seized them. The increasing domination of the central state brought about a shift in the control of prisoners from the individual captor to the sovereign and a consequent regularizing of the economic exploitation of war captives for labor or ransom.

The final development of what three decades ago could be called the "modern view" is attributed by Trimble to the influence of Montesquieu, Rousseau, and Vattel. As amplified by Rousseau in his *Social Contract* (book 1, chapter 4), this view asserted: "War is . . . a relation between state and state in which individuals are enemies only accidentally." Soldiers are enemies while they are bearing arms, but according to Rousseau, "as soon as they lay them down and surrender . . . they become once more merely men whose life no one has any right to take" (Rousseau 1762, as quoted in Trimble 1934, p. 420).

These views became increasingly incorporated into and elaborated in legal theory and in agreements between nations, beginning in 1785 with a treaty between the United States and Prussia. Both in this beginning and in the subsequent attempt at codification by Francis Lieber at the direction of President Lincoln, the United States played a prominent role in the development of humanitarian legal doctrine concerning prisoners and internees. A series of international conventions embodied developing versions of these doctrines. These were formulated by conferences at Brussels in 1874, The Hague in 1899 and 1907, Copenhagen in 1917, and Geneva in 1929 and 1949.

The major principles of these agreements were as follows. First, the prisoner was defined as in the power of the government that held him, rather than of the individuals who were his immediate captors. Second, the captor government was responsible for the safety, humane treatment, food, quarters, clothing, etc. of prisoners, with the standards of well-being of the captor nation's troops as the measure of the adequacy of provisions. Third, the prisoners were to be insulated ("quarantined," in the words of Prugh 1956) from participation in the war; this included guarantees against their exploitation by the captor for war-related functions, while allowing for their secure detention or their parole under obligation not to reassume arms. Finally, the prisoners were assigned certain duties to the captor, including providing true identification of themselves and their rank (age being added by the 1949 Geneva Convention) and abiding by international law and by rules for their detention established by the captor power.

Some ambiguity remained regarding conflict stemming from the assumed patriotic duty and motivation of the captive. Two major areas of continuing conflict between captor and captive were recognized. The first was the prisoner's obligation to escape and to rejoin his own forces if he could overcome the captor's security measures. This right was recognized, and the punishment of recaptured escapees was narrowly restricted by these agreements. The agreements also recognized that a similar game would be played in the area of interrogating prisoners for military information. It was regarded as unrealistic to attempt to prohibit the captor from questioning prisoners for intelligence purposes, but all forms of "mental and physical duress" to elicit intelligence information were forbidden by the agreement of the Geneva Convention in 1949.

The history of actual prisoner treatment during the century that saw the development and acceptance of these legal doctrines showed largely a record of deviation from these theories. In almost all wars public attitudes toward the enemy of the moment were not as benign as they were toward the symbols of humanity that were considered in formulating these international doctrines. The urgencies, shortages, disorganization, and emotions of warfare made deviations the rule rather than the exception, even when governments felt that both morality and self-interest urged abiding by the legal doctrines. With a few exceptions, such as Japanese treatment of Russian prisoners during the Russo–Japanese War, which was long regarded as a demonstration of the practicality of the humanitarian doctrine (Spaight 1911), the international agreements functioned as ideal models that could only remotely be achieved in practice [*see* MILITARY LAW].

**Types of war and prisoner treatment.** Two types of factors account for the extent and nature of the deviations from humanitarian practice that have characterized prisoner treatment in recent warfare. One of these is, essentially, the fortunes of war: that is, the relatively unpredictable outcome of the applications of strategies and resources in conflict that determines how many prisoners are taken by a particular power at a particular time and place. Indeed, in most of the extreme situations that have occurred, the severities of climate, the lack of logistical preparation and resources, and the disorganization of supplies by highly mobile or destructive combat conditions have probably played a greater role than the malevolence of the capturing troops or government. More benevolent intents on the part of the captors might have tremendously ameliorated, but would not have entirely precluded, conditions such as occurred during the U.S. Civil War, during World War II in southeast Asia, or at Stalingrad.

This matter of intent is a vital second factor, however. A possibly broader way of considering it is in terms of how the captor defines his prisoners and his conceptions of what activities toward his prisoners are appropriate. While peculiar features of the national culture of the captor country account for some of these conceptions, in the main they follow from the particular type of war that is taking place. Speier (1941) has presented a social typology of war, in which he suggests that major varying features of warfare can be distinguished according to the social definition of the enemy. "Absolute war" is characterized by the aim of annihilating the enemy, who is a symbol of strangeness, evil, and danger to the community as a whole. It is war fought with no restrictions upon its frightfulness. Prisoners during their brief captivity serve as objects for direct or ritualized expressions of hatred and rage. In "instrumental war," where the object is to gain access to values which the enemy controls, the defeated and captured enemy himself becomes an immediate source of gain, through forced labor, ransom, or blackmail. The extreme opposite of absolute war, which Speier calls "agonistic conflict," is fought under conditions of studied equality and strict and ceremonious norms; in its ideal form, the enemy is treated in the manner of an opponent in a sport.

Rarely has a given war accorded fully with any one of the ideal types of Speier's typology. However, the nature of the particular social conflict and of its objectives (in terms of Speier's models) has been an important determinant of the conception of the enemy and the general orientation to prisoner treatment during war. Thus the factors considered by Speier seem to have played a more important role in prisoner treatment than the particular codifications of principles that were accepted features of international law at the time. The legal doctrines themselves involved the application of the ideologies of what Speier calls "agonistic" war to a conceptual model of the nature of conflict that is close to Speier's "instrumental" type.

**Total war and the prisoner.** Contemporaneously with the later growth of international law concerning prisoners, there took place an accentuation of "nonrational" elements in international conflict. Both nationalistic and political ideologies became more dominant components of war relative to the "instrumental" and "agonistic" ones. In the present century, wars have become more "absolute" or "total," in the sense that the opponents are usually defined as members of an out-group representing everything that is alien and detestable. This form of conflict reached singular intensity during World War II, particularly in the case of German–Soviet and American–Japanese conflict.

The emergent form of war was "total" in an additional sense—there was a pervasive "rationalization" of potential means in the service of nonrational nationalistic and political ideologies. The entire physical and social environment of both one's own and the enemy's society in rationalized total war becomes open to attempted manipulation or elimination in accordance with the doctrinaire objectives of the ideology. Restrictions of a sacred, sentimental, legal, or traditional nature that previously immunized persons, institutions, or physi-

cal objects from the war, or made particular practices unthinkable, lost much of their force. These developments were epitomized by the totalitarian state.

The concept of absolute warfare, furthermore, provided the basic operating and organizational principle of totalitarian societies even in time of peace. Both Nazi and Soviet doctrine embraced the concept of the nation as being at permanent war against hostile elements at home as well as against encircling, hostile powers abroad. A product of this element of totalitarian doctrine was the concentration camp; in conception it is much like the extension of the prisoner-of-war concept to the permanent, civil, ideological war (Abel 1951; Adler 1958). (The term "concentration camp" arose originally in connection with mass political imprisonments of Cubans by the Spanish administration during the Cuban revolutionary era.)

The distinctive features of the recent history of internment practices have reflected both forms of "totalism" (Lifton 1961) that have been discussed: the nonrational and the rationalistic. On the one hand, in total conflict there has been the accentuation of the image of the foe as an individual of another, antagonistic world; he is a non-person meriting extermination, retribution, or, at best, reformation. On the other hand, there has been the rationalistic view of prisoners as an exploitable resource toward the total objective and thus the attempt at rational exploitation of prisoners in order to work toward all conceivable state objectives —economic, political, and military.

In both the Soviet Union during the Stalin era and in Nazi Germany, the blend of the rationalistic and the nonrational was evident in elaborate systems of slave labor. These involved millions of captives, both natives and foreigners. While the regimes paid considerable attention to the value of slave labor to their economies, which became importantly dependent upon this type of manpower, economic exploitation in many respects was secondary to the expression of hostile, paranoidal aggressions against the classes of persons who were captured or arrested. Nevertheless, the intimidation and isolation of potential dissidents often became subservient to filling mounting needs for slave labor. To meet this demand, promiscuous mass arrests, fraudulent judicial procedures, and arbitrary prolongation of sentences were widely employed (Wormser 1954).

Although the concept of absolute warfare is epitomized by totalitarian (particularly communist and Nazi) practice, some observers see the same influences—rationalistic exploitation and ideological nonrationality—as affecting the doctrines of the democratic nations toward war prisoners. The notions of progress that formerly organized historical accounts of captivity have been largely replaced in the post-World War II era by those which implicitly chronicle an "advance toward barbarism" (Veale 1953). Although after World War II the important precedent of punishing mistreatment of civil and military prisoners was established by the United Nations War Crimes Commission (United Nations War Crimes Commission 1948), this punishment itself was viewed by some as retrogression, in that it was punishment visited by conquerors on their captives.

### Behavioral studies of captivity

During the twentieth century, and more particularly since the Nazi period, social scientists have produced an extensive and influential literature on behavior in situations of internment and custody in totalitarian countries. The greatest volume of this material, and perhaps the most influential, developed from the writings of involuntary participant observers in German concentration camps (*Konzentrationslager*, or KZ) during the period 1935–1945. While there have also been some important investigations of relatively more benign recent situations, such as that of Japanese Americans "relocated" (i.e., interned) during World War II (Leighton 1945; Grodzins 1956), and the more-or-less enforced confinement of displaced persons (DP's) in camps in Europe after World War II (Murphy 1955), the greatest attention has been given to the most extremely oppressive and deprivational episodes. In Europe, the continuity of interest in these matters was kept alive after World War II by accounts of political imprisonment and forced labor in the Soviet Union and other east European countries and the prolonged detention of war prisoners in the Soviet Union and China.

These latter writings on captivity in communist countries were closely linked to an earlier interest in what subsequently came to be called "brainwashing." This interest was originally kindled during the Stalin era by accounts of victims of political purges as well as by the show trials of prominent communist figures and, later, "war criminals." The violently self-castigating "confessions" excited a great deal of scholarly speculation (e.g., Hinkle & Wolff 1956; Leites & Bernaut 1954). These events interested scholars both as instances of behavior under conditions of extreme deprivation and also as manifestations of the manipulatability of behavior.

Literature on the KZ's and on Soviet political imprisonment provided perspectives from which the experiences of prisoners of the Chinese communists were interpreted. Special interest was engendered among American, Canadian, and British social scientists by the alarm registered in the government and the press regarding deaths and misbehavior among prisoners of war in Korea in 1950–1953 (Biderman 1963). In France, a parallel interest was occasioned by events surrounding French Union forces captured during the war in Indochina.

**Moral loadings in studies of captivity.** While moral indignation and the dramatic nature of oppressive captivity situations doubtless account for much of the attention such events have received from social scientists, they have also been of interest on purely scientific grounds. Exposing objects to extreme conditions is a basic technique of the sciences for determining their basic properties, and isolating objects from interacting elements with which they are always associated in "the natural state" is another such method. Moral limits on experimentation with humans restrict to a narrow range the environmental conditions that can be investigated in the laboratory. For much of our knowledge of human nature, we are consequently dependent upon "experiments of nature," including those naturally occurring situations in which people are subjected to extremes beyond those which can be produced under controlled experimental conditions, or which isolate them from the environments in which they are usually observed.

Much of the interest in the scientific study of captivity situations involves a view of them as highly significant experiments of nature. However, this orientation is not far removed from folk wisdom regarding the significance of human behavior in crises. There is a close relationship between the meaning of such words as "trial" and "test" in scientific usage and the denotation of crises by these words in common speech. Folk wisdom regards crises as providing critical tests of the moral worth of an individual, as trials of his physical mettle, and as revealing his "true and fundamental nature." Thus, however objective the approach has been, scientific writings on stressful captivity situations almost invariably have focused on aspects of behavior which have the same kinds of significance for human values.

Even investigations of the question of life and death among oppressed prisoners have less frequently been examinations of the physical limits of the viability of the human organism than quests for answers to questions with greater moral loadings. Depending on the writer's outlook and the particular set of events studied, the implicit or explicit aim may be to account for what the observer regards as the remarkable perseverance of the human being through seemingly impossible hardships, for the seemingly mysterious "fatal surrender" to death in conditions apparently readily consistent with physical survival, for the determinants of the differential "fitness" or "worth" of persons that results in some surviving while others die, or for extraordinary loyalty or disloyalty to one's country or cause.

Viewing the matter simply from the standpoint of the strategy of science—a standpoint which probably has little to do with determining these emphases—there are sound reasons for the preoccupation of these studies of prisoners with questions that have distinct value implications, or even moral ones. Many questions about the environmental requirements for the biological survival and normal functioning of the human organism can be answered by experimentation with other organisms having similar biological requirements and similar equipment for biological adaptation. There is some point, then, in the concentration on questions regarding the distinctively human aspects of behavior in these stressful situations. Many of these questions therefore can be directly classed as of this type: Through what range of conditions will a human being continue to display the characteristics of a person?

Physical deprivation is one aspect of the model of captivity that has been of central concern. From a social-psychological standpoint, however, the deprivational environment assumes special significance in the context of the peculiar captor–captive relationships with which we are concerned that are not present in other extremely deprivational situations, such as the aftermaths of natural disasters. The influence that captor personnel have on the prisoners' definitions of the situation and the modes of adaptation open to them is a pervasive differentiating factor in captivity situations.

**Popular images and normative definitions.** Although the abstract doctrines treated in legal-historical discussions have affected the environment of the prisoner, the working concepts of the immediate participants in captivity situations (both captor and captive) derive to a greater degree from less formal sources, particularly mass media, folklore, and extrapolations from everyday experience. The most prevalent popular images are those relating to the inhumanity and barbarity of captors, notably those expressed in wartime atrocity propaganda and in heroic stories of prisoner defiance. The most highly developed of these traditions is the heroic escape (Hall 1954); resistance to inter-

rogation is another frequently portrayed theme (Biderman 1960).

The cold war atmosphere has led to a decline of the image of the prisoner as merely "quarantined" and has accentuated the view of the prisoner as still at war with the enemy. Military indoctrination has accentuated the theme of heroic resistance (Prugh 1956), and in the period since World War II both popular and serious writings have increasingly viewed the challenges of captivity as "loyalty crises" (Biderman 1963; Grodzins 1956).

*Expectations of captives.* From the moment of capture, reality begins to temper the vague expectations and definitions with which the prisoner enters the situation. Since these are derived in the main from popular cultural materials emphasizing "human interest" and ideological values, they have little content that is pertinent to problems of coping with the stressful realities. Nonetheless, it is held that the closer these initial expectations accord to reality, the more successful is the prisoner's adaptation. Deviations of expectations from the realities encountered have primarily been analyzed in terms of some facet of overoptimism or overpessimism (Cohen 1952; Curle 1947).

## Physical privation in captivity

Stressful captivity situations have presented opportunities for the study of the effects on behavior of almost all varieties and degrees of deprivation, and of various combinations of the scarcity of some values and the plenitude of others. Relationships within the prisoner group, as well as those between the captors and the captives, affect the severity of the impact of physical deprivations on particular individuals and on the group as a whole (Hinkle & Wolff 1957; Kogon 1946).

Accounts of captive populations have been used to demonstrate both the hardiness of the human constitution and its fragility. Some accounts stress the omnipotence of the "will to survive" (Bluhm 1948), and others emphasize the ease with which persons surrender themselves to death (Katz 1950). Survival is the most frequently applied criterion for judging success of prisoner adjustment in the extreme situation. Failure to survive is frequently interpreted by prisoners, captors, and other observers as indicative of the moral weakness of individuals or social groups. Examples are the discussions of survival and durable personal and group organization of the Jehovah's Witnesses, a band of children, and some political groups (Kogon 1946) in German concentration camps. In the other direction, the contention that Jews tended to facilitate their own destruction has occasioned much speculation regarding Jewish culture and personality (Bettelheim 1963). The relatively high death rate of American prisoners of war in Korea as compared with that of Turks in the same situation gave rise to speculations about alleged weaknesses of American society at the close of the Korean War (Biderman 1963).

There have been many attempts to ascribe differences in death rates in given situations to differences in age, sex, precapture status, status in camp society, national origin, and mode of attempted adjustment (Bergman 1948). Even with high rates of death, however, poor data and situational variation make most such comparative interpretations tenuous, at best. Conflicting assertions have been ventured regarding the ability of various categories of persons and groups to survive oppressive captivity. In general, the most likely hypothesis asserts that, in the extreme situation, factors affecting the differential exposure to the hardships of captivity are the major source of patterned variance in death rates, rather than varying capacities to withstand these hardships. The most successful adaptational efforts, from the standpoint of survival, are usually those which provide the individual or group with extra measures of sustenance, shelter, and safety, as opposed to those which minimize the impact of a given degree of privation.

**Behavioral effects of privation.** Accounts of stressful captivity have been used to evaluate the effects of various physical privations on behavior. However, the combination of specific physiological reactions with subjective reactions, and their interaction, complicates the problem of evaluating the role of each (E. Cohen 1952; Hinkle 1961; Wolf & Ripley 1947). Many aspects of the behavior of prisoners in extreme situations have been interpreted as manifestations of regression; the most common interpretation is that if normal adult ways of gratification and coping are blocked, a person turns back to pleasure sources and defenses of the childhood period (Bluhm 1948). Analyses of behavior in privational circumstances frequently posit a conflict between "animal" needs and impulses and internalized social values and controls. The failure of prisoners to free themselves from inappropriate cultural standards and needs, on the one hand, and the failure of cultural restraints to govern the pursuit of primitive needs, on the other, are both given as interpretations of maladaptive behavior (Bettelheim 1960; Bloch 1947; Bluhm 1948).

Challenges set by privational circumstances and liberation from previous conflicts are advanced as explanations of frequent observations of a low incidence of neurotic disorders and suicides in privational captivity (E. Cohen 1952). However, some writers find that a pervasive disorder is associated with the confinement and deprivation experienced by prisoner populations; this is a pronounced state of apathy (e.g., see Greenson 1949). Extremely apathetic behavior has been observed in even relatively benign custody circumstances, such as among interned belligerents in Switzerland during World War I; the term "barbed-wire syndrome" was coined to describe this type of apathy. In the extreme situation, high fatalities have been ascribed to the apathetic response pattern. Various terms have been used by prisoners to refer to this pronounced apathetic state: "around the bends" during the U.S. Civil War (Goss 1866); "bamboo disease" among prisoners in the Philippines during World War II (Katz 1946), "give-up-itis" in the Korean War (Biderman 1963), and "muslim" in German concentration camps (Kogon 1946). Somatic disorders associated with severe privation, rather than psychogenic causes, may account for many of these behavioral manifestations; Eitinger (1961) finds organic brain changes highly correlated with behavioral symptoms among former KZ inmates.

## Adaptations to prisoner society

Many of the problems of custody can be ordered by examining those requisites of organized behavior which are initially missing in custody situations and the nonviability of much of the precustody cultural and personality repertoires of the captive. Adaptations of captives can be analyzed either in terms of the deculturation and desocialization of individuals and groups, or in terms of the reestablishment of these lost elements, innovation of substitutes for them, or compensations for their lack (Abel 1951; Bettelheim 1960; Bloch 1947).

A fundamental problem facing the captive is the working out of definitions of his new social and physical environment that will enable him to establish a viable position in relation to this environment. Conceptualizations of this process in terms of adult socialization and cultural innovation are applicable (Cressey & Krassowski 1957–1958). These problems are frequently compounded by the subjection of the prisoner to captors who are from a culture alien to him.

The form that prisoner organization can take is limited by the captor's exploitative and control measures. The type of exploitation may be shaped by the special status the captive occupies in the society of the captor (as in the case of slave labor and domestic propaganda exploitation) or by the captive's status in his own society (as in intelligence and external propaganda exploitation). The degree and nature of the captive's exploitative value is also a major determinant of the conditions under which he lives. Captor control measures vary in the degree of autonomy they allow captive society and inmates. This can range from control of external relationships only, as in the case of some U.S. prisoner-of-war camps in World War II, to the semiautonomy allowed prisoner authorities in a Nazi concentration camp, to communist attempts at total control.

**Accommodation and normative conflict.** Continued interaction of captor and captive personnel tends to break down action that is initially based on formal, official, and stereotyped role models. Complex understandings and a normative structure develop at the levels of direct contact between captors and captives. These accommodations are essential for sustaining mutually necessary relationships, but they conflict with official norms concerning appropriate roles; thus tacit fictions and other mechanisms for coping with the conflict emerge. Moreover, these accommodations create pressures that conflict with internalized norms of political loyalty, the influence on behavior of remote reference groups, the enforcement of loyalty by prisoner groups, and the fear of reprisal after liberation.

Differences in personal characteristics have been found between prisoners whose adaptations to this conflict lean toward active involvement and those who respond in a passive, withdrawing fashion (Leighton 1945, pp. 263–265). While there is a wealth of clinical discussion of personality and background characteristics as determinants of the mode of adjustment of captives, this finding is the major observation of its kind that is based upon systematic, statistical evidence. Attempts to differentiate between American prisoners who collaborated with Chinese captors and those who resisted actively found that both categories resembled each other but that the men in both differed sharply from those whose records bore evidence of neither active collaboration nor resistance. The latter tended to have more apathetic, withdrawing personality features and histories.

The meaning of custody situations for the psychic and social existence of the captor has also been subject to some attention. Arendt (1951) and Bettelheim (1943), for example, regard the concentration camp as a necessary training ground for those who are to enforce inhuman standards in the society as a whole. Leighton (1945) has analyzed the irrational responses to stress on the part of internment camp authorities. Bettelheim (1960, p. 226) has shown the tendency of the persecutor to exaggerate his victim's power.

Organization along military or quasi-military lines constitutes the usual basic or ideal model for the prisoner society. However, problems arising from scarcities (Radford 1945), relationships with the captor (Biderman 1963; Prugh 1956; Schein 1960), and isolation from control and reference groups of the country of origin (Lifton 1961) result in deviations from this form. Predatory forms of organization have developed frequently in conditions of acute scarcity. Conditions perceived as submarginal for survival make for a divisiveness that is surmounted by cohesive group-wide organization only where a consensus regarding supraindividual values provides the basis for the development of an authority system. Group-wide organization may be created on the basis of group survival and welfare (Vaughan 1949), heroic values such as escape and resistance (Hall 1954), and political goals (Schein 1960). The values forming the basis of elite legitimacy, the prison economy, and the captor interventions all affect the scope and form of captive organization (see Abel 1951; Kogon 1946; Leighton 1945; Radford 1945). Processes of social differentiation within the prison negate many status distinctions based on precapture statuses (Vaughan 1949). Modes of adaptation to privation constitute one major basis of social differentiation (Bettelheim 1943; Kogon 1946).

**Psychological continuity and change.** Adaptation to the stressful captivity situation is usually dependent upon a high degree of commitment to the immediate situation and thus involves discontinuities with previous identifications and motivations. In common with all "total institutions," internment institutions employ a variety of "identity-stripping" mechanisms (Lifton 1961). The need for change experienced by the prisoner is dependent upon the degree to which roles are available for him within the prison society that have continuity with his precapture roles. High opportunity for continuity usually exists for certain professions (e.g., physicians, clergymen) and occupations (e.g., cooks), but not for others (e.g., attorneys). Moreover, certain religious, political, and military groupings with cohesive memberships can provide continuities of identity among their representatives in the prison situation. While there is, on the one hand, the need to change, on the other hand, "ideal adjustment" is described by some writers as dependent upon continued identification with "the outside" and resistance to pressures toward change and immersal in the prison milieu. Presumably, overemphasis upon either of these two directions of adjustment can be pathological. The failure to change makes the individual prone to succumb to the immediate physical and psychological stresses of the situation, and overimmersal in the immediate situation leads to eventual frustration and despair or to ego-alien behavior and violations of norms and expectations of the larger society (Bettelheim 1960; E. Cohen 1952; Katz 1950).

The conflict considered above has also been analyzed in terms of the need for maintaining "the integrity of the personality" (for example, see Beck & Godin 1951; Lifton 1961). In the literature on captivity, consciousness of this conflict on the part of prisoners provides many illustrations of individual concepts of "the essential self." Particularly in totalistic captivity situations, manipulative attempts by the captor create pressure toward ego-alien behavior and demands for change which are regarded by the individual as threatening the integrity of the self, or his "ego-identity" (Lifton 1961; Schein et al. 1961). Concepts of "breakdown" and "breaking point"—abrupt and extensive behavioral disorganization from excess stress—have played important roles both as explanations of behavior and as models that are acted upon by persons involved in captivity stresses.

The intensity of the conflicts experienced by prisoners creates problems of psychological defense against anxiety, fear, shame, and guilt. Various aspects of behavior are frequently explained as arising from both universal and idiosyncratic mechanisms of defense against these reactions. The observation that many concentration camp inmates emulated their captors in dress, language, and demeanor suggests the relevance of "identification with the aggressor" as describing a frequent defense mechanism of the captive. Since Bettelheim's use of this concept (1943), which was first developed by Anna Freud (1936), it has been widely employed to account for the behavior of persons in oppressive custody. The regressive consequences of captivity situations facilitate the adoption of this childlike means of neutralizing a threat by incorporating its source. Former prisoners have also discussed deliberate devices they employed to control and manage their own responses to the stresses they experienced, so as to avoid irrational, self-destructive, or guilt-provoking behavior.

## Postcaptivity problems

Some traumata of stressful captivity are found to have lasting effects; in general, rates of morbidity and mortality are much higher among former prisoners than among other comparable populations (Cohen & Cooper 1954; Curle 1947). More ambiguous, however, is evidence regarding the extent to which traumatization affects the ability of former captives to assume normal social roles. The persistence after release of the "withdrawal" reac-

tions and "psychological hardening" characteristic of prisoners in extreme situations has also been the subject of study. One hypothesis asserts that when the pressures of the captivity situation are removed, the intense conflicts hitherto repressed emerge, with a consequent increase in psychological disorder over that characteristic of the internment situation itself (Greenson 1949; Shuval 1957–1958).

Official institutions and primary groups to which the prisoner must relate have definitions and conceptions of the captivity situation and of the former prisoner that differ from those which formed the basis of his own action in the situation. The former prisoner confronts an initial problem of re-evaluating his captivity experiences and himself from the "back-home" perspectives, both those of official institutions and those of individuals and groups to whom he must relate. Former prisoners are frequently subjects of intense scrutiny and special treatment by others because of assumptions that they may have been heroes or traitors or have been deranged by their experiences; thus, a given individual sometimes has to cope in succession with persons who define him in a variety of ways (Biderman 1963; Lifton 1961).

The former prisoner must reassume positions in groups and institutions, such as the family and his occupational group, that have been changing significantly during his absence. Normal social life is dependent upon the motivation and control of behavior by values that may be abandoned as part of adaptation to stressful captivity. Bodies of experience exist in organized programs for the resocialization and "social reconnection" of former prisoners (Curle 1947). During the early 1960s, the long-range effects of imprisonment and deportation have been given extensive consideration in multidisciplinary scientific conferences of the World Veterans Federation and the International Confederation of Ex-Prisoners of War.

ALBERT D. BIDERMAN

[*Directly related is the entry* BRAINWASHING. *Other relevant material may be found in* MENTAL DISORDERS, TREATMENT OF, *article on* THE THERAPEUTIC COMMUNITY; SEGREGATION; SLAVERY; WAR.]

### BIBLIOGRAPHY

ABEL, THEODORE 1951 The Sociology of Concentration Camps. *Social Forces* 30:150–155.

ADLER, H. G. 1958 Ideas Toward a Sociology of the Concentration Camp. *American Journal of Sociology* 63:513–522.

ARENDT, HANNAH (1951) 1958 *The Origins of Totalitarianism*. 2d ed., enl. New York: Meridian.

BECK, F.; and GODIN, W. [pseudonyms] 1951 *Russian*

*Purge and the Extraction of Confession.* London and New York: Hurst & Blackett; New York: Viking.

BERGMAN, R. A. M. 1948 Who Is Old? Death Rate in a Japanese Concentration Camp as a Criterion of Age. *Journal of Gerontology* 3:14–17.

BETTELHEIM, BRUNO 1943 Individual and Mass Behavior in Extreme Situations. *Journal of Abnormal and Social Psychology* 38:417–452.

BETTELHEIM, BRUNO 1960 *The Informed Heart: Autonomy in a Mass Age.* Glencoe, Ill.: Free Press.

BETTELHEIM, BRUNO 1963 [Review of] *Eichmann in Jerusalem: A Report on the Banality of Evil. New Republic* 148, no. 24:23–33. → Discussion appears in Volume 148, no. 26, pages 29–31, and Volume 149, no. 3/4, pages 28–30.

BIDERMAN, ALBERT D. 1960 Social-psychological Needs and "Involuntary" Behavior as Illustrated by Compliance in Interrogation. *Sociometry* 23:120–147.

BIDERMAN, ALBERT D. 1963 *March to Calumny: The Story of American POW's in the Korean War.* New York: Macmillan.

BLOCH, HERBERT A. 1947 The Personality of Inmates of Concentration Camps. *American Journal of Sociology* 52:335–341.

BLUHM, HILDE O. 1948 How Did They Survive? Mechanisms of Defense in Nazi Concentration Camps. *American Journal of Psychotherapy* 2:3–32.

COHEN, BERNARD M.; and COOPER, MAURICE Z. 1954 *A Follow-up Study of World War II Prisoners of War.* Washington: Government Printing Office.

COHEN, ELIE A. (1952) 1954 *Human Behavior in the Concentration Camp.* London: Cape; New York: Norton. → First published in Dutch with a summary in English.

CRESSEY, DONALD L.; and KRASSOWSKI, WITOLD 1957–1958 Inmate Organization and Anomie in American Prisons and Soviet Labor Camps. *Social Problems* 5:217–230.

CURLE, A. 1947 Transitional Communities and Social Re-connection: A Follow-up Study of the Civil Resettlement of British Prisoners of War. *Human Relations* 1:42–68, 240–288.

EITINGER, LEO 1961 Pathology of the Concentration Camp Syndrome: Preliminary Report. *Archives of General Psychiatry* 5:371–379.

FREUD, ANNA (1936) 1957 *The Ego and the Mechanisms of Defense.* New York: International Universities Press. → First published as *Das Ich und die Abwehrmechanismen.*

GOSS, WARREN L. (1866) 1875 *The Soldier's Story of His Captivity at Andersonville, Belle Isle, and Other Rebel Prisons.* Boston: Richardson.

GREENSON, RALPH R. 1949 The Psychology of Apathy. *Psychoanalytic Quarterly* 18:290–302.

GRODZINS, MORTON 1956 *The Loyal and the Disloyal: Social Boundaries of Patriotism and Treason.* Univ. of Chicago Press.

HALL, DAVID O. W. 1954 *Escapes.* Wellington: Department of Internal Affairs, War History Branch.

HINKLE, LAWRENCE E. JR. 1961 The Physiologic State of the Interrogation Subject as It Affects Brain Function. Pages 19–50 in Albert D. Biderman and Herbert Zimmer (editors), *The Manipulation of Human Behavior.* New York: Wiley.

HINKLE, LAWRENCE E. JR.; and WOLFF, HAROLD G. 1956 Communist Interrogation and Indoctrination of "Enemies of the State": Analysis of Methods Used by the Communist State Police (A Special Report). *A.M.A. Archives of Neurology and Psychiatry* 76:115–174.

HINKLE, LAWRENCE E. JR.; and WOLFF, HAROLD G. 1957 The Methods of Interrogation and Indoctrination Used by the Communist State Police. New York Academy of Medicine, *Bulletin* 33:600–615.

KATZ, CHARLES J. 1946 Neuropathologic Manifestations Found in a Japanese Prison Camp. *Journal of Nervous and Mental Disease* 103:456–465.

KATZ, CHARLES J. 1950 Experiences in a Prison Camp as a Background for Therapy. *Mental Hygiene* 34:90–96.

KOGON, EUGEN (1946) 1960 *The Theory and Practice of Hell: The German Concentration Camps and the System Behind Them.* New York: Berkley. → First published in German.

LEIGHTON, ALEXANDER H. (1945) 1964 *The Governing of Men: General Principles and Recommendations Based on Experience at a Japanese Relocation Camp.* New York: Octagon Books.

LEITES, NATHAN; and BERNAUT, ELSA 1954 *Ritual of Liquidation: The Case of the Moscow Trials.* Glencoe, Ill.: Free Press.

LIFTON, ROBERT J. 1961 *Thought Reform and the Psychology of Totalism: A Study of "Brainwashing" in China.* New York: Norton.

MURPHY, HENRY B. M. 1955 Refugee Psychoses in Great Britain: Admissions to Mental Hospitals. Pages 173–194 in Henry B. M. Murphy et al., *Flight and Resettlement.* Paris: UNESCO.

PRUGH, GEORGE S. 1956 Prisoners at War: The POW Battleground. *Dickinson Law Review* 60:123–138.

RADFORD, R. A. 1945 The Economic Organization of a POW Camp. *Economica* New Series 12:189–201.

SCHEIN, EDGAR H. 1960 Interpersonal Communication, Group Solidarity, and Social Influence. *Sociometry* 23:148–161.

SCHEIN, EDGAR H.; SCHNEIER, I.; and BARKER, C. H. 1961 *Coercive Persuasion: A Socio-psychological Analysis of "Brainwashing" of American Civilian Prisoners by the Chinese Communists.* New York: Norton.

SHUVAL, JUDITH T. 1957–1958 Some Persistent Effects of Trauma: Five Years After the Nazi Concentration Camps. *Social Problems* 5:230–243.

SPAIGHT, JAMES M. 1911 *War Rights on Land.* London: Macmillan.

SPEIER, HANS 1941 The Social Types of War. *American Journal of Sociology* 46:445–454.

TRIMBLE, E. G. 1934 Prisoners of War. Volume 12, pages 419–421 in *Encyclopaedia of the Social Sciences.* New York: Macmillan.

UNITED NATIONS WAR CRIMES COMMISSION 1948 *History of the United Nations War Crimes Commission and the Development of the Laws of War.* London: H.M. Stationery Office.

VAUGHAN, ELIZABETH H. 1949 *Community Under Stress: An Internment Camp Culture.* Princeton Univ. Press.

VEALE, FREDERICK J. P. 1953 *Advance to Barbarism: How the Reversion to Barbarism in Warfare and War-trials Menaces Our Future.* Appleton, Wis.: Nelson.

WOLF, STEWART; and RIPLEY, HERBERT S. 1947 Reactions Among Allied Prisoners of War Subjected to Three Years of Imprisonment and Torture by the Japanese. *American Journal of Psychiatry* 104:180–193.

WORMSER, OLGA 1954 Le rôle du travail des concentrationnaires dans l'économie de guerre allemande. *Revue d'histoire de la deuxième guerre mondiale* 4, no. 15/16:81–98.

**INTERPERSONAL INFLUENCE**
*See under* DIFFUSION.

**INTERPERSONAL RELATIONS**
*See* GROUPS; INTERACTION; *and the biography of* SULLIVAN.

## INTERVIEWING

### I
#### SOCIAL RESEARCH

The interview has been defined as a conversation with a purpose, and the purposes for which interviews are conducted are many and various. They include the purpose of therapeutic change, as in the psychiatric interview; the purpose of instruction and appraisal, as in the interviews initiated by a supervisor with a subordinate; and the purposes of selection and assessment, as in the interviews conducted with applicants for jobs or with students applying for admission to universities. In all these situations, there is the transaction of giving and getting information, and the understanding of this transaction as the immediate task of interviewer and respondent. This immediate task, however, is embedded in a larger cycle of purposive activities that define the roles of interviewer and respondent more exactly, reflect the motives of both for undertaking the interview, and stipulate the consequences of the interview for other aspects of their lives.

To label an interview "psychiatric" or "therapeutic," for example, implies that it probably has been initiated by the respondent (or patient) and that his motivation in doing so is to obtain relief from certain symptoms or strains of a mental or emotional sort. Moreover, the interviewer is seen not only as an information getter but also as a direct and powerful source of help; the interview is seen not only as an informational transaction but also as part of the therapeutic experience.

By contrast, the research interview, to which this article is addressed, may be defined as a two-person conversation that is initiated by the interviewer for the specific purpose of obtaining information that is relevant to research. Such an interview is focused on content specified by the usual research objectives of systematic description, prediction, or explanation. Other characteristics of the research interview are more variable. Typically, however, the differentiation of roles between inter-

viewer and respondent is pronounced. The interviewer has not only initiated the conversation; he presents each topic by means of specific questions, and he decides when the conversation on a topic has satisfied the research objectives (or the specific criteria which represent them) and when another topic shall be introduced. In the research interview the respondent is led to restrict his discussion to the questions posed.

The consequences of the research interview for an individual respondent are often minimal and almost always removed in time, space, and person from the interview experience itself. The respondent is asked to provide information about himself, his experiences, or his attitudes to an interviewer who has no direct power or intention to provide therapy, instruction, a job, or any other major tangible reward. If the research interview does contribute to such a reward, it does so through a sequence of events that involves the aggregation of responses from numerous interviews, some process of data reduction and inference, and some additions to the description or explanation of social facts. From this enlarged base of knowledge may come applications or decisions of policy that have great importance for the respondent, but the sequence is complex and often uncertain. Nevertheless, the prospect of ultimate benefit, public or personal, from the accumulation of knowledge is one major basis for respondent agreement to participate in a research interview.

Perhaps the prototypical example of research interviews is provided by the national census. Most countries of the world conduct some kind of population count, and in many countries the census has been expanded to provide with regularity an inventory of social resources and problems. Census interviews usually make only modest demands on interviewer and respondent. They are brief; they ask for demographic data well within the respondent's knowledge and not of a kind that he is likely to regard as confidential. Moreover, the information is requested under circumstances familiar to, or expected by, most respondents, and the request is backed by the legitimate power of the national government.

Similar to the census in most of these respects is a whole class of brief, officially sponsored, information-getting interview surveys. In the United States alone, hundreds of thousands of such interviews are conducted by agencies of government in randomly selected homes each year to provide continuing data on family income, employment and unemployment, health and illness, and other aspects of economic and social welfare.

Almost as widely known as census taking and

other government-sponsored research that involves interviewing are the activities of those private agencies which conduct recurrent interview studies of public opinion on national and international affairs, family life, and other subjects of public interest. The Gallup Poll is typical of private organizations that conduct such surveys and, in the United States and much of Europe, its name has become a general term for describing them. The interviews conducted by such polls resemble those of the census in brevity, simplicity, and the avoidance of very private material. However, public opinion interviewing differs from most government-sponsored surveys in dealing with matters of attitude rather than of fact and in depending on interviewer persuasiveness rather than on legal authority and prestige to obtain respondent cooperation. Market research and studies of readership are usually of like simplicity and brevity, although more elaborate and indirect techniques of interviewing have often been used in such studies.

It is likely that the most ambitious and demanding use of the interview as a research technique has been made by social scientists in the course of psychological, sociological, political, and economic investigations. Such studies often involve interviews of an hour or more, on subjects that may raise difficult problems of recall, potential embarrassment, and self-awareness. Consider as examples the recurring studies of consumer behavior and family income (Katona 1960), the studies of fertility and family planning (Freedman et al. 1959), the studies of sexual behavior (Kinsey et al. 1948), the studies of mental health and illness (Gurin et al. 1960), of political behavior (Michigan . . . 1960), and the many studies of supervisor–subordinate relations and worker attitudes (Argyris 1964; Herzberg et al. 1959; *Organizational Stress* 1964; Likert 1961).

These examples suggest a conclusion that can hardly be questioned: much of the data of social science is generated by means of the interview. Sociologists, psychologists, anthropologists, political scientists, and economists depend on interviews to obtain data for describing the phenomena of interest to them and for testing their theories and hypotheses about those phenomena.

Moreover, the use of the interview in these disciplines is not limited to surveys and other studies done in the field; interviewing is a necessary element in laboratory research as well. Laboratory experiments in psychology and other social sciences typically involve a situation contrived by the experimenter in order to introduce some factor into the experience of the people who are his experimental subjects, and to do so under conditions in which their reactions can be closely studied. That study often requires interviewing as well as observation, physiological measures, and the like. The experimenter depends on the subject to report anxiety or elation, increased confidence or reduced self-esteem, and feelings of acceptance or rejection (see, for example, Asch 1952; Milgram 1965). The interview helps the experimenter to learn whether the intended manipulation of a variable really "took," and if so, whether it had the predicted effects.

In short, the social scientist, from the first nineteenth-century British surveys of poverty (Booth et al. 1889–1891) and the early psychophysical experiments in the laboratory (Boring 1929), has been, willy-nilly, an interviewer. Whether he has been too much an interviewer (Webb et al. 1966) is a question of prime importance for the strategy of social science but not for the present discussion. Like other scientists, the social researcher has attempted to measure rather than merely to describe in qualitative terms, and for him the interview has been the most useful instrument in the measurement process.

## The interview as measurement

We have defined the interview as a conversation with a purpose and have further specified that the purpose with which we are concerned is information getting. The research interview, however, is not after mere information; it has to do with that particular quantitative form of information getting called *measurement*. The interview is one part, and a crucial one, in the measurement process as it is conducted in much of social research. Thus, the use of the interview is subject to the laws of measurement; it can be properly judged by the standards of measurement, and it suffers from the limitations of all measurement processes in degrees peculiar to itself.

The key concept for thinking about the adequacy of measurement is *validity*, defined as the extent to which an instrument and the rules for its use in fact measure what they purport to measure (Kaplan 1964; *Research Methods in Social Relations* 1959). Inferences about validity, however, particularly about interview validity, are too often made on the basis of *face validity*, that is, whether the questions asked look as if they are measuring what they purport to measure. A preferable way of thinking about validity, and a basis for developing tests of validity, is the question of what a given measurement will do. Does the measure do the things that theory and experiment have convinced us it should do (Campbell 1957; Cronbach 1946; Coombs 1964)? For example, does a test that purports to measure intelligence enable us to predict scholastic achievement to some significant degree?

A similar approach to the validation of interview measures involves the comparison of the interview measure with some other measure that has already met the test of validity. This kind of comparison has been called *convergent validity*, in part to distinguish it from other approaches to the validation of constructs. If the two measures in fact agree, there is a presumption of validity for the measure being tested at least as great as that of the measure taken as standard. Thus hospitalization data obtained from interviews might be validated against hospital admission records. When the standard measure has already been validated, the method of convergent validity is powerful. For example, when the results of political surveys correspond to election statistics, or when the results of consumer surveys agree with the volume of actual purchases, we have confidence in the survey measures. The problem of validation becomes more difficult, however, in the case of interview measures of attitudes, for which no independent and objective measures exist in quite the same terms.

Questions of validity and invalidity are only part of the problem of measurement adequacy. A measure is invalid to the extent that it measures something more than or less than it purports to measure. Put another way, the mark of invalidity is bias, which is a systematic or persistent tendency to make errors in the same direction, that is, to overstate or understate the "true value" of an attribute. Scarcely less important than validity is *reliability*, which has to do with the stability and equivalence of a measure (Cronbach 1949). The reliability of an interview measure is defined by such questions as these: If the measure is used repeatedly in the same circumstances, will it yield the same results? If it is used by different interviewers to measure the same attribute, will it produce the same results? Methods for determining the reliability of a measure are to arrange for repetitions of it in identical circumstances ("test–retest reliability") or, if the measure involves numerous items, to compare the results obtained on the basis of one half of the items, randomly selected, with the results obtained by using the other half of the items. The latter method is called the "split-half reliability" test.

The relationship between validity and reliability is complex. For the interview method, however, it is important to remind ourselves that a measure may be valid without being reliable; that is, it may

measure what it purports to, but do so badly. On the average, such a measure obtains the "true value," but its variance is large. Repeated use of the measure in the same circumstances produces values which are random about the mean but vary from it by large amounts.

The question of how to insure or achieve measurement adequacy by means of interview procedures can be answered in several ways. One solution, of course, is to restrict oneself to measures already developed, for which pedigrees of reliability and validity have been established. Many paper and pencil tests and some interview scales have been developed with enough attention to methodological considerations so that such data are available. Examples include numerous personality scales, tests of intelligence and reading ability, the census procedures for ascertaining labor-force status and occupation, measures of political party identification, and others. Unfortunately, in the social sciences standard, well-validated measures are not available for most concepts. As a result the investigator is commonly faced with the need to develop his own measures.

For the investigator who must create his own interview measures, there exists a considerable accumulation of general principles and specific procedures to guide him in the preparation of questions, scales or sets of questions, and questionnaires (Payne 1951; Kahn & Cannell 1957; Richardson et al. 1965). All of these help to achieve validity in measurement. It is also possible to improve validity by including in the data collection measures of potential sources of bias, so that there can be an after-the-fact assessment of the extent of their intrusion and a correction in the raw data. The "lie scale" of the Minnesota Multiphasic Personality Inventory, the Edwards Social Acceptability Scale, and the Mandler–Sarason Test Anxiety Scale are examples of measures that are used for such ex post facto statistical corrections with some success. The achievement of high reliability depends on the same basic principles but is particularly enhanced by specifying the exact wording of the questions to be asked in the interview, as well as the forms and range of behavior that may be used in the interview to evoke response, and by using multiple questions rather than single questions for the measurement of each concept or variable.

In short, adequacy of measurement by means of interviews requires knowledge of the conditions for a successful interview, and the skill to meet those conditions both in the construction of questionnaires or interview schedules and in the conduct of the interview itself. These issues are the subjects of the following sections of this article.

## Conditions for successful interviewing

Interviews are not uniformly successful. Respondents differ in ability and motivation; interviewers differ in skill; and interview content differs in feasibility. While many approaches have been taken to these problems, three broad concepts seem to comprise much of the available research and advice. These are *accessibility* of the required data to the respondent, *cognition* or understanding by the respondent of his role and the informational transaction required of him, and *motivation* of the respondent to take the role and fulfill its requirements. These are not independent factors; they can be thought of as a set of interrelated conditions for attaining an adequate interview, and most of the specific techniques of interviewing (to be discussed in the following section) can be thought of as means of meeting these conditions.

**Accessibility.** The simplest condition for interviewing occurs when the datum which the interviewer requires is completely accessible to the respondent, that is, when he has the information in conscious form, clearly conceptualized in the terms used by the interviewer. This condition is typically met for simple demographic data—age, family size, and the like. To the extent that the required data are accessible to the respondent, the interviewer can turn his attention to problems of cognition and motivation, making sure that the respondent understands what is asked of him and that he is willing to provide the information which he possesses. To the extent that the data are inaccessible to the respondent, this inaccessibility constitutes the first problem in interviewing.

Three major reasons for inaccessibility can be distinguished, each with its own implications for the formulation of questions and the conduct of the interview. First, the material may simply have been forgotten (Bartlett 1932). The respondent may once have been in conscious possession of the required information, but it has receded from conscious recollection. A second kind of inaccessibility has to do with repression; an event is important or recent enough to be remembered, but it involves sufficient emotional stress to have been obliterated from conscious memory. The third category of inaccessibility has to do not with the intrinsic content of the material sought but with the terms or categories in which the interview requires recollection and communication. Problems of language, vocabulary, and understanding are involved, as well as differences in social class, subculture, and region. This aspect of inaccessibility is related to the cog-

nitive conditions for successful interviewing. For example, an interviewer may be so ill-advised as to ask workers to recount recent experiences on the job which were "ego-enhancing" and "ego-threatening." A respondent may be quite insightful and observant, quite able to describe in some detail his experience on the job, and yet be unable to respond meaningfully to this question. Moreover, his difficulties are likely to persist even after the words "ego-enhancing" and "ego-threatening" have been defined for him, because he has not thought of his experiences in terms of such categories.

**Cognitive conditions.** A second requirement for successful interviewing has to do with respondent cognition or understanding. The respondent role is by definition an active, self-conscious one, and the respondent can meet its expectations best when he understands them fully. Specifically, he needs to know what constitutes successful completion of the role requirements and to know the concepts or terms of reference by means of which he is being asked to provide data. Without this understanding, data accessible to the respondent are nevertheless likely to remain unreported because interviewer and respondent lack a common frame of reference, a common conceptual language, or common standards of response adequacy and excellence.

How much understanding of the research enterprise by the respondent is appropriate will vary with the demands being made in the interview, and how much effort the interviewer must devote to the development of such understanding will depend on the extent of the interview demand and the sophistication of the respondent. Typically the respondent need not understand the nature of the measurement being attempted, the construction of scales, or the plans for computer analysis. He should understand the requirements of his own role in the interview—the demands to be made on him, and the criteria for relevance and completeness. To understand these things and to be motivated to accept the role may, in turn, require acquaintance with the over-all aims of the research enterprise, information about its compatibility with the respondent's own goals, and reassurance about its risks. These issues bring us to the third condition for successful interviewing.

**Respondent motivation.** There is general agreement among students and practitioners of interviewing that respondent motivation or willingness to report is a prime condition for successful data collection; it could hardly be otherwise. There is little agreement, however, about the theory or model of motivation that is most appropriate to the interview, and about the major sources of re-

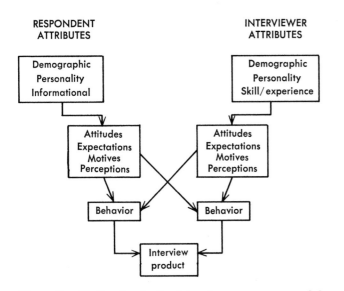

**RESPONDENT ATTRIBUTES**

**INTERVIEWER ATTRIBUTES**

*Figure 1 — Motivation in the interview: a process model*

spondent motivation. Kahn and Cannell (1957) propose a dual emphasis: intrinsic motivation, because the experience and relationship with the interviewer are valued by the respondent; and instrumental motivation, because the respondent sees that the enterprise of which the interview is a part is congruent with his own goals and values. Kinsey and his colleagues (1948) stress altruism as the initial source of respondent motivation, although many of their interview descriptions seem to rely more on the assumption of legitimate authority and the use of medical–scientific prestige. Richardson, Dohrenwend, and Klein (1965) explain respondent motivation in terms of altruism, emotional satisfaction, and intellectual satisfaction. Such partial agreements and discontinuities are hardly surprising; they reflect the more general diversity of motivational theories. The interview is one form of complex molar behavior; attempts to understand

it will inevitably share the contemporary strengths and weaknesses of motivational theory as a whole.

Despite the lack of agreement on any one motivational model, the research evidence on the interviewing process (Hyman et al. 1954; Riesman 1958; Kahn & Cannell 1957; Richardson et al. 1965) strongly urges that respondent motivation be conceptualized in terms that take account of the social situation of interviewer and respondent, the nature of the transaction between them, their perceptions of each other and of their joint task, and the effects of such perceptions. In short, the evidence argues in favor of a motivational model that treats the interview as a social process and regards the interview product as a social outcome. One such model is presented in Figure 1.

This model is compatible with the role-oriented view of the interview. It stipulates that the interview product or outcome is the immediate and joint result of interviewer and respondent behavior; that the behavior of both interviewer and respondent stems from their attitudes, motives, expectations, and perceptions; and that these, in turn, can be understood as reflecting more enduring attributes of demography and personality. The model also emphasizes the interaction of respondent and interviewer. The behavior of the interviewer is perceived by the respondent, and it generates or modifies his attitudes and his motivation to continue the interaction. The respondent is reacting not only to the interviewer's behavior as such, however; he is reacting to it as a cue that evokes role behavior already familiar in other contexts, as well as attitudes already formed. Thus, the respondent may behave toward the interviewer as a polite stranger, a hospitable host, a dutiful citizen, a fellow research worker and scientist, or even an obedient servant or intimidated inferior. The inter-

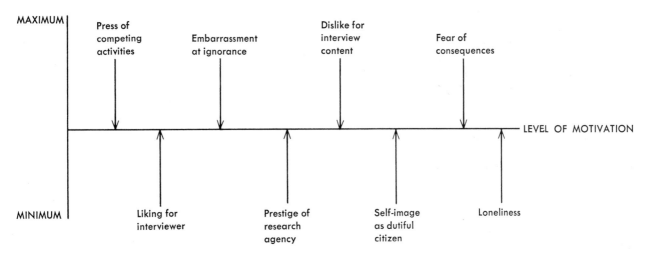

*Figure 2 — Opposing motivational forces in the interview*

viewer's expectations and behavior in turn are a mixed product of his own personality and experience, combined with his immediate reaction to what the respondent is doing.

Such a general model of the interview requires additional specification. It requires, among other things, some means for representing the moment-by-moment state of the respondent's motivation to provide complete and accurate data. The various forces tending, at any point in the interview, to increase or decrease respondent motivation to work in this sense can be well represented by the Lewinian model of the "quasi-stationary equilibrium" (Lewin 1947), in which each factor urging compliance or resistance is depicted as an arrow (force), and the level of motivation is depicted as a horizontal line that is the resultant of the opposing forces. In Figure 2 the factors identified as opposing forces have been taken from current research on the interview process (Fowler 1965; U.S. Department . . . 1965*a*).

## Techniques of data collection

It is clear that the conceptualizations of the interview and of the conditions for success have implications for the specific techniques and procedures to be advocated. We have emphasized the conditions of accessibility, cognition, and motivation, and the role relationship of the interviewer and respondent. It follows, for example, that if the dominant problem in a particular case is accessibility, one thinks in terms of ways in which the demand for data might be limited, of records or documents which might evoke associated recollections, and the like.

The technique of data collection by interview can be usefully separated into two main and related aspects—question formulation (developing a measurement instrument) and interviewing itself (using the instrument). The close relationship of these two aspects of technique is most apparent when the same person is performing both functions in rapid succession, as anthropologists do habitually and other social research workers do at least in the early phases of investigation. Even when question formulation and data collection are conspicuously separated in time and space (as in survey research and opinion polling), the connection remains. The instrument both limits and assists the interviewer, and the interviewer necessarily modifies the instrument and the accompanying rules in the very act of using them.

To relate each bit of detailed practical advice on question formulation and interviewing technique to the above theoretical material would be desirable, but lengthy and difficult. The following sections are based, however, on the same model of the interviewing situation, with special emphasis on respondent–interviewer interaction, role taking, and the attainment of accessibility, understanding, and motivation.

**The formulation of questions.** Of the many ways of describing decisions that the interviewer or research worker must make about the form of questions, two seem particularly useful and important: questions may be open or closed; and they may be direct or indirect in their relationship to objectives. Openness has to do with the form of the response required by a question; an open question invites the respondent to reply in his own words, and a closed question asks him to select, from a series of alternatives, the answer that best approximates his views. The closed question thus controls the form, length, and content of the possible response. The classic example is the trial lawyer's instruction to the witness on the stand that he "answer 'Yes' or 'No.'"

Directness and indirectness have to do with the relationship between the question and the objective, that is, the interviewer's purpose in asking the question. For example, when a respondent is shown an ambiguous picture and asked to tell a story about its meaning for him, so that the story can subsequently be used to infer the intensity of the respondent's need for achievement (Atkinson 1958), we consider the question to be indirect. A direct (but ill-advised) question to meet the same objective would ask the respondent how achievement-oriented he considers himself to be.

*Open versus closed questions.* The intolerant advocacy of one or another of these question forms has been largely abandoned, as Lazarsfeld (1944) long ago proposed it should be. But there remains the problem of how and when to choose one type of question rather than another. At least five considerations are relevant to the choice between open and closed questions: interview objectives, the respondent's information level, the strength of the respondent's opinions on the topic, the respondent's motivation to communicate on the topic, and the interviewer's initial knowledge of these characteristics of the respondent.

With respect to the objectives of the interview, the general principle is that closed questions tend to be more appropriate for straightforward categorizing of respondents according to their agreement or disagreement with some stated point of view. If the interviewer's objectives go beyond such description and include explanatory aims, such as discovering the respondent's particular frame of reference or the process by which he came to his present views, an open question will almost certainly be superior to a single closed one, and perhaps to a combination of several closed questions.

The choice between open and closed questions should also be guided by the probable degree of structuring of the respondent's opinion on or experience with the topic. To the extent that the respondent has done his cognitive work in advance, so to speak, and has formulated his ideas in terms close to those of the question, the closed form is appropriate, as well as economical in terms of the interviewer's time and the respondent's effort. On the other hand, to the extent that the respondent's thoughts are less structured on the topic in question, the interviewer must assist the respondent to recall, order, and perhaps evaluate his experience.

Definitive research on the motivational advantages of open versus closed questions is yet to be done. The closed question demands less effort from the respondent, as well as less self-revelation, and may therefore be less threatening. To the extent that the closed question incorporates extreme alternative responses, it may also make these extremes more admissible (Kahn 1952; Metzner & Mann 1951). On the other hand, the closed question may be restrictive and may also invite an easy, invalid response instead of the more difficult "don't know." Finally, the choice between the closed form and the open form should take into account the interviewer's (or research worker's) advance knowledge of the situation. If he knows relatively little about the range or terms of response he will encounter, he is obviously in a poor position to formulate closed questions, which are meaningful and successful only when their limited alternatives match the respondent's experience, vocabulary, and frame of reference. If these conditions are not met, the open question is likely to be preferable.

*Direct and indirect questions.*   A direct question, as we have said, simply asks for information stipulated by the objectives of the interview; there is a congruence between objective and question that is obvious on inspection. An indirect question is not congruent with its objective in the same sense; it is related by some inference or theory. One of the major reasons for using indirect questions is to obtain information about the respondent that he is incapable of providing directly because it is beyond the limits of his conscious insight. Indirect questions are also used to get around unwillingness or inability to report certain kinds of material directly.

The forms of indirection include the use of the third person, since people are sometimes willing to impute to others feelings and opinions that they will not admit as their own. They also include questions that have the appearance of directness but are interpreted as measuring attributes which the respondent is not aware of as being measured (see, for example, the *F*-scale for the measurement of authoritarianism, as described by Adorno et al. 1950). Finally, indirection may take the form of a purposefully ambiguous stimulus—an ink blot, a picture of uncertain meaning, or the beginning of a sentence which the respondent is asked to talk about spontaneously, to interpret, or to complete.

The indirect approach clearly makes accessible data that would otherwise be inaccessible. The disadvantages of indirection have mainly to do with the problem of validation. Face validity is always risky, but with indirect measures it quickly becomes meaningless.

Apart from the decisions regarding the open or closed form of questions and the direct or indirect means of questioning, there are a number of considerations in question wording and question sequence which bear on the attainment of cognitive understanding, accessibility, and respondent motivation. These are considered briefly below.

*Language.*   The primary criterion in the choice of language is complete and accurate communication of ideas to the respondent. The language of the question must therefore conform to vocabulary that is available to him. This does not mean that the respondent's colloquialisms or regionalisms should be imitated; such efforts are more often ludicrous than convincing. However, it does mean that the basis for communication between interviewer and respondent consists of their shared vocabulary and that questions should be formulated in these terms.

*Frame of reference.*   Inevitably each respondent interprets and replies to a question in terms of his own experience and of his own present concerns and interests. Even the casual greeting "How are things?" leads one person to think of health, another of financial matters, a third of family affairs. A common but undesirable practice in question formulation is to assume the respondent's frame of reference is the same as the interviewer's. More desirable practice is to ascertain the respondent's frame of reference by additional questioning ("Why is that?" "What did you have in mind?") whenever his reply to a major question has not made clear his frame of reference. An alternative procedure is to stipulate the desired frame of reference as part of the question itself. Thus the unqualified "How are things?" might become "How are things going—financially, I mean?" The respondent's frame of reference may be so powerful, however, that it becomes necessary to allow him to answer the question in his own terms before attempting to impose a different frame of reference on him (Bancroft & Welch 1946).

*Avoiding ambiguity.* A common fault in question formulation is the inclusion of two or more propositions in such a way that the meaning of the response is ambiguous. For example, consider the survey question "Do you favor or oppose raising real estate taxes for new schools or highways?" A direct response of "Favor" or "Oppose" is ambiguous with respect to the referent; it may be tax increases in general, schools, highways, or all of these. Avoidance of such ambiguity is simple: the researcher need only keep in mind that each question should have a single and unambiguous referent and should test, with respect to that referent, a single proposition or point of view.

*Recognition versus recall.* Where recall is a problem for respondents, questions can usefully be formulated in terms that require only recognition. Experiments in the psychological laboratory have shown that in studies of memory the process of recognition is an easier task for the subject than the process of recall. Moreover, there is some evidence (Kahn 1952) that the presentation of alternatives covering a wide range also increases the likelihood of respondents' choosing extreme statements and admitting to socially unacceptable opinions or behaviors. Unfortunately, little research has been done to explore the disadvantages of such questions or to document unequivocally their relative reliability and validity under varying conditions of data accessibility.

*Sanctioning.* The problem of defensiveness can be dealt with in many ways, primarily in the interpersonal technique of interviewing rather than in the formulation of questions. Nevertheless, the wording of questions can facilitate or inhibit the respondent's admission to facts or opinions that are in some fashion ego-threatening to him. One means of making such material admissible is to include it in the hypothetical range of alternatives presented to the respondent, as suggested above. Another is to build into the question some phrase of reassurance, some reminder of the purpose of the inquiry, or some factual indication that the "unacceptable" is common and, in this context, acceptable.

*Leading questions.* Avoiding "biased" or "leading" questions is a standard and oversimplified piece of advice in the formulating of questions. By a "leading question" we mean one so formulated

that respondents find it easier or more acceptable to answer in one way than another, or to choose one alternative over another. When such questions are formulated inadvertently and the responses are interpreted without regard to the asymmetrical tendency of the questions themselves, the results are biased. The most common example in survey research is the yes–no type of questions, in which respondents who answer "Yes" are then subjected to a long series of additional questions about time, place, reason, and reaction, while respondents who answer "No" are asked no more on the topic. People learn quickly that it is easy and brief to say "No." Still more crude is the use of question wording that assumes a particular answer and thus forces the respondent to contradict the interviewer in order to formulate a response of his own. The generally accepted principle regarding such questions is that they should be asked only for the purpose of imposing some additional stress on the respondent, for example, in order to identify people who feel strongly enough to assert that the interviewer has assumed wrongly (Smith et al. 1956; Litwak 1956; Kahn & Cannell 1957; Kinsey et al. 1948). The rule of thumb justly favors balanced wording, questions designed to equalize the amount of work and the degree of social acceptability regardless of which alternative a respondent chooses, and avoidance of emotionally loaded words and phrases.

*Organization and sequence of questions.* Issues of organization and sequence of questions, like so much else in interviewing, cannot be settled by generalization but must be resolved in relation to the interview objectives and the characteristics of the population from whom information is sought. Generally, a battery of questions is preferable to a single question, for reasons of both reliability and validity. The more complex the issue and the less tested the approach, the more important it becomes to use multiple questions. When multiple closed questions are used, and the respondent is asked to indicate agreement or disagreement with a stated proposition, it is important to randomize the form of the statements. The purpose of doing so is to randomize the tendency of some respondents to be chronic "yea-sayers" or "nay-sayers" (Couch & Keniston 1960). Similarly, if lists of items are being presented to respondents, the order should be varied, since some respondents show a tendency to select the alternative first presented. [*See* RE-SPONSE SETS.]

The sequence of the topics themselves should be planned to make the total interview experience as meaningful as possible by giving it a beginning, a middle, and an end. More specifically, the early questions should serve to engage the respondent's interest—without threatening or taxing him before he is really committed to the transaction—and to teach him the kind of task the interview represents. The most demanding of questions might well be placed later in the interview, at a point when the respondent's commitment can be presumed to have peaked but fatigue has not yet set in.

**Interviewing technique.** Two major qualifications must be made of any specific set of recommendations respecting interviewing technique. First, the technique of the interviewer is not really separable from the formulation of questions. In almost all situations, the interviewer is in some degree a formulator of questions. In much case study and anthropological work the interviewer formulates and asks questions almost simultaneously; he interacts spontaneously with the respondent. At the other extreme is the injunction to census enumerators to ask each question precisely as worded, to do no improvising of additional questions, and to respond to requests for explanation by repeating the question. As methodological research has shown, there is considerable variation in interviewer technique even under such constrained circumstances (Hansen et al. 1951). The second qualification to recommendations about technique is that the most appropriate advice must differ with the situation—as defined by respondent characteristics, interviewer characteristics, and above all by the task requirements of the interview itself. For example, to develop a close and trusting relationship as a preliminary to a few questions for a school census is ludicrous, whereas to neglect the development of such a relationship in psychiatric diagnosis is equally bad.

It follows that recommendations about technique must be stated in relation to such situational factors. The following recommendations accordingly are based on the situational factors most common in social research (including but not limited to survey research). In such research the respondent is free to give information or refuse it. Moreover, the power of an interviewer over a respondent is limited. He can neither impose formal penalties for nonresponse nor offer a prize for response. The demands on respondent time and effort are significant but not overwhelming, perhaps as little as one-half hour or as much as two hours. The interviewer approaches the respondent as a stranger; the interviewer is identified with some sponsoring agency (university, research institute, or the like) that has at least modest prestige value without possessing legitimate authority or coercive power to demand information. The interviewer must generate and maintain sufficient respondent motivation to meet the interview objectives, and he must direct and control the communication process in the service of those objectives. In general, he does these things by describing the purpose of the interview, treating the respondent with some reasonable show of warmth and interest, indicating directly and approvingly those responses which are relevant and complete, and letting the respondent know also when he is being irrelevant or fragmentary in his answers. These things the interviewer does by building on the specific questions that have been prepared in advance of the interview. He adds supplementary or "probe" questions; he comments on the completeness or inadequacy of a response; he nods, murmurs, and in other ways exerts control over the communications process. Let us consider these behaviors sequentially and specifically.

The introduction of the interview to the respondent is almost wholly dependent upon appeals to extrinsic motivation. An appropriate introduction would include a statement of the purpose of the interview and identification of the sponsoring agency. In some situations this may be introduction enough. If the data requirements and time demands are more than trivial, however, or if the respondent shows curiosity or reluctance, the introduction should also include reassurances to the respondent with respect to the manner in which he came to be selected for interview, the protection and confidentiality which will be accorded his statements, and the specific ways in which his statements will be used. There is a related misunderstanding that the interviewer must be alert for during the early moments of an interview. Many respondents lack experience and knowledge of interviewing for research purposes, but they have no lack of experience at being interrogated for other purposes. To them the appearance of a stranger who wishes to ask questions suggests truant officers, bill collectors, policemen, unwanted salesmen, and a variety of other sources of threat or annoyance. The interviewer will need to look for signs of such misidentification and be prepared to explain and, on occasion, to document his true identity and function.

A remaining problem that arises in the introductory moments of an interview has to do with the ethics of persuasion, particularly in describing the purpose of the interview and the uses to which it will be put. To counsel absolute and complete truthfulness is easy and irreproachable, but there are circumstances in which the effect of such completeness would negate the purpose of the interview. It seems consistent with the ethics of the social sciences in general to resolve such problems by telling the respondent as much as possible without negating the purpose of the interview, by then withholding or generalizing rather than fabricating explanations, and by being uncompromising in letting the respondent know what the interview will require of him.

The development of intrinsic motivation in the interview—emotional and intellectual satisfaction in the process itself—may begin with the introduction, but it matures only as the task and relationship acquire meaning for the respondent. The opportunity to talk to a good listener, to find one's opinions of serious interest to another person, to see that person making a real and successful effort to understand rather than to evaluate or criticize —these are experiences which are rare for many people and which are intrinsically satisfying. Thus, the interviewer should create and maintain an atmosphere in which the respondent feels that he is fully understood and in which he is safe to communicate fully without fear of being judged, criticized, or subsequently identified and disadvantaged. At the same time, the interviewer must focus attention on the content of the communication, encouraging the respondent to consider each topic as deeply, fully, and frankly as the interview objectives require.

The interviewer's means for doing these things are not mysterious; they are his elaborations on the primary (prepared) interview questions and in some respects resemble the processes of mutual influence familiar in informal conversation. Richardson and his colleagues (1965) have referred to them as "encouragements, silences, guggles, and interruptions"; Kahn and Cannell (1957) have called them "controlled nondirective probing"; other authors have used still other terms. The specific behaviors proposed for the interviewer by these various authors are more alike than their terminology. The following is a list of some of these behaviors.

Brief expectant pauses.

Brief expressions of understanding and interest:
  "I see, um-hm."
  "Yes, I understand."

Neutral requests for additional information:
  "How do you mean?"
  "I'd like to know more of your thinking on that."
  "What do you have in mind there?"
  "Is there anything else?"
  "Can you tell me more about that?"

Echo or near repetition of the respondent's words:
  Respondent: "I've taken these treatments for almost six months, and I'm not getting any better."
  Interviewer: "You're not getting better?"

Summarizing or reflecting respondent expressions:
  Examples would follow respondent statements, stating the interviewer's understanding of a key feeling or meaning. Such summaries often begin with phrases like "You feel that———" or "You mean that———"

Requests for specific kinds of additional information:
  "*Why* do you think that is so?"
  "*How* did that become clear to you?"
  "*When* was that?"

Requests for clarification:
  "I'm not clear on that."
  "Could you explain what you mean?"

Repetition of a primary question:
  Interviewer: "What kind of work do you do?"
  Respondent: "I work at the paper mill."
  Interviewer: "I see. What kind of work do you do there?"

To these specific forms of supplementing the primary questions in an interview must be added explanations, reassurances, and further information about the interview.

The separation of such interviewing techniques from the formulation of the major questions that present the topics of inquiry is in some degree arbitrary, of course. This distinction between primary and supplementary or "probe" questions is perhaps least useful in the two extreme forms of the interview, that is, when the interviewer is formulating all questions on the spur of the moment in a completely unstructured situation, and when the interviewer is absolutely restricted to reading prepared questions from a script or schedule. But most interviews are well within these extremes and involve some mixture of predetermined questions and spontaneous interactive elaborations on them. In most social research of scale, this functional distinction is emphasized by a division of labor; the people who conduct the interviews have usually not developed the basic questions to be asked. In such circumstances, it becomes essential to develop an understanding of the complementary functions of question formulation and elaboration or probing, so that they may in fact complement each other instead of producing a validity-destroying and unintended competition.

## Selection and training of interviewers

Evidence for the importance of interviewer selection and training is compelling and of long standing, although much of it is also indirect. It is clear, for example, that a variety of interviewer characteristics—demographic and attitudinal—can affect the interview product. It is less clear under what circumstances and through what chain of events these effects occur. Race and religion have been shown to inhibit responses, particularly when the respondent holds critical views of a minority to which the interviewer apparently belongs (Hyman et al. 1954; Robinson & Rhode 1946). Differences in age and sex between interviewer and respondent have been shown to reduce the communication of some kinds of data (Benney et al. 1956). Moreover, there is evidence that the social class of interviewers is reflected in the data they obtain on political issues (Katz 1942).

The unwanted relationship between interviewers' attitudes and interview data, which was first described by Rice (1929), has been demonstrated repeatedly (Cahalan et al. 1947; Guest 1947; Ferber & Wales 1952). Stanton and Baker (1942) have demonstrated that similar outcomes may result from an "expectation bias," that is, the interviewer's expectations of the respondent. Studies of interviewer personality and its effects are fewer, but one by Richardson (1965), using TAT (Thematic Apperception Test) measures of personality in relation to interviewer performance, suggests that the effective interviewer enjoys people, seeks friendly relations with them, and has insight into the complex of feeling relationships among widely varying types of people.

It is a plausible assumption that most of the characteristics of interviewers that have been shown to create biased data do so via the interviewers' behavior rather than through the reaction of respondents to some nonbehavioral characteristic. In other words, interviewers make characteristic errors which might be avoided to some extent by appropriate techniques and training (Cannell 1953) and by selection on the basis of intelligence (Guest & Nuckols 1950) and other measurable criteria. [*See* ERRORS, *article on* NONSAMPLING ERRORS.]

As yet there is not enough research on the selection and training of interviewers to warrant making definitive statements. However, it appears that the most important consideration in selection is that the interviewer must be seen by the respondent as being "within range" of communication on the interview topic. This does not imply a matching on education, age, sex, or other characteristics but, rather, suggests that the respondent must perceive the interviewer as having sufficient knowledge and understanding so that effective communication between the two is possible.

Evidence for the effects of interviewer training under varying circumstances is sketchy; opinions are strong—and variable. They range from reliance on brief written instructions (characteristic of much commercial opinion polling and market research) to the proposals of Nadel (1951) and Kluckhohn (1945) that interviewers in anthropological research should be psychoanalyzed as well as intensively trained in more specific ways. There is evidence that training makes a difference, some of it indirect and some direct. Cannell (1953) found that carefully trained interviewers produced results that were relatively free of the class and attitudinal biases reported by other investigators; his research, however, did not include experimental comparisons among interviewers differing in training. Richardson (1965) found that intensive training in field methods produced significant increases in measures of interviewing performance and no significant changes in personality measures (TAT). Individual differences in training effects were large, and the performance of individual interviewers before training was a poor predictor of posttraining performance.

To be effective, a training program should place heavy emphasis on interviewing practice. Role playing, observation by experienced persons, and tape recordings are useful, since they provide the opportunity for immediate feedback, which is a most important aspect of training.

Any article on interviewing in social research written today should be tentative in tone. For a number of reasons, the field is in flux. For one thing, some new ideas have been proposed after a long and relatively static period. Webb, Campbell, and their colleagues (Webb et al. 1966) have argued persuasively for less addiction to interviewing among social research workers and more attention to "unobtrusive measures." Richardson, Dohrenwend, and Klein (1965) have presented the opposing notions of "stressed" versus "unstressed" interviews in terms that invite research on the appropriate use of differing techniques. Cannell (see U.S. Department . . . 1965a; 1965b), Fowler (1965), and others have questioned the earlier emphasis on avoidance of interviewer influence and have begun research on the interviewer's functions as teacher and reinforcer of appropriate respondent behavior, as well as permissive encourager of conversation.

A second factor that makes for change in interviewing theory and practice is cultural and historical; the violation of privacy for trivial or questionable purposes has brought the rights and roles of interviewers and respondents under some discussion in the United States. It is a poor time for predicting the outcome of a trend that is so new and that may show vastly different forms in different cultures. Nevertheless, it seems likely that increasing sophistication about the reasons for interviewing and the consequences of the interview is a part of technological and industrial development in its contemporary forms. Whether the increasing sophistication of respondents will make the collection of data by interviewing easier, more difficult, or virtually impossible depends on the visible uses and abuses of the interview. In all but its most extreme and indirect forms, the interviewing technique is ultimately dependent upon a societal record of individual protection, respect for the confidentiality of personal data, and relevant and benign use of information in research, industry, and government.

ROBERT L. KAHN AND
CHARLES F. CANNELL

[*Directly related are the entries* FIELD WORK; OBSERVATION. *Other relevant material may be found in* ETHICS, *article on* ETHICAL ISSUES IN THE SOCIAL SCIENCES; MENTAL DISORDERS, TREATMENT OF, *article on* CLIENT-CENTERED COUNSELING; PROJECTIVE METHODS; REASON ANALYSIS; *and in the biography of* SULLIVAN.]

## BIBLIOGRAPHY

ADORNO, THEODOR W. et al. 1950 *The Authoritarian Personality.* American Jewish Committee, Social Studies Series, No. 3. New York: Harper.

ARGYRIS, CHRIS 1964 *Integrating the Individual and the Organization.* New York: Wiley.

ASCH, SOLOMON E. (1952) 1959 *Social Psychology.* Englewood Cliffs, N.J.: Prentice-Hall.

ATKINSON, JOHN W. (editor) 1958 *Motives in Fantasy, Action, and Society: A Method of Assessment and Study.* Princeton, N.J.: Van Nostrand.

BANCROFT, GERTRUDE; and WELCH, EMMETT H. 1946 Recent Experience With Problems of Labor Force Measurement. *Journal of the American Statistical Association* 41:303–312.

BARTLETT, FREDERIC C. (1932) 1950 *Remembering: A Study in Experimental and Social Psychology.* Cambridge Univ. Press.

BEEZER, R. H. 1956 *Research Methods of Interviewing Foreign Informants.* Technical Report, No. 30. Washington, D.C.: George Washington Univ., Human Resources Research Office.

BENNEY, MARK; RIESMAN, DAVID; and STAR, SHIRLEY A. 1956 Age and Sex in the Interview. *American Journal of Sociology* 62:143–152.

BINGHAM, WALTER; and MOORE, BRUCE V. (1931) 1959 *How to Interview.* 4th ed., rev. New York: Harper.

BOOTH, CHARLES et al. (1889–1891) 1902–1903 *Life and Labour of the People in London.* 17 vols. London: Macmillan.

BORING, EDWIN G. (1929) 1950 *A History of Experimental Psychology.* 2d ed. New York: Appleton.

CAHALAN, DON; TAMULONIS, VALERIE; and VERNER, HELEN W. 1947 Interviewer Bias Involved in Certain Types of Opinion Survey Questions. *International Journal of Opinion and Attitude Research* 1, no. 1: 63–77.

CAMPBELL, DONALD T. 1957 Factors Relevant to Validity of Experiments in Social Settings. *Psychological Bulletin* 54:297–312.

CANNELL, CHARLES F. 1953 A Study of the Effects of Interviewers' Expectations Upon Interviewing Results. Ph.D. dissertation, Ohio State Univ.

COOMBS, CLYDE H. 1964 *A Theory of Data.* New York: Wiley.

COUCH, A.; and KENISTON, K. 1960 Yeasayers and Naysayers: Agreeing Response Set as a Personality Variable. *Journal of Abnormal and Social Psychology* 60: 151–174.

CRONBACH, LEE J. 1946 Response Sets and Test Validity. *Educational and Psychological Measurement* 6: 475–494.

CRONBACH, LEE J. (1949) 1960 *Essentials of Psychological Testing.* 2d ed. New York: Harper.

FERBER, ROBERT; and WALES, HUGH G. 1952 Detection and Correction of Interviewer Bias. *Public Opinion Quarterly* 16:107–127.

FOWLER, F. J. JR. 1965 Education, Interaction, and Interview Performance. Ph.D. dissertation, Univ. of Michigan.

FREEDMAN, RONALD; WHELPTON, PASCAL K.; and CAMPBELL, ARTHUR A. 1959 *Family Planning, Sterility, and Population Growth.* New York: McGraw-Hill.

GORDEN, RAYMOND L. 1954 An Interaction Analysis of the Depth-interview. Ph.D. dissertation, Univ. of Chicago.

GUEST, LESTER L. 1947 A Study of Interviewer Competence. *International Journal of Opinion and Attitude Research* 1, no. 4:17–30.

GUEST, LESTER L.; and NUCKOLS, ROBERT 1950 A Laboratory Experiment in Recording in Public Opinion Interviewing. *International Journal of Opinion and Attitude Research* 4:336–352.

GURIN, GERALD; VEROFF, JOSEPH; and FELD, SHEILA 1960 *Americans View Their Mental Health: A Nationwide Interview Survey.* Joint Commission on Mental Illness and Health, Monograph Series, No. 4. New York: Basic Books.

HANSEN, MORRIS H. et al. 1951 Response Errors in Surveys. *Journal of the American Statistical Association* 46:147–190.

HERZBERG, FREDERICK; MAUSNER, BERNARD; and SNYDERMAN, BARBARA B. 1959 *The Motivation to Work.* New York: Wiley.

HILDUM, DONALD C.; and BROWN, ROGER W. 1956 Verbal Reinforcement and Interviewer Bias. *Journal of Abnormal and Social Psychology* 53:108–111.

HYMAN, HERBERT H. et al. (1954) 1962 *Interviewing in Social Research.* Univ. of Chicago Press.

KAHN, ROBERT L. 1952 A Comparison of Two Methods of Collecting Data for Social Research: The Fixed-alternative Questionnaire and the Open-ended Interview. Ph.D. dissertation, Univ. of Michigan.

KAHN, ROBERT L.; and CANNELL, CHARLES F. 1957 *The Dynamics of Interviewing: Theory, Technique and Cases.* New York: Wiley.

KAPLAN, ABRAHAM 1964 *The Conduct of Inquiry: Methodology for Behavioral Science.* San Francisco: Chandler.

KATONA, GEORGE 1960 *The Powerful Consumer: Psychological Studies of the American Economy.* New York: McGraw-Hill.

KATZ, DANIEL 1942 Do Interviewers Bias Poll Results? *Public Opinion Quarterly* 6:248–268.

KINSEY, ALFRED C. et al. 1948 *Sexual Behavior in the Human Male.* Philadelphia: Saunders.

KLUCKHOHN, CLYDE 1945 The Personal Document in Anthropological Science. Pages 79–173 in Louis R. Gottschalk, Clyde Kluckhohn, and Robert Angell, *The Use of Personal Documents in History, Anthropology and Sociology.* New York: Social Science Research Council.

KRASNER, LEONARD 1958 Studies of the Conditioning of Verbal Behavior. *Psychological Bulletin* 55:148–170.

LAZARSFELD, PAUL F. 1944 The Controversy Over Detailed Interviews—An Offer for Negotiation. *Public Opinion Quarterly* 8:38–60.

LENSKI, G. E.; and LEGGETT, J. C. 1960 Caste, Class and Deference in the Research Interview. *American Journal of Sociology* 65:463–467.

LEWIN, KURT 1947 Frontiers in Group Dynamics. Parts 1–2. *Human Relations* 1:5–41, 143–153. → Part 1: Concept, Method and Reality in Social Science, Social Equilibria and Social Change. Part 2: Channels of Group Life; Social Planning and Action Research.

LIKERT, RENSIS 1961 *New Patterns of Management.* New York: McGraw-Hill.

LITWAK, EUGENE 1956 A Classification of Biased Questions. *American Journal of Sociology* 62:182–186.

MANDLER, GEORGE; and KAPLAN, WARREN 1956 Subjective Evaluation and Reinforcing Effect of a Verbal Stimulus. *Science* 124:582–583.

MERTON, ROBERT K.; FISKE, MARJORIE; and KENDALL, PATRICIA L. (1944) 1956 *The Focused Interview: A Manual of Problems.* Glencoe, Ill.: Free Press.

METZNER, HELEN; and MANN, FLOYD C. 1951 A Limited Comparison of Two Methods of Data Collection: The Fixed-alternative Questionnaire and the Open-ended Interview. Unpublished manuscript, Univ. of Michigan, Institute for Social Research.

MICHIGAN, UNIVERSITY OF, SURVEY RESEARCH CENTER 1960 *The American Voter*, by Angus Campbell et al. New York: Wiley.

MILGRAM, STANLEY 1965 Some Conditions of Obedience and Disobedience to Authority. Pages 243–262 in Ivan D. Steiner and Morton Fishbein (editors), *Current Studies in Social Psychology.* New York: Holt.

NADEL, SIEGFRIED F. 1951 *The Foundations of Social Anthropology.* London: Cohen & West; Glencoe, Ill.: Free Press. → See especially pages 169–176.

*Organizational Stress: Studies in Role Conflict and Ambiguity*, by Robert L. Kahn et al. 1964 New York: Wiley.

PAYNE, STANLEY L. 1951 *The Art of Asking Questions.* Studies in Public Opinion, No. 3. Princeton Univ. Press.

QUAY, HERBERT 1959 The Effect of Verbal Reinforcement on the Recall of Early Memories. *Journal of Abnormal and Social Psychology* 59:254–257.

*Research Methods in Social Relations.* Rev. ed. By Claire Selltiz et al. (1959) 1964 New York: Holt.

RICE, STUART A. 1929 Contagious Bias in the Interview: A Methodological Note. *American Journal of Sociology* 35:420–423.

RICHARDSON, STEPHEN A. 1965 A Study of Selected Personality Characteristics of Social Science Field Workers. Pages 328–358 in Stephen A. Richardson, Barbara S. Dohrenwend, and David Klein, *Interviewing: Its Forms and Functions.* New York: Basic Press.

RICHARDSON, STEPHEN A.; DOHRENWEND, BARBARA S.; and KLEIN, DAVID 1965 *Interviewing: Its Forms and Functions.* New York: Basic Books. → See especially pages 64–65 and 277–278.

RICHARDSON, STEPHEN A.; HASTORF, ALBERT H.; and DORNBUSCH, SANFORD M. 1964 Effects of Physical Disability on a Child's Description of Himself. *Child Development* 35:893–907.

RIESMAN, DAVID 1958 Some Observations on the Interviewing in the Teacher Apprehension Study. Pages 266–370 in Paul F. Lazarsfeld and Wagner Thielens,

Jr., *The Academic Mind: Social Scientists in a Time of Crisis.* Glencoe, Ill.: Free Press.

ROBINSON, DUANE; and ROHDE, SYLVIA 1946 Two Experiments With an Anti-Semitism Poll. *Journal of Abnormal and Social Psychology* 41:136–144.

SALZINGER, KURT; and PISONI, STEPHANIE 1960 Reinforcement of Verbal Affect Responses of Normal Subjects During an Interview. *Journal of Abnormal and Social Psychology* 60:127–130.

SASLOW, GEORGE et al. 1957 Test–Retest Stability of Interaction Patterns During Interviews Conducted One Week Apart. *Journal of Abnormal and Social Psychology* 54:295–302.

SHAPIRO, SAM; and EBERHART, JOHN C. 1947 Interviewer Differences in an Intensive Interview Survey. *International Journal of Opinion and Attitude Research* 1, no. 2:1–17.

SMITH, M. BREWSTER; BRUNER, JEROME S.; and WHITE, ROBERT W. 1956 *Opinions and Personality.* New York: Wiley.

STANTON, FRANK; and BAKER, KENNETH H. 1942 Interviewer-bias and the Recall of Incompletely Learned Materials. *Sociometry* 5:123–134.

U.S. DEPARTMENT OF HEALTH, EDUCATION, AND WELFARE, PUBLIC HEALTH SERVICE 1965a *Reporting of Hospitalization in Health Interviewing Survey: Methodological Study of Several Factors Affecting Reporting of Hospital Episodes.* Prepared by C. F. Cannell et al. Washington: Government Printing Office.

U.S. DEPARTMENT OF HEALTH, EDUCATION, AND WELFARE, PUBLIC HEALTH SERVICE 1965b *Comparison of Hospitalization Reporting.* Prepared by C. F. Cannell et al. Washington: Government Printing Office.

WEBB, EUGENE et al. 1966 *Unobtrusive Measures.* Chicago: Rand McNally.

## II

### PERSONALITY APPRAISAL

Despite the developments in twentieth-century psychological measurements, the interview, the most ancient method for personality appraisal, remains both the most powerful and the least affected by psychometric refinements. The primary appeal of the interviewing method lies in its potential. The interview can provide a broader spectrum of information than any standard procedure and can be focused on classes of information for which no standard procedure is available; entirely in contrast with the sense of a standard procedure, it permits a change in emphasis and an adjustment in observational focus as the goals of appraisal may define or redefine themselves during the course of the interview. The secondary appeal of the interview is its convenience; it can be of any duration. In addition, there is no standard procedure which can be applied in a greater variety of circumstances because the interview requires no equipment, no definite setting, and no response modalities other than verbal; with a telephone it does not even require the physical proximity of the interviewer and the interviewee.

In the appraisal of personality, it is possible to distinguish three kinds of orientation. There is the *normative* orientation, where the manifestation of a quality or an attribute in a given individual is appraised on a comparative basis, using as reference the manner in which the manifestation may be found in a standard population from which the individual in question may have been drawn; this orientation emphasizes individual differences between people. In addition there is the *ipsative* orientation; this is the orientation which attempts to determine the relative strength of various qualities within the individual. It emphasizes intraindividual differences which indicate the relative dominance of qualities within individuals, without providing a basis for comparison between individuals with respect to the normative strength of these qualities. There is also the *idiographic* orientation; this is the orientation which seeks within the individual to identify manifestations or qualities which are distinctive to him but may not be of sufficient general interest or frequency to provide a meaningful basis for either ipsative or normative appraisal.

Regardless of the orientation chosen by the appraiser, it is apparent that the interview may be used in a manner which provides a normative assessment comparable with available psychometric procedures for personality appraisals. The interview is uniquely suitable for determining the relative or intraindividual strength of various motivational components and the relative extent to which the ego employs certain mechanisms of defense. The interview is without peer in the broad screening of atypical idiographic qualities pointing to personality weaknesses which could interfere with proper functioning under certain high-demand situations. While the appeal of the interview remains in its potential, there are situations in which its vulnerabilities make it a second choice to the relatively cumbersome and circumscribed standard psychometric devices. [*See* PSYCHOMETRICS.]

## Vulnerabilities of the interview

**Reliability and validity.**   The interview is not an objective procedure. Any given result may not always be reproducible, and in this sense it is unreliable. The results of an interview may not be reproducible because the individual himself has changed, perhaps in some way which is pertinent to the appraisal, but more probably in his perception of the appraisal interview and the manner in which he should respond. He may have become more fearful, more confident, or more opportunistic in the situation. The interviewer, too, may have changed in consequence of the first interview; he

may have come to see his task in a different way, or he may have developed biasing feelings about the interviewee.

The literature is rich in studies which show that the interviewer is not only a primary stimulus to the interviewee's response (Cairns & Lewis 1962; Cohen et al. 1954; Greenspoon 1955; Kanfer & McBrearty 1962; Verplanck 1955; Williams 1964; Zigler & Kanzer 1962); unless the interview is recorded, he is also the fallible observer and variable recorder of the interviewee's response (Cuadra & Albaugh 1956; Hildum & Brown 1956). He is the interacting participant–observer; his effective role is not only subject to change but is also unknown and ungauged. It is possible, of course, to place restraints on the interviewer's role, to standardize his questions and his responses, and in this way to approach reproducibility. To the extent to which this standardization is obtained, however, the interview loses its unique potential and assumes both the guarantees and the limitations which characterize psychometric standardization.

The issue of reliability as a challenge to interview appraisals is no more disquieting than the issue of validity. The substance of an interview may not be pertinent to its purpose. This paradox is possible because the purposes of the appraisal to which the interview is applied are often poorly defined. Sometimes the interview must both explore and assess so that, in effect, the interview has the confounding task of defining its own purpose.

**Sources of distortion.**   Once the purposes of the appraisal are known, the pertinence of the content of the interview to these purposes remains a matter of considerable uncertainty. The meaning of the content of interview responses is qualified by many factors, and the array of content which emerges in any interview is biased and selected by many influences (Bolster & Springbett 1961; Dohrenwend & Richardson 1963; Gynther 1957; Jones 1954). The amount of any given kind of responsive material may be truncated by the expressive capacity of the interviewee, by the defensive requirements of the interviewee's personality, or by the tolerance of the interviewer for material which is threatening to his own defensive needs. In addition to such limitations there are distortions which may be deliberate, as the interviewee attempts to direct his performance, or may be unconscious, when one unrecognized requirement of his personality interacts with another.

There are also response distortions which accrue from the context. These may have their origins in the meaning of the interview situation to the interviewee, in the setting of the interview with its facilitating or distracting stimulus properties, and in the general set which accrues from concurrent life circumstances and may characterize the interviewee at that particular time only. Aside from the defensive requirements of the interviewee's personality and current influences which affect the content of his responses at the time, the manner in which the interviewee perceives both the interviewer and his responses is subject to perceptual biases or predispositions which may or may not be known by the interviewer. Some of these perceptual characteristics reflect the values, the mores, and the experiences that accrue from the interviewee's subculture and may result in gross distortions or complete failures in communication that may be beyond the control of the interviewer, if not entirely outside his awareness. For similar reasons, the responses of the interviewee may be grossly misconstrued by the interviewer who, because of his ethnic, social, economic, or educational background, may ascribe a mistaken meaning to responses of the interviewee (Douvan 1956; McArthur 1955; Ort 1952; Rankin & Campbell 1955; Rosen 1956; Siller 1957).

**Controlling responses.** Although the interview may be reduced to a standard procedure to assure a modicum of reliability and validity, its greatest value and its greatest challenge may be found when it is used as a *process* for securing and interpreting information. The process is unique in the particular sense that the information which is secured at any one phase may have been selectively sought on the basis of interpretations accruing from information provided by preceding phases. Because of this, most of the current research on the interview is concerned either with the task of selectively controlling the interviewee's response (Cairns & Lewis 1962; Cohen et al. 1954; Ferguson & Buss 1960; Heller et al. 1963; Hildum & Brown 1956; Kanfer & McBrearty 1962; Sarason & Campbell 1962; Verplanck 1955; Williams 1964; Zigler & Kanzer 1962) or with the task of interpreting the implications of these responses (Hathaway 1956; Shrauger & Altrocchi 1964; Taft 1955). Thus the concern with standardizing the selection and interpretation of interview material is relatively minor. The major emphasis is on controlling and comprehending.

The problem of controlling the course of the interview and comprehending the data it generates is a problem of developing adequate descriptive concepts and applying the relevant available theories of human behavior. The ways in which such concepts and theories must function can be appreciated in part by a review of the kinds of data that are available from the interview and that presumably could be pertinent to the task of appraising the personality of the individual.

### Descriptive information

The verbal content alone usually contains a wealth of information which dwarfs the interpretive resources of the interviewer and may greatly surpass the initial purposes of the interview. As reflected in the tradition of oral examinations, the interview is an excellent device for sampling the individual's knowledge. Beyond this, it may provide an exhibit of his verbal facility and his conceptual resources. The content of the interview can provide information concerning the intentions, the attitudes, and the values of the respondent with respect to specific topics. At a more personal level, however, the interview may be used to provide information about the individual's personal circumstances, his background experiences, accounts of how he or others have responded to various experiences and situations, and many other kinds of information which are either directly expressive of the individual's personality or are in some indirect way clues to qualities which are relevant to an understanding of his personality. The verbal content of the interview may also describe the feelings of the individual, including the prevailing moods that characterize his general outlook, the varieties of moods that he can experience, and the intensity and labile sensitivity of these mood changes.

**Nonverbal responses.** In most situations the verbal content is the object of primary interest, but other response modalities or qualities (Domey et al. 1964; Secord & Muthard 1955) provide data of substantial relevance to an appraisal of the personality (Giedt 1955). There are such obvious features as voice intensity, pitch, and adaptive modulation to accompany content and intent (Kramer 1963). There is a host of accessory motor responses. The mobility of the eyes and face, the involvement of the hands and arms, postural adjustments (Dittman 1962; Ekman 1964; Krout 1935; Luriia 1932; Sainsbury 1955), tentative movements of various parts of the body which appear to be a part of the expressive effort, and yet other movements which obviously detract from the manifest communication—such as tics, grimaces, lisps, stammers, and respiratory irregularities—may tell a story that is not necessarily congruent with the manifest verbal content. To be included in this class of information are the temporal features of the individual's behavior, the latency of his responses, the duration (Anderson 1960; Phillips et al. 1961), the number of pauses (Wittenborn et al. 1962), and response variability (Boomer

1963; Dibner 1956; Eldred & Price 1958; Mahl 1956; Pope & Siegman 1962). Beyond this there are those accessory response qualities which must be described as physiological (Malmo et al 1956; Shagass & Malmo 1954). These would include flushing or blanching of the face, perspiration, temperature changes of the hands, tremors, the pounding pulse of excitement, the lassitude of fatigue or boredom, and the respiratory irregularities of tension, with shallow or irregular breathing, deep sighs, or arrested inspirations.

**Situational context.** In addition to the responses themselves, the information from the interview can and should include a description of the stimulus context in which the responses occurred. The most obvious features of the stimulus context would include the questions and the responses verbalized by the interviewer. Nevertheless, it is apparent from several inquiries that the mood (Bolster & Springbett 1961) and the values and expectations (Koltuv 1962; Shrauger & Altrocchi 1964) of the interviewer, as well as the way he feels about the interviewee and the content of the interview, also affect the responses of the interviewee and are a part of the stimulus context (Heller et al. 1963).

In addition, the context includes the manner in which the purposes of the interview are presented of the interviewee's perception are referred to as are expected, that are prudent, or that are permissible for him. Attempts to control these features of the interviewee's perception are referred to as the preliminary *structuring* of the interview and are, in effect, an attempt on the part of the interviewer to instruct the interviewee with respect to what he should expect and how he may respond. There are also the obvious facts concerning the circumstances of the interview, including privacy, assurance of confidentiality, associative distractions within the setting, and incidental distractions during the course of the interview. These all may have a bearing on the interviewee's responses and are, therefore, a part of the total body of information which may be supplied by the interview and may be relevant to the appraisal of the personality.

**Response contexts.** The interview also provides information of a more subtle nature. Most important of these subtler considerations is the sequential context in which a given response occurs. As anticipated in prior statements, where the interview lies in the course of the individual's antecedent and anticipated subsequent experiences is of obvious relevance; where a response lies in the preceding and succeeding verbal content within the interview may be even more informative. The

association may be explicit and unambiguous; more often, however, it is symbolic. It is not sufficient to note the sequential context of verbal responses. The antecedents and the consequences of an autonomic response may reveal more about the personality of the individual than many pages of verbal transcription. A similar implication may be found in the temporal variations in response, e.g., delays, pauses, or accelerations.

The relevant sequential context is not to be found in the responses of the interviewee alone, however; as research reports indicate, and as may be well revealed in almost any recorded interview, where the interviewee's response lies in the sequential context of the interviewer's responses, verbal or nonverbal, overt or covert, has a basic, almost invariable qualifying significance (Greenspoon 1955; Kanfer et al. 1960; Moos 1963; Sarason 1962; Verplanck 1955). For the purposes of appraising personality these sequential features cannot safely be disregarded.

## The interpretive use of information

**Frames of reference.** Assuming that it is possible to guide, if not direct, the genesis of information during the course of the interview to secure the kinds of information that are desired, there remains the question of how this information may be interpreted in order to serve the purposes of personality appraisal. Such a discussion requires some attempt to define and distinguish what is meant by personality, and it should be observed that personality may be viewed from either of two standpoints.

From the more popular standpoint, personality refers to the social stimulus characteristics of the individual, i.e., how people perceive and respond to him. This obviously includes his appearance, the quality of his performance in various situations, and the manner in which he responds to the presence of others. Since these qualities change rather slowly, their appraisal has some value because it may be used to anticipate how the individual will perform in the future and how people may be expected to respond to him in future situations. The principle that appears to govern the accuracy of such predictions assumes that the more similar a future situation is to a present one, the more the individual's future personality qualities will resemble his presently perceived qualities.

There is a second, more sophisticated view of personality, however; in this view, personality refers to the dynamic economy of the individual's motivational adjustment and to both the relative strengths of his basic drives and the skills he has acquired in expressing these drives in the society in which he lives. In response to the demands and opportunities of his society there appears to be a gradual shift in the relative strength of his motives and a somewhat more fluid, although tardy, change in the skills or defensive mechanisms whereby the individual seeks to serve his needs as he negotiates in his society. This lifelong process of acquisition and change tends to be prompt and orderly during years of physical development, but like most other changes it diminishes with advancing age. These changes and acquisitions are sometimes referred to as the socialization of the personality.

There are important advantages in an appraisal of the relative strengths of the individual's motives and an identification of the preferred modes of defense (Weintraub & Aronson 1964) which he employs in the service of these motives. The advantage lies in the general premise that the concepts involved are applicable to virtually all situations. The dynamic theory of personality is sufficiently well developed that once the strengths of motives are assessed and the preferred coping mechanisms are identified, a transcendent understanding of the individual emerges, making it possible to anticipate qualities of the individual's behavior in situations that are quite different from those in which these features of the personality were first known and appraised. On this basis, attempts may be made to anticipate the manner in which the individual would respond in new employment situations, to social threats that he has never known, and to various hypothetical future situations, including life with a prospective spouse. Although such predictions can be made on the basis of a personality appraisal that is built upon an understanding of the dynamic economies of the individual's adjustment, the accuracy of such predictions seems to be highly variable. Some interviewers provide much more accurate predictions than others (Bieri 1955; Campbell et al. 1964; Cronbach 1955; Gage & Cronbach 1955; Koltuv 1962; Landfield 1955; Lundy 1956; Shrauger & Altrocchi 1964; Wittich 1955; Yonge 1956). The various studies of such accuracy serve primarily to confirm that it is a variable which rests upon the individual appraiser; the studies do not clearly illuminate the characteristics of background, temperament, or training that identify the appraisers who will be most accurate. It appears, however, that experience may be an important factor.

The interpretive use of interview information may be seen as guided by several different kinds of considerations. Much of the verbal content of the interview has an obvious relevance to the purposes of appraisal, giving it a quality of face validity which permits its direct interpretive application at a practical, common-sense level.

Many of the physiological manifestations in the interview have an implication for stress—that is, tension, fear, or anxiety—which is almost universal in its significance and for interpretive purposes may be assumed to cut across most national, linguistic, and other cultural differences. Various motoric signs of excitement or indifference and indications of lassitude or fatigue may also have a rather general interpretive significance, although there are subcultural differences in the meaning of the temporal aspects of verbal response. For example, the temporal aspects of responses of Scotch descendants in the Appalachian hills cannot be interpreted on the same basis as they might for certain groups of Spanish-Americans.

*Normative factors.* Most of the information that is generated in the course of the interview cannot be safely interpreted for personality appraisal without some consideration of normative factors. The meaning of the response is greatly qualified by who makes the response, and from this standpoint the most important features of an individual may be defined in terms of the general characteristics of the social or subcultural group or groups with which he may be identified. This is not only true for the meaning of the manifest content of the verbal material but can be true for the symbolic or allusional meaning as well. (This is not to deny that the symbolic significance of some material appears to be almost universal in its implications.)

The normative significance of interview material may present difficulties at several different levels. For example, the way in which language is used by preparatory school students, jazz musicians, or some Negro groups can be seriously misleading if the interviewer is not aware of the peculiarities of denotation and connotation that characterize the group. Perhaps more seriously misleading than the distinctive use of words are the values that are ascribed to certain phrases, gestures, or other communicative expressions. A response that may be viewed as an indication of affectionate acceptance in one social group may be regarded as an expression of rejection or contempt in another.

Almost all of the content of the interview is invested with value implications. The values, attitudes, and affective involvements that may be safely inferred, however, require an application of the appropriate normative reference. For example, in some communities knowledge about the experience and affairs of other members is freely shared

(Zborowski 1951), and the requirements for privacy may be moderate. In other communities certain kinds of experiences, sentiments, and personal knowledge are not shared and the requirements for privacy and confidentiality are extreme, so that the interviewee's loss of privacy is tantamount to a serious loss of face and can be a threatening prospect. There are also important differences in the meaning of an experience. For example, individuals from some groups are tolerant of their blunders and regard themselves as one with the world so that they can safely refer to their own errors as things "that happened." Persons from other groups, however, must regard a blunder as solely their own responsibility, a deficit in their life balance sheet which can never be fully compensated for. Such distinctions that relate to social norms must be a part of the appraiser's awareness, because a specific point of view when manifested in one subculture may indicate an appropriate product of socialization, while the same point of view in another subculture may indicate a crippling neurotic aberration.

*Crucial interviewer skills.* Thus it may be acknowledged that much of the content of the interview has an obvious meaning; that some of the affective expressions, particularly those involving the autonomic nervous system, have an almost universal significance; and that appropriate normative references add substantially to the interviewer's interpretive acuity and greatly reduce the risk of gross misperceptions. Nevertheless, the great burden of the interpretive use of the information provided by the appraisal interview rests on the inferential and deductive skills of the interviewer. Although the powerful use of inference and deduction in personality appraisal may be described as a skill, it rests upon a fairly definitive body of fact and theory concerning the development of the human personality and its functional economy in the interacting requirements of the living organism in its social and physical environment.

The appraisal of the social stimulus characteristics of the individual makes relatively superficial demands on the inferential and deductive acuity of the interviewer. In contrast, however, the assessment of the strength of the individual's drives and the identification of the coping mechanisms employed in commerce with society are primarily products of complex inference and deduction and are subject to error of judgment. Nevertheless, it is the complex inferential appraisal of these qualities which offers the greatest promise of providing a defensible basis for anticipating the responses of the individual in new situations.

**Psychosexual development.** For the most part, the assessment of the relative strength of drive is concerned with attempts to establish the levels of psychosexual development that the individual may have reached in the metamorphosis of his personality and the readiness with which he may regress to earlier, more primitive levels in response to frustration (Fenichel 1945). Level of psychosexual development is primarily a psychoanalytic concept and is based upon the premise that the motivational requirements of the individual evolve through a successive series of stages as the individual's social and interpersonal role is modified from infancy to maturity (Munroe 1955). Where the individual lies on this hypothetical continuum of motivational maturation can often be safely inferred from the manner in which the individual handles himself in the interview, the way he sees others, the role he plays vis-à-vis others, the significance he ascribes to various personal experiences, and the way in which he responds to both the demands of his social environment and his inclination toward affective expression. Whether psychoanalytic theory can always be relied upon to provide an index to the various strengths of the individual's motivational requirement has not been established with scientific rigor, but it seems reasonable to suggest at this time that such a theoretical approach does provide the interviewer with powerful and incisive questions that can guide his inferences and sharpen his deductions so that in the course of his appraisal some of the very best answers may be generated.

**Other aspects of motivation.** Ordinarily, most individuals who are the subject of personality appraisal are part of a middle-class society with its traditional emphasis on achievement (Douvan 1956), and often the aims of appraisal must emphasize achievement striving with its compensatory and competitive features. The dynamic views of personality developed by Alfred Adler (Munroe 1955) and his associates emphasize compensatory striving in response to real or imagined weaknesses relative to the environment. These provide an array of postulates and tenets which may be of great value to the appraiser, particularly as he attempts to formulate useful inferences and provide specific deductions concerning achievement predispositions in the personality of the interviewee. [See Achievement motivation; Individual psychology; *and the biography of* Adler.]

In addition to these general views concerning

the cultural significance of the personality and the dynamic motivational implications of its various manifestations, there is a substantial and rapidly growing body of research-based information which may guide the interviewer as he attempts to assess the motivational requirements of the individual (Feinberg 1953; Handel 1965; Helper 1958; Jourard 1957; Koch 1956; Manis 1958; Payne & Mussen 1956; Peck 1958).

Attempts to infer motivational characteristics of the individual must be made during the course of the interview. The alert and resourceful appraiser will also find or create numerous opportunities to confirm or refute the deductive implications of his inferences. It may be noted that the development of knowledge concerning the individual, like the development of all other integrated bodies of information, requires the reciprocal use of inference and deduction, with the revisions of inference based on attempts at observational verification of the deductions. [See MOTIVATION, *article on* HUMAN MOTIVATION.]

An assessment of the individual's motivational requirements is not enough, however; it is equally important to identify the devices which the individual characteristically employs in expressing or gratifying these motives. These devices contribute in large measure to the social stimulus value of his personality and are the basis for the description of what is ordinarily known as character (Fenichel 1945) and disposition (Mendelson 1960). It is also relevant to predict the individual's response in novel situations, particularly those where the probable motivational components may be anticipated. The capacity of the individual to sublimate primitive drives, the extent to which he evades the energy requirements of challenges by resorting to denial, the projective ascription of culpable motives to others, and the extent to which he displaces affect, particularly hostility, from the stimulating source to some innocuous object are all a part of the coping devices or mechanisms of defense (Haan 1964; Weintraub & Aronson 1964) that may characterize the individual's attempts to handle the insistent requirements of his drives.

As a final comment on the interpretive use of interview information in the appraisal of the personality, it should be noted that in most situations the interviewer is not dependent on the interview information alone. Usually there is supplementary information describing background, education, work history, a statement of current circumstances, the opinions or interests of the referral source, and sometimes the availability of psychological test results. Any such information can have substantial value, either in drawing inferences or in verifying them by providing other sources of data for testing their deductive implications.

## Methods of interviewing

The foregoing review of some of the aims of the interview appraisal, its vulnerabilities, the kind of data on which it is based, and the rational basis by which these data may be applied for the purposes of appraisal can lead to an appreciation of the problems of gathering information by an interview procedure. As familiar forms and conventions of the appraisal interview are reviewed in the following paragraphs, it will be noted that there is some rough correspondence between the manner in which the information is gathered and the manner in which it may be interpreted.

**Standardization.** There have been numerous attempts to develop a standardized interview procedure. The primary aim of such standardization was to increase reliability and validity. In some instances, however, the standardization reflected a distinctive view of personality as well. One of the most important standardized interview procedures was developed by Chapple (1949), an anthropologist who worked with various collaborators on the premise that the important clues in personality were not to be found in the content of the interview but were revealed in characteristic patterns of interaction. Interaction was examined primarily in terms of its temporal aspects, and an interaction chronograph was developed for this purpose. The procedure is one where the observer presses buttons signaling various events and the machine provides a series of scores reflective of such qualities as initiative, tendency to interrupt, and dominance as they may characterize the verbal behavior of the participants in the interview. Several investigators have examined the properties of these interaction scores. Notable among them are G. Saslow, J. D. Matarazzo, and their collaborators, who have provided reassuring indication of reliability and potential validity (Matarazzo et al. 1956; Phillips et al. 1961).

Wittenborn and his colleagues (1962) developed a standard interview procedure which incorporates the principle of scores based on temporal characteristics but is different in its basic orientation in the sense that it comprises a series of standard questions calculated to involve various motivational qualities selected from Henry A. Murray's system of needs (see *Explorations in Personality* 1938). The temporal scoring requires no machine, however, and can be reliably provided by the practiced interviewer counting silently to himself and making marks to indicate periods of speech and silence. The procedure provides excellent inter-observer reliability, and indications of validity may be found in the fact that it generates scores that are correlated with symptom ratings and are sensitive to antidepressant medication.

A further approach to the standard interview is provided by Gleser, Gottschalk, and Springer (1961). This procedure requires only that the interviewee talk about a life experience for an uninterrupted period of five minutes. The recorded interviews are transcribed, and the scoring and analysis are provided by counting the occurrence of psychologically pertinent themes in each communication unit, e.g., one hundred words. The themes that are counted vary with the purposes of the interview, and a detailed application of an anxiety scale has been described.

**Structure.** Often when the purpose of the interview is highly specific, arbitrary restrictions of the content of the interview may be justified. This would obviously be true in a census interview or a simple poll of buying habits, political opinions, or voting intent. In a similar way the taking of testimony is often a highly restricted interview. In many situations the employment interview is equally restricted, but it is possible that such restriction misserves its purpose and may obscure more than it reveals about the candidate.

It is possible to conduct an interview in a somewhat structured manner, thereby guaranteeing that certain types of information are included without being narrowly restrictive or resorting to a question–answer type inquiry (Cline 1955). This is often done by being certain that a standard set of provocative questions is introduced during the course of the interview. Psychiatric case history procedures may follow such a pattern. It is also possible to give the interview an effective structure if the interviewer has well in mind a standard set of questions for which he desires answers. On this basis he can be selectively attentive to the material that is pertinent to his interest. As the interview progresses to its close, he can guide the discussion over remaining areas of pertinence so that answers to his questions may be secured without making the informant fully aware of the selective nature of his interest and without biasing the informant's responses. Thus a standard body of information is secured without the stilted or arbitrary employment of a standard inquiry. This procedure can be developed to yield scores that have a high order

of reliability and validity. For example, Wittenborn and his associates have developed a standard set of questions which may be answered by a social worker on the basis of her interview with the family informants of mental hospital patients. These scores, based on a factor analytic reduction of data, have been found to be useful in identifying patients who will respond favorably or unfavorably to a given treatment (Wittenborn & May 1966).

**Unstructured interviews.** There are also unstructured approaches to the interview. These are, in effect, exploratory in the sense that their content and course are expected to be reflective of the interest, needs, and moods of the respondents and not determined by the a priori interests of the interviewer. The use of such an approach is usually based on the premise that the affectively significant material will find expression in a tolerant, acceptant, protected atmosphere (Rogers 1942). If affective requirements and the huge freight of content which they carry are considered to be important for the purposes of the appraisal, then the acceptant, unstructured approach has much to commend it; the interviewer's task becomes one of encouraging the flow of such material without precipitating an accelerated cathartic reaction which can generate a subsequent defensive refractory phase often known as "resistance." In general, however, the unstructured approach does little to heighten the vigilance of the respondent and generates very little defensive resistance. The permissiveness of the interview situation is never complete. Even the most nondirective interviewer is somewhat selective in the material that elicits from him expressions of sympathy, assurance, understanding, interest, or acceptance. Since such feedback communication from the interviewer tends selectively to reinforce certain kinds of materials and not others, the unstructured interview is never without control, and the literature showing that the response of the interviewee is greatly influenced by his perception of the interviewer is quite substantial.

In some interviews, particularly those employed in psychotherapy, an attempt is made to secure a free association of the respondent's thoughts and feelings. Presumably in this situation the course of the content is guided primarily by the interplay of the individual's needs and his defensive responses to them. Since it appears that the interviewee requires guiding, coaching, encouragement, and correction while attempting to associate freely, a free association may not be entirely "free" and may rest largely on what the interviewer's theoretical persuasion or personal viewpoint leads him to consider to be "free."

Of increasing significance is the use of technical aids in securing a record of the interview. Complete recordings which may be subsequently reviewed, transcribed, or scored are now commonplace. In some situations the use of sound movies is considered to be practical, and closed-circuit television permits the simultaneous use of more than one observer. These devices may have their greatest value in obviating problems of reliability and validity which are always a part of the participant observer situation, both because of the practical limits of the interviewer's observational acuity and the defensive limitations that are generated in him as he responds to the interviewee and is involved in the emerging flow of information.

Much is possible within an interview procedure, but there are barriers to an invariably satisfactory use of the interview as a method of personality appraisal. The greatest barrier appears to lie not in the interview itself but in the fact that right answers to wrong questions do not lead to satisfaction. In the interview method of personality appraisal, it is probable that failure is more often due to the fact that the wrong questions were asked than to the possibility that the wrong answers to these questions may have been proffered. This is the criterion problem. If as much care were taken in formulating the questions that the appraiser is expected to answer as the appraiser ordinarily exercises in providing his answers, the interview as a method of personality appraisal could be viewed with greater confidence. Unfortunately, the same interview, if not the same responses within the interview, must often be used not only to formulate the incisive questions but to provide the definitive answers. Such confounding may lead to unverifiable results because in the appraisal interview, as in all other inquiries, one cannot use the same data both to generate an inference and to test its implications. The difficulties that prompt these reservations are not insuperable. While the traditional use of standard psychometric devices may have attained its maturity, the use of the interview, guided by increasing knowledge of the personality and aided by the data-reducing capacity of modern computers, may now be approaching the threshold of its great development.

J. R. WITTENBORN

[*Directly related are the entries* PERSONALITY MEASUREMENT; PROJECTIVE METHODS. *Other relevant* material *may be found in* PERSONALITY; PSYCHOANALYSIS, *article on* THERAPEUTIC METHODS; *and* PSYCHOMETRICS.]

BIBLIOGRAPHY

ANDERSON, C. W. 1960 The Relation Between Speaking Times and Decision in the Employment Interview. *Journal of Applied Psychology* 44:267–268.

ANISFELD, MOSHE; MUNOZ, STANLEY R.; and LAMBERT, WALLACE E. 1963 The Structure and Dynamics of the Ethnic Attitudes of Jewish Adolescents. *Journal of Abnormal and Social Psychology* 66:31–36.

BIERI, JAMES 1955 Cognitive Complexity–Simplicity and Predictive Behavior. *Journal of Abnormal and Social Psychology* 51:263–268.

BOLSTER, B. I.; and SPRINGBETT, B. M. 1961 The Reaction of Interviewers to Favorable and Unfavorable Information. *Journal of Applied Psychology* 45:97–103.

BOOMER, DONALD S. 1963 Speech Disturbance and Body Movement in Interviews. *Journal of Nervous and Mental Disease* 136:263–266.

CAIRNS, ROBERT B.; and LEWIS, MICHAEL 1962 Dependency and the Reinforcement Value of a Verbal Stimulus. *Journal of Consulting Psychology* 26:1–8.

CAMPBELL, DONALD T. et al. 1964 Varieties of Projection in Trait Attribution. *Psychological Monographs* 78, no. 15.

CHAPPLE, ELIOT D. 1949 The Interaction Chronograph: Its Evolution and Present Application. *Personnel* 25: 295–307.

CLINE, VICTOR B. 1955 Ability to Judge Personality Assessed With a Stress Interview and Sound-film Technique. *Journal of Abnormal and Social Psychology* 50:183–187.

COHEN, BERTRAM D. et al. 1954 Experimental Manipulation of Verbal Behavior. *Journal of Experimental Psychology* 47:106–110.

CRONBACH, LEE J. 1955 Processes Affecting Scores on "Understanding of Others" and "Assumed Similarity." *Psychological Bulletin* 52:177–193.

CUADRA, CARLOS A.: and ALBAUGH, WILLIAM P. 1956 Sources of Ambiguity in Psychological Reports. *Journal of Clinical Psychology* 12:109–115.

DIBNER, ANDREW S. 1956 Cue-counting: A Measure of Anxiety in Interviews. *Journal of Consulting Psychology* 20:475–478.

DITTMANN, ALLEN T. 1962 The Relationship Between Body Movements and Moods in Interviews. *Journal of Consulting Psychology* 26:480.

DOHRENWEND, BARBARA S.; and RICHARDSON, STEPHEN A. 1963 Directiveness and Nondirectiveness in Research Interviewing: A Reformulation of the Problem. *Psychological Bulletin* 60:475–485.

DOMEY, RICHARD G.; DUCKWORTH, JAMES E.; and MORANDI, ANTHONY J. 1964 Taxonomies and Correlates of Physique. *Psychological Bulletin* 62:411–426.

DOUVAN, ELIZABETH 1956 Social Status and Success Strivings. *Journal of Abnormal and Social Psychology* 52:219–223.

EKMAN, PAUL 1964 Body Position, Facial Expression, and Verbal Behavior During Interviews. *Journal of Abnormal and Social Psychology* 68:295–301.

ELDRED, STANLEY H.; and PRICE, DOUGLAS B. 1958 A Linguistic Evaluation of Feeling States in Psychotherapy. *Psychiatry* 21:115–121.

*Explorations in Personality: A Clinical and Experimental Study of Fifty Men of College Age*, by Henry A. Murray et al. 1938 London and New York: Oxford Univ. Press.

FEINBERG, MORTIMER R. 1953 Relation of Background Experience to Social Acceptance. *Journal of Abnormal and Social Psychology* 48:206–214.

FENICHEL, OTTO 1945 *The Psychoanalytic Theory of Neurosis.* New York: Norton.

FERGUSON, DONALD C.; and BUSS, ARNOLD H. 1960 Operant Conditioning of Hostile Verbs in Relation to Experimenter and Subject Characteristics. *Journal of Consulting Psychology* 24:324–327.

GAGE, N. L.; and CRONBACH, LEE J. 1955 Conceptual and Methodological Problems in Interpersonal Perception. *Psychological Review* 62:411–422.

GIEDT, F. HAROLD 1955 Comparison of Visual Content and Auditory Cues in Interviewing. *Journal of Consulting Psychology* 19:407–416.

GLESER, GOLDINE C.; GOTTSCHALK, L. A.; and SPRINGER, K. J. 1961 An Anxiety Scale Applicable to Verbal Samples. *Archives of General Psychiatry* 5:593–605.

GREENSPOON, JOEL 1955 The Reinforcing Effect of Two Spoken Sounds on the Frequency of Two Responses. *American Journal of Psychology* 68:409–416.

GYNTHER, RUTH A. 1957 The Effects of Anxiety and of Situational Stress on Communicative Efficiency. *Journal of Abnormal and Social Psychology* 54:274–276.

HAAN, NORMA 1964 The Relationship of Ego Functioning and Intelligence to Social Status and Social Mobility. *Journal of Abnormal and Social Psychology* 69:594–605.

HANDEL, GERALD 1965 Psychological Study of Whole Families. *Psychological Bulletin* 63:19–41.

HATHAWAY, STARKE R. 1956 Clinical Intuition and Inferential Accuracy. *Journal of Personality* 24:223–250.

HELLER, KENNETH; MYERS, R. A.; and KLINE, L. V. 1963 Interviewer Behavior as a Function of Standardized Client Roles. *Journal of Consulting Psychology* 27:117–122.

HELPER, MALCOLM M. 1958 Parental Evaluations of Children and Children's Self-evaluations. *Journal of Abnormal and Social Psychology* 56:190–194.

HILDUM, DONALD C.; and BROWN, ROGER W. 1956 Verbal Reinforcement and Interviewer Bias. *Journal of Abnormal and Social Psychology* 53:108–111.

JONES, EDWARD E. 1954 Authoritarianism as a Determinant of First-impression Formation. *Journal of Personality* 23:107–127.

JOURARD, SIDNEY M. 1957 Identification, Parent-cathexis, and Self-esteem. *Journal of Consulting Psychology* 21:375–380.

KANFER, FREDERICK; and MCBREARTY, JOHN F. 1962 Minimal Social Reinforcement and Interview Content. *Journal of Clinical Psychology* 18:210–215.

KANFER, FREDERICK et al. 1960 Experimental Modification of Interviewer Content in Standardized Interviews. *Journal of Consulting Psychology* 24:528–536.

KOCH, HELEN L. 1956 Attitudes of Young Children Toward Their Peers as Related to Certain Characteristics of Their Siblings. *Psychological Monographs* 70, no. 19.

KOLTUV, BARBARA B. 1962 Some Characteristics of Intrajudge Trait Intercorrelations. *Psychological Monographs* 76, no. 33.

KRAMER, ERNEST 1963 Judgment of Personal Characteristics and Emotions From Nonverbal Properties of Speech. *Psychological Bulletin* 60:408–420.

KROUT, MAURICE H. 1935 Autistic Gestures: An Experimental Study in Symbolic Movement. *Psychological Monographs* 46, no. 4.

LANDFIELD, ALVIN W. 1955 Self-predictive Orientation and the Movement Interpretation of Threat. *Journal of Abnormal and Social Psychology* 51:434–438.

LUNDY, RICHARD M. 1956 Assimilative Projection and Accuracy of Prediction in Interpersonal Perceptions. *Journal of Abnormal and Social Psychology* 52:33–38.

LURIIA, ALEKSANDR R. 1932 *The Nature of Human Conflicts; or, Emotion, Conflict and Will: An Objective Study of Disorganization and Control of Human Behaviour.* New York: Liveright.

MCARTHUR, CHARLES 1955 Personality Differences Between Middle and Upper Classes. *Journal of Abnormal and Social Psychology* 50:247–254.

MAHL, GEORGE F. 1956 Disturbances and Silences in the Patient's Speech in Psychotherapy. *Journal of Abnormal and Social Psychology* 53:1–15.

MALMO, ROBERT B.; SMITH, A. A.; and KOHLMEYER, W. A. 1956 Motor Manifestation of Conflict in Interview: A Case Study. *Journal of Abnormal and Social Psychology* 52:268–271.

MANIS, MELVIN 1958 Personal Adjustment, Assumed Similarity to Parents, and Inferred Parental-evaluations of the Self. *Journal of Consulting Psychology* 22:481–485.

MATARAZZO, JOSEPH D.; SASLOW, G.; and GUZE, S. B. 1956 Stability of Interaction Patterns During Interviews: A Replication. *Journal of Consulting Psychology* 20:267–274.

MENDELSON, MYER 1960 *Psychoanalytic Concepts of Depression.* Springfield, Ill.: Thomas.

MOOS, RUDOLF H. 1963 The Retention and Generalization of Operant Conditioning Effects in an Interview Situation. *Journal of Abnormal and Social Psychology* 66:52–58.

MUNROE, RUTH L. 1955 *Schools of Psychoanalytic Thought.* New York: Dryden.

ORT, ROBERT S. 1952 A Study of Role-conflicts as Related to Class Level. *Journal of Abnormal and Social Psychology* 47:425–432.

PAYNE, DONALD E.; and MUSSEN, PAUL H. 1956 Parent–Child Relations and Father Identification Among Adolescent Boys. *Journal of Abnormal and Social Psychology* 52:358–362.

PECK, ROBERT F. 1958 Family Patterns Correlated With Adolescent Personality Structure. *Journal of Abnormal and Social Psychology* 57:347–350.

PHILLIPS, JEANNE S. et al. 1961 Relationships Between Descriptive Content and Interaction Behavior in Interviews. *Journal of Consulting Psychology* 25:260–266.

POPE, BENJAMIN; and SIEGMAN, ARON W. 1962 The Effect of Therapist Verbal Activity Level and Specificity on Patient Productivity and Speech Disturbance in the Initial Interview. *Journal of Consulting Psychology* 26:489.

RANKIN, ROBERT E.; and CAMPBELL, DONALD T. 1955 Galvanic Skin Responses to Negro and White Experimenters. *Journal of Abnormal and Social Psychology* 51:30–33.

ROGERS, CARL R. 1942 *Counseling and Psychotherapy.* Boston: Houghton Mifflin.

ROSEN, BERNARD C. 1956 The Achievement Syndrome: A Psychocultural Dimension of Social Stratification. *American Sociological Review* 21:203–211.

SAINSBURY, P. 1955 Gestural Movement During Psychiatric Interview. *Psychosomatic Medicine* 17:458–469.

SARASON, IRWIN G. 1962 Individual Differences, Situational Variables, and Personality Research. *Journal of Abnormal and Social Psychology* 65:376–380.

SARASON, IRWIN G.; and CAMPBELL, JAMES M. 1962 Anxiety and the Verbal Conditioning of Mildly Hostile Verbs. *Journal of Consulting Psychology* 26:213–216.

SECORD, PAUL F.; and MUTHARD, JOHN E. 1955 Personalities in Faces: IV. A Descriptive Analysis of the Perception of Women's Faces and the Identification of Some Physiognomic Determinants. *Journal of Psychology* 39:269–278.

SHAGASS, CHARLES; and MALMO, ROBERT B. 1954 Psychodynamic Themes and Localized Muscular Tension During Psychotherapy. *Psychosomatic Medicine* 16:295–314.

SHRAUGER, SID; and ALTROCCHI, JOHN 1964 The Personality of the Receiver as a Factor in Person Perception. *Psychological Bulletin* 62:289–308.

SILLER, JEROME 1957 Socioeconomic Status and Conceptual Thinking. *Journal of Abnormal and Social Psychology* 55:365–371.

TAFT, RONALD 1955 The Ability to Judge People. *Psychological Bulletin* 52:1–23.

VERPLANCK, WILLIAM S. 1955 The Control of the Content of Conversation: Reinforcement of Statements of Opinion. *Journal of Abnormal and Social Psychology* 51:668–676.

WEINTRAUB, WALTER; and ARONSON, H. 1964 The Application of Verbal Behavior Analysis to the Study of Psychological Defense Mechanisms. 2: Speech Pattern Associated With Impulsive Behavior. *Journal of Nervous and Mental Disease* 139:75–82.

WILLIAMS, JUANITA H. 1964 Conditioning of Verbalization: A Review. *Psychological Bulletin* 62:383–393.

WITTENBORN, J. R.; and MAY, PHILIP R. A. (editors) 1966 *Prediction of Response to Pharmacotherapy.* Springfield, Ill.: Thomas. → See especially Chapter 7 on "Factors Which Qualify the Response to Iproniazid and to Imipramine," by J. R. Wittenborn.

WITTENBORN, J. R. et al. 1962 A Standard Interview as an Aid to Assessment. *Journal of Nervous and Mental Disease* 134:353–360.

WITTICH, JOHN J. 1955 The Generality of the Prediction of Self Reports. *Journal of Consulting Psychology* 19:445–448.

YONGE, K. A. 1956 The Value of the Interview: An Orientation and a Pilot Study. *Journal of Applied Psychology* 40:25–31.

ZBOROWSKI, MARK (1951) 1955 The Children of the Covenant. Pages 352–374 in David C. McClelland (editor), *Studies in Motivation.* New York: Appleton. → First published in Volume 29 of *Social Forces.*

ZIGLER, EDWARD; and KANZER, PAUL 1962 The Effectiveness of Two Classes of Verbal Reinforcers on the Performance of Middle- and Lower-class Children. *Journal of Personality* 30:157–163.

## III

### THERAPEUTIC INTERVIEWING

The therapeutic interview, like any interview, is a structured social situation involving two persons who communicate with each other primarily by means of a shared language. Although communication by verbal symbols is emphasized, it may also be mediated to some extent by bodily movements, tone of voice, rate of speech, inflection, etc. The therapeutic interview differs from other interview situations in its purpose. It is designed to influence the interviewee's feelings, attitudes, or beliefs so as to produce a reduction or amelioration of intrapsychic and/or interpersonal conflict. While the therapeutic interview has evolved as a clinical instrument of major importance in psychiatry, psychoanalysis, clinical psychology, and psychiatric social work, there are significant implications for the study of interpersonal processes in a wide variety of two-person situations.

**Contrasts between therapeutic and other forms of interviews.** The purposes of an interview may vary widely. The situation is commonly regarded as being under the control of one person (the interviewer), who elicits information, expressions of opinion or belief, attitudes, etc. from the second person (the interviewee). Some of the many aims may be to obtain information that the interviewee may possess (as in legal proceedings); to learn his opinions, attitudes, and views on given topics (as in a press interview); to appraise his mental or physical qualifications (as in an employment interview); to gather data for research purposes (as in opinion polling); or to study his mental functioning (as in a psychodiagnostic interview). In all of these situations, the interviewee furnishes the interviewer with something which the latter presumably needs for a purpose that is usually, although not necessarily, understood by the interviewee. At times (in research studies, for example), it may be desirable or even necessary to disguise the true purpose of an interview. The data elicited from the interviewee are typically considered to be under his conscious control. He is free to give information or to withhold it, although some interviews may be specifically designed to gather data that the interviewee is either reluctant to reveal (as in a crime-detection interview) or of which he is not consciously aware (as in a psychodiagnostic interview).

Although the dividing lines are not always sharp, the therapeutic interview differs from the foregoing situations in important respects. Perhaps the most significant difference is that the therapeutic interview is always undertaken with the explicit understanding that the person to be benefited by the interaction is the interviewee, not the interviewer. The interviewer functions in the role of an expert who, by virtue of special training and experience, attempts to provide help in solving a problem in living or in alleviating an emotional disturbance for which the other person consults him. The role relationship, therefore, is one of a professional person to a client who expects to pay for the professional service he receives. It resembles, but is not identical with, the physician–patient relationship. A major difference lies in the role assigned to the patient. In the medical model, the patient passively receives the ministrations of the physician. In contrast, the psychotherapeutic interview generally assigns to the patient a rather active role: he is encouraged by the therapist to become a collaborator and to retain full responsibility for the conduct of his life. In important respects, the relationship is one between equals, one of whom possesses superior knowledge. Following general usage and for lack of better words, the terms "therapist" and "patient" are employed in this article.

**Structure of the therapeutic relationship.** Central to the conception of the therapeutic interview is the development of an interpersonal relationship between patient and therapist. The patient usually approaches the therapist by presenting a "problem" for which he desires help. Often he is anxious, depressed, troubled, or otherwise in distress. By accepting the patient for "treatment," the therapist implicitly (although rarely explicitly) promises relief. Usually he does not give direct advice but approaches the problem indirectly. The therapeutic value of a single interview is rarely tangible; rather the ameliorative influence evolves from *repeated* contacts between therapist and patient. Thus the single therapeutic interview is a link in a chain of meetings often extending over considerable periods of time.

The meetings are structured with regard to time, place, financial arrangements, and the like. Furthermore, the character of the therapist's role behavior is rigorously defined and adhered to. While being attentive, maintaining a friendly interest and a nonjudgmental attitude, and conveying respect, the therapist attempts to remain detached and emotionally uninvolved. His verbal communications are sparing and confined to occasional comments, questions, clarifications, and "interpretations."

The patient, on the other hand, is free to talk about any topic he desires; indeed, he is fully encouraged to express his feelings, attitudes, and concerns. It is his responsibility to introduce topics for discussion and to maintain verbal communication. Thus there results a one-sided personal relationship within a highly impersonal framework, which is unlike any other human relationship in that it fosters an atmosphere facilitating the largest possible degree of self-revelation and disclosure on the part of the patient. The patient is assured by the therapist of the confidentiality of all communications.

## Dynamics of the therapeutic interview

The therapeutic interview is designed to bring about "corrections" in the patient's life experience. Through a variety of techniques that are the province of various systems of psychotherapy (including psychoanalysis), the therapist creates a climate in which the patient has an opportunity to develop greater trust in another person. To accomplish this, he has to unlearn patterns of feelings and behavior that he developed in childhood to cope with early interpersonal difficulties. For example, he may learn that he tends to provoke others into rejecting him, or he may come to realize that he tends to dominate people. These patterns are often exceedingly intricate and refractory to change. Great skill and patience are, therefore, prerequisites for the therapist. In his work he is greatly aided by the patient's unconscious tendency to recreate in any interpersonal situation—and particularly in the therapeutic interview—those early life experiences which have remained problematic and troublesome. This tendency is encompassed by Freud's concept of the transference, which, when properly dealt with by the therapist, becomes the most potent therapeutic force.

The model of the psychoanalytic situation has been chosen to delineate dynamic events in the therapeutic interviews, although other forms of psychotherapy conceptualize the transactions between patient and therapist in different terms.

The arrangements of the therapeutic interview create a "tilted relationship" (Greenacre 1954) in which the communicative flow tends to be directed from the patient to the therapist. The setting capitalizes on important aspects of all human interactions: (1) Whenever two people are repeatedly alone together, some sort of positive or negative emotional bond will develop between them. The depth and intensity of this bond will be partly influenced by the frequency and the length of periods they are in each other's company. (2) In everyone there is a need for human "contact," presumably rooted in the earliest mother–child relationship. The basic need is for sensory contact (warm touch of another body), but it later extends to other sense modalities. (3) The emotional bond develops particularly rapidly if (*a*) the two persons are *alone* together, so that the feelings and spontaneous expressions of one person are not deflected by a group, and (*b*) the patient is *troubled* and comes to the other person for help, the other person having the characteristics of an expert or an authority. (4) Since the patient is admittedly in need of help and the situation is structured in such a way that the therapist is relatively passive, nonparticipating, and more clearly aware of the kinds of transactions to be expected in a situation of this kind, the relationship does not become one of "mutual warming"; rather the patient develops a receptive–expectant (dependent) attitude toward the therapist. The very structure of the therapeutic setting is conducive to a reinstatement of the child–parent relationship; that is, conditions are created in which the patient can take advantage of the tendency inherent in everyone to regress to more primitive, childlike modes of relating to important authority figures.

On the other hand, the tendency to regress is opposed by the realistic aspects of the patient–therapist relationship, which is and always remains a relationship between two adults. Irrespective of the patient's tendency to distort his perception of the therapist and to treat him as a parental figure, the fact remains that the therapist is a real person. His maturity, fair-mindedness, reasonableness, and tact are characteristics that pertain to the present, not the past.

This dual aspect of the relationship, aided by the therapist's interpretations, brings about a process that in psychoanalysis is called "splitting of the ego." Thus, the patient is forced to re-experience and to some extent re-enact the past in the presence of the therapist (that is, the emergence of transference feelings is encouraged), but he is urged at the same time to become a dispassionate observer of these processes and to view them, in alliance with the therapist, as anachronistic occurrences that have largely lost their utility in the present. Accordingly, the patient eventually learns to identify with the therapist as a representative of adult reality and to abdicate his own allegiance to his neurotic impulses and patterns that had dominated him in the past. In this way the patient achieves mastery and conscious control over hitherto ego-alien impulses and strivings, or, stated otherwise, by identifying with the therapist's mature ego, the patient gradually acquires strength of his own (Freud 1940).

Furthermore, by assuming an attitude of neutrality, benevolence, and interest, the therapist gradually wins the patient's confidence. However, while he does not punish, neither does he gratify the patient's excessive and often contradictory needs. The inevitable result is that sooner or later the patient will experience frustration, because the experiencing and the verbal expression of his wishes and expectations are stimulated, but his wishes are not gratified. Frustration is accompanied by impatience, anger, resentment, and hos-

tility, which tend to be directed against the therapist as the person who has become the instigator of the patient's significant feelings and emotions. However, the patient's expectations and wishes rarely express themselves directly and in clearly recognizable form. More typically, they are disguised, rationalized, and distorted in a variety of ways. In other words, the patient unwittingly fights against their recognition.

The manner in which these expectations and wishes express themselves follows the patterns the patient has learned since early childhood in dealing with frustrating situations. For example, he may directly attack the therapist for alleged lack of interest, passivity, and the like. Or, he may try to ingratiate himself by submitting to the therapist for the purpose of winning his favor and acceptance. When all of these maneuvers fail, his anger and hostility against the therapist may be openly experienced. If the feelings become too strong or painful, the patient may become tempted to break off the therapy.

The therapist's approach to this chain of events takes essentially the following course: First, he attempts to demonstrate to the patient that there are feelings emerging in the therapeutic situation that the patient is fighting to keep out of awareness; that is, the therapist identifies the patient's resistances, which are manifested by blocking, talking about trivia, and other diversionary tactics. Second, he tries to identify the character of the resistance and the feelings against which it is directed. Once this interpretive task is accomplished, and as the patient progressively gains more awareness of his behavior, he gradually abandons the resistance and instead experiences the painful affect, which thus far has been warded off. As this process repeats itself, increasingly deeper layers of the patient's defensive system are mobilized, dealt with, and restructured. The study of the patient's dreams and other fantasy materials often proves very valuable in this connection. Gradually the patient improves, and the returns from continuing therapy diminish. Therapy then comes to a close, but only after the patient's dependency on the therapist has been resolved. The process of "weaning" the patient from what he has come to experience as a helpful relationship is frequently very difficult, opposed as it is by strong unconscious forces within the patient (and sometimes within the therapist as well).

**Theoretical differences.** Although the foregoing account represents a schematic account of the process of therapeutic work in terms of the psychoanalytic model, it should be emphasized that there is no unanimity of opinion concerning the essential ingredients of the therapeutic action in the two-person relationship. Similarly, there are marked differences beween therapists with respect to concepts, techniques, and goals in the therapeutic interview. These divergences derive from different conceptions of personality, personality development, and personality change. That is, differences in the therapist's attitudes and techniques are (at least in part) dictated by the theoretical orientation to which he subscribes (Ford & Urban 1963).

In general, theories of therapeutic action may be divided into those that view the action primarily in terms of the *personal relationship* between the two participants and those that rely more heavily on *technical procedures* followed by the therapist to bring about a specific objective. The former group, among whose exponents are the phenomenologists (like Carl Rogers, the existentialists, and adherents of *Daseinanalyse*), stress the patient's self-realization, self-actualization, and freedom to grow, which are believed to be promoted by an interpersonal relationship in which the therapist attempts to understand and to empathize with the patient. Once the therapist's unconditional positive regard and empathic understanding are communicated to the patient (Rogers 1961), he is then able to free himself from the defensive and self-defeating and constricting tendencies that impede his free personality functioning.

The second group of theorists (exemplified by therapists subscribing to one or another form of learning theory) conceptualize the role of the therapist as that of a person who directly and actively attacks and conditions the maladaptive patterns of the patient by deliberately encouraging him to make responses antagonistic to anxiety-provoking situations. Freudian psychoanalysis seems to occupy an intermediate position between these two poles.

A common element in all therapeutic approaches, as Frank (1961) has pointed out, is the existence of a firm belief on the part of the patient in the superior ability of the therapist as a professional helper, and a similarly strong conviction on the part of the therapist that he is able and willing to work with the patient toward the achievement of a particular therapeutic goal. It certainly seems plausible that a therapeutic relationship in which the patient experiences the therapist's acceptance, respect, dedication, and positive regard leads to the development of a high degree of *interpersonal trust*. Once this condition has been created, the therapeutic relationship may come to serve as a vehicle for mediating *learning experiences* of various kinds. These may consist in the extinction of maladaptive patterns of interpersonal relatedness and the learning of more mature and satisfying and less conflictual ones. The therapeutic interview thus constitutes a model for learning experiences in the interpersonal realm. The patient learns how to learn and how to benefit from interpersonal experiences. Clearly, to have therapeutic value, any learning in the therapy situation must generalize to the patient's life outside of therapy. Much remains to be learned about this process of translation.

**The therapist as participant and observer.** The therapist operates within a complex social field, and it is one of the unique aspects of his role that he is both participant and observer (Sullivan 1954). What the therapist learns about the patient's feelings, attitudes, moods, symptoms, conflicts, difficulties in living, etc., is filtered through and influenced by the patient's relationship to the therapist. The therapist, as an objective observer, gathers his data by participating with the patient in a personal relationship, albeit a highly specialized one. He must alternate between the roles of observer and participant. As observer he gathers data that hopefully can be turned to therapeutic advantage, but the data come to him only because he is a participant. As participant, too, he attempts to influence the character of the interaction for the benefit of the patient. He is more likely to be successful in this attempt when the patient's feelings have been mobilized in the situation. At such times, the social field has become fluid and more amenable to modification. In the absence of feeling on the patient's part in the here and now, the therapist's messages are perhaps chiefly didactic. It has been said that the patient needs an experience, not an explanation. Accordingly, the essence of the therapeutic interview is the patient's *emotional experience* with the therapist—what the therapist comes to mean to him on a feeling level.

**Limited objectivity of clinical data.** It is important to note that there can be no purely "objective" data in an interpersonal situation. To be sure, the patient's verbalizations and other modes of communication are or can become objective data. But the patient's state of mind, the meaning of his feelings, as communicated more or less directly to the therapist, must be inferred. In so doing the therapist relies on his clinical experience and theoretical knowledge, but perhaps more importantly on empathy and introspection. Thus, the therapist himself is the most sensitive instrument of observation. However, a concomitant of this process is the observer's subjectivity, which constitutes a potential pitfall in objective research.

### Research and methodological considerations

Since communication between patient and therapist is mediated primarily by linguistic symbols, a first requirement for objective research is to devise conceptual tools that permit the investigator to abstract and quantify relevant aspects of the verbal interchange. Obviously, there are numerous ways of accomplishing this end, and the measures the investigator decides upon are as noteworthy for what they leave out as for what they include. The selection is dictated by theoretical as well as practical considerations, and in a sense it represents a prejudgment of what is important to measure. A system of analysis, therefore, is not a neutral yardstick, and the descriptive measures representing its yield are accordingly circumscribed.

During the past twenty years a large number of content-analysis systems have been developed—some applicable to patient communications, some to therapist communications, some to both. (For references, see Strupp 1962; Auld & Murray 1955; Marsden 1965). Some systems are anchored in a particular theory of psychotherapy, others are theoretically neutral. Ideally, one would like a system that is highly objective and equally sensitive to therapist activities irrespective of theoretical orientation. But these requirements are difficult to meet and perhaps even mutually exclusive.

Of the technical problems inherent in measuring the content of the message exchanged between patient and therapist, probably none is more difficult than the assessment of latent motives and meanings. A large part of the difficulty arises from the fact that (1) linguistic symbols are inadequate to deal with the phenomena to be described, defined, and measured, and (2) psychotherapy as a technique relies heavily on verbal symbols to bring about changes in the affective processes of another person.

In recent years, transactions in therapeutic interviews have been studied from the vantage points of many different theories and by means of a variety of techniques. Apart from the various theories of psychotherapy proper (Ford & Urban 1963), other new departures include communication theory (Ruesch & Bateson 1951); sociology (Lennard & Bernstein 1960); anthropological linguistics (Pittenger, Hockett & Danehy 1960); kinesics, i.e., the study of body motions having communicational value (Dittmann & Renneker 1963).

**Technique and the therapist's personality.** Technique in the interview may be viewed as a theory translated into action. This translation, however, is not made in a vacuum, nor are techniques as a rule slavishly applied. The translation is made by the therapist, who, as a sensitive participant–observer, is responsive to the patient's attitudes, moods, verbal and nonverbal communications, etc.

A number of studies have taken the therapist's communications in actual interviews as a point of departure and investigated various correlates attributable to therapist variables (theoretical orientation, level of experience, etc.). Such studies have been facilitated by the advent of sound recording techniques, combined with a greater willingness on the part of therapists to tolerate external observers who admittedly represent an intrusion into the privacy of a unique and confidential human relationship. From the standpoint of research operations, the development of a variety of systems permitting the quantification of the verbal (and, to some extent, the nonverbal) communication content of the messages exchanged between patient and therapist has rendered research more feasible. In addition to studies dealing with the naturally occurring events in psychotherapy, there have been experimental or quasi-experimental investigations of the therapist's contribution. While such work is more rigorous and permits a wider sampling of patient and therapist variables, its relevance (validity) to actual psychotherapy remains an open question (Conference on Research in Psychotherapy . . . 1962).

At present, it is impossible to assess the nature of the therapist's personal influence in any form of psychotherapy, and it is one of the important objectives of research to elucidate the effects of this variable.

## Outlook

The primary purpose of research is to attain increasingly objective and specific information about the most effective utilization of the patient–therapist relationship for maximum therapeutic gain. This statement implies the need for extending knowledge concerning the precise nature of the psychological influence exerted by the therapist in interaction with a particular patient, including data about the modes of interaction between the two participants, the technical operations employed by the therapist, and the effects of other social, cultural, and psychological factors impinging upon the therapeutic process. The danger of invading the privacy of the therapeutic relationship is a special problem in psychotherapy research.

Modern therapeutic interviewing attempts a systematic and self-conscious manipulation of variables in a human relationship and has thus become, or is striving to become, a scientific discipline. The therapist, for his part, is an applied scientist. In this role, he is an observer of the patient's attitudes, feelings, and patterns of behavior, particularly as they are expressed toward him. He tries to be aware of the impact of these variables upon him as a person and as a participant observer; he notes the immediate or long-range effects of his therapeutic interventions (the therapeutic method) as well as his attitudes, feelings, and behaviors upon the patient; and he is engaged in the process of refining his observations and specifying the nature of his influence. In this endeavor, the psychotherapist (as an applied scientist) joins hands with the psychologist (as a "basic" scientist).

HANS H. STRUPP

[*Other relevant material may be found in* MENTAL DISORDERS, TREATMENT OF; PSYCHIATRY; PSYCHOANALYSIS, *article on* THERAPEUTIC METHODS.]

BIBLIOGRAPHY

ALEXANDER, FRANZ 1950 Analysis of the Therapeutic Factors in Psychoanalytic Treatment. *Psychoanalytic Quarterly* 19:482–500.

AULD, FRANK JR.; and MURRAY, EDWARD J. 1955 Content Analysis Studies of Psychotherapy. *Psychological Bulletin* 52:377–395.

BELLAK, LEOPOLD; and SMITH, M. BREWSTER 1956 **An Experimental Exploration of the Psychoanalytic Process.** *Psychoanalytic Quarterly* 25:385–414.

CONFERENCE ON RESEARCH IN PSYCHOTHERAPY *1958* 1959 *Research in Psychotherapy: Proceedings.* Edited by Eli A. Rubenstein and M. B. Parloff. Washington: American Psychological Association.

CONFERENCE ON RESEARCH IN PSYCHOTHERAPY *1961* 1962 *Research in Psychotherapy: Proceedings.* Edited by Hans H. Strupp and L. Luborsky. Washington: American Psychological Association.

DITTMANN, ALLEN T.; and RENNEKER, RICHARD 1963 Kinesic Research and Therapeutic Processes: Further Discussion. Pages 140–160 in Symposium on Expression of the Emotions in Man, New York, 1960, *Expression of the Emotions in Man.* New York: International Universities Press.

FORD, DONALD H.; and URBAN, HUGH B. 1963 *Systems of Psychotherapy: A Comparative Study.* New York: Wiley.

FRANK, JEROME D. 1959 Problems of Controls in Psychotherapy as Exemplified by the Psychotherapy Research Project of the Phipps Psychiatric Clinic. Pages 10–26 in Conference on Research in Psychotherapy, 1958, *Research in Psychotherapy: Proceedings.* Edited by Eli A. Rubenstein and M. B. Parloff. Washington: American Psychological Association.

FRANK, JEROME D. 1961 *Persuasion and Healing.* Baltimore: Johns Hopkins Press.

FREUD, SIGMUND (1940) 1949 *An Outline of Psychoanalysis.* New York: Norton. → First published in German as *Abriss der Psychoanalyse.*

FROMM-REICHMANN, FRIEDA 1950 *Principles of Intensive Psychotherapy.* Univ. of Chicago Press.

GILL, MERTON; NEWMAN, RICHARD; and REDLICH, FREDRICK C. 1954 *The Initial Interview in Psychiatric Practice.* New York: International Universities Press.

GLAD, DONALD D. 1959 *Operational Values in Psychotherapy.* New York: Oxford Univ. Press.

GREENACRE, PHYLLIS 1954 The Role of Transference: Practical Considerations in Relation to Psychoanalytic Therapy. *Journal of the American Psychoanalytic Association* 2:671–684.

HARPER, ROBERT A. 1959 *Psychoanalysis and Psychotherapy: 36 Systems.* Englewood Cliffs, N.J.: Prentice-Hall.

JANIS, IRVING L. 1958 The Psychoanalytic Interview as an Observational Method. Pages 149–181 in Gardner Lindzey (editor), *Assessment of Human Motives.* New York: Rinehart.

LENNARD, HENRY L.; and BERNSTEIN, ARNOLD 1960 *The Anatomy of Psychotherapy.* New York: Columbia Univ. Press.

MARSDEN, KENNETH G. 1965 Content-analysis Studies of Therapeutic Interviews: 1954 to 1964. *Psychological Bulletin* 63:298–321.

MENNINGER, KARL A. 1958 *Theory of Psychoanalytic Technique.* New York: Basic Books.

MOWRER, ORVAL H. (editor) 1953 *Psychotherapy: Theory and Research.* New York: Ronald Press.

PITTENGER, ROBERT E.; HOCKETT, CHARLES F.; and DANEHY, JOHN J. 1960 *The First Five Minutes: A Sample of Microscopic Interview Analysis.* Ithaca, N.Y.: Martineau.

ROGERS, CARL R. 1957 The Necessary and Sufficient Conditions of Therapeutic Personality Change. *Journal of Consulting Psychology* 21:95–103.

ROGERS, CARL R. 1961 *On Becoming a Person: A Therapist's View of Psychotherapy.* Boston: Houghton Mifflin.

RUESCH, JURGEN; and BATESON, GREGORY 1951 *Communication: The Social Matrix of Psychiatry.* New York: Norton.

STRUPP, HANS H. 1962 Patient–Doctor Relationships: The Psychotherapist in the Therapeutic Process. Pages 576–615 in Arthur Bachrach (editor), *Experimental Foundations of Clinical Psychology.* New York: Basic Books.

SULLIVAN, HARRY STACK 1954 *The Psychiatric Interview.* New York: Norton.

WOLBERG, LEWIS R. 1954 *The Technique of Psychotherapy.* New York: Grune.

# INVENTION

*See* CREATIVITY; INNOVATION; RESEARCH AND DEVELOPMENT; TECHNOLOGY.

# INVENTORIES

## I

### INVENTORY BEHAVIOR

Inventories account for a relatively small portion of a nation's wealth and long term capital formation: they constituted only 8 per cent of U.S. tangible assets in 1958 and 6 per cent of tangible asset accumulation from 1946 to 1958. Yet fluctuations in nonfarm business inventories, which make up roughly three-fourths of total inventories, are an important source of cyclical instability.

The explanation of this paradox (that nonfarm inventories which are relatively unimportant as a part of national wealth and long term wealth-accumulation are nevertheless of strategic importance during business cycles) lies in the fact that firms tend in the course of the business cycle to alter sharply their short term rates of inventory accumulation. Accumulation (investment) is a source of demand for the factors of production, and variations in the rate of accumulation or shifts from accumulation to reduction (disinvestment) are a source of variation in the demand for the factors of production. It is for this reason that attention often focuses on movements in inventory investment rather than on movements in inventories themselves. In the course of the business cycle rates of accumulation change rapidly and cyclically, typically moving upward to a peak of investment in late expansion and downward to a trough of disinvestment in late contraction.

**Functions performed by inventories.** Understanding of the nature of the forces which influence inventory investment must begin with a consideration of the reasons why firms hold stocks. An elaborate literature has dealt with this subject [see INVENTORIES, *article on* INVENTORY CONTROL THEORY]. Mack (1966) has suggested that the functions performed by stocks may be described in a general way by two statements: (1) Stocks support the time required for processes (economic transformation) to be performed. (2) Stocks "buy efficiency" by substituting the lesser cost of carrying stocks for a greater cost of coping with a particular management problem in some other way. With regard to the first statement, not only are certain goods-in-process necessary if production is to take place, but some minimum of purchased materials are needed to cover routine, time-consuming operations related to receipt and warehousing, and some finished stocks must support warehousing and shipping activities. Similar reasons exist for holding quantities of distributors' stocks in trade. All such stocks may be regarded as "sales linked," and management will attempt to vary them with, though not necessarily in proportion to, the level of activity of the firm.

On the other hand, stocks can buy efficiency by making possible economies resulting from larger production or purchase lots, by providing insurance against being "caught short" as a result of unpredictable fluctuations in demand, by smoothing production in the face of predictable fluctuations in sales, by taking advantage of anticipated changes in purchasing conditions, and simply by providing freedom of action under conditions of uncertainty.

At the same time, holding stocks involves costs of storage, insurance, and financing, as well as the risk of obsolescence. The management of inventories is therefore a process of balancing gains from holding additional stocks against their marginal cost.

Such observations indicate that behavior of aggregate stocks will reflect a complex of somewhat dissimilar forces. To the extent that stocks are linked to sales or output they will tend to rise and fall with activity; to the extent that they are held against fluctuations they may move in an inverted fashion relative to sales or output; to the extent that inventory objectives are affected by other factors, such as purchasing conditions, still other patterns may occur. Finally, it should be noted that anticipations may be incorrect and that actual inventory behavior may reflect errors of estimation as well.

Explanation of observed cyclical patterns of inventory behavior must involve, therefore, explanations of why in the light of such a variety of influences there are more or less systematic movements in various types of stocks and in their rates of change.

**Explanations of inventory behavior.** Inventory behavior has long been the concern of business cycle theorists. Prominent among those who dealt with the topic in an earlier day are Hawtrey, Mitchell, Keynes, J. M. Clark, and Kuznets. Clark's work (1917) is of special interest since he first made explicit the implications of any tendency for the stock of inventories to be linked to the volume of sales or output (and inventory investment to the rate of change in the volume of sales or output) and noted how this link would tend to increase the amplitude of business fluctuations and contribute to reversals (i.e., the acceleration principle).

More recent research has tended to be of three general types. The first is largely theoretical and is represented principally by the work of Metzler (1941). In the second, which includes the studies of Abramovitz (1950), Mack (1966), and Stanback (1962), the approach relies heavily upon the analysis of time series representing inventories, sales orders, output, and related activities, but does not impose upon the investigation the constraints inherent in a formal model. The third approach emphasizes the use of econometric models to explore the relationship between inventory movements and various hypothesized causal forces. Among the large number of economists who have done work along these lines are Darling (1961), Holt (see Holt & Modigliani 1961), Klein (see Klein & Popkin 1961), Lovell (see 1961; 1964), Mills (see 1954; 1957), Modigliani (see Modigliani & Sauerlender 1955), and Terleckyj (1960). Some builders of macroeconometric models have included equations designed to forecast levels of inventory investment.

Metzler, drawing upon earlier work of Lundberg (1937), traced out, under a number of assumptions, the results that would occur when businessmen attempt to bring inventories into some desired relationships with sales and thereby set off secondary changes in demand that preclude the desired equilibrium levels of stocks and that result in still further effects on inventory objectives and demand. In his models, desired levels of stocks are related to expected sales (the acceleration principle), and there is income feedback via the consumption function. Consumption expenditures are not lagged but production *is* lagged (i.e., is based upon sales of the previous period plus planned inventory investment, the amount necessary to bring inventories to desired levels). Actual inventory investment in any period is the sum of planned inventory investment plus the unplanned change that is due to actual sales turning out differently from anticipated sales.

A major contribution of the second type of research was to determine the typical patterns of timing, to show the relative importance of movements in manufacturers' inventories during interwar business cycles, and to demonstrate how and why it is that inventory investment plays a more important role in short business cycle phases than in long business cycle phases (Abramovitz 1950).

Work done with postwar data (Stanback 1962) has disclosed a decline in the lag of stocks to sales and a reduction of tendencies toward inverted behavior. In addition, attention has been called to the role of market conditions and unfilled-orders positions in influencing inventory objectives for purchased materials. Recent work (Mack 1966) features still further the role of unfilled orders and finds it important to consider the backlog of orders placed by business enterprises in the same frame of reference as their materials stocks, i.e., to regard stocks on hand and on order as the primary variable to be explained. Variations in the functions that stocks serve are apparent in the different behavior of two important inventory time series: department store stocks and durable-goods purchased-materials stocks.

However, most investigations since the war have taken the form of econometric studies. Some have treated nonfarm inventory investment in the aggregate, others have investigated manufacturers' total inventories or inventories held at different stages of fabrication.

A common property of the models tested in these studies has been a reliance upon the working of the acceleration principle in some form. In some instances a lagged relationship between changes in inventories and in output is assumed; in others the assumption is that the firm attempts only a partial adjustment toward some desired (equilibrium) level of stocks in a given period. In endeavoring to estimate the volume of stocks that firms desire to hold, a variety of influences have been examined, including credit restraint and price anticipations. In general, credit restraint and interest rates do not appear to have played a significant role, although findings have been mixed. Efforts to determine the influence of price anticipations have been inconclusive. The most useful variable by far has been unfilled orders; this variable has been found to be significant in every study in which it has been included. In dealing with the problem of determining firms' planned sales, some investigators have attempted to use estimates based on actual business sales anticipations, although without much success. Until recently, however, such estimates have demonstrated a high degree of inaccuracy (Lovell 1966).

These studies have left many questions unanswered. Criticism has been voiced both in terms of deficiencies of underlying theory and ambiguity of the measured coefficients of relationship. One investigator (Lovell 1964) has stated that "part of the difficulty may arise from certain weaknesses in the accelerator principle. The model assumes that the impact of erroneous anticipations falls either upon output or inventory; making no allowance for the possibility that adjustments in either price or advertising expenditures may shoulder part of the burden." Further, the assumption of profit maximization permits a wide range of choice of hypotheses about modes of behavior. As for ambiguity of findings, it has been suggested (Mack 1964) that investigations based on accelerator-type models do not support the notion that the volume of sales is the primary determinant of inventory investment, since the importance of this variable is rivaled by unfilled orders. Moreover, a variety of coefficients linking inventories to sales have been found, and reaction coefficients indicated by solutions to the estimating equations have been unrealistically long.

**Importance in business cycles.** During post-World War II U.S. business cycles, changes in nonfarm inventory investment (measured as the difference between the amount of accumulation in nonfarm inventories in the calendar quarter of the business cycle peak and that of the trough) have accounted for as much as 176 per cent of total decline in gross national product and never less than 52 per cent of the decline during any recession. These movements have been the single most important source of weakness during recessions.

Changes in inventory investment have played a lesser role during U.S. business cycle expansions, accounting for between 11 and 19 per cent of the increase in gross national product during expansions. Early in an expansion, however, their influence is strong. During the first year of every expansion since 1949 increases in nonfarm inventory investment have accounted for at least 26 per cent of the increase in gross national product.

It is difficult to determine whether or not there is a long term tendency for inventories to play a more important role in business cycles. The data available, which are annual for the prewar years and which go back no earlier than 1919, indicate that changes in inventory investment played a major role in the mild recessions of the 1920s and in the brief but sharp recession of 1937–1938, just as they did in the recent mild recessions. During the prolonged 1929–1932 contraction, when many factors contributed to weakness, their role was relatively small.

Inventory investment changes have been less important during postwar than prewar expansions, but this appears to be due largely to the greater length of expansion phases (Abramovitz 1950, p. 484) coupled with the fact that peaks in inventory investment have occurred earlier in expansion, with the result that change in investment levels when measured from business cycle trough to peak understates the full extent of cyclical rise.

There are factors making for both relatively less and relatively more cyclical sensitivity of inventory investment in recent years. Inventories are smaller today relative to output or sales. During the period 1947–1954 manufacturers' inventory-to-output ratios were about three-fourths of average 1920–1929 levels, and there is evidence of at least comparable declines in distributors' stock-to-sales ratios. Since 1954 declines in stocks to sales or output ratios have continued, although in more recent years such declines have occurred principally in manufacturing. This reduction in size of stocks appears to be the result of adoption of improved management techniques made possible in part by the increased availability of electronic data processing. More effective control may be expected to reduce cyclical sensitivity of total inventory changes unless offset by tendencies for movements in investment in the various types of stocks to move together more closely and in greater conformity to cyclical fluctuations in aggregate demand.

There have been some such tendencies. The proportion of stocks held within the cyclically sensitive, durable manufactures sector is higher than prewar (see below), and there has been a decline in the tendency for manufacturers' stocks, especially finished goods, to move in an inverted pattern following business cycle turns. Moreover, there has been a decline in the share of less cyclically sensitive finished goods and an increase in the share of the more volatile goods in process. These shifts have tended to offset the effect of the reduction in the relative size of inventories.

*Composition and behavior patterns.* The composition of U.S. nonfarm business inventories at the end of 1964 was as follows: manufacturing, 54 per cent; wholesale trade, 15 per cent; retail trade, 24 per cent; other nonfarm, 7 per cent.

The proportion accounted for by manufacturing in the postwar period (average 55 per cent) has been somewhat larger than during the prewar period, when it averaged about 50 per cent. More important, movements in manufacturers' inventory investment have played a larger role than would be expected on the basis of their share of total nonfarm stocks and have tended to dominate movements in nonfarm inventory investment. Changes in manufacturers' inventory investment constituted 56 per cent of total cyclical change in nonfarm inventory investment from 1919 to 1938 and 83 per cent from 1946 to 1960.

To a large extent, explanation of this relatively high degree of cyclical sensitivity lies in the high proportion of durable goods inventories that are held by manufacturers. At the end of 1964 durables constituted 55 per cent of manufacturers' stocks, 41 per cent of wholesale stocks, and 37 per cent of retail stocks. Investment in durable stocks is typically more sensitive mainly because durable goods output and sales are more volatile, which, in turn, is due to the fact that replacement is relatively postponable during recessions. Moreover, inventory investment in the various durable-goods-producing industries moves together in closer conformity to cyclical forces than is true for nondurables. As a result, movements in manufacturers' durable inventory investment have tended to dominate the movements of manufacturers' total inventory investment.

Manufacturing inventories are held at different stages of fabrication (1962 composition was: purchased materials, 36 per cent; goods in process, 30 per cent; finished goods, 34 per cent). Purchased-material stocks in the postwar period have turned roughly coincident with business cycle peaks and lagged from 4 to 8 months at business cycle troughs. Finished goods have lagged 6 to 8 months at cycle peaks and 1 to 11 months at troughs. Goods in process inventory can be analyzed with less confidence because of special problems of adjustment for price variation, but typical timing appears to be a lead or coincident turn at cycle peaks and a coincident turn or short lag at troughs. Taken as a whole, manufacturers' stocks have lagged business cycle peaks by 2 to 4 months; troughs by 1 to 8 months.

Purchased-materials investment shows a high degree of sensitivity to business cycles, particularly for durable goods manufacturing. Leads occur at all cycle turns. The amplitude of investment movements appears to be associated with the level of unfilled orders. When orders are rising at a faster pace than shipments so that the backlog of unfilled orders is growing rapidly, or when the backlog is very large and not significantly diminishing, heavier investment in purchased materials takes place. Consistent with this is the observation that purchased-materials investment movements tend to parallel movements in purchasing agents association data for suppliers reported to be making slower deliveries.

Finished goods investment reaches its peak or trough roughly coincident with the business cycle peak or trough. Even certain types of finished stocks known to be held as buffers against seasonal or irregular fluctuations show very little tendency to move significantly against the business cycle.

Investment in goods in process is cyclically sensitive. Although timing is somewhat irregular, investment turns typically occur at about the same time as turns in purchased materials and ahead of turns in finished goods.

Differences in the behavior of investment in these three types of stocks are not great enough to mute significantly the cyclical sensitivity of manufacturers' inventory investment. Taken as a whole, manufacturers' inventory investment shows decidedly cyclical patterns of movement.

As already noted, wholesale and retail inventory investment play a secondary role in changes of total nonfarm inventory investment. Inventory investment in retailing has moved irregularly, although major movements have agreed roughly in timing with those of manufacturers' inventory investment. Wholesaling inventory investment shows more fully developed cyclical behavior, with timing similar to that noted for manufacturing.

Although gaps remain in our knowledge of the exact nature of the forces influencing inventory investment, research has produced a significant advance in understanding of the nature and importance of inventory movements. Whereas it was previously a matter of controversy whether inventories contributed to business cycles or caused them to be less severe (Whitin 1953, chapter 5), no such doubt exists today. The significance of changes in inventory investment, as distinct from movement in stocks proper, is widely appreciated. Government and trade association data on inventory investment and related variables are closely studied by analysts of business conditions.

Accurate forecasting has proven difficult, partly because it is always difficult to predict a widely fluctuating economic series with the same degree of accuracy as a more stable series. Thus, all other factors being the same, it is more difficult to predict inventory change than the level of consumer spending. Nevertheless, the forecasts that have actually been made in the post-World War II period have typically been significantly more accurate than mere extrapolations (National Bureau . . . 1964).

Knowledge of current and prospective levels of inventory demand makes possible a more accurate evaluation by management of the extent to which the current level of sales is a reflection of final demand rather than inventory accumulation. Such knowledge permits more intelligent planning of operations both for the short run and on a longer range basis. Such forecasts have also been of major importance to government in the development of general economic policy.

Unsolved questions of major importance involve (1) the issue of whether or not reversals in investment movements cause business cycle turns (cf. Burns 1960, p. 14; Darling 1961, part 5; Fromm 1962, p. 88; Stanback 1962, chapter 8) and (2) the problem of what type of government policy, if any, is appropriate to modify inventory investment swings.

THOMAS M. STANBACK, JR.

[*See also* BUSINESS CYCLES; CAPITAL.]

### BIBLIOGRAPHY

ABRAMOVITZ, MOSES 1950 *Inventories and Business Cycles, With Special Reference to Manufacturers' Inventories.* New York: National Bureau of Economic Research.

ALLEN, JULIUS W.; and GENTRY, RICHARD H. 1961 Inventories, Inventory Investment, and Inventory Control: A Selected Bibliography. Pages 203–217 in U.S. Congress, Joint Economic Committee, *Inventory Fluctuations and Economic Stabilization.* Part 3: Income Fluctuations and Economic Instability. 87th Congress, 1st Session. Washington: Government Printing Office. → Contains the most complete bibliography available.

BURNS, ARTHUR F. 1960 Progress Towards Economic Stability. *American Economic Review* 50:1–19.

CLARK, JOHN MAURICE 1917 Business Acceleration and the Law of Demand: A Technical Factor in Economic Cycles. *Journal of Political Economy* 25:217–235.

DARLING, PAUL G. 1961 Inventory Fluctuations and Economic Instability: An Analysis Based on the Postwar Economy. Pages 1–68 in U.S. Congress, Joint Economic Committee, *Inventory Fluctuations and*

*Economic Stabilization.* Part 3: Income Fluctuations and Economic Instability. 87th Congress, 1st Session. Washington: Government Printing Office.

FROMM, GARY 1962 Inventories, Business Cycles, and Economic Stabilization. Pages 35–133 in U.S. Congress, Joint Economic Committee, *Inventory Fluctuations and Economic Stabilization.* Part 4: Supplementary Study Papers. 87th Congress, 2d Session. Washington: Government Printing Office.

HAWTREY, R. G. 1929 *Trade and Credit.* London and New York: Longmans.

HOLT, CHARLES C.; and MODIGLIANI, FRANCO 1961 Firm Cost Structures and the Dynamic Responses of Inventories, Production, Work Force and Orders to Sales Fluctuations. Pages 1–55 in U.S. Congress, Joint Economic Committee, *Inventory Fluctuations and Economic Stabilization.* Part 2: Causative Factors in Movements of Business Inventories. 87th Congress, 1st Session. Washington: Government Printing Office.

KEYNES, JOHN MAYNARD 1936 *The General Theory of Employment, Interest and Money.* London: Macmillan. → A paperback edition was published in 1965 by Harcourt.

KLEIN, LAWRENCE R.; and POPKIN, JOEL 1961 An Econometric Analysis of the Post War Relationship Between Inventory Fluctuations and Changes in Aggregate Economic Activity. Pages 71–89 in U.S. Congress, Joint Economic Committee, *Inventory Fluctuations and Economic Stabilization.* Part 3: Income Fluctuations and Economic Instability. 87th Congress, 1st Session. Washington: Government Printing Office.

KUZNETS, SIMON 1926 *Cyclical Fluctuations: Retail and Wholesale Trade, United States, 1919–1925.* New York: Adelphi.

LOVELL, MICHAEL C. 1961 Manufacturers' Inventories, Sales Expectations and the Acceleration Principle. *Econometrica* 29:293–314.

LOVELL, MICHAEL C. 1964 Determinants of Inventory Investment. Pages 177–224 in Conference on Models of Income Determination, Chapel Hill, N.C., 1962, *Models of Income Determination.* Princeton Univ. Press. → Contains an excellent bibliography of recent work.

LOVELL, MICHAEL C. 1966 Sales Anticipations, Planned Inventory Investment, and Realizations. Unpublished manuscript. → Submitted to the Conference on Investment Behavior, sponsored by the Universities–National Bureau Committee for Economic Research.

LUNDBERG, ERIC (1937) 1954 *Studies in the Theory of Economic Expansion.* New York: Kelley.

McGOULDRICK, PAUL F. 1961 The Impact of Credit Cost and Availability on Inventory Investment. Pages 89–157 in U.S. Congress, Joint Economic Committee, *Inventory Fluctuations and Economic Stabilization.* Part 2: Causative Factors in Movements of Business Inventories. Washington: Government Printing Office.

MACK, RUTH P. 1964 Comments on Lovell, "Determinants of Inventory Investment." Pages 224–231 in Conference on Models of Income Determination, Chapel Hill, N.C., 1962, *Models of Income Determination.* Princeton Univ. Press.

MACK, RUTH P. 1966 Information, Expectations and Inventory Fluctuations: A Study of Materials on Hand and on Order. Unpublished manuscript, National Bureau of Economic Research.

METZLER, LLOYD A. (1941) 1965 The Nature and Stability of Inventory Cycles. Pages 100–129 in American Economic Association, *Readings in Business Cycles.*

Homewood, Ill.: Irwin. → First published in Volume 23 of *Review of Economic Statistics.*

MILLS, EDWIN S. 1954 Expectations, Uncertainty and Inventory Fluctuations. *Review of Economic Studies* 22, no. 1:15–22.

MILLS, EDWIN S. 1957 Expectations and Undesired Inventory. *Management Science* 4:105–109.

MITCHELL, WESLEY C. 1913 *Business Cycles.* Univ. of California Press. → Part 3 was reprinted by the University of California Press in 1959 as *Business Cycles and Their Causes.*

MODIGLIANI, FRANCO; and SAUERLENDER, OWEN H. 1955 Economic Expectations and Plans of Firms in Relation to Short-term Forecasting. Pages 261–361 in Conference on Research in Income and Wealth, *Short-term Economic Forecasting.* Studies in Income and Wealth, Vol. 17. Princeton Univ. Press.

NATIONAL BUREAU OF ECONOMIC RESEARCH, ANNUAL REPORT, 44TH 1964 *The National Bureau Enters Its Forty-fifth Year.* New York: The Bureau. → See the progress report on "General Economic Forecasts" by Victor Zarnowitz.

NURKSE, RAGNAR 1952 The Cyclical Pattern of Inventory Investment. *Quarterly Journal of Economics* 66:385–408.

STANBACK, THOMAS M. JR. 1962 *Postwar Cycles in Manufacturers' Inventories.* New York: National Bureau of Economic Research.

TERLECKYJ, NESTOR E. 1960 *Measures of Inventory Conditions.* National Industrial Conference Board, Technical Paper No. 8. New York: The Board.

WHITIN, T. M. 1953 *The Theory of Inventory Management.* Princeton Univ. Press.

## II
### INVENTORY CONTROL THEORY

Inventory control theory seeks to establish optimal inventory decision rules for individuals and business firms. Inventory decisions may arise in purchasing or in production. A retailer or wholesaler generally must hold stocks of goods to meet the demands of his customers, and he must therefore decide on the quantities of the goods he will purchase and hold and at what point he will place new orders for each good. A manufacturer generally must hold inventories of finished goods because it is not possible (or economical) to synchronize perfectly his sales and his production process. His inventory decisions are therefore closely related to decisions regarding the scheduling of production. A manufacturer must also hold stocks of semifinished goods and stocks of raw materials. Inventory decisions regarding semifinished goods are, again, closely related to the scheduling of production, while those regarding raw materials are related both to production scheduling and to purchasing.

The optimal decision rules established for various inventory problems are not only of prescriptive value; they may also provide useful insights into observed fluctuations of inventories at the microeconomic and macroeconomic levels.

**Historical sketch.** In past decades there were occasional periods of intensive interest in inventory theory, sometimes as the aftermath of forced inventory liquidation. For the most part, the literature consisted of a few articles in business journals that had little impact on business behavior and no impact on economic theory. More recently there has been an upsurge of interest which has far surpassed any of its predecessors with respect to the quantity and quality of the work accomplished and with respect to its over-all effect on business behavior and economic theory. Statisticians and economists have become interested in industrial problems concomitantly with increased attention in business to the techniques of advanced management, including operations research and management science. The development of these latter areas has included much detailed attention to inventory theory. [See OPERATIONS RESEARCH.]

The earliest attempts at developing inventory theory were primarily concerned with the problem of determining economical lot sizes in purchasing or production (discussed below). Raymond's book (1931) is illustrative of these attempts. During World War II, a useful probabilistic model for controlling stocks was developed. Shortly thereafter a probabilistic version of economical lot-size analysis was developed by Whitin (1953), whose book was the first in English that dealt with probabilistic inventory systems in any detail. Several economists and mathematicians have provided rigorous mathematical analyses of inventory systems, the most noteworthy contributions being an article by Arrow, Harris, and Marschak (1951) and the rather abstract mathematical papers by Dvoretzky, Kiefer, and Wolfowitz (1952). The past few years have given rise to more than ten books on inventory theory, as well as chapters dealing with inventories in almost all of the many books on operations research. At the same time, business firms have been stressing the importance of stock control far more than ever before, as evidenced by the many new corporate vice-presidents in charge of inventory control. Several of the formal mathematical approaches to inventory analysis have been applied in practice by business firms.

From the standpoint of the national economy also, inventory theory has received a considerable amount of attention. One important development was Metzler's formulation (1941) of a business cycle theory in which inventory behavior is the primary causal factor. A business cycle study of much empirical and theoretical interest was published by Abramovitz (1950), who showed that changes in inventory investment constituted a major component of the changes in national income in the five business cycles between the two world wars.

## Approaches to inventory theory

There are a wide variety of mathematical analyses of inventory problems. A few different types will be presented here for the purpose of illustration. The mathematical analysis underlying each example will be avoided in order to make the material accessible to readers who are not mathematically oriented.

**The newsboy problem.** Suppose a newsboy is faced with the problem of determining how many papers to stock when his daily sales vary in a probabilistic manner. He buys papers at a unit cost $C$ and sells them at a unit price $P$. He can be reimbursed an amount $R$ for each paper not sold. How many papers should he stock to maximize his daily profit? This problem may be simply formulated in terms of the familiar marginal analysis. Let $p(x)$ be the probability that customers will demand $x$ or more papers. If the $x$th paper is sold, the newsboy makes a marginal profit of $P - C$ on this paper. If it is not sold, the newsboy incurs a marginal loss of $C - R$. Weighting the marginal profit and the marginal loss by their probabilities, $p(x)$ and $1 - p(x)$ respectively, one can readily ascertain that the $x$th paper should be stocked if

$$(1) \quad p(x)\,(P-C) \geqslant (1-p(x))\,(C-R).$$

Simple computations show that condition (1) will be satisfied if $p(x) > (C-R)/(P-R)$. That is, the newsboy should continue to add papers to his stock as long as the probability of selling the marginal paper exceeds a known critical ratio. It can readily be seen that the newsboy should stock more papers the higher the profit margin $(P-C)$ and the lower the loss on papers not sold $(C-R)$. One of the principal lessons is that he should not, in general, stock the number of papers that corresponds to average sales. The existence of random demand changes the basic nature of the problem.

**Economical lot-size problems.** As mentioned before, the earliest inventory problems subjected to mathematical analysis were those involving the determination of economical purchase quantities of goods for inventories. Consider, for example, the case of a retailer who must hold stocks of the goods he sells. There are some inventory costs that decrease as the quantity of inventory goods he orders increases—for example, costs of procurement and costs of receiving. These are usually referred to as "ordering costs." Other inventory costs increase with the size of the quantity ordered, for example, costs of holding inventories—interest, depreciation, obsolescence, etc. These costs are usually referred to as "carrying costs." The problem for the retailer is, when faced with a known demand, to purchase a lot (a quantity of the inventory good) that fulfills demand and minimizes the sum of the ordering and carrying costs.

Let $Y$ be the number of units the retailer sells per year (assumed to be sold at a constant rate during the year). At one extreme, he could purchase $Y$ units at the beginning of the year; at the other extreme, he could purchase $Y/365$ units each day of the year. Obviously the first policy would entail very high carrying costs, and the second policy would entail very high ordering costs. If $S$ is ordering costs per order and $I$ is carrying costs per unit per year (both assumed to be constant), it can be shown that minimum costs will be incurred for lots of size $Q^*$ where

$$(2) \qquad Q^* = \sqrt{\frac{2YS}{I}}.$$

This equation indicates that the optimal lot size varies proportionately with the square root of expected sales and the square root of procurement expenses and varies inversely with the square root of unit inventory carrying costs.

The problem of determining economical lot sizes in manufacturing has been subjected to a similar analysis. In these cases, the lot is the amount to be produced rather than purchased, and $S$ is defined as the cost per setup, i.e., the clerical and other costs of preparing the machines for a production run. The identical formula results. Although many restrictive assumptions are made in deriving them, economical lot-size formulas are perhaps the most widely applied mathematical technique of inventory analysis.

**Probabilistic lot-size models.** Probabilistic lot-size models deal with the problem of determining economical lot sizes when demand is not known with certainty but varies about a given mean in accordance with a known probability distribution. Because of the random variations in demand, it is possible to incur unintended stockouts or shortages. The optimal lot size is the one that minimizes an expected-cost expression which includes procurement costs, carrying costs, and stockout costs. The details of this analysis will not be presented here. The result specifies an optimal reorder-point quantity (a point at which orders will be initiated) as well as an optimal lot size to be ordered. The optimal reorder-point quantity varies directly with the

demand level, demand variance, and shortage penalty, and varies inversely with the unit inventory carrying charges and setup costs. Typically, the optimal lot size is higher in the probabilistic case than in the case of certainty, since the fewer the number of orders placed, the smaller is the expected number of stockouts. Hence the introduction of stockout costs makes it worthwhile to buy in larger quantities.

The mathematical analysis underlying the probabilistic lot-size model is presented at widely different levels of generality and sophistication in the literature. The literature also contains solutions to the lot-size problem for cases of certain and probabilistic demands in which there are variations in average demand over time (Hadley & Whitin 1963).

**Linear programming.** Another technique used for analyzing inventory control problems is linear programming [*see* PROGRAMMING]. Business sales often behave roughly in accordance with a known seasonal pattern. If the fluctuations in sales are met by corresponding fluctuations in production, overtime costs will be incurred. Alternatively, if production is kept relatively constant, the fluctuations in sales may be absorbed by inventory adjustments. Linear programming analysis of the problem makes it possible to determine the production schedule that will meet sales at the minimum combined overtime costs and inventory carrying charges. The approach can be trivially extended to handle other situations in which marginal costs increase as the level of output increases. However, the linear programming approach has not yet been extended to allow for random variations in demand or to include lot-size considerations.

**Linear decision rules.** The linear decision rule approach, developed at the Carnegie Institute of Technology (Holt et al. 1960), takes into account more types of cost factors than does the linear programming approach. Specifically, the approach minimizes a quadratic cost function including regular payroll costs, costs of overtime and idle time, costs of changing the level of the work force, and costs involved in having either too large or too small an inventory level. The quadratic approximation to costs plays a vital role in two ways. First, the derivatives of this function are linear, making it feasible to solve the equations resulting from setting the first derivatives of the function with respect to work force and production levels equal to zero. Second, when the cost function is quadratic, it is possible to consider only average sales, rather than the probability distribution of sales, for it has been demonstrated that the results are identical. The linear decision rules resulting from the solution of the derivative equations are simple linear expressions that can easily be handled in hand computations. The rules indicate the changes in the level of production and work force that are desirable. The derivative equations need only be solved again when cost conditions change.

**Waiting-line theory.** The "queuing" or waiting-line approach to the inventory problem has received a considerable amount of attention in recent years (Morse 1958). The level of inventory serves as the queue, which is depleted by customer demands and increased by production or procurement. Mathematical expressions (or "equations of detailed balance") for the rate of change of the probabilities that the queue is at each of its possible levels or "states" are developed. Under long-run, steady-state conditions these state probabilities remain unchanged, i.e., the probability that there are exactly $x$ items in the queue at a random instant of time remains constant. This implies that each of the equations of detailed balance can be set equal to zero, making it possible to solve for the (steady) state probabilities. These state probabilities, combined with the associated costs of each state, can be used to make simple evaluations of the costs of various inventory policies. The assumption required concerning the nature of demands and/or deliveries is typically quite restrictive, so that the approach cannot be applied to a wide range of problems. [See QUEUES.]

## Inventory theory and the theory of the firm

Classical versions of the economic theory of the firm do not take inventories into account explicitly in any way [see FIRM, THEORY OF THE]. Since inventories are of considerable importance in the actual operation of almost all firms, the theory appears to have serious deficiencies on this score. Only in the case of stationary demand known with certainty and stationary cost conditions can inventories be included in the classical theory. It has been shown that inventory carrying charges and setup costs can be included in the traditional long-run cost curve of the firm, i.e., the envelope of the short-run cost curves, the short-run average cost curves being based on a fixed time between orders, i.e., a fixed lot size (Wagner & Whitin 1958). Some nonstationary inventory situations can be handled by price-discrimination techniques. However, there remain important fundamental differences between inventory theory and classical economic theory. For example, consider the costs included in the linear decision rule example above. Of the several types of costs discussed, only regular payroll costs are taken into consideration by the

classical approach, for under stationary demand conditions there would be no overtime, no idle time, no changes in the work force, and no changes in the average inventory level. The very existence of this inventory approach is based on nonstationarity. No long-run equilibrium is ever achieved. A more realistic theory of the firm must allow for some of these nonstationary aspects.

Another aspect of inventory theory that has relevance for the theory of the firm is the existence of economies of scale in most inventory models. Lot-size analysis indicates that inventory costs vary less than proportionately with sales, and the analysis of reorder-point stocks also gives rise to economies of scale because, by the law of large numbers, stocks held as protection against random variations in demand vary less than proportionately with demand. Thus at least two causes of decreasing average costs are established. The arguments for increasing average costs, which are an essential ingredient of classical economic theory (both the theory of the firm and the theory of the economy), have not been convincing, typically being rather vague statements concerning diseconomies of large-scale management or control. Inventory analysis has much to contribute to problems of returns to scale, including problems of vertical and horizontal integration. Few attempts have thus far been made to complete such analyses. [See ECONOMIES OF SCALE.]

One of the few attempts to incorporate inventory behavior into the theory of the firm was Boulding's reconstruction of economic theory on the basis of balance sheet considerations (1950). "Preferred asset ratios" played a vital role in his analysis, but he spent little time explaining the basic determinants of these ratios.

## Inventory theory and aggregate economics

At the level of aggregate economic analysis, inventory theory is of interest from several standpoints. Its relevance to business cycle theory was mentioned above. In addition, inventory theory can readily be related to Keynesian economics through the three Keynesian motives for holding cash (or goods)—the transactions motive, the precautionary motive, and the speculative motive. According to the transactions motive, it is necessary and desirable to hold some inventories of goods for the purpose of meeting demand. Lot-size analysis provides an approach to determining the quantities that should be held for this purpose in order to minimize the sum of setup costs and inventory carrying charges. The determination of reorder-point quantities involves the precautionary motive. Safety or "cushion" stocks are held to avoid stockouts arising from random sales variations. Finally, inventories may be held for speculative reasons, that is to say, in anticipation of changes in demand or supply conditions. Aggregate levels of stocks held for any of these reasons are of significance in aggregate models of the economy.

Stocks of money have also been subjected to probabilistic inventory analysis. (Here, brokerage fees play the role of setup costs.) For example, the precautionary motive for holding stocks of cash was discussed by Edgeworth in 1888 in connection with the determination of bank reserve ratios.

In a general sense, the behavior of economic aggregates depends upon the behavior of the detailed components of the aggregates, which, in turn, depend quite heavily on inventory considerations. Thus, a better understanding of inventory theory is needed for a more complete theory of aggregate economics.

T. M. WHITIN

### BIBLIOGRAPHY

ABRAMOVITZ, MOSES 1950 *Inventories and Business Cycles, With Special Reference to Manufacturers' Inventories.* New York: National Bureau of Economic Research.

ARROW, KENNETH J.; HARRIS, THEODORE; and MARSCHAK, JACOB 1951 Optimal Inventory Policy. *Econometrica* 19:250–272.

ARROW, KENNETH J.; KARLIN, SAMUEL; and SCARF, HERBERT 1958 *Studies in the Mathematical Theory of Inventory and Production.* Stanford Mathematical Studies in the Social Sciences, No. 1. Stanford Univ. Press.

BOULDING, KENNETH E. 1950 *A Reconstruction of Economics.* New York: Wiley.

BUCHAN, JOSEPH; and KOENIGSBERG, ERNEST 1963 *Scientific Inventory Management.* Englewood Cliffs, N.J.: Prentice-Hall.

DVORETZKY, A.; KIEFER, J.; and WOLFOWITZ, J. 1952 The Inventory Problem: I. Case of Known Distributions of Demand; II. Case of Unknown Distributions of Demand. *Econometrica* 20:187–222, 450–466.

EDGEWORTH, FRANCIS Y. 1888 The Mathematical Theory of Banking. *Journal of the Royal Statistical Society* 51:113–127.

FETTER, ROBERT B.; and DALLECK, WINSTON C. 1961 *Decision Models for Inventory Management.* Homewood, Ill.: Irwin.

HADLEY, GEORGE; and WHITIN, T. M. 1963 *Analysis of Inventory Systems.* Englewood Cliffs, N.J.: Prentice-Hall.

HANSSMANN, FRED 1962 *Operations Research in Production and Inventory Control.* New York: Wiley.

HOLT, CHARLES C. et al. 1960 *Planning Production, Inventories, and Work Force.* Englewood Cliffs, N.J.: Prentice-Hall.

METZLER, LLOYD A. (1941) 1965 The Nature and Stability of Inventory Cycles. Pages 100–129 in American Economic Association, *Readings in Business Cycles.* Homewood, Ill.: Irwin. → First published in Volume 23 of *Review of Economic Statistics.*

MILLS, EDWIN S. 1962 *Price, Output, and Inventory Policy: A Study in the Economics of the Firm and Industry.* New York: Wiley.

MORSE, PHILIP M. 1958 *Queues, Inventories and Maintenance: The Analysis of Operational Systems With Variable Demand and Supply.* New York: Wiley.

RAYMOND, FAIRFIELD E. 1931 *Quantity and Economy in Manufacture.* New York: McGraw-Hill.

STARR, MARTIN; and MILLER, DAVID W. 1962 *Inventory Control: Theory and Practice.* Englewood Cliffs, N.J.: Prentice-Hall.

WAGNER, HARVEY M. 1962 *Statistical Management of Inventory Systems.* New York: Wiley.

WAGNER, HARVEY M.; and WHITIN, T. M. 1958 Dynamic Problems in the Theory of the Firm. *Naval Research Logistics Quarterly* 5:53–74.

WHITIN, T. M. 1953 *The Theory of Inventory Management.* Princeton Univ. Press.

## INVENTORIES, PERSONALITY
*See under* PERSONALITY MEASUREMENT.

## INVESTMENT

I

### THE AGGREGATE INVESTMENT FUNCTION

By "aggregate investment function" we usually mean the relation explaining producers' net acquisition of the capital goods (buildings, equipment, and inventories) that are part of the process of production in the economy as a whole.

The major importance of investment is twofold. First, output in the future depends upon the maintenance of existing means of production. Economic growth, i.e., the increase of the rate of output, depends largely upon investment in excess of the wearing away of existing means of production. Second, the maintenance of "full employment" or, in general, the full utilization of existing resources, requires that aggregate investment plus aggregate consumption equal the total output that would be produced if all individuals who wished to work could find employment. The first aspect of investment was stressed by the classical and neoclassical economists and, usually under the designation "capital accumulation," by Marx and his followers. The second aspect has received major attention in recent years, in large part as a consequence of the work and influence of John Maynard Keynes (1936).

**Investment and saving.** In considering the aggregate investment function, two related issues are generally distinguished: the determinants of investment by individual business units, and the determinants of saving, that is, abstention from current consumption, by those who earn or receive income. By usual accounting definitions (with appropriate adjustments of government accounts), the sum of investment by all producing units must, in fact, be identically equal to the sum of saving by all consumer or income-receiving units. Hence, separate consideration of these issues may seem paradoxical. But separate consideration *is* meaningful because actual aggregate investment or saving is the resultant of two sets of forces, those related to producers' desires to obtain goods and those related to consumers' preferences to forgo the opportunity to obtain goods. The analogy to supply and demand curves is apt and helpful here. The saving function indicates the supply of financial resources that producers may apply to the purchase of capital goods, and the investment function indicates the demand by producers for financial resources with which to buy capital goods. The actual total of investment or of saving (the totals will be identical) is determined by the intersection of the saving and investment schedules, the intersection being the point of equality of these two functions.

With this approach we are able to set to one side the factors affecting investment that relate to the supply of saving, i.e., to the saving or consumption function. Analysis of the investment function itself may be concerned with the rates of investment that would be consistent with various sets of values of the variables that affect the rate of investment, regardless of consistency of these values with the consumption or saving function; or it may concern what could be considered the inverse of the investment function, that is, the sets of values of the variables that would determine a rate of investment equal to some predetermined rate of saving given by the saving function or by policy considerations.

**Investment demand.** Investment demand may be seen as determined by the interaction of the factors that affect the expected profitability of investment, on the one hand, and by those that affect the interest rate (or some other, more appropriate measure of the cost of capital), on the other hand. The expected profitability of a contemplated unit of investment is best viewed as that rate of discount for which the sum of resultant additional expected receipts and expenditures, including the purchase cost, the yield, and the ultimate sale or salvage return, is zero. The relevant cost of capital for the firm that already has command over the resources necessary to finance investment is the rate of return, appropriately adjusted for any differences in risk, that may be enjoyed on alternative uses of these resources. For the firm that must secure command over such resources, the relevant cost of capital relates to the cost of securing funds, again adjusted for the resulting changes in the risk position of the firm. While the cost of capital may therefore differ, depending, among other things, on whether firms are borrowers or users of their own finances, one may wonder whether this distinction carries much weight *in the aggregate*, at least in economies with well-developed financial markets.

The investment demand function may then be reduced to a two-variable relation indicating the rate at which producers would wish to acquire capital goods per unit of time as a function of the rate of interest. Since, at a given rate of interest, producers would wish to acquire all capital goods they would have wished to acquire at higher rates of interest as well as some additional capital goods that are profitable at the given rate, investment demand is presumed to be higher (or at least not lower) the lower the rate of interest.

A stable relation between investment demand and the rate of interest presumes, for one thing, however, a stable relation between "the rate of interest" and the relevant cost, appropriately discounted for risk, of the financial resources required for investment. Further, it requires that the expected marginal profitabilities of investment opportunities remain unchanged.

Largely following Keynes, many economists have stressed, since the great depression of the 1930s, that the rate of interest is not the critical variable determining investment demand. Rather, the critical variables are those determining the expected profitability of investment, especially at the margin, or what is called the "marginal efficiency" of investment. Their view is that investment demand is fairly *inelastic* with respect to the rate of interest. This means that changes in the rate of interest bring about proportionately small changes in investment demand. The logical corollary of the argument is that the expected profitability of additional investment (again, the marginal efficiency of investment) declines rapidly as the rate of investment increases. Investment demand, however, is considered to be highly variable as a result of changes in factors other than the rate of interest, either because of high elasticity of investment demand with respect to these other variables or because these other variables themselves, unlike the (long-term) rate of interest, are subject to great variability.

These views are represented in Figure 1, which shows three investment demand curves, all depicting investment demand ($I_D$) as a declining, relatively inelastic function of the rate of interest ($i$).

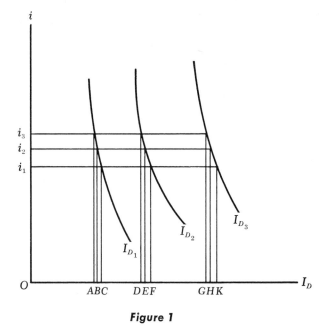

**Figure 1**

determining; otherwise we should have the paradox of entrepreneurs repeatedly acting on the basis of expectations that are persistently falsified by events, and never learning from the unhappy experience. Nevertheless, the equivalence of subjective expectations and objective conditions is limited by imperfect knowledge, risk, and uncertainty, which are endemic to the investment process. The resultant partial independence of expectations from objective factors must be accorded a major role in our inability to use objective data to predict more than a minor fraction of short-run variations in the rate of investment.

With the production function, relative prices, and demand for output constant, one may expect a constant demand for capital stock. Producers' demand for capital goods, that is, investment demand, would consist only of demand to replace capital goods used up in production. Positive net investment demand—demand for capital goods in excess of depreciation—must depend upon expected changes in the production function, prices, or demand for output relative to their values in determining the existing capital stock.

Because of the imperfection of information and heavy discounting for risk and uncertainty, one may expect entrepreneurs to delay action based on expected changes in the determinants of the optimum capital stock until these changes have become very clear. In practice this may mean waiting at least until changes have taken place and, particularly in the case of unanticipated changes, waiting until changed conditions have persisted long enough to generate confidence in their relative permanence. In an uncertain world a good rule of thumb may be to act as if the future will be like some weighted average or projection of the past. Yet it must be recognized that entrepreneurs attempting to maximize profit must be guided ultimately by their view of the future, however much their view of the future may be conditioned by the past and present. With this caveat, we may look to changes in current values of relevant variables for determinants of investment demand. Let us consider in turn the production function, relative prices, and the demand for output.

*Changes in the production function.* Changes in technology, which we may consider to be changes in parameters of the production function, will influence investment if they alter the composition or total of capital goods desired to produce a given output. Changes in the composition of desired capital will serve to make existing capital goods obsolete and may generate an investment demand for purposes of their replacement. A change in the

It may be noted readily that the variation in investment demand along any one investment demand curve that might be occasioned by variation of the rate of interest, as among $i_1$, $i_2$, and $i_3$, is relatively small compared with the variation in investment demand that would be occasioned by shifts from one investment demand curve to another. Thus, the differences within the sets $(A, B,$ and $C)$, $(D, E,$ and $F)$, and $(G, H,$ and $K)$ are relatively small compared to the differences between any one of these sets and any other. Keynes and "Keynesians" have concluded that, since movements of the investment demand curve are likely to be quite large relative to the changes in investment demand that may be induced by movement *along* any one investment demand curve, the effectiveness of monetary action, which might alter the rate of interest, is severely limited.

*Role of expectations.* The factors affecting the expected profitability of investment, that is, the factors indicating which of the investment demand curves in Figure 1 is relevant, may be in part objective and in part subjective. The objective factors affecting expected profitability are technology (the current and future parameters of the production function), relative prices of factors of production (both current and future), and future demand for product. If decision makers could know these with certainty, the investment function would be fully determined. However, these underlying objective elements influence investment demand to the extent and in the manner that they are subjectively perceived by decision makers. It may be argued that in "equilibrium" the objective elements must be production function that changes only the composition of desired capital will have a "one-shot" effect on investment. Once alteration in the composition of capital goods is completed, the rate of investment will be the same as it was previously.

A change in the production function that alters the desired ratio of capital stock to output is likely to have a continuing effect on investment. Again, any accompanying change in the desired or "equilibrium" composition of capital may generate investment until the existing capital stock has experienced the desired transformation. Such investment may be negative in amount if the capital–output ratio of the new equilibrium is less than the capital–output ratio of the previous equilibrium. But in addition, the investment generated by a change in the desired capital–output ratio must be such as to permit the attainment of the new desired stock of capital for any given level of output. If output is constant, a change in the capital–output ratio will also have merely a "one-shot" effect on investment, which will end when the new capital–output ratio is attained. If output is growing, which is probably the more likely case, an increase in the capital–output ratio will increase the equilibrium rate of investment, for more additional capital will then be required for each additional unit of output. Conversely, a decrease in the capital–output ratio will lower the amount of investment associated with any given rate of growth of output.

*Changes in relative prices.* Changes in relative prices may have effects analogous to those induced by changes in the production function because they may induce changes in either the composition or total amount of desired capital (or in both) associated with any given level of output. Changes in relative prices may involve changes in relative wages or other forms of remuneration for different types of labor; changes in the relative prices of other nondurable inputs, such as electric power or gas heat; changes in relative prices of different kinds of capital goods; changes in wage–price ratios; and changes in rates of interest or other ratios of the current prices of goods and services to corresponding prices expected at future dates.

It is probably most useful to think of relative prices as affected by supply conditions. Thus, if individuals come to supply more or less of a certain type of labor, the wage for that type of labor will change. Similarly, changing degrees of monopolistic or oligopolistic power may alter the prices charged both for goods and for labor services. Finally, preferences for present and future consumption may be altered by changes in individual choices or by changes in the distribution of income among those

exercising such choices, so that the supply of saving is affected. This might manifest itself in changes in rates of interest or in other measures of the relative prices of present and future goods.

*Role of interest rates.* Alteration in the relative price of current and future goods, frequently measured, in professional-economics shorthand, by "the rate of interest," merits further consideration. A lower rate of interest, by raising the present discounted expected prices of future output (and input) relative to current input (and output), tends to increase the demand for capital goods generally and, in particular, to increase the demand for long-lived capital goods. Long-lived capital goods are current inputs that promise consequent outputs far into the future. Longer-lived capital, however, must of necessity involve higher ratios of capital to output, as long as we are dealing with economically relevant choices. Capital goods that offer the prospect of lower outputs now as well as in the future would never be chosen. Hence an interest-induced shift to longer-lived capital must be a shift to capital with relatively higher expected outputs in the distant future but with relatively lower current output and lower expected outputs in the near future. Since longer-lived capital is associated with smaller *current* output, a shift to longer-lived capital implies a higher capital–output ratio. Conversely, higher interest rates will militate for a choice of shorter-lived capital and lower capital–output ratios.

It may be further expected that given changes in the rate of interest will have a greater effect on those categories of investment involving relatively longer-lived assets, since changes in the rate of interest will have a greater relative effect on the present values of expected returns from longer-lived assets. Thus, for any given change in the rate of interest, the effect on inventory investment may be expected to be small compared with any possible effect on investment in equipment and, a fortiori, in plant. This must be qualified, however, by the recognition that changes in the short-term rate of interest are what are relevant to immediate effects on inventory investment and that the short-term rate of interest, both in theory and in fact, will fluctuate more than the relatively stable long-term rate which is relevant to fixed investment.

It is this last consideration that has led many economists to conceive of variations in rates of interest as having only a very limited potential for affecting investment. For if it is from the long-term rate that any substantial influence on investment must stem, it is to possible changes in the long-term rate that we must look. But in a free market the long-term rate must reflect expectations of future short-term rates. Investors would hardly be willing to hold long-term securities at prices that implied rates of return lower than their expectations of returns from corresponding successions of shorter-term maturities. In the face of expectations of higher future short-term rates, investors would strive to sell long-term securities until their prices were depressed sufficiently to raise their yields to equality with a weighted average, appropriately adjusted for risks, of current and expected future short-term rates. But this would mean that action by the monetary authority to reduce short-term rates in a recession, for example, could have only a small effect on long-term rates as long as investors continue to anticipate higher short-term rates when the recession is over. Hence, action by the monetary authority to stimulate investment would be stymied by its inability to bring about any substantial reduction in long-term rates.

It is generally suggested that this problem is asymmetrical, in that the monetary authority should always be able to raise interest rates sufficiently to choke off an excess of investment, but it may be argued that something analogous may take place to prevent unlimited increases in the rate of interest. For prospective borrowers might find new flexibility in trade credit and other forms of "near money" when faced with rises in short-term rates above the convenience value of that particular form of bank credit generally known as money.

*The role of risk.*   Once we admit that decision makers are concerned not merely with the mathematical expectation of expected returns but also with maximization of some preference or utility function such that a cost is attached to risk, it becomes clear that investment may be increased by a reduction of the risk faced by the investor. A project promising a 10 per cent return with certainty might be undertaken by a private investor who would reject a project offering a .9 probability of a 15 per cent return along with a .1 probability of a bankrupting, 35 per cent loss, although the mathematical expectation of the latter project is also 10 per cent.

This suggests that investment may be stimulated by two kinds of actions by government. In an economy in which investment is undertaken by privately motivated business, government could undertake measures to reduce the risks confronting the investor. This would, incidentally, argue against countercyclical monetary policy, which would have the effect of increasing uncertainty as to future interest rates. Government intervention to reduce risk facing the individual would be justi-

fied where the true risk to society is less than that to the individual.

In such cases, however, it may be preferable for government itself to undertake the investment rather than endeavor to find an appropriate subsidy or insurance scheme to induce private investment to do so. This issue is inevitably a major one in the case of underdeveloped economies requiring a large amount of interrelated or complementary investment and in the case of major new industries. It is noteworthy that in both of these instances government investment or subsidy has in fact frequently been undertaken. In the United States reference may be made particularly to railroads, commercial aviation, and atomic energy.

In view of the likelihood that risk will be viewed as cumulative over time, so that longer-term projects tend to be viewed as more risky than shorter-term projects, reduction in riskiness will tend to operate in roughly the same manner as a reduction in the rate of interest. It would increase the capital–output ratio and bring about both an initial increase in investment and a continuing increase, to the extent that demand is growing.

*Changes in demand.*   Finally, let us consider the role of changes in demand. Changes in the composition of demand for output will, to the extent capital is specific to particular outputs, generate changes in the desired composition of capital stock. This in turn implies net investment, or the addition of capital at a faster rate than normal replacement, unless the adjustment process is no faster than the wearing out of existing capital. The portion of depreciation charges which represents an allowance for normal obsolescence will tend to include the effects of a changing composition of demand that causes obsolescence of output-specific capital. A more rapid rate of change in the composition of demand may conceivably result in increasing depreciation charges, to reflect consequently more-rapid obsolescence. This would then involve an increase in gross investment which, however, would not constitute a corresponding increase in net investment.

It is important to recognize the possible extent of changes in the composition of demand. A major source of change is geographical movement. People migrating from Mississippi to Illinois or California, or from Amsterdam to Australia, generate an additional demand for services that are particular to their new locations. Housing and public services are, of course, major and conspicuous examples. Idle or excess capacity in one region does not preclude a demand for capital to provide new capacity in another region.

Changes in the rate of aggregate demand are very likely to be of prime importance in the aggregate investment function. Except for limiting effects due to excess capacity or to reductions in the capital intensity of production, an increase in aggregate demand must generate an increased demand for capital stock. In equilibrium terms, the faster the rate of growth of aggregate demand, the greater the rate of investment demand. Indeed, as long as the capital–output ratio remains unchanged, the absorption of a constant proportion of output in investment (a constant ratio of saving to income) requires a constant per cent rate of growth of output and, in turn, of investment itself. To sustain a greater relative rate of investment, there must be a proportionately faster rate of growth of output. Thus, the rate of growth, frequently seen by the classical economists as the essential result of investment, may be viewed, as well, as the critical determinant of investment.

It may readily be calculated that a rate of growth of output of some 4 per cent per annum would account for net investment equal to some 8 per cent of output, if the capital–output ratio took on the not unreasonable value of 2. But in the United States, for example, this would constitute more than 50 per cent of gross private domestic investment. A reduction of the rate of growth of output from 4 per cent to 3 per cent while maintaining the same capital–output ratio would entail a reduction of investment for purposes of expansion from 8 per cent of output to 6 per cent of output and would thus imply a reduction of gross investment of a full 13 per cent—from 15 per cent of output to 13 per cent of output. Conversely, an increase in the rate of growth from 4 per cent to 6 per cent per annum would require, if the capital–output ratio were unchanged, an increase in investment by almost 30 per cent—to 19 per cent of output.

The argument that investment is very largely dependent upon rates of growth relates to the relative magnitudes of effects due to admissible fluctuations in rates of growth and those due to other factors, but it cannot properly be argued that growth-induced investment is independent of these other factors. Thus, the technology or the rate of interest might be such that output would be produced with virtually no capital. Then fluctuations in the rate of growth of output would have little effect on the demand for capital and investment. However, given the capital-intensive methods of production and the fairly stable long-term interest rates associated with advanced economies, there is considerable reason to believe that any major variability in investment must be associated with changes in the relation between demand and capacity in the short run and with changes in the rate of growth in the long run.

Asymmetry has been noted with regard to the determination of positive and negative net investment. In both cases, it has been argued, there is some form of constraint that sets bounds for the rates of investment attainable (Hicks 1950). In regard to positive investment, the limitation (an upper bound) is set by the amount of capacity available to create producers' goods. In regard to negative net investment, the limitation (a lower bound) relates to the speed at which existing plant and equipment can be worn out and inventories can be disposed of, with or without conversion to a form acceptable to nonproducers. The upper bound is usually felt to be sufficiently high to permit a substantial investment boom if increases in aggregate demand or other factors are such as to bring about a great expansion of investment demand. A depression-induced fall in investment demand is frequently held, however, to run quickly into a "floor" to actual investment such that an economic slump, while cushioned, is prolonged by limitation on the rate at which excess stocks of capital can be worked off.

A general formulation of the investment function would probably replace upper and lower bounds by a dynamic adjustment process, subject to cost functions and to the usual maximization criteria by which producers strive to react to changes in their demand for capital. A critical and not implausible element in this dynamic system would be an equation that shows the cost of changes in the capital stock, within relevant ranges, to be an increasing function of the speed at which changes are accomplished (Eisner & Strotz 1964). The costs of transferring resources to producers' goods industries in the face of a boom may become increasingly high and eventually prohibitively high, thus constraining the boom and, if the boom can feed only upon itself, setting the stage for its collapse. In the downturn, the costs of speedy liquidation of assets, recognizing the alternative of more-gradual sale or realization of returns from production in the future, may be such as to curtail even more sharply the rate of disinvestment.

One advantage of this more general formulation is that it makes entirely separate approaches to the study of inventory investment and to the study of investment in plant and equipment unnecessary. Unintended investment, long recognized as an important component of inventory investment, may also be a component of investment in plant and equipment, although the parameters of underlying relations may be such that the role and volatility of unintended investment are significantly different in the two categories. While an increase in sales expected to be "permanent" is likely to bring about inventory investment until a new, consequently higher level of inventory stocks is attained, an unexpected increase in sales will have, as an immediate effect, inventory disinvestment. With no planned increase in output, the unexpected increase in sales must be met out of existing inventory stocks. This initial, unintended disinvestment is then seen to give way to intended investment, to restore a desired stock of inventories. However, a similar analysis can be made with respect to investment in plant and equipment. An unexpected increase in sales will, when followed by an increase in output, result in a more intensive utilization of fixed capital and consequently more-rapid depreciation. Thus, the real capital stock of plant and equipment would be reduced by the unexpected increase in sales, just as was the stock of inventories. This initial, unintended disinvestment in plant and equipment would also give way to positive, intended net investment, in order to restore a desired capital–output ratio.

If technical factors (the nature of the production function) curb the possibility of added real depreciation of capital as a consequence of increased output with the existing capital stock, the analogous treatment of unintended investment in inventories and capital stock may still hold fairly clearly in the case of unexpected decreases in sales. Just as production plans may be executed in the face of a drop in sales, causing unintended inventory investment, so plant and equipment construction and purchase may continue, once initiated, in the face of a decline in sales, even though the additional plant and equipment is redundant. Thus, in a sense very similar to that relating to inventories, total investment in plant and equipment proves more than sufficient to provide the capital stock desired in the light of the new level of sales, and there is (temporary) unintended investment.

**Empirical studies.** Empirical investigation of the investment function has sometimes involved analysis of relations between time series of aggregative data for an entire national economy. More often, however, investment studies have focused on relations, usually also estimated from time series, within particular industries. Recently, increased attention has been given to cross sections of data for individual firms. Some work has also been done with time series data of individual firms.

Explanatory variables in empirical studies have included current and past output, sales, profits, stock yields, interest rates, depreciation charges, stocks of capital, age of capital, capacity, prices of output, prices of labor and of capital goods, "liquidity," value of the firm, and a number of measures of expectations. Investigators have tended to find substantial positive correlations between investment and profits but less certain association between investment and the rate of interest. Tests and estimates of crude forms of the acceleration principle—that the connection between capital and output leads to prime dependence of investment on the rate of change of output—have frequently produced negative results.

A number of recent studies, with varied sets of data, have reported meaningful results with distributed lag formulations of the acceleration principle and of similar capital stock adjustment or capacity adjustment models. It has also proved possible to reinterpret the findings of earlier studies to fit this mold (Eisner & Strotz 1964). In particular, classic work of Tinbergen (1938–1939) and major studies of Klein (1951), purporting to find in profits a prime determinant of investment, can be shown to confirm equally well (or better, depending on one's a priori model) the role of changes in output or the relation of expected demand to capacity. Chenery (1952) obtained good fits for industry time series in relations involving both single first differences of output and a capacity adjustment term. His "capacity model" made the change in capacity in any period some fraction of the difference between desired capacity, which depends upon output, and actual capacity. Koyck (1954), also working with industry time series data, secured positive results with a distributed lag formulation in which coefficients of previous changes in output were assumed, after a certain number of lags, to take on the form of a decaying geometric progression, with the common ratio for successive coefficients estimated from the data. Interestingly, he noted that the acceleration effects were more marked in relatively expanding industries, and in expansionary periods rather than in those of contraction. Meyer and Kuh (1957), working primarily with cross-section data of individual firms within industries, reported positive associations both for profits and for "liquidity" variables and acceleration variables, with the former more important in periods of recession. Eisner (1960), in his examination of a distributed lag accelerator in cross-section data, has reduced profits to the role of a proxy variable for the pressure of demand on capacity. He has reported (1963) that accelerator components may be seen more clearly, and presumably may be better estimated, by isolating "permanent" elements in the sales and output variance to which firms may be expected to respond.

Estimates of inventory–investment relations have been bedeviled by neglect or inability to distinguish between unintended and intended investment. Essentially, increases in anticipated output or sales, as measured by new orders, have been found to be positively correlated with inventory investment. Unexpected changes in sales, as measured, for example, by differences between actual and anticipated sales, show some negative relation to inventory investment. However, the two elements are difficult to separate, since changing sales and output themselves clearly affect expectations and consequent production decisions.

Direct estimates of the aggregate investment function, it is only fair to report, are still in an early, experimental stage. Estimates derived from time series or cross sections at a less than economy-wide level are probably poor substitutes for direct estimates. For one thing, it is far from clear that variances and covariances between relevant variables at a microeconomic level or within particular industries bear sufficiently similar relation to variances and covariances between relevant expectational variables at the macroeconomic level. Is there, after all, any reason why a firm experiencing an increase in its sales relative to sales of other firms in its industry or even to sales in the economy should form the same expectation about future demand as it would if the increase were part of a general aggregative increase? But what is more, one must beware of ever dangerous fallacies of composition in dealing at less than aggregative levels. It remains possible, after all, that changes in demand for individual firms and whole industries may determine investment in those firms and those industries, while investment in the economy as a whole is fairly rigidly contained by the supply of saving.

**Policy implications.** Policy recommendations regarding investment depend in part, of course, on the preference functions of those making the recommendations. Under conditions of full employment, which are usually assumed to obtain in socialist economies but are considered less general in capitalist economies, a higher rate of investment at any point of time implies less current output for consumer use; it also implies a higher rate of growth and, hence, more future output. With less than full employment, a higher rate of investment is likely to cause increased current consumption, as well as increased future output. Decisions as to allocation of resources to provide for current consumption or for future output may be shaped by

market forces, reflecting individual (including business) preferences and the existing distribution of income or, more generally, the existing distribution of control over resources. Or these decisions may be made by some central planning authority, reflecting its own preferences or some function of what are conceived to be the preferences of individuals in the society. No matter how the decisions are made, they should be influenced by the expected productivity of investment which, as we have observed, largely determines the investment function.

In an economy where the physical means of production are privately owned and are acquired for purposes of private profit, some additional issues arise. First, decisions as to the rate of investment and the distribution of investment between physical goods and human skills become decisions affecting directly the distribution of income and wealth. Second, the issue of investment becomes intimately intertwined with the question of maintenance of full employment and, hence, with the essential efficiency of the economic system.

Distributional considerations aside, policy recommendations regarding investment in a capitalist economy should be based closely on one's view of the investment function. If investment is considered highly interest elastic, it may appear reasonable to allow free rein to individual and business saving propensities and to rely upon the rate of interest to equate investment demand and saving at reasonably full employment. This would leave the rate of economic growth at whatever level is consistent with these saving propensities, given the distribution of income, role of risk, and existing institutional arrangements—and the basic natural and technological constraints.

If investment is considered fairly inelastic with respect to the rate of interest and if full-employment saving propensities appear high relative to investment demand, various recommendations for government action come to the fore. There is usually general agreement that, at the very least, monetary policy should be directed at keeping interest rates as low as possible. In addition, in capitalist countries a number of direct fiscal measures have been proposed and applied, chiefly involving some form of increased or accelerated depreciation allowances for tax purposes and direct tax reductions or subsidies dependent upon investment.

The effects of these fiscal measures would appear to depend in part on companion fiscal policies as well as on the nature of the investment function. The direct effect on investment stemming from higher earnings by business corporations should be relatively small unless general principles of profit maximization prove irrelevant. Firms striving to maximize profit should not invest more when earnings are higher, unless their expectations of profit stemming from such additional investment are increased. If the various tax benefits to investment are accompanied by increased taxes elsewhere in order to keep government revenues constant, there is no presumption that aggregate demand will be increased and, therefore, no justification in this direction for expectations of increased profitability from additional investment. Tax benefits or subsidies to investment unaccompanied by other compensating increases in taxes, however, should result in an increase in aggregate demand. For while firms may not raise their own expenditures, the increase in earnings will be reflected in higher dividends or higher values of corporate shares or will be passed on in lower prices, in any event raising appropriately defined real disposable income. The consequent increase in aggregate demand would generate increased demand for capital stock. Investment would then be accelerated until this larger capital stock is acquired. Maintaining the increase in the rate of investment, however, would necessitate further increases in the desired capital stock, such as might be generated by an increase in the rate of tax benefits or subsidies associated with investment.

There is another effect of the usual fiscal benefits related directly to investment. This is to raise the expected profitability of investment for any given demand by making capital goods more attractive relative to other factors of production. The magnitude of this effect may be restricted by limitations of factor substitutability, which would underlie an interest-inelastic investment demand schedule. Thus, a given benefit may raise the expected profitability of all prospective investment by, say, 20 per cent over a five-year period; but if the elasticity of investment demand is only .3, this would raise investment by only 6 per cent. However, to the extent that more capital-intensive methods of production are adopted as a result of tax benefits or other subsidies to investment, the amount of investment required to maintain any given rate of output would be increased, and more investment would thus be generated, year after year, to provide for whatever increases in demand and output are forthcoming.

To those who see investment demand as determined largely by increases in the demand for output, appropriate fiscal measures for raising investment would entail repeated cuts in taxes or increases in government expenditures, so that aggregate demand would continue to grow. Action to bring about repeated increases in aggregate demand would not only sustain investment and employment but would also tend to insure that the growth of the economy be limited only by the growth in capacity permitted by technology and by the increase in supply of factors of production—of labor and capital—under conditions of full employment.

Critics of such a policy might offer as their main objection that it would be difficult, if not impossible, to provide adequate increases in demand without generating chronic, and perhaps accelerating, inflation of prices. This would entail not only serious inequities in the distribution of real income but also losses of efficiency in the productive system that might imply a lower output with full employment than could be obtained with somewhat less than full employment but with the more efficient allocation of resources provided by a stable price system. Counterarguments in favor of governmentally induced increases in demand include the insistence that price inflation can be kept mild enough to avoid threats to efficiency and that the distributional effects of inflation are not necessarily bad (unless one views the current income distribution as necessarily the best) and can in any event be compensated for by other fiscal measures. It is further argued that increased government expenditures on various kinds of social investment (education, research, urban renewal) may actually increase efficiency, as well as provide a more equitable distribution of the benefits of social production and social living.

ROBERT EISNER

### BIBLIOGRAPHY

ABRAMOVITZ, MOSES 1950 *Inventories and Business Cycles, With Special Reference to Manufacturers' Inventories.* New York: National Bureau of Economic Research.

ARROW, KENNETH J.; KARLIN, SAMUEL; and SCARF, HERBERT 1958 *Studies in the Mathematical Theory of Inventory and Production.* Stanford Mathematical Studies in the Social Sciences, No. 1. Stanford Univ. Press.

CHENERY, HOLLIS B. 1952 Overcapacity and the Acceleration Principle. *Econometrica* 20:1–28.

CLARK, JOHN MAURICE (1917) 1949 Business Acceleration and the Law of Demand: A Technical Factor in Economic Cycles. Pages 235–260 in American Economic Association, *Readings in Business Cycle Theory.* Philadelphia: Blakiston. → First published in Volume 25 of the *Journal of Political Economy.*

CONFERENCE ON RESEARCH IN INCOME AND WEALTH 1955 *Short-term Economic Forecasting.* Studies in Income and Wealth, Vol. 17. Princeton Univ. Press.

CONFERENCE ON RESEARCH IN INCOME AND WEALTH 1957 *Problems of Capital Formation: Concepts, Measurement, and Controlling Factors.* Studies in Income and Wealth, Vol. 19. Princeton Univ. Press.

Dean, Joel 1951 *Capital Budgeting: Top-management Policy on Plant, Equipment, and Product Development.* New York: Columbia Univ. Press.

Dieterlen, Pierre 1957 *L'investissement.* Paris: Rivière.

Domar, Evsey D. 1948 The Problem of Capital Accumulation. *American Economic Review* 38:777–794.

Eisner, Robert 1960 A Distributed Lag Investment Function. *Econometrica* 28:1–29.

Eisner, Robert 1963 Investment: Fact and Fancy. *American Economic Review* 53:237–246.

Eisner, Robert; and Strotz, Robert H. 1964 Determinants of Business Investment. Pages 59–233 in Commission on Money and Credit, *Impacts of Monetary Policy: A Series of Research Studies Prepared for the Commission on Money and Credit.* Englewood Cliffs, N.J.: Prentice-Hall.

Haavelmo, Trygve 1960 *A Study in the Theory of Investment.* Univ. of Chicago Press.

Hicks, John R. (1939) 1946 *Value and Capital: An Inquiry Into Some Fundamental Principles of Economic Theory.* 2d ed. Oxford: Clarendon. → See especially Parts 3 and 4.

Hicks, John R. 1950 *A Contribution to the Theory of the Trade Cycle.* Oxford: Clarendon. → See especially Chapters 4, 5, 6, and 10.

Jorgenson, Dale W. (1963) 1965 Capital Theory and Investment Behavior. Pages 366–378 in American Economic Association, *Readings in Business Cycles.* Homewood, Ill.: Irwin. → First published in Volume 53, No. 2, of the *American Economic Review.*

Kalecki, Michael 1954 *Theory of Economic Dynamics: An Essay on Cyclical and Long-run Changes in Capitalist Economy.* New York: Rinehart.

Keynes, John Maynard 1936 *The General Theory of Employment, Interest and Money.* London: Macmillan. → See especially Book 4. A paperback edition was published in 1965 by Harcourt.

Klein, Lawrence R. 1951 Studies in Investment Behavior. Pages 233–277 in *Conference on Business Cycles.* New York: National Bureau of Economic Research. → A paper delivered at a conference held in New York City in 1949.

Koyck, M. 1954 *Distributed Lags and Investment Analysis.* Amsterdam: North-Holland Publishing.

Lutz, Friedrich A.; and Lutz, Vera C. 1951 *The Theory of Investment of the Firm.* Princeton Univ. Press.

Massé, Pierre (1959) 1962 *Optimal Investment Decisions.* Englewood Cliffs, N.J.: Prentice-Hall. → First published as *Le choix des investissements.*

Meade, J. E.; and Andrews, P. W. S. 1938 Summary of Replies to Questions on Effects of Interest Rates. *Oxford Economic Papers* 1:14–31.

Metzler, Lloyd A. (1941) 1965 The Nature and Stability of Inventory Cycles. Pages 100–129 in American Economic Association, *Readings in Business Cycles.* Homewood, Ill.: Irwin. → First published in Volume 23 of the *Review of Economic Statistics.*

Meyer, John R.; and Kuh, Edwin 1957 *The Investment Decision: An Empirical Study.* Harvard Economic Studies, Vol. 102. Cambridge, Mass.: Harvard Univ. Press.

Novozhilov, V. V. (1946) 1956 On Choosing Between Investment Projects. *International Economic Papers* 6:66–87. → First published in Russian.

Robinson, Joan 1956 *The Accumulation of Capital.* Homewood, Ill.: Irwin; London: Macmillan.

Strumilin, S. G. (1946) 1951 The Time Factor in Capital Investment Projects. *International Economic Papers* 1:160–185. → First published in Russian.

Terborgh, George W. 1949 *Dynamic Equipment Policy.* New York: McGraw-Hill.

Tinbergen, Jan 1938–1939 *Statistical Testing of Business-cycle Theories.* 2 vols. Geneva: League of Nations, Economic Intelligence Service. → Volume 1: *A Method and Its Application to Investment Activity.* Volume 2: *Business Cycles in the United States of America: 1919–1932.*

Universities–National Bureau Committee for Economic Research 1954 *Regularization of Business Investment.* Princeton Univ. Press.

## II

### THE INVESTMENT DECISION

Investment is present sacrifice for future benefit. Investment decisions of economic agents include an individual's buying a bond, planting a seed, or undertaking a course of training; a firm's purchasing a machine or constructing a building; and a government agency's building a dam. *Productive* investments (such as planting a seed) necessitate a social sacrifice of current consumption and may be distinguished from *financial* investments (such as purchase of a bond), which reduce to an exchange of titles to consumption between two economic agents.

**Normative and positive theories.** As in other branches of economics, there are normative (how one *should* act) and positive (how one *does* act) theories of the investment decision. In managerial economics and capital-budgeting studies, analysts offer advice as to how private investors should act. The theoretical basis for advice is clearly normative, which is true also of advice offered governments in connection with national or regional planning. The central tradition in investment theory, although also seemingly normative, is positive in aim. The question of how the rational investor *should* act has been given attention in order to generate testable inferences about how investors *do* act—or, since the rationality of investors is not essential, to discover the types of investments that will be successful and so will tend to persist (whatever the actual motivation).

**Basic concepts.** From the point of view of the individual, the investment decision is linked to consumption on the one hand and accumulation of wealth or capital on the other. Consumption in the present and future periods will here be the primitive concept in terms of which the other theoretical terms are defined. Each individual has, at a moment of time, an endowment in the form of a sequence of consumption possibilities or *incomes*, $y_t$, in the various periods: $y_0, y_1, y_2, \cdots, y_t, \cdots$

Here $y_0$ is the "current income"—the amount that can be consumed in the present period without adding to or subtracting from the future income elements in the endowment. *Investment* in any period, $i_t$, is the amount by which consumption, $c_t$, falls short of income: $i_t = y_t - c_t$. By this definition, investment is equivalent to "saving" and may take on negative values (disinvestment).

*Wealth* and *capital* are derivative concepts, referring to time-aggregates of consumption possibilities (incomes). Suppose there is a market in which titles to incomes ("funds") of various dates are exchanged, as through borrowing and lending. Then one dollar of current funds will exchange for $1 + r$ dollars of funds dated one year hence, where $r$ is the annual *rate of interest* (annual compounding assumed). If, for simplicity, it is assumed that the rate of interest is uniform over time, current wealth $W_0$ may be found by discounting the endowment of incomes according to the formula

$$(1) \quad W_0 = y_0 + \frac{y_1}{(1+r)} + \frac{y_2}{(1+r)^2}$$
$$+ \cdots + \frac{y_t}{(1+r)^t} + \cdots .$$

With more frequent compounding (at the semi-annual rate $\frac{1}{2}r$, quarterly rate $\frac{1}{4}r$, etc.), one dollar of current funds would grow to more than $1 + r$ dollars in a year. In the limit, compounding may be said to be continuous, and the discounting equation takes on the form

$$(1') \qquad W'_0 = \int_{t=0}^{\infty} y(t)e^{-rt}\, dt.$$

The discrete formulation (1) and the continuous (1') are both in common use. The amount of wealth reserved for future consumption is denoted *capital*, $K_0$, so that the endowment may be subdivided (using the discrete formulation): $W_0 = y_0 + K_0$.

**Irving Fisher's theory.** The modern theory of investment was set down in classical form by Irving Fisher as part of his great work on interest (1930). Fisher looked at investment as a means of achieving an optimal pattern of consumption over time, rather than as a process of accumulation per se. This view permits the extension of the economic theory of choice into the time dimension, the objects of choice being present and future consumption. The elements needed to determine the individual's investment decision are: (*a*) the *endowment*, in the form of an existing income stream over time; (*b*) the *preference function*, which orders in desirability all possible time-combinations of consumption; and (*c*) the *opportunity set*, which specifies the productive and financial possibilities

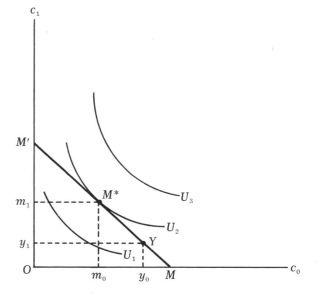

Figure 1 — *Endowment, preference function, and financial investment opportunities*

for transforming the original endowment into other time-combinations. The theory is fully worked out only under the assumption that economic agents act under certainty or possess complete information; uncertainty will be introduced below.

Figures 1 and 2 illustrate artificially simple cases of investment choice, but cases that are instructive and capable of easy generalization. It is assumed that there are only two periods (say, this year and next); each point in either diagram represents a combination of current consumption, $c_0$, and future consumption, $c_1$. The endowment combination, Y, has coordinates $(y_0, y_1)$. The time-preferences are portrayed by the "indifference curves," $U_1$, $U_2$, $U_3$, $\cdots$, each such curve connecting all combinations yielding equal satisfaction.

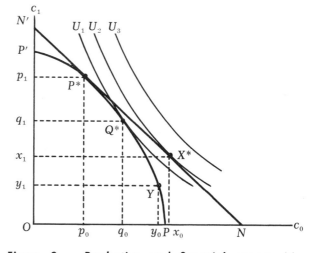

Figure 2 — *Productive and financial opportunities combined*

In Figure 1 there are financial opportunities only —i.e., exchange opportunities with other individuals that leave wealth unchanged. This is expressed in the diagram by the ability to move along a "market line," such as $MM'$, with slope $-(1 + r)$. To move northwest along a market line is to lend (exchange a dollar of $c_0$ for $1 + r$ dollars of $c_1$); to move southeast is to borrow (give up $c_1$ for $c_0$). The line $MM'$ goes through $Y$ and so defines the triangle $OMM'$ as the total opportunity set (set of attainable combinations) for the individual with endowment $Y$. Other market lines, all parallel to $MM'$, would be appropriate with different endowments. Along each market line, wealth, $W_0$, is constant. Any addition to current consumption, $c_0$, by borrowing is balanced by a wealth-equivalent sacrifice of future consumption, $c_1$, in repaying: $W_0 = y_0 + y_1/(1 + r) = c_0 + c_1/(1 + r)$. In Figure 1 the length $OM$ represents $W_0$. The optimum combination of $c_0$ and $c_1$ within the wealth constraint is at $M^*$, where $MM'$ is tangent to the highest attainable indifference curve, $U_2$. The amount invested (lent) is $y_0 - m_0$, the repayment being $m_1 - y_1 = (y_0 - m_0)(1 + r)$.

In Figure 2 the endowment, $Y$, and preference function, $U_1, U_2, U_3, \cdots$, again appear. But here the curve $PP'$ through $Y$ represents *productive* investment (and disinvestment) opportunities: for example, sowing seed to convert $c_0$ into $c_1$. Extensions of productive investments are subject to diminishing returns, shown by the absolutely declining slope of $PP'$ moving up the curve. If there were *only* productive opportunities, the relevant opportunity set would be just $PP'$, and the optimum would be at $Q^*$, where the highest attainable indifference curve touches $PP'$. Robinson Crusoe, who could engage in transactions with nature but not with a capital funds market, was in such a situation; his amount invested would be $y_0 - q_0$. But if there are both productive and financial investments (and disinvestments) available, the opportunity set is greatly enlarged to become the triangle bounded by $NN'$. The optimum is attained in two stages. The "productive solution," $P^*$, is characterized by the attainment of the highest level of wealth, $\hat{W}_0$. Symbolically, $\hat{W}_0 = p_0 + p_1/(1 + r)$. In a more general $n$-period case, the productive solution $P^*$ is such that

(2) $$\hat{W}_0 = p_0 + \frac{p_1}{(1 + r)} + \frac{p_2}{(1 + r)^2} + \cdots + \frac{p_n}{(1 + r)^n}.$$

The investor then "finances" the productive solution by moving along the "market hyperplane" of maximum $\hat{W}_0$ through $P^*$ to find the best time-distribu-

tion of consumption, $X^*$, in terms of his preferences. Thus the capital market permits an increase in productive investment to $y_0 - p_0$. The increase is made possible by the investor's ability to replenish current consumption by borrowing (financial disinvestment) in the amount of $x_0 - p_0$ to attain his optimal time-combination of consumption at $X^*$. Productive investment has increased wealth to $\hat{W}_0 = ON$; the investor has suffered no diminution of current consumption, although in the community as a whole real saving has taken place.

This solution is quite general, but there is an interesting special case. We may think of the original two-period example as an illustration of the "widening" of investment, i.e., increasing the level of current sacrifice to attain greater return at some fixed future date. A different two-period problem involves "deepening" of investment. Suppose that the amount of current sacrifice, $i_0$, is fixed, but the output date is subject to choice (e.g., when to cut a tree). In Figure 3, horizontal distances represent time, $t$, and vertical distances wealth or value, $V_t$, at each moment of time. *Present value*, $V_0$, is indicated by height along the vertical axis (where $t = 0$). The curve $GG'$ represents productive growth of the asset—in the case of a tree, market value of the standing timber. The "discount curves," $D, D', D'', \cdots$, are analogous to the "market lines" of figures 1 and 2. They represent the growth of a specific sum of present dollars by continuous compounding of interest over time, so that wealth is constant along a discount curve. Their general equation is $V_0 = V_t e^{-rt}$, where $V_0$ is the wealth parameter. The optimal investment period $\hat{t}$ is the one that yields maximum wealth or present value $\hat{V}_0$, a result that follows from the general produc-

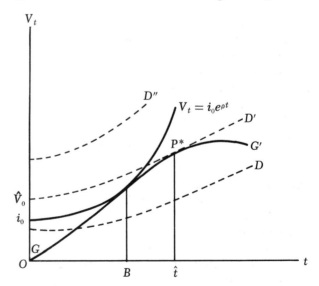

**Figure 3 — The "deepening" decision: optimal length of investment**

tive solution. Here $GG'$ is the relevant productive opportunity set, and the tangency of $GG'$ with the highest constant-wealth curve attainable corresponds to the productive solution $P^*$. The "financing" decision is not shown in Figure 3, since the preference function cannot be displayed on $(t,V)$ axes, but maximizing wealth is a prerequisite for attaining the over-all optimum.

**Decisions of firms and governments.** The theory developed above applies strictly to a maximizing individual; the decisions of other economic agents —in particular, business firms and governments— must be considered also. Firms are instrumentalities of individuals for productive purposes only; they cannot consume. Firms have income streams and, therefore, wealth. But all such wealth is held on account, in the form of capital left by owners —ultimately, by individuals—to generate future income. For the firm, the alternative to investment is not consumption, but distribution of current funds back to the owners. Or there may be inflow of funds to the firm from the owners. Decisions that maximize wealth for the firm maximize wealth for the owners.

Government agencies may also be regarded as instrumentalities of individuals. They may engage in essentially consumptive activities of a communal nature—such as national defense. In other respects, governments may act like productive firms, as in the sale of water or in postal service. Government agencies are not "owned" in any simple sense; they may deliberately pursue ends other than wealth-maximization—for example, redistribution of community income. To the extent that satisfaction of such goals is at the expense of the community's capital, as is ordinary consumption, the goals can be regarded as quasi-consumption objectives. There is, unfortunately, no accepted criterion of social rationality to tell us how far alternative aims should be pursued. Maximizing wealth can be regarded as a partial or limited goal for governments, subject to modification because of competing goals. [*See* BUDGETING.]

**The criterion controversy.** Certain investment criteria employed in business practice, such as rapidity of "payout" (return of capital invested), are obviously erroneous in failing to allow properly for time-discount. Controversy among theorists has centered on the concept variously known as the "internal rate" and the "rate of return" on investment. It is defined implicitly as $\rho$ in the discrete discounting equation

(3)
$$0 = s_0 + \frac{s_1}{1+\rho} + \frac{s_2}{(1+\rho)^2} + \cdots + \frac{s_n}{(1+\rho)^n}.$$

Here the $s_t$ are the successive terms, positive or negative, of the payments–receipts sequence associated incrementally with a particular investment or characterizing an over-all set of investments. In the special "deepening" case illustrated in Figure 3, the corresponding concept under continuous compounding is defined implicitly in

(3′)
$$0 = -i_0 + V_t e^{-\rho t}.$$

Under these conditions $\rho$ represents an average compounded rate of growth.

The plausibility of maximizing growth has led some analysts to propose, as the investment criterion, adoption of the investment set that maximizes over-all $\rho$—in contrast to the *wealth*-maximization criterion of the previous analysis. In terms of the "widening" decision depicted in Figure 2, maximizing $\rho$ would evidently be absurd: both marginal and average $\rho$ on the funds committed are maximized when investment is zero (the highest *rate* of growth is on the first infinitesimal investment). The proposal has some appeal in the "deepening" choice of Figure 3, where investment, $i_0$, is held fixed. The solution of (3′) that maximizes $\rho$ is shown as $t = B$ in Figure 3. The Fisher solution, $t = \hat{t}$, maximizes $V_0$ (which is equal to $V_t e^{-rt}$). Which one is correct depends upon the alternatives envisaged. In Figure 3, $B$ is correct if the deepening opportunity can be reproduced (e.g., on new land) on an ever broadening scale, but only as funds are freed (by cutting the tree, in the example). This turns out to be an uninteresting case, as it implies that the opportunity must be of infinite value if $\rho > r$ (and of no value otherwise). Fisher's solution $\hat{t}$ is correct if the opportunity is a unique one and cannot be (profitably) reproduced after cutting. Another solution, $t = F$, found by the German forester Faustmann, is appropriate when the opportunity can be reproduced over time by cutting and replanting but cannot be profitably broadened. $F$ is found by maximizing the $V_0$ of an infinite sequence of rotations, allowing for cost of replanting; it is a maximum-wealth solution under the stated assumptions. ($F$ is not shown in Figure 3 but would lie between $B$ and $\hat{t}$.) Maximizing wealth, within the opportunities available, is the general (productive) solution.

Quite a different "rate of return" rule was proposed by Fisher himself. He argued that it would be equivalent to maximizing present value if every investment project were adopted for which $\rho$ calculated on the associated incremental payments and receipts exceeded the market interest rate, $r$. (Note that this rule for *comparison* of $\rho$ and $r$ is not at all the same as *maximizing* $\rho$ irrespective of $r$.) Over a wide class of cases Fisher's $(\rho,r)$ comparison rule and his maximum-wealth rule are equivalent. But disparities occur when returns from possible investments are interdependent (options may, for example, be mutually exclusive or, alternatively, complementary); also, in some multiperiod options $\rho$ is ambiguous or undefined—there may be no solution, or multiple solutions, of the defining equation (3). In all such cases the maximum-wealth rule unambiguously indicates the productive solution, making possible the optimum consumption pattern within the opportunities available.

Recent investigations have explored the implications of more general opportunity sets, productive or financial, than are assumed by Fisher. As was just suggested, investment options in the productive opportunity set may be interconnected in various ways, and indivisibilities may also be important. These complexities of the productive set indicate the need for high-speed computational techniques such as linear and especially integer programming. But so long as perfect capital markets can be assumed, the maximum-wealth rule remains appropriate. The effect of imperfect capital markets is to restrict the financial opportunity set; in the limiting (Crusoe) case, there are no financial opportunities —only productive ones. When the financial opportunities cannot be described by "market lines" like $MM'$ and $NN'$, the very concept of wealth becomes ambiguous. Although an optimum can always be obtained, in principle, for any opportunity set and preference function, the great advantage of the wealth concept is that it provides an objective guide to the *productive* solution, independent of the particular agent's time-preferences.

**Empirical evidence.** This economic theory of investment choice is highly abstract and patently neglects some important phenomena bearing on decisions (e.g., uncertainty). Nevertheless, a number of implications drawn from the theory are confirmed by evidence from various realms of experience: (*a*) The theory predicts that, other things being equal, an endowment characterized by a rising income stream will encourage borrowing. This is notoriously true, on the individual level, for prospective heirs with "great expectations"; it is also commonly observed in young physicians and lawyers setting up practice. If the rising income stream applies to a region or nation, the pressure of demand for borrowings should lead to high interest. We find that interest has been high, in fact, in the United States during the nineteenth century, in California after the discovery of gold, and in communities struck unexpectedly by earthquake or hurricane—all cases in which future incomes higher than current levels could be anticipated.

(*b*) By a related argument, borrowing demand, and therefore interest, should be high where the productive opportunities are very favorable. California in the 1850s is again a case in point. More recently, U.S. interest rates were higher in the productive decade of the 1950s than in the stagnant 1930s. (*c*) Divergences in time-preference patterns should also lead to predictable consequences. Fisher credits such groups as the Scots, Dutch, and Jews with a high degree of forethought and concern for posterity, both of which are associated with low time-preference. Interest rates within such groups tend to be low, so that the groups become lenders and investors for the outside world. (*d*) Although highly productive opportunities lead to high interest, high market interest, other things being equal, is (according to the theory) a deterrent to productive investment. We in fact observe in underdeveloped countries many investment opportunities that are technically more productive than those in advanced countries but that nevertheless go unexploited; high interest is one of the reasons, although there may be others (such as political instability or distance from markets). A clearer case occurs when, within such a country, Europeans and natives engage in the same industry; the former will generally have access to lower-interest finance. Accordingly, it has been observed on the Malay peninsula that peasant small holders tap rubber trees of smaller girth than do operators of European plantations there. (*e*) The same example illustrates the theoretical implication that an enlarged financial opportunity set, through increased perfection of and wider access to capital markets, leads to an increased scale of investment if there are productive opportunities available.

In recent years, however, some investigations have cast doubt on one implication of the theory: that interest rates and levels of corporate investment, other things being equal, should be inversely associated. Studies using questionnaire techniques have encountered generally negative responses from businessmen on the role of interest rates in influencing investment decisions. And some statistical investigations of investment magnitudes have been unable to isolate the effect of interest—or, indeed, have indicated a perverse result, high interest being associated with high investment.

Currently, econometric investigators tend to discredit the questionnaire technique, on the ground that it elicits the ideas or rationalizations of businessmen rather than information on their actions. It should be noted, however, that even if the questionnaires are correct and only a minority of businessmen respond to interest rates, the over-all effect may yet be significant. The statistical results raise more complex questions. First of all, a lag probably exists between the forces determining investment and statistically measurable construction and equipping. Second, the effect of expectations should be allowed for. Theoretically, investment should be inversely associated with interest, if other factors (primarily expectations about investment yield) remain unchanged. But with a change in expectations, upward or downward, investment and interest should move *together* in response. The more recent studies that have explicitly allowed for lag and for the disturbing effects of changes in expectations have generally shown the anticipated inverse association of interest and investment.

**The role of uncertainty.**  Uncertainty, which may be understood as a subjective condition characterized by imperfect information about the world, influences all economic decisions. But the present may be relatively well known, whereas the future is always risky. Investment choices, involving as they do present sacrifice for future benefit, are peculiarly sensitive to uncertainty. Among the phenomena left unexplained under the certainty assumption are the nonequalization of the yields of various investment media ("assets") on the market, the mixtures of debt and equity employed in "financing" productive investments, and the value attached to "liquidity."

An *asset* is the source of a future, generally uncertain, stream of potential consumption (income). The productive transformations defined earlier correspond to the formation of *physical* assets. The market transformations correspond to the trading of *financial* assets (securities) that partition the income stream generated by physical assets. As in the case of certainty, the productive decision under perfect markets aims at maximizing wealth. The consumptive (or financing) decision is much more complex, however; risk-preference is involved as well as time-preference.

The traditional formulation of investment choice under risk—due initially to Fisher (1930) and developed more recently by Markowitz (1959)—postulates that the individual prefers high mathematical *expectation* but dislikes high *variability* (as measured, usually, by the standard deviation) of the probability distribution of future income yielded by his portfolio of assets. Making the usual convexity assumption, indifference curves between expected future income, $E(c)$, and standard deviation of future income, $\sigma(c)$, are represented in Figure 4. For a given level of current sacrifice, the $E,\sigma$ opportunity set available to an individual by alternative portfolios of risky assets is shown by the shaded area. Because *diversification* tends to lower

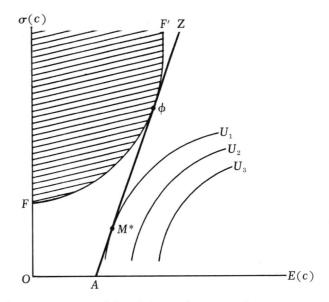

**Figure 4 — Portfolio-choice under uncertainty**

$\sigma$, the portfolios along the efficiency frontier $FF'$ will ordinarily be mixtures of assets. The point $A$ represents a possible portfolio held entirely in a *riskless* ($\sigma = 0$) asset. The "market line" $A\phi Z$, tangent at $\phi$ to the risky opportunity set, represents (in the range $A\phi$) portfolio mixtures of $A$ and $\phi$ made available by the existence of the riskless asset. Depending upon the shape of the preference map, the optimal portfolio $M^*$ may be found anywhere along $A\phi$—and even along $\phi Z$ to the extent that riskless borrowing is possible.

Under the assumption that all investors have identical beliefs about the probability distributions, Sharpe (1964) has obtained important results on the properties of optimal portfolios and asset prices. There will in general be a range of perfectly correlated risky portfolios along $AZ$ (rather than the unique optimum at $\phi$ shown in Figure 4). In equilibrium there may be defined a "price of risk"—a positive linear relation between the per cent return on an asset and the portion of the asset's variability correlated with the fluctuations of optimal portfolios. This formulation explains, therefore, both diversification and the divergences of yield among assets. Furthermore, the analysis can be made operational by assuming, for example, that past history can be used as the basis for probability distributions of future returns. In extending this theory of portfolio-choice (governing the *media* for investment within a wealth constraint) to cover time-choice as well (governing the *scale* of investment, involving in general productive as well as market transformations), greater degrees of current sacrifice will be reflected by a rightward shift of the entire opportunity set of Figure 4.

The assumption that preference attaches to the expectation and standard deviation of probability distributions raises a number of analytical and empirical difficulties. However, it turns out that the $E,\sigma$ formulation can be regarded as an approximation to a formally more satisfactory theory of "time-state-preference" put forward by Arrow (1953). On this latter view, preference attaches not to mathematical properties of probability distributions but to the set of consumption incomes to be received at stated dates and under specified contingencies (states of the world). If, for example, the present is certain but there are two distinct possible future states, $a$ and $b$, the problem (as a direct generalization of Fisher's riskless theory) is to attain an optimal balance among $c_0$ (current certain consumption), $c_a$ (future consumption if state $a$ obtains), and $c_b$ (future consumption if state $b$ obtains). Looking only at the balance between the future contingent claims (to isolate the element of risk-preference), aversion to high $\sigma$ corresponds to convex indifference curves on $c_a$, $c_b$ axes. More precisely, it can be shown that, under the von Neumann–Morgenstern postulates of rational choice, riskless solutions (where $c_a = c_b$, or equivalently where $\sigma = 0$) will be preferred if the prices for the contingent income claims are "fair" (proportionate to the respective probabilities). [*See* DECISION MAKING, *article on* ECONOMIC ASPECTS.]

Under the time-state-preference formulation, the individual will seek a productive optimum that maximizes wealth (certainty-equivalent present value). He will then move along his constant-wealth constraint to locate a preferred distribution of claims over times and states. If a *firm* is investing so as to achieve a wealth maximum, the implication is that (under perfect markets) the specific debt-equity mix chosen to finance the productive solution need not concern the individual owners (their wealth is unaffected). This assertion, which is true only in the absence of external drains (such as corporate income taxes and bankruptcy penalties) on the wealth of the firm, corresponds to a theorem first set forth by Modigliani and Miller (1958).

In the real world, of course, market imperfections (transaction costs) play an important role. In particular, there is reason to believe that there are far too many contingencies to be explicitly traded in markets. Within the limited range of distinct assets that are actually traded, assets represent complex bundles of the contingent dated claims that are the objects of preference. Transaction costs prevent the full attainment of private optimality

in risky markets, and explain the desire for "liquidity."

There are other practical difficulties in applying the maximum-wealth criterion to actual decisions of the firm under uncertainty. It may be far from clear to corporate management, for example, how the market for the firm's securities would respond to a proposed risky investment. Capital-budgeting analysts commonly recommend calculating the effect of incremental investment on corporate wealth somewhat as follows: First, estimate the investment returns, and then discount to find the present value via equation (1)—using for $r$ the "cost of capital" appropriate for the firm's "risk-class." (Alternatively, compare the cost of capital with the $\rho$ calculated on the estimated returns.) Unfortunately, this sort of "practical" advice leaves both the estimate of returns and the cost of capital rather vague. If perfect markets in time–state contingent claims exist, however, it is possible to define rigorously a "cost of capital" for application to the mathematical expectation of returns in present-value calculations. This cost of capital will be the *minimum* expected yield, per dollar invested, demanded by the market before funds will be made available for the time–state pattern of returns envisaged. Thus, the proportionate time–state distribution of asset returns is what defines the "risk-class." Under the $E,\sigma$ approximation, the risk-class is determined simply by $\sigma$ (as evaluated by the market). If the market will commit a dollar to an investment with expected return $1.20 (expected 20 per cent yield) and standard deviation $0.50, an investment with the same standard deviation but 30 per cent expected yield would show positive present value (discounting at $r = 20$ per cent).

It is necessary here to distinguish between the risk-class of the corporation as a whole and the risk-class of a particular incremental investment; the latter is what is relevant for the decision on adoption of the investment. A company whose over-all position was very secure might, by pledging the full credit of the company, finance a risky investment with funds acquired at a low $r$. But if the expected present value of the investment is only barely positive calculated at this $r$, the worsening of the company's over-all risk position will lead to a fall in the market valuation of the company.

**Government investment—normative issues.** Even if a maximum-wealth criterion is accepted for government investment decisions, serious questions persist as to the interest rate, $r$, for use in equation (1). To the extent that present-worth or analogous evaluations of investment options have been applied at all, historic practice in the United States has been to use for $r$ the long-term rate on government debt. (In contrast, a somewhat higher rate seems to have been applied for rationing government investments in postwar France.) But private corporations, unless an investment is exceptionally secure, cannot finance at the low rates of debt securities without incurring at least a partially offsetting loss—equity values falling because of increased riskiness. Numerically, federal borrowing rates in the United States in recent decades have been in the $2\frac{1}{2}$–5 per cent range, whereas the average cost (and yield) of corporate capital, counting income-tax liability, has been in the range of 6 per cent to 20 per cent. The inference has been drawn, consequently, that the U.S. government criterion is too lax. Speaking, for simplicity, in terms of $(\rho, r)$ comparisons, use of such a low $r$ has led to the adoption of government investments that are lower-yielding than marginal private investments.

Two lines of argument have been used to combat this inference. The first is that the high rates deterring private investment reflect a socially irrational aversion to variability risk; since government is in a position to pool many options whose average return thus becomes practically secure, a government discount rate lower than the private discount rate is not inefficient. This argument is fallacious; granted the premises, the opposite conclusion follows. Rather than spend on pooled but still low-yielding government projects, it would be more efficient to subsidize the private investments that, in terms of a comparably secure pooled average over the whole private sector, would yield more.

A weightier argument rests on the concept of *social time-preference*. It is alleged that market interest is too high, biased upward by the time-preferences of the present generation. Since future generations cast no "dollar votes" in current decisions, their concerns are given inadequate consideration in the market. What would be "adequate" consideration requires a social judgment on which opinions differ. (It should be noted that despite the aforesaid bias, almost everywhere in the Western world each generation has in fact sacrificed enough to leave its successor richer than itself.) Adoption of low-yielding investments is, however, an inefficient means of enriching future generations. Much more appropriate would be an increase in aggregate current sacrifice without substituting low-yielding for high-yielding uses of the funds diverted from current consumption. This end could be achieved by a taxation policy penalizing consumption relative to investment.

Finally, governments may, as we have noted, pursue investment objectives inconsistent with wealth-maximization for the community. Government planners may regard investments primarily as levers for altering social structures and attitudes, the rates of growth in specific industrial sectors, domestic distribution of income, or the country's power and prestige in the eyes of others. In underdeveloped countries, in particular, governments may control most of the funds available for investment, and goals alternative to wealth-maximization may dominate their planning. In such countries private markets (especially capital markets) are liable to be highly imperfect; even if this were not the case, the government planners may have little comprehension of or tolerance for the working of private market processes. There has been some discussion among theorists about how it might still be formally possible to apply investment efficiency criteria in which planners' judgments are partially or wholly substituted for market valuations of inputs and outputs and of time-discount. The Soviet system provides an interesting special case. Although explicit interest charges are forbidden on ideological grounds, the practical need to make efficient investment choices has led Soviet economists into discussions of investment criteria that in some ways parallel Western theoretical analyses.

JACK HIRSHLEIFER

[*See also* DECISION MAKING, *article on* ECONOMIC ASPECTS; *and the biography of* FISHER, IRVING.]

### BIBLIOGRAPHY

THEORETICAL AND EMPIRICAL STUDIES

ARROW, KENNETH J. (1953) 1964 The Role of Securities in the Optimal Allocation of Risk-bearing. *Review of Economic Studies* 31:91–96. → First published in French in the *International Colloquium on Econometrics*.

BORCH, KARL 1962 Equilibrium in a Reinsurance Market. *Econometrica* 30:424–444.

FARRAR, DONALD E. 1962 *The Investment Decision Under Uncertainty*. Englewood Cliffs, N.J.: Prentice-Hall.

FISHER, IRVING (1930) 1961 *The Theory of Interest*. New York: Kelley. → The classic work on the investment decision and interest.

HARBERGER, ARNOLD C. (editor) 1960 *The Demand for Durable Goods*. Univ. of Chicago Press; Cambridge Univ. Press. → An empirical study.

HIRSHLEIFER, JACK 1965 Investment Decision Under Uncertainty: Choice–Theoretic Approaches. *Quarterly Journal of Economics* 79:509–518.

JORGENSON, DALE W. 1965 Anticipations and Investment Behavior. Pages 35–92 in James S. Duesenberry et al., *The Brookings Quarterly Econometric Model of the United States*. Chicago: Rand McNally.

LUTZ, FRIEDRICH A.; and LUTZ, VERA C. 1951 *The Theory of Investment of the Firm*. Princeton Univ. Press.

MARKOWITZ, HARRY M. 1959 *Portfolio Selection*. Cowles Foundation for Research in Economics, Monograph No. 16. New York: Wiley. → A major pioneering work on uncertainty and the investment decision.

MASSÉ, PIERRE (1959) 1962 *Optimal Investment Decisions*. Englewood Cliffs, N.J.: Prentice-Hall. → First published as *Le choix des investissements*.

MEYER, JOHN R.; and KUH, EDWIN 1957 *The Investment Decision*. Harvard Economic Studies, Vol. 102. Cambridge, Mass.: Harvard Univ. Press. → An empirical study.

SHARPE, WILLIAM F. 1964 Capital Asset Prices: A Theory of Market Equilibrium Under Conditions of Risk. *Journal of Finance* 19:425–442.

SMITH, VERNON L. 1961 *Investment and Production*. Harvard Economic Studies, Vol. 117. Cambridge, Mass.: Harvard Univ. Press; Oxford Univ. Press.

STIGLER, GEORGE J. 1963 *Capital and Rates of Return in Manufacturing Industries*. National Bureau of Economic Research, General Series, No. 78. Princeton Univ. Press.

CAPITAL BUDGETING AND CRITERION CONTROVERSY

BIERMAN, HAROLD JR.; and SMIDT, SEYMOUR 1960 *The Capital Budgeting Decision*. New York: Macmillan. → A theoretically oriented manual for corporate investment decisions.

CHARNES, A.; COOPER, W. W.; and MILLER, MERTON H. 1959 Application of Linear Programming to Financial Budgeting and the Costing of Funds. Pages 229–255 in Ezra Solomon (editor), *The Management of Corporate Capital*. Glencoe, Ill.: Free Press. → First published in the *Journal of Business,* January 1959.

DURAND, DAVID (1952) 1959 Costs of Debt and Equity Funds for Business: Trends and Problems of Measurement. Pages 91–127 in Ezra Solomon (editor), *The Management of Corporate Capital*. Glencoe, Ill.: Free Press. → First published as a monograph by the National Bureau of Economic Research.

GAFFNEY, MERRILL MASON 1957 *Concepts of Financial Maturity of Timber and Other Assets*. Agricultural Economics Information Series, No. 62. Raleigh: North Carolina State College.

GRANT, EUGENE L.; and IRESON, W. GRANT (1930) 1960 *Principles of Engineering Economy*. 4th ed. New York: Ronald. → An excellent guide to investment planning, designed as an economics text for engineers.

HIRSHLEIFER, JACK (1958) 1959 On the Theory of Optimal Investment Decision. Pages 205–228 in Ezra Solomon (editor), *The Management of Corporate Capital*. Glencoe, Ill.: Free Press. → First published in the *Journal of Political Economy*, August 1958.

LORIE, JAMES H.; and SAVAGE, LEONARD J. (1955) 1959 Three Problems in Rationing Capital. Pages 56–66 in Ezra Solomon (editor), *The Management of Corporate Capital*. Glencoe, Ill.: Free Press. → First published in the *Journal of Business*, October 1955.

MODIGLIANI, FRANCO; and MILLER, MERTON H. (1958) 1959 The Cost of Capital, Corporation Finance and the Theory of Investment. Pages 150–181 in Ezra Solomon (editor), *The Management of Corporate Capital*. Glencoe, Ill.: Free Press. → First published in the *American Economic Review*, June 1958.

PYE, GORDON 1966 Present Values for Imperfect Capital Markets. *Journal of Business* 39:45–51.

SOLOMON, EZRA (1956) 1959 The Arithmetic of Capital-budgeting Decisions. Pages 74–79 in Ezra Solomon (editor), *The Management of Corporate Capital*. Glencoe, Ill.: Free Press. → First published in the *Journal of Business*, April 1956.

SOLOMON, EZRA (editor) 1959 *The Management of Corporate Capital*. University of Chicago Studies in Business, 3d Series. Glencoe, Ill.: Free Press. → An excellent collection of important contributions.

WEINGARTNER, H. MARTIN 1963 *Mathematical Programming and the Analysis of Capital Budgeting Problems*. Englewood Cliffs, N.J.: Prentice-Hall.

GOVERNMENT INVESTMENT DECISIONS

CHENERY, HOLLIS B. 1953 The Application of Investment Criteria. *Quarterly Journal of Economics* 67: 76–96.

ECKSTEIN, OTTO 1961 A Survey of the Theory of Public Expenditure Criteria. Pages 439–504 in Universities–National Bureau Committee for Economic Research, *Public Finances: Needs, Sources, and Utilization*. National Bureau of Economic Research, Special Conference Series, No. 12. Princeton Univ. Press.

HIRSHLEIFER, JACK; DE HAVEN, JAMES C.; and MILLIMAN, JEROME W. 1960 *Water Supply: Economics, Technology, and Policy*. Univ. of Chicago Press.

KHACHATUROV, TIGRAN S. 1958 The Economic Effectiveness of Capital Investments in the USSR. *American Economic Review* 48, no. 2:368–384.

KRUTILLA, JOHN V.; and ECKSTEIN, OTTO 1958 *Multiple Purpose River Development*. Published for Resources for the Future, Inc. Baltimore: Johns Hopkins Press.

McKEAN, ROLAND N. 1958 *Efficiency in Government Through Systems Analysis*. New York: Wiley.

# ISLAM

*Islam* ("the act of submitting [to God]") is the proper and most widely used term for the religion of those who believe that the Qur'ān (Koran) is the true word of God transmitted to mankind as an ultimate revelation through the medium of his Prophet and messenger, Muḥammad. Although the term was used in early periods in the more limited sense of "submission" and seems to have been generally equated with "belief" (*imān*), the meaning today to Muslims and non-Muslims alike is that of the definitive name of a specific religion. The practitioner of the faith is a *Muslim*, a term that also serves as an adjective, but the attributive adjective *Islamic* is preferable in social or cultural contexts, e.g., *Muslim theology*, but *Islamic law* and *Islamic architecture*. The terms *Mohammedan* and *Mohammedanism* are disliked by Muslims because they carry the implication of the worship of Muḥammad as a more than human figure and thus contain the germs of polytheism.

The most recent of the three great monotheisms to have arisen in the Middle East and the last major universal religion to have appeared in history, Islam came into being in the early seventh century in west-central Arabia. Although a good part of the Qur'ān records the preaching of Muḥammad in Mecca in the first two decades of that century, the definitive outlines of Islam as a system of beliefs and as a political organization took shape in Medina after the emigration (*hijrah*) to that city of Muḥammad and a band of his followers in 622. In recognition of the importance of this event, the Muslim calendar reckons events from the first lunar month of that year—July 16, 622, becoming the first day of Muḥarram, A.H. 1. Between that date and the death of Muḥammad in 632, two years after a triumphal return to his newly converted birthplace of Mecca, the new religion established itself throughout most of the Arabian Peninsula, not only as a corpus of religious belief but equally as a political community (*ummah*) provided with its own laws and embryonic governmental and social institutions. The significance and uniqueness of this twin foundation structure is recognized in the well-known dictum, "Islam is a religion and a state," which is interpreted, however, by Muslims in a unitary meaning rather than implying any dualism.

The century following Muḥammad's death saw a far-reaching series of conquests by the new Muslim armies. Their spectacular successes and the way in which ancient communities and seemingly powerful states succumbed with little resistance testify to underlying weaknesses in the existing order but also say something of the fresh appeal Islam had for peoples in the Middle East at a time when they were exhausted by internecine struggles and doctrinal quarrels. However, the large number of conversions to Islam at this period may be said to have stemmed more from socioeconomic causes than from religious motivation, although these in the end had repercussions on both the faith itself and the subsequent nature of the Islamic state. In the Fertile Crescent area and in Egypt the numerous Christian and Jewish communities were legally allowed to continue practicing their religion, but inequalities in taxation which favored Muslims, and the natural social desire to become full members of the body politic with all its advantages, furthered Islamization. In Iran multiple causes conditioned conversion: the desire of the bureaucracy to preserve its privileges, the reluctance of the landed nobility to pay the poll tax, and the wish on the part of the merchant class to have a full share in the material culture of the Islamic empire. In north Africa pagan or semi-Christianized Berbers were more often either genuinely influenced by the tenets of Islam or spontaneously gave their allegiance to the new religion rather than suffer the alternative, loss of life, reserved for those other than "people of the book," i.e., monotheists who possessed scriptures.

In the centuries following its birth Islam was spread by conquest and occupation, organized and at times militant religious activism, and peaceful missionary work. The first wave of expansion was the work of Arabs, largely armies buttressed by new converts in the Middle East and north Africa. By the end of the Umayyad reign (A.D. 750), the frontiers of Islam extended to the Pyrenees in the west and the Indus River in the east. Included in Muslim domains were most of Spain, north Africa, Egypt, the Levant to the frontiers of Anatolia, the Arabian Peninsula, Iran, and part of Turkestan. Once this force had been spent there was relatively little fluctuation in the extent of the House of Islam (*Dār ul-Islām*) until a second wave of military conquest was set under way in the fourteenth century by Turkic peoples who had migrated from central Asia to Iran and Asia Minor and been progressively Islamized over a period of several centuries. One of these groups, the Osmanli, destroyed the remnants of the Byzantine state, took Constantinople in 1453, and established Muslim rule in large areas of southeastern Europe, maintaining it until well into the nineteenth century. These two waves directed at Europe left important cultural legacies in Spain and Sicily and vestigial groups of Muslims in Yugoslavia, Albania, and Bulgaria.

The historical advance of Islam into south and southeast Asia, and later into tropical Africa, has been of another kind. The faith came to these areas at a comparatively late date and was spread more gradually, sometimes by force, but more often through the voluntary conversion of nonmonotheists. Muslim power gained sway in northwest India only after A.D. 1000, and converts in Bengal were not numerous until the sixteenth century. The force of Islam in south Asia in modern times is shown by the success of Muslim demands for the partition of British India and the establishment of Pakistan as a separate state for Muslims. In addition to some ninety million Muslims in that country, a large minority of over forty million is found in India. In south Asia as a whole, Muslims have increased their numbers at the expense of non-Muslims, not only because of the one-way nature of conversion but because of socioeconomic factors, including a greater life expectancy resulting from a higher protein diet, the urban nature of the Muslim population, which somewhat spares it from rural famines, and the fact that widows are permitted to remarry. Proselytization in southeast Asia was mainly the work of Muslim traders who established themselves in Malaya, Sumatra, and elsewhere in the fourteenth century. Gradually Islam spread inland in Sumatra and Malaya and penetrated the farther islands of Indonesia as far as the southern Philippines. Today the Malays of Malaya are overwhelmingly Muslim and the Indonesians are very heavily Muslim, while important minorities exist in Thailand, Burma, and the Philippines. The stronghold that Islam had early obtained in central Asia was the source for the considerable Islamization of Sinkiang and parts of northwestern China in later times. At present it is estimated that as much as one-tenth of the total Chinese population may be considered Muslim.

In Africa, Islam spread unevenly at different periods, but it has continued to make impressive advances in modern times. Although peoples living along the Mediterranean shores of northern Africa were converted in the first wave of Arab conquest, Islam spread more gradually up the Nile and across the trade routes of the Sahara to reach the Chad area and, eventually, in the fifteenth century, northern Nigeria. By sea it moved down around the horn of east Africa to the Somali coast and Zanzibar. An island of resistance exists in the Abyssinian highlands, but Islam is heavily predominant today in Somalia, Zanzibar, and the Sudan, while important minorities exist in coastal Kenya, Tanganyika, and Mozambique. Islamization in west Africa was furthered by brotherhood activity in the eighteenth and nineteenth centuries. Islam has a majority today in Mauritania, Senegal, Mali, Niger, Chad, and probably Nigeria, large minorities in Guinea, Gambia, Sierra Leone, Ivory Coast, Cameroon, and the Central African Republic, and numerous adherents in the other states of west and central Africa as far south as Zambia and Rhodesia.

In all, more than 500 million persons today, one-sixth of humanity, profess themselves to be Muslims, however nominal in practice. Of this number about 125 million are in Africa and almost 400 million in Asia, with scattered communities in Europe and the Americas. Of perhaps greater significance than its present numbers is the fact that Islam, of all the major religions, continues to show the most steady growth. Particularly noteworthy is its progress in regions previously dominated by pagan tribal cultures. Its strong appeal to underprivileged or minority groups everywhere, as has historically been evident in south Asia, is a further factor of political and social importance in this century.

## Fundamentals

The basis of Islam, and the heart of Muslim belief and thought, lie in its holy scripture, the Qur'ān, considered by Muslims to be the direct and true word of God, transmitted by the angel Gabriel to Muḥammad (in Arabic) while the latter was in a state of divine inspiration akin to trance. In this state Muḥammad was ordered to recite (iqrā') the word of God, whence qur'ān, a "recitation." A supplementary source of faith began to emerge after the death of the Prophet as it became clear that the Qur'ān did not provide specific guidance for many of the questions faced by the growing community. In their search for additional guidance, Muslims turned to the life, the habits, and the dicta of Muḥammad in given situations. There thus arose the practice of compiling, recording, and classifying the "tradition" (ḥadīth) of or relating to the Prophet. Out of this material, expressed in the form of short narratives relating specific acts and sayings of Muḥammad through a chain of hearsay, grew the completed product: the customary way of doing (sunnah), which expresses the ideal of behavior for pious, orthodox Muslims, who style themselves "followers of the custom" (ahl al-sunnah)—whence the term Sunnites.

The central importance of Muḥammad in Islam is thus evident. His position as the sole communicant of God's word to man is attested in the basic Muslim profession of faith: "There is no God but God and Muḥammad is His Prophet." This credo, although it does not occur in a single phrase in the Qur'ān itself, has become the foundation of Muslim self-identification. It differentiates the believer from the nonbeliever and Islam from other religions by emphasizing that Muḥammad is not one prophet among many but the seal of the prophets and that the revelation given to him was the ultimate and unchangeable exposition of divine will. The function of the ḥadīth reinforced this position, as may well have been one of its main purposes, by preserving for later generations a portrait of the personality of Muḥammad in warm and simple details which link the believer to him in an atmosphere of pious affection that has grown through the centuries. Through the device of the ḥadīth, which contrasts strongly with the formalism and transcendentalism of the Qur'ān, Muḥammad is kept from becoming a dim historical figure; he emerges as a venerable, just, but understandable human leader of his flock. In this way Islam maintains the principle of the strictest monotheism, while tempering it with a human touch which, to judge by the historical experience, has fulfilled the needs of ordinary Muslims in all ages. It is true that this devotion has sometimes seemed to approach adulation or even outright worship, particularly in the past century, when a new consciousness of Christianity led some Muslim biographers of Muḥammad to present his life in ways that clearly reveal the influence of the story of Jesus. However, both orthodox Muslim thought and the practice of the masses have kept the fine distinction between ceremonial veneration and anthropolatry.

The Qur'ān is divided into 114 chapters, arranged in decreasing order of length. The generally earlier Meccan chapters are distinguishable by their apocalyptic style, their use of a strongly fashioned rhymed prose, their relatively simple subject matter, and their poetic expression of religious symbolism. In their imaginative grasp and their masterly use of Arabic they reveal a genuine prophetic genius. In comparison, the later Medinan chapters, which include moral maxims, legal proscriptions, and historical narratives that are sometimes taken from Christian and Jewish sources, suffer from a dilution of this vigorous style.

The essential dogma of the Qur'ān is that of the unity of God: "Say God is one, God the eternal. He hath not begotten nor was he begotten, and there is none equal to him." The believer is enjoined to accept the envoys of God and the scriptures they have revealed, beginning with Adam and continuing with Noah, Abraham, Moses, and Jesus, to the final revelation of Muḥammad. Running through the entire work are two motifs: one envisions an impersonal, remote, and majestic deity, who evokes in the believer a sense of awe and humility; the other conceptualizes the Divine Spirit in terms of hope and mercy. Among the most numerous epithets for God in the Qur'ān are those describing him as compassionate and merciful, and while a theme of fiery destruction for the sinful is preached in some Meccan verses, others rank among the purest expressions of trust in divine love.

It has long been clear to non-Muslim scholars that to some degree Christian beliefs, Judaism, and the pre-Islamic tradition in Arabia all had a part in shaping Qur'ānic dogma. Contacts with Christian communities in western Asia and Abyssinia were numerous, and Jewish colonies were found throughout the peninsula; in the Yemen, Judaistic movements had held power shortly before Muḥammad's lifetime. Textual criticism of the Qur'ān reveals such borrowings in, for example, the doctrine of the Last Judgment, where not only the concept but the technical terminology is taken from Syriac Christian writings, and in Muḥammad's

gradual incorporation into his revelation of Old Testament stories that would validate his teaching. In Medina, Muḥammad found a large Jewish community, with which a dispute ultimately arose, the source of much of the anti-Judaist polemic in the Qur'ān. Early in the Medina period, however, Muḥammad had incorporated several Jewish practices into Islam, notably 'Āshūrā', the holy day that corresponds to the Day of Atonement, and the direction of prayer toward Jerusalem. The Qur'ān stresses the alleged falsification of the Scriptures by both Jews and Christians but in a way that usually indicates a derivative or insufficient understanding of the original ideas or facts. Among these are the Incarnation, which is categorically rejected, and the Crucifixion, said to be a Jewish distortion of the true event. According to Islamic dogma, another figure was crucified in the place of Jesus, who was himself taken to heaven.

Of prime importance in the formation of Muḥammad's doctrines, however, was the existence of two intertwined strands of tradition in pre-Islamic Arab life. One was the animistic beliefs of tribal society, which ascribed powers to inanimate objects, stones, trees, etc., as well as to certain human categories (soothsayers, sorcerers) and to nonhuman elements (*jinn*). Entangled with this Arab paganism, however, there was an ill-defined monotheism, which may have owed something to Jewish and Christian influences. This was exemplified by prophets (singular, *ḥanīf*) who opposed a nativistic monotheism to the pagan polydemonism, which no longer satisfied the Arabs' desire for a broader religious experience. The *ḥanīf*'s, despite their monotheism, were unwilling to accept Judaism or Christianity as such. The Qur'ān describes Abraham as a *ḥanīf*, and thus asserts itself as a restoration of the true, indigenous Abrahamic monotheism, which had been corrupted by Jewish and Christian beliefs.

The supreme accomplishment of Muḥammad in the Qur'ān was to make use of these two elements but to disentangle them at the same time, thus opening the religious imagination of the Arabs to new horizons without too abruptly cutting away their old cultural and emotional roots. This delicate operation involved simultaneously banning most animistic associations but amalgamating others with the new religion by reinterpreting them in a monotheistic way. This restructuring of pagan practice and terminology can be seen most successfully in the incorporation of the earlier religious pilgrimage to the sacred region of Mecca and the circumambulation of the Black Stone, in the adoption of the ritual sacrifice of sheep, and in the new application of terms that formerly referred to pagan customs but that are clothed in richer and broader monotheistic meaning in the Qur'ān. In this reconstruction, by lifting Arab spiritual values out of the incoherence in which they were enmeshed and by focusing them on the concept of a supreme God who encompassed and stood above all previous formulations, Muḥammad created a distinctive religious edifice. Although it contains elements of earlier faiths, it can be understood only as a unique, new entity possessing its own structure and dynamics.

## Ritual

The practice of Islam consists essentially of a small number of ritual obligations called the "pillars of the faith." These include giving witness, ritual prayer, legal almsgiving, fasting, and the pilgrimage. To profess faith with intention is to become a Muslim and be admitted to all the duties and privileges of the community. While good works are considered to be as commendable as faith itself, orthodox opinion has generally held that testimony alone without any other deed during the lifetime of a believer is sufficient for ultimate salvation. Ritual prayer is formal worship, whose ceremony, postures, gestures, and verbal formulas are strictly laid down by law; it is designed to express adoration of God rather than personal communion with him or petition. It may be noted, however, that the period of meditation following upon the prostrations allows the worshiper an opportunity to enter into a relationship of communion with a spirit of humility. Ritual cleanliness is mandatory and is minutely regulated according to the circumstances. Although the Qur'ān is silent on the subject, five daily prayers have been standard since the earliest period of Islam. Their times vary somewhat but usually come before dawn, just after midday, in midafternoon, after sunset, and at night, usually in the first minutes of darkness—hours seemingly calculated to avoid any hint of sun worship. There is no requirement that ordinary prayer be carried out in the mosque, although it is recommended because ritual purity is better guaranteed within its precincts. The Friday midday prayer, however, should be kept in the mosque; it usually contains several sections and a sermon. Legal almsgiving is today in most Muslim countries an institution of only historical interest, having been superseded almost everywhere by modern legislation. Originally it was a religious tax levied on property according to a detailed formula and payable in kind.

These three pillars of the faith (giving witness, ritual prayer, and almsgiving) have somewhat less influence on Muslim life than might be supposed.

Witness is automatic and often unspoken throughout the lifetime of those who are born to the faith and can conceive of no other. Almsgiving is obsolete, and ritual prayer is to a growing degree slighted or ignored by many modern Muslims, especially in urban areas. This is not true, however, of the remaining two pillars: the fast and the pilgrimage.

Early in the Medinan period Muḥammad instituted a fast on 'Āshūrā', but later he abrogated this and instead ordained abstinence during the entire ninth month of the lunar calendar, Ramadān. During this month, from sunrise to sunset, the faithful must completely abstain from food, drink, tobacco, and sexual intercourse. The fast is compulsory only for adults in good health; pregnant women, children of prepuberty age, the aged and the sick, and bona fide travelers are specifically exempt, although the last must make up the broken fast days. Today the Ramadan fast is without doubt the one ceremony most strictly held to by believers, and it is a basic component of the social cement that holds the community together. While violations are found both among bedouin and rural elements, on the one hand, and in secret in a few modernist and intellectual circles, on the other, townsmen in most Muslim countries tend to keep the fast unanimously. Public opinion strongly reproves individuals who try to avoid the obligation in private and has, even recently, reacted violently to public disregard of it. There appears also to be a discernible connection between rigorous observance and modern nationalism in some countries where Islam was used as a rallying point in the struggle against foreign colonialism, and some states (e.g., Morocco) have inserted penalties for transgressing it in their modern penal codes. In a few Muslim states, however (e.g., Turkey and Tunisia), where the holy law (sharī'ah) has been abolished, the secularist orientation of their nationalism has led the governments to encourage fastbreaking in the interest of national economic imperatives or to consider it a matter of personal conscience.

The pilgrimage to Mecca incorporates in Muslim practice two pagan rites celebrated by the Arabs, one connected with the circumambulation of the Black Stone of the Ka'bah in Mecca, and the other the pilgrimage to the hill of 'Arafāt outside the town. The rites are performed in the twelfth lunar month and now usually include a visit to nearby Medina. The pilgrimage may be described as a conditional obligation; it is incumbent only on Muslims with the necessary means and the physical ability to reach Mecca. Nevertheless, it has remained a vital element in Muslim life throughout the centuries and, even in the most difficult periods of history, attracted numerous pilgrims. Today, with improved communications, increased travel within the Muslim world, and security in the pilgrimage area, it has taken on new dimensions of cultural and even political significance. Mecca has become a meeting place for Muslims from the entire world, and a deep impression is made on many pilgrims by the reaffirmation of their faith in company with cobelievers of every color and nationality. The annual re-enactment of the ceremonies, with the pilgrims as active participants and not simple onlookers, gives them an especially moving character. The returning pilgrim, who is entitled to add the title *ḥājj* to his name, is the object of admiration and congratulations, but more important perhaps is the feeling on the part of those who have remained at home that he brings with him an atmosphere of holiness which is shared by all. At all times the social function of the pilgrimage to the sacred sites has been to serve as a journey to a common hearth fire from which the pilgrims could carry back the renewed and restored flame of faith to their own communities. In this sense, the pilgrimage may be looked on as the counterpart of the fast, for while the fast solidifies the bonds that hold together each community by a common sacrifice, the pilgrimage allows the members of the elites of widely different regions and groups to engage in a spiritual intercourse which strengthens the ties between the various communities of Islam.

## Law and institutions

It is not certain whether the Qur'ān was written down during the lifetime of the Prophet. The tradition indicates that scraps of it were preserved, and an authoritative text was prepared by a commission appointed by the third caliph, 'Uthmān, and copies of this circulated throughout the empire. However, difficulties in reading the imperfectly developed Arabic script and hesitancies in interpretation caused a reform in writing and the adjustment to a standard pronunciation, as well as the recognition of a certain number of reciters whose readings were by compromise accepted as orthodox. Toward the end of the first century A.H. the text as now used was standardized in most details.

During this formative period the administration of justice was carried out somewhat haphazardly by Qur'ānic precepts as they were customarily interpreted by the Arabs, and with the incorporation of some elements of Roman and pre-Islamic law, administrative procedures were modified and more fully incorporated in the embryonic body of legal practice. Toward the end of the Umayyad period, between about A.D. 725 and 750, the Qur'ān and the *sunnah* had become established as the principal sources of Muslim jurisprudence, but there had also grown up a body of jurists and men interested in legal problems who in their experience were finding it necessary to go beyond these sources to devise laws for the community.

Up to this time law and religion were inextricably interconnected and rested upon the infallible revelation of the Qur'ān and its presumably infallible verification in detail by the tradition. The infallibility of these two sources, however, was not of the same order; in fact, the proliferation of narratives in the tradition was such that scholars were aware that many of them were spurious. In order to establish the veracity of the tradition beyond any doubt and reinforce its position as an anchor of the legal system, a science of *ḥadīth* criticism was introduced in the second and third centuries A.H. This placed stress on the reliability of each member of the chain of authorities cited. Biographies of transmitters were compiled and their subjects carefully investigated, after which each narrative (*ḥadīth*) was classified for legal purposes as sound, good, or weak. Many traditions that modern Western scholarship considers highly dubious were classified as sound in this process, for many theologians were at bottom less interested in the historical objectivies of a given tradition than in the practical consequences of its acceptance and application to community life. Later, in the ninth century A.D., *ḥadīth* study developed into a full-fledged scholastic enterprise; the great compilations of al-Bukhārī (d. 870) and Muslim (d. 875) have enjoyed almost universal authority in Islam.

The Qur'ān and the expurgated tradition, however, for all their infallibility, did not supply a definitive body of legal precepts for general use. The jurists of the so-called ancient schools in Iraq, Syria, and Medina devoted themselves to finding a way to generalize the specificity of the original sources, and in so doing they established the foundations of the four great legal schools of orthodox Islam and, more importantly, laid down the framework of Islamic law for all time. The concept of opinion, or common sense, had been applied for some time but was thought to contain the dangers of human irresponsibility. It was favored by the school of Iraq, however, while Medinan jurists, among them Malik Ibn Anas (d. 795), developed the doctrine of the "suitability" of one decision to a fixed point of reference and that of the "association" of one with an anterior case. The problem was resolved by al-Shafīi (d. 820), who completed the system by extending the use of the Prophetic tradition, as opposed to the narrower Medinan tradition, and introduced the more precise concept of analogical reasoning (*qiyās*), by which the principles that had governed decisions in previous cases could be applied to new situations. The actual difference between the schools was not overly great, but the reasoning of al-Shafīi established his work as the third source of Muslim holy law.

The construction of the Muslim legal edifice was completed by the introduction of the principle of consensus (*ijmā*) as the guarantor of legal theory and beyond that of the integrity of the entire framework of Muslim religious thought. The doctrine of *ijmā* has been subsumed in a tradition that relates the saying of Muḥammad, "My community will not agree in error." During the second century A.H. it had been established that the consensus of the community, which meant that of the jurists and scholars dealing with religious and legal matters, was binding. The extension of this concept by these very jurists, to stamp with approval the legal systems they had elaborated, removed the possibility of a revision of their work by later generations and gave final validity to the entire structure. *Ijmā* verifies the authenticity and the proper interpretation of the Qur'ān; it guarantees the correct transmission of the *sunnah* tradition and the proper use of *qiyās*. It covers all aspects of the holy law and admits the validity of distinctions between the orthodox legal schools. Of the highest importance, however, is the fact that consensus itself becomes, as Gibb has noted, "a third channel of revelation" (1949) and is elevated to infallibility itself alongside the Qur'ān and the *sunnah*, which it sanctions. While it is often suggested that the principle of consensus was adopted as a device of convenience by the legal scholars, a broader view leads to the conclusion that the Muslim community's sense of its own divinely instituted and rightly guided nature has always been so highly developed that it produced an unwavering belief in its own charisma and infallibility. The ideal of Islamic law taken as a whole is absolutist and charismatic at its roots and may be considered a reflection of the Islam which Muslims have brought into being, either, as they would believe, through their unerring understanding of God's word or, as Western scholars believe, through their own will and actions.

Islam prides itself on the absence of clergy who might interpose themselves between God and man. While this is true in a formal sense, nonetheless from the earliest periods there have been, as seen, a large body of men dealing with religious problems and their interpretation. In time this turned into an identifiable body of theologians (*'ulamā*) and jurists. The growth of this group is intimately connected with the development of the holy law and the appearance of the orthodox legal schools in the eighth and ninth centuries. At first they were individual members of the still informal religious institution of Islam, but as this solidified they tended to come together as the formal representatives of the community in questions of faith and, in so doing, often found themselves in positions of opposition to the state. From Abbasid times on, however (after A.D. 750), the political authorities attached theologians to themselves and gave many of them official positions, so that overt opposition by members of the religious establishment tended to be muted. With the establishment of religious colleges (singular, *madrasah*) in the eleventh century A.D., in which courses were given and degrees granted, there was a further formalization of the structure, which reached its height in the complex government-supported theological institutions of the Ottoman Empire. Such developments tended inevitably to limit the independence of the religious establishment with respect to the authorities, and there are manifold examples of subservience and abasement. Nevertheless, throughout Islamic history there runs the principle, however often violated, that the religious institution exists apart from and as a check on the ruling institution. The theologian and the jurist were in the end the guardians of the law for the state, although they were independent of it and at times in opposition to it. The most notable limitation on the power of the state at all times has been the theoretical inviolability of official members of the religious institution and of their property. A large quantity of mortmain property lay, and still lies, in their hands, and by these means mosques, schools, hospitals, and the like were supported, and to a certain extent the independence of the judge protected.

## Unity and diversity

Almost from its inception Islam encountered difficulties in adapting the message of Muḥammad to the changed historical circumstances in which the Muslim empire was developing and in formulating a theological statement that would satisfy the diverse elements that were becoming part of the community. The relationship between religion and politics has always been unusually intimate in the Middle East, and this was particularly true in the case of Islam. It is therefore often difficult to separate political from theological questions, and important to understand that the Muslims of the early periods did not consciously do so themselves. Nevertheless, it is fair to say that with rare exceptions conflicts in the formative first decades primarily reflected political and social considerations and the influence of the differing local environments in western Asia to which the faith had spread, rather than theological considerations. It was only later, toward the beginning of the Umayyad period, that religious factors first intervened significantly, and the practice of transferring sociopolitical grievances to the level of theological disputes and challenging the powers that be on those grounds—a practice which was to become a central theme of Islamic history—was initiated.

The first major example of this was the separation of the Kharijites, whose activities were closely linked with what later turned into the principal schismatic movement in Islam, the Shi'ite deviation from orthodoxy. Both groups were found as extremist elements among the fractious nomadic tribesmen who had been settled in garrison towns in Iraq and who made up the troops of 'Ali, the son-in-law of Muḥammad, during his campaign to claim supreme authority after the murder of the third caliph, 'Uthmān, in 656. The Kharijites represented discontented tribesmen whose anarchic spirit resisted being forced into an urban mold and to whom the end of the conquests in their immediate area meant a diminution of booty and of the satisfaction of raiding. The Shi'ah, or "partisans" of 'Ali, on the other hand, were composed of men from Kufa in Iraq who felt alienated from the caliphal establishment, which was the center of power in the Hejaz, and its emanations in Syria.

The quarrel of the Kharijites with the rest of the community lay in the domain of religious practice. They insisted that evildoers within Islam must be rigorously punished and that those Muslims who temporized on the extirpation of evil were themselves guilty of apostasy. This radical point of view led them to withdraw from the armies of 'Ali and eventually, after a series of unsuccessful minor uprisings, to divorce themselves from the community, in which they had no further direct influence. Today they survive in isolated communities in Algeria, Oman, and Zanzibar, without political influence.

The Shi'ite movement was more complex and permanent. Its psychological foundations seem to have been laid first in the personal devotion accorded to 'Ali by his followers and, second, in the sense of rejection and bitterness which accompanied his defeat and death in 661 and the martyrdom of his son Ḥusain in 680. At the same time,

the political bases of the movement were strengthened by the opposition of the Arabs of Iraq to rule from Syria. The movement attracted many recent non-Arab converts, or clients, to Islam, who were seeking equality and fuller integration within the community and who came principally from among Persian and Aramaean elements in Iraq and Iran. From this period begins a cross-linkage of the political and social grievances of non-Arab Muslims with Shi'ism, which culminates in the sixteenth century in the Shi'ite nationalism of the Safavid state in Iran.

The earliest Shi'ism had no distinctive doctrine, and in questions of theology and law individual Shi'ites were indistinguishable from others in the community, with whom they lived, on the whole, harmoniously. However, the political insistence on the legitimacy of 'Ali called into being a doctrine that refused recognition to the first three caliphs who followed Muḥammad and thus challenged orthodox belief. Moreover, the elevation of 'Ali to the position of an infallible and charismatic leader (imām) brought Shi'ism, in later centuries, into sharper conflict with the Sunnite concept of consensus of the community. Gradually a polarization occurred in which Hellenistic remnants in formerly Byzantine areas attached themselves to and influenced the development of orthodox theology, while a variety of sects and ideas from the pre-Islamic Oriental substrata in Iraq, Iran, and later India were grafted onto Shi'ism. Moreover, Shi'ism served as a banner to cover social revolt against the orthodox establishment on more than one occasion.

The further development of Shi'ism may be traced from its character as a volatile opposition movement dependent on strong personal leadership, which contained within itself the seeds of further splitting. Secrecy, concealment of one's true beliefs, the possession of esoteric knowledge by the infallible imām, and a doctrine of messianic return and salvation became the hallmarks of the various Shi'ite subsects. Of these there are three principal groups, each of which has erected the concept of divinely inspired leadership, or "imamism," into basic doctrine, although with differences of interpretation. The Zaidi branch, which is prominent in the Yemen, attributes no superhuman qualities to its imām's and is closest to Sunnite Islam. The majority Imami branch is the state religion of Iran and has many adherents in Iraq and India among other countries. The extreme Isma'ili branch has contributed some of the most extraordinary episodes to Islamic history, among them the odyssey of the Fatimid caliphate in north Africa and Egypt, the activities of the sect of the Assassins (hashshashin), and several revolutionary uprisings in the Middle Ages. The distinctive features of Isma'ilism, which today has a following primarily in India and east Africa, consist of graded instruction in religious mysteries, a distinction between external and internal meaning in all their aspects, and the practice of dissimulation. Several offshoots of Isma'ilism, such as the Druze, the Nusairi, and the Yazidi sects in the Levant, display such extreme syncretism that it is doubtful whether they should be considered fully Muslim.

Counterbalancing the tendencies toward sectarianism in Islam at all times, however, has been a broad current of tolerance which has permitted the main orthodox corpus of the faith to entertain, modify, and assimilate a variety of ideas and, having done so, to allow a wide latitude of diversity to flourish among the individuals and bodies that constitute the community. Historically it has been only those sects which have voluntarily excluded themselves from the orthodox community, like the Kharijites, that are considered heretical. Today, the position of the Shi'ites, the only important heterodox body in Islam, is in general viewed with less rigor than previously. Conversely, Islamic history demonstrates the absorptive and integrationist character of the religion in many instances, the most outstanding of which is the Mu'tazilite movement of the eighth and ninth centuries.

The Mu'tazilah came to prominence about a century after Muhammad's death in reaction against both the extremism of the Kharijites and the corresponding indifference to religious questions on the part of their opposites, the Murji'ites. Mu'tazilism was an intellectual movement whose activity was stimulated by the translations of Greek thought then appearing and by the generally felt need to express and defend Muslim belief in rational terms, especially vis-à-vis recently converted scholars familiar with the canons of Greek logic and philosophy. The Mu'tazilah were the first to try to provide a sound philosophical basis for Islam through forthright discussions of the nature of God, of the Qur'ān, and of man's relationship to God. While maintaining the purest monotheism and chastising any semblance of anthropomorphism, they held two tenets that ran directly counter to orthodox dogma. One was that the Qur'ān was created in time rather than being the uncreated word of God which had been in existence forever. The other, of more general philosophical importance, was a doctrine of free will, which held that it was inconceivable that God should decree the actions of man, induce him into error, and then punish him for it, as the orthodox doctrine of predestination

and the unqualified omnipotence of God asserted. The dispute came to a head in the ninth century, when Mu'tazilite influence held sway briefly. In the end the movement came to grief because of its own rigidity in the face of counterargument and its persistent attempt to force Muslim thought into Greek forms, an effort that was not only opposed by the orthodox theologians but that met with no response from the mass of believers.

The reaction to Mu'tazilism led by al-Ash'ari (d. 935) consolidated the orthodox position and produced a new orthodox scholasticism, which has remained definitive until today. While setting a lasting dogmatic stamp on Islam, the reaction reconciled some Mu'tazilite concepts with orthodox belief and thus strengthened and enlarged the area of consensus. Predestination was maintained, but a doctrine of "acquisition," under which man has contingent responsibility for his deeds, was introduced. The dogma of the absolute omnipotence of God and the orthodox position that right is what God decrees it to be in the Qur'ān—rather than something independently ascertainable by man—were affirmed, but their rigor softened by stressing the intercession of Muhammad in favor of man, something which the Mu'tazilah had rejected. Finally, the relationship of cause and effect propounded by the Mu'tazilah, which in orthodox eyes limited the power of God, was disavowed by means of an atomistic theory according to which all events and substances exist transitorily in time and space only through the inscrutable will of God and not through any inherent connection among themselves.

The intellectual consequences to Islam of the orthodox reformulation begun by al-Ash'ari and completed two centuries later (by al-Ghazāli) were of the greatest importance. Ash'arism marks a rejection of Hellenism and the victory of intuitive faith over rationalism in the struggle to shape Islam. The contribution of the Mu'tazilah in raising the level of intellectual activity in Islam was important, however, as was the work of al-Ash'ari, in finding a way to incorporate many of the basic elements of Greek thought introduced by the Mu'tazilah without undermining the basic dogmas of orthodox Islam.

The will to catholicity in Islam was shown two centuries later in the synthesis achieved by al-Ghazāli (d. 1111) between philosophy and orthodox theology. In the intervening period, largely as another by-product of the importation of Greek thought, Islamic philosophy had come into flower and made a remarkable contribution to the growth of medieval sciences in Europe as well as in the Middle East. Beginning with al-Kindi (d. 873) and continuing through Avicenna (d. 1037) in the east and Averroës (d. 1198) in the west, Muslim philosophers evolved a philosophical interpretation of Islam within a Neoplatonic framework, which they seem to have felt existed outside the sphere of Islamic doctrine rather than in contradiction with it. There is no hint of a conflict in Avicenna, and one of Averroës' most important works is the *Faṣl al-Maqāl* ("Decisive Treatise [on the Harmony Between Religion and Philosophy]"), in which he states that philosophy is the companion and foster sister of the *sharī'ah*. His answer to al-Ghazāli, *Tahāfut al-Tahāfut* ("Inconsistency of the Inconsistency"), reveals his conviction that although reason cannot attain a complete understanding of eternal truths, man has a duty to seek a rational explanation by demonstrative argument. Similarly, the work of Averroës' contemporary Ibn Ṭufail (d. 1185), *Ḥayy Ibn Yaqẓān* ("The Living Son of the Vigilant"), demonstrates that reason and revelation independently lead to the same belief.

Views of this kind were considered dangerously close to heresy by many, and by the eleventh century there was strong hostility on the part of theologians toward such philosophical constructions. The accomplishment of al-Ghazāli was essentially to dam this second tide of Hellenism by reconciling the positions of philosophy and theology, much as al-Ash'ari had stemmed the first by synthesizing orthodox and Mu'tazilite ideas. Moreover, just as al-Ash'ari had defended Sunnite dogma by the use of intellectually superior Mu'tazilite methods of logic, al-Ghazāli upheld it in his major argument against philosophy, *Tahāfut al Falāsifa* ("The Inconsistency of the Philosophers"), with Neoplatonic ideas taken from Avicenna and other followers of Greek thought.

Al-Ghazāli was important also as a living example of synthesis between theology and the mystic (*sūfi*) movement in Islam. Sufism had been, more than any of the other movements of diversity, an intuitive way of practicing Islam through the cultivation of personal religious experience, and Sufi mystics and ascetics are found from very early times. Some of them were considered orthodox, but others, like al-Hallāj (d. 922), were persecuted or even executed. For many, however, the personal communion which lay at the heart of the Sufi movement was felt as complementary to normal orthodox devotion and not contrary to it. Al-Ghazāli turned to Sufism in his later years and in some of his works illuminated the inner meaning of the obligation of Muslim faith. On the basis of personal experience he propounded the necessity of founding belief on the strict observance of these obligations before

turning to seek the inner awakening for which Sufism characteristically strove.

The growth of Sufism had been accentuated in the period after al-Ash'ari, in good part as a reaction to the austereness of orthodox Sunnism. Al-Ghazāli's efforts were temporarily successful, but in the long run they had effects that were unexpected and unwelcome to the orthodox establishment. While orthodoxy was at first given fresh vigor by the new infusion, the acceptance of Sufism within its realm eventually produced a lowering of intellectual standards dealing with the purity of the doctrine. This led in time to a capitulation before the power of popular religion, on the part of both the *'ulamā'* and many temporal rulers, unwilling to offend popular religious susceptibilities. The result was a final *de facto* separation of the two briefly joined streams of Muslim faith. The theologians retreated to the sanctuary of the mosque and the *madrasah*, where they perfected a pedantic system of rote education and intellectual sterility, divorced from the living forces of religion; in consequence, the energies that had been unleashed were left without the guidance provided by rigorous intellectual discipline and soon gave themselves over to excesses of mysticism, saint worship tantamount to pantheism, and cultism often having more to do with pre-Islamic animism than with Islam. In particular, the social evolution of Sufism was marked by the appearance of brotherhoods, associations of mendicants, dervish orders, and mystic fraternities, which since the thirteenth century have significantly changed the nature of Islam as popularly practiced. The subsequent development of Sufism influenced the Islamic world in other ways also. As a result of the devastation accompanying the Mongol conquest and occupation of most of western Asia in the fourteenth century, the orthodox establishment was disrupted and discredited. In these circumstances, in countries as different and distant as Persia and Morocco, it was the popular Sufi movement that upheld the unity of the community and resisted the invader. In so doing, the movement utilized efficiently the personal links cultivated by early Sufi circles, but at the same time it began to take on a more formal organization. Colleges were founded by Sufi sheikhs, and these in turn gave rise to a regular network of affiliated institutions, each called a *ṭarīqah*, or "path." Many of these were regional in their influence, but others spread throughout the Muslim states and were a principal means of cultural interchange in the succeeding centuries. Finally, Sufism took root in the sociopolitical debris left in areas such as Asia Minor and Persia as Mongol rule waned. In the two great empires which from that period until the twentieth century dominated the heartland of the Muslim world Sufism played a significant role. In Anatolia Sufi sheikhs were politically active in the *ghāzi* states, which were organized in corporations often affiliated with a *tarīqah*, and it was out of one such *ghāzi* state that the Ottoman Empire grew. In Iran, Sufism along with Shi'ism contributed to the Iranian national revival from the fourteenth century on, and the Safavid state was founded by Sufi sheikhs attached to the Suhrawardi *tarīqah*.

## Islam and polity

The character of the political institutions of Islam was essentially determined during the lifetime of Muḥammad by the simultaneous emergence of Islam as a faith and as an autonomous political community. In classical Islamic thought, government exists for no other purpose than that of upholding the faith and guaranteeing service to God on earth, and political institutions are designed to safeguard the community in the widest sense from all the perils, spiritual and material, of this existence.

The principal institution by which this design has been carried out is the caliphate, which was instituted when the followers of Muḥammad upon his death selected one of his companions as the rightful successor to the mantle of the Prophet. Since the divine will had been made clear to men in the Qur'ān and expatiated on in the *sunnah* and inasmuch as the correct path for the community is subsumed in the *sharī'ah*, the caliphate has ideally been an executive stewardship bereft of legislative prerogatives. In practice, however, especially in later times, both the use of administrative decrees and the doctrine of consensus became loopholes permitting considerable legislative initiative.

In the first Islamic decades under the leadership of the "rightly guided" caliphs Muslims did not distinguish between the moral authority of the caliphate and the actual power it wielded in its own right. Beginning with the successional quarrel after the death of 'Uthmān in 656, however, a train of events was let loose that greatly influenced Muslim political theory as well as practice. The disaffection of the Kharijites and the Shi'ites called into question the legitimacy of the occupant of the office, and Shi'ite insistence that only a descendant of the Prophet could be caliph was instrumental in forcing Sunnite theologians to work out theories of the caliphate that would withstand such attacks. By the early ninth century, moreover, the increasing fragmentation of the Muslim empire and the seizure of power by regional commanders and adventurers,

first in distant provinces and finally in the capital itself, underlined the split between a limited caliphal authority and the new self-assertive power, which continued in varied forms and disguises from then until modern times. In succeeding centuries some of the greatest legal minds of Islam attempted to explain this divergence in terms consonant with the theological bases of Islam, and their reasoning had crucial consequences for Islamic political history.

The classical exposition of the Sunnite position was made by al-Māwardi (d. 1031), who formalized the legal fictions (*hiyāl*) of the Ash'arites by admitting in cases of necessity the principle that the caliph, whose authority was of divine origin, might delegate this to temporary power holders. By so doing, al-Māwardi took the first step along a dangerous path which led to the collapse of the entire system. Later, al-Ghazāli moved further along it by legitimizing power holders who paid symbolic allegiance to the caliph in ritual prayer, coinage, etc. He tried to forge a synthesis between power and authority by making obedience to any but a manifestly anti-Islamic ruler a virtue because proper leadership was essential to the functioning of the community. The final step was taken after the destruction of the 'Abbāsid caliphate in 1258 with the legitimation of power in itself, on the grounds that all power comes ultimately from God and derives authority from that fact. In this way the difference between good and bad government was reduced through expediency to religious criteria alone; if the ruler protected the faith and carried out his executive responsibilities with respect to the holy law, he should then be obeyed. Such a justification of force offered great incentives to schemers, freebooters, and disgruntled military leaders, for the only criterion of a rightful revolution became its success. But for the mass of the community it eliminated, by its limited definition of injustice, the right to revolt and even the ability to protest effectively against harsh rule.

Having thus completely divorced the power of the emirate from the caliphate, Sunnite jurists were forced into further legal fictions, the most important of which was the doctrine, previously repudiated by the Ash'arites, that the true caliphate had only lasted thirty years, after which there had existed a self-constituted imamate to which caliphal titles were given as pure form. The caliphate came to be viewed, then, like the *sharī'ah*, as an ideal formulation to be constantly aspired to but seldom attained. Sunnite juristic theory was encapsuled by Ibn Khaldūn in the late fourteenth century and a century later by Jalāl ud-Din Dawwāni. They distinguished between secular kingship and the caliphate and insisted that only the righteous ruler who governs according to the *shari'ah* is entitled to style himself caliph.

The caliphate instituted by the Ottoman Empire is thus in strict terms the equivalent of an imamate only, and its resuscitation in the late eighteenth century, after more than two centuries of Ottoman indifference to the title, occurred at a time of declining Ottoman power when the Porte was concerned with reinforcing its symbols of authority. With European encroachments on Muslim lands and the rise of Pan-Islamist sentiment in the nineteenth century, the position of the Ottoman sultan-caliph at the head of the only Muslim state possessing a semblance of power in world politics was reinforced, but its nature was changed. Islamic solidarity grew temporarily on political grounds rather than as the expression of any true revival of the community, and as a political force it had to contend, in the end unsuccessfully, with local or more secular nationalisms among the Turks, the Arabs, the Persians, and other Muslim peoples. Ottoman efforts to rally Islamic solidarity behind the nominal caliph during World War I were fruitless, and the formal abolition of the caliphate by the Turkish Republic in 1924 came during an era of nascent nationalism in many parts of the Muslim world and created little stir except among Pan-Islamists or politicians trying to capitalize on religious issues. A congress of unofficial delegations from many Muslim countries met in Cairo in 1926 but could not agree on the qualifications of a new caliph or the bases for the restoration of the institution.

## Islam and society

The divine commands laid down in the Qur'ān and the *sunnah* not only concern God and man but also order the social relationships among men and are especially explicit about matters pertaining to the family, marriage, divorce, and inheritance. The Muslim family is the re-creation of the Arab family within the ethical confines of Islam. Thus it is authoritarian, patriarchal, polygamous, patrilineal, and largely patrilocal, with vestigial survivals of what appears to be an earlier matrilineal kinship system reflected in the prominent position of the maternal uncle. The role of women has on the whole, despite Muslim apologetics, been subordinate to that of men; this is attested by the Qur'ān, which ranks men above women and allows only half value to the testimony of the latter. The inheritance shares of female heirs are half those allotted to males. However, the counsel of moderation in the treatment of spouses which runs through the Qur'ān gives some weight to those who claim that Muḥammad did in effect lighten the burden

women bore in pre-Islamic times. In practice today many elder women exercise great authority over members of their household, and particularly in urban areas, working women of the lower and lower-middle classes have a considerable degree of autonomy. Nevertheless, in almost every Muslim country, the legal position of the wife is inferior to that of the husband and in many cases is precarious.

Traditional marriage is a contract arranged between heads of households. The consent of the groom is necessary if he is of age (formerly puberty, but now fixed almost everywhere by statute), but not that of the bride, except through her tutor for marriage. The right of compulsory marriage of a daughter by a male parent, formerly common, has been sharply restricted in most countries. Although Muslim law specifies degrees of kinship forbidden for marriage, the union of first cousins is sanctioned and often favored. Muslim males may marry non-Muslim women, but except in those countries where the holy law no longer exists (Turkey and Tunisia) Muslim women may not marry outside their faith.

Polygamy is expressly sanctioned by the Qur'ān, which allows the Muslim to take four wives, and has been widely practiced throughout Islam at all times, but with regional variations and under some social and ethical restrictions. Economic factors alone have always limited the number of polygamous families, most of which are found among the urban well-to-do. Peasants tend, through economic necessity, to be monogamous or to limit themselves to the taking of a second wife, often later in life. Under the influence of Western mores in this century plural marriages have come to be regarded by many Muslims as a sign of backwardness. Many Muslim reformers now claim that the Qur'ānic purpose was to limit the uncontrolled polygamy of pre-Islamic Arabia by imposing a limitation reasonable to the age. Today codes of personal status in countries like Syria and Egypt, which combine features of the holy law with European legislation, have made plural marriage increasingly difficult, although they have hesitated to outlaw it completely, as in Turkey and Tunisia.

Probably a greater impediment to family stability than polygamy has been the classical mode of divorce through repudiation. Traditionally, the husband may repudiate his wife in unilateral fashion by simple pronouncement and repayment of the balance of the dowry. The *shari'ah* mitigates this somewhat by applying numerous conditions, but, in effect, the wife is subject to being divorced, with all the consequent stigma, without any effective legal recourse except under extraordinary circumstances. Successive repudiations are often equivalent to serial polygamy, and they have been and still are widespread in parts of Muslim society, particularly among the poor, where the dowry is inconsequential or nonexistent. In this domain, too, the law is gradually changing; in recent years Egypt, Morocco, and several other countries have made repudiation more difficult, while the more secularly oriented states have outlawed the practice.

Marriage is encouraged in the Qur'ān, and the Christian concept of celibate purity has always been combated; to Muḥammad is attributed the phrase, "No monkery in Islam." Procreation is held up as desirable, and children, especially boys, are welcomed. The male child is closely dependent on his mother and the women of the household. They take care of him until about the age of seven, when he begins his life as a young man, a step traditionally signaled either by his taking up work with his father or an uncle or by his starting religious instruction at school. Circumcision is normally carried out at this time, although in some areas it is practiced shortly after birth. It is not mentioned in the Qur'ān but has become a strictly observed rite throughout Islam, and the festivities surrounding circumcision make it a rite of passage equivalent only to marriage in popular Muslim custom. The traditional religious instruction of the mosque-school, usually limited to rote Qur'ānic studies and the rudiments of mathematics and civics, has been supplemented or replaced now almost everywhere by modern educational facilities, which attract a majority of the children of school age in many Muslim countries. These uniformly supply religious instruction, however, and thus young men even today, in contrast with modern Westerners, possess a detailed knowledge of their scripture, which serves as a further channel for maintaining Islamic solidarity. The education of girls, previously much neglected, has made great strides in recent decades. Nevertheless, many fewer girls than boys attend school, and even fewer go on to higher education. In some countries women are entering the professions in small numbers and working in salaried positions for the first time, but marriage and housekeeping are still considered their proper occupations.

The social ethic of Islam is founded upon a real sense of solidarity and brotherhood. The teachings of the Qur'ān have shaped an ideal Muslim civism rooted in humility before God, piety, frugality, charity toward the less fortunate, and an equality of believers in the face of the majesty of an all-powerful Deity. The transformation from the pre-Islamic Arab character, which laid emphasis on the blood tie, vengeance, and manliness, is complete, although much of the bedouin background persists under the Islamic mantle. A summary list of grave sins reveals the influence of both strains. Ancient tribal feelings about ritual cleanliness, the eating of carrion and forbidden food, sorcery and usury, unlawful sexual relations, and the blood price co-exist with unbelief, refusal to pay legal alms, apostasy, telling falsehoods about the Prophet and his companions, striking a fellow Muslim without cause, not fasting during Ramadan, and the like. Throughout Muslim teaching and writing runs the thread of moderation in all things. The *sharī'ah* is, literally, the "straight path" not only in the sense of righteousness opposed to deviation but also as a golden mean. Moderation and abstinence are often recommended in the Qur'ān, even for acts that are permissible, and the balance they create is disturbed by the sins of greed and pride. Prodigality and lavishness of hospitality are tenacious pre-Islamic survivals in much of the Muslim East today, but they are not encouraged by the tradition. Finally, the doctrine of equality of all believers and frequent intermarriage with slaves and concubines have led to the relative absence of a color bar in Islam, a fact which today has great sociopolitical significance as well as ethical meaning.

Islam has in certain respects stamped its own image on economic institutions or at least emphasized certain characteristics of economic life to the extent that a distinctive coloration was given to them in the classical period within the limits of the Middle East and the Mediterranean.

Classical Islamic society is one of merchants and trade. The socioeconomic causes lying behind the origins of Islam itself concern the conflict of economic interests in Mecca and the question of the trade routes in western Arabia. The social background of Muḥammad and the predominance of the Quraish clan in early Islam insured a continuing emphasis on mercantilism which has never been lost. The *sūq*, properly an assemblage of shops and ateliers and workshops in which the commercial life of the town is grouped, has Greco–Roman antecedents but has evolved in special ways. The economic geography of the city is arranged from the center out in a descending order of virtue: the cathedral mosque surrounded by those trades catering to it, such as candlestick makers, incense shops, booksellers, etc.; followed by the *sūq* of luxury goods, imported wares, and silks; and ending at the gates of the city with the tanneries, slaughterhouses, etc. Extreme specialization and geographical grouping by occupation and organization into guilds or corporations are constants of a pattern that still exists in many areas. The guilds often have ties with Sufi religious orders, and it is common for each to have a patron saint for whom an appropriate annual festival is held. The social function of the guilds counterbalances and complements for the individual that of the extended family and, sometimes but not always, that of the brotherhood or religious order to which he may belong.

As might be expected, Muslim law regulates commercial transactions in detail. It puts its greatest emphasis on the immediacy of transaction, the lawfulness of the thing exchanged, and the good faith of the parties involved. It thus forbids lending for interest and in theory permits only the exchange of quantities and articles of equal value. In due course of economic life, as in other areas, Islam has had recourse to legal fictions in order to avoid the paralyzing effect of the more rigorous Qur'ānic prohibitions. As international trade became important from the ninth century on, double sales, deposit contracts, promissory notes, temporary transfer of property to avoid taxes, and other devices formerly condemned by the tradition were and are widely practiced. Many such commercial customs and banking procedures in fact became models for European financial practices in the Middle Ages.

### Islam today

Since the late eighteenth century Islamic society, in common with other non-Western societies, has been undergoing an onslaught from Western civilization which is reflected in every aspect of its social, economic, political, and religious life. At the time the Western assault began in earnest, this society in its core area of western Asia and the Mediterranean was showing every sign of material and spiritual enervation. The internal and external tribulations of the Ottoman state were symptoms of a deeper illness reflected in the divorce between the medieval tradition and the most rampant elements of Sufism, the intellectual stagnation of the more rational forces within Islam, and an extreme subjectivism of the intuitive elements that had temporarily triumphed and threatened at times to lead Islam into a totally mystic pantheism.

In reaction both to these inner dangers and to the Western menace, Islam appears to have embarked upon a path of revival and restoration. This revival has developed over the past two centuries, hesitantly at first but with a growing sense of concern and self-awareness, accompanied by a still unformed and unformulated effort to search for solutions that will enable Islam to meet the challenges of the present age. The first such manifestation came in the fundamentalist Neo-Hanbalite Wahhābi movement of central Arabia, which arose in protest against the laxness and heresies of Sufi versions of the faith in the mid-eighteenth century and which flourished until it was defeated by Ottoman arms in the early nineteenth century. Its influence survived, however, and not only became the basis of the Sa'ūdi state but has had profound repercussions among revivalist, purifying movements in India and Africa. Although Sufi orders continued to expand in some areas, such as India, Africa, and fringe Muslim territory, in the nineteenth century, the puritan streak embodied in Wahhābism has in the twentieth century taken strong hold in the more purely Arab countries, where in almost all instances the orthodox version of the faith has been reinforced with the encouragement of and sometimes pressure from the authorities.

The confusion of religious and political factors in the Islamic crisis of the nineteenth century gave birth to a revived form of Pan-Islamism, which reflected in part the influence of similar political movements in Europe among the Slavs and Germans. Its message was preached by Jamāl al-Din al-Afghāni (d. 1897) from Egypt but eventually had little impact. One of his pupils, Muḥammad 'Abduh (d. 1905), took that part of it which emphasized the need for a thoroughgoing reform of Islamic thought and intellectual standards and attempted a reformulation of basic orthodox beliefs in order to show that they were compatible with modern life. Although it is too early to assess the ultimate importance of 'Abduh, he remains at this juncture the outstanding reformist theologian of modern times within Islam. One of his disciples, Muḥammad Rashīd Ridā (d. 1935), continued his work but moved from rationalism to a more conservative literalism, while calling for a revived caliphate under Arab, and more specifically, Quraish, guidance. Within the past generation the reaction against Westernization has, if anything, grown stronger, and there has been a proliferation of apologetics among Muslim intellectuals and writers. Much of this has been directed at Christianity, which is seen in a dual light: as a rival faith and as the indirect promoter of Western sociopolitical infiltration into the Muslim world. A conscious sense of competition, as opposed to the medieval Muslim assumption that Islam was infallible and had no rivals, can be discerned today for the first time in Islamic history. Among its manifestations are defenses against alleged attacks on Islam, an extreme defensiveness with respect to social issues on which Islam takes stands different from Western norms—or about which it is felt, however unconsciously, to be backward—and attempts at emulation and justification, represented notably by the biographical literature centering on Muḥammad and the historical literature emphasizing the past glories of Islam and the superiority of medieval Islamic civilization to that of Europe in the Middle Ages. Such attitudes, however, permitted the Indian Muslim reformer Muḥammad Iqbāl (d. 1938) to expound the idea that Muslims were entitled to take the fruits of Western civilization because they originally grew out of Islamic soil. His writings and activities were instrumental in helping to create the state of Pakistan in 1947.

Although it is manifestly impossible to summarize the various trends in modern Islam in well over a score of countries, it might be said that the overriding problem is that of the confrontation of the faith with a secular nationalism which demands that the highest loyalties be given to the state. In its concept and function as a supranational solidarity ethos and as the bearer of an ultimate message to mankind, Islam has so far found it impossible to come to terms with secularist nationalism as it is found in many Muslim countries, just as it has with scientific materialism, whose tenets have made inroads throughout the Muslim world. Several solutions have been tried. The idea of an Islamic state was promulgated in Pakistan but subsequently abandoned. The creation of a secular state in Turkey after World War I was followed a generation later by concessions to religious sentiment of a kind that makes it impossible to consider Turkey fully secular today. And in modern Egypt there is a complex relationship between the religious institution and the state in which traditional religious education has been modernized and laicized while the orthodox institution has been incorporated into the state and made subservient to it for manifestly political ends. In all these endeavors Muslims are being forced to think in terms of an uncompromising dualism for which their previous theological constructions provide no adequate model. Inherent also in these efforts is the clear desire of modern Muslims, at almost any cost, to put a greater social content into their religious formulations. The outstanding examples of this trend may be the efforts being made in Egypt, Indonesia, Syria, Algeria, and other countries to reconcile various forms of socialism with Islam.

CHARLES F. GALLAGHER

[*Directly related are the entries* AFRICAN SOCIETY, *article on* NORTH AFRICA; ASIAN SOCIETY, *article on* SOUTHEAST ASIA; HISTORIOGRAPHY, *article on* ISLAMIC HISTORIOGRAPHY; NEAR EASTERN SOCIETY.]

BIBLIOGRAPHY

ANDERSON, JAMES N. D. 1959 *Islamic Law in the Modern World*. New York Univ. Press.

ARBERRY, ARTHUR J. 1950 *Sufism: An Account of the Mystics of Islam*. London: Allen & Unwin.

ARNOLD, THOMAS W. (1924) 1965 *The Caliphate*. London: Routledge.

ARNOLD, THOMAS W.; and GUILLAUME, ALFRED (editors) (1931) 1952 *The Legacy of Islam*. Oxford Univ. Press.

BROCKELMANN, CARL (1939) 1960 *History of the Islamic Peoples*. New York: Capricorn. → First published as *Geschichte der islamischen Völker und Staaten*. Contains a review of events from 1939 to 1947 by Moshe Perlmann.

COULSON, NOEL J. 1964 *A History of Islamic Law*. Edinburgh Univ. Press.

DANIEL, NORMAN A. 1966 *Islam, Europe and Empire*. Edinburgh Univ. Press.

*The Encyclopaedia of Islam*. New ed. (1913–1938) 1954— Leiden (Netherlands): Brill. → To be published in five volumes.

ETTINGHAUSEN, RICHARD (1952) 1954 *A Selected and Annotated Bibliography of Books and Periodicals in Western Languages Dealing With the Near and Middle East, With Special Emphasis on Medieval and Modern Times*. Washington: Middle East Institute.

GAUDEFROY-DEMOMBYNES, MAURICE (1921) 1950 *Muslim Institutions*. London: Allen & Unwin. → First published as *Les institutions musulmanes*.

GIBB, H. A. R. 1947 *Modern Trends in Islam*. Univ. of Chicago Press.

GIBB, H. A. R. (1949) 1961 *Mohammedanism: An Historical Survey*. 2d ed. New York: Oxford Univ. Press. → A basic source.

GOLDZIHER, IGNÀCZ (1888) 1961 *Muhammedanische Studien*. 2 vols. Hildesheim (Germany): Olms.

JEFFERY, ARTHUR (editor) (1962) 1963 *A Reader on Islam: Passages From Standard Arabic Writings Illustrative of the Beliefs and Practices of Muslims*. New York: Humanities Press.

KORAN *The Koran Interpreted*, by Arthur J. Arberry. 2 vols. New York: Oxford Univ. Press, 1955.

LEVY, REUBEN (1931–1933) 1957 *The Social Structure of Islam*. 2d ed. Cambridge Univ. Press.

*Middle East Journal*. → Published since 1947.

ROSENTHAL, ERWIN I. J. (1958) 1962 *Political Thought in Medieval Islam*. Cambridge Univ. Press.

SAUVAGET, JEAN (1943) 1965 *Introduction to the History of the Muslim East: A Bibliographical Guide*. Berkeley: Univ. of California Press. → First published as *Introduction à l'histoire de l'orient musulman*.

SCHACHT, JOSEPH 1964 *An Introduction to Islamic Law*. Oxford: Clarendon.

SMITH, WILFRED CANTWELL 1957 *Islam in Modern History*. Princeton Univ. Press. → A paperback edition was published in 1959.

VON GRUNEBAUM, GUSTAVE E. (1946) 1953 *Medieval Islam: A Study in Cultural Orientation*. 2d ed. Univ. of Chicago Press.

VON GRUNEBAUM, GUSTAVE E. (editor) 1955 *Unity and Variety in Muslim Civilization*. Univ. of Chicago Press.

WATT, W. MONTGOMERY 1961 *Islam and the Integration of Society*. London: Routledge.

WATT, W. MONTGOMERY 1962 *Islamic Philosophy and Theology*. Edinburgh Univ. Press.

# ISOLATIONISM

Essentially the term "isolationism," when applied to the foreign policies of the United States, suggests a diplomatic tradition at variance with that of other great nations of the modern world. That American behavior in the external realm has not always followed the established patterns of *Realpolitik* is demonstrated repeatedly by the record itself. Yet historians have never agreed on either the nature or the degree of that divergence. Like most broad generalizations, isolationism defies any precise definition. Not even as a form of escapism did isolationism create necessarily unique national responses; for the United States, in attempting to hoard its energy by limiting its commitments abroad, pursued principles universally accepted by prudent statesmen.

Isolationism as a foundation of national policy cannot be divorced from the geographical insulation that the American people enjoyed through much of their history vis-à-vis the great powers of Europe. Yet to the Founding Fathers, isolationism was more than a response to geographic factors or the basis of thoughtless preoccupation with inner-directed and self-sufficient pursuits. The United States never sought the solitude of such hermit nations as Japan and Korea; from its republican beginnings, it created and maintained a commercial empire that blanketed much of the globe. American isolationism was always political and military, never commercial or intellectual.

In an effort to limit the political interests of the United States to the Western Hemisphere and to employ the nation's geographical advantages in the defense of those interests, early American leaders made the avoidance of entangling alliances the keystone of their diplomacy. John Adams, during a conversation with the Englishman Richard Oswald in November 1782, explained his fear of any permanent American commitment to Europe. "It is obvious," declared Adams (*Works*, vol. 3, p. 316), "that all the powers of Europe will be continually manoeuvering with us, to work us into their real or imaginary balances of power. . . . But I think it ought to be our rule not to meddle; and that of all the powers of Europe, not to desire us, or perhaps, even to permit us, to interfere, if they can help it." In his farewell address, George Washington acknowledged the diplomatic and military benefits that accrue from distance. "Why forego the advantages of so peculiar a situation?" he asked ([1753–1796] 1948, p. 641). For Washington, such convictions reflected a realistic judgment

of European power and the conclusion that the young republic would only waste its energies if it engaged in struggles abroad which it could not control.

In their preoccupation with diplomatic flexibility, the Founding Fathers reinforced the doctrine of no entangling alliances with the principle of complete neutrality in relation to Europe's wars. No nation could be completely free that had bartered away its right to be neutral. To thoughtful Americans the avoidance of involvement abroad was a less important consideration than preserving the nation's freedom to carry out the decisions that best defended its interests. If the United States maintained its independence of action more successfully than did the powers of Europe, it did so not because of differences in intent, or even of geographical insulation, but rather because the precise political conditions of Europe in the eighteenth and nineteenth centuries seemed to assure American security. American diplomatists could pursue a policy of isolationism throughout the years 1815 to 1900 because they understood that the European balance of power was adequate for the nation's needs.

Unfortunately this favorable balance, anchored to British power and diplomacy, was ultimately taken for granted and its relationship to American security all but forgotten. By the 1890s, Americans no longer recognized the nation's vital stake in traditional European politics. The restoration of the Continent after the Napoleonic wars created such conditions of stability that the average citizen of the United States, enjoying perennial security at relatively little cost, began to put his faith in the fact of geographic isolation itself. This gradual identification of American security with the Atlantic Ocean, rather than with a British-dominated European balance of power, created the foundations of twentieth-century American isolationism, which viewed less involvement in European affairs as the essence of sound policy. Whatever happened in Europe, ran the burgeoning isolationist argument, it could not challenge the historic security of the American people.

This nation's dramatic entrance onto the world stage at the turn of the century in no way challenged its isolationist habits of thought. The new sense of obligation to expand did not include, except on the part of a brilliant minority of American writers, any gauging of the forces being unleashed by British–German rivalry or any evaluation of the meaning of that rivalry for the American future. Some critics of national behavior, such as Alfred

Thayer Mahan, demanded, but in vain, a closer *rapprochement* with England, if not an actual alliance. Perhaps Lord Bryce (1888, I, p. 310 in 1909 edition) described the prewar attitudes of the American people with precision when he wrote: "America lives in a world of her own. . . . Safe from attack, safe even from menace, she hears from afar the warring cries of European races and faiths. . . . But for the present at least—it may not always be so—she sails upon a summer sea."

That American expansion into the Pacific failed to challenge the nation's isolationist tradition reflects fundamentally the ease whereby the acquisition of Hawaii, Guam, and the Philippines, as well as the establishment of an open-door policy in China, was achieved. Even in the Caribbean, where the nation faced no competing power, the new commitments created the illusion of huge accomplishment at a minimum of financial and military expenditure. Thus the nation could underwrite enthusiastically the policies of expansion into Latin America and the western Pacific while rejecting all involvement in European affairs as an unnecessary and dangerous overcommitment of the resources of the United States. The powerful Asia-first orientation of American isolationism had its inception in the basic conviction, demonstrated by events, that the United States could protect its interests in the Far East at relatively little cost. As late as 1940, when Hitler's armies were sweeping across Europe, Americans were more fearful of Japan than Germany, more determined to defend the integrity of China than that of Norway, the Low Countries, or France.

From 1917 to 1920, Woodrow Wilson's crusade for a new world order attempted to commit the United States to the maintenance of a stable world, which would supposedly resolve the pressures for change in the postwar *status quo* through representative deliberative bodies. Instead it laid the foundation for the violent isolationist reaction of the 1920s, for it was clear by 1919 that Wilson could not uproot the traditions of European power politics. The League of Nations seemed to obligate the nation to action in undefined and unforeseeable contingencies. Its rejection by the Senate, the result of many factors, reflected basically an American disinclination to commit United States military forces to the defense of the Versailles system. Disillusioned by the apparently meager benefits that accrued to the United States from the great involvement of World War I, many Americans accepted the new watchwords of national purpose, "never again."

The powerful isolationism of the interwar years has been subjected to endless scrutiny by American scholars. It was a national phenomenon. Yet its chief strength always seemed to lie in the upper Middle West, especially in the prairie states. For many students, this was the simple dictate of geographic reality. It appeared reasonable that isolationism should center in those regions of the country most remote from world events.

For others, interwar isolationism had a clear economic base. Many western agrarians, for example, long regarding eastern bankers and industrialists as their mortal enemies, attributed the American involvement in World War I to the influence of Wall Street. They disliked England because that nation represented the system of international finance and investment that led the great nations to war. Charles A. Lindbergh, Sr., in his book *Your Country at War and What Happens to You After a War* (1917), blamed the war on profiteering and international bankers. Agrarian isolationists attributed the destruction of progressivism to wartime profits.

This form of liberal economic isolationism reached its climax in 1934 with Senator Gerald P. Nye's investigation of the munitions industry. The public was prepared to hear the worst of the "merchants of death"—those who had profited so handsomely from the war effort. Nye, a former North Dakota newspaper editor, regarded the farmer as the backbone of American society, always beset by the bankers of Wall Street. Gradually, Nye identified the interest of the farmer with those of the citizens of the midwestern villages and even the large midwestern cities, for all such business centers had a clear interest in the welfare of the farmer. All, moreover, were enemies of Wall Street. His investigation of the munitions makers was the logical extension into the field of foreign affairs of his long crusade against the influence of finance capitalism. His conclusions were as much antibusiness as they were antiwar.

In the late 1930s, economic isolationism shifted gradually from liberalism to conservatism. By 1939 many men of wealth stood at the forefront of the American isolationist crusade; they dominated such organizations as the influential America First Committee. Conservatives feared more and more that American involvement in war would further weaken the American free enterprise system. For the isolationist leadership in the Republican party, the program of "America first" was fundamentally an anti-New Deal crusade. Eventually, even Nye discovered that the masses had outbid the farmer for control of governmental policy—that the New Deal spoke largely for the urban dweller. By the late 1930s, he had turned to the conservatives for support in his effort to keep America out of war.

For some Americans, isolationism was largely an expression of the nation's democratic idealism. Its purpose, in short, was to protect the uniqueness of American society against the corrupting influence of European politics. Traditionally this sense of uniqueness was the essence of an affirmative faith. According to Abraham Lincoln, America was the earth's last best hope. The achievement of that promise demanded the rejection of Europe. As John Dos Passos once observed, "Repudiation of Europe is, after all, America's main excuse for being." By the late 1930s, even the desire to protect the uniqueness of American society had turned conservative. For many isolationists, the concepts of progress and change had retreated before the conviction that American society had matured and that Europe, with its radical tendencies, must be avoided. No longer did isolationists view the United States as the changing society in a reactionary world, but as a stable and accomplished society in a revolutionary world. Isolationism was the means whereby the nation would preserve its economic, social, and political institutions against the dangers of experimentation abroad.

Samuel Lubell, from his studies of the elections of 1920 and 1940, concluded that American isolationism was neither geographic, economic, nor idealistic. In *The Future of American Politics* (1951, p. 132) he wrote, "This concept of isolationism must be discarded. It is a myth. The hard core of isolationism in the United States has been ethnic and emotional. . . ." The great Democratic setbacks in 1920, when contrasted with the 1916 returns, he discovered, came in Swedish, German, Norwegian, and Irish districts, revealing an ethnic reaction to Wilson's decision to lead the American people to war against Germany. In 1940 Roosevelt's majority vote dropped roughly 7 per cent from 1936. In 20 counties the losses exceeded 35 per cent; 19 of these were fundamentally German in background. Another 35 counties showed a Democratic drop of 25–34 per cent; in all but four of these, German was either the first or second strongest nationality of origin. The same ethnic factors were present in another 83 of 101 counties where Roosevelt's 1940 vote dropped between 20 and 24 per cent. It was, concluded Lubell, the absence of Germans in the South that limited that region's isolationism.

As war returned to Europe in 1939, the concept of a fortress America became the ultimate intellectual refuge of the nation's isolationist leadership. American security, ran the argument, did not hinge on Britain or the balance of power, but on the United States' capacity to guard the sea lanes. Herbert Hoover announced in February 1939 that the hemisphere was protected by a "moat of 3000 miles of ocean on the East, and 6000 miles on the West" (1940, p. 101). By this isolationist doctrine, the course of war in Europe mattered little. Charles A. Beard wrote: "It was one thing to regard Hitler and Mussolini as madmen at Munich . . . it was another thing to maintain that the United States should pour out the blood of its sons in restraining the dictators after Great Britain, France, Russia and the other powers of Europe had failed to unite against them in diplomacy and coercion" (Beard & Beard 1939, pp. 499–500).

For such men, the outbreak of war in Europe merely affirmed the notion that the United States was invulnerable. "Actually," wrote Oswald Garrison Villard in September 1939, "from the purely military point of view, the security of the United States has been increased by the outbreak of war. And the longer war continues, the safer the United States will be, if it ever was in danger. For with each day that passes, the exhaustion of the contestants will become greater" (1939, p. 324). Whatever the logic of such convictions, they failed to preserve American neutrality. Again, as in 1917, it was the nation's ultimate unwillingness to countenance a British defeat at the hands of Germany that brought it into the European war.

For the vast majority of Americans at mid-century the isolationist tradition was no longer relevant. The disintegration of the alliance with Russia and the acceptance by the United States of a world-wide commitment to the containment of communist power seemed to leave little room for the doctrines of the 1930s. Senator Robert A. Taft, one of the nation's leading proponents of prewar isolationism, declared in 1950: "I don't know what they mean by isolationism; nobody is an isolationist today." Dwight D. Eisenhower observed two years later, "I have long insisted—and do now insist, that isolationism is dead as a political issue."

Yet isolationism was not dead. World War II had demonstrated its obsolescence, but it had not destroyed the emotions and traditions that underlay it. What remained had changed its emphasis, but its significance for the nation was only partially diminished. Contributing to the rebirth of a powerful conservative American isolationism in the postwar era was the conviction that the Roosevelt administration, through its involvement of the country in World War II, had assured the rise of Russia to a position of power. Past Democratic policies, in short, were responsible for the unprecedented insecurity of the American people. Senator Taft charged quite characteristically (1951, p. 6) that "our leaders failed to foresee that the Soviet Union would turn against us after the defeat of Germany and Japan. They made no attempt to insure our future against that eventuality." The vast power revolution of the 1940s appeared to demonstrate that the isolationists of the interwar years were correct in their judgment of the national interest after all.

Aggravated by the postwar dread of communism, American isolationism, more than ever before, placed its emphasis on the uniqueness of American society and the need for protecting that uniqueness from its enemies at home and abroad. For many Americans, the containment policies of the Truman administration were nothing but an assault on the nation's values. The reactionary–nationalist foreign policy elite, as Gabriel Almond (1950) has defined it, attributed American insecurity not to Russian power and aggressiveness, but to the gradual destruction of the traditional American free enterprise system. Beginning with the presidency of Woodrow Wilson, ran its argument, socialism, New Dealism, heavy military expenditures, and high taxes had undermined the strength of the nation. If the United States would return to the old Americanism as it existed before 1914, the nation's external challenges would evaporate. Organizations of the extreme right, such as Merwin K. Hart's National Economic Council, opposed the Marshall Plan as a scheme to "finance socialism in Europe." It termed the United Nations an octopus leading to a "statist, collectivist world." The United States should clear the decks for action "by reducing our government expense and rejecting the whole Truman program for a socialized welfare state." The American Coalition of Patriotic Societies, led by John B. Trevor, agreed that the danger to American security lay in the "nationalist socialist planners." When the nation again returned to its nineteenth-century orthodoxy, it would enjoy security without excessive military expenditures.

If few Americans identified American insecurity abroad so completely with the erosion of American values, a significant body of editors and politicians condemned the nation's commitment to the defense of Europe. Senator Taft, in his book *A Foreign Policy for Americans*, explained his opposition to NATO: "I do not like the obligation written into the pact which binds us for twenty years to come to the defense of any country, no matter by whom it is attacked and even though the aggressor may be another member of the pact . . ." (1951, pp.

88–89). Taft, like other conservative Americans, believed that the essence of American security lay in the domestic economy. He opposed the American commitment to NATO as an overestimation of both the Soviet threat and the defense burden that the American economy could bear. "Just as our nation can be destroyed by war," he declared (1951, p. 14), "it can also be destroyed by a political or economic policy at home which destroys liberty or breaks down the fiscal and economic structure of the United States."

American isolationism in the postwar world continued to harbor its Asia-first tendencies. If the United States had failed in its historic effort to preserve the open door in China by permitting the transfer of political power from Chiang Kai-shek to Mao Tse-tung and the Chinese communists, the answer lay not in the nation's inability to subdue the Chinese revolution but rather in errors of judgment, if not actual treason, within the Department of State. This denial of the vast power revolution in Asia permitted those who favored the reduction of American forces in Europe to demand a show of aggressiveness in Asia without appearing to assume an expensive military burden. The mere return of Chiang to the mainland promised the reestablishment of the open door at little cost.

Perhaps the key development in the history of American isolationism was the shift from a realistic evaluation of both the role of distance from the power centers of Europe and the significance for the nation's security of the European balance of power, to an assumption that the country's security had become absolute and rested on the fact of geographic insulation and the supremacy of the nation's economic and political institutions. So secure did the country appear in the nineteenth century that, according to Abraham Lincoln, it could be injured only from within. Anchored to such assumptions of omnipotence, American isolationism in the twentieth century became identified with a primary concern for the domestic economy, an overestimation of American power, and a belief in the nation's moral superiority, all of which encouraged the tendency toward unilateralism in diplomacy. Isolationism, although a logical consequence of geography and the national experience, was in fact the creation of several generations of writers, editors, and politicians. It triumphed as a political program and achieved a predominant place in American thought simply because no other course of national action could promise so much at such negligible cost. World War II and the events that followed destroyed only the illusion of geographical insulation. The traditional belief that the United States could achieve security at less expense to itself than nations with fewer physical advantages was not destroyed.

NORMAN A. GRAEBNER

[*See also* FOREIGN POLICY; NATIONAL INTEREST; NATIONAL SECURITY.]

### BIBLIOGRAPHY

ADAMS, JOHN   *The Works of John Adams, Second President of the United States.* 10 vols. Boston: Little, 1851–1856.

ADLER, SELIG   1957   *The Isolationist Impulse.* New York: Abelard-Schuman.

ALMOND, GABRIEL A.   (1950) 1960   *The American People and Foreign Policy.* New York: Praeger.

BEARD, CHARLES; and BEARD, MARY   1939   *America in Midpassage.* New York: Macmillan.

BRYCE, JAMES   (1888) 1909   *The American Commonwealth.* 2 vols. New York and London: Macmillan. → An abridged edition was published in 1959 by Putnam.

COLE, WAYNE S.   1953   *America First: The Battle Against Intervention, 1940–1941.* Madison: Univ. of Wisconsin Press.

COLE, WAYNE S.   1962   *Senator Gerald P. Nye and American Foreign Relations.* Minneapolis: Univ. of Minnesota Press.

DE CONDE, ALEXANDER (editor)   1957   *Isolation and Security: Ideas and Interests in Twentieth-century American Foreign Policy.* Durham, N.C.: Duke Univ. Press.

GRAEBNER, NORMAN A.   1956   *The New Isolationism: A Study in Politics and Foreign Policy Since 1950.* New York: Ronald Press.

HOOVER, HERBERT   1940   *Further Addresses Upon the American Road: 1938–1940.* New York: Scribner.

LINDBERGH, CHARLES A. SR.   (1917) 1934   *Your Country at War and What Happens to You After a War.* Philadelphia: Dorrance.

LUBELL, SAMUEL   (1951) 1956   *The Future of American Politics.* 2d ed., rev. Garden City, N.Y.: Doubleday.

LUBELL, SAMUEL   1956   *Revolt of the Moderates.* New York: Harper.

TAFT, ROBERT A.   1951   *A Foreign Policy for Americans.* Garden City, N.Y.: Doubleday.

VILLARD, OSWALD G.   1939   Issues and Men: The United States and the War. *Nation* 149:324 only.

WASHINGTON, GEORGE   (1753–1796) 1948   *Basic Writings of George Washington.* New York: Random House.

WEINBERG, ALBERT K.   1940   The Historical Meaning of the American Doctrine of Isolation. *American Political Science Review* 34:539–547.

## ISRAEL

*See under* NEAR EASTERN SOCIETY.

## ITEM ANALYSIS

*See* PSYCHOMETRICS; RESPONSE SETS.

# J

## JACKKNIFE TECHNIQUE

*See* Errors, *article on* NONSAMPLING ERRORS.

## JACOBSSON, PER

Per Jacobsson (1894–1963), Swedish monetary economist and international public servant, was for more than forty years a leading spokesman for policies of monetary stability and international financial cooperation. The height of his influence was reached during a richly creative period as Managing Director of the International Monetary Fund from November 1956 until his death in May 1963.

Prior to 1956 Jacobsson served for 25 years as Economic Adviser to the Bank for International Settlements in Basel, Switzerland. Here he was an unofficial and confidential counselor to many of the world's leading central bankers and statesmen. His official responsibility centered on the preparation of the bank's *Annual Report*. First published in 1931, the report, under his guidance, became known as the most influential diagnosis of the principal events and forces at work in the world's economy to appear anywhere. Earlier, Jacobsson had served from 1920 to 1928 with the economic and financial section of the League of Nations Secretariat in Geneva, working primarily in the field of public finance. He spent the years 1928–1931 in Sweden, first in public service, and a brief period, 1930–1931, in private business.

Before leaving Sweden in 1920, he had worked and studied, both during the formative stages of his intellectual development at Uppsala University and in the years thereafter, with a remarkable group of Swedish economists, notably Gustav Cassel, David Davidson, Eli Heckscher, and Knut Wicksell. Their emphasis on the influence of monetary factors on the general level of economic activity, and their highly developed analysis of the functions of the rate of interest in influencing investment flows, were identifying characteristics of Jacobsson's own economic thought and writing. His firm grasp of the fundamentals of the Swedish approach may also account, in part, for his ability to evaluate and find appropriate uses for the doctrines developed by Keynes: he avoided both the impassioned rejection and uncritical acceptance which were so common among various of Jacobsson's contemporaries in Europe and the United States.

Although Jacobsson was a prolific writer, highly articulate in four languages (Swedish, English, German, and French), his impact on political economy was greater through his direct influence upon men and events than through his published work. To him as well as to Keynes, economics was a method of thought, not a single body of doctrine. His ability to grasp the doctrine that was suited to the needs of the times, combined with the ebullient good humor with which he presented his views, assured him access to the financial and governmental leaders who were working on the important economic problems confronting nations or the world economy as a whole, and he communicated the essence of his appraisals with telling clarity and directness.

Among his striking predictions that were of special significance for the evolution of public policy was the daring forecast in 1925 that interest rates would soon begin a major decline in the principal countries of the West (1925). After World War II, he was also one of the first to see that massive postwar demand would preclude the postwar depression expected in the United States and elsewhere (Bank for International Settlements 1944, esp. p. 23). In a 1950 lecture, *Monetary Improvements in Europe and Problems of a Return to Convertibility* (1950, pp. 37–43), he rejected the hypothesis of a continuing dollar shortage and indicated the range of fundamental problems that the end of the dollar shortage would produce.

Jacobsson assumed his duties as Managing Director of the International Monetary Fund in November 1956. Shortly thereafter, a large United Kingdom credit from the Fund was instrumental in restoring financial confidence shaken by the Suez crisis. Apart from meeting the immediate financial strains which that crisis produced for several countries, Jacobsson concentrated his attention on containing the continuing world-wide forces of inflation. In that effort, he strongly supported the effective application of the classical doctrines of sharply restrictive monetary policy and high and rising rates of interest in order to check internal expansion and re-establish balance in a country's external accounts. But as the United States achieved reasonable price stability from 1958 on and yet experienced larger and larger balance of payments deficits while unemployment remained unusually high, Jacobsson saw this as an even greater economic problem for the world at the time. With characteristic flexibility, he drew heavily on the doctrines that Keynes had developed during the great depression of the 1930s to help find ways to resolve this new paradox of the 1960s. He stressed the need for greater reliance on fiscal policy and specifically for tax reduction, even though large budget deficits were still continuing, while also urging careful attention to wage costs and the active development of incomes policies.

His activities at the Fund are best described by listing the series of tests which the international financial system met and overcame during the years he served there. For example, on two occasions, in 1957 and 1961, the Fund took a leading part in operations that helped stabilize the position of the pound sterling. In 1962 the Fund provided the principal counterforce that quelled the speculative uncertainties threatening the Canadian dollar. Earlier, in 1958, Jacobsson was convinced, when many others were doubtful, that France was ready for monetary stability. With daring and initiative he led the Fund to its decision to assist France through rigorous application of the classic approach of monetary stability and budgetary restraint. The resulting stabilization of the franc proved to be the major prerequisite for the widespread restoration of European currency convertibility that occurred at the end of 1958.

At the same time that the financial resources of the Fund were substantially expanded to cope more adequately with pressures on the world's leading currencies, Jacobsson also continued to explore ways in which the Fund could most effectively promote the growth and financial stability of the world's less developed nations. His last major effort, in 1963, led to the Fund's decision on "compensatory financing of export fluctuations," by which a new facility was provided for members, particularly for those producing primary materials, to be used at times when their export earnings were adversely affected by a decline in prices and sales.

Jacobsson combined, in unusual measure, a keen analytic faculty with a highly developed sense of what was possible and practical in the financial affairs of nations. He became the spokesman and the conscience for a monetary system that would be able to promote the orderly growth of the world economy.

ROBERT V. ROOSA

[*For the historical context of Jacobsson's work, see* INTERNATIONAL MONETARY ECONOMICS, *article on* INTERNATIONAL MONETARY ORGANIZATION; *and the biographies of* CASSEL; DAVIDSON; HECKSCHER; WICKSELL.]

### WORKS BY JACOBSSON

1925    The Rate of Interest: A Forecast. *Economist* 100: 441–442, 491–492, 529–530, 587–588. → Unsigned articles written by Per Jacobsson as a correspondent.

1950    *Monetary Improvements in Europe and Problems of a Return to Convertibility.* Cairo: National Bank of Egypt.

1958    *Some Monetary Problems: International and National.* Basle Centre for Economic and Financial Research, Publications, Series B, No. 4. Oxford Univ. Press.

1959    *Towards a Modern Monetary Standard.* Univ. of London.

1961    *The Market Economy in the World of Today.* American Philosophical Society, Memoirs, Vol. 55. Philadelphia: The Society.

1963    *The Role of Money in a Dynamic Economy.* New York Univ., Graduate School of Business Administration.

1964    *International Monetary Problems, 1957–1963: Selected Speeches.* International Monetary Fund, Monograph Series, No. 3. Washington: The Fund. → Published posthumously.

### SUPPLEMENTARY BIBLIOGRAPHY

BANK FOR INTERNATIONAL SETTLEMENTS 1944 *Annual Report of the President, Fourteenth.* Basel: The Bank. → See especially Per Jacobsson's opinion on page 23.

EMMINGER, OTMAR 1963 Per Jacobsson in Memoriam (1894–1963). *Weltwirtschaftliches Archiv* 91:5–14.

Montgomery, Arthur 1963 Per Jacobsson och IMF. *Ekonomisk revy* 20:345–353.

Sweden, Statens Krigsberedskapskomission 1918 *Betänkande: Part 1.* Stockholm: Statens Krigsberedskapskomission. → See especially pages 55–143.

## JAENSCH, ERICH

Erich Rudolf Jaensch, German psychologist, was born in Breslau in 1883 and died in Marburg an der Lahn in 1940. After studying physics and mathematics at Göttingen he became a student of G. E. Müller and Hermann Ebbinghaus, to whom he dedicated his first book (1909). In 1913 he was appointed to a chair of philosophy at Marburg and founded the Psychological Institute there.

It is characteristic of Jaensch that in all his work, beginning with his earliest (1909), he moved beyond the particular problem with which he had started to the applications of his results. In this first book, for example, he moved from psychophysical experiments in visual acuity and the like to the pathology of vision. From the simpler visual phenomena he proceeded to experiments on the perception of space (1911) and extended his general discussion into the fields of aesthetics and epistemology. His work on size and color constancies (1914), which later was integrated with his experiments on eidetic imagery (1925), was speculatively extended into a comprehensive theory of psychophysiological development, personality theory, and race psychology, as well as a theory of the structure and development of the world as perceived and known (1923).

In *Über den Aufbau der Wahrnehmungswelt* (1923) Jaensch showed, anticipating Wittgenstein, that the world of perceptual experience is not a product or precipitate of external stimuli alone, or of inner (psychological) contents alone; it is a product of both, in which inner and outer responses interpenetrate. Memory has a stratified structure of primordial and later contents, with both phylogenetic and ontogenetic roots, and these two kinds of content emerge as such in various states of the person (e.g., in dark-adapted vision and under the influence of drugs such as alcohol). A simple example of the differential interpenetration of outer and inner is to be found in tachistoscopic experiments on reading. At one extreme, a briefly exposed mutilated word is "seen" by the subject as a meaningful one, even to the extent that on successive exposures it is reported as being much clearer, "in quite black print," "standing out from the screen"; subjects at the other extreme read letter by letter in an analytic rather than a syn-

thetic way even when the word is long, meaningful, and well known to them. Similarly, in experiments on space orientation, the first type of subject is less "stimulus bound" than is the second (cf. the work of H. A. Witkin).

Outside central Europe, Jaensch is best known through his work on eidetic images (EI). A positive EI is a particularly strong visual afterimage, which has great clarity and which in its most pronounced form is reproduced in the colors of the stimulus object, often in very fine detail. Its frequency is highest in young children. Its opposite is the negative EI, which appears in complementary colors.

While common afterimages (AI) are due to primitive retinal functions and obey Emmert's law (their size is proportional to the distance at which they are projected), EI do not obey this law but tend toward size constancy. Jaensch thus supposed that EI arise from the functioning of centers that are phylogenetically earlier and that they play a part in forming the memory of objects. In memory, of course, objects are constant in size. The development of visual size constancy is therefore explained by supposing that the perceived visual object is a fusion of retinal image and memory "image," which in ontogenesis was first an EI. Similar but more complex evolutionary considerations are put forward to explain the origin of color constancy and the laws of color contrast and transformation.

Having at first classified EI as "sensations" and as not normal, Jaensch thus soon recognized that, instead, they have a conceptual character, that they are an extension or variant of what an adult calls an "idea" or a "memory image of an idea," that attention is necessary for their formation, and that they do occur normally in development.

The intraorganismic functions that generate visual experiences, memories, and ultimately all concepts are stratified. The strata are the products of ontogenetic developmental stages. In phylogenetic development ontogenesis is recapitulated, but different experiences create the unique individual as a variant of basic biopsychological types. The biopsychological typology (see below) in turn led Jaensch to a general theory of concept formation, of the different classes of anomalous color vision, of the ontogenesis of color and movement perception, and finally into a somewhat grandiose explanation of racial and cultural phenomena.

The two extreme types of EI, according to Jaensch and his school, are characteristic of two physical types: the B-type (from Basedow's disease, i.e., hyperthyroidism) and the T-type (since it has tetanoid stigmata). Different chemotherapeutic treatments are needed by these types if they are pathologically exaggerated. Jaensch's brother, a physician and physiologist, based the greater part of his clinical and pharmacological research on the B and T types (Walther Jaensch 1926; 1930).

Jaensch attempted to build a comprehensive theory of personality as well as a typology. His experimental and theoretical writings and those of his school are very extensive; the best coverage in a single volume is in *Grundformen menschlichen Seins* (1929). His typology tries to avoid the arbitrary categorization of clusters of individual differences and is based on general principles and a limited number of dimensions. In modern terms Jaensch could be classified as a cognitive theorist and an ego psychologist.

The main principles Jaensch called *Kohärenz* and *Integration*. By *Kohärenz* he meant the degree to which a person is anchored in and responds to the demands of reality. By *Integration* he meant the degree to which stimuli for one sensory modality or complex stimuli for one molar behavioral modality interact to modify or "integrate" the total response. For example, if a person with a high degree of integration has a depressing experience he will tend to see even a bright sunny day as literally gloomy, suffer other distortions of his pattern and space perceptions, and also show marked physiological effects.

This way of defining *Integration* implies that there are individual differences in the extent of invariance of the structures of perceptual and molar behavioral events. For some persons it is true to say that they exhibit invariant "traits"; for others, "traits" have degrees of invariance depending on context, stimulus, and intraorganismic state. The use here of the word "traits" highlights the degree of similarity between Jaensch's view of the dynamics of behavior and Raymond B. Cattell's view of "source traits." The difference between these theorists is that Jaensch based his theoretical and experimental work on a theory of the relation between the biological and psychological properties of the organism and its stimulus environment, not on a heuristic collection of data treated by the mathematical device of factor analysis.

Jaensch's integrate type is one who might be said to act as a dynamic whole, whose ego has low rigidity. He responds easily to stimuli (physical, verbal, and social), is imaginative and creative, prefers romantic art forms to classic, impressionism to expressionism, expressive movements to the standardized responses of organized games, literature to mathematics, speculative philosophy (e.g., Leibnitz and Plato) to analytic philosophy (e.g., Descartes and Aristotle). At lower levels, he pro-

duces more *W*-responses than *D* or *Dd* on the Rorschach, has high values for the Müller–Lyer illusion, and is percept-dominated in that his perception of objects is not strongly affected by changes of illumination, has low perseveration scores, adapts quickly, and in general is strongly sympathetico-tonic. His physical type tends to be slender, clear-skinned, with large "luminous" eyes (the extreme being the B-type, which has the stigmata of exophthalmic goiter). His imagery is predominantly visual and, like all his actions, strongly influenced by emotional states.

The polar opposite of this I-type is the *des*-integrate type. He prefers expressionistic or other bizarre forms of art, has jerky movements, is analytic instead of synthetic, is cold, detached, and so on. Between these extremes there are several classes of I-types, the two important ones being the "inwardly integrate" or Ii-type and the S-type (so labeled because one of his characteristics is a proneness to synesthesias). The Ii-type has less *Kohärenz* with objective reality than the I-type but has strongly integrated sentiment and value systems; he is the typical German idealistic thinker. The S-type tends to negative cynicism and to destructive skepticism, especially about social and value systems.

Jaensch speculated broadly about the place of these types in various civilizations and their frequencies in various climates. Thus, he thought that the primitive peoples of the Pacific must be integrates and that predominant in southern Europe were the $I_1$ and $I_2$ types, in northern Europe the Ii or inwardly integrate type, in France the S-type.

These unbridled generalizations on a totally insufficient statistical basis led him to support some of the theories of race current in Germany in the 1930–1940 era. Naturally, he regarded the Nordic Ii as the "best" type, while the dominance of the S-type among the Jews destined them for biological reasons to be the destroyers of idealism and *Volksgemeinschaft*. However, he did believe that education could and should play a formative role in assisting the development of children from their early state of labile responsiveness to a higher state of inward integration, and his educational theories would be well accepted in "progressive" schools, which pay attention to the whole child and try to get away from the excessive concentration on the particulate fragments of intellectualized syllabuses, analytic thinking, and passive ingestion.

His "functional" and phylogenetic approach to the study of personality is important for students of existentialist philosophy, as it tried to give existentialism an empirical foundation in the theory of personality and perception. Jaensch always cited the whole range of his work in visual perception and the synesthesias to show in what sense personality is an integration, not a conglomerate, of traits. His biopsychological theories are related to those of Hans Driesch, and much of his logical development of the concept of integration is pertinent to the work of some modern system theorists like Ludwig von Bertalanffy. Similarly, Gordon W. Allport's "functional autonomy" and Ernst Spranger's "styles of living" have affinities with many of Jaensch's concepts.

That Jaensch's work was not taken up by English-speaking psychologists is hardly surprising. It appeared when behaviorism was rapidly gathering strength, when S–R was the most widely accepted concept, when the idea of states of consciousness was rejected, and tendencies to indulge in philosophical "speculations" were firmly suppressed. But now that the nonstatistical work of Piaget is widely accepted and ego psychology is almost respectable, Jaensch's work may once again be studied after half a century of neglect. In one sense he was like present-day factorists, in that he made a large number of different experimental tests instead of merely reporting individual differences in this or that aspect. He was unlike factorists, however, in his continuing effort to reduce the multiplicity of human responses and conscious experiences to, say, three or four functions rather than an indefinitely increasing number of "factors"; above all, Jaensch differed from the factorists in trying to find "functions" that are firmly rooted in the biology of the organism without thereby becoming a reductionist.

O. A. OESER

[*Relevant articles are those on* DEVELOPMENTAL PSYCHOLOGY, *article on* A THEORY OF DEVELOPMENT; PERCEPTION, *articles on* PERCEPTUAL CONSTANCY *and* ILLUSIONS AND AFTEREFFECTS; PERSONALITY: CONTEMPORARY VIEWPOINTS; PROJECTIVE METHODS, *article on* THE RORSCHACH TEST; SYSTEMS ANALYSIS, *article on* PSYCHOLOGICAL SYSTEMS; TRAITS; VISION, *article on* COLOR VISION AND COLOR BLINDNESS.]

### WORKS BY JAENSCH

1909    Zur Analyse der Gesichtswahrnehmungen: Experimentell-psychologische Untersuchungen nebst Anwendungen auf die Pathologie des Sehens. *Zeitschrift für Psychologie* Supplement no. 4.
1911    Über die Wahrnehmung des Raumes: Eine experimentell-psychologische Untersuchung nebst Anwendung auf Ästhetik und Erkenntnislehre. *Zeitschrift für Psychologie* Supplement no. 6.
(1914) 1930    *Über Grundfragen der Farbenpsychologie: Zugleich ein Beitrag zur Theorie der Erfahrung.* Leipzig: Barth.
(1923) 1927–1931    *Über den Aufbau der Wahrnehmungswelt und die Grundlagen der menschlichen Erkenntnis.* 2 vols. 2d ed. Leipzig: Barth.
(1925) 1930    *Eidetic Imagery and Typological Methods of Investigation: Their Importance for the Psychology of Childhood, the Theory of Education, General Psychology, and the Psychophysiology of Human Personality.* New York: Harcourt. → First published in German.
1929    *Grundformen menschlichen Seins.* Berlin: Elsner.
1930a    *Studien zur Psychologie menschlicher Typen.* Leipzig: Barth.
1930b    Über den Aufbau des Bewusstseins. Part 1: Die Kohärenz mit der Aussenwelt in der Kindheit und die Kohärenzpetrefakte in der bleibenden Wahrnehmungsstruktur. *Zeitschrift für Psychologie* Supplement no. 16.
1933    *Neue Wege der Lichtbiologie unter funktionellem und ganzheitlichem Betrachtungsgesichtspunkt.* Leipzig: Barth.

### SUPPLEMENTARY BIBLIOGRAPHY

ANSCHÜTZ, GEORG 1953 *Psychologie.* Hamburg (Germany): Meiner.
JAENSCH, WALTHER 1926 *Grundzüge einer Physiologie und Klinik der psychophysischen Persönlichkeit.* Berlin: Springer.
JAENSCH, WALTHER 1930 Die Hautkapillarmikroskopie am Lebenden. Pages 865–940 in Emil Aberhalden (editor), *Handbuch der biologischen Arbeitsmethoden.* Section 9, part 3, no. 5. Berlin: Urban & Schwarzenberg.
KRUDEWIG, MARIA 1953 *Die Lehren von der visuellen Wahrnehmung und Vorstellung bei Erich Rudolf Jaensch und seinen Schülern.* Meisenheim am Glan (Germany): Hain.
WELLEK, ALBERT 1955 *Ganzheitspsychologie und Strukturtheorie.* Bern: Francke.

## JAMES, WILLIAM

William James (1842–1910), American philosopher and psychologist, secured a permanent place in the history of psychology with the publication of *The Principles of Psychology* (1890), a two-volume treatise that quickly became a basic text. His *Varieties of Religious Experience* (1902), a pioneering study of the psychology of religion, also became a classic. James possessed a vivacity of style that earned him a broad audience both in America and Europe. His outlook was pluralistic, and his remarkable openness to new experience led him to champion many an academically disreputable subject. More often than not, though, subsequent developments have justified his tolerance.

In his later years James devoted most of his attention to philosophy. His works of that period, which propound a pragmatic conception of truth, may at first seem of merely tangential interest to the social scientist. Yet, in fact, they provide an inchoate system for his earlier psychological writings. Near the end of his career James proposed the doctrine of radical empiricism, which contained a new point of view regarding the mind–body problem. Curiously, this often neglected philosophical theory, together with the pragmatic approach to meaning and truth, may eventually prove more important for social science than his text in psychology.

The household in which William James grew up contained three other exceptionally gifted individuals. Henry James, the father, produced a sizable corpus of writings on religious topics. Popularly regarded as an eccentric, he was a beloved friend of Ralph Waldo Emerson and Thomas Carlyle. William's brother, Henry, acquired fame as a novelist. His sister Alice, though, was perhaps the most talented member of the family; her literary contributions, unfortunately, were meager, for she suffered throughout her life from a particularly severe form of the neurasthenia that also afflicted her brothers.

Henry James the elder discouraged his sons from making any premature decisions regarding their vocations. The atmosphere of the household was broadly educative, although William James later complained of a lack of formal precollege schooling. Moreover, three times during his childhood he had the opportunity to travel for prolonged periods in Europe. He attended school and was tutored in England, France, Switzerland, and Germany.

At the age of 18, James decided to pursue a career in painting. He had painted since early childhood, and his skill and interest had long been recognized. The results of experimental lessons with a professional artist, however, were unambiguous: he soon realized not only that his talent was less than his standards demanded but also that his desire to paint was far from insatiable. Having rejected a career as an artist, he seldom looked back. His subsequent work always bore the marks of acute sensory perception and aesthetic imagination, but he consistently subordinated his artistic flair to his moral and metaphysical concerns.

James's university education was marked by doubts about his eventual career and interruptions caused by poor health. When he entered Harvard in 1861, he had decided to become a scientist. After three years as an undergraduate, he convinced himself that he was best suited, not for science in any strict sense, but rather for the broad scientific concerns of medicine. Doubts continued to assail him, however, during his first term at Harvard Medical School.

In March 1865, James interrupted his studies to embark on a field trip to Brazil. Louis Agassiz, the great biologist, led the expedition, and for one year the group investigated the flora and fauna of South America. Returning to Boston in March 1866, James immediately resumed his work at medical school, but the following spring he was again compelled by physical illness and depression to leave Harvard. He departed for Europe and remained there 19 months, eventually receiving his M.D. degree in the spring of 1869.

James's poor health was to plague him for nearly six years. His condition made prolonged work in a laboratory unendurable. Having become interested in experimental physiology, he selected Germany as the place for convalescing. Physically, James "took the cure" at the baths of Teplitz. Academically, he sought it in Dresden, Berlin, and Heidelberg, where he studied under Emil Du Bois-Reymond and Hermann von Helmholtz. His spiritual malaise was alleviated at moments by "a sort of inward serenity and joy in living, derived from reading Goethe and Schiller" (quoted in Perry 1935, vol. 1, p. 273).

The years from 1869 to 1872 were to be his worst. A sense of moral impotence constantly tormented him; thoughts of suicide never wholly departed from his mind. On February 1, 1870, James recorded in his diary: "Today I about touched bottom, and perceive plainly that I must face the choice with open eyes: shall I *frankly* throw the moral business overboard, as one unsuited to my innate aptitudes, or shall I follow it, and it alone, making everything else merely stuff for it? I will give the latter alternative a fair trial. Who knows but the moral interest may become developed" (Perry 1935, vol. 1, p. 322). One of James's most troubling problems was that of determinism and free will. On April 30, 1870, he recorded:

I think that yesterday was a crisis in my life. I finished the first part of [Charles Bernard] Renouvier's second *Essais* and see no reason why his definition of free will —"the sustaining of a thought *because I choose to* when I might have other thoughts"—need be the definition of an illusion. At any rate, I will assume for the present—until next year—that it is no illusion. My first act of free will shall be to believe in free will. (Perry 1935, vol. 1, p. 323)

In Renouvier, James had found comfort, if not an immediate cure for his doubts. Slowly he regained enthusiasm for life in general and for intellectual life in particular. Two events of the 1870s contributed greatly to his recovery. James started teaching at Harvard, and in 1878 he married Alice Howe Gibbens. He viewed the offer of employment from Harvard as a "godsend," welcoming the stabilizing influence of a regular vocation. His first appointment was to an instructorship in physiology, but from the outset he refused to treat physiology, psychology, and philosophy as distinct and separate disciplines. In his lectures, as in his writings, he sought a synthesis of insights and factual contributions from each of the fields.

By correspondence with his European contemporaries James enhanced the intellectual reputation of the United States even more, perhaps, than through his widely acclaimed lectures in Britain and on the Continent. Such men as Hawthorne, Poe, and Emerson had, of course, attracted the attention of Europeans in an earlier era. But no American developed the close ties with English and Continental thinkers that James's articulateness and extraordinary friendliness so naturally created. As a mere sample of his friends one might mention Bergson, Ernst Mach, Renouvier, F. H. Bradley, Giovanni Papini, Kipling, Henry Sidgwick, Herbert Spencer, and Carl Stumpf. James's *Letters* have, accordingly, received considerable attention as a guide to the era. At Harvard, James influenced many of his students and younger colleagues. Prominent among this group were Josiah Royce, Gertrude Stein, George Santayana, Hugo Münsterberg, and G. Stanley Hall.

**Contributions to psychology.**    James began the first chapters of *The Principles of Psychology* during the weeks following his marriage. In 1890, 12 years later, he finally completed the book. The work was both a grand summation of previous developments and a portent of the paths psychology would take in the twentieth century. James anticipated most of the major psychological movements of the succeeding seventy years; in many instances a direct line of influence is traceable. He did not achieve this remarkable breadth of coverage without some sacrifice. Not all of his ideas are operationally verifiable, nor did he present them in a rigorously systematic fashion.

*Functional psychology.*    In its basic assumptions concerning the mind *The Principles* opposed the elementalism of the then current German psychology. James decried the practice of chopping consciousness into "single ideas" with which the investigator could not hope to have immediate acquaintance. Chains, trains, or other compoundings of bits seemed to him inadequate as models. Consciousness is nothing jointed, he argued; it flows. Thus, he preferred such metaphors as "river" or "stream." Every conscious state, he claimed, is a function of the entire psychophysical context. Mind is cumulative, and experience produces alterations in its structure. The psychophysical context must necessarily change over time, precluding exact recurrence. This denial that a mental state can ever recur in a form identical with a past state anticipated one thesis of gestalt psychology.

For James selectivity was an essential characteristic of consciousness. Only a small portion of the potentially effective stimuli enter into a person's awareness [see ATTENTION]. James argued that the choice is made purposively and that the criterion of choice is the relevance of the stimuli to various goals. This concept of relevance is a manifestation of James's functionalism, anticipating the Würzburg theory of set and determining tendency. It was Darwin's profound influence upon James that made the utility of consciousness a fundamental issue in his work. James went so far as to speculate that consciousness evolved to regulate a nervous system that had grown too complex to govern itself.

To the functionalist, psychology is the study of mental operations rather than of mental elements. Habit for James was the structural unit of mental life. The acquisition of a habit consisted in developing a new pathway of discharge in the brain [see LEARNING, *article on* NEUROPHYSIOLOGICAL ASPECTS]. James considered habit the great conservative agent of society. He felt that most personal habits, such as vocalization, pronunciation, gesture, and gait, are fixed by the age of 20. The period between 20 and 30, on the other hand, appeared to him as the critical one for the formation of intellectual and professional habits.

James recognized the implications of his theory for the teaching profession. His *Talks to Teachers on Psychology* (1899) exerted a strong influence upon pedagogical thinkers and contributed to the rapid development of educational psychology in the United States. James emphasized interest and action; he regarded the child as a behaving organism for whom the major task is the formation of sound habits. Transfer of training in memorizing struck him as unlikely. Consequently, he opposed the justification of mechanical drill in one field as a technique for improving retentiveness in another. This rejection of rote memorization had a sharp impact upon American educators. But perhaps more important, as a precursor of the progressive movement, was James's underlying attitude. He sought to persuade teachers to "conceive, and, if possible, reproduce sympathetically in their imagination, the mental life of their pupil as the sort of active unity which he himself feels it to be" ([1899] 1946, p. x).

*Theory of emotions.*    Perhaps the most famous of James's specific doctrines is the James–Lange theory of the emotions. Basically, it asserts that an emotion results from the feeling of certain bodily changes that themselves follow directly from a given stimulus [see EMOTION]. This, of course, is an inversion of the common-sense explanation; James argued that we feel sorry because we cry and afraid because we tremble, not vice versa. The nervous system makes various reflex adjustments to emotional stimuli, leading automatically to bodily changes. Our perception of these changes, mostly in the skeletal muscles and viscera, we call an emotion. This theory was greeted with heavy criticism at its initial presentation, and James modified it several times. Although it has been discredited in its extreme form, the theory served to generate much useful research.

The theory is important historically for its behavior-based approach to the emotions: it makes awareness depend upon response. With this doctrine, as elsewhere in *The Principles*, James achieved a bold anticipation of behaviorism. And, like his behavioristic successors, he recognized the value of controlled, replicable experiments. James himself, however, did not seek detailed experimental corroboration for his theories. Although he was instrumental in establishing one of the first psychology laboratories in the world, he quickly became bored with experimental work. Eventually he recruited Münsterberg from Germany to supervise experimentation at Harvard.

*Theory of the self.* James's chapter on the self in *The Principles* stands as one of the classics of psychological literature. In depth, breadth, and insight it has few rivals. For several decades after its publication, psychologists took little interest in the self; and although some commentators have attributed the avoidance to the prevailing behavioristic temper, others speculate that no one felt that he could add to the Jamesian treatment of the concept. James began with the distinction between the *I*, the self as knower or pure ego, and the *Me*, the self as known or empirical ego. In its widest possible sense, he claimed, a man's *Me* is the sum total of everything that he can designate *mine*. The *material Me* accordingly includes the body, the attire, the immediate family, and property [see IDENTITY, PSYCHOSOCIAL; SELF CONCEPT].

The second constituent of the *Me*, the *social Me*, anticipates modern role theory and, in a sense, the theory of object relations. "Properly speaking," James wrote, *"a man has as many social selves as there are individuals who recognize him* and carry an image of him in their mind" ([1890] 1962, vol. 1, p. 294). He added, however, that since these various individuals can be divided into groups, a man may be said to have as many different social selves as there are distinct groups of people about whose opinion he cares. James's conception of the differ-

ent social selves involved in an individual's interpersonal relations led him to emphasize the conflicts among the individual's social selves. In contemporary social science this individual-oriented model of conflict is useful as a counterweight to sociological conceptions of role and role conflict.

The third constituent of the *Me*, the *spiritual Me*, designates the entire collection of a person's states of consciousness and psychic faculties. James distinguished between this aggregation, which he took as an array of concrete entities, and the complementary self as *I*. The *I* functions as an agent—a knower rather than merely a collection of things known. The significance of this distinction becomes fully clear, however, only in the context of James's philosophical work.

**Philosophical work.**    When James took over the concept of pragmatism and made it famous, he scrupulously gave credit to his friend Charles Sanders Peirce for the notion [see PEIRCE]. The term "pragmatism" derives from the Greek word for action. In 1878, Peirce had introduced the word into philosophy in an article entitled "How to Make Our Ideas Clear." In discussing pragmatism, he had argued that beliefs are really rules for acting and that the meaning of having a belief can only be discovered by assessing its consequences for action. Yet Peirce felt that James had so greatly changed the term's meaning that he soon rechristened his own philosophical method "pragmaticism." This word, he remarked, is so ugly that it should be eternally safe from "kidnappers."

Differences of temperament among philosophers greatly interested James. Indeed, he viewed pragmatism as a method for mediating between contradictory philosophical styles. The history of philosophy, he believed, can be seen as an interminable battle between the "tender-minded" and the "tough-minded" types of thinker. Of the numerous Jamesian dichotomies, this is the most famous ([1907] 1949, pp. 9–20):

| Tender-minded | Tough-minded |
|---|---|
| Rationalistic | Empiricist |
| Intellectualistic | Sensationalistic |
| Idealistic | Materialistic |
| Optimistic | Pessimistic |
| Religious | Irreligious |
| Free-willist | Fatalistic |
| Monistic | Pluralistic |
| Dogmatic | Skeptical |

To James, a man's attitudes in philosophy owe their origin to the balance in him of "two cravings." The first is the sentiment of rationality, the passion for simplicity and labor-saving theoretical formulations (tender-mindedness). The second, called the passion for distinguishing, stresses loyalty to the facts of perception and to principles of clarity and precision (tough-mindedness). James asserted that no system of philosophy can have a chance of universal acceptance if it neglects either craving or if it greatly subordinates one to the other. By referring to sentiment, James brought the individual philosopher's needs into the field of criticism. Like the psychoanalyst, he demanded that an individual's behavior and beliefs be scrutinized within the context of his total life history.

James insisted that we specify what concrete difference the truth or falsity of an idea will make to anyone's life. This theory of truth is contextualist: the final test of an idea's validity is its coherence with the rest of one's experience. The rationalist asserts that ideas are true if they agree with the facts. James accepted this proposition too, but he questioned its fruitfulness. What are the "facts," he asked, with which the ideas agree? Does not our conception of what constitutes the facts in a situation change as our understanding increases? James vigorously condemned both the assumption that truth is an inert, static relation between fact and idea and the doctrine that true ideas merely copy reality. "Truth *happens* to an idea," he said ([1907] 1949, p. 201). Validation is a process—a gradual elucidation of interrelationships and consequences. To the extent that these consequences are desirable, or useful, or good, the idea may be considered valid.

By baldly inserting words like "good" and "desirable" into his descriptions, James sought to stress that true ideas serve as indispensable instruments for effective action. Indeed, he remarked that the quest for truth could hardly stand in such high esteem if truth were not worthwhile, desirable—good for something. A belief is "true" if its consequences—taken in their totality—are good, and the belief must therefore be judged in its total context, as coherent or incoherent with the rest of reality. Of course, James recognized the practical impossibility of assessing all the consequences of a belief; that is why for him verification seemed necessarily a perpetually ongoing process.

James fought against the acceptance of custom and established routine when he felt it restricted the possibilities for satisfaction—for value—in direct personal experience. His theory of truth is, in the widest sense, moral, for it rests ultimately on the proposition that the only legitimate purpose of belief and action is the maximization of good. Thus, the pragmatic principle of verification seemed to James a commandment requiring total commitment and not, as some critics have alleged, a license for selfishness and opportunism.

*Radical empiricism.*   Toward the end of his life James developed the doctrine of "radical empiricism." He came to regard it as more fundamental and more important than pragmatism. Although he viewed radical empiricism as logically independent of pragmatism, he considered the establishment of a pragmatic theory of truth to be of prime importance for achieving the general acceptance of radical empiricism.

It is for its theory of relations that James's doctrine receives the title "radical": relations have the same status in his scheme of reality as do entities. An on-top-of relation (e.g., of a book to a table) is as real for James as the book and the table. With his theory of relations, James argued, the undue stress upon disjunction in classical empiricism has been corrected. Rationalists, of course, have traditionally employed trans-experiential concepts to provide the unity and coherence that the empiricist world picture lacked. James adamantly rejected such concepts, claiming that they permit the dogmatic affirmation of all manner of nonsense. In contrast to both rationalism and empiricism, radical empiricism represents the world as a collection, some parts of which are disjunctively and others conjunctively related. This hanging together, or concatenated union, bears little resemblance to the "each in all and all in each" form of union characteristic of monistic rationalism.

James's radical-empiricist orientation enabled him to approach the mind–body problem in an original and highly suggestive way. The question "Does 'Consciousness' Exist?" (1904), the title of one of his essays, receives an ironic, negative answer. James really was denying that the word "consciousness" stands for an entity. As his initial supposition, James stated simply that there is one primal material in the world, of which everything is composed. He called it "pure experience." If this is granted, one can readily explain knowing as "a particular sort of relation towards one another into which portions of pure experience may enter" ([1904] 1912, p. 4). One of the terms of the relation becomes the knower, while the other becomes the object known. Thus, this scheme of presentation rejects the doctrine of the ultimate duality of experience. In one context a portion of pure experience plays the part of the knower. But with another set of associates it can act as a thing known, an objective content.

The present, as an instantaneous field, constituted "pure experience" for James. "It is only virtually or potentially either object or subject as yet. For the time being, it is plain, unqualified actuality, or existence, a simple *that*" ([1904] 1912, p. 23). For persons who argue that they apprehend the immediate present as "consciousness" (the experience of distinct self) and who claim to feel the free flow of thought within them as sharply distinct from objective reality, James had a surprising answer. He declared that the sense of such a person's thinking, when carefully examined, turned out to consist chiefly of the perception of the regular rhythm of his breathing. James implied that the self is therefore not an ultimate given but a secondary construct.

In the course of his argument James consigned many respectable terms such as "mental," "physical," "subjective," "objective," and even "self," to a derived or secondary status. But a place must be found for such entities elsewhere in a system. It is here that James the pragmatist furnished great aid to James the radical empiricist. For pragmatists, the "reality" of secondary concepts depends upon their capacity to satisfy—to put us on more satisfactory terms with our immediate experience. Unless an "abstraction" fulfills this intensely personal function it is not worthy of acceptance. Each individual by a process of continuous selection and rejection builds from the "blooming, buzzing confusion" of immediate experience his own distinctive *Weltanschauung*. The criterion of its reality is its total utility for his life.

**"Varieties of Religious Experience."**   Characteristically individualistic in his religious interests, James disregarded institutions and focused his attention upon personal religious experience [*see* RELIGION]. His major work in this field was *The Varieties of Religious Experience*, originally delivered as the Gifford lectures of 1901–1902 at Edinburgh. In the introduction to *The Varieties* he admitted that the incidence of abnormal psychical conditions among religious leaders had been high. He even granted that the "pathological" aspects of their personalities had contributed greatly to their prestige and authority. Nonetheless, James insisted that the prevalence of such traits and tendencies does not constitute a refutation of their teachings: "By their fruits ye shall know them, not by their roots."

Just as James divided thinkers into the tough-minded and the tender-minded, he categorized religious believers as healthy-minded or sick-souled. Sick-souledness, he wrote, appears to encompass a wider range of experience.

The method of averting one's attention from evil, and living simply in the light of good is splendid as long as it will work. . . . It breaks down impotently as soon as melancholy comes; and even though one be quite free from melancholy one's self, there is no doubt that healthy-mindedness is inadequate as a philosophical

doctrine, because the evil facts which it refuses positively to account for are a genuine portion of reality; and they may after all be the best key to life's significance, and possibly the only openers of our eyes to the deepest levels of truth.   ([1902] 1963, p. 163).

Regeneration by the conversion experience, James felt, is what enables the sick-souled individual to escape from the dark night of his soul. The theory of subconscious mental processes, which had recently been proposed, appealed to him as highly useful for understanding the sudden shifts in character that often attend conversion experiences. A person with a strongly developed, intrusive subliminal region, James argued, will have a proclivity for hallucinations, obsessive ideas, and automatic actions that seem unaccountable by ordinary experience. As illustrations he cited the phenomenon of posthypnotic suggestion and the findings of Freud, Pierre Janet, and Morton Prince on hysteria. Although James regarded this research as marking the most important advance in psychology during his lifetime, he refused to employ it merely to "explain away" conversion.

From personal experimentation with nitrous oxide James received what he emphatically believed to be a form of mystical experience. Trances and other exceptional mental states occupied his attention for many years. The so-called rational consciousness, he felt, is only one special kind of consciousness, "whilst all about it, parted from it by the filmiest of screens, there lie potential forms of consciousness entirely different" ([1902] 1963, p. 388). Though one can live an entire lifetime without knowing about these forms, James wrote, the proper drug or other stimulus will promptly make them accessible.

For James a basic concern was always the *whole* personality in its functional relationship with its environment. In *The Varieties* he therefore presented many individual case histories. Nothing bears truer witness to his compassion and tolerance than these skillfully rendered descriptions. And nothing provides a better indication of the ultimate aim of his inquiry: transcendence of one's own limitations through familiarity with the entire spectrum of human experience.

**Views on war.**   James's now famous essay "The Moral Equivalent of War" (1910) gained the approval of pacifists and military men alike. In this widely circulated article he did not hesitate to praise the martial ideals of hardihood, daring, and discipline. But he deplored the brutality of war and strove to develop methods for sublimating the urge to fight. One proposal recommended the conscription of youth for work on land development and reclamation projects.

**Interest in psychical research.**    Probably James's most persistent "cause" was his effort to make psychic research scientifically respectable [*see* PARA-PSYCHOLOGY]. He served as president of the Society for Psychical Research for two years and maintained his membership from 1884 until his death. Despite a remarkable ability to scent out quacks and frauds, James never lost his conviction that some of the bizarre phenomena were genuine. Scientists who rejected the data because they failed to conform to prevailing psychological theories lost his professional respect. James's own commitments to empiricism would not permit the discounting of raw data simply to preserve established ideas. Moreover, research—including studies of faith healers—appealed to him on humanitarian grounds. Every possible technique for alleviating suffering deserved investigation, he felt, no matter how unscientific or cranky the claimant.

It is James's perpetual concern with improving the lot of the individual human being that makes him so apt a symbol of American social thought in his era. He denounced not only the attempts of idealists to explain away evil but also the gloomy pessimism of such philosophers as Schopenhauer. For James, meliorism was the only tenable position. Too sensitive not to be acutely aware of social injustice, he nevertheless remained ever uncynical, convinced that sustained, intelligent effort would produce improvement.

As James's work in psychology cleared the way for behaviorism, so his pragmatism, interpreted in a narrow manner and applied to scientific methodology, facilitated the emergence of logical positivism and operationalism. Hard-headed respect for facts and suspicion of rationalistic theorizing in the grand style unquestionably represent one strain in his thought. But he was a nonconformist and clever strategist. Thus, in an era that has witnessed the triumph of rigorous experimentalism, James would surely have directed his polemical skills toward other goals. Individualism, pluralism, and the importance of immediate experience would undoubtedly have received prime stress.

James's high tolerance for ambiguity and his desire to mediate between intellectually opposing temperaments have led to charges of contradiction and betrayal by both sides. Yet constant striving for balance struck him as necessary for the achievement of his fundamental objective: the improvement of the quality of experience of the individual human being. This paramount aim, this human-istic orientation, determined his thinking in metaphysics as well as in religion, in epistemology as on social problems. James was above all a humanitarian and only secondarily a psychologist, philosopher, and gifted man of letters.

WILLIAM D. PHELAN, JR.

[*See also* EMOTION; IDENTITY, PSYCHOSOCIAL; RELIGION; SELF CONCEPT. *Other relevant material may be found in the biographies of* COHEN; COOLEY; DEWEY; HALL; HOLT; JANET; MEYER; MÜNSTERBERG; PARK; TITCHENER.]

### WORKS BY JAMES

(1879–1907) 1948    *Essays in Pragmatism*. Edited with an introduction by Alburey Castell. New York: Hafner. → A paperback edition of several of James's most important essays.

(1884–1906) 1912    *Essays in Radical Empiricism*. New York: Longmans.

(1890) 1962    *The Principles of Psychology*. 2 vols. New York: Smith.

(1892) 1948    *Psychology: The Briefer Course*. Cleveland, Ohio: World. → Gordon Allport edited a paperback version, published in 1961 by Harper.

(1896–1910) 1911    *Memories and Studies*. New York: Longmans.

(1897) 1956    *The Will to Believe, and Other Essays in Popular Philosophy and Human Immortality*. New York: Dover.

(1899) 1946    *Talks to Teachers on Psychology*. New edition with an introduction by John Dewey and William H. Kilpatrick. New York: Holt.

(1902) 1963    *The Varieties of Religious Experience: A Study of Human Nature*. Enlarged edition with appendices and introduction by Joseph Ratner. New Hyde Park, N.Y.: University Books.

(1904) 1912    Does "Consciousness" Exist? Pages 1–38 in William James, *Essays in Radical Empiricism*. New York: Longmans.

(1907) 1949    *Pragmatism: A New Name for Some Old Ways of Thinking*. New York: Longmans. → A paperback edition was published in 1963 by Washington Square Press.

1909    *A Pluralistic Universe*. New York: Longmans.

(1910) 1911    The Moral Equivalent of War. Pages 265–296 in William James, *Memories and Studies*. New York: Longmans.

(1911) 1928    *Some Problems of Philosophy: A Beginning of an Introduction to Philosophy*. New York: Longmans.

*The Letters of William James*. Edited by Henry James, Jr. 2 vols. Boston: Atlantic Monthly Press, 1920.

*William James on Psychical Research*. Compiled and edited by Gardner Murphy and Robert O. Ballou. New York: Viking, 1960.

### WORKS ABOUT JAMES

JAMES, HENRY 1913    *A Small Boy and Others*. New York: Scribner.

JAMES, HENRY 1914    *Notes of a Son and Brother*. New York: Scribner.

PERRY, RALPH B. 1920    *Annotated Bibliography of the Writings of William James*. New York: Longmans.

PERRY, RALPH B. 1935    *The Thought and Character of William James, as Revealed in Unpublished Correspondence and Notes, Together With His Published*

*Writings.* 2 vols. Boston: Little. → Volume 1: *Inheritance and Vocation.* Volume 2: *Philosophy and Psychology.*

SUPPLEMENTARY BIBLIOGRAPHY

BORING, EDWIN G. (1929) 1950 *A History of Experimental Psychology.* 2d ed. New York: Appleton.

DEWEY, JOHN 1934 *Art as Experience.* New York: Putnam. → A paperback edition was published in 1959.

MOORE, E. C. 1961 *American Pragmatism: Peirce, James, and Dewey.* New York: Columbia Univ. Press.

PEIRCE, CHARLES S. (1878) 1955 *How to Make Our Ideas Clear.* Pages 23–41 in Charles S. Peirce, *Philosophical Writings of Peirce.* Selected and edited with an introduction by Justus Buchler. New York: Dover.

WIENER, PHILIP P. 1949 *Evolution and the Founders of Pragmatism.* Cambridge, Mass.: Harvard Univ. Press.

# JANET, PIERRE

Pierre Marie Felix Janet (1859–1947), French physician and psychologist, did much to bring about the close relation that exists in France between the medical and the academic study of mental disorders. He advanced clinical psychology by insisting that a knowledge of academic psychology is indispensable to an understanding of the individual.

Janet studied in both the faculty of letters and the faculty of medicine at the University of Paris. He soon became interested in phenomena related to hypnosis and clairvoyance. This interest brought him into direct contact with Charcot, whose writings he studied, along with those of Hippolyte Bernheim. Janet felt that both Charcot and Bernheim minimized the importance of psychological factors in psychoneurotic manifestations, and he began what was to be a lifelong study of the etiology of the neuroses.

While he was still studying for his doctoral degrees, Janet was invited by Charcot to become director of the psychological laboratory at the Salpêtrière, the largest Parisian mental hospital. In 1889 he received his doctorate in the faculty of letters with a thesis on the psychology of automatic activities (1889), and by 1892 he produced a dissertation for the doctorate in medicine, based on his work at the Salpêtrière.

At the same time that Janet held his post at the psychological laboratory of the Salpêtrière, he taught at the Sorbonne from 1895 to 1902 and then succeeded Théodule Ribot in the chair of psychology at the Collège de France; he continued in this chair until his retirement in 1936. With Georges Dumas, Janet founded the *Journal de psychologie normale et pathologique* in 1904 and edited it until 1937.

The study that served as his dissertation, *The Mental State of Hystericals* (1892–1894), represents Janet's attempt to bring order and system into the classification of the various forms of hysteria and to relate the symptoms exhibited by hysterical patients to then current psychological theories. He became convinced that hysteria is only apparently physical in nature, while in reality it reflects a host of psychological conditions. He described hysteria as a form of mental disintegration, induced by cerebral exhaustion. In hysteria there is a weakening of psychological synthesis, exhibited particularly in a contraction of the field of consciousness and a complete and permanent division of the personality. Hysteria, in general, is deteriorative in nature, and terms such as "degenerative" and "stigmata" are, in Janet's view, applicable in connection with the illness. For the rest of his life Janet's thinking about hysteria remained basically set in the pattern of this early study. Charcot, in a preface to the book, accepted Janet's contention that hysteria is essentially mental and approved of the attempt to relate psychology and medicine more closely.

Early in his career Janet realized that the various stages of hypnosis and the symptoms of hysteria are both products of suggestion. He understood more fully than had Charcot just how important suggestion is in producing the appearance of hysterical symptoms. The fact that hysteria and hypnosis are caused by suggestion does not mean, however, that they are not genuine and important subjects for study. Although hysteria almost disappeared as a disease entity during Janet's lifetime, he attributed this to the fact that patients he would have called hysterics were being designated by other names.

Over the years Janet investigated not only hysteria but also other forms of neuroses, such as phobias and obsessions, which he grouped under the inclusive name of psychasthenia. He saw different patterns as pervasive in normal and abnormal mental life. Normal mental life is a flux of sensations, images, and ideas, cohering in an integrated stream of consciousness; abnormal mental life results from the dissociation of this stream, which in extreme cases splits into two or more streams. In the normal person, integration is achieved; in the neurotic, it is imperfect. Psychic energy and its diminution or depletion was his guiding concept:

Diminution of force and modification of the important relationship between tension and psychological force are becoming elements of vast importance to psychological analysis. . . . One of the most important studies of *l'analyse psychologique* will be the appreciation of the degree of psychic energy of an individual and the extent of his weakness; we know nothing of the nature of this psychic energy, but we must study its manifestations and succeed in measuring it as the physicist measures an electric current without understanding the nature of it.    (1930a, p. 372)

In the 1920s behavioral psychology became predominant. Janet did much to further European behavioristic views, referring to psychology as the science of conduct. He held that every discriminable psychological event is also a discriminable response. But he felt that within a behavioral system a place must and can be found for consciousness and described it as a form of specialized conduct expressed in terms of action. Even after Janet began to write the psychology of conduct, he continued to think in terms of energy and tension. Instead of judging the quantity of energy by assumed mentalistic (psychic) and physical interactions, he judged the patient's energy by the speed, strength, and duration of his actions. If energy is so depleted that actions charged with high tension cannot be performed, mental disorder results.

Janet's approach to psychotherapy was always an eclectic one. In *Psychological Healing* (1919), he advocated a great variety of methods, among them suggestion, hypnosis, rest, confession, education, and moral guidance. When in his "L'analyse psychologique" (1930a) he developed a diagnostic tool for the clinical psychologist—an eclectic case history establishing an individual's unique characteristics—he explicitly made further development of that tool dependent on necessarily unknown but expected advances in both medicine and psychology.

In the early 1900s Janet's work was quite well known in the United States. He lectured at the Harvard Medical School in 1906 and published his lectures the following year as *The Major Symptoms of Hysteria* (1907). The book did much to bring Janet to the attention of American psychologists and psychiatrists. William James' writings in psychology show his awareness of Janet's work, and Morton Prince, who in 1927 founded the Harvard Psychological Clinic for the study of abnormal and dynamic psychology, called Janet's work epoch-making (1914, p. 157). Through his influence on such men as Prince, Janet fostered the union of academic psychology and medical science.

Janet's popularity in the United States waned considerably in the 1920s. Psychologists and psychiatrists were attracted by Watsonian behaviorism and Freudian psychoanalysis respectively. Freud himself disparaged Janet's work, and his followers reacted accordingly.

Many factors contributed to the strained relations between Freud and Janet. Janet considered psychoanalysis to be only one form of treatment, namely, treatment by "mental liquidation," or the dissociation of traumatic memories. He offended Freud by commenting that the term "unconscious" is suitable enough as a metaphor but not as designating an implied entity. Janet further alienated Freud by claiming that psychoanalysis arose directly from Charcot's work and his own (1919). Not only did he claim priority, but he deprecated certain aspects of psychoanalysis: thus, he considered free association "somewhat simple-minded" ([1919] 1925, vol. 1, p. 603) on the grounds that the patient knows he is under observation, and he advised instead watching a patient who does not know he is being observed. In general, because Janet was an eclectic, he could not or would not understand that psychoanalysis constitutes a coherent system of analysis of the personality.

For his part, Freud considered Janet's work to be in an area similar to his own but carried on at a nondynamic, superficial level and without proper regard for the etiological significance of sexual factors. Freud (1910) acknowledged the influence of Charcot's work on hysteria and traumatic memories but resented Janet's wider claims. Janet, an acute and original psychologist, lived to see medical psychology move in an alien direction, as his views were overshadowed by those of Freud.

ROBERT I. WATSON

[*Other relevant material may be found in* CLINICAL PSYCHOLOGY; HYPNOSIS; HYSTERIA; SUGGESTION; *and in the biographies of* CHARCOT; FREUD; JAMES.]

### WORKS BY JANET

(1889) 1930  *L'automatisme psychologique: Essai de psychologie expérimentale sur les formes inférieures de l'activité humaine.* 10th ed. Paris: Alcan.

(1892–1894) 1911  *The Mental State of Hystericals: A Study of Mental Stigmata and Mental Accidents.* With a preface by J. M. Charcot. London and New York: Putnam. → First published in French.

(1903) 1919  JANET, PIERRE; and RAYMOND, FULGENCE *Les obsessions et la psychasthénie.* 2 vols. 3d ed. Paris: Alcan.

(1907) 1920  *The Major Symptoms of Hysteria: Fifteen Lectures Given in the Medical School of Harvard University.* 2d ed. New York: Macmillan.

(1919) 1925  *Psychological Healing: A Historical and Clinical Study.* 2 vols. London: Allen & Unwin; New York: Macmillan. → First published in French in three volumes.

1923  *La médecine psychologique.* Paris: Flammarion.

1930a  *L'analyse psychologique.* Pages 369–373 in *Psychologies of 1930.* Worcester, Mass.: Clark Univ. Press.

1930b  *Autobiography.* Volume 1, pages 123–133 in Carl Murchison (editor), *A History of Psychology in Autobiography.* Worcester, Mass.: Clark Univ. Press.

SUPPLEMENTARY BIBLIOGRAPHY

BAILEY, PERCIVAL 1956 Janet and Freud. A.M.A. Archives of Neurology and Psychiatry 76:76–89.

FREUD, SIGMUND (1910) 1957 Five Lectures on Psychoanalysis. Volume 11, pages 1–56 in The Standard Edition of the Complete Psychological Works of Sigmund Freud. London: Hogarth. → First published as Über Psychoanalyse.

PRINCE, MORTON (1914) 1921 The Unconscious: The Fundamentals of Human Personality, Normal and Abnormal. 2d ed. New York: Macmillan.

SCHWARTZ, LEONHARD 1951 Die Neurosen und die dynamische Psychologie von Pierre Janet. Basel: Schwabe.

# JAPANESE SOCIETY

Japan is the most important, if not the only, example of a non-Western country that has unmistakably entered the category of "modern industrial society." This development has taken place under cultural and historical conditions completely different from those of the "Judeo–Christian" West; thus, for the comparative social scientist, understanding Japan's development poses fundamental and far-reaching questions and explains at least a part of the country's continuing fascination. Are the characteristics of industrial society essentially "culture-bound," so that their extension to non-Western areas is to be explained primarily in terms of "diffusion" or "acculturation"? Or do they result from the "imperatives" of industrial society at various levels of integration, so that they must be seen primarily as points on developmental continua, such as universalism–particularism, diffuseness–specificity, ascription–achievement, and so forth? A related problem that arises is whether "modern industrial society" will eventually become a single societal type, in which national differences are reduced to little more than folkloric marginalia, or whether the terms "American," "French," or "Japanese" will have distinctive meaning even though each be attached to the phrase "industrial society."

However these questions are to be ultimately phrased as research topics, Japan will continue to remain important as a test case of what is distinctive and what is nondistinctive, what is critical and what is noncritical in the process of "development" and "modernization." What is the structure of "readiness" for modern development? What factors facilitate or impede development? Are they cultural—favorable or unfavorable cultural elements, such as individualism, achievement-orientation, secularization, capacity for cooperative action, entrepreneurial outlook, etc.; or are they structural—by-products of the particular form, stage, and degree of integration of the given social structure?

Japan, setting out after the Meiji restoration in 1868 on a path leading toward modernization, turned out to be quick, sure-footed, and steady where so many other countries have wobbled. Historians, social scientists, and economists have naturally attempted to understand where the difference lies. This concern has by now generated a considerable literature, particularly on the comparison between Japan and China, which has helped to clarify many of the critical factors involved in modern development.

## Nation building

For the student of comparative modern development one of the most important conclusions that emerges from these many studies is the significance of national unity as a precondition for success. With respect to this criterion, Japan's preparatory "nation building," a problem that continues to trouble most of the developing nations, was already substantially achieved by 1868. In contrast to other newly emergent states, Japan was a compact and contiguous geographical area, with oceanic borders clearly defined and virtually unchallenged. There were, to be sure, marginal problems with the Russians in the north and with the Chinese over the Ryūkyū Islands, but these never challenged the territorial core, and later they proved to be quite tractable.

**Race.** Within the core geographical area of Japan there were no ethnic, linguistic, religious, or cultural divisions having an organizational or territorial base. Fifteen hundred years before 1868 the islands of Japan had been inhabited by tribes, groups, and clans of diverse ethnic origins. We know from archeological findings, legends, and documentary records that the alliance of Yamato tribes established hegemony by defeating people of Korean descent, Ainus, and other nonrelated indigenous groups, some of southern provenience and others apparently more closely related to the Tungusic tribes of the borderlands of eastern Siberia, Manchuria, and Korea. By the ninth century, Chinese and Korean immigrants had been completely absorbed and the other groups either wiped out or absorbed; only a few tens of thousands of Ainus remained, primarily on the otherwise virtually uninhabited northern island of Hokkaido, as a reminder of the ancient ethnic divisions. Japan, by the nineteenth century a nation of about thirty million people, had been ethnically united for a thousand years.

**Language.** Japanese has its dialects, as do all languages spread widely over a geographical area. Broadly, they can be divided into eastern and western divisions, following a line running through the Chūbu region, which lies between the Kantō region (Tokyo and surrounding area) and the Kinki region (Kyoto, Nara, and Osaka). This east–west dialect division has a long history and appears to correspond with other social and cultural differences independently suggested by archeology, history, and ethnology. Whether this corresponds to some deeper division, perhaps based on greater mainland Asiatic influence in the east and greater southern influence in the west, is an important issue in Japanese prehistory and ethnology. The broad divisions can then be subdivided, depending on the perspective and problem in hand, into at least 12 major dialect groupings, which are at their margins sometimes mutually incomprehensible. The farthest southern dialect, Satsuma, still spoken today in Kagoshima prefecture, is virtually incomprehensible to most other dialect speakers and appears to be closer to Ryūkyūan than to Japanese. But the centrifugal force of these dialect differences, although abetted by a topography highly unfavorable for communication, was strongly counteracted by the early development of a unified national language of literature, religion, and administration. In 1868 the choice of a modified Tokyo dialect for a national language presented no insuperable problems and left no alienated linguistic communities to assert claims for autonomy against an oppressive majority.

**Culture.** Culturally, in spite of variations in detail sufficient to provide happy labors for generations of folklorists, ethnologists, and rural sociologists, Japan was remarkably homogeneous from one end of the islands to the other. The Japanese were aware of themselves as a unified people; some observers would contend that even today cultural homogeneity is a distinctive "characteristic" of Japan. "Despite obvious individual differences," runs one typical statement of this kind, "every Japanese has resembled every other Japanese much more closely than Americans or European individuals have resembled their compatriots. Although the stress on democracy after World War II fostered individual differences, Japan's population continues to be less diversified than Occidental populations." Whether this is so or not remains one of the important questions on the agenda of social science research; nevertheless, insofar as it refers to the problem of the relations between cultural unity and modern development the general proposition remains acceptable.

**Religion.** Although in 1868 Japan had many different religions within her borders—including the indigenous Shinto and its many variants, Buddhism in a wide variety of differing, and sometimes even hostile, sects, Confucianism in both secular and religious dress, and even a small number of Christians—these did not provide the bases for enduring group identifications that precluded a larger, national identification. On the contrary, rather than being exclusive, each religion was considered to have its own area of appropriateness. Except for fanatics or religious professionals, these religions demanded no exclusive commitment. From the standpoint of the ordinary villager, who went to his local community Shinto shrine as well as to a Buddhist temple, religious life was a smooth, seamless whole. One was named at the Shinto shrine, buried in the Buddhist temple, and indoctrinated in Confucian moral precepts.

### Centralization

**The Yamato state.** Although all of the elements classically associated with disunity were present in ample measure, Japan transcended them, and, by 1868, perhaps to a greater degree than most other countries of the world. Japanese history can be read from one point of view as a steady expansion of centralized control. Each attempt at unity was immediately followed by a prolonged period of breakdown, decentralization, and gradual reconstitution of a new and more effective base of centralized power. By the fourth century or thereabouts, some of the Yamato tribes (or clans), later designated "imperial," succeeded with their allies in establishing a tentative sovereignty over the main inhabited parts of the country. This sovereignty was, however, so strongly inhibited by powerful territorial, tribal, and clan chieftains that the imperial clan could only be considered *primus inter pares* rather than the unchallengeable ruler of the nation.

**The Taika reforms.** In the seventh century, another effort was made to strengthen central control, this time looking to flourishing China of the T'ang dynasty for inspiration. The Taika reforms of 645 and the subsequent elaborations in the Taihō Code of 701 and the Yōrō Code of 718 attempted to establish the T'ang principle that all the land belonged to the emperor and was held only on grant from him. In order to reduce the independent power of tribal or territorial chieftains and landed magnates, a centralized bureaucracy was created from which authority was considered to emanate. The system of centralized court bureaucracy, the appointment by the political center of provincial and local governors, the development of a national tax system, and the improvement of communications drew extensively from the Chinese models.

The Yamato state was accordingly transformed from a loose tribal coalition with a poorly defined center of sovereignty into what was, in principle at least, a centralized nation-state under a king (emperor) and a court bureaucracy. Its stability and authority were increased by the establishment of a fixed capital (until then the capital had moved from one temporary site to another upon the death of each emperor)—first in the city of Nara (in 710) and then at the end of the eighth century in the city of Kyoto. With this began the long era of cultural expansion known as the Heian period (794–1185).

**The Heian period.** In spite of the bold centralizing moves, however, the forces of decentralization were never entirely reduced. Gradually throughout the Heian period, and with gathering force after the eleventh century, powerful provincial military houses in control of lands, arms, and men built up their own structures of political alliance, land tenure, and local administration. By the end of the twelfth century, under the leadership of Minamoto Yoritomo, they were able to displace the central court in effective power over the country. The central court and the military estate remained in a situation of uneasy and shifting "dual power" until the fourteenth century, when there was another breakdown of the central power, an attempt at imperial "restoration," followed by a new centralized military power, the Ashikaga shogunate (1336–1573). This new centralized power once again broke down under the pressure of dissident local forces, and Japan was to go through another century of civil war, sometimes quiescent, sometimes in violent eruption, before new centralizing forces appeared. From the latter part of the sixteenth century, three great centralizers appeared in succession—first Oda Nobunaga, then Toyotomi Hideyoshi, and finally Tokugawa Ieyasu.

**The Tokugawa regime.** Ieyasu's military victory in 1600 at Sekigahara marked the beginning of the final premodern phase of centralization. This phase was far more effective and thoroughgoing than the earlier attempts, and it lasted, in effect, until 1868, when it was overthrown by the modernizing coalition gathered under the banner of "imperial restoration." Although the Tokugawa unification was the most effective in Japanese history up to that point, it was still far from complete; the shogunal government permitted substantial powers over almost three-fourths of the country to remain in the hands of powerful territorial barons, the *daimyō*. They held their positions, to be sure, only as vassals of the shogun; and the shogun maintained extensive controls over them, through the system of hostages and compulsory residence

in the court city, called the *sankin-kōtai*, through spying, through the sequestration of strategic areas for his own direct domains (*chokkatsu-chi*), and through the careful placement of personal vassals and family members to control movements by potential enemy lords. Nevertheless, the shogun was, in effect, ruling 100 per cent of the country with only 25 per cent of its tax revenues, land, and manpower. The restoration regime under the Meiji emperor in 1868 swiftly completed the centralization process, replacing the semiautonomous feudal domains with a modern system of prefectures governed by appointed officers.

## Homogeneity and isolation

Many factors had to combine in just the right sequence to bring about political homogeneity. However, in retrospect, it is clear that Japan's insular position perhaps played the most important role. Like England, Japan stood in a marginal position in relation to the great Eurasiatic land mass. But England lies only 20 miles off the nearest point of the European continent, while Japan lies 110 miles away from the nearest point in Korea and several hundreds of miles of dangerous waters away from the main centers of Chinese civilization. The greater distance, under conditions of primitive navigation, made Japan's isolation disproportionately great, perhaps greater than that of any other large nation in the world.

**Military invasion.** Isolation has had, and perhaps continues to have, widely ramifying effects on Japan's development. It did not cut Japan off from all contact with the outside, but it assured that this contact would take place at a relatively slow rate which offered the chance for slow assimilation. Japan was never overwhelmed by massive immigration, military conquest, or alien rule. We have ample evidence of constant traffic, of individuals and small groups, throughout the early centuries of Japan's history—from Korea and China as well as the southerly islands and the southern portions of the Asiatic mainland. Some were accorded high prestige and incorporated within the highest aristocracy (approximately one-third of the aristocratic clans in the early eighth century were estimated to be of Chinese or Korean origin); others were put to work at their crafts or professions, particularly if they were skilled workers, artists, or literate men; others were enslaved or placed in menial occupations. Still others managed to maintain their own communal lives in distant provinces, until the expansion of Japanese state power finally reached them.

We need accept no far-reaching theory of geographical determination, such as has been put forth by some Western and Japanese scholars, to acknowledge that geographical position was important in Japan's development. The most obvious effect of Japan's insular location was protection against being overwhelmed, either by cultural influences, large-scale immigration, or military power. Insularity alone did not guarantee this. Had they wished, the Chinese could have mounted a large enough invasion force to establish some direct political power in the islands. But fortunately for Japan, China has always been a continental power, oriented toward overland expansion. Except for a brief and uncharacteristic episode during the Ming period, from 1368 to 1644, China has never had serious maritime inclinations. The nineteenth-century Western powers could also have invaded Japan. But they did not, and it was perhaps Japan's remoteness and lack of attractive resources that made the venture not worthwhile. The only serious invasion attempts, under the direction of Kublai Khan, ended in disaster for the Mongol invaders when a storm in 1274 and a typhoon in 1281 (the *kamikaze*, or "divine wind") scattered their fleets. Japan was not entirely uninfluenced by the Mongol invasions, but apart from the direct impact on weapons technology and battle tactics most of the effects were indirect, such as pressure on the political structure, strains on feudal ties and obligations, growing awareness of a dangerous outside world, improvement of internal communications and transport facilities, and a temporary drain on food supplies followed rapidly by substantial agricultural improvement. Japan, for its part, had maintained a military garrison on the southern tip of the Korean peninsula until the seventh century. Nine hundred years later, in 1592 and 1597, Japan invaded Korea, leaving behind a legacy of destruction and hatred that is not entirely dissipated even today.

**Patterns of culture contact—China.** This relative isolation meant that Japan was able to absorb outside influences at its own pace. The country had time to experiment; to reject, to adopt, or to modify foreign ideas and objects in accordance with its own understanding and needs.

The confrontation of Japan with China from the sixth century through the ninth century was not imposed by China; it was self-imposed by a Japan seeking for models to strengthen and improve itself. The Japanese desperately sought out the "Chinese learning," importing the treasured bits in large and small packages, often not understanding their contents. The process must be understood as a prolonged searching out and assimilation that went on for centuries, not as a single titanic event.

Buddhism, for example, was first formally introduced from Korea into Japan in 552, when the king of the Korean state of Paekche, in the hopes of securing Japanese support against the enemy Korean states of Silla and Koguryo, sent a goodwill mission to the emperor of Japan. The mission brought with it a statue of the Buddha, several manuscripts of sutras, and some Buddhist paraphernalia, along with the Paekche king's commendation that the religion was the best in the world and eminently suited to the needs of the state—even though he himself did not fully understand it. In 554 men learned in Chinese studies—such as divination, calendar making, Confucianism, medicine, and music—and several Buddhist monks came from Paekche. But it was not until the twelfth or thirteenth century that Buddhism can be said to have become fully assimilated as a popular religion in Japan. Buddhism started as the religion of one of the contending court factions; it was then used by the centralizing Taika reformers against their enemies. For several centuries it remained essentially a religion of the court, the aristocracy, and learned men; and only after the eleventh century did it begin to undergo a full "Japanization" that brought it in understandable form to the common people. During most of that period only specialists and highly learned men who could read and write Chinese could understand even the language of Buddhism. The package was taken in whole, and then only gradually was it picked over, translated into understandable language, and finally assimilated. In the course of this process it underwent many changes, so that Japanese Buddhism differs not only from the south Asian forms but also from the Chinese and Korean forms. [See BUDDHISM.]

**Patterns of response.** Isolation and the absence of land contact with China made it necessary to develop modes of learning at a distance. In addition to going on official missions to China, Japanese scholars and clerics continued to visit China unofficially, and both Chinese and Korean specialists came to Japan on their own or were invited by high authorities and Buddhist temples. Nevertheless, most of the learning took place not through face-to-face contacts but through books, pictures, and artifacts. Material culture was the easiest to absorb; artists, artisans, and architects worked directly from models and designs, reproducing forms and acquiring techniques. On the other hand, "literary" learning required knowledge of Chinese and then textual interpretation.

This process allowed Japan to accommodate foreign culture to its own style. Foreign models could be accepted, but they did not have to be slavishly followed. The fate of the Chinese political principles and codes adopted in the Taika reforms of 645 remains an instructive case study of culture contact and acculturation. The Japanese took over the principle that "all land belongs to the emperor," but they accommodated it to the reality of private control of land; they took over the forms of China's imperial bureaucracy, but adjusted them to the spirit of hereditary aristocracy; they greeted with enthusiasm the Chinese concept of a national conscript army, but allowed private hereditary warriors to take over military functions; they adopted the Chinese concept of promotion through examinations, even creating a university in the eighth century, but they limited entrance to the hereditary aristocratic classes. Sansom writes:

The development of political forms throughout the ninth, tenth, and eleventh centuries may be regarded, from one point of view, as a gradual departure from Chinese models, and the political history of that long period may be summarized by saying that practically all the leading features of the system of government borrowed from China gradually became obsolete, to be displaced by new methods designed to meet new conditions, and at length survived only as empty forms in a feudal society which differed in all its fundamental characteristics from the unworkable scheme of centralized monarchy.   (1958–1963, vol. 1, p. 132)

A similar process can be detected for every cultural import from China: first, there is uncritical acceptance; then differentiation and reinterpretation; later, rejection or modification; and finally, the development of genuine novelty. New art styles brought over by students, artists, or priests from China—or perhaps by Chinese traders in Japanese markets—were immediately copied in Japan, only to be transformed in a short period of time into something that would no longer be recognized by the Chinese originators.

The long experience of isolation may have contributed to that special "national self-consciousness and a sense of inferiority" (Reischauer 1950, p. 109 in the 1957 edition) that most foreign observers feel is characteristic of Japan both as a nation and as a people. Living for more than a millennium in awareness of the great power of China, and later of the West, the Japanese appear to have an inordinate preoccupation with their relative standing on some implicit scale of values. This results in sharply alternating periods of excessive humility and willingness to borrow, on the one hand, and arrogance and total rejection of "foreign" influences, on the other. Although much of this may be due to Japan's modern experience of trying to catch up with the industrialized West, there is strong evidence that these tendencies have a long history and that they have deeper and more tenacious roots than can be explained by the past one hundred years alone. This "widespread self-consciousness," as one author describes it, "seems to make all Japanese acutely aware of just what their status is in relation to those with whom they come into regular contact" (Beasley 1963, p. 310). A full explanation, therefore, would have to take into consideration not only the effects of historical experience but also the inner dynamics of these frustration–aggression and superiority–inferiority cycles in individual and social life.

But however we estimate the causes, it is clear that "nationalist" ideas have a long history in Japan. The isolation, the feeling of separateness, the process of diffusion filtered through books rather than coming through direct contact, may have contributed to making the Japanese, from one point of view, different from any other people in the world.

Analysis of Japan's experience raises, as we have suggested, far-reaching problems for theories of culture contact in general and of modernization in particular. Does the acceptance of certain cultural "items" (or total "culture complexes")—particularly if they come from a "superior" culture—necessarily entail the acceptance of the entire supportive structure of ideas, philosophy, and social organization that go along with them? Is it the case that one cannot accept the one without eventually accepting the rest? We have seen this not to be the case in Japan's borrowings from China. From the seventh century through the ninth century a preliterate, tribal Japan borrowed wholesale from the brilliant civilization of continental China; through this experience it emerged as a completely new nation, not as a mere provincial version of China. The borrowing was selective and critical. The new Japan of the Heian period accommodated Chinese features to traditional institutions and dispositions. Sansom writes: "The power and prestige of a foreign culture seem as if they would overwhelm and transform Japan, but always there is a hard, non-absorbent core of individual character, which resists and in its turn works upon the invading influence" ([1931] 1962, p. 15).

## Continuities

To evaluate this proposition about Japanese culture contact, careful attention must be paid to continuities, as well as discontinuities, in Japan's development. What, then, are some of these "measurable continuities," to use John W. Hall's term (Hall & Beardsley 1965, p. 151), that are of significance for the social scientist concerned with the problems of culture contact and modernization?

"Continuity" does not imply that no changes at all have taken place in the institutions or values concerned. There have, quite obviously, been enormous changes. Nor are we concerned with cultural "survivals"—the fossil leftovers of an earlier age. The seeker for survivals in this sense will find Japan a happy hunting ground. He will find specimens wherever he turns: forms of ritual and prayer retained virtually intact from prehistoric times; forms of dress, food, architecture, poetic technique, and language; court and religious music and dance; practices of the imperial court and ancient Shinto shrines; better examples of T'ang period architecture than remain in China; better examples of Silla period art and architecture than can be found in Korea; surviving shamanistic practices and concepts; ideas of animal possession; customs and techniques associated with rice agriculture that have come down to the present virtually unchanged; and even items of material culture that remain much as they were fifteen hundred years ago. What we are concerned with is whether there are enduring dispositions in forms of organization and cultural values that persist in spite of the profound changes brought about by culture contact and modernization. Scholars profess to find these broad continuities in the remarkable durability of the emperor system, in the techniques of behind-the-scenes rule, and in the long tradition of religious tolerance; art historians find them in the plastic arts and in aesthetic conceptions. Here, however, we shall confine our attention primarily to continuities in a few selected aspects of Japanese social structure.

**The family.** One of the most important of these continuities is the apparently peculiar combination of "familistic" and "feudal" elements in the structure of authority. We know from history that the Japanese familial form was present before Japan became a feudal state and continued after it ceased to be. The ideal Japanese family has always been hierarchical, and internal family relations have provided a model for authority relations in nonkinship groupings. The terms *oya* (parent) and *ko* (child), for example, have been extended in meaning to indicate superiors and inferiors: lord and vassal, boss and henchman, employer and employee, leader and follower.

The traditional Japanese family was ideally organized with the father at the top (in the past he might also have been the head of the ancestral cult), then the heir-presumptive (usually the eldest son), next the remaining males in order of age,

and finally the females in order of descending age. This ideal was realized in actuality more frequently by the elite classes than the common people; statistically, it is likely that more Japanese families have been nonhierarchical and even relatively egalitarian than the contrary. Nevertheless, the elite style represented the ideal that was approached when circumstances made it possible or desirable.

**The extended family.** The Japanese extended family differs somewhat from the extended family systems of neighboring Korea and China; there are no true clans, and membership is not totally defined on a genealogical basis. The Japanese extended family is highly selective, including or excluding individuals and families on the basis of convenience; it is rarely extended in time or size beyond the point where cooperative relations can be usefully carried on; and it can accommodate nonrelatives as if they were "members of the family." Structurally, the Japanese extended family (*dōzoku*) consists of a central stem, the "main house" (*honke*), and its satellite "branch houses" (*bunke*). But the main and branch houses are not equals that come together for their mutual benefit: the branch houses are dependent and subordinate. In return for the main house's "benevolence," the branch owes continuing loyalty, obedience, deference, and service. Hierarchical position within the *dōzoku* is based upon the order of branching and the degree of genealogical distance from the main house. The older branches outrank the newer; branches formed by second sons outrank those of third sons. The *dōzoku* (which might even include "grandchild" branches, subbranches fissioned off from earlier branches, and branches established by various degrees of nonrelatives) forms a unit with an identity of its own persisting over time, sharing the *pietas* of the ancestral deity and even certain elements of common family property.

**Adoption.** A distinctive feature of the Japanese family system was its extraordinary capacity to absorb nonkin. The institution of adoption of non-kin into the individual household was one means of accomplishing this. In the absence of a suitable heir a son might be adopted to assure the continuity and prosperity of the family line. But the adopted son, it is important to note, did not have to be a relative. The most usual case was the "adopted husband" (*yōshi*): a family with no male heirs might "take in" a prospective husband for a daughter; this boy thereupon became the son of the family, took its name as his own, and acquired all the rights and responsibilities that would normally pertain to a real eldest son.

However, the technique of adoption could be used in many other ways as well. A son might be taken into the family, even if not as an heir, to provide additional manpower, whether for a farmer's or a warrior's family; a young man from a high-born but poor family to add luster to his new family; a young man of a well-to-do but low-status family to bring financial support; a promising young man of low birth to be given patronage and protection. Adoption was, and remains to a surprising extent today, an important mode of social mobility; this was even more true during the Tokugawa period, when theoretically no movement across class boundaries was permitted. Historically—to take another example—domestic slavery disappeared in Japan not through formal acts of emancipation but through absorption into the family system by way of adoption. Less admirably, adoption was sometimes used for acquiring servants or other dependent menials. Even after World War II many girls were sold into prostitution under the guise of being adopted as daughters.

**The house.** The *dōzoku* too might contain not only genealogically related branches but also branches originally formed by nonrelatives aggregated to the larger grouping by ties of fictive kinship. This technique of branching and aggregation of both kin and nonkin into hierarchical units appears to have been characteristic of Japan from the very earliest period for which we have records. The *uji* (inaccurately translated as "clan") of the sixth and seventh centuries had as its core a main house and its satellite branch households consisting of patrilineally related persons, along with a much larger number of guilds (*be*) and corporations (*tomo*) composed of nonrelatives. The latter groups were attached to the *uji* in order to perform services, including labor. Allied families of similar composition were often aggregated to the core so that an *uji* became in effect a large federation of genealogically related main-and-branch families and dependent workers organized into units of various kinds. The head of the main family of the *uji* was the leader of the entire ensemble—the patriarch, custodian of the ancestral shrines, commander of the military forces, owner (or at least custodian) of the *uji* property, representative of the group to government and other *uji*, and political boss. His tutelary deity (*ujigami*) was worshiped as the common deity of the entire group, even though the component units might have their own deities. Thus a hierarchy of tutelary ancestral deities developed, ranging from the great deity (*sō-ujigami*) of the main house through the varying degrees of lesser deities (*shō-ujigami*) of the branch houses; this hierarchy corresponded to the main–branch hierarchy.

The militarily and politically powerful families, or "houses" of a later period, such as the Minamoto (or Genji), the Taira (or Heike), and the Fujiwara, were essentially aggregations of the same type. They should not be thought of as huge extended families that somehow managed to produce curiously large numbers of male children (even in the thousands and tens of thousands) able to bear arms, but rather as vast *dōzoku* alliances composed of a main family with its satellite branches (including "servant" and other branch forms) and dependents, allied houses with their branches and dependents that accepted the overlordship of the leading house, and dependent nonkin of varying degrees. Although we know from the frequent shifts of loyalty and alliance that these vast aggregates were often unstable, in principle they were all united in loyalty to the head of the main family and to the promotion of its prosperity, in return for the security of land tenure, protection against enemies, military and political support, etc., provided by the main family.

Despite the undoubted vast changes that have been taking place, the technique of aggregating familial and familylike groupings into cooperating hierarchical units remains recognizable, although it is expressed in different forms, depending upon the kind of situation in which it operates. *Dōzoku* of farmers could obviously not become as large as the great aristocratic and military houses, but they operated on similar structural principles, even if on a much reduced scale. In the case of the great commercial houses, however, the *dōzoku* sometimes attained remarkable size. The Mitsui family, for example, one of Japan's oldest commercial houses, carried on essentially as a *dōzoku* into the beginning of the twentieth century. New units and new enterprises were staffed primarily by means of branch families that consisted either of genealogical relatives (in this case, the branch was called *bunke*) or of adopted relatives (*bekke*). When a promising apprentice or employee was promoted to an executive or managerial position, he was taken into the Mitsui house as a branch family, thereby incurring the expected traditional obligations that obtained between main and branch family. By the end of the Tokugawa period, the Mitsui family is estimated to have had over one thousand branch families.

Early in the nineteenth century, during the period of transition from the apprentice–adoption branch family (that is, the *dōzoku*) system to modern forms of wage labor and bureaucratic management, hired labor was first taken in as "commuting" branch families (*tsūkin-bekke*), as distinct from the traditional "live-in" apprentices in branches. Within a few decades, the newer type became dominant because of growing hostility between the two types of employees, the need to rationalize the system, the difficulty of continuing the traditional seignorial obligations toward a vastly increased work force, and the lack of living space. The area of effective relations between main family and branches was gradually reduced to the inner core of the company, instead of, as hitherto, covering all employees. Even after its early nineteenth-century adjustment, the far-flung Mitsui industrial–commercial empire was held together by a holding company that was, in effect, the family council of the house (*dōzoku*) of Mitsui. This system did not collapse through natural obsolescence or the inability of the traditional *dōzoku* to adapt to modern industrial society; it was dissolved by the American Occupation's antitrust and cartel reform legislation.

**Oyabun–kobun.** It is clear, then, that the essence of the *dōzoku* is not so much the grouping of related families into a larger unit but rather the grouping of individuals and families, whether or not related genealogically, into a functionally cooperating hierarchical organization centering on a main house or its leader. The *dōzoku*, in other words, is a corporate group based upon some work function of such character that it engages a major part of the participating individual's social and economic life and demands his highest loyalty. In some cases the cooperating group is actually a family, even though it may contain nonrelatives; in other cases it acts "as if" it were a family. The underlying principle, which might be considered a constitutive principle of organization and authority in Japan, has been found throughout Japanese history to be extendible to a wide variety of forms of cooperative activity. Japanese groups, even those formed of very heterogeneous elements, tend to take on the generalized form of the "house." In such groups, as Bennett and Ishino put it: "persons of authority assume obligations and manifest attitudes toward their subordinates much as if they were foster parents, and conversely the subordinates behave dutifully and hold feelings of great personal loyalty toward their superiors" (1963, p. 40). Confucian principles of filial piety are equally applicable to actual families and to these familylike groupings.

This extension of familism to nonfamily groupings is another example of what we have characterized as enduring dispositions of values and organizational principles that show remarkable persistence in spite of vast changes in form. The generic type is the hierarchical system called *oyabun–kobun* by Japanese sociologists.

In such groupings, organization and authority follow closely the models of the family, whether of the individual household or of the extended "house." The head is the *oyabun*, or *oyakata* (literally, "father role"), and the subordinates are *kobun*, or *kokata* (literally, "child role"). *Oyabun* can be translated into English by such terms as lord, master, boss, leader, employer, landowner, protector, godfather, and patron; *kobun* can be translated as underling, subordinate, henchman, godchild, vassal, dependent, protégé, worker, employee, tenant, servant, and client. The *oyabun–kobun* relation is central to the authority structure. In more complex forms of organization, different levels of authority can be expressed by other kinship-derived terms, such as *anikibun* (older brother role), *otōtobun* (younger brother role), and *magobun* (grandchild role). An alliance of several *oyabun* groups into a larger grouping might be called *kyōdaibun*, or "brotherhood." The "brotherhood" might take one of two forms—a federation of equals or an expanded *dōzoku* hierarchy. Just as in the main house–branch relationship, the *oyabun*'s benevolence must be repaid in loyalty, obedience, deference, and service.

It is important, however, to make it clear that *oyabun–kobun* can refer to a specific form of organization as well as to a general principle of organization. Even when the specific form is lacking, one often finds that the spirit, or ethos, is present. "Why was it," one Japanese scholar asks, "that in spite of the spread of education and the wholesale introduction of Western thought, even intellectuals, in deciding their everyday conduct, were strongly swayed by patriarchal considerations of social status?" (Tōyama Shigeki, as quoted in Jansen 1965, p. 39). The *oyabun–kobun* relation has shown a remarkable tenacity in spite of the growth of modern institutions. When the form cannot be directly realized, either for ideological or organizational reasons, it is covertly expressed in the form of cliques and patron–client relations.

Just as the family signifies two sharply contrasting sets of attributes—affection, warmth, love, and guidance, on the one hand, and unquestioned patriarchal authority, harsh rule, hierarchy, and exploitation, on the other—an ambivalence attaches to other forms of authority relations. Since World War II *oyabun* has become a bad word, having the unpleasant connotation of "boss." Nevertheless, the *oyabun* type of relation has been very extensive. In many rural areas, for example, landlord–tenant relations were deeply imbued with these principles. In the prototypical cases—the ones usually characterized as most "feudal"—the landlord was usually the head of the main house and the tenant the head of one of the branches.

Characteristically, the rural *dōzoku* centered on the cooperating agricultural unit, which was usually bound by strongly reinforcing experiences and work relations. The process of branching established a ritual and genealogical hierarchy, but this was always linked with the hierarchy of land tenure. Before the Meiji restoration in 1868 the branch held no independent civic position in the community but derived its rights from the position of the main house with respect to participation in community political affairs, access to community common lands, forest, and compost. With the development of modern forms of land ownership after the Meiji restoration, the main house, or *oyabun*, became the modern landlord, and the branch house, or *kobun*, the tenant. Nevertheless, in many parts of the country the relationship remained much more personal than would be expected of a purely economic landlord–tenant relation. Often the tenant owed the landlord not only rent but many other obligations as well—agricultural and industrial labor, personal service, deference, obedience. He would bow deeply to the landlord when they met; work on his lands and property in accordance with a fixed schedule or when called upon; bring tribute and gifts on ceremonial occasions; seek the landlord's advice and permission in major enterprises, even such personal ones as marrying off a son or a daughter; and he would support the civic and political activities of the landlord. In return, he counted upon the landlord to assist him in time of need, protect him, and give him guidance and patronage. The overlapping among the traditional hierarchical systems—the main house was often the landlord and the *oyakata* as well—tended to reinforce their separate authorities. Where these three arrangements coincided—that is, where the landlord, the person with most political influence, and the head of the main house were one and the same person—the system was strongest and corresponded most closely to what is described as "feudalistic" in Japanese agriculture prior to land reform. The more the authority systems tended to separate out, so that the landlord, the *oyakata*, and the head of the main family were three separate persons, the more the community appeared "modern." Although the American-sponsored land reform, conducted from 1947 to 1949, abolished landlordism and thereby weakened the structure of rein-

forcing obligations on which the system rested, patron–client relations continue to be important in rural areas, even if in attenuated form.

To a remarkable extent, even in modern times, these intrafamilial and extended family relations provide a model for extrafamilial groupings. Why this should be is the subject of much controversy. Many scholars argue that the only mode of "human relations" known to the Japanese is familial; no ethic has developed for dealing with outsiders, or "strangers." Others argue that the explanation must be sought in the deeper realms of notions of sacred hierarchy, ancestral *pietas*, and relations to ancestral deities.

Whatever the reason, *oyabun–kobun* relations can be found in a wide variety of organizations. Characteristically, the head is the benevolent father, the subordinates are loyal and obedient children; and the relation between them is not only functional, specific, and economic, but personal and diffuse as well. The relationship may last for the duration of specific tasks, over the lifetime of individuals, or even for many generations. Some well-known Tokyo gangs can boast an ancestry of over three hundred years and enumerate 14 or 16 generations, just as would a great family of artists, actors, or craftsmen. Generation after generation the same main family provides the *oyabun*, and the same subordinate families provide *kobun*. Until the labor reforms of 1945–1947 and before economic growth altered the employment market, a great part of Japan's casual labor, especially in stevedoring and construction, was organized under labor bosses who, in return for strict obedience and a cut of the workers' wages, undertook to keep the men employed or to look after them when they were out of work. The labor gangs were, incidentally, also useful in political campaigning, for minor intimidation, for fighting the growing union movement, and for furthering the personal political ambitions of the boss or of his own higher patrons (*ō-oyabun*, or "great bosses"). Modern labor employment practices, labor unions, social security, and unemployment insurance have still not fully ended the influence of labor bosses.

*Oyabun–kobun* (or *oyakata–kokata*) relations are found widely in other traditional sectors of Japanese life and economy. In many areas that specialize in coastal fisheries, for example, the owners of nets, boats, and fishing rights are not only employers in the economic sense but also *oyakata*, parental figures accepting extralegal obligations for the welfare and personal needs of their workers and their families. Until the end of the nineteenth century, when modern powered boats and improved nets were introduced, the coastal fisheries were carried on mainly by family groups. Single families or, as operations became more complicated, groups of neighboring families who were usually related to each other formed a *kumi* (association). The head of the senior family was the fishery leader, and he was the *oyakata*. As in the rural villages, there was a typical overlap of authority systems: the upper classes owned the boats, nets, and fishery-rights; they were the *oyakata*, the heads of the main houses in the extended family network, and the political leaders of the community. This familial flavor has carried over even into modern fishery operations: where possible, junior relatives are employed through the extended family system and nonrelatives enter the work group as pseudo relatives. Seasonal labor for large-scale fishery operations, such as manning the giant nets used in the annual herring runs, are often organized by labor bosses.

The principle of house organization is also strong in the traditional theater arts and entertainments. Kabuki, for example, is conducted not by companies but by "families" that continue in the art generation after generation, often having to adopt heirs in order to maintain the great traditions of the family. The principal actors, who bear the great theatrical names, are the *oyakata* of their troupes. The entire system of organization, including the administration, the relations between the chief actors and their juniors, the form of payment within the group, and its social and moral life, is permeated by the *oyakata–kokata* principle. Similarly, in the traditional Japanese dance and music, each major style and tradition is carried on by a particular family, and the disciples (apprentices, students) are considered the "children" of the house "father" (master, leader). [See PATERNALISM.]

## Principles of Japanese social structure

**Leaders and followers.** In most organizations interpersonal relations are those between the leader and his follower or followers. In more complex organizations, however, the ties between top and bottom are established through subordinates—the leader, his followers, and his followers' followers. The first-degree subordinates stand in the closest relation to the leader, and his ties with the lower degrees are mediated through them. Each first-degree follower therefore becomes a subleader, capable of mobilizing his own retainers. Since each individual's primary tie is with his immediate leader, the horizontal relations among individuals of similar status within the organization tend to be weak. The result is that equal-status consciousness is weaker than consciousness of status within the vertical system of ties of the organization as a whole. Although many organizations, particularly in modern times, may start out on egalitarian principles or with emphasis on horizontal ties, mature organizations in Japan inevitably tend toward the strong vertical emphasis and the weak horizontal emphasis. The mature group presumes clear, single linkages (described by one Japanese anthropologist as "univalent") between all individuals in the group and high emotional involvement in group life and aims. The web of vertical linkages forms a kind of family, centering on its leader–parent, a unit of common destiny, and the groundwork of the individual's identity, commitment, and meaning in life.

**Styles of leadership.** As in a family, members consider that they are not working for an employer alone but also for the enhancement of the group. Thus, although the leader commands their devotion and effort, it is as the symbol of the group as a whole that he does so. He is the embodiment of the linking principle that holds the separate individual linkages together. If they work for him, he must also work for them. The members accept a high degree of self-sacrifice for the group (or its symbol, the leader) and an exceptional invasion of their private life space; the leader, in turn, is expected to be benevolent, emotionally concerned, solicitous, and attentive to the needs and views of the members. Although in many situations it is easy to mobilize instant and unhesitating obedience, at whatever self-sacrifice, continuing arbitrary authority is difficult. One type of leader is little more than a figurehead acting only on the initiative of his subordinates. Another is the mediator whose effectiveness comes from his ability to find the consensus, or the acceptable point of compromise among the leader–follower groups that form his organization. Arbitrary dictatorial authority is too constrained by internal organizational principles to be common in Japanese history; where it is found, it is usually limited in duration, or else it leads to the collapse of the group. The opposite style, in which higher authority simply ratifies plans and decisions prepared and approved by subordinate authority networks, is more common. The informal authority webs of an organization often defeat, or at least neutralize, the formal tables of organization which presume that orders pass down from the top, through the executive staff, and are then translated by the "ranks" into action.

**Cooperation and competition.** Within the group, the prevailing norms are harmony, agreement, consensus, and cooperation. But between groups cooperation is very difficult; there competition is unrelenting and often of an awesome ferocity. But there are important structural points of competitive stress within apparently harmonious organizations as well. Since, as we have noted, the larger organizations cannot, in the very nature of the personalized leader–follower relation, form a single continuous vertical linkage system, nodules, or factions, are formed at different status points made up of small leader–follower groupings, so that the larger organization tends to take on the character of a federation of groups rather than a seamless, continuous whole. This makes for continuous conflict, factionalism, and fission. Competition among the factions is often intense, and the factions' capacity to work together is correspondingly weak unless the top leadership is exceptionally skillful. Within each small faction there is competition between individuals close to each other in status; their primary affective ties are not to each other but rather to the leader. An ambitious subordinate leader may try to elevate the status of his group by expanding his influence, stimulating factional rivalries, and even forming alliances with other groupings. If a subordinate becomes more powerful than the leader (as, for example, a branch shop becoming more prosperous than the main store, a branch family becoming wealthier than the original main house, a subsidiary outstripping the parent company, a feudal military vassal winning more battles and acquiring more fighting retainers than his lord), he might very well challenge the top leader or withdraw from the group entirely to go off on his own. In such cases, the original associates often become the bitterest of enemies.

**Rank consciousness.**    The result of this system of vertical linkages is that individuals are aware of their status within groups but they are not much concerned with their horizontal linkages with individuals of similar status position in other groups or in society as a whole. Some Japanese social scientists would argue from this that class or status consciousness therefore cannot exist in Japan. The essential status awareness does not pertain so much to society as a whole—as relations between employers and employees or tenants and landlords—as it does to single institutions, groups, and areas organized on principles of vertical stratification. The individual's identity is not that of his occupation, individual qualities, or even of family lineage, but rather his organization and his position within it. An individual first reveals his identity to others in terms of his institutional or group affiliation—X-company, X-government bureau, university, faction, etc.—rather than as being an engineer, political scientist, typist, or journalist. (The feudal

warrior, before entering single combat, would challenge his opponent by citing his pedigree: "I am Wada Shōjirō Yoshishige, 17 years old, grandson of Miura Taisuke Yoshiaki, not far removed from a princely house, the 11th generation from Prince Takamochi, descendant of the Emperor Kammu; let anyone come, be he general or be he retainer, I am his man"; quoted in Nakamura [1948–1949] 1964, p. 418). Society tends to be seen as made up of parallel vertical-linkage groups, each internally harmonious but bitterly at war with each other. Movement from one parallel escalator to another is extremely difficult; the move is as emotionally difficult as changing one's family, and the individual capable of such a move is never fully trusted. This fundamental social perception helps explain what looks suspiciously like "company unionism" in Japan, in spite of the apparent militancy and political "progressivism" of the trade unions. Local unions are organized on a company, or plant, rather than on an industry-wide basis. This seems to reflect recognition of the "work place" as the ground of the individual's identity.

**"We" and "they."**    The structural dispositions of Japanese organization bring about a sharp distinction between "we" and "they," between in-group and out-group. Relations between groups are rarely easy and informal; rather, they are like high-level diplomatic negotiations. Since they are accompanied by so much emotion and suspicion, they must be swathed in protective layers of protocol. It follows that it is hard to form stable, large groupings, and this has been the case throughout Japanese history, whether the federation of *uji* in the archaic period, the formation of alliances of military houses during the feudal eras, the establishment of relations among *daimyō* (feudal lords), the cooperation of factions within a political party, or the merger of companies competing in the same market areas.

The "go-between," the mediator between two groups, has therefore always played an important role. "We" and "they" are always rivals if not actually enemies. Face-to-face conflict, or even disagreement, arouses such deep emotions and structural strains that the go-between becomes essential. It is easier for people to accommodate themselves to "strangers"—that is, all "others" as seen from the perspective of one's own group of identification—through proper introductions and the mediation of the go-between. Even modern young people who contemptuously reject the idea of marriages arranged by marriage brokers (the so-called "arranged marriage" versus the modern "love marriage") still prefer, or at least are willing out of deference to parental feelings, to accept a formal marriage sponsor on the actual occasion of the wedding.

Related to the go-between is a preference for indirection. In the most intimate of relations explicit statement is not necessary: wordless understanding is the mode; or hints and fragments of sentences may serve as pointers, even though outsiders may find them completely incomprehensible. The effect of the structural tensions of Japanese organization is constant sensitivity to relative status, self-consciousness, delicately graded responsiveness to the most minimal alterations of atmosphere, and concern with "face." These preoccupations loom so large in relations among people that communication is often a delicate probing or feeling out, a search for hidden meanings and implications, a groping for limits rather than the transmission of the apparent content of the communication.

**Loyalty and achievement.** Since the individual's fundamental identity is with his vertically stratified functional group, which lives in a dangerous world surrounded by other similar groups—rivals or enemies, but at least strangers—loyalty is and has always been one of the principal values of Japanese society. The loyal individual, who willingly sacrifices personal interests, has always been one of the admired heroes of Japanese history. Although personal loyalty has often been converted into institutionalized loyalty—that is, loyalty between statuses rather than between individuals—in the preferred form there is a strong personal, emotional element. Leaders should act like leaders, just as followers should act like followers. That is, they should follow the Confucian principle of *meibun*, each person acting appropriate to his status. While a strict interpretation makes this a conditional relation—authority derives from virtue; in the absence of virtue, authority is not legitimate—the heroic ideal is unlimited loyalty. The leader who does not hold up his end of the bargain may continue to receive loyalty, but not forever. Lords who scamped their obligations have been attacked, deserted, and even overthrown; the retainer hurt by his lord's indifference or lack of virtue felt free to end his feudal ties. In the case of many of the young samurai and *rōnin* (men of samurai lineage without feudal ties) who carried through the Meiji restoration, from 1867 to 1868, the insistence upon *meibun* justified their apparent disloyalty.

Paradoxically, throughout Japanese history there has been constant emphasis on the values of achievement. Although achievement-orientation and loyalty are not necessarily incompatible, potential conflict may be seen in the hypothetical cases of the completely loyal but utterly incapable fellow and the man of ability who cannot fit into the team. The classic solution has been, and tends to remain, the encouragement of achievement within the framework and in the larger interests of the group. Within this framework ambition is permitted, competition tolerated, achievement applauded, merit rewarded, and ability cultivated. The "primacy of political values," which Bellah (1957) described for the institutions of the Tokugawa period, still holds today: priority is given to the continuity of the group, the enhancement of its position, and the furtherance of its broad aims rather than to specific ends and individual benefits. The loyal but incapable individual (whether this comes about through age, disability, loss of skill, or physical weakness) is protected by the group: he may be assigned tasks commensurate with his abilities, given a sinecure, or pastured out and looked after.

Not all groups in Japan manifest these principles in the same way and in the same degree. The principles will be more evident in large organizations rather than small ones, old organizations rather than new ones, and the higher ranks rather than the lower ranks. Moreover, many Japanese may never have contact with such groups, either because they live relatively isolated lives or because the groups with which they are affiliated are too small to permit the full play of all these operative principles. Nevertheless, this is the general form that all fully matured groups in Japan tend to approximate.

## Conclusion—tradition and modernity

Most social scientists are willing to concede that Japan may so far have been able to retain many features of its traditional order and system of values alongside the industrialization of its economy, but they would tend to consider this condition transitional or "unstable" (as Veblen argued in 1915); the "discrepancies," they feel, are bound to disappear. Veblen wrote:

It should, then, confidently be presumed, [that the Japanese will] presently and expeditiously . . . fall in with the peculiar habits of thought that make the faults and qualities of the western culture—the spiritual outlook and the principles of conduct and ethical values that have been induced by the exacting discipline of this same state of the industrial arts among the technologically more advanced and mature of the western peoples . . . as soon as her people shall have digested the western state of science and technology and have assimilated its spiritual contents, the "Spirit of Old Japan" will, in effect, have been dissipated. All that will remain will be ravellings of its genial tradition [and a] vapor of truculence [floating] through the adolescent brains of Young Japan.    (Veblen [1915] 1964, pp. 254–255)

Fifty years after these predictions, the same statement can still be made, and we are still waiting upon the event. As Schumpeter has argued:

Social structures, types and attitudes are coins that do not readily melt. Once they are formed they persist, possibly for centuries, and since different structures and types display different degrees of this ability to survive, we almost always find that actual group and national behavior more or less departs from what we should expect it to be if we tried to infer it from the dominant forms of the productive process.    (1942, pp. 12–13 in 1962 edition)

While many scholars would be prepared to acknowledge that this incomplete fusion of modern industry and important elements of the traditional order may be relatively enduring, they are almost instinctively inclined to feel that the equilibrium must be an unstable one. A few have tried to explain so-called "pathological" features of Japanese development, such as militarism and aggression, as a result of the persistent tension, the instability of the relationship between modernity and tradition. However, the history of Japanese culture contact suggests the equally plausible interpretation that the tension, if tension it be, is as stable as in Western countries undergoing change and that traditional culture and social-relational norms have affected the way in which elements of industrial society are accepted and rejected.

Whatever cross-section we take at any given moment during the course of modernization presents a fascinating spectacle of apparent contradiction. We seem to see a mosaic of past and present, fragmentation of the total society into old and new sectors, old patterns persisting in their entirety or in parts, new patterns displacing the old or reorganizing total areas of experience, old patterns governing the form of acceptance of new ones, fusions between old and new, and even the emergence of totally new hybrid patterns incorporating elements of both. Moreover, since the adult participants in the process have usually had their basic conditioning and socialization in an earlier era, they often appear to carry over older attitudes and modes of perception into new situations. As Parsons has argued, modernization (or in its more specific form, "rationalization") has uneven impact on "different elements in the social structure. . . . It tends to divide elements of the population according to whether they tend toward . . . more 'progressive' or 'emancipated' values of patterns of conduct, or the more conservative 'backward,' or traditional patterns" ([1938–1953] 1963, p. 118).

The experience of Japan suggests a position intermediate between the extreme formulations of "cultural determination of modern forms" and the "imperatives of modern industrial society." Some, but not all, effects of industrialization are instant and almost "inevitable"; some, but not all, can be widely accommodated to traditional modes of organization and traditional values. As Plath has put it, ". . . the past century has brought Japanese society and culture closer than ever to the West in form as well as in function. Nevertheless there continue to be customs and values and social forms such that the configuration is uniquely and characteristically Japanese. It is a Japanese modernism and not simply a Western one. Unless we see both of these facts at once we cannot begin to understand it, much less evaluate it" (1964, pp. 191–192).

After many years of life in Meiji Japan, the great English scholar, Basil Hall Chamberlain, wrote:

Old Japan is dead and gone, and Young Japan reigns in its stead, as opposed in appearance and in aims to its predecessor as history shows many a youthful prince to have been to the late king, his father. . . . Nevertheless . . . it [is] abundantly clear to those who have dived beneath the surface of the modern Japanese upheaval that more of the past has been retained than has been abandoned. . . . The national character persists intact, manifesting no change in essentials. Circumstances have deflected it into new channels, that is all.    ([1890] 1939, p. 6)

It is still possible to say much the same thing today.

HERBERT PASSIN

[Other relevant material may be found in FEUDALISM; MODERNIZATION.]

## BIBLIOGRAPHY

ABEGGLEN, JAMES 1958 The Japanese Factory: Aspects of Its Social Organization. Glencoe, Ill.: Free Press.

ASAKAWA, KANICHI 1903 The Early Institutional Life of Japan: A Study in the Reform of 645 A.D. Tokyo: Shueisha.

BEARDSLEY, RICHARD; HALL, JOHN W.; and WARD, ROBERT E. 1959 Village Japan. Univ. of Chicago Press.

BEASLEY, WILLIAM G. 1963 The Modern History of Japan. New York: Praeger.

BELLAH, ROBERT N. 1957 Tokugawa Religion: The Values of Pre-Industrial Japan. Glencoe, Ill.: Free Press.

BENEDICT, RUTH 1946 The Chrysanthemum and the Sword: Patterns of Japanese Culture. Boston: Houghton Mifflin.

BENNETT, JOHN W.; and ISHINO, IWAO 1963 Paternalism in the Japanese Economy: Anthropological Studies of Oyabun–Kobun Patterns. Minneapolis: Univ. of Minnesota Press.

BLACKER, CARMEN 1964 The Japanese Enlightenment: A Study of the Writings of Fukuzawa Yūkichi. Cambridge Univ. Press.

BORTON, HUGH 1955 *Japan's Modern Century.* New York: Ronald.

BURKS, ARDATH W. (1961) 1964 *The Government of Japan.* 2d ed. New York: Crowell.

CHAMBERLAIN, BASIL H. (1890) 1939 *Things Japanese: Being Notes on Various Subjects Connected With Japan, For the Use of Travellers and Others.* 6th ed., rev. London: Routledge.

COOPER, MICHAEL (editor) 1965 *They Came to Japan: An Anthology of European Reports on Japan, 1543–1640.* Berkeley: Univ. of California Press.

CRAIG, ALBERT M. 1961 *Chōshū in the Meiji Restoration.* Harvard Historical Monographs, Vol. 47. Cambridge, Mass.: Harvard Univ. Press.

DORE, RONALD P. 1958 *City Life in Japan: A Study of a Tokyo Ward.* Berkeley: Univ. of California Press.

DORE, RONALD P. 1959 *Land Reform in Japan.* Oxford Univ. Press.

DORE, RONALD P. 1965 *Education in Tokugawa Japan.* Berkeley: Univ. of California Press.

HALL, JOHN W. 1955 *Tanuma Okitsugu, 1719–1788: Forerunner of Modern Japan.* Harvard–Yenching Institute, Monograph Series, Vol. 14. Cambridge, Mass.: Harvard Univ. Press.

HALL, JOHN W. 1966 *Government and Local Power in Japan, 500 to 1700: A Study Based on Bizen Province.* Princeton Univ. Press.

HALL, JOHN W.; and BEARDSLEY, RICHARD K. 1965 *Twelve Doors to Japan.* New York: McGraw-Hill.

HENDERSON, DAN F. 1965 *Conciliation and Japanese Law: Tokugawa and Modern.* 2 vols. Association for Asian Studies, Monographs and Papers, Vol. 13. Seattle: Univ. of Washington Press.

JANSEN, MARIUS B. 1961 *Sakamoto Ryōma and the Meiji Restoration.* Princeton Univ. Press.

JANSEN, MARIUS B. (editor) 1965 *Changing Japanese Attitudes Toward Modernization.* Princeton Univ. Press.

JAPAN, SAIKŌ SAIBANSHO 1964 *Court and Constitution in Japan: Selected Supreme Court Decisions, 1948–60.* Edited by John M. Maki. Seattle: Univ. of Washington Press.

JOÜON DES LONGRAIS, FRÉDÉRIC 1958 *L'Est et l'Ouest: Institutions du Japon et de l'Occident comparées (six études de sociologie juridique).* Tokyo: Maison Franco-Japonaise.

KEENE, DONALD 1952 *The Japanese Discovery of Europe: Honda Toshiaki and Other Discoverers, 1720–1798.* London: Routledge.

LEVINE, SOLOMON B. 1958 *Industrial Relations in Postwar Japan.* Urbana: Univ. of Illinois Press.

LOCKWOOD, WILLIAM W. (1954) 1958 *The Economic Development of Japan: Growth and Structural Change, 1868–1938.* Princeton Univ. Press.

LOCKWOOD, WILLIAM W. (editor) 1965 *The State and Economic Enterprise in Japan: Essays in the Political Economy of Growth.* Princeton Univ. Press.

NAKAMURA, HAJIME (1948–1949) 1964 *Ways of Thinking of Eastern Peoples.* Rev. ed. Honolulu: East–West Center Press. → First published in Japanese.

OLSON, LAWRENCE A. 1963 *Dimensions of Japan: A Collection of Reports Written for the American Universities Field Staff.* New York: American Universities Field Staff.

PARSONS, TALCOTT (1938–1953) 1963 *Essays in Sociological Theory.* Rev. ed. New York: Free Press. → See especially pages 275–297, "Population and the Social Structure of Japan." A paperback edition was published in 1964.

PASSIN, HERBERT 1965 *Society and Education in Japan.* New York: Columbia Univ., Teachers College.

PASSIN, HERBERT 1966 Intra-familial Linguistic Usage in Japan. *Monumenta nipponica* 21:91–113.

PLATH, DAVID W. 1964 *The After Hours: Modern Japan and the Search for Enjoyment.* Berkeley: Univ. of California Press.

REISCHAUER, EDWIN O. (1950) 1965 *The United States and Japan.* 3d ed. Cambridge, Mass.: Harvard Univ. Press.

REISCHAUER, EDWIN O. 1955 *Ennin's Travels in T'ang China.* New York: Ronald.

ROSOVSKY, HENRY 1961 *Capital Formation in Japan, 1868–1940.* New York: Free Press.

SANSOM, GEORGE B. (1931) 1962 *Japan: A Short Cultural History.* Rev. ed. New York: Appleton.

SANSOM, GEORGE B. 1950 *The Western World and Japan: A Study in the Interaction of European and Asiatic Cultures.* New York: Knopf.

SANSOM, GEORGE B. 1958–1963 *A History of Japan.* 3 vols. Stanford Univ. Press.

SAUNDERS, ERNEST DALE 1964 *Buddhism in Japan, With an Outline of Its Origins in India.* Philadelphia: Univ. of Pennsylvania Press.

SCALAPINO, ROBERT A. (1953) 1962 *Democracy and the Party Movement in Prewar Japan: The Failure of the First Attempt.* Berkeley: Univ. of California Press.

SCALAPINO, ROBERT A.; and MASUMI, JUNNOSUKE 1962 *Parties and Politics in Contemporary Japan.* Berkeley: Univ. of California Press.

SCHUMPETER, JOSEPH A. (1942) 1950 *Capitalism, Socialism, and Democracy.* 3d ed. New York: Harper; London: Allen & Unwin. → A paperback edition was published by Harper in 1962.

SHELDON, CHARLES D. 1958 *The Rise of the Merchant Class in Tokugawa Japan, 1600–1868: An Introductory Survey.* Association for Asian Studies, Monographs, No. 5. Locust Valley, N.Y.: Augustin.

SHINODA, MINORU 1960 *The Founding of the Kamakura Shogunate, 1180–1185.* With selected translations from the *Azuma Kagami.* New York: Columbia Univ. Press.

SILBERMAN, BERNARD S. 1964 *Ministers of Modernization: Elite Mobility in the Meiji Restoration, 1868–1873.* Tucson: Univ. of Arizona Press.

SMITH, THOMAS C. 1955 *Political Change and Industrial Development in Japan: Government Enterprise, 1868–1880.* Stanford Univ. Press.

SMITH, THOMAS C. 1959 *The Agrarian Origins of Modern Japan.* Stanford Univ. Press.

STEINER, KURT 1965 *Local Government in Japan.* Stanford Univ. Press.

TSUNODA, RYŪSAKU; DE BARY, THEODORE W.; and KEENE, DONALD (editors) (1958) 1964 *Sources of the Japanese Tradition.* 2 vols. New York: Columbia Univ. Press.

VEBLEN, THORSTEIN (1915) 1964 The Opportunity of Japan. Pages 248–266 in Thorstein Veblen, *Essays in Our Changing Order.* Edited by Leon Ardzrooni. New York: Kelley.

VOGEL, EZRA F. 1963 *Japan's New Middle Class: The Salary Man and His Family in a Tokyo Suburb.* Berkeley: Univ. of California Press.

VON MEHREN, ARTHUR T. (editor) 1963 *Law in Japan: The Legal Order in a Changing Society.* Cambridge, Mass.: Harvard Univ. Press.

## JEFFERSON, THOMAS

Thomas Jefferson (1743–1826), premier philosopher of American democracy, was born in Shadwell, Virginia. The first son of a leading planter, he grew up in a simple society a stage removed from the frontier and was educated to the responsibilities of leadership in the Virginia manner. He attended the College of William and Mary, 1760–1762, and thereafter studied law with the learned George Wythe at the provincial capital of Williamsburg, being admitted to the bar in 1767. He became a proficient scholar in English law and also in the Greek and Roman classics. The latter, together with his study of modern rationalists (Locke, Bolingbroke, Shaftesbury, Lord Kames, and others, primarily English and Scottish) undermined his inherited Anglican faith and converted him to a deistic natural religion. Natural religion, English law, and ancient philosophy were the wellsprings of his political thought.

First elected to the Virginia legislature in 1769, Jefferson played a prominent part in the coming of the American Revolution. His "Summary View of the Rights of British America," 1774, was one of the earliest denials of the English Parliament's right to legislate for the American colonies. In 1776, as a Virginia delegate to the Continental Congress, he drafted the Declaration of Independence, a brilliant first statement of the principles of American government and, indeed, of democratic revolution the world over. The Declaration appealed to "the Laws of Nature and of Nature's God" for justification of American independence.

The fundamental principles of Jefferson's political theory were included in the philosophical second paragraph of the Declaration of Independence. The principles were not original. They were Lockean by and large, and so generally accepted by American patriots in 1776 that Jefferson himself later said he had only attempted "to place before mankind the common sense of the subject" (letter to Henry Lee, May 8, 1825, in *The Writings of Thomas Jefferson*, vol. 16, p. 118). But the founding of American independence upon the philosophy of the rights of man helped to make the first great colonial revolt of modern times the first great democratic revolution as well.

Jefferson is not to be considered primarily as a political theorist but rather as an enlightened statesman engaged in the practical task of implementing liberal principles in the government of the new nation. Political philosophers, although they had written of "the sovereignty of the people," had not considered the mundane means and contrivances necessary to realize it. Jefferson joined with other American leaders in working out the solution to this problem. It was found, basically, in the constitutional convention, a product not of abstract theory but of developing practice in the American states under the trying conditions of the Revolutionary War. In 1776 Jefferson drafted a constitution for his native state. The reforms it sought, its notably democratic provisions for suffrage and representation, were in advance of republican opinion, and it had little influence on the frame of government ultimately adopted. Subsequently, as a member of the Virginia House of Delegates, 1776–1779, he achieved a number of far-reaching reforms in connection with a general revision of the laws of the commonwealth. The laws of entail and primogeniture were abolished, the criminal code liberalized, the Anglican church disestablished, and religion freed of all state connection. Jefferson wrote the Virginia Statute for Religious Freedom, finally passed in 1786 under the auspices of his good friend and closest political associate, James Madison. Religious freedom he regarded as an absolute right. Its exercise, being wholly a matter of private conscience, injured no one and admitted neither protection nor support from the state. He rejected toleration, which implied an official or preferred religion, and demanded complete religious liberty together with entire separation of church and state. Despite the anticlerical tone of his argument, its animus was friendly, not hostile, to religion and thus unlike the anticlericalism of European liberals. Religious freedom was ostensibly the subject of the famous statute; actually, however, Jefferson widened its scope and made it a ringing manifesto of freedom of inquiry in all fields of intellectual endeavor.

Jefferson's faith in democracy and human progress was one with his faith in education. The people were the only safe depositories of their liberties and happiness, always provided they were sufficiently educated. And he wrote characteristically: "If a nation expects to be ignorant and free, in a state of civilization, it expects what never was and never will be" (letter to Colonel Charles Yancey, January 6, 1816, in *ibid.*, vol. 14, p. 384). Education is, therefore, a paramount responsibility of republican government. His Bill for the More General Diffusion of Knowledge, 1779, provided for three distinct grades of education, the whole system rising like a pyramid from its base in the elementary schools of the local communities to its summit in the state university. (The bill was rejected by the Virginia legislature.) In his theory and plan of public education, Jefferson made one of his most enduring contributions to the democratic polity.

Jefferson was governor of Virginia during two difficult war years, 1779–1781. Then he retired for a few years and completed most of his only book, *Notes on the State of Virginia,* first published in Paris in 1785. Although primarily a work of natural history, which established his reputation as a scientist and philosopher on two continents, it also circulated his political ideas. He was elected to Congress from his state in 1783. There he drafted the Ordinance of 1784, the first plan of government for the immense western domain extending to the Mississippi River. It called for the organization of these lands into many new republican states; after progressing through easy stages of "territorial" government, they would be admitted to the Union on equal footing with the original states. Reflecting the anticolonialism of the new nation, Jefferson's plan laid the basis for an expanding nation—"an empire of liberty"—in the multiplication of self-governing states.

Jefferson's statesmanship was often informed by the reason of the Enlightenment. His plan for the introduction of the decimal system in the nation's coinage, adopted in 1785, was a landmark in world monetary history. Later, as secretary of state, he followed up the principles earlier enunciated in his report on weights and measures of 1790. Here he proposed a comprehensive system of weights, measures, and currency, all based on a universal standard derived from nature and grounded in the simplest arithmetic. The idea was a commonplace of the Enlightenment, but seldom had statesmen acted as natural philosophers. Congress did not adopt Jefferson's plan; only revolutionary France, by adopting the metric system, registered progress in this area.

As American minister to France, 1785–1789, Jefferson witnessed the coming of the French Revolution. Closely associated with liberal circles in Paris, he sympathized with their aspirations for reform of the Bourbon monarchy but did not believe France was ready for a republican government on the American model. His observation of French society convinced him that although the principles of human rights were universally valid, the form of government must be tailored to the conditions of a given society. The main effect of his experience abroad was to make him better aware of the unique advantages of American society and to strengthen his commitment to the national union as an instrument of American power and freedom in a hostile world. Yet the progress of the French Revolution also tended to

give greater intellectual organization to his political beliefs; and this was eventually reflected in the ideology of the Democratic Republican party which he later led.

In 1789, in the midst of revolutionary ferment, he wrote a long epistolary disquisition on the idea " 'that the earth belongs in usufruct to the living'; that the dead have neither powers nor rights over it" (letter to James Madison, September 6, 1789, Jefferson [1760–1826] 1904–1905, vol. 6, pp. 3–4). It was evidently a favorite idea of Jefferson's Paris physician, an elderly Englishman and friend of *philosophes,* Dr. Richard Gem. But it had been germinating in Jefferson's mind for some time, primarily as a response to the European situation, where the laws of property had so far trespassed upon human rights as to make misery an endemic disease, to negate the "sovereignty of the living generation," and to invite violent revolution as the only remedy. Consulting the mortality tables, he calculated the life of a generation (19 years) and then argued that none could impose its constitution and laws upon another, or contract debts to be paid by another, or bind its successors by obligations of any kind. This formulation of the principle that generations, as well as individuals, have natural rights, together with the mathematical application of it to the fundamental conditions of civil society, was at once the most original and the most radical of Jefferson's political ideas. Thomas Paine took it up, perhaps independently, and employed it in his famous controversy with Edmund Burke on the French Revolution. Although he was addressing a foreign situation, Jefferson advocated the doctrine for America as well. It became a permanent fixture of his thought and, while never applied with any exactitude, it entered into the progressive spirit of American institutions.

As the first secretary of state, 1790–1793, under the new national government, Jefferson made important contributions to the law of nations. Believing that sovereign nations are bound by the same moral code as individuals, he worked for the establishment of liberal rules of conduct and the extension of free and pacific intercourse in international affairs. From the principle of popular sovereignty he deduced a new test of the legitimacy of a government: The will of the nation substantially declared. He considered expatriation a natural right, advocated a system of mutual naturalization, worked for free trade, sought concerted action against piratical enemies of mankind, and, in 1793, defined the rights and duties of neutrals more clearly than had been done before. All this expressed his sense of the bonds among nations. His hopes for international cooperation were disappointed, of course, and increasingly he himself was forced to curtail the international references of his political creed and to concentrate on securing the peace and independence of the United States against the dangers of European war and politics.

He was elected president in 1800 after a bitter partisan campaign between Federalists and Democratic Republicans. As vice-president from 1797 to 1801 he had become the acknowledged head of the Republicans in opposition to policies, so he believed, of centralization, economic privilege, war, and political coercion in the Federalist administration. The passage of the Alien and Sedition Acts in 1798 provoked him to draft the Kentucky Resolutions, which asserted the right of a state to "nullify" unconstitutional acts of the federal government. He had long associated responsible republican government with the decentralization and diffusion of political power, involving in the United States strict adherence to the federal constitution and protection of the reserved rights of the states. The Kentucky Resolutions were an extreme statement of this "states' rights" doctrine. Directed against oppressive legislation, they were fraught with unfortunate consequences for the American Union that Jefferson did not anticipate in 1798 [see CONSTITUTIONAL LAW]. His party leadership had more constructive effects. The Federalist party was a "government party," narrowly based on elite groups and intolerant of opposition. Jefferson and his friends went outside the government to build a more broadly based political organization. The success of the Democratic Republicans in 1800 was revolutionary in the sense that it set the course for continuing democratic change in the American political system. Through agitation of public opinion, party organization, and popular elections, change without destruction became possible. The significance, both historical and theoretical, of this development is not lessened by the fact that it was largely unconscious and only brought to completion at a later day.

Jefferson's presidency, 1801–1809, is chiefly memorable for, first, the Louisiana Purchase, 1803, which gave vast new scope to the "empire of liberty," and, second, the Embargo Act, 1807–1809, which employed economic coercion on an unprecedented national scale to enforce American claims upon the belligerent European powers. It failed, although not without demonstrating the utility of "peaceable coercion" in international disputes.

Jefferson retired to Monticello—the superb architectural expression of his genius—in 1809. A Virginia farmer and agriculturist, he owned and worked several plantations. His last years were devoted to the establishment of the University of Virginia, which he conceived, planned, and supervised in every detail. He died at Monticello on the fiftieth anniversary of American independence, July 4, 1826.

MERRILL D. PETERSON

[*See also* DEMOCRACY; PRESIDENTIAL GOVERNMENT.]

### WORKS BY JEFFERSON

(1760–1826) 1950—    *Papers*. Vols. 1—. Edited by Julian P. Boyd. Princeton Univ. Press. → To be published in 60 volumes.

(1760–1826) 1904–1905    *Writings of Thomas Jefferson*. Collected and edited by Paul L. Ford. 12 vols. New York: Putnam. → Known as The Federal edition.

*The Writings of Thomas Jefferson*. 20 vols. Edited by Andrew A. Lipscomb and A. Ellery Bergh. Washington: Thomas Jefferson Memorial Association of the United States, 1905.

### SUPPLEMENTARY BIBLIOGRAPHY

BOORSTIN, DANIEL J.    1948    *The Lost World of Thomas Jefferson*. New York: Holt.

CHINARD, GILBERT    (1929) 1939    *Thomas Jefferson: The Apostle of Americanism*. 2d ed. rev. Boston: Little. → A paperback edition was published in 1952 by the University of Michigan Press.

KOCH, ADRIENNE    (1943) 1957    *The Philosophy of Thomas Jefferson*. Gloucester, Mass.: Smith.

LEHMANN, KARL    1947    *Thomas Jefferson: American Humanist*. New York: Macmillan.

MALONE, DUMAS    1948–1962    *Jefferson and His Time*. 3 vols. Boston: Little. → Volume 1: *Jefferson the Virginian*. Volume 2: *Jefferson and the Rights of Man*. Volume 3: *Jefferson and the Ordeal of Liberty*.

PETERSON, MERRILL D.    1960    *The Jefferson Image in the American Mind*. New York: Oxford Univ. Press. → A paperback edition was published in 1962.

WILTSE, CHARLES M.    1935    *The Jeffersonian Tradition in American Democracy*. Chapel Hill: Univ. of North Carolina Press. → A paperback edition was published in 1960 by Hill & Wang.

# JELLINEK, GEORG

Georg Jellinek (1851–1911), German jurist, was born in Leipzig, the son of a rabbi and scholar. In 1857 the family moved to Vienna. Jellinek studied philosophy, history, and law there and in Heidelberg and Leipzig. In 1872 he received a doctorate in philosophy from the University of Leipzig and in 1874 a doctorate in law from the University of Vienna. He worked for almost two years as an Austrian civil servant while he continued his studies and in 1879 received his *venia legendi* from the law faculty in Vienna. After appointments in Vienna, Berlin, and Basel, in 1890 Jellinek became professor of constitutional and international law and political science at the University of Heidelberg, where he remained until his death.

In 1883 Jellinek married Camilla Wertheim, the daughter of an Austrian professor of medicine. Their son Walter (1885–1955) was professor of constitutional and administrative law in Kiel and Heidelberg.

Jellinek's friends included Wilhelm Windelband, Ernst Troeltsch, Max Weber, and Erwin Rohde, and together they helped shape the intellectual climate of Heidelberg at the turn of the century. Jellinek was a good teacher as well as a prolific and stimulating scholar who was praised for his erudition and his moral sensitivity.

Jellinek's first writings dealt with philosophical problems. In *Die sozialethische Bedeutung von Recht, Unrecht und Strafe* (1878) he characterized the law in a famous phrase as embodying the "ethical minimum," i.e., in an objective sense, a set of elementary moral norms that are indispensable for living in society, and, in a subjective sense, the minimum of "morality" embodied in legal precepts that the members of a society demand. He next published a series of monographs on constitutional law and the law of nations. These monographs are marked by a systematic and somewhat formalistic mode of interpretation. They culminate in Jellinek's favorite book, *System der subjektiven öffentlichen Rechte* (1892), which was a significant contribution to the German theory of the constitutional state. In this book he developed his well-known classification of subjective rights in relation to particular "statuses"; thus he distinguished *status passivus* (which entails general subjection to the state), *status negativus* (which assures rights of protection against the state), *status positivus* (which grants rights to positive actions by the state), and *status activus* (which guarantees rights of political participation, especially voting).

Jellinek also wrote on the history of political ideas. In his widely known book *The Declaration of the Rights of Man and of Citizens* (1895), for which Princeton University awarded him an honorary degree, he put forward the thesis that the French Declaration of the Rights of Man of 1789 was not written under the influence of Rousseau but rather under the influence of the American bill of rights, which had its origin in the struggle for the liberty of conscience and religion. This thesis of Jellinek's still commands attention.

Jellinek's work culminated in his monumental synthesis, *Allgemeine Staatslehre* (1900). The most significant feature of this book is its division into two distinct parts—a sociological and a "jur-istic" one. This division derives from Jellinek's Neo-Kantian views. The "is" is separated from the "ought" and leads to a corresponding methodological dichotomy. Jellinek's theory of the state is dualistic insofar as he saw no intrinsic correlation between the investigation of social reality and the elaboration of judicial concepts. However, there is a degree of methodological monism in his thinking insofar as he considered both the formation of the law and the validity of the law to be based on social-psychological facts. The link between the "is" and the "ought" is formed by the principle of the "normative force of the factual." But Jellinek did not believe that law originates *ex ipso facto bruto*. For the factual to have normative force requires general acceptance that what is ought to be; for Jellinek it was self-evident that the law must agree with the ethical minimum.

The theory and the sociology of the state owe much to Jellinek, who greatly influenced German legal science. His work in the history of legal science contributed toward the weakening of the jurisprudence of concepts that (under the influence of C. F. von Gerber and P. Laband) had prevailed in German public law. But because he did not transcend the antimetaphysical relativism and voluntarism of his Neo-Kantian system, he was unable to provide clear guidelines for jurists trying to find their way between the one-sided positions of a pure normativism and a sociological positivism that minimizes the normative force of the law.

ALEXANDER HOLLERBACH

[*For the historical context of Jellinek's work, see* JURISPRUDENCE; LAW; POLITICAL THEORY; POSITIVISM; *and the biographies of* BRECHT; KANTOROWICZ; KELSEN; WEBER, MAX.]

### WORKS BY JELLINEK

(1872–1910) 1911 *Ausgewählte Schriften und Reden.* 2 vols. Edited by Walter Jellinek. Berlin: Häring.

(1878) 1908 *Die sozialethische Bedeutung von Recht, Unrecht und Strafe.* 2d ed., rev. Berlin: Häring.

1880 *Die rechtliche Natur der Staatenverträge: Ein Beitrag zur juristischen Construction des Völkerrechts.* Vienna: Hölder.

1882 *Die Lehre von den Staatenverbindungen.* Berlin: Häring.

(1887) 1964 *Gesetz und Verordnung: Staatsrechtliche Untersuchungen auf rechtsgeschichtlicher und rechtsvergleichender Grundlage.* Aalen (Germany): Scientia.

(1892) 1964 *System der subjektiven öffentlichen Rechte.* 2d ed. Darmstadt (Germany): Wissenschaftliche Buchgesellschaft.

(1895) 1901 *The Declaration of the Rights of Man and of Citizens: A Contribution to Modern Constitutional History.* New York: Holt. → First published as *Die Erklärung der Menschen- und Bürgerrechte.*

(1900) 1960 *Allgemeine Staatslehre.* 3d ed., rev. & enl. Bad Homburg (Germany): Getner.

1906  *Verfassungsänderung und Verfassungswandlung: Eine staatsrechtlich-politische Abhandlung.* Berlin: Häring.

### SUPPLEMENTARY BIBLIOGRAPHY

BRECHT, ARNOLD 1959 *Political Theory: The Foundation of Twentieth-century Political Thought.* Princeton Univ. Press. → See especially pages 220–221.

EMERSON, RUPERT 1928 *State and Sovereignty in Modern Germany.* New Haven: Yale Univ. Press. → See especially pages 59–63, 71–73, 83–85, 107–111.

HALLIS, FREDERICK 1930 *Corporate Personality: A Study of Jurisprudence.* Oxford Univ. Press. → See especially pages 189–216 on "The State as Presupposition of Law: Georg Jellinek [and] The Law as Presupposition of the State: H. Krabbe."

HOLUBEK, REINHARD 1961 *Allgemeine Staatslehre als empirische Wissenschaft: Eine Untersuchung am Beispiel von Georg Jellinek.* Bonn (Germany): Bouvier.

JELLINEK, CAMILLA 1931 Georg Jellinek: Sein Leben. Volume 7, pages 136–146 in *Neue österreichische Biographie: 1815–1918.* Vienna: Amalthea.

JELLINEK, WALTER 1911 Georg Jellineks Werke. *Archiv des öffentlichen Rechts* 27:606–619.

KELSEN, HANS (1911) 1923 *Hauptprobleme der Staatsrechtslehre entwickelt aus der Lehre vom Rechtssatze.* Tübingen (Germany): Mohr. → See especially pages 482–491.

LUKAS, JOSEF 1931 Georg Jellinek: Sein Werk. Volume 7, pages 147–152 in *Neue österreichische Biographie: 1815–1918.* Vienna: Amalthea.

NELSON, LEONARD (1917) 1949 *Die Rechtswissenschaft ohne Recht: Kritische Betrachtungen über die Grundlagen des Staats- und Völkerrechts, insbesondere über die Lehre von der Souveränität.* 2d ed. Göttingen (Germany): Verlag "Öffentliches Leben." → See especially pages 6–68.

TROELTSCH, ERNST 1912 [Review of] Jellinek, Georg, *Ausgewählte Schriften und Reden. Zeitschrift für das Privat- und Öffentliche Recht der Gegenwart* 39:273–278.

WEBER, MAX (1911) 1926 Zu G. Jellineks Gedächtnis. Pages 481–486 in Marianne Weber, *Max Weber: Ein Lebensbild.* Tübingen (Germany): Mohr.

WINDELBAND, WILHELM 1911 Zum Geleit. Volume 1, pages 5–12 in Georg Jellinek, *Ausgewählte Schriften und Reden.* Berlin: Häring.

ZWEIG, EGON 1914 Georg Jellinek. Volume 16, pages 147–154 in *Biographisches Jahrbuch und Deutscher Nekrolog.* Berlin: Reimer.

# JEVONS, WILLIAM STANLEY

William Stanley Jevons (1835–1882), one of the greatest and most original of English economists, was born in Liverpool. His father was an iron merchant and engineer who constructed one of the first iron boats and also wrote on economics and legal subjects; his mother was a daughter of the historian William Roscoe. Both parents were Unitarians. At the age of 15 Jevons was sent as a boarder to University College School, London, and a year later he entered University College. Although

he studied chemistry and botany there, it was during these London years that his interests, always wide-ranging, first turned to the study of society. "It was in 1851," he later wrote, "that I first began, at the age of sixteen, to study the industrial mechanism of society" (1905, p. vii). He used to go for long walks through the poorest parts of Dickensian London, observing the condition of the people—as Alfred Marshall was later to do in the great industrial cities. At 17 he wrote of "wanting very much to get Mayhew's *London Labour & London Poor*, as that is the only book I know of to learn a little about the real condition of the poor in London" (1886, p. 29). Already he was imbued with a sense of mission: "I began to think that I could and ought to do more than others. A vague desire and determination grew upon me" (1886, pp. 12–13). He later described this as a determination "to be *powerfully good*, that is to be good, not towards one, or a dozen, or a hundred, but towards a nation or the world" (1886, p. 96).

In 1853, when still under 19, Jevons was offered a very responsible and well-paid post as assayer at the newly established mint at Sydney, Australia. The collapse of the family firm in the 1847–1848 crisis had left his family in straitened circumstances, and he reluctantly, through a sense of duty, accepted the offer. The combination of leisure and solitude during his five years in Sydney provided, for one as powerfully inner-directed as Jevons, ideal conditions for the development of his great intellectual originality and capacity for independent thought. Meteorology became a main interest, and a paper on the climate of Australia was one of his first publications (1859). He also continued his early interests in urban problems and in conducting social surveys; he planned a work entitled "Notes and Researches on Social Statistics or the Science of Towns." He completed some sections on Sydney, but he did not publish anything, nor did he ever return to his "science of towns."

In 1857 political economy began to become his main interest. As an economist, Jevons was entirely self-taught and the originality of his thought is apparent from his first work. He had no reverence for the prevailing classical orthodoxies and from the beginning saw economic problems in what was to be the characteristically neoclassical manner, that is, as problems of valuation and optimal allocation. In a letter of February 1858 he wrote to his sister:

I am glad you find political economy tolerable. *The Wealth of Nations* is perhaps one of the driest on the subject. You will perceive that *economy*, scientifically speaking, is a very contracted science; it is in fact a sort of vague mathematics which calculates the causes and effects of man's industry, and shows how it may best be applied. . . . I have an idea, which I do not object to mention to you, that my insight into the foundations and nature of the knowledge of man is deeper than that of most men or writers. In fact, I think that it is my mission to apply myself to such subjects, and it is my intention to do so. . . . Thoroughly to understand the principles of society appears to me now the most cogent business.   (1886, p. 101)

Jevons' first articles were concerned with railway and land problems in New South Wales (1857a; 1857b). One of the books he read in 1857 was Dionysius Lardner's *Railway Economy*. Lardner knew Cournot's work, and his analysis of the profit-maximizing rates for railways had close similarities with Cournot's treatment of monopoly. Some elements of Cournot's pioneering marginal analysis presumably filtered through to Jevons. However, Jevons was not to be concerned with the theory of the firm, the great achievement of Cournot, but with utility and the consumer. In fact, though Jevons doubtless owed a little to Bentham and to one or two other lesser-known English utility theorists, such as Richard Jennings, there can be no doubt as to the high and substantial degree of independent originality in his marginal utility theory.

**Jevons' academic career.**   Jevons returned to England in 1859 and resumed his studies at University College for his B.A. and M.A. degrees. He came back from Australia not only with the means to carry on his studies but also with a stock of ideas, which he was to develop in his next few years of remarkable pioneering achievement in London and Manchester.

In October 1863 he took up a post as tutor at Owens College, Manchester (later. the University of Manchester), and was thus launched on an academic career, being appointed in 1866 as professor of logic and mental and moral philosophy and of political economy. The range of his official titles was no wider than his interests and contributions to knowledge. He married a daughter of the founder of the *Manchester Guardian* in 1867 and stayed in Manchester until 1876, when he moved to University College, London. He always found lecturing a great strain and resigned his chair in 1880.

**Writings, 1859–1871.**   Jevons' work between the time he returned to England and the publication of his fully developed theory of value, *The Theory of Political Economy* (1871), can be roughly divided into three categories: the first formulation of his theory of value, a group of papers on monetary statistics, and a full-length book on public policy, *The Coal Question* (1865).

In 1860 he wrote his brother that "in the last few months I have fortunately struck out what I have no doubt is *the true Theory of Economy*, so thorough-going and consistent, that I cannot now read other books on the subject without indignation. . . . One of the most important axioms is, that as the quantity of any commodity, for instance, plain food, which a man has to consume, increases, so the utility or benefit derived from the last portion used decreases in degree" (1886, p. 151). Jevons wrote up his theory of value in a paper to the British Association for the Advancement of Science in 1862; it was entitled "Notice of a General Mathematical Theory of Political Economy" and was first printed four years later. Little or no recognition was given to this first statement of Jevons' theory of value—and, indeed, his later, much fuller, statement in *The Theory of Political Economy* (1871) was at first also neglected.

Jevons' early and finest papers in monetary statistics were published in this period: "On the Study of Periodic Commercial Fluctuations" (1884), also submitted to the British Association in 1862, which included a pioneering analysis of seasonal variations; and perhaps the greatest of all his works, "A Serious Fall in the Value of Gold Ascertained, and Its Social Effects Set Forth" (1863). In the decade or so following the mid-century gold discoveries in California and Australia, there had been much controversy regarding their effects on the level of prices. Some economists, John Ramsey McCulloch and William Newmarch, for example, held that no significant rise in the general level of prices had taken place. Jevons, in his 1863 pamphlet, provided a precise estimate of the fall in the value of gold, that is, 9 per cent between 1848 and 1860, which was later shown to have been remarkably accurate. In so doing he made one of the greatest single contributions to the technique of constructing price index numbers [*see* INDEX NUMBERS]. Indeed, according to Keynes, on the subject of index numbers Jevons "made as much progress in this brief pamphlet as has been made by all succeeding authors put together" (Keynes [1933] 1951, p. 269). Jevons also touched, in this work, on the subject of economic crises, which he then seemed inclined to explain in terms of periodically excessive and disproportional investment—along similar lines as James Wilson. But when he returned to the problem in subsequent essays, he developed his theory that periodic sunspots cause bad harvests and hence economic depressions. His statistical evidence for this theory was never very convincing, but the theory may have had more plausibility for explaining Britain's depressions in the middle decades of the nineteenth century than it would seem to have had for subsequent periods.

Jevons' mainly statistical papers in the fields of money, prices, and fluctuations were collected post-humously in *Investigations in Currency and Finance*. They indicate that he was a pioneer in the graphic presentation of economic and financial statistics, adapting for the charting of the economic "weather" the methods used in his meteorological studies. Like Marshall and Pareto, Jevons was one of the few leading late nineteenth-century neoclassical exponents of deductive marginal analysis who also made valuable contributions to statistical and descriptive economics, in "an attempt"—as he put it in some notes for an introduction to the *Investigations*—"to substitute exact inquiries, exact numerical calculations, for guess-work and groundless argument" ([1863–1884] 1964, p. xxiv).

*The Coal Question* (1865), Jevons' first full-length book, brought him a wider measure of fame and certainly succeeded in its aim of rousing public opinion. In it he warned his countrymen that British coal deposits were exhaustible and that the cost of coal would rise as the best and easiest seams were used up. Jevons did not foresee the development of other major sources of power—just as Malthus had not foreseen the development of great overseas supplies of food. But the book certainly shows prophetic insight into the inevitably temporary nature of Britain's coal-based industrial leadership, then at its peak. He also foresaw the rising industrial power of the United States. The work is a masterly tract in applied economics and an achievement in a quite different genre from his contributions to economic theory and monetary statistics.

**Jevons' theory of political economy.**   Jevons had conceived the essentials of his theory of value by 1860 and had written them up briefly in his 1862 paper to the British Association; little notice, however, was taken. For some years he turned to a wide range of other subjects and from 1866 to 1870 was absorbed in problems of logic and scientific method.

The publication in 1870 of Fleeming Jenkin's "The Graphic Representation of the Laws of Supply and Demand," and subsequent correspondence with Jenkin, seems to have stimulated Jevons to publish more fully his ideas on the theory of value and so to establish his priority with regard to the new approach. *The Theory of Political Economy* was rapidly written (though not perhaps as rapidly as John Stuart Mill's *Principles*) and published in October 1871. Although it was not fully appreciated when it was first published, this book opened a new

epoch in the history of economic thought, and it is the work for which Jevons is best known. Though it has many brilliantly original and challenging passages, its argument is imperfectly or incompletely developed at various important points. Much was left to be worked out in subsequent decades, and even the central concept of utility was soon to be fundamentally called in question. Nevertheless, Jevons did in fact provide a new point of departure for economic analysis.

Jevons' theory of utility and value was subjectively highly original. Compared with the other two pioneers of the marginal utility theory in the early 1870s, Carl Menger and Léon Walras, Jevons had much less to build on. Menger knew the works of Friedrich Hermann, Albert Schäffle, and Hans Mangoldt, and Walras had behind him the whole French tradition of utility and scarcity theory. When Jevons came in 1879 to write the preface to the second edition of his *Theory*, he too had become acquainted with this literature and gave a masterly survey—itself a pioneer achievement in economic scholarship—of the contributions to marginal analysis and utility theory by his predecessors and contemporaries. Of course, neither the marginal concept nor the analysis of the relation of utility to value was absolutely novel in 1871. It was simply that the coincidence in the early 1870s of Jevons, Menger, and Walras, each almost simultaneously publishing his version of the theory, could, in due course, be seen as the opening of a new period in economic theorizing. As Walras wrote to Cournot in 1874: "M. Jevons et moi avons amené la question à un point tel, qu'elle ne pourra bientôt plus être écartée par les économistes" ("Jevons and I have brought the matter to the point where economists will soon be unable to ignore it"; Walras & Cournot 1873–1875).

*The Theory of Political Economy* begins on a note of revolutionary challenge to classical orthodoxy, and particularly to John Stuart Mill's *Principles*. Jevons expressed complete confidence in the substantial correctness of his proposition that "value depends entirely on utility." At the same time, he made enthusiastic claims for mathematical methods that were then highly controversial. He started on markedly Benthamite lines with the theory of pleasure and pain, then proceeded to the theory of utility. For Jevons, as for Menger, Walras, and Marshall, but not for Edgeworth, the utility function for a commodity is related to the quantity of that commodity only. He formulated the law of diminishing utility and then proceeded to deduce the utility-maximizing allocation formula for the consumer, establishing the pattern for much of the subsequent neoclassical theorizing. Jevons did not use the concept of marginal utility but rather that of "the final degree of utility," or marginal utility (that is, the utility of the marginal increment) divided by the size of the marginal increment. In his words: "The keystone of the whole Theory of Exchange, and of the principal problems of Economics, lies in this proposition—*The ratio of exchange of any two commodities will be the reciprocal of the ratio of the final degrees of utility of the quantities of commodity available for consumption after the exchange is completed*" ([1871] 1957, p. 95).

Jevons' analysis of market exchanges, however, is highly unsatisfactory. He attempted to generalize the analysis of two-party, two-commodity barter to apply to a competitive market. Although he contributed to the development of a precise definition of competitive conditions through his "law of indifference," his use of the concept of trading bodies, with their collective marginal utilities, was mistaken.

Jevons concluded his chapter on exchange with an eloquent attack on labor and cost-of-production theories of value:

The fact is, that *labour once spent has no influence on the future value of any article: it is gone and lost for ever.* In commerce bygones are for ever bygones; and we are always starting clear at each moment, judging the values of things with a view to future utility. Industry is essentially prospective, not retrospective; and seldom does the result of any undertaking exactly coincide with the first intentions of its promoters. (*ibid.*, p. 164)

He then provided his own summary of the determination of values:

But though labour is never the cause of value, it is in a large proportion of cases the determining circumstance, and in the following way: *Value depends solely on the final degree of utility. How can we vary this degree of utility?—By having more or less of the commodity to consume. And how shall we get more or less of it?—By spending more or less labour in obtaining a supply.* According to this view, then, there are two steps between labour and value. Labour affects supply, and supply affects the degree of utility, which governs value, or the ratio of exchange. In order that there may be no possible mistake about this all-important series of relations, I will re-state it in a tabular form, as follows:

*Cost of production determines supply;*
*Supply determines final degree of utility;*
*Final degree of utility determines value.*
(*ibid.*, p. 165)

This typically and brilliantly incisive summary led Keynes to comment that Jevons chiseled in stone while Marshall knitted in wool. Nevertheless,

two criticisms of Jevons' conclusion—both actually first suggested by Marshall—can be made. The first is that it does not seem consistent with Jevons' basic proposition that value depends solely on final degree of utility; in fact, as traced back by Jevons, it is the classical cost of production that is the first determinant. Second, the determinants of value have, in any case, to be sought not in one-way causal chains but in mutual determination and interdependence.

Jevons' *Theory of Political Economy* provides a sketch of only one half of the field of microeconomic analysis—the theory of the consumer. Jevons attempted no theory of the firm. But his theories of labor and capital are both significant. That of labor supply states an allocation principle according to which the marginal disutility of labor, which after a point increases, is balanced against the diminishing marginal utility of the product. The free laborer "will cease to labour just at the point when the pain becomes equal to the corresponding pleasure gained. . . . In this, as in the other questions of Economics, all depends upon the final increments, and we have expressed in the above formula *the final equivalence of labour and utility*" (*ibid.*, pp. 176–177). The concept of "the free laborer" involves the often unrealistic assumption that the individual can continuously adjust his supply of labor and does not have to supply it in large, indivisible units.

Jevons' theory of capital or "capitalization" anticipates in important respects the theory expounded so voluminously in 1889 by Böhm-Bawerk [*see* BÖHM-BAWERK]. Jevons stated that capital has two dimensions, the quantity and the period of time for which it is invested, and that, in Böhm-Bawerk's terminology, an increase in capital amounts to "a lengthening of the period of production": "*Whatever improvements in the supply of commodities lengthen the average interval between the moment when labour is exerted and its ultimate result or purpose accomplished, such improvements depend upon the use of capital*" ([1871] 1957, pp. 228–229). It is in his theory of capital that Jevons came nearest to stating a marginal productivity theory: "The rate of interest depends on the advantage of the last increment of capital, and the advantages of previous increments may be greater in almost any ratio" (*ibid.*, p. 256).

In the preface to the second edition Jevons hinted at a marginal productivity theory by remarking that distribution is entirely subject to the principles of value. Except in his theory of capital and interest, however, he did not work out this idea.

Jevons' ideas met with little acceptance in his

lifetime. Cairnes, Marshall, and Sidgwick were all in various ways coolly skeptical. Simon Newcomb in the United States was one of the few to give them some recognition, although he justifiably felt that Jevons' *Theory* was not as outstanding an achievement as Cournot's *Recherches*. Nor was Jevons the founder of a school of disciples, as were Menger and Marshall, although P. H. Wicksteed later emerged as an enthusiastic propagator of what he regarded as Jevons' theoretical revolution.

Nevertheless, from 1871, as we can now see, a new pattern had been set for economic theorizing. Exchange and allocation became the central problem in a much more exclusive way than previously. Economic analysis was built up logically on the foundation of the maximizing individual. This permitted much more precision and a great development of mathematical formulation; but it made also for greater abstraction and a narrowing of focus, compared with classical political economy.

**Economic and social reform.** In his *Lecture Notes on Types of Economic Theory* (1949), Wesley C. Mitchell described Jevons as primarily an economic "scientist," more interested in developing detachedly the methods and criteria of the natural sciences in the social and economic field than in immediate practical reforms. It is true that his great contributions both to statistical and analytical economics have this scientific emphasis. But in his youth he certainly showed a deeply "engaged" reforming approach to social problems, and he continued throughout his tragically abbreviated career to contribute to the discussion of the practical problems of social reform. He concerned himself especially with questions of state control and management, supporting the nationalization of telegraphs but opposing that of the railways.

Considering his temperament, upbringing, and family and social background, it is not surprising that Jevons was a sturdy individualist. Indeed, the opening words of his first article on political economy (published in Australia in 1857), were: "Freedom for all commercial transactions is the spirit of improved legislation." In his inaugural lecture at Manchester (1866) he warned that the greatest danger was that the "working classes, with their growing numbers and powers of combination, may be led by ignorance to arrest the true growth of our liberty, political and commercial." A trade union, he held, could benefit its members only at the expense of their fellow workers outside the union and of consumers generally. Jevons was critical also of both public and private charity, and of the incipient social services, as weakening the initiative and self-reliance of the people. In his presidential address to the British Association for the Advancement of Science in 1870, he welcomed the great Education Act of that year, which established elementary education in Britain, but he complained that pauperism was "almost as prevalent as ever," holding that that was "precisely what Malthus would have predicted of a population which, while supplied with easily earned wealth, . . . [is] bribed by the mistaken benevolence of the richer classes into a neglect of the future" ([1870] 1962, p. 27). He argued that although, according to his calculations, the tax burden then was spread roughly in proportion to incomes, those poorer families who consumed only "moderate quantities of tobacco and spirituous liquor" were not contributing proportionally or sufficiently. He therefore recommended that it would be "inexpedient to proceed further in the reduction of the customs and excise duties" ([1870] 1962, p. 34).

It seems that Jevons may have somewhat modified these rigorous views in his later years. At any rate, like Cairnes and Sidgwick, he rejected the laissez-faire maxim, then widely regarded as the orthodox lesson of political economy, and he called for a systematic analysis of economic policy:

While population grows more numerous and dense, while industry becomes more complex and interdependent, as we travel faster and make use of more intense forces, we shall necessarily need more legislative supervision. If such a thing is possible, we need a new branch of political and statistical science which shall carefully investigate the limits to the *laissez-faire* principle, and show where we want greater freedom and where less. . . . Instead of one dictum, *laissez-faire, laissez-passer*, we must have at least one science, one new branch of the old political economy. ([1876] 1905, pp. 203–206)

Jevons' main contribution to economic policy lies in *The State in Relation to Labour* (1882), published in the year of his death. Here he reasserted his proposition that trade unions can improve the position of their members only at the expense of the rest of the community. But he recognized that "one result which clearly emerges from a calm review is that all classes of society are trades-unionists at heart, and differ chiefly in the boldness, ability and secrecy with which they push their respective interests" (1882, p. vi). He placed his hopes for the future, perhaps rather optimistically, in industrial partnership, which would bind the interests of the employer and workman more closely together. In *The State in Relation to Labour*, Jevons developed a much more cautious, empirical, and antidogmatic approach to the principles of policy than was suggested by some of his earlier attitudes. In fact, in his conclusion to that work he gives us one of the finest and most eloquent statements of English empiricism:

It is clear that there can be no royal road to legislation in such matters. We cannot expect to agree in utilitarian estimates, at least without much debate. We must agree to differ, and though we are bound to argue fearlessly, it should be with the consciousness that there is room for wide and *bona fide* difference of opinion. We must consent to advance cautiously, step by step, feeling our way, adopting no foregone conclusions, trusting no single science, expecting no infallible guide. We must neither maximise the functions of government at the beck of quasi-military officials, nor minimise them according to the theories of the very best philosophers. We must learn to judge each case upon its merits, interpreting with painful care all experience which can be brought to bear upon the matter. (1882, p. 166)

**Logic and the principles of science.** The wide range not only of Jevons' interests but of his important contributions to knowledge is as remarkable as his path-breaking, fundamental originality of thought. He wrote almost as much on logic and scientific method as on political economy, in both fields publishing valuable, widely read textbooks as well as major original works. *The Principles of Science* (1874) has been recognized as a pioneer work, in important respects well ahead of its time. Especially notable was his development of the fundamentals of formal logic on the lines of George Boole, and his construction of a machine, still extant (a "logical piano," as Ernest Nagel called it) for the mechanical solution of deductive problems—an anticipation of modern computing machines (see Jevons [1874] 1958, p. xlix). Jevons also developed the hypothetico–deductive approach, expounded more recently by Karl Popper, in that he rejected the Baconian conception of scientific enquiry as starting from the accumulation of facts and stressed the role of conjectures and hypotheses. "Inductive investigation," he wrote, "consists in the union of hypothesis and experiment" (*ibid.*, p. 525).

Jevons was drowned in a swimming accident at an age (46) when many great thinkers—for example, Marshall—had not completed a fraction of the work for which they were subsequently renowned. Among the books he left unfinished are a treatise on religion and science, in which he stressed their complete compatibility, an edition of *The Wealth of Nations*, to be prefaced by a survey of the history of economic thought, and an examination of Mill's philosophy. But the greatest loss, certainly for economists, was the unfinished

*Principles of Economics*, some fragments of which were subsequently published under the editorship of Henry Higgs (1905). In this comprehensive work he would almost certainly have worked out further the marginal analysis of which he had been the pioneer, combining it with his essential contributions to the explanation of commercial fluctuations and with a treatment of that new branch of the subject, which he had called for, dealing with the principles of economic policy. Keynes, on first meeting Jevons' work at the age of 22, wrote: "I am convinced that he was one of *the* minds of the century. He has the curiously exciting style of writing which one gets if one is good enough" (Harrod 1951, pp. 106–107). This is no overstatement of the case. For breadth, variety, originality, and incisive penetration, Jevons' work as economist, statistician, logician, and philosopher is among the greatest of modern times.

T. W. HUTCHISON

[*See also* UTILITY; *and the biographies of* MANGOLDT; MARSHALL; MENGER; MILL, *article on* ECONOMIC CONTRIBUTIONS; NEWCOMB; WALRAS; WICKSTEED.]

### WORKS BY JEVONS

1857a The Public Lands of New South Wales. *Empire* (Sydney) June 23.

1857b Comparison of the Land and Railway Policy of New South Wales. *Empire* (Sydney) April 7.

1859 Climates of Australia and New Zealand. *Waugh's Australian Almanack* (Sydney) [1859]:1–52.

1862 Notice of a General Mathematical Theory of Political Economy. British Association for the Advancement of Science, *Reports* 32:158–159.

(1863) 1964 A Serious Fall in the Value of Gold Ascertained, and Its Social Effects Set Forth. Pages 13–111 in W. Stanley Jevons, *Investigations in Currency and Finance*. New York: Kelley.

(1863–1884) 1964 *Investigations in Currency and Finance*. With a preface by Stanley H. Jevons. New York: Kelley. → Published posthumously.

(1865) 1906 *The Coal Question: An Inquiry Concerning the Progress of the Nation, and the Probable Exhaustion of Our Coal-mines.* 3d ed., rev. Edited by A. W. Flux. London and New York: Macmillan.

1866 *An Introductory Lecture on the Importance of Diffusing a Knowledge of Political Economy.* Manchester (England): No publisher given.

(1870) 1962 Economic Policy. Pages 25–40 in British Association for the Advancement of Science, Economic Science and Statistics Section, *Essays in Economic Method: Selected Papers . . . 1860–1913.* London: Duckworth. → First published as "Address to the Section of Economic Science and Statistics" in Volume 40 of the Association's *Reports.*

(1871) 1957 *The Theory of Political Economy.* 5th ed. New York: Kelley. → Pages xi–lii contain the preface to the second edition. A list of Jevons' economic writings appears on pages 315–321.

(1874) 1958 *The Principles of Science: A Treatise on*

*Logic and Scientific Method.* With a new introduction by Ernest Nagel. New York: Dover.

(1876) 1905  The Future of Political Economy. Pages 185–206 in W. Stanley Jevons, *The Principles of Economics: A Fragment of a Treatise on the Industrial Mechanism of Society and Other Papers.* London and New York: Macmillan.

(1882) 1910  *The State in Relation to Labour.* 4th ed. With an introduction by Francis W. Hirst. London: Macmillan.

(1884) 1964  On the Study of Periodic Commercial Fluctuations. Pages 1–11 in W. Stanley Jevons, *Investigations in Currency and Finance.* New York: Kelley.

1886  *Letters & Journal of W. Stanley Jevons.* Edited by his wife, H. A. Jevons. London: Macmillan. → Published posthumously. A remarkable Victorian document, showing Jevons' intellectual development.

1905  *The Principles of Economics: A Fragment of a Treatise on the Industrial Mechanism of Society and Other Papers.* With an introduction by Henry Higgs. London and New York: Macmillan. → Published posthumously.

### SUPPLEMENTARY BIBLIOGRAPHY

BLACK, R. D. COLLISON 1962  W. S. Jevons and the Economists of His Time. *Manchester School of Economic and Social Studies* 30:203–221.

HARROD, ROY FORBES 1951  *The Life of John Maynard Keynes.* London: Macmillan. → A paperback edition was published in 1963 by St. Martins.

KEYNES, JOHN MAYNARD (1933) 1951  William Stanley Jevons. Pages 225–309 in John Maynard Keynes, *Essays in Biography.* New York: Horizon. → A paperback edition was published in 1963 by Norton.

KÖNEKAMP, ROSAMOND 1962  William Stanley Jevons (1835–1882): Some Biographical Notes. *Manchester School of Economic and Social Studies* 30:251–273.

MAYS, WOLFE 1962  Jevons' Conception of Scientific Method. *Manchester School of Economic and Social Studies* 30:223–249.

MITCHELL, WESLEY C. 1949  *Lecture Notes on Types of Economic Theory.* 2 vols. New York: Kelley. → See especially Chapters 2–8 in Volume 2.

WALRAS, LÉON; and COURNOT, A. (1873–1875) 1952  La correspondance complète de Cournot et Walras. *Économie appliquée* 5:5–33.

# JOCHELSON, VLADIMIR

*See the article on* BOGORAZ, VLADIMIR G., STERNBERG, LEV Y., AND JOCHELSON, VLADIMIR.

# JOHNSON, ALVIN

Alvin Johnson has a place in the social sciences as an encyclopedic scholar, an innovator in adult education, and an outstanding writer and humanist.

He was born in December 1874 on a farm in Nebraska. His father, Jens Jensen Deyrup, had changed his name to John Johnson at the suggestion of an immigration officer when he arrived in the United States from his native Denmark. His mother had also emigrated from Denmark; her parents were members of the Danish aristocracy. It was probably of lasting influence on Johnson that he was the son of a pioneer farmer and of a mother who had intellectual ambitions for her son. He managed his father's farm from his thirteenth to his eighteenth year but while on the farm studied science and Latin. After a year's premedical course at the University of Nebraska, he changed to the classics, with particular emphasis on languages, and he taught Greek at the same university for one year.

When the Spanish–American War broke out he enlisted, and his appalling experiences in a military camp quickened his awareness of social problems. After his discharge he began to study economics and political science at Columbia University, where he came under the influence particularly of John Bates Clark and Edwin R. A. Seligman.

Johnson thereafter held a number of academic positions in economics at various universities and colleges, including Bryn Mawr, Columbia, Nebraska, Texas, Chicago, Stanford, and Cornell.

As a scholar, Johnson described himself as an "exile from the world of the classics—to the fields of economics and politics" (1952). Nevertheless, some of his essays are a direct outgrowth of his intimate familiarity with the languages and life of ancient societies. An example is the delightful article "Cleopatra and the Roman Chamber of Commerce" (1949a) and also the moving plea for a new "social democracy" in his "Faith of a Skeptic" ([1949b] 1954, p. 178–191).

In economics, Johnson might be characterized as a neoclassicist with strong social and institutional undertones. Articles written several decades ago dealing with the relationship between ethics and economics, or with intangible investments and technological unemployment, are still very timely. The early papers on economics show the promise of an original theoretician. However, Johnson responded to the challenges of a revolutionary age and applied most of his energies in his later life to his tasks as publicist, educator, and organizer in the social sciences.

In 1917 he joined Herbert Croly, Walter Lippmann, and others as a staff member of the *New Republic.*

At the end of World War I Johnson was one of a group of liberals who began to deliberate the desirability of establishing an academic institution wholly independent of academic accreditation and degrees. This group was joined by some outstanding men from Columbia University, including Charles A. Beard, Wesley Mitchell, and James Harvey Robinson, who left Columbia partly because of a conflict over an issue of academic freedom. They established the New School for

Social Research in New York City in 1919. When the New School got into difficulties after a few years, Johnson was asked to take over the active directorship in 1922, and he molded the school into an institution for adult education. Previous schools for adult education were either on an elementary level or had a decided focus on technological and professional improvement. The New School was probably the first institution in America designed to enable mature adults to deal with the intellectual challenges of the time. The emphasis of the school was on the social sciences, but an effort was made to integrate the social sciences with other disciplines and to incorporate the various arts into the curriculum.

In 1929 Johnson took on the additional burden of associate editorship of the *Encyclopaedia of the Social Sciences*, with Seligman as editor in chief. Seligman conducted all external relations with foundations and other domestic and foreign organizations, while Johnson primarily directed the staff work. He became, indeed, the main architect and the guiding force of that ambitious project which, as its founders expressed it, sought to achieve a "comprehensive synthesis" of the separate social sciences. While this ideal could not be fully attained, the *Encyclopaedia* under Johnson's direction did achieve an impressive degree of coherence among the several elements of the social sciences, which were defined by Seligman as "those mental or cultural sciences which deal with the activities of the individual as a member of a group" (1930, vol. 1, p. 3). Whatever merits or defects this comprehensive definition had, it was largely the imprint of Johnson's broad vision which brought about a work characterized by Irving Dilliard as "the United States' most distinguished contribution to international scholarship" (1954/1955, p. 93). At Johnson's instigation, and as the result of the subsequent efforts of many other scholars, the present encyclopedia came to be prepared.

The vitality and the creative force with which Johnson had endowed both the New School and the *Encyclopaedia* were applied to a new purpose in 1933. When the Nazis came to power in Germany, the lives and the creative work of many scholars were menaced. Johnson sensed earlier than others that Nazism was a threat not only to individuals but also to the values of European academic life as such. He took prompt action with plans for a "university in exile," not only to save lives and offer work opportunities for individuals but also as a means of preserving at least a nucleus of the kind of free scholarship that had flourished at the German universities. He also anticipated that the quality of intellectual life in the United States would gain by the establishment of an academic institution of this kind. With the New School as a base of operation, financial support was soon mobilized and, through connections with European scholars already established by the *Encyclopaedia*, the initial faculty of the "university in exile" was selected and recruited. The faculty became, officially, the Graduate Faculty of Political and Social Science of the New School for Social Research. Later, Johnson was instrumental in bringing to the United States scholars from Italy, Austria, France, and other countries in which academic freedom had been suppressed by dictatorial regimes.

It may be that Johnson's most significant contribution to the social sciences was his success in mobilizing domestic and foreign talents and developing the New School into a center of intellectual and artistic pursuits, both on the level of general adult education and of graduate and postgraduate study. The graduate faculty in itself has become one of the largest graduate schools specializing in the social sciences. Johnson was also the founder and for many years the editor of the journal *Social Research*, which published much of the work of members of the graduate faculty at the New School and also served as a link between the New School and American scholarship in general.

Johnson's many other activities included travels as an economic expert for the U.S. Reclamation Service, the establishment of experimental agricultural settlements for refugees in North Carolina, and an assignment from the governor of New York to formulate laws and procedures to prevent discriminatory practices in that state.

Johnson's contributions to the social sciences received recognition in the form of many honors. He was elected president of the American Economic Association in 1936 and received honorary degrees from several American and foreign universities (including Heidelberg). He was also honored by several foreign governments for his role in safeguarding European scholarship.

Besides his activities as an economist, editor, and organizer of adult education, Johnson had time for belletristic writings: he wrote several novels and, with particular success, many short stories. Some of these fictional writings and also his autobiography are a very real addition to the social history of the midwestern United States. Beyond these manifold contributions to the social sciences in the broadest meaning of the concept is the impact Johnson has made as a great humanitarian.

GERHARD COLM

[*See also the biography of* SELIGMAN, EDWIN R. A.]

### WORKS BY JOHNSON

1903   *Rent in Modern Economic Theory: An Essay in Distribution.* New York: Macmillan; London: Sonnenschein.

(1905–1949) 1954   *Essays in Social Economics.* Albany: Boyd. → A selection of articles published by Alvin Johnson and presented to him on the occasion of his eightieth birthday by the Graduate Faculty of Political and Social Science of the New School for Social Research.

(1909) 1922   *Introduction to Economics.* Rev. ed. Boston: Heath.

1914   *The Professor and the Petticoat.* New York: Dodd. → A satirical novel.

1919   *John Stuyvesant Ancestor, and Other People.* New York: Harcourt. → Sketches and short stories, many of which first appeared in the *New Republic.*

1934   *Deliver Us From Dogma.* New York: American Association for Adult Education.

1936a   *Spring Storm.* New York: Knopf.

1936b   Andrew Carnegie: Educator. *Journal of Adult Education* 8:5–9.

1938   *The Public Library: A People's University.* New York: American Association for Adult Education.

1945   *Liberal Education: Fact and Fiction.* New York: New School for Social Research.

1946   *The Clock of History.* New York: Norton.

1949a   Cleopatra and the Roman Chamber of Commerce. *American Scholar* 18:417–424.

(1949b) 1954   Faith of a Skeptic. Pages 178–191 in Alvin Johnson, *Essays in Social Economics.* Albany: Boyd.

1952   *Pioneer's Progress: An Autobiography.* New York: Viking. → A paperback edition was published in 1960 by the University of Nebraska Press.

1961   *The Battle of the Wild Turkey, and Other Tales.* New York: Atheneum.

1962   *Ideas Are High Explosives: A Selection of Editorials From the "New School Bulletin," 1945–1961.* New York: Privately printed.

1963   *A Touch of Color, and Other Tales.* New York: Atheneum.

1965   *New World for Old.* New York: Privately published.

### SUPPLEMENTARY BIBLIOGRAPHY

DILLIARD, IRVING 1954/1955 Portrait: Alvin S. Johnson. *American Scholar* 24:88–95.

SELIGMAN, EDWIN R. A. 1930 What Are the Social Sciences? Volume 1, pages 3–7 in *Encyclopaedia of the Social Sciences.* New York: Macmillan.

U.S. BUREAU OF RECLAMATION 1929 *Economic Problems of Reclamation: Economic Aspects of Certain Reclamation Projects.* Washington: Government Printing Office.

# JOHNSON, CHARLES S.

Charles Spurgeon Johnson (1893–1956) was a sociologist who did pioneering work in the field of human relations, a prolific writer, an editor, an adviser to governmental and philanthropic groups, and the president of Fisk University from 1946 to 1956.

A graduate of Virginia Union University, he received his sociological training at the University of Chicago, primarily through an unusual apprenticeship which he served under Robert E. Park. At the University of Chicago men such as Park, W. I. Thomas, and Ellsworth Faris were seeking to study race relations with the techniques of sociology, that is, as a specific problem in social interaction and collective action. They wished to study the character of racial and cultural contact in all cultures with heterogeneous populations, rather than just as a particular aspect of American society.

In view of the nature of his training at Chicago, it is not surprising that one of Johnson's major sociological contributions was his demonstration that the emotion-ridden subject of race relations could be studied by sociologists from an objective and scientific point of view. His first major research in this field resulted in the classic work *The Negro in Chicago: A Study of Race Relations and a Race Riot* (1922). This work effectively combined personal documents and statistical data; it documented in an objective fashion the riot itself, the events leading up to it, and the misconceptions, misinformation, and attitudes upon which the events were based.

The bulk of Johnson's sociological contributions was made during that period in which he served as chairman of the department of social sciences at Fisk University, 1928–1947. His sociological studies covered a wide range of Negro life, but he was perennially concerned with the depressed status of the Negro within American society and the implications of this status for the Negro's personality development and for the nation's image of itself as a democratic society. Johnson excelled in his ability to document the reactions of Negroes of varying socioeconomic classes to their racial status.

In *Shadow of the Plantation* (1934) Johnson related the social and cultural influences of the plantation to the social patterns and personality development of Negroes who lived in this type of agricultural situation. In *The Negro College Graduate* (1938), for which he received the Ainsfield award, he attempted to synthesize the social as well as the educational philosophy of the Negro college graduate. In *Patterns of Negro Segregation* (1943) he attempted to delineate the class structure of the Negro community and to describe the differential behavioral responses of the various classes.

Johnson's concept of the "folk Negro" as a social category cutting across class lines was new, as was his critical view of the caste theory of race relations. In *Growing Up in the Black Belt* (1941) Johnson took issue with the then current view of some social scientists that race relations in America constituted a caste system. Unlike a caste system, the Southern race system lacked both religious sanctions and the mutual acceptance of a fixed status; it was also highly unstable, with Negroes constantly changing and redefining their own status in relation to whites.

Johnson was also noted for his ability to marshal facts effectively as an aid to the solution of practical problems. From 1943 to 1948 he edited the *Monthly Summary of Events and Trends in Race Relations* (later called *Race Relations*), a report that carried an interpretive account of the month's events; it had developed out of a confidential assignment from President Franklin D. Roosevelt to write a monthly report on race relations.

Perhaps Johnson's most influential practical contribution was his development of the "community self-survey of race relations," a technique for allowing the people of a community to discover for themselves facts about human relations in the community. [*See* RACE RELATIONS.]

Johnson rendered important services to the American government, and to various philanthropic foundations, social agencies, and international organizations. In 1930 he served as the American member of an international commission of the League of Nations that inquired into the existence of forced labor in Liberia. In 1946 he went to Japan as one of the advisers on the reorganization of the Japanese educational system. He also served as one of the social science consultants to the legal staff of the National Association for the Advancement of Colored People (NAACP) at the time of the historic United States Supreme Court decision on school segregation in 1954.

Before becoming chairman of the social sciences department at Fisk University, Johnson served as director of research and investigation for the National Urban League. At that time he established *Opportunity*, a journal of Negro life. This magazine, which contained sociological research, short stories, poetry, literary criticism, and graphic art, became during the 1920s a leading medium of expression in what has come to be called the "Negro Renaissance."

In 1946 Johnson was appointed president of Fisk. Under his leadership the university became a national and international center for research and study, attracting some of the nation's foremost teachers and scientists. It became the first predominantly Negro institution to meet Phi Beta Kappa's qualification criteria.

Johnson was a prolific writer. At the time of his inauguration as president of Fisk, a bibliography compiled by the Fisk University library (1947) listed 17 books of which he was author or coauthor,

14 other books to which he had contributed chapters, and more than 60 articles. Although Johnson was not primarily a textbook writer, one of his major sociological contributions, *The Negro in American Civilization* (1930), became an influential textbook in the field of race relations.

Throughout his career Johnson received many honors, including honorary degrees from Virginia Union University and the University of Glasgow, as well as from Columbia, Harvard, Howard, and Lincoln universities. Edwin R. Embree in *Thirteen Against the Odds* said of him: "Charles Johnson has one of America's great careers in scholarship and statesmanship" (1944, p. 70). His former teacher, Ernest W. Burgess, placed him as a social scientist of the first rank (1956, p. 321).

PRESTON VALIEN

[*See also the biographies of* PARK *and* THOMAS.]

### WORKS BY JOHNSON

1922  *The Negro in Chicago: A Study of Race Relations and a Race Riot.* Univ. of Chicago Press.
1930  *The Negro in American Civilization: A Study of Negro Life and Race Relations in the Light of Social Research.* New York: Holt.
1934  *Shadow of the Plantation.* Univ. of Chicago Press.
1938  *The Negro College Graduate.* Chapel Hill: Univ. of North Carolina Press.
1941  *Growing Up in the Black Belt: Negro Youth in the Rural South.* Washington: American Council on Education.
1943  *Patterns of Negro Segregation.* New York: Harper.

### WORKS ABOUT JOHNSON

BURGESS, ERNEST W. 1956 Charles Spurgeon Johnson: Social Scientist, Editor and Educational Statesman. *Phylon* 17:317–321.
EMBREE, EDWIN R. 1944 Charles S. Johnson: A Scholar and Gentleman. Pages 47–70 in Edwin R. Embree, *Thirteen Against the Odds.* New York: Viking.
FISK UNIVERSITY, NASHVILLE, TENN., LIBRARY 1947 *Charles Spurgeon Johnson: A Bibliography.* Nashville: The Library.
GARDINER, GEORGE L. (compiler) 1960 *A Bibliography of Charles S. Johnson's Published Writings.* With an Introductory Note by Anna Bontemps. Nashville: Fisk Univ. Library.

# JONES, ERNEST

Ernest Jones (1879–1958) was one of a small band of pioneers who first espoused the teachings of Freud and who succeeded in developing a worldwide organization devoted to the advancement of those ideas. From about 1906, when he first took an active interest in the new science of psychoanalysis, Jones was its acknowledged leader in the English-speaking countries.

Of the deeper motives that led him to accept this

scientifically adventurous career there is little record, save a few remarks in his short volume of memoirs (1959). He was born in Rhosfelyn, Glamorgan, a village on the Gower Peninsula of south Wales. Of modest parentage (his father was a self-made man), Jones quickly absorbed the aspirations to success that prevail in impoverished and provincial principalities and that have driven the Welsh to frequent eminence. A rather puny and ailing child, he soon showed signs of precocity, went early to the village school, where he was recognized as a boy "of parts," proceeded to Swansea Grammar School, thence to University College, Cardiff, and finally to University College Hospital in London. In 1901, at the age of 21, he received his M.B. and B.S. from the University of London and three years later his medical degree. Although he became a member of the Royal College of Physicians in 1904, prejudice against psychoanalysis delayed his becoming a fellow of the College until 1942.

Like many other brilliant students, Jones preferred a hospital career to private practice in Harley Street. The gradual shifting of his interests, from clinical medicine to neurology and neuropathology, then to general psychiatry, and finally to psychoanalysis, is clearly indicated by the list of his appointments. After the usual post as house physician (at University College Hospital), he became clinical assistant to the Ophthalmic Hospital and the National Hospital for Nervous Diseases, and then registrar and pathologist at the West End Hospital for Nervous Diseases. Finally he obtained the post of lecturer in practical neurology at the London School of Clinical Medicine. When it appeared that he could not rise further professionally in London, he emigrated, in 1908, to Canada, where the University of Toronto and the Toronto General Hospital offered him more satisfactory positions. By this time he was a full-fledged psychiatrist and had begun to experiment with psychoanalytic techniques. He had first met Freud before he moved to Canada, and when Freud came to lecture at Clark University in 1909, Jones met him a second time. After this meeting, Jones decided to devote himself exclusively to psychoanalysis and to return as soon as possible to England.

Jones's organizational efforts on behalf of psychoanalysis were prodigious: he set up professional organizations both in America and, after his return in 1913, in England; he edited the *International Journal of Psycho-analysis;* and he was a leading founder of the Institute of Psycho-analysis in London and cofounder and first director of the London Clinic of Psycho-analysis. His intensive committee work on a British Medical Association inquiry into the workings of psychoanalysis led to the recognition of the science by this conservative and sometimes hostile body. After this victory he played an increasingly active part in the affairs of the International Psycho-analytic Association and often acted as president, finally retiring with the honorary title of "perpetual president."

Thoroughly versed in psychoanalytic method, Jones was at the same time closely conversant with the methodologies not only of academic psychology and sociology but also of natural science in general and organic medicine in particular. He was able to dovetail the results of his excellent research with the structure of psychoanalytical and psychological theory. Although a great deal of his early work was necessarily didactic, as for example his classic essay on dreams, he broke new ground in his monographs on suggestion, on the nature of symbolism, on anal-character formation, and on the obsessional neuroses (see *Papers on Psycho-analysis,* 1913).

It is possible, however, that in the long run Jones will be best remembered for his contributions to applied psychoanalysis. Here, as in his research interests, his range was extremely wide and gave him ample opportunity to display his almost obsessive erudition. His contributions to literary and artistic problems and puzzles, to the understanding of folklore and myth, of various aspects of religious belief and practice, of linguistics, and of a host of other social and cultural subjects were always illuminated by a wealth of apposite examples. Literary critics find his essay on Hamlet (1949) and his biography of Freud (1953–1957) especially noteworthy. The Freud biography, an immense compendium of facts as well as a sustained characterological and intellectual study, is sufficient to secure him a lasting reputation.

Keen and nimble of wit and endowed with unusual tenacity of purpose, Jones was able to overcome the inevitable setbacks to which pioneers are subject. No one could have been better suited to lead what proved to be a scientific crusade in the face of bitter and prolonged opposition. Psychoanalysis afforded him a disciplined outlet for an unusual degree of filial piety: his scientific allegiance to Freud was greatly reinforced by personal devotion, and he rendered tribute to his mentor by every expedient of scientific defense. Oblivious of unpopularity, he was more concerned with the well-being of the psychoanalytic movement than with success in professional diplomacy.

EDWARD GLOVER

[For the historical context of Jones's work, see Psy-CHOANALYSIS; and the biography of FREUD. For discussion of the subsequent development of Jones's ideas, see OBSESSIVE–COMPULSIVE DISORDERS and PSYCHOANALYSIS, article on EGO PSYCHOLOGY.]

## WORKS BY JONES

(1913) 1948  *Papers on Psycho-analysis.* 5th ed. London: Baillière.

(1923) 1951  *Essays in Applied Psycho-analysis.* 2 vols. London: Hogarth.

1949  *Hamlet and Œdipus.* London: Gollancz. → The revision of an essay published in 1910 in the *American Journal of Psychology* under the title "The Œdipus Complex as an Explanation of Hamlet's Mystery." A paperback edition was published in 1954 by Doubleday.

1953–1957  *The Life and Work of Sigmund Freud.* 3 vols. New York: Basic Books. → Volume 1: *The Formative Years and the Great Discoveries*, 1953. Volume 2: *Years of Maturity*, 1955. Volume 3: *The Last Phase*, 1957.

1959  *Free Associations: Memories of a Psycho-analyst.* New York: Basic Books.

## SUPPLEMENTARY BIBLIOGRAPHY

Ernest Jones [obituary].  1958  *British Medical Journal* [1958]:463–465.

Ernest Jones [obituary].  1958  *Lancet* [1958], no. 1:438–439.

# JOURNALISM

By the conventional definition of the word "profession," the occupation of journalist is not a profession at all. Although an increasing number of practitioners are trained in academic institutions, no such formal training is required either to secure a job or to fill it well; some highly successful journalists have been men of slight formal education. In the United States, furthermore, there is no system of licensure or certification of journalists; unlike a lawyer or a physician, the journalist requires as the only certification of his competence the willingness of someone to pay for his product. Concomitantly, his professional activities are not policed by any official body of the profession; he cannot be formally restrained from practice by his peers. Many nations have some kind of system of registration or licensing; although experience and demonstration of competence may be specified as a requirement in these countries, the purpose of such registration often is to make surveillance by political authorities easier or to control entrance into what is essentially a trade union.

The tendency to view the journalist as a member of a profession seems to rest largely on the recognition of the importance of his work; he is seen as a man of high responsibility more than as the inheritor of a long tradition of meritorious performance. This ascription of responsibility, in turn, seems to rest upon the general belief that the mass media have much influence in society. The fact that the nature or extent of this influence is hard to demonstrate empirically (see Klapper 1960) seems to have little effect upon the newsman's willingness to assume it and the rest of society's readiness to concede it.

**Who are the journalists?**  "Journalism" is a word of broad and varied meaning; so is "journalist." As used in this article, the word "journalist" or "newsman" refers to a person whose primary occupation is the gathering, writing, and editing of material which consists largely of the reporting or interpretation of current events. Such a definition leaves out many persons professionally involved in mass communications: advertising and public relations men, those on the "business side," and several kinds of part-time contributors, ranging from "stringers," who provide routine coverage of minor news on a piecework basis, to the intellectuals who contribute to the "culture" pages of the great dailies of western Europe. But the essential characteristics of these complex systems of mass communication would seem to be best demonstrated by the full-time employees who provide the bulk of the product.

The lack of systematic study of the intellectual is frequently noted by sociologists and other students of society; the profession of journalism is no exception. There is more information available on the profession in the United States than in any other country, but even these data are skimpy and drawn largely from surveys which were often designed primarily for some other purpose. Studies of organizational characteristics and role behavior have been confined almost entirely to the United States, and there have been few of these. There is a sizable body of writing about the profession from European, British, and Soviet sources, but the larger part of this literature tends to be abstractly analytical and to center upon such concepts as journalists' rights and responsibilities. The autobiographical writings of newsmen—and there have been hundreds of such volumes—frequently provide valuable personal insights and impressions; for example, the works of Lincoln Steffens (1931), Eric Sevareid (1946), Webb Miller (1936), Vincent Sheean (1935), and T. S. Matthews (1960).

## Selection and recruitment

Available evidence indicates that most professional journalists in the United States come from the upper socioeconomic bracket; various studies (see, for instance, Rosten 1937; Deutschmann 1957; 1958) of discrete groups of practicing journalists show percentage ranges from 40 to 80 per cent with fathers in the professional, managerial, or proprietary occupational groups. There is some slight evidence (Kimball & Lubell 1960) that there is an increasing representation of "blue-collar" background in those now choosing the field, but substantially journalism in the United States remains a field of work for those who settle for the same, or in some cases lesser, social position. It is not a profession, apparently, which particularly recommends itself to the poor-but-bright boy as a channel of upward mobility. Most young people who choose the field do so early, many by the twelfth grade, most of the rest by the junior year in college. A study of 1,500 high school upperclassmen who worked on high school papers (Kimball & Lubell 1960) indicates that two factors are most important in choosing journalism as a career; the beliefs that the work is "interesting" and that it is "useful to society." These students ranked the field well below the classic professions in prestige, economic security, prospects for good family life, and financial reward. An idealistic commitment, then, was of major importance to these students in their choice, and other studies and observation tend to confirm the finding. "Scratch a reporter," the phrase goes, "and you find a reformer." The feeling that the work provides an opportunity for self-expression also appears to be an important element in occupational choice. The problem of accommodation of idealized expectations to institutional realities is characteristic of many people in the profession.

There is no substantial body of information on either the socioeconomic origins or the reason for career choice among journalists outside the United States, but some cautious inferences can be made. Most western European journalists, as defined here, completed their formal academic training with the secondary school; their lack of higher education may indicate family backgrounds in which higher education is not a normal expectation. Further, the press on the continent of Europe is highly politicized, and the journalist is generally a member of a trade union. The young man who chooses this career in such a context has a more specific definition of "usefulness to society," perhaps, but within that definition he would seem to share a sense of social purpose. He is not likely to be a social climber; seldom in Western society does the ordinary working journalist have high status. The journalist in the U.S.S.R. is likely to be chosen for the profession rather than choosing it himself; in either case, as Alex Inkeles (1950) points out, his identity as a party worker is more important than any specific assignment. Since there are few journalists in new and developing countries, recruiting for the profession is much more important than studying it. The role of the mass media in national development is generally assumed to be critical (for example, see Schramm 1964), but in much of Africa and Asia the only really professional newsmen are, or were, the Anglo–European employees of foreign-owned newspapers. New men have to be recruited, trained, and set to work; often they will have to be drawn from a pool of potential leaders that is tragically small. It is significant that most of the journalists of an atypical "new" nation, Israel, were men of long professional experience, which was often gained in Europe (Gill 1959). It is precisely the lack of this kind of resource that cripples the building of news organizations in most developing countries and sets great problems for national leadership in deciding where scarce resources of competence should be assigned. It also means, however, that the journalist in these nations begins with high status and has great opportunity for making it higher.

### Training for the profession

Hard data on the educational background of journalists are difficult to find for any country, including the United States. The U.S. Census of 1960 projects a total of about 110,000 persons in the category "editors and reporters" and indicates that about 40 per cent have had four or more years of college (U.S. Bureau of the Census 1963). There are no census data on the number among these who studied journalism. A 1965 survey, based on a relatively small sample and with slightly different categories, indicated that 58 per cent of "news-editorial staff" had college degrees and that about half of these had concentrated in journalism (Odendahl 1965). Compared with data from a similar study done in 1954, there seems to have been a small increase in the percentage of working newsmen with college degrees (particularly advanced degrees), but the percentage with journalism degrees has remained about the same. These findings are contrary to the general assumption, on the part of both the profession and journalism educators, that the percentage of journalism degrees has been increasing, modestly but steadily, since the establishment of the first American school of journalism at the University of Missouri in 1908.

After considerable early hostility to the idea of training for journalism in college, American publishers and broadcasters have come to look upon such programs as a primary source of new personnel. Today, U.S. education for journalism puts heavy stress upon the traditional liberal arts and social sciences and thus upon the newsman's need to know something about many fields of knowledge. Accrediting procedures, as set out by the American Council on Education in Journalism, suggest that programs should contain no more than 25 per cent of the total course work in journalism; in practice, the figure seldom runs over 30 per cent. Most schools and departments provide training in the essential skills of writing and editing; some have elaborate facilities, including photographic laboratories, wire-service machines, and laboratory newspapers. Most teachers of journalism at the college level have substantial professional experience, either before or concomitant with their teaching careers, but PH.D.s with primary training in research are beginning to come into the field as well. Although there is a good deal of variety among journalism schools and departments, ranging from some which are concerned largely with preparing the student to fit smoothly into current jobs to some which are largely research-oriented, there is little evidence to support the common charge that such programs are mainly preoccupied with teaching "techniques."

The U.S. newsman without academic training in journalism learns his trade, in most cases, on the job, in a process generally too casual to be referred to as an apprenticeship. On metropolitan dailies, he may start as a copy boy; elsewhere, as a reporter beginning with simple and routine assignments. He thus acquires perceptions of his role in the news bureaucracy, and of the social setting of institutionalized mass communications while he is learning the rudiments of the craft. The academically trained journalist, on the other hand, has been exposed to a wider and more systematically organized view of the structure and workings of the mass media. There is no significant evidence concerning the differential effects, if any, of these kinds of preparation. There is no longer much debate about the value of academic training in journalism, although many editors may casually downgrade it; and there is little tendency for newsrooms to polarize into journalism-school versus non-journalism-school cliques. The newsman seems to advance in position and salary largely in terms of "how well he does his job"—in other words, the ease with which he adapts to his superior's view of his proper role.

From its American origins, formal education for journalism has become common in the rest of the world, although the geographical pattern is spotty and the types of programs and their institutional settings vary widely. After World War II the Soviet Union developed five-year degree programs in ten of its major universities; those in Kiev, Lvov, and Moscow are the most elaborate (Khudiakov 1958). In addition, an extensive program of short courses brings working newsmen in for refresher work or updating; night school courses also are available in larger cities. Given the objectives of the Soviet system of mass communication, the content of this instruction is highly political, but it also emphasizes craft skills. Journalism education in the People's Republic of China is structurally similar to the Soviet system; in 1965 three Chinese universities were known to offer journalism degree programs (United Nations . . . 1965).

Ten universities in Japan offer journalism degrees or certificates, and curricula resemble those in U.S. universities. The widest variety of types of journalism is available in Latin America; the 57 entities on that continent that offer training for the profession range from small privately owned commercial schools to national universities. Some of the latter (for example, the University of Chile) closely resemble the larger U.S. schools of journalism, and this seems to be the general direction of development on the continent.

Each of the major countries of continental Europe has some kind of academic journalism training, but these generally have little resemblance to the American or Soviet pattern. Some programs have a university base (for example, L'École de Journalisme, University Louvain; Istituto di Pubblicismo, University of Rome; Institut für Publizistik, Free University of Berlin). Broadly speaking, university-anchored entities tend to be oriented toward research and descriptive analysis; there is a common feeling among European academicians that training for the profession is not appropriate to the regular university curriculum. Practical training in craft skills tends to be concentrated in special establishments which are staffed by former or part-time professionals and often involve a kind of concurrent internship on participating newspapers. These are essentially vocational schools, with programs of one or two years' length (for example, Le Centre de Formation des Journalistes, Paris; Werner-Friedmann Institut, Munich; Institut pour Journalistes, Brussels). Some idea of the limited impact of these training programs can be gained from France, where in 1959, 200 of about 8,000 registered professional journalists had received formal professional training (Voyenne 1959). There is no recognized academic training for journalists in the United Kingdom, but entry into the profession requires completion of a nation-wide formal apprenticeship program under the direction of the National Council for the Training of Journalists, in which all newspapers participate (Dodge 1965).

New and underdeveloped nations give the development of a cadre of capable journalists a high priority, and most of the countries of Africa now are establishing programs of instruction. There were eight programs on the continent in 1965, including three in universities. In addition, various international agencies, such as UNESCO, the International Press Institute, and the African–American Institute, have been involved, especially in providing short-term practical courses. One of India's ten institutions offering training for journalism goes back to 1941, but the remainder are post-World War II. Most are postgraduate, which means that admission is difficult and enrollments are small.

Generally, underdeveloped countries are attempting to enlarge their resources of competent newsmen. International organizations are providing assistance; the United States example is often relied upon, and American teachers of journalism have been involved in the operations of many overseas programs since 1945. The academic preparation of journalists is a growing trend, but in most countries the workers so trained will be a small percentage of the professional force for several more decades.

## Job orientation of the professional

The profession of journalism has been defined here as a field of full-time work concerned with the processing of information related to current affairs. The popular stereotype of the newsman is the reporter, who gathers information and then writes a news story. Although writers of popular fiction have made this a colorful and exciting role (at least in the United States; interestingly, the journalist seldom appears as hero in other cultures), it consists largely of routine: the daily checking of regular sources, the writing of standard accounts of happenings which themselves become standardized because they are written about. Like most other aspects of the profession, the relationship between the reporter and his regular sources has been little studied. Frequently the objectives of the reporter and the source, as well as their conception of the basic function of the news outlet, are in opposition; the source sees the newspapers' chief function as giving publicity and avoiding controversy; the reporter sees it as the exposure of conflict (Edelstein & Schultz 1963; Nimmo 1964).

**The news-handling hierarchy.** At the top of the news-handling hierarchy in a newspaper is the managing editor (in news broadcasting, a news director). The managing editor supervises the work of various specialized editors who do the actual supervision of news personnel: city editor, wire editor (who is responsible for the choice and processing of material received from news agencies), sports and society editors. This supervisor gives the reporters under his direction their daily assignments, generally with a rough indication of the length desired, and passes judgment on the stories when they come in; he may order them rewritten, discard them altogether, or accept them. The processing of this copy is done on "the desk" by copy editors, who cut, correct for style and mechanics if necessary, and write headlines. Large daily newspapers also have rewrite men on the desk; these are writers who take material over the telephone from reporters and then write the actual stories.

There are, then, three discrete roles: that of news gatherer–writer, that of copy editor and headline writer, and that of supervisor. This tight triumvirate represents the basic news-handling process in daily and weekly newspapers; in weekly news magazines; and, generally in simpler form, in broadcast journalism. In almost every setting it functions under demanding conditions: close personal relationships with constant interaction; continual decision making, little of it consciously centered on policy considerations, much on accumulated perceptions of role relationships; constant pressure of time which hinders careful consideration and revision either before or after the story is written.

Journalists other than these basic news handlers —editorial writers, columnists, and various feature specialists—often work under less stringent demands of time and sometimes in simpler hierarchies, but the essential dimensions of their roles are the same.

**Professional advancement—up or out?** The newsman's opportunity for upward mobility within the news business is limited. There is an ancient saw in the newspaper field that deskmen are old reporters whose feet have given out; many men on the desk did begin as reporters. Supervisory editors —again, within the news-handling triumvirate— almost invariably have been either reporters or deskmen and in many cases have had experience as both. There is some evidence (Jones & Swanson 1954) that this structure does tend to reward ability, that is, that supervisory personnel rank higher on standard tests which would seem to measure competence. The most significant measure of mobility, however, is not the process of internal promotion but the tendency to move into other kinds of work. Studies of the American newspaper field repeatedly have indicated a tendency to work in the field for a relatively short time and then move on to other activities (see, for instance, Deutschmann 1957; 1958). The median age of editorial personnel in American newspapers is apparently somewhere around 35. A study of nonmetropolitan newspapers indicated that more than 70 per cent of news-handling personnel had been on their jobs for less than five years. It has been estimated that one of every three newspapermen in their thirties who are now on the job will leave it.

This problem of departing manpower has been a major concern of newspaper publishers, particularly in the United States, and projections indicate a worsening situation in the future. It is complicated by the fact that only about 5 per cent of those who leave the news business ever come back; occupational movement is almost entirely outward. For this reason, recruitment of new staff members and of journalism students has received considerable attention from both the industry and journalism's academicians. During the past decade, journalism schools have regularly reported three to five times as many jobs available as graduates to fill them.

Evidence indicates that most of these newsmen do not leave the field of mass communication; there is substantial movement into such fields as public relations, advertising, and industrial editing (Keinzle 1963). The essential pattern of the shift is from news handling into areas in which skills already acquired are still useful. However, a substantial number of newsmen remain in the field, find great satisfaction in it, and never seriously contemplate leaving. Those who made a career decision early and had college training in journalism are most likely to be in this category. Studies of job satisfaction among those who do stay show, as the salient element, the continued finding of the work as "interesting."

Why do newsmen leave the field? Investigation tends to show a predictable cluster of complaints: low pay, unsatisfactory conditions of work (for reporters on small newspapers and broadcasting operations, in particular, hours are often long and irregular), and boredom with routine. Certainly money is important in the decision to move out; although news personnel salaries in the United States have risen considerably in the past decade —a study for the National Science Foundation (Bureau of Social Science Research 1963, p. 53) showed journalists tenth in median income ($5,130) two years after college graduation in a list of forty representative occupations—there generally is more money to be had in writing press releases and speeches or putting out employee magazines. There is also less pressure and a more predictable pattern of daily living.

**Job satisfaction and institutional pressures.** The structure of institutionalized mass communications in the United States and the role of the individual in it also affect the satisfaction the newsman finds in his job. In many ways the characteristic internal organization of the news business conforms to the standard sociological descriptions of bureaucracy. A premium is put upon the organization's technical efficiency, with great emphasis upon accuracy, speed, continuity, and sharply defined lines of authority with control from the top. There is little time for experimentation which may lead to waste; responses must be predictable; the basic learning of the first few weeks on the job is the establishment of such responses. From the individual's point of view, the most significant effect of bureaucracy is, of course, its tendency to capture the people in it and substitute its own structure for individual creativity or the coherent pursuit of values. The profession of journalism in the United States is particularly vulnerable to this kind of ossification.

There has been relatively little study of the journalist's relation to the framework and context of his work. One elite group has been studied in some detail: the Washington correspondents (Rosten 1937; compare such later treatments of the topic as Rivers 1960; Cohen 1963; Nimmo 1964). This group is too small, as well as too much of an elite, to be taken as representative of the profession, but certain fundamental conclusions parallel those which can be deduced from scattered studies of other groups (see, for instance, Gieber 1960; Judd 1961; Deutschmann 1957; 1958; White 1950; Breed 1955). No two of these studies (with the exception of Rivers' updating of Rosten) have been organized in such a fashion as to provide rigid comparability, and the variety of data involved is capable of various interpretations. Certain conclusions, however, are highly persuasive.

Many, if not most, persons who choose journalism as a profession do so in part because of their social values. They feel it is a way to do something about the world; it promises to be a useful occupation, in the highest sense of the word "useful." Yet the day-to-day practice of the profession cannot be set against this goal for measurement. The newsman feels his first obligation is to his audience, but his view of that audience is curiously vague and generalized; there is a striking unanimity of findings on this point. He feels that his job is the molding of public opinion, but he is of necessity vague about what constitutes a "public or what a supposed public is thinking." Therefore, he is content to satisfy the bureaucracy: as one of Judd's respondents put it, "if the city editor will accept a story, it is good enough for everyone" (Judd 1961, p. 39).

The journalist is seldom told specifically in advance how to decide what is news or how to handle it once he decides. His decisions are subject to revision by those in other roles, but generally after the fact; as Rosten (1937) first pointed out, the newsman learns what *not* to do from the stories that are rewritten or go unused. He therefore operates, in the classic bureaucratic fashion, within an unmistakable pattern of control, that is, control through structure. This is even true of publications generally assumed to be almost idiosyncratically reflective of a single personality: a writer for *Time* magazine, for example, is seldom told how to handle a story when it is assigned to him.

*Politics and the newsman.*   More often than not, the American newsman is out of political sympathy with his employer; there is an old joke that publishers are Republicans but reporters are Democrats, and there is some evidence to confirm this. For example, a majority of U.S. newspapers have consistently supported the Republican candidate for president in the period 1936–1960, but informal preference polls of reporters assigned to cover the campaigns have regularly turned up majorities favoring the Democrat. Even if the reporter sees himself as not a party man, he is generally aware of a difference between himself and the top of the hierarchy on a liberal–conservative scale. There is little he can do about this; if he produces the wrong responses, he simply interferes with the efficiency of the organization, and if he does it frequently enough it will either isolate or reject him. The greatest force for conservatism which he faces is not the political commitments of his superiors, in any case, but the very nature of the organization.

*Occupational isolation.*   He also lacks reinforcement by factors outside the organization in which he works. Max Weber pointed out that journalists have no clear-cut social classification (Weber 1919); recent rankings of occupations by the general population (National Opinion Research Center 1947; compare Reiss et al. 1961, p. 263) indicate that the editor or reporter falls somewhere in between the white-collar and blue-collar rankings in public prestige. In the United States the newsman has no formal certification of his competence; other than by the first amendment to the constitution and some minor state legislation, he has no special status under the law. There are various codes of ethics in the profession, but these tend to be both vague and ignored (only one attempt has been made to expel a member of the American Society of Newspaper Editors under that organization's code of ethics, which is perhaps the best-known such statement in American journalism, and the attempt aborted). If he works on a metropolitan daily, he may be a member of a trade union; the American Newspaper Guild, an AFL-CIO affiliate, dominates newsrooms in some of the largest cities, but most newsmen have no such connection.

Given this lack of formalized "outside" values and reinforcing reference groups, the professional journalist comes close to the prototype of the intellectual in a bureaucracy (Merton [1949] 1957, pp. 207–224) and seems to fit the familiar pattern of displacement of goals: ". . . a transference of the sentiments from the *aims* of the organization onto the particular details of behavior required by the rules. Adherence to the rules, originally conceived as a means, becomes transformed into an end-in-itself" (p. 199). Walter Gieber (1963) has shown in addition that in some cases this phenomenon extends to the point where the newsman may see the same public issue from two quite different points of view, evaluating it in one way as a newsman and quite differently as a citizen of the community. The day-to-day process of gathering, writing, and editing the news, however, represents an almost classic case of bureaucratization.

The extent to which this domination of the news-handling operation by organizational structure is related to the continued movement out of the field of journalism as it has been defined here is not clear, and blithe assumptions would be unwarranted. No amount of analysis can belie the fact that many newsmen (apparently about half) remain in their jobs throughout their careers, find them stimulating and intellectually rewarding, and do excellent work.

## Journalism outside the United States

The newsman in countries other than the United States is generally in a somewhat different position. Although the internal structure and basic functioning of the organization are the same, there are external points of reference—repositories of values, in a sense—which overlap and frequently conflict with the primary organization. Most journalists in Europe and Latin America (and, needless to say, in the communist-bloc countries) are members of trade unions or their equivalent. For example, 90 per cent of British journalists are members of the National Union of Journalists (NUJ).

Journalists' trade unions not only establish, through negotiation, rates of pay, working conditions, and fringe benefits; in some cases they provide encouragement for independence. Thus the British NUJ offers "full financial support to any member who may be victimised for refusing to do work 'incompatible with the honor and interests of the profession'" (Kenyon 1948, p. 15). In France, reinforcement is provided by the law of 1935, which contains a "conscience clause" specifying that a newsman who leaves a job because the political line of his employing newspaper has become unpalatable is entitled to the same benefits as those who lose their jobs involuntarily, including severance pay (Voyenne 1962).

Further, almost all countries outside the United States have a body of press law. This is not necessarily desirable; such laws do, however, provide a solid definition of the society's expectations of the profession, as well as a special status. The last twenty years have also seen a sharp rise in the number of what are generically often referred to as courts of honor. These are national bodies, of varying composition, which hear complaints by the public against the press (and, in some cases, by the press against outside individuals) and, if the evidence warrants, issue formal censure against specific offenders. These bodies, of which the British Press Council is perhaps the best known, include representatives of the profession in their membership, and although their powers are generally limited to the formal pronouncement of censure, they are generally agreed to have influence. More than fifty countries now have some such entity; the idea has never been seriously considered in the United States.

**American and foreign journalists compared.** Commonwealth, European, Latin American, and communist-bloc journalists, then, operate within a much more sharply defined context and a more formalized value system than their American colleagues. Non-American journalists may still be members of a mass communications bureaucracy; but a significant difference may rest in the fact that they are oriented toward not one bureaucracy, but several, and that these bureaucracies frequently contend with each other. The existence of national newspapers in such countries as England and Japan helps define the job; the newsman begins in the provinces and works up by traditional steps to the top bracket. By contrast, the U.S. newsman can become a national figure only by becoming a columnist for more than one paper.

There are no substantial data concerning job satisfaction or mobility rates in the profession outside the United States. Casual observation might lead to the conclusion that a much higher percentage of European journalists, in particular, remain in their jobs permanently, but this may not be true. Even if it is, other factors might explain this fact, particularly the very modest development in most other countries of the service fields into which American journalists ordinarily move—public relations, advertising, industrial editing, and journalism teaching. Newspaper owners in Europe have begun to note the loss of personnel to these areas.

It would be specious to contend that the unique bureaucratization of the profession of journalism in the United States is entirely negative in its effects. This would imply that the press in the United States is of low quality and destined to go lower, and such is hardly the case; indeed, it is generally considered, as a whole, the best press system in the world. The increasing traffic from overseas to American schools of journalism, and the increasing use of the American model in journalism elsewhere, speaks for itself.

WILLIAM E. PORTER

[See also COMMUNICATION, MASS.]

### BIBLIOGRAPHY

BREED, WARREN 1955 Social Control in the Newsroom: A Functional Analysis. *Social Forces* 33:326–335.

BUREAU OF SOCIAL SCIENCE RESEARCH, WASHINGTON, D.C. 1963 *Two Years After the College Degree: Work and Further Study Patterns; Report on a 1960 Survey of 1958 College Graduates.* Prepared for the National Science Foundation. Washington: Government Printing Office.

COHEN, BERNARD C. 1963 *The Press and Foreign Policy.* Princeton Univ. Press.

DEUTSCHMANN, PAUL 1957 The Michigan Newspaperman: The Manpower Problem. Unpublished manuscript, Michigan State Univ., Communications Research Center.

DEUTSCHMANN, PAUL 1958 The Michigan Newspaperman: Attitudes Toward the General Field of Newspaper Work. Unpublished manuscript, Michigan State Univ., Communications Research Center.

DODGE, JOHN 1965 Britain Re-jigs Its Training Scheme. *Journalism Quarterly* 42:466–470.

EDELSTEIN, ALEX S.; and SCHULTZ, J. BLAINE 1963 The Weekly Newspaper's Leadership Role as Seen by Community Leaders: Weekly Editor's Role in Offering Opinion Leadership and in Initiating Community Projects. *Journalism Quarterly* 40:565–574.

GIEBER, WALTER 1960 How the "Gatekeepers" View Local Civil Liberties News: Various Factors Which Influence the "Fate" of the Civil Rights News Story. *Journalism Quarterly* 37:199–205.

GIEBER, WALTER 1963 The Private vs. the Public Role of the Newsman. Unpublished manuscript, San Francisco State College, Department of Journalism.

GILL, RAFAEL E. 1959 Journalists in Israel: A Statistical Portrait. *Journalism Quarterly* 36:57–62.

INKELES, ALEX (1950) 1958 *Public Opinion in Soviet Russia: A Study in Mass Persuasion.* 3d printing, enl. Russian Research Center Studies, No. 1. Cambridge, Mass.: Harvard Univ. Press.

JONES, ROBERT L.; and SWANSON, CHARLES E. 1954 Small-city Daily Newspapermen: Their Abilities and Interests. *Journalism Quarterly* 31:38–55.

JUDD, ROBERT P. 1961 The Newspaper Reporter in a Suburban City. *Journalism Quarterly* 38:35–42.

KEINZLE, GEORGE 1963 The Role of the Journalism Schools to the Graduate. *The APME Red Book* 16: 40–45.

KENYON, A. (editor) 1948 *Entry Into Journalism: A Guide for Students, and for Educationists and Others Advising on Careers.* London: Medallion Press.

KHUDIAKOV, E. L. 1958 Training Facilities in Different Countries: Union of Soviet Socialist Republics. Pages 197–206 in United Nations Educational, Scientific and Cultural Organization, *The Training of Journalists: A World-wide Survey on the Training of Personnel for the Mass Media.* Press, Film and Radio in the World Today Studies. Paris: UNESCO.

KIMBALL, PENN T.; and LUBELL, SAMUEL 1960 High School Students' Attitudes Toward Journalism as a Career: 2. *Journalism Quarterly* 37:413–422.

KLAPPER, JOSEPH T. 1960 *The Effects of Mass Communication.* Glencoe, Ill.: Free Press.

MATTHEWS, THOMAS S. 1960 *Name and Address: An Autobiography.* New York: Simon & Schuster.

MERTON, ROBERT K. (1949) 1957 *Social Theory and Social Structure.* Rev. & enl. ed. Glencoe, Ill.: Free Press.

MILLER, WEBB 1936 *I Found No Peace: The Journal of a Foreign Correspondent.* New York: Simon & Schuster.

NATIONAL OPINION RESEARCH CENTER 1947 *National Opinion on Occupation: Final Report of a Special Opinion Survey Among Americans 14 and Over.* Survey No. 244. Univ. of Chicago Press.

NIMMO, DAN D. 1964 *Newsgathering in Washington: A Study in Political Communication.* New York: Atherton.

ODENDAHL, ERIC 1965 College Backgrounds of Staffs of American Daily Newspapers. *Journalism Quarterly* 42:463–464.

REISS, ALBERT J. JR. et al. 1961 *Occupations and Social Status.* New York: Free Press.

RIVERS, WILLIAM L. 1960 The Washington Correspondents and Government Information. Ph.D. dissertation, American Univ.

ROSTEN, LEO C. 1937 *The Washington Correspondents.* New York: Harcourt.

SCHRAMM, WILBUR L. 1964 *Mass Media and National Development: The Role of Information in the Developing Countries.* Stanford (Calif.) Univ. Press.

SEVAREID, ERIC 1946 *Not So Wild a Dream.* New York: Knopf.

SHEEAN, VINCENT 1935 *Personal History.* Garden City, N.Y.: Doubleday. → British edition published as *In Search of History.*

STEFFENS, LINCOLN 1931 *The Autobiography of Lincoln Steffens.* New York: Harcourt.

UNITED NATIONS EDUCATIONAL, SCIENTIFIC AND CULTURAL ORGANIZATION 1965 *Professional Training for Mass Communications.* Reports and Papers on Mass Communications, No. 45. Paris: UNESCO.

U.S. BUREAU OF THE CENSUS 1963 *Census of Population: 1960.* Subject Reports: Occupation by Earnings and Education. Final Report PC(2)-7B. Washington: Government Printing Office.

VOYENNE, BERNARD 1959 Les journalistes. *Revue française de science politique* 9:901–934.

VOYENNE, BERNARD 1962 *La presse dans la société contemporaine.* Paris: Colin.

WEBER, MAX (1919) 1946 Politics as a Vocation. Pages 77–128 in Max Weber, *From Max Weber: Essays in Sociology.* Translated and edited by Hans H. Gerth and C. Wright Mills. New York: Oxford Univ. Press.

WHITE, DAVID M. 1950 "The Gatekeeper": A Case Study in the Selection of News. *Journalism Quarterly* 27: 383–390.

# JUDAISM

The word "Jew" can refer to a member of either of two kinds of collectivities. First, it is sometimes used to refer to any person of Jewish parentage, that is, anyone born of people who are identified as descendants of the group described in Biblical and post-Biblical sources; this criterion of descent does not necessarily entail a particular common attitude on the part of those to whom it applies. The word is also applied to an adherent to a body of beliefs —Judaism—who performs the religious practice required by it.

Absolute monotheism is the main tenet of Judaism. Religious practice consists primarily in abiding by the body of prescriptions and prohibitions laid down by the Supreme Being, the details of which are to be found in the traditional literature as it is interpreted by the duly authorized persons, the rabbis. In non-Orthodox practices of Judaism the adherence to details of this ritual is selective.

The Jews formed a definite society in the Palestine of the Near East sometime between the years 1200 and 600 B.C. The Jewish people, or at least the prophets and their devotees, manifested a sense of religious consciousness which set the Jews apart from other nations and attributed to them a special religious mission. This self-image involved a belief in a covenant which, once contracted between God and the ancestors of the existing Jewish society, rendered the observance of the divine revelation incumbent on the whole society. The prophetically foretold events of the sixth century, such as the deportation of the Jews to Babylonia and their subsequent restoration to Palestine by the Persians, strengthened the belief that the Jewish nation was under the special care of divine providence and led to ideas of the future redemption of the nation.

During the second commonwealth, which followed the restoration to Palestine and which lasted until A.D. 70, Jews came into political and cultural contact with the West. During this period Jewish communities were also established outside Palestine, in Babylonia and Egypt. These encounters with other cultures sharpened the Jews' feelings of ethnic and cultural distinctiveness and made their sense of religious mission more acute. Both in Palestine and abroad, Jewish society was, in principle, based on traditions contained in the law and prophetic teachings, which were then being collected and canonized. These were supplemented by and adapted to current conditions by means of the oral law, a large and somewhat fluid body of interpretations and independent teachings and prescriptions, which claimed to be coeval with the written law itself and to have been handed down by word of mouth through the ages. The oral law did not remain uncontested and its fluid character invited widespread variations; alongside the mainstream of Judaism there appeared different denominations and sects, such as the Samaritans, Sadducees, Essenes, and Kumerans (perhaps identical with the Essenes). With the exception of the Samaritans, however, these sects were not separated from the political framework of the nation.

After the Jews ceased to be a self-governing society, they continued to believe that the old covenant remained in force and continued to maintain and develop the national religious tradition which subsequently served as the framework of existence for all Jewish communities during the Middle Ages.

The loss of political autonomy was accompanied by the cessation of the internal sectarianism which had been characteristic of the second commonwealth. Pharisaism, the major sect of that period, now achieved complete ascendancy and provided the set of beliefs and practices which came to be known as Rabbinic Judaism and which became the belief system of all Jewry. Only the Karaites (a sect in Babylonia which rejected, in principle, the use of the oral law in the interpretation of the Bible) challenged the authority of Rabbinic Judaism during the early Middle Ages. Otherwise, throughout this period what variations there were, were those of interpretation and custom as, for example, the Sephardic (Spanish) as against the Ashkenazi (German) traditions in Europe or various local traditions in the Near East, such as the Yemenite. Only in the beginning of modern times—in the late seventeenth century—was the consensus of religious belief within the Jewish people disrupted, first by the sudden appearance of antinomian and mystical sects and then by the gradual spread of rationalism.

The number of Jews during different historical periods is roughly estimated as follows: for Biblical times 2 million; at the end of the second commonwealth 5 to 8 million (accounting for 10 to 12 per cent of the population of the Roman Empire); during the Middle Ages 2.5 million, remaining at that level until the second half of the eighteenth century; from the end of the nineteenth century it remained at 15 million, until the Nazi holocaust, when a loss of 5 to 6 million was sustained. The present estimate is 12 million, of whom 5.5 million live in the United States, 1.5 million in Israel, some 3 million in Russia and other communist countries, 1 million in western Europe, and 1 million elsewhere.

## Rabbinic Judaism

Rabbinic Judaism is historically the most widespread and most representative form of Judaism. It accepts the canonized books of the Hebrew Bible as divine revelation and accords them uncontested authority. The same holds true of the substance of the oral tradition. Both written and oral law, however, are not simple sources to be directly consulted by the believer for guidance. Their interpretation lies in the hands of experts, that is, the sages or rabbis who are, in a more or less formal fashion, authorized by their predecessors. This uninterrupted transmission of oral law from teacher to student since the time of Moses is one of the cardinal tenets of the belief system of Rabbinic Judaism.

The rules and content of interpretation are themselves included in the tradition and are relatively stringent when they touch upon practical affairs, such as moral, ritual, or civic matters (halachah). In the area of belief and dogma, however, the body of teaching (agadah) is less strictly defined in both method and in content. Both types of teachings were incorporated into the basic texts of Rabbinic Judaism—the Mishnah and the Gemara, which together constitute the Talmud (both the Palestinian version, edited in the third century, and Babylonian, edited in the fifth). The Mishnah is a terse summary, in Hebrew, of the full corpus of Jewish law as it had crystallized by the second century of the Christian era. The Gemara is a quasi-stenographic report, in Aramaic, of the discussions and lengthy elaborations of the Mishnah as they occurred in the Palestinian and Babylonian academies in the subsequent centuries. The text is further interspersed with lengthy discussions of formulated exegesis and folklore. The whole body of religious teachings is commonly designated by the name torah, a term which strictly speaking refers only to the first five books of the Old Testament, that is, the Pentateuch.

The authoritative Mishnah and Gemara were subjected to reinterpretation, partly as a consequence of the inherent dialectic of textual interpretation and partly as an outgrowth of religious–judicial decisions on new and problematic realities. From commentaries, novellae, and responsa, layer after layer was added to the law, and as a consequence the *halachah* was repeatedly codified. Correspondingly, religious thinkers brought its theoretical teachings into alignment with various contemporary philosophical systems. Both intellectual activities—juridical and philosophical—were dependent on interpretation of given sacred texts by qualified authorities and remained scholastic in nature.

Alongside these two branches of religious learning there developed since Talmudic times, especially during the Middle Ages, the esoteric lore of the mystics known as the *cabala*. Starting with gnostic-like ideas, it developed emanative theories of the godhead and reinterpreted much of the tradition in this light. The main book of the *cabala* is the pseudographic Zohar, written in Aramaic in thirteenth-century Spain and attributed to one of the Talmudic sages of the second century. Although opposed by some rationalists ever since and looked upon with suspicion by some halachists, it nevertheless found widespread acceptance, especially since the late Middle Ages, when it strongly influenced both religious thinking and practice.

**The natural universe.**    Judaism did not define its own beliefs dogmatically. The Jewish outlook on the nature of the universe, man, and the like must be derived from an analysis of sources rather than by citation of authoritative statements.

For the Jew, the universe is the creation of God and it runs its course according to laws implanted in it by the Creator. Interference by man with the course of natural events by use of magic is perhaps possible but is outlawed by religious proscription. The Creator himself is capable of changing the course of nature, and it is assumed that such changes did indeed occur in the remote past—Biblical miracles are in principle taken literally. New interventions by the Creator, while possible, are not expected. Nature is therefore taken, for all intents and purposes, as a stable and reliable entity. This stability does not exclude, however, the control of God over the natural processes which determine human life. The welfare of man on earth is dependent on his moral and religious behavior. Longevity, the blessing of children, prosperity, and health are thought to be dependent upon one's merit. This presupposes the divine direction of events. The obvious logical and experimental difficulties of this position are noted and have been discussed in theological and philosophical terms. In effect, however, neither the constancy of nature nor the providence of God is repudiated.

This conception of the relationship between nature, God, and man leaves man sufficient scope to work out his own destiny. Man is regarded as free to choose the morally good and religiously desirable. Rabbinic Judaism is aware of the evil impulse in man both as an impediment to the performance of good and as a constant source of temptation. This, however, is capable of being overcome by human will, and divine support is vouchsafed to aid in the struggle. The concept of original sin is not unknown but is peripheral and does not infringe upon the capacity of man to determine his own fate both in this world and in the world to come.

The attitude of Rabbinic Judaism to the world does not preclude quietism, but it is more conducive to activity. Man's moral responsibility requires him to provide for his own needs and for the needs of those who are dependent on him.

The conception of God as transcendent does not preclude contact with him. Revelation and prophecy, like miracles, however, have been relegated by Judaism to remote times, and they are viewed as having ended with the close of the Biblical era. Although the claims of individuals throughout later periods to have had visions or other supernatural contacts with another world were not discounted, they never received recognition as authoritative guides to religious conduct. Such guidance is to be derived exclusively from the accepted body of revealed law through the medium of rational interpretation.

**The conduct of life.**    Religious precepts in Judaism are traditionally divided into prohibitions and positive commandments. The first represents a system of religious taboos or restrictions which lend to Jewish life the air of restraint but not of outright ascetic character. They limit gratification but do not seek to suppress it. Dietary laws prescribe the exclusion of some ("unclean") animals from the Jewish menu and dictate the manner of preparation of certain foods—the slaughtering and salting of meat and the separation of milk and meat products, for example. Within these limits the partaking of food is limited only by the general injunction against gluttony. As against the days of fast, there are festivals on which the enjoyment of a meal is a religious duty. All sexual or even erotic contact outside marriage is proscribed, and marriage is prescribed, preferably at an early age. Within marriage, sexual intercourse is limited by an additional period of purification after the cessation of menstruation. Yet sexual intercourse is not limited to the purpose of propagation but includes the mutual satisfaction of man and woman.

The execution of religious rites is part of the fulfillment of the positive commandments. Prayer, preferably together with the community, must be recited three times a day. The Pentateuch is read during the Sabbath and festival services, and on festivals special rites are also performed. On the Feast of Tabernacles (Sukkoth), for example, originally a harvest festival, the worshiper is required to hold four kinds of plants during the services. On the New Year (Rosh Hashanah) the ram's horn (shofar) is sounded. The special rites of Passover, such as the partaking of unleavened bread (matzah) and the narration of the exodus from Egypt, take place within the family. Special significance is attributed to the rite of circumcision, since it initiates the eight-day-old male child into the covenant of Israel. Although devoid of any special rite, the Day of Atonement (Yom Kippur) with its full-day fast and prayers occupies a special place in the Jewish religious calendar, for it is dedicated to repentance which, if genuine, is, according to the rabbinic outlook, capable of atoning for sins. The periodic unity of the community in prayer and ritual has been a major factor in social cohesion, while the family is similarly strengthened by being the locus of the religious performance.

Positive as well as negative commandments are obligatory on males above the age of 13 and females above the age of 12. Women are exempted from some of the positive commandments, as they are also excluded from the study of the law beyond an acquaintance with the precepts necessary for religious practice. Women are not participants in the religious community, nor do they take active part in the communal rites, although they may attend such services, seated in sections apart from the men. They may, however, acquire religious merit by fulfilling the special duties connected with the Jewish home and by aiding their husbands and sons in the fulfillment of religious obligations, especially the study of the law.

The fulfillment of religious precepts, both positive and negative, is the basic means of religious justification (in the Weberian sense) in Rabbinic Judaism. The degree of piety is established by the conscientiousness and exactitude of religious observance—the time and effort lavished upon an observance to give it an aesthetic character above and beyond its technical requirements and the intensity and devotion with which the commandment is actually performed.

In addition to being attached to religious duties in the strict sense of the word, religious merit is attributed to communal good works. Communal works are highly esteemed, as is every aid to those in need, such as extending hospitality to strangers, visiting the sick, and, above all, attending the dying and eulogizing and burying the dead. Correct behavior in business relations and abstention from deceptive speech and practices are also religiously valued. In places where the letter of the law conflicts with equity, the individual is admonished to forgo his legal rights. Thus moral behavior also becomes a source of religious justification.

**Rabbinical learning and practice.** Besides emphasizing the practical need for knowledge of the law (Torah) as a guide to religious observance and communal practice, Rabbinic Judaism regards the study of the law as an end in itself and one of the most basic of religious duties. Therefore, it advocates the dedication of one's time to the study of the Torah and exclusive devotion to it, even at the cost of reducing all other activities to a bare minimum.

Since early Pharisaic times there developed an elite which tried to live up to these demands. This was first achieved by the leading of an austere and even ascetic life in a society of peasants or artisans where work could be limited to provide for the necessities of life. In Mishnaic and Talmudic times, both direct and indirect support were provided by the community to members of the learned elite. They were often exempted from taxation and given certain minor business concessions: where they were concentrated in academies, as in Babylonia during Talmudic times, for example, these institutions were supported by voluntary contributions, and in the early Middle Ages a tax was levied on the Jews within their districts. Generally, despite variations arising from the different environments in which they existed, all Jewish communities followed these patterns. In the earliest stages of a Jewish settlement, men of learning were not to be found, but after having consolidated itself economically, a particular community usually attracted scholars from other, longer-established Jewish communities in the Diaspora.

The status of the elite varied according to prevailing economic conditions. In Yemen, where Jews remained an artisan class, no systematically supported elite developed and learning was cultivated as a part-time occupation of the intellectually oriented. In France and Germany, where the Jews became money lenders, their economic activity left much time free for independent study by "laymen," alongside that taking place in the communally supported institutions devoted exclusively to the study of the texts and the training of young persons in their interpretation. In Muslim and Christian

Spain the academies were supported by rich court-iers. In addition to the support of the very rich, the academies of Poland in the sixteenth and seven-teenth centuries could rely on the support of the less wealthy but still prosperous middle class. The intellectual elite became dependent upon the court Jews (the permanent financial agents of the abso-lute rulers of German principalities), who emerged in the seventeenth and eighteenth centuries. In all periods there were instances of wealthy families supporting a scholar among their own kin and sometimes even sustaining a whole academy which had grown up around him.

The door to the intellectual elite was, both in principle and in the final analysis, open to all, though naturally the time required to master the complex data made it easier for the well-born and well-to-do to attain the necessary intellectual level. In several instances this conjunction of ad-vantages, circumstances, and hereditary talent re-sulted in learned family dynasties.

The support of those who devoted themselves to study was regarded as one of the highest religious virtues. The contributor was viewed as participat-ing vicariously in the activity of the learned. Even after the maintenance of scholars had become common, exceptional individuals still adhered to the old ideal and refused to accept any remunera-tion for their studies. Indeed, one of the greatest authorities of medieval Jewry, Maimonides (1135–1204), lodged a formal protest against the in-stitution of private or communal support of the learned. For the average scholar, however, neither such protests nor his own qualms were of much avail, as both the changed economic conditions and the ever-increasing body of material to be mastered made full-time study imperative and necessitated what may be called a division of labor between the economically active and the learned.

The disapprobation which had adhered to the acceptance of payment by scholars had been at-tached also to the acceptance of payment for any services rendered in the exercise of religious au-thority. It was originally assumed that teaching, preaching, serving as a judge, or functioning in any other religious capacity was to be done gratui-tously. Later, payment for such services was legal-ized and morally defended. When such functions were concentrated in the hands of one person, spontaneously by virtue of his intellectual and moral pre-eminence or formally by election by the community, the communal rabbinate arose. This occurred noticeably in Christian Spain in the thir-teenth to the fifteenth centuries and in Germany and Poland in the fifteenth and sixteenth centuries.

In the course of time a fixed salary was guaranteed in addition to various emoluments.

Any action of a scholar or rabbi in matters of ritual or in the performance of marriage or di-vorce drew its authority from his halachic ex-pertise. If an error could be shown, the action could be invalidated. As no formal hierarchy existed, invalidation could be achieved only by appeal to some informally acknowledged higher rabbinic au-thority or by bringing the matter before the as-sembled opinion of the learned. On all levels, once decisions were made, discussions were conducted upon formal legal categories. Although theoreti-cally the validity of any act depended solely upon its technical agreement with an external frame of reference (*halachah*), in practice it drew much of its authority from the fact that it came from one who was regarded as being charismatic in conse-quence of his knowledge of and sustained contact with divine law and lore.

**Relations with other religions.**   Judaism makes no claim to universal allegiance and demands it only from those born of a Jewish mother. It holds the door open, however, to those who wish to join it out of conviction. The ritual of conversion re-quires circumcision and immersion for the male and the latter for the female. In pre-Christian times Jewish proselytes were common and in some places perhaps converted en masse. The attitude toward converts is somewhat ambivalent, but the possi-bility of their joining the faith has never been seri-ously contested. Proselytes from among the Chris-tians were accepted at times even in Christian countries where such conversion was forbidden by the political authorities. Jewish activity for gain-ing converts was perhaps vigorous at times, but at no time did Judaism achieve the dimensions of a missionary religion.

The claim of religious superiority has tradition-ally been maintained toward Christianity, which was first regarded by Judaism as simply another form of idolatry. Jews who became Christians fell under the category of heretics (*min*) or renegades (*mumar*). Insofar as Christianity claimed to be the true party to the Abrahamic or Sinaitic cove-nant, it was viewed as a usurper. In business and social affairs the Jews in Christian countries sought viable and amicable relationships with the population, and many restrictions originally insti-tuted with respect to paganism were declared in-operable in relation to Christianity. Gradually this also led to a lenient attitude toward Christianity itself. Maimonides, for example, declared that the spread of Christianity paved the way for the ulti-mate universal acceptance of the true faith. One of his followers in the fourteenth century exonerated Christianity from any charge of paganism. This tolerant attitude has gained more and more acceptance since the sixteenth century. Islam, being dogmatically unequivocal as to its monotheism, has been regarded as less contradictory than Christianity to Judaism. Toward the other world religions Rabbinic Judaism has had no occasion to take a stand.

**Society and polity.** Rabbinic Judaism takes the division of society between rich and poor for granted. Poverty may be viewed as a divine punishment for one's sins, as a testing of the righteous by God, or simply as a result of misfortune; but at any rate poverty is not a state in which one ought to remain intentionally. A premium is placed upon economic independence, not so much as an indication of divine grace but rather as the circumstance in which man is most free to serve God. Fundamentally Judaism is indifferent to the manner of self-support. Indirectly, however, through the high evaluation of study, the choice of profession has historically been religiously influenced. Occupations which left time free for study were preferred. This led in earlier societies to the preference of artisanship over agriculture and in later times to trade over manual labor. A religious impetus for acquiring wealth derived from the fact that wealth could be used for performing good deeds, especially the support of scholars. Striving for wealth could have derived some of its motivation from religious sources, but economic activity could not become a calling, as it was in certain Protestant sects. Economic success could only be a contributory factor to religious justification but not the basis of it.

It is more difficult to elicit the thoughts of Rabbinic Judaism in the field of politics. The necessity of government in general is acknowledged in the maxim "Were it not for fear of the government a man would devour his neighbor alive." But the manner of establishing the government is not set forth. Talmudic literature reflects the conception of a hereditary kingdom guided by the prescriptions of the law and limited somewhat by the High Court (Sanhedrin). Since the Jews did not long retain political independence and the foreign body politic within which the Jews existed had to be accepted, there was no incentive for the further development of political thought. Jewish communities adapted themselves to the prevailing political conditions. The political authority of the Christian prince was at no time challenged; it was acknowledged from the outset. In practical matters a similar attitude was adopted toward Islam. Concern for political matters was confined to communal affairs, which were conducted by the acknowledged elders or elected officials under general rabbinic supervision.

## Heterodoxy and sectarianism

**The Karaites.** The religious unity of the Jews lasted from the first to the seventeenth century with only one major deviating sect—the Karaites. This sect arose in the seventh century in Babylonia, under Arab rule and probably under Arab influence. Its members rejected the authority of the oral law and based their beliefs upon the direct interpretation of the Scriptures. The sect spread to Palestine, Egypt, and other Mediterranean countries with some outposts in the Crimea, Poland, and Lithuania. Although strongly opposed by the rabbinates, the Karaites at no time rejected the basic conception of Judaism as an institutionalized revealed religion whose observance was incumbent upon all members of the Jewish people, and they rejected the rival religions of Christianity and Islam. The links between the two communities were not severed, and intermarriage was at times countenanced and even legalized. In modern times the sense of common nationality drew the two groups together, although in Israel the Karaites view themselves, and are viewed, as a sect apart.

**Sabbatai Zevi.** Jewish tradition had foreseen a radical change in the status of religious law in the Messianic era. According to the widely held view, with the appearance of the Messiah the religious commandments would no longer be held binding. Throughout the Middle Ages, Messianic expectations evoked Messianic pretenders, but as they were quickly disproved, the possible implications for religious practice were not realized. Different, however, was Sabbatai Zevi, who came from Smyrna, Turkey, and who from 1665 to 1666 succeeded in keeping all Jewry in suspenseful waiting for the final call. He introduced new religious rites and partook in forbidden food in order to demonstrate by deed the end of the old era and the commencement of the new. When called to account by the Turkish authorities for causing mass upheavals, Sabbatai Zevi, to save his life, converted to Islam. A number of his followers accepted this as a necessary stage in the process of redemption, and in the course of theological justification for the converted Messiah, heretical theologies arose which were linked with the prevailing dualistic doctrines of the *cabala*. These gave rise to a number of sects, some of which were syncretisms of Judaism and Islam and lived on the margin of Jewish society, while others, although remaining within the confines of the Jewish community, were of a heretical and even antinomian or nihilistic character. These groups led a more or less clandestine existence among Jews in Turkey, Poland, Bohemia, and Moravia, thus disrupting the age-old religious unity of the Jewish people.

**Hasidism.** Sabbataianism at the very least served as a catalyst in engendering the great mystical movement of Hasidism, which arose in Poland in the middle of the eighteenth century. Originating in the small rural communities of Podolia, this movement centered on popular religious leaders of lower rank, wandering preachers, popular healers, and the like. Its first leader, Israel Ba'al Shem-Tov (who died in 1760) possessed an extraordinary gift for communicating his mystical experiences to his followers. During his lifetime the movement was still a local one, but in the following decades, under his disciples, it spread throughout eastern Europe and was checked only where it encountered savage opposition, as in Lithuania, for example. Hasidism did not challenge the validity of religious law, and except for some minor changes in liturgy and ritual, the accepted body of law and custom was left intact. What Hasidism did introduce was a new overriding religious value —that of communion with God, which was to be achieved either through enthusiasm or contemplation. The Hasidic leader was expected to have attained this "union" and to communicate it to his followers. Thus, a new type of religious leader arose whose legitimation did not stem primarily from his knowledge of the law but from his charismatic qualities. A new "community" was thus formed upon the basis of personal contact and was not bound by traditional territorial divisions. Those who could settle around the leader did so, while those who could not returned regularly to participate in the religious experiences of the community. In the course of time the leader was viewed not only as the guarantor of religious experience but also as a figure whose intervention was essential for the material well-being of the individual. The followers who gathered around provided for his support and that of his household, which often took on the dimensions of a court. And as in courts, the succession tended to become hereditary. The new religious leadership did not supplant the traditional rabbinical type, but it did encroach upon its authority.

Hasidism also had a deep impact upon many nonreligious aspects of life. It lessened the ascetic tendencies in Jewish living and encouraged emotional self-expression in the form of storytelling and song. It also loosened religious and communal disciplines and sanctioned the quiescent attitude toward the demands of practical life. It was a religious movement, but its total impact was to produce a new Jewish mentality.

## Modern Judaism

While Hasidism was altering Jewish society in eastern Europe from within, Jewry in western Europe was being transformed by forces from without. The theory and practice of separateness, which had been the way of Jewish life, was becoming progressively less tenable. Intellectual, social, and political forces were, in the course of a century, from 1750 to 1850, transforming Europe from a semifeudal society into a society of classes having a relatively high mobility. The status of Jewry within this new framework had to be redefined, and internally the old tradition had to be adapted to the new conditions.

The idea of Jewish political and social emancipation was originally conceived by John Toland in England in 1714, spelled out in detail in 1781–1783 in Germany by Ch. W. Dohm, and first implemented during the French Revolution. In the United States, Jewish equality was implied in the constitution. In the following decades the idea of emancipation spread to all countries of western Europe, and by 1870, after much struggle and some reverses, political emancipation was an accomplished fact.

Alongside these social and political changes, intellectual contact with European thought took place. In the last third of the eighteenth century, the first Jewish secular intellectuals appeared, headed by Moses Mendelssohn. They were deeply influenced by the doctrines of the Enlightenment and later by other European intellectual currents.

Judaism was confronted by rationalism and later by historical criticism. These, together with the social and political adjustments, led to a disintegration of the old conceptual as well as concrete framework of Jewish existence. In the ensuing chaos, many intellectuals and members of the upper class abandoned Judaism and perfunctorily embraced Christianity. Later, as the intellectual turmoil subsided, the main trends of modern Judaism emerged—Reform, Orthodox, and what came to be known as Conservative.

**Reform Judaism.** Reform Judaism started in Germany in the second decade of the nineteenth century, found followers in other European countries, such as England, Holland, and Hungary, and spread widely in the United States, where it assumed its most radical and thoroughgoing form. It rejected ritual, especially the restricting observances, and retained only ceremonies with obvious symbolic meanings. Liturgy was purged of elements of an archaic and nationalistic character, such as the prayer for the institution of sacrifices and the ultimate return of the Jews to their homeland. Instead, Messianism was interpreted as a belief in human progress. Of the prayers retained, some were translated into the vernacular, and the service was adapted to modern taste. As to doctrine, Reform Judaism emphasizes the ethical aspects of religion and advocates an enlightened but absolute monotheism, stressing in this way its difference from Christianity. Relinquishing tradition in principle, the Reform trend did not substitute any other source of authority for guidance in religious theory or practice. For this reason there is no unanimity among Reform Jews on just how much of the tradition is to be retained. The Reform rabbi is not expected to lay down the law for the community but rather to serve as preacher whose task is to officiate at ceremonies and guide the congregation to religious contemplation and elevation.

**Orthodox Judaism.** Orthodoxy, on the other hand, retained the authority of *halachah* and claimed allegiance to all details of Jewish observance and rites. In theory at least, an Orthodox rabbi is prepared to answer all questions concerning the permissible and the forbidden arising out of modern conditions while adhering to the traditional modes of halachic interpretation. In dogma, no concessions are made either to criticism of the verbatim revelation of the Pentateuch or to criticism of the substantive reliability of the oral tradition. Orthodoxy therefore remains antagonistic toward critical examination of the literary sources of religion. This did not prevent one German group under the guidance of S. R. Hirsch, regarded as the founder of modern Orthodoxy, from advocating the acquisition of and participation in secular culture. The old Talmudic institutions having disappeared, Hirsch attempted to secure the loyalty of the youth not by the study of the law's minutiae but through an understanding of and identification with the principles of Jewish doctrine and observance.

Eastern Europe in the early nineteenth century witnessed a renaissance of Talmudic academies, but as midcentury drew near, the impact of rationalism was being felt. To counterbalance the increasingly secular and assimilationist environment, an ethical–religious movement (Mussar), founded by Rabbi Israel Lipkin of Salant, arose, which sought to assure identification with Jewish values and commandments through continuous introspection. A third trend in Orthodoxy was noticeable in Hungary, where the clash with the Reform led the Orthodox leadership to advocate a radical seclusion from modern life and a proscription of any secular study. Hasidism, despite serious inroads of secularism, maintained its communal cohesion. All these ideologies are still operative in our day, especially in the United States, England, and modern Israel.

**Conservative Judaism.** The greater part of Jewry, while not accepting tradition as absolutely valid, adheres nevertheless to some parts of it because of religious sentiments or need for identification. This attitude assumed the nature of a principle for some thinkers and historians of the Breslau school in Germany and for the Conservative movement in the United States. Having perceived in the past a process of development in religion, they accept this notion as a legitimate course to be pursued in the present. However, they expect the process to be organic and continuous and reject outright changes based on rationalistic considerations. Conservatism neither accepts *halachah* in the strict sense of the word nor repudiates it. Accordingly it has made some adaptations in religious services and practice but more on an *ad hoc* basis than on any clear-cut principle.

These three main trends in modern Judaism have assumed the character of denominations. They are centered on synagogues, and these are connected by nation-wide and even world-wide organizations. They also maintain seminars for the training of teachers and rabbis. In Continental Europe in the nineteenth century such organizations were necessary, as one's formal affiliation with the Jewish community was prescribed by the secular state. However, in English-speaking countries, in France since 1905, and in Germany since the end of World War I, such associations have been on a voluntary basis.

Since then, the usual manner of identification with Judaism has been through affiliation with one of the religious organizations or by observance of some religious practice. A third way, though less common, is the personal acceptance of a certain religious outlook which is defined as Jewish. Such a school of thought is represented by Martin Buber, who interpreted prophetic Judaism and especially Hasidism in the light of an existentialist philosophy. Buber was not committed to any observance nor was he associated with any synagogue, but he was satisfied to be affiliated on the basis of his theoretical exposition of the Jewish religion. Buber has had a marked influence among affiliated and nonaffiliated Jews alike. [*See the biography of* BUBER.]

**Secular Judaism.** It is paradoxical but historically understandable that there evolved ways of Jewish identification which are religiously indifferent or even antireligious. This development originated in eastern Europe during the latter half of the nineteenth century where, in spite of the disintegration of the traditional religious framework, Jewry remained a distinct ethnic group, linguistically and socially set apart from the populace. In this environment Yiddish and Hebrew literature of a secular nature prepared the ground for national social movements with distinctly Jewish objectives—such as Zionism and the socialist movement of the Bund. These movements drew their objectives from the persecutions in eastern Europe and the rise of anti-Semitism in western Europe. However, large segments within secular Judaism based their ideologies upon a reinterpretation of Jewish history: behind the religious unfolding of Judaism through the ages there always had been an ethical or social doctrine which, by the progress of human thought, then came to the forefront. The ethical interpretation was represented by Achad Haam (pseudonym of Asher Ginzberg) and the social one by Ber-Borochoff, both leading figures of modern nationalistic movements. Achad Haam, especially, believed in the revitalization of ancient Judaism through the establishment of a Jewish state and society which, although secular, would have a historical continuity with traditional Judaism because of its ethnic identity with it. A secular interpretation of Judaism is the premise of the contemporary national culture of Israel.

In other countries, too, trends combining ethnic and cultural aspirations together with some religious content could be discerned. Most conspicuous perhaps is the reconstructionist movement of Mordecai M. Kaplan in the United States, which prefers to define Judaism in terms of civilization rather than in terms of religious dogma or law.

Not all those who are considered by themselves or by others as Jews would subscribe to any of the above-mentioned outlooks, whether religious or secular. There are Jews who are indifferent to any Jewish content yet still have strong feelings of group identity, expressed in such ways as contributing to Jewish causes. Others disavow Judaism entirely, and some even conceal their origins. Irrespective of how assimilated a Jew may be, he is nevertheless commonly regarded by Jews and gentiles alike as a Jew until he joins a non-Jewish church, a fact which reflects the original ethnic–religious connotation of the term. Converts to Judaism, being few in number, are easily absorbed by the community.

**The Jewish community.** Any assessment of the numerical division of Jewry among the above-mentioned groups remains conjectural. The three religious movements in the United States, for example, claim to include some 60 per cent of the 5½ million American Jews. Each group claims about 1 million members. While affiliation with the Reform movement clearly indicates the renunciation of strict religious observance, affiliation with Orthodoxy and Conservatism does not indicate the degree of adherence to religious practice. It is certain that the number of those who strictly abide by the law comes nowhere near that of the formally affiliated. In Great Britain, with the exception of some ultra-Orthodox and a few Reform congregations, all the synagogues are officially connected with the Orthodox chief rabbinate, but no more than 5 per cent of the half million British Jews could possibly be viewed as strictly observant. In France, out of a slightly smaller population, even fewer Jews are observant. Other countries conform to a similar pattern. In eastern European countries, especially in Russia, religious activity is barely tolerated, and Jewish observance and even circumcision is practiced by only a small fraction of the 3 million Jews.

Israel is a case apart. If judged by the number of those voting for religious political parties, Orthodox Jewry would total 15 per cent of the population; if judged by those sending their children to religious schools, they would total 37 per cent. Both figures are correct, as they reflect various aspects of religious attachments. Reform Judaism and Conservatism for all practical purposes are not represented institutionally. Nonetheless, gradations of observance are to be found among the populace. The nation is also divided on the issue of church and state. Since the time of the British mandate no secular marriage or divorce exists, and religious communities (Christian, Muslim, and Jewish) are subject to their respective religious courts. This is resented by the antireligious segments of the population and criticized by some religious elements as well. The tension is heightened by the generous leavening provided by the extremely orthodox (some of whom go so far as to deny the authority of the state) and militantly antireligious minorities in Israel.

**Contemporary relevance of religion.** Having found that Jewry in modern times adopts a selective attitude toward its traditional religion, we may ask whether this religion still retains some influence. Allowing for variations according to time and place, Jewry in modern society presents a certain sociological profile which may roughly be described as follows: It is a social unit with a clear sense of group identity and a strong leaning toward endogamy, family cohesion, and group solidarity. Concentrated largely in certain sectors of the economy, it constitutes a comparatively striving group within it. Socially it tends to move within its own circles, culturally to have a comparatively high level of education, and politically to reveal a leaning toward the more liberal trends and parties of its country.

All these traits can be understood in light of past history and the present situation as a consequence of the memory of former persecutions and as a reaction to contemporary economic and social prejudice. Yet it is still possible that religion has its share in maintaining some of these group characteristics. Two forces are at work, and we must clearly distinguish between the restrictive tendencies of specific religious requirements and the general *Weltanschauung* of Judaism.

Religious restrictions, such as Sabbath observance, dietary laws, and, among some groups, opposition to secular knowledge, confine their followers in the choice of occupation, in the extent of social intercourse with the environment, and in the identification with the surrounding culture. They act directly upon the believer and are operative only insofar as one submits to them; thus, their impact is most noticeable among the Orthodox and becomes progressively less as one moves across the religious spectrum.

The effects of the Jewish *Weltanschauung* are less direct, more diffuse and general, and thus much more difficult to gauge. It is commonly held that Jewish intellectualism of the medieval period (until the eighteenth century) has influenced the development of modern society. The absence of religious restrictions upon the acquisition of wealth may have fostered Jewish economic striving. Finally, the idea of social justice, found abundantly in Jewish sources and dwelt upon by modern exponents of Judaism, strengthened the impulse toward social reform which had probably been engendered by the situation of the Jews as a permanent minority.

Be that as it may, religion continues to serve as a source of social cohesion. For while it is true that during the modern period Jewish society developed many secular institutions of social and quasi-political activity (Zionism, for example), which presented opportunities for group identification, never-theless religious organizations remain to this day the most ubiquitous and all-embracing. In this capacity, Judaism, even in its most diluted form, serves the purpose of communal self-preservation.

JACOB KATZ

[*See also* ANTI-SEMITISM; CANON LAW; NEAR EASTERN SOCIETY, *article on* ISRAEL; ZIONISM. *Other relevant material may be found under* RELIGION.]

### BIBLIOGRAPHY

BAECK, LEO (1921–1938) 1958 *Judaism and Christianity: Essays*. Philadelphia: Jewish Publication Society of America. → A paperback edition was published in 1961 by World.

BAER, YITZHAK F. (1936) 1947 *Galut*. New York: Schocken. → First published in German.

BARON, SALO W. (1937) 1965 *A Social and Religious History of the Jews*. 10 vols., plus index. 2d ed., rev. & enl. New York: Columbia Univ. Press.

BARON, SALO W. (1942) 1945 *The Jewish Community: Its History and Structure to the American Revolution*. 3 vols. Philadelphia: Jewish Publication Society of America.

EPSTEIN, ISIDORE 1954 *The Faith of Judaism: An Interpretation for Our Times*. London: Soncino.

FINKELSTEIN, LOUIS (editor) (1949) 1960 *The Jews: Their History, Culture and Religion*. 2 vols. 3d ed. New York: Harper.

GINSBERG, LOUIS (1901–1941) 1955 *On Jewish Law and Lore: Essays*. Philadelphia: Jewish Publication Society of America. → A paperback edition was published in 1962 by World.

GUTTMANN, JULIUS (1933) 1964 *Philosophies of Judaism: The History of Jewish Philosophy From Biblical Times to Franz Rosenzweig*. New York: Holt. → First published in German.

JACOBS, LOUIS 1964 *Principles of the Jewish Faith: An Analytical Study*. London: Vallentine.

KAPLAN, MORDECAI M. (1934) 1957 *Judaism as a Civilization: Toward a Reconstruction of American-Jewish Life*. Enl. ed. New York: Reconstructionist Press.

KATZ, JACOB 1961 *Tradition and Crisis: Jewish Society at the End of the Middle Ages*. New York: Free Press.

MOORE, GEORGE F. 1927–1930 *Judaism in the First Centuries of the Christian Era*. 3 vols. Cambridge, Mass.: Harvard Univ. Press.

SCHECHTER, SOLOMON (1896–1924) 1958 *Studies in Judaism: A Selection*. New York: Meridian.

SCHOLEM, GERSHOM G. (1941) 1961 *Major Trends in Jewish Mysticism*. 3d rev. ed. New York: Schocken.

WIENER, M. 1933 *Jüdische Religion im Zeitalter der Emanzipation*. Berlin: Philo.

## JUDD, CHARLES H.

Charles Hubbard Judd (1873–1946), American psychologist, was born in India of missionary parents and came to America in 1879. He received his B.A. at Wesleyan in 1894 and his PH.D. at Leipzig under Wilhelm Wundt in 1896. After seven years as professor of psychology at Yale, he accepted the position of head of the department of education at the University of Chicago, where he remained until his retirement in 1938. His vigorous leadership at Chicago made a marked contribution to the development of education as a field of graduate study, changing its content from a set of courses on the philosophy of pedagogy to a program based on a substantial body of research findings.

Judd's graduate work with Wundt gave him a strong and persistent interest both in language, especially the psychology of reading, and in experimental methods of research. Early in his career, as director of the psychological laboratory at Yale, and later at Chicago, he stressed the importance of objective laboratory studies in the creation of what he called "a science of education." He was chiefly concerned with the mental processes involved in studying various school subjects. His pioneer laboratory research on eye movements in reading (Judd et al. 1905) stimulated more than one hundred published studies in the following twenty years, and other books and monographs that he published between 1903 and 1927 had a wide influence on teaching in elementary and secondary schools.

Throughout his writings Judd emphasized the importance of social psychology in the study of education. He believed that the contributions of animal psychology to education had been grossly overrated and that those of social psychology were of much greater significance. He held that "social institutions," such as language, numbers, tool consciousness, and systems of exchange are the accumulated abstractions of the human race, made possible by the immense cerebral development of the human brain as compared with animal brains. Through language and mathematics, the crucial subjects of education, the intellectual inventions of the human mind are revealed to the individual learner.

Judd's position on social psychology was first presented in his *Genetic Psychology for Teachers* (1903) and developed in much greater detail in his *Psychology of Social Institutions* (1926). In 1936, in his *Education as Cultivation of the Higher Mental Processes*, he made more explicit his theory that more can be learned about mental life by studying experience than by speculating about neural connections. He believed that the psychology of his time devoted too much attention to what he called the "path" theory of neural activity and too little to the "pattern" theory, since significant human responses operate to a greater extent through the higher mental processes of abstraction and generalization than through the simple connections that mediate the stimulus–response behavior of

animals. His research was devoted to the detailed analysis of these higher mental processes.

The primary target of Judd's criticism was the early work of E. L. Thorndike on transfer of training. Judd held that Thorndike's connectionism tended to reduce the higher mental processes to aggregations of simpler processes. For example, he asserted that Thorndike's view led teachers of arithmetic to think of the subject as a collection of specific items to be learned through drill rather than to look on arithmetic as a highly abstract and systematic form of learning. Judd rejected not the concept of transfer, but Thorndike's mechanism of transfer: he believed in the possibility of transfer through the learning of widely applicable generalizations rather than through the connection of different situations by identical elements. His position on transfer was an outgrowth of his fundamental view of the higher mental processes. He emphasized learning as an organization of experience, with the possibility of transfer increasing as the higher levels of generalization are reached.

Although Judd was a psychologist by training, his long career as head of the department of education at Chicago brought him in direct contact with all the major issues of educational administration. He exerted an important influence on school organization over a period of three decades. In addition, as editor of two major periodicals in the field of education, the *School Review* and the *Elementary School Journal*, Judd was able to give his views on education wide currency.

GUY T. BUSWELL

[*For the historical context of Judd's work, see the biography of* THORNDIKE; *for discussion of the subsequent development of his ideas, see* EDUCATIONAL PSYCHOLOGY; LEARNING, *article on* TRANSFER; VISION, *article on* EYE MOVEMENTS.]

## WORKS BY JUDD

1903    *Genetic Psychology for Teachers.* New York: Appleton.
1905    JUDD, CHARLES; MCALLISTER, C. N.; and STEELE, W. M.   General Introduction to a Series of Studies of Eye-movements by Means of Microscopic Photographs. *Psychological Monographs* Vol. 7, no. 29.
1915    *Psychology of High School Subjects.* Boston: Ginn.
1926    *Psychology of Social Institutions.* New York: Macmillan.
1927    *Psychology of Secondary Education.* Boston: Ginn.
1936    *Education as Cultivation of the Higher Mental Processes.* New York: Macmillan.

## WORKS ABOUT JUDD

BUSWELL, GUY T. 1947  Charles Hubbard Judd: 1873–1946. *American Journal of Psychology* 60:135–137.
FREEMAN, F. N. 1947  Charles Hubbard Judd. *Psychological Review* 54:59–65.

# JUDICIAL PROCESS

*The articles under this heading deal with judicial institutions and processes. Closely related are* ADJUDICATION *and* JUDICIARY. *A detailed guide to further topics will be found under* LAW.

## I
### INTRODUCTION

The judicial process is a set of interrelated procedures and roles for deciding disputes by an authoritative person or persons whose decisions are regularly obeyed. The disputes are to be decided according to a previously agreed upon set of procedures and in conformity with prescribed rules. As an incident, or consequence, of their dispute-deciding function, those who decide make authoritative statements of how the rules are to be applied, and these statements have a prospective generalized impact on the behavior of many besides the immediate parties to the dispute. Hence the judicial process is both a means of resolving disputes between identifiable and specified persons and a process for making public policies.

## Development of the concept

For centuries hundreds of writers in thousands of articles and books have tried to determine what is the essence of the judicial or adjudicatory process, what distinguishes it from the legislative and administrative processes. During the last several centuries this exercise in political taxonomy has taken on special urgency and normative concerns. For under the doctrine of separation of powers it became improper for legislatures to engage in the judicial process—issuance of bills of attainder, for example—or for judges to assume functions that are thought to be within the scope of the legislative process.

The classic doctrine of separation of powers divided the world of political activity into the three familiar divisions based both on what was thought to be the behavior of political actors and on what were thought to be the requirements for the maintenance of liberty. The judiciary was assigned the function of applying the laws that the constitution makers and the legislatures had created and that the administrators enforced.

Today political analysts have abandoned these categories in favor of a continuum. At one pole is the legislative process for making law (formulating norms) and at the other the administrative and judicial processes for administration or applying the law (individualizing the norm). (These categories are analytic, and the activities are not necessarily performed by agencies with corresponding labels.) As to the distinction between the administrative and judicial, some writers—such as Hans Kelsen and Otto Kirchheimer—insist that these processes cannot be distinguished functionally and that it is more or less a historical accident whether some disputes are assigned to what are known as courts whereas others are assigned to what are known as administrative agencies. Others, such as Roscoe Pound, insist that the difference grows out of the fact that administrators are not obliged to make their decisions by following prescribed procedures or in accord with legal doctrines. Administration is seen by these writers as power and discretion, whereas adjudication is rational and controlled. The dispute here is but a facet of an ever-recurring discussion to which we will return later.

**The orthodox theory.** According to what is variously called the "mechanical," "slot-machine," "photographic," "formalistic," "conceptual," or "orthodox" theory of the judicial process, judges, like doctors or scientists, are trained technicians who apply their specialized knowledge to discover answers to legal disputes. Judging is to be sharply distinguished from politics. Political forces determine what the rules are; the judge merely applies the given rules to the facts. If the judges come across a novel situation for which there is no agreed upon rule, by a process of analogy and logic they discover what rule should be applied; to this extent, and to this extent only, they may be said to create rules. Some commentators have even gone further: to them the judicial process is a self-contained world with its own dynamics and is totally divorced from the political system. And even those who recognize that legal rules and judicial decisions are related to the political community insist that the judges and the law they apply are neutral among competing interests within the community. The judge is a spokesman for the more enduring values of the society, not merely the wishes of those who are for the moment governing it. As the noted English barrister Sir Carleton Kemp Allen phrased it:

Our law has had its political vicissitudes, and at certain periods of its history it has been threatened with degradation into an instrument of government; it might, indeed, have suffered that dismal fate but for the resistance of men like Sir Edward Coke. But today there is nothing more repellent to Anglo-Saxon legal instinct than the corruption of law by political "ideology." (Allen [1927] 1964, p. 56)

**The realists' criticism.** This formalistic conception of the judicial process has always been questioned. But beginning toward the end of the last century, and with great zeal in this century, there has been a mounting criticism of it. The attack has come from many sources and from many different writers. The skeptics represent a wide variety of different kinds of analyses, many of which contradict one another, and it is difficult to present the skeptics' views as a consistent whole. They are often grouped together under the label of "legal realists," although at times this appellation is reserved for a smaller number of American writers of the 1920s and 1930s. Using the term "realists" in its broadest sense to include all who are skeptical of the traditional analysis, we might mention three of the major assertions:

(1) Legal rules do not determine judicial decisions. "The theory that rules decide cases seems for a century to have fooled, not only library-ridden recluses, but judges" (Llewellyn 1934, p. 7). "[The] half explanatory, half apologetic reference to the judge's subservience to the law is at best a playful protective device; at worst it testifies to his unwillingness to understand his own role in the social process" (Kirchheimer 1961, p. 187).

The point here—and about it there remains much confusion—is not that there are no legal rules or that there is always uncertainty as to what the law requires. The skepticism relates to the extent to which rules determine judicial decisions. There are rules, for example, conferring jurisdiction on courts and making their decisions authoritative. Clearly understood laws govern the great bulk of human transactions; most men know what they must do if they wish the contracts they make to be valid and enforceable by courts. Most legal conflicts do not give rise to litigation, since the law provides relatively precise answers to most questions without the necessity of bringing the matter before a judge. Furthermore, often the judge is not asked which rule should be applied but what happened, that is, to determine who did what to whom. And in other instances, especially at the trial level, the judge's function is to legitimize a transaction by applying a rule about which there is no dispute. No judge is likely to make a decision in such a case contrary to the widely accepted rule; if he did so his decision would not long survive, and he would be unmasked as an incompetent. In this sense he has no discretion, and the rule does provide a guideline.

However, when a judge must resolve a conflict and there is a dispute as to which rule should be applied, the traditional explanation of the judicial process is misleading. According to this explanation judges look to past precedents or to constitutions, statutes, or codes and find the proper rule to resolve the dispute. But there are conflicting precedents and an infinite variety of factual situations to which the uncertain precedents can apply. Nor do constitutions, statutes, and codes provide certain guidelines. "Much of the jurisprudence of this century has consisted of the progressive realization (and sometimes the exaggeration) of the important fact that the distinction between the uncertainties of communication by authoritative example (precedent), and the certainties of communication by authoritative general language (legislation) is far less firm than this naive contrast suggests" (Hart 1961, p. 123).

(2) The formal theory of interpretation and the fiction of legislative intent are methods of "paying lip service to the prevailing myth of statutory interpretation and to the equally mythical notion that judicial legislation is both unconstitutional and improper. . . . Attempts to hide that fact [of the creative function of statutory interpretation] behind a cloak of verbiage are fatuous at best. And the judicial creative activity applies, to some degree at least, to all statutes" (Miller 1956, p. 34).

Judges do and must make law. But this is not to say that when judges make law they are acting improperly, for such lawmaking is inherent in their function. A judge may be neutral between the parties to a lawsuit and dedicated to the principles of his craft, but he must choose; and the difference between one judge's choice and another's does not stem from any difference in their technical knowledge of the law, but from their differing response to the conflicting values which the case presents.

To recognize that judges make law is not to conclude that they are "free" to make any laws they wish; and while one strand of the realist ferment emphasizes the choice-making, creative role of the judge, another searches for the variables that condition and restrict that choice.

(3) The decisions are not personal choices of the judges, accidental, arbitrary, or divorced from the rest of the political system. Although some American realists of the 1930s seemed to suggest that judicial rulings were determined by the personality traits of the jurists—which some wag labeled the "breakfast-food theory" of jurisprudence—most writers have concluded that to add personality to precedent does not substantially advance our understanding of the judicial process.

Statutory directions, traditional procedures, the demands of the judicial role, and the organizational and political connections between the judicial process and the political system set limits to and give a direction to judicial decision making.

Underlying much of the work of the realists is the view that since judges must inevitably choose between competing values, awareness of the fact that they are making such choices, some knowledge on which to base these choices, and concern for the social consequences of the choice are desirable.

During the 1920s and the 1930s the American legal realists emphasized empiricism and attacked formal legal concepts, and they made what seemed to be sharp distinctions between the "is" and the "ought." But there was no agreement among them whether judicial or any other values could be established by objectively demonstrable standards. A relativist position toward value questions did not—and does not—necessarily follow from a realist analysis of the judicial process, although many critics of realism have so charged. It is true that many realists, especially those writing prior to World War II, were skeptical that judges were any better equipped than legislators or administrators to determine these value questions. And they felt that many judges had too simple-minded a conviction that they had some special insight into justice.

The realist "ferment" of the 1920s and 1930s had important political consequences, especially in the United States. At the time American, English, and Canadian judges were striking down or restricting the scope of social welfare legislation, were generally hostile to positive government relating to economic matters, and were not particularly zealous in protecting civil liberties. The judges looked askance upon administrative agencies and wherever possible insisted that decisions of administrators be subject to review by judges.

During the 1920s and 1930s realists were critical of the particular policy choices the judges were then making. Legal realism became a tool to attack judicial decisions and to reduce the role of the judges. Within the context of the realist analysis the statement that the judges were making policy did not necessarily carry any critical content for, as realism taught, such policy making is inherent in the judicial process. But the " 'forward-looking scholar' (who was most likely to be abreast of the thinking in the neighboring discipline) found grist aplenty in the current product of the appellate courts to disapprove and to 'show up' as being by no means inherent in the scheme of our

law" (Llewellyn 1960, p. 13). Realism tore off the mask of detachment behind which judges, consciously or more likely without understanding what they were doing, manipulated legal symbols in behalf of their own limited concepts of the public interest. And in addition to furnishing ammunition with which to attack the laissez-faire judicial decision in the 1930s, realism had strong overtones critical of judicial restraints on political and legislative majorities. Not surprisingly, liberals tended toward a realist evaluation of the judicial process, to favor restrictions on the scope of judicial authority, and to be critical of the courts as policy instruments.

On the other side conservatives not surprisingly used the orthodox explanations of the judicial process to defend the restrictive judicial rulings, to urge judicial control of legislative and administrative agencies, and to stress the desirability of judicial checks on popularly elected and politically accountable decision makers. Although conceding that some judges might act improperly and permit their own political predispositions to influence their rulings, the conservatives contended that these were exceptions. Proper judges merely applied the law as given to them by the constitution, the legislatures, or past judicial decisions. The judicial decisions under attack, they argued, were not to be considered either as conservative or liberal, either proemployer or antiworker, but in accord with eternal verities. And, the conservatives argued, to suggest that judicial decisions reflected the judges own economic and social views was dangerously misleading, destroyed public confidence in the courts, and undermined the concept of an independent nonpolitical judiciary.

**The post-1945 period.** By the end of World War II these attitudes toward the judicial process began to alter. Within the democratic nations, especially the United States and England, judges—many of whom had been educated in the period of the realist ferment—were now supporting governmental regulation of the economy and at the same time protecting civil liberties. At least in the United States, this alteration in the stance of the federal judges seemed to be based on political factors making it probable that this liberal tone would have stability. For the first time in American history conservatives, who now had a louder voice within legislative chambers than they had within judicial halls, were raising doubts about the desirability of judicial restraints on legislators and administrators. Still clinging to the concepts of mechanical jurisprudence, the conservatives charged that the judges were making decisions based on "sociology" and not on law. On the other side, liberals began to repudiate some of the conclusions drawn from realism and, building on more orthodox explanations of the judicial process, to defend judicial review as a device to protect and keep open the democratic processes. In 1960 the major leader of the realist ferment wrote, "jurisprudence [in the 1930s] promptly became a football of politics, study of the courts' processes of deciding was suddenly taken as an attack on decency of the court's operation, issues were distorted, energies were wasted. . . . One looks around, after war and foreign danger have sweated some of this silliness out of us, and sees a vastly different scene. . . . The danger lies now in altogether different quarters" (Llewellyn 1960, pp. 14–15). The danger now is that men will lose confidence in their judges, thinking that they operate without regard to generalizable standards.

A group of scholars for whom there is as yet no label but who may be called the "neo-orthodox" have redirected attention not to how the judicial process is like the legislative but to how it differs. The whole purpose of the judicial process, they argue, is to permit knowledge and argument to lead to a reasoned decision. To reduce the analysis of the judicial process to the same terms that are used to describe the legislative process is to strip the judicial of what distinguishes it from the other ways to order human affairs. Although it is not to be assumed that judges are superhuman logicians or even that their decisions always are the deductive application of legal rules, nonetheless their decisions are products of a different set of conditions than are those of political actors who are directly accountable to political majorities and who are assigned different tasks and different roles.

Some skeptics of the orthodox ideology concede that the judges sometimes do make value choices and that the law does not necessarily determine their behavior. Nonetheless, they argue, the policy-making activity of the judges is an exception to the general course of judicial business and stems primarily from giving judges the power of judicial review.

Whether a synthesis between the realist and formalist concepts of the judicial process will result and whether such a synthesis will provide a better tool for understanding the dynamics of the judicial process is yet to be determined. As it stands, in the world of scholarship the formalist view has been modified, and the statement of the realist position is no longer so shrill. Among sophisticates the orthodox explanations of judicial behavior are no longer in good standing. On the other hand,

there is no longer much shock value in pointing out that the judges are men and like all men are subject to limited perspectives. Few scholars now deny that the judicial process operates within and is conditioned by the political system and that judges make policy, but because of their adjudicatory function they make policy in special ways. Outside the world of scholarship, the orthodox position still holds. The prevailing expectations still require judges to state their decisions as controlled by statutes or precedents, and the official explanation of public men and practicing lawyers remains that the law is independent of the judges and controls their behavior.

## Organization of the judicial process

The organization of the judicial process is determined by its purpose: to adjudicate particular kinds of disputes. (There must be a conflict between parties presenting the judges with a "yea" or "nay" choice.) By definition, among the factors that distinguish adjudication from the other techniques of dispute deciding—bargaining, electioneering, voting, fighting—is that each side in the conflict is entitled to be heard by an outsider to the dispute who is to make his decision solely on the evidence presented to him and in accord with a standard of right and wrong.

In democratic societies adjudication is based on an entirely different set of expectations than those that underlie the legislative or executive functions. What the majority wishes is what the legislators should decide. But adjudication calls for decisions in accord with standards of right, to be made by persons who are free to apply these standards without concern for the popularity of their decisions. Adjudication rests on the conviction that some kinds of differences are best resolved by an appeal to a specially qualified elite.

Based on these expectations and in accord with its defined function, the judicial process is deliberately organized to "disconnect" it from the rest of the community. The judicial system ordinarily does not have direct lines of accountability to the political authorities. (In some American states where judges are elected for short terms obviously this is not so.) This independence of the judicial system from the community is based on the need for dispute deciders who are not subject to outside instructions or coercion. Both realist and orthodox analyses support this independence in order that those who come before the judges may have a hearing by a tribunal free to make a decision on the basis of the evidence and arguments presented to it. The orthodox ideology has the additional advantage of squaring this judicial independence with the principles of democratic politics, for portraying the judges as technicians who do not participate in the resolution of policy conflicts makes it unnecessary to hold them politically accountable.

Selection procedures and tenure arrangements vary from nation to nation, but their design is to reduce considerations of partisan politics and to maximize attention to professional qualifications. Although lay participation still survives in the form of jury and lay judges, the definition of the "best qualified" now carries the expectation that the judges will be men trained in law. As early as the seventeenth century the celebrated Lord Coke told King James that since he lacked knowledge of the "artificial reason and judgment of the law" even the king was not entitled to decide cases but must act through his law-trained officers. Nowadays the legal profession has much to say as to who among them shall be selected as a judge, even if the actual selection process vests the final choice in political authorities. (The Supreme Court of the United States is to a considerable extent an exception in that the president exercises something like a personal prerogative in choosing justices for this Court.) Once selected, judges are expected to perform in accordance with professional standards, and they are measured by these standards: judges are members of a distinctive professional group who look to that group for their prestige.

More important than the formal constitutional and institutional arrangements in disconnecting the judicial from the rest of the political system are the factors growing from the judicial role. This role conditions and restricts the way the judges should behave and limits how others should behave in their relations with the judges. Once appointed to the bench a judge is expected to withdraw from active partisanship, to refrain from taking public positions on controversial issues, and to conduct himself so that there can be no suggestion that his official behavior is in any way influenced by his own personal concerns or attachments. His role makes it improper for any groups to make out-of-courtroom contacts or to use any of the normal methods of influencing political decision makers. To do so is not only improper but in many instances illegal.

The "disconnectedness" of the judicial process from the political system, however, is only relative. Changes in the rest of the system affect the nature of the decisions that will be made. Like all who make decisions affecting the fate and fortunes of the community, judges exercise their discretion not only within the confines of the requirements of the judicial process itself but within the context of the political system of which it is a part. What distinguishes judicial from other kinds of political actors is not that the judges are outside the system but that they are related to it in a different fashion than are the other decision makers.

## Courtroom access and judicial scope

Since judges are expected to approach each case with an open mind, in all nations they lack authority to initiate proceedings for if permitted to do so, it is felt, they would be compelled to prejudge the case. "It is the fact that such application [of person claiming rights] must be made to him, which distinguishes a judge from an administrative officer" (Gray [1909] 1963, p. 114). Of greater significance, however, than the fact that the judges may not start lawsuits is the fact that an ordinary individual through a regular lawsuit may raise fundamental questions of public policy. Whereas only those with some political strength may command legislative attention, a single individual may compel a judge to make a ruling. The litigant may be concerned only with his own problems: to secure ownership of a piece of property, to dissolve a marriage contract, or to stay out of prison; but the decision he secures will create or confirm a rule that governs the behavior of many persons other than himself.

In the Anglo–American nations there are no distinctions between courts created to adjudicate disputes and those established to hear conflicts involving questions of "high politics." The higher appellate courts, however, operate under rules specifying that they are not to hear cases merely to do justice between litigants but only where the public interest is paramount. Nonetheless, they are organized like and function as ordinary law courts. Civil law nations do attempt to distinguish more sharply between courts created to adjudicate lawsuits and those established to deal with questions of more general public significance. In the German Federal Republic and in Italy, for example, special courts deal with constitutional questions. Their jurisdiction does not depend on the ordinary litigant but may be invoked by public authorities. In France a separate court system deals with disputes between citizens and administrative officials.

There are limits to courtroom access. Generally speaking, only those who are able to persuade the judges that they are personally and directly involved in a dispute may seek a judicial resolution of it, and there are some kinds of disputes judges will not attempt to decide. The technical rules and rationalizations to distinguish between "justiciable" and "nonjusticiable" issues vary from nation to nation and time to time. The widest range of subjects are dealt with by courts in nations such as the United States, Australia, and Canada, where the constitution is a legal as well as a political document, that is, a document subject to construction by judges. In the United States judges have the broad jurisdiction characteristic of the common-law countries, plus the authority to treat the constitution as a legal instrument. The Supreme Court of the United States has been squarely in the middle of almost every major political conflict that has arisen within the American republic. But even in the United States the judicial process has played a minor role in some areas: conflicts over control of the machinery of government; price policies for the distribution of goods and services; and the whole area of American relations with foreign nations.

Civil law nations attempt to restrict the impact of decisions to the immediate cases, and except in a few nations—and here only since World War II —constitutional documents are not considered to be subject to judicial construction. The French judiciary, for example, has never been the pivot for any major political interest. It is impossible to cite a single judicial ruling that has had a substantial impact on the political life of that nation, which is all the more remarkable in view of the highly divisive nature of French politics.

Litigation as a device for making policy depends upon the ability to formulate a lawsuit that presents judges with a yea or nay choice. However, for some issues a day in court is easier to secure than a day before the legislature. The "chips" for winning the judicial "game" are different from those for winning the legislative "game," since judges are related to the political community in a different fashion than are legislators. Groups who lack electoral strength may, therefore, find it more profitable to resort to litigation than to legislation. However, without some political strength in the community, major alterations of public policy through litigation are as unlikely as through legislation. For the chance of securing favorable judicial rulings is not unrelated to the political configurations of the community. Unpopular minorities whose activities have been restricted by legislation seldom have more success before the courts than they have had before the legislature. Yet in many nations because of such factors as federalism, bicameralism, election district geography, rules of debate in the legislature, and so on, even relatively widely supported values may not secure legislative expression. The judicial process thus provides a forum for raising issues in a different context from the one provided by legislative or executive decision makers.

## The formal requirements

By definition adjudication is distinguished from other techniques of dispute deciding in that it calls for the open presentation of evidence and reasoned argument before impartial judges who are to make their decisions in accord with the evidence and arguments presented to them and in accord with established standards. Courts exist to settle lawsuits, and this function imposes certain requirements on judicial procedures. Whether these requirements accurately describe how judges behave is for the moment irrelevant, for they have a significance divorced from consideration of whether they are descriptively accurate.

Judicial decisions are expected to be based only on the information formally fed into the system. In contrast legislators and administrators (except when they are expected to perform as judges) may secure information whenever and however they please, may contact rival claimants in private, and are under no obligation to give each claimant an opportunity to respond to the other side. Judges, however, are forbidden to discuss a case or to gather evidence outside the formal proceedings. Although in the misleadingly named "inquisitorial system" of civil-law countries, judges have somewhat more leeway in making independent investigations, they too operate under narrowly prescribed procedures designed to exclude from consideration any facts or arguments except those which the participants have presented in formal proceedings. (The doctrine of "judicial notice" provides an exception. Judges are permitted to make rulings in light of knowledge that is so widely known and acceptable that it may be taken into account without being formally presented to them.)

Perhaps the most important single formal requirement is that judicial decisions be based on reason. All decision makers are expected to act on the basis of the best available knowledge and to make decisions that conform to the rules of logic and rationality. But no other political actors are expected to perform solely in terms of reasoned argument. The legislative process provides for an infusion of knowledge and argument into the proceedings, and the legislator's decisions are not without supporting reasons; but the ultimate outcomes are without apology recognized as determined by political power. They are better explained as part of the political situation. Few expect that any series of legislative or administrative decisions enacted over a course of time will form an internally consistent series of logically interrelated policies, but this is precisely what is expected from the judicial process. Judges are required to phrase their decisions and explain them in a technical language that conceals any subjective elements. Their decisions must be justified as the single right answer, required by precedent or statutory command, and consistent with the whole corpus of the law.

Students of the legislative process have not thought it profitable to analyze debates on the floor of the chamber in order to account for the legislative decision. They assume that most of the significant data is the behavior that takes place outside the formal proceedings. In contrast, and in response to the formal model, the main staples of research concerning the judiciary are the evidence presented, the arguments before the courts, and the judge's formally stated reasons for his decision. The judicial decision is approached as a product of a controlled debating contest.

Recognizing that to focus on each decision isolated from its political situation, and with awareness that judicial decisions do not depart too far from the configuration of political power with the community, scholars have started to look at other materials and to develop models for analysis other than the traditional debating society framework. Nonetheless, they cannot ignore the fact that the judicial process is deliberately created and specifically designed to reduce the impact of political forces and to maximize evidence and reasoned choice. And the freedom of the judge from direct political accountability and the expectation that he will base his decision on arguments presented to him help to explain why the same individual will behave differently and support different values as a judge than as a legislator. The judicial process does make it possible for interests that lack large numbers of votes or controlling legislative representation to win favorable decisions.

The requirement that the judge base his decision on evidence and reasoned argument shades into the requirement that he be impartial. Again, other political decision makers are also expected to be impartial—it is contrary to the mores for a legislator or an executive to participate in decisions where he has an immediate financial stake in their outcome—but again the standards of impartiality required for judges are of a different order.

Judicial impartiality between the immediate parties to a lawsuit is obviously required if the judges are to be able to function as outsiders to the dispute. If a judge is under obligation to one of the parties or if he shares the fate of one of the litigants, he clearly cannot be dispassionate and neutral. This kind of impartiality is easy to achieve. At the next level of impartiality, although a judge may share some of the characteristics of one of the disputants—they both may be white southerners or both may be from the middle class—the judge is obliged to make a decision uninfluenced by such factors. Since judges are recruited from among the educated members of the community and are likely to be from among the dominant social classes, and since they ordinarily are not directly accountable to the electorate, the impact of the class structure upon the judicial system cannot be ignored. Whether judges do permit factors of personal bias, prejudice, or subconscious predispositions to influence their rulings is an empirical question, but that they will not do so is the working assumption of all established judicial systems in the free nations. And in an open society it is generally easy to secure agreement that judges have met these requirements of fairness and have made their decisions uninfluenced by personal, partisan, or class considerations.

There is no difference between the realist and orthodox analysis with respect to the desirability and possibility of securing judicial impartiality in the sense of neutrality between and even-handed treatment of all parties. It is at the level of value choosing that the realist and traditionalist analyses differ. According to the traditional descriptions of the judicial process the judge can and should be neutral between competing concepts of the public interest. He should be an uncommitted man, the servant of the legal system, a mouthpiece of the law. If the law favors one interest over another, it is because the legislature has so ordained or the logic of the situation so demands. The realists, on the other hand, although agreeing that the judicial process requires and in fact secures neutrality as between parties to a lawsuit, insist that however desirable it might be in fact, it is impossible to secure a system in which the judges will be complete ciphers in the process of balancing competing claims to justice. The judicial role, the statutory directions, and the precedents may well structure the judge's choice, but his is a positive and creative participation in the determination of which values the laws will reflect.

Judges must explain decisions. Other decision makers are often called on to justify their actions and to put their decisions into the rhetoric of the public well-being. But only judges are compelled to provide detailed, formally stated, and—at the appellate level—frequently written justifications of why they decided as they did. The fact that a judge knows that he will have to justify his ruling and expose his arguments to the critical attention of a professional audience of his peers has an impact on the decision he makes which is easy to see, difficult to measure, and little studied. The formally written opinion, of course, tidies up a much more complex decision-making process. Many students have been concerned with the various forms of reasoning judges use and have wondered whether they make decisions first and then seek rules to justify them, or whether they move from general rules to the particular dispute.

### Judicial rulings as political forces

A judicial opinion justifying a decision, especially of an appellate court, itself becomes a factor in the political process. For the opinion is both an explanation of a particular decision and instruction to law officers, including subordinate judges, as to how they should dispose of similar disputes. And these opinions, like statutes, are themselves subject to a variety of constructions.

Both the traditional and realist analysis of the judicial process tend to emphasize the finality of a judicial ruling. Chief Justice Charles Evans Hughes's famous quip that the constitution is what the judges say it is is frequently cited to demonstrate that although the Congress may pass a law, it is the Supreme Court which determines whether it will be applied. To the same point is the often quoted remark by Gray, one of the intellectual fathers of the realist movement: "Statutes are . . . sources of Law . . . not part of the Law itself" (Gray [1909] 1963, p. 125). In the same tradition Kirchheimer writes, "The validity of a norm does not follow from its existence, but from the fate it suffers in the administrative and judicial process" (Kirchheimer 1961, p. 187).

In all political systems where there is any measure of stability, a judicial decision normally disposes of the dispute between the parties to the lawsuit. In fact, review of a particular decision outside the judicial system (except for executive pardons) is thought to violate the doctrine of separation of powers. And in all nations it is accepted that court decisions *ought* to be obeyed, that rulings of courts are *authoritative*, and that the policies pronounced by judges, especially those who serve on appellate courts, *ought* to guide the behavior of all, especially those who administer the law.

But whether the rulings announced, as distinguished from the resolution of the particular lawsuit, become the standard that controls the behavior of others is no more—perhaps even less—assured for judicially created rules than for legislatively created laws. Judicial constructions do not neces-

sarily end a policy dispute and are no more self-applying than are statutes. What a judicial ruling will mean in the next "individualization" and the next is just as open to the push and pull of the political process, of which the judicial process is a part, as is a legislatively announced rule. What Gray said of statutes can also be said of judicial rulings: "They are sources of the Law . . . not the law."

The precise impact of judicially proclaimed rules has only recently been investigated. At this stage we can only report in terms of the most sweeping generalizations and cannot trace with any assurance the mechanics that determine which particular judicial rulings are likely to be translated into substantial alterations in behavior. Since judges have no direct command of political or military force and depend on the executive for the enforcement of their decrees, judicial constructions have been of little significance when challenged by totalitarians in control of the legislative and executive agencies. It is impossible to cite a single instance in which judges have been able to defend democratic institutions against onslaught by antidemocrats who have taken or been given legislative authority: not in Nazi Germany, not in fascist Italy, not in the Soviet Union, not in Latin American nations. Although the judges in the Union of South Africa were able to dull the edges of the restrictive apartheid laws for almost a decade, ultimately they were forced to capitulate. After a totalitarian system has been established the rules produced by the judiciary are not likely to conflict with those coming from the legislature.

Some have felt that if the judges are authorized to defend the basic constitution, then they are better able to maintain democratic institutions. Undoubtedly the hope that this might be so accounts for the creation in many of the nations established after World War II of constitutional courts empowered to declare legislative acts unconstitutional.

In stable democratic nations the differing institutional arrangements and the freedom to form differing combinations of political groups often result in conflicts between judicial and legislative agencies. But there is little in the history of these nations to suggest that judicial rulings are likely to endure in the face of determined legislative opposition. For by design courts are not as responsive to the political forces of the community as are the legislatures. (Here we are referring to legislative officials with a nationwide constituency. Compared to regional officials, national judges are more likely to reflect dominant political forces than are the local authorities, and the history of judicial victories over such regionally accountable officials confirms this generalization.) "Except for short-lived transitional periods when the old alliance is disintegrating and the new one is struggling to take control of political institutions, the Supreme Court is inevitably a part of the dominant national alliance. . . . By itself, the Court is almost powerless to affect the course of national policy" (Dahl 1957, p. 293).

Yet it would be wrong to conclude that judges are merely passive instruments reflecting current sentiments and tools of the dominant political groups. For judges themselves are active members of the governing elites and create as well as respond to the political situation. And within stable democratic regimes where the community is divided, judicial support for particular values will often be the critical factor in their emergence as the controlling rules of the community. To have the judges on one's side and to have their stamp of legitimacy for one's course of conduct can be an important political asset. Most of the time the judicial rulings will "stick," although without significant political support they will not stick for long. The key word, of course, is "significant," and with additional research we may be able to specify the conditions under which the law announced by the judges will control the behavior of the community.

J. W. PELTASON

### BIBLIOGRAPHY

ABRAHAM, HENRY J. 1962 *The Judicial Process: An Introductory Analysis of the Courts of the United States, England, and France.* New York: Oxford Univ. Press.

ALLEN, CARLETON KEMP (1927) 1964 *Law in the Making.* 7th ed. Oxford: Clarendon.

AUERBACH, CARL A. et al. (1956) 1961 *The Legal Process: An Introduction to Decision-making by Judicial, Legislative, Executive and Administrative Agencies.* Rev. ed. San Francisco: Chandler.

BENTLEY, ARTHUR F. (1908) 1949 *The Process of Government: A Study of Social Pressures.* Introduction by H. T. Davis. Bloomington, Ind.: Principia Press.

BERMAN, HAROLD J. (1950) 1963 *Justice in the U.S.S.R.: An Interpretation of Soviet Law.* Rev. & enl. ed. Cambridge, Mass.: Harvard Univ. Press. → First published as *Justice in Russia: An Interpretation of Soviet Law.*

CAHN, EDMOND 1955 *The Moral Decision.* Bloomington: Indiana Univ. Press.

CARDOZO, BENJAMIN N. (1921) 1960 *The Nature of the Judicial Process.* New Haven: Yale Univ. Press.

DAHL, ROBERT A. 1957 Decision-making in a Democracy: The Supreme Court as a National Policy-maker. *Journal of Public Law* 6:279–295.

FRANK, JEROME (1930) 1949 *Law and the Modern Mind.* New York: Coward.

FULLER, LON L. 1934 American Legal Realism. *University of Pennsylvania Law Review* 82:429–462.

GLUCKMAN, MAX (1955) 1967 *The Judicial Process Among the Barotse of Northern Rhodesia.* 2d ed. Manchester Univ. Press.

GRAY, JOHN C. (1909) 1963 *Nature and Sources of the Law.* 2d ed. Boston: Beacon.

HART, HERBERT L. A. 1961 *The Concept of Law.* Oxford: Clarendon.

HAZARD, JOHN N.; and SHAPIRO, ISAAC 1962 *The Soviet Legal System: Post-Stalin Documentation and Historical Commentary.* Dobbs Ferry, N.Y.: Oceana.

HOEBEL, E. ADAMSON 1954 *The Law of Primitive Man: A Study in Comparative Legal Dynamics.* Cambridge, Mass.: Harvard Univ. Press.

HURST, JAMES W. 1950 *The Growth of American Law: The Law Makers.* Boston: Little.

JACKSON, RICHARD M. (1940) 1964 *The Machinery of Justice in England.* 4th ed. Cambridge Univ. Press.

JACOB, HERBERT 1965 *Justice in America.* Boston: Little.

*The Jurisprudence of Interests: Selected Writings of Max Rümelin [and others].* Edited by Magdalena Schoch. 1948 Cambridge, Mass.: Harvard Univ. Press.

KELSEN, HANS (1945) 1961 *General Theory of Law and State.* New York: Russell. → The author's reformulation of ideas previously expressed in his works published in German and French between 1925 and 1934.

KING, JEROME B. 1965 Constitutionalism and the Judiciary in France. *Political Science Quarterly* 80:62–87.

KIRCHHEIMER, OTTO 1961 *Political Justice: The Use of Legal Procedure for Political Ends.* Princeton Univ. Press.

LLEWELLYN, KARL N. (1930) 1951 *The Bramble Bush: On Our Law and Its Study.* New York: Oceana.

LLEWELLYN, KARL N. 1931 Some Realism About Realism: Responding to Dean Pound. *Harvard Law Review* 44:1222–1264.

LLEWELLYN, KARL N. 1934 The Constitution as an Institution. *Columbia Law Review* 34:1–40.

LLEWELLYN, KARL N. 1960 *The Common Law Tradition: Deciding Appeals.* Boston: Little.

LLEWELLYN, KARL N. 1962 *Jurisprudence: Realism in Theory and Practice.* Univ. of Chicago Press.

MILLER, ARTHUR S. 1956 Statutory Language and the Purposive Use of Ambiguity. *Virginia Law Review* 42:23–39.

MILLER, ARTHUR S.; and HOWELL, RONALD F. 1960 The Myth of Neutrality in Constitutional Adjudication. *University of Chicago Law Review* 27:661–695.

MURPHY, WALTER F.; and PRITCHETT, C. HERMAN (editors) 1961 *Courts, Judges, and Politics: An Introduction to the Judicial Process.* New York: Random House.

PELTASON, JACK W. 1955 *Federal Courts in the Political Process.* Garden City, N.Y.: Doubleday.

ROSS, ALF (1953) 1959 *On Law and Justice.* Berkeley: Univ. of California Press. → First published in Danish.

SCHUBERT, GLENDON 1965 *Judicial Policy-making: The Political Role of the Courts.* Chicago: Scott, Foresman.

SHAPIRO, MARTIN 1964 Political Jurisprudence. *Kentucky Law Journal* 52:294–343.

VON MEHREN, ARTHUR 1956 The Judicial Process: A Comparative Analysis. *American Journal of Comparative Law* 5:197–228.

WECHSLER, HERBERT 1959 Toward Neutral Principles of Constitutional Law. *Harvard Law Review* 73:1–35.

## II

### COMPARATIVE ASPECTS

The judicial process consists in the hearing by impartial persons of a complaint by one party to a dispute and of a defense by the other party, together with their witnesses, followed by a decision that one or the other has the superior claim. Such decisions markedly affect the fortunes and even the lives of members of a society. Hence, there has been considerable discussion of the judicial process and of the general beliefs and personal factors which influence that process, both in preliterate societies and in literate societies. In the Western world, historians and jurisprudents have considered carefully the effects of key decisions. Biographies of judges have investigated their social and personal characteristics, and these have been further illuminated by the autobiographical records and introspections of some great judges. In recent years sociological and psychological studies have introduced new techniques and new interests, so that the study of the judicial process is now considerably diversified. Judges are no longer regarded as engaged in a purely intellectual process of applying normative rules to various situations; the relation between judges and their changing social and cultural milieus is examined in various ways.

While research on the relation of judges and judicial decision to the social and cultural milieu still dominates the outlook of European scholars, the existence in the United States of local, state, and federal courts, each with its political ties, and above all the split decisions of the United States Supreme Court on constitutional issues, have led Americans to focus greater attention on the types of decisions made by particular courts and particular judges or alliances of judges, and on the prediction of those decisions, sometimes with the use of mathematical or quasi-mathematical models. This tendency has been encouraged by the growth of sociometry, small-group sociology, and social psychology in the United States.

There are presumably powerful social and emotional reasons why most judges were for so long regarded by non-Marxist jurisprudents as sacrosanct—wise and impartial arbiters. In this view, the occasional weak, foolish, and even corrupt judges were exceptions who proved the rule. Marxists, of course, saw judges as largely operating in the interests of the ruling class. Nevertheless, it is strange that it took so long before the realistic appreciation by practicing lawyers of judicial "biases" ousted from Anglo-Saxon jurisprudence what Seagle (1941) satirically called the worship of Our Lady of the Common Law, a phrase used by Cardozo and others before him. Now there is a tendency to go to the other extreme and to preach that the only illuminating way to study the judicial process is to concentrate on the actions and motivations of single judges and the interaction between judges in multijudge courts (see editorial comments in Schubert 1964). Study of this key process of

social control seems still to arouse considerable emotion and to prevent some scholars from recognizing the multiple complexities of judicial decision making and the many different sociological and behavioral scientific methods of analysis that are applicable.

One type of analysis of the judicial process is that which examines how judges bring to bear the various norms current in the society on a variety of disputes, each of which is potentially unique. These norms are of many different kinds, for they range from "scientific laws" that are believed to govern the behavior of men, animals, insects, and things, through rules whose breach automatically constitutes an offense, to a whole range of general moral precepts. The task of the judge is to select from the variety of rules of different types those which are most likely to give what he considers to be justice in the case and to apply these in terms of a logic which is acceptable to other judges, to the public, and, he hopes, to the litigants. There are, of course, situations in which the judge may merely enforce a decision against one litigant in the interests of a conquering group over a conquered, or of a strong ruling class over a subordinated class. But part of the symbolic accretion of the law is that often the end result of the judicial process has been a decision which claims to represent something called at least law, and usually justice as well. The extent to which judges aim at establishing this claim is therefore one of the first empirical problems which has to be investigated; and the assertion of this claim also has to be checked against the degree of homogeneity of social interests in the population served by the court. The ethics of the judicial position itself often seem to influence judges' behavior.

Unhappily, records of the reasoning of judges in cases in the classical world and in the early Middle Ages of Europe are too meager to provide adequate material to set in comparison with the detailed records we have of the public argumentation of judges since fuller law records have been kept. It is here that research on the judicial process in tribal societies has added new dimensions to the investigation of the judicial process. Llewellyn and Hoebel's study (1941), from old people's reports, of how the Cheyenne dealt with disputes has been followed by a number of detailed studies of judicial reasoning in various tribes. In general these studies present accounts of judicial reasoning in what were relatively homogeneous societies with stable economies, yet societies differing markedly in certain of their cultural premises or jural postulates (Hoebel 1954). Even in these relatively simple situations, judges have to deal not only with standardized situations but also with new types of disputes, precipitated perhaps by slight changes in the environmental situation, or by the idiosyncratic actions of individuals, or by some unique constellation of the complex components that go into making up the interactions between human beings in any sociocultural milieu. If after one Cheyenne has murdered another he has to be banished and the sacred arrows of the tribe have to be cleansed, what is to be done with a woman who kills her father when he tries to rape her, or, on the other hand, with a woman who by unjustified ill-treatment causes her daughter to commit suicide? An investigation of this sort of case led Llewellyn and Hoebel into an illuminating analysis of basic Cheyenne values and of how they were changed and developed to meet new crises, yet were believed to persist. These scholars emphasized, too, how key situations of this kind might contribute to the evolution of political authority, of which judicial action is often a part (Llewellyn & Hoebel 1941, pp. 160, 179).

Men, judges and laity alike, may be (as some argue) guided basically by economic and social interests of which they are perhaps not fully aware. In Europe and America, there has consequently been an emphasis upon the often subconscious motivations that influence judicial behavior (Schubert 1964). But men everywhere interact through language in order to conceptualize their sociocultural and personal aims and values. It would therefore seem unwise to exclude the semantic and structural analysis of the words and the patterned arrangement of words into the arguments of the judicial process: these symbolic relations are something more than a mere veil concealing the real spurs to judicial decision. There must, therefore, be an investigation of the types of words used in the formulation of disputes and decisions, in the full social context of each word, whether it be a key concept of law (such as right, duty, property, etc.) or a simple word defining types of action or relationships between persons. In certain judicial institutions, such as the United States Supreme Court, where most of the decisions of individual judges are recorded in detail and where to some extent the formulas in which decisions are couched, and what they represent, can be taken for granted, students are able to concentrate on how the judges, each with his own social outlook, vary in their decisions on particular issues. These students attempt to apply different theories, such as the theory of games, to predict the strategy a judge may follow in different situations to achieve his ends, and

they formulate mathematical models which will predict, both for behavioral theory and for practicing lawyers, the probable decisions of particular judges or benches of judges on certain kinds of disputes (Schubert 1964). This work is important, both for an understanding of the judicial process and as a general contribution to various branches of sociology and social psychology. But it takes large sets of facts—such as the structure of American society—for granted and does not analyze the interaction between that society and the judicial process.

For tribal courts we still often lack detailed knowledge of the sociocultural milieu, and in most instances we also lack detailed records of cases, including examination of evidence and judicial decisions. The cases out of which Llewellyn and Hoebel and a number of other lawyers and anthropologists have made remarkable studies of American Indian law are mostly recalled from distant times. Barton's classic work on the Ifugao (1919) and Kalinga (1949) of the Philippines also gives only the bare bones of cases, which were heard by mediators rather than judges. Pospisil (1958) had the opportunity to record in detail judicial and negotiating processes in a New Guinea tribe before the advent of foreign rule, and Berndt (1962) studied a New Guinea tribe shortly after foreign rule was established; but neither of them has yet published sufficiently detailed records of the process of argumentation toward decisions. The best records come from Africa; these include Schapera's work on the Tswana (1938), which gives almost complete reports on two cases, Gluckman's report on ten cases of the Barotse (1955), and Epstein's records from African Urban Courts established by the former Northern Rhodesian government (1954). Colson (1962, chapter 4) provides one good record of a case of negotiation of settlement among the Tonga, and Gulliver (1963) reports on a few such cases among the Arusha. Bohannan's study *Justice and Judgment Among the Tiv* (1957) and Howell's *A Manual of Nuer Law* (1954) give brief summaries of cases, rarely reporting cross-examination.

Two contrary attitudes have been adopted in analyzing tribal judicial processes. Bohannan (1957) has insisted that each people has its own folk system of concepts in terms of which the study of non-Western judicial processes and institutions should be made. He has insisted that it is essential not to use the folk concepts of Western jurisprudence to handle the folk systems of other cultures, for, being a folk system themselves, they cannot constitute an analytical system. In contrast, Gluckman and Epstein (and to a lesser extent Llewellyn and Hoebel, and earlier, Barton) have set their analyses against the type of analyses made of Western judicial processes, in order to highlight both similarities and differences. To pursue this comparison, they have used concepts, such as the reasonable man and reasonable expectations, right and duty, which are used in Western jurisprudence (see Gluckman 1955; Epstein 1954).

There are involved here major problems for all sociological and anthropological comparisons, since similar problems arise in the cross-cultural analysis of religious beliefs and other cultural phenomena. The constant use of local vernacular terms (for example, the use of Latin, German, French, Tiv, or Barotse terms when writing in English) makes reading and discussion difficult for those who do not know the language concerned. In fact, Bohannan in practice has to use English concepts to cover Tiv situations; for example, he emphasizes that Tiv law classifies all actions under the rubric of "debt" and not as contracts or torts, without discussing the relation of this Tiv conception to the dominance of actions in debt in early and middle English law, in ancient Chinese and Babylonian law, etc., and without considering why there should be this apparent similarity (see Gluckman 1965a, chapter 8). And in practice he uses English words, such as right and duty, throughout his analysis.

It is clear that, as Bohannan insists, the first step in ethnographic reporting of the judicial process, in the West as elsewhere, must be to state clearly the local concepts and the manner in which they are used by litigants and their representatives and witnesses to present evidence to the judges and by judges in cross-examination on evidence and in coming to decision. The presentation of these folk concepts, in action, should be clearly separated from the analysis itself. Here it might be clearer, as Ayoub (1961) implies, if one were to invent a set of neologisms, in order to escape from the cultural accretions of key folk concepts in the researcher's own language. Unfortunately no one has yet proposed such a set of neologisms. Gluckman's attempted solution was to propose that, for English, a whole series of relevant words be chosen and stipulated to have specific meanings for analysis. If the same words are used as translations of the folk concepts of the people under study, it would be advisable, experience shows, to use printing devices (such as italics or capitals) to indicate where they are being employed for analysis, as against reporting.

The prime necessity in this field is clearly for detailed reporting of the whole course of a trial, with careful attention to what specific folk concept is used in each context. In recent years jurisprudents have concentrated attention, and often criticism, on the multiple meanings and fringe meanings of key judicial concepts, such as law itself, justice, crime, property, right, duty, negligence, guilt, and innocence. These concepts are not necessarily vague: they may have what Curtis called "a precise degree of imprecision" (1954, p. 71). This is also a characteristic of religious symbols. The study of religious symbolism clearly involves an examination of the multivocality of each symbol, the manner in which it ramifies in its social and emotional referents, and the manner in which it evokes both emotional and social responses. Similarly, the concepts of law have to be investigated to find out how parties, witnesses, and judges use the multivocality of these concepts in order to fit the facts of varied disputes into the rules of law and to advance, respectively, pleas and decisions, which are claimed to state where justice lies.

An important problem is immediately raised by the fact that concepts in law refer not only to states of fact but also to implied moral evaluations of human actions and possibly also the motivations which are believed to lie behind those actions. In developed systems of law, written pleadings by the parties, usually presented through their counsels, have to be stated according to particular formulas which strip away what is believed to be irrelevant and present only those facts which have "forensic" (to avoid the multivocal "legal") value in terms of those normative rules which, it is argued, apply to the dispute. At some stages in the history of law, failure to set pleadings in a rigidly prescribed form might invalidate a claim, and in modern Western law, indictments may still be thrown out if not properly drafted. Facts at these stages of forensic development therefore come before the judges already processed to conform with certain forensic, and possibly also moral, norms. Many scholars have stressed that this preliminary processing entails that, to understand the judicial process, research should be done on the preliminary work of police and counsel before disputes come to court, a field little investigated.

Tribal societies—even those like Ashanti, where oaths are sworn to establish jurisdiction—seem to lack this period of preliminary processing of the facts in dispute. Litigants are allowed to state their respective claims in apparently full, and often seemingly irrelevant, detail. While they do so, the judges play a role similar to that of counsel in more developed systems, sifting and processing the facts and issues (Gluckman [1955] 1967, chapter 9). It is necessary to watch carefully the extent to which judges allow seeming irrelevance, by analyzing their interruptions and the weight they attach to the various types of facts laid before them. This leads to an investigation of what is conceived to be the task and aim of judges in specific types of disputes: what is irrelevant in a dispute between people who are relative strangers to each other may be very relevant in a dispute between spouses or closely related kinsmen, if the judges are attempting to reconcile the parties and enable them to resume living and working together. This is the common situation in tribal courts, and these may therefore work in ways more akin to Western marriage counselors, lawyers, arbitrators, and industrial conciliators than to Western judges in court.

Most scholars who study social control comparatively emphasize that the establishment of courts is a key phenomenon in the development of law (e.g., Seagle 1941; Stone 1946). The conception of a court here involves that all parties to a dispute should be heard by the court's judges, who normally refuse to give a verdict until both sides of a case have been presented. Litigants present their evidence and the supporting evidence of witnesses. Litigants and their representatives then cross-examine their opponents and opposing witnesses to try to break down the other case. Judges may enter into cross-examination, although they do so in varying degrees in different societies. Techniques of cross-examination require careful investigation of the extent to which direct evidence, hearsay evidence, and circumstantial evidence are distinguished; the weight which is accorded to impartiality; and the manner in which these distinctions and other devices are employed to test and perhaps to destroy particular versions of events.

In Zambia, Epstein and Gluckman found that in practically all the cases they heard tried, the litigants and their supporters framed their versions of events in such a way as to present themselves as "reasonable men." These researchers thus reported the occurrence in Zambian African law of a folk concept which can be translated as parallel to a Western folk concept. Furthermore, they raised the "reasonable man" to the status of an analytical concept which they saw as crucial in the process of judicial cross-examination and decision. By presenting themselves as reasonable men who conformed to the modes of behavior and the standards of their society, and who thus accepted the same premises of "rightdoing" as the judges, litigants exposed themselves to attack by the judges, who

seized on discrepancies within their accounts, and between their accounts and those of eyewitnesses. In many cases this enabled judges to destroy a version which appeared to be reasonable and to convict a litigant on the basis of his own story. Thus, in the course of cross-examination they would begin to come to a decision by setting up the standard of how a reasonable incumbent of the role under review would behave in particular circumstances.

Epstein's work, published in a series of papers, has escaped the attention of most other scholars; but Gluckman's use of the reasonable man has been severely criticized because it imparts an allegedly vague concept from the Western folk system that is of chief importance in the complex law of negligence. None of the critics has as yet discussed the cases analyzed thus by Gluckman to show that the process of judicial cross-examination and decision can be better understood by using some other set of concepts. On the other hand, Gluckman (1965b) has discussed Tiv cases reported by Bohannan, and other negotiations in societies without courts, to argue that these can be more successfully analyzed by emphasizing how both parties and judges (or other outsiders) operate with some concept of the reasonable man.

For example, in an Arusha case reported by Gulliver (1963, pp. 243 ff.), a father-in-law sued his son-in-law for cattle still due under the marriage payment. At several negotiations, the father-in-law insisted that he was reasonable in bringing suit, for he and his son had debts of their own to meet. He refused to take away his daughter from her husband, as he was entitled to do in law, because the man was a good husband to the daughter, a good father to her children, and a good son-in-law to him. The son-in-law contended that although he had cattle, he needed them for milk and to plough for food for the plaintiff's grandchildren. How could a good grandfather cause his grandchildren to fall into want? Similarly, when it was found that the son-in-law was planning to use cattle to buy land, he countered that he needed the land to get food for the plaintiff's grandchildren, of which a good grandfather should approve. And so forth. If within the concept "good" we include, as we must, the idea of "reasonable," then we understand how a compromise was reached by negotiation in terms of the rights and duties of a complex of roles, applied in terms of reasonable conformity according to people's poverty and the demands on them, within certain overriding rules and moral ideas (for a discussion of this whole problem, see Gluckman 1965b; [1955] 1967, chapter 9).

Many disputes, both in tribal and in more developed systems of law, hinge on the manner in which a person has fulfilled the obligations of a particular role and the degree of conformity in the "range of leeway" (Llewellyn & Hoebel 1941, p. 23) that is allowed to him. This degree of conformity can be determined only when all his obligations are considered in the light of his wealth, strength, etc., as he runs his personal economy in meeting the demands of all those linked to him. That is, the "reasonable man" is here used to try to illuminate how certain key concepts in sociological analysis (role, role expectations, selection of goals) appear through a dispute in the judicial process. Even if it is unwise to use this particular concept, the problems thus raised are crucial, since the dispute is often over degree of conformity; and some means of handling these problems must be devised. This statement on degrees does not deny that certain actions are per se unlawful, although it may even then be possible to demonstrate connections with reasonable demands on incumbents of given roles. In comparative studies it must be recognized that varying standards, customs, etc., may assemble into stereotypes of roles, perhaps not consistently held by all judges (or all jurymen). Disagreement will increase as a society becomes more heterogeneous. Thus, during World War II Barotse judges felt themselves to be helpless when arguing the justice of a levy for war funds with members of the Watchtower sect (Jehovah's Witnesses), who were pacifists (Gluckman [1955] 1967, p. 158). A British jury refused to convict a man of breaches of national insurance law, because some members reacted to what they felt to be the bureaucratic behavior of a civil servant; and members of another jury felt themselves helpless in a case of receiving because, being middle-class, they did not know whether working-class people sold goods to one another in public houses (Devons 1965).

The next stage in the analysis of the judicial process is to examine how judges move from evaluation of evidence to decision. Here there is obviously scope for considerable personal variation. It is worth examining the ways in which the alleged logical steps involved are discussed; and what is striking is the extent to which extremely complex processes of public ratiocination—whether they be rational argument, or rationalization, or both—are described in metaphorical terms. Both in the Western world and in some African cultures, men speak metaphorically of the processes of making decisions: sifting or weighing the evidence, clinching an argument, coming to land, judicial "hunches," and so forth. These metaphorical expressions show

how greatly the conclusions on the evidence by different judges may vary, and how the judges may be strongly influenced by principles and prejudices derived from their social positions or their personal experiences. It must be emphasized that the actual concepts and logic used in judicial decision have to be analyzed to work out how it is possible for idiosyncratic interpretations nevertheless to be stated in some kind of acceptable form.

Central to the judicial process is the manner in which norms stated in general terms are brought to bear on a great variety of disputes, each of which is in some senses unique. The norms which are deployed thus may be well-known rules or codes defining righteous and wrongful conduct, particular customs of patterns of behavior, examples of "rightdoing" derived from everyday life, or previous decisions of the courts. There has to be an assessment of how judges select from these norms, which are not necessarily consistent with one another.

But some disputes may be unprecedented, whether because social conditions have changed or because of some extraordinary combination of events. When judges attempt to cope with disputes without precedents, they often have to develop existing law. In *The Nature of the Judicial Process* (1921, pp. 30–31) Cardozo examined how these gaps in the law are filled in the United States. He defined four methods by which judges meet the general problem of applying existent law, more strongly marked when situations are unprecedented: (1) the line of logical progression—the rule of analogy or the method of philosophy; (2) the line of historical development—the method of evolution; (3) the line of the customs of the community—the method of tradition; and (4) the lines of justice, morals, and social welfare—the method of sociology.

There may well be other methods, and these may not be the most appropriate for sociological analysis. However, Gluckman (1955) was able to apply Cardozo's categories to Barotse judicial decisions and to show that the kind of logic with which Barotse developed their law to meet the new situations raised by changes consequent on colonial rule could be comprehended in Cardozo's categories.

For example, when men began to go to work for Europeans in distant areas, the Barotse authorities ruled that if a man was away two years, his wife was entitled to a divorce. In one such case, when the absent husband's kin pleaded that he continually sent his wife blankets, clothes, and money, the court held: "This woman did not marry a blanket." A month later the husband returned: he had been on his way home at the time of the suit. His father-in-law insisted on the husband's making another marriage payment to regain his "divorced" wife. The court rescinded its previous decision, on the grounds that had it known the husband had started for home, it would not have granted a divorce. The purpose of the statute requiring husbands to return was to strengthen marriages: therefore, the court interpreted "return home" as meaning "start for home." The court also objected to what it considered the wife's father's "unjust enrichment." These decisions exemplify what Cardozo called the method of sociology. At the same time, it must be noted that the Barotse always had frequent divorce and that both the law and the decisions in this case are along the lines of traditional custom.

By contrast, when the southern Bantu tribes, among whom divorce was very rare, have faced the problems of absentee husbands, they have not granted divorce to wives of long-absent husbands, but their courts have held that, after a certain reasonable period, a "grass widow" may take a lover in order to bear children. It is against tribal policy for a woman's fertility to be idle. The absent husband is denied damages for adultery, and under the rule that children belong to the man who gave cattle for their mother, the adulterine children are his, and not the adulterer's. The logic of justice, morals, and social welfare combine with different traditions and customs to give varied judicial solutions to similar problems (see Gluckman [1955] 1967, pp. 141–142, 284–290; Schapera 1938, p. 157).

MAX GLUCKMAN

[See also LAW, article on LAW AND LEGAL INSTITUTIONS; LEGAL SYSTEMS, article on COMPARATIVE LAW AND LEGAL SYSTEMS; POLITICAL ANTHROPOLOGY; SANCTIONS.]

### BIBLIOGRAPHY

AYOUB, VICTOR 1961 Review: The Judicial Process in Two African Tribes. Pages 237–250 in Morris Janowitz (editor), Community Political Systems. International Yearbook of Political Behavior Research, Vol. 1. New York: Free Press.

BARTON, ROY F. 1919 Ifugao Law. University of California Publications in American Archaeology and Ethnology, Vol. 15, No. 1. Berkeley: Univ. of California Press.

BARTON, ROY F. 1949 The Kalingas: Their Institutions and Custom Law. Univ. of Chicago Press.

BERNDT, RONALD M. 1962 Excess and Restraint: Social Control Among a New Guinea Mountain People. Univ. of Chicago Press.

BOHANNAN, PAUL 1957 Justice and Judgment Among the Tiv. Oxford Univ. Press.

CARDOZO, BENJAMIN N. (1921) 1960 The Nature of the Judicial Process. New Haven: Yale Univ. Press.

COLSON, ELIZABETH 1962 The Plateau Tonga of Northern Rhodesia: Social and Religious Studies. Manchester Univ. Press.

CURTIS, CHARLES P. 1954 It's Your Law. Cambridge, Mass.: Harvard Univ. Press.

DEVONS, ELY 1965 Serving as a Juryman in Britain. Modern Law Review 28:561–570.

EPSTEIN, ARNOLD L. 1954 Juridical Techniques and the Judicial Process: A Study in African Customary Law. Rhodes-Livingstone Papers, No. 23. Manchester Univ. Press.

FRANK, JEROME (1930) 1949 Law and the Modern Mind. New York: Coward.

GLUCKMAN, MAX (1955) 1967 The Judicial Process Among the Barotse of Northern Rhodesia. 2d ed. Manchester Univ. Press.

GLUCKMAN, MAX 1965a The Ideas in Barotse Jurisprudence. New Haven: Yale Univ. Press.

GLUCKMAN, MAX 1965b Reasonableness and Responsibility in the Law of Segmentary Societies. Pages 120–146 in Hilda Kuper and Leo Kuper (editors), African Law: Adaptation and Development. Berkeley and Los Angeles: Univ. of California Press.

GLUCKMAN, MAX 1965c Politics, Law and Ritual in Tribal Society. Oxford: Blackwell; Chicago: Aldine.

GULLIVER, PHILIP H. 1963 Social Control in an African Society; a Study of the Arusha: Agricultural Masai of Northern Tanganyika. Boston University, African Research Studies, No. 3. Boston Univ. Press; London: Routledge.

HOEBEL, E. ADAMSON 1954 The Law of Primitive Man: A Study in Comparative Legal Dynamics. Cambridge, Mass.: Harvard Univ. Press.

HOWELL, PAUL P. 1954 A Manual of Nuer Law. Oxford Univ. Press.

LLEWELLYN, KARL N.; and HOEBEL, E. ADAMSON 1941 The Cheyenne Way: Conflict and Case Law in Primitive Jurisprudence. Norman: Univ. of Oklahoma Press.

POSPISIL, LEOPOLD 1958 Kapauku Papuans and Their Law. Yale University Publications in Anthropology, No. 54. New Haven: Yale Univ. Press.

SCHAPERA, ISAAC (1938) 1955 A Handbook of Tswana Law and Custom. 2d. ed. Oxford Univ. Press.

SCHUBERT, GLENDON (editor) 1964 Judicial Behavior: A Reader in Theory and Research. Chicago: Rand McNally. → Contains an excellent selection of articles on judicial behavior and good bibliographical references.

SEAGLE, WILLIAM (1941) 1946 The History of Law. 2d ed. New York: Tudor. → First published as The Quest for Law.

STONE, JULIUS (1946) 1950 The Province and Function of Law; Law as Logic, Justice, and Social Control: A Study in Jurisprudence. Cambridge, Mass.: Harvard Univ. Press. → The 1950 reprint incorporates a few corrections and changes.

## III

### JUDICIAL ADMINISTRATION

The administration of justice is a vital concern of any civilized community. Upon the proper functioning of the courts depends not only the enforcement of rights and liabilities, such as those between individuals, but also the protection of the individual against arbitrary government and the protection of society itself against the lawless individual.

This article concentrates on judicial administration in the United States. This is not because similar problems do not exist elsewhere, but because their complexion varies so much from one nation to another that a comparative study would not be meaningful unless it took into account in each nation the structure of government, the character of the legal profession, and similar matters beyond the scope of any brief treatment. However, a few references to comparative material are included in the bibliography.

Despite its importance, little systematic study was given to judicial administration in the United States until recent years. Lawyers, judges, and law professors were preoccupied with rules of law and with the procedure for translating them into concrete decisions; they devoted relatively little attention to the over-all functioning of the judicial machinery. Political scientists also tended to avoid the subject, concentrating their concern upon the legislative and executive branches of government on the theory that the judicial branch was the special preserve of the legal profession. This left the field to politicians, legislators, and a few others confronted with such specific tasks as selecting judges or establishing courts. Understandably, their tendency was to approach each problem *ad hoc*, without seeing it in context and without much research into historical or comparative experience or into empirical data.

The beginning of sustained attention to the subject probably dates from a now famous speech by Roscoe Pound to the American Bar Association in 1906, entitled "The Causes of Popular Dissatisfaction With the Administration of Justice." To the then complacent members of that body, he spoke some harsh truths about "waste," "delay," "inefficiency," "archaic judicial organization" and "obsolete procedure." There followed an awakening of interest in the subject in the law schools of the nation—an interest that has continued and is still growing and in which university political scientists and sociologists have recently joined.

Before long, public-spirited members of the bench and bar began to take notice. The chief vehicle for their early efforts at reform was the American Judicature Society, formed in 1912. In the 1930s, the organized bar began to lend its strength to the growing movement, largely as the result of the enthusiasm of Arthur T. Vanderbilt, who was destined to become not only president of the American Bar Association, the American Judicature Society,

and the Institute of Judicial Administration, as well as chief justice of New Jersey, but also the acknowledged leader of the entire movement.

In 1934 Congress passed a statute giving power to the United States Supreme Court to make rules of civil procedure for the federal district courts. This was an important step forward, not only because federal procedure badly needed revising but also because of the precedent of vesting in the courts themselves the power to regulate their own methods of operation. The new rules went into effect in 1938, and have been amended from time to time. They have become a model for procedural reform in the various states.

In 1937 the American Bar Association took a stand against the popular election of judges and in favor of a method of selection that would de-emphasize political considerations; and in the same year that association undertook the formulation of "minimum standards of judicial administration" (American Bar Association 1938). These standards were promulgated the following year as a guide for states in improving their court systems, and since then the state committees of the American Bar Association have worked for their implementation. The association has continued to enunciate goals for judicial administration and to work toward them, as is evidenced by its promulgation in 1962 of a model judicial article for state constitutions. Many state and local bar associations have similarly contributed their efforts.

The major problems in judicial administration center on (1) the personnel of the courts, (2) the institutional framework within which they operate, and (3) the procedures they follow. All of these problems are interrelated.

## Personnel

**Selection of judges.** Most judges in the United States are popularly elected, but the voters seldom have much interest in the contests or knowledge of the persons for whom they are voting, being content to leave such matters to political leaders. In the federal system, and in a few states, the judges are appointed, but even here, politics tends to play a dominant role. One approach toward de-emphasizing political considerations (without eliminating them entirely) is to require that a judicial appointment be made from a list presented to the governor (or other appointing official) by a nonpartisan nominating commission; and to require that after a probationary period of service, the appointee shall run against his own record, not against any other candidate. The choice that appears on the ballot is simply whether Judge X shall, or shall not, be retained in office. This plan is known by various names, the most familiar of which is the Missouri plan, Missouri being one of the first states to put it into effect. Similar plans are now in operation in Kansas, Alaska, California, Alabama, and Iowa; and movements are under way for the adoption of the idea in still other states.

**Judicial tenure, retirement, and removal.** The tenure of judicial office is one of the factors affecting recruitment of the proper men to become judges, because an office that carries tenure for life or for a long period of years is obviously more attractive than one that carries a short tenure. At the same time, it is important that men do not remain on the bench after their powers have failed or if they have demonstrated by their conduct that they are not fit to hold office. The direction of reform, therefore, has been toward making tenure long, but at the same time providing for retirement or removal under the proper conditions and by a simple and effective procedure. Impeachment, involving legislative accusation and trial, has proved to be a cumbersome and generally ineffective method of getting rid of unfit judges and, consequently, has in some states been replaced or supplemented by removal machinery operated and controlled by the highest judicial officers of the state.

When judges retire from active service because of age or ill-health, adequate financial provision should be made for their retirement. In the federal system, a judge receives full pay for life upon retirement at age 70 after serving for 10 years, or at age 65 after service of 15 years, but this is a far-off ideal for many states. In some states, there is no financial provision at all for retirement, with the result that judges are almost forced to stay on the bench long after their powers have failed; in others, retirement plans exist but are inadequate.

**Judicial salaries.** The more generous judicial salaries are, within limits, the more likely they are to attract able lawyers and therefore improve the functioning of the judicial system. Throughout the United States, disparities in salary are striking, with one judge receiving two or three times the amount of money that another receives in a different place for performing much the same work. The movement has been toward generally increased salaries in recent years, but great disparities remain. In the federal courts, the salaries of district (trial) judges have tripled since World War I (going from $7,500 in 1919 to $22,500 in 1955) and appear likely to rise again soon. They seem to be tied (in the minds of congressmen, at least) to the salaries paid members of Congress. In some states,

the federal salaries are substantially higher than those paid state judges, but in a few others, like New York, they are substantially lower than the state salaries.

**Judicial training.** Some nations have a career judiciary in which members of the legal profession choose between the bench and the bar at an early age. Those who become judges receive specialized training—either formal education or apprenticeship—for their work and then progress by a regular system of advancement through the hierarchy of courts. In the United States, no such system prevails. Judges ordinarily are chosen from the practicing bar at a fairly advanced age and assume office (either at high or low levels) without the benefit of special training for their new work. Because of this system of selecting judges, because there is no regular system of promotion, and because even experienced judges sometimes need help in orienting themselves when they assume new duties or when they are confronted by major changes in the law or in court organization, training programs for judges have become popular in recent years.

Such programs had their origin in conferences where judges got together informally to discuss common problems and needed improvements in the law or to listen to speeches. These informal meetings have gradually been converted into, or supplemented by, more formalized programs of judicial education. The pioneer project was the Appellate Judges Seminar, inaugurated by the Institute of Judicial Administration in 1957 and held for two weeks each summer. Each year it provides a program for 20 to 25 of the appellate judges of the nation. In 1962, under the aegis of the Joint Committee for the Effective Administration of Justice, an organization sponsored by 14 national organizations interested in judicial administration and headed by Justice Tom C. Clark of the United States Supreme Court, the same idea was extended on a large scale to trial judges of state courts of general jurisdiction. It has held many two-day or three-day seminars throughout the nation. Other seminars are held for new federal district judges under the auspices of the Judicial Conference of the United States; and still others are conducted for juvenile court judges, traffic court judges, and justices of the peace. The movement is continuing to grow and expand, as is evidenced by the establishment in 1964, on what was hoped to be a permanent basis, of the College of Trial Judges, to be conducted four weeks each year for new judges of state trial courts of general jurisdiction. Further in the future is the possibility of establishing a training program for lawyers who are not yet judges, but who have ambitions in that direction.

**Elimination of lay judges.** Some judges have not even received a law school education to qualify them to act as lawyers. These typically are justices of the peace, handling small traffic cases, other minor criminal cases, and small civil claims; but sometimes they are also found in probate courts, administering the estates of persons who have died. In England, the justice of the peace is a highly respected official, but in the United States the office has been degraded and has become the object of widespread criticism. Too often it is given as a reward to the politically faithful whose only qualifications are services rendered, or to be rendered, to the party in power. It is not surprising, therefore, that a movement is under way in many states to replace justices of the peace and lay probate judges with legally trained, full-time professional judges. Where this is politically feasible, efforts are being made to require that justices of the peace be lawyers or at least to provide training programs for them along the lines of the programs for regular judges described above. In a considerable number of states such reforms have already been accomplished. In Maine, for example, in 1960 the justices of the peace were eliminated and replaced by a system of full-time, legally trained judges.

**The jury.** During the last fifty years the civil jury has virtually disappeared in England. In the United States it still flourishes, its greatest use being in personal injury negligence cases. The right to trial by jury is guaranteed by state constitutions (for state court cases) and in the federal constitution (for federal court cases)—but only in those situations where a jury had been traditionally used, namely, actions developed in the common law courts of England. The typical constitutional provision is that the right shall "remain inviolate," meaning that it is not extended to actions either historically tried without a jury or newly created by statute. In consequence, many civil actions are today tried without a jury.

Some judges and lawyers believe that the jury is no longer justified even in the limited group of civil actions where it is still used. They point out that juries are the cause of many of the law's delays, that they greatly increase the expense of litigation, that they introduce uncertainty into the judicial process, and that they frequently disregard and set at nought the governing law. Consequently, from time to time there is talk about the desirability of getting rid of the jury in civil cases—a movement that thus far has not progressed very much. More

successful have been indirect efforts to curtail the use of the jury by encouraging waiver of the constitutional right or by making the party demanding this method of trial pay some of the extra costs entailed thereby. Currently under serious consideration is a proposal to take automobile accident cases out of the courts and entrust such claims to administrative tribunals modeled after workmen's compensation boards.

In criminal cases, the jury is still used extensively both in England and the United States. The grand jury, however—the one that makes accusations of crime, as distinguished from the petit jury, which determines guilt or innocence—has disappeared in a number of states, having been replaced by a procedure, which is less cumbersome, whereby the district attorney, on his own responsibility, makes the accusations that bring men to trial.

Important efforts have been made, and are being made, to improve the method of selecting jurors for both civil and criminal cases. The goal is to secure more intelligent, better educated juries, that is, juries more fairly representative of the community. Notable in this regard have been United States Supreme Court decisions outlawing systems of jury selection that involve the systematic and intentional exclusion of Negroes and similar minority groups. Sometimes independently of such decisions and sometimes as a result of them, administrative improvements in the method of selecting juries have been made.

**The bar.** The proper functioning of the courts depends not only upon the judges and jurors but also, and perhaps equally, upon the performance of the bar. If the bar is capable, conscientious, and responsible, the quality of justice is likely to be good; if not, the quality of justice is likely to be deficient, for the Anglo–American system is predicated in very large part upon lawyers presenting to the court the raw materials, both factual and legal, that will be needed for decision.

Three developments in recent years have tended to increase and improve the services rendered by the bar. One is the inauguration of new methods of supplying legal service to those who are unable to pay for it, beyond the traditional practice of having a judge appoint a member of the bar to represent an indigent defendant accused of a serious crime. Legal aid societies, which offer the services of lawyers to indigent persons in both civil and criminal cases, have been established in many communities; and in some counties, public defender systems have been created, whereby publicly appointed and compensated officers defend indigent defendants. The trend toward more adequate legal representation for indigents has been greatly stimulated by a series of Supreme Court decisions holding that the right to counsel in criminal cases is guaranteed by the U.S. constitution.

Another development of importance has been the improved education of lawyers. Not only have the undergraduate law schools been greatly improved and standards for admission to the bar tightened but systems of postgraduate legal education have also been developed in university law schools and in bar-controlled programs of continuing legal education.

A third development of significance is the strengthening of bar associations, which maintain a degree of discipline over the conduct of individual lawyers and provide a vehicle for the discharge of professional responsibilities. An increasing number of such associations have become "integrated," meaning that membership in them has become mandatory, with all lawyers in the state paying dues and having a voice in their affairs. As a result, such bar associations can speak with a high degree of authority.

## Court organization

Court structure in the United States is far from simple. Instead of a single system of courts such as in England or France, 51 separate systems are in operation—one for each of the 50 states and another for the federal government. To a large extent, the federal courts duplicate the work of the state courts, but Americans have become so accustomed to the idea of a dual system of courts that there is little likelihood of such duplication being eliminated or even substantially reduced.

A much more likely area of reform is the court structure of any given state, where there frequently is great complexity and disorganization. Jurisdiction all too often is fragmented among a motley conglomeration of disparate courts, operating independently of one another and doing cumbersomely and inefficiently what could, and should, be done simply in a unified system. Many states have radically simplified their court structure, reducing the number of courts and eliminating duplication.

Many states have also established machinery for the unified operation of their courts, providing for conferences of judges to discuss common problems and vesting administrative authority over the entire system in a single judge (usually the chief justice of the highest court), giving him the responsibility of relocating, if necessary, the entire judicial manpower of the state by temporary assignment of judges from one locale or one court to another. For these administrative tasks, he is provided with assistants, who collect statistics, prepare reports, conduct studies, and the like.

A prime objective of improved administration is to combat delay. Many courts, particularly those in metropolitan areas, are suffering from chronic congestion. In these courts, it may take as long as three, four, or five years for a case to reach trial. Efficient, businesslike administration, with free transferability of judges and cases, is thought by many to be a key remedy for this malady.

As in many other areas, the federal courts took the lead in judicial administration, too, with the inauguration in 1922 of the Judicial Conference of the United States and the establishment in 1939 of the Administrative Office of the United States Courts. These provide models for states wishing to improve the administration of their own courts, and they have been extensively copied.

## Procedure

Until the nineteenth century, the regulation of procedure was largely in the hands of the courts, which devised their own rules and changed them from time to time as they saw fit. Then legislatures began to take over the function, in part because the rules developed in the courts of England had become excessively rigid, unrealistic, and unsuited to the needs of litigants, necessitating a radical change, and in part because of the general increase of legislative power and activity during this era. One of the great legislative achievements was the promulgation of the Field Code of New York in 1848, abolishing ancient forms of procedure, providing a uniform procedure for all types of action, and merging into a single court of general jurisdiction the powers that theretofore had been exercised separately by the common law courts and the chancery or equity courts.

Time proved, however, that legislative regulation of procedure was not satisfactory, for reasons well stated by Judge Cardozo: "The legislative, informed only casually and intermittently of the needs and problems of the courts, without expert or responsible or disinterested or systematic advice as to the workings of one rule or another, patches the fabric here and there, and mars often when it would mend" (1921, pp. 113–114).

As a result of such criticisms, the tendency has been to restore procedural rule-making power to the courts. This has been accomplished in many states as well as in the federal government, where Congress delegated to the Supreme Court rule-making power over the lower federal courts. The rules promulgated by the Court pursuant to this authority (covering both civil and criminal cases) are brief and simple, de-emphasizing technicalities and procedural niceties in favor of greater concentration on the merits of litigation. They have provided an inspiration and model for procedural reform in many of the states.

While great strides have been made during the twentieth century toward simplified and improved procedure, there are still many areas that urgently demand attention. One is the law of evidence, which tends to be unduly complicated and to exclude relevant and reliable information for reasons so technical that they are meaningful only to tradition-minded lawyers. Another is the reaching of a proper balance between the right to a fair trial and the right to a free press. Newspaper, television, and radio coverage of the facts of some cases prior to trial is so extensive and spectacular that it makes virtually impossible a fair trial. Still another is restoring to the trial judge his historic power to control the trial, including the power to comment on the evidence and thus guide and help the jury in determining questions of fact. These few examples, far from being a catalogue of what remains to be done, merely suggest the range and nature of the many problems to be faced.

## The future

In recent years there has been a growing recognition that the administration of criminal justice requires and deserves, at the least, attention equal to that given to the handling of civil litigation. One of the reasons is that the United States Supreme Court has devoted much attention to the subject, making clear, in a long series of decisions, that criminal justice in many of the states falls below the minimum requirements of decency and fair play guaranteed by the federal constitution. In the 1950s the American Bar Foundation engaged in major research into the functioning of criminal law in the United States. This study is expected to result in the publication of several detailed volumes of description and criticism. In 1964 a new effort was launched by the American Bar Association, in conjunction with the Institute of Judicial Administration, to formulate minimum standards of criminal justice similar to the Minimum Standards of Judicial Administration of 1938. Many additional research projects, generously supported by foundation grants, are being carried on in schools of law and departments of sociology in a number of American universities.

Increasing interest in criminal law also may be responsible, in part, for another significant recent development: the utilization of new methods and techniques of research in the law. The emphasis today seems to be upon empirical, quantitative methods borrowed from the social science disciplines, supplementing the older emphasis upon books, theory, and a priori reasoning. Increasingly of late, men from university faculties other than the law schools have been interesting themselves in problems of judicial administration.

Finally, growing attention is being paid to the comparative aspects of judicial administration. As men have become conscious of the fact that, in general, one nation may learn from another, so also have they become increasingly aware that much is to be learned by comparative study in the field of judicial administration. Recent interchanges between British and American jurists on appellate procedure and on the administration of criminal justice have yielded excellent results for both countries and are likely to continue.

DELMAR KARLEN

### BIBLIOGRAPHY

AMERICAN BAR ASSOCIATION 1938 *Minimum Standards of Judicial Administration.* Volume 63, pages 517–656 in American Bar Association, *Annual Report.* Chicago: The Association.

BERMAN, HAROLD J. (1950) 1963 *Justice in the U.S.S.R.: An Interpretation of Soviet Law.* Rev. & enl. ed. Cambridge, Mass.: Harvard Univ. Press. → First published as *Justice in Russia: An Interpretation of Soviet Law.*

CARDOZO, BENJAMIN 1921 A Ministry of Justice. *Harvard Law Review* 35:113–126.

DAVID, RENÉ; and DE VRIES, HENRY P. (1957) 1958 *The French Legal System: An Introduction to Civil Law Systems.* Dobbs Ferry, N.Y.: Oceana.

ELLIOTT, SHELDON D. 1959 *Improving Our Courts: Collected Studies on Judicial Administration.* Dobbs Ferry, N.Y.: Oceana.

GSOVSKI, VLADIMIR; and GRZYBOWSKI, KAZIMIERZ (editors) 1959 *Government, Law and Courts in the Soviet Union and Eastern Europe.* Vol. 1. New York: Atlantic.

HAYNES, EVAN 1944 *The Selection and Tenure of Judges.* Newark, N.J.: National Conference of Judicial Councils.

JACKSON, RICHARD M. (1940) 1964 *The Machinery of Justice in England.* 4th ed. Cambridge Univ. Press.

KARLEN, DELMAR 1963 *Appellate Courts in the United States and England.* New York Univ. Press.

KLEIN, FANNIE J. 1963 *Judicial Administration and the Legal Profession.* Dobbs Ferry, N.Y.: Oceana.

MAYERS, LEWIS (1955) 1964 *The American Legal System: The Administration of Justice in the United States by Judicial, Administrative, Military, and Arbitral Tribunals.* Rev. ed. New York: Harper.

MILLAR, ROBERT W. 1952 *Civil Procedure of the Trial Court in Historical Perspective.* New York University, Law Center.

ORFIELD, LESTER B. 1939 *Criminal Appeals in America.* Boston: Little.

ORFIELD, LESTER B. 1947 *Criminal Procedure From Arrest to Appeal.* New York Univ. Press.

Pound, Roscoe (1906) 1963 *The Causes of Popular Dissatisfaction With the Administration of Justice.* Chicago: American Judicature Society to Promote the Efficient Administration of Justice.

Pound, Roscoe 1940 *Organization of Courts.* Boston: Little.

Pound, Roscoe 1941 *Appellate Procedure in Civil Cases.* Boston: Little.

Schubert, Glendon (editor) 1963 *Judicial Decision-making.* International Yearbook of Political Behavior Research, Vol. 4. New York: Free Press.

Vanderbilt, Arthur T. 1949 *Minimum Standards of Judicial Administration.* New York University, Law Center.

Vanderbilt, Arthur T. 1955 *The Challenge of Law Reform.* Princeton Univ. Press.

Warren, George 1942 *Traffic Courts.* Boston: Little.

Willoughby, William F. 1929 *Principles of Judicial Administration.* Washington: Brookings Institution.

Zeisel, Hans; Kalven, Harry Jr.; and Buchholz, Bernard 1959 *Delay in the Court.* Boston: Little.

## IV
### JUDICIAL REVIEW

Judicial review, considered functionally, is one method for resolving disputes over constitutional boundaries. (Constitution, in this article, means the set of rules, whether or not written, which is considered by most members of a community to define authoritatively the fundamental political relationships within that community.) In any political system, no matter how developed or Westernized, the boundaries separating constitutionally permissible behavior from that which is constitutionally proscribed are imprecise enough to cause occasional controversy. The task of resolving such constitutional boundary conflicts is commonly assumed by one or more of a variety of political or quasi-political structures, for example, parties, religious associations, legislatures, judicial bodies, military establishments, or political executives. But in only a few countries do judicial bodies actually play much of a part in settling constitutional boundary disputes. These certainly include Australia, Canada, and the United States. Something of a case can be made for adding several others, among them Austria, Argentina, Brazil, Colombia, India, Ireland, Mexico, Japan, Switzerland, Italy, Norway, and the German Federal Republic (West Germany).

Authorities tend to disagree on whether judicial review exists in a given country, largely because no two scholars appear to hold identical views as to what judicial review is or how it should be defined (cf., e.g., Abraham 1962; Black 1960; Corwin 1932; Haines 1914). Nevertheless, some definition is essential as a point of departure. The following is offered as somewhat less troublesome than most: *Judicial review is the process whereby a judicial body determines the constitutionality of activity undertaken by a country's national legislature and by its chief political executives.*

The above definition requires three assumptions to which some might take exception. Each needs to be made explicit. First, the body exercising judicial review need not be an integral part of the ordinary system of law courts, as is the case in the United States, Canada, Australia, Japan, Norway, Ireland, and India. Therefore, countries that make use of special constitutional tribunals (Austria, Italy, and the German Federal Republic) are not *ipso facto* excluded from the roster of those having judicial review (Cole 1959; Rupp 1960).

The second assumption is that a judicial body's refusal to enforce or otherwise legitimize official conduct constitutes judicial review only when the ground for doing so is that the country's constitution has been violated. Thus, refusing to sanction an official's conduct because it exceeds the authority delegated to him by ordinary statute or by an administrative superior (the doctrine of *ultra vires*) is not considered a species of judicial review.

The third assumption is that the range of behavior reviewed must cover national (rather than merely regional or local) legislative and executive action. Switzerland, as a result, is not considered to have judicial review because its Federal Tribunal can determine the constitutionality of only cantonal but not federal legislation. Mexico is currently a somewhat similar case. Its writ of *amparo*, however important in protecting individuals against unconstitutional action by minor officials and local ordinances, is no longer seriously invoked against high officials or national policies of the Institutional Revolutionary Party (PRI), which has dominated Mexican politics since the late 1920s (Busey 1964, pp. 38–40).

**Development of judicial review.** On whatever else they may differ, virtually all students of judicial review agree that the phenomenon is an innovation of the American federal system. One can, of course, point to certain antecedents (Haines 1914, pp. 29–121 in 1932 edition). Among these are (1) the centuries-old natural-law doctrine that even kings and legislatures are bound by a higher or fundamental law; (2) Coke's famous, if questionable, dictum in Dr. Bonham's case that "when an act of parliament is against common right and reason, or repugnant, or impossible to be performed, the common law will controul it, and adjudge such act to be void" (Coke [1610] 1826, p. 375); (3) the experiences with councils of censors and revision in Britain's American colonies before the American Revolution; and (4) a small fistful of state court decisions before the drafting of the constitution in 1787. Although some discussion of judicial review took place at the constitutional convention of 1787, at the state ratifying conventions, and in the Federalist Papers, no direct link between these antecedents and the beginnings of the American practice under the constitution has been firmly established (Beard 1912; Corwin 1938; Mason 1962). Indeed, decades of combing the relevant records and papers have served to leave even the intentions of the framers concerning judicial review as elusive as a will-o'-the-wisp.

Whatever the intentions of the Founding Fathers may have been, the American doctrine of judicial review received its classic statement from the pen of John Marshall in *Marbury* v. *Madison* (1 Cranch U.S. 137, 1803). In that celebrated decision, a section of the Judiciary Act of 1789, which authorized the Supreme Court to mandamus officers of the United States, was held unconstitutional. Chief Justice Marshall chose to build his argument for judicial review not upon a foundation of precedent and practice but upon one of close reasoning and lofty rhetoric. The heart of his position may be stated as a set of three propositions: (1) The constitution is a higher law, superior to ordinary law such as statutes, ordinances, and the common law; (2) In a conflict between the constitution and ordinary law, the constitution must prevail; (3) If in litigation properly before a court of law the court in question finds a conflict between the ordinary law on which one party relies and the constitution, that court must refuse to enforce the ordinary law.

The first two propositions were accepted without much dissension, but the third point was hotly disputed at the time and for several decades thereafter. The principal objection was that Marshall had overridden the distinction between the legal and the political.

The striking implications of Marshall's third proposition become more apparent on analysis of the governmental functions which courts ordinarily perform (Almond & Coleman 1960, pp. 3–64). The most characteristic of these is *rule adjudication*—the peaceful resolution of conflicts arising from the application of general rules to particular situations. After evaluating both the evidence presented and the relevance of the statutes or regulations applied, courts decide whether punishment or relief is appropriate. In countries where the judiciary possesses any measure of independence, rule adjudication customarily includes the authority to invoke the doctrine of *ultra vires*. This practice, however, does not constitute a subset of judicial review as defined above.

Their active role in rule adjudication involves courts willy-nilly in another governmental function, that of *rule making*. This is so because precisely what a given rule means is often a central issue in a legal dispute and as such must be determined by the court involved. The need to engage in rule making via statutory construction, as English judges have on occasion effectively demonstrated, offers courts opportunities to frustrate legislative-executive policy for substantial periods of time (Laski 1926; Allen 1927, pp. 402–504 in 1951 edition; McWhinney 1956, pp. 31–48). Ultimately, the more political branches will have their way in practice as well as in theory, but the judicial impact on public policy in the short run can be rather substantial. Yet this judicial braking, or "indirect judicial review" as it is sometimes called, is a far cry from what John Marshall had in mind in *Marbury* v. *Madison*.

What Marshall claimed was that courts, in carrying out their age-old task of assisting in the peaceful settlement of disputes by applying previously established general rules to particular situations, were free to do even more than reshape through imaginative statutory interpretation. They could, in effect, go behind legislative and executive prescriptions by independently assessing the constitutional authority of the more political branches to make them. This doctrine, once firmly established, won for the United States courts a major role in defining and maintaining the boundaries separating legitimate governmental action from that which is constitutionally proscribed.

**Judicial review and federalism.** Marshall's opinion in *Marbury* v. *Madison* is universally regarded as the classic justification for judicial review. Although the doctrine of federalism is not involved in that case at all, the relationship between federalism and judicial review is hardly casual. Dicey may have been guilty of overstatement when he maintained that judicial review is a necessary element of a federal state ([1885] 1961, but cf. Bryce [1888] 1909, pp. 242–261, who took the opposite view); however, it is nonetheless true that almost every contemporary federal polity has a judicial body with some authority for mediating conflicts between its central and regional systems. This is as true of Austria and the German Federal Republic, with their special constitutional courts, as it is of Australia and the United States. Switzerland, as noted above, is something of an exception, for its Federal Tribunal is empowered to evaluate only the constitutionality of cantonal statutes.

The reason why federal states generally make use of judicial bodies in resolving boundary controversies is no mystery when the essence of federalism is considered. In a federal polity there are two major political subsystems, the central and the regional. In each of these subsystems the governmental structures and the functions they perform are authorized by a source largely independent of the other subsystem. Each is free to do its work without serious threat of intervention from the other. With arrangements such as these, a federal system must almost of necessity possess a written document, or constitution, which outlines in more or less realistic fashion the subsystem boundaries. This constitution must, in addition, be treated as more basic than ordinary law in two regards. First, the constitution prevails whenever there is a conflict between it and an ordinary legislative or executive action and, second, the constitution cannot be unilaterally altered by either subsystem. Resolving controversies which arise over the subsystem boundaries delineated in such a written document requires a relatively impartial governmental structure experienced in the techniques of textual exegesis. Judicial bodies are especially well suited for this purpose. Indeed, as experience in Argentina, Australia, Canada, and the United States suggests, even the absence of a specific constitutional authorization for judicial review in a federal system is not apt to prove a deterrent to judicial participation in boundary definition.

Although federal states tend by their very nature to utilize judicial review in solving central–regional boundary controversies, a judicial body, once relegated this authority, may extend its jurisdiction to almost any section of the constitution—and even seek to assume the role of its general guardian. When the basic law contains vague restrictive clauses like "due process" and "equal protection," as in the constitution of the United States, judges are handed generous opportunities for opposing public policy which does not meet their approval. In Australia, for instance, although section 92 of the constitution is clearly aimed at the border duties which had so sorely troubled the Australian colonies in prefederation days, it has been used by the High Court to invalidate important state and federal legislation designed to institute social and economic planning.

As a rule countries which are truly federal in practice have some form of judicial review; and unitary systems leave constitutional boundary problems to nonjudicial instrumentalities. However, there are at present several exceptions, notably,

Norway, Ireland, Japan, and Italy. Each of these unitary systems has a written constitution whose restrictions on legislative and executive conduct are to some extent monitored by a judicial body. Just when the Norwegian Supreme Court first assumed the power of judicial review is open to question, but it has exercised this power, however cautiously, since the last decade of the nineteenth century (Torgerson 1963, pp. 221–225). In Ireland judicial review was established by the constitution of 1937. Here, too, the Supreme Court's action has been characterized by self-restraint; but there can be no question that the doctrine of judicial review is an integral part of the Irish political process (McWhinney [1956] 1960, pp. 152–169). Review in Japan (Nathanson 1958) and Italy (Cole 1959) is a post-World War II phenomenon, and in the case of Japan it is directly attributable to American occupation authorities. It is probably too early to say that the institution of judicial review is firmly established in either country, although there is no current indication that the appropriate courts in either are disposed to let it wither on the vine. But in any case, judicial review of a meaningful kind has been practiced more or less effectively in enough unitary systems to demonstrate that it is a viable, although clearly not essential, method of dealing with their constitutional boundary problems.

**Impact of judicial review.** The success that judicial bodies have enjoyed in having their constitutional interpretations accepted has been the subject of a great deal of scholarly attention, and some broad generalizations are possible. An interpretation which is strenuously opposed by a determined legislative–executive coalition, for example, will not stand for long. Ultimately the judicial institution must yield. If it does not do so gracefully by abandoning its earlier position, then the written constitution will be formally amended, or the composition or the powers of the judicial body itself will be altered. Argentina represents the extreme case (Blanksten 1953, pp. 123–129).

After a series of head-on clashes with Juan Perón, whose supporters controlled both the Senate and the Chamber of Deputies, impeachment proceedings were instituted against all five members of the Supreme Court of Justice. Rather than suffer further through this trying ordeal, Chief Justice Roberto Repetto resigned. His four associates stayed on to be impeached by the Chamber and subsequently removed from office by the Senate.

Even in the United States, where judicial review is most firmly entrenched, the Supreme Court has consistently come out second-best in direct confrontations with a strong executive–legislative coalition.

When political power is badly fractionalized, however, judicial interpretations will generally stand, even though they are highly controversial and have vast consequences (Murphy 1962). Dozens of post-World War II decisions by the United States Supreme Court in cases involving Negroes, criminal defendants, and persons actually or allegedly associated with the communist movement illustrate this point.

Generalizations such as these admittedly do not constitute precise statements of the relationships among the relevant variables. And there is precious little evidence that much energy is being directed to so refining them. Hardly more attention has been given to measuring rigorously the impact on the community of judicial review in a particular decision or set of decisions. Sorauf's study of the United States Supreme Court's released-time cases, a noteworthy exception, barely scratches the surface (1959; see also Dahl 1957). The methodological difficulties inherent in rigorously assaying either the circumstances under which judicial interpretations will be accepted or the impact of judicial review are formidable indeed. Nevertheless, until more strenuous efforts have been made to overcome these methodological problems, it would be unduly pessimistic to suggest that they are insurmountable.

JOSEPH TANENHAUS

[See also ADMINISTRATIVE LAW; CONSTITUTIONAL LAW; CONSTITUTIONS AND CONSTITUTIONALISM; FEDERALISM; LAW.]

### BIBLIOGRAPHY

*An extensive bibliography is appended to the article by Corwin 1932; unless cited in the above text, these references are not repeated in the bibliography. The best single source of information on judicial review in the non-English-speaking world is the quarterly* American Journal of Comparative Law, *which frequently publishes articles on judicial review by leading authorities.*

ABRAHAM, HENRY J. 1962 *The Judicial Process: An Introductory Analysis of the Courts of the United States, England, and France.* New York: Oxford Univ. Press.

ALLEN, CARLETON K. (1927) 1964 *Law in the Making.* 7th ed. Oxford: Clarendon.

ALMOND, GABRIEL A.; and COLEMAN, JAMES S. (editors) 1960 *The Politics of the Developing Areas.* Princeton Univ. Press.

*American Journal of Comparative Law.* → Published since 1952.

BEARD, CHARLES A. (1912) 1962 *The Supreme Court and the Constitution.* With an introduction and bibliographies by Alan F. Westin. Englewood Cliffs, N.J.: Prentice-Hall.

BLACK, CHARLES L. 1960 *The People and the Court: Judicial Review in a Democracy.* New York: Macmillan.

BLANKSTEN, GEORGE I. 1953 *Perón's Argentina.* Univ. of Chicago Press.

BRYCE, JAMES (1888) 1909 *The American Commonwealth.* 3d ed., 2 vols. New York and London: Macmillan. → An abridged edition was published in 1959 by Putnam.

BURGOA, IGNACIO (1943) 1957 *El juicio de amparo.* 4th ed. Mexico City: Porrúa.

BUSEY, JAMES L. 1964 *Latin America: Political Institutions and Processes.* New York: Random House.

CAHN, EDMOND N. (editor) 1954 *Supreme Court and Supreme Law.* Bloomington: Indiana Univ. Press.

COKE, EDWARD (1610) 1826 Dr. Bonham's Case. Volume 4, part 8, pages 355–383 in Great Britain, Courts, *The Reports of Sir Edward Coke.* London: Butterworth.

COLE, TAYLOR 1959 Three Constitutional Courts: A Comparison. *American Political Science Review* 53:963–984.

CORWIN, EDWARD S. 1932 Judicial Review. Volume 8, pages 457–464 in *Encyclopaedia of the Social Sciences.* New York: Macmillan.

CORWIN, EDWARD S. (1938) 1957 *Court Over Constitution: A Study of Judicial Review as an Instrument of Popular Government.* Gloucester, Mass.: Smith.

DAHL, ROBERT A. 1957 Decision-making in a Democracy: The Supreme Court as a National Policy-maker. *Journal of Public Law* 6:279–295.

DICEY, ALBERT V. (1885) 1961 *Introduction to the Study of the Law of the Constitution.* 10th ed. With an introduction by E. C. S. Wade. London: Macmillan; New York: St. Martins. → First published as *Lectures Introductory to the Study of the Law of the Constitution.*

GERMANY (FEDERAL REPUBLIC), BUNDESVERFASSUNGSGERICHT 1963 *Das Bundesverfassungsgericht.* Karlsruhe (Germany): Müller. → Contains studies of the Federal Constitutional Court of the West German Republic by leading authorities, including some of its members. Among the contributors are Justices Rupp, Leibholz, Höpker-Aschoff, and Wintrich.

GRANT, J. A. C. 1954 Judicial Control of Legislation: A Comparative Study. *American Journal of Comparative Law* 3:186–198.

HAINES, CHARLES GROVE (1914) 1959 *The American Doctrine of Judicial Supremacy.* 2d ed., rev. & enl. New York: Russell.

LASKI, HAROLD J. 1926 Judicial Review of Social Policy in England: A Study of Roberts *v.* Hopwood et al. *Harvard Law Review* 39:832–848.

LINARES QUINTANA, SEGUNDO V. 1953– *Tratado de la ciencia del derecho constitucional argentino y comparado.* Vol. 1– . Buenos Aires: Editorial Alfa.

McWHINNEY, EDWARD (1956) 1960 *Judicial Review in the English-speaking World.* 2d ed. Univ. of Toronto Press.

McWHINNEY, EDWARD 1962 *Constitutionalism in Germany and the Federal Constitutional Court.* Leiden (Netherlands): Sythoff. → Deals exclusively with the Bundesverfassungsgericht.

MASON, ALPHEUS T. 1962 *The Supreme Court: Palladium of Freedom.* Ann Arbor: Univ. of Michigan Press.

MURPHY, WALTER F. 1962 *Congress and the Court: A Case Study in the American Political Process.* Univ. of Chicago Press.

NATHANSON, NATHANIEL L. 1958 Constitutional Adjudication in Japan. *American Journal of Comparative Law* 7:195–218.

ROCHE, JOHN P. 1952 Executive Power and Domestic Emergency: The Quest for Prerogative. *Western Political Quarterly* 5:592–618.

ROSSITER, CLINTON L. 1951 *The Supreme Court and the Commander in Chief.* Ithaca, N.Y.: Cornell Univ. Press.

RUPP, HANS G. 1960 Judicial Review in the Federal Republic of Germany. *American Journal of Comparative Law* 9:29–47.

SORAUF, FRANK J. 1959 Zorach v. Clauson: The Impact of a Supreme Court Decision. *American Political Science Review* 53:777–791.

TANENHAUS, JOSEPH 1956 The Supreme Court and Presidential Power. Pages 106–113 in American Academy of Political and Social Science, *The Office of the American Presidency.* Philadelphia: The Academy.

TORGERSON, ULF 1963 The Role of the Supreme Court in the Norwegian Political System. Pages 221–244 in Glendon A. Schubert (editor), *Judicial Decision-making.* New York: Free Press.

# JUDICIARY

*The articles under this heading deal primarily with the study of judges. Closely related are the articles on* ADJUDICATION *and* JUDICIAL PROCESS. *A detailed guide to further topics will be found under* LAW.

| | |
|---|---|
| I. JUDICIAL BEHAVIOR | *Glendon Schubert* |
| II. JUDICIAL VALUES | *Walter F. Murphy* |
| III. JUDICIAL DISCRETION | *Wallace Mendelson* |
| IV. JUDICIAL RECRUITMENT | *John R. Schmidhauser* |

## I
### JUDICIAL BEHAVIOR

Judicial behavior is part of the broader approach in political science that has come to be called behavioralism. The aims, theory, and methods of the study of judicial behavior are in general the same as those which characterize the field of political behavior; what distinguishes judicial behavior from behavioralism generally is its specific focus upon the decision making of judges.

All complex modern polities, all those of the past concerning which historical records are available, and all contemporary underdeveloped and primitive polities rely upon adjudication processes as a major technique for resolving conflicts among individuals and groups in order to maximize acquiescence on the part of all persons affected by particular disputes and, at the same time, to minimize recourse to force and violence on the part of the disputants and their allies. Consequently, the ways in which adjudication processes are structured, the ways in which they function, and the effects contingent upon their outputs are major questions of political theory and practice. All polities endeavor to protect the functionaries of their adjudication processes by the establishment of statuses, rituals, and secret languages which have the effect of shielding them from widespread public scrutiny and understanding.

In the United States, and apparently in many other polities as well, the mystique of adjudication is maximal for courts and judges. As a direct consequence, attempts to understand courts and judges on the basis of the formal categories, concepts, and justifications that constitute the central elements of the judicial process itself have served largely to reinforce the inaccessibility of the nominal object of study. So long as social science was limited, in its investigation of courts and judges, to the philosophical system of Aristotelian logic, the historical method of collating the manifest content of legal documents, the legal theory of Austinian positivism, and the empiricism of a political science that confined itself to institutional analysis, there was only a limited possibility of acquiring knowledge beyond the replication of the rites, symbols of status, and formal language of discourse employed by the judges themselves.

Behavioralism in public law builds upon the traditional lore, while at the same time checking its reliability and validity by focusing upon the human characteristics of judges as decision makers. This requires an investigation of judges as discrete individuals, as members of social groups, and as actors in social systems. The goal of the study of judicial behavior is to acquire valid, reliable, and precise knowledge of the extent to which the actions of judges conform to and/or deviate from the social expectations that constitute the substantive content of the norms that define the ideals of judicial systems. It becomes necessary, therefore, to analyze not only who judges are, what they do, and when and how they act but also *why* they make their choices.

## History

Public law was one of the first components to become recognized during the nineteenth century as a part of the emerging academic discipline of political science (Schubert 1966). Until the middle of the twentieth century it evinced minimal response to the influence of the other, more recently evolved social sciences: psychology, sociology, and anthropology; and only since the mid-1950s has it been possible to trace a sustained behavioral development that surpasses the discrete efforts of individual scholars. Since 1960, however, the results of research in judicial behavior lead one to conclude that this is a lasting development. Judicial behavior seems certain to bring about fundamental and widespread changes in both teaching and publication in political science. Moreover, it is likely that the influence of judicial behavior upon the other social sciences will be greater than the influence that has been exercised by traditional public law because of the greater relevance of the content and because of the greater number of open channels of communication maintained by the behavioral approach.

Most scholars agree that the classic essay on the subject of judicial behavior is that of Charles Grove Haines (1922), who debunked the prevailing theory of mechanical jurisprudence, surveyed the empirical research, begun in 1914, on variations in magisterial sentences in the New York City courts, and suggested the probably crucial role that social and psychological variables have in influencing judicial decisions. Haines's essay included no empirical data of its own, and a decade elapsed before an attempt was made to supply, in part, the kind of evidence that would be relevant to a test of the propositions implicit in his suggestions. In 1933, Rodney Mott, Spencer Albright, and Helen Semmerling published their report of research in which they had compiled descriptive data for a national sample of U.S. state judges, with findings concerning 16 quantifiable characteristics (such as "attendance at a standard law school," "number of fraternal orders to which the judge belonged," and "size of town in which the judge was born"). Soon thereafter, Mott (1936) reported an extensive survey evaluating the professional reputation of the federal and state supreme courts. He used such indices as the opinions of law professors, and he made a sociometric analysis of the extent to which state supreme courts cited each other and were cited by the United States Supreme Court. Gaudet (1938) followed up the data on New York magistrates with studies of his own on individual variations in the sentencing behavior of judges. Many other descriptive studies, including some which reported quantified data, were published by lawyers during the two decades following World War I, but these diverse empirical analyses, which typify the legal-realist movement in American jurisprudence, were not sufficiently articulated with any systematic body of theory about human behavior to make any enduring contribution to the development of a science of judicial behavior. Perhaps the best of these studies was the Frankfurter and Landis (1927) analysis of the United States Supreme Court's administration and jurisdictional decision making, which was followed up in the *Harvard Law Review* during the subsequent decade by a series of annual articles by Frankfurter and various collaborators.

A quite different line of potential development which was strongly influenced by Freudian psychology was charted by a few pre-eminent jurisprudents, especially Harold Lasswell, who reported psychiatric case studies of three types of judges (1948, pp. 64–88), and Jerome Frank (1930). Both Lasswell and Frank were intimately familiar with the theory and practice of psychoanalysis; but notwithstanding the imaginative facility with which each of them discussed the idea of psychoanalytic study of judicial behavior, neither undertook the empirical research that would be necessary to test the many hypotheses that each suggested.

A third approach was charted by Felix S. Cohen (1935), who criticized the excesses of both the Neo-Freudian acolytes—the "bellyache school of jurisprudence"—and the more traditional exponents of "slot-machine jurisprudence." A truly realistic jurisprudence, Cohen pointed out, could not be content with bare-footed empiricism but must anchor its work in sociological theory: every judicial decision is a social event and can be understood only in terms of the complex patterning of influences that have produced it and the equally complex set of consequences to which it contributes. Cohen's essay was important as a sophisticated and persuasive statement of a theoretical position; the evidence to support it, however, was to come from others. One step in that direction was made by E. Adamson Hoebel, an anthropologist, and Karl N. Llewellyn, a leader of the "realists" among the law professors, who together published the results of their field investigation among the survivors of the Cheyenne Indians (Llewellyn & Hoebel 1941). This unique endeavor reconstructed the judicial function and the "law-ways" among the primitive tribal societies who had ruled the northwestern plains of the United States until about half a century before. The work is important to judicial behavior because it suggests that the organization and policy output of the judicial process is a function of the basic need of social self-preservation in cultures as vastly different as those of the Cheyenne in 1850 and of the United States today.

The transition to the contemporary period in which behavioralism in public law has emerged as a distinct movement was marked by two publications authored by colleagues at the University of Chicago. The first of these was political scientist C. Herman Pritchett's study (1948) of the relation between small groups and political attitudes among the justices of the United States Supreme Court during the decade following President Franklin Roosevelt's endeavor to "pack the Court" with a majority of justices of his choice. Pritchett used a modified form of cluster-bloc analysis to investigate the dissenting voting behavior of the justices. By making an independent examination of their voting in several substantive areas (such as civil liberties, the civil rights of criminal defendants, and governmental regulation of business and labor), he was able to demonstrate that the Court persistently divided into liberal and conservative blocs. Moreover, by extending his analysis of dyadic agreement in dissent to include the five terms preceding the 1937 reformation, he was able to demonstrate that such blocs existed when the Court was dominated by a conservative majority as well as later when its decision making was controlled by a more liberal majority.

Although a decade elapsed before a generation of younger scholars began to pick up where Pritchett left off, there can be no doubt that his ideas and findings became widely disseminated among students of the Supreme Court in political science and in the law schools. His work became the basis for the standard interpretation of the behavior of the justices during the period since the advent of the New Deal.

The other research that emanated from Chicago, also a study of the United States Supreme Court, was designed and carried out by a leading psychometrician, Louis L. Thurstone. Thurstone and Degan (1951) undertook what was by far the most methodologically sophisticated investigation of judicial behavior up to that time, utilizing factor analysis of a correlation matrix based upon dyadic agreement and disagreement with the majority in voting upon the decisions of the Court in the 1944–1945 terms. From a substantive point of view, however, their findings were limited by their inability to postulate a nonstatistical criterion for attributing substantive meaning to the frame of reference they postulated.

The intimate functional relationship between the exploratory studies of Pritchett and that of Thurstone and Degan was demonstrated over a decade later, when Schubert (1962a) used Pritchett's data on judicial attitudes and Thurstone and Degan's factor measurements in order to provide a substantive interpretation of the relationships among the ideal points representing the justices in multidimensional psychological space. This reinterpretation of the earlier data was made possible by the intervening progress that had been made in research into the theory of judicial decision making.

## Analysis

Recent research in judicial behavior has depended upon the construction of new interdisciplinary bridges to psychology and sociology—especially social psychology—and to anthropology and economics, to a lesser extent. For methodological rigor, it has turned to mathematics and statistics. The influence of these sister social sciences has by no means been uniform, however, nor has all the research resulting from these influences been of equal value in either quantity or quality.

In order to observe the different influences, we shall compare the most relevant subfields of these other disciplines, in the sequence that corresponds to the degree of theoretical and methodological rigor they provide in the definition, control, and measurement of the variables that constitute the focus of inquiry in research. Thus, the order of our consideration will be from the most subjective to the most objective of the major theoretical approaches that characterize the field of judicial behavior.

**Projective psychology.** Although the influence of Freudian and Neo-Freudian psychology has been strong in other fields of behavioral science, it has been hardly discernible in recent research in judicial behavior. The seminal theorizing of Frank and Lasswell has borne no empirical fruit, at least thus far. Few judges seem to have taken Frank's advice to become psychoanalyzed (as he had been); and no studies have been published that have employed any of the other methods—such as direct observation—recommended by Lasswell.

**Cultural anthropology.** Apart from Llewellyn's collaboration with Hoebel, the research in primitive law has been done by anthropologists—many of whom have been English. The only relevant writing by a political scientist appears to be James G. March's review (1956) of a book by English anthropologist Max Gluckman. The March article is important for the theoretical analysis it includes. (For an American anthropologist's reaction to the same book and to the related body of research in judicial behavior in primitive tribes, consult Hoebel 1961; see also Gluckman 1965a and 1965b, chapter 5.) In comparison with the Freudian contribution, there has been considerably more empirical research done in judicial behavior in primitive societies.

Such work is relevant to a better understanding of judicial behavior in more complex societies because it directs attention to the fundamental similarities of human behavior in adjudicatory roles, and it facilitates discrimination of the effect of cultural differences upon the definition of such roles. Hence, the study of primitive law by social anthropologists may well prove to be of importance to further theoretical and methodological developments in the scientific study of judicial decision making.

**Sociology—systems theory.** General systems theory and structural–functional analysis are developments in American sociological theory associated with the writings of Talcott Parsons, Edward Shils, Robert K. Merton, Marion J. Levy, and Charles P. Loomis. This kind of abstract conceptual model building has been related to the study of judicial behavior by several political scientists. Herndon (1962) has suggested the possibility of developing a general framework for empirical research in state judiciaries on the basis of an "action theory" of judicial behavior. His paper specifies a number of questions that might appropriately be investigated in order to collect empirical data relevant to the requirements of the theory. Ulmer (1961) has made similar suggestions, although with particular reference to study of the United States Supreme Court; his article reports the findings of his own exploratory research in applying the theory in an analysis of the relationship between leadership by the chief justice and dissension in voting behavior among the justices, over a 70-year period. Schubert (1965a) has used systems theory as the framework for a description and analysis of the national judicial system in the United States.

**Sociology—interest groups.** One way of attempting to operationalize Felix S. Cohen's suggestions concerning the desirability of tracing out the antecedents and consequences of judicial decisions would be to investigate the attempts of organized groups to influence both the decision making of courts and the responses to their decisions. Various groups might articulate their activities to all stages of the adjudicatory process, for example, the generation of disputes, the sponsorship and management of litigation, affiliation (through such devices as *amicus curiae* participation) with litigation controlled by other parties, opposition to the enforcement of judgments, and attempts to gain or deny access to alternative decision-making processes (such as legislation).

As it happened, however, the source of inspiration for such studies in public law was not Cohen. Instead, some students of the judicial process turned to the theory of Arthur F. Bentley and made

a very valuable contribution to the study of judicial decision making. In its way, Bentleyan theory is just as mechanical as the legal theory of Austinian jurisprudence; but it did direct the attention of investigators to a different range of data. Instead of limiting description to the formal processes of courts, Bentleyanism pointed toward a focus upon the host of ancillary and informal activities that go on outside the courtroom. The result was a shift of emphasis from the legal aspects of politics to the political aspects of lawmaking by judges. It also led to research designs that took investigators out of the law library and into the field. The best and most succinct statement of the Bentleyan approach as applied to the analysis of judicial behavior is that of Jack W. Peltason (1955). An example of the kind of empirical research that has been produced by the Bentleyan approach is Peltason's field study (1961) of the role of federal district judges in enforcing the Supreme Court's school desegregation decision; another example is Danelski's study (1965) of the complex interplay of influences and interests in the selection of even a single judge.

Empirical research in interest-group activity impinging upon the judicial process was also undertaken by political scientists who did not purport to follow Bentley's theory—for instance, Clement Vose in his analysis (1959) of the successful campaign of the National Association for the Advancement of Colored People to induce the United States Supreme Court to facilitate access by Negroes to urban housing. Among other recent studies that embrace the judicial-process approach is that of Krislov (1965); several studies have emphasized the political relations of state and local judiciaries (Sayre & Kaufman 1960, chapter 14; Vines & Jacob 1963; Jacob & Vines 1965).

**Sociology—political socialization.** Haines and Mott had suggested that studies of the background characteristics of judges would be particularly valuable for gaining insight into the underlying bases for judicial choice, providing that such data could be quantified and assembled systematically for sets of judges and also that theories and methods could be developed for testing the influence of such background characteristics upon the decision-making behaviors of judges. Schmidhauser (1959) undertook to measure the predominant characteristics of United States Supreme Court justices collectively. Nagel, in a series of articles (e.g., 1962) investigated the relation between judicial attitudes and specific background characteristics. He found, for example, that Democratic judges voted more liberally than Republican judges, and Catholic judges more liberally than Protestant judges. Schmidhauser (1962) has reported a study of United States Supreme Court justices in which he investigated the interrelations among half a dozen background variables (political party affiliation, previous judicial experience, experience as a corporation lawyer, parental-family socioeconomic status, family tradition of judicial service, and geographical origins) and two decisional variables (adherence to precedent and tendency to dissent). Among his more interesting findings was that contrary to the prevailing beliefs and expectations of both lawyers and politicians, Supreme Court justices who had previous judicial experience voted *less* frequently in accord with the canon of *stare decisis* than did justices without experience in the lower courts.

**Social psychology—small groups.** Pritchett's bloc-analysis method of studying subgroups in the United States Supreme Court has been used in several subsequent investigations by other scholars. Snyder (1958) studied ideological differences and change among Supreme Court justices on the basis of a sample of cases involving the interpretation by the Court of amendments to the constitution. Ulmer (1965) subsequently made a somewhat more refined study of the same subject, using for data all votes in decisions accompanied by opinions during the 1946–1961 terms. Schubert (1960*a*) used bloc analysis to study the 1953–1957 terms of the United States Supreme Court and also the 1954–1957 terms of the Michigan Supreme Court; his findings demonstrated, *inter alia*, that for the elective justices of the Michigan Supreme Court, there was a very high correlation between liberal voting and Democratic party affiliation but for the appointed justices of the United States Supreme Court, there was no significant correlation between liberalism and partisan affiliation. Ulmer (1960*a*) studied the civil liberties decisions of the 1958 term of the United States Supreme Court, using phi-correlation coefficients, which take into consideration both agreement and disagreement in the voting of a pair of justices. Loeb (1965) has found that blocs of judges on the Court of Appeals of the District of Columbia differ, as do equivalent blocs on the United States Supreme Court, in their attitudes toward civil liberties questions.

Ulmer used dominance matrices to study leadership in the Michigan Supreme Court, which he measured on the sociometric basis of the extent to which each justice accepted the opinions written by every other justice (Schubert 1963*a*, chapter 1). The annual survey articles on the Supreme Court, appearing in such leading journals for their respective professions as the *American Political Science Review* (until 1961) and the *Harvard Law Review*, began in the 1950s to include summary statistics on dissenting behavior as well as on work load; and the Supreme Court section of *United States Law Week* has gone further, including (since 1944) in its annual survey article a matrix of dyadic agreement in dissent.

**Social psychology—judicial attitudes.** The research on judicial attitudes has built upon the theory of cumulative scaling of attitudes developed during World War II by Samuel A. Stouffer and his associates, and in particular by Louis Guttman. The possibility of using cumulative scaling to study the attitudes of Supreme Court justices apparently was first suggested by Jessie Bernard (1955) and by Joseph Tanenhaus in a paper in 1956. Most of the empirical research using this method, and developing the implications of the theory for the analysis of judicial attitudes, has been done by Schubert (1960*a*; 1965*b*), Ulmer (1960*a*; 1960*b*), and Spaeth (chapter 4 in Schubert 1963*a*). Ulmer established the probability that a single-scale variable—attitude toward the civil liberties—has tended to determine the voting of Supreme Court justices in this field of the Court's policy making. Schubert (1965*b*) demonstrated that approximately two-thirds of the Court's decisions on the merits, during a period of almost two decades (1946–1963), involved one or the other of two basic dimensions of liberalism: political or economic. Spaeth found that justices who were sympathetic toward labor were correspondingly antipathetic toward business and that many putative legal variables (such as federalism and deference to administrative expertise) appeared to have little or no influence upon the voting behavior of the justices when they were asked to decide cases that raised questions of economic liberalism.

**Psychometrics—judicial ideologies.** Psychometric research on judicial ideologies has built upon the exploratory factor analysis of the Supreme Court by Thurstone and Degan (1951) and the writings of Louis Guttman in the theory of cumulative scaling (1954; see Stouffer et al. 1950, chapters 2, 3, 6, 8, 9), together with the theoretical work of other leading psychometricians such as Clyde H. Coombs (1964). Schubert (1965*b*) has reported investigations for 17 terms of the Supreme Court, in which he utilized factor analysis of correlation matrices based upon dyadic agreement and disagreement, in voting with the decisional majority and in dissent, in order to position the ideal points representing the justices in three-dimensional psychological space. These dimensions were found to represent the dominant ideologies that determined the attitudes of Supreme Court justices: (1) the social ideology of equalitarianism; (2) the political ideology of libertarianism; and (3) the economic ideology of individualism. Schubert showed that such distinct attitudes as political liberalism and economic liberalism could be measured by cumulative scaling but that the interrelations among attitudes can best be studied at the ideological level and within the multidimensional frame of reference that factor analysis makes possible. His major empirical findings were that Supreme Court justices during the period since the end of World War II have been divided among three ideological types; and the homogeneity of the point of view of the liberal type is the basic explanation for the emergence of social equalitarianism (racial integration, civic equality, and legislative reapportionment) as the core of both the attitudes of the liberal justices and the most important policy making by the Supreme Court during the 1950s and 1960s.

**Econometrics—game theory.** Relatively little use has been made of game theory as an approach to the study of judicial decision making. Schubert (1960a) has described two experimental game models of Supreme Court decision making, and in a subsequent reformulation he utilized symbolic logic as a more precise language for the specification of the rules of strategy to be followed by the players (1962b). By comparing the actual voting behavior of the justices with the requirements of rational play, he demonstrated that the correlation between theory and practice was positive and very high. The justices of the Supreme Court may not have conceived of themselves as playing a game when they participated in the decisions in these cases, but they nevertheless behaved with the strict rationality that would be required of competing players who wished to maximize their possible gains, and minimize their possible losses, in terms of control over the Court's policies. Murphy (1964) has discussed the implications of such rational strategies for Supreme Court behavior, including decision making by the justices, both individually and collectively.

**Statistics—predicting decisions.** A recent study has undertaken to reanalyze some of the extensive data that were collected, during the periods 1915–1916 and 1918–1930, on the sentencing behavior of the judges of the magistrates court of New York City. Somit, Tanenhaus, and Wilke (1960), by taking advantage of the large number of judges and volume of cases included in the reports, were able to test two hypotheses: (a) that considerable difference in sentencing behavior will be found among judges handling fundamentally similar cases; and (b) that each individual judge's behavior will be generally self-consistent over a substantial period of time. The data strongly supported the first hypothesis but contradicted the second: the New York City magistrates tended not only to differ widely from each other but also to be individually inconsistent through time.

Tanenhaus, Schick, Muraskin, and Rosen (chapter 5 in Schubert 1963a) have collaborated in a study of the jurisdictional decision making of the Supreme Court in certiorari cases. By extensive statistical sampling of thousands of cases over a period of almost a decade and subsequent use of multiple-regression analysis, they were able to denote three criteria (or "cues," as the authors termed them) that were most likely to result in the grant of certiorari by the Court: (1) the support of jurisdiction by the solicitor general of the United States; (2) the presence of a civil liberties issue; and (3) previous judicial conflict in a case, in the form of either dissenting votes or the reversal of a trial court by an intermediate appellate court. The odds were about eight to two that the Court would grant certiorari in a case containing all three cues. Obviously this kind of knowledge would be useful to an attorney who wanted to predict the likelihood that the Supreme Court would accept jurisdiction, if requested to do so, in a case that he might wish to bring (or to oppose having brought) up from a lower court.

Fred Kort has developed a method for utilizing content analysis of judicial opinions as the basis for predicting decisions of courts. Kort (chapter 6 in Schubert 1963a) used factor and regression analysis in order to predict how a court will decide a case, depending upon the fact patterns (which Kort identifies by the content analysis of opinions and votes in samples of similar cases). Most interestingly, in terms of the importance attributed to *stare decisis* in traditional legal theory, Kort was able to predict with almost the same degree of accuracy going backward in time as going forward, which suggests that the underlying basis for the high degree of consistency in voting behavior observable in the decision making of many appellate courts is not a function of respect for legal precedent but rather results from the high degree of cognitive structure in the attitudes of the justices, both individually and collectively.

The methodological weakness in Kort's procedures is the reciprocal of the weakness in Schubert's psychometric approach. Kort can (in effect) locate with precision in a multidimensional psychological space the stimulus points representing the questions raised for decision by cases, but the most that he can say about the ideal points of the justices is that a majority lie on one or the other side of a hyperplane that transects the space. Schubert's method locates the judicial respondents but not the case stimuli. The development of procedures that would locate points representing both the pending cases and the justices in the same joint space would make possible more precise prediction of outcomes and also would provide a more useful model for the development of a more general sociopsychological theory of judicial decision making.

Several recent studies have attempted to evaluate the comparative utility of various statistical procedures for predicting decisional outcomes. Grunbaum and Newhouse (1965) discuss factor analysis, partial correlation, and multiple regression; Nagel (1965) compares the postdictive power of correlation, multiple regression, and discriminant analysis; while Schubert (1965c) uses correlation, cluster, and factor analysis to compare the opinion with the voting behavior of a single judge. All three of these studies are focused upon data drawn from decisions of the United States Supreme Court.

## Prospects

An examination of the approaches to research in judicial behavior indicates that they may conveniently be divided into two groups. Freudian psychology, anthropology, and sociology are less rigorous in theory and method and may be characterized as focusing upon judicial *attributes*—the background factors that affect the beliefs and attitudes of judges and thereby the decision-making processes of courts. Social psychology, psychometrics, econometrics, and statistics are more rigorous and focus upon the decision-making process itself—that is, how and why judges make the decisions they do.

Another way to classify these approaches is according to the relative emphasis that each has received in contemporary research in judicial behavior. It is clear that the greatest contribution has been made in the study of interest groups, political socialization, small groups, attitudes, and statistical prediction. Less work has been done in systems theory, ideology, and game theory; and practically no further attempts have been made in recent years to use Freudian or anthropological approaches for the study of judicial behavior.

The discussion of the empirical research that has been done thus far makes it evident that the most work, and the most sophisticated work, has focused upon the United States Supreme Court. This emphasis can readily be explained on expediential

grounds relating to the greater visibility and accessibility of data regarding the decision-making process of that court. Nevertheless, several scholars have criticized what they regard as an overconcentration of attention upon the United States Supreme Court (Jacob & Vines 1965; Schubert 1963a, chapter 10), as well as the methods employed in some of the recent research (Shapiro 1964, chapter 1; Becker 1966). The relevant theoretical and methodological issues are discussed further in the symposium "Frontiers of Legal Research" (1963) and in recent works by Schubert (1965a; 1966).

The lack of discussion and research in judicial behavior outside the United States shows that behavioralism in the study of judges remains largely an indigenous American movement which has only recently begun to spread to other countries (see chapter 7 by Aubert and chapter 8 by Torgersen in Schubert 1963a; and Hayakawa 1962). The extent to which substantive findings about judicial behavior reflect the cultural influences of the American system necessarily remains virtually unknown. What is most needed, therefore, is an extension of the focus of inquiry to include comparative analyses of lower courts and of adjudication processes in cross-cultural settings.

Consideration of the predictability of judicial decisions must ultimately confront an underlying question of normative theory, which has sharply divided the legal profession from judicial behavioralists (see Schubert 1963b). Legalists, for reasons of tradition, training, and vocational need, emphasize the importance of predicting the outcome in the individual case. Behavioralists are more interested in understanding the factors that explain significant continuities in the decision making of judges, and therefore what they seek to predict is how most judges will behave in the decision of most cases most of the time; for their purposes some small margin of error must be tolerated, and an adequate test of their theories is provided by statistical probability theory and measures. Aggregates necessarily consist of discrete items; but success in the prediction of the outcome in any individual case is neither a necessary nor a sufficient condition for evaluating the acceptability of behavioral research theory and methods. On the other hand, the accurate prediction of behavior in the aggregate is an essential—if in some present fields an ultimate—test of the validity and reliability of research in judicial behavior. The natural scientist who studies the effect of a filtering screen in a cathode-ray tube cannot predict *which* electrons will pass through the filter; but he can and must be able to predict how many electrons will penetrate, when, why, how, and with what effect. It may not be unreasonable to stipulate an equivalent standard for judicial behavioralists, at least at the present stage of development of the social sciences.

GLENDON SCHUBERT

[*See also* POLITICAL BEHAVIOR; PUBLIC LAW.]

### BIBLIOGRAPHY

*For further discussion and additional references to the literature, see the introduction and the bibliography in Schubert 1963a. The research published during the period 1955–1962 is summarized in greater detail in a bibliographical article, Schubert 1963c. Examples of studies of historical significance and of all ten analytical types (including many of the references cited in the present article) are reprinted in Schubert 1964.*

BAADE, HANS W. (editor) (1963) 1964 *Jurimetrics.* New York: Basic Books. → First published in Volume 28 of *Law and Contemporary Problems.*

BECKER, THEODORE L. 1966 *Political Behavioralism and Modern Jurisprudence: A Working Theory and Study in Judicial Decision-making.* Chicago: Rand McNally.

BERNARD, JESSIE 1955 Dimensions and Axes of Supreme Court Decisions: A Study in the Sociology of Conflict. *Social Forces* 34:19–27.

COHEN, FELIX S. 1935 Transcendental Nonsense and the Functional Approach. *Columbia Law Review* 35: 809–849.

COOMBS, CLYDE H. 1964 *A Theory of Data.* New York: Wiley.

DANELSKI, DAVID J. 1965 *A Supreme Court Justice Is Appointed.* New York: Random House.

FRANK, JEROME (1930) 1949 *Law and the Modern Mind.* New York: Coward.

FRANKFURTER, FELIX; and LANDIS, JAMES M. 1927 *The Business of the Supreme Court: A Study in the Federal Judicial System.* New York: Macmillan.

Frontiers of Legal Research. 1963 *American Behavioral Scientist* 7, no. 4. → Special issue.

GAUDET, FREDERICK J. 1938 Individual Differences in the Sentencing Tendencies of Judges. *Archives of Psychology* 32, no. 230.

GLUCKMAN, MAX 1965a *The Ideas in Barotse Jurisprudence.* New Haven: Yale Univ. Press.

GLUCKMAN, MAX 1965b *Politics, Law and Ritual in Tribal Society.* Oxford: Blackwell; Chicago: Aldine.

GRUNBAUM, WERNER F.; and NEWHOUSE, ALBERT 1965 Quantitative Analysis of Judicial Decisions: Some Problems in Prediction. *Houston Law Review* 3:201–220.

GUTTMAN, LOUIS 1954 The Principal Components of Scalable Attitudes. Pages 216–257 in Paul F. Lazarsfeld (editor), *Mathematical Thinking in the Social Sciences.* Glencoe, Ill.: Free Press.

HAINES, CHARLES G. 1922 General Observations on the Effects of Personal, Political, and Economic Influences in the Decisions of Judges. *Illinois Law Review* 17: 96–116.

HAYAKAWA, TAKEO (1962) 1964 Civil Liberties in the Japanese Supreme Court. Pages 325–334 in Glendon Schubert (editor), *Judicial Behavior: A Reader in Theory and Research.* Chicago: Rand McNally. → A partial reprinting of "Legal Science and Judicial Behavior, With Particular Reference to Civil Liberties in the Japanese Supreme Court," published in the *Kobe University Law Review*, No. 2, pages 1–27.

HERNDON, JAMES (1962) 1964 The Role of the Judiciary in State Political Systems. Pages 153–161 in Glendon Schubert (editor), *Judicial Behavior: A Reader in Theory and Research.* Chicago: Rand McNally. → Paper delivered at the Midwest Conference of Political Scientists, April 1962.

HOEBEL, E. ADAMSON 1961 Three Studies in African Law. *Stanford Law Review* 13:418–442.

JACOB, HERBERT; and VINES, KENNETH N. (editors) 1965 *Politics in the American States: A Comparative Analysis.* Boston: Little. → See especially Chapter 7 on "Courts and Political and Governmental Agencies."

KRISLOV, SAMUEL 1965 *The Supreme Court in the Political Process.* New York: Macmillan.

LASSWELL, HAROLD D. 1948 *Power and Personality.* New York: Norton.

LLEWELLYN, KARL N.; and HOEBEL, E. ADAMSON 1941 *The Cheyenne Way: Conflict and Case Law in Primitive Jurisprudence.* Norman: Univ. of Oklahoma Press.

LOEB, LOUIS S. 1965 Judicial Blocs and Judicial Values in Civil Liberties Cases Decided by the Supreme Court and the United States Court of Appeals for the District of Columbia Circuit. *American University Law Review* 14:146–177.

MARCH, JAMES G. 1956 Sociological Jurisprudence Revisited: A Review (More or Less) of Max Gluckman [*The Judicial Process Among the Barotse of Northern Rhodesia*]. *Stanford Law Review* 8:499–534.

MOTT, RODNEY L. 1936 Judicial Influence. *American Political Science Review* 30:295–315.

MOTT, RODNEY L.; ALBRIGHT, S. D.; and SEMMERLING, H. R. 1933 Judicial Personnel. American Academy of Political and Social Science, *Annals* 167:143–155.

MURPHY, WALTER F. 1964 *Elements of Judicial Strategy.* Univ. of Chicago Press.

NAGEL, STUART S. 1962 Testing Relations Between Judicial Characteristics and Judicial Decision-making. *Western Political Quarterly* 15:425–437.

NAGEL, STUART S. 1965 Predicting Court Cases Quantitatively. *Michigan Law Review* 63:1411–1422.

PELTASON, JACK W. 1955 *Federal Courts in the Political Process.* Garden City, N.Y.: Doubleday.

PELTASON, JACK W. 1961 *Fifty-eight Lonely Men: Southern Federal Judges and School Desegregation.* Introduction by Paul Douglas. New York: Harcourt.

PRITCHETT, C. HERMAN (1948) 1963 *The Roosevelt Court: A Study in Judicial Politics and Values, 1937–1947.* New York: Octagon Books.

SAYRE, WALLACE S.; and KAUFMAN, HERBERT 1960 *Governing New York City: Politics in the Metropolis.* New York: Russell Sage Foundation.

SCHMIDHAUSER, JOHN R. 1959 The Justices of the Supreme Court: A Collective Portrait. *Midwest Journal of Political Science* 3:1–57.

SCHMIDHAUSER, JOHN R. 1962 *Stare Decisis,* Dissent and the Background of the Justices of the Supreme Court of the United States. *University of Toronto Law Journal* 14:194–212.

SCHUBERT, GLENDON 1960a *Quantitative Analysis of Judicial Behavior.* Glencoe, Ill.: Free Press.

SCHUBERT, GLENDON 1960b *Constitutional Politics: The Political Behavior of Supreme Court Justices and the Constitutional Policies That They Make.* New York: Holt.

SCHUBERT, GLENDON 1962a A Solution to the Indeterminate Factorial Resolution of Thurstone and Degan's

Study of the Supreme Court. *Behavioral Science* 7: 448–458.

SCHUBERT, GLENDON 1962*b* Policy Without Law: An Extension of the Certiorari Game. *Stanford Law Review* 14:284–327.

SCHUBERT, GLENDON (editor) 1963*a* *Judicial Decisionmaking*. International Yearbook of Political Behavior Research, Vol. 4. New York: Free Press.

SCHUBERT, GLENDON 1963*b* Judicial Attitudes and Voting Behavior: The 1961 Term of the United States Supreme Court. *Law and Contemporary Problems* 28: 100–142.

SCHUBERT, GLENDON 1963*c* Behavioral Research in Public Law. *American Political Science Review* 57:433–445.

SCHUBERT, GLENDON (editor) 1964 *Judicial Behavior: A Reader in Theory and Research*. Chicago: Rand McNally.

SCHUBERT, GLENDON 1965*a* *Judicial Policy-making: The Political Role of the Courts*. Chicago: Scott, Foresman.

SCHUBERT, GLENDON 1965*b* *The Judicial Mind: The Attitudes and Ideologies of Supreme Court Justices, 1946–1963*. Evanston, Ill.: Northwestern Univ. Press.

SCHUBERT, GLENDON 1965*c* Jackson's Judicial Philosophy: An Exploration in Value Analysis. *American Political Science Review* 59:940–963.

SCHUBERT, GLENDON 1966 The Future of Public Law. *George Washington Law Review* 34:591–661.

SHAPIRO, MARTIN 1964 *Law and Politics in the Supreme Court: New Approaches to Political Jurisprudence*. New York: Free Press.

SNYDER, ELOISE C. 1958 The Supreme Court as a Small Group. *Social Forces* 36:232–238.

SOMIT, ALBERT; TANENHAUS, JOSEPH; and WILKE, WALTER 1960 Aspects of Judicial Sentencing Behavior. *University of Pittsburgh Law Review* 21:613–620.

STOUFFER, SAMUEL A. et al. 1950 *Measurement and Prediction*. Studies in Social Psychology in World War II, Vol. 4. Princeton Univ. Press.

THURSTONE, LOUIS L.; and DEGAN, J. W. 1951 A Factorial Study of the Supreme Court. National Academy of Sciences, *Proceedings* 37:628–635.

ULMER, S. SIDNEY 1960*a* The Analysis of Behavior Patterns on the United States Supreme Court. *Journal of Politics* 22:629–653.

ULMER, S. SIDNEY 1960*b* Supreme Court Behavior and Civil Rights. *Western Political Quarterly* 13:288–311.

ULMER, S. SIDNEY (editor) 1961 *Introductory Readings in Political Behavior*. Chicago: Rand McNally. → See especially pages 167–189 on "Homeostatic Tendencies in the United States Supreme Court" by S. Sidney Ulmer.

ULMER, S. SIDNEY 1965 Toward a Theory of Sub-group Formation in the United States Supreme Court. *Journal of Politics* 27:133–152.

VINES, KENNETH N.; and JACOB, HERBERT 1963 *Studies in Judicial Politics*. Tulane University Studies in Political Science, Vol. 8. New Orleans, La.: The University.

VOSE, CLEMENT E. 1959 *Caucasians Only: The Supreme Court, the NAACP, and the Restrictive Covenant Cases*. Berkeley: Univ. of California Press.

## II

### JUDICIAL VALUES

Most legal theories in the Western tradition have been characterized by a search for objectivity, for clear, all-inclusive, and logically arranged rules of conduct administered by informed, intelligent, and impartial judges. This quest, of course, has not been and never will be completely successful. The important question, however, given the imperfections of human nature, is the degree of success in achieving a "rule of law" rather than one of whim or caprice. Various nations have attempted to attain comprehensive sets of rules [*see* LEGAL SYSTEMS]. This article is concerned with the extent to which the values of individual judges impinge on their applications of those rules to specific cases. For reasons that will be brought out in the second section, most of this exposition will focus on American judges.

### Values and judicial choice

Judges cannot help but be influenced by the traditions and values of the society in which they have been reared. "The great tides and currents," Cardozo wrote, "which engulf the rest of men, do not turn aside in their course, and pass the judges by" ([1921] 1960, p. 168). This influence is not of itself evil. A judge who did not believe in justice, in fair play, or in respect for the dignity of man would be an intolerable official in a free society. But agreement on general values implies neither agreement on how those general values may be applied nor agreement on more specific values. Moreover, despite Cardozo's assurance, many judges, as older men in a society, may resist tides of social change and be left stranded on sparsely settled ideological islands.

In deciding individual cases judges must choose. They must choose between opposing litigants, between competing claims to abstract justice, between conflicting principles of jurisprudence, between different public policies that may flow from a decision, and thus often between specific values. Hopefully, as men of strong character, judges are impartial toward litigants. But it is unlikely that any intelligent man who has been active in public affairs—and judges in common law countries are rarely selected from recluses—will not have formed strong convictions about what specific values are necessary to his society and what policy courses are best for his nation. Nor is it likely that such a man will be indifferent to the jurisprudential theories that compete within the Western legal tradition.

The statutes, executive orders, and constitutional provisions that judges apply are rarely so clear as not to admit of two or more reasonable interpretations in difficult cases. Terms like "equal protection," "due process," "cruel and unusual punishment," and "commerce among the several states" are no more self-defining than the concept of the "reasonable man." Cold, deductive logic may be the cement that binds together the words of judicial opinions; but the critical decision may be the selection of a major premise rather than deductions from that premise. In Holmes's oft-quoted phrase: "The felt necessities of the time, the prevalent moral and political theories, intuitions of public policy, avowed or unconscious, even the prejudices which judges share with their fellow-men, have had a good deal more to do than the syllogism in determining the rules by which men should be governed" ([1881] 1963, p. 5).

Thus, in many cases the wording of legal documents creates a wide range of choice for judges. Where, then, do they secure unequivocal guidance for their decisions? Lower court judges may look to appellate courts. Appellate court judges may look to their own past decisions for help. But *stare decisis* often supplies little more than general admonishments. As a distinguished British jurist has written: "On the whole, it is a sign of an incompetent lawyer or Judge that he is over-impressed by citation of particular authority. Authority is but a guide to juridical understanding—a servant, not a dictator" (Slesser 1962, p. 28). There may be no case strictly in point; there may be several decisions in point, but they might be incompatible in doctrine if not in result. Compromises among judges of the highest court, where an institutional opinion has been published, may have blurred the precise principles that underpinned a relevant decision; where the judges spoke seriatim they may have followed mutually conflicting or even contradictory principles. Or there may be a case and an opinion directly in point, but the resulting general rule may have been eroded by changing conditions.

Nor can the "intent of the framers," either of a constitution or a statute, always be a reliable guide, even on the assumption that courts should decide current problems according to the wisdom of the past. First of all, since the framers could not have foreseen all social and economic changes, it is probable that on many issues they had no intent at all. Second, even where the framers foresaw problems of the future, it is no easy task to discover exactly how they planned to cope with these difficulties. The materials from which judges are asked to divine the intent of the framers of the U.S. constitution, Justice Robert H. Jackson once quipped, are "almost as enigmatic as the dreams Joseph was called upon to interpret for Pharaoh" (concurring opinion in *Youngstown Sheet & Tube Co. v. Sawyer*, 343 U.S. 579, 634, 1952; see also Anderson 1955). Since legislators are aware that judges may scan the record of debates to discern intent, that record may reflect little more than a series of tactical maneuvers whose real purpose is to deceive in order to make a partisan point.

Where general principles of jurisprudence are unclear, constitutional, statutory, or administrative phrases vague, precedents unimpressive, and history uncertain, a judge's discretion is at its maximum. In such instances his decisions create new law and very possibly new policy. The guidance for his creativity, as both Cardozo ([1921] 1960, p. 113) and Frankfurter (1934, p. 480) remarked, must come from his reading of life itself. In this process a judge's personal values cannot help but have a great impact. Indeed, a judge's very perception of his alternatives—or even his realization that, in fact, alternatives are open—will inevitably be heavily influenced by his values. Cantril has pointed out that "a person sees what is 'significant,' with significance defined in terms of his relationship to what he is looking at" (1957, p. 121).

To a judge with one set of values, a case may have to be decided by balancing the interests of an individual citizen against those of the government. To a second judge with a somewhat different set of values, the same case may also involve balancing, but balancing the interests of the country as a whole in freedom against its interests in security. A third judge, with his own set of values, may see the decision in the case as requiring an application of what is to him a straightforward command of a constitutional or statutory provision.

A judge's values may influence him consciously or unconsciously. Since his values affect his perception, he may not be aware of their impact. Few men would be so brash as to claim that they fully understand themselves. On the other hand, a judge may be made aware of at least some of his values. His colleagues if he is on a collegial court or his superiors if he is a trial judge may delight in pointing out to him some of his predilections; so too may his staff as well as professional scholars. Furthermore, if he is a serious, reflective person, introspection may help him analyze himself and enable him to maintain some degree of control over the impact of his values on his decisions.

A judge who is aware of his values may consciously work to see them achieved in judicial decisions and in public policy, but this is not to say that a judge can effectively implement his value preferences. A U.S. judge, even a Supreme Court justice, who deliberately set out to attain those decisional and policy goals demanded by his values would face a network of checks (Murphy 1964, chapter 2). As one of nine judges on a collegial tribunal, a Supreme Court justice would need the assent of four of his colleagues both for a favorable decision and an opinion of the Court. As a member of an appellate tribunal that can hear only a minute proportion of the lawsuits brought in the country, he is heavily dependent on a bureaucracy of state and federal court judges to carry out decisions in cases reviewed by the Supreme Court and also to apply the same principles to thousands of similar cases. The Supreme Court is also subject to numerous political checks by Congress and the president. In addition, because the aura of sacredness that has so often surrounded the Court has been one of the major sources of judicial power, public opinion can operate as a check on one justice's—or nine justices'—ability to translate individual values into public law and policy. Lower court judges in the United States are liable to similar and more restrictive institutional and political limitations, as are judges of most other nations.

The last set of checks on a judge's capacity to allow free play to his value preferences is an internal one. As a complex man, a judge is likely to have a complex value system. Policy goals, role concepts, personal ambitions, convictions about ethics and morality, may interact to form a tangled web rather than a pyramid of preferences. The tidy picture of a neat value hierarchy may be a useful model for some purposes, but it is questionable how closely this model fits human beings in the real world. Where difficult cases are involved—where a judge's range of choice is widest—there is apt to be a serious conflict within his value system, if the term "system" with its connotation of ordered relations is not misleading here. Deep respect for decisions made by legislators may be among a judge's values, and it may conflict with the demands of some of his other values, thus leading him to agonizing and not always consistent decisions. Even granting that judges' pleas for self-restraint are apt to be most strident when coming from those who agree with a policy the court has been asked to negate, it does not follow that a judge may not feel strong internal conflict or that he may not opt for a different decision as a judge than he would if he were a legislator, or an executive official, or a private citizen.

The gist of the matter is that given the vagueness of many legal rules and the complicated nature of the factual situations presented, a judge often has considerable leeway for choice. And the common law system has always given him—or burdened him with—such leeway. It is not improbable that the civil law also provides leeway. Because he is a human being his perception of alternatives as well as his selection among alternatives will be influenced by his values. But a judge has leeway, not license. "He is not," as Cardozo pointed out, "a knight-errant, roaming at will in pursuit of his own ideal of beauty or of goodness" ([1921] 1960, p. 141). A judge cannot give free rein to his values unless they are widely shared by the general community or at least by the elements within that community who wield effective political power.

## The search for methodology

In the United States during the 1920s and 1930s, a group of legal realists, especially Karl Llewellyn (1928–1960) and Jerome Frank (1930), stimulated scholarly investigation of the impact of personal values on judicial decision making. Of course, the fact that values influence judicial action is hardly a recent discovery. Jefferson complained that John Marshall used the constitution as "nothing more than an ambiguous text, to be explained by his sophistry into any meaning which may subserve his personal malice" (*Writings*, vol. 12, p. 392). In defense against the assaults of the Jeffersonians, Marshall enshrined in U.S. law the great myth of mechanical decision making, that "courts are the mere instruments of the law, and can will nothing" (*Osborn* v. *U.S. Bank*, 9 Wheaton 738, 866, 1824).

The legal realists and political scientists like Edward S. Corwin (1914; 1925; 1934) diverted discussion of the influence of judicial values away from partisan attacks against particular decisions and helped direct criticism into more general lines of analysis. The impact of this scholarship, although not always its immediate intent, was to demonstrate the pervasive effect of the judge's values on his decisions. Biographical studies, such as those by Beveridge of Marshall (1916–1919), Swisher of Field (1930) and Taney (1935), Fairman of Miller (1939), and Mason of Brandeis (1946), Stone (1956), and Taft (1965), provide fascinating life histories of individual judges as well as revealing accounts of the role of the Supreme Court in U.S. politics. Since these biographies were done by political scientists and lawyers rather than by social psychologists, they illustrate the nature of the various judges' jurisprudence more than they analyze in a systematic fashion the values that the judges brought to their office and the effect of those values on their decisions.

The fundamental problems in linking values and decisions are obviously ones of methodology: first, how to discover a judge's values and, second, how to measure their impact on his decisions. In 1918 Schroeder asserted that judges might be psychoanalyzed through their opinions. Schroeder's approach has not yet been demonstrated as feasible for broad investigations, although Lasswell (1930*a*; 1930*b*) has published some suggestive work on this subject. The fact that opinions of appellate courts—and it is at this level that opinions are most readily available—are frequently group products inhibits the general usefulness of this method, as does the apparent lack of interest by psychiatrists competent to analyze legal documents. On the other hand, Schroeder's proposal is not far removed from content analysis, a technique, discussed below, that offers some promise if applied to writings authored by one man.

Quantitative analysis of large numbers of decisions is another possible way of getting at the link between values and choices. In 1922 Haines used the statistics of the city magistrates court in New York to show how some judges had, in huge masses of cases, handled similar issues very differently from other judges. In a series of books and articles, Pritchett used the votes of Supreme Court justices to rank these judges on their attitudes toward certain values as well as to indicate the propensity of some justices to vote together on particular issues (1948; 1954).

Other scholars, most notably Schubert, have refined and extended Pritchett's statistical methods, using such devices as Guttman scales to rank the justices more precisely in regard to their values (1959). This technique offers a unidimensional explanation of voting behavior; that is, votes on a given issue are analyzed to support or refute a hypothesis that value $x$ is crucial or trivial to Judge A, or that reactions to value $y$ explain the votes of some—or all—of the judges studied. Among the more serious drawbacks of a unidimensional explanation is that many cases involve several values. In an effort to repair this defect, Schubert has attempted to construct multidimensional scales (1962; 1963*a*; 1965). These early formulations are interesting, but it is as yet too early to ascertain how fruitful they will be.

A related shortcoming of scaling is that, as Pritchett pointed out about his own work (1954, p. 191), such statistics are relational. At most they indicate only that Judge A is apt to defend value $x$ more often than does Judge B. Moreover, analysis of scalograms often suffers from circular reasoning. As Shapiro remarked, "Consistency in voting behavior is used to infer the attitude, and then the attitude is used to explain the consistency" (1964, p. 14). Scaling also shares a weakness of all methods that rely on counting votes: judges, at least appellate court judges, frequently suppress dissent-

ing votes for tactical reasons (Brandeis 1957; Murphy 1964). Thus, while votes may indicate the values held by a judge, the precise extent varies with the individual judge and the circumstances in which he finds himself. Congruence of votes and values is also affected by the kinds of values a judge holds. Loyalty to his court and colleagues, for instance, may overcome attachment to a policy value and help squelch a dissent.

Taking a different tack, Nagel (in Schubert 1964, pp. 234–259) has tried to discover the extent to which judges' social and political background characteristics correlate with their decisions. He reports, for example, that judges who were Democrats before coming to the bench are somewhat more prone than judges who were Republicans to favor: (1) the defendant in criminal prosecutions; (2) free speech in civil liberties cases; (3) labor in labor–management controversies; (4) the employee in employer liability litigation; and (5) the government in tax and regulation of business cases.

This evidence, although interesting, is not conclusive. Because Nagel's work has been of a pioneering nature, he has had to work with small samples of judges, broad categories of background characteristics, and relatively unsophisticated statistical techniques. As work progresses in this area and research methods are more refined, one may be able to speak with firmer assurance of the probable impact of a judge's general background on his jurisprudential orientation.

Another means of studying the influence of values on decision making is through examination of a judge's private letters, memoranda, and draft opinions. Chief Justice William Howard Taft, for example, wrote long and candid letters every week to his family, explaining in great detail what was going on within the Court. Chief Justice Harlan F. Stone and Justice Frank Murphy kept a number of memoranda in which they or other justices offered to change votes or to suppress separate opinions if certain compromises in the style and substance of opinions could be reached. Murphy and Justice Harold H. Burton kept notes at the supposedly secret conferences of the justices. These notes purported to reveal what the justices said in private about some of the cases they had to decide.

These papers help pierce the veil of secrecy that shrouds much of judicial decision making, but like quantitative analysis their use is subject to serious limitations. First, only a few substantial collections of judges' papers are open to all scholars, and to date no judge has allowed unrestricted access to his files while still on the bench. Second, what is said in a letter or a memorandum may reflect what a judge wants to recall—again his perception would be influenced by his values—or wants others to recall, rather than what actually transpired. Third, a judge can use notes to his brethren as tactical instruments to persuade or to bargain; what he says he wants, what he really wants, and what he will accept may be very different. Last, a hasty remark at a conference or even a memorandum may represent a tentative position rather than a firm judgment.

A possibility that may greatly further systematic study of judicial values is that of content analysis of a judge's personal correspondence or of his lone concurring or dissenting opinions (cf. the technique used by White 1947). As of this writing, however, only one such attempt has been made—and that, admittedly, was a preliminary investigation (Danelski 1964).

Although not completely restricted to the United States, the realistic approach to the study of courts and law has had its major impact on U.S. scholars. The civil law's reliance on finely detailed codes supposedly narrows the discretion of the judge, and the civil law's prohibition against dissenting or concurring opinions multiplies problems of discovering relationships between behavior and values. Moreover, the continued prevalence in most of the Commonwealth nations of analytical jurisprudence and a mechanical theory of judicial decision making has inhibited realistic investigation of the judicial process in those countries.

Nevertheless, numerous worthwhile studies are available in English on judicial behavior in other countries. Among the more important are those of Hayakawa on Japan (see Schubert 1964, pp. 325–334), Sollie (1958), Aubert (see Schubert 1963b, pp. 201–219), and Torgensen (see Schubert 1963b, pp. 221–244) on Norway, and McWhinney's general investigation of the common law nations (1956) and his more specialized study of Germany (1962). In addition, there appears to be a growing interest in comparative analysis among U.S. political scientists, and an increasing concern among foreign scholars about the actual way their own judges arrive at decisions and influence public policy.

## Values and jurisprudence

It is from the inevitable impact of a judge's values on his decisions that the really important problems in jurisprudence flow. First, how can a judge limit this impact and to what extent should he try? Should he not attempt to foster certain kinds of values? As was noted earlier, a judge who did not believe in justice or fair play would be an intolerable official in a free society. But suppose a judge discovers—and the process of discovery is by no means obvious—that his specific values are in conflict with those which dominant public opinion or the opinion of more popularly representative members of government is currently supporting. Should he pursue his own values? Or should he play the role of the tribune and reflect as best he can the will of the people and their legislative or administrative representatives? Does a judge have the moral or legal right to try to lead public or official opinion toward what he feels are more worthwhile values? If he does have such a right, what are its limits?

WALTER F. MURPHY

BIBLIOGRAPHY

ANDERSON, WILLIAM 1955 Intention of the Framers: A Note on Constitutional Interpretation. *American Political Science Review* 49:340–352.

BEVERIDGE, ALBERT J. 1916–1919 *The Life of John Marshall.* 4 vols. Boston: Houghton Mifflin. → Volume 1: *Frontiersman, Soldier, Lawmaker, 1755–1788.* Volume 2: *Politician, Diplomatist, Statesman, 1789–1801.* Volume 3: *Conflict and Construction, 1800–1815.* Volume 4: *The Building of the Nation, 1815–1835.*

BRANDEIS, LOUIS D. 1957 *The Unpublished Opinions of Mr. Justice Brandeis: The Supreme Court at Work.* Selected and edited by Alexander M. Bickel. Cambridge, Mass.: Belknap Press. → Published posthumously.

CANTRIL, HADLEY 1957 Perception and Interpersonal Relations. *American Journal of Psychiatry* 114:119–126.

CARDOZO, BENJAMIN N. (1921) 1960 *The Nature of the Judicial Process.* New Haven: Yale Univ. Press.

CORWIN, EDWARD S. (1909–1952) 1964 *American Constitutional History: Essays.* New York: Harper.

CORWIN, EDWARD S. 1914 *The Doctrine of Judicial Review: Its Legal and Historical Basis, and Other Essays.* Princeton Univ. Press.

CORWIN, EDWARD S. 1925 Constitution v. Constitutional Theory. *American Political Science Review* 19:290–304.

CORWIN, EDWARD S. 1934 *The Twilight of the Supreme Court: A History of Our Constitutional Theory.* New Haven: Yale Univ. Press.

DANELSKI, DAVID J. 1964 Values as Variables in Judicial Decision-making: Notes Toward a Theory. Unpublished manuscript. → A paper delivered at the 1964 annual meeting of the Midwest Conference of Political Scientists.

FAIRMAN, CHARLES 1939 *Mr. Justice Miller and the Supreme Court: 1862–1890.* Cambridge, Mass.: Harvard Univ. Press.

FRANK, JEROME (1930) 1949 *Law and the Modern Mind.* New York: Coward.

FRANKFURTER, FELIX 1934 Supreme Court, United States. Volume 14, pages 474–482 in *Encyclopaedia of the Social Sciences.* New York: Macmillan.

HAINES, CHARLES G. 1922 General Observations on the Effects of Personal, Political, and Economic Influences in the Decisions of Judges. *Illinois Law Review* 17:96–116.

HOLMES, OLIVER WENDELL (1881) 1963 *The Common Law.* Cambridge, Mass.: Harvard Univ. Press.

JEFFERSON, THOMAS *The Writings of Thomas Jefferson.* 20 vols. Washington: Thomas Jefferson Memorial Association of the United States, 1905.

LASSWELL, HAROLD D. (1930a) 1960 *Psychopathology and Politics.* New ed., with afterthoughts by the author. New York: Viking.

LASSWELL, HAROLD D. 1930b Self-analysis and Judicial Thinking. *International Journal of Ethics* 40:354–362.

LLEWELLYN, KARL N. (1928–1960) 1962 *Jurisprudence: Realism in Theory and Practice.* Univ. of Chicago Press. → See especially pages 431–465 on "A Realistic Jurisprudence: The Next Step."

MCWHINNEY, EDWARD (1956) 1960 *Judicial Review in the English-speaking World.* 2d ed. Univ. of Toronto Press.

MCWHINNEY, EDWARD 1962 *Constitutionalism in Germany and the Federal Constitutional Court.* Leiden (Netherlands): Sythoff.

MASON, ALPHEUS T. 1946 *Brandeis: A Free Man's Life.* New York: Viking.

MASON, ALPHEUS T. 1956 *Harlan Fiske Stone: Pillar of the Law.* New York: Viking.

MASON, ALPHEUS T. 1965 *William Howard Taft: Chief Justice.* New York: Simon & Schuster.

MURPHY, WALTER F. 1964 *Elements of Judicial Strategy.* Univ. of Chicago Press.

PRITCHETT, C. HERMAN (1948) 1963 *The Roosevelt Court: A Study in Judicial Politics and Values, 1937–1947.* New York: Octagon Books.

PRITCHETT, C. HERMAN 1954 *Civil Liberties and the Vinson Court.* Univ. of Chicago Press.

SCHROEDER, THEODORE 1918 The Psychologic Study of Judicial Opinions. *California Law Review* 6:89–113.

SCHUBERT, GLENDON (1959) 1960 *Quantitative Analysis of Judicial Behavior.* Glencoe, Ill.: Free Press.

SCHUBERT, GLENDON 1962 The 1960 Term of the Supreme Court: A Psychological Analysis. *American Political Science Review* 56:90–107.

SCHUBERT, GLENDON 1963a Judicial Attitudes and Voting Behavior: The 1961 Term of the United States Supreme Court. *Law and Contemporary Problems* 28:100–142.

SCHUBERT, GLENDON (editor) 1963b *Judicial Decision-making.* International Yearbook of Political Behavior Research, Vol. 4. New York: Free Press. → See especially pages 201–219 on "Conscientious Objectors Before Norwegian Military Courts" by V. Aubert and pages 221–244 on "The Role of the Supreme Court in the Norwegian Political System" by Ulf Torgerson.

SCHUBERT, GLENDON 1963c Behavioral Research in Public Law: Bibliographical Essay. *American Political Science Review* 57:433–445. → This bibliographical article contains a fine discussion of some of the literature on judicial behavior published up to 1962. The discussion, however, is largely limited to writings employing quantitative research techniques.

SCHUBERT, GLENDON (editor) 1964 *Judicial Behavior: A Reader in Theory and Research.* Chicago: Rand McNally. → See especially pages 234–259 and 325–334.

SCHUBERT, GLENDON 1965 *The Judicial Mind: The Attitudes and Ideologies of Supreme Court Justices, 1946–1963.* Evanston, Ill.: Northwestern Univ. Press.

SHAPIRO, MARTIN 1964 *Law and Politics in the Supreme Court: New Approaches to Political Jurisprudence.* New York: Free Press.

SLESSER, HENRY H. 1962 *The Art of Judgment, and Other Studies.* London: Stevens.

SOLLIE, FINN 1958 Courts and Constitutions: A Comparative Study of Judicial Review in Norway and the United States. Ph.D. dissertation, Johns Hopkins Univ.

SWISHER, CARL B. (1930) 1963 *Stephen J. Field: Craftsman of the Law.* Hamden, Conn.: Shoe String Press.

SWISHER, CARL B. (1935) 1961 *Roger B. Taney.* Hamden, Conn.: Shoe String Press.

WHITE, RALPH K. 1947 Black Boy: A Value-analysis. *Journal of Abnormal and Social Psychology* 42:440–461.

## III
### JUDICIAL DISCRETION

Surely the basic judicial value in the Anglo–American legal tradition is the Rule of Law. Yet the meaning or application of the law in concrete settings is often plagued with doubt. One reason for this is that lawmakers are handicapped by the limitations of human foresight. They cannot anticipate all the combinations and permutations of circumstance. Likewise, the law must reveal itself in ordinary language, which is plagued with imprecision. Moreover, competing claims in a free society often reflect not merely incompatible interests but differing conceptions of right and wrong. Inevitably in such a setting the essence of the legislative process is compromise and accommodation. This is apt to find expression in terms more suggestive than precise and sometimes more calculated to avoid clear commitments than to embrace them. Moreover, as Plato observed, laws by definition are general rules; this is their essence and their weakness. Generalities falter before the complexities of life. They must usually concern themselves more with form than with substance. That is why, in Plato's view, law is far inferior to the wise discretion of a philosopher-king, who could give each man his due—whereas law must be satisfied to prescribe what is due in abstract categories regardless of much that is unique in the men and events that they embrace. Recognizing the problem of generality, Aristotle rejected the Platonic all-wise ruler: "To invest men with authority is to introduce a beast, as desire is something bestial, and even the best of men in authority are liable to be corrupted by anger." Law, in contrast, "is intelligence without passion" (*Politics* III, 16, 1287a32).

**The common law.** The Anglo–American legal tradition synthesizes the wisdom of Plato and the wisdom of Aristotle. Having rejected the philosopher-king in favor of the Rule of Law, it calls him back to limited service as judge. In this capacity he is expected to fill the gap between the generalities of law and the specifics of life.

Of course, the meaning and application of some legal rules are unambiguous. Indeed, they may be sufficiently clear to preclude litigation. Others are so vague, so lacking in standards, as to foreclose judicial decision. Justice Oliver Wendell Holmes ventured to suggest that when a judge refers a negligence question, for example, to a jury, "he avows his inability to state the law" and recognizes that "while if a question of law is pretty clear we [judges] can decide it, as it is our duty to do, if it is difficult it can be decided better by twelve men at random from the street" (Holmes [1885–1918] 1952, p. 234). Putting such problems to a jury is not unlike leaving inscrutable constitutional provisions for application by the political branches of government (e.g., *Luther* v. *Borden,* 48 U.S. 1, 1849).

Between these extremes, where the law is neither so clear nor so vague as to preclude adjudication, judges must find standards for decision as best they can. By the common-law tradition their guide in doubtful cases is not justice, but what Holmes called "the actual feelings and demands of the community, whether right or wrong" (Holmes [1881] 1963, p. 36). Other great lawyers have expressed the same thought in somewhat different terms. "Law accepts as the pattern of its justice the morality of the community whose conduct it assumes to regulate" (Cardozo 1928, p. 37). A judge must "manifest the half-framed purposes of his time" (Hand [1952] 1960, p. 14). "Whatever is *contra bonos mores et decorum,* the principles of our law prohibit . . ." (Lord Mansfield in *Jones* v. *Randall,* 98 E.R. 707, 1774). It is "the duty of the Court to keep the rules of law in harmony with the enlightened common sense of the nation" (Pollock 1929, p. 295). The "sober second thought of the community . . . is the firm base on which all law must ultimately rest" (Stone 1936, p. 25). In short, judicial law must express "the views and feelings that may fairly be deemed representative of the community as a continuing society" (Frankfurter 1954, p. 237).

It comes to this: When doubtful matters cannot be avoided by referring them to juries or to the political processes, judges shall decide them in accordance with the standards and values of "the reasonable man." This common-law creature symbolizes the community, as do jury and legislature. He is an "external standard" for the guidance of a troubled court—the common denominator of the views just quoted.

The Anglo–American synthesis of Plato and Aristotle thus insists upon the Rule of Law, yet recognizes the necessity of judicial discretion: a discretion which it limits by an ancient common-law device—the reasonable man. In this manner it seeks to accommodate the traditions of the past and the comfort of the present, society's need for stability and its need for change.

Some insist that, whatever the proclaimed standard, a judge cannot escape his own values—his own personal bias. Yet we know that men differ widely in the ability to rise above this limitation, and as Learned Hand insists, "the incredulity which seeks to discredit that knowledge is a part of the crusade against reason from which we have already so bitterly suffered" (Hand [1952] 1960, p. 218). In the long view, surely the common law itself is a monument to the belief that the judicial process can attain a high degree of objectivity, that the reasonable-man standard is an effective guide for those who strive for detachment.

Others insist that even if judicial neutrality is possible, it is not desirable, that the community ought to have the benefit of the moral insights of its great judges (Cahn 1951, pp. 838 ff.). Hand's answer expresses the orthodox tradition, "[The judge] is not to substitute even his juster will [for that of the community]; otherwise it would not be the common will which prevails, and to that extent the people would not govern" (Hand [1952] 1960, p. 109).

**American constitutional law.** Inspired by the common-law tradition, American constitutional law has insisted (with some lapses) that dubious acts of the political branches of government shall not be adjudged invalid unless a court is prepared to hold that no reasonable man could support them (Thayer 1893, pp. 129 ff.). Here again the ultimate standard is the views and feelings that may fairly be deemed representative of the community as a continuing society. Yet the Platonic ideal dies hard, and from time to time Platonists have found their way to the bench. In modern terminology they are called "activists." Judges of this persuasion do not deny their duty of deference to community values when the law is dubious. They seem, however, to have a special ingenuity for dissipating doubt. Where others are torn between alternate paths, they are apt to find unmistakable guidance in the wisdom and purpose of the Founding Fathers or in some "higher law." Platonists on the bench do not avow, they merely practice, activism. When Justice Field needed a constitutional device for imposing laissez-faire upon the states, he found it in the natural rights of the Declaration of Independence—which he insisted had been incorporated in the constitution's fourteenth amendment (*Butchers' Union Co.* v. *Crescent City Co.,*

111 U.S. 746, 1884). Modern libertarian activists find that Field was quite wrong, that the fourteenth amendment was designed to absorb not the Declaration but the bill of rights (dissenting opinion in *Adamson* v. *California*, 332 U.S. 68 ff., 1947). This permits them to escape, as Field did, the traditional, community-oriented value system of the Supreme Court's majority (*Palko* v. *State of Connecticut*, 302 U.S. 319, 1937). They, too, may eventually prevail—if only temporarily.

Of course, a judge may be as creative in determining the consensus of the community as in discovering the "true meaning" of the Founding Fathers. Yet there is a major difference: the Founding Fathers can neither protest nor clarify their views. Given the modern activist's progressive bent, surely he would not accept past "purposes" as generally binding. Moreover, in view of the changing and contradictory intentions that have been attributed to the Fathers, their views with respect to modern problems would seem to be at least as uncertain as our own. Perhaps, when the activist pleads past purposes to support his conception of present needs, he does so because he is reasonably sure his views would not be presently acceptable on their own merits. In any event, the difference between activism and the more orthodox common-law tradition is a difference in emphasis, as that between Plato and Aristotle.

Some "legal realists" (among others), insisting that political choice is inherent in the judicial process, argue that judges should abandon the ideal, or pretense, of objectivity. In short, courts should courageously exercise their discretion to achieve social justice—as they see it (Braden 1948, p. 594). In this view, of course, both the reasonable-man and the Founding Fathers approaches are at best vehicles of self-deception—at worst "noble fictions" that hide the inevitable process of judicial legislation.

Ultimately, law is not a basket of ready-made answers, but a technique for solving an endless flux of social problems. "[It] is always approaching, and never reaching, consistency. It is forever adopting new principles from life at one end, and it always retains old ones from history at the other, which have not yet been absorbed or sloughed off" (Holmes [1881] 1963, p. 32). Under a façade of formal symmetry the judicial process must synthesize established rules, pragmatic needs, and moral yearnings. It must honor reasonable expectations born of the past and yet allow adequate *Lebensraum* for the present and the future. In the long run it cannot defy or ignore the basic values of the community that it serves. There is no other reliable sanction for law and order in a democratic society.

WALLACE MENDELSON

[*See also the biographies of* BRANDEIS; CARDOZO; HOLMES.]

### BIBLIOGRAPHY

BRADEN, GEORGE D. 1948 The Search for Objectivity in Constitutional Law. *Yale Law Journal* 57:571–594.

CAHN, EDMOND N. 1951 Authority and Responsibility. *Columbia Law Review* 51:838–851.

CARDOZO, BENJAMIN N. (1921) 1960 *The Nature of the Judicial Process.* New Haven: Yale Univ. Press.

CARDOZO, BENJAMIN N. 1928 *The Paradoxes of Legal Science.* New York: Columbia Univ. Press.

CHAFEE, ZECHARIAH 1947 Do Judges Make or Discover Law? American Philosophical Society, *Proceedings* 91:405–420.

DICEY, ALBERT V. (1905) 1962 *Lectures on the Relation Between Law and Public Opinion in England During the Nineteenth Century.* 2d ed. London and New York: Macmillan.

FRANKFURTER, FELIX 1954 Some Observations on the Nature of the Judicial Process of Supreme Court Litigation. American Philosophical Society, *Proceedings* 98:233–239.

FRIEDMANN, WOLFGANG (1945) 1960 *Legal Theory.* 4th ed. London: Stevens.

HAND, LEARNED (1952) 1960 *The Spirit of Liberty: Papers and Addresses.* 3d ed., enl. Collected and with an introduction and notes by Irving Dilliard. New York: Knopf.

HOLMES, OLIVER WENDELL (1881) 1963 *The Common Law.* Cambridge, Mass.: Harvard Univ. Press.

HOLMES, OLIVER WENDELL (1885–1918) 1952 *Collected Legal Papers.* New York: Smith.

POLLOCK, FREDERICK 1929 Judicial Caution and Valour. *Law Quarterly Review* 45:293–306.

POUND, ROSCOE 1921 *The Spirit of the Common Law.* Boston: Jones.

POUND, ROSCOE 1959 *Jurisprudence.* 5 vols. St. Paul, Minn.: West. → Volume 1: *Jurisprudence: The End of Law.* Volume 2: *The Nature of Law.* Volume 3: *The Scope and Subject Matter of Law.* Volume 4: *Application and Enforcement of Law.* Volume 5: *The System of Law.*

STONE, HARLAN F. 1936 The Common Law in the United States. *Harvard Law Review* 50:4–26.

THAYER, JAMES B. 1893 The Origin and Scope of the American Doctrine of Constitutional Law. *Harvard Law Review* 7:129–156.

## IV

### JUDICIAL RECRUITMENT

The process of judicial recruitment embodies those factors that bear directly or indirectly upon the choice of the officials who man the courts of a given nation or its political subdivisions. Judicial selection has been considered the first great problem that arises in any judicial system. Solutions to this problem and to the closely related subject of judicial tenure have varied in accordance with the prevailing theoretical conceptions of the nature of justice and practical considerations reflecting the distribution of political power in the society.

Dawson, in his *History of Lay Judges* (1960), underscores the fact that the evolution of the manor courts in England and the seignorial courts in France was seriously influenced by power struggles between monarchs seeking greater national control and local lords fighting to maintain or expand local autonomy. In these countries the specialization of legal skills and the organization of lawyers led to the monopolization of judicial posts by lawyers and was a matter not only of prime political consequence but also of great significance in the historical development of judicial recruitment. The relatively unique historical experience of England permitted the survival of lay judges for a considerably longer time than was true in the rest of western Europe.

These references to the historical analysis by Dawson illustrate one of the approaches to the study of legal institutions presently employed by western European students. Much of the research and writing available on the process of judicial selection and tenure is limited to the western European and American experiences, and even here there are great lacunae. The development of these institutions has not been definitely explored for every western European nation. Neither has the process of further historical exploration and reinterpretation of the British evidence been completed. Except for material of a formal descriptive nature, little research in depth has been conducted on non-Western legal systems (Washington Foreign Law Society 1956; Yanaga 1956).

Within the Western tradition there remains much emphasis upon formal description. But a penchant for relating institutional practice (such as mode of recruitment and relative stability of tenure) to qualitative evaluation (such as the relative prestige and influence of specific courts) has long characterized some of the more perceptive scholars in England, France, and the United States. James Kent, for example, argued:

The judiciary of the United States has an advantage over many of the State Courts, in the tenure of the office of the judges, and the liberal and stable provision for their support. The United States are, by these means, fairly entitled to command better talents, and to look for more firmness of purpose, greater independence of action, and brighter displays of learning. The federal administration of justice has a manifest superiority over that of the individual states, in consequence of the uniformity of its decisions, and the universality of their application. Every state court will naturally be disposed to borrow light and aid from the national courts, rather than from the courts of other individual states, which will probably never be so generally respected and understood.  ([1826–1830] 1844, vol. 1, pp. 443–444)

Perceptive, albeit impressionistic, hypotheses concerning the relationship of the social, economic, and political background of judges to decision-making behavior aroused intense academic, as well as political, interest in judicial recruitment and tenure in America. Historically, this intellectual focus was a concomitant of the political reappraisal that characterized the Populist and Progressive movements. Karl N. Llewellyn's "On Warranty of Quality, and Society" was a study of interaction between economic background, legal ideology, social function, and judicial personality. Thomas Reed Powell's work provided yet another example. Articles such as his "Judiciality of Minimum Wage Legislation" (1924) concentrated upon the ideological commitments of the individual justices. Among political scientists, Cortez A. M. Ewing (1938) and Charles Grove Haines contributed to this intellectual current. Western European examples are not lacking; although, as the work of Piero Calamandrei (1935) demonstrates, such treatments often tended toward eulogistic formalism. The influence of Louis L. Thurstone, the University of Chicago psychologist, upon some of his colleagues in political science gave impetus to the development of systematic appraisal of judicial selection and tenure. The work of Rodney L. Mott and his associates (1933) was seminal in this respect. Mott undertook exploratory investigations of the chronological pattern of changes in the characteristics of selectees of several American courts (1936). Employing modifications of Thurstone's factor analysis, Mott also devised a method for measuring quantitatively the relative influence and prestige of state and federal highest appellate courts (1948).

The widespread American adoption of elective judicial selection methods (often with relatively brief tenure) in the nineteenth century was followed by a counterrevolution spearheaded by the American Bar Association. A veritable torrent of opinion concerning the relative merits of the appointive or elective mode of judicial selection has flooded law journals and professional legal publications for over half a century. However, since much of the academic as well as professional writing on this controversy has been exhortive, little factual material has been available on the actual nature of these systems, other than institutional descriptions of the sort now supplied periodically by the Council on State Governments.

Beginning in the late 1930s, research of an analytic quantitative nature has added several dimensions to modern investigation of American judicial recruitment and tenure. Herndon (1962) has documented that approximately 56 per cent of the judges serving on 36 elective state courts (1948–1957) were first chosen by appointment rather than popular election. Ewing (1938) and Schmidhauser (1960) each investigated, in the late 1930s and 1950s respectively, the social, educational, and political backgrounds of members of the Supreme Court of the United States. Nagel provided a comprehensive series of articles demonstrating that regardless of variations in tenure and methods of selection certain background factors, such as political party affiliation, do consistently influence decision making on the major state appellate courts. Nagel (1961) also found that the ideological differences between Democratic and Republican judges were consistent with partisan differences found in voting behavior studies and congressional voting behavior.

Attention has also been focused upon chronological age, particularly age at judicial oath-taking and at the termination of judicial service (Donahue & Tibbitts 1962). Data drawn from the United States Courts of Appeals, the United States Supreme Court, and several highest state appellate courts indicate variations in such age patterns that suggest the need for more research on regional differences. Exploratory study of the relationship of judicial background to institutional tradition rather than decision-making tendency indicated that commonly held notions about the significance of such factors as prior judicial experience need serious modification. For instance, judges thoroughly experienced in the American tradition of appellate decision making prior to serving on the United States Supreme Court felt less compulsion to adhere to *stare decisis* and were more prone to dissent than inexperienced colleagues (Nagel 1962).

The comparatively recent flowering of American behavioral studies of judicial recruitment and tenure (Schubert 1960) has not resulted in the accumulation of a body of data sufficient for definitive analysis even among the American states; and far less has been completed quantitatively with respect to western European or non-Western processes. To the extent that the new modes of analysis provide the means for challenging cross-cultural research, students of judicial personnel are at the threshold of a potentially great research opportunity.

JOHN R. SCHMIDHAUSER

## BIBLIOGRAPHY

ABRAHAM, HENRY J. 1962 *The Judicial Process: An Introductory Analysis of the Courts of the United States, England, and France.* New York: Oxford Univ. Press.

CALAMANDREI, PIERO (1935) 1942 *Eulogy of Judges.* Princeton Univ. Press. → First published in Italian under the title *Elogio dei giudici: Scritto da un avvocato.*

CARR-SAUNDERS, ALEXANDER; and WILSON, P. A. 1933 *The Professions.* Oxford: Clarendon.

DAWSON, JOHN P. 1960 *A History of Lay Judges.* Cambridge, Mass.: Harvard Univ. Press.

DONAHUE, WILMA T.; and TIBBITTS, CLARK (editors) 1962 *Politics of Age.* University of Michigan Conference on Aging, 1961. Ann Arbor: Univ. of Michigan.

EWING, CORTEZ A. M. 1938 *The Judges of the Supreme Court, 1789–1937.* Minneapolis: Univ. of Minnesota Press.

HAYNES, EVAN 1944 *The Selection and Tenure of Judges.* Newark, N.J.: National Conference of Judicial Councils.

HERNDON, JAMES 1962 Appointment as a Means of Initial Accession to Elective State Courts of Last Resort. *North Dakota Law Review* 38:60–73.

KENT, JAMES (1826–1830) 1844 *Commentaries on American Law.* 4 vols. 5th ed. New York: The Author. → A fourteenth edition was published in 1896 by Little, Brown of Boston.

LLEWELLYN, KARL N. 1936–1937 On Warranty of Quality, and Society. *Columbia Law Review* 36:699–744; 37:341–409.

MOTT, RODNEY L. 1936 Judicial Influence. *American Political Science Review* 30:295–315.

MOTT, RODNEY L. 1948 The Measurement of Judicial Personnel. *New York University Law Quarterly Review* 23:262–277.

MOTT, RODNEY L.; ALBRIGHT, S. P.; and SEMMERLING, H. R. 1933 Judicial Personnel. American Academy of Political and Social Science, *Annals* 167:143–155.

NAGEL, STUART S. 1961 Political Party Affiliation and Judges' Decisions. *American Political Science Review* 55:843–850.

NAGEL, STUART S. 1962 Ethnic Affiliations and Judicial Propensities. *Journal of Politics* 24:92–110.

POWELL, THOMAS REED 1924 The Judiciality of Minimum Wage Legislation. *Harvard Law Review* 37:545–553.

SCHMIDHAUSER, JOHN R. 1960 *The Supreme Court: Its Politics, Personalities and Procedures.* New York: Holt.

SCHUBERT, GLENDON 1960 *Quantitative Analysis of Judicial Behavior.* Glencoe, Ill.: Free Press.

WASHINGTON FOREIGN LAW SOCIETY 1956 *Studies in the Law of the Far East and Southeast Asia.* Washington: The Society.

YANAGA, CHITOSHI 1956 *Japanese People and Politics.* New York: Wiley.

# JUGLAR, CLÉMENT

Clément Juglar (1819–1905), French economist, was the son of a physician and himself a doctor. He made a good record at medical school, culminating in a noteworthy thesis on the influence of heart disease on the lungs. The fact that he began his career as a doctor left a deep imprint on his method of analyzing economic phenomena. He was devoted to experimental science all his life and applied to the field of economics his care for exact, precise, and measurable facts.

The change in his career was apparently caused by the political and economic events of 1848. The shift was not sudden, however; he had already written several articles on trends in French population statistics from 1772 to 1849. These articles form a link between his interests as a physician and his interests an an economist, since they are based on a search for the relationship of demographic phenomena, such as births, marriages, deaths, etc., to the country's wealth. It is not surprising that as a former physician Juglar should see an analogy between changes in France's wealth and fluctuations in human health. Wealth is not a constant: it oscillates and is subject to serious depressions; it results from the common life of many cells, some of which must occasionally be eliminated, not without pain, in order for life to continue.

Starting with this fundamental image Juglar was attracted to the study of economic crises. He had already set forth his early formulation of the problem in two articles (1856; 1857) when the subject of commercial crises was proposed for a contest by the Académie des Sciences Morales et Politiques. In 1862 Juglar submitted *Des crises commerciales et de leur retour périodique en France, en Angleterre et aux États-Unis* ("Commercial Crises and Their Periodic Recurrence in France, England, and the United States") and won. It was expanded and republished together with a series of articles in 1889; it is Juglar's main work and made him the first cycle theorist.

Before Juglar, efforts had been made to find the causes of crises—the sudden and visible occurrence of such events as rapidly falling prices, stock market crashes, commercial failures, unemployment, etc. Such crises were attributed to many different factors, among them bad harvests, wars, and excessive issuance of paper money. Juglar considered crises within the larger framework of the economic cycle, of which the crisis is but one phase. He looked for an explanation of cycles, or the fact that crises appear at approximately regular intervals after a phase of prosperity and preceding a phase of liquidation; each of these phases contains within itself the succeeding one. In a period of prosperity prices rise and production increases. In a crisis, which is felt in all sectors of the economy, prices fall, whereupon health is gradually restored. As a crisis is liquidated, the economy, and particularly credit, may be said to be healed.

Juglar's search for an explanation of cycles was

made in three stages. To begin with, in order to analyze the phenomenon scientifically he gave a clear and precise history of economic crises in Great Britain, France, and the United States, which he built up from a large number of economic time series (prices, interest rates, gold prices, central bank balances, etc.). Second, on examining these statistical series and studying their minima and maxima, Juglar discovered an almost uniform periodicity, with the cycles breaking down into phases (between 1803 and 1882 he found 14 cycles with an average duration of six years). Only in the third stage of his analysis did he try to construct an explanatory theory of the cycle. He considered crises, since they exist potentially in the period of prosperity, as inevitable. Prosperity gives rise not only to optimistic activity but also to the abuse of credit and the saturation of consumption. Crises are the direct result of the excesses of prosperity; they are a necessary purge of the economic system and occur when fear replaces euphoria. The basic reason for these crises lies in human nature, which is as much given to excesses of confidence as it is to excesses of fear.

Juglar's political attitude toward business cycles is liberal (laissez-faire). Nothing should be done to try to prevent a crisis *because it is necessary*. It is useful, however, to predict a crisis in order to attenuate the effects of surprise. Juglar himself became "the prophet of crises": his studies of the uneven growth of the portfolios of banks and of their metallic reserves make him a forerunner of the constructors of economic barometers.

All modern work on the business cycle has its starting point in Juglar; he was a precursor both as theoretician and as statistician. Methods and data have become richer, and the purpose of business cycle theory has changed from merely trying to foresee a crisis to trying to prevent it. Nonetheless, Schumpeter rightly named the 7-year to 11-year cycles after the man who blazed the trail for the study of economic fluctuations.

Juglar taught statistics in Paris at the École Libre des Sciences Politiques; he founded the Société de Statistique de Paris; he was a member of the Comité des Travaux Historiques et Scientifiques (Section des Sciences Économiques et Sociales) attached to the Ministère de l'Instruction Publique et des Beaux Arts; he was also a member of the Institut International de la Statistique and vice-president of the Société d'Économie Politique, Paris. In 1892 he was elected to the Académie des Sciences Morales et Politiques.

Juglar, a sincere and somewhat austere Catholic, regarded moral progress as more important than material progress; however, he did have a certain interest in social problems and accepted the presidency of the Société d'Économie Sociale, Paris. He was also a cultivated amateur of painting and classical music.

ANDRÉ MARCHAL

[*For discussion of the subsequent development of Juglar's ideas, see* BUSINESS CYCLES; *and the biographies of* AFTALION; KONDRATIEFF; SCHUMPETER.]

### WORKS BY JUGLAR

1856   Des crises commerciales. *Annuaire de l'économie politique et de la statistique* 13:555–581.

1857   Situation comparée de la Banque d'Angleterre et de la Banque de France, d'après les comptes rendus officiels pendant les crises commerciales depuis 1799. *Journal des économistes* Second Series 16:262–263.

(1862) 1889   *Des crises commerciales et de leur retour périodique en France, en Angleterre et aux États-Unis.* 2d ed. Paris: Guillaumin. → Partially translated as *A Brief History of Panics and Their Periodical Occurrence in the United States;* published by Putnam in 1916.

1865   BANQUE DE FRANCE, PARIS *Extraits des enquêtes parlementaires anglaises sur les questions de banque, de circulation monétaire et de credit.* Translated and published under the supervision of Paul J. Coullet and Clément Juglar. 8 vols. Paris: Furne.

1868   *Du change et de la liberté d'émission.* Paris: Guillaumin.

1884a   *Les banques de dépôt, d'escompte et d'émission: Résumé comparé de leur histoire et de leur organisation.* Nancy (France): Berger–Levrault.

1884b   La crise de New-York: Les chèques certifiés; les certificats du clearing-house. *L'économiste français* 12, no. 2:191–192.

1891   Crises commerciales. Volume 1, pages 641–650 in Léon Say and Joseph Chailley-Bert (editors), *Nouveau dictionnaire d'économie politique.* Paris: Guillaumin.

### WORKS ABOUT JUGLAR

BEAUREGARD, PAUL   1909   Notice sur la vie et les travaux de M. Clément Juglar. Académie des Sciences Morales et Politiques, *Revue des travaux . . . et comptes-rendus de ses séances* 171:153–179.

*Des crises commerciales . . . ,* par Clément Juglar [A Book Review of]. 1890   *Journal of the Royal Statistical Society* 53:158–159.

MANGELSDORF, FRIEDRICH-SIEGMUND   1930   *Clément Juglars Krisenbarometer: Seine Grundlagen und seine Bedeutung.* Berlin: Möller & Borel.

# JUNG, CARL GUSTAV

Carl Gustav Jung (1875–1961), founder of analytical psychology, was born the son of a clergyman in Kesswil (Thurgau canton, Switzerland) on Lake Constance. At the age of four he went to Basel, which he regarded as his hometown: his mother was born there, and he went to school and received his doctorate in medicine there. Several of his ancestors on his mother's side were also Protestant theologians, including his grandfather and great-grandfather. His paternal great-grandfather, however, was a Roman Catholic *Kirchenrat* (member of a consistory) in Mainz, and his grandfather was in his eighteenth year when he was converted by Schleiermacher to Protestantism. This heritage of concern with religious problems may have been the source of the questioning always characteristic of his work. Despite an inclination toward the humanities, his ancestors on his father's side also included physicians who exercised an enduring influence on Jung's intellectual development. His paternal grandfather, an aesthete and poet, was exiled from Germany for his revolutionary views; he was called to the chair of surgery in the University of Basel in 1822 through the intercession of Alexander von Humboldt and later founded the first insane asylum there, as well as the Anstalt zur Hoffnung, a home for mentally retarded children.

As a young man, Jung was full of enthusiasm for biology, zoology, and paleontology; it was only later that he shifted to medicine. At the same time, philosophy and the history of religion excited him, and the list of great men who had a decisive influence upon him is a long one; it includes Heraclitus, Plato, Aristotle, St. Augustine, St. Thomas Aquinas, Meister Eckhart, Paracelsus, Böhme, Joachim of Floris, Goethe, Carus, Hölderlin, Nietzsche, Schopenhauer, and Freud, to name but a few. From as early as 1898 until the end of his life, occultism and mysticism interested him, as did the study of mythology. Thus, his lifework has that significant double aspect that ties it, on the one hand, to the natural sciences and, on the other, to the humanities. As he saw it, this was the only way to do justice to the multilayered structure of the psyche.

**Early career in psychiatry.**   Jung began as an assistant to Eugen Bleuler at Burghölzli, the psychiatric clinic of the University of Zurich. In 1902 the degree of doctor of medicine was conferred upon him for his dissertation, "On the Psychology and Pathology of So-called Occult Phenomena" (1902). His later fundamental notion that there is in every individual a natural predisposition toward a "totality of the psyche" is first set forth here. He left for Paris that same year, studying with Pierre Janet for a semester, and then went to London to broaden his knowledge of psychopathology. In 1903 he married Emma Rauschenbach of Schaffhausen, who was his loyal companion and scientific collaborator until her death in 1955. With her he moved to their permanent home situated in a large garden in Küsnacht on the shore of Lake Zurich, where he lived until his death.

Around the time of his marriage, Jung, together

with a few associates, began his systematic investigations at the Burghölzli, the first fruits of which were his publication of *Studies in Word-association* in 1904 and 1909. The method of testing that he elaborated in these studies was used to reveal affectively significant groups of ideas in the unconscious region of the psyche. To designate them, he coined the term "complexes," which has since become part of our everyday language. The association test made him known throughout the world (it won him, among other things, an honorary degree conferred by Clark University in the United States). Today it is still part of the diagnostic equipment of mental hospitals and courts, and it is used for training in personality diagnosis and for vocational guidance of all kinds. It likewise provided the initial impetus for his closer acquaintance in 1907 with Sigmund Freud, in whose work on the interpretation of dreams Jung found his own ideas and observations to be essentially confirmed and furthered.

Jung is generally regarded as a disciple, and an unfaithful one, of Freud. This is not at all correct. Jung did accept Freud's findings and methods in the years of their close association, but the decisive underlying concept of Jung's work may be traced back to the very beginnings of his career, many years before he met Freud. Today we know that the role of a lifelong disciple was inconceivable for Jung; his own stature would soon have broken such bonds. Thus it was that their collaboration could last but a short time; nevertheless, it did last from 1907 to 1913. After a joint lecture tour through the United States in 1909 and four years (1909–1913) as an editor of the Bleuler–Freud *Jahrbuch für psychologische und psychopathologische Forschungen* and as the president of the International Psycho-analytic Society, which he himself founded, Jung's path branched off in a different direction. This was foreshadowed as early as 1912 in his book *Wandlungen und Symbole der Libido* (*Symbols of Transformation*, 1902–1959, vol. 5), in which he sought to elaborate the symbolic meaning of the dreams and fantasies of a young woman by the use of mythological parallels. With this book Jung advanced to a new position. He was unable to accept many of Freud's most essential doctrines, such as the theory of wish fulfillment and the theory of infantile sexuality. To distinguish his own doctrine from Freud's "psychoanalysis" and Adler's "individual psychology," he thenceforth called his theory "analytical psychology." Later he himself called its theoretical aspect "complex psychology," because of the complexity of its subject, but today only the earlier designation is employed.

Jung's radically different approach was based in the last analysis on a *Weltanschauung* that differed from Freud's. Freud's positions remained grounded in the theories of cognition of the nineteenth century, while Jung's were linked with that of the twentieth, which has brought with it revolutionary innovations in so many branches of science, especially modern physics and depth psychology.

After publishing numerous studies on psychiatric problems, among which his paper "The Psychology of Dementia Praecox" (1907) and several other of his articles anticipate modern interpretations of schizophrenia, Jung gave up his work at Burghölzli in 1909 and in 1913 resigned his lectureship at the University of Zurich, which he had held since 1905, to devote himself entirely to his private medical and psychotherapeutic practice, scientific research, writing, and travel.

**Travels and spiritual explorations.**   In 1912–1913 Jung traveled repeatedly to France, Italy, and the United States; his travels ended with World War I. In addition to his military duties, Jung entered upon a period of intensive soul-searching and strenuous empirical scientific endeavor. Then there followed other voyages of discovery to study the psychology of primitive peoples by direct contact with them. In 1920 Jung was in Tunis and Algiers, in 1924–1925 among the Pueblo Indians of New Mexico and Arizona, in 1925–1926 among the inhabitants of Mount Elgon in Kenya, and later in Egypt. He was aiming, in particular, to uncover the analogies between the unconscious psychic contents of modern Western man and certain manifestations of the psyche in primitive peoples, as well as of their myths and cults. He also studied Asian culture, for the religious symbols and phenomenology of Buddhism and Hinduism and the teachings of Lao-tzu, Confucius, and Zen always had special significance for him. He traveled to India twice, the second time in 1937.

Jung's most important works appeared in rapid succession, covering ever-widening spheres. In addition to psychiatry, he became more and more involved in Greek and other mythologies, patristics and Christian mysticism, gnosis and cabala, and above all alchemy, turning in his later years to modern physics and parapsychology. Everywhere he sought parallels and illuminating insights that provide a deeper understanding of the creative products of the human soul and its eternally recurring basic forms and statements. Above all, however, it was in the symbolism of alchemy and Hermetic philosophy that he found astounding correspondences to the psychic developmental process of the human being. Then there were the important problems of current events, which he treated with an uncanny clearsightedness, thus investing the chaos of our world with new meaning. To the very end his sense for medical problems led him to pursue the targets sighted in his early works: his last paper on schizophrenia (1958a) takes up an old theme, again pointing out the possible physiological etiology of this disease. He strove constantly to penetrate the deeper meaning of delusions and to interpret the material presented in schizophrenia, which is characteristically rich in symbols, and so became one of the champions of the psychotherapeutic approach to the treatment of schizophrenia.

**Basic contributions.** Only when we survey the nearly two hundred longer and shorter works of Jung do we realize the tremendous scope of the unique pioneering work he accomplished. His writings have been translated into nearly all European languages and into some Asiatic ones. We shall confine ourselves here to listing in brief form some of his most important principles and concepts.

The following concepts are both original and fundamentally significant:

(*a*) A new formulation of the *libido concept,* which refers not only to sexuality but to the whole of vital energy, which flows through the psyche in incessant motion, sometimes rising, sometimes diminishing, making possible a functional approach to psychic events.

(*b*) The concept of the psyche as a *self-regulating system,* in which the conscious and the unconscious realms are compensatorily related.

(*c*) The heuristic concept of the unconscious, which distinguishes between the contents of the *personal* unconscious and the contents of the *collective* unconscious: the personal unconscious includes material that originates in ontogenesis, and the collective unconscious includes material that originates in phylogenesis, i.e., those patterns of behavior, or actions and reactions of the psyche, that are determined by race and that Jung termed *archetypes.* They are imperceptible potentialities that manifest themselves as perceptible archetypal patterns and processes (or symbols) only under certain psychic conditions. They occur in man's dreams, visions, and fantasies and have been expressed in the myths, religious concepts, fairy tales, sagas, and works of art of all epochs and all cultures. Moreover, Jung explicitly stressed the relationship between archetype and instinct.

(*d*) The concept of the process of *individuation,* i.e., of "the evolution of the psyche to its wholeness," its way of maturing, in which the archetypes appear both as structural elements and as regulators of the unconscious psychic material and constitute particularly dynamic factors. The phases of this process are characterized by the confrontation of the conscious with some typical components of the unconscious realm (shadow, animus–anima, the great mother, the wise old man, the self, etc.). From the perspective of wholeness, which is always kept in mind, both the first and the second halves of life receive their appropriate significance.

(*e*) The special consideration and development of the *religious function* of the psyche, which is an integrating element in mental health, its repression and neglect causing psychic disturbances.

(*f*) The differentiation between two *attitude types:* the *extrovert* (oriented toward the external world) and the *introvert* (oriented to the internal world) and of four *functional types,* which are characterized by the primacy of thought, intuition, feeling, and sensation respectively.

(*g*) The *interpretation of dreams,* using the elements of the subject's dreams as representations of intrapsychic data, thus gaining insight into the subject's projections and facilitating the remission of symptoms. In contrast to the causal–reductive interpretation of Freud, attention is centered on the future-oriented aspect of unconscious processes.

(*h*) The positive conception of *regression* in particular and of *neurosis* in general. Jung gave the latter concept a new content by freeing it from attachment to the biological and instinctual and by giving it, as well as regression, a deeper spiritual sense.

(*i*) *Synchronicity,* i.e., the meaningful coincidence of an interior and an external event, as a principle that explains acausal connections, such as presentiments, prophetic dreams, fortuitous events, etc.

(*j*) The method of *active imagination,* a stimulation of the symbol-making ability of the psyche to create spontaneous products in which the unconscious contents are concretized in the form of words, musical sounds, painting, drawing, sculpture, dance, etc., and are able to resolve psychic disturbances.

**Honors and offices.** It is not surprising that these great achievements were appreciated both at home and abroad, earning Jung official positions and honors. Honorary doctorates were conferred on him by Clark, Fordham, Yale, and Harvard universities in the United States; by Oxford in England; by the universities of Calcutta, Benares, and Allahabad in India; and finally by the University of Geneva and the Federal Institute of Technology in Zurich. Jung was awarded the city of Zurich's literature prize in 1932, and in 1938 he was elected honorary fellow of the Royal Society of Medicine in England. He was made an honorary member of the Swiss Academy of Medical Sciences in 1944. His academic appointments included the professorship of medical psychology at the University of Basel, which he held for only a brief period because of his health, and the titular professorship of philosophy in the faculty of philosophical and political sciences of the Federal Institute of Technology in Zurich, 1933–1941/1942.

Jung was elected honorary president of the German Medical Society for Psychotherapy in 1930, and from 1933 to 1939 he was president of the International Society for Psychotherapy, during which time he also edited the international periodical *Zentralblatt für Psychotherapie und ihre Grenzgebiete*. He was also chairman of the board of trustees of the Lehrinstitut für Psychotherapie in 1939 and, until his death, of the Swiss Society for Practical Psychology, which he had founded in 1935. In 1948 he founded the bilingual (English and German) C. G. Jung Institute in Zurich, to which he entrusted the continuation and dissemination of his teachings and research and the training in psychotherapy of the new generation.

**Jung the man.** Justice would not be done to the genius of Jung if we were to try to understand only the scientific and professional aspects of his career. His was an extraordinary personality, combining the keenest contradictions. Contemplativeness and childlike cheerfulness, delicate sensibility and robust simplicity, cold reserve and true devotion, rigor and tolerance, humor and severity, aloofness and love for mankind, were equally prominent traits in his makeup. Except when he was troubled by the birth pangs of a new book, he generously shared his insights and explanations, both in conversation and in letters.

Freud unlocked the door to modern psychical research and psychotherapy. Jung penetrated into the psyche still deeper, shedding light on the impersonal, primeval forces that the twentieth century has confronted with horror and fear. In his untiring effort to solve intractable riddles, he constantly repeated this warning:

I am convinced that exploration of the psyche is the science of the future. . . . This is the science we need most of all, for it is gradually becoming more and more obvious that neither famine nor earthquakes nor microbes nor carcinoma, but man himself is the greatest peril to man, just because there is no adequate defense against psychic epidemics, which cause infinitely more devastation than the greatest natural catastrophes. (Jung 1944)

JOLANDE JACOBI

[For the historical context of Jung's work, see PSYCHO-ANALYSIS *and the biographies of* BLEULER; FREUD;

JANET. *For further discussion of Jung's ideas, see* ANALYTICAL PSYCHOLOGY. *Other relevant information may be found in* DREAMS; FANTASY; LITERATURE, *article on* THE PSYCHOLOGY OF LITERATURE; RELIGION.]

WORKS BY JUNG

(1902) 1957 *On the Psychology and Pathology of So-called Occult Phenomena.* Pages 3–88 in Carl Gustav Jung, *Collected Works.* Volume 1: Psychiatric Studies. New York: Pantheon. → First published as *Zur Psychologie und Pathologie sogenannter occulter Phänomene.*

(1902–1959) 1953— *Collected Works.* Vols. 1— Edited by Herbert Read et al. New York: Pantheon. → Volume 1: *Psychiatric Studies,* 1957. Volume 3: *The Psychogenesis of Mental Disease,* 1960. Volume 4: *Freud and Psychoanalysis,* 1961. Volume 5: *Symbols of Transformation,* 1956. Volume 7: *Two Essays on Analytical Psychology,* 1953. Volume 8: *The Structure and Dynamics of the Psyche,* 1960. Volume 9, Part 1: *The Archetypes and the Collective Unconscious,* 1959. Volume 9, Part 2: *Aion: Researches Into the Phenomenology of the Self,* 1959. Volume 10: *Civilization in Transition,* 1963. Volume 11: *Psychology and Religion: West and East,* 1958. Volume 12: *Psychology and Alchemy,* 1953. Volume 14: *Mysterium Coniunctionis,* 1963. Volume 16: *The Practice of Psychotherapy,* 1954. Volume 17: *The Development of Personality,* 1954. Forthcoming volumes include Volume 2: *Experimental Researches;* Volume 6: *Psychological Types;* Volume 13: *Alchemical Studies;* Volume 15: *The Spirit in Man, Art, and Literature;* and final volumes on his minor works, bibliography, and index.

(1904–1909) 1918 *Studies in Word-association: Experiments in the Diagnosis of Psychopathological Conditions Carried Out at the Psychiatric Clinic of the University of Zurich, Under the Direction of C. G. Jung.* London: Heinemann. → First published as *Diagnostische Assoziationsstudien.*

(1906) 1941 *Die psychologische Diagnose des Tatbestandes.* Zurich: Rascher.

(1907) 1960 *The Psychology of Dementia Praecox.* Pages 1–151 in Carl Gustav Jung, *Collected Works.* Volume 3: *The Psychogenesis of Mental Disease.* New York: Pantheon. → First published as *Über die Psychologie der Dementia Praecox: Ein Versuch.*

(1909–1946) 1953 *Psychological Reflections: An Anthology of the Writings of C. G. Jung.* Selected and edited by Jolande Jacobi. New York: Pantheon.

(1910) 1954 *Psychic Conflicts in a Child.* Pages 8–35 in Carl Gustav Jung, *Collected Works.* Volume 17: The Development of Personality. New York: Pantheon. → First published as "Über Konflikte der kindlichen Seele."

(1913) 1961 *Theory of Psychoanalysis.* Pages 83–226 in Carl Gustav Jung, *Collected Works.* Volume 4: Freud and Psychoanalysis. New York: Pantheon. → First published as *Versuch einer Darstellung der psychoanalytischen Theorie.*

(1916–1945) 1948 *Über psychische Energetik und das Wesen der Träume.* Zurich: Rascher. → Contains six essays, all of which appear in translation in Volume 8 of Jung 1902–1959 as *The Structure and Dynamics of the Psyche.*

(1917) 1953 *The Psychology of the Unconscious.* Pages 1–117 in Carl Gustav Jung, *Collected Works.* Volume 7: Two Essays on Analytical Psychology. New

York: Pantheon. → First published as *Die Psychologie der Unbewussten Prozesse.*

(1921) 1959 *Psychological Types.* London: Routledge. → First published as *Psychologische Typen.*

(1922–1931) 1959 *Modern Man in Search of a Soul.* London: Routledge. → First published as *Seelenprobleme der Gegenwart.*

(1926) 1954 Analytical Psychology and Education: Three Lectures. Pages 65–132 in Carl Gustav Jung, *Collected Works.* Volume 17: The Development of Personality. New York: Pantheon. → First published as *Analytische Psychologie und Erziehung.*

(1928) 1953 The Relations Between the Ego and the Unconscious. Pages 119–239 in Carl Gustav Jung, *Collected Works.* Volume 7: Two Essays on Analytical Psychology. New York: Pantheon. → First published as *Die Beziehungen zwischen dem Ich und dem Unbewussten.*

(1929) 1962 Commentary. Pages 77–137 in T'ai i chin hua tsung chih, *The Secret of the Golden Flower: A Chinese Book of Life.* New York: Harcourt. → First published as "Europäischer Kommentar."

(1929–1934) 1947 *Wirklichkeit der Seele: Anwendung und Fortschritte der neueren Psychologie.* Zurich: Rascher.

(1930–1940) 1950 *Gestaltungen des Unbewussten.* Zurich: Rascher.

(1932) 1958 Psychotherapists or the Clergy. Pages 325–347 in Carl Gustav Jung, *Collected Works.* Volume 11: Psychology and Religion: West and East. New York: Pantheon. → First published as *Die Beziehungen der Psychotherapie zur Seelsorge.*

(1935) 1958 Psychological Commentary on *The Tibetan Book of the Dead.* Pages 509–526 in Carl Gustav Jung, *Collected Works.* Volume 11: Psychology and Religion: West and East. New York: Pantheon. → First published as "Psychologischer Kommentar zum *Bardo Thödol.*"

(1935–1947) 1954 *Von den Wurzeln des Bewusstseins: Studien über den Archetypus.* Zurich: Rascher.

(1936–1945) 1946 *Aufsätze zur Zeitgeschichte.* Zurich: Rascher.

(1938) 1958 Psychology and Religion. Pages 3–105 in Carl Gustav Jung, *Collected Works.* Volume 11: Psychology and Religion: West and East. New York: Pantheon. → First published in English.

(1940) 1959 The Psychology of the Child Archetype. Pages 151–181 in Carl Gustav Jung, *Collected Works.* Volume 9, Part 1: The Archetypes and the Collective Unconscious. New York: Pantheon. → First published as "Zur Psychologie des Kind-Archetypus."

(1941) 1959 The Psychological Aspects of the Kore. Pages 182–203 in Carl Gustav Jung, *Collected Works.* Volume 9, Part 1: The Archetypes and the Collective Unconscious. New York: Pantheon. → First published as "Zum psychologischen Aspekt der Kore-Figur."

1942 *Paracelsica: Zwei Vorlesungen über den Arzt und Philosophen Theophrastus.* Zurich: Rascher.

(1942–1946) 1953 *Symbolik des Geistes: Studien über psychische Phänomenologie.* Zurich: Rascher.

(1943) 1954 The Gifted Child. Pages 135–145 in Carl Gustav Jung, *Collected Works.* Volume 17: The Development of Personality. New York: Pantheon. → First published as "Der Begabte."

(1944) 1962 Epilogue. In Carl Gustav Jung, *L'homme à la découverte de son âme.* 6th ed. Geneva: Éditions du Mont-Blanc.

(1946) 1954 Psychology of the Transference. Pages 163–321 in Carl Gustav Jung, *Collected Works.* Volume 16:

The Practice of Psychotherapy. New York: Pantheon. → First published as *Die Psychologie der Übertragung.*

(1952a) 1958 Answer to Job. Pages 355–470 in Carl Gustav Jung, *Collected Works.* Volume 11: Psychology and Religion: West and East. New York: Pantheon. → First published as *Antwort auf Hiob.*

(1952b) 1960 Synchronicity: An Acausal Connecting Principle. Pages 417–519 in Carl Gustav Jung, *Collected Works.* Volume 8: The Structure and Dynamics of the Psyche. New York: Pantheon. → First published as "Synchronizität als ein Prinzip akausaler Zusammenhänge."

(1957) 1963 The Undiscovered Self (Present and Future). Pages 245–305 in Carl Gustav Jung, *Collected Works.* Volume 10: Civilization in Transition. New York: Pantheon. → First published as *Gegenwart und Zukunft.*

(1958a) 1960 Schizophrenia. Pages 256–271 in Carl Gustav Jung, *Collected Works.* Volume 3: The Psychogenesis of Mental Disease. New York: Pantheon. → First published in German.

(1958b) 1963 Flying Saucers: A Modern Myth. Pages 307–433 in Carl Gustav Jung, *Collected Works.* Volume 10: Civilization in Transition. New York: Pantheon. → First published as *Ein moderner Mythos: Von Dingen, die am Himmel gesehen werden.*

(1958c) 1963 A Psychological View of Conscience. Pages 437–455 in Carl Gustav Jung, *Collected Works.* Volume 10: Civilization in Transition. New York: Pantheon. → First published as "Das Gewissen in psychologischer Sicht."

SUPPLEMENTARY BIBLIOGRAPHY

ADLER, GERHARD 1948 *Studies in Analytical Psychology.* New York: Norton.

CLARK, ROBERT ALFRED 1953 *Six Talks on Jung's Psychology.* Pittsburgh, Pa.: Boxwood.

FORDHAM, MICHAEL 1957 *New Developments in Analytical Psychology.* London: Routledge.

FORDHAM, MICHAEL (editor) 1963 *Contacts With Jung: Essays on the Influence of His Work and Personality.* London: Tavistock.

GLOVER, EDWARD (1950) 1956 *Freud or Jung?* New York: Meridian.

HARDING, M. ESTHER 1948 *Psychic Energy: Its Source and Goal.* With a foreword by C. G. Jung. New York: Pantheon.

JACOBI, JOLANDE (1940) 1951 *The Psychology of C. G. Jung.* Rev. ed. New Haven: Yale Univ. Press. → First published in German. A paperback edition was published in 1962 by the Yale University Press.

JACOBI, JOLANDE (1957) 1959 *Complex, Archetype, Symbol in the Psychology of C. G. Jung.* New York: Pantheon. → First published in German.

JACOBI, JOLANDE 1966 *The Way to Individuation.* London: Hodder & Stoughton.

JUNG INSTITUT, ZURICH 1955 *Studien zur analytischen Psychologie C. G. Jungs.* 2 vols. Zurich: Rascher.

PROGOFF, IRA 1953 *Jung's Psychology and Its Social Meaning.* New York: Julian.

## JUNOD, HENRI ALEXANDRE

Henri Alexandre Junod (1863–1934), missionary and anthropologist, was born of Swiss Protestant parents in the canton of Neuchâtel, Switzerland. He spent 26 years as a missionary among the Thonga tribes of southern Africa, and his book, *The Life of a South African Tribe* (1912–1913), has been universally acclaimed as one of the greatest monographs in African ethnography.

Although his professors at the Collège Latin and the Gymnase in Neuchâtel expected him to have a brilliant career in science and natural history, Junod decided to dedicate his life to the service of God. He was ordained in 1887, following theological studies in Neuchâtel, Basel, and Berlin. At the request of the council of the Mission Romande he left on his first missionary tour of Africa in 1889, returning to Switzerland in 1896. After three other tours—1899–1903, 1904–1909, and 1913–1920—Junod spent the last 14 years of his life as agent for the Mission Romande in Geneva. During that time he also wrote up his anthropological material and participated in scientific discussions.

Soon after his arrival in Africa, Junod began to apply his scientific skills to the study of the life around him. With the help of an illiterate instructor he made a systematic analysis of Ronga, one of the numerous Thonga dialects (see 1896). While giving religious instruction at the school for evangelists in Rikatla and later in Shilouvane, Transvaal, he kept careful records of the tales his students told him and of the customs they described, and he analyzed these records. In his early years in Africa his interest in natural history persisted, and he collected plant specimens, insects, and butterflies. (His collection of southeast African butterflies is preserved in museums in Lausanne, Lourenço Marques, and South Africa; various specimens bear his name.) It was not until 1895 that he seriously shifted from entomology to ethnography.

Junod was familiar with the work of his major contemporaries in anthropology, that of Frazer, Tylor, Herbert Spencer, Gobineau, Frobenius, Schmidt, Boas, and Lévy-Bruhl, and he corresponded with many of these men. He used Frazer's questionnaire, designed especially for collecting ethnographic material on matters of taboo. His use of van Gennep's framework for analyzing *rites de passage* remains a model for many students. While he did not explicitly acknowledge men like Durkheim, René Hubert, and Marcel Mauss, their influence is evident in his major book on the Thonga.

Junod's aim was to test general theories against the body of factual material that he was accumulating: he analyzed and interpreted the customs and religion of the Thonga in the light of prevailing evolutionary theory. Compared to more recent students of the Thonga, Junod wrote extensively on religion and ritual to the neglect of political structure and institutions, law and legal institutions, and economic systems.

In his approach to field observation Junod was a pioneer. He was among the first Africanists to concentrate on the details of the life of a single people and so came to hold in south African ethnography an esteemed position similar to that held by R. S. Rattray in west African ethnography. It was his conviction that to be truly scientific, ethnographic description must be limited to one well-defined tribe and that the data must be related only to a limited locality, since in a single tribe there are different clans, and customs vary among these clans. He felt, therefore, that the geographical classification of facts is of the greatest importance.

Junod desired to "write the facts carefully and to describe them accurately." He had an eye for what was significant to the people in a particular society and vividly described such customs as the moving of a village, and such rituals as the destruction of a hut after death. At the time and in the area of south Africa that he was studying, traditional aspects of culture had as yet been little touched by the advent of the white man and could therefore be isolated and precisely defined. He never shrank from recording customs that were morally repugnant to him. He was not satisfied with simply reproducing verbatim the description of customs by his informants but always attempted to set the described custom in its place in the dynamic processes and trends of social life, knitting it into what Malinowski called the "all-embracing manifestation" of that social life.

On the evidence of his field material Junod questioned many widely held anthropological theories. In an article entitled "Le noir africain: Comment faut-il le juger?" (1931) he suggested that Gobineau's treatise on racial inequality might have been modified had he known that Africans share the dolichocephalic characteristic with the "noble Aryan." He suggested also that denigrators of African languages might well profit from memorizing ten of the Bantu's loveliest proverbs, and he cast doubt on the validity of Lévy-Bruhl's theory that primitive man has a "prelogical and magical mind."

Junod was concerned with more than his avocation—the scientific study of the Thonga; he also devoutly desired to help them. He realized that in order to achieve this vocational goal it was necessary for him to understand the meaning behind the observable facts he was recording. Facts isolated for scientific ends had to have coherence in moral and religious terms: all items of a people's culture or social life must be seen in their interrelation, and all have a purpose. His approach is admirably illustrated in his article "Le sacrifice dans l'ancestolâtrie sud-africaine" (1932). He attacked those scholars, notably Alfred Loisy (1920), who claimed that sacrifices are meaningless and without value; that a ritual sacrifice is nothing but a "sacred action . . . lost in the void" and never more than "magical action at the point of departure." Fundamental to Junod's attack was his religious theory of life, which held that man, whether primitive or civilized, eternally reaches for God and continuously expresses this sentiment of absolute dependence. Junod argued that ritual sacrifices are primitive man's way of satisfying his need to express child–father dependency, extending it through time in the worship of his gods—his ancestors. To Junod the ancestor cult is but a phase in the evolution of religion toward the notion of God and is not antithetical to this notion. Ritual sacrifices are thus a meaningful and necessary element of a stage of evolution. The scientists of Junod's time had little use for the transcendental dimensions he constantly introduced into scientific discussions, and Junod was well aware of their views. More recently, his departure from the largely mechanistic analysis of human phenomena has acquired great relevance for social science.

VIOLAINE JUNOD

[*For the context of Junod's work, see* AFRICAN SOCIETY, *article on* SUB-SAHARAN AFRICA; RELIGION; RITUAL; *and the biographies of* DURKHEIM; FRAZER; GENNEP; LÉVY-BRUHL; MAUSS; SMITH, WILLIAM ROBERTSON.]

### WORKS BY JUNOD

1896   *Grammaire ronga suivie d'un "Manuel de conversation et d'un vocabulaire ronga-portugais-français-anglais."* Lausanne (Switzerland): Bridel.

1897   *Les chants et les contes des Ba-Ronga de la baie de Delagoa.* Lausanne (Switzerland): Bridel.

1898   *Les Ba-Ronga: Étude ethnographique sur les indigènes de la baie de Delagoa.* Neuchâtel (Switzerland): Attinger.

(1907) 1932   *Elementary Grammar of the Thonga–Shangaan Language.* 2d ed. Lausanne (Switzerland): Mission Suisse dans l'Afrique du Sud.

1911   *Zidji: Étude des moeurs sud-africaines.* Saint-Blaise (Switzerland): Foyer Solidariste.

(1912–1913) 1962   *The Life of a South African Tribe.* 2 vols. New Hyde Park, N.Y.: University Books. → Volume 1: *Social Life.* Volume 2: *Mental Life.*

1931   Le noir africain: Comment faut-il le juger? *Africa* (London) 4:330–342.

1932   Le sacrifice dans l'ancestolâtrie sud-africaine. *Archives de psychologie* 23:305–335.

### SUPPLEMENTARY BIBLIOGRAPHY

CHATELAIN, C. W. (compiler) 1909   *Pocket Dictionary: Thonga (Shangaan)–English, English–Thonga (Shangaan).* Preceded by an elementary grammar by Rev. H. A. Junod. Lausanne (Switzerland): Bridel.

JUNOD, HENRI PHILIPPE 1934   *Henri-A. Junod: Missionnaire et savant; 1863–1934.* Lausanne (Switzerland): Mission Suisse dans l'Afrique du Sud.

LOISY, ALFRED 1920   *Essai historique sur le sacrifice.* Paris: Nourry.

# JURISPRUDENCE

Jurisprudence has had controversial definitions since classical times. To avoid recapitulating the history of these learned disputes, the broadest possible connotation of the term that is permissible under current usage will be adopted here. In civil law countries "jurisprudence" is a technical term referring to a settled course of judicial decision. This usage is also known in the common law countries. Indeed, in the United States, the term "jurisprudence" is a general honorific designation for the more ordinary term "law." Jurisprudence as an academic subject in the United States can mean the study of law as an autonomous science (analytical jurisprudence); or of the nature of justice (philosophical jurisprudence); or of the relation of law to society (sociological jurisprudence). In civil law countries, philosophical jurisprudence is usually called "philosophy of law"; sociological jurisprudence, "sociology of law," and analytical jurisprudence is subsumed under the general category of "positivism."

## Historical perspective

Two main sources of jurisprudential thought and experience emerge from antiquity. These are the philosophical speculation of the Greeks and the legal and administrative practice of the Romans. The speculative genius of Plato issued in the *Republic* and *The Laws.* Aristotle consolidated this body of philosophical thought and brought to it the strength of empirical observation in his treatises on ethics and on politics.

Greek speculation on the nature of law centered on the question of whether law exists by nature or by convention. The Greek philosophers examined this fundamental question so thoroughly that it is hard to find instances of contemporary speculation that escape the bounds set by the Greek thinkers.

Roman law, on the other hand, had an autonomous development based on a millennium of judicial experience and administrative practice. Greek philosophical theories permeated the essence of Roman law, but the slow, steady accumulation of legal experience and its crystallization into general principles of law and finally into codification gave Roman law its enduring character. For the Romans, jurisprudence always remained an eminently practical study.

These two sources, namely, Greek theories of the nature of justice and Roman experience in political administration, became, after religion, the most dominant aspect of medieval culture. The idea of the Holy Roman Empire with the Corpus Juris Civilis as a statute binding all Christendom and the Roman Catholic church with its manifold forms of law as spiritual authority for all Christians formed a coherent theoretical structure.

St. Thomas Aquinas divided law into the eternal, the divine, the natural, and the human. It will be noted that two of these, the eternal law and the natural law, are theories of the nature of justice. The divine law and the human law are ordained or posited. We thus see the divisions of antiquity continued in the form of notions of law that exists by nature and law that is ordained, whether by God or by man.

This distinction survived the Renaissance revolutions in science and government. Indeed, the great political revolutions were waged in the name of a secularized law of nature abstracted from the mind of man and considered the true mark of his humanity. Reason, as higher law, was held to legitimize revolt against the dictates of sovereign will.

This fundamental divergence of opinion on the nature of law came down to the twentieth century, the English-speaking common law countries heavily committed to the view that law is the ordainment of a lawfully constituted sovereign; and the civil law countries alternating between a social scientific view of law as positive enactment and law as existing in some sense independently of human disposition.

## Methods of jurisprudence

The basic methods of modern investigators in the legal field are either speculative analysis or empirical investigation. The dominant trends in modern jurisprudence are toward natural law as a matter for speculation and toward the empirical study of law as one of the behavioral sciences.

**Analytical jurisprudence.** The principal method throughout the world by which legal materials are studied is the method of analysis. Authoritative legal prescriptions are collected, compared, contrasted, and synthesized. This activity, stemming from the most ancient times when its practice was hardly separate from religious exegesis, still goes on in the same way and accounts for all but a small fraction of scholarly activity in the field of law. Monographs, treatises, encyclopedias, digests, pamphlets, and books on all aspects of the law pour out in forms that are not too different from those that were extant in the classical period of ancient Rome.

This immense legal product is in turn material for analytical jurisprudence, which attempts to raise the level of abstraction. In addition to this secondary material, analytical jurisprudence also concerns itself with primary legal data, that is, statutes, cases, executive orders and decrees, and other legal prescriptions.

In earlier days, the method of analysis was felt to constitute an autonomous science of law. Its organon, in turn, was taken to be Aristotelian logic, even though many of the fundamental classifications long antedated Aristotle, having been derived from religious and theological sources. Authoritative Roman models were Gaius' Institutes and, for later times, the Corpus Juris itself, especially its Institutes.

Analytical jurisprudence seeks to impose upon the body of authoritative legal materials the logical constraints of clarity, consistency, coherence, and nonredundancy. It attempts to discover basic legal conceptions, basic legal categories, and basic legal truth propositions. It inherits these ideals from traditional logic.

Modern developments take two forms. The first, exemplified pre-eminently in the work of Hans Kelsen (1945), is speculative analysis of what is taken to be the inherent *structure* of legal systems. In Kelsen's work, the analysis discloses a hierarchy of authoritative norms in terms of which legal prescriptions can be arranged. Kelsen's basic materials were primarily those of civil law [*see* KELSEN]. It differs from traditional common law analysis, such as that of John Austin, which followed more or less the categories, classifications, and conceptions used in the law historically [*see* AUSTIN]. Yet more different is the contemporary work of H. L. A. Hart (1961) and his followers, which, although basically analytical, accepts much of the work of sociological jurists (to be discussed) and analyzes law by means of the methods of the Oxford school of analytical philosophy (see Fuller 1958).

Modern logic is slowly making its influence felt in the second type of analytical jurisprudence, that which is coming to be called juristic logic. The powerful tools of symbolic logic, which have remade modern mathematics and which form the theoretical basis of much work in the behavioral sciences, such as game theory and information theory, are only beginning to have an effect on law. Law and electronics is another facet of analytical jurisprudence that is being developed as a result of the current explosion in computer technology (Cowan 1963).

**Philosophical jurisprudence.** Philosophy has had so pervasive and enduring an influence on the study of law that in many countries jurisprudence is called the philosophy of law. Roscoe Pound has written on this subject for more than half a century, and his voluminous writings (1959) should be referred to for its history and development [see POUND]. It is perhaps not too much to say that every important system of philosophy has or has had its correlate in a philosophy of law.

Law consists of a body of obligations and a body of facts. According to whether attention is focused on one or the other, philosophical emphasis shifts. Where obligation is thought of as paramount, one easily finds himself led to the ideal element of law, to theories of justice, to idealistic philosophy, to ethics, and to value theory. Where the factual element obtrudes, one turns his attention to authoritative legal materials, to positivism, to empirical philosophy, to epistemology, and to science.

Needless to say, good sense invariably suggests a synthesis (Jenkins 1959), but this sensible opinion does not have an opportunity to get itself heard until the warring factions reach a high state of tension. Then in the history of philosophy, as in the history of the philosophy of law, the grand syntheses present themselves.

At the present the two major opponents, natural law and positivism, are in a relatively high state of dialectical opposition, but no over-all synthesis is apparently in the offing, despite the heroic efforts of Lon Fuller (1964). A report on the present state of the philosophy of law, then, must necessarily be in terms of the opposition of the ideal and the factual elements in law.

*Idealism.* As a philosophical movement, idealism has two main facets: idea-ism and ideal-ism. It emphasizes the importance of ideas in man's knowledge of the world and of ideals in human action. It brings such leading notions as unity, coherence, rationality, and the power of reflection to the task of understanding the world and formulates ideals of justice, the value of the good, and the worth of reason and human dignity in the study of law and morals. In the common parlance of the jurists, it is said to be concerned with the law as it ought to be rather than with the law as it is. This last point is shared with the doctrine of natural law. Where idealism still exerts influence on the philosophy of law, it is chiefly in the form of Neo-Kantianism and Neo-Hegelianism.

*Natural law.* There is a universal temptation to use the ancient term "natural law" as the antithesis of all positivistic, pragmatic, and even analytical theories of the nature of law. Natural law assumes the existence of basic inherent principles of justice which, especially in times of social stress, are assumed to be paramount over ordained legal pre-scriptions. It also serves as a constant critique of the existing law. That it takes itself to be of more profound significance than the body of law which it criticizes is perhaps not altogether unexpected.

Natural law theories are presently of great and growing importance throughout the entire jurisprudential world. Where the treatment of natural law is secular it becomes a theory of value and hence has much significance for the behavioral sciences. Natural law is the form which the perennial undeclared war between law and ethics takes. In periods of religious orthodoxy, ethics aligns itself with religion and attacks the secular character of law as a conflict-resolving agency of the community. In such periods, lawyers are apt to be clerics.

Where law becomes secular, ethics tends to become humanistic. The ultimate source of ethical obligation is seen to be human reason itself. A rationalistic ethics emerges and with it rationalistic natural law. All species of revolt against the coercive power of positive legal enactments tend to call themselves natural law. Indeed, much of what one would be tempted to call a balanced view between the law as it is and the law as it ought to be is very likely to be considered a species of natural law. To the extent that secular theories of value are currently mixed up with theories of natural law, the latter becomes of consequence to students of the behavioral sciences [see NATURAL LAW].

*Phenomenology.* This brand of philosophy is compounded of idealism, empiricism, and subjectivism. It aims to deal only with phenomena and thus distrusts all noumenal, or nonexperienceable, entities. Phenomenology seeks to make knowledge clear and distinct, not by means of rational intuitions but by the intuitions of experience. It attempts to bring to consciousness all the unconscious elements of knowledge by an intensive reflection upon the stream of experience. It is thus a radical subjectivism that has its counterparts in art and in the humanistic studies. For social science it is important in its emphasizing of subjectivity and consciousness, elements the social sciences, with their orientation toward natural science, often find convenient to neglect. The influence of phenomenology on law is hard to assess. Law, like behavioral science, is heavily oriented toward objective behavior. Since this leads to a slighting of the subjective element of human behavior, rapport between phenomenology and law is effected more closely in the civil law countries, with their long history of attachment to idealistic philosophies, than in the more objectively oriented countries of the common law.

*Existentialism.* This species of idealism is more an aesthetics and an ethics than an epistemology.

It does not ask how we acquire knowledge but, rather, how we should live. Its concern is with human existence and the aesthetic and moral dilemmas with which existence confronts the individual. Its disdain for metaphysics does not make it any the less an idealism, for the last thing it will accept in justification of human action is any existing state of affairs. It is interested, in brief, in what the concrete single human being ought to do with his life. Existentialism is fascinated with some legal problems, particularly those that raise problems of ultimate moral obligation. Its influence on law may become very great, since law has a profound concern for the individual, since it sets the stage for most of the moral dilemmas that modern man faces, and since it is very badly in need of an aesthetic. Nevertheless, existentialism is more an intellectual movement than a systematic philosophy, and its influence on law and the behavioral sciences is too diffuse for accurate assaying.

*Positivism.* This philosophical system which emphasizes attachment to facts, data, secular values, and scientific humanism has had its counterpart in law since the Greek classical period. Presently, its revolutionary effect in opposition to natural law is almost spent. Hence, its importance today is felt as a guiding principle in empirical research in law. In the United States, the current form of positivism is pragmatism. Legal positivism is a philosophical attitude that favors only the examination of authoritative legal materials as actual legal existents. Its attitude toward value theory is either to exclude it from the domain of law or to reduce value to fact [*see* POSITIVISM].

*Pragmatism.* Pragmatism is the American variant of positivism. It is the most pervasive influence in the field of American jurisprudence. All sectors of the American jurisprudential continuum are heavily influenced by the national bias for action-oriented, practical determinations both in law and in ethics.

*Realism.* Philosophical realism was thought in antiquity to be concerned with the reality of universals. Its opposite was nominalism, for which these universals were only names. In this understanding, natural law theories were taken to be realistic. In modern times, and especially in the philosophy of law, realism is understood as the opposite of conceptualism. Modern realism has become empiricism, whether psychological or sociological. It has a strong positivistic bent [*see* LLEWELLYN].

*Dialectical materialism.* The philosophical movement of dialectical materialism has become as closely identified with communism as is scholasticism with the Roman Catholic church. Its materialism stems from that branch of materialistic philosophy which holds that all ideas and motivations, in a word, consciousness, result from matter, the physical universe, and from human action. Its dialectic is based on the Hegelian philosophy which seeks in world history the principles by which change occurs both in the material world and in human consciousness. Developments of the theory of dialectical materialism are inseparable from the history of Soviet political–legal thought [*see* MARXISM].

**Sociological jurisprudence.** Sociological jurisprudence originated in the United States chiefly under the direction of Roscoe Pound, whose works should be consulted for a very extended treatment of the subject. Briefly, it is a program for the integration of law and the social sciences, which aims at creating the conditions under which law may move from a body of authoritative and quasi-autonomous principles to a body of scientific knowledge of the behavior of human beings under the conditions of law.

Sociological jurisprudence attempts to substitute for such basic legal conceptions as right and duty such social psychological conceptions as interest, need, desire, or drive. This movement has had the effect of undermining the primacy of legal conceptions and the autonomy of legal study. It relativizes the foundations of law and prepares the way for a study of the social origins of law and the social effects of legal prescriptions in action.

Sociological jurisprudence has not yet made law a social science. Currently, it is under attack from natural law, which it attempts to neutralize by changing natural law into a secular problem of the nature of human value. More important than the active opposition of natural law theorists to sociological jurisprudence is the immense conservatism of the legal profession itself. Being a substantial body of professional workers administering an age-old apparatus for settling human conflict on traditional lines, the legal community does not directly oppose the attempts to make law a science. It simply ignores them. This means that legal theorists can very rapidly get out of touch with their base in the living law. Theory can quickly outrun practice with the consequent effect that it becomes empty abstraction. Still, to the extent that it does remain in touch with its sources in the law, sociological jurisprudence is having a cumulative effect throughout the world, particularly on the teaching profession and more particularly in sections of the world where social science itself shows signs of development. The climate needed for the development of social science is the one in which socio-logical jurisprudence may be expected to thrive.

Sociological jurisprudence leads to empirical data gathering of the sort practiced in the behavioral sciences. It favors empirical research by jurisprudential theorists and the use of behavioral science learning in the law [see JUDICIARY, *article on* JUDICIAL BEHAVIOR].

### Trends in jurisprudence

World-wide movements in jurisprudence are so complex that one hesitates to speak with any degree of confidence about them. At most, one can try to indicate general trends in various countries or parts of the world, based upon surveys by area specialists (see Friedmann 1945; Friedrich 1955; Szladits 1955–1962; 1959).

**The United States.** Pragmatism with its action-oriented pluralistic approach is still the dominant philosophical influence in the United States (Llewellyn 1928–1960). It is strongly opposed by various shades and degrees of natural law theory, both neoscholastic (Brown 1960) and secular. The prominence of value theory studies in all the behavioral sciences has led to the emergence of different kinds of natural law theories. These movements can be followed in the pages of the excellent *Natural Law Forum*, published by the University of Notre Dame.

Sociological jurisprudence led in the United States to extreme pluralism and skepticism about the existence of fundamental legal conceptions and about the existence of uniformity in the disposition of legal matters. There has been a reaction (Llewellyn 1960; Wasserstrom 1961) against the excesses of this extreme atomicity. There is much evidence that the use of social science materials and methods in the study of law is in for a broad proliferation (Cohen et al. 1958; Jones 1962).

There is some work being done in analytic jurisprudence at the philosophical level (Kelsen 1957; Shuman 1963). Of course, the immense business of analyzing and commenting upon the various aspects of the legal process, represented in the main in the law reviews, shows no sign of abating.

Although the judicial process is still the dominant concern of most legal theorists in the United States, there is a growing interest in comparative law (Hall 1963) and in international law, particularly as this last subject is related to prospects for lasting international peace. These subjects readily link law and political theory. The work of Lasswell and Cleveland (Conference on Science, Philosophy, and Religion . . . 1962) and McDougal and his

colleagues (1961; 1963) on policy science is very influential among U.S. students of international law and relations. Space law, on the other hand, appears still to be only an extrapolation from traditional doctrines of international law.

The legal community has not yet shown much interest in the possible relevance of decision theory and game theory for the study of law, although political scientists and other behavioral scientists are embracing the newer technology, including computer capabilities (Cowan 1963). As decision theory advances more deeply into the area of actual (nonrational) human decisional behavior, it may be expected to encounter the trials and tribulations that have beset legal decision making from the beginning of history. The application of electronics, especially computer technology, to law is burgeoning.

Political theorists are showing increasing fondness for the application of factor analysis to the decisions of appellate courts (Schubert 1960), notably the Supreme Court of the United States. Many other connections between law and science, such as law and medicine, law and psychiatry, law and social science methods of proof, are coming in for increasing attention. Symbolic logic is being applied to the notions of obligation, command, and imperatives in general (Cowan 1963). And philosophers are becoming increasingly interested in the relation of law to ethics (Nakhnikian 1957. For general references about U.S. jurisprudence, see *Annual Survey of American Law;* Bodenheimer 1962; Hurst 1960; Hall 1958; Coing 1952; Patterson 1953; Reuschlein 1951.)

**Great Britain and the Commonwealth.** It is fortunate that the Anglo–American tradition of analytical jurisprudence is being kept alive in England (Hart 1953; Guest 1961; Dias & Hughes 1957), even though it has almost disappeared in the United States. The work of H. L. A. Hart (1954; 1961) continues in the spirit of Austinian positivism, but it has greatly expanded the subject matter beyond the relatively simple notion of "law as the command of a sovereign." Hart and his associates bring to analytical jurisprudence much of the wealth of technique of philosophical analysis without, however, getting lost in either finespun semantic speculations or the intricacies of modern symbolic logic. It might be said of this work that its structure is a sort of layman's logic of scientific method applied to the body of legal prescriptions and to the social matrix in which they are embedded [see DUTY].

Aside from this dominant note of analytical

jurisprudence there is much evidence of the influence of sociological and realistic jurisprudence in the work of other legal philosophers in Great Britain. The academic furor centering about the work of Hart at Oxford seems, unfortunately, to have somewhat obscured this important development. In the course of time it should become easier to obtain a more balanced view, as a result of which social scientists will begin to perceive more clearly those elements of jurisprudential development in Great Britain that should be of interest to them.

*Canada.* The dominant analytical jurisprudential outlook in Canada (see McWhinney 1958) has long been enriched by influences of realistic jurisprudence in the United States. Many teachers of law were attracted to the sociological views of Roscoe Pound and to the "revolutionary" exploits of the new realists. The basic economic and cultural developments of the country paralleled to a certain degree those of the United States, thus making reception of its jurisprudential views natural.

On the other hand, since Canada carries both the civil law (Quebec) and the common law as competing and cooperative factors in its exploding economy, the Canadian student of jurisprudence is forced to give attention to comparative law as a living reality and, therefore, as a basic factor in any theory of the nature of law. Here the natural positivistic bent of the common law lawyer must be reconciled with the normal preference of the Catholic civil law lawyer for the natural law.

*Australia.* A very vigorous recent movement in jurisprudence in Australia stems from the work of Julius Stone, whose monumental *Province and Function of Law* (1946) introduced sociological jurisprudence to the country. Stone's later work in international law is heavily charged with jurisprudential elements. Analytical jurisprudence is represented by the work of George W. Paton (1946).

In addition to the main currents of analytic and sociological jurisprudence, attention is being given to juristic logic by I. Tammelo and to natural law by W. L. Morison and others (Lumb 1960). Indeed, the whole gamut of jurisprudential thought seems to be represented in this thriving legal philosophical community.

**Latin America.** Throughout Latin America, as in all countries outside the area of the English and American common law, legal philosophy is a standard part of the law curriculum. There is, therefore, an immense amount of activity in what in the United States is called jurisprudence. Fortunately, there are useful surveys in English: the work of Josef L. Kunz (1954) and a thoroughly documented historical survey of value theory in Latin America by Luis Recaséns-Siches (1958).

The familiar dispute between positivism and natural law goes on with variations introduced by differences in national economy and culture. The basic philosophical movements of Europe are taken up in Latin America in pristine form and then modified to meet specific needs. Even positivism is taken in a purer form there than in related movements in the common law countries. Neo-Kantian and Neo-Hegelian philosophies are still exerting considerable influence. In the newer movements of phenomenology and existentialism the Latin American legal theorists exhibit their extreme sensitivity to the intellectual and philosophical climate of continental Europe. For example, even Neo-Thomist thought is combined with phenomenology to produce a new brand of natural law (Recaséns-Siches 1958).

There is not much evidence of sociological jurisprudence or activity in empirical data gathering or other techniques of the social sciences connected with the philosophy of law. These activities, where they exist, are more likely to be regarded as part of the sociology of law.

**Germany.** The furious attack waged by natural law theorists (Maihofer 1962) on German legal positivism after the fall of the Nazi regime seems to be waning. After World War II, positivism and logical positivism were so thoroughly in disrepute that the natural law sector in turn was forced to accommodate all shades of legal philosophical opinion in the country. The result was that natural law fell into many discordant parts, each, however, adhering to some "higher law" theory or other. The secular-minded soon began to talk about value theory rather than natural law. Religiously oriented natural law theorists, whether Catholic or Protestant, found themselves embracing some aspects of phenomenology or existentialism. Since almost everyone tried to crowd into the natural law tent, Catholic and Protestant natural law theorists came to study even Marxist dialectical materialism—not, however, with the avowed purpose of adopting it.

In the 1960s the positivistically inclined scholars were gaining prominence. Their position is that higher law theories, while they may and indeed must serve as a critique of the justness of positive enactment, are nevertheless not able to take the place of that which they criticize. Law is "after all" what is positively ordained, they say, and therefore must merit study in its own name. There is no doubt that this movement is destined to grow.

Much of what is called sociological jurisprudence in the United States is studied in Germany as the sociology of law or perhaps as just plain sociology. The legal community is beginning to notice the possibilities of law and electronics, and it is even conceivable that this subject might receive attention from the legal philosophers.

Meanwhile, Germany continues to export the whole range of her developed theories of the philosophy of law to the civil law countries. This is accompanied by a corresponding interest on the part of German legal philosophers in their traditional legal philosophical movements. The most important of these are still Neo-Kantianism, Neo-Hegelianism, natural law theories (secular and religious), phenomenology, existentialism, dialectical materialism, and even logical positivism. This well-settled, traditional, legal philosophical activity, in abeyance under the Hitler regime, picked up immediately after World War II and is once more in full swing. At the present time, no new philosophical movement, and hence no new legal philosophical movement, is evident. But the ingredients of the older systems apparently can be agglomerated indefinitely. The philosophical situation, to sum it up in a word, is eclectic. (For general references about German jurisprudence, see Bodenheimer 1954.)

**Italy.** It is reported (Bobbio 1959) that the legal philosophers and the "jurists" seem to be drawing more closely together. Philosophers of law in Italy have always prided themselves on the purity of their interest in philosophy, leaving the study of jurisprudence to the jurists.

The fascist regime in Italy, like that in Germany, had used positivistic theories of law to bolster its *de jure* claims to sovereign competence. The fall of Mussolini precipitated the same reaction against legal positivism in the form of a resurgence of the always influential natural law. Indeed, there is even a movement to formulate natural law as already existing law in the same sense as positive law but paramount to it. This position, in all probability too radical for a civil law country, is likely to be abandoned unless the position of the judiciary is strengthened to a point commensurate with that in the United States.

What is reported to be taking place in Italy is a gradual abandonment of extreme legal formalism and conceptualism. This may prepare the way for something like sociological jurisprudence, although this is more likely to result from the activities of the jurists and the sociologists of law than from those of the legal philosophers.

The philosophy of law is still very much concerned with Neo-Kantianism and Neo-Hegelianism, with phenomenology and existentialism, and with the various shades and degrees of natural law, both religious and secular.

**France.** Recent developments in the philosophy of law in France are far from spectacular. Indeed, there seems to be a widespread tendency for the various schools to draw closer together on the basis of a rather commonsensical notion that extremes ought to be avoided. This does not result in a philosophical eclecticism. Paradoxically, the conventional philosophies as such are not favored by the legal philosophers. The tendency is rather toward a kind of secular scholasticism. The common core of agreement seems to be a general existentialist concern that law base itself squarely on man and man's life in society. Rationalism comes under frequent attack in the land of Descartes. It has not succeeded in giving birth to a rapport between modern logic and the law. Comte, although still defended, is often looked upon as the creator of a formal, sterile, nonliving positivism. Natural law is criticized as otherworldly. And, finally, even the prevailing existentialism is condemned for its excesses.

One interesting aspect of this widespread agreement by the legal philosophers in favor of common sense is paralleled in the behavior of the French jurists. There is discernible in the course of judicial decision a greater willingness to get rid of the remnants of the rigid formalism for which the French courts have long been criticized in the interests of a more adequate concern for the needs of society (Savatier 1948; Carbonnier 1955–1957). The French appear to have concluded that the condition of humanity is to be one of permanent crisis. Not only legal philosophy but also the very forms of law, therefore, must be plastic enough to reflect the movements of people engaged in continuous political and social upheaval. The law must keep its eye fixed steadily on its subject matter, man himself.

This does not mean that traditional movements are neglected (Batiffol 1960). Natural law, especially among the Catholic philosophers, continues to be cultivated. There is much attention paid to the philosophical explication of basic legal conceptions and of the definition of law. And, of course, the more or less "orthodox" forms of existentialism and phenomenology, French and German, maintain their pressure on all schools.

Despite the widespread criticism of positivism referred to above, it would be impossible to over-emphasize the immense importance of the positivistic outlook in the daily life of the law, of its jurists, and, finally—despite their vigorous protests —of the philosophers of law themselves. Positivism is deeply ingrained in the very substance of the legal process, French or otherwise. It seems to be the essence of legal professionalism. After every excursion into newfangled philosophical movements, the law turns back to the mundane business of setting its own house in order. Any current philosophy that seems to encourage practical attention to detail is apt to be seized upon as a principle for ordering legal affairs. Scholasticism, empiricism, positivism, and (in the United States) pragmatism all serve this purpose. Hence, although Comtean positivism is outmoded, its influence is still ubiquitous. In fact, this is true in greater or less degree for all countries under the influence of the civil law, for codification and positivism are natural bedfellows.

**Scandinavia.**   The dominant legal philosophy in Scandinavian countries is legal positivism or, as it is usually called, realism (Olivecrona 1951; 1959; Ross 1957). The legal philosophical specialty is a very subtle form of psychological realism. The general orientation is empirical. There is also an interest in juristic logic. As might be expected, there exists an ' "idealistic" reaction (Castberg 1955) against the prevailing realism; it takes the form of an insistence upon the claims of value theory in a rounded philosophy of law.

There is an excellent source on legal philosophical movements in *Scandinavian Studies in Law*, first published in 1957 and continuing to date. The studies are in English. There are also two surveys of Scandinavian legal philosophy available in United States publications (Castberg 1955; Orfield 1956). These volumes should be consulted for an understanding of the ramifications of legal philosophy in the various countries included under the rubric "Scandinavia." The leading legal philosophers today are Karl Olivecrona, Alf Ross, and Otto Brusiin.

**Soviet Union.**   Legal philosophy in the U.S.S.R. has always been intimately connected with the theoretical work of the founders of communism, Marx and Engels, with the philosophy of dialectical materialism, and with the power struggles of political factions within the Soviet Union (Ginsburgs 1961; Jaworskyj 1960). Hence, a general outline of the legal philosophy of the U.S.S.R. is known to most educated laymen in the West. In a sense, legal philosophy is the party line, for the questions of the nature of the state, of the relation between the state and its citizens, and of the doctrine of law as the chief instrument by which a ruling class (including the proletariat) consolidates power are all problems in the philosophy of law. So, too, are the questions of the withering away of the state and of the possibility of socialism in one country. In brief, legal philosophy is the very business of the Soviet political partisan.

Information on these general political aspects of Soviet legal philosophy is not hard for outsiders to find. When, however, it comes to the intricacies of legal philosophy and to the part it plays in legal education, in the formation and training of the legal administrators of society, and in the form and content of civil and criminal law, we find only scattered pieces of information. Two sources of study of dialectical materialism as a philosophical position and of its influences in official and academic life in the U.S.S.R. are available. One is the Institute for East European Studies at the University of Fribourg, the other, the Research Commission of the German Evangelical Academies at Tübingen.

Articles examining the foundation of Soviet law are contained in the introduction to a symposium on Marxist–Soviet ethics and jurisprudence (Noonan 1963). The articles in this symposium stress how little is known in noncommunist countries about Soviet philosophy. Still less is known, it might be added, about the Soviet philosophy of law. What is known of this subject antedates in the main the recent revolutionary changes in the climate of intellectual and academic opinion in the Soviet Union.

The available Soviet literature gives no hint of a theory of "higher law" or principle of morality which could be taken to override the positive enactments of the state. Such notions would be condemned as idealism. Yet, dialectical materialism is a dynamic philosophy, and change is not only envisioned it is deemed necessary, subject of course to the fundamental principles of materialism. These principles are the primacy of matter over mind and of the objective forces of production over human consciousness. Not only can human laws change to meet these conditions they must do so.

The exigencies of politics rather than any limitations of the philosophical doctrine of dialectical materialism are the normal constraints on the proliferation of alternative philosophical theories about the nature of law. In one sense, Soviet legal philosophy could be called positivitic. This term, however, is not very helpful since the very idea of principled resistance to ordained law is apparently not even entertained. I have the impression that empirical studies of the actual workings of Soviet legal institutions are encouraged. To be scientific, however, such studies must await the development of scientific sociology in the U.S.S.R. It also appears that since logic and mathematics are very highly developed in communist countries, partly because of their apparently nonpolitical character, the relation of law and science will probably come in for consideration in the near future. There is some evidence that Soviet legal philosophers are becoming interested in cybernetics and in law and electronics. (For general references about jurisprudence in the Soviet Union, see *Soviet . . . 1951.*)

**Japan.** There is a great and growing interest in Japan in all types of legal philosophy (Yagi 1959; Konishi 1960; Tabata 1961; Sawai 1962). The German legal philosophical theories receive continued attention. This includes the whole range from Neo-Kantian and Neo-Hegelian idealism, which has long interested the Japanese, to phenomenology and existentialism. Interest in logical positivism continues unabated.

Since World War II and the adoption of the new Japanese constitution, British and American theories have been receiving widespread attention. Philosophical analysis from England and especially sociological jurisprudence from the United States are attracting the notice of the younger scholars. This is part of a larger interest in the sociology of law, which in Japan, as in other civil law countries, has always been considered a discipline quite separate from the philosophy of law. However, here as elsewhere, legal philosophy is becoming more practical and sociology of law more theoretical. Consequently, the two disciplines are drawing somewhat closer together. There is much interest in the application of empirical methods to the study of legal phenomena. Scalogram analysis of judicial decisions (Hayakawa 1962) is receiving some attention and even experimental jurisprudence has a following.

One of the greatest currents of legal thought in Japan is the study of Marxist theories of law, despite the great difference in the political structure of Japan and the U.S.S.R.

THOMAS A. COWAN

[*See also* LEGAL REASONING; LEGAL SYSTEMS; *and the biographies of* AUSTIN; EHRLICH; JELLINEK; KANTOROWICZ; KELSEN; POUND; RADBRUCH. *A detailed guide to other relevant material may be found under* LAW.]

### BIBLIOGRAPHY

*Annual Survey of American Law.* → See especially the section on "Jurisprudence" in the annual issues since 1944.

*Archiv für Rechts- und Sozialphilosophie.* → Published since 1907.

*Archives de philosophie du droit,* New Series. → Published since 1952.

BATIFFOL, HENRI 1960 *La philosophie du droit.* Paris: Presses Universitaires de France.

BOBBIO, NORBERTO 1959 Trends in Italian Legal Theory. *American Journal of Comparative Law* 8:329–340.

BODENHEIMER, EDGAR 1954 Significant Developments in German Legal Philosophy Since 1945. *American Journal of Comparative Law* 3:379–396.

BODENHEIMER, EDGAR 1962 *Jurisprudence: The Philosophy and Method of the Law.* Cambridge, Mass.: Harvard Univ. Press.

BROWN, BRENDAN F. (editor) 1960 *The Natural Law Reader.* Dobbs Ferry, N.Y.: Oceana.

CARBONNIER, JEAN (1955–1957) 1960–1962 *Droit civil.* 2 vols., 3d ed. Paris: Presses Universitaires de France.

CASTBERG, FREDE 1955 Philosophy of Law in the Scandinavian Countries. *American Journal of Comparative Law* 4:388–400.

COHEN, JULIUS; ROBSON, REGINALD A. H.; and BATES, ALAN 1958 *Parental Authority: The Community and the Law.* New Brunswick, N.J.: Rutgers Univ. Press.

COING, HELMUT 1952 Tendencies in Modern American Legal Philosophy: A Survey. *Georgetown Law Journal* 40:523–561.

CONFERENCE ON SCIENCE, PHILOSOPHY, AND RELIGION IN THEIR RELATION TO THE DEMOCRATIC WAY OF LIFE, 1960 1962 *The Ethic of Power: The Interplay of Religion, Philosophy, and Politics.* Edited by Harold D. Lasswell and Harlan Cleveland. New York: Harper.

COWAN, THOMAS A. 1963 Decision Theory in Law, Science, and Technology. *Rutgers University Law Review* 17:499–530. → Also published in Volume 140, pages 1065–1075, of *Science.*

DIAS, R. W. M.; and HUGHES, G. B. J. 1957 *Jurisprudence.* London: Butterworth.

FRIEDMANN, WOLFGANG (1945) 1960 *Legal Theory.* 4th ed. London: Stevens.

FRIEDRICH, CARL J. (1955) 1958 *The Philosophy of Law in Historical Perspective.* Univ. of Chicago Press. → First published in German.

FULLER, LON L. 1958 Positivism and Fidelity to Law. *Harvard Law Review* 71:630–672.

FULLER, LON L. 1964 *The Morality of Law.* New Haven: Yale Univ. Press.

GINSBURGS, GEORGE 1961 Objective Truth and the Judicial Process in Post-Stalinist Soviet Jurisprudence. *American Journal of Comparative Law* 10:53–75.

GUEST, ANTHONY G. (editor) 1961 *Oxford Essays in Jurisprudence.* Oxford Univ. Press.

HALL, JEROME 1958 *Studies in Jurisprudence and Criminal Theory.* Dobbs Ferry, N.Y.: Oceana.

HALL, JEROME 1963 *Comparative Law and Social Theory.* Baton Rouge: Louisiana State Univ. Press.

HART, HERBERT L. A. 1953 Philosophy of Law and Jurisprudence in Britain (1945–1952). *American Journal of Comparative Law* 2:355–364.

HART, HERBERT L. A. 1954 Definition and Theory in Jurisprudence. *Law Quarterly Review* 70:37–60.

HART, HERBERT L. A. 1961 *The Concept of Law.* Oxford: Clarendon.

HAYAKAWA, TAKEO 1962 Legal Science and Judicial Behavior With Particular Reference to Civil Liberties in the Japanese Supreme Court. *Kobe University Law Review,* International Edition 2:1–27.

*Hōgaku kyōkai zasshi* (Journal of the Jurisprudence Association). → Published since 1888.

HURST, JAMES W. 1960 *Law and Social Process in United States History.* Ann Arbor: Univ. of Michigan Law School.

JAWORSKYJ, MICHAEL  1960  Soviet Critique of the "Bourgeois" Philosophy of Law. *Osteuropa-Recht* 6:9–34.

JENKINS, IREDELL  1959  The Matchmaker: Or, Toward a Synthesis of Legal Idealism and Positivism. *Journal of Legal Education* 12:1–32.

JONES, ERNEST M.  1962  Some Current Trends in Legal Research. *Journal of Legal Education* 15:121–138.

KELSEN, HANS  (1945) 1961  *General Theory of Law and State.* New York: Russell.

KELSEN, HANS  1957  *What Is Justice? Justice, Law, and Politics in the Mirror of Science: Collected Essays.* Berkeley: Univ. of California Press.

KONISHI, MINORI  1960  A Report on Legal Philosophy in Japan in the Year 1958. *Japan Annual of Law and Politics* 8:5–12.

KUNZ, JOSEF L.  1954  Contemporary Latin-American Philosophy of Law: A Survey. *American Journal of Comparative Law* 3:212–232.

LLEWELLYN, KARL N.  (1928–1960) 1962  *Jurisprudence: Realism in Theory and Practice.* Univ. of Chicago Press.

LLEWELLYN, KARL N.  1960  *The Common Law Tradition: Deciding Appeals.* Boston: Little.

LUMB, R. D.  1960  Recent Developments in Legal Theory in Australia. *Archiv für Rechts- und Sozialphilosophie* 46:97–114.

McDOUGAL, MYRES S.; and FELICIANO, FLORENTINO P.  1961  *Law and Minimum World Public Order: The Legal Regulation of International Coercion.* New Haven: Yale Univ. Press.

McDOUGAL, MYRES S.; LASSWELL, HAROLD D.; and VLASIC, IVAN A.  1963  *Law and Public Order in Space.* New Haven: Yale Univ. Press.

McWHINNEY, EDWARD  1958  New Frontiers in Jurisprudence in Canada. *Journal of Legal Education* 10:331–337.

MAIHOFER, WERNER (editor)  1962  *Naturrecht oder Rechtspositivismus?* Bad Homburg (Germany): Gentner.

NAKHNIKIAN, GEORGE  1957  Contemporary Ethical Theories and Jurisprudence. *Natural Law Forum* 2:4–40.

NOONAN, JOHN T. JR.  1963  Introduction. *Natural Law Forum* 8:1–6. → The principal part of this issue is devoted to discussions of Marxist–Soviet ethics and jurisprudence.

OLIVECRONA, KARL  1951  Realism and Idealism: Some Reflections on the Cardinal Point in Legal Philosophy. *New York University Law Review* 26:120–131.

OLIVECRONA, KARL  1959  The Legal Theories of Axel Hägerström and Vilhelm Lundstadt. *Scandinavian Studies in Law* 3:125–150.

ORFIELD, LESTER B.  1956  A Survey of Scandinavian Legal Philosophy. *Wisconsin Law Review* [1956]:448–480, 585–624.

*Österreichische Zeitschrift für öffentliches Recht.* → Published from 1946 to 1948.

PATON, GEORGE W.  (1946) 1951  *A Text-book of Jurisprudence.* 2d ed. Oxford: Clarendon.

PATTERSON, EDWIN W.  1953  *Jurisprudence: Men and Ideas of the Law.* New York: Foundation Press.

POUND, ROSCOE  1959  *Jurisprudence.* 5 vols. St. Paul, Minn.: West. → Volume 1: *Jurisprudence: The End of Law.* Volume 2: *The Nature of Law.* Volume 3: *The Scope and Subject Matter of Law.* Volume 4: *Application and Enforcement of Law.* Volume 5: *The System of Law.*

RECASÉNS-SICHES, LUIS  1958  Juridical Axiology in Ibero-America. *Natural Law Forum* 3:135–169.

REUSCHLEIN, HAROLD G.  1951  *Jurisprudence; Its American Prophets: A Survey of Taught Jurisprudence.* Indianapolis, Ind.: Bobbs-Merrill.

*Rivista internazionale di filosofia del diritto.* → Published since 1921.

ROSS, ALF  1957  Tû-Tû. *Scandinavian Studies in Law* 1:137–153.

SAVATIER, R.  (1948) 1952–1959  *Les métamorphoses économiques et sociales du droit civil d'aujourd'hui.* 3 vols., 2d ed. Paris: Dalloz.

SAWAI, KIYOSHI  1962  Legal Philosophy in Japan: 1960 Term. *Japan Annual of Law and Politics* 10:13–17.

*Scandinavian Studies in Law.* → Published annually since 1957 under the auspices of the Stockholm University faculty of law. See especially the bibliography on jurisprudence in Volume 5, 1961, pages 160–162.

SCHUBERT, GLENDON A.  1960  *Quantitative Analysis of Judicial Behavior.* Glencoe, Ill.: Free Press.

SHUMAN, SAMUEL I.  1963  *Legal Positivism: Its Scope and Limitations.* Detroit, Mich.: Wayne State Univ. Press.

*Soviet Legal Philosophy.*  1951  Cambridge, Mass.: Harvard Univ. Press.; Oxford Univ. Press.

STONE, JULIUS  (1946) 1950  *The Province and Function of Law; Law as Logic, Justice, and Social Control: A Study in Jurisprudence.* Cambridge, Mass.: Harvard Univ. Press.

SZLADITS, CHARLES  1955–1962  *A Bibliography on Foreign and Comparative Law: Books and Articles in English.* 2 vols. Published for the Parker School of Foreign and Comparative Law, Columbia University. Dobbs Ferry, N.Y.: Oceana. → Volume 1 contains a bibliography up to 1953, published in 1955; Volume 2, from 1953 to 1959, published in 1962.

SZLADITS, CHARLES  1959  *Guide to Foreign Legal Materials: French, German, Swiss.* Published for the Parker School of Foreign and Comparative Law, Columbia University. Dobbs Ferry, N.Y.: Oceana.

TABATA, SHINOBU  1961  Current Theory in Jurisprudence. *Doshisha Law Review*, International Edition 4:29–38.

WASSERSTROM, RICHARD A.  1961  *The Judicial Decision: Toward a Theory of Legal Justification.* Stanford (Calif.) Univ. Press.

YAGI, TETSUO  1959  The Trend in the Field of Philosophy of Law in Japan in 1957. *Japan Annual of Law and Politics* 7:1–15.

# JURY

*See* JUDICIAL PROCESS.

# JUSTICE

In the beginnings of recorded ethical and legal thought the term "justice" was used as equivalent to righteousness in general. Justice comprised the whole of virtue and complete conformity with the approved pattern of moral conduct. For purposes of rational analysis the classic philosophers, following Aristotle, preferred to restrict the term's reference to a particular virtue, distinguishing, for example, between justice and equity or between justice and charity. Nevertheless, in common usage justice still retains significant traces of its original comprehensiveness. For this reason, the very broad concepts presented in the Hebrew Bible and in Plato's *Republic* continue to be important.

## Justice as general virtue

**The Bible.** Aside from questions of theodicy and apologetics, the vast cultural influence of the Hebrew Bible has not been attributable to precision of concept or dialectical consistency. In certain passages, the Scriptures seem to indicate that justice alone is sufficient to comprehend the entire scheme of divinely ordained behavior; in others, they place justice in various combinations of primary virtues, e.g., along with loving-kindness and reverence. Moreover, the emphasis shifts markedly from the Pentateuch, which can give a misleading impression of equating justice with mere obedience to ordained rules, to the prophetic books, which can give an opposite (and equally misleading) impression of rejecting all fixed rules in favor of rather vague ideals and general standards. Presented as they are in continual synthesis with a developing religion and in assumed involvement with divine purposes and sanctions, the Biblical teachings reach us not as definitions but as exhortations and exemplary episodes, not as abstract concepts but as practical, concrete, and progressive insights.

Taken as a whole and with due allowance for multiplicity of periods and authors, the Bible affords the following imperfectly conceptualized insights for secular application: (1) that (*a*) general standards of justice or righteousness (such as not oppressing one's neighbor) may become too vague in outline and arbitrary in use without the specification that comes from definite rules (such as a prohibition against taking a man's upper millstone in pawn); (*b*) on the other hand, rules may become too inflexible and rigid without the emollient influence of general standards; (*c*) on occasion (e.g., the ostensible rules prescribed in Leviticus 25 for the jubilee year) a legislator may attempt to inculcate ideal standards of justice under the guise of declaring legal regulations; and (*d*) further, a people's ethical sensibility may evolve to the point where it prompts a re-examination and a reinterpretation of inherited rules; (2) that in order to be considered just, a system of ethical or legal ordinances requires not only a conceived authoritative command but also a conceived popular consent, acceptance, or mutual covenant; (3) that justice imposes a duty to perform group and individual acts of social reparation, welfare, and assistance; (4) that justice comprises the functionally related principles of impartiality and probity in rendering judgment, reciprocity in interpersonal transactions (including limited retaliation for violence), and equality of elementary rights not only between members of diverse economic classes but also between nations and races; and (5) that the emotional manifestation of justice consists in passionately abhorring all forms of oppression, exploitation, and cruelty, and its behavioral manifestation consists in denouncing and combating them.

Since the Biblical corpus, like Plato's works, postulates a constant endeavor to edify the people and guide them into ways of virtue, it is suitable to add (6) that both Hebraic and Hellenic geniuses emphasized the potency of justice as a pedagogic influence. The Hebrew seers saw justice instilling rectitude, benevolence, and mutual trust among the populace, whereas Plato expected it to teach public order, private self-discipline, and the supremacy of reason. These educational doctrines might have been taken more seriously during ensuing centuries if high secular and ecclesiastical officials had provided more impressive examples.

**Plato.** The exposition of Plato's thought reversed the Biblical sequence, moving from reliance on the discretion of the guardians, in the *Republic*, through a transitional discussion, in the *Statesman*, to reliance on detailed legal prescriptions, in the "second-best state" of the *Laws*. Although various modern scholars have rightly criticized the provisions for rigorous censorship and inquisition in Plato's final dialogue, they have given him less credit than they might for replacing the dangerous notion of all-wise, unfettered philosopher–kings with a rule of laws.

In the *Republic*, justice regulates and equilibrates the other virtues. Whether "writ small" within the individual psyche or "writ large" in the workings of the political state, its functions are to achieve harmony and to maintain equilibrium. To do these things, reason must rule within the psyche, and reason's embodiment (the elite guardians) must rule within the state. Justice results from each element in society doing the appropriate task, doing it well, and doing it only. Here again Plato's recent critics have been less than generous; although rightly condemning the *Republic*'s hierarchic structure as undemocratic, they have said little about its anticipating modern sociological systems that base social solidarity on a deliberate separation of social functions.

Influenced perhaps by Plato's imposing metaphysical dualism, subsequent philosophers, with few exceptions, have concentrated on the tension between (*a*) justice as an impartial application of established substantive rules and (*b*) justice as an ideal criterion or reformer or nullifier of such rules. In sharp contrast to common usage, most of them have neglected the extremely important subject of procedural justice. True, Plato decreed some procedural regulations in the *Laws*, but he gave them no role in a theory of justice; the Jewish sages who composed the Mishnah did much the same, though with greater sophistication. But common usage has surpassed the philosophers and sages. It reflects an infinitude of experience not merely in passing judgment but also in being judged, which can leave a searing and instructive impression. According to common experience in every species of economic and social activity, the problem of justice is at least as likely to arise out of, say, being condemned without a hearing as out of being condemned under an unfair substantive rule. In short, if it lacks a procedural aspect, any concept of justice may readily become a mockery. [*See* PLATO.]

## Procedural justice

**The paradigms.**  Procedural justice consists in employing correct methods to develop rules of conduct, to ascertain the facts of a particular case, or to devise a total appreciation absorbing rules and facts into a final, dispositive judgment. Among the classic philosophers, only Aristotle and Thomas Aquinas showed sufficient awareness of the functional relations between standards and rules, evidence and facts, and facts and judgments to inquire with care into the principles of procedural justice. Their respective contributions were derived from two main sources: (*a*) the empirical wisdom of the times, and (*b*) the practices and nomenclature of the law courts.

Each of these sources reached a turning point in the eighteenth century. Empiricism then began its evolution into modern utilitarianship, pragmatism, and instrumentalism, while court practices began slowly to adapt themselves to modern ideals of human dignity and political democracy. Moreover, as former provinces of philosophy gradually became specialized into the new sciences of economics, psychology, sociology, and anthropology, these offered new guides, of varying degrees of dependability, for the progress of procedural justice.

As for fact-finding (i.e., the threshold process of sifting conflicting evidence and ascertaining what to believe about a unique and unrepeatable past event), the evolving methods of the law courts still presented an indispensable paradigm of judgment. Jeremy Bentham's bold criticism of the English courts of his day helped to effect a gradual rationalization of judicial procedure. But other eminent utilitarians made no comparable contribution. In

point of fact, the explicit utilitarian and scientific emphasis on generality of rules and propositions served to exclude an adequate concern for particular transactions. [*See* BENTHAM.] Bentham apart, the philosophers and social scientists can be said to have elevated the quality of procedural justice only through their influence on the general culture.

Since the eighteenth century, despite innumerable errors and injustices in the law courts, judicial procedure has undergone noteworthy reforms and advances. The procedural criteria compendiously known as "due process of law" have improved sufficiently in the United States of America and other mature democracies to offer a worthy paradigm for the exercise of ethical judgment. By and large, they make it possible to speak without embarrassment of "due process of moral decision."

**The requirements.**  In the law courts, the main requirements of due process, or procedural justice, are the following: No one must be accused of violating a rule of behavior unless he could have ascertained the existence and meaning of the rule before he committed the challenged act. When accused, a person is entitled to know the charge against him, to know the evidence adduced in support of the charge, and to have a fair opportunity to collect and present his own evidence. The judge or other arbiter must be disinterested, unbiased, and attentive. If the accusation is grave, the accused is entitled to the assistance of a counsel and advocate (who in cases of informal charges like those that are bandied about in family life may be an advocate pleading within the self-same psyche that makes the accusation). Moreover, even if a person has been found guilty, procedural justice requires that some way be afforded to reconsider the case later and correct any serious error that comes to light.

Two influences have impelled the recent improvements in this paradigm. Foremost has been the rapid emergence of what may be called the "consumer perspective," i.e., the view of law, morals, and justice in the perspective of the many who are subject to them instead of the few who officially declare and administer them. The second influence has consisted in a growing awareness of the gross imperfections inherent in fact-finding processes. Articulated by Judge Jerome Frank in his philosophy of "fact-skepticism," this awareness has inspired, on the one hand, a variety of procedural reforms in the courts and, on the other hand, a growing resistance to irreversible sanctions, such as the death penalty.

**Relation to substantive justice.**  In undervaluing the procedural aspect of justice, general philosophers have likewise neglected its influence on substantive rules. Granted that an impartial administration of justice can comport theoretically with an oppressive system of substantive law, the general experience of mankind demonstrates that this is true only in theory. In actual fact, procedural injustice not only accompanies substantive injustice; it also aggravates its cruelty. Procedural justice has the opposite influence; sooner or later it prompts and promotes advances in substantive justice. Thus, whereas unfair trials have aggravated the laws that discriminate against Negroes in certain American communities, fair trials and impartial tribunals have committed other American communities to the full vindication of equality and human dignity.

## Major philosophies of substantive justice

**Aristotle.** Although Aristotle treated justice as a particular virtue, and the one most necessary to a state's welfare, he recognized the prevalence of general justice in popular usage. Some interpreters believe that he reserved a role for it in his taxonomy of legal justice over and above the familiar categories of (*a*) "distributive" and (*b*) "corrective" (or "remedial" or "commutative") justice. Distributive justice applies to the allotment of honor, wealth, and other social goods and should be proportionate to civic merit; corrective or commutative justice, which may apply in the first instance to private, voluntary exchanges outside the law courts, is confided peculiarly to the judiciary, whose duty is to restore a middle point of equality whenever it is lacking between the parties. Commentators have taken the distinction between the two rather too literally, for it is evident that when the law grants or denies a commutative claim to recover damages for a specified type of injury (i.e., when it grants or denies a "cause of action"), it performs an act of distributive justice.

More characteristic of Aristotle's profound practical wisdom were the several ways in which he delineated the antitheses and tensions (later to be called antinomies) of justice. Profiting by the insights of Plato, he produced a model for almost every subsequent assertion of value-relativism and for almost every subsequent effort to overcome or limit it. All later treatments of justice are indebted to him—even those that gainsay him by reducing justice to a list of immutable, universal, dogmatic precepts and those that gainsay him by seeking to expel justice from the realm of legal theory.

On the one hand, no philosopher has surpassed Aristotle's tributes to the rational dignity of authoritative textual rules, which provide "justice accord-

ing to law"; on the other, none has surpassed the keenness with which he criticized the inflexibility of legal precepts and their frequent unsuitability to the exigencies of a concrete case. His demand for individualization in the application of law, his appeal to judicial discretion, and his invocation of the magnanimous spirit of equity are as pertinent now as ever, yet so is his statement (quoted too often from *Politics* 1287*a* without its contextual limitations) that he "who commands that law should rule may thus be regarded as commanding that God and reason alone should rule; he who commands that a man should rule adds the character of the beast."

Although he occasionally adopted the usage of his day and condemned a practice such as usury as being "against nature," he furnished a merciless exposé of natural-law terminology, which he reduced to mere rhetoric and advocacy. One gathers that at bottom he rejected perceptual natural law and subscribed to a very general natural justice whose manifestations were much influenced by conventional and contingent data.

In moving away from Plato's dualism, which would serve to exalt justice and denigrate positive law, Aristotle treated justice as immanent in the workings of law and thus gave it a markedly more effective function. Since immanent justice necessarily evokes difficult antitheses and tensions, it is to Aristotle's enduring credit that, unlike most of his successors, he candidly left the unresolvable unresolved. [*See* ARISTOTLE.]

**Thomas Aquinas.** In Thomas Aquinas' treatment of justice, most of Aristotle's insights reappeared—modified, however, by the intervening influences of Stoic natural law, Christian doctrine, and the institutional interests of the medieval church in its conflict with the Holy Roman Empire. The result was a most ingenious amalgam, Christian throughout, yet susceptible of widely divergent uses. With one hand, Aquinas gave Cicero and the church fathers all they could have desired of eternal, divine, and ecclesiastical authority for the precepts of natural law; with the other, he explicated and underscored those variable, local, and contingent factors that must come into play whenever a precept of natural law is applied to the regulation of concrete human transactions. The "immutable" precepts in such a system would not necessarily stultify judgment.

In discussing the dangerous question whether a subject was in duty bound to obey or resist an unjust law, Aquinas adopted a prudent middle course. He demanded absolute resistance to any ordinance that might violate the divine good or divine law (of which, of course, the church was sole authoritative arbiter). If a law was unjust by being contrary to human good (e.g., a law imposed on subjects not for the common good but for the ruler's cupidity, or one that exceeded the legislator's authority, or one that imposed disproportionate burdens on members of the community), Aquinas held that it was not binding in conscience but that subjects should submit to it in order to avoid public scandal or disturbance. We need scarcely add that in practice these propositions have engendered many diverse and conflicting interpretations. [See AQUINAS.]

**Kantians.**  Kant and his disciples have elucidated the concept of justice only tangentially. After giving a baldly positivistic definition of "just" and "unjust" in the *Metaphysic of Morals*, Kant devoted his *Philosophy of Law* (*Rechtslehre*) to analyzing right or law (*Recht*), not justice (*Gerechtigkeit*). His practical observations on legal and political rules and institutions were generally unimpressive. Hence his continuing influence on theories of justice has been due to (*a*) the sharp dichotomy between cognition and volition in his critical philosophy, which has had a markedly skeptical impact, and (*b*) the quality of rigorous objectivity, reciprocity, and universality in his ethical maxims (e.g., the categorical imperative and the admonition against using man merely as a means). Although the maxims do not appear to advantage in most of the concrete examples that Kant provided, their general tone has remained edifying. But as Huntington Cairns (1949) has made clear, Kant's conclusions embodying ethical or legal content do not follow necessarily from the premises of his *Rechtslehre*. [See KANT.]

In the twentieth century, Rudolf Stammler (1911) attempted ingeniously but without success to articulate the governing maxims of just law, his formulation merely elaborating notions of reciprocity such as the anthropologist Bronislaw Malinowski (1926) was reporting more or less simultaneously from the Trobriand Islands. In an idealistic treatment that concluded, in Kantian manner, that justice was a quality not of social arrangements but of the human will, Bertrand de Jouvenel (1955) disclosed new values in the time-worn Stoic definitions of the concept. (Ulpian had defined justice as a species of *voluntas*, which Cicero had amended to *habitus animi*.) Gustav Radbruch—a most impressive Neo-Kantian whose philosophic posture shifted radically after the rise and fall of Hitler Germany—conducted an unsurpassed examination into the antinomies of justice (1914).

Applying Kant's critical epistemology, Hans Kelsen reiterated strongly over a period of years that justice is an irrational ideal. [See KELSEN.] "However indispensable it may be for volition and action of men, it is not subject to cognition" (1945, p. 13). Although like many other Kantians and Neo-Kantians Kelsen, as a jurist, supported a variety of just causes, his "pure theory of law" exerted a skeptical, and occasionally cynical, influence in this regard, particularly in central Europe and Latin America. Only at an unfortunately late date—after he had retired from teaching—did his readers learn that the above often-quoted words of dismissal referred exclusively to "*absolute* justice" (such as a supernatural authority might ordain) and that the author never intended to deny or disparage a humane conception of "relative justice" (cf. 1958, p. 1056).

**The English utilitarians.**  Dangerous errors in the theory of justice have resulted from the rhetorical practice of calling it "the end of law"—as though the extremely complex social, intellectual, and institutional mechanism called law served only a single purpose and end. Since monisms inevitably beget rival monisms, which seek to absorb or destroy them, it is not strange that the concept of justice, taken in monistic relation to law, was uncongenial to the classic English utilitarians. The respective reactions evinced by Hume, Bentham, Austin, and Mill provide a chapter of unusual interest.

Hume, concerned mainly with the coherence and concinnity of utilitarian morals, was content to enlist justice in its service by submitting that "public utility is the *sole* origin of justice." Not so Bentham. The adversaries of reform having misused the phrase "natural justice" too heinously to allow it room among utilitarians, he denounced it and all similar terms as mere invective and darkening of the intellect. Austin, a conservative utilitarian who had suffered special disappointments of his own, echoed Bentham on this score.

It was Mill alone who, having once subdued justice to the Procrustean bed of utilitarianism, waited to ascertain what he could observe while holding it there and insisting that "the just" was only a particular species of "the useful." More clearly than any previous philosopher, Mill saw that because human beings experienced a primal need for security from attack they attributed a special moral value to the claim on their fellow creatures to join in making them safe, and that the felt intensity of the need distinguished this claim from common cases of utility and made it differ from them in kind.

Mill erred. He neglected procedural justice and

preventive justice; often he leaped from the single individual to the whole of mankind without regard to intermediate groups, institutions, or national societies; and he made social utility the sole and final arbiter whenever men might differ with other men (as they almost invariably have and will) in their opinions of concrete justice.

Nevertheless, Mill was the first to discern some of the elemental psychic and emotional forces that impel men to strive for justice. "Justice," he wrote, "is a name for certain classes of moral rules, which concern the essentials of human well-being more clearly, and are therefore of more absolute obligation, than any other rules for the guidance of life" (*Utilitarianism*, chapter 5). Others, from Heraclitus to Schopenhauer, had indicated in various ways that philosophers would profit from exploring the dynamics of injustice. Although Mill's monistic utilitarianism blocked certain avenues of exploration and distorted some of his findings about justice, he deserves to rank among the concept's foremost elucidators. [*See* MILL.]

**Marx, Engels, and the Soviet jurists.** Unlike Saint-Simon and various other socialist theorists, and unlike many of their own disciples, Marx and Engels allowed no place for "justice" in their analysis of economic relations. Like Bentham, they ridiculed the term, regarding it as a mere mask for capitalist exploitation and hypocrisy. In their view, its main defects were that: (1) since criticism of the capitalist system as "unjust" focused characteristically on inequalities or unfairnesses of *distribution*, it tended to obscure the essential nature of exploitation, which, they submitted, was a direct corollary of the capitalist mode of *production*; and (2) since any attempt to rectify "injustices" on the distributive side must assume that some sort of equilibrium could be found between the irreconcilable forces in capitalist society, socialists who advocated "social justice" were misrepresenting the nature of the class conflict, diverting the workers from revolutionary uprisings, and postponing the achievement of total victory. Thus, in both its distributive and its equilibrium-maintaining implications they treated the concept as irrelevant and inept if not dangerous. [*See* ENGELS; MARX.]

During the 1920s the most creative Soviet jurist of the period, Evgenii B. Pashukanis, elaborating Marx and Engels' analysis, argued that the notion of equality was a product of assumptions attached to the exchange of commodities under earlier stages of economic development and that morality, law, and the state, at least as theretofore known, were mere features of bourgeois society. Pashukanis regarded the concept of justice as interchangeable with that of equality—except that the former might afford greater possibilities for disguising inequalities. His theories having been denounced by Stalin, Pashukanis simply disappeared from life during the purges of 1937; after Stalin's death the list of those who were posthumously rehabilitated included his name (see Pashukanis 1927).

Although later Soviet writers cannot be said to have employed the term "justice" as a concept of juristic discourse, they have preserved certain limited aspects of its reference in their accepted phrase "socialist legality." The principle of socialist legality requires all state organs as well as citizens to comply strictly with the provisions of Soviet legislation; it does not negative the taking of extraordinary measures against persons branded as class foes. Although during the post-Stalin era the climate of juristic discussion has by no means been stable, much less libertarian, there are unmistakable demands for greater procedural regularity and for a measure of popular participation in certain organs of state activity. Grounds for guarded optimism may be found when the government evinces a willingness to experiment, currently exemplified by the "comrades' courts," which involve lay citizens in adjudicating minor social infractions for the purpose of discouraging deviant behavior. Nevertheless, the old imperial or official perspective still prevails among Soviet jurists; even if some of them look beyond the libraries and see the masses, they seldom notice the individuals who make up the masses.

## Justice as active process

Unaffected by the Neo-Kantian, utilitarian, and Marxist criticisms, common usage continues to treat "justice" as denoting some of the greatest of human needs and worthiest of social enterprises. Philosophers miss the reference of the term insofar as they fail to observe the occasions when it becomes relevant to the concrete experience and discourse of individuals and social groups. No concept would be adequate that identified justice with a merely ideal relation or static condition or list of preceptual standards. In common experience, men turn to the vocabulary of justice when they confront a real or imagined instance of injustice. The ethical and biological functions of justice become evident in *the sense of injustice*.

The sense of injustice is an indissociable blend of reason and empathy, evolutionary in its manifestations. It is not mere intuition or some mystical law-instinct (*Rechtsgefühl*). Without reason, the sense of injustice could not identify the transactions that provoke it, nor could it serve the interests of social utility; without empathy it would lack its emotive heat and its capacity to impel men to act.

It derives logical and social justification from its efficacy, for it succeeds precisely to the extent that in any given case the relevant circumstances have been understood, felt, and appreciated. It is an immanent working factor not only within the institutions of law but throughout the cosmos of interpersonal transactions.

The sense of injustice is the equipment by which a human being discerns assault, recognizes oppression of another as a species of attack upon himself, and prepares defense. Among its facets, which should not be taken as categories, are the demands for equality, desert, human dignity, conscientious official behavior including due process of decision, confinement of government to its proper functions, and fulfillment of the common expectations of the given society. The sense of injustice does not provide a formula to relieve men of the duty of deliberation and decision nor does it deprive them of their corresponding freedoms. Generally, it assists the decisional process rather by barring a course that is wrong than by selecting among courses that are right.

In this perspective, "justice" means the active process of preventing or remedying what would arouse the sense of injustice. Thus the experience of the sense of injustice is itself a dramatic species of social transformation, because it incites men to join with one another in perceiving danger, in resisting it, and in exulting over an achieved success —all of which are public acts of solidarity. Justice then is more than a static equilibrium or a quality of the human will; it is, as common usage has always hinted, an active process or agenda or enterprise. The meaning of the term comes alive whenever one confronts injustice and "does" justice.

EDMOND CAHN

[See also the articles listed under LAW.]

### BIBLIOGRAPHY

*For a discussion of the Bible, see* Finkelstein 1949, *Volume 2, especially Chapter 15 by Mordecai M. Kaplan. For an exposition of Plato's thought, see* Cairns 1949, *Chapter 2, and references supplied there. For a discussion of the paradigms, see* Cahn 1955, *Chapter 9, and Aristotle's* Rhetoric. *For an explanation of the requirements of justice, see* Frank 1949; Cahn 1961, *Chapter 7. For Aristotle's thought, see his* Ethics *and* Politics, *as well as the often neglected* Rhetoric. *For Thomas Aquinas' treatment of justice, see his* Summa theologica I–II, 2, 94–96. *For the Kantian concept, see Kant's* Philosophy of Law, *summarized in* Cairns 1949, *Chapter 12;* Stammler 1911; Malinowski 1926; Jouvenel 1955, *Chapter 9;* Radbruch 1914; *and* Kelsen 1945 *and* 1958. *For the English utilitarians, see Hume's* Enquiry Concerning the Principles of Morals, *Chapter 3, Appendix 3;* Bentham's *The Limits of Jurisprudence Defined;* Austin's *The Province of Jurisprudence Determined, Lecture 2; and* Mill's *Utilitarianism, Chapter 5. For references to Marx and Engels, see* Tucker 1963, *Chapter 15; and for the ideas of E. B. Pashukanis see* 1927; *for later Soviet theorists, see* Soviet . . . 1951. *For an analysis of justice as an active process, see* Cahn 1949, 1955, *and* 1961.

CAHN, EDMOND 1949 *The Sense of Injustice.* New York Univ. Press. → A paperback edition was published in 1964.
CAHN, EDMOND 1955 *The Moral Decision.* Bloomington: Indiana Univ. Press.
CAHN, EDMOND 1961 *The Predicament of Democratic Man.* New York: Macmillan.
CAIRNS, HUNTINGTON 1949 *Legal Philosophy From Plato to Hegel.* Baltimore: Johns Hopkins Press.
FINKELSTEIN, LOUIS (editor) (1949) 1960 *The Jews: Their History, Culture and Religion.* 2 vols., 3d ed. New York: Harper.
FRANK, JEROME 1949 *Courts on Trial.* Princeton (N.J.) Univ. Press → A paperback edition was published in 1963.
FRIEDMANN, WOLFGANG (1945) 1960 *Legal Theory.* 4th ed. London: Stevens.
GILBY, THOMAS 1958 *Principality and Polity: Aquinas and the Rise of State Theory in the West.* London: Longmans.
JOUVENEL, BERTRAND DE (1955) 1957 *Sovereignty: An Inquiry Into the Political Good.* Univ. of Chicago Press. → First published in French as *De la souveraineté: À la recherche du bien politique.*
KELSEN, HANS (1945) 1961 *A General Theory of Law and State.* New York: Russell. → The author's reformulation of ideas previously expressed in works published in German and French between 1925 and 1934.
KELSEN, HANS 1958 Letters. *New York University Law Review* 33:1056–1058.
MALINOWSKI, BRONISLAW (1926) 1961 *Crime and Custom in Savage Society.* New York: Harcourt. → A paperback edition was published in 1959 by Littlefield.
PASHUKANIS, E. B. 1927 *Obshchaia teoria prava i Marksizm* (General Theory of Law and Marxism). Moscow: Izdatel'stvo Kommunisticheskoi Akademii. → For a partial English translation, see *Soviet Legal Philosophy* 1951.
POUND, ROSCOE 1951 *Justice According to Law.* New Haven: Yale Univ. Press.
RADBRUCH, GUSTAV (1914) 1950 *Gustav Radbruch: Legal Philosophy.* Pages 43–224 in *The Legal Philosophies of Lask, Radbruch, and Dabin.* Translated by Kurt Wilk. 20th Century Legal Philosophy Series, Vol. 4. Cambridge, Mass.: Harvard Univ. Press. → First published in German. The 1950 edition was translated from the revised and rewritten edition of 1932. A sixth German edition, edited by Erik Wolf, was published in 1963.
*Soviet Legal Philosophy.* 1951 Cambridge, Mass.: Harvard Univ. Press; Oxford Univ. Press. → A collection of major classics by V. I. Lenin and others, translated by Hugh W. Babb and published under the auspices of the Association of American Law Schools.
STAMMLER, RUDOLF (1911) 1925 *The Theory of Justice.* New York: Macmillan. → First published in German.
TUCKER, ROBERT C. 1963 Marx and Distributive Justice. In Carl J. Friedrich and John W. Chapman (editors), *Justice.* Nomos 6. New York: Atherton.
VECCHIO, GIORGIO DEL 1952 *Justice: An Historical and Philosophical Essay.* Edited by A. H. Campbell. Edinburgh Univ. Press. → First published in Italian; also translated into German and French.

# JUVENILE DELINQUENCY
*See* DELINQUENCY.

# K

## KANT, IMMANUEL

Immanuel Kant (1724–1804) was born in Königsberg (then in East Prussia) and spent his entire life there. He studied at the University of Königsberg and taught there from 1755 until a few years before his death.

Kant's philosophy lies between empiricism and rationalism. He took from Hume the idea that man is "nothing but a bundle or collection of perceptions which succeed each other with inconceivable rapidity" (Hume 1739–1779, p. 320 in 1826 edition), and from Spinoza the concept that ideas are independent of experience. Yet he could accept neither a pure rationalism nor a pure empiricism; his primary work, the *Critique of Pure Reason*, begins as follows: "There can be no doubt that all our knowledge begins with experience . . . but it does not follow that it all arises out of experience" ([1781] 1950, p. 41). In this and another major work, *Prolegomena to Any Future Metaphysics* (1783), he was concerned to find the "valid source" of human knowledge, the way of establishing truth.

Kant's particular concern was to determine whether what he called synthetic a priori judgments are possible, that is to say, whether it is possible to establish necessary and universal connections among objects. Convinced that mathematics provides such synthetic a priori propositions, he sought to prove that it is possible in like manner to obtain knowledge of the laws of nature.

Newton's construction of scientific and mathematical theories suggested to Kant the process by which such knowledge might be acquired: "Accidental observations, made in obedience to no previously thought-out plan, can never be made to yield a necessary law, which alone reason is concerned to discover. Reason . . . must approach nature in order to be taught by it. It must not, however, do so in the character of a pupil who listens to everything that the teacher chooses to say, but of an appointed judge who compels the witnesses to answer questions which he himself has formulated" ([1781] 1950, p. 20 in Preface to 1787 edition).

Man, according to Kant, approaches experience in terms of basic *Anschauungen* (kinds of intuition) that are themselves not derived from experience and are not subject to empirical proof; these intuitions are space, time, and causation. Together with four categories (quantity, quality, relation, and modality), these intuitions are the basis of all understanding. Knowledge is merely an application of these categories, or a priori concepts, to sense perceptions, which are intuitively structured in time and space. Human knowledge is limited to these spatial and temporal phenomena; it does not extend to what is behind phenomena, that is, to the noumena, or things-in-themselves.

**Influence on psychology.** Much controversy in psychology developed as a result of Kant's distinction between the self as a thing-in-itself, or noumenon, and the self as a phenomenon. Since the first self is the transcendental unity of self-consciousness or apperception, it is inaccessible to inquiry except by introspection; its sole expression is moral judgment. According to Kant, only the phenomenal self can be the subject of empirical studies, and so it becomes part of anthropology ("Anthropologie in pragmatischer Hinsicht" 1798). This empirical or pragmatic psychology deals with what an observer can know about mental processes. Kant's dichotomy between what an individual may know of his own mind (noumenon) and what others may know of him (phenomenon) gave rise to the controversy between the introspectionist and the behaviorist approaches to psychology.

For the introspectionists, awareness of oneself, *Bewusstsein* or consciousness, became the core concept and introspection the chief method. Their subject of study was inner experience, and introspection provided the only means of access to the data. The behaviorists rejected this method, relying exclusively on observation of the overt behavior of the phenomenal self.

While Kant's "anthropology" (i.e., psychology) does not contain many new ideas, his critique of the concept of soul was a significant departure both from the Judaeo–Christian tradition and from Platonic philosophy. "The concept," he wrote, "is therefore quite void as regards all hoped-for insight into the cause of appearances and cannot at all serve as a principle of explanation of that which inner or outer experience supplies" ([1783] 1951, p. 79).

**Social theory.** Kant's social theory was based on the concept of progress, the source of progress being the inner conflict between man's sociability and his selfishness. Kant called this antagonism the "unsocial sociability." Man, according to Kant, "has an inclination to socialize himself by associating with others"; but he is also driven by antisocial forces. Kant's conception of the positive dynamic consequences of man's conflict are well expressed in this passage: "Man wishes concord; but Nature knows better what is good for his species, and she will have discord. . . . The natural impulses that urge man in this direction, the sources of that unsociableness and general antagonism from which so many evils arise, do yet at the same time impel him to new exertion of his powers, and consequently, to further development of his natural capacities" ([1784–1795] 1891, pp. 11–12).

The social order that Kant recommended, based as it was on this analysis of man's nature, would permit a maximum of individual freedom and competition, yet would have enough power to restrain this freedom whenever it threatened to produce oppression or anarchy. He proposed a similar system for international affairs; each separate state should be free to run its own affairs, but a supranational federation of sovereign states would have enough power to regulate international relations and prevent war.

Kant believed not only in political progress—the history of the human race could be viewed as a development toward a perfect political constitution —but also in moral progress. The stages in man's moral development are anomy, heteronomy, and autonomy. In the natural, primitive, anomic state, impulses were naive, innocent, and uncontrolled.

Civilization began when man broke with the natural state and accepted externally imposed moral law; this is the stage of heteronomy. Ultimately, there will be moral autonomy, a state of absolute freedom, in which the individual will obey only a self-imposed law, the "moral imperative."

BENJAMIN B. WOLMAN

[*For the historical context of Kant's work, see the biographies of* HUME *and* SPINOZA. *For discussion of the subsequent development of Kant's ideas, see* GESTALT THEORY; PHENOMENOLOGY; PSYCHOLOGY, *article on* EXISTENTIAL PSYCHOLOGY; *and the biographies of* DURKHEIM; HEGEL; HERING; KOFFKA; KÖHLER; KÜLPE; LOTZE; MÜLLER, GEORG ELIAS; STUMPF; WEBER, MAX; WERTHEIMER; WUNDT.]

### WORKS BY KANT
(1781) 1950 *Immanuel Kant's Critique of Pure Reason.* Translated by N. Kemp Smith. New York: Humanities. → First published in German.
(1783) 1951 *Prolegomena to Any Future Metaphysics.* New York: Liberal Arts. → First published in German.
(1784–1795) 1891 *Kant's Principles of Politics, Including His Essay "On Perpetual Peace."* Edited and translated by W. Hastie. Edinburgh: Clark. → First published in German.
(1798) 1907 *Anthropologie in pragmatischer Hinsicht.* Volume 7, pages 117–333 in *Kant's gesammelte Schriften.* Berlin: Reimer.
*Kant's gesammelte Schriften.* 22 vols. Berlin: Reimer, 1900–1942.

### SUPPLEMENTARY BIBLIOGRAPHY
BRETT, GEORGE S. (1912–1921) 1962 *Brett's History of Psychology.* Edited and abridged by R. S. Peters. London: Allen & Unwin; New York: Macmillan.
CASSIRER, ERNST 1918 *Kants Leben und Lehre.* Berlin: Cassirer.
HUME, DAVID (1739–1779) 1964 *The Philosophical Works.* 4 vols. Edited by Thomas Hill Green and Thomas Hodge Grose. Aalen (Germany): Scientia.
PATON, HERBERT J. (1936) 1951 *Kant's Metaphysic of Experience: A Commentary on the First Half of the Kritik der reinen Vernunft.* 2 vols. London: Allen & Unwin.
SPINOZA, BENEDICT (1677) 1950 *Ethics.* Translated by A. Boyle. London: Dent; New York: Dutton.
WELDON, THOMAS DEWAR (1945) 1958 *Kant's* Critique of Pure Reason. 2d ed. Oxford: Clarendon. → First published as *Introduction to Kant's* Critique of Pure Reason.
WOLMAN, BENJAMIN B. (editor) *Historical Roots of Contemporary Psychology.* New York: Harper. → Contains an essay by Wolman on "Immanuel Kant and His Impact on Psychology." Scheduled for publication in 1968.

## KANTOROWICZ, HERMANN

Hermann Kantorowicz (1877–1940), German jurist, was born in Posen (Posznan). After receiving his secondary education at the Louisen Gymnasium in Berlin, he proceeded to study law at Berlin, Geneva, and Munich, and he obtained his doctorate of laws in 1904 from the University of Heidelberg with a dissertation on the history of criminal law. After devoting several years of study in Italy to the history of European jurisprudence, he was appointed in 1907 as *Privatdozent* to teach criminal law, the philosophy of law, and the history of law in the University of Freiburg (Breisgau). He was made an associate professor in 1913 and full professor of auxiliary juridical sciences in 1923. In 1927 he gave a seminar at Columbia University, New York. The following year he was appointed professor of criminal law at the University of Kiel. After the Nazi government dismissed Kantorowicz in 1933, he became a professor in the graduate faculty of the New School for Social Research, New York, and he also lectured at the College of the City of New York, the London School of Economics, All Souls College, Oxford, and at Cambridge. In 1937 he was appointed assistant director of research in law at Cambridge, where he died in 1940.

Kantorowicz early turned to the problems of method in jurisprudence. His controversial pamphlet *Der Kampf um die Rechtswissenschaft* appeared in 1906 under the pseudonym of Gnaeus Flavius. This pamphlet aimed at uniting the growing number of those who emphasized the legislative aspect of judicial decisions into a militant movement for the "doctrine of free law" (*Freirechtslehre*). The pamphlet proclaimed that a judge must not only apply the rules of law to individual cases but should also create law whenever there is a hiatus in a statute. This, then, constituted a challenge to legal positivism, which based jurisprudence on the logical subsumption of any particular case under the law. Kantorowicz felt that as a consequence of positivist legal theory the dictates of justice were frequently ignored and the demands of social reality were neglected, and he tagged the legal-positivist judge as a "subsumption automaton." He combined his criticism of positivism in law with a critique of "analytical jurisprudence," which at that time still tended to dominate legal thinking, and asserted that abstract logical deduction does not suffice for the exposition of the rules of law and the formation of juridical concepts. He also maintained that judicial decisions and jurisprudence should take the emotions into account.

The study of the sources of law was also enriched by Kantorowicz. In addition to formal law, especially statute law, he considered "free law" to be such a source. (Free law consists not only of custom and usage but also of judicial opinions and the authoritative statements of legal scholars.) Supporting the validity of statute law, Kantorowicz refused to accept any judicial decision *contra legem* as a source of law. He regarded the judge's commitment to the statutes to be a constitutional guarantee of the individual's freedom and legal security and believed that only where there is a hiatus in a statute should the judge exercise his juridical creativity.

The new free-law school of thought acquired more and more adherents and made a major contribution to the defeat of legal positivism. In his *Aus der Vorgeschichte der Freirechtslehre* (1925), Kantorowicz traced the development of this trend from antiquity to the nineteenth century. He pointed out that the doctrine of free law was founded upon new methods and findings in the philosophy of law, in the study of juridical method, and in the study of the psychology of the judge. The influence of Neo-Kantianism is clearly perceptible in Kantorowicz' writings on the philosophy of law and the theory of juridical method. Kantorowicz felt indebted, above all, to the Heidelberg philosopher Emil Lask. And his doctrine is akin to that of Gustav Radbruch, the Heidelberg legal philosopher, who had long been his close friend.

Like Radbruch, Kantorowicz espoused a relativism of values. In his "Staatsauffassungen" (1924a) and in "Legal Science" (Kantorowicz & Patterson 1928), Kantorowicz tried to specify the place of the science of law among the sciences. In his theory of science, he distinguished sciences of facts, sciences of meaning, and sciences of value. Although he finally classified jurisprudence among the sciences of value, he attempted to take into account its many aspects. In his posthumous book, *The Definition of Law* (1958), Kantorowicz dealt with the basic question, "What is law?" and demarcated law from other norm areas, "normal law" in particular. His definition of law is "a body of rules prescribing external conduct and considered justiciable" (*ibid*, p. 21).

Kantorowicz was one of the first German professors of law to espouse sociology, and he did so enthusiastically. Before his time Jhering, Gierke, Duguit, Gumplowicz, Menger, and others had emphasized the social aspect of the law. Kantorowicz was especially indebted to Max Weber for his sociological insights. Following in the latter's footsteps, Kantorowicz tried to introduce sociology into jurisprudence. In a lecture entitled *Rechtswissenschaft und Soziologie* (1911), delivered at a Frankfurt convention of sociologists, he established limits for the two disciplines based on his classification of the sciences: jurisprudence was to be a science of values and sociology a science of facts. He urged that the two sciences, jurisprudence and sociology, complement each other. His "Aufbau der Soziologie"

(1923) outlined the nature of sociology and located it among the sciences in such a way as to allow full play to all its tendencies, whether philosophically oriented or empirical.

In his article "Some Rationalism About Realism" (1934), Kantorowicz took issue with the empirical tendency then dominant in the United States. He criticized the views of the legal realists, who held that the factual takes precedence over the normative and were more concerned with what the courts were doing than with what could be deduced from the norms of the laws. He stressed that the "law is not what the courts administer, but the courts are the institutions which administer the law" (1934, p. 1250). Kantorowicz also charged the realists with laying too much stress on the notion of the social determination of all law and with regarding jurisprudence exclusively as an empirical sociological science. Kantorowicz' essay was credited with having a moderating influence upon the realist tendency in American legal science.

Kantorowicz made significant contributions to the history of law as well as to legal theory. Throughout his career he wrote and edited books about the history of Italian criminal law in the Middle Ages and the early Renaissance (1904; 1919; 1907–1926; 1938). He also studied the history of the sources of Roman law in the Middle Ages. His painstaking work in the field of the history of law is evident in his writings *Entstehung der Digestenvulgata* (1910) and *Einführung in die Textkritik* (1921). Finally, Kantorowicz was concerned with the nature and significance of the historical school of law of the nineteenth century. He was greatly attracted to the ideas of F. C. von Savigny, the founder of the historical school, as indicated by *Was ist uns Savigny?* (1912) and "Savigny and the Historical School of Law" (1937). He also wrote about other nineteenth-century representatives of legal science, such as Jhering and Max Conrat.

Kantorowicz was a leading student of criminal law. At an early date he realized the great significance of comparative criminal law in the evolution of jurisprudence. He also took a stand on the reform of German criminal law, trying to strike a balance between the "classical" and "sociological" schools of criminal law. In his book *Tat und Schuld* (1933), he developed the concept of universal doctrines of criminal law by taking a critical attitude toward the German science of criminal law. This book clearly shows how broad Kantorowicz' concepts were and how much he was imbued with a constitutional way of thinking. [See CRIMINAL LAW.]

Kantorowicz was a militant throughout his life

and was passionately concerned with the problems of politics. In works such as *Germany and the League of Nations* (1924b) and *The Spirit of British Policy and the Myth of the Encirclement of Germany* (1929) he was primarily concerned with the problems of foreign policy and the idea of world peace.

THOMAS WÜRTENBERGER

[*See also* JURISPRUDENCE; PUBLIC LAW. *Other relevant material may be found in the biographies of* LLEWELLYN; POUND; RADBRUCH; SAVIGNY; WEBER, MAX.]

### WORKS BY KANTOROWICZ

1904 *Goblers Karolinen-Kommentar und seine Nachfolger.* Berlin: Guttentag.

1906 *Der Kampf um die Rechtswissenschaft,* by Gnaeus Flavius [pseud.]. Heidelberg: Winter.

1907–1926 *Albertus Gandinus und das Strafrecht der Scholastik.* 2 vols. Berlin: Guttentag; de Gruyter.

1910 *Entstehung der Digestenvulgata: Ergänzungen zu Mommsen.* Weimar: Böhlaus Nachfolger.

1911 *Rechtswissenschaft und Soziologie.* Tübingen: Mohr.

1912 *Was ist uns Savigny?* Berlin: Heymann.

1919 DIPLOVATATIUS, THOMAS *De claris iuris consultis.* Edited by Hermann Kantorowicz and Fritz Schulz. Berlin: de Gruyter.

1921 *Einführung in die Textkritik: Systematische Darstellung der textkritischen Grundsätze für Philologen und Juristen.* Leipzig: Dieterich.

1923 Der Aufbau der Soziologie. Volume 1, pages 73–96 in *Hauptprobleme der Soziologie: Erinnerungsgabe für Max Weber.* Munich and Leipzig: Duncker & Humblot.

1924a Staatsauffassungen: Eine Skizze. Volume 1, pages 102–114 in *Jahrbuch für Soziologie.* Karlsruhe: Braun.

1924b *Germany and the League of Nations.* Westminster and London: Fabian Society.

1925 *Aus der Vorgeschichte der Freirechtslehre.* Mannheim: Bensheimer.

1928 KANTOROWICZ, HERMANN; and PATTERSON, EDWIN W. Legal Science: A Summary of Its Methodology. *Columbia Law Review* 28:679–707.

(1929) 1931 *The Spirit of British Policy and the Myth of the Encirclement of Germany.* London: Allen & Unwin. → First published in German.

1933 *Tat und Schuld.* Zurich and Leipzig: Füssli.

1934 Some Rationalism About Realism. *Yale Law Journal* 43:1240–1253.

1937 Savigny and the Historical School of Law. *Law Quarterly Review* 53:326–343.

1938 KANTOROWICZ, HERMANN; and BUCKLAND, WILLIAM W. *Studies in the Glossators of the Roman Law: Newly Discovered Writings of the Twelfth Century.* Cambridge Univ. Press.

1958 *The Definition of Law.* Edited by A. H. Campbell. With an introduction by A. L. Goodhart. Cambridge Univ. Press. → Written in 1938; first published posthumously.

# KATZ, DAVID

David Katz (1884–1953), experimental psychologist associated with the universities of Göttingen, Rostock, and Stockholm, is best known as a proponent of the phenomenological method in psychology and as a contributor of research in a wide variety of experimental fields, notably in visual and tactual perception, motivation, and animal and child behavior. Although he was not identified with a specific "school" of psychology, he was one of the leaders of the post-World War I revolt against the atomistic and associationistic tradition of the nineteenth century. His *Gestalt Psychology* (1944), while an exposition and critique rather than a defense of that position, reveals a systematic point of view close to that of Max Wertheimer, Wolfgang Köhler, and Kurt Koffka.

Katz was a native of Kassel, Germany, where he received his early education. He studied at Göttingen, Munich, and Berlin, receiving his doctorate at Göttingen under G. E. Müller in 1906 and serving as Müller's assistant until he was promoted to the rank of *Privatdozent* in 1911. In 1914 he volunteered for military service, being assigned first to ambulance duty and later to a range-finding unit in the artillery. In both assignments he succeeded in combining research with his military duties. At the end of the war he initially returned to Göttingen but in 1919 was called to a newly established chair of psychology and education at the University of Rostock in Mecklenburg, where he remained until his dismissal by the Nazis in 1933 because of his Jewish origins. From then until 1937 he was supported as a refugee research scientist in England, first with T. H. Pear at Manchester and later in Cyril Burt's department at the University of London. In London, too, through the good offices of Julian Huxley, he was provided with facilities for animal research in the London Zoological Gardens. In 1937 he was appointed to the chair of pedagogy (which at that time included psychology) at the University of Stockholm, a post which he held until his retirement in 1952. While in Stockholm Katz served as organizing secretary of the Thirteenth International Congress of Psychology, which met there in 1951. His posts included a visiting professorship at the University of Maine in 1929, the Hitchcock Lectureship at the University of California in 1950, and a postretirement visiting professorship at the University of Hamburg. He was married in 1919 to Rosa Heine, also a pupil of G. E. Müller's, who collaborated with him in many of his researches.

Although Katz will probably be remembered primarily for his application of the phenomenological method to experimental psychology, his fertile imagination and his experimental ingenuity yielded important, frequently pioneering contributions to a wide variety of psychological fields. In addition to his classic studies of color and touch, these contributions included: studies in educational and child psychology (Katz & Katz 1928); a long series of animal experiments, many of which are summarized in *Animals and Men* (1937); an approach to the theory of motivation based on the analysis of hunger and appetite; investigations of vibratory and other relatively unnoticed forms of perception (1930); studies in the psychology of thinking (1953); and miscellaneous contributions to experimental instrumentation. His laboratory in Rostock became one of the most active and productive in pre-Hitler Germany, and his influence on the development of experimental psychology in Sweden was great.

G. E. Müller was undoubtedly the dominant influence during Katz's formative years as a psychologist. During the early years of this century Müller's institute in Göttingen rivaled that of Wilhelm Wundt in Leipzig as a center for experimental research and as a mecca for young psychologists from other countries. Müller ruled his laboratory with an iron hand. His own research interests were primarily in psychophysics, perception, and memory, and his pupils were likely to begin their research in one of these fields. Among the students with whom Katz was associated were the Dane Edgar Rubin, the Hungarian Géza Révész, the American Lillien Martin, the Englishmen William McDougall and Charles Spearman, and the Germans Narziss Ach and E. R. Jaensch, all of whom learned from Müller the discipline of the laboratory but most of whom moved far from Müller's rigorously analytic psychology. For Katz, and probably also for Révész and Rubin, an equally important influence came from the philosopher Edmund Husserl and through him from the phenomenological movement that was gaining strength in German philosophy. Katz attended Husserl's lectures and also became friendly with Max Scheler, both of whom showed a lively, although not uncritical, interest in the new experimental psychology.

The appeal of Husserl's phenomenology to the psychologist lay in its insistence on a free and unbiased, yet rigorous description of the phenomena of experience. It was antipositivistic in its rejection of the reductive atomism of the nineteenth-century associationists, but not antiscientific. Husserl held out the hope that philosophy itself could eventually become a rigorous science (*strenge Wissenschaft*). The phenomenological method involved the deliberate suspension or "bracketing" (*einklammern*) of presuppositions as to the nature, composition, and origin of experience. Katz employed this method in his descriptive and experimental analyses of the world of color (1911) and the world of touch (1925). To be suspended was the prevailing nineteenth-century theory of perception, identified with

Hermann von Helmholtz and with the earlier English empiricists, as a composite of primary, meaningless, sensory elements modified or interpreted through central associative or intellectual processes. Such a theory, Katz pointed out, involves a prejudgment of the nature of perception that automatically and arbitrarily excludes from investigation some of its most interesting phenomena. In addition to the traditional descriptive categories of hue, brightness, and saturation, the phenomena of color may be ordered along such dimensions as mode of appearance (*Erscheinungsweise*), pronouncedness (*Ausgeprägtheit*), insistence (*Eindringlichkeit*), transparency, inherence, and stability; and similarly the world of touch (*tasten* —to touch actively) has many properties and dimensions not included in the traditional categories of pressure, pain, and temperature. For Katz the study of perception must include the whole world of things, events, and relations as they are naively apprehended, including the phenomena of meaningful organization, expression, and intentionality. Katz's experiments, particularly those on phenomenal constancy, now rank as classics in the field of perception.

ROBERT B. MACLEOD

[*For the historical context of Katz's work, see* GESTALT THEORY; PHENOMENOLOGY; *and the biographies of* HUSSERL; KOFFKA; KÖHLER; MÜLLER, GEORG ELIAS; WERTHEIMER. *For discussion of the subsequent development of Katz's ideas, see* SKIN SENSES AND KINESTHESIS; *and* VISION, *article on* COLOR VISION AND COLOR BLINDNESS.]

### WORKS BY KATZ

(1911) 1935  *The World of Colour.* London: Routledge. → First published in German as *Die Erscheinungsweisen der Farben und ihre Beeinflussung durch die individuelle Erfahrung.* A revised and enlarged edition was published in 1930 as *Der Aufbau der Farbwelt.*

1913  *Psychologie und mathematischer Unterricht.* Leipzig: Teubner.

1921  *Zur Psychologie des Amputierten und seiner Prothese.* Leipzig: Barth.

1925  *Der Aufbau der Tastwelt.* Leipzig: Barth.

1928  KATZ, DAVID; and KATZ, ROSA *Gespräche mit Kindern.* Berlin: Springer.

1930  *The Vibratory Sense, and Other Lectures.* Orono: Univ. of Maine Press.

1937  *Animals and Men: Studies in Comparative Psychology.* English translation by Alice I. Taylor and Herbert S. Jackson from David Katz's manuscript. London and New York: Longmans.

(1944) 1950  *Gestalt Psychology: Its Nature and Significance.* New York: Ronald Press. → First published as *Gestaltpsychologie.*

1952  Autobiography. Volume 4, pages 189–211 in *A History of Psychology in Autobiography.* Worcester, Mass.: Clark Univ. Press.

1953  *Studien zur experimentellen Psychologie.* Basel: Schwabe.

# KAUṬILYA

No authentic contemporary or even nearly contemporary account of the life of Kauṭilya, also known as Chánakya and Vishṇugupta, is available to us. All that we know of him is derived from traditions current about five centuries after his death. According to these traditions he was a very learned orthodox Bráhmaṇa of eastern India who was highly versed in politics. He served the Nanda kings of Magadha (South Bihar) but, becoming alienated from them, helped Chandragupta to seize their throne. Chandragupta, the founder of the Mauyra dynasty of Magadha, appointed Kauṭilya his prime minister and by following his counsel made himself a great emperor.

Chandragupta is undoubtedly a historical person. According to the Roman historian Justin, Chandragupta established his kingdom by driving out the Greek governors whom Alexander had left in charge of the territories he had conquered in India. After Alexander's death his general Seleucus marched with an army to India to recover the lost territories. He actually crossed the Indus but was obliged to make peace by ceding to Chandragupta vast territories, roughly corresponding to modern Afghanistan and Baluchistan, that were still in Greek possession. Chandragupta ruled over a vast empire that extended from the Hindu Kush all the way to Assam and probably included a large part of the Deccan. His reign probably covered the last quarter of the fourth century B.C.

According to tradition Kauṭilya played an important role as Chandragupta's prime minister. But to what extent Kauṭilya actually helped his imperial master to acquire or maintain his vast empire cannot be determined exactly. His chief claim to fame is the composition of a treatise known as the *Arthaśāstra*, which deals with the art of government in a very comprehensive manner. It has been mentioned and quoted by many writers down to the fifteenth century. But although the work was regarded as the authoritative treatise on the subject, no copy of the text was known to modern scholars until the discovery of a manuscript at the beginning of this century. It is a big book, containing 150 chapters divided into 15 sections. This manuscript was at first unanimously accepted as the genuine text of the long-lost treatise of Kauṭilya, but doubts have since been expressed by many scholars. Without going into the details of this question one may reasonably take the view that the text is the *Arthaśāstra* of Kauṭilya with minor modifications introduced in later times.

Proceeding on this basis we may note in the first place the information that we may gather about

Kauṭilya himself from the internal evidence of the *Arthaśāstra*. He was highly intellectual and well-read in the Hindu religious scriptures and in works on polity and other allied subjects. Since the book not only discusses political theories but also gives elaborate details of the administrative system, Kauṭilya evidently had that familiarity with the detailed work in various branches of administration that we would expect from one who held the high office of prime minister of a great empire. He was thoroughly conversant with the minute details of legal principles and of the administration of justice, with military science (including rules of warfare, strategy, offensive and defensive weapons, fortifications, battle array, etc.), and with the principles governing interstate relations, corresponding to modern international law. At the same time he showed practical knowledge of agricultural operations, maritime trade and commerce, both inland and foreign, the working of mines, animal husbandry, forestry, the textile industry, and even distillery operations, not to speak of sundry minor trades and occupations.

The *Arthaśāstra* also throws light on some special characteristics that distinguish Kauṭilya from other Indian statesmen and writers on polity. In the first place, he had a very rational mind and did not blindly accept the current views based on faith and tradition. The ancient Hindus held that the Vedas constitute the sole source of law; more liberal writers added, as supplementary sources, the conduct and customs of holy men. But Kauṭilya laid down four distinct sources of law, namely, sacred scriptures; the rules he laid down in the *Arthaśāstra;* customs; and edicts of kings. Each of these he considered more authoritative than the one preceding it. He explicitly stated that when sacred law is in conflict with the rational law, reason shall be held authoritative. No other Hindu writer before the nineteenth century had the courage to assert openly that the law made by the state or supported by reason may supersede the injunction of sacred texts. The bold statement of Kauṭilya shows that he did not regard politics as ancillary to religion.

Second, according to Kauṭilya, moral considerations have no place in politics. He advised the king to follow only that policy calculated to increase his power and material resources, and he felt no scruple in recommending dubious and sometimes highly unjust and immoral means to achieve that end. For this purpose he sketched an elaborate system for recruiting spies and training them.

Third, Kauṭilya preached the ideal of a strong centralized monarchy, which would gradually develop into an all-India empire, established by the ruthless conquest of smaller states, particularly the republican and oligarchic states that existed in large numbers in those days and were considered to be very powerful.

Kauṭilya often showed a surprisingly modern outlook. His view of the origin of kingship anticipates Locke's theory of contract. "People," he said, "elected Manu to be their king, to protect them from the evils of anarchy, and agreed to pay him taxes." Fed by this payment, kings took upon themselves the responsibility of maintaining the safety and security of their subjects. His conception of the different elements necessary to constitute a state is even more modern; it fulfills the requirements of twentieth-century international law for the recognition of a state.

More surprising is the fact that Kauṭilya preached a kind of state socialism, or state capitalism. The state, in his opinion, should conduct mining operations and carry on trade in commodities manufactured from mineral products, as well as producing and trading in various other commodities, including textiles, timber, and fishery and agricultural products.

To Kauṭilya, the ideal state was something like a modern welfare state. He clearly required the state to provide for the maintenance of children, childless women, and old, infirm, and diseased persons, who have no natural guardians to protect them. As a corollary it was provided that a person who was able to maintain his parents, wife, children, and minor brothers and neglected to do so, should be punished. Punishment was also to be inflicted upon a person who took to the ascetic life without making provision for the maintenance of his wife and sons. This was all the more surprising in a society that regarded ascetics with the highest veneration and held asceticism to be the *summum bonum* of life.

If we regard the extant *Arthaśāstra* as indeed mainly the handiwork of Kauṭilya, we must attribute to him keen intellect, versatile knowledge, wide experience of men and affairs, and bold, original ideas. He must also have been an able minister, a clever politician, and a great statesman—albeit without any moral scruples—whose only concern was with the development of the power and resources of an empire whose interests were entrusted to his care. We can easily visualize him devoting himself to the service of his imperial master with zeal and sincerity, undeterred, or rather unfettered, by considerations of either religion or morality.

R. C. MAJUMDAR

[*For the historical context of Kauṭilya's work, see* IN-DIAN POLITICAL THOUGHT; *also consult the biography of* MACHIAVELLI *for similar ideas in a different context.*]

### BIBLIOGRAPHY

BHANDARKAR, DEVATTA R. 1929 *Some Aspects of Ancient Hindu Polity.* Lecture delivered February 1925. Benares (India) Hindu University.

BRELOER, BERNHARD 1927–1934 *Kauṭalīya-Studien.* 3 vols. Bonn: Schroeder.

*The History and Culture of the Indian People.* Volume 2: The Age of Imperial Unity. (1951) 1960 Bombay (India): Bharatiya Vidya Bhavan.

KAUṬILYA *Kauṭilya's Arthaśāstra.* 3d ed. Translated by Dr. R. Shamasastry with an introductory note by the late Dr. J. F. Fleet. Mysore (India): Wesleyan Mission Press, 1929.

MODELSKI, GEORGE A. 1964 Kauṭilya: Foreign Policy and International System in the Ancient Hindu World. *American Political Science Review* 58:549–560.

# KAUTSKY, KARL

Karl Kautsky (1854–1938), socialist theoretician and social scientist, was born October 16, 1854, in Prague, the son of a Czech painter and an Austrian actress and novelist. Kautsky was throughout his life, by temperament and interests, above all a social scientist. His social science was not the politician's tool in his drive for power; rather, he became influential in politics only to the extent that his approach and findings met needs existing in the socialist movement.

While attending the University of Vienna and working as a journalist for the small Austrian Social Democratic party, Kautsky, influenced by the works of J. S. Mill, H. T. Buckle, and especially Darwin, groped for a theory of history along natural science lines. In 1880 he joined some German socialists, in exile in Zurich, as a writer and as a student of the writings of such anthropologists as Herbert Bancroft, J. J. Bachofen, and Lewis Henry Morgan. He became a Marxist under Eduard Bernstein's guidance, and in 1881 he visited Marx and Engels.

In 1883, Kautsky founded the monthly (weekly from 1890) *Die Neue Zeit* in Stuttgart, an event that marks the beginning of Marxism as a school of thought. As its editor until 1917, he published contributions from socialist thinkers all over the world as well as hundreds of his own articles. From 1885 to 1890, he worked in London in close contact with Engels. His *Economic Doctrines of Karl Marx* (1887), in numerous German and foreign editions, made Kautsky largely responsible for Marxism's early spread. He also applied the Marxian method in some original historical studies—*Thomas More and His Utopia* (1888), *Foundations of Christianity* (1908), and a study of the precursors of modern socialism (1895). A book on class conflicts during the French Revolution (1889) stressed the complexity of social conflicts and modified the concept of the class struggle by emphasis on divisions within classes, a recurring theme in Kautsky's thought, somewhat akin to the interest-group approach of modern political science.

In 1891, Kautsky drafted the "theoretical part" of the German Social Democratic party's (SPD) Erfurt program. This first major Marxist party program and his widely translated commentary, *Das Erfurter Programm* (1892), established him, after Engels, as the leading Marxist theoretician in the Socialist International. He moved to Berlin in 1897.

Kautsky was one of the first Marxists to formulate theories of imperialism (beginning in *Die Neue Zeit* in 1898) and agricultural development (*Die Agrarfrage* 1899a; see also 1919a). Unlike Rudolf Hilferding and Lenin, but more like Schumpeter, Kautsky saw imperialism as the product not of industrial capitalism but of preindustrial, especially aristocratic, elements that remained strong in modern society. He traced these elements back to prehistoric times when nomadic conquerors of peasant societies sought unlimited territorial expansion. In agriculture, Kautsky could, at the turn of the century, find no general tendency for large enterprise to replace small enterprise, but he considered large enterprise to be potentially more productive. He therefore favored a socialist program that advocated conversion of large estates into communal or cooperative enterprises, and he expected that individual peasant enterprises would eventually voluntarily join such cooperatives.

When Bernstein attacked the SPD's "revolutionary" doctrine, Kautsky became the chief defender of "orthodox" Marxism (see his *Bernstein und das sozialdemokratische Programm* 1899b; *The Social Revolution* 1902). He advocated reformist practice and revolutionary, but not insurrectionary, goals. Such a program served to integrate those German and other Continental socialist parties which, despite their sharp conflict with their militarist-bureaucratic regimes, appealed to the working classes by demanding reforms. With the Revisionists, Kautsky believed that socialism could be realized only through parliamentary democracy (see his earlier *Parlamentarismus und Demokratie* 1893), but unlike them he did not expect democracy to grow peacefully in the German empire (*The Road to Power* 1909). He insisted on a "revolutionary," i.e., oppositional, strategy, because compromises with the so-called bourgeois parties supporting the imperial regime would endanger labor's political unity. In the same period, Kautsky edited Marx's manuscript notes for a fourth volume of *Capital*, entitling the volume *Theorien über den Mehrwert* (1905–1910).

In 1910, Kautsky, in the "Marxist center" of the SPD, attacked as impatient and reckless the radical advocates of revolutionary mass strikes, led by Rosa Luxemburg. Their polemics (reviewed in Kautsky 1914*a*) foreshadowed the clash between the social-democrats and the communists. The former saw the party as an instrument to prepare the workers for their inevitable rise to power, while the latter saw it as a revolution-making "shock troop."

During World War I, Kautsky opposed both the SPD majority's support of the German government and the Spartacists' call for revolution against all "bourgeois" governments. Although resisting a party split as long as possible, he did join the new Independent Social Democratic party (USPD), to oppose the SPD's war policy. Between 1915 and 1918, in studies of the problem of nationalities, he advocated national self-determination and rejected the inevitability of imperialist expansionism under capitalism. After the German revolution at the end of the war, he served as a secretary of state for foreign affairs in the SPD–USPD coalition of November–December 1918. He collected the German documents on the outbreak of the war (1919*b*; see also his book on the origins of World War I, 1919*c*) and was chairman of the government's socialization commission. Kautsky's views of the political and economic transition to socialism (*The Labour Revolution* 1922) became the basis of the reunited SPD's Heidelberg program.

Soon after the Bolshevik Revolution, Kautsky denounced all attempts to introduce socialism in a backward society by violent minority action as a betrayal of Marxism and democracy that would lead to dictatorship and eventual collapse (*The Dictatorship of the Proletariat* 1918). Called a renegade by Lenin and Trotsky, he replied in *Terrorism and Communism* (1919*d*) and in a book on democracy, dictatorship, and forced labor (1921*a*; see also 1925; 1930). In late 1920, Kautsky visited Menshevik-governed Georgia to study an underdeveloped country with a strong intelligentsia and a substantial urban working class (1921*b*).

At 70, Kautsky returned to Vienna to engage in research. He had always been interested in anthropology, ecology, and demography, fields straddling the social and natural sciences; and he aimed at developing a conceptual framework encompassing both these areas of science. He attempted this in his first, as yet non-Marxian book on the influence

of population growth on the progress of society (1880), in his later work on reproduction and development in nature and society (1910), in *Are the Jews a Race?* (1914*b*), and also in his natural science explanation of ethics as a response of man and certain animals to the requirements of life in society (1906). Later Kautsky systematized and elaborated his ideas about social and natural science in his monumental work on the materialist conception of history (1927). He regarded the Marxian theory of history as the application, in principle value-free, of the methods of science to the study of society. He rejected the Hegelian dialectic with its teleological overtones and substituted for it, as the basis for the law of development for which he had searched all his life, the process of adaptation to a changing environment. In organic nature, species change to adjust to a slowly changing natural environment; in human society, man adjusts by changing his environment himself, which in turn requires further adjustment by further changes, including both technical and social ones, in an unending process that is history.

With the rise of fascism in Germany and Austria, Kautsky critically analyzed various proposed socialist counterstrategies (1933; 1934). His last major publications were two of four projected historical works on war (*Krieg und Demokratie* 1932; *Sozialisten und Krieg* 1937) and an edition of his correspondence with Engels (1935). Of a large-scale autobiography (1960) only the part covering his life until 1883 was completed by March 1938, when Kautsky fled from the Nazis to Amsterdam. He died there on October 17, 1938.

JOHN H. KAUTSKY

[*For the historical context of Kautsky's work, see the biographies of* BACHOFEN; BERNSTEIN; DARWIN; ENGELS; LENIN; LUXEMBURG; MARX; MILL; TROTSKY.]

### WORKS BY KAUTSKY

1880    *Der Einfluss der Volksvermehrung auf den Fortschritt der Gesellschaft.* Vienna: Bloch & Hasbach.

(1887) 1936    *The Economic Doctrines of Karl Marx.* New York: Macmillan. → First published as *Karl Marx' ökonomische Lehren.*

(1888) 1959    *Thomas More and His Utopia.* New York: Russell. → First published as *Thomas More und seine Utopie.*

1889    *Die Klassengegensätze von 1789.* Stuttgart (Germany): Dietz. → Also published in 1908 as *Die Klassengegensätze im Zeitalter der französischen Revolution.*

1892    *Das Erfurter Programm in seinem grundsätzlichen Theil erläutert.* Stuttgart (Germany): Dietz. → Translated into English in 1910 as *The Class Struggle (Erfurt Program).*

(1893) 1911  *Parlamentarismus und Demokratie.* 2d ed., rev. & enl. Stuttgart (Germany): Dietz. → First published as *Der Parlamentarismus, die Volksgesetzgebung und die Sozialdemokratie.*

(1895) 1947  *Die Vorläufer des neueren Sozialismus.* 2d ed., enl. 2 vols. Stuttgart (Germany): Dietz. → Reprinted from the second edition of 1909.

1899a  *Die Agrarfrage: Eine Übersicht über die Tendenzen der modernen Landwirtschaft und die Agrarpolitik der Sozialdemokratie.* Stuttgart (Germany): Dietz.

1899b  *Bernstein und das sozialdemokratische Programm: Eine Antikritik.* Stuttgart (Germany): Dietz.

(1902) 1916  *The Social Revolution.* Chicago: Kerr. → First published as *Die soziale Revolution.*

1905–1910  MARX, KARL *Theorien über den Mehrwert: Aus dem nachgelassenen Manuskript* Zur Kritik der politischen Ökonomie. 3 vols. in 4. Edited by Karl Kautsky. Stuttgart (Germany): Dietz. → Enlarged and revised from Marx's preliminary manuscript, written between 1861 and 1863, for a fourth volume of *Capital.* A selection was published in 1952 by International Publishers as *Theories of Surplus Value: Selections.*

(1906) 1914  *Ethics and the Materialist Conception of History.* Chicago: Kerr. → First published as *Ethik und materialistische Geschichtsauffassung.*

(1908) 1953  *Foundations of Christianity.* New York: Russell. → First published as *Der Ursprung des Christentums.*

1909  *The Road to Power.* Chicago: Bloch. → Also published as *Der Weg zur Macht.*

1910  *Vermehrung und Entwicklung in Natur und Gesellschaft.* Stuttgart (Germany): Dietz.

1914a  *Der politische Massenstreik.* Berlin: Vorwärts.

(1914b) 1926  *Are the Jews a Race?* New York: International Publishers. → First published as *Rasse und Judentum.* Translated from the second German edition of 1921.

(1918) 1964  *The Dictatorship of the Proletariat.* Ann Arbor: Univ. of Michigan Press. → First published as *Die Diktatur des Proletariats.*

1919a  *Die Sozialisierung der Landwirtschaft.* Berlin: Cassirer.

(1919b) 1924  GERMANY, AUSWÄRTIGES AMT *Outbreak of the World War.* German documents collected by Karl Kautsky and edited by Max Montgelas and Walther Schücking. New York: Oxford Univ. Press. → First published as *Die deutschen Dokumente zum Kriegsausbruch.*

1919c  *Wie der Weltkrieg entstand: Dargestellt nach dem Aktenmaterial des Deutschen Auswärtigen Amts.* Berlin: Cassirer.

(1919d) 1920  *Terrorism and Communism.* London: Allen & Unwin; National Labour Press. → First published as *Terrorismus und Kommunismus.*

1921a  *Von der Demokratie zur Staatssklaverei.* Berlin: Freiheit.

1921b  *Georgia: A Social-Democratic Peasant Republic; Impressions and Observations.* London: International Bookshops. → First published as *Georgien: Eine sozialdemokratische Bauernrepublik; Eindrücke und Beobachtungen.*

(1922) 1925  *The Labour Revolution.* New York: Dial; London: Allen & Unwin. → First published as *Die proletarische Revolution und ihr Programm.*

1925  *Die Internationale und Sowjetrussland.* Berlin: Dietz.

1927  *Die materialistische Geschichtsauffassung.* 2 vols. Berlin: Dietz. → Volume 1: *Natur und Gesellschaft.* Volume 2: *Der Staat und die Entwicklung der Menschheit.*

(1930) 1931  *Bolshevism at a Deadlock.* London: Allen & Unwin. → First published as *Der Bolschewismus in der Sackgasse.*

1932  *Krieg und Demokratie.* Berlin: Dietz.

(1932–1937) 1946  *Social Democracy versus Communism.* Edited and translated by David Shub and Joseph Shaplen. New York: Rand School Press.

1933  *Neue Programme.* Vienna: Prager.

1934  *Grenzen der Gewalt.* Carlsbad (Czechoslovakia): Graphia.

(1935) 1955  *Friedrich Engels' Briefwechsel mit Karl Kautsky.* 2d ed. enl. Edited by Benedikt Kautsky. Vienna: Danubia. → First published as *Aus der Frühzeit des Marxismus.*

1937  *Sozialisten und Krieg: Ein Beitrag zur Ideengeschichte des Sozialismus von den Hussiten bis zum Völkerbund.* Prague: Orbis.

1960  *Erinnerungen und Erörterungen.* Edited by Benedikt Kautsky. The Hague: Mouton.

### SUPPLEMENTARY BIBLIOGRAPHY

BLUMENBERG, WERNER  1960  *Karl Kautskys literarisches Werk.* The Hague: Mouton. → A bibliography listing 1,800 original works and over 900 translations.

BRILL, HERMANN  1954  Karl Kautsky. *Zeitschrift für Politik* New Series 1:211–240.

*Ein Leben für den Sozialismus: Erinnerungen an Karl Kautsky* 1954 Hannover (Germany): Dietz.

*Karl Kautsky: Der Denker und Kämpfer* 1924 Vienna: Wiener Volksbuchhandlung. → Special issue of *Der Kampf.*

*Karl Kautsky zum 70. Geburtstage.* Edited by R. Hilferding. 1924 Berlin: Dietz. → Special issue of *Die Gesellschaft.*

KAUTSKY, JOHN H.  1951  *The Political Thought of Karl Kautsky.* Ph.D. dissertation, Harvard Univ.

KAUTSKY, JOHN H.  1961  J. A. Schumpeter and Karl Kautsky: Parallel Theories of Imperialism. *Midwest Journal of Political Science* 5:101–128.

MATTHIAS, ERICH  1957  Kautsky und der Kautskyanismus. Volume 2, pages 151–197 in *Marxismusstudien.* Edited by Iring Fetscher. Tübingen (Germany): Mohr.

RENNER, KARL  1929  *Karl Kautsky.* Berlin: Dietz.

## KELLEY, TRUMAN L.

Truman Lee Kelley (1884–1961) was highly influential in the introduction of statistical methods into psychological studies. His work also gave considerable impetus to the rise of psychometrics within the field of psychology.

Kelley was born in Whitehall, Muskegon County, Michigan. His early interests led him to study mathematics at the University of Illinois, where he received his A.B. in 1909. His first career in mathematics, although short-lived (he was an instructor of mathematics at the Georgia Institute of

Technology, 1909–1910, and in a high school and junior college in Fresno, California, 1911–1912), became the keystone of his later career, which started when he turned to the new field of psychometrics. He received an A.M. in psychology from the University of Illinois in 1911 and his PH.D. from Columbia University in 1914. His mentors at Columbia were Edward L. Thorndike and Robert S. Woodworth. It was through the medium of psychometrics that Kelley carried forward into education and guidance the kind of work that Thorndike and Woodworth had done in experimental psychology. His later studies of the bearing of capability, accomplishment, and interest on the practical affairs of men took form while he was still a graduate student; it was in this period that he wrote *Educational Guidance* (1914).

The political and economic turmoil that coincided with Kelley's years at the University of Texas, 1914–1917, and at Teachers College, Columbia University, 1917–1920, made certain government authorities more receptive to the application of statistics to practical affairs in education and work. Kelley pursued his interest in such application through service as psychological consultant to the Committee on Classification of Personnel, United States Army, and to the Surgeon General's Office. In these appointments Kelley was able to use his ideas on the statistical treatment of data to predict, by means of psychological tests, the performance of men on one job or another.

Kelley moved to Stanford University in 1920 as assistant professor of education. He became professor of education and psychology in 1926. Lewis M. Terman, a colleague at Stanford, joined Kelley and Giles M. Ruch in preparing and publishing the Stanford Achievement Test Battery, a series that has remained in good repute throughout several revisions over forty years. This series of achievement tests was a step toward Kelley's general goal of providing a practical system of assessing and describing the performance of men during the years of minimum required education.

Kelley's *Statistical Method* (1923*a*), an influential book, encapsulated much of his prior work in statistics for educational and psychological purposes. The text was well grounded in the statistics of correlation and regression. Kelley elaborated these basic ideas with his own emphases on the normal distribution, curve fitting, time series, standard errors, and multiple and partial correlation. At this time he was already very much concerned with enabling others to apply and compute statistics accurately, a concern that led eventually

to his publication of *The Kelley Statistical Tables* (1938). All these themes were given further consideration in later publications; they were to be the major topics of his work.

Kelley usually considered statistics and applications simultaneously. The interaction led to his reputation in psychometrics; his still classic *Interpretation of Educational Measurements* (1927) clearly shows evidence of this interaction. The book contains Kelley's ideas about the reliability and validity of test scores and offers evaluations of then existing tests. Other psychometricians have been quick to appreciate the importance of publishing professional judgments about mental and educational tests, and their subsequent work has superseded Kelley's earlier evaluations of specific tests. Nevertheless, his theory of reliability endures today in much of its original outline.

Kelley developed his theory of the multidimensionality of intellect in interrelation with Spearman's work on a single general factor of intelligence. He extended Spearman's tetrad criteria for determining the number of factors needed to explain relations between variables to pentad criteria (1928). [*See* INTELLIGENCE AND INTELLIGENCE TESTING.] His belief in a multidimensional intellect also carried him forward to provide his solution of the principal components problem in factor analysis in *Essential Traits of Mental Life* (1935). This book was published during his tenure as professor of education in the Graduate School of Education at Harvard University, a tenure which began in 1931 and lasted until his retirement in 1950.

At about the same time that Kelley published a general solution for the principal axes problem, Harold Hotelling, with whom Kelley consulted, also published such a solution [*see* FACTOR ANALYSIS]. Kelley, unlike Hotelling and others, insisted that judgments of the importance of mental functions should be incorporated in an analysis of principal axes when the analysis is originally designed. If a group of people is tested on a set of tests, a series of scores for every person who took the set of tests is obtained. Psychometricians are interested in the factor structure of the abilities, which gives rise to the observed correlations among the several tests contained in the set. Most psychologists, and particularly L. L. Thurstone, preferred to ascertain this structure from the set of observations alone. The Thurstone school claimed that this makes the structure empirical and that it can therefore be tempered at the user's discretion with the knowledge of how he has modified and analyzed the information. Kelley, on the other hand, claimed that his procedure would focus attention on the importance of psychological processes as well as on the accuracy of statistical analysis and that Thurstone's method might produce many accurate but inconsequential factors. Although Kelley insisted that one be aware of the problem of accuracy, he valued usefulness above accuracy.

Kelley insisted on completeness of the correlation matrix if work in education was to be solidly grounded. He favored a system of principal components; Thurstone, a system of primary mental abilities. Kelley analyzed the *total* variance of the matrix of test intercorrelations (as augmented even by the psychologist's judgments); Thurstone analyzed only the *communalities* (or commonness) of test correlations. Whereas Thurstone advocated the rotation of what he called "simple structure," Kelley advocated the rotation of test axes in orthogonal terms. Kelley's incorporation of judgment in his conception of science is evident in his series of lectures published as *Scientific Method* (1929). These ideas endured in his efforts to define the components of mental functioning by simultaneous analysis of sets of criteria and sets of predictors. This technique, known as canonical correlation analysis, appeared in *Talents and Tasks* (1940). Hotelling again published a similar solution at about the same time, but in his solution he did not incorporate judgments of importance as did Kelley.

Kelley's constant concern with making psychometric methods useful led him, in a series of papers on psychophysical scaling, to try to define a unit of measurement appropriate for everyday tasks in schools and personnel departments. When others were no longer interested in the concept Kelley continued to regard the "just noticeable difference" useful in this connection. In 1940 he contributed the idea of a ridge route norm, a general way of establishing a norm for a grade with control for age. These norms became a part of the Stanford Achievement Tests, as did the K (for Kelley) scores derived by his student and eventual coauthor, Eric F. Gardner.

Kelley extended his series of achievement measurements for use in education with *Tests and Measurements in the Social Sciences* (1934), of which he was coauthor. His other test, outlined in the *Activity Preference Report* (1954), grew from a project commissioned by the National Defense Research Committee during World War II, a project to which Kelley devoted his time while also serving as consultant to the secretary of war.

Kelley was active in professional organizations as well as in scholarship. He served as president of the Psychometric Society in 1938–1939 and also as vice-president of the American Statistical Association in 1926 and Section Q of the American Association for the Advancement of Science in 1928. He was a cofounder of the national honorary education society, Kappa Delta Pi.

DAVID V. TIEDEMAN

[*For the historical context of Kelley's work, see the biographies of* THORNDIKE; THURSTONE; WOODWORTH. *For discussion of the subsequent development of his ideas, see* PSYCHOMETRICS.]

### WORKS BY KELLEY

1914    *Educational Guidance: An Experimental Study in the Analysis and Prediction of Ability of High School Pupils.* New York: Columbia University, Teachers College.

(1923a) 1924    *Statistical Method.* New York: Macmillan.

1923b    KELLEY, TRUMAN L.; RUCH, G. M.; and TERMAN, L. M. *Stanford Achievement Test: Test Forms A and B.* Yonkers-on-Hudson, N.Y.: World Book.

1926    *The Influence of Nurture Upon Native Differences.* New York: Macmillan.

1927    *Interpretation of Educational Measurements.* Yonkers-on-Hudson, N.Y.: World Book.

1928    *Crossroads in the Mind of Man: A Study of Differentiable Mental Abilities.* Stanford (Calif.) Univ. Press.

(1929) 1932    *Scientific Method: Its Function in Research and in Education.* New York: Macmillan.

1934    KELLEY, TRUMAN L.; and KREY, AUGUST C. *Tests and Measurements in the Social Sciences.* New York: Scribner.

1935    *Essential Traits of Mental Life.* Cambridge, Mass.: Harvard Univ. Press.

(1938) 1948    *The Kelley Statistical Tables.* Rev. ed. Cambridge, Mass.: Harvard Univ. Press.

1940    *Talents and Tasks: Their Conjunction in a Democracy for Wholesome Living and National Defense.* Cambridge, Mass.: Harvard Univ. Press.

1947    *Fundamentals of Statistics.* Cambridge, Mass.: Harvard Univ. Press.

1954    *Activity Preference Report.* Cambridge, Mass.: Educational Research Corporation.

### SUPPLEMENTARY BIBLIOGRAPHY

FLANAGAN, JOHN C. 1961    Truman Lee Kelley. *Psychometrika* 26:343–345.

## KELSEN, HANS

In the history of modern legal thought, Hans Kelsen has aroused more response—ranging from enthusiastic acceptance to vehement rejection—than any other jurist. He was born in 1881 in Prague. His prolific writings, spanning a period of nearly sixty years, have been published in 24 languages. Kelsen's earlier work was devoted mainly to basic problems of law and the state; it is in this area that his theories have aroused passionate controversy. In his middle and later periods, his range of interests broadened, resulting in significant contributions to the philosophical and historical analysis both of political ideas and systems (such as democracy, parliamentary government, socialism, communism) and of such great political thinkers as Plato and Aristotle. His personal acquaintance in Vienna with Sigmund Freud combined with his lifelong interest in psychology resulted in numerous writings that examine the relation of psychology and social psychology to basic conceptions of law and the state. A student of religion and theology, Kelsen also examined some key conceptions of the state and of justice and natural law in the light of the Old and New Testaments. Finally, toward the end of his career he devoted a great deal of study to anthropology and early ("precivilized") history, focusing his interest on the slow development of basic categories of thought, such as of causality in the physical world and of responsibility (or "imputation") in the ethical realm. His investigations in this field were related to his persistent interest in the structure of the norm—above all, the legal norm, but also of the ethical and moral norm.

Among the early intellectual influences on Kelsen's thought, Kant must be given first place, although it was Kantianism as renewed by Neo-Kantians like Hermann Cohen and Ernst Cassirer. Just as Kant had sought to establish, through his critical method, the possibilities and limitations of knowledge of the external physical world—leaving to the physical scientists in the various branches of learning the task of finding concrete knowledge —so Kelsen attempted to do the same in the field of law. Beginning with his first major work (1911*a*), Kelsen sought to develop a general theory of positive law as a system of fundamental categories and concepts, which would enable the practitioner (lawyer, judge, legislator) or the analyst (jurist, law teacher) of a particular legal order to attain a scientifically correct understanding of his subject matter. From Kant (and even more from the Neo-Kantians) Kelsen acquired a deeply felt sense of the importance of methodological purity: according to this view, the method of cognition determines the object of cognition. Since the "thing in itself" (*Ding an sich*) is unknowable, the object of cognition is logically "created" by the knowing subject. In this sense, the nature known to the scientist is nothing but an object of cognition "created" by the science of nature, a logically constructed system of functions and relations.

Kelsen attempted to construct a theory of law along Kantian lines which would enable legal science to come to grips with legal phenomena.

However, whereas Kant confined his critical epistemology to natural science (treating law in his *Metaphysics of Ethics*), Kelsen sought to supplement Kant by constructing a normative epistemology, defining the nature and structure of the legal order and of a critical legal science. Cassirer's main influence on Kelsen's thinking lay in pointing the way toward resolving the age-old dualism between substance and function. In his pioneering philosophical books, *Substance and Function;* and *Einstein's Theory of Relativity* (1910–1921), Cassirer emphasized the general tendency in modern science to dissolve traditional concepts of science— such as matter, force, energy, atom—into nonsubstantive concepts of relations, functions, and events. Similarly, Kelsen showed in his juristic analysis that traditional concepts like state, person, and similar substantive terms are nothing but reifications or personifications of relationships. The traditional problems of the relations between state and law, for example, are, according to Kelsen, insoluble because they are based on the false *dualism* of state and law: since state and (national) law are identical, the relations between them cannot be a subject of discussion. Likewise, the traditional problems of physical versus moral (or legal) person (such as the corporation) are based on the opposite false assumption of the *identity* of "person" in the physical–biological sense and "person" in the legal sense. Since, for Kelsen, "person" in the legal sense is nothing more than the sum total of legal rights and duties regulating human behavior, it makes no conceptual difference whether such legal norms define the behavior of one physical person or of many. The term "person" in the law thus never connotes a particular physical person but is merely a substantive reification or metaphorical personification of a complex of norms. Kelsen similarly resolved other traditional dualisms which are based on false premises, such as the dualism between law and administration, or between creation of the law (legislation) and finding of the law (adjudication).

## Definition of law

In defining the meaning of law, Kelsen attempted to determine whether there is any one element common to all legal systems at all times and places and at every level of cultural development. Politically colored definitions of law invariably introduce substantive elements: thus, in a democratically oriented definition of law, a legal order is not "really" law unless a minimum of personal liberty is safeguarded. Similarly, to Marxist jurists a legal system that maintains private property in the means of production is not law, but naked bourgeois force. In his search for a conception of law that is based on scientific universality rather than on political particularism, Kelsen defined law in its most general meaning as an "ordering of human behavior" ([1934] 1960, p. 31), as a "specific technique of social organization" ([1945] 1961, p. 5). He emphasized the *how* (the function of law)—which can be universally valid—rather than the *what* (or contents of the law)—which cannot be so valid. However, other systems of norms (such as morality and religion) also seek to regulate human behavior. Therefore, Kelsen identified a specific characteristic of the legal method of ordering human behavior that both morality and religion lack: the element of physical force. Law is thus a *coercive order of human behavior.* Such an order can be (in its political orientation) liberal or totalitarian, capitalist or collectivist, but it is a legal order if it is a coercive order of human behavior. Kelsen, in his definition of law, thus dispensed with the traditional elements of justice, reason, or morality that so frequently were attached to the definitions of law as "the voice of reason" (Aristotle, the Stoics) or as an "ordinance of reason for the common good" (Thomas Aquinas). To introduce the criterion of justice or reason as a definitional element into the conception of law either serves the political purpose of legitimizing or sanctifying the existing legal system or of attacking it in the name of a "higher" law which is not realized in the existing system.

## The legal norm

The constitutive element of law as a coercive social order is the "norm," or the rule that somebody *ought* to act in a prescribed way. In Kelsen's conception, legal norms always belong to the realm of the "ought," although linguistically this may sometimes be hidden, such as in the phrasing of a criminal statute that a thief "will" be punished in such and such a way. Yet this linguistic inexactitude does not conceal the fact that the statutory legislator "is no prophet" ([1945] 1961, p. 45) and is not predicting events but prescribing what ought to happen in a predetermined situation, such as theft. Kelsen stressed that the "ought" in the norm created by the legislator or in the legal rule has no ethical, moral, or natural-law connotations, but is merely a "functional connection" ([1934] 1960, p. 109) or "mode of thinking" (1911*b*, p. 6). Following Kant and the Neo-Kantians, he sharply distinguished the causal from the normative connection between two sets of facts or actions. The causal connection (whether in the physical or social sphere) is expressed in the formula: "If A,

then B." In the normative connection, the formula runs: "If A, then B shall be." From the fact that something will be, one cannot logically deduce that it shall be, nor can one deduce from the fact that something shall be that it actually will be. He held that the modal, logical categories of the "is" and the "ought" are not susceptible of further definition or simplification, since they are basic categories of our mind. However, this axiomatic character of the "ought" applies only to its functional aspect; the content of the "ought," that is, the content of a specific legal order, cannot be directly perceived or rationally discovered, since it is the result of acts of will.

The structure of the legal norm clearly shows its difference from the moral norm. A moral norm might run thus: "Thou shalt not steal," but, because the moral order is not a coercive order, it does not attach a punitive consequence to the act of stealing. By contrast, the structure of the legal norm (regardless of its linguistic expression) runs thus: "If a person steals, he ought to be punished by the competent organ or agent of the state." The illegal act (crime or tort) is called by Kelsen the "delict"; the consequence threatened by the norm in its second half is called the "sanction." In Kelsen's ingenious conception of the structure of the norm, the legal order is concerned not with human behavior that is in accord with the law but with behavior that is in opposition to it. The "ought" in the legal norm refers to the sanction to be applied to contralegal behavior—to the action prescribed for the state authority by the sanction. The contralegal (illegal or unlawful) behavior—the first structural half of the norm—is but a condition for the sanction. Kelsen emphasized that the condition on the basis of which the sanction ought to be applied is not necessarily an act. A person may be punished for what he *is*, not for what he *does*. For example, when a totalitarian state imprisons or murders members of a particular social class, political entity, religion, or race; or when a nontotalitarian state imprisons citizens of enemy nationality resident in its territory at the outbreak of war.

By viewing unlawful behavior, the delict, as the condition of the sanction, Kelsen attained a double objective of analysis. First, he removed the last traces of natural-law or ethical criteria from the concept of positive law, since legally prescribed or permitted behavior is no longer posited or prescribed by the law as a positive command (in the sense in which this is done in morality or religion). Instead, legal behavior is "downgraded," as it were, to the mere logical level of a condition; the behavior which according to the legal norm (of national law) ought to follow is the sanction of the state authority. Second, Kelsen's structuring of the norm also enabled him to solve the problem, or apparent problem, of how a norm can be said to be valid in case of illegal behavior. "The delict," Kelsen wrote, "is neither a violation nor a negation of the law. It is conduct determined by the law as a condition of the sanction, likewise determined by the law" (1952, p. 7). For this reason, Kelsen also objected to the usual formulation according to which a sanction is attached to certain types of human behavior because it is a delict. The more accurate way would be to reverse this formulation: a certain type of human behavior is a delict because a sanction is attached to it. "There is no delict in itself" ([1945] 1961, p. 51).

**Imputation.** The relationship between the elements of the legal norm—delict and sanction—is called by Kelsen "imputation" (*Zurechnung*). Whereas in nonnormative propositions (if A, then B) the principle of connection between A and B is causality, in the legal norm (if A, then B ought to be) it cannot be causality, since in actual fact A is not always followed by B (such as when a thief escapes legal punishment), or B may take place although A did not occur (such as when a sanction is imposed for an act which in fact did not happen and a person is punished for a crime he did not commit). Imputation thus does not connote the relation of a person and his action, but the relation between the sanction and that action. In the case of a child, for example, who has committed murder, this action can be "imputed" to him according to the principle of causality, but legally it cannot be imputed to him, because such action by a child does not entail a sanction.

The clarification of the difference between causality and imputation also enabled Kelsen to throw some new light on the problem of determinism and free will. Kelsen rejected the widespread view that man is subject to a moral or legal order because his free will enables him to break the chain of causality and establish a new chain of conduct. According to this hypothesis, man's will is not the result of other causes, but only a cause which brings forth effects. Therefore, so this widespread view holds, if man fails to exercise his free will and to choose the right course of action, he is responsible for the moral disapproval or legal sanction attached to his morally wrong or legally delinquent conduct. Kelsen rejected this hypothesis of free will on the ground that every human action is causally determined, although our methods of knowing may not always be refined enough to ascertain the causes. Moreover, Kelsen pointed to the fact that the very establishment of a legal order influencing and regulating human behavior presupposes that human conduct is causally determinable, that is, not free. The function of the legal order (as of any normative order) is to induce men to be motivated by ideas and perceptions in accord with the conduct prescribed by the legal (or moral) order. If the legal order fulfills this function, men then "will" to do what they legally ought to do, and their so willing serves as a cause of their actions in harmony with the law. The legal order (like any normative system) is thus based on the supposition not of free will, that is, causal nondeterminacy, but of causal determinacy. On the latter supposition, if a person acts illegally, such a delict is imputed to him, or, more correctly, the sanction is imputed to his action (the delict). Kelsen also rejected the customary formulation according to which man is "imputable" (or legally responsible) because he is free, and substituted for it the opposite formula: man is free because he is "imputable," because legal consequences—awards or punishments—can be attached to his actions. In this conception, freedom and causality do not exclude each other, since the legal order assumes the causal determinacy of human action and therefore prescribes that certain actions ought to be followed by corresponding sanctions. From a fundamentally epistemological viewpoint, too, there can be no contradiction between causality in the physical realm and freedom in a normative order (like law or ethics), for there can be no contradiction between a system based on the "is" and a system based on the "ought." The proposition, "If A, then B," is contradictory to the proposition, "If A, then not B," but is not contradictory to the proposition, "If A, then B ought to be."

**Validity.** The validity of the norm is most conspicuous in the case of illegal conduct. In a theft, for example, the norm against stealing does not lose its validity because the act of stealing has occurred, and the judge is required to apply the sanction against the delict. But even if the thief escapes and no judicial sanction can be prescribed, the norm still retains its validity. The validity of a norm thus does not imply that the conduct it prescribes is always followed but only that it has binding force. To know whether a specific norm is valid, we must therefore inquire in what way that norm is derived from other norms, since an "ought" can only be derived from another "ought." Thus, the individual norm invoked by a judge against a thief is considered legal if it can be derived from a general statute prescribing sanctions against the delict of theft. If we ask why the general statute is legal, we find that it, in turn, can be derived from the legal authority of the legislative body. The legal validity of the body must again be derived from a norm: we find that under the constitution, the legislative body is authorized to make such general norms. In trying to discover the validity of the constitution, we find that it cannot be derived from any higher legal source since it is itself the highest legal source from which all other (lower) norms are derived. If the validity of the highest legal norm cannot be derived from another legal norm, it can only be derived from a nonlegal norm, or "basic" norm," as Kelsen called it. This basic norm is presupposed to be valid but is not itself a norm of positive law. In brief form, the basic norm prescribes that conduct ought to be in accord with the constitution. Without such a presupposed norm conferring validity upon the constitution, the latter would have no legal character and the norms below the constitution—legislative, judicial, and executive—would have no legal character either, since a norm can be derived only from another norm.

### The basic norm

The basic norm thus supplies the legal order with a principle of unity. It makes it possible to consider a human act as legally binding if it can be integrated into an entire system of norms, ultimately deriving its validity from the presupposed basic norm. However, although the basic norm is presupposed, it is not arbitrarily presupposed, for the legal order upon which the basic norm confers validity must on the whole be effective, although individual conduct may be contrary to the law. Kelsen applied here the principle of "cognitive economy." According to this principle, physical laws are constructed under the postulate that the largest number of facts be explained by the simplest possible formula. Similarly, in the normative sphere, that basic norm should be presupposed according to which the largest number of behavioral phenomena can be subsumed under the legal order that seeks to regulate them. To assume the validity of British law in the United States after the success of the American Revolution makes it impossible to interpret acts of citizens or state organs as legal, since from the viewpoint of British law prior to 1776 such acts have no, or very little, legal significance.

The concept of the basic norm led Kelsen to the dynamic view of the law as hierarchically held together. In traditional legal thought, the main emphasis had been put on the difference between the creation of the law and the application of the law. This approach led, in Roman law countries, to a virtual identification of statute with law as such, while in common law countries the tendency was in the opposite direction—to identify law with

judicial decision. In viewing the legal order as a hierarchical system that culminates in the highest norm, the basic norm, Kelsen dismissed the sharp distinction between law creation and law application. Most legal norms both apply and create law. The constitution itself applies a norm in relation to the basic norm but creates law in relation to the legislative process. The parliamentary statute applies law in relation to the constitution but creates law in relation to the executive and the judiciary. The administrative or judicial organ applies the statutory law but creates administrative or judicial norms. Only the first and the last stages of the law are necessarily not dual in character. The basic norm as a presupposed norm is pure law creating, not applying any superior norm. At the other end of the legal system, the execution of the legal sanction in a concrete case is pure application of the law, without creating new norms. If, apart from the basic norm and the final act of law enforcement, every legal norm is both law applying and law creating, the higher norm appears as a frame within which several more specific lower norms may be created. The difference between the legislator and the judge is quantitative rather than qualitative. In the case of the legislator, the superior norm—the constitution—prescribes mainly the procedure of creating statutory law, although some determination of contents, too, may be included (such as a listing of fundamental rights removed from legislative interference). In the case of the judge, the superior norm—the statute—also prescribes the content of the frame within which he may move, but in either case the legislator or judge has discretion with respect to the manner of creating the lower norm.

The act of filling the frame of the superior norm is an act of will rather than of intellect, a political act rather than a cognitive act. In choosing one of the possible interpretations or applications of the superior norm—the constitution in the case of the legislator, the statute in the case of the judge—both legislator and judge act as politicians, not as logicians. This position of Kelsen was anticipated by Justice Oliver Wendell Holmes when he spoke of the fallacy "that the only force at work in the development of law is logic," and went so far as to say that the alogical element is "the very root and nerve of the whole proceeding" (Holmes [1897] 1952, p. 180).

### Limits of legal analysis

From the very beginning, Kelsen sought to demarcate his "pure theory of law" against two areas into which legal analysis has frequently been drawn: psychology and sociology on the one hand

and ethics and politics on the other. Initially he rejected the possibility of a sociology (or psychology) of law, if law is to be conceived as a normative order. He later conceded that a sociology of law is possible, if the object of such inquiry is the "is" rather than the "ought." The sociologist, for example, can legitimately investigate what social or economic motives or interests have induced a legislative body to pass a particular law, what motives induce persons to adapt their behavior to legal norms, or what social pressures or influences are behind judicial decisions. But, Kelsen argued, all such sociological and psychological analyses deal with causal phenomena parallel to the law, not with the law itself as a normative system.

The defense of legal analysis against the intrusion of ethical and political criteria appeared to Kelsen, particularly in the middle and later phases of his intellectual development, even more important than the defense against the intrusions of sociological methods into legal theory. The degradation of social science in the totalitarian systems of communist and fascist states strengthened Kelsen's conviction that scientific investigation must be kept free from political intrusion in the form of particular value preferences, natural-law doctrines, conservative rationalizations, or revolutionary challenges of positive law. The theoretician or analyst of the social or legal order is not a social authority. His task is to understand society, but not to remake it politically. Analysis of the law—as of any other social institution—belongs to the realm of *rational cognition*, not to irrational *political will*. Rational cognition cannot, Kelsen argued, solve the problem of conflicting values, since values are subjective, based on emotional rather than cognitive factors. In numerous writings on natural law, Kelsen insisted that neither a rationalistic nor a metaphysical–religious natural-law doctrine has ever been able to formulate absolute values or universally valid principles of justice on which general agreement can be attained. Social progress, Kelsen held, consists in making the idea of justice relative: peace through compromise of conflicts of interest and of the values such conflicts reflect. Whereas absolute justice is impossible and its pursuit, if persistent, must result in great sacrifices of human dignity and even of human life, the relative justice of social (and international) peace is attainable and, if practiced, is socially less costly in terms of human life and dignity.

The position of philosophical relativism—both in the theory of knowledge and the theory of values—has often led to the charge that relativism is amoral or immoral, since it denies the possibility of demonstrating absolute standards of truth or value. Kelsen categorically rejected this charge in his farewell lecture, "What Is Justice?" given on his retirement in 1952, from the University of California, at which institution he concluded his formal career as a teacher. Relativism, Kelsen held, does not claim that there are no values but only that there are no absolute values, no one valid system. Relativism thus compels the individual to make his own choice between competing systems of values and prevents him from delegating his moral responsibility to a superior authority, be it religious or political. "The fear of personal responsibility is one of the strongest motives of the passionate resistance against relativism. Relativism is rejected and—what is worse—misinterpreted, not because it morally requires too little, but because it requires too much" (Kelsen 1957b, p. 22). However, while Kelsen admitted he could not provide an answer that is absolutely true to the question "What is justice?" he did not hesitate to answer this question from his own viewpoint as a scientist. "Since science is my profession, and hence the most important thing in my life, justice, to me, is that social order under whose protection the search for truth can prosper. 'My' justice, then, is the justice of freedom, the justice of peace, the justice of democracy—the justice of tolerance" (1957b, p. 24).

Kelsen's antimetaphysical position in his theory of knowledge as applied to his legal theory, combined with his relativistic, liberal value orientation in his political views, thus places him in the great tradition of modern thought that is identified with John Locke, David Hume, Immanuel Kant, and Bertrand Russell. The social sciences have, since the middle of this century, been engaged in a renewed effort to shed ideology as incompatible with science, since ideology is ideas in the service of interest rather than cognition. In his tireless struggle against the subservience of legal and political science to ideological, political interests Kelsen has made a lasting contribution to the growing process of establishing the social sciences as bodies of cognitive knowledge rather than as tools of political or ideological manipulation.

WILLIAM EBENSTEIN

[*For the historical context of Kelsen's work, see* INTERNATIONAL LAW; JURISPRUDENCE; POSITIVISM; *the biography of* CASSIRER; *for discussion of ideas that influenced his thought, see* KANT.]

WORKS BY KELSEN

1905    *Die Staatslehre des Dante Alighieri.* Vienna and Leipzig: Deuticke.

(1911a) 1960    *Hauptprobleme der Staatsrechtslehre entwickelt aus der Lehre vom Rechtssatze.* 2d ed. Aalen (Germany): Scientia.

1911*b*   *Über Grenzen zwischen juristischer und soziologischer Methode.* Tübingen (Germany): Mohr.

(1920*a*) 1960   *Das Problem der Souveränität und die Theorie des Völkerrechts: Beitrag zu einer reinen Rechtslehre.* 2d ed. Aalen (Germany): Scientia.

(1920*b*) 1923   *Sozialismus und Staat: Eine Untersuchung der politischen Theorie des Marxismus.* 2d ed., enl. Leipzig: Hirschfeld.

(1920*c*) 1929   *Vom Wesen und Wert der Demokratie.* 2d ed., rev. Tübingen (Germany): Mohr.

1923   *Österreichisches Staatsrecht: Ein Grundriss entwicklungsgeschichtlich dargestellt.* Tübingen (Germany): Mohr.

(1923–1957) 1964   *Aufsätze zur Ideologiekritik.* Edited with an introduction by Ernst Topitsch. Neuwied am Rhein (Germany): Luchterhand.

1925   *Allgemeine Staatslehre.* Berlin: Springer.

1926   *Das Problem des Parlamentarismus.* Vienna: Braumüller.

1933   *Staatsform und Weltanschauung.* Tübingen (Germany): Mohr.

(1934) 1960   *Reine Rechtslehre.* With Supplement: Das Problem der Gerechtigkeit. 2d ed., enl. & rev. Vienna: Deuticke. → The final and most comprehensive statement of Kelsen's "pure theory of law." Contains a bibliography of Kelsen's works.

1942   *Law and Peace in International Relations: The Oliver Wendell Holmes Lectures, 1940–1941.* Cambridge, Mass.: Harvard Univ. Press.

(1943) 1946   *Society and Nature: A Sociological Inquiry.* London: Routledge.

1944   *Peace Through Law.* Chapel Hill: Univ. of North Carolina Press.

(1945) 1961   *General Theory of Law and State.* New York: Russell.

1948   *The Political Theory of Bolshevism: A Critical Analysis.* University of California Publications in Political Science, Vol. 2, No. 1. Berkeley: Univ. of California Press.

(1950) 1951   *The Law of the United Nations: A Critical Analysis of Its Fundamental Problems.* With Supplement. New York: Praeger.

1952   *Principles of International Law.* New York: Rinehart.

1955   *The Communist Theory of Law.* New York: Praeger; London: Stevens.

1957*a*   *Collective Security Under International Law.* U.S. Naval War College, International Law Studies, Vol. 49. Washington: Government Printing Office.

1957*b*   *What Is Justice? Justice, Law, and Politics in the Mirror of Science; Collected Essays.* Berkeley: Univ. of California Press.

#### SUPPLEMENTARY BIBLIOGRAPHY

CASSIRER, ERNST (1910–1921) 1953   *Substance and Function; and Einstein's Theory of Relativity.* New York: Dover. → First published as *Substanzbegriff und Funktionsbegriff* in 1910 and *Zur Einsteinschen Relativitätstheorie* in 1921. The 1953 edition is a translation of both books.

EBENSTEIN, WILLIAM (1938) 1945   *The Pure Theory of Law.* Madison: Univ. of Wisconsin Press. → An extensive revision of William Ebenstein's *Die rechtsphilosophische Schule der reinen Rechtslehre.*

ENGEL, SALO (editor) 1964   *Law, State, and International Legal Order: Essays in Honor of Hans Kelsen.* Knoxville: Univ. of Tennessee Press.

HOLMES, OLIVER W. (1897) 1952   The Path of the Law.

Pages 167–202 in Oliver W. Holmes, *Collected Legal Papers.* New York: Peter Smith. → First published in Volume 10 of the *Harvard Law Review.*

LIPSKY, GEORGE A. (editor) 1953   *Law and Politics in the World Community: Essays on Hans Kelsen's Pure Theory and Related Problems in International Law.* Berkeley: Univ. of California Press.

VERDROSS, ALFRED (editor) 1931   *Gesellschaft, Staat und Recht: Untersuchungen zur Reinen Rechtslehre.* Vienna: Springer.

# KEY, V. O., JR.

V. O. Key, Jr. (1908–1963) played a central role in the development of a more empirical or behavioral approach in American political science. Key was a Texan and received much of his education in Texas, for two years at McMurry College in Abilene and then at the University of Texas, where he obtained his B.A. in 1929 and his M.A. in 1930. Key then went to the University of Chicago for his doctoral work.

The Chicago school of political science, led by Charles E. Merriam and his student (and later colleague) Harold D. Lasswell, was diverse in its interests but united in its aim to explore new methods of studying political and administrative behavior. The department pioneered in the use of statistics, the use of field methods, the study of the role of psychology in politics, and, above all, the study of power and power relations. In this stimulating environment Key wrote, under Merriam's direction, his dissertation, *The Techniques of Political Graft in the United States.* In it he dealt with graft not as a legal or moral problem but as one of many forms of social control and influence.

After teaching for a short time at the University of California at Los Angeles, Key moved to Washington, D.C., in 1936. There he was first associated with the Social Science Research Council and then served as a staff member of the controversial National Resources Planning Board. In 1938 he joined the faculty of Johns Hopkins University, but World War II brought him back to Washington for several years' service with the U.S. Bureau of the Budget. His Washington experience served as a valuable supplement to his academic training by exposing him to the actual processes of decision making at the national level.

Key's central concern with the process of governing was made clear in 1942 in the first edition of his pioneering text, *Politics, Parties, and Pressure Groups.* Instead of being a mere chronicle of party history, the book presented a broad analysis of the functions of different elements in the political process. Key examined the sections and interest groups that contend for power and dealt with the roles of the party system and of the electorate. Finally, he discussed the role of force and violence, the uses of pecuniary sanctions, and education (or socialization) as a form of political control [see INTEREST GROUPS].

Shortly after World War II Key assumed direction of research for a major study of the electoral process in the South. The project led to *Southern Politics in State and Nation* (1949), which was promptly hailed as a classic as well as a harbinger of a new era in political science writing. It received the Woodrow Wilson Foundation award for 1949 and inspired a number of subsequent regional studies.

In order to find meaningful patterns in Southern politics, Key analyzed local election returns and conducted extensive interviews with participants in politics and with observers. He showed that the underlying pattern in many primary elections was one of conflict between counties with a high proportion of Negroes (then nonvoting) and counties with fewer Negroes. The race issue had a far more potent appeal in the former counties than in the latter. In general, the issues in the primary election contests of the one-party South had to do with support for the "local" candidate or with the personal qualifications of candidates rather than with substantive political problems. Key suggested that this fragmented style of politics, conducted without the stabilizing influence of party label, probably made it difficult to develop sustained popular support for any federally sponsored programs and, hence, probably worked to the long-run advantage of the haves as against the have-nots (1949, p. 307).

Soon after the publication of *Southern Politics*, Key accepted an appointment to Yale University as Alfred Cowles professor of government and chairman of the political science department. But he much preferred research to administrative duties, and in 1951 he moved to Harvard, where he held the Jonathan Trumbull professorship of American history and government. Although troubled by ill health he continued to work at a remarkable pace. In 1958 he was elected president of the American Political Science Association.

Key hoped that the use of quantitative methods in political science might be extended, and to this end he produced a basic guide to statistics, using illustrative material drawn from political data. This was published in 1954 as *A Primer of Statistics for Political Scientists*. It combined a general introduction to statistics with shrewd advice on research strategy.

In 1956 Key published his *American State Poli-*

*tics*, a study which examined the functioning of two-party states by the use of aggregate election returns. He gave particular attention to the effects of the separation of powers and of the direct-primary method of nomination on state parties [see ELECTIONS, *article on* ELECTORAL SYSTEMS].

Even while he was working on state politics, Key's interests were turning to the application of survey research to the study of politics. He had long been dissatisfied with the early sociological approach to the study of voting, and in the paper "Social Determinism and Electoral Decision" (1959) he and Frank Munger criticized the idea that social characteristics determine political preference. Key and Munger suggested that this theory did not take into account the independence of such political factors as party identification, and they maintained that it is the very events of politics that make some social factors important at one time but not at another.

Key believed that ultimately "the concern of the student of politics must center on the operation of the state apparatus" (1960, p. 55) and not on the individual voter, and that although the sample survey is "a powerful observational instrument," it is difficult to use this instrument in such a way that it sheds light on "significant questions of politics." He noted that it was "a truly formidable task to build a bridge from observation of the atoms of the political system to the system itself" (1960, p. 55).

Although he recognized the difficulties in adapting the survey research method to the study of what is politically relevant, Key felt that the effort was worthwhile. *Public Opinion and American Democracy* (1961) grew out of his attempt to get at the politically relevant by reanalyzing previously gathered survey material. He sought, insofar as secondary analysis permitted, to explore the patterns and distributions of opinions, the ways opinions are formed, and the properties they have. But he was aware that "these endeavors are bootless unless the findings about the preferences, aspirations, and prejudices of the public can be connected with the workings of the government system" (1961, p. 535), and his ultimate concern, therefore, was to find the links between mass opinion and the operation of the system. To do this, he concluded, "we have had to go beyond the survey data and make assumptions and estimates about the role and behavior of that thin stratum of persons referred to variously as the political elite, the political activists, the leadership echelons, or the influentials" (1961, p. 536) [see PUBLIC OPINION].

Although his health became progressively worse, Key set to work to analyze the survey findings which had accumulated from 1936 to 1960, in order to uncover the broad nature of electoral decision. At the time of his death he had almost completed the study, subsequently published as *The Responsible Electorate* (1966). Here he sought to show that American presidential elections are tests of the public's judgment of a party's past performance in office rather than mandates for one of two competing party platforms. Drawing on the large samples used in Gallup polls, Key showed the extent to which people who switch from one party to the other usually move in a direction consistent with their expressed policy preferences. Similarly, voters standing by their previous choices are also generally being consistent. This suggests a rather greater degree of voter rationality than is commonly inferred from the average voter's inability to articulate his policy preferences.

While Key's own work was received with great respect, his basic emphasis on combining empirical techniques with concern for the significant questions of politics was by no means a universal one at the time of his death. Many of those political scientists who shared his empirical bent found it easier to do microscopic studies of the individual voter than to unravel the connections between voters and the political system. When these links are successfully established, scholars will appreciate the extent to which Key was ahead of his time.

H. Douglas Price

[*For the context of Key's work, see* Parties, political; Political science; Public opinion; Voting; *and the biography of* Merriam.]

#### WORKS BY KEY

1936   *The Techniques of Political Graft in the United States.* Univ. of Chicago Libraries.

1937   *The Administration of Federal Grants to States.* Chicago: Public Administration Service.

1939   Key, V. O.; and Crouch, Winston W. *The Initiative and the Referendum in California.* Berkeley: Univ. of California Press.

1940   The Lack of a Budgetary Theory. *American Political Science Review* 34:1137–1144.

(1942) 1964   *Politics, Parties, and Pressure Groups.* 5th ed. New York: Crowell.

1943   The Veterans and the House of Representatives: A Study of a Pressure Group and Electoral Mortality. *Journal of Politics* 5:27–40.

(1946) 1959   Legislative Control. Pages 312–333 in Fritz M. Marx (editor), *Elements of Public Administration.* 2d ed. Englewood Cliffs, N.J.: Prentice-Hall.

1949   *Southern Politics in State and Nation.* New York: Knopf.

1954   *A Primer of Statistics for Political Scientists.* New York: Crowell.

1955a   The Erosion of Sectionalism. *Virginia Quarterly Review* 31:161–179.

1955b   A Theory of Critical Elections. *Journal of Politics* 17:3–18.

1956   *American State Politics: An Introduction.* New York: Knopf.

1958   The State of the Discipline. *American Political Science Review* 52:961–971.

1959   Secular Realignment and the Party System. *Journal of Politics* 21:198–210.

1959   Key, V. O.; and Munger, Frank J. Social Determinisim and Electoral Decision: The Case of Indiana. Pages 281–299 in Eugene Burdick and Arthur J. Brodbeck (editors), *American Voting Behavior.* Glencoe, Ill.: Free Press.

1960   The Politically Relevant in Surveys. *Public Opinion Quarterly* 24:54–61.

1961   *Public Opinion and American Democracy.* New York: Knopf.

1966   *The Responsible Electorate: Rationality in Presidential Voting, 1936–1960.* Edited by Milton C. Cummings, Jr. Cambridge, Mass.: Harvard Univ. Press. → Published posthumously.

# KEYNES, JOHN MAYNARD

I.   Contributions to Economics          *R. F. Harrod*
II.  Contributions to Statistics        *Dennis V. Lindley*

## I

### CONTRIBUTIONS TO ECONOMICS

It is probably agreed that the impact of John Maynard Keynes (1883–1946) on the development of economic theory was greater than that of any other economist in the first half of the twentieth century. There remains some difference of opinion as to whether or not the large reconstruction of economic theory that he attempted is valid and will endure. However, even those most critical of his work acknowledge that he made many valuable specific contributions.

Keynes is also significant for having been, outside the sphere of economics, a liberal thinker and intellectual leader. His *Economic Consequences of the Peace* (1919) contains a powerful and detailed exposure of the plans put forward at the Paris Peace Conference to impose heavy reparations on Germany. The economic arguments alone, skillful as they were, would probably not have won world-wide fame for this book had it not also made an impassioned plea for magnanimity toward a fallen foe. By publishing this invective against the policy of the Allies only a few months after he himself had been the principal representative of the British government in Paris, Keynes showed he was willing, for a righteous cause, to sacrifice the possibility of a successful career, at least for many years ahead and even, as some thought, forever. Thereafter he was looked to as a liberal leader who could be relied on to fight for good causes, internationally as well as in Britain.

During World War II, Keynes was the principal formulator of British views regarding postwar economic reconstruction, and he served as the leading British representative both at the Bretton Woods Conference in 1944 and at the still more important bilateral discussions between the Americans and the British a year earlier in Washington. Thus he may be regarded as a cofounder of the International Monetary Fund and of the International Bank for Reconstruction and Development, especially of the former. It should be noted, however, that it was American thinking somewhat more than Keynes's that determined the final form of the International Monetary Fund.

## The revolution in economic theory

When Keynes was a student, the influence of Alfred Marshall was paramount in English economics, especially at Cambridge, Keynes's university. Marshall had sought to bring together and weld into a definitive system all that was valuable in the English classical school from Adam Smith to John Stuart Mill. Further, Marshall was a joint originator of the later nineteenth-century developments in the classical system, which are also associated with the names of Jevons, Menger, and Walras. These developments involve a much more extended use of marginal analysis and stress the interdependence of the processes of price formation throughout the economy. Marshall, combining the older British tradition with these newer elements, offered a general theory of value, which he believed likely to be permanent. Consequently, he saw the task of the next generation of economists not as a fundamental reconstruction of economic theory but as the application of the general principles he had established to the various specialized fields of inquiry.

Keynes fully accepted this program and decided to work in the field of money. In his first book, *Indian Currency and Finance* (1913), he furnished a penetrating analysis of how the Indian system actually worked. He explained the nature of a gold exchange standard (or a sterling exchange standard). As a member of the Chamberlain Commission on Indian currency in 1913, he argued, in an appendix to the commission's report, for the need of a country like India to have a central bank.

The ideas that lay behind Keynes's criticisms of the proposals for German reparations were shared by most contemporary economists; Keynes became their spokesman by virtue of his fine powers of polemic and his practical experience in the British Treasury. He was also fully in line with his fellow economists in condemning the evils of inflation and expressed his view with characteristic forcefulness: "Lenin is said to have declared that the best way to destroy the Capitalist System was to debauch the currency. . . . Lenin was certainly right. There is no subtler, no surer means of overturning the existing basis of society" ([1919] 1920, pp. 235–236).

Nor did Keynes depart far from contemporary opinion when, after the Americans and British had brought their inflations to an end in 1920, he stressed the evils that might arise from the opposite process of deflation, at least if it were carried too far. And he was still in line with such respected contemporaries as Irving Fisher, Gustav Cassel, and R. G. Hawtrey when he became an advocate for a monetary system that would ensure stability in the general price level. But thereafter one may begin to detect a slight departure from accepted theory, both in Keynes's opposition to the proposal that Britain should re-establish the prewar gold parity for sterling (as it did in 1925), on the ground that this would lead to more deflation, and in his recommendation that sterling should not return to any fixed parity with the dollar, on the ground that the British authorities would then have complete freedom to maintain the stable purchasing power of sterling in terms of goods.

During and after the deflation of 1920–1921, Britain experienced very heavy unemployment. Keynes early began to advocate public works as a remedy for the situation. While he did have some support among his fellow economists, they were inclined to regard public works as a somewhat unsatisfactory "first aid" measure. The even more strictly orthodox view, known in Britain as the "Treasury view," was that public works do not tend to increase employment at all, since they merely divert funds to the public sector that would otherwise be used by private enterprise to produce an equal amount of employment in the private sector. One way of regarding the "Keynesian revolution" in economic theory is to consider it as the refutation, at the most fundamental level of abstract theory, of the view that public works cannot provide additional employment. The three most salient features of the Keynesian revolution are his theory of employment, his theory of interest, and his theory of wages. He also developed a new theory of money.

**Theory of employment.** Keynes held that the level of employment depends on the level of demand, which has two main components—the propensity to invest and the propensity to consume.

Income receivers tend to use a certain proportion of their income for consumption; the remainder is saved. If, when the economy is reasonably fully employed, the amount of money that income receivers tend to save exceeds the amount of money required by those responsible for investment, then the total demand will be insufficient to sustain full employment. A recession will result, leading to a low-level equilibrium at which the saving from the reduced incomes is no greater than the amount required for investment. If, on the other hand, at a reasonably full level of employment income receivers save less than is required for investment, inflationary pressures will develop. The main period of Keynes's important work as a theorist, from 1921 to 1939, was one in which the tendency toward depression was preponderant; and it was accordingly upon this tendency that Keynes concentrated his attention.

It was Keynes's conviction that if the propensity to invest is too low, relative to the propensity to save, depression will be endemic and there will be no natural forces in the system tending to restore the equilibrium of full employment. This was a departure of the first magnitude from the old orthodoxy, according to which there will be such natural forces, whether they operate through Say's law or otherwise.

**Theory of interest.** It is an essential feature of Keynes's thought that he rejected the classical argument that if the propensity to save is excessive, relative to investment requirements, it will bring interest rates down, thereby stimulating fresh investment and, perhaps, reducing the propensity to save. Keynes asserted that the conditions described above do not in themselves suffice to bring down interest rates. For the classical school, a response in the rate of interest is the essential mechanism by which Say's law operates to sustain full employment; if an increasing thriftiness of income receivers and a corresponding fall in consumption reduce demand, the rate of interest will fall by whatever amount is needed to stimulate investment demand, so that the extra investment demand will exactly fill the gap left by the reduced consumer demand. Keynes denied that this happens.

He put forward the view that the rate of interest is governed by the balance between the community's need for liquidity and the amount of liquidity furnished to it by the workings of the banking system, or ultimately by the policy of the central bank. If, on the occasion of an increase in thriftiness, as defined above, there is no change in the balance between the demand for and supply of liquidity, there will be no change in interest rates. An equili-

brium between investment and saving will then be secured, not by a fall in interest rates, but by a fall in employment, activity, and income. This decline will continue until some fresh factor begins to operate. Such a factor can, by deliberate policy, be introduced by the central bank, which can do something to remedy the situation by increasing liquidity and thus bringing the interest rate down to the level required to stimulate investment by an appropriate amount. The difference between the older school and Keynes is that the former thought that interest rates will fall automatically to an appropriate level by the operation of natural forces while Keynes did not.

One further point must be made here. Keynes held that even appropriate action taken by the central bank with regard to the interest rate would not necessarily secure full employment, for one or both of two reasons. (1) Because of "liquidity preference," there is probably a level below which the interest rate will not fall, however much liquidity the banking system supplies. Thus there are limits to the power of the central bank to reduce the interest rate. (2) If the prospects of profitable investment have become bad, as a result, for instance, of a severe and prolonged slump, a fall in interest rates may not have a sufficiently powerful effect in stimulating investment to restore employment to a satisfactory level. In this case public works are indispensable.

According to Keynes, there is no reason why the investment constituted by public works should in the least degree diminish the investment undertaken by private enterprise, provided that the central banks ensure that the rate of interest remains low; on the contrary, public works should increase private investment. For, if the increased incomes resulting from public works improve prospects, this may give private enterprise an incentive for making more investment also. If aggregate investment, namely public and private together, rises, then, given a certain propensity to consume, aggregate demand will rise and employment will increase. It should be noted that aggregate demand will increase by an amount greater than the increase in investment. The rise in employment and income resulting from the extra investment will give rise to a higher consumer demand. The relation of the total increase of demand to the increase in demand constituted by the extra investment is known as "the multiplier."

A subsidiary but very important point about Keynes's theory of interest may be noted. Distinguished economists, including Marshall, had argued that the prospect of inflation will inevitably raise the rate of interest, on the ground that if prices are rising by, say, 3 per cent, £103 will have the same real value at the end of a year as £100 had at the beginning. Consequently, if one receives back only £103 on a £100 loan, one will have received no real interest at all. Therefore the rate of interest has to be higher than the expected rise in prices. Keynes's theory implicitly denies this. Cash and bonds are both expressed in money; interest arises because one form is liquid and the other is not; interest remunerates for the sacrifice of liquidity. Interest is thus independent of whether prices are expected to rise or fall, since in this regard one's position is not affected by whether one holds cash or bonds. If one wants a hedge against inflation one must transfer one's capital into real property, equities, etc. Thus, the prospect of inflation will affect the relative yield on equities and bonds but will not affect the rate of interest, which merely expresses the difference between two forms of monetary assets.

**Theory of wages.** Keynes totally rejected the classical argument that if there is unemployment, wages will fall and that if trade unions, etc., prevent this fall, such rigidity is the cause of protracted unemployment. Some have wrongly supposed that in rejecting this position Keynes based his reasoning on the de facto inflexibility of wages. Rather, he held that a downward movement of wages will have no positive effect on employment, given a situation in which the propensity to invest and the propensity to consume are insufficient. A fall in wages will merely be matched by a downward movement of prices, leaving incentives to business as insufficient as they were before.

Keynes recognized exceptions to this, however. If there is a fixed rate of foreign exchange, the downward movement of wages can stimulate exports, to the extent that foreign prices remain at their previous level. In addition, a downward movement of wages can cause a decreased demand for liquidity to satisfy the "transactions motive." Provided that the banking authorities are careful not to reduce the supply of liquidity at the same time, this change in the balance between the demand for and supply of liquidity will cause a fall in interest rates, which may in favorable circumstances increase employment. It should be noted that an increased supply of liquidity by the authorities can produce precisely the same effect as a downward movement of wages, but in a much less painful manner.

**Quantity theory of money.** The orthodox school was inclined to argue that a deficient aggregate effective demand cannot cause prices to fall, nor can an excessive one cause prices to rise, provided the authorities keep the money supply level. Keynes did not accept the quantity theory of money in this form. He asserted that the propensity to consume and the propensity to invest are "real" propensities and independent of the money supply; if aggregate demand is excessive, prices *will* tend to rise, whether the money supply is increased or not; and conversely, if aggregate demand is deficient, prices will fall. Furthermore, Keynes held that increases in factor rewards in excess of increases in productivity will cause prices to rise, whether the money supply is increased or not and whether aggregate effective demand is excessive or not. His position is clearly evident in the equations he presented in *A Treatise on Money* (1930, pp. 135–138).

While Keynes did not suppose the money supply to have the direct effect on prices that is postulated by some quantity theorists, he by no means thought that the money supply is unimportant. For by increasing the money supply (supply of liquidity) the authorities can bring down interest rates, and conversely, by decreasing it, raise the interest rates. If the fall in interest rates is sufficient to stimulate investment and thus aggregate demand, then the increase in money supply will tend to increase activity. If the economy is initially very much underemployed, this increase may have little or no effect on prices. But if employment initially is at a higher level, then the increased supply of money will tend, in the roundabout way described, to raise prices.

**Acceptance of Keynes's views.** One must ask to what extent Keynes's various views have been generally accepted by economists. With regard to the issue that originally produced the Keynesian reconstruction of economic theory, there are few now who would hold that a program of public works will cause an equivalent reduction in the investment undertaken by private enterprise. More widely, Keynes's analysis of aggregate demand, as governed by the propensity to consume and to invest as well as by export opportunities and governmental expenditures, is now generally adopted by those responsible for economic policy, in such countries as have policy makers. It may be noted here that in the last twenty years much work has been done in providing and elaborating national income statistics, which constitute the essential tool for developing public policy on the basis of Keynesian theory. It was largely due to Keynes's initiative in the British Treasury during World War II that British national income statistics were compiled and published.

Since the various parts of Keynes's general theory on employment are logically interconnected, one would suppose that those who accept his theory of aggregate demand would also feel bound to accept the other theories linked with it. However, it appears to be more often the case that at a particular point of time economists concurrently hold views that are not necessarily consistent; indeed, it was Marshall's exceptional achievement to have gained even temporary acceptance for an integrated and mutually interdependent theory covering a large part of economics.

One part of the Keynesian system that has aroused much controversy is the theory of interest. Keynes put it forward in a rather aggressive spirit vis-à-vis traditional economics, and even some of his close followers have held that he did not give enough thought to integrating it with what is valid in traditional theory, namely the statement of the relationship of interest to the demand for and supply of savings. These followers believe that Keynes could have kept intact his doctrine that actual market interest rates are determined in the short period by the demand and supply of liquidity without discarding the valid part of traditional theory. A related problem, which has created crosscurrents of opinion and some confusion, is the influence of the money supply on the interest rate.

Accompanying Keynes's pure theory of interest was his judgment that it would be very important in the future to have low interest rates and an ample supply of liquidity—international as well as national. Insofar as this view concerns liquidity inside national borders, at least, it had little practical importance during the decade following World War II, when so many countries were subject to inflationary pressures. Since then, however, the situation has changed, and Keynes's followers tend to hold that had his views been accepted, some countries would have profited from having lower interest rates and a more ample supply of internal liquidity. Keynes would certainly be much disappointed by the fact that liquid reserves for international settlement have fallen considerably, in comparison with the prewar period, despite the existence of the International Monetary Fund, which he himself did so much to establish.

**Social implications.**    In certain wider social implications, Keynes's economic theories touch on the part that central governments should play in economic matters. There are two ways of interpreting his views on government control. According to one view, his stress on the need for state interference makes him almost a socialist. But he can also be regarded as a passionate libertarian and a strong believer in the value of individual initiative and enterprise. Indeed, he himself believed that his

doctrines could be regarded as a lifeline for private enterprise: if state interference provided the right framework, then the values of free enterprise and choice were much more likely to be fully realized. Keynes held that the adoption of his scheme of thought was an alternative to full-blown socialism, and, indeed, the only available alternative, since systems of undiluted laissez-faire were bound to break down in modern conditions.

Keynes did not restrict state interference to the minimum necessary to sustain full employment. If there were problems (for instance, poverty) to be cured, he was impatient with those who thought that nothing should be done that violated alleged "laws of economics." He advocated international projects for stabilizing commodity prices, and he believed that in certain cases cartels or other forms of industrial rationalization were desirable, even if they could be implemented only by state action.

In his early days Keynes was, like all liberals, a fervent believer in free trade. Later he saw the possibility of conflict between free trade and full employment. Although he had been opposed to the return of Britain to the gold standard in 1925, he was reluctant to advocate a departure when the slump began, partly because he believed it would be bad conduct toward foreigners who had put their trust in sterling (by holding it). He was pleased, however, when external events compelled Britain to depart from the gold standard in 1931, and he felt that this change gave great scope for a better policy of managed currency.

Keynes dissented when the assembled delegates at the World Economic Conference in London in 1933 pressed for measures removing the trade restrictions that had mushroomed as a consequence of the world slump. He thought it was idle to recommend such measures unless at the same time international liquidity was much increased, and instead he recommended an issue of international gold notes. As balance of payments difficulties continued, he came to favor protectionist measures as a lesser evil than deflation, or as a shield for the inflationary measures that would have to be taken to restore full employment. Keynes took the same position during World War II; he felt that Cordell Hull's efforts to get international agreement for a return to a much greater freedom of international trade would be in vain and, in particular, unacceptable to Britain unless the problem of international liquidity were solved by some agency such as the International Monetary Fund.

In his last work Keynes expressed optimism about the feasibility of returning to greater freedom of trade. He had never felt that his doctrines concerning aggregate demand and full employment were inconsistent with the classical doctrine that, given the right framework, individual enterprise and the international division of labor would ensure the best allocation of productive resources. But all this depends on an adequate supply of international liquidity, that is, a larger supply than existed before the war. In actuality, the supply has become smaller.

## Keynes's life

Keynes was born in Cambridge in 1883. His father, John Neville Keynes, was a fellow of Pembroke College, Cambridge, and the author of *Formal Logic* and *The Scope and Method of Political Economy*. (Both these books were for some years considered clear and up-to-date expositions of their respective subjects.) Keynes's mother, Florence, was the daughter of a Congregationalist divine called John Brown, who wrote an authoritative life of Bunyan. She was one of the earliest students of Newnham College, Cambridge. Throughout her life she devoted herself to a multitude of good works, and she served a term as mayor of Cambridge. In Keynes's home there was ceaseless discussion of intellectual matters. The family hero was Henry Sidgwick, philosopher and economist, who at one time had resigned his fellowship at Trinity College as a protest against religious requirements. John Neville Keynes was always in close touch with Alfred Marshall. The Keynes family went to a Congregationalist church in Cambridge, but in his adult life Keynes did not adhere to any religious creed.

Keynes won a scholarship at Eton, where he received the best education available in England. He next obtained a scholarship at King's College, Cambridge. There he specialized in mathematics and in his final examination was twelfth on the list for the whole of Cambridge. His official tutors do not appear to have contributed much to his intellectual development, but the influence of Cambridge was very great indeed.

First and foremost must be mentioned a secret society known as "The Apostles," to which Keynes was very soon elected. It was a highly select society, only two or three undergraduates being chosen each year. Former undergraduates retained their membership and came to the meetings from time to time, especially if they were teaching at Cambridge. The society had an implicit code that had a profound influence on many of its members for the rest of their lives. It may best be summarized as consisting of absolute intellectual integrity and unworldliness in the conduct of one's life. The code may be thought to have amounted almost to a kind of religion.

In the past the Apostles had had such members as Tennyson, Sidgwick, and Clerk Maxwell. In Keynes's time the most influential senior member was G. E. Moore, the philosopher, and his philosophical views had an influence that can be detected, certainly in Keynes's *Treatise on Probability* (1921), and possibly in his economics also. Of the junior members, the man who had the greatest influence on Keynes, both as an Apostle and as a close friend, was Lytton Strachey, biographer and essayist. Strachey brought within Keynes's horizon a higher form of culture than was available in his quiet academic home or in Cambridge generally. He had some influence on Keynes as a writer of prose: Keynes's *Economic Consequences of the Peace* is as fine an example of polemic writing as anything produced in his generation. It was Strachey also who introduced Keynes to a circle that took a passionate interest in artistic matters. This circle of close friends at Cambridge included Leonard Woolf and Clive Bell. These friendships lasted through life. In London the group, containing also Roger Fry, Duncan Grant, and Virginia Woolf, was for many years commonly known as "Bloomsbury."

After obtaining his degree, Keynes spent an additional year at Cambridge, studying economics under Alfred Marshall and A. C. Pigou for the British Civil Service Examination. He was second in the examination. Since there was only one vacancy in the Treasury that year, Keynes opted for the India Office. He was bored there for the most part, but his experience doubtless prompted his specializing in Indian currency when, after two years, he returned to Cambridge to teach economics.

During these years and for some time thereafter Keynes directed the greater part of his energy to the study of probability theory. A dissertation on this subject gained him a fellowship at King's College. The *Treatise on Probability* was published in 1921, but was completed for the most part before World War I. This substantial volume still holds a certain place in the literature on the subject. It has a very lengthy bibliography, not only of then recent works but also of those of earlier date. Some curious items in the list probably reflect Keynes's lifelong interest in collecting first editions, mainly of philosophical or economic works, but later branching into general Elizabethan literature. He discovered and was able to prove the authenticity of a hitherto unknown writing by David Hume.

Keynes's idea in writing the treatise was to do

for inductive logic something analogous to what Russell and Whitehead had done for deductive logic in their *Principia mathematica*. He brought his mathematical expertise to the task as well as his immense learning in various byways of probability theory. His central doctrines are still of interest, especially to the philosophers as distinct from the technicians of probability theory [*See* KEYNES, JOHN MAYNARD, *article on* CONTRIBUTIONS TO STATISTICS.] Under the influence of G. E. Moore, Keynes held that probability is a concept that can be comprehended intuitively and requires no definition; this made the book somewhat unsatisfactory to the following generation of scholars.

Shortly after World War I broke out Keynes was taken into the British Treasury, where he rapidly rose. In the later part of the war he was in supreme control of the external work of the Treasury—foreign exchange control, U.S. loans, etc. At the Paris Peace Conference he was the principal Treasury representative, a position from which he eventually resigned in protest. He then returned to Cambridge, where he continued his lecturing and teaching; he also became bursar of King's College. He wrote a follow-up volume to the *Economic Consequences*, called *A Revision of the Treaty*, in 1922, and a more theoretical work entitled *A Tract on Monetary Reform* in 1923.

Soon after the war, in the autumn of 1919, Keynes embarked upon a career of finance. Borrowing a few thousand pounds from members of his family, he used the funds to deal in foreign exchange and in commodities and, in due course, in stock exchange securities. After repaying his debts, he built up a capital of about half a million pounds during the interwar period. He also constituted himself a financial adviser to firms, sometimes working with O. T. Falk. From 1921 to 1938 Keynes was chairman of the National Mutual Life Insurance Company, and his annual speeches became important events. As bursar of King's he greatly increased the endowment of that college.

He had a very active career as a journalist in the decade following the war, being editor of the massive *Manchester Guardian* supplements on "Reconstruction in Europe" and writing frequently for *The Nation*, of which he was chairman from 1923 to 1929. From 1911 to 1945 Keynes served as editor of the *Economic Journal*.

In 1925 Keynes married Lydia Lopokova, a famous Russian ballerina who had been trained in the Imperial Ballet in St. Petersburg but had been for most of her professional life in the Diaghilev Ballet. It was an extremely happy marriage. After his marriage, Keynes spent a considerable part of

his time in his small country house, to which farming land was attached, in Sussex in the village of Firle. He took a great interest in farming and carried through various improvements.

In politics Keynes was a Liberal, and in the 1920s he did much work on behalf of the Liberal party. Although a close friend of Asquith and his family and very bitterly opposed to Lloyd George at the Paris Peace Conference, he began to believe as the years wore on that Lloyd George was the man to revive the fortunes of the Liberal party. Lloyd George was willing to take up Keynes's ideas about public works. Together with H. D. Henderson, Keynes wrote a pamphlet called *Can Lloyd George Do It?* (1929).

When the Labour party took office under Ramsay MacDonald, Keynes was brought back somewhat into public affairs. He became a member of the Economic Advisory Council in 1930 and of the so-called Macmillan Committee on Finance and Industry, a considerable part of whose classic report he wrote himself.

In 1930 Keynes published *A Treatise on Money*, his most comprehensive work on monetary theory. In the following years he devoted most of his energy to writing *The General Theory of Employment, Interest and Money* (1936), which sets out explicitly what may be called the Keynesian revolution. (His had been a lone voice against retrenchment as the proper cure for the great slump, as early as the crisis year of 1931, and he was thus the first person to recommend what is now called the doctrine of "built-in stabilizers.") Some may think it unfortunate that the *General Theory* has somewhat overshadowed the *Treatise on Money;* the latter has a much greater range of interest and a wealth of ideas.

In the 1930s Keynes also devoted much attention to collecting books and modern paintings. He founded the Arts Theatre at Cambridge, of which the university and the borough of Cambridge became joint trustees. Even during World War II Keynes continued his interest in artistic questions. In 1942 he became chairman of the newly founded Committee for the Encouragement of Music and the Arts, which was later renamed the Arts Council of Britain and which has played a notable part in the encouragement of the arts in Britain ever since.

When World War II broke out Keynes wrote a pamphlet entitled *How to Pay for the War* (1940); he may be regarded as the author of the scheme for "postwar credits," which was adopted. He was taken back into the Treasury, and although he did not have administrative responsibility, as in World War I, his advice was sought on a wide range of day-to-day financial problems arising from the war.

The discussion of article 7 of the projected Mutual Aid Agreement in 1941 led Keynes to give part of his time to the problems of postwar reconstruction. The first draft of his plan for a "Clearing Union," i.e., the original British version of what became the International Monetary Fund, was composed that autumn. He also drafted an elaborate scheme for international buffer stocks, in order to stabilize commodity prices; in 1943 this scheme aroused interest in Washington also.

In addition to his important work in establishing the International Monetary Fund, in Washington in 1943 and the following year at Bretton Woods, Keynes made a number of journeys to the United States during the war to discuss the current financing of the war and reconstruction problems. One of his last major tasks was the negotiation in Washington of the large U.S. loan to Britain during the autumn of 1945. The problems involved were very intricate, and Keynes found himself in disagreement not only with the Americans across the table but also with the directives he received from the British authorities in London. His health had already been damaged by a severe coronary thrombosis in 1937, and the tension of the meetings was a great strain.

At the first meeting of the International Monetary Fund and the International Bank, in 1946 in Savannah, Georgia, Keynes came into sharp conflict with Fred Vinson, secretary of the U.S. Treasury. Some of the decisions taken at the meeting dashed his hopes for the future of these institutions, upon which he had lavished so much work. The emotional strain was great. Back at his home in Sussex, Keynes died on Easter Sunday 1946.

R. F. HARROD

[For the historical context of Keynes's work, see the biographies of CASSEL; FISHER, IRVING; HAWTREY; KEYNES, JOHN NEVILLE; MARSHALL; PIGOU; WHITEHEAD; for discussion of the subsequent development of his ideas, see CONSUMPTION FUNCTION; INCOME AND EMPLOYMENT THEORY; INTEREST; LIQUIDITY PREFERENCE; MONEY, article on QUANTITY THEORY.]

### WORKS BY KEYNES

(1913) 1924  *Indian Currency and Finance.* London: Macmillan.

(1919) 1920  *The Economic Consequences of the Peace.* New York: Harcourt; London: Macmillan.

(1921) 1952  *A Treatise on Probability.* London: Macmillan.

1922  *A Revision of the Treaty: Being a Sequel to* The Economic Consequences of the Peace. New York: Harcourt; London: Macmillan.

1923  *A Tract on Monetary Reform.* London: Macmillan.

1929  KEYNES, JOHN MAYNARD; and HENDERSON, H. D. *Can Lloyd George Do It? An Examination of the Liberal Pledge.* London: The Nation and Athenæum.

(1930) 1958–1960  *A Treatise on Money.* 2 vols. London: Macmillan. → Volume 1: *The Pure Theory of Money.* Volume 2: *The Applied Theory of Money.*

1936  *The General Theory of Employment, Interest and Money.* London: Macmillan. → A paperback edition was published in 1965 by Harcourt.

1940  *How to Pay for the War: A Radical Plan for the Chancellor of the Exchequer.* New York: Harcourt; London: Macmillan.

SUPPLEMENTARY BIBLIOGRAPHY

DILLARD, DUDLEY D.  1948  *The Economics of John Maynard Keynes: The Theory of a Monetary Economy.* Englewood Cliffs, N.J.: Prentice-Hall.

HANSEN, ALVIN H.  1953  *A Guide to Keynes.* New York: McGraw-Hill.

HARRIS, SEYMOUR E. (editor)  (1947) 1965  *The New Economics: Keynes' Influence on Theory and Public Policy.* New York: Kelley.

HARRIS, SEYMOUR E.  1955  *John Maynard Keynes: Economist and Policy Maker.* New York: Scribner.

HARROD, R. F.  (1951) 1963  *The Life of John Maynard Keynes.* London: Macmillan; New York: St. Martins.

KLEIN, LAWRENCE R.  (1947) 1963  *The Keynesian Revolution.* New York: Macmillan.

KURIHARA, KENNETH K. (editor)  1954  *Post-Keynesian Economics.* New Brunswick, N.J.: Rutgers Univ. Press.

LEKACHMAN, ROBERT (editor)  1964  *Keynes' General Theory: Reports of Three Decades.* New York: St. Martins.

## II
## CONTRIBUTIONS TO STATISTICS

Keynes took his degree in mathematics: it was therefore natural that his fellowship thesis should be on a mathematical subject. He chose probability as the topic, and out of this thesis grew *A Treatise on Probability* (1921), his single great contribution to the subject. Of the five parts of this large book, the second attempts to reduce to logical formulas the fundamental theorems of the probability calculus, a mathematical exercise in the tradition of Whitehead and Russell that has had little influence. Another part of the book is historical and bibliographical; the bibliography lists 600 items. Keynes's passion for collecting reveals itself in this admirable compendium, which brought Todhunter's and Laurent's earlier historical treatments of logic up to date. A third feature is a fine critique of some views of probability that were held then and are still popular. Among these are the idea of probability as a subjective degree of belief in a proposition, given the evidence, and the notion of probability as a limiting frequency associated with a certain type of infinite sequence.

The main contribution of Keynes is the argument that probability is a primitive idea—a logical relation between a proposition and the evidence bearing on the truth of the proposition. Thus, with the subjectivists, he held that it is a relation between propositions and evidence; but he supported the frequentists in thinking that it is an objective notion. His conception of probability was pursued with great thoroughness and in a style worthy of attention for its literary merits. For Keynes, the purpose of probability theory is to systematize inference processes. He therefore attempted to formulate certain rules of probability and to develop a calculus. Furthermore, he tried to develop the logical foundations of statistical arguments.

Keynes's viewpoint and the program were novel and important. They have had a great influence on probabilists and statisticians. Unfortunately, they were marred by a serious restriction that Keynes imposed in refusing to admit that all probabilities can be compared. He was prepared to assume only that probabilities are partially ordered. Related to this difficulty is his refusal to recognize that a numerical measure of probability is always appropriate. As Ramsey was later to point out (1923–1928), this refusal to introduce numbers is surprising in view of Keynes's obvious knowledge of Russell's work on the correspondence between order relations and numbers. But without numbers, progress is difficult if not impossible.

In a biographical essay on Ramsey, Keynes (1933, p. 300) later withdrew his objections and admitted the correctness of Ramsey's view of probability as expressed in terms of bets. He also admitted Ramsey's argument that the rules of probability are logical deductions from proper betting behavior, and not primitive axioms. In the hands of Savage, Ramsey's work has led to many interesting developments in what is now often called Bayesian probability, which is having an increasing influence on practical statistics. It is interesting to note that while Keynes was working on the treatise, Jeffreys (1939), also in Cambridge, was developing a similar objective, logical theory. But since he admitted numbers, he made much more progress on the calculus than did Keynes. According to Jeffreys, both he and Keynes were influenced by W. E. Johnson, a lecturer in philosophy at Cambridge.

DENNIS V. LINDLEY

[*Directly related are the articles on* BAYESIAN INFERENCE *and* PROBABILITY.]

### WORKS BY KEYNES

(1921) 1952 *A Treatise on Probability.* London: Macmillan. → A paperback edition was published in 1962 by Harper.

(1933) 1951 *Essays in Biography.* New ed. Edited by Geoffrey Keynes. New York: Horizon Press. → A paperback edition was published in 1963 by Norton.

#### SUPPLEMENTARY BIBLIOGRAPHY

JEFFREYS, HAROLD (1931) 1957 *Scientific Inference.* 2d ed. Cambridge Univ. Press.

JEFFREYS, HAROLD (1939) 1961 *Theory of Probability.* 3d ed. Oxford: Clarendon.

RAMSEY, FRANK P. (1923–1928) 1931 *The Foundations of Mathematics and Other Logical Essays.* New York: Harcourt.

SAVAGE, LEONARD J. 1954 *The Foundations of Statistics.* New York: Wiley.

## KEYNES, JOHN NEVILLE

John Neville Keynes (1852–1949), English logician, economist, and university administrator, was a leading contributor to the methodology of economics. In *The Scope and Method of Political Economy* (1891) Keynes combined a mastery of formal logic with erudition in economics to produce perhaps the best statement of the logical character of classical economics ever made. Although tolerant of other points of view and other approaches, he championed the traditional British abstract, positive, and primarily deductive approach that characterized classical and neoclassical economics. Keynes was sympathetic to the use of mathematics and statistics in economics, but he did not foresee the usefulness of econometric methods. He afforded an important place to economic history, but not as an integral part of the science of political economy. His work has significance for the social sciences generally, but he rejected Comte's view of political economy as a branch of sociology, the master social science.

Keynes was born in Salisbury and graduated from University College, London. He entered Pembroke College, Cambridge, where he studied mathematics for a year before concentrating in moral sciences. He received the B.S. degree in moral sciences in 1876 and in the same year became a fellow of Pembroke College, as well as an honorary fellow of University College, London. Political economy was still part of the moral sciences tripos when Keynes was a student at Cambridge, and when he lectured in political economy and in logic it was as a member of the moral sciences faculty. Keynes was sufficiently well regarded as an economist for his name to have been advanced for the chair in political economy at Oxford and for Alfred Marshall to have urged his appointment in 1890 as first editor of the *Economic Journal* (both appointments eventually went to F. Y. Edgeworth). Keynes took an M.A. degree and subsequently received an sc.d. degree from Cambridge University in 1891.

In addition to his scholarly career as teacher and author, Keynes became the leading administrator of Cambridge University. He was elected to the powerful council of the University Senate in 1892 and became its secretary the following year. In 1910 he was appointed registrary of the university and held this position until his retirement in 1925.

Keynes's *Studies and Exercises in Formal Logic* (1884) is a general treatise widely used as a textbook for several decades. He viewed logic as a normative science, similar in this respect to ethics and aesthetics, concerned with the general principles of valid thought—that is, with how we ought to think and only indirectly with how we actually think. He presented some of the most complicated problems of formal logic without resort to technical mathematical symbolism at a time when symbolic logic was coming to the forefront. Keynes's *Formal Logic* was not an important original contribution to knowledge, but its influence was considerable because the author's masterful exposition brought a difficult subject within the reach of many who were technically not equipped to wrestle with mathematical and symbolic logic.

In *The Scope and Method of Political Economy* Keynes defined political economy as a positive science concerned with the production, distribution, and accumulation of wealth, or alternatively, as "the science which treats of the phenomena arising out of the economic activities of mankind in society" (1891, p. 101). He wrote at the time of the well-known controversy over method (*Methodenstreit*), in which Carl Menger and Gustav Schmoller were the principal protagonists. Like most British economists, Keynes felt the *Methodenstreit* exaggerated the mutual exclusiveness of the historical–descriptive and the theoretical–analytical approaches. He saw the need to combine induction and deduction, analysis and synthesis, a posteriori and a priori reasoning.

In the logical method of political economy Keynes distinguished three stages. (1) Initially the economist observes the facts of the actual world, to gain insight into economic relations. (2) From clearly stated premises drawn from prior observation, he then formulates by deductive inference the general laws of political economy. (3) These laws in turn are tested by inductive verification. Only the second stage is strictly deductive, and it is meaningful only in relation to the antecedent and subsequent, primarily inductive, stages. Consequently, economics is both deductive and inductive in method.

As compared with his British predecessors, Nassau Senior and John Elliott Cairnes, Keynes appears to have compromised with the historical school [*see the biographies of* CAIRNES *and* SENIOR]. It is well to note, however, that the compromise is more apparent than real, more a matter of toleration than of acceptance of a broader scope for economics. Since economic theory is concerned with general laws, and since only deduction can yield general laws, the second stage is for Keynes the most significant one. Keynes's scope and method lent itself readily to Marshall's equilibrium theory of normal conditions, but not, for example, to Veblen's concept that the central task of economic science is to explain cumulative economic change. In emphasis, Keynes adhered to the deductive phase as the focus of pure theory.

Keynes neglected the important question of how economists choose the "relevant" observations upon which the "general" laws are based. His system contains nothing resembling what Joseph Schumpeter called "vision," which is related to ideology and which lies behind significant innovations in economic theory. Keynes denied that an important connection exists between laissez-faire and classical economics and thus missed the point that it was precisely their value-laden premises that enabled Adam Smith and David Ricardo, for example, to formulate powerful theoretical arguments for laissez-faire and free trade and to be justly acclaimed as great innovators in classical economics. Keynes's third stage, the appeal to fact for testing the deduced general laws, is also more complicated than he supposed if one considers the selective and pragmatic nature of the premises upon which the general laws rest.

Keynes wrote as a logician about the scope and method of economics, about how economists ought to think and not how they actually do think, and his work has the merits and shortcomings of that approach. Ironically, his methodological tenets must have been more handicap than asset to his son, John Maynard Keynes, whose polemical orientation against laissez-faire led him to formulate a new system of political economy.

DUDLEY DILLARD

[*For the historical context of J. N. Keynes's work, see the biographies of* MENGER *and* SCHMOLLER.]

WORKS BY KEYNES

(1884) 1906  *Studies and Exercises in Formal Logic, Including a Generalisation of Logical Processes in Their Application of Complex Inferences.* 4th ed. London: Macmillan.

(1891) 1955  *The Scope and Method of Political Economy.* 4th ed. New York: Kelley.

(1894*a*) 1963  Analytical Method. Volume 1, page 38 in *Palgrave's Dictionary of Political Economy*. Rev. ed. New York: Kelley.

(1894*b*) 1963  A Posteriori Reasoning. Volume 1, page 43 in *Palgrave's Dictionary of Political Economy*. Rev. ed. New York: Kelley.

(1894*c*) 1963  Applied Economics. Volume 1, page 44 in *Palgrave's Dictionary of Political Economy*. Rev. ed. New York: Kelley.

(1894*d*) 1963  A Priori Reasoning. Volume 1, pages 47–48 in *Palgrave's Dictionary of Political Economy*. Rev. ed. New York: Kelley.

(1894*e*) 1963  Deductive Method. Volume 1, pages 523–526 in *Palgrave's Dictionary of Political Economy*. Rev. ed. New York: Kelley.

SUPPLEMENTARY BIBLIOGRAPHY

BROAD, C. D.; and PIGOU, A. C. 1950  John Neville Keynes. *Economic Journal* 60:403–408.

KEYNES, FLORENCE A. 1950  *Gathering Up the Threads: A Study in Family Biography*. Cambridge: Heffer.

# KIDDER, ALFRED V.

Alfred Vincent Kidder (1885–1963) was recognized as the leading American archeologist of his time. His major achievements lie in two fields: the Southwestern culture area of the United States and the territories of the Old and New Maya empires in Mexico and Central America.

Although he appeared to be a typical New Englander, he was born in Marquette, on the Upper Peninsula of Michigan. His father was Alfred Kidder, a Bostonian seeking his fortune in the Michigan iron mines, and his mother was Kate Dalliba of Chicago. Kidder received all his academic degrees from Harvard: A.B., 1908; A.M., 1912; and PH.D., 1914.

Inspired by Roland B. Dixon, Alfred M. Tozzer, Frederic Ward Putnam, George A. Heisner, W. C. Farabee, and Vilhjalmur Stefansson, he began his field work in the San Juan drainage in New Mexico, Colorado, and Utah in 1907. There he met Edgar L. Hewitt, Byron Cummings, Neil Judd, Sylvanus G. Morley, and Jesse L. Nussbaum. The enthusiasms generated by these contacts in Cambridge and the Southwest were responsible for his decision to become an archeologist instead of a physician. His doctoral thesis was the first effective application of pottery typology to the problems of prehistory in the American Southwest.

Kidder was responsible for the first thoroughgoing systematization in American archeology. In *An Introduction to the Study of Southwestern Archaeology*, published in 1924 and still constantly used, he elaborated his conception of the development of the prehistoric Basket Maker culture into the historically known Pueblo cultures of the American Southwest. He also presented his ideas at the first Southwestern Archaeological Conference, held at his excavation headquarters near Pecos, New Mexico (1927*a*).

In the course of a series of expeditions to the canyons and mesas of northeastern Arizona, in the company of Samuel J. Guernsey, and to the excavation of the large pueblo of Pecos, the system known as the Pecos Classification of archeological units was set up. Although the original, developmental phases have been modified by discoveries made since the classification was first presented at the 1927 Pecos conference, the classification did establish a framework subsequently used by all workers in the Pueblo area. The conference has also continued and at present attracts annually some two hundred students of Southwestern anthropology.

In 1910 Kidder married Madeline Appleton of Boston, and thereafter she regularly accompanied him as an assistant on his expeditions. The Kidders were noted for their ability to transform students into productive scholars and amateur archeologists into professionals. They also participated enthusiastically in the communities where they worked, assisting in the establishment of departments of anthropology in the colleges and universities of the area, state and regional archeological societies, the Laboratory of Anthropology at Santa Fe, the Museum of Northern Arizona at Flagstaff, and the Gila Pueblo Museum at Globe, Arizona.

For a quarter of a century, beginning in 1907 on Alkali Ridge in southeastern Utah, Kidder was a field worker par excellence, although he also held research and curatorial appointments in the department of anthropology and the Peabody Museum at Harvard and at the Robert Singleton Peabody Foundation for Archaeology at Phillips Academy in Andover, Massachusetts. Among the students whom the Kidders encouraged and trained at Pecos were many who went into the Middle American field, and eventually Kidder's own interests shifted to that field. Although at that time an actual relationship between Mexican and Pueblo culture was not susceptible to proof, Kidder was sure that many of the elaborate, civilizing manifestations in the Pueblo culture must have diffused from the Valley of Mexico and beyond. He therefore kept a close watch on the work of his former students (who included George C. Vaillant, Samuel K. Lothrop, Karl Ruppert, and Oliver Ricketson) and of his contemporary, Morley, who was excavating the famous Maya site, Chichén Itzá, in Yucatan.

Kidder began his long association with Phillips Academy when in 1915 he undertook for them the excavation of the old pueblo of Pecos, New Mexico. After his 1926 appointment as research associate of the Carnegie Institution of Washington in the capacity of adviser to its archeological program in Middle America, he still continued his official connection with Andover. In 1929 he was appointed chairman of the division of historical research in the Carnegie Institution, but he kept his office in Andover until 1935, when he moved it to Frisbie Place in Cambridge.

With official responsibility for the outstanding archeological research program in the New World south of the United States, Kidder's first step was to make it interdisciplinary. In addition to the standard archeological program, he initiated studies in ethnology, social anthropology, linguistics, medicine, physical anthropology, colonial history, geology, geography, ethnobiology, and agronomy. There resulted a comprehensive survey of Maya cultural history that is a highly important addition to our knowledge of the American past. Under Kidder's direction the Carnegie Institution's research program was extended to the Guatemalan highlands. Kidder himself constantly visited and worked with the expeditions, particularly the one at the great early Maya site of Kaminaljuyu, near Guatemala City. Under his leadership many outstanding Americanists were encouraged and supported.

Kidder rendered many services to his profession: for example, he was chairman of the division of anthropology and psychology of the National Research Council in 1926/1927; president of the Society for American Archaeology in 1937 and of the American Anthropological Association in 1942; and a principal founder of the Institute of Andean Research. Also, he served in an advisory capacity to such bodies as the Committee for the Recovery of Archaeological Remains, the Southwest Museum of Los Angeles, and the Peabody Museum of Natural History at Yale. Among the honors he received were the first Viking Fund Medal for archeology and the Drexel Medal of the University of Pennsylvania. Honorary degrees were conferred on him by the universities of New Mexico and Michigan, the National University of Mexico, and the San Carlos University, Guatemala. Upon his retirement from his post at the Carnegie Institution in 1950, an independent committee of archeologists set up the Alfred Vincent Kidder Medal, to be awarded every three years in perpetuity for outstanding achievement in the fields of Southwestern and Middle American archeology.

J. O. BREW

[*For the historical context of Kidder's work, see* ARCHE-OLOGY; *and the biographies of* DIXON; PUTNAM; TOZZER; *for discussion of the subsequent development of his ideas, see the biography of* VAILLANT.]

WORKS BY KIDDER

1910    Explorations in Southeastern Utah in 1908. *American Journal of Archaeology* 14:337–360.

1915    Pottery of the Pajarito Plateau and of Some Adjacent Regions in New Mexico. American Anthropological Association, *Memoirs* 2:407–462.

1916    The Pottery of the Casas Grandes District, Chihuahua. Pages 253–268 in *Holmes Anniversary Volume: Anthropological Essays.* Washington: Bryan.

1919    KIDDER, ALFRED V.; and GUERNSEY, SAMUEL J. *Archaeological Explorations in Northeastern Arizona.* Smithsonian Institution, Bureau of American Ethnology, Bulletin No. 65. Washington: Government Printing Office.

1921    KIDDER, ALFRED V.; and GUERNSEY, SAMUEL J. *Basket-maker Caves of Northeastern Arizona.* Harvard University, Peabody Museum of American Archaeology and Ethnology, Papers, Vol. 8, No. 2. Cambridge, Mass.: The Museum.

(1924) 1962    *An Introduction to the Study of Southwestern Archaeology: With a Preliminary Account of the Excavations at Pecos.* Rev. ed. New Haven: Yale Univ. Press.

1926    Archaeological Work by State Agencies in 1925. Edited by Alfred V. Kidder. *American Anthropologist* New Series 28:679–694.

1927a    Southwestern Archaeological Conference. *Palacio* 23:554–561.

1927b    Early Man in America. *Southwest Museum Masterkey* 1, no. 5:5–13.

1930–1950    Annual Report of the Chairman, Division of Historical Research. Carnegie Institution of Washington, *Year Book.*

1931    *The Pottery of Pecos.* Volume 1: The Dull-paint Wares. New Haven: Yale Univ. Press.

1932    *The Artifacts of Pecos.* Papers of the Southwestern Expedition, No. 6. New Haven: Yale Univ. Press.

1936    Speculations on New World Prehistory. Pages 143–152 in R. H. Lowie (editor), *Essays in Anthropology Presented to A. L. Kroeber. . . .* Berkeley: Univ. of California Press.

1937    A Program for Maya Research. *Hispanic American Historical Review* 17:160–169.

1938    The Prehistoric New World. *Think* 4, no. 7:28,48.

(1940) 1962    Archaeological Problems of the Highland Maya. Pages 117–125 in *The Maya and Their Neighbors.* Salt Lake City: Univ. of Utah Press.

1945    Excavations at Kaminaljuyu, Guatemala. *American Antiquity* 11:65–75.

SUPPLEMENTARY BIBLIOGRAPHY

HARRISON, MARGARET W. 1947 A. V. Kidder. *Boletín bibliográfico de antropología americana* 9:337–342.

Alfred V. Kidder. 1950 *Palacio* 57:10–11.

Alfred Vincent Kidder. 1963 Volume 13, pages 161–170 in Harvard University, Peabody Museum of Archaeology and Ethnology, Library, *Catalogue.* Part 1: Authors. Boston: Hall. → A bibliography.

# KINESICS

Kinesics is the science of body behavioral communication. Any person who has "learned how to behave in public" and is at all aware of his response to the awkward or inappropriate behavior of others recognizes the importance of body motion behavior to social interaction. It is more difficult to conceive that body motion and facial expression belong to a learned, coded system and that there is a "language" of movement comparable to spoken language, both in its structure and in its contribution to a systematically ordered *communicative system.*

Communication is a term used to describe the structured dynamic processes relating to the interconnectedness of living systems. As such, it has much of the indefiniteness and usefulness of terms like "gravity," "electromagnetic field," or, perhaps, "metabolism" in their respective phenomenological contexts. While communication studies must investigate certain biological, social, and cultural processes, communication is an essential *aspect* of, not a master category for, such processes. Communication is a multichannel system emergent from, and regulative of, the influenceable multisensory activity of living systems. The spoken and the body motion languages thus are *infra*communicational systems that are *interdependently merged* with each other and with other comparable codes that utilize other channels; they are operationally communicative. Emphasis upon communication as a multichannel system stresses the difficulty of final objective appraisal of the relative or specific importance of spoken language to communication before we know more about communication. It is unproductively tautological to argue from the fact that language is characteristic of humans to the position that language is the central or the most important communicative code utilized by humans. All infracommunicational channels are equally necessary to the whole of which they are dependent subsystems. To attempt to weigh their relative importance to cultural continuity without more evidence than is now available is somewhat like arguing whether sex or food is more important to speciational continuity.

Communication is a continuous interactive process made up of multileveled, overlapping, discontinuous segments of behavior. The interaction of communication does not cease when interactants lapse into silence, to begin again with the onset of phonation; other channels continue communicative operations even when the auditory–aural channel is not in use. Humans move in relatively orderly fashion while they vocalize and when they are silent; they can perceive the regularity in the visible movement of others (or at least become aware when it is irregular) and proprioceptively in themselves. They can smell, taste, touch, and otherwise register perception of themselves and their surroundings. When regularities appear, they are not simply mechanical, "automatic," or happenstantial. Research with visible body motion is

convincing us that this behavior is as ordered and coded as is audible phonation. Like language, infra-communicational body motion behavior is a structured system that varies from society to society and must be learned by the membership of a society if it is to interact successfully.

It is as yet unclear how taste, smell, touch, heat, and cold, to speak only of the sensory potential of the more obvious communicative channels, are structured and utilized. However, as we gain control of the theory and the methodology (including the technology) prerequisite to their isolation and description, these should prove to have decipherable codes. Body behavioral communication has been the subject of extensive research and major theoretical formulations contributed by descriptive and structural linguists. Yet much of the structural analysis of body motion behavior had to await the development of the movie camera and the slow-motion projector before elements of kinesic structure could be isolated and demonstrated as significant. Comparably, even the preliminary investigation of the relationships between linguistic and kinesic structure discussed below could not be tested and demonstrated until the linguist and the kinesicist gained control of the sound movie, the tape recorder, the slow-motion projector, and the speech stretcher. Engineers are confident that the technology for recording the behavior of other sensory channels is now within the range of possibility. However, such developments are not likely until there is sufficient sophistication about the essential nature of these channels so that the investigator is not drowned in an ocean of insignificant data. Just as linguistic research laid bare data for kinesic investigation, linguistics and kinesics, as they exhaust their respective behavioral fields, should point the way for definitive research in the other communicative channels.

It is within this conceptual framework that some of the results of communicational body motion research are sketched below. The scientific investigation of human body motion communication is a recent development. While a bibliography of thousands of items could be developed which attest to the fact that the graphic artist, the writer, the story teller, the dancer, and the ethnographer have long noted the fact that men gesture, posture, move, and grimace in interesting, significant, and unusual fashions, it does not seem that anyone prior to the twentieth century suspected the structured, languagelike nature of human body behavior.

## Contemporary study

Darwin is often seen as the father of modern communicative studies of body motion. Yet neither in his *Expression of the Emotions in Man and Animals* (1872) nor anywhere else does he seem to have made the qualitative jump between his brilliant observations of animal and human body motion and expression and these as related to ordered communicative systems. Franz Boas is said by his students to have laid the groundwork for Sapir's brilliant intuition that body motion was coded and that this code had to be learned for successful communication (Sapir 1931; 1933). Efron (1941), another of Boas' students, conclusively demonstrated the culture-bound nature of southeastern European, Jewish, and Italian gestural complexes. From these insights and from others provided through psychoanalysis and psychiatry, LaBarre (1947) reviewed the literature to discuss "phatic" communication and the "pseudo languages" that preceded and surrounded vocal language. However, the beginning of the scientific investigation of the *structured* nature of body motion communication was marked by the publication of the *Introduction to Kinesics* (Birdwhistell 1952).

More directly relevant to the development of kinesics was the theoretical and methodological progress of the modern descriptive linguists, who in their penetrating and exhaustive analysis of human vocalic behavior presented a model that could be used for the investigation of other kinds of behavior (Bloomfield 1933; Sapir 1921; Trager & Smith 1951). One stimulus to investigate the meaningful variability of human body behavior came from the culture shock induced by the difference between Kutenai and American gestural and expressional patterning. Body motion research gained maturity and discipline under responsible linguistic tutelage. The recognition that a bilingual Kutenai moved in a consistently and regularly different manner when speaking Kutenai than when speaking English could not be understood until systematic analysis of the structure of American kinesics was undertaken.

**Context and meaning.**    From the outset of kinesic research, investigators have been distracted by the temptation to pursue the phantom of "meaning." Each new form or segment of structure isolated during investigations provoked the question, "What does it mean?" Even linguists, long since chastened by the relative sterility of their own explorations into the semantics of speech forms, seemed to cherish the hope that the kinesicist might present them with an "expressionary" or a kinecography that would list specific gestural, expressional, or movement complexes, together with their exclusive meanings. It is true that when informants are questioned they may give the investigator an extensive listing of such forms and a range of meaning for each. Cross-cultural comparison quickly reveals that an Arab from Beirut, a Chinese from Taiwan, and a Harlem Negro respond quite differently to apparently identical body behaviors. It can be easily established that these differences in response are cultural rather than idiosyncratic; different cultures exploit the potential for body motion in differing ways. Data are accumulating in the literature; particularly worthy of note is the work of Gordon Hewes (1955), who has compiled an extensive cross-cultural listing of body posture. However, like other studies of the specialized gestures of particular groups (Saitz & Cervenka 1962), these belong more properly in the province of ethnographic studies than in the area of kinesics or communication studies. Such lists often have the same relationship to kinesic anthropology that dictionaries do to linguistic anthropology—they are suggestive, but of indirect relevance.

Structural analysis of even the apparently most discrete facial expression (the "smile" or the "frown"), the apparently most explicit gesture (the "nod" or the "head shake"), or the apparently most indicative posture ("military uprightness" or "sag") show reports of such behavior to be impressionistic summaries of quite complex and systematically varying particles of activity that are, more importantly, always dependent upon other behaviors. The assemblage of component body behaviors that is reported by informants cannot stand alone any more than the phoneme can stand alone in functional speech behavior. Furthermore, while some informants may have quick responses as to the "meaning" of such behaviors and others may be goaded into choosing more likely "meanings" from a dichotomous battery, when these body behaviors are studied in a natural social setting they prove to depend upon the range of stimuli available in the larger contexts of interactive behavior in which they appear. It appears that these nonlexical forms have the same variability of semantic function as do "words." Whatever it is we mean by "meaning," it is a term which covers the relationship between an isolated event and its appropriate spectrum of surrounds.

Research into the nature of body motion communication over the past decade has proceeded in two differing but intimately related directions. An attempt has been made to isolate the significant forms of communicative body motion behavior and, in separate research operations, to gain perspective upon the nature of the levels of context in which these forms function. These latter operations, ultimately concerned with meaning, have been termed *context analysis*. While research in this area remains exploratory, it is promising. In differing ways, the studies of Goffman (1963), that of Hall (1959), and that of Ruesch (Ruesch & Kees 1956) have been pioneering. Their work points toward the rich data that await the investigator who would systematically describe the structural logic of interpersonal activity in precise social settings. More cogent to context analysis is the work of Scheflen (1965). He and others who have followed his lead report the isolation of interactional units characteristic of the psychotherapeutic situation. Such studies give promise that minutes-long sequences of communicative behavior may be as structurally marked as are syntactic sentences ($\frac{1}{2}$ to 4 or 5 seconds in duration) or the kinesic constructions that are contained within triple-cross kinesic junctures (ranging between 5 seconds and 2 or $2\frac{1}{2}$ minutes). These larger regular shapes of behavioral sequences increase the possibility of objectively measuring the function of particular communicative elements in contextual contrasts. Discovering the structural aspects of the interactive process is necessary to the objective definition of the "meaning" of the integral units, the messages carried by the communicative system. From the point of view of context analysis, *meaning* is the behavioral difference occasioned by the presence or the absence of a particular cue at a particular level of context. The range of meaning of a particular cue is governed by the range of contexts in which the cue can be observed to occur.

**Units and structure of body motion.**  Kinesics has been concerned with the exhaustive description and analysis of the American kinesic structure. Structural linguists have traditionally approached their data through the word and then, in one set of operations, engaged in morphological and phonological research, and, in another set, moved toward the isolation and description of lexemes and syntax. More recently, linguists have sought to analyze the longer sequences of discourse. Using an analogous model, kinesic studies have demonstrated that the "gesture" is a *bound morph* (a stem form) and have gone on to analyze the position and activity of such forms. The tentative descriptions of kinemorphology prepared the ground for analysis of behavior into the component *kines* and *kinemes*. As research proceeded, it became increasingly evident that the American kinesic pattern, at least, was not simply a sequence of these complex kinemorphs (kinemorphic stem plus suffixes). By conventions of junction, these wordlike forms are combined into sentencelike sequences.

Clearly, kinesic forms at each ascending level of analysis resemble linguistic forms in their duality of patterning (Hockett 1960). Just as syntactic sentences do not dangle isolated in nature, these extended, linked sequences of body motion behavior, the *complex kinemorphic constructions*, do not exhaust the potentials of body activity in communication. These again are building blocks for still longer sequences of behavior, evident in operation but which have thus far resisted analysis. Kinesic forms at each level of analysis (*kinelogical*, *kinemorphological*, and *kinesyntactic*) have distinctive contrastive identity as significant forms and also operate as items of structure.

Over the past century, acoustic phoneticians have developed a sufficient theory and an increasingly complex and reliable technology for the description of the physiological behavior that underlies the production of significant sounds utilized in human speech. It should not be surprising that some students confuse the activity of the apparatus for phonation with the linguistic process. At the present preliminary stage of kinesic research, it is even more difficult to keep the prekinesic activity of the body separate from the structured activity utilized in the kinesic code. Just as we are so impressed with the activity of the lips, the teeth, the tongue, the lungs, the larynx, the pharynx, etc., that we think of them as emitting speech, it is difficult not to be so preoccupied with musculature, bones, fatty tissue, the vascular system, and skin that we think of these as emitting body motion language. Rather these must be regarded as sources of potentials for behavior which are selectively regulated to form the kinesic code. The arm and hand of the telegrapher are of no direct consequence to the telegraphic code.

**An example of kinesic communication.**  As long as the kinesic anthropologist can remain sufficiently disciplined so that he does not confuse the particular activity of a particular part of the body with the code that makes use of certain activities of that body part in certain situations, he can profitably examine the body as an instrument specifically adapted for interactive behavior. Seemingly identical body movements supply the activity for quite different cue classes. To keep the example as simple as possible, movement of the eyebrows is the activity selected for discussion, and only the variables of context and duration are described. The specialized kinesic terminology and annotational conventions may prove confusing to the reader, but the examples chosen should be sufficiently familiar to soften the technicality of the illustration.

One of the more easily detectable *kines* (least perceptible units of body motion) is that of eyebrow lift and return (here transcribed as bb∧∨). At times such movement is fleeting; I have been able to detect and record brow movement lasting but thousandths of a second. For instance, the brows may be raised in certain contexts and held for a short duration before returning to the zero or base position. Such positioning may operate as one of the allokines (again using the linguistic analogy, the allokines would be, as allomorphs are, members of a class of events that can be substituted for one another) of the junctural *kineme* (the least cue class) of (/k//). This bilateral eyebrow raise is quite comparable to, and may during phonation co-occur with, the linguistic single bar of terminally raised pitch, appropriate to the context of "doubt" or "question" or as a signal to repeat a message. If we ignore the duration of the action and attend only to the spatial movement of the brows, an identical movement of the brows may be seen in the circumvocal behavior of speakers who select the brows for kinesic stress functions. Intensive experimentation on the relationship between spoken and moved American has demonstrated that there are four degrees of kinesic stress (Birdwhistell 1965). The brows form one of the positional allokines of the kinemes of stress. Other allokines are provided by the head, hand, foot, or body nodding, or the lid closure that accompanies speech.

Thus, the kine eyebrow raise (bb∧) may be allokinic with the kines of superior head nod (h∧) or hand nod (/∧), members of the class kineme of kinesic single bar (/k//) in one context position and an allokine of the form degrees of kinesic stress (/primary, secondary, unstressed, or destressed/) in another. These two allokinic roles do not exhaust the cue potential of the brows. Furthermore, with the same muscular involvement, the (bb∧) may be an allokine of the kineme, the first degree of eyebrow raise (/bb$^1$/), which combines with other circumfacial kinemes to form a kinemorph.

I fully appreciate the reader's difficulty in picturing these abstractions. The point made here may be comprehended if the reader will conceive of a conversation in which an animated speaker is being attended to by an interested auditor. The eyebrows of the speaker rise and fall as he speaks (kinesic stress kinemes). From time to time, the speaker's eyes "focus" upon the face of the auditor and he pauses in his speech and raises his brow (/k//). He may continue vocalization following the single head nod (/hn/) of the auditor. During one sequence of the conversation, the auditor may "de-expressionalize" into the complex kine-

morph of dead pan (// O //); the speaker, without signaling response, may continue vocalization until the auditor raises his brows (/bb$^1$/), while sustaining the dead pan (// O //), to form the kinemorph $\left( // \dfrac{bb^1}{O} // \right)$. At this point, the speaker hesitates in his speech flow, drops his head and lids $\left( // \dfrac{h\vee\wedge}{oo\vee\wedge} // \right)$, and after several vocal false starts repeats part of his lexication. In the situations that we have observed, several conversationalists returned in discourse correction to the topic under discussion at the onset of the auditor's dead pan (// N → O //).

These three kinesic activities do not exhaust the cue potential of the eyebrows. Like the scalp, the eyebrows, while mobile in position in the young, gradually become relatively stationary in *base* placement (the point from which movement is initiated and the point of return following movement). As measured at the most superior aspect of the hirsute brow, there is a possible range of almost one-half inch for brow placement. While the diakinesic (comparable to language dialect) range is less marked in Americans, any observant traveler in England can mark the contrast between the high placement of the brows among people of certain regional and economic groups (many Englishmen look to the American as though they were perpetually surprised) and the low brow placement in other areas and at different socioeconomic levels (so-called beetle-browed). Such brow and scalp placement is learned behavior and is, on the one hand, an aspect of unique identity, and thus part of signature behavior, and, on the other, contributes to the common appearance of family, group, and regional members. The latter represents signature behavior at another level. From this example of certain eyebrow behaviors and from this view of communication it becomes clear that communicative units may vary in duration from milliseconds to years. It may be argued that individual appearances, such as diakinesic variation, are not to be classified as communicative behavior. Such a position, focusing on short sequences, would also deny the communicative role of dialect and individual speaking style. However, any regular and systematically variable learned behavior that redundantly contributes to the definition of an aspect of the code is in itself part of a larger code and must be understood if we are to comprehend the structure of the interactive process. As we have long realized intuitively, there is more that goes on in any conversation than is present in the immediate interaction. It is the researcher's duty to adapt his observations to the shapes of nature.

## Future research

Kinesics has been preoccupied with the description and analysis of body positions and movements. It has been possible to isolate and test thirty-four kinemes in the American kinesic system. While such a prediction is risky, there may be no more than fifty base units in the system. However, as kinesic research proceeds to gain security from cross-cultural studies it is going to have to pay systematic attention to other body associated phenomena. Such matters as the oiliness, wetness, and dryness of the skin, tension and laxity of the skin and musculature, variable and shifting vascularity in the skin's surface, and shifts in the underlying fatty tissue are all going to have to be studied intensively and systematically. All of our present observations, and these have been extensive but crude and nonconclusive, lead us to believe that these are coded in both long and short durational cue complexes. While at the moment these behaviors are assigned to paralanguage, a catchall category for insufficiently analyzed behavior, there seems every reason to believe that they will be subject to isolation, analysis, and communicative assignment. In this perspective particular attention must be paid to the work of Hall and Westcott. Using what may be an unnecessarily limiting dyadic model, Hall, in his conception of *proxemics* (Hall 1963), places emphasis on the human use of space arrangements as a coded system of transactional process. His work forces attention on all primary telecommunicative processes. Westcott (1964), in his discussion of *streptistics*, is attempting to order the various channels and their operative codes in structural relation to each other. These approaches, when taken together with the accumulating data from kinesic and linguistic anthropology, lay the groundwork for communication analysis.

RAY L. BIRDWHISTELL

[*Directly related are the entries* COMMUNICATION; COMMUNICATION, ANIMAL; ETHNOGRAPHY; LANGUAGE, *article on* LANGUAGE AND CULTURE.]

### BIBLIOGRAPHY

BIRDWHISTELL, RAY L. 1952 *Introduction to Kinesics.* Univ. of Louisville (Ky.) Press.

BIRDWHISTELL, RAY L. 1959 Contribution of Linguistic–Kinesic Studies to the Understanding of Schizophrenia. Pages 99–123 in Symposium on Schizophrenia, San Francisco, 1958, *Schizophrenia: An Integrated Approach.* New York: Ronald Press.

BIRDWHISTELL, RAY L. 1961 Paralanguage: 25 Years After Sapir. Pages 43–63 in Conference on Experimental Psychiatry, Western Psychiatric Institute and Clinic, 1959, *Lectures on Experimental Psychiatry.* Univ. of Pittsburgh Press.

BIRDWHISTELL, RAY L. 1962 Critical Moments in the Psychiatric Interview. Pages 179–188 in Tenth Anniversary Symposium on Biological, Psychological and Sociological Approaches to Current Psychiatric Problems, State Research Hospital, Galesburg, Ill., 1960, *Research Approaches to Psychiatric Problems: A Symposium.* New York: Grune.

BIRDWHISTELL, RAY L. 1965 Communication Without Words. Unpublished manuscript.

BLOOMFIELD, LEONARD (1933) 1951 *Language.* Rev. ed. New York: Holt.

DARWIN, CHARLES (1872) 1965 *The Expression of the Emotions in Man and Animals.* Edited by Francis Darwin. Univ. of Chicago Press.

EFRON, D. 1941 *Gesture and Environment.* New York: Kings Crown Press.

GOFFMAN, ERVING 1963 *Behavior in Public Places.* New York: Free Press.

HALL, EDWARD T. 1959 *The Silent Language.* Garden City, N.Y.: Doubleday. → A paperback edition was published in 1961 by Fawcett.

HALL, EDWARD T. 1963 A System for the Notation of Proxemic Behavior. *American Anthropologist* New Series 65:1003–1026.

HEWES, GORDON 1955 World Distribution of Certain Postural Habits. *American Anthropologist* New Series 57:231–244.

HOCKETT, CHARLES F. 1960 Logical Considerations in the Study of Animal Communication. Pages 392–430 in Symposium on Animal Sounds and Communication, Indiana University, 1958, *Animal Sounds and Communication.* Washington: American Institute of Biological Sciences.

INDIANA UNIVERSITY, CONFERENCE ON PARALINGUISTICS AND KINESICS, BLOOMINGTON, IND., 1962 1964 *Approaches to Semiotics, Cultural Anthropology, Education, Linguistics, Psychiatry and Psychology.* Edited by Thomas A. Sebeok, Alfred S. Hayes, and Mary C. Bateson. Janua linguarum, Series maior, No. 15. The Hague: Mouton.

LABARRE, WESTON 1947 The Cultural Basis of Emotions and Gestures. *Journal of Personality* 16:49–68.

LABARRE, WESTON 1954 *The Human Animal.* Univ. of Chicago Press. → See especially pages 165–168 on "Paralinguistics," and page 349 on "Kinesics."

RUESCH, JURGEN; and KEES, WELDON 1956 *Nonverbal Communication.* Berkeley: Univ. of California Press.

SAITZ, ROBERT L.; and CERVENKA, EDWARD J. 1962 *Colombian and North American Gestures: A Contrastive Inventory.* Bogotá: Centro Colombo Americano.

SAPIR, EDWARD A. (1910–1944) 1949 *Selected Writings in Language, Culture, and Personality.* Edited by David G. Mandelbaum. Berkeley: Univ. of California Press.

SAPIR, EDWARD A. 1921 *Language: An Introduction to the Study of Speech.* New York: Harcourt.

SAPIR, EDWARD A. 1931 Communication. Volume 4, pages 78–80 in *Encyclopaedia of the Social Sciences.* New York: Macmillan.

SAPIR, EDWARD A. 1933 Language. Volume 9, pages 155–168 in *Encyclopaedia of the Social Sciences.* New York: Macmillan.

SCHEFLEN, ALBERT E. 1965 *Stream and Structure of Communicational Behavior: Context Analysis of a Psychotherapy Session.* Behavioral Studies Monograph

No. 1. Philadelphia: Eastern Pennsylvania Psychiatric Institute.

TRAGER, GEORGE L.; and SMITH, HENRY L. JR. (1951) 1962 *An Outline of English Structure*. Washington: American Council of Learned Societies.

WESCOTT, ROGER W. 1964 Strepital Communication: A Study of Non-vocal Sound Production Among Man and Animals. Unpublished manuscript.

## KINESTHESIS

*See* SKIN SENSES AND KINESTHESIS.

## KING, GREGORY

Gregory King (1648–1712), the son of a mathematician who was also a landscape gardener, was born at Lichfield. He got his early education at home, at the Free School, and as clerk to the antiquary Sir William Dugdale, whose service he entered at the age of 14 and with whom he spent several years traveling in the English counties on heraldic surveys. He was a well-informed topographer and surveyor; he assisted in the production of *Itinerarium Angliae: Or, a Book of the Roads*, 1675; and for a while he supported himself by mapmaking, engraving, and surveying. He was a skilled and well-known genealogist and became successively Rouge Dragon, registrar of the College of Arms, and Lancaster herald. He was a successful practicing accountant; he taught bookkeeping as a young man and in later life became secretary to the comptroller of army accounts and to the commissioners of public accounts. Finally, he was a distinguished political arithmetician. His autobiography (which, however, ends in 1694) was reproduced by James Dalloway as an appendix to *Inquiries Into the Origin and Progress of the Science of Heraldry in England* (1793).

It is as a statistician that King makes his claim to fame as a social scientist although, so far as we know, he did not become interested in political arithmetic until 1695. In that year he published a broadsheet summarizing the rates of duties payable under the Act of 1694, which levied taxes on marriages, births, burials, bachelors, and childless widowers. Possibly King had been involved in designing the statistical inquiries that were essential to the assessment of these taxes: he was certainly interested in the results, which were immensely significant sources of demographic information in an age when the size and trend of the population was a matter of great political interest and much speculation. There is no record of his having published any other work relating to political arithmetic during his lifetime, although his work was well known among his contemporaries and his estimates were freely used and quoted by Charles Davenant.

Unlike most of his contemporary political arithmeticians, King was a scholar rather than a politician. Perhaps this was why he never published his estimates, being content to make them freely available as a basis for economic policy-making or analysis rather than using them to support his own special pleadings. He was primarily interested in finding the exact truth about the dimensions of the national economy, so far as the available data would let him. It is evident from the notes and communications which have survived that he was completely honest about the limitations of his material and amazingly methodical in his use of it, and the more modern scholars have probed his methods and uncovered new sources of his notes, the more they have tended to admire his results. His famous "Scheme of the Income and Expences of the Several Families of England," given in his *Natural and Political Observations and Conclusions Upon the State and Condition of England* (1696), and his international comparisons of national income and expenditure for England, France, and Holland in his *Of the Naval Trade of England Aº 1688 and the National Profit Then Arising Thereby* (1697) were based essentially on guesswork, but as explicit statements of the views of a particularly well informed observer they are profoundly revealing. They inspired comparable calculations by Patrick Colquhoun in the early nineteenth century and became bench mark data of immense value to students of long-term growth.

All King's estimates were made with an accountant's meticulous concern for internal consistency, and in this respect his national income estimates were in advance of any calculations made in this field until the mid-twentieth century. It is possible to extract from the national income and balance of payments estimates given in his two tracts, supplemented with additional estimates quoted by Davenant, a complete, articulated set of double-entry social accounts as well as an abundance of detail on the content of national income, output, and expenditure in 1688 and 1695. He also made estimates of the national capital, its content, and its rate of increase through the seventeenth century. His population estimates were based on careful analyses of actual enumerations for particular places, corrected for technical errors and adjusted to a national basis, on assumptions that modern demographers (basing their judgments on the results of nineteenth-century census enumerations) have found to be both consistent and plausible. His schedule of the relation between changes in the price of wheat and deviations from the normal wheat harvest, which was originally published by Davenant and became known as "Gregory King's Law," represents a piece of demand analysis of a kind that we find in no other source until the early twentieth century.

PHYLLIS DEANE

### WORKS BY KING

*There are manuscripts and calculations by King in the British Museum, the Public Record Office (London), the Bodleian Library (Oxford), and the Library of the London County Council.*

1695 *A Scheme of the Rates and Duties Granted to His Majesty Upon Marriages, Births, and Burials, and Upon Batchelors and Widowers, for the Term of Five Years from May 1, 1695.* London: A broadsheet.

(1696) 1936 Natural and Political Observations and Conclusions Upon the State and Condition of England. Pages 12–56 in *Two Tracts by Gregory King.* Edited by George E. Barnett. Baltimore: Johns Hopkins Press. → The manuscript of 1696 was first published in 1802 in George Chalmers' *An Estimate of the Comparative Strength of Great-Britain.*

(1697) 1936 Of the Naval Trade of England A° 1688 and the National Profit Then Arising Thereby. Pages 60–76 in *Two Tracts by Gregory King.* Edited by George E. Barnett. Baltimore: Johns Hopkins Press. → The manuscript of 1697 was first published in 1936.

1793 Some Miscellaneous Notes of the Birth, Education, and Advancement of Gregory King. Appendix 2 in James Dalloway, *Inquiries Into the Origin and Progress of the Science of Heraldry in England.* Gloucester (England): Raikes. → The autobiography covers the years 1648 to 1694.

### SUPPLEMENTARY BIBLIOGRAPHY

DEANE, PHYLLIS 1955 The Implications of Early National Income Estimates for the Measurement of Long-term Growth in the United Kingdom. *Economic Development and Cultural Change* 4:3–38.

GLASS, D. V. 1946 Gregory King and the Population of England and Wales at the End of the Seventeenth Century. *Eugenics Review* New Series 38:170–183.

GLASS, D. V. 1950 Gregory King's Estimate of the Population of England and Wales, 1695. *Population Studies* 3:338–374.

REES, J. F. 1932 Gregory King. Volume 8, page 565 in *Encyclopaedia of the Social Sciences.* New York: Macmillan.

YULE, G. UDNY 1915 Crop Production and Price: A Note on Gregory King's Law. *Journal of the Royal Statistical Society* 78:296–298.

# KINGSHIP

The word "king" is derived from the Old English *cynn* and seems to have been first used for the chiefs or representatives of the cognatic kin groups, or "kins," into which Anglo-Saxon society was organized. This use of the term seems to lack religious reference, these early "kings" having apparently been primarily arbitrators, leaders, and warriors. Later, the word came to be used to translate the names for rulers in other European languages (such as the Greek *basileus* and the Latin *rex*) with whom ritual and religious functions were explicitly associated. Research into non-Western cultures has demonstrated that the association of religious or magical significance with what is usually called kingship is practically universal. The term "kingship" applies not only to those states that, like most modern or recent European monarchies, are considerable in size and population, but also to those many smaller traditional polities that center on a sovereign—or formerly sovereign—ruler or head. These chieftaincies, which are usually hereditary, differ only in scale and complexity from the more familiar Western kingships.

**Rituals of kingship.** Sir James Frazer was the first to develop the theme of kingship's ritual or sacral nature, and his famous work *The Golden Bough* (1890) begins with the Roman legend of the priest–king of Nemi, whose reign ended when he was slain by his successor. Frazer showed that in many ancient states, as well as in contemporary preindustrial societies, kings were commonly thought of either as priests or mediators between gods and men or as gods themselves. Thus the ancient Egyptian kings manifested the divine essence or force upon earth (Frankfort 1948, pp. 107–108), and kings were frequently identified with a sun deity, as in ancient Egypt, the Inca state of preconquest Peru, and Japan.

In considering the religious, or sacred, aspect of kingship it is important to remember that ritual is essentially symbolic; like other kinds of ritual, royal ritual is an institutionalized way of saying something that is thought to be important. Although ritual is basically expressive, it is also instrumentally effective. We not only have to ask, therefore, what are the social consequences of royal ritual, but we must enquire what it symbolizes. Since a single rite may have different levels of meaning, kingly ritual may be examined in four broad aspects.

First, there are myths of origin, symbolic statements about the beginnings of particular kingships. I referred above to the widespread identification of kings with the sun, from which many royal lines are supposed to be descended. Elsewhere, kings are thought to be descended from other nonhuman powers or gods. Thus in certain of the Bantu kingdoms of Uganda the traditional rulers are believed to be the descendants of a wonderful race, half men and half gods, who occupied the land many generations ago and then mysteriously disappeared.

Such myths are best regarded as a kind of ritual rather than as a kind of history, and they dramatically affirm the uniqueness and distinctiveness of the royal lines to which they refer. Their social importance is that they validate and so tend to sustain the systems of royal authority and prestige to which they relate.

The second important aspect of royal ritual (with the one next referred to, the central component in Frazer's concept of "divine kingship") is the mystical identification of the king with the territory and people over whom he reigns. It is widely believed in many cultures that the king should not be allowed to suffer any physical defect or to become old and feeble, for if this should happen the country itself would suffer corresponding injury. Like the priest–king of Nemi, many traditional rulers are, or are believed to be, ceremonially killed when they grow ill or old and their powers begin to wane. It is the belief in the ruler's death rather than the practice itself that is important, for it shows how kingship may be conceived of as primarily a ritual, symbolic office and not as a merely secular institution.

The third aspect, which is associated with the foregoing, is the expression, in a huge variety of rites and ceremonials, of the king's uniqueness—his difference from and superiority to ordinary people. Accession always involves some ceremony of crowning or anointing, which effectively consecrates or makes sacred the person of the king. He thus becomes imbued with a special ritual or symbolic value and is set apart as different from other men. Very often there is a special court language or vocabulary to refer to the king and his activities; this usage has been reported from regions as remote from one another as ancient Siam and central Africa. The king's distinctiveness may also be marked by the use of special prepositional forms by, and of, him—such as the "royal plural" and the use of the third person in addressing him. Often no part of his body may be allowed to touch the earth, as in the Ashanti kingdom of Ghana, and in many kingdoms he must not be seen eating and drinking by ordinary men. Sometimes certain ritually impure foods are forbidden to him. Always there is a regalia of ritually important objects associated with kingship. Some kings have been permitted to practice brother–sister incest, universally forbidden to ordinary people. Where, as is not often the case, such kings have been permitted to have children it may be claimed that such incest is a means of preserving the purity and distinctiveness of the royal line.

It is a characteristic of symbolism that the virtue or power attributed to what is symbolized comes to be ascribed to the symbol itself. Thus a special kind of potency comes to be associated with the king's unique ritual status. Polynesians believe that the *mana* of their rulers can kill ordinary men, and in the old Malayan kingdoms it was thought a breach of royal taboo could doom the offender. Sometimes this potency can be beneficial rather than, or as well as, malevolent; thus in England in the Middle Ages to touch the king or even his garment was believed to be a cure for scrofula, "the king's evil." Very commonly the king's potency is conceived of as a power to influence nature. For example, many traditional African kings were rainmakers; when the rain failed, the king was often blamed for willful neglect. Because he did not use his ritual powers for his people's welfare, he might be deposed or even killed. Similar usages are reported from other parts of the world; the early Swedish kings are said to have been killed if the crops failed.

The fourth broad aspect of royal ritual is the king's secular authority. Almost universally the king's accession to secular power over other men is symbolized by the handing to him on his accession a sword, scepter, or (as in early Egypt) a shepherd's crook. In some coronation rites the king's power over other men is symbolically expressed by a mock combat with an opponent who is, of course, defeated. The ancient Egyptian kings performed a rite of discharging arrows toward the four cardinal points of the compass, symbolizing the extent of their worldly domain, and the king of Bunyoro in western Uganda performs a similar rite on accession, exclaiming as he does so: "Thus I shoot the countries to overcome them!"

**Secular kingship.** Some early "kings" were also heads or representatives of kin groups, and some were war leaders, rather than priests or leaders in ritual. In such cases kingship was evidently a political office rather than a ritual or priestly one, though it seems that invariably symbolism and rite accrete around such office, whether or not they have contributed to its *raison d'être*. In all kingships, loyalty to the person of the king has been the supreme political value, and this has found expression in a variety of ceremonial usages; prostration or obeisance, hand-kissing, declarations of fealty, and so on. Where kingships have been secular in origin (e.g., due to military conquest) it has often been found expedient to "desecularize" them; witness the sedulous fostering of the notion of the "divine right of kings" in Jacobean England. Even wholly nonsecular or ritual kingships can have political importance, for although the king may discharge no governmental or administrative role, he may nonetheless provide a focus and symbol for his people's sense of national or tribal identity and so form an indispensable expression of their political unity.

Where kings are secular rulers their judicial or arbitrative role may be important. The notion of the "king's justice," often regarded as his private and personal possession, is widespread. Indeed, it appears that some kingships have developed in consequence of this need for arbitration. Students of tribal histories, principally in Africa, have recorded traditions of the emergence of royal dynasties from an original arbitrator, often of a different tribe from that of his subjects (and so presumed to be more impartial than any of them could be), who was invited to live among them and settle their disputes. The king's judicial or regulatory function may form a key element in the maintenance of social control in smaller-scale societies. Like other aspects of his power, a king's legal or regulative functions may also be expressed symbolically. In ancient India and elsewhere the comparison between the king's role and the sun's orderly course, seen as a vital regulatory force in the world, was explicit. In modern monarchies, where judicial function, like other governmental activity, has become the concern of nonroyal specialist bodies, the judicial role of kings has, of course, become obsolete; but it may survive, at least formally, in the convention that the king instigates judicial proceedings against malefactors (*Rex* v. *John Smith*) and in such institutions as the "king's pardon."

The economic aspect of kingship is usually most important in those societies which are small enough in scale for the king or chief to maintain some kind of personal relationship with all, or at least with a considerable number, of his subjects. In such polities the king is also the wealthiest man in the kingdom, but his wealth takes the form of services and material goods rendered as tribute to him by his subjects, and he does not retain it for his own private use. Rather he redistributes his wealth among his people in the form of feasts, gifts for favorites, and help for the needy. This constant circulation of goods and services from the periphery to the center and outward again may, at least until the intrusion of a cash economy and the consequent availability of a variety of new things to spend money on, form the basis of a system of relationships of closely knit interdependence between ruler and subjects. Many traditional small-scale states in Africa, southeast Asia, and elsewhere have exemplified this type of economic kingship until very recent times. But with increasing economic specialization, the advent of money, and the spread of centers of production and distri-

bution throughout the community, kings' economic significance, like their judicial importance, has declined almost to vanishing point.

We can conclude that although Frazer's evolutionary theory of the development of kings from priests may account for the historical origins of some kingships, it certainly does not explain all of them. Many traditional kingships have been symbolic or emblematic rather than secular, and they may have originated for this reason. But there is plenty of evidence that many other kingships have come into existence for quite other reasons, such as the conquest of a formerly segmentary society by superior force, the voluntary acceptance of an independent outside arbitrator, and the emergence, in a variety of possible conditions, of one individual or kin group in a segmentary community as *primus inter pares*. Shaka's kingship over the Zulu was of this last type.

But in whatever way different kingships have originated, essential to all of them is their symbolic, expressive quality, and it was Frazer's great merit to have perceived and stated this. For the majority of their subjects all kings are symbols: they symbolize the kingdom they reign over and its people, its prosperity and security, even its very existence. As is commonly the case with symbols, values ascribed fundamentally to what is symbolized run over into the symbol itself; in the institution of kingship they are expressed in a proliferation of rite and ceremony. Like all ritual, the primary aim of royal ritual is expression, but just because it is expressive it is often thought to be instrumental as well. In a certain sense, then, all kings are "divine"; but some kingships are more divine than others.

A number of factors have played a part in the decline of the importance of kingship throughout the modern world: the increased size and complexity of modern administrative organization; the destruction of the old interpersonal bonds of loyalty and dependence which linked the rulers of small-scale polities with their subjects; the introduction of modern economic systems and the consequent breakdown of traditional rulers' monopoly of economic power. But probably the most important factor is the rejection, characteristic of modern literate and scientifically oriented industrial societies, of traditional "expressive" values in favor of modern "instrumental" ones. Often, in earlier times, it was enough that the "divine king" should merely exist in a good moral and physical condition. Nowadays kings who are not at the same time rulers (and few are) are widely regarded as anachronisms, retained, if they are retained at all, for sentimental rather than practical reasons. To those who no longer ascribe to kings their traditional potency as symbols, they are bound to seem an unnecessary and expensive luxury. In any case, it may well be held that modern government is too complex a business to be left to hereditary monarchs whose claim to rule is based on ascribed rather than achieved qualification. No doubt most men will continue to create symbols in order to represent the often inarticulate values they cherish. But evidently the institution of kingship has, for most people, ceased to fulfill this role.

J. H. M. BEATTIE

[*Directly related are the entries* MONARCHY; POLITICAL ANTHROPOLOGY; STATELESS SOCIETY.]

### BIBLIOGRAPHY

BLOCH, MARC (1924) 1961 *Les rois thaumaturges.* Paris: Colin.
FIGGIS, JOHN N. (1896) 1922 *The Divine Right of Kings.* 2d ed. Cambridge Univ. Press. → First published as *The Theory of the Divine Right of Kings.* A paperback edition was published in 1965 by Harper.
FRANKFORT, HENRI 1948 *Kingship and the Gods: A Study of Ancient Near Eastern Religion as the Integration of Society and Nature.* Univ. of Chicago Press.
FRAZER, JAMES (1890) 1955 *The Golden Bough.* 3d ed., rev. & enl. 13 vols. New York: St. Martins; London: Macmillan. → An abridged edition was published in 1922 and reprinted in 1955.
HOCART, ARTHUR M. 1927 *Kingship.* Oxford Univ. Press.
King. 1915 Volume 7, pages 708–732 in *Encyclopaedia of Religion and Ethics.* New York: Scribner. → Contributions by eight authors.
SELIGMAN, CHARLES G. 1934 *Egypt and Negro Africa: A Study in Divine Kingship.* The Frazer Lecture for 1933. London: Routledge.

# KINSEY, ALFRED C.

Alfred Charles Kinsey (1894–1956) was undoubtedly the most famous American student of human sexual behavior in the first half of the twentieth century. In Europe at the turn of the century, Richard von Krafft-Ebing, and then Albert Moll, Havelock Ellis, Magnus Hirschfeld, and Sigmund Freud had opened up to exploration this hidden area of man's life, chiefly by the presentation of individual case histories and philosophical speculation. In the United States in the period between 1929 and 1940 Katherine B. Davis, Gilbert V. Hamilton, Robert Latou Dickinson, Lewis M. Terman, and Carney Landis had made investigations of certain segmental aspects of sex, but it remained for Kinsey to survey a broad range of human sexual behavior based on thousands of face-to-face interviews.

Kinsey obtained an undergraduate degree from Bowdoin in psychology and a doctorate at Harvard in 1920 in biology. He then went to Indiana University where he concentrated on the field of taxonomy, studying the Cynipidae (gall wasps). This study ultimately resulted in important contributions to evolutionary theory.

He began his sex research, unassisted, in 1938. Its importance was soon recognized and his personally financed week-end field trips to nearby cities to gather sex histories became instead three-week interviewing tours, supported by grants, on which he was accompanied by research associates. Clyde Martin and Wardell Pomeroy were among the first staff members to join him in interviewing. Support at first came from the National Research Council and the Medical Division of the Rockefeller Foundation. Indiana University, under the leadership of President Herman B Wells, lent solid backing to Kinsey's sex research, gradually relieving him of teaching duties to facilitate his work.

In 1948 *Sexual Behavior in the Human Male* was published. It aroused unanticipated interest in the general as well as the academic public, and Kinsey's name became synonymous with the study of sex. Five years later the companion volume, *Sexual Behavior in the Human Female*, was completed. In 1947 the Institute for Sex Research was established as a nonprofit corporation affiliated with Indiana University, and the staff was gradually augmented to a dozen or more. By this time an authoritative library dealing with sex had been developed and staffed, and valuable supplementary materials such as diaries, daily sexual calendars, art collections, cine, photographs, and other erotic source materials had been collected. In 1950 the United States Customs challenged the right of the institute to import erotica for scientific study and confiscated a collection of material purchased abroad. A case based on these seizures was decided in the Federal District Court of New York in 1957 in favor of the institute's right to add to its holdings for research uses.

Following Kinsey's death in 1956, the institute continued the scientific study of sex, publishing the third and fourth volumes, *Pregnancy, Birth and Abortion* in 1958 and *Sex Offenders: An Analysis of Types* in 1965.

The two major Kinsey volumes have set a framework that has encouraged further research into man's sexual behavior—even yet a largely unexplored area. Kinsey's chief contributions to this field of study are (1) a quantified, thorough description of the sexual behavior of a large number of individuals of both sexes and of diverse social status; (2) the discovery of an unexpected range of individual and social class variation; (3) a correction of various misconceptions, chiefly those concerned with childhood sexuality, female responsiveness, and homosexuality; (4) a demonstration that human sexual behavior can be investigated objectively and openly, thus paving the way for subsequent research.

The work of Kinsey and his staff, while praised highly by many scientists, was severely criticized by others. Such was the interest that a committee of the American Statistical Association was appointed to appraise the data in the 1948 book, and although it pointed out certain methodological weaknesses, it acknowledged the general importance of the data (Cochran et al. 1954; Hyman & Sheatsley 1948). As a novice in the field of social science, Kinsey had clearly made some methodological errors, but in the years since the volumes were published scientist and layman alike have increasingly accepted them for what they were meant to be, an attempt to survey the approximate range and norms of sexual behavior. Up to the present time no research of comparable scope in this field has been instigated by other groups, and the eighteen thousand histories in the Institute for Sex Research at Indiana University form a backlog of basic data on sex which has still not been fully exploited. The institute that Kinsey founded is now supported in part by the National Institute of Mental Health. Under the directorship of Paul Gebhard, research in sexual behavior is continuing, and the basic data are being made available to other scholars in the field.

CORNELIA V. CHRISTENSON

[*Other relevant material may be found in* INTERVIEWING, *article on* SOCIAL RESEARCH; SEXUAL BEHAVIOR; *and in the biography of* ELLIS.]

### WORKS BY KINSEY

1941    Homosexuality: Criteria for a Hormonal Explanation of the Homosexual. *Journal of Clinical Endocrinology* 1:424–428.

1948    KINSEY, ALFRED C.; POMEROY, WARDELL B.; and MARTIN, CLYDE E. *Sexual Behavior in the Human Male.* Philadelphia: Saunders.

1953    KINSEY, ALFRED C.; POMEROY, WARDELL B.; MARTIN, CLYDE E.; and GEBHARD, PAUL H. *Sexual Behavior in the Human Female.* Philadelphia: Saunders.

### SUPPLEMENTARY BIBLIOGRAPHY

COCHRAN, WILLIAM G. et al. 1954 *Statistical Problems of the Kinsey Report on* Sexual Behavior in the Human Male. Washington: American Statistical Association.

DEUTSCH, ALBERT (editor) 1948 *Sex Habits of American Men: A Symposium on the Kinsey Report.* New York: Prentice-Hall.

ERNST, MORRIS L.; and LOTH, DAVID 1948 *American Sexual Behavior and the Kinsey Report.* New York: Greystone.

GEDDES, DONALD P. (editor) 1954 *An Analysis of the Kinsey Reports on Sexual Behavior in the Human Male and Female.* New York: Dutton.

HIMELHOCH, JEROME; and FAVA, SYLVIA F. (editors) 1955 *Sexual Behavior in American Society: An Appraisal of the First Two Kinsey Reports.* New York: Norton.

HYMAN, HERBERT H.; and SHEATSLEY, PAUL B. 1948 The Kinsey Report and Survey Methodology. *International Journal of Opinion and Attitude Research* 2: 183–195.

INDIANA UNIVERSITY, INSTITUTE FOR SEX RESEARCH 1958 *Pregnancy, Birth and Abortion,* by Paul H. Gebhard, W. B. Pomeroy, C. E. Martin, and C. V. Christenson. New York: Harper.

INDIANA UNIVERSITY, INSTITUTE FOR SEX RESEARCH 1965 *Sex Offenders: An Analysis of Types,* by Paul H. Gebhard, J. H. Gagnon, W. B. Pomeroy, and C. V. Christenson. New York: Harper.

# KINSHIP

## I
### INTRODUCTION

Kinship is one of the universals in human society and therefore plays an important role in both the regulation of behavior and the formation of social groups. Kinship systems depend on the social recognition and cultural implementation of relationships derived from descent and marriage and normally involve a set of kinship terms and an associated set of behavioral patterns and attitudes which, together, make up a systematic whole. All societies distinguish various categories of relationship by descent or consanguinity, and most societies distinguish relationships by marriage or affinity as well. Although dictionary definitions differentiate these relationships, it is convenient to extend the term "kinship" to cover both kinds. The resulting network of social relations may constitute almost the whole social structure in some of the simpler societies or be a relatively small part of a highly complex structure, as in modern industrial societies. In either case, however, the system of kinship and marriage plays an important role in maintaining group cohesion and solidarity and in orienting the individual members to the social maze. The use of the term "system" implies that there is a complex relation of interdependence between the component parts: the social categories and the associated rights and duties.

Kinship systems are found to vary in different societies with respect to a number of characteristics: (1) the extent to which genealogical and affinal relationships are recognized for social purposes; (2) the ways in which relatives so recognized are classified or grouped in social categories; (3) the particular customs by which the behavior of these relatives is regulated in daily life; (4) the various rights and obligations which are mediated through kinship; and (5) the linguistic forms which are used to denote the various categories of kin. Often the domain of kinship is clearly marked off, but there are frequently metaphorical and other extensions which result in related systems or subsystems. [*See* KINSHIP, *articles on* DESCENT GROUPS *and* PSEUDO-KINSHIP.]

The near universality of the nuclear or elementary family and its role in mating and reproduction have made it a focus for studies of kinship. Here are found the "primary" relationships of parent and child, husband and wife, and brothers and sisters, and it is possible to construct a network of genealogical relationships encompassing the whole society by extension from this nucleus. But the processes of mating and reproduction are regulated in all human societies by incest rules and social convention, and although the resulting domestic family group is often based on physiological parenthood, it is the social recognition of parenthood that provides a child with a legitimate position in society. Thus, it is often convenient to distinguish the *pater*, or social father, from the *genitor*, or physical father, and sometimes it may even be necessary to distinguish the culturally assumed *genitor* from the actual biological father. Moreover, in some African societies women may play the role of "social fathers," marrying and "begetting" children with the aid of a biological father.

The family of orientation into which a child is born is often part of a larger extended family which includes many additional relatives. When an individual marries, he and his spouse may establish a new family of procreation or may join a larger family structure. Normally he acquires a new set of relatives by marriage, but in those cases where marriage is specified in terms of a particular category of relatives, his affinal relations may also be his consanguineal ones. In a few instances, as among the eighteenth-century Nayar of southern India, the family of husband, wife, and children did not exist as a social unit, and kinship was correspondingly modified. These examples indicate that the kinship system may or may not coincide with the genealogical network; in every case, the degree of relationship is a matter for empirical investigation.

The kinship categories found in various societies often cut across the distinctions that seem logical in Euro–American societies. In the latter, lineal relatives are set off from the collateral uncles and aunts, and the relatives through the father and the mother are treated in parallel fashion. But in many societies throughout the world the terms for father, mother, brother, sister, and so on may be widely extended instead of being restricted to the immediate family group. In some cases the extension is by generation, the term for father being extended to his brothers and male cousins as far as genealogical relatives are remembered, and analogously for other relatives. In other cases the extensions may be vertical, in terms of unilineal descent groups, so that all the members of a particular lineage or clan may be classed as "fathers" and "father's sisters," or "mothers" and "mother's brothers," regardless of generation or even of genealogical connection. The resulting kinship systems often have a wide range, sometimes encompassing the entire social group, in contrast to the narrow range of many Western systems. The particular patterns of grouping kinsmen show considerable variety, and each must be understood in its own terms before it can be compared with systems based on other principles of grouping.

The patterns of behavior that prevail between relatives define their relationships and as such are an integral part of the kinship system. In almost all societies the family is responsible for the care and support of children during their period of dependency and for their education and training for adult life. These tasks involve both love and affection and authority and discipline. The potential conflicts and ambivalences are often resolved by the allocation of authority to one parent or the other or to some relative outside the immediate family. The relationships established in the family group are affected by generation and relative age and by similarities or differences of sex. Those members of the parental generation who are in a position of authority are entitled to obedience and respect; others may share an intimacy without subordination. Friendship and support are expected of brothers and sisters, although often there are restrictions on behavior between a brother and a sister after puberty. With relatives outside the family group there is frequently a greater variety of behavior patterns, some seemingly based on the model of relationships within the family but others representing obligatory joking or teasing, on the one hand, or extreme respect or avoidance, on the other.

During the long period of socialization within the family or domestic group, the child gradually learns the proper attitudes and behavior patterns toward his various relatives. These patterns are present in the society in terms of cultural ideals and as behavioral norms, and their observance is reinforced in a variety of ways. There is considerable evidence that in most societies children learn the essentials of kinship rather early. At marriage an individual normally acquires a whole new set of affinal relatives to whom he must make varying adjustments, depending on the patterns of residence and interaction. Marriage is frequently an alliance between two groups of kin and may be mediated by exchanges of property as well as of spouses. The individual's relation to his spouse's relatives is often an intensification of the attitudes of respect or familiarity he has toward his own parents and siblings. Thus he may avoid his mother-in-law for a period and may be required to joke roughly with his brothers-in-law and sisters-in-law. Some societies prescribe marriage with a particular category of kin, usually "cross-cousins" (children of a brother and a sister), so that one's new affines are also consanguineal relatives and the new behavioral adjustments are more easily handled. Such societies intensify the bonds between existing relatives at the expense of securing a new set of relatives by means of marriage. In these societies the opposition between "consanguinity" and "affinity" is often present, despite the formal absence of distinct affinal terms.

In most societies the rights and obligations of members are channeled, in part at least, through the kinship system. Thus, the right to membership in a descent group may depend on the proper marriage of the parents, in which the procreative rights in the wife have been formally transferred to the husband and his lineage. Similarly, rights to the utilization of land or other kinds of property may sometimes be secured only through membership in "corporate" descent groups which are both integral parts of the kinship system and units in the larger social structure. Succession to various offices or status positions usually depends on kinship, even though the offices are controlled by descent groups or associations. Even the rights to residence in one locality or another may be specified in kinship terms. Rights normally imply obligations or duties and are concerned with the larger society and its continuation, even though phrased in kinship terms. Many center on marriage and the resulting family and involve domestic service, labor, sexuality, procreation, and support, among other things. Where rights and duties are codified in legal or jural terms they are more easily seen, but they are an integral part of kinship behavior.

In all societies, kinship is marked by a set of relationship terms that define the universe of kin

and that may be extended metaphorically to non-kin and even to various aspects of the world of nature. Kinship terms have been the center of much interest on the part of both anthropologists and linguists, and considerable progress has been made in their classification and analysis. In most societies, kinship terms are utilized in daily life, both in reference and in direct address, and often their use is required by custom. The terminological system frequently represents a distinctive subset of the lexicon, and the linguist can provide greater understanding of it by componential analysis, formal analysis, and historical reconstruction of earlier forms. There is a basic logic to kinship terminology, in that particular terms do not imply a status position so much as a relationship: the use of a particular term implies its reciprocal. Thus, if you call a man "father," he responds with "son." On the other hand, parallel terms in different societies may or may not have the same significance or meaning. Social anthropologists have been more concerned with the set of behavioral patterns between relatives and have tended to consider the terms used as linguistic tags representing or symbolizing the particular expected behaviors and attitudes between pairs or groups of kin. But the two systems are not always in a one-to-one relationship, and it is more profitable scientifically to consider them in a relationship of dynamic interdependence and to examine the discrepancies as possible evidence for social and cultural change.

The kinship system, in turn, has various and complex relations with the other social institutions that together make up the total social system, or social structure. Because kinship enters into economic, political, legal, and ritual relationships in various societies, there is sometimes a tendency to ignore or underestimate its significance. The function of kinship terminology in interaction is a symbolic one. When it is used it defines for the participants the general mode of behavior to be followed in particular social situations. The universality and enduring character of kinship suggest its importance in binding men and women together in society and providing a foundation for the building of more specific social structures.

## Historical development

The scientific study of kinship systems is only a century old, but in that brief period it has engendered more controversy and a greater variety of theoretical formulations than have most aspects of human society. The early studies concentrated on the terminological systems, for the most part, and utilized them as evidence for historical relationships or as survivals of assumed earlier stages of society based on promiscuity and group marriage. The reactions against such "conjectural" history led to a denial of the sociological significance of kinship terms and to an attempted explanation in terms of psychological principles. This, in turn, resulted in a renewed attempt to understand kinship in terms of the behavioral system and with reference to the ongoing society. More recently, some progress has been made in studying changes in kinship systems over time. One recurring difficulty has been the limited number of societies for which there is adequate information on kinship systems, but this situation is improving rather rapidly. A further difficulty has been that the preliminary classifications have been based on limited criteria, and there has been a tendency to study kinship piecemeal and to search for simplified formulations in terms of causal relationships rather than to treat the complex whole.

The foundations for the study of kinship were laid by L. H. Morgan in his *Systems of Consanguinity and Affinity of the Human Family* (1871). [*See the biography of* MORGAN, LEWIS HENRY.] In this work, the result of more than a decade of concentration on kinship, Morgan assembled data on the terminological systems he was able to collect or secure for nearly every major area of the world. He grouped the terminologies into two great classes, the "descriptive" systems, which he ascribed to the Aryan, Semitic, and Uralic linguistic families, and the "classificatory" systems, which he thought were characteristic of the American Indians, the Polynesians, and many of the peoples of Asia. The "classificatory" systems merged lineal with collateral relatives in varying degrees, in contrast to the Euro–American systems, which isolated lineal relatives in the terminology. As W. H. R. Rivers noted later (1914, p. 4), no discovery in the whole range of science can more certainly be credited to one man than the discovery of the classificatory system of relationship to Morgan.

Morgan's early interest in kinship systems was a historical one. Discovering in 1858 that the Ojibwa Indians had a pattern of grouping relatives that was almost identical with that of the Iroquois, who spoke a quite different language, he came to the view that kinship patterns were highly stable and set out to collect kinship terminologies in order to demonstrate that the American Indians were of common descent and had originally come from Asia. When he found an almost identical system among the Tamils of India, he felt he had proved his historical hypothesis. But in the meantime, the discovery of the Hawaiian (Malayan) pattern of

terminology, which was classificatory to an even greater degree, led him to explain it as a result of assumed earlier forms of marriage for which there was no existing evidence. The resulting evolutionary development of social institutions and cultural stages presented in *Ancient Society* (1877) aroused extended controversies which long obscured Morgan's important contributions to the study of kinship.

In America, the criticisms by Kroeber in his "Classificatory Systems of Relationship" (1909) were the most influential and far-reaching [*see* KROEBER]. He found the distinction between "descriptive" and "classificatory" misleading and suggested that kinship terminology be analyzed, instead, in terms of some eight "psychological principles" based on the difference of generations, the distinction of lineal and collateral relationships, the difference of age within a generation, the sex of the relative, the sex of the speaker, the sex of the connective relative, the distinction of blood and affinal relationship, and the condition of life of the connecting relative. Kroeber came to the conclusion that terms of relationship reflect psychology rather than sociology and are determined primarily by language—hence they could be utilized for sociological inferences only with great caution.

In England J. F. McLennan had dismissed kinship terms as a mere set of mutual salutations, in the process of defending his own evolutionary formulations for society. But Rivers, who had become interested in kinship during the Torres Strait expedition of 1898–1900, where he had developed the "genealogical method" for collecting accurate data on various aspects of social organization, returned to Morgan's basic ideas as a result of his studies of Melanesian society. In *Kinship and Social Organisation* (1914) he proposed that kinship terminology is rigorously determined by social conditions and particularly by forms of marriage and hence can be utilized to reconstruct the recent history of social institutions. These hypotheses and the accompanying illustrations have become one starting point for the modern study of kinship systems. [*See* McLENNAN *and* RIVERS.]

Lowie has been the most influential American ethnologist concerned with the study of kinship. Accepting Rivers' position that kinship terminology is related to social usages, but influenced by Kroeber as well, he sought to test the hypotheses that had been proposed against the available ethnographic information. His own comparative studies of the Plateau Shoshoneans and the Hopi Indians led him to the conclusion that the kinship system of the latter is functionally connected with their clan system. [See LOWIE.] He summed up his general position in a statement that is still valid:

Relationship terms are studied by the anthropologist not merely as so many words inviting philological analysis and comparison, but as correlates of social custom. Broadly speaking, the use of a specific kinship designation, *e.g.,* for the maternal as distinguished from the paternal uncle, indicates that the former receives differential treatment at the hands of his nephews and nieces. Further, if a term of this sort embraces a number of individuals, the probability is that the speaker is linked to all of them by the same set of mutual duties and claims, though their intensity may vary with the closeness of the relationship. ([1929] 1959, vol. 19, p. 84)

In England Malinowski and Radcliffe-Brown have been most influential figures in the development of kinship studies. Malinowski, as a result of his study *The Family Among the Australian Aborigines* (1913) and his extended field research in the Trobriand Islands, emphasized the importance of the family as the "initial situation" for the development of kinship, from which attitudes and terminology could be widely extended. He also called attention to the significance of "sociological fatherhood" in a matrilineal society that did not recognize the genetic role; but he was more concerned with the function of kinship and other social institutions in fulfilling individual needs. [See MALINOWSKI.] Radcliffe-Brown, an early student of Rivers, is the central figure in the modern study of kinship systems. He was the first to develop the conception of the kinship system as composed of both terminology and patterns of social behavior and to see kinship as an integral part of the larger social structure. As a functionalist he was concerned with the significance of institutions in maintaining the social system, but he went further and attempted to discover basic structural principles that were relevant to a variety of different terminological groupings and social usages. [See RADCLIFFE-BROWN.]

By the end of the 1920s the preliminary classification of kinship terminologies was well underway. Morgan's twofold classification was remodeled by Rivers, and Gifford (1922) had utilized Kroeber's categories for the classification of Californian Indian terminologies. Spier's classification (1925) of North American Indian terminologies into eight empirical types, based on the patterns of grouping for cross-cousins, was particularly influential. Lowie (1929) proposed a world-wide classification into four major types, based on the treatment of relatives in the parental generation.

These were soon followed by Radcliffe-Brown's classification (1931) of Australian social systems into two main types, in each of which kinship, preferential marriage, and clan groupings were systematically interrelated.

During the following decade a number of field studies were carried out by students of Malinowski and Radcliffe-Brown in which kinship received more adequate treatment. Firth's studies of the Tikopia (1936), Warner's on the Murngin (1930), Evans-Pritchard's on the Nuer (1951), Fortes' on the Tallensi (1949), Tax's on the Fox (1937), Hallowell's on the Ojibwa (1937), Eggan's on the Plains and Pueblo Indian groups ([1937*b*] 1962, pp. 35–95; 1950), and Spoehr's studies of the southeastern Indian tribes (1941; 1942; 1944) are among those researches that have contributed to the development and modification of the structural–functional approach.

The clearest statement of this approach is found in Radcliffe-Brown's Introduction to *African Systems of Kinship and Marriage* (1950), in which he was concerned with the general comparative and theoretical study of kinship organization as an arrangement which enables persons to cooperate with one another in an orderly social life. In this discussion he compared and contrasted the cognatic system of the early Teutonic peoples with the agnatic lineage systems of ancient Rome and many modern African tribes and indicated the relevance of the principles of "the unity of the sibling group" and "the unity and solidarity of the lineage" for various aspects of social life. Here he was particularly concerned with the significance of unilineal descent in bringing about corporate kin groups that continue beyond the life of individual members and may control resources, exact vengeance, regulate marriage, and engage in ritual. He saw marriage as essentially a rearrangement of social structure and discussed in detail the significance of marriage in various African societies. For a worldwide classification of kinship systems he proposed four types: father-right, mother-right, cognatic systems, and double lineage systems, each of which has a number of varieties.

## Current development of kinship studies

In the modern period there have been a number of new directions in the study of kinship which involve both method and theory. Some of these include cross-cultural comparisons involving statistical and correlational techniques; others involve linguistic analyses building on Kroeber's earlier categories or utilizing formal analyses; still others utilize models of various types, some derived from linguistics and others from mathematics. These studies have stimulated a great amount of new research and promise to broaden our knowledge of kinship phenomena in various directions.

Of particular significance is Murdock's cross-cultural study of family and kinship organization in about 250 societies throughout the world, presented in *Social Structure* (1949). Utilizing the postulational method and statistical analysis he found that kinship terminologies are primarily determined by such sociological factors as descent and residence, with marriage rules of lesser importance. He then established six types of kinship terminology, based in part on Spier's earlier classification, and combined these with rules of descent and residence to give 11 major types of social organization. A proposed order of social change, beginning with changes in the residence pattern, was then tested against the evidence from linguistic reconstructions and other data and was found highly reliable. "It seems clear," Murdock wrote, "that the elements of social organization, in their permutations and combinations, conform to natural laws of their own with an exactitude scarcely less striking than that which characterizes the permutations and combinations of atoms in chemistry or genes in biology" (1949, p. 183).

Murdock's study represents a notable advance in the application of social science methodologies to the study of social organization, but there has also been considerable criticism of the sampling involved, the statistical techniques used, and the data selected for analysis. He responded with the more adequate "World Ethnographic Sample" (1957) and with a revised classification (1959, pp. 135–140) of five major types of social organization, based primarily on descent and residence patterns. He also modified his assumptions about the primary role of residence in bringing about social change.

The contributions of Lévi-Strauss to the study of kinship systems are of a different character, and in *Les structures élémentaires de la parenté* (1949) and *Structural Anthropology* (1958) he presents some highly original views on the nature of social structure in general and kinship in particular. "Social structure," for Lévi-Strauss, is in itself concerned not with the empirical reality of social relations but with models which give rise to them, and he discusses the relevance of mechanical models (those on the same scale as the phenomena) and statistical models (where the elements of the model are on a different scale) for various problems, particularly those of communication. With regard to kinship he views the terminology and the system of attitudes as representing quite different orders

of reality: "The modalities of behavior between relatives express to some extent the terminological classification, and they provide at the same time a means of overcoming difficulties and contradictions resulting from this classification" ([1958] 1963, p. 310), a dialectic which is responsible for change in both systems. Lévi-Strauss also proposes a somewhat different unit for kinship studies from the elementary family, which is favored by Malinowski, Radcliffe-Brown, Murdock, and others. He believes "the relationship between 'brothers-in-law' is the axis around which kinship structure is built" ([1958] 1963, p. 46) and thus adds the wife's brother to the family unit. All kinship structures are constructed on this "kinship atom," primarily by the organization of a series of oppositions between attitudes of familiarity and reserve. The resulting kinship system "does not consist in the objective ties of descent or consanguinity between individuals. It exists only in human consciousness; it is an arbitrary system of representations, not the spontaneous development of a real situation" (*ibid.*, p. 50).

The principle of reciprocity, as manifested in various forms of exchange in social life, is central to Lévi-Strauss's view of social institutions. Kinship in human society is established and perpetuated through specific forms of marriage, and marriage as a form of exchange involves the circulation of women. He is, therefore, particularly concerned with what he calls "elementary structures," or those characterized by preferential marriage with a particular category of kin, usually a "cross-cousin." In this respect, Lévi-Strauss has attempted the analysis of matrilateral cross-cousin marriage systems, which are found in Australia and in southeastern and eastern Asia as well as in a few other regions, and he sees the resulting dual structure of "wife-giving" and "wife-receiving" groups reflected in many other aspects of society and culture.

This complex and original contribution (summarized in English in de Josselin de Jong 1952) has stimulated a number of important studies and engendered considerable controversy. Homans and Schneider, in *Marriage, Authority, and Final Causes* (1955), essay an alternate explanation based on Radcliffe-Brown's theory of sentiments. Needham attacked this strongly in *Structure and Sentiment* (1962) and went on to make a number of reformulations of what he calls "prescriptive" marriage systems. Leach, in *Rethinking Anthropology* (1961), shows the considerable influence of Lévi-Strauss, as does Dumont, whose *Hierarchy and Marriage Alliance in South Indian Kinship* (1957) emphasizes the importance of treating certain categories of relatives as affinal rather than consanguineal.

[*See* MARRIAGE, *articles on* COMPARATIVE ANALYSIS *and* MARRIAGE ALLIANCE.]

In recent years a number of anthropologists and linguists have returned to Kroeber's analysis (1909) of kinship terminologies and have developed a more sophisticated approach, called "componential analysis." The general framework for componential analysis derives from linguistic theory, and the kinship vocabulary is regarded as constituting a paradigm which can be analyzed in the same manner as other paradigmatic sets in a language. Currently Lounsbury and others are attempting to construct theories using a limited number of ordered roles similar to those of "generative grammar." The resulting "formal account" specifies (1) a set of primitive elements and (2) a set of rules for operating on these to generate a model which represents the empirical data (see Lounsbury 1964).

Goodenough (1956) treats Kroeber's categories as essentially social components, but Lounsbury's (1956) and Buchler's (1964) analyses are based upon strict genealogical reckoning and operate in terms of the primary relations in the nuclear family and their extensions to more distant relatives. Lounsbury assumes that "the primary function of kinship terminologies is to delineate the relation of ego to the members of his personal kindred in such a way as to express some socially and legally important aspect of each of these relationships" (1964, p. 382). Friedrich, in "Semantic Structure and Social Structure: An Instance from Russian," is concerned with seeing their interrelationships: "The semantic network symbolizes and is generated by the social network. Covariation between both networks is significant because it can lead to yet more general inferences about native concepts" (1964, p. 132). And H. C. Conklin, in "Ethnogenealogical Method," illustrates the steps which may be taken from ethnographic description to final analysis:

The sequence I have followed has led us from specific–to–general–to–abstract–to–correlational substatements of Hanunóo ethnography. We have moved from individuals occupying established genealogical positions in a well-recognized kin net, to the examination of types of kin classes, to the analysis and articulation of the defining features, or significata, which underlie the whole category system; and finally to a brief consideration of one set of significant nonterminological correlates of the more highly structured parts of this system.   (1964, p. 50)

In this procedure he finds that the natives own "model" of their system is an important part of the data.

The utilization of mathematical models for the elucidation of kinship structures has had a long history, beginning with Galton (1889) and continuing with Weil's appendix (1949) to Lévi-Strauss's monograph and, most recently, H. C. White's application of matrix algebra (1963). White is particularly concerned with prescriptive marriage systems, such as the Kariera, Arunta, Murngin, and Purum, but it remains to be demonstrated whether the logical manipulation of kinship categories and marriage rules adds greatly to our understanding of kinship systems. [*See* COMPONENTIAL ANALYSIS.]

## Comparative studies

The comparative study of kinship systems as wholes, and in relationship to ecological and historical factors as well as to other aspects of social structure, has had a more limited development. The initial model for such studies was Radcliffe-Brown's *Social Organization of Australian Tribes* (1931), which has been carried further by *African Systems of Kinship and Marriage* (Radcliffe-Brown & Forde 1950). For North America, Eggan (1955; 1966) has been concerned with the classification and interpretation of kinship systems in a number of regions, utilizing the method of controlled comparison and attempting to study changes over time, and P. Kirchhoff has provided a preliminary survey of the kinship systems in South America (1931; 1932).

On the basis of a detailed analysis of the Cheyenne and Arapaho kinship systems, Eggan ([1937*b*] 1962) proposed a preliminary classification of the kinship systems of the Plains region of North America into two major types: (1) a "generational" type and (2) a "lineage" type. The tribes of the High Plains, who were organized in terms of bilateral bands composing a camp circle and lived as seminomadic hunters, were—with one exception —also organized in terms of a wide-ranging "classificatory" kinship system, in which generation and sex were emphasized. The tribes of the Prairie Plains to the east, on the other hand, were organized in terms of unilineal descent and lived in permanent villages, from which they went on periodic buffalo hunts; but they depended on horticulture for their basic subsistence. Their kinship systems were also "classificatory," in that lineal and collateral relatives were merged in the terminology, but they utilized the lineage principle to provide a wide extension to the system. There were two subtypes: (*a*) the "Omaha" system, associated with patrilineal descent, and (*b*) the "Crow" system, associated with matrilineal descent.

A comparison of these two major types indicated that each represented an adjustment to the ecological and social conditions of their respective regions and that the "generational" systems of the High Plains were based on the relationship of brothers, which was functionally of great importance in Plains life; whereas the Prairie Plains tribes utilized the lineage principle to provide greater stability and continuity over time. By examining the historical backgrounds of the High Plains tribes it became evident that tribes coming into the Plains with different social systems ended up with similar systems. The Crow Indians are a test case. They split off from the Hidatsa several hundred years ago and gave up their village-dwelling, agricultural life in North Dakota for the seminomadic life of the High Plains. Their social system and kinship organization are intermediate, partaking of both types. It seems probable that the conditions of life in the High Plains favored a more amorphous and mobile type of social organization, which could vary to meet changing ecological and social conditions. As Prairie Plains peoples moved out onto the High Plains to take advantage of the greater efficiency of the horse in hunting buffalo, they modified their kinship systems in the direction of a "generational" type.

North and east of the Great Lakes, the Algonkian-speaking peoples have been shown by Hallowell (1937) to have had kinship systems based on cross-cousin marriage, and he has proposed that the contemporary variants are intelligible as a result of modifications resulting from acculturative processes and local conditions. Eggan (1955) has extended this hypothesis to northern Algonkian groups moving into the Plains region and to the Dakota groups. The central Algonkian tribes have been shown by Callender (1962) to have shifted from an earlier kinship system based on cross-cousin marriage to a lineage-based system of the Omaha type, as these tribes moved southward into the Prairie Plains and expanded in population with the adoption of horticulture.

The Omaha and Crow subtypes of kinship systems are not limited to North America but are seen there in their most typical form. The Omaha systems are generally associated with patrilineal lineages or clans, and often with a dual division of the society, while the Crow systems are associated with matrilineal lineages or clans. In either case the essential feature is that the lineage or clan is treated as a unit for kinship purposes, an individual considering all his kinsmen through the mother or father as of the same kind. This utilization of descent groups for kinship extensions results in both a wide range and a continuity to the social system.

In the southeastern region of North America, where all the major tribes were organized in terms of a Crow-type kinship system, preliminary studies of the Choctaw terminology collected for Morgan suggested to Eggan (1937a) that changes due to acculturation has been underway in all of the southeastern tribes up to 1860 and that the degree of change in kinship terminology was related to the degree and type of acculturative pressures. A field study of the modern descendants by Spoehr (1941; 1942; 1944; 1947) not only confirmed these hypotheses but provided demonstrations of the processes by which the Crow type systems shifted to a generational pattern over the period of a century of acculturation.

In the southwestern region the Western Pueblos have all been found to have a simple specialized type of social structure based on matrilineal lineages and clans and a Crow type of kinship system. The Eastern Pueblos, however, though participating fully in the general Pueblo culture patterns, have a quite different social structure, based on a dual organization and a bilateral "nonclassificatory" kinship system which emphasizes generation and relative age (Eggan 1950). A number of hypotheses have been advanced to account for this major difference in a single culture type. Here, Dozier's (1954) study of the Hopi–Tewa, a group of Eastern Tewa who migrated to the Hopi region around A.D. 1700 and who have rearranged their kinship system to conform to the Hopi model, analyzes an important instance of acculturation between Indian groups. The southern Athabaskan groups, made up of the Navajo and the various Apache tribes, show a further series of changes in kinship, not only from their northern relatives in Canada but from one another as well.

These brief summaries can only suggest the kinds of comparative regional studies of kinship systems which have been developed on the basis of structural–functional assumptions, with the added controls of ethnohistory, linguistic reconstruction, and ecological factors. Along with them have been such studies as Bruner's (1955–1956) on the actual processes of change in Mandan–Hidatsa kinship terminology under contemporary reservation conditions, where certain of the factors affecting choice of Indian or Euro–American kinship models have been clarified.

A different type of comparative study is exemplified by Schneider and Gough's *Matrilineal Kinship* (1961), which grew out of a cooperative Social Science Research Council summer seminar organized by Schneider, with the additional participation of Colson, Aberle, Fathauer, Basehart, and Sahlins. The distinctive features of matrilineal descent groups are first stated in theoretical terms and in contrast to their patrilineal counterparts. They are then examined against nine matrilineal systems which are presented in detail, and more broadly, against a larger number of cases available from Murdock's "World Ethnographic Sample" (1957). Here, with descent held as a constant, the variations in group structure, residence, kinship, and marriage are examined in terms of structural theory, cultural ecology, and evolutionary development. Of particular significance for kinship theory is the discussion of the strength of the brother–sister relationship in matrilineal societies as against the husband–wife bond, and its manifold effects on the kinship structure, especially with regard to the tensions between a man and the matrilineal descent group over control of his wife and children, which had earlier been analyzed by Richards (1950). The considerable variety of types of kinship structures associated with matrilineal descent (and the corresponding variety associated with patrilineal and cognatic descent) indicate problems for future research.

### Future developments

Kinship theory is set in the broader framework of social and cultural anthropology, as is indicated in the article on culture, where Singer discusses the structural versus the cultural analysis of kinship systems in terms of the controversies between Kroeber and Radcliffe-Brown. [*See* CULTURE.] In the perspective of modern kinship studies the position of Radcliffe-Brown has been the more productive, and Kroeber has partly modified his original position: "As part of language, kin term systems reflect unconscious logic and conceptual patterning *as well as* social institutions" ([1901–1951] 1952, p. 172). The current interest of linguists in the componential analysis of kin term systems has clarified certain aspects of terminology but at the expense of rejecting the advances made by treating kinship as a social system. One promising move in this direction would be to include social components, such as locality and lineage grouping, along with those of generation, relative age, sex, and so on (see Leach 1961; Friedrich 1964). Lévi-Strauss has been impressed with the relevance of structural linguistics to the study of kinship:

Like phonemes, kinship terms are elements of meaning: like phonemes they acquire meaning only if they are integrated systems. "Kinship systems," like "phonemic systems," are built by the mind on the level of unconscious thought. Finally, the recurrence of kinship patterns, marriage rules, similar prescribed attitudes between certain types of relatives, and so forth, in scattered regions of the globe and fundamentally different societies, leads us to believe that, in the case of kinship as well as linguistics, the observable phenomena result from the action of laws which are general but implicit. ([1958] 1963, p. 34)

But granted that the principles of duality and of reciprocity may be basic, their relevance to many social systems has not yet been demonstrated. For Radcliffe-Brown the recurrence of particular features in the diversity of kinship systems throughout the world was evidence of a limited number of general structural principles, such as the equivalence of siblings and lineage solidarity, which were combined in varying ways.

But if Kroeber's reformulation is to be more than a compromise, it will be important to relate systematically the linguistic, cognitive, and sociological aspects of kinship in order to develop a more comprehensive theory. Thus, the formal rules by which Lounsbury generates Crow- and Omaha-type terminological systems are related to Radcliffe-Brown's sociological principles, as Lounsbury notes (1964, p. 357). And the principle of duality may find more general expression in the relations of ego to alter and in the attitudes of respect and familiarity than in the more specific matrimonial arrangements and dual organizations of society.

The emphasis on descent systems with reference to kinship has been balanced in recent years by a greater concern with bilateral or cognatic systems, but the precise relationships between these two types are not yet clear. Both lineage-based and bilateral kinship systems are faced with similar problems but solve them in somewhat different ways. The historical changes noted above suggest that greater efficiency in adaptation to particular ecological situations may be an important factor. Whether there are broad evolutionary changes is not yet clear. The early formulations of Morgan have been discredited but no large-scale evolutionary sequence with regard to kinship systems has been developed to take their place. L. A. White (1939, pp. 569–570) has proposed a more limited development to account for the Iroquois–Dakota kinship terminology in relation to the Omaha and Crow types: "When the clan system is young and weak the kinship system will be of the Dakota–Iroquois type, regardless of the sex in which descent is reckoned. As the clan system develops, however, and comes to exert its influence more and more upon the social life of the tribe, the Dakota–Iroquois terminology will be transformed into the Crow type in a matrilineal society and into the Omaha type in a patrilineal society." Murdock's study (1949) lends considerable statistical support to this view. It is clear, however, that the Dakota type of kinship system can develop in association with cross-cousin marriage without the presence of any clan organization (Eggan 1955). Where we find the classic Omaha and Crow kinship systems they are generally associated with well-developed "corporate" patrilineal and matrilineal groups, respectively, but not all societies with well-developed corporate lineage groups have Omaha or Crow kinship systems. For North America there is some evidence for a cyclical oscillation between kinship systems based on a generational principle of organization and those based on a lineage principle. These are the two major axes for the classification of kin, and Murdock has provided a theoretical formulation of change in social structures to be tested against the empirical evidence. Here, studies of the type made by Krader (1963) with regard to the Turkic and Mongol kinship systems and by Friedrich (1963) with regard to the historical development of the Russian kinship system will be particularly important.

Studies of Euro–American kinship systems have so far been concerned primarily with terminological patterns and their historical development. However, Schneider and Firth are engaged in a large-scale comparative study of kinship in Chicago and London, respectively, which should both yield new and important results and bring our knowledge of kinship systems in contemporary industrial society up to the level of those of nonliterate groups.

Our knowledge of affinal kinship—the relationships established through the marriage tie—has been seriously neglected in most studies of kinship systems. Some societies, such as the Ifugao in the northern Philippines, reduce the significance of the affinal tie almost to the vanishing point, in contrast to consanguineal relationships; others build much of their social structure on the relationships between spouses. The contributions of Lévi-Strauss, Dumont, and Needham to our understanding of affinity in cases of preferential or prescriptive cross-cousin marriage, where affinal terminology is disguised in the consanguineal system, have been mentioned. But there is as yet no comprehensive classification of affinal kinship terminology, nor any general theory of the nature of affinity, although Aginsky (1935) long ago called attention to the importance of the problem. Friedrich (see Goodenough 1964, pp. 131–166) has provided a beginning with his detailed analysis of the Russian affinal system.

We can look forward to a continued flow of empirical data on kinship and to a continuing dialogue between studies utilizing analytic variables and statistical methods, on the one hand, and intensive studies of a more limited range but concerned with kinship systems as wholes and in their ecological and historical contexts, on the other. Out of this dialectic should come more adequate concepts and classifications, as well as a greater understanding of the phenomena of kinship and the processes relevant to its development. At a more general level, such studies also furnish a body of data to clarify the relations between culture, as a set of ideas and symbols, and social structure, as a system of social interaction. Kinship organizes social relations in terms of cultural patterns.

FRED EGGAN

BIBLIOGRAPHY

AGINSKY, B. 1935 The Mechanics of Kinship. *American Anthropologist* New Series 37:450–457.

BEATTIE, J. H. M. 1964 Kinship and Social Anthropology. *Man* 64:101–104.

BRITISH ASSOCIATION FOR THE ADVANCEMENT OF SCIENCE (1874) 1954 *Notes and Queries on Anthropology.* 6th ed., rev. London: Routledge.

BRUNER, EDWARD M. 1955–1956 Two Processes of Change in Mandan–Hidatsa Kinship Terminology. *American Anthropologist* New Series 57:840–850; 58:554–556.

BRUNER, EDWARD M. 1956 Primary Group Experience and the Processes of Acculturation. *American Anthropologist* New Series 58:605–623.

BUCHLER, I. R. 1964 Measuring the Development of Kinship Terminologies: Scalogram and Transformational Accounts of Crow-type Systems. *American Anthropologist* New Series 66:765–788.

CALLENDER, CHARLES 1962 *Social Organization of the Central Algonkian Indians.* Milwaukee Public Museum Publications in Anthropology, No. 7. Milwaukee, Wis.: The Museum.

CONKLIN, HAROLD C. 1964 Ethnogenealogical Method. Pages 25–55 in Ward H. Goodenough (editor), *Explorations in Cultural Anthropology: Essays in Honor of George Peter Murdock.* New York: McGraw-Hill.

DOZIER, EDWARD P. 1954 *The Hopi–Tewa of Arizona.* Berkeley: Univ. of California Press.

DUMONT, LOUIS 1957 *Hierarchy and Marriage Alliance in South Indian Kinship.* London: Royal Anthropological Institute of Great Britain and Ireland.

EGGAN, FRED 1937a Historical Changes in the Choctaw Kinship System. *American Anthropologist* New Series 39:34–52.

EGGAN, FRED (1937b) 1962 The Cheyenne and Arapaho Kinship System. Pages 35–95 in *Social Anthropology of North American Tribes.* 2d ed., enl. Univ. of Chicago Press.

EGGAN, FRED 1950 *Social Organization of the Western Pueblos.* Univ. of Chicago Press.

EGGAN, FRED (1955) 1962 Social Anthropology: Methods and Results. Pages 485–551 in *Social Anthropology of North American Tribes.* 2d ed., enl. Univ. of Chicago Press.

EGGAN, FRED 1960 Lewis H. Morgan in Kinship Perspective. Pages 179–201 in Gertrude E. Dole and Robert L. Carneiro (editors), *Essays in the Science of Culture, in Honor of Leslie A. White* .... New York: Crowell.

EGGAN, FRED 1966 *The American Indian: Perspectives for the Study of Social Change.* Chicago: Aldine.

EVANS-PRITCHARD, E. E. 1951 *Kinship and Marriage Among the Nuer.* Oxford Univ. Press.

FIRTH, RAYMOND W. 1930 Marriage and the Classificatory System of Relationship. *Journal of the Royal Anthropological Institute of Great Britain and Ireland* 60:235–268.

FIRTH, RAYMOND W. (1936) 1957 *We, the Tikopia: A Sociological Study of Kinship in Primitive Polynesia.* 2d ed. London: Allen & Unwin. → A paperback edition was published in 1963 by Beacon.

FORTES, MEYER 1949 *The Web of Kinship Among the Tallensi: The Second Part of an Analysis of the Social Structure of a Trans-Volta Tribe.* Oxford Univ. Press.

FREEMAN, J. D. 1961 On the Concept of the Kindred. *Journal of the Royal Anthropological Institute of Great Britain and Ireland* 91:192–220.

FRIEDRICH, PAUL 1963 An Evolutionary Sketch of Russian Kinship. American Ethnological Society, *Proceedings* [1962]:1–26.

FRIEDRICH, PAUL 1964 Semantic Structure and Social Structure: An Instance From Russian. Pages 131–166 in Ward H. Goodenough (editor), *Explorations in Cultural Anthropology: Essays in Honor of George Peter Murdock.* New York: McGraw-Hill.

GALTON, F. 1889 Note on Australian Marriage Systems. *Journal of the Royal Anthropological Institute of Great Britain and Ireland* 19:70–72.

GIFFORD, EDWARD W. 1922 *California Kinship Terminologies.* University of California Publications in American Archaeology and Ethnology, Vol. 18. Berkeley: Univ. of California Press.

GOODENOUGH, WARD H. 1956 Componential Analysis and the Study of Meaning. *Language* 32:195–216.

GOODENOUGH, WARD H. (editor) 1964 *Explorations in Cultural Anthropology: Essays in Honor of George Peter Murdock.* New York: McGraw-Hill.

GREENBERG, JOSEPH H. 1949 The Logical Analysis of Kinship. *Philosophy of Science* 16:58–64.

HALLOWELL, A. IRVING 1937 Cross-cousin Marriage in the Lake Winnipeg Area. Pages 95–110 in Philadelphia Anthropological Society, *Twenty-fifth Anniversary Studies.* Edited by Daniel S. Davidson. Publications of the Philadelphia Anthropological Society, Vol. 1. Philadelphia: Univ. of Pennsylvania Press.

HASSRICK, ROYAL B. 1944 The Teton Dakota Kinship System. *American Anthropologist* New Series 46:338–347.

HOCKETT, CHARLES F. 1964 The Proto Central Algonquian Kinship System. Pages 239–258 in Ward H. Goodenough, *Explorations in Cultural Anthropology: Essays in Honor of George Peter Murdock.* New York: McGraw-Hill.

HOMANS, GEORGE C.; and SCHNEIDER, DAVID M. 1955 *Marriage, Authority, and Final Causes: A Study of Unilateral Cross-cousin Marriage.* Glencoe, Ill.: Free Press.

JOSSELIN DE JONG, JAN P. B. DE 1952 *Lévi-Strauss's Theory on Kinship and Marriage.* Mededelingen van het Rijksmuseum voor Volkenkunde, No. 10. Leiden (Netherlands): Brill.

KIRCHHOFF, PAUL 1931 Die Verwandtschaftsorganisation der Urwaldstämme Südamerikas. *Zeitschrift für Ethnologie* 63:85–193.

KIRCHHOFF, PAUL 1932 Verwandtschaftsbezeichnungen und Verwandtenheirat. *Zeitschrift für Ethnologie* 64:41–71.

KRADER, LAWRENCE 1963 *Social Organization of the Mongol–Turkic Pastoral Nomads.* Indiana University Publications, Uralic and Altaic Series, Vol. 20. The Hague: Mouton.

KROEBER, ALFRED L. (1901–1951) 1952 *The Nature of Culture.* Univ. of Chicago Press.

KROEBER, ALFRED L. 1909 Classificatory Systems of Relationship. *Journal of the Royal Anthropological Institute of Great Britain and Ireland* 39:77–84.

KROEBER, ALFRED L. 1917 *Zuñi Kin and Clan.* American Museum of Natural History, Anthropological Papers, Vol. 18, part 2. New York: The Museum.

LEACH, EDMUND R. 1961 *Rethinking Anthropology.* London School of Economics and Political Science, Monographs on Social Anthropology, No. 22. London: Athlone.

LÉVI-STRAUSS, CLAUDE 1949 *Les structures élémentaires de la parenté.* Paris: Presses Universitaires de France.

LÉVI-STRAUSS, CLAUDE (1958) 1963 *Structural Anthropology.* New York: Basic Books. → First published in French.

LOUNSBURY, FLOYD G. 1956 A Semantic Analysis of the Pawnee Kinship Usage. *Language* 32:158–194.

LOUNSBURY, FLOYD G. 1964 A Formal Account of the Crow- and Omaha-type Kinship Terminologies. Pages 351–393 in Ward H. Goodenough (editor), *Explorations in Cultural Anthropology: Essays in Honor of George Peter Murdock.* New York: McGraw-Hill.

LOWIE, ROBERT H. (1916) 1960 Historical and Sociological Interpretation of Kinship Terminologies. Pages 65–74 in Robert H. Lowie, *Selected Papers in Anthropology.* Berkeley: Univ. of California Press.

LOWIE, ROBERT H. 1917 *Culture and Ethnology.* New York: Boni & Liveright.

LOWIE, ROBERT H. (1929) 1959 Relationship Terms. Volume 19, pages 84–90 in *Encyclopaedia Britannica.* 14th ed. Chicago: Benton.

LOWIE, ROBERT H. (1934) 1960 The Omaha and Crow Kinship Terminologies. Pages 100–110 in Robert H. Lowie, *Selected Papers in Anthropology.* Berkeley: Univ. of California Press.

LOWIE, ROBERT H.; and EGGAN, FRED 1963 Kinship Terminology. Volume 13, pages 407–409 in *Encyclopaedia Britannica.* Chicago: Benton.

MALINOWSKI, BRONISLAW (1913) 1963 *The Family Among the Australian Aborigines: A Sociological Study.* New York: Schocken.

MALINOWSKI, BRONISLAW (1913–1941) 1963 *Sex, Culture and Myth.* London: Hart-Davis.

MALINOWSKI, BRONISLAW 1930 Parenthood: The Basis of Social Structure. Pages 113–168 in Victor F. Calverton and Samuel D. Schmalhausen (editors), *The New Generation: The Intimate Problems of Modern Parents and Children.* New York: Macaulay.

MATTHEWS, G. H. 1959 Proto-Siouan Kinship Terminology. *American Anthropologist* New Series 61:252–278.

MORGAN, LEWIS H. 1871 *Systems of Consanguinity and Affinity of the Human Family.* Smithsonian Contributions to Knowledge, Vol. 17, Publication No. 218. Washington: Smithsonian Institution.

MORGAN, LEWIS H. (1877) 1964 *Ancient Society.* Cambridge, Mass.: Harvard Univ. Press.

MURDOCK, GEORGE P. 1949 *Social Structure.* New York: Macmillan. → A paperback edition was published in 1965 by the Free Press.

MURDOCK, GEORGE P. 1957 World Ethnographic Sample. *American Anthropologist* New Series 59:664–687.

MURDOCK, GEORGE P. 1959 Evolution in Social Organization. Pages 126–143 in Anthropological Society of

Washington, *Evolution and Anthropology: A Centennial Appraisal.* Washington: The Society.

MURDOCK, GEORGE P. (editor) 1960 *Social Structure in Southeast Asia.* Viking Fund Publications in Anthropology, No. 29. Chicago: Quadrangle Books.

NEEDHAM, RODNEY 1962 *Structure and Sentiment: A Test Case in Social Anthropology.* Univ. of Chicago Press.

PARSONS, TALCOTT 1943 The Kinship System of the Contemporary United States. *American Anthropologist* New Series 45:22–38.

PEHRSON, ROBERT N. 1954 Bilateral Kin Groupings as a Structural Type: A Preliminary Statement. *Journal of East Asiatic Studies* 3:199–202.

RADCLIFFE-BROWN, A. R. (1931) 1948 *The Social Organization of Australian Tribes.* Glencoe, Ill.: Free Press.

RADCLIFFE-BROWN, A. R. 1950 Introduction. Pages 1–85 in A. R. Radcliffe-Brown and Daryll Forde (editors), *African Systems of Kinship and Marriage.* Oxford Univ. Press.

RADCLIFFE-BROWN, A. R. 1952 *Structure and Function in Primitive Society: Essays and Addresses.* London: Cohen & West; Glencoe, Ill.: Free Press.

RADCLIFFE-BROWN, A. R.; and FORDE, DARYLL (editors) 1950 *African Systems of Kinship and Marriage.* Oxford Univ. Press.

RICHARDS, AUDREY I. 1950 Some Types of Family Structure Amongst the Central Bantu. Pages 207–251 in A. R. Radcliffe-Brown and Daryll Forde (editors), *African Systems of Kinship and Marriage.* Oxford Univ. Press.

RIVERS, WILLIAM H. R. 1914 *Kinship and Social Organisation.* London School of Economics and Political Science, Studies, No. 36. London: Constable.

SCHAPERA, ISAAC (editor) 1963 *Studies in Kinship and Marriage, Dedicated to Brenda Z. Seligman* . . . . Royal Anthropological Institute of Great Britain and Ireland, Occasional Papers, No. 16. London: The Institute.

SCHMITT, KARL; and SCHMITT, IVA 1952 *Wichita Kinship: Past and Present.* Norman: Univ. of Oklahoma Book Exchange.

SCHNEIDER, DAVID M. 1964 The Nature of Kinship. *Man* 64:180–181.

SCHNEIDER, DAVID M.; and GOUGH, KATHLEEN (editors) 1961 *Matrilineal Kinship.* Berkeley: Univ. of California Press.

SERVICE, ELMAN R. 1962 *Primitive Social Organization: An Evolutionary Perspective.* New York: Random House.

*Social Anthropology of North American Tribes.* Edited by Fred Eggan. 2d ed., enl. (1937) 1962 Univ. of Chicago Press.

SPIER, LESLIE 1925 *The Distribution of Kinship Systems in North America.* University of Washington Publications in Anthropology, Vol. 1, No. 2. Seattle: Univ. of Washington Press.

SPOEHR, ALEXANDER 1941 *Camp, Clan and Kin Among the Cow Creek Seminole of Florida.* Anthropological Series, Vol. 33, No. 1. Chicago: Field Museum of Natural History.

SPOEHR, ALEXANDER 1942 *Kinship Systems of the Seminole.* Anthropological Series, Vol. 33, No. 2. Chicago: Field Museum of Natural History.

SPOEHR, ALEXANDER 1944 *The Florida Seminole Camp.* Anthropological Series, Vol. 33, No. 3. Chicago: Field Museum of Natural History.

SPOEHR, ALEXANDER 1947 *Changing Kinship Systems: A Study in the Acculturation of the Creeks, Cherokee and Choctaw.* Anthropological Series, Vol. 33, No. 4. Chicago: Field Museum of Natural History.

SPOEHR, ALEXANDER 1950 Observations on the Study of Kinship. *American Anthropologist* New Series 52: 1–15.

TAX, SOL (1937) 1962 The Social Organization of the Fox Indians. Pages 243–282 in *Social Anthropology of North American Tribes.* 2d ed., enl. Univ. of Chicago Press.

TAX, SOL (1955) 1962 From Lafitau to Radcliffe-Brown: A Short History of the Study of Social Organization. Pages 445–481 in *Social Anthropology of North American Tribes.* 2d ed., enl. Univ. of Chicago Press.

TITIEV, MISCHA 1943 The Influence of Common Residence on the Unilateral Classification of Kindred. *American Anthropologist* New Series 45:511–530.

WALLACE, ANTHONY F. C.; and ATKINS, JOHN 1960 The Meaning of Kinship Terms. *American Anthropologist* New Series 62:58–80.

WARNER, W. LLOYD 1930 Morphology and Functions of the Australian Murngin Type of Kinship. *American Anthropologist* New Series 32:207–256.

WEIL, ANDRÉ (1949) 1963 On the Algebraic Study of Certain Types of Marriage Laws (Murngin's System). Pages 151–157 in Harrison C. White, *An Anatomy of Kinship: Mathematical Models for Structures of Cumulated Roles.* Englewood Cliffs, N.J.: Prentice-Hall. → First published in French.

WHITE, HARRISON C. 1963 *An Anatomy of Kinship: Mathematical Models for Structures of Cumulated Roles.* Englewood Cliffs, N.J.: Prentice-Hall.

WHITE, LESLIE A. 1939 A Problem in Kinship Terminology. *American Anthropologist* New Series 41:566–573.

## II

### DESCENT GROUPS

The analysis of descent groups is a special aspect of the study of kinship. In the majority of preindustrial societies, kinsfolk are more than a narrow category of persons linked to an individual actor by filiation and siblinghood. They constitute a series of social groups that dominate the domestic organization and the process of socialization, the use and transfer of property, the settlement of disputes, religious activities such as ancestor worship, and certain political relationships. Because these kin groups influence so many aspects of social life, their structure and recruitment are highly important variables in the organization of technologically simpler societies. It is not surprising therefore that in the last thirty years descent groups have been intensively studied by comparative sociologists and that there has been much discussion of the meaning of the term *descent*.

Comparative sociologists have generally accepted Rivers' distinction between *inheritance*, the transmission of property; *succession*, the transmission of office; and *descent*, the transmission of kingroup membership. These three aspects of the authorized transmission of property, office, and group membership from one generation to the next are not entirely parallel. Inheritance, as usually understood, refers to transmission after death; the total process of transmission between holder and heirs, which includes certain types of transfer of property at marriage (as in the dowry), is referred to as *devolution.* Second, whereas succession and inheritance (or devolution) do not necessarily imply transfer between kin, descent does; it signifies group membership of a special kind, handed down, like property and office, from generation to generation.

Looking at the process of intergenerational transmission, from the standpoint of the junior generation, an individual can receive any particular set of rights in the following ways: (1) *agnatic* transmission, deriving exclusively from paternal kin; (2) *uterine* transmission, deriving exclusively from maternal kin; (3) *bilateral* (ambilateral) *inclusive* transmission, deriving from paternal and maternal sources; and (4) *bilateral* (utrolateral) *exclusive* transmission, deriving from either the paternal or maternal kin, depending on extraneous factors such as residence.

In any particular society, the inheritance of property, succession to office, and recruitment to kin groups usually follow the same mode of transmission. Indeed, the importance of descent groups lies in the fact that membership usually entails a claim upon basic productive and reproductive resources, as well as channeling succession to roles and offices. But this is not always the case. Moreover, some differences arise in the transmission of these various rights from the fact that office is rarely divisible and its transmission is necessarily selective, whereas all members of a society usually belong to one of the series of kin groups. Property may be partible or impartible, and certain objects, such as weapons and cooking pots, are, like office, often sex-linked; on the other hand, the membership of kin groups is, in a sense, always partible and very rarely sex-linked. Moreover, it is allocated to individuals at birth (or soon after), not simply through birth.

## Unilineal descent groups

Rivers used descent to refer only to kin groups whose members are recruited unilineally (or "unilaterally," to use his own term); that is to say, groups such as clans, which are recruited either through male (agnatic) or through female (uterine) links. However, *unilineal descent groups* (UDGs) of this kind are not defined by the manner of recruitment alone; all the members of a particular group are also related to one another by common unilineal descent. A military regiment like the Fanti *asafo* company in Ghana or an occupational group like the widespread groups of Numu blacksmiths in west Africa may be recruited exclusively by ties of paternal kinship; they do not constitute a UDG unless the members are themselves linked with one another by similar ties and see themselves as having a common ancestry.

When these links are demonstrable and can be genealogically plotted, the group is known as a *lineage;* when the links are not demonstrable and descent is "putative," the group is known as a *clan.* Some authors have attempted to establish the Roman term *gens* for a patrilineal UDG and *clan* for the matrilineal type, but most authorities prefer *patriclan* (or *patrilineage*) and *matriclan* (or *matrilineage*).

**Distribution of UDGs.** UDGs are found in all types of preindustrial economy and in all regions of the world; they occur among the aboriginal hunters of Australia and among the pastoralists of central Asia; among the shifting agriculturalists in Africa and among the irrigation farmers in India. They occur most frequently in pastoralism, then in agriculture, then in hunting and gathering, and only marginally in industrial communities. Ethnographic samples (Murdock 1957; 1963; Aberle 1961) support the hypothesis of those writers (for example, Lowie 1948; Radcliffe-Brown 1950; Forde 1947) who pointed to a positive association between the presence of descent groups and the amount and type of property to be transmitted. Forde (1947) observed that only when a certain threshold of stability and density of settlement is reached do the tendencies for unilineal transmission give rise to UDGs. Like other large-scale kin groups, they tend to have less importance where membership no longer provides rights in the means of production (i.e., when economies have become commercialized or industrialized). Descent groups also lose importance when their function in offense and defense is minimized by a highly centralized political system, and they no longer serve as a focus for ongoing local ties when spatial and social mobility increases.

As with all the wider ties of kinship, the disappearance of UDGs is linked with the growth of economic and social individualism in industrial societies, where a person tends to have direct ties with the political and economic agencies, mediated by specialized associations such as trade unions and political parties rather than by multifunctional units such as kin groups. In general, the role of UDGs diminishes with the importance of governmental institutions. Patriclans were important within the state systems of the Zulu, early Rome, and China; matriclans played a significant part in the kingdoms of Ashanti and the Congo. But their characteristic functions of defense and retaliation were subsumed under central administrations. For example, homicide, a matter for self-help by the kin group in stateless and weakly centralized societies such as the bedouin tribes or Anglo-Saxons, became a criminal offense, dealt with by the king's court.

**Corporate groups.** The functional importance of UDGs and similar social groups is sometimes expressed by the use of the term "corporate." Following legal usage, Sir Henry Maine described the early Roman *gens* as a corporation in order to indicate its character as a property-holding unit that "never died." But the word has also been used (*a*) to translate Weber's *Verband* (a group with a hierarchy of legitimate authority); (*b*) for a group that regularly meets in either plenary or representative session; and (*c*) for a compact, localized group (as distinct from either a dispersed, or a nonlocalized, group, which often has few functions). The need for differentiating the part played by kin groups in different societies is recognized in the recent study of matrilineal systems edited by Schneider and Gough. The authors refer to UDGs as "descent units," while the term "descent group" is used for "that descent unit or portion thereof which engages as a whole in activities with respect to which decisions must be made from time to time and in which all adult male members do not have equal authority" (1961, p. 4); the descent group, essentially a decision-making, or "organized," group, is compared with what has elsewhere been called a "corporate descent group." Murdock (1960) makes a similar distinction between corporate, occasional, and circumscriptive kin groups. The criteria that various writers have used to define "corporate groups" appear too general and too confused for most analytic purposes. The term can be restricted to certain aspects of the property-holding function, or else set aside altogether.

**Subdivision of UDGs.** While UDGs are usually segments of the society, in the sense that they are exclusive and exhaustive parts, they are rarely monolithic. Clans are often divided into smaller units (subclans) and into genealogically based units of at least five generations. In a patrilineal society, this basic lineage usually consists of a man's father, grandfather, son, and grandson— that is, the forebears and descendants whom he actually encounters during his lifetime; it is this five-generation unit around which most systems of

kinship terminology are constructed. But lineages may have a much greater generation depth; among the Nuer of the Sudan, twelve to fourteen generations are reported, and lineages of similar spread occur among other pastoral peoples of the Middle East, such as the contemporary bedouins and the Hebrews of the first millennium B.C.

The genealogy of a lineage differs in function from a chiefly pedigree. The latter acts as a validation of rights to an exclusive office; the former serves as a calculus for the relationship of group members. Consequently, a correlation exists between depth and span—that is, between order of segmentation and number of living members. Adjustment between the two is made by "telescoping" and similar mechanisms. Those ancestors whose presence in the genealogy is inessential for the reckoning of contemporary relationships gradually disappear from memory.

Morphologically, order of segmentation equals depth of genealogy, all levels of which have some importance for social action. But certain levels act as points of reference for specific subgroups of greater functional significance, for example, in the context of ceremonial food sharing, or landholding, or payments of compensation for homicide. The terms *maximal lineage* and *minimal lineage* are used sometimes for the morphological, and sometimes for the functional, differentiation of groups; terms for intermediate units, such as *major lineage*, *minor lineage*, and *nuclear lineage*, refer to the functional ordering of groups.

In such a merging series of subgroups of increasing inclusiveness, two groups that stand in contraposition at one level of segmentation merge when opposed to a group of a higher order of segmentation. This process of segmentation is one of opposition and identification and occurs in any series of "nesting" groups, whatever the political system; counties and cantons conflict on many local issues but unite when national interests are involved. But these processes have a greater importance when centralized administration is absent; hence, stateless societies that have a polysegmental structure (i.e., an extensive merging or nesting series), and particularly those based upon a developed lineage organization, are often known as *segmentary societies*, although the term *acephalous* is less ambiguous.

Some lineage systems extend to the limits of the society itself: the Tiv of eastern Nigeria all regard themselves as descendants in the male line of an eponymous ancestor, and the genealogy of his progeny lays out the complete outline of descent group structure. Sahlins (1961) sees the function of these all-inclusive lineages as one of predatory expansion. It is clear that the deeper the genealogy, the larger the lineage and hence the greater the possibility of mobilizing support on particular issues. But this mobilization may be equally as necessary in situations of defense as of offense. Extensive lineage ties are of particular significance where the population is sparse, and where local groups are bound to be small and therefore able to provide little support in emergencies. They are often important in pastoral societies where ecological conditions demand transhumance and thus the passage of flocks through the territory of one's neighbors; the existence of ongoing ties of descent between such groups facilitates the movements that such a way of life demands.

*Systems of double UDGs.* UDGs are found in 60.6 per cent of the 483 societies in the "Ethnographic Atlas" (Murdock et al. 1963). In some societies (4.6 per cent), two sets of UDGs (patrilineal and matrilineal) are found side by side. In certain cases, one set of UDGs has relatively little significance. In others, both sets of UDGs have important functions; among the Yakö of eastern Nigeria, both sets are vehicles for the transmission of property (Forde 1950) and are therefore corporate, in Maine's sense. Some writers have confined the term "double descent system" to those cases where both sets of UDGs are seen as property-holding corporations and refer to other systems where two sets occur as unilineal systems with secondary (or complementary) UDGs (Goody 1961).

In such full-fledged double descent systems, the two sets of UDGs have more or less differentiated roles. While both sets are exogamous at some level, rights to particular kinds of property are split. By this division, the basic means of production are vested in the patriclans, while other wealth (money, livestock) is linked to the matriclans. Thus, in agricultural economies with full double descent systems, land passes within the patriclan and movable property within the matriclan. As women marry out, the core of the local group consists of male agnates.

*Systems of matrilineal descent.* The "Ethnographic Atlas" shows a considerable predominance of patrilineal over matrilineal systems of UDGs: patrilineal UDGs (40.4 per cent), matrilineal UDGs (15.7 per cent), double UDGs (4.6 per cent), UDGs absent (39.3 per cent).

From many standpoints, agnatic transmission is more straightforward than uterine transmission, since dominant sex roles and descent links coincide. For the dominant sex (i.e., for males), the links are direct, running from father to children.

Daughters move away at marriage, for virilocal residence overwhelmingly prevails where patrilineal UDGs occur. In this case, offspring belong to the UDGs of the husbands.

On the other hand, in matrilineal systems the sex that counts in the reckoning of group membership is nevertheless the inferior one in most social situations. It is men who hold the major positions of authority in domestic and political activities; yet socially the UDG reproduces itself through its female members, who, because of the incest taboo, must take outsiders as husbands or lovers. In the UDG, there is a greater interdependence of brothers and sisters.

If brothers and sisters remain together, as they traditionally did among the Nayar of southwest India, the elementary family cannot exist as a residential unit. But more usual than this duolocal solution to the "matrilineal puzzle" (the problem of combining exogamy and local descent continuity) are two other alternatives: (1) the woman joins the man (*virilocal* marriage); or (2) the man joins the woman (*uxorilocal* marriage). In the uxorilocal solution, as among the Hopi Indians of the southwestern United States, members of the dominant sex are living with affines and hence separated from their own matriclansfolk and "estate." The virilocal solution leaves the men with their own clansfolk, but the children are now separated from their UDG. In societies with localized matrilineal UDGs, this form of marriage must be accompanied by "child return," i.e., change of residence at adolescence or the uxorilocal marriage of at least one male member of the group of full siblings.

The nonresidential Nayar solution is rare (4 per cent of the matrilineal systems in the 1957 sample); residence with the wife's kin is the most common (49 per cent), followed closely by residence with the husband's kin (avunculocally—with his maternal kin—26 per cent; patrilocally—with his father—18 per cent). There is some tendency for avunculocal residence to be associated with the more stratified societies. However, it should be added that these residence types are rarely found in "pure" form; different patterns predominate, depending upon the position in the developmental cycle of the domestic group (e.g., Ashanti), the order in the sibling group (e.g., Yao), the relative status of husband and wife, and upon other factors.

Comparative studies show that matrilineal UDGs are associated with horticulture more frequently than with other types of economy. Although they are often found in stable fishing communities, they are virtually absent from pastoral economies—"the cow is the enemy of matriliny, and the friend of patriliny" (Aberle 1961). Matrilineal UDGs tend to disappear with the development of plough and irrigation agriculture; and, like all UDGs, they are absent from industrialized societies.

*Secondary recruitment.* We have so far assumed that descent groups are recruited according to a single criterion, which derives not simply from the observer's classificatory schema but also from the ideology of the group itself. But probably all societies use additional modes of entry to increase the size of the group, to provide a particular member with an heir, or to regularize an individual's change in domicile when this becomes anomalous in terms of the organization of UDGs. This last procedure is comparable to changing one's nationality.

Various methods other than birthright are used to assimilate an individual into a descent group (Maine's "legal fictions"). Assimilation may occur directly by the adoption of members of the relevant sex (i.e., males in patrilineal descent groups) or by the purchase of slaves. More often the assimilation is indirect: a woman in a patrilineal descent group is used to recruit personnel by contracting a form of limited marriage whereby all, or some, of her offspring are attached to her own natal UDG rather than to her husband's (the "appointed" daughter of China, India, and the Middle East); alternatively the daughter may simply stay at home and produce children by a lover ("institutionalized illegitimacy"); a woman may "marry" another woman, who in turn takes a *cicisbeo* and breeds children for the female husband (as in Dahomey); or a servant or slave girl can substitute for the infertile wife (as Bilhah did for Rachel).

However, assimilation is rarely complete, and social situations such as sacrifices to ancestors may resurrect the differential status of members recruited by secondary means. Where the secondary mode of recruitment is by *complementary filiation* (that is, through the parent excluded from the reckoning of descent), and where this is widely practiced, the group is, in fact, recruited bilaterally, although *de jure* group ideology may impose a fiction of common unilineal descent upon the members. But, like recruitment itself, ideology is also a variable. In some societies, patrilineal attachment to the group may be expressed as a preference rather than an imperative, while other modes of recruitment are openly accepted, although of lower status. Here, we come close, *de jure* as well as *de facto*, to kin groups of a cognatic kind; neither in terms of recruitment nor of ideology (and this is as true of function as of form) can a hard and fast line be drawn between descent and other kin groups.

**Monosexual kin groups.** In the discussion of UDGs we have assumed that recruitment of the sibling group is inclusive; in other words, in patrilineal systems both male and female children belong to the father's UDG. But this is not the only way in which kin groups may be recruited and organized. Logically, the sibling group may be differentiated according to sex and age. Such monosexual groups may be differently organized for men and women; among the Apinayé of central Brazil, the brother belongs to a group of agnatically related males, the sister to a group of women linked by uterine ties. Or men may be linked cross-sexually to their mothers, and women to their fathers, to produce the alternating or cross-sexual system of the "rope" described by Mead for the Mundugumor of northern New Guinea. But such arrangements seem always to be ancillary to other more important sets of kin groups (Maybury-Lewis 1960). Monosexual groups do not stand on their own, since the continuity of all kin groups must depend upon both sexes; and, therefore, the most significant kin groups in a society demand control of both sexes to ensure their character as ongoing units.

A further possibility exists, at any rate for agnatic systems: only one sex is organized on a monosexual basis (i.e., the males), leaving the females as a free floating element. But such an arrangement appears to run counter to the importance of the sibling group (brothers and sisters) in childhood and adolescence, and particularly to the sexual and marital prohibitions placed upon full and, commonly, classificatory sisters (i.e., sisters of fellow clansmen). The closest approximation to this logical possibility is the situation reported to exist in some agnatic systems of east Africa, societies in which a woman is "incorporated" in her husband's kin group, either immediately upon marriage or after she has borne children (Southall 1959). In early Rome, according to Maine, the wife was considered *in manum viri* and was, in law, the daughter of her husband. The resultant unit would correspond to a segment of what Murdock calls a "clan," a compromise as distinct from a consanguineal kin group, for which he uses Lowie's term "sib."

All patrilineal systems transfer some rights in the woman from the bride's to the groom's kin group, i.e., rights *in genetricem* (over her procreative powers) and usually the right of bride removal. The very fact of virilocal residence is bound to place her in a structurally ambiguous position.

Rather than using a simple dichotomy between UDGs that "incorporate" spouses and those that do not, it seems better to treat the degree of transfer of rights as a continuous variable and to make some assessment of the extent of formal assimilation and alienation of spouses, and the degree of their participation in the activities of the two groups involved. The limiting case would be the complete severance of a spouse from his or her natal group, but except in slave marriages it seems doubtful if this situation occurs in practice. Certainly the evidence from Africa, Rome, and China is equivocal here. The construction of such a scale would make it easier to interpret the divorce statistics of patrilineal systems where incorporation has been linked with rare divorce and nonincorporation with higher divorce rates (Fallers 1957). But unless the concept of "incorporation" is broken down, one cannot be sure that it does not already involve a consideration of the ease and frequency of divorce.

## Cognatic kin groups

Unilineal descent is not the only means by which kin groups are organized and recruited. Societies lacking UDGs are frequently referred to as bilateral (or cognatic). In such societies (and in unilineal systems) we find groupings based upon ties traced unrestrictedly, through *both* males and females at one time, or restrictedly through one parent or the other, with the particular selection depending upon nonkinship factors.

Ties traced through *both* males and females give rise to fluctuating *personal kindred* and *descending kindred.* The first is based upon the network of ties that radiate out from any individual, through kin of both sexes, and then descend from these ascendants to collateral kin. The most inclusive of these circles coincides with a man's relatives, i.e., the whole field of consanguineal kinship, but less inclusive groups may emerge as significant social units. Personal kindreds, such as the sib in Anglo-Saxon England, are necessarily ego-orientated; each man's grouping differs from the next (except a full brother), and the units are not true segments of the society. There is some discussion as to whether affines should be included in the definition of a kindred as such (see Freeman 1961, who uses "kindred" for the category of cognatic kin and speaks of the sib as a "kindred-based group"); for cross-cultural analysis, the problem is simply a matter of selecting a verbal tool, but for the analysis of a single society it is a question of establishing what happens in a particular case.

Like other cognatic kin groups, personal kindreds do not consist only of persons linked to a central actor by specific genealogical connections; two individuals may regard themselves as cousins simply because their respective fathers did. The distinction between genealogical and derived kinship is the basis of the formal distinction between lineage and clan.

The descending kindred is quite a different kind of unit. Unlike the personal kindred, membership is traced from an ancestor, ancestress, or an ancestral pair. Since ties are reckoned through both males and females, the resultant groupings are overlapping in terms of membership; but the members all see themselves as belonging to the same unit ("the descendants of X"). In the first respect, they resemble kindreds, in the latter a UDG.

Goodenough (1955) refers to such groups as "unrestricted nonunilineal descent groups" (Bohannan's "omnilineal descent group") and points out that they emerge mainly in the context of claims on fixed resources, especially ancestral land. Such nonunilineal descent groups (NDG, or Murdock's "cognatic descent group") become restricted by the introduction of additional criteria of entry, such as residence, parents' residence, or the use of land rather than claims on land. If these alternatives are exclusive (as usually with residence), then the result will be a restricted kin group that is a true segment of the society; each individual is normally allocated to one such unit and one alone, as with UDGs.

Where membership of a restricted NDG is either nonexclusive (i.e., plural membership is allowed) or reversible (i.e., a man may alternate between the kin groups of his father and his mother), then the group is said to be *ambilateral* (Firth 1957). It is *utrolateral* where membership is exclusive and irreversible, as in the case of the Iban *bilek.*

Where the membership of a restricted UDG is organized around a geneaology, the group (a *ramage*) is, from this standpoint, the morphological equivalent of the lineage.

On the question of the similarities and differences between UDGs and restricted NDGs has turned the discussion as to whether groups of the latter type are properly called descent groups. Most American scholars adopt the wider usage, but some British authorities, such as Fortes and Leach, follow Rivers in making unilineality an essential criterion. They do this because first, "bilateral" groups may involve additional nonkinship criteria of eligibility. Second, these criteria involve choice or optation. It should be remarked that it is the existence of prescribed alternatives, rather than choice, that is important here; the selection of alternatives may derive from factors outside the control of the individual involved as in the case of parental residence. Third, the membership of these bilateral groups may overlap. Last, the processes of segmentation, fission, etc., are very different where the genealogical links consist of both males and females.

Whether descent is taken to refer only to UDGs or to include other ancestor-oriented kin groups is, however, not of great importance. What matters is that groups of this kind are of basic significance in the social structure of a large number of nonindustrial societies. Because of their importance in the domestic, political, economic, and religious spheres, an understanding of the way they work and a knowledge of the principles of recruitment and organization are central not only to the understanding of particular societies but of human history itself and of the problems arising from the rapid social change of recent times. Their importance is explicitly recognized by the fact that preindustrial societies are often classified by the types of kin group present, in particular by the presence of patrilineal or matrilineal descent groups, of both (double descent), or of neither (bilateral). This typology, while requiring much refinement, has had considerable relevance for explaining differences in such fields as domestic groups (Fortes 1958), incest rules (Goody 1956), rates of divorce (Gluckman 1950), relationship between adjacent generations (Malinowski 1927; Goody 1962), and developing agricultural organizations (Hill 1963).

JACK GOODY

[*Directly related are the entries* FAMILY, *article on* COMPARATIVE STRUCTURE; MARRIAGE, *article on* COMPARATIVE ANALYSIS.]

### BIBLIOGRAPHY

ABERLE, DAVID F. 1961 Matrilineal Descent in Cross-cultural Perspective. Pages 655–727 in David M. Schneider and Kathleen Gough (editors), *Matrilineal Kinship.* Berkeley: Univ. of California Press.

BOHANNAN, PAUL J. 1963 *Social Anthropology.* New York: Holt.

DAVENPORT, WILLIAM 1959 Nonunilinear Descent and Descent Groups. *American Anthropologist* New Series 61:557–572.

DURKHEIM, ÉMILE (1893) 1960 *The Division of Labor in Society.* 2d ed. Glencoe, Ill.: Free Press. → First published as *De la division du travail social.*

EVANS-PRITCHARD, E. E. (1940) 1963 *The Nuer: A Description of the Modes of Livelihood and Political Institutions of a Nilotic People.* Oxford: Clarendon.

FALLERS, L. A. 1957 Some Determinants of Marriage Stability in Busoga. *Africa* 27:106–123.

FIRTH, RAYMOND W. 1957 A Note on Descent Groups in Polynesia. *Man* 57:4–8.

FORDE, DARYLL 1947 The Anthropological Approach in Social Science. *Advancement of Science* 4:213–224.

FORDE, DARYLL 1950 Double Descent Among the Yakö. Pages 285–332 in A. R. Radcliffe-Brown and Daryll Forde (editors), *African Systems of Kinship and Marriage.* Oxford Univ. Press.

FORTES, MEYER 1945 *The Dynamics of Clanship Among the Tallensi: Being the First Part of an Analysis of the Social Structure of a Trans-Volta Tribe.* Published for the International African Institute. Oxford Univ. Press.

FORTES, MEYER 1953 The Structure of Unilineal Descent Groups. *American Anthropologist* New Series 55:17–41.

FORTES, MEYER 1958 Introduction. Pages 1–14 in Jack Goody (editor), *The Developmental Cycle in Domestic Groups.* Cambridge Papers in Social Anthropology, No. 1. Cambridge Univ. Press.

FREEMAN, J. D. 1961 On the Concept of the Kindred. *Journal of the Royal Anthropological Institute of Great Britain and Ireland* 91:192–220.

GLUCKMAN, MAX 1950 Kinship and Marriage Among the Lozi of Northern Rhodesia and the Zulu of Natal. Pages 166–206 in A. R. Radcliffe-Brown and Daryll Forde (editors), *African Systems of Kinship and Marriage.* Oxford Univ. Press.

GOODENOUGH, WARD H. 1955 A Problem in Malayo–Polynesian Social Organization. *American Anthropologist* New Series 57:71–83.

GOODY, JACK R. 1956 A Comparative Approach to Incest and Adultery. *British Journal of Sociology* 7:286–305.

GOODY, JACK R. 1961 The Classification of Double Descent Systems. *Current Anthropology* 2:3–26.

GOODY, JACK R. 1962 *Death, Property and the Ancestors: A Study of the Mortuary Customs of the Lodagaa of West Africa.* Stanford (Calif.) Univ. Press.

HILL, POLLY 1963 *The Migrant Cocoa-farmers of Southern Ghana: A Study in Rural Capitalism.* Cambridge Univ. Press.

LOWIE, ROBERT H. (1948) 1960 *Social Organization.* New York: Holt.

MAINE, HENRY J. S. (1861) 1960 *Ancient Law: Its Connection With the Early History of Society, and Its Relations to Modern Ideas.* Rev. ed. New York: Dutton; London and Toronto: Dent. → A paperback edition was published in 1963 by Beacon.

MALINOWSKI, BRONISLAW (1927) 1953 *Sex and Repression in Savage Society.* London: Routledge; New York: Harcourt. → A paperback edition was published in 1955 by Meridian.

MAYBURY-LEWIS, DAVID 1960 Parallel Descent and the Apinayé Anomaly. *Southwestern Journal of Anthropology* 16:191–216.

MURDOCK, GEORGE P. 1949 *Social Structure.* New York: Macmillan.

MURDOCK, GEORGE P. 1957 World Ethnographic Sample. *American Anthropologist* New Series 59:664-687.

MURDOCK, GEORGE P. 1960 Preface. In George P. Murdock (editor), *Social Structure in Southeast Asia.* Viking Fund Publications in Anthropology, No. 29. Chicago: Quadrangle Books. → Papers presented at a symposium held at the ninth Pacific Science Congress, Bangkok, Thailand, 1957.

MURDOCK, GEORGE P. et al. 1963 Ethnographic Atlas. *Ethnology* 2:109–133, 249–268, 402–405, 541–548.

RADCLIFFE-BROWN, A. R. 1950 Introduction. Pages 1–85 in A. R. Radcliffe-Brown and Daryll Forde (editors), *African Systems of Kinship and Marriage.* Oxford Univ. Press.

RICHARDS, AUDREY I. 1950 Some Types of Family Structure Amongst the Central Bantu. Pages 207–251 in A. R. Radcliffe-Brown and Daryll Forde (editors), *African Systems of Kinship and Marriage.* Oxford Univ. Press.

SAHLINS, MARSHALL D. 1961 The Segmentary Lineage: An Organization of Predatory Expansion. *American Anthropologist* New Series 63:322–345.

SCHNEIDER, DAVID M.; and GOUGH, KATHLEEN (editors) 1961 *Matrilineal Kinship.* Berkeley: Univ. of California Press.

SOUTHALL, A. W. 1959 A Note on Local Descent Groups. *Man* 59:65–66.

## III

### PSEUDO-KINSHIP

Pseudo-kinship includes those relationships in which persons are described or addressed by kin terms (or terms derived from the idiom of kin) but do not stand in such a relationship by virtue of the principles, however they happen to be conceptualized, of descent or marriage. It has been suggested that any relationship which employs a kin term is kin, and in that case there would be no pretext for the notion of pseudo-kinship. Nevertheless, such a viewpoint does not evade the need to distinguish between such relationships and consanguineal or affinal kinship. Every society has rules for ascribing kin status to its members, but these do not determine a relation of pseudo-kinship, which depends always upon the individual will of, at least, the initiator.

Three types of pseudo-kinship can be distinguished. (1) There is, first of all, the figurative usage of kin terms, which may be little more than a convention of speech or which may, on the other hand, designate a status within the society or within a specific context. (2) There are also customs whereby a person is given the status of kin by attribution rather than by birth—and this is commonly called "fictive" or "artificial" kinship. (3) There are also institutions which, in some ways, resemble kinship and are named by analogy with it, yet which possess a separate nature and accord a distinct status. These are sometimes regarded, rightly, as ritualized forms of friendship.

These three categories merge into one another; a figurative usage becomes an attribution of status when it enjoins behavior appropriate to kin, while the fiction of attributed kin status is no more than an analogy once the pseudo-kin are differentiated from the genuine. Again, ritualized friendship can exist without any analogy to kinship at all, as in the bond-friendship of Tikopia (Firth 1936), and the institutionalized "best friend" is sometimes no more than a trading partner. Trading partnership, on the other hand, may involve a relationship which carries the analogy with kinship to the point of imposing a bar to the intermarriage of descendants (Gorer 1938).

**Figurative usage.** Kin terms are used figuratively in many societies for the purpose of stressing some particular quality associated with kin. They may be employed momentarily, as when an old man is addressed as "grandad" in order to imply intimacy and age difference and when "son" or "daughter" is used to underline the seniority of the speaker. They may be particular to a given relationship, as when children are encouraged to address friends of their parents who adopt an avuncular role as "aunt" or "uncle." Usages similar to all of these are found in other parts of the world.

Such usages are clearly distinguished from genuine kinship even when they are required by convention, since the kin relationship to the person addressed is irrelevant. They are mere expressions of attitudes, part of the common currency of personal relations. They imply a quality of behavior rather than a status, fraternity rather than the relationship of sibling. Kin terms may also provide a conventional title, as in the case of the Catholic priesthood, lay brotherhoods, or guilds, or in connection with a role in a festival, as in the Pawnee Hako (Fletcher 1904). Here the quality of the role begs an analogy with kinship.

**Fictive or artificial kinship.** Whether kinship is a purely social tie or whether it has any necessary biological basis is a question which has been much discussed, and the point of view taken necessarily affects what is to be regarded as pseudo-kinship. However, it seems advisable to consider as genuine kin those to whom the custom of the society ascribes such status, whatever the criteria for ascription may be, and to regard as pseudo-kin those who achieve the role otherwise. The distinction is not always easily made in societies such as the Eskimo, which appear to ascribe kin status on the basis of residence in a given household. When a person is adopted into a kin status to which he was not born, the definition of kinship becomes even more complex. He may acquire the status permanently and thus be established as a member of a kin group. The adopted individual becomes almost equivalent to one who was born into that status, is linked to all its members through ties of kinship, and addresses them by kin terms. In Western as in Far Eastern civilization, the desire for an heir is the common motive for such adoptions.

In Japan, the *mukoyōshi,* "groom-foster-son" as it has been translated, is adopted as a husband for the daughter when there is no son or no suitable son to whom the patrimony can be entrusted. Such an institution is reminiscent of the custom of the French peasantry, expressed in the phrase *entrer gendre* (to go in as a son-in-law), which defines the position of the bridegroom who joins the family farm in order to succeed his father-in-law. In Japan, however, there are other forms of adoption: the adoptive daughter who is later married to a "groom-foster-son," even the *kaiyōshi*, "buyer-adoptive-son," who takes over the patrimony of a bankrupt family and acquires kin status in it. A tenant can also become an adoptive son, and his descendants form a branch of the family which adopted him (Nagai & Bennett 1953; Norbeck & Befu 1958; Befu 1962). It must be pointed out that the fiction here is not complete, in the sense that the adoptive child does not become equivalent in every way to one born into the status. Though he uses the terminology of kinship to all the members of his adoptive parents' kin, he is distinguished from the natural legitimate progeny in that his rights of inheritance are not always equivalent to theirs, and he retains his ties to his natural kin. Moreover, the very fact that he marries the daughter of his adoptive parents demonstrates that the groom-foster-son is not equated to a natural son with regard to the prohibition of incest. The *oyabun–kobun* complex is to be distinguished from adoption in that it sets up a whole system of artificial kinship, quite separate from natural kinship, which endows a structure of patronage in economic and political life with the ritual and terminology of kinship. Bennett and Ishino (1963) have termed this "simulated kinship."

Slaves of warlike tribes in Africa and North America were often adopted into the lineage of their captor and thereby acquired kin, but they did not by the same token acquire the status of son in all its aspects. Such a custom can be viewed as a way of providing a kin affiliation for those who have none in a society where this is essential for the conduct of social relations. Fictive kinship is also established for specific purposes, as for example in Islam, where it allows a man access to women who are not kin.

On the other hand, adoption may establish a person as a member of the family equivalent to its offspring, as commonly in Western civilization. In some societies, however (e.g., M. G. Smith 1962, p. 90), upbringing from infancy defines the status of child rather than procreation; filiation has dispensed with the supposition of physical maternity. In other societies, paternity is defined by social rather than genetic criteria—a fact which has led anthropologists to distinguish between "pater" and "genitor." In neither case could one speak of fictive kinship, since by definition the kinship is genuine. The genitor may at the same time receive recognition as kin.

Genealogical relationships frequently involve a certain number of fictions whereby the record of descent is adapted so as to conform with the reality of the groups who believe themselves to share a common ancestor. In certain cases all the members of a single small community are addressed and referred to by a kin term, and their behavior is modeled upon that appropriate for kin, regardless of any putative cognatic tie. The tie of neighborship is thus given the value of a tie of kinship. This may be maintained even across differences of caste in India, as Freed (1963) has shown.

Finally, we may describe as fictive kinship the instances where persons who are related genealogically in one way adopt the forms of address and behavior prescribed for a different relationship. This is commonly the case where their roles in a household have constrained the members to mutate their kin ties to conform to their mutual behavior.

**Ritual kinship.** There exist, throughout the world, institutions which establish ties analogous to kin ties. The participants recognize a bond which is likened to, though it is not confused with, kinship. These are commonly defined under the headings of blood brotherhood and ritual coparenthood, or *compadrazgo*, and they are all best classified as ritual kinship. To refer to them as "fictive kinship," as many authors have done, is to invite confusion, since no fiction is involved; these institutions are conceptually distinct from and frequently contrasted with natural kinship (Tegnaeus 1952, p. 13). Too often the ethnographer has written that persons tied by ritual kinship are "as brothers," yet a closer look at the ethnography shows that they are not "as brothers" in any real sense (cf. Beidelman 1963). In order to use the word "fictive," we must ascertain that the pseudo-kinsman does in fact acquire, at least in a relevant context, a status similar to that of the natural kinsman. Moreover, just as there are fictive forms and usages of consanguineal kinship, so there are of ritual kinship—and we can hardly speak of fictive "fictive kinship." In fact, the role of the ritual kinsman often resembles that of the brother-in-law rather than the brother.

*Blood brotherhood.* Early studies of blood brotherhood (e.g., W. R. Smith 1885, pp. 47–58) were dominated and obscured by the assumption that primitive peoples regarded kinship, just as Westerners do, as a matter of blood. Even those who perceived that it was the magical associations of blood which accounted for its use in rituals continued to class together, as blood brotherhood, types of relationship which have in common only this detail of the rite which initiates them. Thus the discussions as to whether blood brotherhood was to be explained as a form of kinship, a legal contract, or a political alliance reinforced by a magical curse, a private pact, or a peacemaking ceremony were fundamentally confused, for blood can be used in many different rites (Evans-Pritchard 1933). The intimate identification implied by the exchange of blood represents a bond between two persons which gives each a mystical hold over the fidelity of the other. This bond does not as a rule entail the acquisition of ties with his kin. Indeed, in some instances the pact thus established remains secret; this is particularly the case where it is made for the purpose of political conspiracy or entry into a secret society. Such a pact is also found in certain marriage ceremonies and in love pacts (Sousberghe 1960).

On the other hand, such pacts are frequently a means of cementing peaceful relations or economic cooperation. They are therefore made with potentially hostile strangers, such as those early explorers of Africa who are often pictured entering into blood covenants, and between tribal chiefs whose followers are thereby committed to refrain from hostilities. The pact of blood may also be used to end a feud or a personal enmity. Depending upon the recognized extension of the tie engendered in this way, it serves to guarantee amicable terms between tribes, kin groups, families, or individuals. In this sense the blood pact may be put to the same purpose as alliance through marriage, as it is commonly a means of formalizing an instrumental or a purely affective relationship between two men. It is rarely found between two women, since the status of women commonly precludes such independence of action.

Covenanted comradeship depends upon the individual will of the participants (though they may be subject to their parents' approval in this, or they may be committed to such a relationship in infancy by the parents). Yet it is almost always irrevocable. It prescribes reciprocal gifts and mutual trust, feelings of amity and the obligation of mutual assistance. In some instances it imposes an incest prohibition between the children of the comrades and even between their descendants; in others it enjoins a preference for their union. This type of comradeship is initiated by a rite which commonly involves the invocation of divine powers who bear witness. The rite itself consists in exchanging some personal substance, which is very frequently blood but also may be saliva, semen,

and the like, or in the ingestion of some sanctified substance in common, a "loving cup" of blood or wine, for example, or an exchange of sacrifice. Foster brotherhood may sometimes create a similar tie. Thus, by analogy, a man could establish a tie of sacrosanct amity among the Caucasian tribes by pressing his lips to the breast of the mother of his enemy, an act which obliged the latter to forgo vengeance. Among the Plains Indians of North America, men who had sexual relations with the same woman thereafter called each other "brother," a custom which may not be unconnected with the levirate.

A relationship similar to blood brotherhood may be initiated by a rite which centers upon the role of sponsor to certain persons, festivals, or celebrations, the passage together through a religious rite, or the exchange of sanctified gifts. Thus, ritual kinship may be established in central India when groups of young people "hear Ram's name" together from a teacher (guru); they are then considered to be ritual brothers and sisters (Mayer 1960, pp. 139 ff.). The tie thus established bears a resemblance to Christian coparenthood. It is a particular form of a relationship which exists throughout India between a guru and his disciples, who are regarded as spiritual children to him and spiritual brothers and sisters to each other.

*"Compadrazgo," or coparenthood.* The most fully documented form of ritual kinship in the literature of anthropology is coparenthood. It derives from the Christian notion of spiritual kinship, one of the three kinds of affinity, the other two being affinity through blood and through marriage. Spiritual affinity originated in the sacrament of baptism and grew to be separate from natural affinity in the early Middle Ages, when parents were forbidden to stand as sponsors to their own children. The dogmatic basis for this development was provided by the opposition between natural generation, through which the sin of Adam was transmitted, and spiritual regeneration, through which it was cleansed. A corresponding opposition is found in those customs in which a spiritual parent must replace the physical parent. Spiritual kinship involves ties of two sorts, both of which impose an impediment to marriage: that which is established between godparent and godchild and that between godparent and natural parent, the coparents, who address each other and are referred to as *compadres* (Spanish), *compari* (Italian), *koumbari* (Greek), *kum* (Serbian and Russian). The pretexts for establishing such ties vary. The Roman Catholic religion now recognizes spiritual affinity only as arising from the rites of baptism and confirmation, and only between the officiant

and the child and between the godparent and god-child. Wider extensions of spiritual affinity are still recognized by the Eastern Catholic rites and by the Eastern Orthodox churches. The Council of Trent (1545–1563) greatly restricted the range of this regard to the persons between whom spiritual affinity was recognized (two spiritual parents of the same child, the children of *compadres*) and to the number of godparents. Spiritual affinity between coparents has lapsed in twentieth-century dogma in the Roman church, though not in the Eastern churches.

The social functions of this institution are to be distinguished from its spiritual function. In many parts of the world, popular custom ignores dogma and institutes the social bond of *compadrazgo* through rites which give rise to no spiritual affinity in the eyes of the church, though in the eyes of custom they may imply an incest prohibition. Thus in Spain the marriage godparents have no liturgical significance but have considerable social significance (except in Catalonia); conversely, the god-parents of confirmation required by the church frequently have no social functions. The baptismal godparents ·should act as godparents in the first communion and, according to the custom of certain regions, at the godchild's marriage. A variety of preferential rules governs the selection of the godparents; sometimes they prescribe a member of the family of one or other parent. Sometimes the landowner is viewed as the appropriate godfather for the tenant's child, and sometimes simply a friend becomes godparent (Foster 1953; Pitt-Rivers 1958). The significant differences are that in Italy and the northern half of Spain the tie between *compadres* is generally regarded as less important than that between godparent and godchild and that in Italy the godparent of confirmation is given more importance than the baptismal godparent (Anderson 1957).

On the whole the quality of the relationship of *compadre* is similar, although in Italy the spiritual rather than the material aspect is stressed; it is even regarded as preferable to choose someone with whom there will be no business entanglements. In both countries it is a relationship of trust, mutual assistance, affection, and respect—coparents traditionally use the formal third person in address. It is said that one can deny one's *compadre* nothing, but the reciprocal duties are not stipulated. The duties of the godparent are more explicit, though they vary from place to place. In sum, they involve payment for the ceremony of fiesta, gifts of amulets and first articles of clothing, aid in starting out in life, and special duties in the case of godchild's death during childhood—in fact,

whenever the individual destiny of the child is at stake. The godparent also has the theoretical obligation to act as guardian in the case of the death of the parents. In exchange, the godchild owes only respect, obedience, and affection. The relations between *compadres*, on the other hand, are always conceived of as relations of equality, even where they cut across class barriers. Indeed their significance in such cases is precisely that they provide a tie of intimacy between persons of different classes which is not otherwise possible. Thus within the *compadrazgo* there are ritual relations between superior and inferior (godparent–god-child) or between equals (coparents), and there are social relations of ritualized friendship between equals and also of patronage between social classes. (Mintz & Wolf 1950). Therefore it is not surprising that the terminology of the *compadrazgo* should have acquired a slang usage to describe the maneuvers of intrigue, particularly in politics.

Coparenthood (*kumstvo*) in southeastern Yugoslavia establishes a lasting bond between two extended families (*zadruge*) through the customary obligation to renew the relationship, which is inherited from father to son. In this way a collective tie is maintained from one generation to the next. Ritual kinship is recognized, and the appropriate term used, between all members of the two families.

The bond of *compadrazgo* takes on its widest extension and its fullest significance in Latin America, as Tylor (1861, p. 251) was the first to note. The tie between *compadres* is generally of greater importance than that between godparent and godchild. It is sometimes recognized not only between the *compadres*, as hitherto defined, but also between each one of them and the ascendants of the other (certain Indians regard it as a relationship involving all the members of each family). In addition, the occasions on which *compadrazgo* is formed are many more than in Europe. Thus, baptism may provide the infant with up to three or even more pairs of godparents (*padrinos de pila, de ceremonia, de arras, de vela*, or *de evangelios*), all of whom become *compadres* of the parents. Fresh godparents are chosen for other occasions, particularly the *rites de passage* of the child. *Compadrazgo* may be formed on such pretexts as the first hair or nail cutting of a child, the ceremony when it is first carried astride the hip of an adult, a daughter's ear piercing (this is found in Italy also), the dedication of a house, an altar, a religious image, a rosary, or a new truck, a healing ceremony, or simply the cosponsoring of a fiesta.

There are degrees of seriousness attached to different forms. *Compadrazgo* with the godparents of the font (*padrinos de pila*) tends to be treated as the most serious and sacred, while that which is established with the sponsor of a fiesta or the "godparent" at the blessing of a truck is no more than fictive *compadrazgo* which entitles the participants to call each other "*compadre*" as long as they feel well disposed but which is unlikely to be recognized by their ascendants. An influential man often has more *compadres* than he can remember. The degree to which *compadrazgo* implies a genuine affective tie whose sacred character is respected, rather than a perfunctory affability—and the distinction is inevitable in communities where middle-aged people are nearly all *compadres* of one sort or another—is sometimes expressed by the term "*compadres de corazón*" (*compadres* of the heart), which is reserved for relationships of true friendship and is usually ritualized by one of the more serious forms.

It is not easy to determine where to draw the line between genuine ritual kinship and fictive ritual kinship. Seen from the liturgical point of view, all the customary forms which do not involve spiritual affinity are fictive, but, if the authority of custom is accepted, then any form of *compadrazgo* established on a generally recognized pretext is genuine. Nevertheless, custom recognizes that some pretexts imply a more binding relationship than others, and it is wiser perhaps to regard the distinction here as a continuum rather than a dichotomy.

**The structure of ritual kinship.**  All the forms of ritualized friendship, whether or not they use the terminology of kinship, derive not from birth but from the mutual feelings of individuals, guaranteed by the magical power of blood or the sacrosanctity of the rite. Even where there are preferential rules as to the choice of ritual kinsmen, it is subject always to the existence of the appropriate sentiments. This is true even in the extension of the *compadrazo* to the parents of *compadres;* the relationship is established only when they exchange the ritual embrace, and it is always therefore possible to avoid. Ritual kinship commonly forms a series of dyadic or triadic ties, not an extended structure (cf. Foster 1963, p. 1285). Unlike natural kinship, it has no origin in descent from the past and no projection into the future where kin relations grow apart and realign themselves in the course of the domestic cycle. Even in the few cases (mainly blood brotherhood) where children take over the ritual kin ties of parents and the tie possesses a collective aspect, ritual kinship does not become part of the structure of kinship. This is illustrated by a provision concerning the collective Serbian *kumstvo:* a marriage between two families linked in this way brings the relationship to an end. Its restricted range and independence of other ties render it apt for the purposes of assuring or restoring peace, for when two of a man's ritual kinsmen fight each other, he must remain friendly with both, since his ties with each are equivalent and independent. Equally, ritual kinship avoids being implicated in the internal dissensions of the kinship structure, for it involves no structural issues. It does not depend upon a network of rights and duties, but upon a reciprocal claim to favor and benevolence; it makes requests (not demands) and gifts (not payments) even where custom may define what these should be, and it is reinforced by supernatural sanctions only. The quality of the relationship differs from that of kin relations; "All that is mine is thine," is the principle which inspires both the blood brother and the *compadre,* as in fact they say on occasions, but, even where rights are collectively vested in a kin group this is not the language of kinship. Indeed, where ritual kinship is superimposed upon natural kinship it endows the relationship between the two persons with a sacredness which it did not previously possess; for this reason blood brothers are sometimes said to be "closer than real brothers" and *compadre* frequently replaces a kin term in address, even, in parts of Latin America, brother or father.

We may ask why ritual kinship so often employs the language of consanguineal kinship, especially brotherhood. It does so by analogy with the ideal of brotherly love rather than with the reality of brotherly behavior, which opens with sibling rivalry and becomes in time subject to the dissonant demands of new families of procreation and the disintegration of the family of origin. By contrast, the tie of ritual kinship is immutable and free of ambivalence. Hence we can see that while adoptive kinship supplements the kinship structure, becoming, thanks to a fiction, what cognatic kinship *is,* ritual kinship complements it; it *is* what cognatic kinship aspires to, but *cannot, be.*

This statement should not blind us to the fact that ritual kinship is not always what it is thought it ought to be. It is as liable to exploitation as any form of friendship. Like friendship, it depends upon a balance of reciprocal favor. Its function is to provide through the attachment of personal feelings a basis for trust between individuals, which may or may not be put to the service of political or economic ends.

The institutions of ritual kinship do not flourish in modern urban society. In Europe, they lost their significance, save in the south, before the industrial revolution; "god-sib" became gossip, and *commère* came to mean the same. The south of Europe uses the words in the same figurative sense, and the institution retains its full significance today only in the rural areas. The same is true in principle of Latin America, though the influx of peasants into the cities has obscured the fact. Blood brotherhood is rapidly vanishing in Africa. Considering the varied social functions which the different forms of ritual kinship fulfill, it would be hard to enumerate all the causes of this development, but it appears that ritual kinship requires the environment of the closed community and particularistic rather than universal relations (Eisenstadt 1956). The *oyabun–kobun* system of Japan is exceptional in this regard in representing an adaption of a traditional form of ritual kinship to fulfill a function in modern industrial organization.

In summary, pseudo-kinship is a residual category that includes a number of very different institutions which have in common only the fact that they are likened to kinship by the people themselves. To sort out this rag bag into sociological categories the following distinctions were required: whether the relationship is universal or particularistic; momentary, temporary, restricted as to context, or continual and permanent; dictated by custom or voluntary; extended to the kin of the primary participants or purely individual; and whether it entails a role within the kinship system or one contrasting with the role of kin.

The analytical distinctions may be clear, but the facts are sometimes ambiguous, and this occurs especially when the institution is found in transition. Pseudo-kin relations change their nature, and those which were once sacred are abused and devaluated; words which once denoted ritual kin extend to senses in which the original meaning is lost.

JULIAN PITT-RIVERS

[*See also* ADOPTION; PATERNALISM.]

### BIBLIOGRAPHY

ANDERSON, G. 1957 Il Comparaggio: The Italian Godparenthood Complex. *Southwestern Journal of Anthropology* 1:32–53.

BEFU, HARUMI (1962) 1963 Corporate Emphasis and Patterns of Descent in the Japanese Family. Pages 34–41 in Pacific Science Congress, Tenth, Honolulu, 1961, *Japanese Culture: Its Development and Characteristics.* Edited by Robert J. Smith and Richard K. Beardsley. Chicago: Aldine.

BEIDELMAN, THOMAS O. 1963 The Blood Covenant and the Concept of Blood in Ukaguru. *Africa* 33:321–342.

BENNETT, JOHN W.; and ISHINO, IWAO 1963 *Paternalism in the Japanese Economy.* Minneapolis: Univ. of Minnesota Press.

CORBLET, JULES 1881–1882 *Histoire dogmatique, litur-gique et archéologique du sacrement de baptême.* 2 vols. Paris: Palmé.

EISENSTADT, SHMUEL N. 1956 Ritualized Personal Relations. *Man* 56:90–95.

EVANS-PRITCHARD, E. E. 1933 Zande Blood-brotherhood. *Africa* 6:369–401.

FIRTH, RAYMOND W. 1936 Bond-friendship in Tikopia. Pages 259–272 in *Custom Is King: Essays Presented to R. R. Marett on His Seventieth Birthday.* London: Hutchinson.

FLETCHER, ALICE C. 1904 The Hako: A Pawnee Ceremony. U.S. Bureau of American Ethnology, *Twenty-second Annual Report, 1900–1901,* part 2.

FOSTER, GEORGE M. 1953 Cofradia and Compadrazgo in Spain and South America. *Southwestern Journal of Anthropology* 9:1–28.

FOSTER, GEORGE M. 1963 The Dyadic Contract in Tzintzuntzan: Patron–Client Relationship. *American Anthropologist* New Series 65:1280–1294.

FREED, STANLEY A. 1963 Fictive Kinship in a North Indian Village. *Ethnology* 2:86–103.

GORER, GEOFFREY 1938 *Himalayan Village: An Account of the Lepchas of Sikkim.* London: Joseph.

HAMMEL, EUGENE A. 1966 Ritual Co-parenthood (Kumstvo) in Serbia. Unpublished manuscript, Univ. of California, Department of Anthropology.

MAYER, ADRIAN C. 1960 *Caste and Kinship in Central India: A Village and Its Region.* London: Routledge; Berkeley: Univ. of California Press.

MINTZ, SIDNEY W.; and WOLF, ERIC R. 1950 An Analysis of Ritual Co-parenthood. *Southwestern Journal of Anthropology* 6:341–368.

NAGAI, MICHIO; and BENNETT, JOHN W. 1953 A Summary and Analysis of *The Familial Structure of Japanese Society,* by Takeyoshi Kawashima. *Southwestern Journal of Anthropology* 9:239–250.

NORBECK, EDWARD; and BEFU, HARUMI 1958 Informal Fictive Kinship in Japan. *American Anthropologist* New Series 60:102–117.

PITT-RIVERS, JULIAN 1958 Ritual Kinship in Spain. New York Academy of Sciences, *Transactions* 2d Series 20, no. 5:424–431.

SMITH, MICHAEL G. 1962 *Kinship and Community in Carriacou.* New Haven: Yale Univ. Press.

SMITH, WILLIAM ROBERTSON (1885) 1903 *Kinship and Marriage in Early Arabia.* New ed. London: Black.

SOUSBERCHE, LÉON DE 1960 Pactes de sang et pactes d'union dans la mort chez quelques peuplades du Kwango. Académie Royale des Sciences d'Outre-mer, Brussels, Classe des Sciences Morales et Politiques, *Mémoires* New Series 22, no. 2.

TEGNAEUS, HARRY 1952 *Blood-brothers.* Stockholm: Statens Etnografiska Museum.

TYLOR, EDWARD B. 1861 *Anahuac: Or, Mexico and the Mexicans, Ancient and Modern.* London: Longmans.

# KJELLÉN, RUDOLF

Rudolf Kjellén (1864–1922), Swedish political scientist, politician, and publicist, was born in a vicarage on Torsö, an island in the lake of Vener, and was raised in a conservative Lutheran atmosphere typical of the period. He studied at the University of Uppsala, where he came under the influence of Oscar Alin, professor of political science and one of the conservative leaders of the Swedish Senate.

Kjellén taught at the University of Gothenburg from 1891 until 1916, when he became professor of political science at Uppsala. From 1905 to 1908 and again from 1911 to 1917 he was a free conservative member of the Swedish parliament. His integrity and eloquence were highly appreciated, but his political importance may have been diminished by a rhetoric too high-flown for the dispassionate Swedish parliament.

Many influences shaped his thought. He was touched both by the realistic European literature of the 1880s and by the romantic Swedish poetry of the 1890s. The strong Linnaean tradition in Swedish culture and his own hobby, ornithology, made him particularly receptive to the current biological modes of thought. Many ideas were suggested to him by the works of the geographer Friedrich Ratzel. The imperialistic theories of Heinrich von Treitschke and John R. Seeley and the imperialistic struggles among nations at the turn of the century changed his conception of the state. He came to see it not simply as a *Rechtssubjekt*, a legal abstraction, but as a reality, an organism.

Kjellén felt it was the business of historians and political scientists to study the state. He read Seeley's *Expansion of England* (1883) and was impressed with the assertion that history must be "scientific in its method"; this was an idea common to many social scientists at that time, such as Comte, Marx, and Spencer. Later, Seeley extended this aim to the political sciences (*Introduction to Political Science*, 1896), referring explicitly to Linnaeus as a master of "description and classification." Although it is not clear whether Kjellén read Seeley's *Introduction*, he certainly shared his approach to political science. In fact he once confessed that it was his ambition to be known as a forerunner of some future Linnaeus of the political sciences.

Kjellén published a statement in 1901 (see reprint in [1916] 1924), asserting that the primary task for political science is to give a systematic account of modern states and the laws that governed their development. In *Stormakterna* (1905) he followed his earlier programmatic statement with a realistic analysis of the great powers of the time. In discussing the factors which caused their development he tended (following Ratzel and Lamprecht, but not going as far as H. T. Buckle) to stress the material ones over the psychological.

During World War I, Kjellén was much preoccupied with the dangers of Russian expansion and the decline of European power and, under the spell of Nietzsche and Sombart, he predicted the replacement of the old values of liberty, equality, and fraternity by duty, order, and rectitude. After the war he returned to more systematic writing, developing the principles of an organic system of political science in *Staten som lifsform* (1916), *Schweden* (1917), and finally in *Grundriss zu einem System der Politik* (1920). *Schweden* represents the application of his system to a modern state.

The study of the political organism (the state) has the following aspects:

(1) *Geopolitik*, a term inspired by Ratzel's *politische Geographie*, describes those conditions and problems of the state which originate in its geographic characteristics;

(2) *Oecopolitik* deals with the economic factors which influence the position and power of the state;

(3) *Demopolitik* deals with the racial and ethnic composition of the state and the problems caused by that composition;

(4) *Sociopolitik* analyzes the social groups and classes of the state and the way in which they affect its unity;

(5) *Kratopolitik* describes and analyzes the constitutional law and the constitutional life of the state, discussing institutions and organizations such as political parties and pressure groups.

Like many modern sociologists, Kjellén gave much attention to terminology. Although material considerations were always of primary importance in his investigations, he did occasionally use as romantic a term as *Volksgeist* (borrowed from the German historical school).

At the time of his death Kjellén was working on a book in which he hoped to give a systematic exposition and analysis of the different forms of constitutions and their inherent tendencies. He was particularly interested in the tendency of democracies to move toward Caesarism.

Kjellén's importance to Swedish political science can be seen in the change of emphasis in the literature from a juridical point of view to a political one. However, his influence in Germany was far greater than it ever was in Sweden. *Geopolitik* became in Germany an ideological slogan, sometimes rather remote from the social scientific context in which Kjellén had developed the concept.

There were many conflicting tendencies in Kjellén's personality. He was an idealist, but he tried to construct a naturalist conception of the state. He was a moralist with a great respect for Ibsenian individualism and humanistic ideas, but he also had great understanding of the politicians "beyond good and evil" and of the imperialists with their tough-minded methods.

GEORG ANDRÉN

[*For the historical context of Kjellén's work, see* POLITICAL SCIENCE; *and the biographies of* LAMPRECHT; RATZEL; SOMBART; TREITSCHKE.]

### WORKS BY KJELLÉN

1897    *Om den svenska grundlagens anda.* Göteborg, Högskola, Göteborg högskolas årsskift, 1897: no. 5. University of Gothenburg.

(1905) 1911–1913    *Stormakterna: Konturer kring samtidens storpolitik.* 4 vols., 2d ed. Stockholm: Gerber. → Volume 1: *F.d. stormakter samt Österrike-Ungern och Italien.* Volume 2: *Frankrike och Tyskland.* Volume 3: *Det Brittiska världsriket.* Volume 4: *Förenta staterna; Ryssland; Japan; Slutsatser.*

(1914) 1933    *Die Grossmächte vor und nach dem Weltkriege.* 24th ed., rev. & enl. Edited by Karl Haushofer. Leipzig: Teubner. → First published as *Samtidens stormakter.*

1914–1915    *Politiska essayer: Studier till dagskrönikan (1907–1913).* 3 vols. Stockholm: Gerber. → Volume 1: *Internationell politik och geopolitik.* Volume 2: *Samhälls- och författningspolitik.* Volume 3: *Svensk statsrätt och svensk geopolitik.*

(1916) 1924    *Der Staat als Lebensform.* 4th ed. Berlin: Vowinckel. → First published in Swedish as *Staten som lifsform.*

1917    *Schweden.* Munich: Oldenbourg. → Published as *Sverige* the same year.

1920    *Grundriss zu einem System der Politik.* Leipzig: Hirzel.

1921    *Dreibund und Dreiverband: Die diplomatische Vorgeschichte des Weltkriegs.* Rev. ed. Munich: Duncker & Humblot. → First published as "Die Koalitionspolitik im Zeitalter 1871–1914" in *Schmollers Jahrbuch.*

### SUPPLEMENTARY BIBLIOGRAPHY

ARRHÉN, ERIK 1933    *Rudolf Kjellén och "unghögern": Sammanställning och diskussion.* Stockholm: Seelig.

ELVANDER, NILS 1961    *Harald Hjärne och konservatismen: Konservativ idédebatt i Sverige, 1865–1922.* Stockholm: Almqvist & Wiksell.

HAUSSLEITER, OTTO 1925    Rudolf Kjelléns empirische Staatslehre und ihre Wurzeln in politischer Geographie und Staatenkunde. *Archiv für Sozialwissenschaft und Sozialpolitik* 54:157–198.

KIHLBERG, MATS; and SÖDERLIND, DONALD 1961    *Två studier i svensk konservatism: 1916–1922.* Stockholm: Almqvist & Wiksell.

SEELEY, JOHN R. (1883) 1931    *The Expansion of England: Two Courses of Lectures.* London: Macmillan.

SEELEY, JOHN R. (1896) 1923    *Introduction to Political Science: Two Series of Lectures.* London: Macmillan.

VOGEL, W. 1926    Rudolf Kjellén und seine Bedeutung für die deutsche Staatslehre. *Zeitschrift für die gesamte Staatswissenschaft* 81:193–241.

# KLEIN, MELANIE

The psychoanalyst Melanie Klein (1882–1960), nee Reizes, was born in Vienna. Her father, brought up in a strictly orthodox Jewish family and origi-nally trained to be a student of the Talmud, broke away from this tradition at the age of 37, studied medicine, and later practiced as a dentist. Her mother was the daughter of a rabbi. Melanie was the youngest of four children. Her only brother, five years her senior and an intelligent and gifted young man, had a deep influence on her, but he died when he was only 25.

At the age of 14, Melanie decided to study medicine, but she became engaged at 17 and gave up her plans for a medical career. She never lost her interest in medicine, however, and always regretted that she had not become qualified as a doctor. When she was 21, she married Arthur Klein, an industrial chemist; the marriage was not a happy one. They had three children, a daughter and two sons. A few years before World War I, the family moved to Budapest; there Melanie Klein came across one of Freud's books, which immediately interested her greatly. Later, she started a personal analysis with Sándor Ferenczi, the principal Hungarian analyst at that time, and, encouraged by him, she began to think about the application of psychoanalysis to young children. In July 1919 she read her first paper, entitled "The Development of a Child" (1921), before the Hungarian Psychoanalytic Society. Two years later, invited by Karl Abraham, the president of the Berlin Psychoanalytic Society, she settled in Berlin with her children; her husband's business interests took him to Sweden, and their separation eventually led to divorce.

From the time she moved to Berlin Melanie Klein devoted herself fully to psychoanalytical practice and research. She was deeply impressed and influenced by the work of Abraham—perhaps most notably by his work on the early stages of infantile development. Early in 1924 she went into analysis with him, but the analysis was terminated by his fatal illness in the summer of 1925. After his death she carried on regular daily self-analysis.

Soon after her arrival in Berlin she began to develop her technique of analyzing children. Her first contributions to the Berlin society aroused considerable interest as well as considerable controversy there and abroad, and in 1925 Ernest Jones, the president of the British Psycho-analytic Society, invited her to give a course of lectures in London. In 1926 she accepted an invitation from the British society to settle permanently in London. There her work developed, and her clinical and theoretical approach was widely accepted by other analysts. Indeed, the members of the British society were often referred to by analysts outside England as the "British school of psychoanalysis" to differentiate the work that was developing in London under Melanie Klein's influence from that in other centers, particularly in Vienna.

The differences arose mainly from the significance for all later development that the British analysts attributed to early infantile anxieties and unconscious fantasies occurring in the first year of life and from their contention that these anxieties and fantasies can be explored in the transference situation. These differences were acknowledged by the British and the Viennese groups of analysts, and in 1936 exchange lectures (Riviere 1936; Waelder 1937) were arranged in order to clarify the different points of view. When in 1938 many Viennese analysts settled in London, the conflicts of opinion became more marked and threatened to cause a split within the British society. However, unity was preserved by the creation of two separate streams of training within the main teaching course. As the awareness of the importance of Melanie Klein's work developed, an increasing number of students and analysts turned to her for training analyses and supervision, and there grew up round her a group of analysts who became close colleagues. Her views have greatly influenced psychoanalytic thinking both within and outside Great Britain, and in several countries groups have formed that have attempted to base their work on her views.

**Child analysis.** During the years from 1921 to 1934 Melanie Klein developed her technique of analyzing children (1955a). Her aim was to create a psychoanalytic setting for children similar to that created by Freud for the treatment of adult patients, a setting in which the patient is free to develop a transference relationship to the analyst and to use free association, so that the therapeutic result depends purely on interpretative work. To achieve this she provided the child with a simply furnished room containing a box of small toys and other play materials. Since the child expresses himself in play more than in words, she analyzed free play (1929), treating it as free association, and showed that one can achieve an analytical relationship with the child, using neither re-education nor reassurance. This approach distinguishes Melanie Klein's work from other attempts at child analysis in which re-education and reassurance play an important part.

From the beginning her interest focused on the child's anxieties and his defenses against them. This emphasis on anxiety led her ever deeper into the unconscious fantasy life of the child. She also insisted not only on interpreting the child's positive transference but on uncovering and interpreting the negative transference which was hidden behind his anxieties. Her emphasis ran counter to the then current psychoanalytic tenet that interpretations should not go very deep and should not be given frequently (1955a). Some of the main differences in approach were expressed in a symposium on child analysis held in 1927 (see 1927). Her technique led to the understanding of early infantile fantasies, anxieties, and defenses, all of which were at that time still largely unexplored.

When she was analyzing small children she found that many of the processes and structures described by Freud had their roots in much earlier periods of life than he had postulated. For instance, a little girl patient, only two years and nine months old, was found to have a strong superego, a structure that Freud believed was not built up until about the fifth year; and the same child had a complicated and long-standing triangular relationship to her parents (Oedipus complex), whereas Freud believed that the Oedipus complex did not come into being until about three or four years of age. In trying to understand anxiety Melanie Klein came to recognize that aggression and cruelty play a much greater role in the child's mind than had been assumed by Freud. She found that the infant's fantasies of sadistic attacks on the mother's breasts and the inside of her body and the resultant paranoid fears of retaliation seem to dominate the infant's relation to the mother during the first year. Her discoveries in this period culminated in the publication in 1932 of *The Psycho-analysis of Children*, in which she described her technique with three different age groups of children and elaborated her findings on the early anxiety situations of infancy and their effects on the development of the ego and superego, on the sexual development of boy and girl, and on other aspects of normal growth and neurotic illness.

**Manic–depressive states.** Beginning in 1934, Melanie Klein's contributions were increasingly influenced by her work with adult patients. Her views on early anxiety situations were clarified and extended. She made an important contribution to the psychopathology and treatment of manic–depressive states by elaborating on the nature of depression and the relation of manic defenses to the depressive conflict (see 1937). In addition, she presented a detailed reconstruction of infantile phases of development in the first year, an understanding of which she regarded as basic for the comprehension of psychotic illnesses in adult life. She introduced the concept of the paranoid and of the depressive position. In the paranoid position, extending over the first three to four months, the infant perceives his mother mainly as a part object (breast) that is either very good or very bad, and the anxiety situations have a paranoid character. The depressive position begins to develop in the fourth or fifth month. During the depressive position the whole relationship to the mother undergoes significant changes that are important for normal development: the infant begins to recognize that the good, satisfying mother and the bad, frustrating mother are the same person. He also sees her as a whole object on whom he can depend. When he experiences anger in situations of frustration, he becomes afraid of destroying and losing her as a good object. Therefore, the anxiety experienced has a depressive character. Guilt feelings for harm done to the love object make their appearance and assist the drive for reparation. Normally, most of the anxieties and mechanisms of the early paranoid phase become modified during the depressive position. Melanie Klein believed that the development of the capacity to love and establish normal object relations depends on the ability to reach and work through the depressive position. These ideas were further elaborated on and related to the subject of mourning in a paper of 1940, in which she also extended her research into manic states and manic defenses. In 1945, in a detailed clinical and theoretical paper, she related her work on the paranoid and depressive positions to the Oedipal conflicts of both the boy and girl.

**Projective identification.**    The discovery of the depressive position as a phase on which normal development depends increased Melanie Klein's interest in studying in greater detail the factors in very early development that may lead to a failure to work through the depressive position. In 1946 she read a paper, "Notes on Some Schizoid Mechanisms," before the British Psycho-analytic Society, an important milestone in her work. She presented there a detailed investigation of the earliest infantile position, which she now renamed the paranoid–schizoid position. She confirmed her previous observations that paranoid anxieties and the splitting of objects are characteristics of this phase, but she also introduced the concepts of ego splitting and projective identification. Projective identification, a more complicated mechanism than projection as described by Freud, is a process by which good or bad parts of the self are split off and projected into an object, initially the mother, who then becomes identified with these parts of the self. This results not only in the ridding by the self of unwanted parts but also in a sense of depletion of the personality. It is likely to lead to paranoid anxieties about being invaded by the object into

whom the projection had taken place. Excessive projective identification can lead to severe difficulties in establishing both one's own identity and normal relations with others. The concepts of ego splitting and projective identification have thrown new light on the understanding of the psychoses, particularly schizophrenia, and have profoundly stimulated psychoanalytic research into these conditions. Melanie Klein described the mechanism of projective identification in some detail in 1955, using a novel by Julian Green to illustrate its operation (see 1955*b*).

Melanie Klein was always concerned with the origin of the conscience, or superego, maintaining that it is built up from the beginning of life by the introjection of objects into the ego. As these internal objects are colored by the child's projection of his impulses, particularly his destructive ones, the superego has at first mainly a persecutory character. Melanie Klein's work on the depressive position showed how guilt feelings develop because of a change in the character of the internal objects representing the superego, namely a lessening of their persecutory quality. In 1948 she wrote a paper, "On the Theory of Anxiety and Guilt" (see 1948*a*), in which she linked the views of Freud and Abraham on the superego with her own investigation into paranoid and depressive anxieties and their relation to guilt. In 1952 she published an account of her work on the emotional life of the infant, in which she described the two infantile positions and their relation to one another, and a further paper on infant observation.

**Envy.**    In 1955 Melanie Klein read a paper, "Envy and Gratitude," to the International Congress of Psycho-analysis in Geneva; she later published this in an enlarged version as a book (see 1957). She had always emphasized the importance of the sadistic, envious feelings in the relationship of the infant toward his parents. However, in 1955 she deepened and widened her original concept of envy as the primary source of aggression, directed initially against the mother and her breast. She now stressed that aggressive envy is capable of interfering from the beginning in the development of good and satisfying object relations and may severely inhibit the development of the capacity to love, which in turn is linked with the capacity to feel gratitude. The concept of envy has important theoretical and clinical implications in that it illuminates infantile states of confusion and increases our understanding of splitting processes, particularly projective identification. In addition, Melanie Klein illustrated how excessive envy interferes in the therapeutic process: primary envy is one of the main causes of the negative therapeutic reaction—the tendency to relapse repeatedly after some progress in treatment has been made.

Her conception of envy has become one of the major controversial aspects of her work, even though many analysts see it as making severe mental conditions accessible to the psychoanalytic approach.

During the last years of her life she concentrated largely on reconstructing, from detailed notes taken after each session, the analysis of a child whom she had treated in 1941 for four months. Although this narrative (1961) does not make use of some of her later discoveries, it is a unique example of her work as a practicing analyst.

Melanie Klein's contributions on infantile development have thrown a new light on the understanding of normal and abnormal mental states and so have made a major contribution to psychoanalytic theory and therapy. Apart from her revolutionizing influence on psychoanalysis, her work has directly and indirectly exerted a profound influence on psychiatry, psychology, child upbringing, and infant care, and, more remotely, on such disciplines as sociology, anthropology, and art criticism.

HERBERT A. ROSENFELD

[*For the historical context of Klein's work, see the biographies of* ABRAHAM; FERENCZI; FREUD; *for discussion of the subsequent development of her ideas, see* DEPRESSIVE DISORDERS; DEVELOPMENTAL PSYCHOLOGY; INFANCY; MENTAL DISORDERS, *article on* CHILDHOOD MENTAL DISORDERS; PARANOID REACTIONS; PSYCHOANALYSIS, *article on* EGO PSYCHOLOGY.]

### WORKS BY KLEIN

(1921) 1948 The Development of a Child. Pages 13–67 in Melanie Klein, *Contributions to Psycho-analysis: 1921–1945*. London: Hogarth. → First published in Volume 1 of *Imago*.

(1927) 1948 Symposium on Child-analysis. Pages 152–184 in Melanie Klein, *Contributions to Psycho-analysis: 1921–1945*. London: Hogarth. → First published in Volume 8 of the *International Journal of Psychoanalysis*.

(1928) 1948 Early Stages of the Oedipus Conflict. Pages 202–214 in Melanie Klein, *Contributions to Psychoanalysis: 1921–1945*. London: Hogarth. → First published in Volume 9 of the *International Journal of Psycho-analysis*.

(1929) 1948 Personification in the Play of Children. Pages 215–226 in Melanie Klein, *Contributions to Psycho-analysis: 1921–1945*. London: Hogarth. → First published in Volume 10 of the *International Journal of Psycho-analysis*.

(1930a) 1948 The Importance of Symbol-formation in the Development of the Ego. Pages 236–250 in Melanie Klein, *Contributions to Psycho-analysis: 1921–1945*. London: Hogarth. → First published in Volume 11 of the *International Journal of Psychoanalysis*.

(1930b) 1948 The Psychotherapy of the Psychoses. Pages 251–253 in Melanie Klein, *Contributions to Psychoanalysis: 1921–1945*. London: Hogarth. → First published in Volume 10 of the *British Journal of Medical Psychology*.

(1932) 1959 *The Psycho-analysis of Children*. 3d ed. London: Hogarth. → First published as *Psychoanalyse des Kindes*.

(1933) 1944 The Early Development of Conscience in the Child. Pages 64–74 in Sandor Lorand (editor), *Psychoanalysis Today*. New York: International Universities Press.

(1937) 1948 A Contribution to the Psychogenesis of Manic–Depressive States. Pages 282–310 in Melanie Klein, *Contributions to Psycho-analysis: 1921–1945*. London: Hogarth. → First published in Volume 16 of the *International Journal of Psycho-analysis*.

(1940) 1948 Mourning and Its Relation to Manic–Depressive States. Pages 311–338 in Melanie Klein, *Contributions to Psycho-analysis: 1921–1945*. London: Hogarth. → First published in Volume 21 of the *International Journal of Psycho-analysis*.

(1945) 1948 The Oedipus Complex in the Light of Early Anxieties. Pages 339–390 in Melanie Klein, *Contributions to Psycho-analysis: 1921–1945*. London: Hogarth. → First published in Volume 26 of the *International Journal of Psycho-analysis*.

(1946) 1952 Notes on Some Schizoid Mechanisms. Pages 292–320 in *Developments in Psycho-analysis*, by Melanie Klein et al. Edited by Joan Riviere. London: Hogarth. → First published in Volume 27 of the *International Journal of Psycho-analysis*.

(1948a) 1952 On the Theory of Anxiety and Guilt. Pages 271–291 in *Developments in Psycho-analysis*, by Melanie Klein et al. Edited by Joan Riviere. London: Hogarth. → First published in Volume 29 of the *International Journal of Psycho-analysis*.

1948b *Contributions to Psycho-analysis: 1921–1945*. International Psycho-analytic Library, No. 34. London: Hogarth.

1952a Some Theoretical Conclusions Regarding the Emotional Life of the Infant. Pages 198–236 in *Developments in Psycho-analysis*, by Melanie Klein et al. Edited by Joan Riviere. London: Hogarth.

1952b On Observing the Behavior of Young Infants. Pages 237–270 in *Developments in Psycho-analysis*, by Melanie Klein et al. Edited by Joan Riviere. London: Hogarth.

1955a The Psycho-analytic Play Technique: Its History and Significance. Pages 3–22 in Melanie Klein, Paula Heimann, and R. E. Money-Kyrle (editors), *New Directions in Psycho-analysis*. London: Tavistock.

1955b On Identification. Pages 309–345 in Melanie Klein, Paula Heimann, and R. E. Money-Kyrle (editors), *New Directions in Psycho-analysis*. London: Tavistock.

1957 *Envy and Gratitude*. New York: Basic Books.

1961 *Narrative of a Child Analysis*. London: Hogarth. → Published posthumously.

### SUPPLEMENTARY BIBLIOGRAPHY

RIVIERE, JOAN (1936) 1952 On the Genesis of Psychical Conflict in Earliest Infancy. Pages 37–66 in *Developments in Psycho-analysis*, by Melanie Klein et al. Edited by Joan Riviere. London: Hogarth. → First published in Volume 17 of the *International Journal of Psycho-analysis.*

WAELDER, ROBERT 1937 The Problem of the Genesis of Psychical Conflict in Earliest Infancy. *International Journal of Psycho-analysis* 18:406–473.

## KLUCKHOHN, CLYDE

Clyde Kluckhohn (1905–1960) made his major contributions to the social sciences in his works on Navajo ethnography and in his theoretical writing on culture pattern and value theory. He also did pioneering work in the field of culture and personality, engaged in some research in linguistics and human genetics, and wrote a few papers in archeology.

Born in Le Mars, Iowa, Clyde Kluckhohn was adopted by Katherine and George Wesley Kluckhohn. He prepared for college at the Lawrenceville School in New Jersey and began his undergraduate studies at Princeton. Ill health interrupted his studies, and an experience followed which had a profound effect upon his later career. His family sent him to a ranch in New Mexico where the nearest neighbors were Navajo Indians. Young Kluckhohn developed an immediate interest in these Indian neighbors and began to learn to speak Navajo and to try to understand their customs. He obviously had both a persistent curiosity about exotic customs and a deep sensitivity to the nuances of alien ways of life—two qualities essential for an anthropologist. He fell in love with the Southwest and its people, undertook a long pack trip to the Rainbow Bridge, and published his first book, *To the Foot of the Rainbow* (1927), when he was only 22 years old. He returned to undergraduate work by enrolling at the University of Wisconsin, where he took his A.B. in 1928. He studied at the University of Vienna, where he had experience with psychoanalysis, in 1931–1932, and at Oxford, where he studied with R. R. Marett as a Rhodes scholar in 1932. From 1932 to 1934 he served as assistant professor of anthropology at the University of New Mexico. He completed his PH.D. in anthropology at Harvard in 1936. During this decade he kept in close touch with the Navajos, making a number of pack trips to completely unexplored country on Wild Horse Mesa in southern Utah and writing his second book, *Beyond the Rainbow* (1933), about these experiences.

In 1935 Kluckhohn was appointed an instructor of anthropology at Harvard, and the rest of his academic career was spent at Harvard, where he rose to full professorship and chairmanship of the department and became a stimulating teacher for several academic generations of students. He was also one of the founders of the Department of Social Relations and the first director of the Russian Research Center at Harvard.

Through all these years he seldom passed up an opportunity to return to the Southwest for field work among the Navajo, for it was there that he was most relaxed and there that his most creative intellectual work was done. He took great pride in his ability to speak fluent Navajo—an extremely difficult language for a person brought up speaking an Indo-European language—and in the close rapport he developed with hundreds of Navajo. From these Navajo studies came a number of classic monographs and a large number of articles in the specialized journals. Between 1936 and 1948 he also served as director of the "Ramah Project," which involved some 15 graduate students and colleagues from Harvard and elsewhere who published many technical monographs and articles. The project's goal was to make a long-range, intensive study of a small community, Ramah, New Mexico, in order to describe very precisely the patterns of Navajo culture and to analyze the processes of change. In 1949 he became the key founder and member of the advisory board (along with J. O. Brew and Talcott Parsons) of the "Comparative Study of Values in Five Cultures Project," which undertook far-ranging field operations among the Navajo, Zuñi, Spanish-American, Mormon, and Texan communities that were located in proximity to Ramah. This project, sponsored by the Laboratory of Social Relations and the Peabody Museum at Harvard, financed by a grant from the Rockefeller Foundation, and directed by John M. Roberts and Evon Z. Vogt, involved 37 field workers from a variety of the behavioral sciences and produced a large number of theoretical and empirical monographs and papers covering the ethnography and the value systems of the five cultures that were under investigation.

Kluckhohn's own Navajo research was characterized by painstaking attention to ethnographic detail combined with sophisticated theoretical analysis. He was clearly a most gifted field worker, and his continuing relationships with the Navajo permitted a level of understanding of their intricate patterns of life that cannot be achieved by field work that extends over only a season or two of investigation. He was also a vociferous reader in seven languages and was able to keep abreast of current developments in anthropology and also in sociology, psychology, and philosophy, both in the United States and abroad. This scholarly sophistication was applied to the analysis of much of his

Navajo data, especially to his classic study *Navaho Witchcraft* (1944). This monograph was a landmark in the combined use of theories drawn from the social structuralists, the psychoanalysts, and the psychologists specializing in "learning theory," in order to demonstrate how beliefs about witches functioned as both scapegoat and social control mechanisms in Navajo society.

As an anthropologist, Kluckhohn was far more than an eminent authority on the Navajo. He was deeply concerned that anthropologists develop their theories and refine their methods to a point where they could begin to think of anthropology as a science. However, it is extremely difficult to characterize his theoretical position. Rather than develop a tight theoretical scheme, he was eclectic in theoretical matters. This precluded his founding a "school" with "disciples," and hence a focused effort to develop a particular type of anthropology. Instead he had the virtue of cultivating and encouraging novel and oftentimes "off-beat" ideas in his students. Curiously, the theories that he developed himself had little in common with those of the anthropologists with whom he studied during his graduate student days: his early professors in Vienna, Robert R. Marett at Oxford, or Alfred Tozzer, Roland B. Dixon, and Earnest A. Hooton at Harvard. Rather, two things appear to have happened. From the very beginning, he ranged well beyond the field of anthropology for ideas and insights. He also responded strongly to the influence of four men with whom he never studied as a graduate student: Edward Sapir, Franz Boas, Ralph Linton, and Alfred Kroeber. Sapir clearly stimulated his interest in culture pattern theory, as did Linton. He came to have great admiration for the contributions of Boas. And in the last 15 years of his life he developed a very close intellectual and personal relationship with Kroeber. Although the relationships were not as close, Kluckhohn was an admirer of the contributions of Ruth Benedict and Robert Redfield, whose intellectual interests were very similar to the ideas he was working on at the time of his death.

Kluckhohn's most impressive contributions on culture pattern and value theory are found in a series of brilliant papers on levels and types of patterning in culture and on value systems, and in brief form in his semipopular *Mirror for Man* (1949). In his work on patterns, he made notable contributions to the understanding of "covert" or "implicit" patterns in culture, i.e., regularities in behavior of which the members of a society may be minimally aware but which are nonetheless patterned to the same extent as the customs that are

quite explicit (on this subject, see especially 1941; 1943; and, with W. H. Kelly, 1945). His theoretical work with values took two forms: a search for universal values and the development of a series of categories derived from Roman Jakobson's emphasis upon the importance of binary oppositions in the structure of language. The papers on universal values (see especially 1952; 1953; 1955) played a critical role in the shift in anthropological thinking from the view that all cultures are relative to the position that, despite wide differences in customs, there are certain fundamental human values common to all the diverse cultures of the world. The application of "binary distinctive features" analysis to value systems was just beginning to emerge in his writings in the last few years of his life (see especially 1956; 1958). It is too early to judge whether this method of analysis will provide a lasting contribution to the study of values, but it was at the least a pioneering attempt to bring some order into what has been and will continue to be one of our most difficult areas of study in the social sciences.

EVON Z. VOGT

[*For the historical context of Kluckhohn's work, see* ANTHROPOLOGY; ETHNOGRAPHY; VALUES; *and the biographies of* BENEDICT; BOAS; KROEBER; LINTON; SAPIR.]

### WORKS BY KLUCKHOHN

1927    *To the Foot of the Rainbow.* New York: Century.

1933    *Beyond the Rainbow.* Boston: Christopher.

(1937–1960) 1962    *Culture and Behavior: Collected Essays.* Edited by Richard Kluckhohn. New York: Free Press. → Contains a bibliography of Kluckhohn's works.

1938    KLUCKHOHN, CLYDE; and WYMAN, LELAND C. Navaho Classification of Their Song Ceremonials. American Anthropological Association, *Memoirs,* No. 50.

1940    KLUCKHOHN, CLYDE; and WYMAN, LELAND C. An Introduction to Navaho Chant Practice. American Anthropological Association, *Memoirs,* No. 53.

(1941) 1960    Patterning as Exemplified in Navaho Culture. Pages 109–130 in *Language, Culture and Personality: Essays in Memory of Edward Sapir.* Salt Lake City: Univ. of Utah Press.

1943    Covert Culture and Administrative Problems. *American Anthropologist* New Series 45:213–227.

1944    *Navaho Witchcraft.* Cambridge, Mass.: Peabody Museum.

1945    KLUCKHOHN, CLYDE; and KELLY, W. H. The Concept of Culture. Pages 78–105 in *The Science of Man in the World Crisis.* Edited by Ralph Linton. New York: Columbia Univ. Press.

(1946) 1951    KLUCKHOHN, CLYDE; and LEIGHTON, DOROTHEA (CROSS) *The Navaho.* Oxford Univ. Press.

1947    LEIGHTON, DOROTHEA (CROSS); and KLUCKHOHN, CLYDE *Children of the People: The Navaho Individual and His Development.* Cambridge, Mass.: Harvard Univ. Press.

1949 *Mirror for Man: The Relation of Anthropology to Modern Life.* New York: McGraw-Hill.

1951 McCOMBE, LEONARD *Navaho Means People.* Photographs by Leonard McCombe, text by Evon Z. Vogt and Clyde Kluckhohn. Cambridge, Mass.: Harvard Univ. Press.

1952 Universal Values and Anthropological Relativism. Volume 4, pages 87–112 in *Modern Education and Human Values.* Univ. of Pittsburgh Press.

1952 KLUCKHOHN, CLYDE; and KROEBER, ALFRED L. *Culture: A Critical Review of Concepts and Definitions.* Cambridge, Mass.: Peabody Museum.

(1953) 1961 Universal Categories of Culture. Pages 89–105 in Frank W. Moore (editor), *Readings in Cross-cultural Methodology.* New Haven: Human Relations Area Files Press.

1955 Ethical Relativity: Sic et Non. *Journal of Philosophy* 52:663–677.

1956 Toward a Comparison of Value-emphases in Different Cultures. Pages 116–132 in Leonard D. White (editor), *The State of the Social Sciences.* Univ. of Chicago Press.

1958 The Scientific Study of Value, and Contemporary Civilization. American Philosophical Society, *Proceedings* 102:469–476.

SUPPLEMENTARY BIBLIOGRAPHY

PARSONS, TALCOTT; and VOGT, EVON Z. 1962 Clyde Kay Maben Kluckhohn: 1905–1960. *American Anthropologist* New Series 64:140–148. → Includes a bibliography of Kluckhohn's works.

## KNAPP, GEORG FRIEDRICH

Georg Friedrich Knapp (1842–1926), economic historian and theorist, was born in Giessen and studied in Munich, Berlin, and Göttingen. Early in his career, as head of the statistical office of the city of Leipzig, he revealed a considerable mastery of statistics by publishing the first systematic theory of mortality measurement (1868). From 1867 to 1874 he taught at the University of Leipzig, and during this period he published other works in which he applied mathematical methods to demographic problems (1871; 1874).

When Knapp accepted a new academic appointment at the University of Strassburg, where he was to remain until 1919, he also shifted his scholarly interests. He turned to agricultural history and produced his classic study of the emancipation of the peasants and the rise of a class of rural workers (1887). Although focusing primarily on Prussia, the study was a comparative one: Knapp compared the agricultural economic systems of the long-settled parts of Prussia and of western Germany, the estate economy (*Gutsherrschaft*) and landlordship (*Grundherrschaft*), respectively. Under landlordship, the seignorial owner possessed his own demesne, exercising the right of *dominium directum* over peasant holdings, claimed certain labors from the peasants, and enjoyed political and juridical authority over the villagers. In the estate economy, the noble owner operated his estate as a unit of production and tended to absorb the landholdings of the peasants, reducing them to a servile labor force working on the estate. Knapp found that landlordship was the prevailing system in most of western Germany, while the estate economy was predominant in the old provinces of Prussia. Moreover, the farther one moved east, the larger were the landed estates of the nobility and the worse the condition of the peasants and cottagers.

The dwindling of peasant holdings was accompanied by a decline in the size of the peasant population and so became a problem for the Prussian monarchy, whose military policies required a steady supply of peasant-born soldiers. Legislation was used to halt the increase in the size of noble estates and to stabilize the number of peasant farms. However, royal protection was contingent on serfdom, and, as Knapp showed, the nobility emancipated the peasants in order to absorb peasant holdings.

Peasants were eligible for emancipation—that is, for obtaining unencumbered property rights over their holdings—if they (a) owned a team of oxen or horses; (b) had their landholdings listed on the tax roll; and (c) had inherited usufruct rights over several generations. In return for freedom, the peasants had to compensate the nobility for its lost rights. Although this compensation could take the form of cash, in most cases the peasants paid by giving up from one-third to one-half of their landholdings. Peasants who lacked the qualifications for emancipation were separated from their lands in other ways: owners either refused to continue leases or raised the rentals and other obligations to such an extent that peasants defaulted in their payments and forfeited their land. In the event, they were little worse off than the "emancipated" peasants, and both groups of peasants came to constitute, Knapp concluded, the first real working class. The chief consequence of emancipation was to enhance the power of the *Junker* class that was to dominate the political life of Prussia for a century.

Another important discovery that emerged from Knapp's studies in economic history was that of the patriarchic organization of work on the estates. Rather than working as straight wage earners, impoverished peasants became cottagers who were paid primarily in kind and were thereby chained to the landed estate. Knapp's analysis of such economic systems as the estate economy had an impact on Max Weber, who developed further Knapp's theory that landed estates are a special form of capitalist enterprise with a patriarchic organization of work. Knapp's ground-breaking work in economic history became a model for many later studies.

Late in his career, Knapp's interests shifted again, this time to monetary theory. At the age of 63 he published his most controversial book, *The State Theory of Money* (1905). He singled out the function of money as a medium of exchange and thus saw its value as created by the state and accepted by the members of a nation-state. Issue by the state and acceptance by governmental fiscal agents gave money "validity" and general acceptance at face value. Knapp's critics have pointed out that popular respect for money depends not only on its creation by the state but also on its quantity and its consequent purchasing power; Knapp should not, therefore, have omitted the discussion of the role of the state in regulating the supply of money. Although it was a deliberate omission, it unfortunately prevented him from dealing with the criteria for determining the necessary money supply or from examining the ways in which the state could influence the public acceptance of domestic money.

Although Knapp's monetary theories became known internationally, his contribution was rejected by most professional economic theorists in Germany. Wieser accepted the *Nennwertbefehl* (the authority of the state to establish legal tender) only in the case of the hypothetical isolated state; neoliberals condemned Knapp as a monetary interventionist; only Max Weber incorporated the chartal (nominalistic) theory of money into his social economics. Outside of Germany, however, some of the followers of Keynes and of Pigou have developed an increasing intellectual sympathy for Knapp's ideas, since his "institutional" approach is a necessary precondition for their monetary theories and policies.

ARTHUR SCHWEITZER

[*See also* LAND TENURE; MANORIAL ECONOMY.]

### WORKS BY KNAPP

1868    *Über die Ermittlung der Sterblichkeit aus den Aufzeichnungen der Bevölkerungs-statistik.* Leipzig: Hinrichs.
1871    *Die neueren Ansichten über Moralstatistik.* Jena: Mauke.
1874    *Theorie des Bevölkerungs-wechsels: Abhandlungen zur angewandten Mathematik.* Brunswick (Germany): Vieweg.
(1887) 1927    *Die Bauernbefreiung und der Ursprung der Landarbeiter in den älteren Teilen Preussens.* 2 vols. 2d ed. Munich: Duncker & Humblot. → Volumes 2 and 3 of the *Ausgewählte Werke.*
(1891) 1909    *Die Landarbeiter in Knechtschaft und Freiheit.* 2d ed., enl. Leipzig: Duncker & Humblot.
1897    *Grundherrschaft und Rittergut.* Leipzig: Duncker & Humblot.
(1905) 1924    *The State Theory of Money.* 4th ed., enl. London: Macmillan. → First published as *Staatliche Theorie des Geldes.*
1925    *Einführung in einige Hauptgebiete der National-ökonomie.* Munich: Duncker & Humblot. → Volume 1 of the *Ausgewählte Werke.*
1958    KNAPP, GEORG F.; and BENDIXEN, FRIEDRICH *Zur staatlichen Theorie des Geldes; Ein Briefwechsel: 1905–1920.* Veröffentlichungen der List Gesellschaft, Vol. 10. Basel: Kyklos.
*Ausgewählte Werke.* 3 vols. Munich: Duncker & Humblot, 1925–1927.

### SUPPLEMENTARY BIBLIOGRAPHY

DÖRING, HERBERT (1921) 1922    *Die Geldtheorien seit Knapp.* 2d ed., enl. Greifswald (Germany): Bamberg.
GUTMANN, FRANZ 1932    Georg F. Knapp. Volume 8, page 578 in *Encyclopaedia of the Social Sciences.* New York: Macmillan.
SCHRÖDER, ERICH 1928    *Wert, Preis und Geld bei Knapp und Elster.* Rostock (Germany): Winterberg.
SCHUMPETER, JOSEPH A. 1926    Georg F. Knapp 1842–1926. *Economic Journal* (London) 36:512–514.

# KNIES, KARL

The economist Karl Knies (1821–1898), one of the founders of the German historical school, was born in Marburg (Lahn), the son of a police official. He read history, philosophy, and theology at the University of Marburg and in 1846 was awarded a doctorate and the rights of a docent in history and government.

Caught up in the political ferment of the mid-1840s, Knies increasingly turned his attention to current social issues, including problems of political economy. By doing so he was following in the footsteps of his mentor, Bruno Hildebrand, then professor of government at Marburg. As a champion of the liberal cause and as the scholar who later wrote the programmatic *Die National-ökonomie der Gegenwart und Zukunft* (1848), Hildebrand exerted an influence upon Knies that appears to have been profound.

In 1848 the liberal German government that had been swept into office by the revolution appointed Knies to a professorship at the technical college in Kassel and entrusted him with the reorganization of that institution. His appointment ended, of course, with the triumph of absolutism; moreover, when Knies refused to sign a loyalty oath, the reactionary government removed him from the teaching post he still held at Marburg.

Politically suspect to the authorities and without means of support, Knies went into exile in Switzerland, accepting a teaching post in the technical college at Schaffhausen. Continuing his research activities despite difficulties, he remained abroad for about three years. Eventually, in 1855, he was able to return to Germany when the University of Freiburg (Breisgau) offered him the chair of political science (*Staatswissenschaften*).

In this new environment Knies was to prove himself not only as a teacher and scholar but also as a popular public figure. Although he was a "foreigner" and a Protestant, in 1861 Baden's Catholic population elected him a deputy to the second chamber. There he distinguished himself as a foe both of clericalism and of the still existing feudal laws which hampered freedom of economic activity. During the next year he was chosen prorector of the university and, at the same time, appointed by the ducal authorities to the directorship of the newly created board of education. In the latter capacity Knies was assigned the reorganization of Baden's entire educational system. He proposed that secular control replace much of clerical supervision, but in spite of support by large sections of the population and by the majority of the teaching profession, Knies was unable to implement his reforms. He soon became the victim of political intrigue and was relieved of his directorship. Disappointed by these experiences, Knies gladly accepted a chair in government at the University of Heidelberg. He remained in Heidelberg for the rest of his life. Throughout the next thirty years, from 1865 to 1896, Knies's seminar was one of the principal centers for the study of political science in Germany.

Despite his political activities and personal hardships, Knies produced many and varied academic works. During the 1850s his studies ranged from a comparison of modern statistics and old-fashioned political arithmetic (1850) to monographs about the impact of the railways (1853*a*) and the telegraph system (1857) on the world at large and the German states in particular. These latter two studies demonstrate the thoroughness of research and the willingness to approach a problem from several vantage points so typical of Knies's work. At the same time, they betray Knies's somewhat limited vision; he saw the entire world in relation to the issue of German unity.

The force of mid-nineteenth century nationalism is inseparable from the genesis of the historical method in German political economy. When in 1853 Knies published *Die politische Ökonomie vom Standpunkte der geschichtlichen Methode*, his distaste as a patriot for the cosmopolitanism of the classical school is obvious. In the same spirit, Knies deprecated the dominant role of individual self-interest in the classical system, not only for being one-sided but also for being "subversive" with respect to his conception of a social order—an organically evolving community, which at each stage of its development requires a particular form of economic analysis.

Knies noted inconsistencies in the work of List, Roscher, and even Hildebrand, but he shared their basic ideals and assumptions regarding the social process: he wanted to develop an economic approach and, by implication, an economic policy which would reconcile the peculiarities of German society with the requirements of economic progress. Knies and many of his contemporaries harbored all kinds of petty bourgeois fears that liberal capitalism on the rampage would inevitably lead to a socialist nightmare. Given the power constellation of imperial Germany, it is not surprising that Knies's methodology and viewpoint became official doctrine in most German institutions of higher learning.

Anyone who reads Knies's voluminous writings on capital, money, and credit is bound to be impressed by his scholarship, theoretic ability, and pedagogical skills. Yet when he tackled specific economic problems he was unable to live up to the methodology prescribed by the historical school. As Henry Sidgwick put it in his presidential address to Section F of the British Association:

When Knies, for instance, is discussing the nature and functions of capital, money and credit . . . the lenders and borrowers, whose operations are contemplated, exhibit throughout the familiar features of the old economic man . . . we find everywhere the old economic motives assumed and the old method unhesitatingly applied. The proof of the pudding . . . is in the eating; but our historical friends make no attempt to set before us the new economic pudding which their large phrases seemed to promise. It is only the old pudding with a little more ethical sauce and a little more garnish of historical illustrations. (Sidgwick [1885] 1962, p. 88)

HERBERT KISCH

[*For the historical context of Knies's work, see* ECONOMIC THOUGHT, *article on* THE HISTORICAL SCHOOL; *and the biographies of* HILDEBRAND; LIST; ROSCHER.]

### WORKS BY KNIES

1850   *Die Statistik als selbständige Wissenschaft: Ein Beitrag zu einer kritischen Geschichte der Statistik seit Achenwall.* Kassel (Germany): Luckhardt.

1853*a*   *Die Eisenbahnen und ihre Wirkungen.* Brunswick (Germany): Schwetschke.

(1853*b*) 1930   *Die politische Ökonomie vom geschichtlichen Standpunkte.* New ed., enl. Leipzig: Buske. → First published as *Die politische Ökonomie vom Standpunkte der geschichtlichen Methode.*

1857    *Der Telegraph als Verkehrsmittel: Mit Erörterungen über den Nachrichtenverkehr überhaupt.* Tübingen (Germany): Laupp.

(1873–1879) 1931    *Geld und Credit.* 3 vols. Leipzig: Buske → Volume 1: *Das Geld.* Volumes 2 and 3: *Der Credit.*

SUPPLEMENTARY BIBLIOGRAPHY

Böhm-Bawerk, Eugen von    (1884–1912) 1959    *Capital and Interest.* 3 vols. South Holland, Ill.: Libertarian Press. → First published as *Kapital und Kapitalzins.* Volume 1: *History and Critique of Interest Theories,* 1884. Volume 2: *Positive Theory of Capital,* 1889. Volume 3: *Further Essays on Capital and Interest* was first published as appendices to Volume 2 of the 1909–1912 edition, and was printed in a separate volume in 1921.

Cohn, Gustav    1899    Karl Knies. *Economic Journal* 9: 489–492.

Eisermann, Gottfried    1956    *Die Grundlagen des Historismus in der deutschen Nationalökonomie.* Stuttgart (Germany): Enke.

Hildebrand, Bruno    (1848) 1922    *Die Nationalökonomie der Gegenwart und Zukunft, und andere gesammelte Schriften.* Jena: Fischer.

Kalveram, Gertrud    1933    *Die Theorien von den Wirtschaftsstufen.* Leipzig: Buske.

Karl Friedrich, Grand Duke of Baden    1892    *Carl Friedrichs von Baden brieflicher Verkehr mit Mirabeau und Du Pont.* 2 vols. Edited with an Introduction by Karl Knies. Heidelberg (Germany): Winter.

Lifschitz, Feitel    1914    *Die historische Schule der Wirtschaftswissenschaft.* Bern: Stämpfli.

Schumpeter, Joseph A.    (1954) 1960    *History of Economic Analysis.* Edited by E. B. Schumpeter. New York: Oxford Univ. Press.

Sidgwick, Henry    (1885) 1962    The Scope and Method of Economic Science. Pages 73–97 in British Association for the Advancement of Science, Economic Science and Statistics Section, *Essays in Economic Method.* Edited by R. L. Smyth. London: Duckworth.

Von Mises, Ludwig    (1912) 1953    *The Theory of Money and Credit.* New ed., enl. Translated by H. E. Batson. New Haven: Yale Univ. Press. → First published as *Theorie des Geldes und der Umlaufsmittel.*

Weber, Max    (1903–1906) 1952    Roscher und Knies und die logischen Probleme der historischen Nationalökonomie. Pages 1–145 in Max Weber, *Gesammelte Aufsätze zur Wissenschaftslehre.* 2d ed., rev. & enl. Tübingen (Germany): Mohr.

Weber, Max    (1903–1919) 1952    *Gesammelte Aufsätze zur Wissenschaftslehre.* 2d ed., rev. & enl. Tübingen (Germany): Mohr.

Werner, Ulrich    1938    *Der Einfluss der lutherischen Ethik auf die Sozial- und Wirtschaftsauffassung von Roscher und Knies.* Berlin: Ebering.

## KNIGHT, FRANK H.

Frank Hyneman Knight was born on a farm in McLean County, Illinois, in 1885. He received a motley education; his higher degrees commenced with a B.A. from Milligan College (Tennessee) in 1911, followed by two degrees (B.A. and M.A.) from the University of Tennessee in 1913, and a PH.D. from Cornell University in 1916. His major subjects ranged from chemistry, through German literature, to economics and philosophy. At Cornell he studied under Allyn Young, who was perhaps the only man to have exerted an important direct influence on Knight's economic ideas. His academic career included appointments at Cornell, Chicago, and Iowa before he finally returned in 1928 to the University of Chicago. Knight served as president of the American Economic Association in 1950, and in 1957 he was awarded the association's Francis Walker medal.

Knight has always lived primarily in the world of ideas, and he has not compromised his commitment by becoming involved in governmental service or in quasi journalism. He has never been much concerned with defending his own works, once completed, and in these works one senses the struggle of a man who seeks first of all to set his own thinking straight rather than to preach the gospel or to enhance his own professional stature. Frank Knight, the scholar–critic, the self-made intellectual, is a product of the American Midwest, and it is difficult to imagine that he could have emerged from the more sophisticated culture of the eastern seaboard.

**"Risk, Uncertainty and Profit."**    Knight's first major work, *Risk, Uncertainty and Profit* (1921), was written as a doctoral dissertation at Cornell in 1916. It won second prize in the Hart, Schaffner and Marx essay competition in 1917 and after rewriting was published as a book.

The motivation for this work, as with so much of Knight's writing, was the desire for clarification. Ambiguities remained in the formal neoclassical theory of economic organization, notably in relation to the role and meaning of pure profit and its connection with predictive knowledge. Critical of the lack of precision that seemed to be present in the Marshallian treatment, Knight made explicit the distinction between rent, which is a distributive share in the ordinary sense, and profit, which results from imperfect knowledge. In order to do this he was forced to spell out, in considerable detail, the features of a system in which competition is perfect, and his treatment represents, in a sense, the apogee of neoclassical theorizing. He fully recognized and stated quite explicitly that the model of perfect competition is an idealization of reality, not a description.

Lesser theorists who followed Knight overlooked this essential point and erroneously expected real world institutions to match up descriptively with the idealized model. Their overly simplistic comparisons of theoretical perfection and observed reality have permitted the critics of a competitive economic order to undermine effectively much of its general social support, especially when comparisons failed to consider the flaws of alternative arrangements. Since the rigorous formulation of the idealized competitive model, by Knight and others, did lend itself to this misinterpretation, it is appropriate to ask whether the relevant theory could have been so formulated as to prevent these results. The answer is, of course, that rigorous construction of the model was essential to the development of economic science as it exists.

To construct this model of the perfectly competitive economy, Knight explained profit as the result of uncertainty, which he distinguished sharply from risk. This step involved the differentiation, in degree, between those possible events which can be insured against, to which an objective probability calculus can be applied, and those possible events to which such a calculus cannot be applied. This important distinction between risk and uncertainty found its way quickly into the general structure of theory, and it represents one of Knight's more specific contributions to the standard body of doctrine.

Developments since 1921 in the theory of probability have tended to reduce somewhat the sharpness of the differentiation between risk and uncertainty, at least in any formal sense. The fact remains, nonetheless, that there exist certain uninsurable uncertainties in the institutional environment of modern business operation. Moreover, the distinction retains its formal validity, despite modern notions of probability, when it is recognized that insurance against the possibility of making wrong decisions removes all content from decision itself. To this extent, therefore, genuine Knightian uncertainty must exist in a world where decisions must be made and where decisions may be erroneous. As Knight quite explicitly stated in this early work, where there is no genuine uncertainty, there are no decisions [see DECISION MAKING, article on ECONOMIC ASPECTS; ECONOMIC EXPECTATIONS].

**Theory of economic organization.** Several generations of students at the University of Chicago obtained their "vision" of the whole economic process only after encountering Henry Simons' syllabus (for Economics 201, his course in introductory economic theory) and Frank Knight's monograph, *Economic Organization* (1933). The latter was first prepared in the early 1920s at Iowa, and it was later duplicated at Chicago. It was intended solely for student use, and it is in no sense an ordinary textbook, yet it contains the elements of theory that helped to establish for Chicago its

eminence in neoclassical economics. There is little in the monograph that is wholly original; its value is in its critical emphasis on key points, its clarification of ambiguous concepts and notions, and, finally, its integrated approach to the economy as a social organization.

In this monograph Knight used his now-familiar double dichotomy of the whole subject field, the sharp distinction between statics and dynamics on the one hand, and between the individual and the social economy on the other. He spelled out in some detail the five functions of an economic system, an approach that has since found its way into many introductory textbooks. He also used the image of the wheel of wealth or income, another standard textbook feature. He emphasized the central position of the economic principle—equalization of returns at the margin. Further, he stated the law of variable proportions, classifying the first, second, and third stages of the production function, and distinguished between the meanings of the law of diminishing returns. Finally, he stressed opportunity cost, a characteristic feature of his economic theory.

Many of the points made in this small monograph had been discussed, earlier and more thoroughly, in *Risk, Uncertainty and Profit* and in journal articles. But for Chicago graduate students, *Economic Organization* was the first encounter with Knight's basic thought. The monograph was not widely circulated beyond Chicago, and Knight's early theoretical contributions became known primarily through his first book and a series of important papers in the 1920s. His influence was notable at the London School of Economics, where, largely at the urging of Lionel Robbins, Knight's work became a necessary part of reading for an economics degree.

**Theory of capital.** In his early theoretical writings Knight accepted without much question the Austrian theory of capital, which utilizes the time period of production as the common denominator for abstract capital. Later he emphatically rejected this theory, and in the 1930s he published a series of important papers designed to show the fallacies inherent in the Austrian view.

Knight held that the Austrian theory is based more or less directly on the classical Ricardian model of an agricultural economy in which capital stock is conceived of as the subsistence for labor over the year until a new crop is harvested. This model of an economy, along with the classical tendency to "explain" all payments as rewards for "pain," produced the notion that the return to capital is a payment for waiting and that capital itself is nothing more than labor embodied in storable product. It is the capital theory that emerges from this model, which attempts to measure the quantity of abstract capital in terms of the time period between input and output, namely roundaboutness in production, that Knight flatly rejected. Capital, he asserted, is not embodied labor; there is no measurable time period of production, and an increase in the quantity of abstract capital need not amount to a lengthening of the production process. While Knight's criticism does not entirely apply to the more sophisticated versions of the Austrian theory, it did much to undermine the more elementary versions of the period-of-production approach.

Knight's own theory of capital is based on a consistent application of the theory of opportunity cost. The rate of return is determined by the real yield on capital investment at the margin, and the economy in equilibrium is adjusted so that the return is equalized in all uses. The long-run demand for investment is extremely elastic at ruling rates of return. There is little need for the tortuous reasoning involved in the Austrian theory, since the rate of return can be explained more straightforwardly.

This theory of capital has been somewhat neglected by other economists. This is largely due to the fact that attention has shifted away from abstract capital theory since the 1930s, so much so that it is now difficult to say just what pure theory of capital the majority of economists do accept. It is to be expected that when the attention of economists does return to this theory, Knight's contribution will be critically re-examined [see CAPITAL].

**The methodology of economics.**    Knight is the economist as philosopher, not the economist as scientist. Economic theory is for him an idealized construction, a logical system, not an explanatory science. His work represents the search for logical contradictions rather than for conceptually refutable hypotheses, although these two approaches can lead to quite similar results, as evidenced best by Knight's work on realism and its relevance for the theory of demand.

His conception of economic theory as relevant to idealized rather than actual behavior enables Knight to be both an abstract theorist and a severe critic of the "economic" explanation of human behavior. Theory allows prediction to the extent that men do, in fact, act in terms of economic motives and to the extent that they do not make errors. But since, in fact, these motives do not exclusively, or perhaps even primarily, determine behavior, and since there is no way of observing the extent to which they do, theory cannot be operational in the modern methodological sense. Theory can help in the understanding and explanation of behavior, but not in the scientific prediction of behavior.

**Limitations of economics as a science.**    Although he has written several books, Knight is essentially an essayist, and much of his work has taken the form of essays in "criticism of established dogma." It has been suggested that he is the ideal book reviewer, and in a real sense his whole work can be interpreted as a continuing review of the books that are written or read uncritically by so many others. Nowhere is this quality of Knight's work more evident than in *The Ethics of Competition* (1921–1935), a collection of essays (most of which had been previously published) edited by a group of his students.

The pervasive concern here is with the limits that must be placed on the economic way of looking at behavior, on the limitations of economics as a science. Knight's avowed skepticism of any extended application of theory places him alongside the American institutionalists. This question-ridden, almost answerless, set of essays shows that he is that rare theorist who is also an institutionalist, an institutionalist who is not a data collector.

In a classic discussion, he denied the givenness of human wants, emphasizing the continual emergence of wants in creative interplay with the environment. Central to Knight's conception of economic order are the game elements in economic behavior, the deliberate setting of goals designed to make the process of achieving them interesting in itself. This conception, in turn, leads to considerations and more questions regarding the establishment of rules for economic and social behavior, the formation of the social constitution.

**Social philosophy.**    Knight's concern with the larger issues of social philosophy is clear in his 1935 essay "Economic Theory and Nationalism" (in 1921–1935). Although written in the mid-1930s, the essay has remained relevant. Basically Knight is a pessimist, and his interpretation of the historical process is a tragic one. Liberalism, as a system of order, failed to realize what it might have become, partly because of its own excesses; socialism emerged as its replacement. While regretting the failure of what might have been, Knight nonetheless conveys perceptively the values inherent in systems alternative to liberalism, and he especially stresses the human desire to be part of a larger organic whole, suggesting the modern necessity of a "social" religion. This essay distills features of national socialism that transcend the disastrous experiments of the 1930s and 1940s, and its predictions continue to be relevant.

Knight's concern with the larger issues of social philosophy is also evident in a second volume of essays, *Freedom and Reform* (1929–1946), which, like its predecessor, was published by students. His shift toward philosophical issues, toward ethics, morals, and values, arises out of his developing conviction that these are the important issues for modern society. The economic problem, as such, is one of Western man's lesser worries; its removal will leave the problem of social order largely unchanged. The difficulties that twentieth-century man confronts are not centrally intellectual; scientific progress offers no panacea.

One of Knight's many crusades has been against the view, which he associates with John Dewey, that science in some instrumental sense can be used to solve social problems in a community of free men. Knight believes that science applied instrumentally implies control, whereas the social problem is one of attaining consensus, of securing mutual agreement. The "social engineer," so prevalent in the background of modern economic models, has no place in Knight's approach to social problems.

Modern man's central problem, according to Knight, is a moral one. Historical liberalism has destroyed conventional religion and has provided no effective substitute for it; as a consequence, men have turned all too quickly to nihilism or to the deification of the state. What men need, therefore, is a common morality founded on truth, honesty, mutual respect, and "good sportsmanship," the ethics that liberalism should have produced but somehow failed to.

It is noteworthy that Knight believes the prospects for a society embodying the liberal ethics improved, if only slightly, in the years after World War II. In his most recent book, *Intelligence and Democratic Action* (1960), he assesses somewhat more optimistically the possibility of a man's applying critical intelligence to his relationships with other men in organized political society. He warns against romanticism in all its varieties, and he calls for an education of the will rather than of the intellect, an education that must, above all, inculcate the critical attitude that is based on a respect for truth. "The distinctive virtue for men in a free society, the essence of the whole liberal view of life, is truth-seeking."

Surveying the history of Western civilization since the Enlightenment, Knight sees no clear indication that man can rise to the challenge presented by the liberation of his own mind. But in his later writings especially, one senses his increased willingness to leave this question open.

Knight's attitude toward organized religion is directly related to his commitment to truth-seeking. As he sees it, the very exercise of critical intelligence requires a willingness to examine all things objectively, to hold nothing sacrosanct. Religion is designed to "fence off" certain areas of inquiry and to ask that the individual accept certain precepts on faith. This represents the antithesis of the critical attitude, which Knight deems so essential. He insists that religious dogma is not different from other dogma and that it should be subject to the same critical scrutiny.

Knight's revulsion from religious dogma resulted from his overexposure in early life to the hell-fire and brimstone of prairie evangelism. His reaction against religious orthodoxy was, perhaps, an essential ingredient in his intellectual development: having rejected it, the less rigid dogma encountered in the world of scholarship became easy prey to the Midwestern skeptic.

**Assessment.** In his critical attitude and outlook, in his abhorrence of nonsense even in its most sophisticated forms, Frank Knight has much in common with David Hume, although Hume does not appear to have directly influenced Knight's thought. These two critics share a determination to cut through the metaphysical–linguistic fuzziness that enshrouds the human mind.

Knight is no social reformer in the ordinary sense of this term. He believes that reform, improvement, in social order can come only through man's acquisition of an ability, and a willingness, to use his own mind. Knight's emphasis is always on changing man's way of thinking about social problems rather than on changing social institutions in order to solve problems.

Knight has no "disciples" as such, and those who have been most influenced by his work are as likely to criticize him as others are. This is because as a teacher he has been almost uniquely willing to look for merit in all questions and because he has refused to accept any final answers. His attitude has always been that all principles have their limits, that most of them are both right and wrong, that they hold more or less, and that judgment can never be dispensed with. This is the central point in his 1950 presidential address to the American Economic Association (1951).

Scorning both the relativist and the absolutist, Knight finally insists on the relevance of the "relatively absolute absolutes," a position that makes him refuse to interpret matters in terms of black or white, yet, at the same time, allows him to hold steadfastly that man can, and must, use his own good judgment in making distinctions among the various shades of gray.

JAMES M. BUCHANAN

WORKS BY KNIGHT

(1921) 1957   *Risk, Uncertainty and Profit.* London School of Economics and Political Science, Series of Reprints of Scarce Tracts in Economic and Political Science, No. 16. New York: Kelley. → A paperback edition was published in 1965 by Harper.

(1921–1935) 1951   *The Ethics of Competition, and Other Essays.* New York: Kelley.

(1928–1951) 1956   *On the History and Method of Economics: Selected Essays.* Univ. of Chicago Press.

(1929–1946) 1947   *Freedom and Reform: Essays in Economics and Social Philosophy.* New York and London: Harper.

1932   Interest. Volume 8, pages 131–144 in *Encyclopaedia of the Social Sciences.* New York: Macmillan.

(1933) 1951   *The Economic Organization.* With an article, "Notes on Cost and Utility." New York: Kelley. → A paperback edition was published in 1966 by Harper.

1934   Profit. Volume 12, pages 480–486 in *Encyclopaedia of the Social Sciences.* New York: Macmillan.

1943a   The Ideal of Freedom: Conditions for Its Realization. Pages 87–118 in Charner M. Perry (editor), *The Philosophy of American Democracy.* Univ. of Chicago Press.

1943b   The Meaning of Freedom. Pages 59–86 in Charner M. Perry (editor), *The Philosophy of American Democracy.* Univ. of Chicago Press.

(1945) 1948   KNIGHT, FRANK H.; and MERRIAM, THORNTON W. *The Economic Order and Religion.* London: Routledge.

1951   The Rôle of Principles in Economics and Politics. *American Economic Review* 41:1–29.

1960   *Intelligence and Democratic Action.* Cambridge, Mass.: Harvard Univ. Press.

# KNOWLEDGE, SOCIOLOGY OF

The sociology of knowledge may be broadly defined as that branch of sociology which studies the relation between thought and society. It is concerned with the social or existential conditions of knowledge. Scholars in this field, far from being restricted to the sociological analysis of the cognitive sphere as the term would seem to imply, have concerned themselves with practically the entire range of intellectual products—philosophies and ideologies, political doctrines, and theological thought. In all these areas the sociology of knowledge attempts to relate the ideas it studies to the sociohistorical settings in which they are produced and received.

Assertions as to how social structures are functionally related to categories of thought and to specific sets of ideas have a long history. At the beginning of the seventeenth century, Francis Bacon outlined the general territory when he wrote about

impressions of nature, which are imposed upon the mind by the sex, by the age, by the region, by health and sickness, by beauty and deformity, and the like, which are inherent and not extern; and again, those which are caused by extern fortune; as sovereignty, nobility, obscure birth, riches, want, magistracy, privateness, prosperity, adversity, constant fortune, variable fortune, rising *per saltum, per gradus,* and the like.   ([1605] 1958, p. 170)

This is indeed the field that later systematic sociology of knowledge claimed as its province.

A variety of European thinkers of the seventeenth, eighteenth, and early nineteenth centuries may be considered among the precursors of the sociology of knowledge. Several of the *philosophes* of the Enlightenment (Condorcet in particular) inquired about the social preconditions of different types of knowledge, and Auguste Comte's famous "law of three stages," asserting the intimate relationship between types of social structures and types of knowledge, might well be considered a contribution to the sociology of knowledge. It nevertheless remains true that systematic development of the sociology of knowledge as an autonomous enterprise rather than as a by-product of other types of inquiry received its main impetus from two trends in nineteenth-century European sociological thought: the Marxian tradition in Germany and the Durkheimian tradition in France. Although neither these two mainstreams—nor their tributaries—are by any means identical in their fundamental assumptions, they are the starting point of most theorizing in the field.

## Marx and the German tradition

In his attempt to dissociate himself from the panlogical system of his former master, Hegel, as well as from the "critical philosophy" of his former "young Hegelian" friends, Karl Marx undertook, in some of his earlier writings, to establish a connection between philosophies and the concrete social structures in which they emerged. "It has not occurred to any of these philosophers," wrote Marx in *The German Ideology,* "to inquire into the connection of German philosophy with German reality, the relation of their criticism to their own material surroundings" (Marx & Engels [1845–1846] 1939, p. 6). This programmatic orientation once established, Marx proceeded to analyze the ways in which systems of ideas appeared to depend on the social positions—particularly the class positions—of their proponents.

In his struggle against the dominant ideas of his time, Marx was led to a resolute relativization of these ideas. The eternal verities of dominant thought appeared upon analysis to be but the direct or indirect expression of the class interests of their exponents. Marx attempted to explain ideas systematically in terms of their functions and to relate the thought of individuals to their social roles and class positions: "The mode of production in material life determines the general character of the social, political and spiritual processes of life. It is not the consciousness of men that determines their existence, but on the contrary their social existence determines their consciousness" ([1859] 1913, pp. 11–12). While Marx was mainly concerned with uncovering the relationships between bourgeois ideas and bourgeois interests and life styles, he nevertheless explicitly stated that the same relation also held true with regard to the emergence of new dissident and revolutionary ideas. According to the *Communist Manifesto,*

What else does the history of ideas prove, than that intellectual production changes its character in proportion as material production is changed? The ruling ideas of each age have ever been the ideas of its ruling class. When people speak of ideas that revolutionize society, they do but express the fact that within the old society the elements of a new one have been created, and that the dissolution of the old ideas keeps even pace with the dissolution of the old conditions of existence. (Marx & Engels 1848, p. 91 in 1964 paperback edition)

In their writings of a later period, Marx and Engels were to qualify their somewhat sweeping initial statements, which had most often been made in a polemical context. They were thus led to grant a certain degree of intrinsic autonomy to the development of legal, political, religious, literary, and artistic ideas. They now stressed that mathematics and the natural sciences were exempt from the direct influence of the social and economic infrastructure. Moreover, they now granted that the intellectual superstructure of a society was not simply a reflection of the infrastructure but rather could in turn react upon it.

While the original Marxian thesis reinterpreted in this fashion became a considerably more flexible instrument, it also lost some of its distinctive qualities. Interpreted rigidly, it tended to lend itself to use as a rather crude tool for debunking all adverse thought; interpreted flexibly, it became difficult to distinguish from non-Marxian attempts at the functional analysis of thought. Also, as Merton has pointed out ([1949] 1957, p. 479), when the Marxian thesis is stated in so flexible a

manner, it becomes impossible to invalidate it at all, since any set of data may be so interpreted as to fit it.

Despite these difficulties, Marxian modes of analysis in this field, as in so many others, exerted a powerful—if often subterranean—influence on subsequent German social thought. Major portions of the work of Max Weber can be seen as attempts on the part of this greatest of all German sociologists to come to terms with the Marxian inheritance and particularly with the Marxian assertion of the essentially epiphenomenal character of knowledge and ideas. The twin heritage of Marx and of Nietzsche (particularly the latter's "debunking" attack on Christianity as a slave philosophy of *ressentiment*-laden lower-status groups) loomed very large in the mental climate of pre-World War I Germany. But it remained for two German scholars, Max Scheler and Karl Mannheim, to develop a corpus of theory that represents the first systematic elaboration of the sociology of knowledge as a new scientific discipline. Even though it followed upon the work of Max Scheler, Karl Mannheim's contribution will be dealt with first, since it is more directly tied to the main themes of Marxian thought.

**Mannheim and universal relativism.**  Mannheim undertook to generalize the Marxian interpretation so as to divest it of polemical elements; thus he attempted to transform into a general tool of analysis what for Marx had been primarily a means of attack against adversaries. Mannheim wished to create a tool that could be used as effectively for the analysis of Marxism as for any other system of thought. While in the Marxian formulations attention was called to the function of ideology in the defense of class privileges and to the distortions and falsifications of ideas that flowed from the privileged class position of bourgeois thinkers, Marx's own ideas were held by Marxists to be true and unbiased by virtue of their being an expression of classes that had no privileged interests to defend. According to Marx, the defenders of the *status quo* were inevitably given to false consciousness, while their critics, being affiliated with the emerging working class, were exempt from such distorting influences and hence had access to "true consciousness"—that is, to nondistorted historical truth. Mannheim's orientation, in contradistinction, allowed for the probability that all ideas, even "truths," were related to, and hence influenced by, the social and historical situation from which they emerged. The very fact that each thinker is affiliated with particular groups in society—that he occupies a certain status and enacts certain social roles—colors his intellectual outlook. Men "do not confront the objects of the world from the abstract levels of a contemplating mind as such, nor do they do so exclusively as solitary beings. On the contrary they act with and against one another in diversely organized groups, and while doing so they think with and against one another" (Mannheim [1929–1931] 1954, p. 3).

Mannheim was thus led to define the sociology of knowledge as a theory of the social or existential conditioning of thought. To him all knowledge and all ideas, although to different degrees, are "bound to a location" within the social structure and the historical process. At particular times a particular group can have fuller access to the understanding of a social phenomenon than other groups, but no group can have total access to it. (At times, though, Mannheim expressed the hope that "detached intellectuals" might in our age achieve a "unified perspective" free of existential determination.) The task of the new discipline was to ascertain the empirical correlation between intellectual standpoints and structural and historical positions.

From its inception Mannheim's thesis encountered a great deal of criticism, especially on the grounds that it led to universal relativism. It has been said that the notion of relativism, or relationism—the term that Mannheim preferred—"is self-contradictory, for it must presuppose its own absoluteness. The sociology of knowledge . . . must assume its own validity if it is to have any meaning" (Dahlke 1940, p. 87). If it is assumed that all thought is existentially determined and hence all truth but relative, Mannheim's own thought cannot claim privileged exemption.

Mannheim did indeed lay himself open to such attacks, especially in his earlier writings; however, it seems that he did not mean to imply that "existential determination" (*Seinsverbundenheit*) is a kind of total determination that leaves no room for an examination of ideas in other terms. He explicitly stated that in the social sciences, as elsewhere, "the ultimate criterion of truth or falsity is to be found in the investigation of the object, and the sociology of knowledge is no substitute for this" ([1929–1931] 1954, p. 4). No matter what the imprecisions and methodological shortcomings of Mannheim's theoretical statements are judged to be, he left a number of concrete studies on such topics as "Conservative Thought" ([1922–1940] 1953, pp. 77–164) and "Competition as a Cultural Phenomenon" ([1923–1929] 1952, pp. 191–229) which have been recognized as important contributions even by those who have been critical of Mannheim's theoretical apparatus.

**Scheler's "real factors."** Marx laid primary stress on economic and class factors in the determination of ideas; Mannheim expanded this conception to include other groupings such as generations, status groups, and occupational groups. Max Scheler went still further in widening the range of factors that influence thought forms. According to Scheler, there is no constant independent variable that determines the emergence of ideas; but rather, in the course of history, there occurs a sequence of "real factors" that condition thought. In nonliterate groups, blood and kinship ties constitute the independent variable; later, political factors; and, finally, in the modern world economic factors are to be considered as the independent variables to which thought structures have to be related.

Scheler rejected what he considered the "naturalism" and relativism of previous theorizing in the field and asserted that there exists an atemporal, absolute order of values and ideas—that is, a realm of eternal essences, which is totally distinct from historical and social reality. At different moments in historical time and in different cultural systems, different "real factors" predominate. These real factors "open and close, in determinate ways and determinate order, the sluice gates of the stream of thought," so that different aspects of the eternal realm of essences can be grasped at particular points in time and in particular cultural systems (1926). Thus Scheler thought that he had succeeded in reconciling sociocultural relativity with the Platonic notion of an eternal realm of unchanging essences.

Scheler's theory of eternal essences is metaphysical and hence not susceptible to scientific validation. However, his proposal to widen the range of existential factors that may be seen as the source of particular systems of ideas is testable and potentially fruitful for research. Scheler's own studies provide important examples of the fruitfulness of this type of inquiry: for example, his studies on the interrelations between the hierarchical medieval world of communal estates and the medieval conception of the world as a hierarchy culminating in God, between the content of Plato's theory of ideas and the formal organization of the Platonic Academy, and between the rise of mechanistic models of thought and the rise of bourgeois, *Gesellschaft* types of society. (For a different view of Scheler, see Ranulf 1938.)

### French contributions

Émile Durkheim's contributions to the sociology of knowledge form only a relatively small part of his total work. Although some of his statements in this area are mixed with epistemological speculations that most experts would consider rather dubious, he nevertheless did some of the most vital pioneering work in the field. In his attempt to establish the social origin and functions of morals, values, and religion, and in explaining these as different forms of "collective representations," Durkheim was led to consider a similar social explanation of the basic forms of logical classification and of the fundamental categories of thought themselves.

Durkheim attempted to account for the origins of spatial, temporal, and other classifications among nonliterate peoples and concluded that these classifications closely approximated the social organization of these peoples (Durkheim & Mauss 1903). The first "classes," he suggested, were classes of men, and the classification of objects in the world of nature was but an extension of the social classification already established. All animals and natural objects were classified as belonging to this or that clan, phratry, or residential or kinship group. He further argued that, although scientific classifications have now largely become divorced from their social origins, the very manner in which we classify things as "belonging to the same family" still reveals the originally social origins of classificatory thought.

In his last major book, *The Elementary Forms of the Religious Life* (1912), Durkheim returned to these earlier ideas and attempted a sociological explanation of all fundamental categories of human thought, especially the concepts of time and space. These, he claimed, are not only transmitted by society, they are social creations. Society is decisive in the genesis of logical thought by forming the concepts of which that thought is made. The social organization of the primitive community is the model for the primitive's spatial organization of his surrounding world. Similarly, temporal divisions into days, weeks, months, and years correspond to periodical recurrences of rites, feasts, and ceremonies: "A calendar expresses the rhythm of the collective activities, while at the same time its function is to assure their regularity" ([1912] 1954, p. 10).

These Durkheimian notions have been challenged frequently. It has been pointed out, for example, that Durkheim slighted the importance of the rhythm of natural phenomena by his overemphasis on social rhythms (Sorokin 1928, p. 477). More fundamentally, Claude Lévi-Strauss has argued that society "cannot exist without symbolism, but instead of showing how the appearance of symbolic thought makes social life altogether pos-

sible and necessary, Durkheim tries the reverse, i.e., to make symbolism grow out of society. . . . Sociology cannot explain the genesis of symbolic thought, but has just to take it for granted in man" (1945, p. 518).

Durkheim failed to establish the social origins of all categories of thought, but it is important to recognize his pioneering contribution to the study of the correlations between specific systems of thought and systems of social organization. It is this part of Durkheim's contribution, rather than some of the more debatable epistemological propositions found in his work, that has influenced later developments in the sociology of knowledge. Thus the eminent Sinologist Marcel Granet (1934) used Durkheimian leads when he related the conceptions of time and space in ancient Chinese thought to such social factors as the ancient feudal organization and the rhythmic alterations of concentrated and dispersed group activities. Jane Harrison (1912) and Francis Cornford (1912) renovated classical studies by tracing Greek religious notions and philosophical ideas to their origins in tribal initiation ceremonies and to the clan structure of the Greek tribes. Finally, Maurice Halbwachs (1925) attempted to establish how even such apparently private and intimate mental activities as dreams and memories need for their organization a stable reference in the group life in which individuals participate. [*See* Durkheim; Granet; Halbwachs.]

## American sociology of knowledge

The work of the major American pragmatists—Peirce, James, and Dewey—abounds with suggestive leads for the sociology of knowledge. To the extent that pragmatism stressed the organic process by which every act of thought is linked to human conduct and thus rejected the radical distinction between thinking and acting which had informed most classical philosophy, it prepared the ground for consideration of the more specifically sociological links between social conditions and the thought processes. Insofar as the pragmatists stressed that thought is in its very nature bound to the social situation in which it arises, they set the stage for efforts to inquire into the relations between a thinker and his audience. Insofar as they rejected the traditional view according to which an object of thought was to be sharply distinguished from the thinking subject and stressed the intimate transactions between subject and object, they prepared the ground for the specifically American contributions to the sociology of knowledge.

Pragmatic philosophy is not the only American

intellectual trend to influence the development of the sociology of knowledge. American historical scholarship, especially the work of Charles A. Beard and Vernon L. Parrington, appropriated for its own uses a number of the orientations of European sociology of knowledge—especially of its Marxian variety—in efforts to develop new perspectives on American politics and letters by self-consciously relating currents of thought to economic interest and social condition. Many of these strains of ideas had only an indirect impact on American sociology. In contrast, two major American thinkers, Thorstein Veblen and George Herbert Mead, directly and explicitly influenced American sociology of knowledge.

Veblen's emphasis on habits of thought as an outcome of habits of life and his stress on the dependence of thought styles on community organization are well known. Perhaps less well known is Veblen's relatively systematic effort to relate styles of thought to the occupational roles and positions of their proponents. "The scheme of thought or of knowledge," he wrote, "is in good part a reverberation of the schemes of life" ([1891–1913] 1961, p. 105); hence, those engaged in pecuniary occupations are likely to develop thought styles that differ from the styles of those engaged in industrial occupations. Magical as well as matter-of-fact ways of thinking find their proponents among groups of men differentially located in the social structure and in the economic process. Moreover, Veblen's savage polemics in his *Higher Learning in America* (1918) should not be read as polemics alone. The work is also, and perhaps above all, a seminal contribution to the sociological study of the organization and functioning of the American university.

Finally, George Herbert Mead's social behaviorism, with its insistence that mind itself is a social product and is of social origin, provided the social psychological basis for some of the assertions of previous theorists. For Mead, communication was central to an understanding of the nature of mind: "Mind arises through communication by a conversation of gestures in a social process or context of experience" (1934, p. 50). Even when certain epistemological positions of Mead are not accepted, it would seem very difficult to deny his claim that if determinants of thought other than society itself exist, they can structure mind only through the intermediary of the social relations in which it is necessarily enmeshed. [See MEAD.]

**Contemporary trends.** As the sociology of knowledge has been incorporated into general sociological theory both in America and in Europe, it has often merged with other areas of research and is frequently no longer explicitly referred to as sociology of knowledge. Its diffusion through partial incorporation has tended to make it lose some of its distinctive characteristics. Thus, the works of Robert K. Merton (1949) and Bernard Barber (1952) in the sociology of science, the works of E. C. Hughes (1958), T. H. Marshall ([1934–1949] 1950, chapter 4), Theodore Caplow (1954), Oswald Hall (1948), Talcott Parsons (1938–1953), and others in the sociology of the professions and occupations, and—even more generally—much of the research concerned with social roles may be related to, and in part derived from, the orientations of the sociology of knowledge. Many practitioners of what is in fact sociology of knowledge may at times be rather surprised when it is pointed out that, like Monsieur Jourdain, they have been "talking prose" all along.

Given this wide variety of research in which at least certain leads of the sociology of knowledge have been utilized, it is difficult to delineate the distinctive characteristics of contemporary or near contemporary developments in the sociology of knowledge in the United States. Yet one characteristic seems salient. While in the European tradition attention tended to be centered upon the production of ideas, with the axiomatic assumption that different strata of society produce different types of ideas, modern American research is more concerned with the consumption of ideas and the ways in which different strata of society use standardized thought products. To some extent, as Merton has pointed out ([1949] 1957, pp. 440 ff.), the sociology of public opinion and mass communication has pre-empted the place of the sociology of knowledge in the contemporary United States.

Nevertheless, recent American contributions have by no means been limited to this field. There has been a significant attempt at stocktaking and at discussing methodological questions left unresolved by the European tradition. Merton's writings in this area represent the most sophisticated codification of the problems faced by the sociology of knowledge. Among other notable contributions to the methodology and theoretical clarification of the sociology of knowledge are those of the philosopher Arthur Child and the sociologists Hans Speier (1938), Gerald DeGré (1943), Kurt H. Wolff (1959), Werner Stark (1958), and C. Wright Mills (1963).

Among substantive American contributions, the work of Pitirim A. Sorokin is of special note (1937–1941; 1943). Blending an earlier European tradition of large-scale speculation with American statistical research techniques, Sorokin developed a characteristically idealistic theory of the sociology of knowledge. Rejecting the prevalent conceptualizations that consider social classes or other social and economic groups as the independent variable in the functional relations between thought and society, Sorokin considers variant "cultural mentalities" or cultural premises as the key variables. He attempts to show that the periodic dominance of three major cultural tendencies—the ideational, the idealistic, and the sensate mentality—can account for the fluctuations of types of knowledge that have marked history. Although his argument often seems to involve a kind of circular reasoning, and although the neglect of the existential roots of thought can hardly be justified in view of the promising results already achieved by Sorokin's predecessors, the many contributions by Sorokin and some of his students—in, for example, the sociology of science or the elucidation of the notion of social time—remain noteworthy.

Florian Znaniecki's neglected but important study, *The Social Role of the Man of Knowledge* (1940), represents, like Sorokin's work, a fruitful blending of the European tradition with American contributions. Znaniecki introduces the notion of the "social circle," that is, the audience or public to which a thinker addresses himself. He thus links the sociology of knowledge with research on publics and audiences that was pioneered by the Chicago school of sociology (for example, see Park 1904). Znaniecki shows that thinkers—at least in differentiated societies—are not likely to address their total society but rather only selected segments or publics. The thinker is related to a social circle; and this circle expects him to live up to certain of its demands, in exchange for which it grants him recognition and support. Men of knowledge anticipate the demands of their public; and they tend to form self-images, select data, and seize upon problems in terms of their actual or anticipated audiences. Men of knowledge may thus be classified in regard to their social roles and their publics. Hence it becomes possible to understand the emergence of such special roles as that of sage, technologist, and scholar in terms of the differentiated publics to which they address themselves. [*See* INTELLECTUALS.]

It is impossible to discuss or even enumerate within the confines of this article the recent American studies which either directly or indirectly contribute to the further development of the sociology of knowledge. This state of affairs may itself be an indicator of the continued strength of this research orientation. A few references will have to suffice.

Research in the field of social role, the sociology of science, the professions and occupations, and the sociology of communications and public opinion has already been mentioned. In other areas can be listed the studies exploring the relations between minority status and originality of intellectual perspective, to which Veblen (1919) made significant contributions, and of which the recent work by Melvin Seeman (1956) seems an excellent example; the studies in the history of sociological or philosophical theories, in which conceptualizations derived from the sociology of knowledge have been utilized—for example, the works of C. Wright Mills on pragmatism (1964); the studies that relate thought styles of American academic men to the structure and functioning of the American academy—such as Logan Wilson's *Academic Man* (1942), Lazarsfeld and Thielens' *Academic Mind* (1958), an analysis of social scientists' reactions to the threats posed by the McCarthy era, and Caplow and McGee's *Academic Marketplace* (1958); general studies of the settings and contexts in which intellectuals play their peculiar roles, such as Lewis Coser's *Men of Ideas* (1965); and Fritz Machlup's large-scale study, *The Production and Distribution of Knowledge in the United States* (1962). More detailed studies—such as Peter Berger's recent attempt to account for the popularity of psychoanalysis in America (1965) and John Bennett's study of divergent interpretations of the same culture by different social scientists in terms of their divergent backgrounds and social perspectives (1946)—have also been very much in evidence in recent years.

The sociology of knowledge was marked in its early history by a tendency to set up grandiose hypothetical schemes. These contributed a number of extremely suggestive leads. Recently its practitioners have tended to withdraw from such ambitious undertakings and to restrict themselves to somewhat more manageable investigations. Although this tendency has been an antidote to earlier types of premature generalizations, it also carries with it the danger of trivialization. Perhaps the sociology of knowledge of the future will return to the more daring concerns of its founders, thus building upon the accumulation of careful and detailed investigations by preceding generations of researchers.

LEWIS A. COSER

[*Directly related are the entries* MARXIST SOCIOLOGY; SOCIAL STRUCTURE, *article on* SOCIAL STRUCTURAL ANALYSIS. *Other relevant material may be found in* LITERATURE, *article on* THE SOCIOLOGY OF LITERATURE; SCIENCE; *and in the biographies of* BACON;

DEWEY; DURKHEIM; HALBWACHS; JAMES; MANNHEIM; MARX; PEIRCE; SCHELER; SOROKIN; VEBLEN; WEBER, MAX; ZNANIECKI.]

### BIBLIOGRAPHY

*For extensive bibliographies on the sociology of knowledge, see* Merton 1949; Mannheim 1929–1931; Maquet 1949; *and* Wolff 1959.

BACON, FRANCIS (1605) 1958 *The Advancement of Learning.* Edited with an introduction by G. W. Kitchin. London: Dent; New York: Dutton.

BARBER, BERNARD 1952 *Science and the Social Order.* Glencoe, Ill.: Free Press.

BENNETT, JOHN W. (1946) 1956 The Interpretation of Pueblo Culture: A Question of Values. Pages 203–216 in Douglas G. Haring (editor), *Personal Character and Cultural Milieu: A Collection of Readings.* 3d ed., rev. Syracuse Univ. Press. → First published in Volume 2 of the *Southwestern Journal of Anthropology.*

BERGER, PETER L. 1965 Toward a Sociological Understanding of Psychoanalysis. *Social Research* 32:26–41.

CAPLOW, THEODORE 1954 *The Sociology of Work.* Minneapolis: Univ. of Minnesota Press.

CAPLOW, THEODORE; and MCGEE, REECE J. 1958 *The Academic Marketplace.* New York: Basic Books. → A paperback edition was published in 1961 by Wiley.

CORNFORD, FRANCIS M. 1912 *From Religion to Philosophy: A Study in the Origins of Western Speculations.* New York: Longmans. → A paperback edition was published in 1957 by Harper.

COSER, LEWIS A. 1965 *Men of Ideas: A Sociologist's View.* New York: Free Press.

DAHLKE, H. OTTO 1940 The Sociology of Knowledge. Pages 64–89 in Harry E. Barnes, Howard Becker, and Frances B. Becker (editors), *Contemporary Social Theory.* New York: Appleton.

DEGRÉ, GERALD L. 1943 *Society and Ideology: An Inquiry Into the Sociology of Knowledge.* New York: Columbia Univ. Press.

DURKHEIM, ÉMILE (1912) 1954 *The Elementary Forms of the Religious Life.* London: Allen & Unwin; New York: Macmillan. → First published as *Les formes élémentaires de la vie religieuse, le système totémique en Australie.* A paperback edition was published in 1961 by Collier.

DURKHEIM, ÉMILE; and MAUSS, MARCEL (1903) 1963 *Primitive Classification.* Translated and edited by Rodney Needham. Univ. of Chicago Press. → First published as "De quelques formes primitives de classification" in *L'année sociologique.*

GRANET, MARCEL (1934) 1950 *Le pensée chinoise.* Paris: Michel.

HALBWACHS, MAURICE 1925 *Les cadres sociaux de la mémoire.* Paris: Alcan.

HALL, OSWALD 1948 Stages of a Medical Career. *American Journal of Sociology* 53:327–336.

HARRISON, JANE ELLEN (1912) 1927 *Themis: A Study of the Social Origins of Greek Religion.* 2d ed., rev. Cambridge Univ. Press.

HUGHES, EVERETT C. 1958 *Men and Their Work.* Glencoe, Ill.: Free Press.

LAZARSFELD, PAUL F.; and THIELENS, WAGNER JR. 1958 *The Academic Mind: Social Scientists in a Time of Crisis.* A report of the Bureau of Applied Social Research, Columbia University. Glencoe, Ill.: Free Press.

LÉVI-STRAUSS, CLAUDE 1945 French Sociology. Pages 503–537 in Georges Gurvitch and Wilbert E. Moore (editors), *Twentieth Century Sociology.* New York: Philosophical Library.

MACHLUP, FRITZ 1962 *The Production and Distribution of Knowledge in the United States.* Princeton Univ. Press.

MANNHEIM, KARL (1922–1940) 1953 *Essays on Sociology and Social Psychology.* Edited by Paul Kecskeméti. London: Routledge. → See especially pages 77–164 on "Conservative Thought."

MANNHEIM, KARL (1923–1929) 1952 *Essays on the Sociology of Knowledge.* Edited by Paul Kecskeméti. New York: Oxford Univ. Press. → See especially pages 191–229 on "Competition as a Cultural Phenomenon."

MANNHEIM, KARL (1929–1931) 1954 *Ideology and Utopia: An Introduction to the Sociology of Knowledge.* New York: Harcourt; London: Routledge. → First published in German. A paperback edition was published in 1955 by Harcourt.

MAQUET, JACQUES J. (1949) 1951 *The Sociology of Knowledge, Its Structure and Its Relation to the Philosophy of Knowledge: A Critical Analysis of the Systems of Karl Mannheim and Pitirim A. Sorokin.* Translated by John F. Locke. Boston: Beacon. → First published in French.

MARSHALL, T. H. (1934–1949) 1950 *Citizenship and Social Class, and Other Essays.* Cambridge Univ. Press.

MARX, KARL (1859) 1913 *A Contribution to the Critique of Political Economy.* Chicago: Kerr. → First published as *Zur Kritik der politischen Ökonomie.*

MARX, KARL; and ENGELS, FRIEDRICH (1845–1846) 1939 *The German Ideology.* Parts 1 and 3. With an introduction by R. Pascal. New York: International Publishers. → Written in 1845–1846, the full text was first published in 1932 as *Die deutsche Ideologie* and republished by Dietz Verlag in 1953.

MARX, KARL; and ENGELS, FRIEDRICH (1848) 1963 *The Communist Manifesto.* New York: Russell. → A paperback edition was published in 1964 by Washington Square Press.

MEAD, GEORGE H. 1934 *Mind, Self and Society From the Standpoint of a Social Behaviorist.* Edited by Charles W. Morris. Univ. of Chicago Press. → Published posthumously.

MERTON, ROBERT K. (1949) 1957 *Social Theory and Social Structure.* Rev. & enl. ed. Glencoe, Ill.: Free Press. → See especially Part 3 on "The Sociology of Knowledge" and Part 4 on "The Sociology of Science."

MILLS, C. WRIGHT 1963 *Power, Politics and People: The Collected Essays of C. Wright Mills.* Edited and introduced by Irving Louis Horowitz. New York: Oxford Univ. Press. → See especially pages 423–438 on "Language, Logic and Culture," pages 439–452 on "Situated Actions and Vocabularies of Motive," and pages 453–456 on "Methodological Consequences of the Sociology of Knowledge."

MILLS, C. WRIGHT 1964 *Sociology and Pragmatism: The Higher Learning in America.* Edited with an introduction by Irving Louis Horowitz. New York: Paine-Whitman. → A revision of Mills's unpublished doctoral dissertation.

PARK, ROBERT E. 1904 *Masse und Publikum: Eine methodologische und soziologische Untersuchung.* Bern: Lack & Grunau.

PARSONS, TALCOTT (1938–1953) 1963 *Essays in Sociological Theory.* Rev. ed. Glencoe, Ill.: Free Press.

RANULF, SVEND (1938) 1964 *Moral Indignation and Middle Class Psychology: A Sociological Study.* New

York: Schocken. → The appendix contains a well-documented attack on Scheler's theory of resentment.

SCHELER, MAX (1926) 1960 *Die Wissensformen und die Gesellschaft.* 2d ed., rev. Bern: Francke.

SEEMAN, MELVIN 1956 Intellectual Perspective and Adjustment to Minority Group Status. *Social Problems* 3:142–153.

SOROKIN, PITIRIM A. 1928 *Contemporary Sociological Theories.* New York: Harper. → A paperback edition was published in 1964 by Harper as *Contemporary Sociological Theories Through the First Quarter of the Twentieth Century.*

SOROKIN, PITIRIM A. (1937–1941) 1962 *Social and Cultural Dynamics.* 4 vols. Englewood Cliffs, N.J.: Bedminster Press. → Volume 1: *Fluctuation of Forms of Art.* Volume 2: *Fluctuation of Systems of Truth, Ethics, and Law.* Volume 3: *Fluctuation of Social Relationships, War, and Revolution.* Volume 4: *Basic Problems, Principles, and Methods.*

SOROKIN, PITIRIM A. (1943) 1964 *Sociocultural Causality, Space, Time: A Study of Referential Principles of Sociology and Social Science.* New York: Russell.

SPEIER, HANS (1938) 1952 The Social Determination of Ideas. Pages 95–111 in Hans Speier, *Social Order and the Risks of War: Papers in Political Sociology.* New York: Stewart.

STARK, WERNER 1958 *The Sociology of Knowledge: An Essay in Aid of a Deeper Understanding of the History of Ideas.* London: Routledge; Glencoe, Ill.: Free Press.

VEBLEN, THORSTEIN (1891–1913) 1961 *The Place of Science in Modern Civilisation, and Other Essays.* New York: Russell.

VEBLEN, THORSTEIN (1918) 1957 *The Higher Learning in America: A Memorandum on the Conduct of Universities by Business Men.* New York: Sagamore.

VEBLEN, THORSTEIN (1919) 1948 The Intellectual Pre-eminence of Jews in Modern Europe. Pages 467–479 in Thorstein Veblen, *The Portable Veblen.* Edited with an introduction by Max Lerner. New York: Viking.

WILSON, LOGAN (1942) 1964 *The Academic Man: A Study in the Sociology of a Profession.* New York: Octagon.

WOLFF, KURT H. 1959 The Sociology of Knowledge and Sociological Theory. Pages 567–602 in Llewellyn Gross (editor), *Symposium on Sociological Theory.* New York: Harper.

ZNANIECKI, FLORIAN 1940 *The Social Role of the Man of Knowledge.* New York: Columbia Univ. Press.

# KOFFKA, KURT

Kurt Koffka (1886–1941) was a German psychologist who, with Max Wertheimer and Wolfgang Köhler, was responsible for the development of gestalt psychology. Koffka was born in Berlin of a family that had been distinguished for more than a generation in the legal profession. His enrollment at the University of Berlin in 1903 as a student of philosophy represented a break with family tradition, but he found himself at home in this field and received the degree of doctor of philosophy in 1908. His thesis, entitled "Experimental-untersuchungen zur Lehre vom Rhythmus" (1909;

"Experimental Investigations of Rhythm") was done under Carl Stumpf at Berlin. During this period Koffka spent a year, from 1904 to 1905, in Edinburgh, perfecting his command of English and familiarizing himself with British psychology, then largely a part of philosophy and physiology. This experience made it easier for him than for many of his German colleagues to renew international contacts at the end of World War I and later to introduce to the English-speaking world the theory that he had helped develop.

During 1908/1909 he was assistant in the psychological laboratory of Johannes von Kries in Freiburg, and in 1909/1910 he was assistant in Würzburg, first to Oswald Külpe and then, after Külpe left for Bonn, to Karl Marbe. This was the period when studies of "imageless thought" were under way at Würzburg, which meant that Koffka was brought into contact there with work that raised questions about the then dominant elementarism of German psychology. His first book, published in 1912 and entitled *Zur Analyse der Vorstellungen und ihrer Gesetze* ("Regarding the Analysis of Images and Their Laws"), reflected the Würzburg approach and was dedicated to Külpe.

In 1910 there came a major turning point in Koffka's development as a psychologist. He went to Frankfurt am Main, where he formed his lasting association with Wertheimer and Köhler. Koffka and Köhler were already there as assistants to Friedrich Schumann when Wertheimer arrived, full of ideas for experiments that he wanted to carry out in the Frankfurt laboratory. During the months that followed, Koffka and Köhler served as the principal subjects for these experiments and joined in discussions of the results. This work led to Wertheimer's paper on the perception of movement that marked the birth of gestalt psychology in 1912.

In 1911, after three semesters at Frankfurt, Koffka became *Privatdozent* at Giessen and in 1918 extraordinary professor. Except for intervals during World War I when he was engaged in military research, he remained at Giessen until 1924. At that time he began the series of visits to the United States that led to his permanent residence in that country. During the year 1924/1925 he was Schiff professor at Cornell and in the spring of 1925 participated with Köhler, as a representative of the gestalt movement, in the series of lectures at Clark University that was published as *Psychologies of 1925* (1926). In 1926/1927 he was at the University of Wisconsin and in 1927 was appointed, for a period of five years, to the newly established William Allan Neilson chair at Smith

College. At the end of this period he remained at Smith, teaching, continuing research, and writing, until his death in 1941. During his tenure at Smith, he spent the summer of 1932 in Uzbekistan on an expedition sponsored by the Soviet government and the year 1939/1940 at Oxford.

**Publications.** During the first few years after 1912, Koffka found himself the spokesman for the gestalt psychologists. Wertheimer did not find it easy to bring his ideas to publication, and Köhler was doing work which served to broaden the theoretical base of gestalt psychology but which did not directly answer the criticism that arose as the impact of the new theory was felt. Koffka had already formalized his position as a gestalt psychologist in 1913 when he began to edit a series of publications entitled *Beiträge zur Psychologie der Gestalt* ("Contributions to the Psychology of the Gestalt"). There were 25 *Beiträge* in all, the first four published originally as part of the *Zeitschrift für Psychologie* (between 1913 and 1919) and the remaining 21 in the *Psychologische Forschung*. The latter journal began to appear in 1921 as the special organ of the gestalt group, largely in German but with some contributions in other languages. Some of the *Beiträge* were also collected in separate volumes, the early ones under that name, and those from the period of 1930 through the final number in 1932 as *Smith College Studies in Psychology*. It was in this series that Koffka presented new experimental work, for example, in 1915 the work of his student, A. Korte, in which the spatial and temporal relationships of stimuli that produce perceived motion were studied; four years later his own treatment of these factors (1919*a*); and in 1922 F. Wulf's study of changes in successive reproductions of visual figures.

In 1915 Koffka answered criticisms of gestalt theory in a paper entitled "Zur Grundlegung der Wahrnehmungspsychologie: Eine Auseinandersetzung mit V. Benussi" ("Foundations of Perception: A Discussion With V. Benussi"), and in 1919 came "Über den Einfluss der Erfahrung auf die Wahrnehmung" (1919*b*; "Regarding the Influence of Experience on Perception"). The first direct presentation of gestalt theory to American psychologists was his article entitled "Perception: An Introduction to the Gestalt-Theorie," which appeared in the *Psychological Bulletin* in 1922.

In 1921 Koffka published *Die Grundlagen der psychischen Entwicklung: Eine Einführung in die Kinderpsychologie* and in 1924 the English translation, entitled *The Growth of the Mind* (1921), with revised editions in 1925 (German) and 1928 (English). His final major work, *Principles of Ge-*

*stalt Psychology*, was published in 1935 and is the most comprehensive application of gestalt thinking to the field of psychology.

**Koffka's contribution.** It is impossible to treat Koffka's contribution without taking into account the unique collaboration that produced the gestalt movement. The men whose names were originally connected with it formed a closely knit triumvirate, and to some extent it is impossible to attribute particular aspects of the theory to one rather than another. Nevertheless, the three were very different in personality and intellectual style. Each played his own role in the group and made his own contribution. In the course of years they differed on details of the theory and in the kinds of investigations they made, but they remained in agreement on its fundamentals and each continued to value the contributions of the others.

The movement itself came into being as a protest against the reductionist theories that were then current. These theories assumed that if psychology was to be a science, it must find ways of analyzing its subject matter into constituent elements. Experience was taken as the starting point, but the elements into which it was broken down were often completely lacking in the quality of the experience that was being studied. For example, until Wertheimer's studies, movement was commonly treated as the experience of a succession of states of rest, states that showed none of the essential character of movement.

Gestalt theory, on the other hand, contended that the real subject matter of psychology is to be found at the level of experience itself and that when experience is analyzed in laboratory studies, the analysis should be in terms of "natural" units at that level: for example, in order to study the experience of movement and relate it to environmental factors, it is necessary to study movement itself and not states of rest.

The empirical work from which the theory was first developed was done in the field of visual perception, and much of the effort of the gestalt movement continued to be in that area. This was especially true of Koffka, who did not go as far afield in his experimental work as Köhler did, for example, in his studies of apes, or as Köhler's students did in their work on memory.

Although Koffka, with his students, was responsible for a large body of experimental work, it is likely that his most important contribution will remain his systematic application of gestalt principles—first to the field of mental development in *The Growth of the Mind* (1921) and, 14 years later, in the *Principles of Gestalt Psychology* (1935), to a broad field ranging from perception to social values.

*The Growth of the Mind* is an attempt to apply evidence supporting the gestalt point of view to the field of developmental psychology. In it, Koffka argued that the infant's first experience is of organized wholes, of relatively vague and undifferentiated figures perceived against a still less differentiated ground, rather than the "blooming, buzzing confusion" of William James's classic formulation. The infant's first responses are to gross features of the environment, like facial expression, rather than to "simple," fixed stimulus patterns, and the process of development, depending both on inner maturation and on experience, involves a gradual increase in structure and differentiation of this originally vague field. A considerable portion of the book consists of Koffka's arguments against the trial-and-error model of learning and his exposition of Köhler's studies of problem solving. This book did a great deal to shift the emphasis in educational theory and practice from rote learning to "insight" and understanding.

In the *Principles of Gestalt Psychology*, Koffka used the gestalt point of view to bring together the large amount of work done by members of the gestalt group and their students, as well as work like Kurt Lewin's, which took much of its original orientation from gestalt principles and further extended the range of application of gestalt theory. At the same time Koffka reinterpreted experimental work that had been used to support other points of view and argued against theoretical explanations that he found unacceptable. Koffka felt that an adequate theory must be able to deal with many aspects of life, and he ended his introductory chapter with:

If psychology can point the way where science and life will meet, if it can lay the foundations of a system of knowledge that will contain the behavior of a single atom as well as that of an amoeba, a white rat, a chimpanzee, and a human being, with all the latter's curious activities which we call social conduct, music and art, literature and drama, then an acquaintance with such a psychology should . . . repay the time and effort spent in its acquisition.   (1935 p. 23)

It is likely, however, that the book's greatest contribution is its treatment of the topics of perception, on the one hand, and of learning and memory, on the other. In discussing perception, Koffka dealt extensively with the work done on perceptual constancy and on the problems involved in the fact that cognition is often closer to the "real" object than are the proximal stimuli through which cognition is mediated. His answer to the question, "Why do things look as they do?" was, ". . . because of the field organization to which the proximal stimulus distribution gives rise," and he admitted that the answer, instead of closing a chapter in psychology, only served to open one (1935, p. 98).

That answer involves most of the central problems of gestalt theory, including those of learning and memory, with which Koffka concerned himself again and again. The first publications of the gestalt group, as part of their attack on the one-sided empiricism of the dominant theories of their day, had emphasized cases in which organizational gestalt factors outweigh experience. Their emphasis on these factors left the movement open to the criticism that gestalt theorists disregarded experience entirely. Koffka made a frontal attack on this criticism in his paper on the influence of experience on perception (1919*b*). At this time, he was principally concerned with refuting the prevailing assumption that the effect of experience is merely to alter or add to an event that occurs when stimuli affect an organism. Instead, he contended, the frequent occurrence of particular events creates *dispositions* for similar events to occur at a later time, even when the stimuli then present do not in themselves call them forth; and when these later events occur, they represent psychological processes in their own right, with underlying physiological activity that must possess the same character as that which was related to the original events.

He again treated questions regarding the influence of experience on later events in *The Growth of the Mind*, especially in his distinction between the problem of *achievement*, or how the first performance of an act comes about, and the problem of *memory*, or the way in which later performances depend upon earlier ones. In the *Principles* he reaffirmed the importance of past experience in such statements as the following: "Although we have attacked traditional empiricism incessantly we have insisted ourselves on the all-pervasive influence of experience" (1935, p. 421). In this final work, he postulated a trace theory that distinguishes the arousal of the correct process, the trace left by that process, presumably in the tissue of the central nervous system, and finally the effects of this trace on later processes. The circularity of the relationship between process and trace in this theory is suggestive of parts of Piaget's developmental theories. Koffka said, ". . . new processes occur in systems already endowed with traces; it is this fact alone that makes mental *development* intelligible." And in the same paragraph: "Thus by processes making traces and traces [affecting] processes, the system is bound to develop . . . if we mean by development the production of ever new processes" (1935, pp. 541–542).

The chapters in the *Principles* specifically related to memory (and forgetting) draw on a long series of investigations and present a theory in which it is postulated that the formation of trace systems, alterations that occur over time in these trace systems, and the stability and availability of traces all follow laws that have been found valid for perception. His treatment of the availability of traces as a factor in forgetting comes close to current ideas about the retrieval of stored information. Wertheimer's principles of grouping and Köhler's studies of memory contributed to the foundation on which this final theoretical exposition of Koffka's was built.

Koffka's somewhat abstract style and his detailed, often legalistic, arguments against theories that even in 1935 seemed primarily of historical importance somewhat lessened the immediate impact of the book. Koffka himself, in his concluding sentences, admitted that many of his special hypotheses needed further verification. Nevertheless, the book stands as a creative integration by a psychologist with a wide and detailed knowledge and, as such, may well remain a classic.

GRACE M. HEIDER

[*For the historical context of Koffka's work, see* PHENOMENOLOGY *and the biographies of* KÖHLER; KÜLPE; STUMPF; WERTHEIMER. *For discussion of the subsequent development of his ideas, see* FIELD THEORY; GESTALT THEORY; PERCEPTION, *article on* PERCEPTUAL CONSTANCY; THINKING; *and the biography of* LEWIN.]

### WORKS BY KOFFKA

1909    Experimental-untersuchungen zur Lehre vom Rhythmus. *Zeitschrift für Psychologie* 52:1–109.

1912    *Zur Analyse der Vorstellungen und ihrer Gesetze.* Leipzig: Quelle & Meyer.

1915    Zur Grundlegung der Wahrnehmungspsychologie: Eine Auseinandersetzung mit V. Benussi. Beiträge zur Psychologie der Gestalt, No. 3. *Zeitschrift für Psychologie* 73:11–90.

1919a    Zur Theorie einfachster gesehener Bewegungen: Ein physiologisch–mathematischer Versuch. Beiträge zur Psychologie der Gestalt, No. 4. *Zeitschrift für Psychologie* 82:257–292.

1919b    Über den Einfluss der Erfahrung auf die Wahrnehmung. *Die Naturwissenschaften* 7:597–605.

(1921) 1928    *The Growth of the Mind.* New York: Harcourt. → First published as *Die Grundlagen der psychischen Entwicklung: Eine Einführung in die Kinderpsychologie.*

1922    Perception: An Introduction to the Gestalt-Theorie. *Psychological Bulletin* 19:531–585.

(1926) 1928    Mental Development. Pages 129–143 in *Psychologies of 1925.* 3d ed. Edited by Carl Murchison. Worcester, Mass.: Clark Univ. Press.

1935    *Principles of Gestalt Psychology.* New York: Harcourt.

### SUPPLEMENTARY BIBLIOGRAPHY

HARROWER-ERICKSON, M. R.   1942   Kurt Koffka: 1886–1941. *American Journal of Psychology* 55:278–281.

KÖHLER, WOLFGANG   1942   Kurt Koffka: 1886–1941. *Psychological Review* 49:97–101.

KORTE, ADOLF   1915   Kinematoskopische Untersuchungen. Beiträge zur Psychologie der Gestalt, No. 2. *Zeitschrift für Psychologie* 72:194–296.

MURCHISON, CARL   1929   Bibliography of Koffka's Work. Pages 131–132 in *Psychological Register.* Worcester, Mass.: Clark Univ. Press.

WERTHEIMER, MAX   1912   Experimentelle Studien über das Sehen von Bewegung. *Zeitschrift für Psychologie* 61:161–265.

WULF, FRIEDRICH   1922   Über die Veränderung von Vorstellungen (Gedächtnis und Gestalt). Beiträge zur Psychologie der Gestalt, No. 6. *Psychologische Forschung* 1:333–373.

## KÖHLER, WOLFGANG

Wolfgang Köhler, psychologist and philosopher, was one of the founders of the gestalt school of psychology. While the scope of his intellectual contributions was extremely broad—ranging from theoretical physics and brain physiology to epistemology and ethics, and from neurophysiology to personality—most of his work was focused on developing and testing the principles of gestalt psychology.

Köhler was born in Reval (now Tallinn), Estonia, in 1887 and grew up in Wolfenbüttel, Germany. After receiving his doctoral degree from the University of Berlin in 1909, he went to the University of Frankfurt as assistant in the psychological laboratory and became a *Privatdozent* in 1911. It was at Frankfurt that he began to work with Max Wertheimer and Kurt Koffka, and the three of them laid the foundations of gestalt psychology. Köhler spent the years from 1913 to 1920 as director of the anthropoid research station of the Prussian Academy of Sciences on Tenerife. He became director of the psychological laboratory at the University of Berlin in 1921 and professor of psychology and philosophy the following year. In 1935 he moved to the United States and became a professor of psychology at Swarthmore College, where he remained until his retirement in 1955. He died in 1967.

Köhler received numerous honors. He was president of the American Psychological Association and the recipient of its Distinguished Scientific Contribution Award; he gave the William James lectures at Harvard in 1934; and he was elected a member of the National Academy of Sciences.

The gestalt movement may be considered to date from Wertheimer's 1912 paper describing his investigations of apparent movement. Köhler and Koffka had served as subjects for these experiments. The movement began as a protest against the then prevailing views of analytic introspectionism; later it opposed the various forms of associationist and behaviorist psychology. It is fair to say that Köhler was a member of the "opposition" throughout his career. [*See* GESTALT THEORY.]

**Perception.** To demonstrate that organization is a basic function that is not dependent on associations of peripheral events, the gestalt psychologists employed several strategies. One was the logical analysis of contradictions and hidden assumptions in traditional theories. Thus, with regard to perception, Köhler analyzed the "constancy hypothesis," an assumption that is implicit in much psychological theorizing but not always recognized (1913). The constancy hypothesis assumes a one-to-one correspondence between local peripheral stimulation and the perceptual experience. Accordingly, if peripheral stimulation on various occasions is the same, the resulting perception should in all cases be the same; conversely, differences in peripheral stimulation should result in differences in perceptual experience. However, since the expected correspondences did not occur, some explanation was required. The most plausible one seemed to be that past learning experiences had supplied information not contained in the retinal stimulation. The gestalt psychologists discarded the constancy hypothesis and argued that local stimulation does not determine perceptual experience. They asserted instead that the effective stimulus for a given perception is relational in character: what is seen in a given region is determined not only by the stimulation arriving from that area but also by interaction among stimuli arriving from neighboring or surrounding areas. Experimental research revealed that many perceptions depend on such stimulus relationships. When the effective stimulus is defined in relational terms, reference to past experience is often unnecessary. [*See* LEARNING, *article on* DISCRIMINATION LEARNING; PERCEPTION, *article on* PERCEPTUAL CONSTANCY; *see also* Zuckerman & Rock 1957.]

Another tactic used to throw doubt on traditional explanations of behavior was to demonstrate particular perceptual phenomena in animal subjects, to which judgments or unconscious inferences presumably cannot be attributed. Thus Köhler (1915) demonstrated size constancy in the perception of objects by hens and chimpanzees. In another series of experiments (1918) Köhler proceeded to show

that the perception of relations and of structural aspects is a primitive, basic function. A hen was presented with two gray samples: a lighter one, *A*, and a darker one, *B*. After the animal was trained to respond to *B*, further investigations were made to determine whether the animal had learned a response to the absolute shade of *B* or to structural features of a particular arrangement—i.e., to *B* as the darker of the two samples. The animal was presented with a new pair of samples consisting of *B* and of *C*, *C* being darker than *B*. The majority of the hens chose *C*. Köhler obtained similar results with chimpanzees, using size as a stimulus factor as well as degree of brightness. These experiments supported the gestalt view of the priority of structural properties in perception and learning. This problem (transposition discrimination) has given rise to a large experimental literature, and attempts have been made to account for the results without accepting the gestalt view of structure. [*See* LEARNING, *article on* DISCRIMINATION LEARNING; *see also* Spence 1937.]

**Learning.** The concept of organization was not limited by gestalt psychologists to the realm of perceptual events; rather their aim was to show that similar structural principles are valid for learning, memory, thinking, and other mental functions. Learning had traditionally been viewed as the building up of associations. An association was defined as a bond or link in the mind between two (or more) mental contents, *A* and *B*; they are so linked that activation of *A* will lead to the recall of *B*. The two most important factors involved in the formation of such a bond were held to be contiguity and frequency.

In his *Gestalt Psychology* Köhler offered several criticisms of associationist psychology. First, he attacked the law of association by contiguity as being a purely mechanical principle:

Two processes A and B happen to occur together and, whatever the nature of A and B may be, a bond is formed between them! I do not know a single law in physics or chemistry which could in this respect be compared with the law of contiguity. . . . There are no examples of interaction in which the nature of the interacting factors plays no part. And yet, in the classical law of association by contiguity, the nature of the things which become associated is tacitly ignored. ([1929] 1947, pp. 258–259)

Köhler argued that the nature of the *A* and *B* involved is essential in determining the facility with which an association between them will be established. For example, pairs of meaningful words are associated more readily than are pairs of nonsense syllables, because the former can more easily be organized into a unified whole (see Epstein et al. 1960). In addition, Köhler asserted that the subject presented with contiguous items does not receive them passively; were this the case, very few associations would be formed. Instead, the subject strives actively to tie the items together and may employ various strategies in order to accomplish this task. Köhler then attempted to derive association from the principles of perceptual organization; in 1941 he reported experiments designed to verify his thesis and concluded, "It seems no longer probable that association is an indifferent bond between merely contiguous items. Our evidence tends to support the view that associations are after-effects of specific organization or interaction" (1941, p. 502).

**Recall.** The associationist conception of recall neglected an important issue: the functional relation between two items. Köhler (1940) revived and extended an argument made by the nineteenth-century Danish philosopher Höffding: to say merely that the later presentation of mental content *A* leads to the recall of the associated item *B* omits a necessary prior step. Before *B* can be recalled, the present perception (*A'*) must be related to the memory trace of *A*. As Köhler explained Höffding's view, "any recall on the basis of a previous association presupposes . . . a more immediate process," the tendency of one mental process to select another, "for which there is no other reason than their kinship" (1940, p. 127). Accordingly, a memory trace can be aroused not only via a previously established connection but also by a present perceptual process on the basis of the similarity of process and trace.

Köhler maintained that the activation of a memory trace by a percept is analogous to the grouping which occurs in the perceptual field because of similarity or, more specifically, *distinctive* similarity. This means that two objects in the visual field will be readily seen as a pair if they are similar to each other and at the same time different from other objects present; if the same two objects are presented in a field containing other similar units, they will not spontaneously be grouped together. Contact between trace and percept is simply an extension of this principle into the temporal dimension. This reasoning was subjected to, and substantiated by, experimental tests (see Köhler & Restorff 1933–1935, part 2; Bartel 1937).

It is unfortunate that neither the Höffding argument nor the experiments confirming it are widely known among American psychologists. The explanation of recognition is a core problem in psychology; an explanation based on the similarity between process and trace has important implications for a variety of issues. On the basis of the Höffding function Duncker (1945) explained the emergence into awareness of specific memory contents during problem-solving processes. Wallach analyzed the implications of the recognition function for the problem of the influence of past experience on perception (1949) and studied the effects of memory modalities on recognition (Wallach & Auerbach 1955). Other implications of Köhler's argument are discussed by Rock (1962).

Better known in the United States is the work of Köhler and Restorff on the role of organizational factors in the realm of memory traces (1933–1935, part 1), which shows that the distinctive item in a list is recalled better than the items that are similar to each other. Köhler and other gestalt psychologists have used this hypothesis to account for many phenomena of learning and retention. Thus, they maintain that the difficulty of learning nonsense syllables is due to their homogeneity, which makes it difficult to group and organize the material; that retroactive and proactive inhibition is caused by the crowding of similar traces; and that the serial-position effect occurs because the items at the beginning and the end of a list are more isolated than those in the middle and are therefore better learned and retained. [See FORGETTING.] Other investigators have called into question the validity of these perceptual analogies. In a more recent paper defending his views Köhler recommended that the Restorff experiments be replicated (1958a).

**Problem solving.** Köhler's most famous work is, of course, his study of the mentality of apes (1917), based on investigations conducted at the anthropoid research station in Tenerife on problem solving in chimpanzees. Köhler reported detailed observation on the chimpanzees' use and fabrication of simple tools (probably most widely noted is the account of the success of an ape named Sultan in fitting together two short sticks to fashion one stick long enough to reach the goal object); on the role of chance, play, and imitation; on the chimpanzees' ability to build structures (the box-stacking problem); on the role of perceptual aspects of the problem situation, etc. Contrary to some secondary accounts of this work, Köhler was interested not only in demonstrating the apes' capacity for insightful solutions but also in determining why the animals failed completely in certain situations (for example, in string-pulling tasks). In addition to the experimental data, Köhler reported many qualitative observations of chimpanzee behavior.

The polemical part of *The Mentality of Apes* was aimed at E. L. Thorndike's treatment of learning and problem solving in animals. Thorndike had concluded that no evidence can be found of insightful solutions. According to him, a correct response is made in the course of random trial-and-error activity; on repeated trials this response is gradually strengthened in a purely automatic and mechanical way, simply because the animal receives a reward shortly after it makes the correct response. Thorndike's law of effect has been widely accepted as an explanation of learning in animals and man, and it was the foundation of Clark Hull's attempt to construct a systematic theory of behavior. Köhler argued that the puzzle-box situation with which Thorndike confronted his animals is inherently incomprehensible, permitting no "survey of the whole arrangement" ([1917] 1956, p. 23) and thus no possibility of problem solving. A true test for insight requires a situation that is both intelligible and "completely *visible* to the animals. For if essential portions of the experimental apparatus cannot be seen by the animals, how can they use their intelligence faculties in tackling the situation?" (*ibid.*, p. 23). [*See articles on* PROBLEM SOLVING; HULL; THORNDIKE.]

According to Köhler, intelligence can be characterized as detour behavior—the ability to reach a goal by roundabout means. Thus, many of the problems he used in his research were varieties of detour: the goal object was so far away that it could be reached only by use of a stick; or the object was so high up that the animal had to pull over a box to a place directly under it in order to reach the object by standing on the box. Köhler concluded that the chimpanzees' solution behavior cannot be described as random trial and error with gradual mastery of the task. Instead, the behavior indicated insight, that is, the perception of properties of the object in relation to certain traits of the problem situation. Solution often comes about suddenly and seems to reflect reorganization of the perceptual field.

Some aspects of this work have given rise to controversy. Köhler has been accused of using the term "insight" to explain, rather than to describe, certain kinds of behavior. A careful reading of his book reveals that this charge is unwarranted, and some years later Köhler himself said, by way of refutation: "Apparently some readers interpreted this formulation as though it [insight] referred to a mysterious mental agent or faculty which was made responsible for the apes' behavior. Actually nothing of this sort was intended when I wrote my report" ([1929] 1947, p. 341). Again, Köhler is criticized for divorcing insight from the learning history of the animal and giving the impression that problem solving is independent of past experience. Yet Köhler's experimental procedure—start-

ing with simpler problems and proceeding to more complex ones—shows that he realized that solution of the present problem depends on skill and knowledge acquired in the past. One criticism for which there is some justification is that Köhler too sharply distinguished insightful learning from trial-and-error learning.

**Neurophysiology of perception.** Köhler's interest in the physical processes in the brain dates back to the years on Tenerife. There he wrote a treatise (1920) tracing the parallels between examples of dynamic self-distribution in physics and the nature of perceptual processes and thus began a search for the neurological correlates of perceptual experience. He did not concern himself with the microstructure of the nervous system but concentrated on the macrophysical processes that might take place in neural tissue, processes that are not subject to the constraints normally thought to be effected by the cellular structure of this tissue. These macroscopic processes thus would transcend the conventional picture of brain activity as a pattern of nerve impulses running along individual fibers and shunted from pathway to pathway. Rather, the processes would, at the cortical level, distribute themselves freely in the nervous tissue. Their nature would depend on the laws of physics and on the physicochemical characteristics of nerve tissue rather than on its microanatomy, while the specific form they would assume and their rough localization would depend on the pattern of nerve processes originating in the sense organ.

It was to this end that Köhler directed his work on figural aftereffects. Figural aftereffects are those distortions of shape and displacement that occur after a subject has been given a prolonged exposure to a specific form pattern. Their existence fits well with the idea that the neurophysiological correlate of pattern vision is to a degree free from microanatomical constraints. Under favorable conditions such distortions or displacements can be quite conspicuous and can therefore be measured by compensation or by matching.

By experimentation Köhler established a single rule that permits prediction of the directions, but not the magnitudes, of the displacement of the aftereffect: There will be a receding from areas where contours or boundaries of an inspection figure have previously been located. This rule also applies to Gibson's form-adaptation phenomena, the first figural aftereffects to have been discovered (Gibson 1933).

Köhler's explanation of figural aftereffects is based on his assumption that direct currents are generated in the cortex at the boundaries between areas of different neural excitation. Such boundaries are the cortical correlate of differences in intensities of stimulation, that is, of retinal contours. The cortical-current theory is hard to test. A demonstration of the existence of direct currents generated in the cortex and dependent on stimulation does not suffice. The role of direct currents in pattern vision needs to be demonstrated. The demonstrations attempted by Lashley (Lashley et al. 1951) and by Sperry (Sperry & Miner 1955; Sperry et al. 1955) were not successful, but their negative results were not conclusive. Köhler (1965) correctly criticized Lashley's technique and found good cause to doubt Sperry's results. The electric-current theory has not been developed to the point where predictions about figural aftereffects or other perceptual phenomena can be made so specific that they can be tested by psychological experimentation. Until more is known about nerve tissue as a medium for direct current, such a development will not be possible.

CARL B. ZUCKERMAN AND HANS WALLACH

[See also LEARNING, article on NEUROPHYSIOLOGICAL ASPECTS; PERCEPTION, article on ILLUSIONS AND AFTEREFFECTS. Other relevant material may be found in the biographies of ANGYAL; BÜHLER; GOLDSTEIN; KATZ; KOFFKA; LASHLEY; WERTHEIMER.]

### WORKS BY KÖHLER

1913    Über unbemerkte Empfindungen und Urteilstäuschungen. *Zeitschrift für Psychologie* 66:51–80.
1915    Aus der Anthropoidenstation auf Teneriffa: 2. Optische Untersuchungen am Schimpansen und am Haushuhn. Akademie der Wissenschaften, Berlin, Physikalisch-Mathematische Klasse, *Abhandlungen* [1915]:no. 3.
(1917) 1956    *The Mentality of Apes.* 2d ed., rev. London: Routledge. → First published in German. A paperback edition was published in 1959 by Random House.
1918    Aus der Anthropoidenstation auf Teneriffa: 4. Nachweis einfacher Strukturfunktionen beim Schimpansen und beim Haushuhn über eine neue Methode zur Untersuchung des bunten Farbensystems. Akademie der Wissenschaften, Berlin, Physikalisch-Mathematische Klasse, *Abhandlungen* [1918]: no. 2.
(1920) 1924    *Die physischen Gestalten in Ruhe und im stationären Zustand.* Erlangen (Germany): Philosophische Akademie.
(1926) 1928    An Aspect of Gestalt Psychology. Pages 163–195 in *Psychologies of 1925: Powell Lectures in Psychological Theories.* 3d ed. Worcester, Mass.: Clark Univ. Press. → Lecture delivered on May 1, 1925.
(1929) 1947    *Gestalt Psychology.* Rev. ed. New York: Liveright. → A paperback edition was published in 1947 by New American Library.
1930    Some Tasks of Gestalt Psychology. Pages 143–160 in *Psychologies of 1930.* Edited by Carl Murchison. Worcester, Mass.: Clark Univ. Press.
1933–1935    KÖHLER, WOLFGANG; and RESTORFF, HEDWIG VON Analyse von Vorgängen im Spurenfeld. 2 parts. *Psychologische Forschung* 18:299–342; 21:56–112. →

Part 1: Über die Wirkung von Bereichsbildungen im Spurenfeld, by Hedwig von Restorff. Part 2: Zur Theorie der Reproduktion, by Wolfgang Köhler.
1938    *The Place of Value in a World of Facts.* New York: Liveright.
1940    *Dynamics in Psychology.* New York: Liveright.
1941    On the Nature of Associations. American Philosophical Society, *Proceedings* 84:489–502.
1944    Value and Fact. *Journal of Philosophy* 41:197–212.
1944    KÖHLER, WOLFGANG; and WALLACH, HANS Figural After-effects: An Investigation of Visual Processes. American Philosophical Society, *Proceedings* 88:269–357.
1947    KÖHLER, WOLFGANG; and EMERY, DAVID Figural After-effects in the Third Dimension of Visual Space. *American Journal of Psychology* 60:159–201.
1950    Psychology and Evolution. *Acta psychologica* 7: 288–297.
1952    KÖHLER, WOLFGANG; HELD, RICHARD; and O'CONNELL, DONALD An Investigation of Cortical Currents. American Philosophical Society, *Proceedings* 96:290–330.
1957    KÖHLER, WOLFGANG; and ADAMS, PAULINE A. Perception and Attention. *American Journal of Psychology* 71:489–503.
1958a    Perceptual Organization and Learning. *American Journal of Psychology* 71:311–315.
1958b    The Present Situation in Brain Physiology. *American Psychologist* 13:150–154.
1959    Gestalt Psychology Today. *American Psychologist* 14:727–734.
1965    Unsolved Problems in the Field of Figural After-effects. *Psychological Record* 15:63–83.

### SUPPLEMENTARY BIBLIOGRAPHY

BARTEL, HELLMUT 1937    Über die Abhängigkeit spontaner Reproduktionen von Feldbedingungen. *Psychologische Forschung* 22:1–25.
DUNCKER, KARL 1945    On Problem-solving. *Psychological Monographs* 58, no. 5.
EPSTEIN, WILLIAM; ROCK, IRVIN; and ZUCKERMAN, CARL B. 1960    Meaning and Familiarity in Associative Learning. *Psychological Monographs* 74, no. 4.
GIBSON, JAMES J. 1933    Adaptation, After-effect and Contrast in the Perception of Curved Lines. *Journal of Experimental Psychology* 16:1–31.
LASHLEY, K. S.; CHOW, K. L.; and SEMMES, JOSEPHINE 1951    An Examination of the Electrical Field Theory of Cerebral Integration. *Psychological Review* 58:123–136.
POSTMAN, LEO; and RILEY, DONALD 1957    A Critique of Köhler's Theory of Association. *Psychological Review* 64:61–72.
ROCK, IRVIN 1962    A Neglected Aspect of the Problem of Recall: The Höffding Function. Pages 645–659 in Jordan M. Scher (editor), *Theories of the Mind.* New York: Free Press.
SPENCE, KENNETH W. 1937    The Differential Response in Animals to Stimuli Varying Within a Single Dimension. *Psychological Review* 44:430–444.
SPERRY, R. W.; and MINER, NANCY 1955    Pattern Perception Following Insertion of Mica Plates Into Visual Cortex. *Journal of Comparative and Physiological Psychology* 48:463–469.
SPERRY, R. W.; MINER, N.; and MYERS, R. E. 1955    Visual Pattern Perception Following Subpial Slicing and Tantalum Wire Implantations in the Visual Cortex.

*Journal of Comparative and Physiological Psychology* 48:50–58.

WALLACH, HANS 1949 Some Considerations Concerning the Relation Between Perception and Cognition. *Journal of Personality* 18:6–13.

WALLACH, HANS; and AUERBACH, EMANUEL 1955 On Memory Modalities. *American Journal of Psychology* 68:249–257.

ZUCKERMAN, CARL B.; and ROCK, IRVIN 1957 A Reappraisal of the Roles of Past Experience and Innate Organizing Processes in Visual Perception. *Psychological Bulletin* 54:269–296.

## KONDRATIEFF, N. D.

Nikolai Dmitrievich Kondratieff (also transliterated Kondrat'ev) was one of the outstanding Russian economists and statisticians of the 1920s. He is known outside Russia almost exclusively for his work on long cycles. However, Kondratieff's writings in the field of agricultural economics and his contribution to the development of economic planning in the Soviet Union are of considerable historical interest; with one exception, none of his work in these fields is available in English.

He was born in 1892. After brief service, at the age of 25, as deputy minister for food in the provisional (Kerensky) government, Kondratieff's professional career was almost entirely associated with the Moscow Business Conditions Institute (Kon'iunkturnyi Institut), which he founded and directed during the entire period of its existence, from 1920 to 1928.

A considerable part of Kondratieff's work at the Business Conditions Institute (which included editing its bulletin) was devoted to obtaining better statistical information on farming and the place of farming in the Soviet economy. His original work in this area consisted, among other things, in the elaboration of a set of price indices for products sold and purchased by farmers, the so-called "peasant indices."

In the early 1920s, Kondratieff drafted the first five-year plan for agriculture. His official position brought him in close contact with the various groups in charge of developing economic policies, including the first five-year plan. In internal and public discussions, Kondratieff argued for policies that would not place undue burdens on farmers —that is, against the setting of unrealistically high goals. His endeavor to analyze current economic conditions and prospects objectively and his skepticism as to the possibilities of global and detailed planning brought Kondratieff into conflicts with official policies. In 1930 he was arrested and made to appear (in 1931) as a witness at one of the political trials of the enemies of the Stalinist regime. Although he was alleged to be the head of a clandestine "Working Peasants' party," Kondratieff was never brought to open trial but was kept in prison, where he died on an unknown date. After the end of the Stalin era some of the surviving associates of Kondratieff were "rehabilitated" and returned to professional work, but Kondratieff's pioneering contributions still await recognition in the Soviet Union.

Although, in the words of Schumpeter, it was Kondratieff "who brought the phenomenon [of the long cycles] fully before the scientific community and who systematically analyzed all the material available to him on the assumption of the presence of a Long Wave, characteristic of the capitalist process" (Schumpeter 1939, vol. 1, p. 164), actually the existence of long cycles was surmised by several economists prior to World War I. Among academic economists, Aftalion, Pareto, Lenoir, and Spiethoff all made reference to long cycles in one way or another; among socialist writers, Parvus and J. van Gelderen suggested their existence. S. De Wolff published an article on long waves two years after Kondratieff's 1922 book.

Kondratieff used the term "long waves" rather than "long cycles" and always referred to his findings as merely a hypothesis. His view on the existence of regular recurring long swings in economic life began to take shape in 1919–1920, and the hypothesis was first formulated, together with a tentative dating of the swings, in a study published in 1922. A fuller statement, supported by statistical analysis to which very little was added in subsequent publications, appeared in 1925 ("The Long Waves in Economic Life," published in Germany a year later and in 1935, in an abridged version, in English). Outside the Soviet Union, knowledge of Kondratieff's work in this field is derived almost exclusively from these two translations.

The analysis of smoothed deviations from the trend of a collection of 36 annual price, value, and physical quantity series for the United States, the United Kingdom, France, and Germany led Kondratieff to suggest the following dating of long waves: (1) From the end of the 1780s (or beginning of the 1790s) to 1844–1851, with a peak in 1810–1817; (2) from 1844–1851 to 1890–1896, with a peak in 1870–1875; and (3) a rise from 1890–1896 to 1914–1920, when a decline "probably begins" (1928a).

Kondratieff held the existence of long waves as "at least very probable." He conceded that the period covered by the statistical data was not long enough "to enable us to assert beyond doubt the cyclical character of waves" ([1925] 1935, p. 112). He doubted, however, that strict uniform periodicity existed—any more than in any other social or economic phenomena.

Kondratieff did not provide a complete theory to explain the causes of long cycles; instead, in his subsequent book (1928a), he merely enumerated certain relevant factors, such as significant changes in technology following major inventions and discoveries, wars and social upheavals, and gold discoveries. He did not show what causal relationships exist between these developments and the dynamics of timing of long cycles. In another publication (1928b; not translated and therefore largely unknown outside the Soviet Union), Kondratieff advanced a theory that long swings reflect spurts in the reinvestment of fixed capital. Kondratieff's hypothesis was immediately violently attacked by Soviet economists, with D. I. Oparin perhaps the most able opponent (see 1928a).

The statistical evidence for long cycles presented by Kondratieff was critically examined by G. Garvy (1943), who concluded that the waves identified by Kondratieff are, in part at least, the result of the specific techniques of statistical analysis used, that the dating of many of the turning points is arbitrary, and that the statistical data used by Kondratieff are limited in time and scope.

Kondratieff's name has become familiar to non-Russian economists mainly because Schumpeter attached it to the long cycle which forms part of his own three-cycle model of economic fluctuations. Some of the work on long cycles, particularly in western Europe, continues to be associated with Kondratieff's hypothesis (for details, see Imbert 1956; Weinstock 1964). Studies of more limited scope have attempted to identify long cycles in specific activities, such as shipbuilding, transportation, and building construction, or to identify general cycles of longer duration than business cycles but shorter than the "Kondratieff cycle." Long swings in prices have also been the subject of numerous studies.

GEORGE GARVY

[For the historical context of Kondratieff's work, see the biographies of AFTALION; PARETO; SPIETHOFF. For discussion of the subsequent development of Kondratieff's ideas, see TIME SERIES, article on CYCLES; and the biography of SCHUMPETER.]

### WORKS BY KONDRATIEFF

1922    Mirovoe khoziaistvo i ego kon'iunktury vo vremia i posle voiny (The World Economy and Its Condition During and After the War). Vologda (Russia): Oblastnoe Otdelenie Gosudartsvennogo Izdatelstva. → Con-

tains the first sketch of Kondratieff's theory of long cycles.

(1925) 1935    The Long Waves in Economic Life. Review of Economic Statistics 17, pt. 2:105–115. → First published in Russian in Volume 1 of Voprosy kon'iunktury.

(1927) 1964    Critical Remarks on the Plan for the Development of the National Economy. Pages 438–451 in Nicolas Spulber (editor), Foundations of Soviet Strategy for Economic Growth: Selected Soviet Essays, 1924–1930. Bloomington: Indiana Univ. Press. → First published in Russian.

1928a    Bol'shie tsikly kon'iunktury (Major Economic Cycles). Moscow: Krasnaia Presnia. → Includes Oparin's critique of Kondratieff's theory.

1928b    Dinamika tsen promyshlennykh i sel'skokhoziaistvennykh tovarov (The Dynamics of Industrial and Agricultural Prices). Moscow, Kon'iunkturnyi Institut, Voprosy kon'iunktury 4:5–83. → See pages 179–184 for a summary in English.

### SUPPLEMENTARY BIBLIOGRAPHY

DE WOLFF, S. 1924 Prosperitäts- und Depressionsperioden. Pages 13–43 in Der lebendige Marxismus: Festgabe zum 70. Geburtstage von Karl Kautsky. Jena (Germany): Thüringer Verlagsanstalt.

GARVY, GEORGE 1943 Kondratieff's Theory of Long Cycles. Review of Economic Statistics 25:203–220. → Contains numerous bibliographical references to the Russian critical literature on Kondratieff's work.

IMBERT, GASTON (1956) 1959 Des mouvements de longue durée Kondratieff. Aix-en-Provence (France): Pensée Universitaire. → Contains an extensive bibliography.

SCHUMPETER, JOSEPH A. 1939 Business Cycles: A Theoretical, Historical, and Statistical Analysis of the Capitalist Process. 2 vols. New York and London: McGraw-Hill. → An abridged version was published in 1964.

WEINSTOCK, ULRICH 1964 Das Problem der Kondratieff Zyklen: Ein Beitrag zur Entwicklung einer Theorie der "langen Wellen" und ihrer Bedeutung. IFO- Institut für Wirtschaftsforschung, Munich, Schriftenreihe, No. 58. Berlin and Munich: Duncker & Humblot. → Contains an extensive bibliography in several languages.

# KOPPERS, WILHELM

Wilhelm Koppers (1886–1961), founder and president of the Institute of Ethnology at the Unisity of Vienna, was active as a professor, author, editor, and field worker.

Born in Menzelen near Xanten, Germany, Koppers was educated at the Mission Seminaries of the Societas Verbi Divini (S.V.D.), St. Michael's in Steyl, Holland, and St. Gabriel's in Mödling, Austria. He joined the S.V.D. in 1901 and was ordained a Roman Catholic priest in 1911. Prevented by illness from undertaking missionary work, he devoted his life instead to scientific research. After being trained in philosophy and theology in Rome in 1911–1912, he concentrated in ethnology and Sanskrit and obtained his PH.D. in Vienna in 1917.

He became a *Privatdozent* at the University of Vienna in 1924 and was appointed to a chair of ethnology in 1928.

When, as a result of Koppers' efforts, the Institute of Ethnology and Physical Anthropology at the University of Vienna was split into two separate institutes, Koppers was appointed president of the Institute of Ethnology (Institut für Völkerkunde). He served as president from 1929 to 1938 and again from 1945 to 1957, contributing to its development into one of the leading ethnological institutes in Europe. Many ethnologists studied under his guidance, among them Christoph von Fürer-Haimendorf, Clyde Kluckhohn, Robert Lowie, Masao Oka, Douglas Oliver, Helmut Petri, and Stephan Wurm. After Koppers became president emeritus in 1957, he maintained an active interest in the institute and continued to give his regular lectures.

Koppers published more than two hundred works, of which four were books. He was coeditor of *Anthropos* for ten years and editor for eight. He founded and edited *Wiener Beiträge zur Kulturgeschichte und Linguistik* in 1930 and *Acta ethnologica et linguistica* in 1950. He made field trips to Tierra del Fuego in 1920–1921 and to central India in 1938–1939, and the material he collected from these field trips appears in numerous publications. He was one of the organizers of the International Congresses of Anthropological and Ethnological Sciences and a member of many learned societies.

The range of Koppers' scholarly interests was broad. He was a student of Father Wilhelm Schmidt, professor of ethnology and linguistics at the Mission Seminary of St. Gabriel, and later collaborated with him for 18 years in the editing of *Anthropos*. Schmidt was a leading proponent of *Kulturkreis* theory, and Koppers began as a disciple. By 1931, however, Koppers had begun to depart from the theories of *Kulturkreis* (see his 1931 review in *Anthropos* of O. Menghin's *Weltgeschichte der Steinzeit*). He considered the *Kulturkreis* a working hypothesis but not a method for obtaining satisfactory explanations of cultural phenomena. He preferred the historical method because it can be used for any ethnological problem and for any period in history.

In studying cultural phenomena, Koppers first made a minute analysis of all the elements to be found in a culture area and then, by means of comparative studies, looked for parallelisms and possible diffusion. This comparative approach marked a departure from the older *Kulturkreis* criteria of quantity, quality, time, and continuity. Koppers recommended close cooperation with other disciplines, especially history, prehistory, and archeology. Since historical records and verbal traditions cover only a comparatively short period of the history of mankind, a relative chronology has to be used to order ethnological data. He acknowledged the importance of functionalism and of structural studies as supplementary methods for obtaining a comprehensive knowledge of cultural phenomena.

Koppers' ethnosociological, economic, and religious investigations among tribes of hunters and food gatherers resulted in many discoveries about the origin and growth of human society. He studied the role of the individual in primitive society, as well as that of the family and of the local group; he sought to explain the origin of the state; and he tried to develop an interpretation of the earliest stages of mankind on a universal and historical basis.

Anna Hohenwart-Gerlachstein

[*See also* Culture area; Ethnology; History, *article on* culture history; *and the biographies of* Frobenius; Graebner; Schmidt.]

### WORKS BY KOPPERS

1915–1916   Die ethnologische Wirtschaftsforschung: Eine historisch–kritische Studie. *Anthropos* 10:611–651; 11:971–1079.

1924   Die menschliche Wirtschaft. Pages 375–681 in *Der Mensch aller Zeiten: Natur und Kultur der Völker der Erde.* Volume 3: Völker und Kulturen; Part 1: Gesellschaft und Wirtschaft der Völker, by W. Schmidt and W. Koppers. Regensburg (Germany): Habbel.

1928   Individualforschung unter den Primitiven, im besonderen unter den Yamana auf Feuerland. Pages 349–365 in *Festschrift, publication d'hommage offerte au P. W. Schmidt: 76 sprachwissenschaftliche, ethnologische, religionswissenschaftliche, prähistorische und andere Studien.* Edited by W. Koppers. Vienna: Mechitaristen-Congregations-Buchdruckerei.

1931   [A Review of O. Menghin's] *Weltgeschichte der Steinzeit. Anthropos* 26:223–243.

1937a   Historische und ethnologische Methodik. Pages 13–19 in Wilhelm Schmidt, *Handbuch der Methode der kulturhistorischen Ethnologie.* Münster (Germany): Aschendorff.

1937b   Die Quellen der Ethnologie und ihre methodische Behandlung. Pages 81–117 in Wilhelm Schmidt, *Handbuch der Methode der kulturhistorischen Ethnologie.* Münster (Germany): Aschendorff.

1948   *Die Bhil in Zentralindien.* Wiener Beiträge zur Kulturgeschichte und Linguistik, Vol. 7. Horn (Austria): Berger.

(1949) 1952   *Primitive Man and His World Picture.* London and New York: Sheed & Ward. → First published in German.

1951a   Der historische Gedanke in Ethnologie und Religionswissenschaft. Volume 1, pages 79–109 in Franz König (editor), *Christus und die Religionen der Erde: Handbuch der Religionsgeschichte.* Vienna: Herder.

1951b   Der älteste Mensch und seine Religion. Volume 1, pages 115–160 in Franz König (editor), *Christus und die Religionen der Erde: Handbuch der Religionsgeschichte.* Vienna: Herder.

1952  Der historische Gedanke in Ethnologie und Prähistorie. Pages 11–65 in *Kultur und Sprache.* Wiener Beiträge zur Kulturgeschichte und Linguistik, Vol. 9. Vienna: Herold.

1954  International Symposium of Anthropology (New York, 9.–20. Juni 1952.): Eine ethnologisch–historische Würdigung. Anthropologische Gesellschaft in Wien, *Mitteilungen* 83:40–60.

1955a  Diffusion: Transmission and Acceptance. *Yearbook of Anthropology* 1:169–181.

1955b  Ethnologie und Geschichte. *Anthropos* 50:943–948.

1957  Das Problem der Universalgeschichte im Lichte von Ethnologie und Prähistorie. *Anthropos* 52:369–389.

1959  Grundsätzliches und Geschichtliches zur ethnologischen Kulturkreislehre. Pages 110–126 in Österreichisches Symposion, First, Wartenstein (Castle), 1958, *Beiträge Österreichs zur Erforschung der Vergangenheit und Kulturgeschichte der Menschheit, mit besonderer Berücksichtigung Mitteleuropas.* Horn (Austria): Berger.

SUPPLEMENTARY BIBLIOGRAPHY

Burgmann, Arnold 1961 Professor Dr. Wilhelm Koppers SVD. *Anthropos* 56:721–736.

Luzbetak, Louis J. 1961 Father Wilhelm Koppers, S.V.D. *Anthropological Quarterly* 34, no. 3:164 only.

# KŐRÖSY, JÓZSEF

József Kőrösy (1844–1906) was a pioneer Hungarian statistician. He was born in Pest, where his father was a merchant. The family moved to the country to take up farming, but Kőrösy's father died when he was six, and he returned to Pest for his education. Financial difficulties forced him to take a job immediately upon graduating from secondary school. After working first as an insurance clerk, he became a journalist and wrote a column on economics. Although he never regularly attended a university and was almost entirely self-taught, he nevertheless acquired both proficiency in languages and advanced knowledge in his professional specialty.

The articles that Kőrösy wrote on economics revealed his excellent sense for statistics and attracted attention. Therefore, in 1869 when a municipal statistical office was first set up in Pest, Kőrösy was appointed director. Only two years had passed since Károly Keleti had set up the Hungarian national statistical service. Prior to that time there had been no such service provided for Hungary; the Austrian government statistical service in Vienna had been responsible for all data relating to Hungary and had furthermore treated most of these data as confidential. Consequently there had been little opportunity for the development of statistical thought in Hungary.

Kőrösy was a research scholar as well as an official statistician—a rare combination—and he turned the Budapest statistical office into a model research institution. (Budapest was formed in 1873, and Kőrösy's office at that time became the statistical office for the new city.) Data were collected covering nearly every aspect of Budapest life. Publications by the office included both methodological experiments and pragmatic analyses, usually written by Kőrösy. He edited the statistical publications of Budapest and was in charge of publishing the first comparative statistics relating to big cities (for vital statistics, see 1874; for finances, see 1877; and so forth).

From 1883 on, Kőrösy was also a reader at the University of Budapest; he lectured there in the field of demography. He was a member of many statistical organizations and of other scientific societies and the recipient of numerous honors and awards, both at home and abroad.

Kőrösy contributed voluminously to the statistical and demographic literature of his age, and his contributions covered a wide range of subjects. His studies of Budapest included detailed analyses both of the city's population census and of mortality. He also used Budapest data to study patterns of contagious diseases, pauperism, public education, construction, taxation, and—with newly developed indicators—corporation profits.

His most outstanding papers from the methodological point of view were those in which he developed the first "natality" (or fertility) tables. These tables and other investigations showed the relationship between the parents' ages and the viability of the newborn infant, as well as the effect of the ages of spouses and the length of their marriage on fertility and family size.

Kőrösy also made important contributions to the problem of obtaining reliable mortality tables. Although his "individual method" of constructing generation mortality tables was not practicable, his proposals make him a precursor of modern cohort analysis. The individual method is an extremely laborious one: Kőrösy planned to follow the life histories of a certain number of persons by using a separate chart for each individual, a sort of perpetual register from birth to death; the charts would then be used to construct mortality tables. In this way precise and valuable data could be obtained, but the method was far too costly to be the final solution to the problem of compiling mortality rates, as Kőrösy believed it was (Saile 1927, pp. 237–238). Other pioneer research by Kőrösy dealt with the hereditary character of certain illnesses and with the effects of weather, housing conditions, educational level, and income level on morbidity and mortality.

Kőrösy tried many methodological innovations, most of which were successful. For example, his ingenious coefficients of relative intensity of morbidity or mortality enabled him to point out connections between phenomena when the size and distribution of the basic population are unknown. And although he was working at a time when the use of mathematics in statistics was not yet commonplace, the indexes he introduced for measuring association are very similar to those developed later by Pearson and Yule (see Jordan 1927, p. 337; Goodman & Kruskal 1959). He also had a great deal to do with introducing standardized descriptions of the causes of death—here he worked with Bertillon—and was active in attempts to standardize population censuses internationally. Along with Ogle in Britain and Koch in Germany, Kőrösy introduced the standardized death rate, which mitigates the problem of comparing over-all death rates in populations of diverse age distributions (Kőrösy 1892–1893; Annual Summary . . . 1883; Hamburg, Statistisches Landesamt 1883).

The statistics collected by Kőrösy's office did much to lower the death rate in Budapest, in part by making clear the need for improved health standards. Battling against false statistics and erroneous methods, he fought for the use of smallpox vaccine (see Westergaard 1932, pp. 253–254).

In doctrine he stood close to Wilhelm Lexis, although he was ahead of Lexis in his knowledge of the laws of demography. Although Kőrösy did not write textbooks on either statistics or demography, his collaborators and students, most notably Gusztáv Thirring, built on the extensive and sound foundations he laid.

LAJOS THIRRING

[For the historical context of Kőrösy's work, see SOCIOLOGY, article on THE EARLY HISTORY OF SOCIAL RESEARCH; VITAL STATISTICS; and the biography of LEXIS; for discussion of the subsequent development of his ideas, see STATISTICS, DESCRIPTIVE, article on ASSOCIATION; and the biographies of PEARSON and YULE.]

#### WORKS BY KŐRÖSY

1871  Pest szabad királyi város az 1870, évben: A népszámlálás és népleirás eredménye. Budapest: Ráth. → Also published in 1872 in German by the same publisher.
1874  Welche Unterlagen hat die Statistik zu beschaffen um richtige Mortalitäts-tabellen zu gewinnen? Berlin: Engel. → Reprinted in section 1 of International Statistical Congress, Ninth, Budapest, 1876, Programme.
1877  Statistique internationale des grandes villes. Deuxième Section: Finances. Budapest: Ráth; Paris: Guillaumin.
1881  Projet d'un recensement du monde. Paris: Guillaumin.
1885  On the Unification of Census Record Tables. Journal of the Royal Statistical Society Series A Jubilee Volume: 159–170.
(1887) 1889  Kritik der Vaccinations-statistik und neue Beiträge zur Frage des Impfschutzes. Berlin: Puttkammer & Mühlbrecht.
1892a  Mortalitäts-coëfficient und Mortalitäts-index. Institut international de statistique, Bulletin 6, no. 2:305–361.
1892b  Wissenschaftliche Stellung und Grenzen der Demologie. Allgemeines statistisches Archiv 2:397–418.
1892–1893  Einfluss des Alters der Eltern auf die Vitalität ihrer Kinder. Volume 10, pages 262–263 in International Congress of Hygiene and Demography, London, 1891, Transactions. London: Eyre & Spottiswoode.
1894  Über den Zusammenhang zwischen Armuth und infectiösen Krankheiten und über die Methode der Intensitätsrechnung. Zeitschrift für Hygiene und Infectionskrankheiten 18:505–528.
1896  An Estimate of the Degrees of Legitimate Natality as Derived From a Table of Natality Compiled by the Author From His Observations Made at Budapest. Royal Society of London, Philosophical Transactions Series B 186:781–875.
1900  La statistique des résultats financières des sociétés anonymes. Paris: Dupont.
1906  Über die Statistik der Ergiebigkeit der Ehen. Institut International de Statistique, Bulletin 15, no. 2: 404–416.

#### SUPPLEMENTARY BIBLIOGRAPHY

Annual Summary of Births, Deaths, and Causes of Death in London and Other Large Cities. 1883 Great Britain, General Register Office, Weekly Return of Births and Deaths in London and in Twenty-two Other Large Towns of the United Kingdom 54:i–lv.
GOODMAN, LEO A.; and KRUSKAL, WILLIAM H. 1959 Measures of Association for Cross Classifications: II. Further Discussion and References. Journal of the American Statistical Association 54:123–163.
HAMBURG, STATISTISCHES LANDESAMT Statistik des Hamburgischen Staats [1883], Heft 12.
J. A. B. 1907 Dr. Joseph Kőrösy.—M. G. Olanesco. Journal of the Royal Statistical Society 70:332–333. → The author of the article is J. A. Baines.
JORDAN, CHARLES 1927 Les coefficients d'intensité relative de Kőrösy. Société Hongroise de Statistique, Revue 5:332–345.
LAKY, DÉSIRÉ 1939 Les représentants académiciens de la grande époque de la statistique hongroise. Société Hongroise de Statistique, Journal 17:365–378.
SAILE, TIVADAR A. 1927 Influence de Joseph de Kőrösy sur l'évolution de la statistique. Budapest: Magyar Tudományos Akadémia.
THIRRING, GUSZTÁV 1907 Joseph de Kőrösy. Institut International de Statistique, Bulletin 16, no. 1:150–155.
WESTERGAARD, HARALD L. 1932 Contributions to the History of Statistics. London: King.

# KOYRÉ, ALEXANDRE

Alexandre Koyré (1892–1964), historian of science, was born in Taganrog, Russia. His family was well-to-do—his father, an industrialist, had interests in the Baku oil fields—and there was no need for Koyré to worry about a career after he had completed his secondary studies in Tiflis and Rostov-on-Don. In 1908 he went to Göttingen, where he remained for three years, taking courses with Husserl and Hilbert; he then went to Paris for another three years of study, especially under Bergson, Picavet, and Léon Brunschvicg. In 1914 he enlisted in the French army. The Russian Revolution destroyed his financial resources, and at the end of the war he had to find a profession. At the École Pratique des Hautes Études, where he had been appointed as instructor, he obtained a diploma, with a thesis entitled *Essai sur l'idée de Dieu et les preuves de son existence chez Descartes* (1922). He was married in that same year. Later he received a doctoral degree from the University of Paris with a thesis on the philosophy of Jacob Boehme (1929).

After a year as *maître de conférence* at Montpellier, from 1929 to 1930, Koyré returned to Paris as instructor at the École Pratique des Hautes Études, where he taught until his retirement. In the 1930s he was on several occasions visiting professor in Cairo. During World War II he taught at the New School for Social Research in New York, and after the war at the University of Chicago, Johns Hopkins University, and the University of Wisconsin. In 1956 he was appointed a member of the Institute for Advanced Study at Princeton. He served as director of the Centre de Recherches d'Histoire des Sciences et des Techniques, connected with the École Pratique des Hautes Études, and as permanent secretary of the Académie Internationale d'Histoire des Sciences. He was honored by the Académie des Sciences, the Académie des Sciences Morales et Politiques, the History of Science Society, and the Centre Nationale de la Recherche Scientifique.

From 1933 on, when his first studies in philosophy and religion convinced him of the unity of human thought, Koyré made this conception of unity the guiding principle in his research into scientific thought. It was as a philosopher and scholar that he studied sixteenth-century and seventeenth-century astronomy, mechanics, and mathematics: from Tartaglia to More, from Copernicus to Newton. The date of the appearance of his *Etudes galiléennes*, 1939, is a crucial one for the history of science.

The following precepts characterize Koyré's method:

(1) It is important to go back to original texts, as far as possible in their original languages, without converting their terms or their methods into a modern idiom.

(2) Scientific works should be related to their intellectual context, which means (*a*) a comprehensive scrutiny of the relevant literature, rather than the more or less arbitrary selection of extracts; (*b*) investigation of the works of minor and unknown writers, as well as of those of the great authors; (*c*) finding out what the scientists themselves made of their own discoveries and what opinions, however false, their contemporaries had of the value of these discoveries; (*d*) an appreciation of the originality of a thinker's contribution, rather than its reduction to an outgrowth of the work of his precursors.

(3) The shifts in an author's point of view should be followed attentively.

(4) Errors and failures should be studied as carefully as successes, so that the development of thought may be grasped "dans le mouvement même de son activité créatrice"—in the very process of its creative growth.

(5) Within the basic unity of human thought, scientific thought has a special character, and this should be revealed by focusing study on scientific works, rather than straying into psychological, economic, or other explanations of how they came about.

These theoretical and methodological precepts reflect Koyré's conception of the history of science, which may be summed up as follows:

(1) The realm of ideas is fundamentally one, and it has priority over other areas of human activity. Experience is secondary, although the positivists have never understood this. Koyré was a Platonist and liked to consider Galileo's work, for example, as an experimental verification of Platonism.

(2) In Koyré's Platonic conception of science, and contrary to the Aristotelian view, there is a progressive mathematization of the physical world, "from the world of the approximate to the universe of the exact."

(3) The progress of thought is orderly, which means both that the world of ideas is timeless and that the creative potential of thought is realized in time.

(4) Thought progresses from confusion to clarity by virtue of errors that are overcome. As Kepler had admonished: "Know then that it is errors that show us the road to truth."

Koyré's influence was delayed but has been increasing. In France, scholars at the Centre de Recherche d'Histoire des Sciences et des Techniques—Pierre Costabel, René Taton, F. Russo— have been carrying on his work; in the United States, the generation of historians of science whose careers began just before or during World War II—Marshall Clagett, I. Bernard Cohen, Charles C. Gillispie, Henry Guerlac, John Murdoch —owes a debt to Koyré.

YVON BELAVAL

[*See also* SCIENCE, *article on* THE HISTORY OF SCIENCE. *Other relevant material may be found in  the biography of* SARTON.]

### WORKS BY KOYRÉ

1922  *Essai sur l'idée de Dieu et les preuves de son existence chez Descartes.* Paris: Leroux.

1929  *La philosophie de Jacob Boehme.* Paris: Vrin.

1938  *Trois leçons sur Descartes.* Cairo, Université Égyptienne, Faculté des Lettres, Publications, No. 20. Cairo: Imprimerie Nationale.

1939  *Études galiléennes.* Actualités scientifiques et industrielles, Nos. 852, 853, and 854. 3 vols. in 1. Paris: Hermann. → Volume 1: *À l'aube de la science classique.* Volume 2: *La loi de la chute des corps: Descartes et Galilée.* Volume 3: *Galilée et la loi d'inertie.*

1953  An Experiment in Measurement. American Philosophical Society, Philadelphia, *Proceedings* 97:222–237.

1955  *A Documentary History of the Problem of Fall From Kepler to Newton: De Motu Gravium Naturaliter Cadentium in Hypothesi Terrae Motae.* American Philosophical Society, Transactions, N.S. Volume 45, part 4. Philadelphia: The Society.

1957  *From the Closed World to the Infinite Universe.* Baltimore: Johns Hopkins Press.

1961  *La révolution astronomique: Copernic, Kepler, Borelli.* Paris: Hermann.

1962  *Études d'histoire de la pensée philosophique.* Paris: Colin.

*Newtonian Studies.* Cambridge, Mass.: Harvard Univ. Press, 1965—.

### WORKS ABOUT KOYRÉ

BELAVAL, YVON 1964 Les recherches philosophiques d'Alexandre Koyré. *Critique* 20:675–704.

COHEN, I. BERNARD; and TATON, RENÉ 1964 Hommage à Alexandre Koyré. Preface in *Mélanges Alexandre Koyré publiés à l'occasion de son 70e anniversaire.* Volume 1: L'aventure de la science. Paris: Hermann.

COSTABEL, PIERRE; and GILLISPIE, CHARLES C. 1964 In Memoriam: Alexandre Koyré (1892–1964). *Archives internationales d'histoire des sciences* 17, no. 67:149–156.

HERIVEL, J. 1965 Alexandre Koyré [Obituary]. *British Journal for the History of Science* 2:257–259.

*Mélanges Alexandre Koyré publiés à l'occasion de son 70e anniversaire.* 2 vols. 1964 Paris: Hermann.

RUSSO, F. 1965 Alexandre Koyré et l'histoire de la pensée scientifique. *Archives de philosophie* 23, no. 3:337–361.

## KRAEPELIN, EMIL

Emil Kraepelin was born in 1856 in Neustrelitz and died in 1926 in Munich, where he had been professor of psychiatry and director of the psychiatric clinic since 1903. He wrote extensively on problems of criminality, opposing the beating of offenders and capital punishment. He was opposed to drinking and smoking, both of which he disliked for eugenic reasons: he thought that alcohol and nicotine undermined the national health and rendered Germany less fit for international competition. He was, however, in favor of sex and marriage, if only for purposes of drive reduction and procreation; he rejected romantic and less materialistic notions regarding the social institution of marriage. His intense nationalism survived World War I, and his view that classification is fundamental to the development of psychiatry as a science survived the advent of Freudian psychology, which he opposed with irony and sarcasm. Kraepelin is best known in psychiatry for his contribution to the classification of mental disorders, particularly the psychoses. There may have been some hereditary predisposition which led him to choose nosology as his main concern; his brother Karl became a well-known botanist.

Kraepelin's enormous influence was exerted in part through his many pupils, at least a dozen of whom achieved international reputations, but mainly through his great *Compendium der Psychiatrie* (1883). The work was first published in 1883, when the author was *Privatdozent* in Leipzig; it went through nine editions, the last of which was not completed because of Kraepelin's sudden death. The crucial advance in Kraepelin's thinking was made in the 1899 (sixth) edition, where he defined and clearly opposed the two great psychotic disease-complexes—dementia praecox and manic–depressive insanity. Modern systems of classification, in spite of many slight changes, still fundamentally resemble Kraepelin's final ordering. No doubt there were predecessors who anticipated, and successors who improved upon, his ideas; nevertheless, Kraepelin remains the main architect of modern nosology.

Kraepelin's nosological contributions are well known; less well known, but possibly even more original and important, are the experimental studies inspired or carried out by him in which methods and designs of the psychological laboratory were applied for the first time to the problems and theories of the psychiatric clinic. As a young student of 21, Kraepelin became friendly with Wilhelm Wundt, who is widely regarded as the founder of experimental psychology and who must probably be credited with the creation of the first psychological laboratory. In 1882, four years after he had obtained his medical degree, Kraepelin returned to Leipzig with the expressed desire of working near Wundt. Flechsig, the director of the Leipzig clinic, was offended by Kraepelin's obvious preference for scientific work in the psychological sphere and terminated his appointment. Wundt advised the young man against concentrating on psychology entirely, and after Kraepelin spent some time in the Nervenpoliklinik under W. Erb, a position he owed to Wundt's support, he became a senior physician there. He had turned away from academic work, where he thought he had no future; however, he was thought of more highly than he had imagined and in 1885 was appointed professor in Dorpat. Six years later he was called to Heidelberg.

Kraepelin's application of psychological methods was a pioneering adventure in two directions. In the first place, he used objective tests to determine the psychological deficits of mental patients. Where previously everything had been surmise, observation, and subjective guesswork, he introduced objectivity, measurement, and demonstration. It is not always appreciated just how advanced some of Kraepelin's work was. For instance, his interest in work curves and work decrement led him to anticipate such phenomena as reminiscence, blocking, and reactive inhibition—all fundamental to modern learning theory, but now mostly credited to much later writers. It is probably this failure of modern workers in the fields of learning theory, personality research, and abnormal psychology to realize the extent and quality of Kraepelin's contribution that has prevented his being recognized as the father of "clinical psychology." The dedication of the recent *Handbook of Abnormal Psychology* to him may be a fitting act of restitution.

Kraepelin's second great contribution was inspired by his already noted execration of tobacco and alcohol, which led him to pioneering work in the field now christened "psychopharmacology." He was the first to test the effect of drugs on human behavior by means of established laboratory techniques, and while his tests and experimental designs were no doubt primitive by modern standards, his conclusions have usually been supported by later workers. Again, the originality of his work has not received the appreciation which it deserves; possibly the fact that his contributions have not been translated into English has something to do with this neglect.

The whole outlook of Kraepelin has, of course, been submerged by the rising tide of "dynamic" psychology, psychoanalysis, and "personalism." The obvious antagonism between the careful, scientific, biological outlook of Kraepelin and the speculative, uncritical, humanistic–literary outlook of the modern schools has led to a temporary eclipse of Kraepelinian modes of work and approach, particu-

larly in the United States. In England and France, and particularly in Germany, there has not been anything like this swing of the pendulum, and it is likely that the demonstrated failure of psychoanalysis to lead to successful cures even in its own chosen field—that of the neuroses—will bring back to favor the fundamentally sounder approach of Kraepelin.

H. J. Eysenck

[*For the historical context of Kraepelin's work, see the biography of* Wundt; *for discussion of the subsequent development of his ideas, see* Depressive disorders; Mental disorders; Mental disorders, treatment of; Psychosis; Schizophrenia.]

### WORKS BY KRAEPELIN

(1883) 1909–1915   *Psychiatrie*. 8th ed., rev., 4 vols. Leipzig: Barth. → First published as *Compendium der Psychiatrie*.

1885   Zur Psychologie des Komischen. *Philosophische Studien* 2:128–160; 327–361.

1886   Über Erinnerungsfälschungen. *Archiv für Psychiatrie und Nervenkrankheiten* 17:830–843.

1892a   *Über die Beeinflussung einfacher psychischer Vorgänge durch einige Arzneimittel*. Jena (Germany): Fischer.

1892b   Die Abgrenzung der Paranoia. *Neurologisches Zentralblatt* 795.

1899   Neuere Untersuchungen über die psychischen Wirkungen des Alkohols. *Münchener medizinische Wochenschrift* 46:1365–1369.

(1901–1905) 1913   *Lectures on Clinical Psychiatry*. London: Baillière. → First published in German.

(1917) 1962   *One Hundred Years of Psychiatry*. New York: Citadel Press. → First published in German.

### SUPPLEMENTARY BIBLIOGRAPHY

American Psychiatric Association 1959   *Epidemiology of Mental Disorder: A Symposium Organized by the American Psychiatric Association to Commemorate the Centennial of the Birth of Emil Kraepelin*. Publication No. 60. Washington: American Association for the Advancement of Science.

Boor, Wolfgang de 1954   *Psychiatrische Systematik: Ihre Entwicklung in Deutschland seit Kahlbaum*. Berlin: Springer.

Kahn, Eugen 1956   Emil Kraepelin: 1856–1926–1956. *American Journal of Psychiatry* 113:289–294.

Kahn, Eugen 1959   The Emil Kraepelin Memorial Lecture. Pages 1–38 in American Psychiatric Association, *Epidemiology of Mental Disorder*. Washington: American Association for the Advancement of Science. → Includes four pages of bibliography.

Kolle, Kurt 1957   *Kraepelin und Freud: Beitrag zur neueren Geschichte der Psychiatrie*. Stuttgart (Germany): Thieme.

# KRETSCHMER, ERNST

Ernst Kretschmer (1888–1964), German physician and psychologist, was born in Wüstenrot near Heilbronn, the son of a Württemberg pastor. The diversity of physical and mental constitutions that existed in Kretschmer's own family, especially the difference in temperament between his parents, may very well have planted the seed for his best-known work *Physique and Character* (1921). His mother was sensitive, humorous, artistic, and lively; while his father, a profound thinker and idealist philosopher, was so Spartan, sober, dry, and laconic that he appeared to lack aesthetic sensibility. It does seem significant that Kretschmer was initially most successful in elaborating the pyknic–cyclothymic group of types to which his mother belonged. Beyond this he did best in developing the contrast between cyclothymic and schizothymic temperaments; his father was an almost pure example of a schizothyme.

Kretschmer studied philosophy at the University of Tübingen but after two semesters switched to medicine. He also studied medicine in Munich, where he was greatly influenced by Emil Kraepelin, and at the Eppendorf Hospital in Hamburg. He had intended to establish himself as a physician in a hospital or clinic and had no thought of an academic career. However, his doctoral dissertation, *Wahnbildung und manisch–depressiver Symptomkomplex* (1914), a notably mature work for a beginner, had attracted the attention of Robert Gaupp, a Tübingen psychiatrist and one of Kretschmer's professors. Gaupp, who saw the special quality of Kretschmer's mind, arranged—almost against Kretschmer's wishes—a regular position for him in his clinic.

After three months in Gaupp's clinic, Kretschmer volunteered for military service. Despite his limited clinical experience, his first assignment was to establish a neurological department in the Bad Mergentheim military hospital. The immediate practical problems of treating his patients forced him to read deeply on neurology and the theories of neuroses and hysteria. His study and his therapeutic work led him to do research on the regularities underlying hysterical phenomena. The first and most important of these regularities is the law of the arbitrary intensification of reflexes. From his observation of a long and complex series of phenomena he also developed an important new approach to neuropsychological science which he called multidimensional thinking, multidimensional diagnosis, and multidimensional therapy. Accordingly, he sought rigorously in his research to establish the etiology of particular pathological elements as well as their interrelations in a clinical picture.

In 1918 Kretschmer left Bad Mergentheim to become a *Privatdozent* at Tübingen. His inaugural lecture was on the influence of psychiatry on the development of modern ethical conceptions. In this lecture he traced the influence of scientific thought on the development of ethical norms and showed the consequences of this influence for psychiatric reports, pedagogy, and criminology. He ended with the plea that the goals of education be defined according to each individual's constitutional limits and that society be protected from the uneducable.

Kretschmer was a prolific author and, from 1919 on, wrote a book almost every year. The publication of *Physique and Character* in 1921 was enthusiastically acclaimed by Gaupp and others; unfortunately, Kretschmer's name came to be too exclusively linked with this book. It gave rise to violent scientific feuds which were to flare up again during the Nazi period. Differences in social philosophy undoubtedly accounted for the polemics— often passionate—against Kretschmer's theories; yet his concept of types has gradually become part of popular culture and has been prominent in some contemporary psychological research. Most notably, William Sheldon has devised sophisticated photographic and anthropometric techniques to assess constitutional components and has attempted to relate constitution to temperament (Sheldon 1940). Hans J. Eysenck has also carried out research on this subject (1950).

In 1926 Kretschmer left Tübingen to become professor of psychiatry and neurology at the University of Marburg (Lahn). In this position he demonstrated that he was a good judge of men. He picked able young assistants and gave them the freedom to do research in the direction for which they were best suited. F. Mauz developed the use of constitutional types for diagnostic purposes, while W. Enke introduced new constitutional–biological concepts into experimental psychology.

From 1946 until his retirement as director of the Neurological Clinic of the University of Tübingen in 1959, Kretschmer was concerned chiefly with the development and elaboration of research on the constitutional biology and psychopathology of childhood and youth. He analyzed variations in the rate of development of children, the various crises of puberty, the inherent regularities of sexual development, and the findings on the blood chemistry, endocrinology, and pharmacology of constitutional types. He also worked out new techniques of hypnosis and psychotherapy.

As he had done in 1918, Kretschmer again boldly took up ethical and religious problems, especially in his *Psychotherapeutische Studien* (1949). This book was followed by fundamental work on the diagnosis of compulsive criminals, with recommendations for modifications in the criminal law that would permit adequate treatment of these criminals. In connection with the developmental patterns he had discovered, he set forth new approaches to guidance in puberty crises and schizophrenia. He also pointed to the gains that could accrue in preventive medicine from having more knowledge of the tendencies toward disease of different constitutional types.

In the field of the healthy personality Kretschmer called attention to the significance of the constitution in mental achievement. This connection is of particular importance to those responsible for the selection of people according to their potential for achievement and for subsequent fulfillment of that potential. Proper selection is facilitated by tailoring the demands as closely as possible to the specific inherent achievement potential of a given constitution.

W. ENKE

[For the historical context of Kretschmer's work, see the biography of KRAEPELIN; for discussion of the subsequent development of his ideas, see PSYCHOLOGY, article on CONSTITUTIONAL PSYCHOLOGY.]

### WORKS BY KRETSCHMER

1914    Wahnbildung und manisch–depressiver Symptomkomplex. Berlin: Reimer. → Reprinted from Volume 71 of the Allgemeine Zeitschrift für Psychiatrie.

(1918) 1950    Der sensitive Beziehungswahn. 3d ed. Heidelberg (Germany): Springer.

1919    Psychogene Wahnbildungen bei traumatischer Hirnschwäche. Annalen für Gewerbe und Bauwesen 84: 272–300.

(1921) 1936    Physique and Character: An Investigation of the Nature of Constitution and the Theory of Temperament. New ed., rev. London: Routledge. → First published in German.

(1922) 1952    A Text-book of Medical Psychology. London: Hogarth. → First published in German. The twelfth German edition was published in 1963 by Thieme.

(1923) 1960    Hysteria, Reflex, and Instinct. New York: Philosophical Library. → First published in German.

(1929) 1931    The Psychology of Men of Genius. New York: Harcourt. → First published as Geniale Menschen. References to music, poetry, and the visual arts, which pervade all of Kretschmer's work, are particularly apparent in this book.

1936    KRETSCHMER, ERNST; and ENKE, WILLI. Die Persönlichkeit der Athletiker. Leipzig: Thieme.

1949    Psychotherapeutische Studien. Stuttgart (Germany): Thieme.

1963    Gestalten und Gedanken: Erlebnisse. Stuttgart (Germany): Thieme.

### SUPPLEMENTARY BIBLIOGRAPHY

ENKE, W.    1964a    Ernst Kretschmer zum 75. Geburtstag. Fortschritte der Medizin 81, no. 23:913 only.

ENKE, W.    1964b    Prof. Dr. med., Dr. phil. h.c., Dr. med. h.c. Ernst Kretschmer: In Memoriam. Fortschritte der Medizin 82, no. 13:477 only.

EYSENCK, HANS J.    (1950) 1954    Cyclothymia and Schizothymia as a Dimension of Personality: Historical Review. Pages 162–188 in Howard Brand (editor), The Study of Personality: A Book of Readings. New York:

Wiley; London: Chapman. → First published in Volume 19 of the Journal of Personality.

SHELDON, WILLIAM H.    1940    The Varieties of Human Physique: An Introduction to Constitutional Psychology. New York: Harper.

# KRIS, ERNST

Ernst Kris (1900–1957), art historian and psychoanalyst, was born in Vienna, the son of an attorney. In 1922 he received a PH.D. in the history of art from the University of Vienna. He served as assistant curator at the Kunsthistorische Museum and contributed important studies to the history of crystals, gems, cameos, gold work, and handicraft. In 1929 he was invited to study and catalogue the Milton Weil collection of postclassical cameos at the Metropolitan Museum in New York City.

In 1927 Kris married Marianne Rie, whose father, Dr. Oskar Rie, was the pediatrician for Sigmund Freud's children. Kris met Freud and became an active participant in the psychoanalytic movement in Vienna.

**Psychoanalysis and art.**    Kris brought to psychoanalysis his profound knowledge of art and from 1933 wrote many articles applying psychoanalytic concepts to the study of art, which in 1952 were collected in a book, Psychoanalytic Explorations in Art. The introductory chapter, written especially for this volume, is entitled "Approaches to Art" and begins significantly with a section on "The Contribution of Psychoanalysis and Its Limitations," in which he stressed the need to validate hypotheses by documentation and clinical observation.

Kris sought to elucidate the relation of the life of the artist to his work, the role of art as communication, and, basic to any psychoanalytic study, the role of unconscious psychic forces in the creative act. His writings on art include biographical essays, the consideration of aesthetic problems, and several papers on the "art" of the insane in which he contrasted the spontaneous productions of the insane and the artist. The artist has the capacity to bring to consciousness what others, less gifted, keep repressed; in the insane, however, there is an uncontrolled irruption of unconscious mental content. In the case of the artist, the inspirational phase of the creative act, "regression in the service of the ego," is followed by a second phase, "elaboration," in which the artist's ego molds his imagery and thought into a created work that will evoke an aesthetic response in his audience (1939). To the extent that the psychotic has lost the necessary ego capacity for elaboration, his productions do not communicate and can be understood only if they are analyzed in the same manner as the imagery of a dream. Kris's demonstration of the role of ego functions in artistic creation led him to question the common association of artistic creativity and mental illness. He asserted that "Clinical experience . . . demonstrates that art as an aesthetic—and therefore as a social—phenomenon is linked to the intactness of the ego. Although there are many transitions, the extremes are clear" (Pappenheim & Kris 1946*b*, p. 28).

**Analysis of wartime broadcasts.**    With the rise of Nazism in Austria, Kris migrated to England. During the war he served in the British Broadcasting Corporation, using psychoanalytic principles in the analysis of Nazi radio broadcasts. In an article, "The 'Danger' of Propaganda" (1941), Kris described the factors that enter into the suggestibility of persons exposed to propaganda and also explained the techniques used by the German broadcasters to create in the listener a sense of infantile passivity and uncertainty, while at the same time portraying the German as a powerful and omniscient parental figure. Kris demonstrated that the best way to deal with propaganda is to reduce the passivity and uncertainty of the listener by giving him as many facts as is possible without jeopardizing national security. Subsequently he carried on similar work in the United States. In 1944 he published, with the collaboration of several other authors, *German Radio Propaganda: Report on Home Broadcasts During the War* (Kris & Speier 1944). A number of shorter papers on this theme appeared in different journals (see "Writings of Ernst Kris" 1958).

**Studies in psychoanalytic theory.**    In his later years Kris's interests centered on basic problems of psychoanalytic psychology, which he approached by clinical studies and by direct observation of child behavior and child development. His papers form a detailed elaboration and confirmation of early theories formulated by Freud. Some of these studies were carried out in collaboration with two other prominent psychoanalysts, Heinz Hartmann and Rudolph M. Loewenstein. In particular, Kris was concerned with the interrelationships and development of the different functional units of the psyche that are denoted structurally as id, ego, and superego. He made fundamental studies of the manifestations of instinctual drive impulses, the concept of psychic energy, and the ego functions involved in adapting the instinctual drives to the demands of reality, such as defenses and sublimation (Hartmann et al. 1946*a*; Kris 1950*a*; 1951).

Kris approached basic problems of psychology, such as thought processes and memory, from the viewpoint of clinical psychoanalysis. Papers especially characteristic of his approach are "On Preconscious Mental Processes" (1950*b*) and "The Recovery of Childhood Memories in Psychoanalysis" (1956), in which he related these fundamental psychological problems to the nature of the psychoanalytic process, all the while enriching his theoretical considerations with clinical examples. In these papers Kris indicated the relation of infantile experience to adult personality structure, the significance of the concept of psychic trauma in childhood, and the role of ego defenses in thought and memory.

Kris saw psychoanalysis as a scientific discipline and sought validation of psychoanalytic propositions by detailed observation in the psychoanalytic situation and by direct observation of children. He considered the psychoanalytic interview, despite the many variables, especially the involvement of the analyst–observer, to be a useful tool for scientific study and one which would increasingly be sharpened (1947). He initiated two research projects, the Child Study Center at the Yale University Medical School and the Gifted Adolescent Research Project at the New York Psychoanalytic Institute.

Unlike Gesell, who simply observed children and set up scales of development, Kris studied the dynamic factors which influence development, both normal and pathological. Kris's emphasis was on child–parent relationships, the effects of parental attitudes on behavior, and the interrelation of constitutional and environmental factors. His studies are intensive and focused on individuals, rather than being concerned with the collection of statistics. In Kris's view, the study of a child begins before it is born, with the observation of the mother: of her reaction to the pregnancy and to the prospect of having a child (Kris 1955; Ritvo et al. 1963).

The gifted-adolescent project at the New York Psychoanalytic Institute was carried out by placing in full psychoanalytic treatment with different analysts a number of carefully chosen individuals who had demonstrated talents in various fields. The analysts met with Kris in monthly seminars to discuss their findings. This study is now inactive and did not go far enough to yield definitive results; however, it did indicate the closeness of sublimation to the instinctual life and the importance of identification with parental figures in the development of talent (Loomie et al. 1958).

An important aspect of Kris's activities in psychoanalysis both in Europe and the United States was his editorial work. In 1933 Freud invited him, along with Robert Waelder, to edit *Imago*, a journal devoted to the application of psychoanalysis to other disciplines. Kris was also one of the editors of the German edition of Freud's writings (1924–1934). With Anna Freud and Marie Bonaparte, he edited Freud's letters to Wilhelm Fliess, which Princess Bonaparte had rescued from destruction by the Nazis; the letters were published in 1950 under the title *Aus den Anfängen der Psychoanalyse*. Kris stressed the need for a publication devoted to child psychology, with the result that the widely read annual, *The Psychoanalytic Study of the Child*, eventually appeared.

Psychoanalysis as a scientific discipline is still in the phase of its development where personal contact between teacher and student plays an important role. Thus, Kris's influence as a teacher of psychoanalysis both in New York and at Yale was immeasurable. His contributions to psychoanalytic theory and practice and his emphasis on the unremitting need for validation have become integral parts of psychoanalytic thought in the United States.

DAVID BERES

[*For the historical context of Kris's work, see* PSYCHOANALYSIS; *for discussion of the subsequent development of his ideas, see* AESTHETICS; ATTITUDES, *article on* ATTITUDE CHANGE; CREATIVITY, *article on* PSYCHOLOGICAL ASPECTS; LITERATURE, *article on* THE PSYCHOLOGY OF LITERATURE; PROPAGANDA; PSYCHIATRY, *article on* CHILD PSYCHIATRY.]

### WORKS BY KRIS

1939   On Inspiration. *International Journal of Psychoanalysis* 20:377–389.
1941   The "Danger" of Propaganda. *American Imago* 2: 3–42.
1944   KRIS, ERNST; and SPEIER, HANS *German Radio Propaganda: Report on Home Broadcasts During the War.* Oxford Univ. Press.
1946a   HARTMANN, HEINZ; KRIS, ERNST; and LOEWENSTEIN, RUDOLPH M. Comments on the Formation of Psychic Structure. *Psychoanalytic Study of the Child* 2:11–38.
1946b   PAPPENHEIM, ELSE; and KRIS, ERNST The Function of Drawings and the Meaning of the "Creative Spell" in Schizophrenic Artists. *Psychoanalytic Quarterly* 15:6–31.
1947   The Nature of Psychoanalytic Propositions and Their Validation. Pages 239–259 in Sidney Hook and Milton R. Konvitz (editors), *Freedom and Experience.* A New School for Social Research publication. Ithaca, N.Y.: Cornell Univ. Press.
1950a   Notes on the Development and on Some Current Problems of Psychoanalytic Child Psychology. *Psychoanalytic Study of the Child* 5:24–46.
1950b   On Preconscious Mental Processes. *Psychoanalytic Quarterly* 19:540–560.
1951   The Development of Ego Psychology. *Samiska* 5: 153–168.
1952   *Psychoanalytic Explorations in Art.* New York: International Universities Press. → Contains modified versions of Kris 1939; 1946b; 1950b.
1955   Neutralization and Sublimation: Observations on Young Children. *Psychoanalytic Study of the Child* 10:30–46.
1956   The Recovery of Childhood Memories in Psychoanalysis. *Psychoanalytic Study of the Child* 11:54–88.
1962   Decline and Recovery in the Life of a Three-year-old: Or, Data in Psychoanalytic Perspective on the Mother–Child Relationship. *Psychoanalytic Study of the Child* 17:175–215. → Published posthumously.

### SUPPLEMENTARY BIBLIOGRAPHY

FREUD, SIGMUND   1924–1934   *Gesammelte Schriften.* 12 vols. Leipzig, Vienna, and Zurich: Internationaler Psychoanalytischer Verlag.
LOOMIE, LEO S.; ROSEN, VICTOR H.; and STEIN, MARTIN H. 1958   Ernst Kris and the Gifted Adolescent Project. *Psychoanalytic Study of the Child* 13:44–63. → Contains five pages of discussion.
RITVO, SAMUEL et al.   1963   Some Relations of Constitution, Environment, and Personality as Observed in a Longitudinal Study of Child Development: Case Report. Pages 107–143 in Albert J. Solnit and Sally A. Provence (editors), *Modern Perspectives in Child Development: In Honor of Milton J. E. Senn.* New York: International Universities Press.
Writings of Ernst Kris.   1958   *Psychoanalytic Study of the Child* 13:562–573.

## KROEBER, ALFRED L.

Alfred Louis Kroeber was born in Hoboken, New Jersey, in 1876. He died in Paris in 1960, on his way home from a conference at Burg Wartenstein in Austria on "Anthropological Horizons," which he had both organized and chaired. His life span almost coincides with the rise of academic anthropology in the United States and with its emergence as a professionalized field of scholarly investigation. To this development Kroeber contributed greatly. He received in 1902 the first PH.D. in anthropology awarded by Columbia University and the second in the United States awarded for a dissertation in ethnology. He developed one of the major university-affiliated anthropological museums, in San Francisco (now in Berkeley), one of the early departments of anthropology—at the University of California—and a major monographic publication series. His own publications between 1896 and 1961 exceed five hundred items, almost all of them professional in content. (For a complete bibliography, see Steward 1962, pp. 217–253.)

The professional and personal aspects of Kroeber's life are unusually integrated. Many of his recurring scholarly interests and viewpoints are related to his own experience and were established at an early age. Kroeber's parents were Protestants of German ancestry. Although they spoke English as fluently as German, German was the language of the home. The milieu was the upper-middle-class German environment of New York City in the late nineteenth century, in which liberal intellectual interests and a deep concern with literature, music, and art were taken for granted. Kroeber early became familiar with Greek and Latin and attributed his enduring interest in linguistics to his childhood contact with four languages. For his early education he was tutored by Dr. G. Bamberger, first principal of the Ethical Culture School. Bamberger not only gave Kroeber a lively appreciation of ancient Greece but also aroused in him an avid interest in natural history. A short time later, Kroeber and a group of boys founded a "scientific society"; they collected fossils, minerals, and biological specimens and read "papers" to each other. Kroeber remained oriented toward natural history and biology, and implicit or explicit biological analogies run through his later work.

After a period at private preparatory schools Kroeber entered Columbia at the age of 16. In his sophomore year he took a deep interest in English literature and was the leader of a group that founded an undergraduate literary magazine; indeed, his first publication, in 1896, appeared in the *Columbia Literary Monthly*. The felicitous style of much of his writing stems from his continuing literary interests. His first formal contact with anthropology was Franz Boas' language seminar; of his first eight anthropological publications, four deal with folk tales, three with decorative art and symbolism, and only one with ethnology.

One reason for Kroeber's choice of anthropology as a career was almost certainly idealistic: he felt that no other subject could do as much to clear away taboos and confused thinking and so aid man's progress. Throughout his life Kroeber maintained liberal political and social viewpoints, but these were expressed mainly in an enormous interest in and sympathy with people. He believed that political and activist commitments prevent objectivity and he espoused no causes until the 1950s, when he became involved with the California Indians in the land claims cases. In the 1930s, when, for the first time, the Bureau of Indian Affairs, under John Collier, employed anthropologists, a step widely hailed by young (and unemployed) anthropologists, Kroeber disapproved and even refused to recommend students to Collier. He observed that if the Indian service truly wanted scientific research it should contract with the universities to have it done independently. The problems of independence in research and freedom of publication for government-employed anthropologists which he anticipated continue to preoccupy the professional associations.

Kroeber is sometimes referred to as the last anthropologist able to make significant contributions to all the subfields of anthropology. This is true insofar as he was interested in the unity of anthropology as a discipline. But he considered himself first of all an ethnologist, and his central concern was with the nature of culture and the search for an understanding of its processes. Whatever he did outside the field of ethnology was either the product of an incidental if acute perception of problems or was ultimately related to his concern with culture. The methods he utilized, the kinds of problems he was most interested in, and the explanatory principles he developed were all strongly conditioned by his historical bent, his familiarity with biology, and his humanistic training.

When Kroeber entered anthropology, previous work had already established the importance of culture in explaining dissimiliarities of behavior found in societies around the world. Anthropologists, at least, accepted the primacy of culture, although others in the field of social science and the public did not. Consequently, much remained to be done in assembling the evidence against simplistic biological, racist, or environmentalist explanations. To this task Kroeber devoted part of his energies, particularly in his earlier years. He believed that it is necessary to understand the biological and environmental aspects of man's existence in order to establish the nature and scope of culture.

In some ways Kroeber's most influential book was his *Anthropology* (1923). During the period in which anthropology first gained extensive recognition as a professional discipline and the number of anthropologists began to grow rapidly, this work was the only textbook. It also was a major source from which scholars in other fields as well as the general public learned about anthropology. The first edition deals at length with the inadequacies of biological and environmental explanations of man's customary behavior, including an admirable and compact summary of the evidence up to that time against racist interpretations of human differences. The 1948 second edition bears the subtitle "Race, Language, Culture, Psychology, Prehistory"; for Kroeber, these were the main subjects of anthropology. A very large part of the book deals with historical problems and the growth of civilizations.

## Anthropological research

**Physical anthropology.** Kroeber's only substantive contributions to physical anthropology, made early in his career, are two routine and, by modern standards, quite unimportant anthropometric studies. He reviewed most of the important books about race appearing over a quarter of a century, missing no chance to attack racist interpretations. In 1928 he reviewed an early book on body types by Franz Weidenreich and suggested it might offer a way out of "the relative sterility into which the study of races has got itself" (see 1928*a*). In 1920 he published *Three Essays on the Antiquity and Races of Man* (see 1920*a*); this material was later incorporated in revised form into his *Anthropology*. Although modern genetics was not available to him, he strongly emphasized evolutionary interpretations of fossil man and race origins. In 1928, in the *Quarterly Review of Biology*, he anticipated a currently active research field in a paper on subhuman cultural beginnings (see 1928*b*) and in 1934 he called attention to the importance of blood-group classifications (see 1934*a*). Kroeber's contributions to physical anthropology, then, consist primarily of critical evaluations, new interpretations, and the identification of new fields of research importance.

**Linguistics.** In the field of linguistics Kroeber's contribution was substantial and long-continuing. Much of his work stemmed from his research in California, but he also wrote on the relationships among Australian languages, and he suggested several Middle American language groupings. His early interests were primarily historical, and, partly in collaboration with Roland Burrage Dixon, he grouped the California Indian languages into a number of larger families. At the same time he pioneered studies of dialect surveys among aboriginal American Indians, publishing significant material as early as 1906 and 1907. Characteristically, in the last work he wrote on California Indian languages (published posthumously in 1963), entitled *Yokuts Dialect Survey*, he incorporated research that began in 1900.

Kroeber's 1907 paper on the Yokuts anticipates some aspects of modern glottochronology and lexicostatistics in its use of basic word lists and attempts at statistical treatment. This is acknowledged by Morris Swadesh, who developed his glottochronological and lexicostatistical methods while associated with Kroeber at Columbia University. Kroeber also explored statistical approaches with Charles D. Chrétien at Berkeley (e.g., "Quantitative Classification of Indo–European Languages" 1937). The 1963 Yokuts work includes lexicostatistical analyses and a chronological comparison of Yokuts with Athapascan.

Kroeber was concerned primarily with historical relationships within and between languages, but he also published some essentially analytical papers concerned with such problems as incorpo-

ration or noun composition. These are by no means at the level of modern structural analysis, and it is primarily for this reason that Kroeber often denied that he was a linguist. It was the very precise methodology of linguistics that interested him, and he speculated upon ways of developing similar techniques in ethnology. In the growing literature on the Hokan, Penutian, and Athapascan language families his work will continue to be basic.

**Archeology.** Kroeber's research interests in American archeology developed slowly. His contributions to California archeology, the region of his greatest ethnographic interests, are almost nil. In part this was because he perceived no significant historical depth in the archeological record. Despite early work under departmental auspices, particularly on Uhle's excavations in the Emeryville shellmound, which suggested chronological development, Kroeber saw these changes as insignificant. Like virtually all archeologists in the early years of this century, he did not attribute any great time depth to the aboriginal peopling of the New World; he recognized regional differences but not cultural change.

Kroeber's first significant contribution to archeology was the seriation of sites near Zuni on the basis of surface shard collections (1916*a*). Without Kroeber's knowledge, Kidder (1915) had used a similar approach a year or so earlier, and Nelson (1916) had established time differences in the Tano area through stratigraphic excavation [*see* KIDDER]. The data published in these three papers gave a major impetus to the recognition of time perspective in American prehistory. Kroeber's paper showed his appreciation of the cultural implications of minor variations in archeological materials, a view he had earlier rejected for California data. His statistical approach set in motion a still expanding use of statistics in archeology.

For a time Kroeber retained some interest in the Southwest, and his "Native Culture of the Southwest" (1928*c*) was the first to emphasize the important difference between Hohokam and Anasazi traditions. His archeological work, however, focused on Mexico and Peru. After a short visit to Mexico, which resulted in the first documentation of subperiods in the Mexican Archaic (now the Preclassic) period through controlled stratigraphic excavation and the seriation of surface materials, he centered his efforts on Peru. This decision was influenced in part by the Uhle collections in the University Museum. Uhle had suggested chronological depth for his materials. Kroeber, working in part with graduate students, analyzed and published articles on the Uhle collections, refining and extending the Uhle chronology. Uhle's materials lacked extensive stratigraphic evidence; he had, however, carefully classified very rich grave goods. Kroeber applied a method of sequential dating to these goods, arranging them according to stylistic similarities. Then, by comparing these materials with materials from other coastal valleys, he developed a complex time sequence. Although modified by later stratigraphic work, much of Kroeber's relative chronology still is useful. Later he undertook two major field campaigns in Peru for the Field Museum of Natural History.

Kroeber played a part in introducing controlled excavational techniques, original seriational techniques, and the use of stylistic analysis for chronological or cultural historical purposes to American archeology. His interpretative contributions in archeology are primarily the extension of theoretical viewpoints he had developed in ethnology, while his analytical categories are derived from the humanities.

**Ethnography.** Kroeber viewed himself primarily as an ethnographer and ethnologist. He did not, however, teach ethnographic methodology to his students (as, indeed, he had never taught archeological methodology). He simply expected his students to become knowledgeable through the literature and the diverse problems they encountered, always recognizing that each situation requires special adaptations. Those of his students who became involved in archeology had to teach themselves the most elementary mapping, excavating, cataloguing, and preservation techniques. Students in ethnology might be advised to take plenty of paper and pencils or not to become involved with reservation factions. Yet at various points they did learn the necessity of identifying the native viewpoint; of recording native terms, particularly for conceptual materials; of maintaining a holistic viewpoint and an awareness of the interrelatedness of culture—before any of these ideas were "discovered" by the methodologists of a later generation.

As an ethnographer Kroeber was thorough and showed great ability in establishing field rapport. His notebooks are meticulous and orderly. He returned to some groups, such as the Yurok and Mohave, time and again over almost a lifetime. Surprisingly, however, he never wrote a "complete" ethnography. His most extensive reporting on a single tribe is perhaps his early work on the Arapaho; his several publications deal with decorative symbolism (1901), ceremonial organization and religion (1902–1907), and tales and language (1916b). He paid little attention to social organization, technology, or ecological adaptations.

Kroeber's characteristic approach is clearest in California ethnography, where he made his major contributions. When he first visited California in 1900, the California Indians were little known and of little interest to anthropologists. At the time of his death probably no comparable area of the world had such a large anthropological literature, a substantial portion written by Kroeber himself. His major contribution is the *Handbook of the Indians of California* (1925), a work of more than a thousand pages, containing much previously unpublished data. Not only does the work summarize the information then known, but it also delineates cultural areas and discusses their historic implications. In the *Handbook* and in some independent short monographs Kroeber gave many excellent "abridged" but holistic ethnographic descriptions of the tribes he knew best. These are often beautifully written and perceptive, but they are far from detailed ethnographies. Most of his some seventy papers on California ethnography deal with ethnological problems, utilizing his ethnographic data. Pomo basketry (1905), for example, is dealt with in the context of California basketry, not Pomo culture; Yurok kin-term systems are described and compared with those of their neighbors (1934b). Publications on the Mohave Indians range from a preliminary sketch in 1902 to a work on Mohave pottery in 1955 (see Kroeber & Harner 1955).

## General theory

Kroeber's substantive contributions alone would make him a memorable figure in anthropology; but his influence, both in anthropology and in the social sciences more generally, derives primarily from his theoretical views. It is not easy to evaluate these so soon after his death, and the difficulty is compounded by the fact that many of his theoretical formulations are embedded more or less incidentally in a profusion of phenomenological data. They are rarely presented as theory in the grand style, but rather as interesting hypotheses. Many of his earlier theoretical interests concerned kinds of problems that are no longer central. In any case, his publications appeared over a period of sixty years, and he rarely bothered to note changes in his views or to organize his developing theoretical views into an overarching, coherent, or consistent design. Moreover, he rarely attempted to defend his theoretical views; when he encountered opposition to them, his tendency was to seek to reconcile divergent views or to let the future decide who was right. The notable exception is *The Nature of Culture*, published in 1952. Most of the book consists of reprints of earlier papers or selections therefrom, arranged and annotated by Kroeber himself to indicate the development of his major theoretical interests.

**The nature of culture.** Kroeber's most systematic theoretical treatments deal with the nature of culture and its processes. These themes dominated his more important courses as well as several of his major monographs. Singer has pointed out that Kroeber's approach to culture was in terms of patterning rather than in terms of structure, and that culture was for Kroeber a global concept. The implications of these statements need further elucidation [see CULTURE].

For Kroeber, as for many of his contemporaries, the term "culture" is referable to pan-human phenomena; hence ultimate explanations must deal not only with the cultures of specific societies but also with culture as a universal human characteristic. Each culture possesses unique aspects of content and pattern which require explanation but represent only a temporary historical eddy in the pan-human sea of culture. Each culture to some degree shares aspects of content and pattern with other cultures, and if several adjacent cultures are surveyed from a sufficient distance, regional patternings emerge. In a different sense Kroeber also saw patterning in the distribution, association, and clustering of traits which crosscut cultures and even regions. While specific cultures are the basic units, the full understanding of culture must include explanations of elements and patternings which transcend the specific culture. Kroeber's concern with the distribution of traits is one basis for the criticism of his "particularistic" view of culture. Paradoxically, Kroeber tended to view such anthropologists as Malinowski as overly particularistic because of their failure to relate the cultures they studied to the regional cultures in which they are embedded, and he was skeptical of Malinowski's grand leap from his particularistic study of the Trobriands to universal generalizations; not only did he find the term "savages" offensive, but for him Malinowski's *Sexual Life of Savages in Northwest Melanesia* gave evidence only of the sexual life of the Trobriand Islanders.

**Cultural units.** Kroeber was particularistic also in his search for basic cultural units of study. This preoccupation was reinforced by, but antedated, the development of such basic units as phonemes and morphemes in linguistics. Since language is a cultural phenomenon, similar units should be discoverable in other aspects of culture. This aspect of Kroeber's work and thought perhaps reached its apogee in the extensive compilation of cultural element distributions. A large part of the surviving cultures of the western United States were resurveyed by means of standard trait lists, and not only presences but also absences were recorded, in order to permit statistical measures of relationship between groups. Such measures of relationship could also be used, in his view, to establish historical depth, both for relationships and for traits or trait complexes.

The culture element distribution lists are heaviest on material culture and lightest on social organization, where at the time the identification of units was less advanced. Had recent work of the social structuralists been available, Kroeber no doubt would have perceived many more units of social structure. In any case, the culture element distribution studies produced much less than Kroeber hoped for, and he himself made little use of them. Field workers found the trait-list approach confining, and at least part of the ethnographic data they collected turned out to be unsuitable for tabular listing. As a result, many of the reports contain extensive ethnographic footnotes or appendices. These, in conjunction with the trait lists, provide a rich body of material.

**Use of statistics.** The culture element survey program illuminates Kroeber's encouragement of the use of statistical approaches to ethnographic and linguistic data. The methods are essentially those of cluster analysis; had factorial or multivariate analysis been available, the results might have been more striking and Kroeber's interest might have remained more active. As it is, the statistical interest in ethnography has remained confined to only a few of Kroeber's students. [See ETHNOLOGY; see also CLUSTERING.]

A major purpose of Kroeber's statistical studies and the culture element surveys was to provide more objective classification methods; this purpose was related to his interest in the culture area, which he saw as a classification device that could also be useful in historical reconstruction. However, Kroeber was well aware that even though a high degree of objectivity might be reached in mapping the geographical clusterings of culture traits (culture areas), historical inferences based on this classification, especially when blurred by diffusion, are less reliable. (See 1935 for a statement by Kroeber of the purpose of the culture element surveys.)

**Culture areas.** Kroeber's first use of the culture area, in 1904 ("Types of Indian Culture in California"), antedated Clark Wissler's first publication by two years. From the beginning Kroeber insisted that culture areas lack absolute boundaries and that the centers of cultural climax are as much the result of the "drawing in" of culture elements as they are centers of origination and dispersal. For Kroeber the culture area is similar to the biotic area of the biologist, whose definition depends upon the scale of the units compared; from a continental view culture areas may be identified as very large units; from a more microscopic view, they break down into subareas or provinces, depending upon the intensity of analysis.

In his major contribution dealing with culture areas, *Cultural and Natural Areas of Native North America* (1939), Kroeber outlined 6 grand areas, 56 areas, and 43 subareas. Here he also declared, "The concept of a culture area is a means to an end. The end may be the understanding of culture processes as such, or of the historic events of culture" (p. 1). He also claimed he was dealing in cultural wholes—meaning, apparently, patterns or configurations—rather than in traits or complexes, "which always constitute only a fraction of the entirety of any one culture" (p. 2). In this work Kroeber attempted to relate his various levels of culture areas to natural areas and produced a number of new and significant relations between ecology and types of social organization. While recognizing that cultures are rooted in nature he made the categorical and significant statement that "the immediate causes of cultural phenomena are other cultural phenomena" (p. 1). Later, in 1947, he wrote that culture areas are really not areas but kinds of cultures which are geographically limited.

**Diachronic explanation.** Kroeber explained cultural processes diachronically: events cannot occur without process or process without events, which introduces time as a factor in all events. For analytical purposes, history may at times be ignored, but the ultimate explanations of culture for him had to include the factor of time. Hence the explanation of culture and its processes in his *Anthropology* is almost entirely historical. And where documentary or archeological evidence was lacking or inadequate, Kroeber relied heavily on historical inference or reconstruction based primarily on distributional data.

At the same time, Kroeber reacted as strongly against simplistic evolutionary explanations and the excesses of the *Kulturkreise* and the heliolithic schools as did the British social anthropologists. He did not believe that methods of historical inference can be used mechanically or that the results express more than degrees of probability, and in his *Anthropology* he discussed this problem in detail.

The basis for most of Kroeber's reconstructions is the process of diffusion or borrowing. All cultures, almost self-evidently, are in large part composed of elements borrowed from other cultures however much they may be reworked, adapted, and fitted into distinctive patterns. But not all things that are similar are necessarily borrowed, and in his *Anthropology* Kroeber characteristically opened his chapter on diffusion with a discussion of the couvade, a set of similar behavioral restrictions placed upon the father at the birth of a child, found in Europe among the Basques and in Brazil among some Indians. Kroeber argued that the couvade is not the result of diffusion; instead it may be a response to a universal human experience. Thus "independent invention," "parallelism," and "convergence" are equally possible explanations of similarities, along with diffusion. In any given case a selection between alternative explanations can be made only after weighing probabilities in the light of certain principles.

Kroeber modeled his approach to diffusion and historical reconstruction on that used by paleontologists to infer relative age; their inferences are based on the distribution of flora and fauna. Kroeber's approach emerges most clearly in his article "Historical Reconstruction of Culture Growths and Organic Evolution" (1931). He compared cultures to biotas, or assemblages of plants and animals, and culture areas to faunal areas such as the Holarctic or Neotropical. In both anthropology and biology geographical continuity of distribution strengthens the case for diffusion, and their age–area interpretations are subject to restraints. A botanist will not infer the relative age of pines and grasses from their distribution; the anthropologist must not compare textile arts with a religious cult. Analogies, particularly at a conceptual level, are not evidence of borrowing. Detailed structural similarities do strengthen the case for borrowing, but the principle of limited possibilities must be borne in mind. If borrowing is postulated, particularly of isolated traits without continuous geographic distributions, then absences or failures to borrow must also be considered and explained. Degeneration or simplification and the relative stability of elements through time and space also may be relevant. In short, although diffusion is a common process, no case of similarity is to be considered as diffusion on a priori grounds.

The diachronic and distributional problems that are central in much of Kroeber's thought and research are somewhat remote from much of modern anthropology; nevertheless, the problems cannot be avoided if universalistic explanations of culture are to be reached. Archeologists have been more influenced by Kroeber's ideas and concerns than have others in recent years. The area co-tradition concepts first advanced by the late Wendell Bennett for Peru are in the Kroeber tradition. In ethnology, Evon Vogt has recently developed a refined genetic approach to the analysis of culture areas, and similar stirrings of interest in historical reconstructions are visible among recent anthropologists. On the other hand, some of the more enthusiastic diffusionists, particularly those among archeologists, have ignored many of Kroeber's methodological cautions. They have been taken to task recently by John H. Rowe (1966) in "Diffusionism in Archaeology."

**Cultural configurations.** Kroeber felt strongly that individual cultures must be considered as wholes, although he never developed a holistic approach that satisfied him. He was sympathetic to Ruth Benedict's patterns or configurations of culture and constantly used these terms himself, although he was dissatisfied with Benedict's approach and conclusions. Along with these terms he often referred to "style," a word he appears never to have defined. He used it most commonly in relation to aesthetic productions, and when he occasionally extended it to other human activities he seems to have meant a distinctive mode of expression or action. His major use of the term was in his analysis of Peruvian art styles (1951).

By the term "patterns" or "configurations" Kroeber customarily meant recurring clusters of phenomena. Sometimes the terms are used to describe the spatial distribution of concrete clusterings; more importantly, in explaining the peaks or climaxes in the history of culture areas and the differential frequency of geniuses at different times and places. His major work on this subject, *Configurations of Culture Growth* (1944), attempts to identify, for nations and areas of the Old World, culminations or peaks in various fields of aesthetic and intellectual endeavor. These peaks are characterized by the emergence of large numbers of exceptional individuals. Kroeber suggested that the appearance of these geniuses is the result of the emergence of new patterns, their exploitation until possibilities have been exhausted, and their subsequent decline and disintegration until some productive new pattern is formed either in the same or some other area. These patterned phenomena he related to other aspects of culture and suggested that certain historic and repetitive configurations of growth and change may be identified.

Others (e.g., Spengler, Toynbee) have attempted to establish regularities in explaining the rise and fall of civilizations. Kroeber's distinctive contribution is his assumption that the distribution of superior ability in a population remains approximately constant. He explained the appearance and recognition of genius and the flourishing of civilizations in cultural terms.

**"The Superorganic."** Allied to his conviction that culture is to be explained in cultural terms was Kroeber's long-standing objection to reductionism. This viewpoint appears many times in his work but is most explicitly stated in "The Superorganic" (1917a) and in "So-called Social Science" (1936). In both articles Kroeber argued for a hierarchy of phenomena, ranging from the inorganic, organic, and psychic to the superorganic, or sociocultural. Kroeber's main thesis is that at each level some phenomena may be reducible or explainable in terms of the level below, but some cannot be so explained.

Kroeber's "Superorganic" drew criticism immediately from Edward Sapir and A. A. Goldenweiser and more recently from Melford Spiro, David Bidney, and others [see GOLDENWEISER *and* SAPIR]. The concept has been attacked as mystical and as sheer reification because it fails to predict variations in individual behavior and because it is deterministic. This controversy has been reviewed recently by David Kaplan (1965), who has argued forcefully in favor of the superorganic by moving the discussion from the ontological to the methodological arena. Most critics of the superorganic, said Kaplan, have in mind psychological questions, although psychological theories cannot explain most cultural phenomena. For example, such a concept as "lineage" cannot be derived from psychology as we now know it; it is of cultural origin, and anthropologists have used it to ask and to answer meaningful and nonpsychological questions.

Kroeber himself in *The Nature of Culture*, in commenting on the two articles that dealt with the controversial concept, proceeded to withdraw those statements which appeared to attribute real existence to culture and pointed out that in the second he had substituted "sociocultural" for "superorganic." However, he clearly regarded as basically sound his insistence upon seeking cultural explanations for cultural facts.

**Anthropology and psychology.** Kroeber's antireductionist views are widely interpreted as reflecting his opposition to psychological interests in anthropology, to the rise of the culture and personality approach, and to modern psychological anthropology. Actually Kroeber had a lively interest in psychology, his minor subject as a graduate student. He first brought psychoanalysis to the attention of anthropologists with his reviews of papers by Jung in 1918, and in 1920 he reviewed Freud's *Totem and Taboo*, albeit very negatively (see 1920*b*). He underwent a brief analysis himself, and in 1921 and 1923 he maintained an office and practiced psychoanalysis with some success in San Francisco. Many years later he encouraged Erik Erikson's work with the Yurok. In the meantime he tolerated and in some cases encouraged those of his students who became interested in psychological problems, and several early doctoral candidates at Berkeley were virtually forced into psychology minors.

In spite of Kroeber's positive attitude toward psychology, he soon came to feel that the preoccupations of the academic psychology of the time with experimental and animal behavior problems reduced the value of the subject for anthropologists. Moreover, having tested psychoanalytical theories thoroughly before most anthropologists had even "discovered" them, he found them unsatisfactory for the explanation of cultural phenomena, however much he continued to find them interesting and at times amusing. Although the second edition of *Anthropology* includes a section on psychology, and in *The Nature of Culture* Kroeber included five papers he considered to be "psychologically slanted," he kept himself aloof from the work of Kardiner, Linton, and others engaged in the development of culture and personality theories. The only book he reviewed in this field was *Personality in Nature, Society, and Culture* (1949). The review is thorough and friendly but mildly skeptical. In surveying the field (see the 1950 article in *The Nature of Culture*), he agreed that an explanation of culture on the psychological level is necessary, but he warned that the problem of providing such an explanation is enormously complex; culture, he believed, had illuminated personality far more than the reverse. One difficulty, he felt, was that many "enthusiasts" in the culture and personality field knew so little about culture.

**Functional analysis.** In contrast to his "particularistic" approach in dealing with culture elements and culture complexes and their distributions, Kroeber was uneasy when confronted with nonhistorical social science approaches in anthropology. The dissection of features of a particular culture and their analysis apart from the total context, he felt, would yield limited and perhaps misleading results. Yet he had no such qualms about isolating culture traits in his comparative studies or identifying complexes for cross-cultural studies.

Indeed, some of his own important contributions in social organization are essentially attempts at isolating items of culture, and he published several important studies in kinship which contradict his own position. An early paper entitled "Classificatory Systems of Relationship" (1909) proposes important studies in kinship which contradict fication of kin, which some regard as the first step toward componential analysis. [*See* COMPONENTIAL ANALYSIS.]

Kroeber's study of Zuñi kinship and clan organization, "Zuni Clan Functioning" (1917*b*), which became part of a larger monographic study published by the American Museum of Natural History (see 1917*c*), broke ground in that it emphasized the variety of functions of the clans and disproved some notions about their origins; the larger monograph showed that the nuclear family kept important functions within a clan-organized society. Kroeber himself deprecated this work, indicating that he had included it in his collected papers only because it is primarily functional in approach, in contrast to his other papers on kinship. Much more important to him was his insistence upon the complexity of causation and the importance of historical, linguistic, and psychological variables as well as of sociological variables. In *The Nature of Culture* he included an exchange of views with A. R. Radcliffe-Brown on this subject. Modern kinship studies have gone beyond Kroeber and in different directions, but the questions he raises are still significant and partly unanswered [*see* CULTURE; KINSHIP].

The papers in *The Nature of Culture* also are significantly related to a problem still vital in discussions of cultural stability and change. Extreme functional and structural approaches have insisted on the interrelatedness of all aspects of culture. In "Basic and Secondary Patterns of Social Structure" (1938) and in later papers Kroeber wrestled with the fact that some aspects of social organization and culture seem more stable than others. Ultimately, he identified four cultural segments: real culture, value culture, societal aspects, and language. Each he suggested has varying modalities of change and may have an independent history.

Kroeber's sense of the uniqueness of culture perhaps kept him from structural analyses on a cross-cultural basis. He could, on occasion, use thoroughly functional concepts in his descriptive analyses (see for example his section on the Yurok in the *Handbook of the Indians of California*), but his habit of mind and his interest led him back continually to the natural-history approach of classical biology and a humanistic emphasis upon patterns and styles.

## Stature in anthropology

It is far too soon to estimate Kroeber's impact upon anthropology and the social sciences. Many of the problems he struggled with, even though far from solved, are no longer fashionable. Yet his emphasis on multiple causation and the importance of historical and linguistic variables may yet prove a way out of the blind alleys encountered in the closed and static systems of functionalism and structuralism. His recurrent concern with the importance of linguistic factors and the methods of linguistic analysis has been rediscovered in the development of componential analysis and of "modern" ethnography.

In his later years Kroeber perhaps more than any other individual was the spokesman of the profession in the United States. He played an important role in organizing the 1951 International Symposium on Anthropology and he organized the 1960 Conference on Anthropological Horizons, both sponsored by the Wenner–Gren Foundation for Anthropological Research.

The regard in which Kroeber was held and the reasons for his eminence rest on several characteristics. On the personal level he was a man of great breadth of interests and a deep concern with what other people thought or were doing. He was primarily an anthropologist's anthropologist, in that he wrote almost exclusively for his professional colleagues. Most important, however, was his lifelong curiosity about new fields, new approaches, and new problems. This curiosity repeatedly led him to enter a new field, topic, or problem on which little had been written or which lacked systematization. In part, but only in part, this was a function of the youth of the field. In many cases, Kroeber's entry into a field or topic was marked by a single paper which he never followed up. Nevertheless, in almost every case the field was never the same again after Kroeber's foray into it. People could disagree with what Kroeber did and said but they could not ignore it.

RALPH BEALS

[*Directly related are the entries* ANTHROPOLOGY, *article on* THE FIELD; CULTURE, *article on* THE CONCEPT OF CULTURE; ETHNOLOGY; HISTORY, *article on* CULTURE HISTORY; INDIANS, NORTH AMERICAN; *and the biography of* BOAS.]

### WORKS BY KROEBER

1901 Decorative Symbolism of the Arapaho. *American Anthropologist* New Series 3:308–336.

1902 Preliminary Sketch of the Mohave Indians. *American Anthropologist* New Series 4:276–285.
1902–1907 The Arapaho. 4 parts. American Museum of Natural History, *Bulletin* 18:1–230, 279–454. → Part 1: General Discussion. Part 2: Decorative Art and Symbolism. Part 3: Ceremonial Organization. Part 4: Religion.
1904 Types of Indian Culture in California. California, University of, *Publications in American Archaeology and Ethnology* 2:81–103.
1905 Basket Designs of the Indians of Northwestern California. California, University of, *Publications in American Archaeology and Ethnology* 2:105–164.
1906 The Yokuts and Yuki Languages. Pages 64–79 in *Boas Anniversary Volume: Anthropological Papers Written in Honor of Franz Boas.* New York: Stechert.
1907 The Yokuts Language of South Central California. California, University of, *Publications in American Archaeology and Ethnology* 2:165–377.
1909 Classificatory Systems of Relationship. *Journal of the Royal Anthropological Institute of Great Britain and Ireland* 39:77–84.
(1916a) 1952 Zuni Culture Sequences. Pages 230–232 in Alfred L. Kroeber, *The Nature of Culture.* Univ. of Chicago Press.
1916b Arapaho Dialects. California, University of, *Publications in American Archaeology and Ethnology* 12: 71–138.
(1917a) 1952 The Superorganic. Pages 22–51 in Alfred L. Kroeber, *The Nature of Culture.* Univ. of Chicago Press.
(1917b) 1952 Zuni Clan Functioning. Pages 182–186 in Alfred L. Kroeber, *The Nature of Culture.* Univ. of Chicago Press.
1917c *Zuñi Kin and Clan.* American Museum of Natural History, Papers, Vol. 18, part 2. New York: The Museum.
1918 [Reviews of] *Analytical Psychology* and *The Psychology of the Unconscious,* by C. G. Jung. *American Anthropologist* New Series 20:323–324.
1920a *Three Essays on the Antiquity and Races of Man.* Berkeley: Univ. of California Press. → First published for use as readings in a course.
1920b *Totem and Taboo: An Ethnologic Psychoanalysis. American Anthropologist* New Series 22:48–55.
(1923) 1948 *Anthropology: Race, Language, Culture, Psychology, Prehistory.* New ed., rev. New York: Harcourt. → First published as *Anthropology.*
1925 *Handbook of the Indians of California.* Smithsonian Institution, Bureau of American Ethnology, Bulletin No. 78. Washington: Government Printing Office.
1928a [Review of] *Rasse und Körperbau,* by Franz Weidenreich. *American Anthropologist* New Series 30: 158–160.
1928b Sub-human Culture Beginnings. *Quarterly Review of Biology* 3:325–342.
1928c Native Culture of the Southwest. California, University of, *Publications in American Archaeology and Ethnology* 23:375–398.
(1931) 1952 Historical Reconstruction of Culture Growths and Organic Evolution. Pages 57–62 in Alfred L. Kroeber, *The Nature of Culture.* Univ. of Chicago Press.
1934a Blood-group Classification. *American Journal of Physical Anthropology* 18:377–393.
1934b Yurok and Neighboring Kin Term Systems. California, University of, *Publications in American Archaeology and Ethnology* 35:15–22.
1935 Preface. Pages 1–11 in Stanislaw Klimek, *Culture*

*Element Distributions: 1. The Structure of California Indian Culture.* California, University of, Publications in American Archaeology and Ethnology, Vol. 37, No. 1. Berkeley: Univ. of California Press. → The first of a series of culture element surveys.

(1936) 1952   So-called Social Science. Pages 66–78 in Alfred L. Kroeber, *The Nature of Culture.* Univ. of Chicago Press.

1937   KROEBER, A. L.; and CHRÉTIEN, CHARLES D. Quantitative Classification of Indo–European Languages. *Language* 13:83–103.

1938   Basic and Secondary Patterns of Social Structure. *Journal of the Royal Anthropological Institute of Great Britain and Ireland* 68:299–309.

1939   *Cultural and Natural Areas of Native North America.* California, University of, Publications in American Archaeology and Ethnology Vol. 38. Berkeley: Univ. of California Press.

1940   The Work of John R. Swanton. Pages 1–9 in Smithsonian Institution, *Essays in Historical Anthropology of North America, Published in Honor of John R. Swanton.* Smithsonian Miscellaneous Collections, Vol. 100. Washington: The Institution.

1944   *Configurations of Culture Growth.* Berkeley: Univ. of California Press.

1947   Culture Groupings in Asia. *Southwestern Journal of Anthropology* 3:322–330.

1949   [Review of] *Personality in Nature, Society, and Culture,* edited by Clyde Kluckhohn and Henry A. Murray. *American Anthropologist* New Series 51:116–118.

(1951) 1952   Great Art Styles of Ancient South America. Pages 289–296 in Alfred L. Kroeber, *The Nature of Culture.* Univ. of Chicago Press.

1952   KROEBER, ALFRED L.; and KLUCKHOHN, CLYDE *Culture: A Critical Review of Concepts and Definitions.* Harvard University, Peabody Museum of American Archaeology and Ethnology, Papers, Vol. 47, No. 1. Cambridge, Mass.: The Museum. → A paperback edition was published in 1963 by Vintage.

1955   KROEBER, A. L.; and HARNER, MICHAEL J. *Mohave Pottery.* Anthropological Records, Vol. 16, no. 1. Berkeley: Univ. of California Press.

1963   *Yokuts Dialect Survey.* Anthropological Records, Vol. 11, no. 3. Berkeley: Univ. of California Press. → Published posthumously.

*The Nature of Culture.* Univ. of Chicago Press, 1952. → Contains articles published between 1901 and 1951.

### SUPPLEMENTARY BIBLIOGRAPHY

DRIVER, HAROLD E.   1962   *The Contribution of A. L. Kroeber to Culture Area Theory and Practice.* Indiana University Publications in Anthropology and Linguistics, 18. Baltimore, Md.: Waverly.

HERSKOVITS, MELVILLE J.   1948   *Man and His Works: The Science of Cultural Anthropology.* New York: Knopf.

HYMES, DELL   1961   Alfred Louis Kroeber. *Language* 37:1–28.

KAPLAN, DAVID   1965   "The Superorganic": Science or Metaphysics? *American Anthropologist* New Series 67:958–976.

KIDDER, ALFRED V.   1915   Pottery of the Pajarito Plateau and of Some Adjacent Regions in New Mexico. American Anthropological Association, *Memoirs* 2:407–462.

NELSON, NELS C.   1916   Chronology of the Tano Ruins, New Mexico. *American Anthropologist* New Series 18:159–180.

ROWE, JOHN H.   1962   Alfred Louis Kroeber, 1876–1960. *American Antiquity* 27:395–415.

ROWE, JOHN H.   1966   Diffusionism in Archaeology. *American Antiquity* 31:334–337.

STEWARD, JULIAN H.   1962   Alfred Louis Kroeber: 1876–1960. Volume 36, pages 191–253 in National Academy of Sciences, Washington, D.C., *Biographical Memoirs.* New York: Columbia Univ. Press. → A bibliography of the publications of Alfred Louis Kroeber, compiled by Ann J. Gibson and John H. Rowe, appears on pages 217–253. It has also been published in Volume 63 of the *American Anthropologist* New Series.

## KROPOTKIN, P'ETR

P'etr (Peter) Alekseevich Kropotkin (1842–1921), anarchist theoretician and leader, came from an ancient Russian aristocratic family. He received an excellent education, which included several years in the Imperial Corps of Pages. As a graduate of that school he could have had a brilliant career at the court; but inspired by egalitarian principles (which led him, while still a boy, to drop his princely title) and love of adventure, he applied instead for service in Siberia. He spent five fruitful and exciting years there, from 1862 to 1867, in the course of which he had much opportunity to observe human and animal life under conditions of virtually complete freedom. He also engaged in geographic exploration. His reports on the topography of Asia, published after his return to St. Petersburg, earned him immediate scholarly recognition and opened doors to a distinguished academic career. But Kropotkin once again rejected the path of personal advancement. The reading of socialist literature had persuaded him to dedicate his life to the cause of social justice. This intention was strengthened by a brief visit to Switzerland in 1872, during which he met some of the leading figures of European socialism as well as the anarchist workers of the Jura region. He returned to Russia a convinced anarchist and joined a clandestine circle engaged in propagandizing among laborers. When the police broke up the circle two years later, Kropotkin was arrested and confined. In 1876, after a dramatic escape from the prison hospital, he made his way to western Europe, where he remained (mostly in England) until 1917.

Kropotkin's social theory concentrated on rebutting Darwinist explanations, which, be it noted, never found favor among Russian intellectuals. To the notions of "struggle for existence" and "survival of the fittest" he opposed the conception of "mutual aid"; and he did so not on ethical but on what he believed to be scientific grounds.

He began to have doubts about Darwinism while

still a young officer in Siberia. He departed for Siberia strongly impressed by the *Origin of Species*, published three years earlier, and eagerly sought there additional evidence of "struggles for existence." To his great surprise, he soon discovered that such struggles played a relatively minor role in animal life. Instead, he noted numerous instances of solidarity in coping with nature and with man. Firsthand observations of peasant and Cossack communities in the Siberian wilderness strengthened his belief in the importance of cooperation. Afterwards, in the course of studying the history and situation of the working class in Russia and western Europe, he was again struck by the prevalence of solidarity within the species.

These vague ideas crystallized into theory in the early 1880s, under the direct stimulus of the Russian zoologist Karl F. Kessler. Kessler, in a report delivered in 1880, argued on the basis of extensive scientific observation that cooperation and not conflict determine the relations between individuals of the same species and constitute the vital factor of the evolutionary process. Kropotkin promptly applied these views to social questions and advanced the view that custom and voluntary agreement, rather than law and normative authority, represent the creative forces in history (1885; 1886). In 1888, when Thomas Huxley published his "Struggle for Existence," in *Nineteenth Century*, Kropotkin replied there with a series of essays (1890–1896) which were later gathered into a separate volume called *Mutual Aid: A Factor in Evolution*; this book became his most celebrated work.

The principal thesis of *Mutual Aid* is the proposition that "sociability is as much a law of nature as natural struggle" and that "under *any* circumstances [sociability is] the greatest advantage in the struggle for life." In other words, the "fittest" are not those strongest individually, but those most adept at cooperation. Creatures that learn to cooperate become the most numerous and the most prosperous; those that fail to do so are doomed to decay. To prove this contention Kropotkin traced evidence of voluntary cooperation from lower forms of animal society through the primitive tribe, village community, and medieval guild to various modern associations. The basis of mutual aid is an instinctive sense of solidarity which, he emphasized, does not derive from love but, on the contrary, provides the basis for love. Kropotkin contrasted voluntary associations with institutions of state and law, which embody predatory instincts and facilitate exploitation. He believed the "governmental," "Roman" principle must with time inevi-

tably yield to the voluntaristic one. Although he did not deny the efficacy of the competitive element in evolution, Kropotkin felt it had been greatly overrated by Darwin's followers.

The society which he envisaged was one of free associations, in which the means of production as well as the products themselves would be held in common, and every citizen would receive according to his needs (1892). This system he called "anarchist communism," in contrast to Marxism, which he regarded as "statist" and indelibly tainted with authoritarian elements. Like many Russian contemporaries, notably Nikolai K. Mikhailovskii, Kropotkin objected strenuously to the intensified division of labor characteristic of modern times as deleterious to human character and pleaded for conditions under which everyone could engage in both mental and physical labor (1899).

In the summer of 1917 Kropotkin returned to Russia. He supported the provisional government and opposed the Bolsheviks. When Lenin seized power Kropotkin withdrew from public life and settled in the country near Moscow, where under conditions of extreme hardship he spent his last years writing a history of moral ideas (1922). Occasionally he emerged from isolation to protest publicly against Lenin's dictatorial measures, such as the taking of hostages. He died convinced that Bolshevism was doomed because it had failed to evolve a grand ethical ideal capable of appealing to the masses.

Kropotkin based his ethical theory, as he did his whole social theory, on the notion of "mutual aid." The necessity for cooperation among individuals of the same species in coping with their environment inevitably develops in them a sense of justice. Justice entails an appreciation of the rights of other individuals and a respect for equality. It induces the individual to sacrifice his personal interests for those of the community. Morality is merely a highly developed conscious and articulated form of this sense of justice. The development from mutual aid through justice to morality is an intrinsic and necessary process of social evolution. All three constitute manifestations of an instinct for self-preservation, mutual aid being the most rudimentary and most deeply rooted, and morality being the highest and least secure of these instincts. Societies which fail to undergo the evolution from mutual aid to morality are doomed to decline and disappear.

Kropotkin's particular achievement was to provide the anarchist theory with a scientific foundation. Drawing on a rich knowledge of zoology and history (among his writings is a history called *The Great French Revolution: 1789–1793*, 1893), he could persuasively argue the great importance of spontaneous, voluntaristic, and associational factors in the evolution of both animals and men and thus endow anarchism with some of the qualities of scientific "inevitability" that helped so much to popularize the views of Engels and Marx. In his own life he personified that combination of thought and action which he preached in his writings. His idealism, his love of life, and the incorruptibility which he displayed even under the most adverse circumstances endowed him with an irresistible charm to which even Oscar Wilde succumbed: he once called Kropotkin one of the two happy men he had known.

RICHARD PIPES

[See also ANARCHISM. Other relevant material may be found in COOPERATION; MARXISM; SYNDICALISM; UTOPIANISM.]

### WORKS BY KROPOTKIN

1885    Paroles d'un révolté. Paris: Marpon & Flammarion.
1886    Law and Authority: An Anarchist Essay. London: International.
(1890–1896) 1955    Mutual Aid: A Factor of Evolution. Boston: Extending Horizons. → Thomas Huxley's "The Struggle for Existence" is included in both the original 1902 and the 1955 publication.
(1892) 1926    The Conquest of Bread. New York: Vanguard. → First published in French.
(1893) 1927    The Great French Revolution: 1789–1793. 2 vols. New York: Vanguard. → First published in French.
(1898–1899) 1930    Memoirs of a Revolutionist. Boston and New York: Houghton Mifflin. → First published in the Atlantic Monthly as "The Autobiography of a Revolutionist."
(1899) 1913    Fields, Factories and Workshops: Or, Industry Combined With Agriculture and Brain Work With Manual Work. Rev. & enl. ed. New York and London: Putnam.
(1922) 1924    Ethics: Origin and Development. New York: MacVeagh. → First published in Russian.

### SUPPLEMENTARY BIBLIOGRAPHY

JOLL, JAMES  (1964) 1965    The Anarchists. Boston: Little.
NETTLAU, MAX  1927    Der Anarchismus von Proudhon zu Kropotkin: Seine historische Entwicklung in den Jahren 1859–1880. Berlin: Kater.
WOODCOCK, GEORGE; and AVAKUMOVIĆ, IVAN  1950    The Anarchist Prince: A Biographical Study of Peter Kropotkin. London and New York: Boardman.

# KULISCHER, EUGENE

Eugene M. Kulischer was born in Kiev, Russia, in 1881 and died in Washington, D.C., in 1956. In the intervening years he fled from Russia in 1920, from Germany in 1936, and from occupied France in 1941. Even before he himself became a displaced person (a term that he coined), the work of the Russian historian V. O. Kluchevsky had turned his attention to the historical role of migration. Kulischer's father and brother were also influenced by Kluchevsky, and all three of them wrote on the subject, although only the volume by the two brothers, Kriegs- und Wanderzüge (1932), now appears to be available in American libraries.

Reviewing the broad sweep of history, Kulischer noted that peoples have always moved about, sometimes because of war, sometimes in search of food, and often for both reasons. Perhaps such movements were more visible in Russia than elsewhere, because of the many migrations from central Asia. These movements have tended to occur irregularly over time and have been influenced by a wide variety of factors. They were described by Kulischer as "disorderly," unlike the relatively "orderly and peaceful" population movements that western European and American demographers observed in their homelands. However, Kulischer's emphasis on irregularity should not be permitted to obscure the extent to which his assessment of the basic factors in migration overlaps that of other demographers.

Kulischer believed that explanations of changes in the size of the population within a specified geographic area, as well as changes in other characteristics of the population, must be subsumed under a general theory of social change. He considered the following items as intimately related: population, technology, the economic structure, natural resources, the political structure, political developments (including wars), and the psychology of man; each affects the others and is in turn affected by them. Kulischer chose to begin his own analysis of social change by studying population, moving from this to other subjects, but as he saw it, it was equally feasible to begin, for example, with technology and ultimately to deal with population. Within the field of population Kulischer's point of departure was the study of migration. His major propositions can be expressed as follows.

(1) If technology (including ethnotechnics) remains unchanged, then the economic structure is also likely to remain unchanged, and within a specified geographic area population will continue to grow as long as there are unused natural resources. When the natural resources are used up, the population will attempt to migrate. If vacant lands are accessible, the migration is peaceful and the process of population growth continues; if the neighboring lands are occupied, war ensues.

Subsequent events depend on who wins the war. If the attackers win, the attacked may flee (unless they are killed in large numbers or taken as slaves);

as the attacked group flees, it may, in turn, attack its neighbors, thereby setting off a chain reaction that ultimately affects populations thousands of miles away. If the attackers are beaten off with heavy losses, the population may be so depleted that the original land area will again suffice to support the population and the need for migration will be eliminated; if the attackers are beaten off with slight losses, they may attack another neighboring group, and thus the process is repeated.

(2) If technology changes, the economic structure is also likely to change, and population adjustments will occur. If the economic base expands, population will expand, and if the economic base contracts, population will likewise contract. Hence, adjustments in the economy may be substitutes for migration and war.

(3) Population will not necessarily increase to the limits of the economic base, as in the Malthusian view. The standard of living to which the population aspires will be of importance in determining ultimate population size.

(4) There are three different types of technological innovation which can affect population movements differently: those which directly increase the economic base; those which improve means of communication and travel and therefore make migration easier; those of a military nature which make it easier for one population to attack another.

(5) Changes in population size may affect the economy; for example, if there are not sufficient people in an area to utilize the natural resources, an increase in the number of people may lead to greatly increased production which, in turn, will support an even larger population. But if increases in population are not accompanied by commensurate increases in production, the larger population in itself may eventually reduce the population-supporting capacity of the economy and thus lead to a reduction in the population.

(6) Changes in the political and social structure independent of economic changes (such as the expulsion of a religious minority) may also affect the other variables—population size, migration, etc.

(7) Superimposed on these human factors is a whole host of possible changes in the natural environment (climatic changes, earthquakes, etc.) which can affect the population-supporting capacity of an area and/or the size of the population in that area.

(8) Finally, Kulischer believed that there is one, and only one, invariable characteristic of human relationships: As long as one group is better

off economically than another or people are not as well off as they think they should be, trouble will erupt sooner or later. For this reason strife has been continuous in history, and viewing the world in the mid-twentieth century, Kulischer could foresee no end to this strife. The world might become peaceful only if the politicians, who are supposed to lead, and the people, who are supposed to follow, came to understand the sources of past strife.

In one form or another there recurs in all of Kulischer's writings the statement that migratory movements "are expressions of a trend towards equalization of economic density, which is the ratio between the number of inhabitants and the resources at their disposal" (Kulischer & Price 1963, p. 463). Although it seems fair to say that he overstressed this point, nevertheless he cannot be charged with having proposed a single-cause theory of history and of human nature. Indeed, it may be argued that the foregoing eight points constitute a complex theory of social change rather than an oversimplified explanation of all human action in terms of migration. Migration was the most obvious form of social change to Kulischer, possibly because he had experienced it so directly. Yet even though he began with migration, he ended with technology, politics, and the entire complex of human social structure and relations.

A. J. Jaffe

[*Directly related are the entries* Migration *and* Refugees. *Other relevant material may be found in* Population, *article on* population theories; War, *article on* the study of war.]

## WORKS BY KULISCHER

1932 Kulischer, Alexander; and Kulischer, Eugene M. *Kriegs- und Wanderzüge: Weltgeschichte als Völkerbewegung.* Berlin: Gruyter.

1943a *The Displacement of Population in Europe.* Studies and Reports, Series O, No. 8. Montreal: International Labor Office.

1943b Planned Migrations and the International Labour Office. *World Economics* 1, no. 1–2:82–89.

1948 *Europe on the Move: War and Population Changes, 1917–1947.* New York: Columbia Univ. Press.

1949 Displaced Persons in the Modern World. American Academy of Political and Social Science, *Annals* 262: 166–177.

1953 Teeming Asia and the West. *Political Science Quarterly* 68:481–491.

1963 Kulischer, Eugene M.; and Price, Daniel O. Migration. Volume 15, pages 463–473 in *Encyclopaedia Britannica.* Chicago: Benton.

## SUPPLEMENTARY BIBLIOGRAPHY

Jaffe, A. J. 1962 Notes on the Population Theory of Eugene M. Kulischer. *Milbank Memorial Fund Quarterly* 40, no. 2:187–206.

Roof, Michael K. 1956 In Memoriam: Eugene M. Kulischer. *R.E.M.P. Bulletin* 4:41–44.

# KÜLPE, OSWALD

Oswald Külpe (1862–1915), founder of the "Würzburg school" of psychology, was born in Kandau, Courland (now Latvia), the son of a notary public. He attended the Gymnasium in Libau and for two years was privately tutored. After he began his university education he had considerable difficulty deciding whether his major interest lay in history or in psychology. In 1881 he registered at the University of Leipzig to study history, but once he was there his interests were directed toward psychology and philosophy by Wilhelm Wundt, whose laboratory had been established just two years previously. After a year at Leipzig, Külpe left for a semester of study at Berlin, undecided whether to throw in his lot with the Berlin historians Theodor Mommsen, Johann Kirchhoff, and Hermann Diels, or with Wundt. When he left Berlin he did study more psychology but not immediately with Wundt; instead he went to study with G. E. Müller at Göttingen and during his three semesters there began a dissertation on the theory of sensual feelings. Once more he was drawn to history and studied that subject for a year at Dorpat, but in 1886 he returned to Wundt. The following year he obtained his doctorate under Wundt, with the dissertation he had first worked on under Müller (1887).

Külpe remained in the Leipzig laboratory for eight years. He wrote his habilitation thesis on the doctrine of the will in recent psychology (1888), was appointed to the faculty as a docent, and after the departure of James M. Cattell became Wundt's assistant. He continued to be immersed in the experimental work of Wundt's laboratory and published an article on simultaneous and nonsimultaneous motion (1891–1892).

As Wundt himself became more and more involved in ethnopsychology (*Völkerpsychologie*), it fell to Külpe to write a systematic exposition of experimental psychology. He discussed the book, chapter by chapter, with Ernst Meumann, James R. Angell, and Edward B. Titchener, then students at Leipzig; it was published as *Grundriss der Psychologie* in 1893. There is nothing in the *Grundriss* concerning thinking, which was then not accessible to experimentation; rather, following Richard Avenarius, Külpe defined psychology as the science of those experiences that are dependent upon an experiencing individual and outlined the experimental findings of that science.

Once Külpe had been appointed full professor at Würzburg in 1894, he proceeded, with all the energy and tenacity at his command, to set up an institute for psychological experimentation. He was supported by Karl Marbe, who had become a docent at Würzburg in 1894. After two years Külpe was granted the use of a few rooms by the library, and it was there that he and Marbe began to experiment, without assistants, staff, or funds. It was only after Külpe had declined appointments both to Münster and Stanford that he was able to secure government grants, and he then hired Ernst Dürr as his first assistant. Five years later, in 1909, Külpe accepted an appointment at Bonn, and his assistant Karl Bühler went with him. His successor at Würzburg was Marbe, and Marbe's first assistant was Kurt Koffka.

**The Würzburg school.** There is little in Külpe's own writings that would lead one to associate him with the Würzburg school, so clearly identified with the psychology of thinking. Except for a brief article (1912*a*), he wrote nothing on this subject, and yet there is no doubt whatever that he was the founder of the Würzburg school. He inspired all the work that made Würzburg famous in psychology, and when he left for Bonn, no further work was done at Würzburg on the experimental psychology of thought processes. Until then Külpe was both the intellectual leader of the Würzburg institute and its most willing experimental subject. During his 13 years at Würzburg more than fifty experimental investigations were published. His aim was to develop an experimental approach to the problem of thought, equivalent to that which Hermann Ebbinghaus had developed for memory.

The findings that Mayer and Orth published in 1901 on the qualitative nature of associations suggested that thought consists of a course of associations and that it is a process that permits description. The method by which it was to be made experimentally accessible was introspection: the description of thought. At about the same time Marbe published his investigation of judgment (1901), and it excited much attention. It showed that the sources of judgment lie concealed beneath all the known phenomena of consciousness and that sensation, imagination, and feeling are not involved in judgment. The individual does not know how he comes to make a judgment; a rational conclusion may follow an irrational process of thought. These Würzburg findings began basically to undermine Wundt's concept of consciousness. The implication of the investigations was that thought is imageless and that it depends on such conscious attitudes (*Bewusstseinslagen*) as doubt, certainty, etc., rather than on images and sensations.

Another member of the Würzburg group, H.

J. Watt, obtained related results with constrained associations, which he investigated by the method of fractionation. He found that a task does not stimulate an "intention" to perform it, but that the "decision" to perform the task produces a quasi-unconscious "determining tendency." Narziss Ach appreciated the significance of this determining tendency in everyday life, and he subjected it to systematic experimental observation, seeking to measure the intensity of an act of will by the strength of the associations that have to be overcome. August Messer, who had previously been at Giessen, and Karl Bühler, who had worked in the laboratory of Carl Stumpf at Berlin, came to Würzburg in 1905 and 1907 respectively and developed the theory of imageless thought. Bühler's introspective method, in particular, exposed the experimental study of thought processes to criticism and thereby aroused the world-wide interest of psychologists.

During his years at Bonn Külpe wrote important works on philosophy. In 1913 he accepted a call to the University of Munich, where his sudden death two years later broke off his work on a new systematic exposition of experimental psychology.

W. J. REVERS

[For the historical context of Külpe's work, see the biographies of MÜLLER, GEORG ELIAS, and WUNDT. For discussion of the subsequent development of his ideas, see GESTALT THEORY; THINKING; and the biography of BÜHLER.]

### WORKS BY KÜLPE

1887    Zur Theorie der sinnlichen Gefühle: Inaugural Dissertation. Altenburg: Geibel.

1888    Die Lehre vom Willen in der neueren Psychologie: Habilitationsschrift. Leipzig: Engelmann.

1891–1892    Über die Gleichzeitigkeit und Ungleichzeitigkeit der Bewegungen. Philosophische Studien 6:514–535; 7:147–168.

(1893) 1901    Outlines of Psychology, Based Upon the Results of Experimental Investigation. 2d ed. London: Sonnenschein; New York: Macmillan. → First published as Grundriss der Psychologie: Auf experimenteller Grundlage dargestellt . . .

(1895) 1901    Introduction to Philosophy: A Handbook for Students of Psychology, Logic, Ethics, Aesthetics and General Philosophy. London: Sonnenschein; New York: Macmillan. → First published as Einleitung in die Philosophie.

(1902) 1913    The Philosophy of the Present in Germany. London: Allen. → First published as Die Philosophie der Gegenwart in Deutschland: Eine Charakteristik ihrer Hauptrichtungen, nach Vorträgen, gehalten in Ferienkurs für Lehrer 1901 zu Würzburg.

1910    Erkenntnistheorie und Naturwissenschaft. Leipzig: Hirzel.

1912a    Über die moderne Psychologie des Denkens. Pages 297–331 in Oswald Külpe, Vorlesungen über Psychologie. Edited by Karl Bühler. 2d ed., rev. & enl. Leipzig: Hirzel.

1912b    Contribution to the History of the Concept of Reality. Philosophical Review 21:1–10.

1912c    Psychologie und Medizin. Leipzig: Engelmann.

1912–1923    Die Realisierung: Ein Beitrag zur Grundlegung der Realwissenschaften. 3 vols. Leipzig: Hirzel.

### SUPPLEMENTARY BIBLIOGRAPHY

ACH, NARZISS 1905    Über die Willenstätigkeit und das Denken; eine experimentelle Untersuchung mit einem Anhange: Über das Hippsche Chronoskop. Göttingen: Vandenhoeck & Ruprecht.

BORING, EDWIN G. (1929) 1950    A History of Experimental Psychology. 2d ed. New York: Appleton. → See especially pages 396–410 on "Külpe Before Würzburg" and pages 433–435 for a bibliography.

BÜHLER, KARL 1907–1908    Tatsachen und Probleme zu einer Psychologie der Denkvorgänge. Archiv für die gesamte Psychologie 9:297–365; 12:1–123. → Part 1: Über Gedanken. Part 2: Über Gedankenzusammenhänge.

FLUGEL, JOHN C. (1933) 1964    A Hundred Years of Psychology: 1833–1933. With an additional part: 1933–1963, by Donald J. West. New York: Basic Books.

MARBE, KARL 1901    Experimentell-psychologische Untersuchungen über das Urteil: Eine Einleitung in die Logik. Leipzig: Engelmann.

MAYER, A.; and ORTH, J. 1901    Zur qualitativen Untersuchung der Association. Zeitschrift für Psychologie und Physiologie der Sinnesorgane 26:1–13.

MESSER, AUGUST 1906    Experimentell-psychologische Untersuchungen über das Denken. Archiv für die gesamte Psychologie 8:1–224.

MURPHY, GARDNER (1929) 1949    Historical Introduction to Modern Psychology. Rev. ed. New York: Harcourt. → See especially pages 225–233 in the 1949 edition on the Würzburg school.

ORTH, JOHANNES 1903    Gefühl und Bewusstseinslage: Eine kritisch-experimentelle Studie. Berlin: Reuther & Reichard.

WATT, H. J. 1905    Experimentelle Beiträge zu einer Theorie des Denkens. Archiv für die gesamte Psychologie 4:289–436.

# KULTURKREIS SCHOOL

See DIFFUSION, article on CULTURAL DIFFUSION; and the biographies of FROBENIUS; KOPPERS; SCHMIDT.

# L

## LABOR ECONOMICS

*See* EMPLOYMENT AND UNEMPLOYMENT; LABOR FORCE; LABOR RELATIONS; LABOR UNIONS; WAGES.

## LABOR FORCE

### I
### DEFINITIONS AND MEASUREMENT

"Labor force" is a term used specifically to refer to data collection procedures developed in the United States during the late 1930s and currently being used in that and a few other countries. A more general term, and one more suited to the scope of this article, would be "working force"; this is more or less equivalent to what United Nations labor statisticians call the "economically active population." But whatever term we finally choose, it should be emphasized from the start that there are many methods of collecting statistics about workers and that any way of referring to all the workers in one country necessarily reflects one or more of these methods.

**Definition of terms.** In its most generalized form the *working force* is conceived as that portion of the population which is economically active. The definition of "economically active" in any particular society must in turn be regarded in terms of the organization of work characteristic of the culture. In primitive societies the working force is hardly distinguishable from the total population. The low level of technology requires the participation of virtually the entire population in the common tasks of producing goods and services necessary for subsistence. With the growth of a market economy in the course of economic development, the working force becomes clearly distinguishable from the total population. The working force may thus be said to be a function of the socioeconomic structure of society.

In every culture, most persons are engaged, a good part of their lives, in activities that may be considered as work. But such activities may or may not qualify them for inclusion in what may be regarded technically as part of the working force. For example, in the United States the services performed by housewives, although highly desirable from a societal point of view, are not regarded as economic. Housewives are therefore excluded from what is measured as the working force because such work is outside the characteristic system of work organization or production. Moreover, their inclusion in the working force, for purposes of economic analysis, would not help policy makers to solve the significant economic problems of American society. Thus, the concept of working force underlying statistical measurement is an artifact, created to serve purposes of social analysis, and can be defined only in terms of economic and social structure.

*Manpower* is a broader term than working force; it not only includes the latter but generally also includes the potential or maximum available working force which might come into being in accordance with economic, social, or political considerations. *Gainful workers* (or *gainfully occupied*), as well as *labor force,* refers to specific ways of collecting data. *Labor supply*, as it is used in economics, is conceived in the sense of a hypothetical schedule showing how much labor would be offered at each level of wages.

## Emergence of a modern working force

The previous observation that the working force in a modern industrialized country is only a portion of the total population can be seen most clearly by comparing its working force conditions with those that would obtain in a country or tribe in the complete absence of industrialization or industrializing influences (see Table 1).

**Table 1 — *Working force conditions in modern industrialized and in nonindustrialized countries***

|  | Modern industrialized | Nonindustrialized |
|---|---|---|
| Technological development | Very high | Very low |
| Division of labor | Highly developed | Almost none |
| Control of means of production | Centralized | Dispersed |
| Exchange economy (based on cash) | Highly developed | None |
| Free contract system | Highly developed | None |

The main point of contrast here is that industrialization frees many workers from the production of food and other goods essential for physical survival. Nothing, however, is implied about the form of government under which production takes place; industrial technology seems to require a centralized form of control regardless of whether the means of production are state-owned or in private hands. By contrast, in a completely nonindustrialized economy each worker tends to control and even own his individual means of production, even if his productive capacity goes little beyond subsistence level. The crucial variable would appear to be the presence or absence of money or its equivalent as a standardized medium of exchange. There is yet another important difference between these two types of society. Nonindustrial societies, as Sir Henry Maine pointed out long ago, lack not only actual contracts but even the very notion of "free contract"; the individual's labor activities are predetermined by the culture. Exactly the opposite is true of industrial societies, in which the worker enters into a free contractual relationship with his employer (there may, of course, be other constraints on him, but they are not the absolute constraints of culture).

We can visualize the process by which the modern working force emerges by starting with a nonindustrialized society which meets two conditions: it is large enough to be able to use a division of labor, and its population has unfilled wants for

goods and services. Although the latter condition can probably be found among all peoples, it is clear that isolated tribes of a few hundred people cannot fulfill the first condition.

If this process does get under way (and there seems to be no reason why it *must* begin), then the combination of division of labor and technological advancement results in the establishment of technologically complex economic institutions in which control rests in the hands of a few managers rather than with the individual workers. A highly developed exchange economy based on cash must now exist, and the worker must be free to offer his services for cash hire as he sees fit. Thus, he receives cash payment for producing a highly specialized item or service and then can use this cash for purchasing at will items or services produced by other specialized workers.

As the end result of this process we have the *labor market*, or that specialized portion of the market place in which the person is free to offer his services for cash hire. The farmer or own-account worker represents the special case of the individual who may offer his goods or labor services simultaneously to several buyers. Those persons, then, who voluntarily offer their services for hire in the labor market and who thereby participate (or attempt to participate) in the production of the gross national product, form the *working force*. Accordingly, those persons who, for whatever reason, do not offer their services for hire in the labor market, thereby automatically exclude themselves from the working force.

Slaves or serfs also are not part of the working force, according to the above definition. Amasa Walker recognized this when he wrote:

What is labor? The voluntary efforts of human beings to produce objects of desire. . . . Involuntary or uncompensated efforts are not to be classed as labor. They are merely the result of the use of a given amount of capital. Slaves are owned, like horses or oxen; and what value they confer is from their employment as so much capital. This distinction is not unimportant, because we shall see that capital is controlled by other laws than those which govern labor.   (Walker [1866] 1872, pp. 18–19; compare Jaffe & Stewart 1951)

**Social policy and working force analysis.** Of overriding importance in the emergence and development of working force analysis was its connection with social policy determination. At times and in places where governments were unconcerned about unemployment, set no minimum wages or maximum working hours, or otherwise saw no problems to be solved which involved the people who produced the goods and services, there was little interest in working force analysis. In particular, where people were born into preordained social positions and occupations, there were no working force problems to solve. The son of a serf in medieval Europe was born to be a serf and work in a manner in accordance with customs and procedures known to everyone. The government might have been concerned with whether it had enough serfs or whether the serfs had enough to eat, but never with whether the serf was employed or unemployed.

In the United States the need for governmental action with regard to the working force became particularly acute during the great depression of the 1930s. If the government were to adopt any policies in an effort to cut down the volume of unemployment, information about the numbers and characteristics of the unemployed and the employed had to be available. This social policy need explains the direction in which the field has since progressed.

## Data collection in the United States

Three sets of procedures for collecting statistics about the American working force are now employed; the first two furnish the statistics most often used. They can be described briefly and in general terms as follows:

**Labor force procedures.** Members of households are interviewed by the U.S. Bureau of the Census enumerators and queried about work experiences during a specified week. These questions are asked either at the time of the monthly sample survey, when some 35,000 households are covered, or at the time of the decennial census.

Each person living in the household who is aged 14 and over is classified as employed, unemployed, or not in the labor force by means of the following procedure. ($a$) First of all, he or she is asked: What was your main activity last week—working for pay or profit, looking for work, or something else? ($b$) Those who replied "looking for work" or "something else" are then asked whether, in addition, they also worked for pay or profit during the past week. If the answer is yes, then they are also included among the employed. ($c$) If the answer to the question of whether a person had worked for pay or profit is no but the reply to question ($a$) had been that he or she was "looking for work," the person is included among the unemployed. ($d$) If the person answers no to the question about pay or profit but had originally replied "something else" to question ($a$), then it is asked whether he or she looked for work last week. If the answer is yes, the person is included among the unemployed. ($e$) If the answer to question ($d$) is no, the person is

asked whether there was a job or business from which he or she was temporarily absent last week. ($f$) If the answer to question ($e$) is yes, the person is included among the employed. ($g$) If the answer to question ($e$) is no, the person is classified as not in the labor force.

The "labor force" thus consists of persons *employed* for pay or profit during the specified week, plus persons who sought work during that week, the *unemployed*. All others aged 14 and over are categorized as *not in the labor force* (U.S. President's Committee . . . 1962).

Certain additional distinctions are made. The decennial censuses include everyone aged 14 and over; the members of the armed forces, however, are shown separately from the civilian population. The monthly sample surveys cover only the civilian population, omitting those who are residents of institutions (jails, hospitals, old people's homes, etc.). Both series distinguish, among the unemployed, between those who have worked previously and those who were seeking their first job; those unemployed who had worked previously, plus the employed, are the *experienced labor force*.

Persons in the experienced labor force are then asked questions about various other matters, including their occupation, industry, type of remuneration (self-employed, wage or salary worker, unpaid family worker), and hours worked per week. The unemployed are asked how many weeks they have spent looking for work. Additional questions are asked from time to time covering other aspects, such as earnings last year, multiple job holding, and so forth.

**Establishment employment statistics.** Payroll information is obtained each month from a sample of firms in all industries except agriculture. Items included are number of persons on the payroll and number of "production," or nonsupervisory, workers, together with hours worked and pay received by the production workers. More information is provided for production workers in manufacturing than for workers of any type in other nonagricultural industries. These monthly establishment data approximate the corresponding figures obtained by the labor force procedures described in the preceding section.

The two sets of statistics, labor force and establishment, have different uses. The former provide information about the personal and job characteristics of workers in the *total* United States; only a minimum of information is available for the country's regions or for the various industries. The establishment data, on the other hand, provide almost no information about the characteristics of the workers but do provide data on employment for state and local areas and for detailed industries.

**Other by-product data.** Certain other series of data covering one or another part of the American working force are available as by-products of administrative procedures. One such series comes from the reports which employers file on payroll pension deductions for workers under the Federal Old Age and Survivors Insurance Program; the series naturally covers only the employed. A series of unemployment data is available as a by-product of the operations of the unemployment insurance program. A count is obtainable weekly of the numbers of persons drawing unemployment insurance benefits. The figures on unemployment so derived range between one-third and one-half of the figures as reported by labor force procedures. Counts are also available of the numbers of persons for whom unemployment insurance has been paid, thus providing information about employment.

Many other administrative programs are available which, as a by-product of their primary operations, furnish information about one part or another of the American working force. Thus additional statistics are available on employment in coal mining, agriculture, government, schools and colleges, and a number of other segments of the economy.

In general, these by-product statistics tend to be rather specialized and therefore most useful for analysis of particular aspects of the working force rather than for over-all working force analysis. For example, if one is particularly concerned with college teachers he would turn to the data provided by the Office of Education, supplemented by the decennial census data, rather than to the monthly labor force statistics.

## Data collection in other countries

Several other countries have adopted the United States labor force procedures in whole or in part. These are: Japan, Italy, Canada, Federal Republic of Germany, France, Philippines, Sweden, and Panama. Since both the length of time that these surveys have existed and their detailed mode of operation vary considerably from one country to another, we cannot discuss each country separately in this article. Some of them conduct monthly surveys, some quarterly, and some less often or irregularly. Information about employment and unemployment is generally asked as of one week, sometimes for a period of one month. The minimum age of those questioned varies from country to country in accordance with customary beginning working ages. In all countries samples of households are interviewed. In addition, there is some

tendency to incorporate labor force procedures into the population censuses, which are generally taken every ten years.

Other countries, such as Great Britain, have highly developed public employment offices and all-inclusive establishment reporting; they therefore rely on these two administrative programs to furnish the available working force statistics. Thus, the public employment offices provide counts of the numbers of persons seeking jobs (the "unemployed"), while the establishment reporting, including the reporting of payroll deductions for the various social welfare programs, produces statistics on employment.

A variety of other statistical collection programs is in use; many of them are somewhat haphazard. Most countries that take occasional population censuses obtain some information about their working forces, though the information varies in usefulness. Some countries collect information only for selected segments of their working force, such as employees in factories hiring twenty or more workers; other countries have other procedures.

The safest general statement to make is that most countries, with the exception of some of those which adopted the labor force procedures or have highly developed public employment offices and establishment reporting, do not have working force data of any real use for public policy information. In summary, for the majority of the world's people, no useful working force statistics are available.

**Measurement of underemployment.** One innovation which some countries are trying to introduce through modifications of the labor force procedures is the measurement of underemployment. In effect, these countries are trying to subdivide the information on the employed into two groups: those *fully employed* and those *underemployed*. Obviously these two terms are relative; the dividing line can be placed at any point in between total unemployment and working busily for 120 hours a week and 52 weeks in the year at top pay.

The procedures which have been tried in an effort to measure underemployment fall into three types: (*a*) arbitrary efforts to allocate workers in accordance with the number of hours worked per week (or some other time period); (*b*) use of amount of time which the person had *wanted* to work, so that the underemployed are defined as those who worked less time than they had wanted; (*c*) some assessment of the worker's desire to change his job because of the poor quality of present employment, including low earnings, little opportunity to use skills, and so on (United Nations 1958).

On the basis of the experiences to date (1964) we can only conclude that there is no uniquely correct way of measuring underemployment: alternative measures provide alternative statistics. The most important factor is the use of identical procedures over time within any given country, so that changes can be measured. In fact, only changes over time *can* be measured, never absolute levels. If there is any more nearly "correct" measure of underemployment for a particular country, it is that definition which best fits the social, economic, and political context—if such a definition can be determined. This leads to the conclusion that it is impossible to have so-called "internationally comparable" measures of underemployment unless several countries happen to be identical in all manpower respects.

## International comparability

Similar collection procedures need not produce similar and comparable working force statistics. This is so, as we have pointed out previously, because the working force—its concept and measurement—is an artifact created to serve a specific purpose within a specific social, economic, and political context. Where societies are organized differently, have different values and goals, and government or private policy makers are concerned with different problems, then different concepts and procedures may be needed. If the same procedures are employed, the net result may be the provision of useless and meaningless statistics for some of the countries.

This can be illustrated by applying the labor force procedures to a semisubsistence population living at very low levels. When subjected to the barrage of questions as previously described, these semisubsistence workers will all turn out to be "employed farmers"; very few will report being unemployed even though they and their families may be living at the edge of starvation. For example, to say that there is virtually no unemployment among Panamanian farmers in 1960 (about 1 per cent) and therefore that they are better off than American workers, among whom unemployment in 1960 was about 5.5 per cent, is meaningless. The working force problems which Panamanian policy makers must consider are quite different from the problems with which United States policy makers must deal, although there is some overlap.

Even when ostensibly similar countries are being compared in terms of employment and unemployment, working force statistics, although obtained by identical procedures, may be noncomparable. For example, in the United States workers tend to work a full week of 40 hours and try to maximize their pay. There seems to be comparatively less interest among American workers, as contrasted with European ones, to spread the work so that more people may have jobs, although at lower pay. American workers, on the contrary, seem anxious to maximize their earnings even if, as a result, some workers become unemployed. Now unemployment can always be eliminated if there is enough spread-the-work; note the labor force procedures for ascertaining unemployment. Therefore, if in one country there is somewhat more of a tendency to spread the work than in another country, the resulting unemployment statistics will not be comparable in the sense of being equally useful for policy determination.

Even the size of the working force may vary from one country to another because of social or economic conditions which could tend to make the statistics noncomparable. Application of the labor force procedures in a country in which the population knows that it is extremely difficult to find jobs will result in many persons replying that they neither worked nor sought work; therefore, they are "not in the labor force." In another country, however, if the people are more optimistic, or more determined, more may seek work and thereby increase the number of unemployed and the size of the labor force. Yet the unemployment problems with which the policy makers in the two countries may have to contend may be quite similar.

In summary, working force statistics are most useful for dealing with the problems of a specific country and for determining the changes that have occurred there over time. They are much less useful, in their present state, for comparing the working force situation in two or more countries; and this difficulty, because it is inherent in the nature of the problem, will not be solved by mere technical improvement in data gathering procedures.

A. J. JAFFE

[*Directly related are the entries* ECONOMIC DATA; EMPLOYMENT AND UNEMPLOYMENT. *Other relevant material may be found in* AGRICULTURE, *article on* LABOR; ECONOMY AND SOCIETY; INDUSTRIALIZATION.]

### BIBLIOGRAPHY

*For detailed statements about methods used by the U.S. Bureau of the Census, see* U.S. Bureau of Labor Statistics 1964; U.S. President's Committee to Appraise Employment and Unemployment Statistics 1962. *An earlier report which also provides much information on measurement procedures in the United States is* Ducoff & Hagood 1947. *For discussion of the measurement of the working force in other countries, including internationally recommended measurement procedures, see* United Nations, Statistical

Office 1958; International Labour Office 1959. *Concepts of the working force are explored in considerable depth in* Jaffe & Stewart 1951; Lederer 1932. *The measurement of underemployment is included in* Jaffe 1959. *Attempts at comparison of the working force in the United States and other countries are given in* Myers & Chandler 1962a, 1962b. Walker 1866 *is an interesting mid-nineteenth-century treatise.*

Ducoff, Louis J.; and Hagood, Margaret J. 1947 *Labor Force Definition and Measurement.* New York: Social Science Research Council.

International Labor Office 1959 *The International Standardisation of Labour Statistics.* Studies and Reports, New Series, No. 53. Geneva: The Office.

Jaffe, A. J. 1959 *People, Jobs and Economic Development.* Glencoe, Ill.: Free Press.

Jaffe, A. J.; and Stewart, Charles D. 1951 *Manpower Resources and Utilization: Principles of Working Force Analysis.* New York: Wiley.

Lederer, Emil 1932 Labor. Volume 8, pages 615–620 in *Encyclopaedia of the Social Sciences.* New York: Macmillan.

Myers, Robert J.; and Chandler, John H. 1962a International Comparisons of Unemployment. U.S. Bureau of Labor Statistics, *Monthly Labor Review* 85: 857–864.

Myers, Robert J.; and Chandler, John H. 1962b Toward Explaining International Unemployment Rates. U.S. Bureau of Labor Statistics, *Monthly Labor Review* 85: 969–974.

United Nations, Statistical Office 1958 *Handbook of Population Census Methods.* Volume 2: Economic Characteristics of the Population. New York: United Nations.

U.S. Bureau of Labor Statistics 1964 *Concepts and Methods Used in Household Statistics on Employment and Unemployment From the Current Population Survey.* Washington: Government Printing Office.

U.S. President's Committee to Appraise Employment and Unemployment Statistics 1962 *Measuring Employment and Unemployment.* Washington: Government Printing Office.

Walker, Amasa (1866) 1872 *The Science of Wealth.* 7th ed. Philadelphia: Lippincott.

## II

### PARTICIPATION

The labor force participation rate of a population is defined as the proportion of the population that is either employed or in search of employment in the labor market during a given period of time. Labor force statistics of many countries contain information about participation rates of the total population and of various population groups. The data reveal large differences in labor force rates among population groups in the same economy. Available time series also reveal sizable and often contrasting changes in labor force participation rates in the various population groups.

Some of the differences in labor force participation among age, sex, and marital-status groups, prevailing at a given time in a given country, are easily understood. It is much more difficult to interpret the diverse patterns of long-run and short-run *changes* in labor force participation. In this article an attempt is made to interpret labor force trends in the light of economic theory and of the growing empirical research in this area.

Table 1 illustrates the patterns of labor force participation of population groups in the United States, classified by age and sex, in the years 1900, 1930, and 1963. The table contains some rather sharp and divergent trends among the several age–sex classifications. Roughly similar trends, varying in magnitude, have been observed in many other countries.

**Table 1 — Participation in the labor force by age and sex, United States, 1900, 1930, and 1963 (per cent of each group in labor force)**

|  | MALES | | | FEMALES | | |
|---|---|---|---|---|---|---|
|  | 1900 | 1930 | 1963 | 1900 | 1930 | 1963 |
| 14 and over | 85.7 | 82.1 | 77.7 | 20.0 | 23.6 | 36.5 |
| 14–19 | 62.1 | 40.1 | 36.5 | 26.8 | 22.8 | 24.6 |
| 20–24 | 90.6 | 88.8 | 86.8 | 31.7 | 41.8 | 47.3 |
| 25–34 | 94.9 | 96.0 | 97.0 | 19.4 | 27.1 | 36.7 |
| 35–44 | 94.5 | 95.7 | 97.8 | 15.0 | 21.7 | 45.4 |
| 45–54 | 92.8 | 93.8 | 96.0 | 14.2 | 19.7 | 51.0 |
| 55–64 | 86.2 | 86.5 | 86.3 | 12.6 | 15.3 | 40.0 |
| 65 and over | 63.1 | 53.9 | 28.5 | 8.3 | 7.3 | 9.5 |

Sources: For 1900 and 1930 data, Bancroft 1958, Table D-1a, p. 207. For 1963 data, U.S. Bureau of Labor Statistics 1963, Table A-12, p. 7.

Economic analysis can provide insights into only some of the factors influencing labor force participation, such as incomes and relative prices. Since noneconomic considerations bulk large in labor force behavior, as in other spheres of human behavior, only a partial understanding can be achieved by this analysis. It is fair to add that even within these limitations such an analysis can never be definitive, nor does it represent a full consensus of specialists in this field of study. The present discussion contains a set of hypotheses for which the degree of empirical verification varies widely. It is, therefore, to be viewed not only as a summary of current research, but in part also as an agenda for future research.

At the outset, it is important to recognize the distinction between the theoretical concept of a quantity of labor supplied by a given population and the empirical measurement of labor force participation. The notion of a quantity of labor supplied by a given population is broad, and hence ambiguous, unless the purpose for which this labor is supplied is specified and the units in which the quantities are to be measured are defined. Labor force surveys, however, are quite specific: they purport to measure the quantity of labor supplied for gainful employment or self-employment in the labor market. They measure this quantity by a simple count of people who are so employed or in search of such employment during a given short period. By this definition, the surveys focus on labor markets, on short periods of observation, and on the number of participants—without regard to the *extent* of participation in terms of hours of work or in terms of periods longer than the survey week. All these restrictions must be kept in mind in applying the broad language of economic analysis to the narrowly defined empirical measurements of labor force participation.

The starting point for this examination, as for most economic analysis, is the problem of individual choice in allocating scarce resources among alternative uses. In this case, it is the problem of allocating time among alternative uses. The simplest set of such alternatives is a dichotomy: time used in production (work) and in consumption (leisure). [*See* LEISURE; TIME BUDGETS.] Using this dichotomy, the effect of the wage rate on the quantity of labor supplied, measured in time units, can be analyzed in terms of the demand for leisure time, which is viewed as a consumption good. Standard demand analysis predicts the effects of changes in relative prices and in income on consumption: a rise in price of a good relative to prices of other goods leads to a decrease in its consumption—that is, a "substitution effect" in favor of other goods; a rise in income normally (excepting "inferior" goods) leads to an increase in consumption—the "income effect." Since the price of leisure is the forgone wage, a rise in the wage rate makes leisure more expensive, inducing the worker to work more; in effect, to "purchase" less leisure. At the same time, however, an increase in the wage rate increases income, which leads to increased "purchases" of leisure, that is, to decreased hours of work. Which of the two effects triumphs cannot be determined a priori. It depends on the relative preferences of individuals between utilities afforded by the purchasing power of wages and those resulting from the availability of leisure time (Robbins 1930).

**Adult males.** According to a widely accepted hypothesis, the income effect of the demand for leisure is stronger, on the average, than the substitution effect, so that an increase in the wage rate normally results in a decreased amount of work (Douglas 1934). This hypothesis, known as the "backward-bending" supply curve of labor, can be used to explain the secular decline in the work week in many countries by the secular growth in

real incomes per capita (Lewis 1956), provided some oversimplifications are deemed empirically inconsequential. The major one is the use of a dichotomy: "work" is work in the labor market; all other activities are defined as "leisure." This oversimplification is perhaps not too severe in the case of adult males in industrial societies. Since the analysis does not specify the period over which the allocation of time is made, it leads to the following generalization: Looking at the lifetime behavior of individual males, and abstracting for the moment from learning processes, aging, and family life-cycle developments, we would expect the fraction of the lifetime devoted to work to decrease as real income and wealth per capita rise.

This fraction, however, can shrink in more than one way: hours worked per week or per year may decline with no change in participation; the converse may be true; or both may decrease. Thus, granted that growth in income affects the length of the work week, does it follow that it also affects labor force participation? For the relevant population group, adult males (say, aged 25 to 60 in the United States), there are economic considerations that lead to a negative answer. According to these, income changes affect hours of work, but not labor force participation, of adult males. Table 1 shows that this is in fact the case: in contrast with the sharp secular declines in participation of young and old males and with an increase in the participation of adult women, the attachment of adult males to the labor force has remained very strong and about the same in 1963 as in 1900. These high and unchanging levels of labor force participation are characteristic of adult males in many other parts of the world.

With labor income being the main source of income, it is not surprising that adult males, most of whom are the main earners in the family, are continuously attached to the labor force. The preference to absorb the gains in leisure in the form of shorter work weeks or paid vacations, rather than in the form of temporary withdrawals from the labor force, reflects, in part, a preference for steady patterns of consumption over time. By and large, such preferences hold for total consumption as well as for the consumption of leisure. The latter directly implies a preference for steady employment. A steady rate of total consumption is more easily achieved with steady employment, giving steady incomes, than with fluctuating incomes. Moreover, interruptions of employment impose reemployment costs on workers and on employers. These costs can be quite sizable, particularly where some degree of skill is involved, since interruptions of employment adversely affect the maintenance and development of skill and of a work career.

In order to extend the analysis to younger and older males, the economic effects of age must be brought into the picture. To isolate the effect of age, abstract for the moment from training processes. The important phenomenon is then the relation between age and worker productivity. At early ages productivity rises with physical and mental growth. At the other extreme, physiological effects of aging eventually bring about a decline in productivity. With wage rates reflecting productivity, it appears that leisure is less costly at younger and older ages than in the middle years. Differences in the cost of leisure, therefore, call for a greater concentration of work in the middle years and a reduction of it at young and old ages. However, assuming the same hours, currently obtainable earnings vary proportionately with the wage rate. Hence, if labor force behavior responded to current income in the manner specified by the backward-bending supply curve, the cost of leisure effects would be more than offset by income effects. This would predict that the young and old would work more than those in the middle years. Such a conclusion is, of course, at variance with observed facts.

But, to the extent that assets and credit are available to the individual, it is clear that current income is not an effective constraint on consumption decisions. The relevant variable to which consumption standards are related is the long-run income position. This is a widely accepted explanation of consumer behavior. The case for a similar income concept as a determinant of labor supply is equally compelling (Lewis 1956; Mincer 1962a). With this income concept in mind, it becomes advantageous, in view of variations in the cost of leisure, to distribute the consumption of leisure disproportionately toward young and old ages. This tendency is reflected in shorter hours, intermittent participation, or total absence from the labor force at the two extremes of working life.

An important implication of this analysis, still assuming the validity of the backward-bending supply curve, is that secular growth in real income tends to raise the age of entry into the labor force, lengthen the span of retirement, and/or increase the frequency of part-time and part-period work at the two extremes of age. As Table 1 shows, the age distribution of the male labor force in the United States and the secular changes in the various age groups are consistent with this analysis. Such patterns, including the progressive elimination of child labor and earlier retirements, are well known in countries that have experienced long periods of growth in real per capita income.

This does not mean that the explanations here advanced are incontrovertible or that they are sufficient. Other factors, some of them economic, are involved and must be considered.

**Older males.** A part of the sharp secular decline in participation rates of older males (65 and over) in countries like the United States might be explained by increasing longevity, one of the benefits of economic growth. But this factor is quantitatively unimportant: While the 65-and-older group grew in relation to total population, there was little change in the age distribution within the older group in the United States (Long 1958).

The growth in size of the older group relative to the younger population may have had some adverse effects on their earnings and employment opportunities, particularly in view of the lower average educational background of older people. Very little evidence is as yet available to shed light on this matter. Some decline in participation rates is undoubtedly associated with the relative decline of employment in agriculture. But participation rates have declined, and quite sharply, among older males in both urban and rural areas (Long 1958). There is little evidence to suggest that the reduction in participation rates is due to a deterioration in health *at given ages*. However, rising health standards, which are particularly responsive to growth in income, may mean that a worker on the border line of physical fitness is less inclined to continue working today than in the past. Contributing to this effect has been the decline in occupations permitting a gradual tapering off of activity, such as self-employment.

A financial factor of some importance is the more recent growth of the benefit provisions of public old-age security programs, public assistance benefits, and private retirement plans. This factor constitutes a reinforcement of the previously emphasized income effect of rising real earnings. This is true to the extent that the redistribution of consumption from younger to older ages is strengthened by these programs—that they increase the net volume of savings available for retirement. There are reasons to believe that this is the case, in view of the income redistribution effects and tax incentives built into these programs. Moreover, the provisions often make eligibility for benefits conditional upon giving up gainful work, or make the benefit a declining function of the income earned during the benefit years. Such provisions reduce the cost of leisure in old age and encourage the withdrawal of old people from the labor force. Indeed, in the United States as elsewhere, the declining trend in labor force participation of older people has accelerated since the 1930s, when such programs were introduced, extended, and liberalized.

The discussion thus far implies that the low and declining participation rates of older people are largely voluntary, proper account being taken of health levels and standards. It is held by many that this view is inadequate, that many old people retire involuntarily, and that declining employer demand for older people is an important force in the secular reduction of their labor force participation.

Unquestionably, many individuals in good health are retired either as a consequence of being laid off or of compulsory retirement upon reaching a certain age. However, neither layoff nor compulsory retirement age need result in withdrawal from the labor force, if the worker seeks and manages to find another job. But evidence abounds to the effect that this is particularly difficult for the older worker. Unemployment rates are higher and the duration of unemployment longer for older people. The available data indicate that, in the short run, reductions of older men in the labor force are closely associated with unemployment for the economy as a whole, as well as among industries and occupations (Jaffe & Stewart 1951).

Over the long run, however, aggregate unemployment rates have not been increasing. To what extent, if at all, they have been increasing for older males cannot be ascertained from the available record. The difficulties encountered by older workers in hiring and such practices as compulsory retirement are often described as discriminatory. Little empirical evidence exists on whether such discrimination has been increasing. Nor is it clear why discrimination, if viewed as a cultural or psychological factor, should have been growing over time.

However, a certain amount of plausibility for the discrimination hypothesis is suggested by economic factors, the most important of which is the difficulty of downward adjustment of wages to individual changes in productivity. Wage adjustments to the decline in productivity of older workers are difficult because of wide individual differences in the time at which productivity starts declining, and because of the morale-disrupting effects that continuous downward adjustments would bring about. Firms therefore find it most economical to estimate an average age at which productivity declines are likely to require significant reductions in wages and to provide for compulsory retirement at that age. The larger the work force of a firm, the more economical this procedure from a management point of view.

Moreover, to the extent that training on the job is important and is partly financed by the firm, hiring of older people frequently becomes disadvantageous. Firms engaging in such training are also likely to be large and to have seniority schemes, pension plans, and policies of hiring younger people for low-level jobs and promoting them from within. Thus, the growth in average size of firms, and the secular upgrading of skills in the labor force resulting from growth in education and in associated training on the job, may contribute to a spread of compulsory retirement and of discriminatory hiring practices.

All of the forces enumerated above may be assumed to have been at work in some degree: rising incomes, public and private security programs, and health standards on the supply side; as well as declining demand, which is related to the same technological and educational trends that raised incomes and reduced supply. The relative importance of these factors and the validity of their interpretation must await further empirical exploration.

**Young males.** In most industrial countries, child labor is a thing of the past. Legislation requiring school attendance is widespread, and the compulsory age for such attendance has been progressively raised. But even above those ages we find that labor force participation of young people is much lower than in the adult age groups. There is little doubt that the participation rate of teenage males, as well as those in their early twenties, is lower in more industrially advanced countries than in others, and that it has been shrinking historically.

It is clear that school enrollment and its historical growth are the basic facts in labor force behavior of young people. Indeed, using recent U.S. data, if school enrollment is added to the labor force of young males (ages 14–19) who are not at school, a total of over 90 per cent of the population of the group is obtained, almost as high as the labor force participation rate of adult males. And, historically, the declines in the labor force of young males have almost precisely matched their inflows into classrooms (Long 1958).

These are facts, not explanations. Can these facts be explained in terms of income and price effects on the demand for leisure? The answer is

"Yes," provided education is considered a specific component of the leisure category, a time-intensive form of consumption. It must be recognized, however, that neither the variables entering the demand for education nor the magnitudes of responses (elasticities) to changes in income and in prices are precisely the same as in the demand for the general category of leisure time. To use an analogy, the demand variables and the price and income elasticities are not the same in the consumption of meat as in consumption of all food.

The price, or cost, of education consists of two parts: the forgone wage and the actual direct costs, such as tuition. At a moment of time and at a given age and education level, the cost of education (of the same quality) is roughly the same for all students; hence, one would expect to find a positive relation between (parental or community) income and the fraction of young people enrolled in school. Empirical estimates based on cross-section data indicate a very strong effect of family income on education of children. This suggests that historical income growth is a powerful force in the growth of education. Over time, however, the growth in income is associated with a growing cost of education. Opportunity costs, that is, forgone wages of young people, may have risen as fast as average family incomes; but direct costs of educational outlays probably increased at a slower rate. The net result of the price and income movements —growth in education—can be interpreted in the same manner as the decline in the work week: the strong income effect dominates the price effects working in the opposite direction.

The validity of this simple analysis hinges on the proviso that education is viewed as a consumer good. True, education is often valued for its own sake, and in a literal sense the shift from conditions of child labor to school constitutes a gain in leisure for the young. But this view disregards the effects of education on market productivity. The effects of education on earning power and on upward social mobility are well known. Unquestionably, they play a part in motivating the demand for education. With this focus, education can be viewed as an investment activity, a process of investing in an income-producing asset [see CAPITAL, HUMAN].

To the extent that education is considered an investment rather than a consumption good, the analysis of the determinants of its growth, which underlies the changes in labor force participation of the young, must be revised. Investment demand is not influenced solely by costs of the investment goods, nor is income of the investor very relevant in a properly functioning capital market. Although a cost attaches to an increment of education, there is also a return to be expected, in the form of an augmented future income. From this point of view, what matters in the decision between school enrollment and labor force participation is not the cost of education, but the rate of return on it. If education and its growth were to be interpreted entirely as a consumption phenomenon, money rates of return could be high, low, or even negative. And, whatever the initial level of rates, a secular spread of education generated by forces unconcerned with monetary investment yields would have tended to depress these rates. Empirical research in the United States indicates that during the last several decades, rates of return to education have been neither low nor declining, despite massive educational growth (Becker 1960; Mincer 1962b). The inference which these data seem to suggest is that of a steady movement of (young) manpower resources into educational investment in response to a continuously growing demand for an educated, skilled labor force.

With rates of return on educational investment higher than in alternative pursuits, the influx of young people into classrooms is limited only by such barriers as insufficient ability, income, and information. Income is a limiting factor, since finance for educational investments is not readily obtainable in capital markets. Hence, the secular growth in income has increasingly facilitated the growth of education. Public subsidies to education have reinforced this effect. At high school and higher levels there has been a tendency to transfer some of the traditional training functions of firms (apprenticeships, engineering and business preparation) to schools. Labor force participation is thereby decreased without any real change in the activity of the young worker.

Why are educational alternatives important in the labor force behavior of young people, and unimportant in other age groups? The answer is provided by the investment aspect of education. A given increment of education benefits younger people more than older ones because of the longer remaining life over which these (monetary and nonmonetary) gains accrue. One application of this analysis, of some relevance to underdeveloped countries, is that improvements in health and increased longevity, even without an initial growth in income, are likely to bring about increases in educational investments, hence decreased labor force participation of young people.

**Women.** The two-way allocation of time between work in the labor market on the one hand,

and leisure or education on the other, is a severe but tolerable oversimplification in the analysis of labor force behavior of males. The dichotomy is an oversimplification of a more general condition in which the allocation of time is a three-way choice between leisure, paid work in the labor market, and production outside the market. The last is the most important activity of all population groups in primitive societies where product and labor markets are not yet developed. In advanced societies, where work at home is a shrinking sector of economic activity, the biological and cultural specialization of functions in the family continues the assignment to women of the major responsibility for the care of home and household. Hence the much smaller labor force participation of women than of men in most societies, except in those agricultural countries where census practices count all women living on the farm as employed. Since the demand for home care varies over the life cycle of the family, reaching its peak at the childbearing and child-rearing stages, it is not surprising that single women past school age have the highest rates of participation and mothers of young children have the lowest rates.

The family context of labor force behavior that is brought to the fore in the discussion of women leads to the following generalization in the economic analysis of labor supply:

The amount of work supplied by a family member to the market depends not only on *his* (or her) market wage rate, but also on the *total* income position of the family, on the individual's productivity in household work and other activities outside the market, on prices of market substitutes for household goods and services, and on family tastes. Since income has a positive effect on the demand for leisure, a higher family income implies a smaller total amount of work (at home and in the market) supplied by family members. In the case

of adult men, the effect of a rising real income has been to decrease their hours of work in the market, this being the major sector of their work activity. There is little reason to believe that the gains in the amount of leisure resulting from growth in real (family) income have been different for women than for men (Mincer 1962a).

But while the total amount of work of women shrank as much as that of men, the distribution of the smaller total shifted, historically, from home to market. In many countries this shift has been so strong that the amount of work in the market has been growing absolutely, sometimes at a spectacular rate. In the United States, between 1890 and 1960, labor force rates of all females 14 years and over rose from about 18 per cent to 35 per cent. In the same period, rates of married women rose from 5 per cent to 30 per cent. (See Table 2.) Real income per family tripled in this period.

These shifts are explainable by the historical changes in the other variables. Increases in female wage rates in industry, which were at least as rapid as those of males in the United States, and declines in relative prices of market substitutes for home goods and services (such as food preparation and labor-saving appliances) meant that increasingly larger quantities of goods and services needed by the home could be obtained by an hour's work in the market than by an hour's work at home. Indeed, the decline in family size, which is often considered an independent explanatory factor facilitating the shift of women's activities to the labor market, may have been in part induced by the same growing market wage, the growing opportunity cost of child care.

The reality and importance of these factors have been substantiated by empirical research (Long 1958; Mincer 1962a). The evidence indicates that for women with similar earning power, labor force participation rates respond negatively to their hus-

*Table 2 — Participation in the labor force of women by marital status and age, United States, 1890 and 1960 (per cent of each group in labor force)*

|  | 1890 | | | | 1960 | | | |
|---|---|---|---|---|---|---|---|---|
|  | All | Single | Married | Other* | All | Single | Married | Other* |
| 14 and over | 18.2 | 36.9 | 4.5 | 28.6 | 34.8 | 44.1 | 30.5 | 40.0 |
| 14–19 ⎱ | | | | | 25.5 | 25.3 | 25.3 | 37.3 |
| 20–24 ⎰ | 27.0 | 33.6 | 6.4 | 54.7 | 44.3 | 73.4 | 30.0 | 54.6 |
| 25–34 | 16.8 | 53.4 | 4.7 | 53.6 | 34.5 | 79.9 | 27.7 | 55.5 |
| 35–44 | 12.7 | 46.1 | 4.4 | 48.4 | 42.4 | 79.7 | 36.2 | 67.4 |
| 45–54 | 12.5 | 39.6 | 3.8 | 35.9 | 48.4 | 80.6 | 40.5 | 68.2 |
| 55–64 | 11.4 | 30.9 | 2.9 | 23.4 | 35.2 | 67.0 | 24.3 | 50.7 |
| 65 and over | 7.6 | 16.5 | 2.1 | 10.0 | 10.1 | 21.6 | 5.9 | 11.0 |

* Widowed and divorced.

Sources: For 1890 data, Durand 1948, Table A-7, pp. 216–217. For 1960 data, U.S. Bureau of Labor Statistics 1961, Table B, p. A-8.

bands' incomes: the more husbands earn, the less wives work. But for families with a similar income position of husbands, the more the wife is capable of earning in the market, the more she works. Indeed, the positive response of the woman's labor force participation to her market wage rate is substantially stronger than her negative response to her husband's income. This dominance of the substitution effect over the income effect is the basic behavioral characteristic capable of explaining much of the secular growth in the female labor force (Mincer 1962a).

The neglect of this factor can create confusion in the interpretation of observed moment-of-time and over-time relationships. The negative relation between labor force participation of women and family income in the cross section appears to be inconsistent with the historical growth of the female labor force. Only when the other factors, such as the sharp rise in women's market wage rate, are taken into account is the inconsistency resolved (Mincer 1962a).

The smaller increase in labor force participation of single women compared with the growth of participation of married women in the historical record of the United States is explainable by the same analysis. Roughly speaking, with responsibilities of single women in the household sector being intermediate between those of married women and mothers on the one hand and males in the family on the other, the result is intermediate.

It is interesting to note that in the United States the secular changes in participation rates of older women (65 and over) and of young girls (14–19) contrast with the changes in the labor force of other adult women and with the changes observed in corresponding age groups of males. The participation rate of elderly women is very small and has remained roughly constant over time. The growing incentives to participate in the labor market play a part in counteracting the declines observed in elderly males. These incentives may include the effect of the market wage rate, but there are additional ones: with growth in the proportion of households limited to nuclear families, and with increasing longevity, the demand for work at home by women whose children have established their own homes shrinks rapidly. These developments not only counteracted the factors that would otherwise have led to a decline in participation of older women but also contributed to the spectacular growth in labor force participation of women aged 45 and over.

Young girls (aged 14–19) had much lower participation rates than did boys in 1900. Over time these rates declined but little, in contrast with the steep decline in labor force participation of teenage boys. The difference cannot be ascribed to a lesser growth in school enrollment of girls. Whereas 36 per cent of the girls in this age group were enrolled in school in 1900, almost twice as large a percentage (60 per cent) were in school in 1963. Both figures are almost precisely the same as for young boys in this age group. However, whereas most of the boys not in school (62 per cent) were in the labor force in 1900, only 27 per cent of the girls not in school were in the labor force in 1900; the remainder, 37 per cent, presumably were helping out at home. In 1960, 25 per cent of the girls were in the labor force, a small decline compared to 1900. The largest shift was from home to school, with the potential shift from home to market more than offset by the shift from market work to school. In terms of economic analysis, these relative shifts in supply are intelligible as responses to the highest rates of return beckoning in education, the lowest in the household, and intermediate ones in the labor market. This ranking is consistent with the previously analyzed behavior of young males and of adult women. But such interpretations, particularly those regarding young girls and elderly women, remain in the realm of hypotheses as long as systematic studies designed to explore the magnitudes of suggested behavioral parameters have not been carried out.

**International comparisons.** A few remarks regarding international comparisons are in order. Differences in national statistical practices and in concepts regarding labor force membership create great difficulties in interpreting such comparisons. Despite these distortions, surveys of a variety of national censuses (see "Women in the Labour Force," 1958; "The World's Working Population," 1956) reveal a rough conformity with the labor force developments that were analyzed here on the basis of U.S. data.

Thus, in all parts of the world over 90 per cent of men between the ages of 20 and 64 are economically active, and the proportion has remained virtually unchanged over the years. In industrial countries the percentage of young persons in the labor force has tended to decline. Indeed, gainful employment of children under 14 has almost disappeared in many of these countries. But children and young people form a considerably larger proportion of the labor force in nonindustrialized countries. The proportion of old people (65 and over) in the labor force is generally lower in industrially advanced countries than in others. It has been declining in most of the advanced countries.

Differences in statistical practices are particularly obstructive in comparisons of labor force participation of women. In most countries their attachment to the labor force is weak, and the difficulties of distinguishing between their "economic" and "noneconomic" activities, particularly in nonindustrial countries, result in diverse and arbitrary statistical classification. Still, when the agricultural sector is separated out, it appears that the upward trend in the female labor force has been shared by a number of industrial countries, with the United States and Canada experiencing the sharpest rise.

The general consistency of these data with the analytical economic structure sketched in this article, however, should not conceal the wide diversity in levels and rates of change in labor force participation of the specific population groups in the various countries. Intensive analyses of local economic and social conditions will be required to clarify these phenomena.

JACOB MINCER

#### BIBLIOGRAPHY

BANCROFT, GERTRUDE 1958 *The American Labor Force: Its Growth and Changing Composition.* New York: Wiley. → Published for the Social Science Research Council and the U.S. Bureau of the Census.

BECKER, GARY S. 1960 Underinvestment in College Education? *American Economic Review* 50, no. 2:346–354.

DOUGLAS, PAUL H. 1934 *The Theory of Wages.* New York: Macmillan.

DURAND, JOHN D. 1948 *The Labor Force in the United States, 1890–1960.* New York: Social Science Research Council.

JAFFE, ABRAM J.; and STEWART, C. D. 1951 *Manpower Resources and Utilization: Principles of Working Force Analysis.* New York: Wiley.

LEWIS, H. G. 1956 Hours of Work and Hours of Leisure. Pages 196–206 in Industrial Relations Research Association, *Proceedings of the Ninth Annual Meeting.* Chicago: The Association.

LONG, CLARENCE D. 1958 *The Labor Force Under Changing Income and Employment.* National Bureau of Economic Research, General Series, No. 65. Princeton Univ. Press.

MINCER, JACOB 1962a Labor Force Participation of Married Women. Pages 63–97 in Universities–National Bureau Committee for Economic Research, Conference, Princeton, N.J., 1960, *Aspects of Labor Economics.* National Bureau of Economic Research, Special Conference Series, No. 14. Princeton Univ. Press.

MINCER, JACOB 1962b On-the-job Training: Costs, Returns, and Some Implications. *Journal of Political Economy* 70 (Supplement): 50–79.

ROBBINS, LIONEL 1930 On the Elasticity of Demand for Income in Terms of Effort. *Economica* New Series 10:123–129.

U.S. BUREAU OF LABOR STATISTICS 1961 *Marital and Family Characteristics of Workers, March 1960.* Special Labor Force Report, No. 13. Washington: Government Printing Office. → First published in the *Monthly Labor Review*, April 1961.

U.S. BUREAU OF LABOR STATISTICS 1963 Statistical Tables: Section A. Labor Force, Employment, and Unemployment. U.S. Bureau of Labor Statistics, *Employment and Earnings* 9, no. 4.

Women in the Labour Force. 1958 *International Labour Review* 77:254–272.

The World's Working Population: Some Demographic Aspects. 1956 *International Labour Review* 73:152–176.

### III
#### MARKETS AND MOBILITY

In its broadest sense, the labor market embraces all those institutions and processes relating to the purchase, sale, and pricing of labor services. Its principal actors are: the individual worker, with his more or less unique pattern of abilities, skills, and preferences for various kinds of work and various combinations of rewards; workers' organizations, which have as their purpose the improvement of labor's economic and social position through collective bargaining, mutual aid, and political action; the individual employer, with his more or less distinct pattern of manpower needs, hiring preferences, and personnel policies; associations of employers, with the (not necessarily exclusive) purpose of promoting employer interests in labor relations; and government. In addition to its role as employer, the last-named plays a part in the labor market as regulator of employment conditions (for example, through minimum-wage legislation), organizer (by such means as the public employment service), formulator of the law of union–management relations, and general economic planner.

The relative influence of these actors as well as the specific functions of each vary considerably from country to country and even from sector to sector within each country. Their interaction, within the framework of the pattern of output and the character of technology in the economy, determines both the allocation of labor among alternative productive uses and the conditions of employment (including the pattern of rewards for work).

Of central importance in the labor marketing process is the *mobility* of labor, that is, the shifting of human resources into and out of the labor force and among firms, occupations, industries, and geographic localities. These kinds of movement of workers embrace all the processes whereby labor supply adjusts to changes in the level and composition of the demand for labor. Analysis of labor mobility, therefore, becomes a means of studying and evaluating the total operation of the labor market. In addition to its relevance to the process of labor allocation, mobility can also be studied with reference to its contribution to individual goal fulfillment, as well as in the context of the class structure of society. Since occupation is an important criterion of social class, the ease or difficulty of "climbing the occupational ladder" is indicative of the relative "openness" or fluidity of class structure and has implications for the assessment, interpretation, and prediction of sociopolitical change [*see* SOCIAL MOBILITY].

**Concepts of the labor market.** The labor market, like many other useful abstractions, is easier to talk about than to define. Conceptually, it is the area within which a given set of supply-and-demand schedules operates to determine wages and other terms of employment. Consider, for a moment, an island with neither immigration nor emigration, small enough so that workers are completely indifferent to the location of their workplace. Assume further that the following conditions are fulfilled: neither workers nor employers combine for purposes of influencing the terms of employment; all workers have the same skill and are equally efficient; all employers are indifferent as to the particular employees they hire, being interested solely in minimizing labor costs; employees continuously decide for whom to work on the basis of wages alone, being solely interested in maximizing their income; and workers have complete knowledge of wage rates being paid by all employers. Under these circumstances, not only would the island constitute a well-defined labor market, but the market would be the perfectly competitive one of traditional economic theory. Workers would be in continuous competition for available jobs; employers would be in continuous competition for labor; and the result would be a tendency toward wage uniformity throughout the island. Wage differentials could not persist because workers in lower-paying firms would make themselves available to higher-paying firms, thus causing wages to rise in the former and to fall in the latter until all wages were equal.

In such an oversimplified model the market is defined by the area within which the uniform wage prevails or—what amounts to the same thing—by the area within which workers move among jobs. Indeed, traditional economic theory treats wage determination and labor mobility or allocation as continuously interrelated processes. Wage differentials, which are presumed to measure differences in contribution to the social product, induce the movement of workers in the direction of higher-paying jobs, and this movement continues until the wage differentials either disappear (for identical work) or (in the case of different occupations) are just large enough to compensate for the relative disutilities of different kinds of work. Thus, in this idealized version of the "market," the end result is a "perfect" allocation of labor for, given the pattern of consumer preferences for final goods and services, the pattern of worker preferences for alternative types of work, and the existing technology, consumer satisfactions could not be enhanced by moving a single worker from where he is to any other job [*see* WAGES, *article on* THEORY].

The difficulty of defining a labor market operationally stems largely from differences of opinion as to how strongly the competitive forces of the foregoing model actually operate. On the one hand, at least since Cairnes (1874, pp. 65–68), the concept of "noncompeting" occupational groups has been recognized. This suggests the necessity for thinking in terms of a system of *submarkets* for labor. Also, evidence for the United States has revealed labor market behavior on the part of both employers and workers that differs significantly from that postulated by the traditional theory; as a consequence, substantial wage differentials for comparable work persist not only among local areas but within communities. Thus Reynolds (1951, p. 83) has stated that most employed workers are not "in the market," in the sense of being aware of or interested in alternative jobs, and that as a consequence, each firm constitutes "virtually a separate labor market."

On the other hand, irrespective of the *strength* of competitive forces, there is no question of their existence. Workers can and do move among firms within a community, among communities, regions, and, indeed, nations; they even move from one "noncompeting group" to another. From this standpoint, it is meaningful to talk about "*the* labor market," even if one recognizes the existence of related "submarkets," within each of which the conventional forces of supply and demand operate with somewhat greater (although by no means perfect) vigor.

Perhaps the best summary of all this is Kerr's observation that labor markets have "vague and varying contours but no ultimate limits short of those for American society itself. . . . Most labor markets are . . . indefinite in their specification of the sellers and the buyers. Such a labor market is merely an area, with indistinct geographical and occupational limits within which certain workers customarily seek to offer their services and certain employers to purchase them" (1954, pp. 92–93).

**Dimensions of labor mobility.** As has been indicated, the movement of workers among jobs and labor market areas is at the core of the operation of the labor market mechanism. The short-run supply of labor adjusts to changes in the volume and pattern of labor requirements by movements of workers into and out of the labor force, between employment and unemployment, and among firms, occupations, industries, or localities. For analytical purposes, therefore, corresponding categories of mobility have been used to classify the types of labor market changes made by workers: labor force mobility, employment mobility, interfirm mobility, occupational mobility, industrial mobility, and geographic mobility. Although these types of movement exhaust all possible sources of change in the number, location, and function of human resources utilized in the productive process, they clearly do not represent mutually exclusive categories of labor market transactions, since a single job change frequently represents a combination of two or more of the types of movement described above.

How a particular job change is classified in the foregoing schema obviously depends upon the way in which occupations, industries, and geographic areas are classified. The broader and less detailed the occupational classification system, the fewer will be the occupational shifts registered. Some studies have treated as occupational and industrial moves only shifts between major occupation groups, such as professional, managerial, and clerical, and between major industry divisions; while others have used more detailed occupational and industrial categories. In the case of geographic movement, the concept has generally referred to a change in job status that would normally necessitate a change of residence. Sometimes this is defined in terms of a minimum distance between the two jobs; but sometimes it is taken to be any job change across county, state, or regional lines.

**Data and measurement.** Most mobility studies have focused upon the employment experience of a sample of workers over some period of time. Work histories have been obtained either by questionnaire or interview from the workers themselves, from employers' personnel files, or from social insurance records. If motivational factors in job decisions are to be analyzed, interviews with workers are virtually indispensable.

Mobility may be defined as the actual movement of workers or as their willingness or propensity to move, given the opportunity and incentive to do so. The latter definition is more closely related to the basic assumption of conventional theory that workers are responsive to differentials in "net economic advantage." However, it poses serious difficulties of measurement, since "propensity to move" has no operational meaning except in terms of specific circumstances and incentives. Generally, therefore, conclusions with respect to workers' propensities to move have been inferred from the *voluntary* job changes they actually make. Use has also been made of hypothetical questions such as: "If you were offered a job with another company doing the same work you are now doing for 10 per cent more pay, would you take it?"

Measurements of mobility have generally been made in terms of number of jobs held or number of job shifts of various kinds made during the period under consideration. Results may be presented in terms of average number of jobs per worker or in terms of frequency distributions of workers according to the number of job shifts they have made. When such measures are used and if comparison is to be made among different groups of workers, account must be taken of differences in time spent in the labor force. Otherwise differences in mobility of various groups may reflect only differences in labor market exposure rather than differences in employment stability or work attachment. Another frequently used measure of mobility involves comparing the worker's job status at the beginning and end of a specified period, ignoring any changes that might have occurred in the interim. Finally, length of service in the current job has also been used as an inverse measure of mobility. In this case, also, there must be some method of standardizing length of labor force exposure.

**Amount and character of labor mobility.** Systematic investigation of the amount and character of labor mobility and of the functioning of labor markets has been carried on much more extensively in the United States than in most other countries. The relative paucity of comparative data for other parts of the world makes confident generalizations about international differences difficult, although it appears that the amount of job movement in the United States is considerably greater than in most European countries and that this is a product not only of a larger volume of voluntary movement in the United States than in Europe but also of a greater incidence of layoffs (Palmer 1960, pp. 520–524). Apart from this, European studies that have investigated the same questions have produced findings that are generally consonant with those for the United States (Organization for Economic Cooperation and Development 1965, *passim*).

Studies of the extent of job shifting among American workers have revealed a substantial amount of flexibility, as well as considerable stability, in work attachments. Scattered evidence relating to the 1940s and 1950s suggests that the proportion of job changers each year might have been as high as one-fourth or even one-third of the total number of employees (Parnes 1960, p. 17).

The only comprehensive data covering the entire labor force, however, are more recent sample surveys conducted by the Bureau of the Census, which show that both in 1955 and 1961 about one-tenth of all workers changed employers at least once (Wolfbein 1964, pp. 267–276). How much of this difference reflects a real decline in the mobility of the labor force and how much results simply from differences in coverage and methods of measurement of the studies is not certain. Whatever the size of its mobile segment, however, the labor force also has substantial proportions of workers with strong job attachments. Thus, over one-third of all those employed at the beginning of 1963 had been continuously associated with the same employer (or self-owned business) for at least 10 years.

Not all job movement, of course, is voluntary; the proportion of the total that results from layoff is very sensitive to the level of aggregate demand for labor. For example, during the prosperous 1920s about three-fourths of all separations in United States manufacturing industries were voluntary, but during the depressed 1930s voluntary quits had shrunk, on the average, to one-fourth of all separations and in certain years approached the vanishing point. In 1961, one-third of the job shifts made by a national sample of the United States labor force represented a voluntary attempt to improve status as compared with over two-fifths in 1955 when the unemployment rate was considerably lower.

The degree of flexibility in labor supply depends upon the *kinds* of shifts made by workers as well as upon their number. The evidence is fairly conclusive that most job shifts made by American workers are "complex"—that is, involve a simultaneous change of employer, occupation, and industry. Even when the very broadest of categories are used, a substantial proportion of job changes are across occupational and industrial boundaries. Only one-third of the job changes made by the United States labor force in 1961 involved no change in major occupation group or major industry division, while over one-third involved a simultaneous change in *both*.

As might be expected, geographic movement is considerably less common than job changes across industrial or occupational lines. Even unemployed workers are frequently reluctant to leave their home communities because of such factors as home ownership, family and community ties, the expense involved in moving, and ignorance of labor market conditions elsewhere. Nevertheless, although less frequent than industrial or occupational moves, geographic movement is by no means inconsequen-

tial in the United States. In the 1950s and early 1960s the annual number of males in the labor force who changed their residence from one county to another was relatively stable at between 6 and 7 per cent of the male labor force, and about half of these moves were across state lines.

**The correlates of mobility.** The incidence of mobility is by no means evenly distributed among the labor force. There is a pronounced inverse relationship between age and all types of mobility. Not only do older workers change jobs less frequently than younger workers, but their job shifts are less likely to involve changes in occupation and industry. In part, this relationship between age and mobility reflects the job shopping that is characteristic of the early labor market experience of young workers; in part it reflects the discrimination in hiring against older workers, which makes them more reluctant to quit their current jobs. But an additional important explanation is the fact that older workers are more likely than younger ones to have accumulated long tenure in their jobs, which not only provides greater protection against layoffs but also acts as a powerful restraint on voluntary separation. There is abundant evidence that workers with long service do not lightly give up the job security provided by their seniority. Other perquisites associated with seniority (vacations, choice of shifts, pensions) have some influence also, as does the psychological comfort of a familiar routine and a familiar circle of associates.

Evidence on the relative mobilities of men and women is not entirely conclusive. Most studies have shown greater mobility among men, but the interpretation is clouded by the fact that women's attachment to the labor force is generally less continuous than men's, so that they have less potential for job changes during a given period of time.

Mobility rates vary among major occupational groups, tending to decline as one moves up the socioeconomic hierarchy. Thus, professional workers and managers generally make considerably fewer job changes than do laborers. Part, though not all, of the differences result from differentials among these groups in the incidence of layoffs. Occupational differences also exist in the *pattern* of job changes. For example, professional workers are more likely than other occupational groups to make geographic moves, reflecting the broader scope of the market for professional services. On the other hand, because of their substantial investment in training, they show a much higher than average attachment to occupation.

The combined influence of all the factors whose effect on mobility has been investigated seems to account for only a small proportion of the total variation in mobility among individuals. It appears, therefore, that variation in mobility is attributable in large measure to personality traits or circumstances that cannot be ascertained as readily as those that have already been investigated. This is an area of research that has hardly been touched.

**Labor market decisions of manual workers.** Studies designed to test empirically the traditional economic theory of wage determination and labor allocation generally have focused on the extent to which the attitudes and actual labor market behavior of workers are consistent with the assumptions of rationality on which the theory is based. Most of this research has related primarily to manual workers; there is need for additional study of white-collar groups to identify whatever differences may exist between white-collar and blue-collar labor markets.

A wide variety of factors in addition to wages has been found to be important in conditioning workers' job decisions. The physical characteristics of the workplace, the nature of the relation between the employee and his supervisors and fellow workers, the security and steadiness of his job, "fairness" of treatment, and the degree of interest of the employee in his job have all been identified as being important. Thus, the influence on workers' job choices of relative wage rates, or even of differentials in "net economic advantage," appears to be more diluted than the conventional theory suggests.

Numerous studies have investigated the reasons for voluntary quits, which are a fairly direct indicator of the extent to which workers change jobs in response to perceptions of "net economic advantage." To begin with, there is mounting evidence that most voluntary separations by manual workers are made before the worker has obtained a new job, which means that only a minority of voluntary separations occur as the result of the worker's being "attracted into" a better job. Second, only a minority of voluntary job changes, it appears, can be explained mainly in terms of dissatisfaction with wages; far more important is dissatisfaction with such intrinsic characteristics of the job as its physical working conditions and the degree of interest the worker has in it.

There is conclusive evidence that manual workers rely chiefly on informal and more or less haphazard means of finding jobs (random gate application, advice from friends and relatives) as contrasted with more formal and systematic methods (public and private employment exchanges). Also, the extent of workers' knowledge about alter-

native job opportunities in the local labor market area has generally been found to be quite meager. It may be concluded that most manual workers who are employed and reasonably satisfied with their jobs—which includes the vast majority—are not "in the labor market" in the sense of knowing about (or even being interested in) the existence and characteristics of other jobs in the locality. Even unemployed workers rarely "shop" for jobs in the sense of making careful comparisons of the characteristics of alternatives; rather, they tend to take the first satisfactory job that comes along, which frequently is the first one offered.

To summarize, empirical studies have tended to confirm the view that workers, far from being concerned exclusively or even primarily with "net economic advantage," have multiple and complex goals, that their job "choices" are bounded by considerable degrees of ignorance of alternatives, and that the typical worker is a "satisficing" rather than a "maximizing" man—all contrary to the postulates of economic theory.

**Employer policies and mobility.** The recruiting methods, hiring practices, and personnel policies of employers tend to explain and to reinforce the pattern of labor market behavior that prevails among workers. For example, most employers appear to use informal recruitment methods, relying on gate applications and recruitment through their existing work forces rather than on public or private employment agencies or newspaper advertisements. This makes the labor market quite different from the competitive ideal in which all workers could choose among all job vacancies and all employers could select from among all candidates. Other common employer hiring practices also tend to insulate the firm from the external market. One of these is the formal or informal hiring specifications that most firms appear to have, which prevent certain groups of workers from effectively competing for certain jobs. Another is the policy of promoting from within, for to the extent that a firm follows this policy rigidly there is contact between the internal and external labor markets only at the base of the occupational ladder.

*Wage differentials.* The net effect of the labor market behavior of workers and employers is to permit interfirm wage differentials in local labor markets that are both larger and more persistent than competitive theory would suggest. It is nevertheless important to inquire to what extent labor supply considerations affect employer wage policies and tend to reduce differentials. For example, do low-wage firms have difficulty in recruiting and maintaining an adequate labor supply? Is there a tendency for low-wage firms or areas to lose workers to the higher paying establishments or areas? Most empirical investigations of local labor markets, particularly those by Reynolds (1951) and Lester (1954), have answered these questions largely in the negative, although all studies show some traces of the traditional economic forces. Moreover, whatever may be true within local labor market areas, the pattern of *geographic* mobility is consistent with the prediction of conventional theory that movement will occur from areas of lesser to areas of greater economic opportunity. However, how strong this tendency is and whether the chief explanatory construct is wage differentials or simply differences in job availability are still unsettled questions.

**Some policy implications.** Despite evidence of wide differences between actual labor market behavior and that postulated by conventional economic theory, there is a difference of opinion among economists with respect to how much "damage" such evidence does to the theory. Rottenberg (1956) contended, for example, that the true measure of a theory is not the validity of its assumptions but whether it yields valid predictions, and he argues that conventional theory *does* describe tendencies that are actually observable in the labor market. On the other hand, the empirical evidence, while not ruling out completely the existence of the kinds of market forces described by conventional theory, indicates that they are considerably attenuated.

So long as the issue is put in these terms it is not likely to be resolved merely by additional research. Yet the issue is of profound importance because of its implications for policy. For instance, if the unrestricted operation of "market forces" is conceived to produce a precisely determinate wage structure and an ideal allocation of labor, then the intrusion of "artificial" influences such as trade unionism or government wage regulation means, by assumption, a misallocation of labor resources. But if the market, even in the absence of such "interferences," would produce only a rather broad range of wage rates for a given type of work, there is no a priori reason for supposing that the "manipulation" of wages, at least within limits, makes matters any worse (or better). The weight of the empirical evidence would seem to make the latter interpretation far more tenable than the former.

HERBERT S. PARNES

[*See also* MIGRATION; OCCUPATIONS AND CAREERS; WAGES.]

BIBLIOGRAPHY

CAIRNES, JOHN ELLIOT 1874 *Some Leading Principles of Political Economy Newly Expounded.* London: Macmillan.
ELDRIDGE, PAUL; and WOLKSTEIN, IRWIN 1956 Incidence of Employer Change. *Industrial and Labor Relations Review* 10:101–107.
FISHER, LLOYD H. 1951 The Harvest Labor Market in California. *Quarterly Journal of Economics* 65:463–491.
JAFFE, ABRAM J.; and CARLETON, R. O. 1954 *Occupational Mobility in the United States: 1930–1960.* New York: King's Crown Press.
JEFFERYS, MARGOT 1954 *Mobility in the Labour Market: Employment Changes in Battersea and Dagenham.* London: Routledge.
KERR, CLARK 1954 The Balkanization of Labor Markets. Pages 92–110 in E. Wight Bakke et al., *Labor Mobility and Economic Opportunity.* New York: Wiley.
LESTER, RICHARD A. 1954 *Hiring Practices and Labor Competition.* Research Report Series, No. 88. Princeton Univ., Industrial Relations Section.
MYERS, CHARLES A.; and SHULTZ, GEORGE P. 1951 *The Dynamics of a Labor Market: A Study of the Impact of Employment Changes on Labor Mobility, Job Satisfactions, and Company and Union Policies.* Englewood Cliffs, N.J.: Prentice-Hall.
ORGANIZATION FOR ECONOMIC COOPERATION AND DEVELOPMENT 1965 *Wages and Labour Mobility: A Report by a Group of Independent Experts on the Relation Between Changes in Wage Differentials and the Pattern of Employment.* With a foreword on the "Implications of the Study for Incomes Policy," by Pieter de Wolff. Paris: The Organization.
ORGANIZATION FOR ECONOMIC COOPERATION AND DEVELOPMENT 1966 *Wages and Labor Mobility.* Supplement No. 1: Abstracts of Selected Articles. Paris: The Organization.
PALMER, GLADYS L. 1954 *Labor Mobility in Six Cities: A Report on the Survey of Patterns and Factors in Labor Mobility, 1940–1950.* New York: Social Science Research Council.
PALMER, GLADYS L. 1960 Contrasts in Labor Market Behavior in Northern Europe and the United States. *Industrial and Labor Relations Review* 13:519–532.
PALMER, GLADYS L. et al. 1962 *The Reluctant Job Changer: Studies in Work Attachments and Aspirations.* Philadelphia: Univ. of Pennsylvania Press.
PARNES, HERBERT S. 1954 *Research on Labor Mobility: An Appraisal of Research Findings in the United States.* Bulletin No. 65. New York: Social Science Research Council.
PARNES, HERBERT S. 1960 The Labor Force and Labor Markets. Pages 1–42 in Industrial Relations Research Association, *Employment Relations Research: A Summary and Appraisal.* Publication No. 23. New York: Harper.
RAIMON, ROBERT L. 1962 Interstate Migration and Wage Theory. *Review of Economics and Statistics* 44:428–438.
REYNOLDS, LLOYD G. 1951 *The Structure of Labor Markets: Wages and Labor Mobility in Theory and Practice.* New York: Harper.
ROTTENBERG, SIMON 1956 On Choice in Labor Markets. *Industrial and Labor Relations Review* 9:183–199.
RUNDBLAD, BENGT G. 1964 *Arbetskraftens rörlighet: En studie av en lokal arbetsmarknad.* Stockholm: Almqvist & Wiksell.

Silcock, H. 1954 The Phenomenon of Labour Turnover. *Journal of the Royal Statistical Society* Series A 117:429–440.

Wilcock, Richard C.; and Sobel, Irvin 1958 *Small City Job Markets: The Labor Market Behavior of Firms and Workers.* Urbana: Univ. of Illinois, Institute of Labor and Industrial Relations.

Wolfbein, Seymour L. 1964 *Employment and Unemployment in the United States: A Study of the American Labor Force.* Chicago: Science Research Associates.

## IV
### HOURS OF WORK

Hours of work have usually been considered analytically only insofar as they are performed by the "economically active" population—the work done for pay or profit is distinguished from that done, notably by housewives, for the direct benefit of the household. The hours of work are also distinguished from those of leisure, in that work is considered to be done for the sake of its product rather than for any satisfactions it yields directly, although in practice much activity during hours of work and leisure alike yields returns of both sorts.

The observed changes in hours of work, so delimited, depend on whether we measure them by the day, the week, or the year. Divergences between the day and the year come about through changes in weekly holidays and half holidays, especially the weekend; those between the week and the year, through changes in public holidays, vacations, absenteeism, sickness, and stoppages. A given total of hours will have different significance, according to the pattern in which those hours are arranged within the day, week, and year and the variability of that pattern. The total hours of work performed by a given household or community depend in part on what proportion of its members engage in the various kinds of work measured.

**The trend of prevailing hours.** Insofar as men work for themselves and not under a contract of employment, they let their hours be fixed by the task rather than by the clock. If hours are fixed by the job to be done, they are liable to vary widely in the course of the year, especially in arable farming; but they may be kept up in the slack seasons by the taking on of other kinds of work, either at home or in places of temporary migration. The worker who fixes his own hours has tended to alternate between idleness and overtime—as did, typically, the domestic weaver. In the newly emergent economies today, workers are helped to adapt to the unfamiliar ways of industry by being required to complete a fixed task each day, rather than work for fixed hours.

Those who work for employers have long had their hours fixed. In Europe in the Middle Ages, guilds, municipalities, or statutes often specified hours, commonly from sunrise to sunset, with a limited break for food and rest at noon and perhaps one other break. The shorter working day in winter carried a lower wage. Over the year, the average was probably around 10½ hours a day, with a six-day week. But the yearly hours were reduced by saints' days and other holidays: the number observed in practice varied from place to place and time to time, but often as many as 90 to 100 days in all were not worked. The yearly total would then be around 2,750 to 3,000 hours, an average of about 54 hours a week.

With the Reformation, the observance of saints' days decreased. The rise in the numbers competing for jobs at that time would in any case have given employers an opportunity to reduce the number of holidays, some of which had been holidays with pay. But it was with the advent of modern industrialism, whether in Britain and the United States in the late eighteenth century or in Germany and Japan in the late nineteenth, that work hours were indeed extended. The motive was to use as fully as possible the greater capital per worker that the new methods required, and again employers were able to enforce longer hours because of the growth in the job-seeking population. The means chosen were reductions of the difference between summer and winter hours and of the number of holidays: the 12-hour day became common throughout the year, and there were few holidays besides Sunday, so that the yearly hours of work may be put at 3,500 to 3,750. But the hours the average worker actually completed were reduced by sickness and by absenteeism—especially after payday.

Since the 1830s the hours of work in the industrialized economies have been progressively reduced. Although the changes have been only roughly synchronous, even in economies at the same stage of development, and although there have been wide divergences within any one economy, some marked traits appear in common. One of the most striking is the extent of the reduction—from, say, 3,500 hours a year to 2,200 or less. The reduction has been effected by limiting normal daily hours to eight; shortening the week, first through a half holiday and more recently by an approach to the five-day week; and the instituting of paid vacations, which now extend to two, three, and four weeks. The chief immediate cause of these changes has been the pressure of organized labor: the differential effects of trade unionism may well be seen more clearly in hours than in pay. This pressure has also made itself felt in legislatures, where it has met with support, as well as resistance, from other parts of society: some notable reductions of hours have been brought about by statute. Reductions have also owed not a little to the initiative and example of particular employers.

In recent years there has been a rise in the proportion of part-time workers—to as much as one-tenth of the American labor force outside agriculture, for example; and whether part-time workers are included or not now has a marked effect on reported average hours of work. Increasing urbanization has lengthened the journey to work, so that total time claimed by work has not been reduced so much as time on the job. Recent years have also been marked in some countries by a persistent excess of hours worked over standard hours, due in great part to the persistence under full employment of levels of demand that before 1940 used to bring overtime only in the more active phases of the trade cycle.

*The timing of reductions of hours.* Hours have been changed much less often and less gradually than pay: they have commonly remained unchanged for long periods and then been reduced substantially in a movement that runs through many industries in the course of only a few years. The infrequency of change is understandable because small reductions in hours often call for extensive reorganization; and even where small reductions can be effected readily, they are not as likely to attract the worker as the rise in earnings that the employer would be equally ready to concede. When hours are regulated by collective bargaining, union members must adopt a common line, but their preferences are likely to be various; Moses (1962) has shown that it is then easier to reach agreement to claim higher earnings rather than shorter hours. On these grounds, we should expect reductions to come about only when workers' preferences for them had had some time to build up and the scope for them had become fairly wide.

Given such a period of gestation, reductions seem to have been induced by two very different states of the economy—by exceptional prosperity, but also by a check to expansion. In the first situation, the recent rise in earnings will have intensified any accumulated preference for shorter hours; a substantial reduction in hours can now be afforded without loss of earnings; and the bargaining power of labor is great enough to force employers to grapple with the difficulties of reorganization. In the second situation, the immediate impulse comes from the wish to "spread the work"—to have each man do less work, rather than have

some men thrown out of work altogether—both as the best palliative for a recession of employment and as the fair way to realize the fruits of technical progress. Probably it is by a mounting threat of unemployment that most reductions of hours have been occasioned in the past, just as the prospects of automation have prompted proposals for reductions recently; although, however they were occasioned, reductions must also be seen as a way of drawing on the rise in productivity achieved in the years preceding them. There are other reasons why, at the time of a check to expansion, a reduction in hours accompanied by such a rise in hourly rates as will maintain weekly earnings should be conceded by employers more readily than a rise in hourly rates with unchanged hours: when production has recently dropped, employers can very likely reduce hours without a further reduction in output, and they do not have to finance a bigger wage bill until production rises again.

*Hours prevailing at the present time.* The general level of hours and the differences between economies in the mid-1950s are illustrated in Table 1. By 1963, in the United States the average actual weekly hours, outside agriculture, were below 40 (although this included part-time jobs), and paid vacations were mainly from two to four weeks, depending on length of service. In western Europe normal weekly hours remained higher, the average in Scandinavia, for instance, being generally 45, but there was a pronounced movement, especially in larger organizations, toward the 40-hour week. Paid vacations were generally from two to two and a half weeks but were tending to lengthen, notably in France, where four weeks had been adopted widely. In the Soviet Union standard weekly hours and paid vacations were much the same as those of the United States, although hours worked per household were greater; the aim had

**Table 1 — *Estimated annual normal hours, about 1956*** *

| | HOURS |
|---|---|
| Egypt | 2,632–2,696 |
| Switzerland | 2,384–2,416 |
| Netherlands | 2,320–2,352 |
| West Germany | 2,296–2,320 |
| Italy | 2,288 |
| Soviet Union | 2,248 |
| Sweden | 2,212 |
| United Kingdom | 2,152–2,192 |
| United States | 1,984 |
| New Zealand | 1,928 |
| France | 1,920 |
| Australia | 1,888–1,912 |
| Indonesia | 1,880–1,904 |

* Excluding overtime and hours paid for but not worked.

*Source:* International Labour Conference 1958.

been set of reaching a 35-hour week in 1968. In the emergent economies weekly hours were generally longer: the standard of 48 hours was representative, but many exceptions were recognized, and enforcement was uneven. Nonetheless, these economies had escaped the earlier connection between industrialization and inhumanly long hours. Rather, the connection that does suggest itself in a survey of these economies is between shorter hours and higher participation rates. Shorter hours —including more part-time jobs—make it easier for more members of a household to take jobs; and reciprocally, a given standard of living can be maintained with shorter hours per worker when the participation rate is higher.

**Industrial and occupational differences.** Differences between industries are now seldom large or persistent, save that service industries tend to have rather longer hours than manufacturing, and in agriculture hours are generally even longer. There is some tendency to offset differences in standard hours by differences in overtime. The most salient occupational difference has long been that between white-collar workers and manual workers, weekly hours being shorter and vacations longer for the former. But some of the longest hours are worked in managerial, administrative, and professional occupations, by those who fix their own hours or often work beyond regular office hours. So far as work requires mental exertion and initiative and the worker identifies himself with it, the line between work and leisure becomes hard to draw and the adverse effects of sustained long hours on productivity tend to be avoided by periods of vacation rather than by limitation of the working day and week.

Shorter hours will go with lower wage rates to the extent that there is a tendency for the market to equalize net advantages of different jobs and that more leisure is seen as a net advantage. Shorter hours will go with higher earnings to the extent that one group of workers is able to secure better terms than another and realizes the advantage in the form of both leisure and earnings. Thus, the generally higher pay and shorter hours of white-collar workers as compared with manual workers may be ascribed to the relative scarcity in past periods of workers with any secondary education, which enabled the white-collar workers to get better terms of both kinds. With an alleviation of that scarcity, as a result of the social changes of the last half century, both pay and hour differentials have been reduced.

In comparing the hours in different jobs, we must regard not only the total but also the pattern

in which given hours are arranged in the day, week, and year. Where processes or output have to be continuous, shifts are worked—there may be three shifts of eight hours, for example, or four of six hours. These arrangements involve night work— which is widely prohibited for women and juveniles. Fuller utilization of manufacturing equipment is provided by the double day shift, with one shift, say, from 6:00 A.M. to 2:00 P.M., the other from 2:00 P.M. to 10:00 P.M. Automation tends to bring more shift work. Workers may remain on one shift indefinitely or (more often) change shifts according to a rota. The roster of duties is often a distinctive and onerous feature of the service industries, where staffs may have to work evenings and weekends, meet morning and evening peaks of demand by working split shifts, and start and finish at times that vary widely from one day or week to another; there may also be periods when, although not at work, they must remain on call. Long-distance transport keeps men away from home for some periods when they are not actually working. In some jobs the work load varies seasonally, and short time alternates with overtime. Although shift working proves congenial to some workers because it provides more free time in daylight or other amenities, any departure from the usual working day and week raises difficulties for the worker and his family in their domestic and social activities. In negotiations it is usual to recognize that compensation is due for such departures: it may take the form not only of a higher hourly rate of pay but also of a smaller total of weekly hours or a longer vacation.

The individual worker may have opportunities to vary his own hours by working part time, doing voluntary overtime, or taking a second job. The growth of part-time jobs in recent years has been associated especially with an increase in the number of married women who work outside the home. When unemployment was rife, working overtime was regarded as taking work away from other men, and the higher rates that had to be paid for overtime were meant to be a deterrent to employers; under full employment, this objection, although still encountered, has weakened, and opportunities for overtime are now widely regarded as an advantage in a job. The practice of taking a second job (sometimes loosely referred to as "moonlighting"), within the usual weekday hours, in the evenings, or on weekends, has increased with the coming of shorter daily hours and the five-day week.

**Choice of hours.** Any one worker has some choice between shorter hours and higher earnings, insofar as he can choose between jobs and vary the hours he works in a given job; and a collective choice of this kind is implicit in most negotiations about terms of employment. The considerations that make up the theory of such choice were well set out by Marshall (1890). These considerations do not enable us to predict the kind of effect that a rise in the rate of return to labor will have upon the number of hours the worker prefers to work. Such a rise increases the worker's purchasing power, including his power to purchase leisure, but it raises the opportunity cost of the unit of leisure. It increases the quantity of commodities he can obtain by working a further hour, but at the same time it increases the quantity of commodities obtainable by working a given number of hours, and so lowers his valuation of a unit increment of commodities. If the first factor predominates, he will prefer longer hours; if the second, shorter. Which effect will in fact predominate depends, among many other things, on the strain put on him by his present hours; on his stage of life—whether he is young or old, or whether he is raising a family; on the attractions of the alternative activities open to him—including work in his home and, especially in emergent economies, on his own holding; and on whether he and his fellows are content with a customary standard of living or are consciously raising their standards and have such goals before them. Where standards are stationary, a rise in the rate of pay will result in a reduction of hours worked. This was thought to be a general feature of the emergent economies, but wider experience has shown it to be only transitory in them or to be confined to certain groups. But the long-run supply curve of labor has certainly shown itself to be backward-sloping in the developed economies, in that their workers have chosen to draw on rises in productivity for both some increment of commodity income and some shortening of hours. Long (1958) gives the following estimates of percentage changes in the hours of the standard work week associated with a 1 per cent rise in real disposable income per hour:

| United States | 1890–1950 | − 0.27 |
| Great Britain | 1911–1951 | − 0.39 |
| Canada | 1921–1941 | − 0.34 |
| Germany | 1895–1950 | − 0.92 |

**Hours and productivity.** The existence of a choice between higher earnings and shorter hours implies that output varies directly with hours. But just how it does so is hard to determine even for manual workers, whose product can be measured. Observations in comparatively controlled conditions have indicated that a change in hours may

take many months to accomplish its effects on productivity, and the majority of changes have taken place in conditions far from controlled. Most extensions of hours in the present century have coincided with the exceptional incentives and difficulties of wartime; or reductions have occurred when there has been slack to take up or technical progress to draw upon; and reductions in themselves have often enforced a change of methods. The record suggests strongly, however, that at least where the rate of output depends on the effort and attention of the worker, hours in excess of 48 a week do not add to output in the long run—the worker adjusts his rate of working, so as to spread a given fund of energy over the longer hours, and the rates of spoilage, accident, sickness, and absenteeism are all higher. Except in work requiring special exertion and endurance, however, it seems probable that reductions of hours below 48 a week will be accompanied, other things being equal, by nearly proportionate reductions in output. But this holds good only at one place and time; there is reason to believe that as time goes on, a labor force that works shorter hours will develop its capabilities as it broadens its interests and education. Long hours were seen to wear men out by the age of 40; shorter hours, even where they decrease output in a given year, may raise it over a man's life. The hours set free, moreover, although they do not add to the measured national product, are used in practice to add something to the unmeasured amenities of households and to the goodness of life.

E. H. PHELPS BROWN AND M. H. BROWNE

[*See also* EMPLOYMENT AND UNEMPLOYMENT; LABOR FORCE, *article on* PARTICIPATION; LEISURE; TIME BUDGETS; WAGES, *article on* WAGE AND HOUR LEGISLATION.]

### BIBLIOGRAPHY

DANKERT, CLYDE E. 1962 Shorter Hours in Theory and Practice. *Industrial and Labor Relations Review* 15: 307–322.

DANKERT, CLYDE E.; MANN, FLOYD C.; and NORTHRUP, HERBERT R. (editors) 1965 *Hours of Work.* Industrial Relations Research Association, Publication No. 32. New York: Harper.

FLORENCE, P. SARGANT 1924 *Economics of Fatigue and Unrest and the Efficiency of Labour in English and American Industry.* London: Allen & Unwin; New York: Holt.

FOURASTIÉ, JEAN 1965 *Les 40,000 heures.* Paris: Laffont.

Hours of Work in the United States and Abroad. 1963 U.S. Bureau of Labor Statistics, *Monthly Labor Review* 86:925–934.

INTERNATIONAL LABOR OFFICE, GENEVA *Year-book of Labour Statistics.* → Published since 1935/1936.

INTERNATIONAL LABOUR CONFERENCE, FORTY-SECOND SESSION 1958 *Report No. 8: Hours of Work.* Geneva: International Labor Office.

Long, Clarence D. 1958 *The Labor Force Under Changing Income and Employment.* National Bureau of Economic Research, General Series, No. 65. Princeton Univ. Press.

McCormick, Brian 1959 Hours of Work in British Industry. *Industrial and Labor Relations Review* 12: 423–433.

Mann, Floyd C.; and Hoffman, L. Richard 1960 *Automation and the Worker: A Study of Social Change in Power Plants.* New York: Holt.

Marris, Robin 1964 *The Economics of Capital Utilisation: A Report on Multiple-shift Work.* Cambridge Univ. Press.

Marshall, Alfred (1890) 1961 *Principles of Economics.* 9th ed. 2 vols. New York and London: Macmillan. → See especially Book 1, Chapter 1, paragraph 2; Book 6, Chapter 2, paragraphs 2 and 3, Chapter 12, paragraph 8, Chapter 13, paragraphs 3–6; mathematical appendixes 10 and 12.

Millis, Harry A.; and Montgomery, Royal E. 1938 *Labor's Progress and Some Basic Labor Problems.* New York: McGraw-Hill.

Moses, Leon 1962 Income, Leisure and Wage Pressure. *Economic Journal* 72:320–334.

Northrup, Herbert R.; and Brinberg, Herbert R. 1950 *Economics of the Work Week.* Studies in Business Economics, No. 24. New York: National Industrial Conference Board.

Rae, John 1894 *Eight Hours for Work.* London: Macmillan.

Solovyov, L. 1962 The Reduction of Employees' Working Hours in the Soviet Union. *International Labour Review* 86:31–41.

Zeisel, J. 1958 The Work Week in American Industry: 1850–1956. U.S. Bureau of Labor Statistics, *Monthly Labor Review* 81:23–29.

# LABOR MARKETS

*See under* Labor force.

# LABOR RELATIONS

## I

### COLLECTIVE BARGAINING

The content and the scope of collective bargaining vary from country to country. The issues in collective bargaining, broadly speaking, relate to wages, hours of work, various benefit provisions, and other terms and conditions of employment. Also involved are questions concerning the recognition and status of unions and collective bargaining procedures.

This article will first discuss briefly some broad differences in the content and scope of collective bargaining in different countries. It will then consider selected collective bargaining issues in the United States. Collective bargaining in the United States, while not extended to as large a proportion of employees as in some other countries, has developed the labor agreement more intensively than elsewhere and hence covers directly a wide range of issues. A concluding section will indicate some developing characteristics and changing issues in various countries.

### Institutional environment

Questions and problems about the terms and conditions of employment arise in any industrialized or industrializing society. As John T. Dunlop points out (1958, p. 4), any industrial society, regardless of its political form, creates distinctive groups of managers and workers. Such societies develop industrial relations systems, which he analyzes in terms of three sets of actors—managers, organized workers, and specialized governmental agencies—and three environmental forces—technological conditions, market constraints, and power relationships in the society.

Although all developing countries create some form of industrial relations system, the power relationship in the society may preclude or drastically limit collective bargaining between managers and freely organized and freely led unions. In command societies without private ownership of the means of production, worker organizations are instruments of the state and are largely restricted in function to encouraging higher employee productivity and administering welfare programs. Even among such societies, however, significant differences can be found in the power and status of worker groups. A very interesting variation seems to exist in Yugoslavia (Dunlop 1958, chapter 7), where workers' councils have substantial power within a system of control which cannot as yet be described as stable. Despite these variations, collective bargaining, as the term is usually used, can hardly be said to prevail in the absence of private ownership and the right to strike.

In countries with private ownership of property but with dictatorial or semidictatorial forms of government, unions have elements of freedom within a highly restrictive political environment. A union movement may provide a useful ally for a dictator in breaking or countering the entrenched power of a landed aristocracy. The allegiance of workers has been obtained and preserved in such countries by various social reforms and legislative codes protecting employees. Although the unions achieve certain goals and employers are considerably restricted, the unions at the same time are likely to have imposed leadership and to be under the ultimate control of the dictator. A limited and weak form of collective bargaining may exist, with both unions and employers restrained and regulated by the power of the state. Collective bargaining under Perón in Argentina and Vargas in Brazil are illustrations of this (Alexander 1962). Apart from particular governmental variations, labor movements in underdeveloped countries commonly are highly political in character and intimately associated with the revolutionary and nationalistic aspirations of the people. A significant impetus to political action is the economic weakness associated with mass underemployment.

In democratic industrialized societies, trade unions function both as collective bargaining and as political institutions. In western Europe unions have, to a considerable extent, been associated with ideological, religious, and revolutionary movements and have reflected the pluralistic political pressures within the countries. Some such union movements have been predominantly political in character and have had limited effectiveness as collective bargaining institutions. Trade unions in France and Italy historically have been cast in this mold. The opposite extreme is to be found in the United States, where unionism has functioned overwhelmingly as a collective bargaining institution, with insignificant ideological aspirations and minimal political objectives. The more middle ground, where unions have been strong both as political institutions and as bargaining institutions, is illustrated by the examples of Sweden and Great Britain.

**Goals in democratic industrial societies.** In democratic industrialized societies organized workers may seek to achieve their goals and objectives by means of political and legislative action or through collective bargaining with private employers. Various general goals may be related to the alternative means. For this purpose general goals may be classified as (1) wage and hour protection and improvement; (2) social benefits and enhanced security through medical and health plans, unemployment compensation, pension plans, and related arrangements; and (3) detailed regulation and determination of conditions of employment, including layoff, promotion, job and personal compensation, discipline and discharge, and other working rules and policies.

All three of the above general goals may be sought primarily through collective bargaining. If so, collective bargaining will be broad in scope and the issues multifarious. This has been the manner in which collective bargaining has developed in the United States since World War II. During this period unions have developed from a small proportion of the labor force—organized by crafts—into an industrial form of union organization, encompassing the large mass-production industries and embracing a large proportion of blue-collar employees. The labor agreement reflects the change that has taken place, evolving from a relatively simple document to a complex web of rules governing many aspects of employment.

In all countries in which collective bargaining has meaningful status the first general goal, wage and hour protection and improvement, has been sought both through negotiation with employers and, less importantly, through minimum-wage laws and other types of legislative enactment. Where unions have been relatively weak as collective bargaining institutions, wage and hour legislation appears to have had a greater relative economic impact. Whereas wage legislation is thus in some degree an alternative means, the most central aspect of and issue in collective bargaining has been various facets of wage determination.

The second goal noted, social benefits and enhanced security, has been sought and achieved in most countries through legislation rather than through collective bargaining. The socialistic political parties, with which unions in Europe have been predominantly associated, have evolved primarily into political advocates of the welfare state. Although unemployment compensation and old-age or retirement benefits have historically been primary legislative objectives, the most important area of development and expansion in the years since World War II has been public systems of medical care. The Scandinavian countries have been outstanding in reducing death rates and providing comprehensive medical care. The United States, on the other hand, developed state old-age and unemployment benefits much later than Europe and retains essentially a private system of medical care. In the postwar years, however, there has been developed through collective bargaining an extensive private "benefit package" that has raised issues about cost and content.

The third goal, detailed regulation and determination of conditions of employment, has been uniquely developed through collective bargaining in the United States. This appears to be the result not only of the weak political orientation of the labor movement but also of the decentralized company-level and plant-level system of bargaining that is characteristic of the United States. Bargaining on an industry-wide basis, or even on a broader confederation basis, which tends to prevail in Europe, appears not to lend itself to, or for other reasons not to focus on, this type of issue. However, to varying extents in different countries this third goal has been sought through legislation. Labor codes, sometimes containing very detailed administrative provisions with respect to employment conditions, are to be found in some European and South American countries and elsewhere, as in India. On the other hand, where this type of legislation is less completely developed, employers are free to establish detailed employment rules and policies, although these are qualified to a growing extent by the emergence of various forms of collective bargaining at the plant level.

Thus, although it can be said that every industrialized or industrializing country has an industrial relations system and that all such systems are concerned with the determination of wages and other terms and conditions of employment, the scope and the content of collective bargaining vary widely from country to country. The existence of a large and broadly based labor movement is not synonymous with a highly comprehensive and strong system of collective bargaining. Such a labor movement may be strong politically but weak economically. Although political strength cannot overcome the economic and technological constraints of a society, it may achieve certain employee goals and impose detailed regulations upon employers. A large labor movement may be relatively weak *both* politically and economically. This appears to be the case in Japan, where the multitude of plant unions, bargaining locally, impose few restraints upon employers and where the union federations, although decidedly active politically, have not achieved extensive political power. Various degrees of economic and political strength and various degrees of economic and political orientation create considerably different systems of collective bargaining. This must be recognized but cannot be dealt with in this article. (In addition to the two works previously cited, examples and analyses of variations in systems of collective bargaining among countries are to be found in other references in the bibliography.)

### Issues in the United States

Through collective bargaining, unions challenge management's right to make unilateral decisions that affect the terms and conditions of employment. This challenge takes two forms. One form is the negotiation of written labor agreements that establish both general and quite specific rules governing the employment relationship. The second form of challenge is the protest against particular day-to-day decisions and actions of management as not being in conformity with the provisions of the labor agreement. This latter challenge is carried out through a grievance procedure established by the labor agreement. Whereas management retains various rights and unilaterally establishes and maintains some labor relations policies, the total union challenge creates an enlarged web of rules that is jointly determined and binding both for the two parties to the agreement (the union and the management) and for the individual employees.

Issues in collective bargaining in the United States have not remained static. The modern labor movement, with greatly enlarged union membership, began in the political and economic climate of the great depression of the 1930s. It was then that the heart of American industry was organized and began to operate under collective bargaining. The process of collective bargaining has been evolutionary. It has gone through an organizing stage, characterized by violent hostility, and a contract development stage, characterized by continued but diminished hostility, and in recent years has given evidence of a stage of increased accommodation and more orderly relationships. Issues that seriously divided the parties some years ago are now in large measure resolved. This process of resolution will be noted in the discussion of particular issues. New issues arise as older issues are resolved, however. There is always a conflict frontier, although this should not obscure the substantial progress that has been made.

**Wages and related benefits.** The size of the "economic package" is the most obvious, persistent, and perhaps inevitable issue that divides the parties. The typical economic package consists of a wage increase and benefit liberalizations. Unions have consistently introduced and improved benefit plans. This drive for benefit improvement has increased the cost of such wage supplements from an insignificant amount in 1940 to roughly one-quarter of total employment costs. Conflict has been primarily related to the additional cost of improved benefits, although the appropriateness of each new benefit has also engendered some controversy. Particular benefits and the related issues will be discussed below [*see also* WAGES, *article on* FRINGE BENEFITS].

The cost and income implications of benefits will not be discussed here. [*For a discussion of the entire subject of the effect of unions on the general level of wages in the United States and on relative wage levels in different industries and in different occupations, see* LABOR UNIONS, *article on* INFLUENCE ON WAGES.] It should be noted in passing that there has been considerable argument about the effect of unions on the process and problem of inflation and about the power of unions to increase the relative wage level for particular groups of organized employees. The only aspect of wages that will be treated in this article, and this treatment will be brief, will be the compensation structure in the plant. It should be emphasized, however, that controversy over wages and costs tends to overshadow other issues in most particular instances of union–management negotiation.

The following sections will discuss (1) the grievance procedure and arbitration, (2) discipline and discharge, (3) the use of seniority, (4) the plant compensation structure, (5) hours of work and vacation and holiday provisions, (6) supplementary unemployment benefits, severance pay, and subcontracting, (7) pension and medical benefits, (8) recognition and union security, and (9) other labor agreement provisions. None of these subjects can be discussed in depth. (A more extensive treatment is to be found in Slichter et al. 1960.)

**Grievance procedure and arbitration.** As previously mentioned, a major form of union challenge to management is alleged contract violation. Employees have the right to present grievances in the first instance to the departmental foreman or equivalent first-line supervisor and to be represented by a union steward or committeeman. If the grievance is not resolved at this first step, it may be carried to higher stages, involving union and management representatives of successively higher levels. Grievance procedures are found with two, three, four, and more steps in the appeal procedure. Grievance procedures have been refined to require that grievances be written, that they allege violation of specific sections of the labor agreement, and that written appeals and answers be given within stated time intervals. Written briefs are commonly used in arbitration.

The most notable change that has taken place over the years has been the general acceptance of arbitration as the terminal step in the grievance procedure. Arbitration gives a neutral individual, selected by the parties, the right to make final and binding decisions on unresolved grievances submitted to him. Prior to World War II arbitration was found in only a few labor agreements and was an important issue between the parties. Unions sought such provisions, and management resisted them. Today, however, most managements favor arbitration, and provision for it is to be found in over 90 per cent of labor agreements.

There is no doubt that managements in large part accepted arbitration to induce unions to accept "no-strike" clauses—that is, clauses that prohibit strikes during the term of the agreement. In addition, the combined effect of arbitration and no-strike clauses was to allow management to discipline employees for taking part in "wildcat" strikes—those prohibited by the contract. Furthermore, arbitration was limited to grievances involving the application or interpretation of the labor agreement, thus restricting the arbitrator's authority. Finally, any particular decision could be modified or negated by subsequent negotiation.

Arbitration is important because it resolves by a private judicial process conflict that arises during the term of the labor agreement. It gives meaning and support to the development and application of labor relations policies. Its scope has necessarily increased as labor agreement provisions have multiplied and become more complex. Its significance goes beyond the making of particular decisions by the arbitrator because both parties are restrained by arbitration precedents and by knowledge of how an arbitrator would probably rule if a particular issue were to be carried to him. No other country is known to have developed a system of private grievance arbitration as extensive as that in the United States.

**Discipline and discharge.** Perhaps the greatest contribution unions have made to the security of the individual employee has been their substantial assistance in the elimination of arbitrary discipline and discharge. This has been done not by elaborate labor agreement provisions but typically by the simple restriction of the grounds for discipline and discharge to "for cause" or "for just or proper cause."

Such simple restriction might not have been effective had it not been coupled with arbitration. In arbitration the burden of proving cause is upon the employer. In response to this union challenge and unilaterally with the development of personnel policies, employers created systems of corrective discipline. These involve oral and written warnings and disciplinary layoff prior to discharge, except in the case of serious acts considered to warrant immediate discharge. The systems emphasize corrective behavior rather than punishment. But the essence of the enhanced job security of the individual employee is to be found in the fact that the employer may not take action that will not be supported as fair and reasonable by a neutral arbitrator.

**Seniority.** Seniority, the according of preference on the basis of length of service with the employer, has two distinct uses in labor agreements. One use may be called benefit seniority. For example, the amount of vacation and the amount of pension to which an employee is entitled are commonly based on seniority. Seniority is used in this manner primarily because entitlement to benefits on such a basis is regarded as equitable, but this use is also a union bargaining device, initially to obtain liberal benefits for long-service employees and subsequently to extend these benefits to employees with lesser service.

The second use of seniority, which may be called competitive-status seniority, is to select one employee rather than another for layoff or promotion or for various other purposes. Seniority is widely accepted at present as the major criterion for layoff; it is more controversial and qualified in its other competitive-status applications.

Seniority systems regulating layoff are highly varied and frequently quite complex. Seniority may be defined, measured, and applied in different ways and combinations—job seniority, department seniority, occupational-group seniority, plant seniority, and company seniority. In actual application, seniority can be more or less qualified by requiring that the employee have the ability to perform particular jobs. Description and analysis of various layoff systems can be found elsewhere (see Slichter et al. 1960, chapter 6).

The principle of seniority appeals to unions and employees as a criterion for making competitive decisions affecting employees because it is regarded as fair, reasonable, objective, and hence nondiscriminatory. It is further supported because it establishes job security for long-service employees. The principle is resisted by management as being contrary to the logic of making business decisions and employee rewards on the basis of efficiency. It is argued that seniority weakens employee motivation to contribute to the goals of the organization and adds to cost by requiring more extensive training and retraining of employees. As stated earlier, management has commonly come to accept the principle of seniority with respect to layoff but has preferred narrow and small units of application, to reduce training costs and internal employee turnover. Unions have worked for broader units of application, typically for plant-wide application. Some constructive compromises have been worked out that minimize internal employee turnover and resulting training costs but that still give plant-wide protection through a labor pool. Layoff provisions at present are seriously controversial only in a minority of instances.

Although management is content to accept seniority as the primary criterion for layoff, it is less content to do so in the case of promotion, even though in practice in most unionized companies a high proportion of promotions go to the senior man.

Labor agreement provisions commonly do not make seniority the single criterion for promotion and frequently provide that seniority shall govern only when skill and ability are equal. But protests in the grievance procedure, when exceptions to seniority are made, have led many managements to promote on the basis of seniority except for rare and unusual cases.

The most controversial applications of competitive-status seniority have been to temporary transfers of employees to meet day-to-day and short-term production needs. Considerable loss in flexibility in the use of manpower can be caused by such requirements, with very little true enhancement of the job security of senior employees. In general, both employees and management now accept seniority as the criterion for permanent layoff and as a factor to be given heavy weight in promotion. However, there is controversy when the use of seniority entails excessive management costs, as it does when it is applied too minutely to the numerous employee shifts caused by short-term changes in production schedules and by employee absence. Controversy also exists where the particular seniority system causes high-cost chainlike movement of employees in the process of layoff.

The quite elaborate development of seniority sections in labor agreements appears to be a characteristic of collective bargaining mainly in the United States. Although custom and practice may impose comparable restrictions upon employers in some other countries, and legal protection may also exist, formal seniority requirements are not commonly found in labor agreements elsewhere.

**Plant compensation structure.**    There has been considerable progress in rationalizing wage structures. Whereas rationalization programs typically have been initiated by management, the prospect of unionization, or grievance experience subsequent to unionization, has been a strong motivating influence. Unionization places management in a position in which it must be able to justify and defend the wage rates paid for particular jobs and to particular individuals.

The problem of justification has been most severe where technological developments create rather minute division of labor and therefore many roughly similar but specialized jobs. Rationalization has taken the form of job evaluation, which analyzes and rates the content of jobs in terms of their skill and responsibility requirements and in terms of unfavorable working conditions and the degree of physical effort required. The result of job evaluation has been to create a logical, simplified wage structure, with all jobs classified by job content into a relatively small number of labor grades and with each labor grade having an attached single wage rate or wage-rate range.

The significance of job evaluation to union–management relations is that it creates a stable wage structure together with orderly change in particular wage rates. Prior to the acceptance and introduction of job evaluation, wage-inequity grievances were brought up during the term of the labor agreement and typically in large numbers. Wage rates for particular jobs became a most troublesome and hectic grievance problem. Acceptance of job evaluation requires agreement that jobs have been equitably classified and that, consequently, wage rates for particular jobs will not be changed unless job content changes. If job content changes or if new jobs are created, orderly change is achieved since evaluation principles have been accepted for the determination of the wage rate for the new or revised job. Disagreement may be resolved, if necessary, through arbitration. The almost complete acceptance of job evaluation, or its near equivalent through more informal procedures, has gone far in the resolution of the issue of the determination of wage rates for particular jobs.

Job evaluation developed in the United States primarily as an application of scientific management. Its use was greatly stimulated by the spread of collective bargaining. Evaluation is much less common in other countries, although it is attracting greater interest abroad and its application is increasing. The most extensive development is in the Netherlands, where through union endorsement it has been utilized in a program to rationalize the wage structure of the entire country.

The compensation of individual employees, when paid by the hour, has tended in the United States to move in the direction of less discrimination between individuals. Many job evaluation plans, and other wage structures, pay all employees working on a particular job the identical wage rate. Probably more than half of the evaluation plans, however, establish a wage-rate range for each labor grade, within which individual employees are compensated. Some managements desire to compensate individuals within the rate range in accordance with merit and ability, but under union pressure seniority tends to govern; workers get automatic or nearly automatic increases in pay at fixed points in time and in this way progress along a pay scale to the maximum rate for the job.

Whereas the issues of job compensation and individual compensation by the hour have been to a great extent resolved, piece-rate and wage-incentive compensation frequently involve controversy. Similarly, there can be controversy over production standards and manning requirements under systems of hourly compensation that have been coupled with employee efficiency requirements. In other words, there has been only limited agreement between managements and unions about the application of industrial engineering principles to the determination of production standards. In recent years acute conflict has sometimes developed when management has attempted to increase the general level of employee efficiency and effort.

The level of effort, manning requirements, and various so-called restrictive work rules, although not usually thought of as part of the plant compensation structure, are crucial determinants of labor cost. Under the reduced competitive pressures of World War II and the high levels of demand that prevailed in the early postwar years, efficiency declined in many companies as employees sought and achieved looser production standards. In the later postwar years, as competition intensified and excess capacity developed, management endeavored to reduce cost by improving employee efficiency. This competitive drive intensified union–management conflict in a significant number of situations.

**Hours of work; vacation and holiday pay.** A long-standing traditional goal of unions has been to reduce the hours in the standard workday and work week. But in the years since World War II there has been very little change in the standard 40-hour week and 8-hour day. In the earlier years of this period there were significant, but not numerous, instances in which hours in excess of this standard were reduced to it. There have also been a few instances in which weekly hours have been reduced to levels below 40, but there has been no general drive to achieve such a reduction.

The goal of increased leisure has been achieved during this period by the introduction of paid vacations and paid holidays. There has been a steady, progressive liberalization of vacation and holiday provisions. A three-week vacation for employees with 10 or 15 years of service is now common, and numerous labor agreements provide for four weeks of vacation for those with 25 (or, in some instances, fewer) years of service. Seven or eight paid holidays during the year are now quite common.

An interesting question for the near future is whether there will be a strong demand for a shorter work week without reduction in the weekly wage. The recent relatively high unemployment rates stimulated interest in increasing employment by this device. On the other hand, the most recent novel negotiation has been in the steel industry, where an optional savings, retirement, and extended vacation plan has been introduced. In the related metal container industry, a sabbatical-leave type of vacation plan has been negotiated. These plans continue the trend toward reduced hours of work per year rather than per week.

Overtime payment has been negotiated for work on paid holidays and for hours beyond the standard day and week. In many labor agreements these provisions are quite complex. The original purpose of penalty overtime rates of pay was to discourage excess hours of work. While the rates continue to serve this purpose, liberal payment has tended to make such work attractive for many employees. Liberalization of overtime payment arrangements has been sought largely to increase take-home pay.

**Unemployment benefits and severance pay.**  Privately financed and trusteed supplementary unemployment benefit plans were negotiated in 1955 in the automobile industry. The plan that became the basis for agreement was developed by the Ford Motor Company as a counterproposal to the demand of the United Automobile Workers union for a guaranteed annual wage. The union's demand for a guaranteed annual wage was perhaps the most controversial benefit issue in the postwar years. Although the unemployment plan as negotiated did not fully satisfy the union's demands, the employer's objections to it were considerably reduced because it was integrated with public unemployment benefits and because the employer could achieve limited liability through trust-fund financing.

In subsequent years the automobile plan, or a variation of it, has been negotiated by larger employers in many industries. The benefit amount has been liberalized, and the maximum duration of benefits has been extended in many instances from 26 to 52 weeks. Various provisions for short-work-week benefits have also been introduced. Liberalizations bring the plans closer to the original objective of the unions, and the extension of maximum benefits to 52 weeks, plus other administrative modifications, has diminished somewhat the integration of private plans with public unemployment benefit systems. Less common than the automobile industry plan, but nevertheless important, are negotiated savings-fund plans, from which employees may draw in emergencies, including unemployment.

A severance-pay plan was added to the automobile industry supplementary unemployment benefit plan in 1958. Severance-pay plans have also been negotiated in other industries, and since 1960 have been spreading rapidly. The amount of such pay varies with seniority and is logically related to, and payable for, permanent severance.

**Job security and subcontracting.**  The entire subject of job security has been a major issue in collective bargaining in recent years. Its increased importance in negotiation may be attributed to higher levels of unemployment associated with some sluggishness in the rate of economic growth and to widespread fear of the disemployment effect of automation and a quickened pace of technological change. Although supplementary unemployment benefits, severance pay, and early retirement have been the primary manifestations of emphasis on job security, there also has been (1) limited experimentation with "automation funds," which have given employers the right to make certain work-rule and technological changes in return for contributions on their part to trust funds providing specialized employee benefits, (2) some broadening of seniority units governing layoff and recall, and some growth of retraining provisions, and (3) an intensification of the issue of subcontracting.

Subcontracting is controversial in principle. Employers regard freedom to subcontract work as a fundamental business right. Any form of restriction of this right is resisted. In addition to the controversy this causes between unions and management, subcontracting causes conflict among unions. In order to maintain or enlarge employment opportunities for their members, industrial unions wish to limit subcontracting. The employment of craft-union construction employees, however, depends in part on the freedom of industrial employers to subcontract construction work. Industrial union–craft union rivalry is intensified by this conflict of interest in employment opportunities with respect to construction and maintenance work. Unemployment intensifies all aspects of the subcontracting issue.

**Pension and medical benefits.**  Unions did not initiate private hospitalization, surgical, and medical group-benefit plans. Nor did they initiate private pension plans. Group life insurance, sickness and accident compensation, hospital and surgical and medical plans, and pension plans were pioneered by employers as an important part of their developing personnel policies and programs. In the postwar years, however, unions sought these benefits through negotiation and gave added impetus to expanding their coverage. Unions achieved more liberal plans not only by increasing benefit amounts but also by adding to the kinds of medical services provided and by the extension of coverage to employees' dependents and, more recently, to retired employees. The entire private welfare structure has been considerably extended, although pension plans cover fewer employees than do hospitalization and medical plans.

Employers typically have not disagreed about the desirability of most benefit plans. On this issue employers cannot be cast in the role of the employees' antagonists. The issue in negotiation has essentially been the degree and cost of particular liberalizations of those benefit plans. It is also not very probable that great conflict will develop in the future.

There is, however, a growing potential issue in the medical field between the direct provision of hospital and medical services and the now more common insurance approach to such benefits. Some unions have, usually through a joint union–management trustee mechanism, established various kinds of clinical, diagnostic, medical, and hospitalization services. The United Mine Workers union, for example, through its trusteed welfare fund, operates 18 memorial hospitals. Direct-service medical plans tend to be opposed by the professional medical associations and to arouse the hostility of various opponents of "socialized medicine." Some of the large industrial unions are becoming more and more interested in the direct-service approach to medical care. Employers tend to favor continuation of insured or similarly financed programs. The method of providing medical services to the entire community is likely to become an increasingly active political issue in the United States, and this issue will involve elements of union–management controversy. [See MEDICAL CARE, article on ECONOMIC ASPECTS.]

Another potential problem involves the investment policy to be followed with respect to pension reserves. Private pension reserves are today quite large and within the next ten years will increase to enormous size. The investment of such reserves, except with respect to plans utilizing the joint union–management trustee device, has been under the control of the employer or a trustee selected by him. The large industrial unions are questioning this unilateral control. Some such unions see opportunities to further various social projects by the investment of such funds. As pension reserves become larger, investment control and policy may become increasingly controversial [see PENSION FUNDS].

It can be argued with conviction, although it cannot be proved, that unions have stimulated the quite rapid growth of private benefit plans. It is also clear that in the United States the importance of private plans (relative to that of public plans providing similar benefits) is greater than in most, if not all, other countries. Although public provision of medical benefits may become an increasingly important political issue in the United States, a combined private and public approach to welfare benefits, with public plans providing only minimum benefits of all types, appears firmly established.

**Recognition and union security.** The United States is one of the few countries with a tradition and practice of the exclusive representation of employees in a bargaining unit by a single union. This tradition became a legal principle of representation with the passage of the Wagner Act in 1935. In most countries various unions have members among the employees of a particular employer.

Unions in the United States, going beyond the concept of exclusive representation, have also sought, and in about three-fourths of union contracts have achieved, compulsory union membership for all employees in the bargaining unit. The most prevalent form of compulsory membership, and the strongest form now compatible with federal law, is a union-shop labor agreement provision requiring membership in the union within 30 days after employment. There are, however, 18 states that prohibit by right-to-work laws any form of compulsory union membership. There is also a qualification in federal law limiting the compulsory discharge of an employee under a union-shop clause to refusal to pay union dues and regularly required initiation fees.

Union-shop and other union security provisions in labor agreements are not common in most countries and are not usually sought by unions, no doubt because such provisions are not consistent with the tradition of multiple-union membership and representation (no attempt is made here to analyze differences in such underlying traditions).

In all countries a most severe controversy between management and unions has historically been the direct issue of recognition. It appears that the struggle over recognition was more severe in the United States than in many other countries, although this is open to debate. What is clear is that this issue has become less important as unions have achieved greater social and political status. In the United States, and in some other countries, recognition is a legal right. In the United States, the issue of recognition now hinges on the ability of a union to win a majority vote among the employees in an appropriate bargaining unit as determined by the National Labor Relations Board.

The issue of the union shop is still a controversial one, although much less so than in the recent past. Compulsory union membership is important to unions today perhaps as much for symbolic as for other reasons. Management likewise objects to compulsory membership on principle, as being contrary to democratic traditions.

There are other provisions in labor agreements relating to union status that at times become serious issues. Union representatives may be given special protection against layoff and may have other special rights and responsibilities relating to their duties as representatives. The number of representatives may itself be an issue. In general, however, minor union-status rights and regulations have been fairly well resolved.

**Other labor agreement provisions.** No attempt will be made to discuss in detail labor agreement provisions other than those discussed above. Most labor agreements contain a management-rights clause, and all agreements contain termination and renewal provisions. Agreements have in the past been of one-year duration, but recently two-year and three-year agreements have been typical.

The major point to note is that agreement provisions vary by industry and in accordance with the attitudes and problems of the negotiating parties. Variations in technology and in economic conditions give rise to variations in the content of agreements. Some examples can serve to indicate some of these differences. In the casual-employment trades, such as construction, seniority provisions are rare. Hiring is usually done through the union in a manner designed to equalize employment opportunities for those actively working at the trade. Craft-union agreements, while not containing seniority provisions, do contain detailed provisions relating to work jurisdiction. In the transportation industries there are usually detailed provisions relating to the composition of crews and to the scheduling of work. In any hazardous industry there are likely to be special provisions relating to safety.

Thus, it is clear that the particular economic and technological conditions in an industry influence the subjects of negotiation and the content of agreements. The problems and attitudes of the parties in negotiation are even more important sources of variation in agreements. Some agreements are much longer and more detailed than other agreements. Agreements grow in scope and content depending upon the problems encountered and the desire of the parties to operate with detailed agreement provisions.

## Changing issues

As we have mentioned, issues in collective bargaining in the United States have not remained static but have gone through an evolutionary process. Labor agreements have been greatly expanded, hostility has declined, and union–management relationships are more orderly. In 1937, the first agreement between the United States Steel Corporation and the Steel Workers Organizing Committee was three typed pages long. Today the basic agreement is some sixty printed pages long, with various lengthy supplementary agreements and many binding arbitration precedents. This expansion has been typical in the history of labor agreements.

The expansion of labor agreements has greatly limited management's right to act unilaterally. Collective bargaining has created a system of constitutionalism or of industrial jurisprudence. Employees have the right of protest through grievances and through negotiation. Employers have been forced to develop industrial relations policies. Autocratic capitalism has been greatly modified by collective bargaining, including its indirect influence upon nonunionized employers, which has thereby contributed to the continued acceptance of private property and private enterprise.

Labor agreements in the United States are today quite fully developed in their noneconomic or administrative aspects. The frequency and extent of change in these provisions of the agreement have been greatly reduced. In the years since the Korean War, in the more competitive economic environment that has existed, conflict has related primarily to the endeavor of management to restore efficiency where costly practices were felt to exist, to the endeavor of unions to enhance job security, and to the amount of economic adjustment that was felt to be appropriate.

Unions in the United States have not, in principle, accepted the concept of wage restraint. Competitive unionism, with strong independent national unions negotiating with many employers on a decentralized basis, is not conducive to the acceptance of such restraint. Conflict, however, has been most prevalent in the more important pattern-setting negotiations, namely, the key negotiations with one or more large employers in the major industries.

Strikes continue to be, therefore, an integral aspect of collective bargaining even though they have declined in frequency during the postwar years. Strikes are also much less violent than in earlier periods. Employers rarely attempt to operate plants during strikes, picketing is largely symbolic, and deep-seated employee hostility is rarely involved. But at the same time there appears to be less public tolerance of strikes. Union aspirations do not elicit the degree of public sympathy and support they formerly aroused. Although free collective bargaining cannot operate without the right to strike or to take a strike, and although strikes are their own best deterrent by forcing more responsible future behavior, the pressure of public opinion is encouraging a reduction of militancy.

A reduction of militancy would be greatly facilitated in the United States by a higher degree of union–management consensus on appropriate limits to economic adjustments. The range and the degree of economic conflict are much broader in the United States than, for example, in Sweden (Johnston 1962). Reducing economic conflict is a major question for the future of collective bargaining in the United States, although its importance can be exaggerated. Pressures in this direction may lead to greater centralization in the bargaining structure and to more active governmental intervention in major disputes.

### Issues in Europe

The parties to collective bargaining in Europe have, at least in some countries, consciously practiced wage restraint; it is hazardous, however, to predict their future course. Perhaps it is reasonable to expect that a consciously developed and applied wage policy will continue to be an integral part of the growing role of economic planning emerging in European countries.

Issues in collective bargaining in Europe appear at present to relate to the stronger development of collective bargaining on a local plant and company basis. Although employees in European countries have had representation through works councils and similar arrangements, which are frequently established by law, collective bargaining as known in the United States has been weak or nonexistent at the local plant level. Systems of collective bargaining have been highly centralized as compared to those in the United States.

In a study of collective bargaining in four European countries (France, Italy, West Germany, and England), Arthur M. Ross (1962a; 1962b; 1962c) found considerable evidence of the increased importance of decentralized collective bargaining in three of them. (It is presently of little significance only in France.) A major question is the extent to which future collective bargaining in Europe may shift to a more decentralized structure and, as one conse-

quence, place greater emphasis upon company-level issues, which have long been important in the United States. It would be naive to expect collective bargaining not to retain significant differences among countries. Abstracting from differences within Europe, it may well be true that collective bargaining in Europe is contending with problems arising from growing decentralization, while in the United States the issues may relate largely to growing centralization [*see* LABOR UNIONS, *article on* LABOR MOVEMENTS AND COLLECTIVE BARGAINING IN EUROPE].

Issues in collective bargaining cannot be stereotyped. They cannot be dissociated from their varied political, economic, and social environments and from the dynamic changes in these environments. And the process of collective bargaining is evolutionary, resolving some issues but facing new issues under constantly changing conditions. Although it is easy to be critical of the results, particularly some of the apparent economic consequences, on balance collective bargaining appears to have contributed to social progress.

E. ROBERT LIVERNASH

#### BIBLIOGRAPHY

ALEXANDER, ROBERT J. 1962 *Labor Relations in Argentina, Brazil, and Chile.* New York: McGraw-Hill.

DUNLOP, JOHN T. 1958 *Industrial Relations Systems.* New York: Holt.

GALENSON, WALTER 1961 *Trade Union Democracy in Western Europe.* Berkeley and Los Angeles: Univ. of California Press.

HARBISON, FREDERICK H.; and MYERS, CHARLES A. 1959 *Management in the Industrial World: An International Analysis.* New York: McGraw-Hill.

JOHNSTON, T. L. 1962 *Collective Bargaining in Sweden: A Study of the Labour Market and Its Institutions.* Cambridge, Mass.: Harvard Univ. Press.

ROSS, ARTHUR M. 1962a The New Industrial Relations in Britain. *Labor Law Journal* 13:492–501.

ROSS, ARTHUR M. 1962b Prosperity and Labor Relations in Europe: The Case of West Germany. *Quarterly Journal of Economics* 76:331–359.

ROSS, ARTHUR M. 1962c Prosperity and Labor Relations in Western Europe: Italy and France. *Industrial and Labor Relations Review* 16:63–85.

SLICHTER, SUMNER H.; HEALY, JAMES J.; and LIVERNASH, E. ROBERT 1960 *The Impact of Collective Bargaining on Management.* Washington: Brookings Institution.

## II

### STRIKES

Strikes—collective stoppages of work, intended to influence those who depend on the sale or use of the products of that work—are almost as old as work itself. They can take various forms and are only one of many restrictive weapons in the armory of labor conflict; others are black lists, union labels and boycotts, bans on piecework or on overtime, going slow or working to rule, and other practices, including sabotage.

Most of these methods, and strikes in particular, are obviously available only to workers who have some social cohesion or tradition of common action. They are, therefore, by no means the only expressions of unrest among industrial workers; other recognized symptoms are a high rate of labor turnover, of sickness or accidents, of absenteeism—or, again, of workplace pilfering, since this may be inspired by resentment, rather than need. Alternatively, workers may take refuge individually in escapist amusements or they may feel goaded to collective political activity. Strikes alone, therefore, are a poor measure of industrial discontent. A decline in their number or severity may merely mean that discontent is finding expression in other ways or possibly not at all; the form it takes at any given time is determined by a little-understood combination of economic, technological, institutional, and psychological factors.

However, strikes are not only among the most obvious and dramatic symptoms of industrial unrest, they are also the best documented of these symptoms. Strike statistics are not based on limited inquiries but on more or less complete counts, and since they usually started as a branch of crime statistics, are available for most industrial countries over many years. Wherever a protest against working conditions has overtones of a protest against the prevailing regime, strikes are still tainted with criminality. (Indeed, one of the reasons totalitarianism is deplored is that it views strikes as subversive.) Elsewhere, strikes have outlived their criminal origins and have, in degree, become institutionalized as one of the acknowledged sanctions of collective bargaining. Political action apart, strikes are probably the most effective of the methods of pressure available to workers, although under full employment the *threat* to strike has been held to be more effective still.

This is not to say that they generally succeed or that their success—indeed, any of their consequences—can often be assessed convincingly (Chamberlain & Schilling 1954). Almost every attempt to quantify the various aspects of strikes— not only their effects but also their causes and even their number or severity—is beset with problems that reflect the elusiveness of the strike phenomenon. Apart from a very few case histories, some press reports, and a good deal of partisan literature, official figures provide the main source of information. It therefore seems best to summarize the shortcomings of this last-named source.

## Classifying and measuring strikes

In the first place, it has proved impossible, when recording strikes, to separate them from lockouts (the analogous weapon of employers). Few disputes, it is true, appear nowadays to take the form of lockouts; but the dichotomy is blurred because both strikes and lockouts may be anticipations of or responses to the threat of the other. Labor statisticians are therefore faced with the same sort of dilemma in distinguishing them as are jurists in deciding between aggressive and defensive actions in international politics.

Again, the classification of strikes according to their main cause is questionable and often subjective. Not only are most strikes (like other human actions) determined by many things, the relative importance of which may change as time goes on, but the apparent main issue may turn out to be almost irrelevant. The precipitating cause may seem so slight in relation to the feeling engendered that one is driven to the conclusion that, as in other conflicts, the choice of a *casus belli* is often comparatively arbitrary.

The effects of strikes are even harder to pinpoint. Any classification of even the immediate results of strikes is dubious, for since the range of possible demands and concessions is wide and bluffing is common, the concepts of victory, defeat, and compromise can be extremely hazy. In any case, the immediate results of a strike may be little guide to its long-term effects, and few people can afford to wait until the long term is up before making an assessment. The analysis of strikes by their results has therefore been generally abandoned.

Another doubtful distinction is the distinction between those directly and indirectly involved. Normally the category "indirectly involved" has had to be limited to workers employed at the establishment where the strike occurs, which limitation is itself unrealistic; but the distinction is shakier than this, since, in order to find out who really favored the strike, a psychologist would presumably need to interview each worker—and, as people's views change, the numbers directly and indirectly involved would change from one day to the next. (For a discussion of this and other problems of enumeration and classification, see International Labor Office 1926; Peterson 1938.) Nor is it practicable to distinguish between "economic" and "political" strikes or even between official (union-supported) and unofficial strikes. All these concepts are clear enough as abstractions but break down if they are made the basis of classification.

**Strike statistics.** There are, moreover, difficulties in sheer counting. Figures of "working days lost" or "man-days idle" can hardly be accurate if, as often happens in big strikes, men drift back day by day. Such figures are bound to be incomplete in any case, because no trustworthy assessment can be made of the effects of a strike in other industries or even factories. On the other side, no appropriate allowance can be made for working days that would have been lost anyway, through unemployment, accidents, sickness, or absenteeism. Nor can these figures be adjusted to show the self-compensating effects by which the losses caused by even the biggest strikes may be made up by extra overtime, improved morale, or even—if, say, pieceworkers strike because their supplies of material are inadequate—by improved efficiency.

Difficulties are inherent in even the simplest strike data. It is hard to interpret a change in the number of strikes when a one-day stoppage of a handful of workers and a shutdown involving hundreds of thousands for weeks or months each counts as one strike. For this reason, any average of the size or length of strikes over a period may be misleading. Again, not only is one strike unlike another, but one man-day idle is also unlike another. A total of 600 man-days idle might relate to a strike of 600 men for one day, to a strike of 100 men for six days, or to six one-day strikes of 100 men apiece, and so on. These are not the same thing, even if they happen in the same factory, and they are still less similar if they happen in different factories or in different branches of industry or are subject to the innumerable other circumstantial differences of industrial life—let alone differences in the general economic, social, and political climate.

## Industrial strike patterns

Some generalizations, however, are possible, despite the complexity of the problem and the limitations of the evidence. There are, for instance, clues to the relative propensity of different groups of workers to strike. We cannot assess the propensity of workers to strike rather than, say, to remain absent or change their jobs; only a few, limited studies have been made of the connection of absenteeism with labor turnover and with strikes in particular industries at particular times, and some have found a long-term alternation between industrial and political action in certain countries.

Nevertheless, we can contrast the striking of particular groups of workers with their own performance at other times, as well as with that of groups of workers in different industries, regions, or countries. Some similarities have been noted in the industrial strike patterns of many countries; for instance, coal miners and dock workers strike most. While interpretation must remain speculative, the following socioeconomic explanations have been suggested (Kerr & Siegel 1954). The workers most prone to strike have traditionally lived in isolation from other groups of workers, retaining their own codes of behavior, doing much the same kind of work (work of low status in the eyes of outsiders), and often suffering severe unemployment with little hope of finding new jobs in other industries. On the other hand, the more "peaceful" workers have lived more as individuals integrated into a complex society, in places where industry has been more diversified and jobs more interchangeable and where the effects of economic depression have, therefore, been less catastrophic. Since industrial strike patterns can transcend national frontiers in this way, it is not surprising that, within countries, industrial influences on striking should appear stronger than regional influences (Knowles 1952, chapter 4).

**Fluctuations in strike activity.** However, long-term industrial strike patterns have little relevance to the marked fluctuations in strike activity, which are a feature of the experience of all countries. If we ask in what specific situations workers are most likely to strike, we have to distinguish between the *immediate* causes of strikes, the *conditioning* causes, and the *underlying* causes; the causation of any given strike will involve all three.

*Immediate causes.* The evidence on the *immediate* causes of strikes is, as we have seen, intrinsically dubious. The prevalence of particular issues varies not only between industries and countries but also over time, and any apparent trend has to be interpreted with caution. Thus, a relative decline in, say, strikes on wage issues may reflect the successful development of procedures by which these issues can be negotiated or it may merely reflect a political situation in which wage strikes are less acceptable, in which case they may masquerade as strikes on other issues. Thus, a corresponding relative increase in strikes about questions of discipline or working arrangements may or may not indicate good prospects for fuller joint consultation, improved factory welfare, or a more sophisticated industrial psychology. The interpretation of the evidence on immediate causes is, therefore, mainly a matter of making sense of it in the light of what we already know about the situation; in itself, it provides little illumination.

*Economic cycles.* We are on slightly stronger ground in inquiring into the *conditioning* causes of strikes. The chief of these, probably, is the economic cycle of boom and depression: the prospects for workers of forcing concessions seem better, and the penalties of failure less, when profits and employment are rising. But our available basic data—number of strikes, of workers involved, and of man-days idle and the average size and length of strike that derive from these—each have a different significance in a given context, and the series tend to move differently.

Thus, it is fluctuations in the number or frequency of strikes that, as many studies have shown, exhibit the best correspondence with cyclical economic fluctuations. In the past this reaction has been clearest in Britain, Germany, and Canada, but there have been traces of it in several other countries (Forchheimer 1948–1949). Despite the shortcomings mentioned, the number of strikes does give some indication of the number of separate points of friction, and it is not surprising that this series should be more responsive to economic events than the others. The numbers of man-days idle and of workers involved and the other indicators of duration and severity are more likely to be affected by noneconomic imponderables, such as the character of trade union leadership and policy. The limits of economic determinism in explaining strike movements must always have been fairly narrow; moreover, these movements are less spontaneous than they were, owing to institutional developments such as the growth in the power of unions to control strikes, the development of negotiating machinery and dispute procedures, and the advance of labor law in general. Nor are economic fluctuations themselves as violent or compulsive as they were before 1939.

*Other conditioning causes.* There is evidence that other conditioning causes—the seasonal working of some industries, the emergencies of war, the timing of vacations, the spread of trade union membership, and perhaps even the weather (although any effect of the latter is probably largely secondary, since the weather affects seasonal economic activity in the first place)—have had perceptible impacts on strikes. Moreover, strikes themselves can be infectious; at any rate, correspondences have been found between strikes in one industry and strikes in others. But one cannot isolate the effect of "infection" on particular industries from that of the trade cycle on all of them; that is, it is difficult to determine how far a correspondence between the strikes of, say, coal miners and metal workers is due to "strike fever" and how far the

upswing of the trade cycle encourages each group of workers independently. The same sort of ambiguity obscures the association of strikes with the degree of trade union membership, for membership has also tended to fluctuate with the trade cycle. But even where a large proportion of strikes is unsupported by unions, the degree of union membership seems likely to affect striking, if only because the organized are better equipped to strike than the unorganized. The independent influence of political agitators on striking generally is hard to assess; a few noteworthy strikes apart, there are grounds for believing it to have been small in most countries at most times.

*Underlying causes.* Several studies of industrial relations have stressed the *underlying* causes of strikes, even though these usually have to be inferred because they seldom become explicit (see especially Great Britain 1917; Kornhauser et al. 1954, part 2; Griffin 1939, chapters 3 and 4). Bad living conditions, which are slow to change; the decline of craftsmanship; the growing size and impersonality of firms; new forms of industrial fatigue, due to the grueling monotony of repetitious work; the isolation of the trade union rank and file from their increasingly specialized officials; the remoteness and delay of centralized collective bargaining; the collaboration of union leaders with employers and government—all these may, it is suggested, promote unrest, quite apart from the evident conflicts of interest which some labor ideologies assume to be unresolvable. All these things emphasize the worker's inferiority: his comparative propertylessness, his difficulty in changing his job, his ignorance of the value of his labor, his liability to dismissal, and his impotence to control the stresses of his work. The implication is that even improved social welfare may be inadequate to compensate for the worker's growing social anonymity.

In this light, it is perhaps suggestive that, for instance, wage strikes—probably still the most common form of strike the world over—seldom indicate poverty below subsistence level, if only because the worst-paid workers usually lack the organization, resources, and energy for such a protest. Despite trade union argumentation, it seems doubtful whether real-wage considerations have played much part in strikes; at any rate, money-wage cuts have probably been resisted more vigorously, even when real wages were rising, than money-wage advances have been demanded to keep pace with a fall in real wages. Strikes for wages scaled to "what the trade can bear" or to the wages of other workers suggest a desire for social justice that reflects the worker's sense of inferiority rather than his poverty; and industrial psychology has asserted that inferiority compensation finds its classic expression in striking (Viteles 1953, p. 68). An important and related aspect of strikes is that they represent a complete break with the restrictions of everyday routine. Thus, American strikers have called themselves "vacationists," and Belgian miners have referred to striking as "pit holidaying"; in Britain "playing" was a traditional euphemism for striking, and the Spanish word for strike also means leisure, recreation, or merrymaking. There are significant analogies in other languages.

It is true that generalizations about strikers' feelings of frustration and inferiority, the symbolic aspect of their demands on occasion, their unconscious susceptibility to economic and political pressures, and so on, do not carry us far beyond the obvious. Those who stress the apparent irrationality of strikers tend to be skeptical of any attempt to analyze causes of strikes; although human behavior is seldom wholly rational, this does not preclude rationality in interpretation. What is needed is a far greater number of case studies than anyone has yet thought it worthwhile to undertake.

### Strike-restricting legislation

It is often asked whether more could not be done to avoid, prevent, or suppress strikes by means of legislation; and there is no doubt that legal provisions in this field need regular overhaul, since out-of-date statutes can make for hard cases in the courts and may serve to bring the law into contempt. As has been said, striking used to be considered a form of crime, but strikes have gradually been legitimized in democratic countries by enactments conferring the freedom to strike. However, this freedom is hedged, and the weight of legal restriction, as well as its direction, varies a good deal in different countries (see Colloquium on Labour Relations and the Law 1965 for an international survey of the legal position regarding strikes). In some cases it is the means employed in strikes that are restricted; in some it is the ends sought; and in some it is both. Direct political strikes apart, any strikes likely to result in a serious interruption of vital services or in danger to life, valuable property, or public order are generally proscribed. But beyond this there is little international agreement on permissible methods or objectives. The emphasis of antistrike legislation relates sometimes to the infringement of established principles implied in such terms as "fair labor practices" or "social adequacy," sometimes to specific offenses, such as the breach of contracts of employment or the contravention of legally en-

forceable collective agreements, and sometimes to activities associated with strikes, for example, picketing and such incidental abuses as intimidation and violence. In other cases procedural delays may be interposed or ballots insisted on, with penalties for nonobservance. On paper the United States approach appears the most legalistic and the British the least so.

**Practical difficulties.** However, the law can mean very much more (or very much less) than the paper it is written on, and what it means in practice is apt to vary with circumstances. In general, the greater reluctance to enforce legislation against strikers than against other lawbreakers is due to the obvious practical difficulty of imposing penalties on large bodies of men without causing greater dislocation than do the strikes themselves; the alternative of punishing the leaders or instigators alone may incur the same risk, by turning them into martyrs. For this reason, antistrike legislation has often appeared to be designed as a deterrent to striking rather than as a punitive response to strikes; a punitive expedition can be a costly confession of failure.

The lesson of wartime experience, as well as of experience since 1945, would seem to be that the viability of strike-restricting legislation depends upon the provision and willing acceptance of legally supported "alternatives" to striking, such as conciliation or arbitration. The comparative absence of legal restrictions in Britain has reflected the "maximum abstention" of the law in industrial relations generally, although a *cause célèbre*, *Rookes* v. *Barnard* (1964, A.C. 1129), reopened in 1964 the question of further limiting the freedom to strike.

### Collective bargaining in democracies

While strikes have, in effect, been domesticated to an important extent, and while the need to maintain the freedom of workers to protest by striking is widely acknowledged, strikes as a means of keeping up pressure are less acceptable than they were. Many European countries, at any rate, are living on narrower margins than they were before the two world wars, and their industries are therefore in some ways more interdependent. Hence, the potential dislocation of strikes has become of greater public concern: big strikes, and even small strikes of key workers, are more apt to have political repercussions, and the state therefore has an increasing interest in preserving or restoring industrial peace.

The question is, in fact, wider than this; for as the state increasingly concerns itself with economic matters—import and export policies, the determination of industrial priorities, and the like —it has a growing stake in the results of collective bargaining in general. Strikes apart, collective bargaining may result in settlements that infringe upon a government's view of what is economically permissible; and several Western governments have felt constrained to try to implement a wages or incomes policy that involves interference with or even direct participation in industrial negotiation.

In some countries—notably in Germany, Scandinavia, and Holland—the whole system of collective bargaining had, in any case, to be recast after the disruption of World War II, and it was therefore possible to provide for the state's concern with industrial bargains by making the appropriate institutional changes and thereby, incidentally, to create an atmosphere in which strikes were less acceptable and, in consequence, legal restriction less irksome. In those countries, however, where the wartime constraints were eventually removed and the earlier practices restored, the problem of accommodating the national interest has proved more difficult.

In any event, the problems posed by strikes are subordinate to the wider problems posed by the continuance, unmodified, of "free collective bargaining." Strikes are, after all, a recognized sanction in the process of collective bargaining, and although they can undoubtedly embarrass the government on occasion, it does not seem practicable or desirable to try to legislate them away, so long as other bargaining practices remain unaffected. In democratic societies plain repression could bring worse evils than strikes as we know them— for instance, political instability or chronic industrial apathy.

**Impact of strikes.**    The economic effect of strikes in practice, severe as this might be in theory, should not be exaggerated even now. If "working days lost" is taken as a crude indicator of lost output (although this is like estimating air raid damage by reference to the bomb tonnage dropped, irrespective of target, accuracy of bombing, or type of bomb), the reduction of such loss in most countries during the present century is marked. The loss of working days through strikes is usually very small when considered in relation to the size of the labor force concerned. Thus, for the ten years 1954–1963, the annual averages per worker of working days lost through strikes in mining, manufacturing, construction, and transport were as follows: United States, 1.05; Italy, .82; India, .70; Canada, .61; Belgium, .50; Japan, .41; Australia, .39; France, .33; United Kingdom, .30; Norway, .29; West Germany, .07; Netherlands, .05; Sweden,

.01 (International Labour Organisation 1964). Only in the United States was the loss as great as one day per worker per year; in most cases it was no more than a few hours, and it may be significant that Sweden, Holland, and Germany (where there has been change and development in collective bargaining) were among those with the lowest averages.

At all times other causes of "loss," such as unemployment, inefficiency at all levels, sickness, and absenteeism, would, on a similar reckoning, be far more telling. Of course, the unpredictable shock effect of strikes may, as is no doubt intended, be felt more severely than the "running-sore" type of loss, and some abnormally big strikes have perceptibly jolted whole economies before now. But in the past the economic effects (if not the social and political effects) of even the biggest strikes have been fairly short lived: stocks were high, and the time "lost" was in effect taken out of the time during which workers would have been idle in any case rather than out of production time. However, economic conditions have changed, and it would be frivolous to dismiss the effects that strikes might have under the conditions of fuller employment and lower stocks that have prevailed in European countries since World War II. It cannot be too much emphasized that the economic climate in which strikes occur provides the most significant weighting of any figures of time or output loss.

**Changing patterns of bargaining.**    To sum up, strikes are a complex phenomenon whose character, causes, and effects are difficult to assess and whose incidence is hard to predict or control. They are no more than the visible tip of the iceberg of industrial unrest. Historically, they have been undertaken primarily as a means of bringing pressure to bear on an employer to redress particular grievances, although the impulse to strike springs from deeper roots. In practice, they are a challenge not only to the employer's authority but sometimes also to that of a trade union leadership and increasingly, as the public has come to be more immediately involved in economic matters, to that of the state itself. In most industrial countries it has been possible to reduce the scale and duration of strikes in general, although big strikes still occur. Some groups of workers are traditionally prone to strike more than others; and strikes appear to have been more sensitive to economic fluctuations than to direct pressure, although institutional changes have undoubtedly contributed to reducing their severity. In democratic countries there are evident practical limits to the adoption of purely preventative or punitive measures, and freedom to strike is part of the accepted tradition of collective bargaining.

A modification of this tradition—in the direction, for instance, of tripartite bargaining, with the provision of alternative sanctions—might well, as the experience of some countries already suggests, be reflected in a further diminution of strikes. Apart from this, any widespread improvement in managerial techniques should have its effect, as also should certain wider social policies, such as the diversification of single-industry areas. It is nevertheless unlikely that strikes will be wholly obviated. Socially, they are still a kind of safety valve: they still have the function—in some ways an increasingly important function—of calling immediate attention to weaknesses in the working of the ever more complex machinery by which industry is regulated. If on balance they are an evil, they may still be one of the better of many possible evils.

K. G. J. C. KNOWLES

[See also INDUSTRIAL RELATIONS; LABOR UNIONS; WORKERS.]

BIBLIOGRAPHY

CHAMBERLAIN, NEIL W.; and SCHILLING, JANE M. 1954 *The Impact of Strikes: Their Social and Economic Costs.* New York: Harper. → One of the more ambitious attempts to estimate the effects of strikes.

COLLOQUIUM ON LABOUR RELATIONS AND THE LAW, LONDON, 1962 1965 *Labour Relations and the Law: A Comparative Study.* Edited and with an introduction by Otto Kahn-Freund. London: Stevens.

FORCHHEIMER, K. 1948–1949 Some International Aspects of the Strike Movement. Oxford, University of, Institute of Statistics, *Bulletin* 10:9–24, 294–304; 11: 279–286.

GALENSON, WALTER (editor) 1952 *Comparative Labor Movements.* Englewood Cliffs, N.J.: Prentice-Hall.

GREAT BRITAIN, COMMISSION OF ENQUIRY INTO INDUSTRIAL UNREST 1917 *Report of the Commissioners for Wales, Including Monmouthshire.* Papers by Command, Cd. 8668. London: H.M. Stationery Office.

GRIFFIN, JOHN I. 1939 *Strikes: A Study in Quantitative Economics.* New York: Columbia Univ. Press.

INTERNATIONAL LABOR OFFICE 1926 *Report on Methods of Compiling Statistics of Industrial Disputes.* Studies and Reports Series N: Statistics, No. 10. Geneva: The Office.

INTERNATIONAL LABOUR ORGANISATION 1964 International Comparison of Days Lost Through Industrial Disputes. Great Britain, Ministry of Labour, *Gazette* 72:419 only.

KERR, CLARK; and SIEGEL, ABRAHAM 1954 The Inter-industry Propensity to Strike—An International Comparison. Pages 189–212 in Arthur W. Kornhauser, Robert Dubin, and Arthur M. Ross (editors), *Industrial Conflict.* New York: McGraw-Hill.

KNOWLES, K. G. J. C. 1952 *Strikes: A Study in Industrial Conflict, With Special Reference to British Experience Between 1911 and 1947.* Oxford, University of, Institute of Statistics, Monograph No. 3. Oxford: Blackwell; New York: Philosophical Library. → See especially pages 143–239 on "Conditions and Causes of Strike Activity."

KORNHAUSER, ARTHUR W.; DUBIN, ROBERT; and ROSS, ARTHUR M. (editors) 1954 *Industrial Conflict.* New York: McGraw-Hill.

PETERSON, FLORENCE 1938 *Strikes in the United States: 1880–1936.* U.S. Bureau of Labor Statistics, Bulletin No. 651. Washington: Government Printing Office. → Discusses problems of enumeration and classification.

ROSS, ARTHUR M.; and HARTMAN, PAUL T. 1960 *Changing Patterns of Industrial Conflict.* New York: Wiley.

TISSEMBAUM, MARIANO R. et al. (editors) 1951 *La huelga.* 3 vols. Santa Fé (Argentina): Universidad Nacional del Litoral, Facultad de Ciencias Jurídicas y Sociales.

VITELES, MORRIS S. 1953 *Motivation and Morale in Industry.* New York: Norton.

## III
### SETTLEMENT OF INDUSTRIAL DISPUTES

All industrial disputes are eventually settled, either with or without recourse to strikes, lockouts, boycotts, and other forms of economic pressure. Generally it is in the interest of employers and workers to avoid or limit the loss of profits and wages resulting from industrial conflict. Likewise, it is in the interest of society as a whole to minimize the number of work stoppages and the duration of those which do occur. Consequently, more or less elaborate techniques of dispute settlement have been developed in every country where collective bargaining is practiced.

The nature of dispute-settling mechanisms varies with the historical background and political philosophy of the country, with the type of dispute, and with the magnitude of economic loss which is threatened or suffered.

In the mature industrial societies of North America and western Europe, freedom of economic action, including the right to strike, has always been valued highly. Public intervention in labor–management disputes is therefore relatively limited. There is a clear trend toward more frequent governmental involvement, however, motivated not only by the desire to avoid the direct economic loss resulting from work stoppages but also by increased concern over the terms of settlement and their potentially inflationary consequences. The tradition of free collective bargaining has always been weaker in South America and the Asian countries. As a result, there is more continuous and systematic surveillance over industrial disputes on the part of those governments. The new countries of Africa, which are undertaking to promote economic development under forced draft, have generally held a tight rein on labor–management relations in order to prevent interference with planning goals. In communist countries, the workers and the employing enterprises do not have freedom of action against each other, although individual and group grievances within a limited range are recognized.

A typology of industrial disputes relevant to the techniques of settlement is more easily formulated for mature industrial countries than for those in the early stages of development. Disputes are not always clearly confined and demarcated in the latter countries. Political and economic motives may be interwoven, as in the case of strikes against foreign enterprises during periods of anticolonial agitation. Controversies may spill over from one trade or industry to another without regard for organizational lines, as in the case of the shorter-hours movement in the United States during the nineteenth century. In mature industrial societies, however, disputes generally involve specifically defined issues between specific organizations of employers and workers. As the level of development rises, disputes become less emotional and ideological, and hence more businesslike and realistic.

There are three principal types of disputes in mature economies. First are problems of institutional status: attempts to organize in the face of employer hostility, demands for recognition and collective bargaining rights, and jurisdictional conflict between competing labor unions. Second are matters involving substantive terms of employment —usually set forth in collective agreements—such as wages, hours, paid holidays and vacations, protection against discharge and layoff, etc. Third are questions involving the obligations and entitlements of the parties under existing collective agreements. Practice in the United States illustrates how these types of disputes are often subject to different methods of settlement. Problems of institutional status are under the jurisdiction of the National Labor Relations Board; disputes over substantive terms of employment are referred to government mediators; and grievances over alleged violations of collective agreements generally go to private arbitration if the parties cannot resolve them through direct negotiation.

Finally, disputes of critical importance--those threatening to create a national emergency, those involving key sectors of the economy—are often handled differently from routine controversies. Extraordinary procedures may include investiga-

tion by a fact-finding board, referral to special commissions and mediation bodies, and legislative handling by the national parliament.

## Settlement techniques

The principal techniques of dispute settlement include mediation, arbitration, investigation, and adjudication. These will be discussed in turn.

**Mediation.** Mediation is a diplomatic procedure which endeavors to settle a controversy by assisting the parties to reach a voluntary agreement. The ultimate decision is made by the parties themselves.

The mediator (sometimes called a conciliator) is generally a government official with prior experience in labor–management relations. Depending on the particular situation confronting him, he will draw from a battery of diplomatic techniques. He will furnish information to the parties that assists them in evaluating the probable consequences of alternative decisions; he will serve as a channel of communication when direct communication is unfeasible; he will offer a recommendation if he believes there is sufficient likelihood of its acceptance.

The mediator's basic task is to find a solution acceptable to both parties rather than to determine the rights and wrongs of the problem. His recommendations are therefore based on his expectations of what arrangements will stabilize relations between the parties for the period immediately ahead. The parties may accept his recommendation, use it as the basis for some other settlement, or reject it altogether. Thus, mediation may not result in an adjustment of conflicting interests. On the other hand, parties often submit to mediation where they would be unwilling to empower an outsider to make a binding decision. Furthermore, since the final decision is left to the parties themselves, they cannot complain that their bargaining freedom has been impaired or that they have been forced into a settlement that is unacceptable to them.

To minimize the risk of complete failure, the laws of some countries empower the government to initiate arbitration or other mandatory proceedings if mediation breaks down, especially in the case of disputes substantially affecting the public interest. Traditionally, mediation has been a voluntary process initiated at the request, or at least with the consent, of the parties. In some countries, however, recent legislation requires that the parties submit to mediation proceedings before they can resort to a test of economic strength. If mediation fails, the next step may be compulsory investigation or compulsory arbitration; or the parties may be left to their own devices.

**Arbitration.** Arbitration is a judicial process under which one or more outsiders render a binding decision based on the merits of the dispute. Arbitration is generally distinguished from adjudication by labor courts or administrative tribunals, but the same type of dispute referrable to arbitration in one country may be sent to a labor court in another.

Voluntary arbitration is initiated by consent of the parties but leads to a final and binding decision. The prevailing view holds that an agreement to arbitrate implies a willingness to abide by the award, even though this is not expressly stated.

Voluntary arbitration is suited to any type of dispute, including those involving basic terms of employment, interpretation of existing agreements, and interunion controversies. The greatest use of voluntary arbitration in the United States is in handling grievances alleging the violation of collective agreements. Arbitration is seldom employed for this purpose in other countries but is often used to establish basic terms of employment when direct agreement between the parties cannot be secured.

Compulsory arbitration rests on the force of law rather than on advance acceptance by contract. Certain clauses of labor disputes, or all unresolved controversies, are referred to an arbitration board. Where compulsory arbitration applies, the parties are forbidden from resorting to strikes or lockouts. In some countries, compulsory arbitration in peacetime is quite exceptional. For example, the only recourse to this technique in the United States during recent years was the congressional enactment of 1963 requiring that the long-standing dispute over working rules in the railroad industry be submitted to a three-man board appointed by the president. At the other extreme, compulsory arbitration is routine under the statutes of Australia and New Zealand; and as already noted, South American and African countries make widespread use of this technique.

Compulsory arbitration laws commonly apply to controversies that threaten to interfere with economic and social stability or with the provision of vital community services, such as transportation, education, and medical care. It is difficult, however, to define precisely all the areas in which work stoppages would jeopardize the public interest. Under these circumstances the statutory definition of disputes that must be submitted to compulsory settlement is so vague and elastic in many countries that the government can prevent the exercise of the freedom to strike whenever it wishes. On the other hand, work stoppages have continued to occur in countries with compulsory settlement systems, even in the economic sectors covered by the legislation, because of either reluctance or inability to enforce the antistrike provisions. The duration of these stoppages is typically rather short, however.

**Investigation.** Investigation, or "fact-finding," is a kind of halfway house between mediation and arbitration. The controversy is referred to a group of distinguished and impartial persons which inquires into the merits of the issues and makes recommendations for settlement. While the recommendations are not binding on the parties, they are intended to serve as the focus of public opinion and of pressure from government authorities, and thereby to pave the way to an agreement.

Compulsory investigation statutes generally cover disputes in essential industries or otherwise affecting the public interest. In some countries a standing tribunal is used, while in others a different board is appointed for each case. It might be noted that for the type of dispute typically covered by these statutes, the term "fact-finding" is something of a misnomer. There are all too many facts in the situation—a welter of conflicting statistics on comparative wage rates, price trends, profit levels, productivity movements, etc. The task of the expert board is to select those facts which it considers most pertinent and call them compellingly to the attention of the public.

Investigation is generally used for the purpose of preventing damaging strikes, but in recent years expert groups have been established in the United Kingdom to advise whether important bargaining agreements will have an inflationary impact. While investigation is generally reserved for the most important cases, it is employed routinely in some countries, such as Canada and India.

**Adjudication.** Adjudication means a mandatory settlement of industrial disputes by courts of justice or administrative tribunals with specialized jurisdiction in the labor–management field. Adjudication is used either for ascertaining the legal rights of the parties under regulatory statutes or for interpreting and applying the terms of collective agreements. The former is exemplified by the National Labor Relations Board in the United States, which makes rulings regarding alleged unfair practices under the Labor–Management Relations Act, and the latter by the "labor courts" which serve as an important element of dispute-settlement machinery in most of the European and Latin American countries.

The line between adjudication and arbitration is not always clear, especially in countries like Australia and New Zealand, where basic terms of employment are set by "courts of arbitration" using formal, legalistic procedures. The difference is that the "labor courts" are interpreting and applying a pre-existing text, such as a collective bargaining agreement or a statute governing minimum wages, while the courts of arbitration are establishing employment conditions to apply in the future and thus in effect are performing a legislative function. But when the same courts of arbitration are called upon to interpret their previous awards, or to settle disputes over the application of collective agreements which have been directly negotiated by the parties, then their functions are indistinguishable from those of a European or Latin American labor court.

### Selected country and regional practices

The foregoing description of dispute-settling mechanisms is necessarily analytical. A review of the practices in a few countries and regions will show how the different techniques are combined into a more or less coherent system reflecting the influence of prevalent ideology, political structure, and industrial experience.

**United States.** In the United States, the principle of unfettered collective bargaining, including recourse to economic pressure, remains strong. The basic ground rules of allowable conduct are set forth in the Labor–Management Relations Act and are enforced by the National Labor Relations Board. But except for protecting unions and employers against unfair practices by the other side, the government leaves them substantial freedom of decision.

For most disputes over agreement provisions, government intervention is limited to the provision of mediation services. These are supplied by approximately three hundred mediators on the staff of the Federal Mediation and Conciliation Service; by numerous state mediation agencies, which tend to handle smaller and more localized situations; and by the National Mediation Board, which has jurisdiction in the railroad and airline industries.

To resolve disputes over the interpretation of collective agreements, the United States has a unique system of private arbitration. About 95 per cent of the agreements provide that grievances which cannot be settled by direct negotiations will be submitted to arbitrators. The binding effect of their decisions is enforced by law because of the previous consent of the parties to be bound. Most arbitrators are practicing attorneys or university professors, although a few dozen are engaged in full-time arbitration practice. Only in the railroad industry does the government supply arbitration services through the National Railroad Adjustment Board.

A limited group of emergency disputes are subject to compulsory investigation before economic pressure may be exercised. Under the Labor–Management Relations Act, a threatened or existing work stoppage which will "imperil the national health or safety" may be enjoined for 80 days. A board of inquiry is appointed by the president and makes a report at the beginning and at the end of the period. The board of inquiry is not permitted to make recommendations, however. This procedure was used in 24 cases between 1947 and 1966. The special procedure for the railroad and airline industries is similar, except that emergency boards do make recommendations for settlement. Finally, a number of state laws provide for compulsory investigation of disputes affecting essential services, such as hospitals and public utilities.

**Canada.** In Canada, dispute-settlement practices resemble those in the United States up to a point. Controversies over bargaining rights are dealt with by the Canadian Labour Relations Board. Collective agreements contain arbitration clauses providing for final arbitration of disputes over their interpretation or application; in fact, federal legislation so requires.

The Industrial Relations and Disputes Investigation Act of 1948, however, provides for much more pervasive intervention than is practiced in the United States. Strikes and lockouts are prohibited until the parties have exhausted the possibilities of mediation and have additionally submitted their case to a special "board of conciliation" appointed by federal authorities. The board of conciliation is actually an investigating body which makes a report and recommendations to the minister of labor. The parties are not permitted to begin a work stoppage until they have considered the report for seven days. This procedure, it should be noted, applies not only to emergency cases but also to the generality of labor disputes. It is widely believed by students of industrial relations that there is excessive government intervention in Canada and that labor and management should be encouraged to discharge their own responsibilities, and take their own risks, in the great majority of cases.

**Sweden.** Dispute-settlement procedures in Sweden represent the greatest reliance on private decision-making processes, and the least involvement of the government, to be found in any major country. Bargaining rights are protected, and the range of allowable activities is defined, not by statute, but by arrangements between the central union and employer federations which date back to 1906.

Conflicts over the terms of collective agreements are unregulated by law, except that mediators may enter into bargaining situations on their own initiative. There is no legislation concerning arbitration and investigation of major disputes, and in fact there have been virtually no work stoppages of any substantial size during recent decades.

Sweden does have a labor court, which has jurisdiction to interpret collective agreements and to rule on alleged violations. Recourse to the labor court has never been very great, and the number of cases declined from 103 in 1945 to 39 in 1960.

**Latin America.** In terms of the degree of state intervention, Latin American countries are at the opposite end of the spectrum from the United States and Sweden. Labor organizations have been oriented principally toward political activity. The tradition of authoritarian management and the persistence of bitterness between social classes have also inhibited the development of stable bargaining relations. In fact, some conditions of work regulated by bargaining agreements in the United States and western Europe (such as paid vacations, holiday pay, and discharge and layoff of workers) are commonly the subject of legislation in Latin America.

In most Latin American countries, strikes and lockouts are prohibited until compulsory mediation procedures have been exhausted. In several countries—including Argentina, Brazil, Ecuador, and Peru—disputes are generally submitted to compulsory arbitration if mediation efforts are unsuccessful.

The resolution of disputes over the application of collective agreements is entrusted to labor courts throughout most of Latin America. In some countries, employers and unions are prohibited from entering into agreements restricting the jurisdiction of the labor courts. In a minority of countries, however, industrial relations have attained a sufficient degree of maturity that the employers and unions have developed their own grievance procedures with the consent and encouragement of government.

**Africa.** Dispute-settlement procedures in the newly independent nations of Africa reflect a number of influences. One is the residue of institutions and practices established during the colonial period. This factor explains some of the differences between English-speaking and French-speaking countries. The British colonial governments endeavored

to promote collective bargaining and voluntary mediation, while those of France emphasized more elaborate legal codes and compulsory mediation and arbitration. A second influence is the weakness of the unions and their dependence on the public authorities. Finally, African governments generally believe that the resource base for economic development is so slim that they cannot afford to permit prolonged and costly work stoppages. Under these circumstances, labor–management relations are subject to stringent regulation in most of the African countries.

ARTHUR M. ROSS

### BIBLIOGRAPHY

BRAUN, KURT 1955 *Labor Disputes and Their Settlement.* Baltimore: Johns Hopkins Press.

INDUSTRIAL RELATIONS RESEARCH ASSOCIATION 1955 *Emergency Disputes and National Policy.* Edited by Irving Bernstein, Harold R. Enarson, and R. W. Fleming. New York: Harper.

INTERNATIONAL LABOUR ORGANISATION 1964 *Industrial Relations in Certain African Countries.* Geneva: The Organisation.

KORNHAUSER, ARTHUR; DUBIN, ROBERT; and ROSS, ARTHUR M. (editors) 1954 *Industrial Conflict.* New York: McGraw-Hill.

ROSS, ARTHUR M.; and HARTMAN, PAUL T. 1960 *Changing Patterns of Industrial Conflict.* New York: Wiley.

STURMTHAL, ADOLF F. (editor) 1957 *Contemporary Collective Bargaining in Seven Countries.* Ithaca, N.Y.: Cornell Univ., Institute of International Industrial and Labor Relations.

## IV
### DEVELOPING COUNTRIES

One characteristic of newly developing regions is the wide diversity of forms of economic organization. Associated with these variations are many different ways of utilizing labor. Typically, labor is self-employed in family enterprises. But there are also various forms of work for others, ranging from primitive forms of group cooperation, through traditional forms of dependency, to wage relationships. Wage labor can be found in traditional agriculture, in handicraft and small workshop activities, and in modern enterprises. These comments are intended to suggest that it is not easy to disentangle all the elements of what might properly be encompassed within the context of labor relations in developing countries.

In order to avoid an overly extended discussion, the present analysis is restricted to labor relations problems in the typically small modern sectors of the economies of the developing countries where enterprise is relatively large and where a substantial number of workers are employed by individual employers. Even with this limitation, the issue is complicated by social, cultural, geographic, and economic variations which distinguish one society from another. Discussion is further complicated by the rapidity of changes in the developing countries and the constant need to experiment with adjustments to the issues arising out of the novel relations between employers, employees, and the state. Enormous diversity and continuous change impose on this brief statement a high degree of abstraction and generalization.

However its productive activities are organized, a traditional society provides few, if any, of the characteristics on which modern types of enterprise depend. The transition to a developing economy with increasing numbers of large business units requires fundamental changes in the existing systems of work relationship. Labor must be recruited; it must be trained to new skills; it must develop responsiveness to new forms of work regulation and to more rigorous standards of performance. Furthermore, it must adjust to a much more structured and bureaucratized system, which is substantially more impersonal than was ever encountered in the traditional order. Typically, these adjustments have to be made in a relatively novel urban environment. Even in socialist economies the relationships are mediated through monetary–market institutions.

Detailed empirical research on this process has tended to be very limited until recently, and even now it is inadequate. Lacking solid evidence, observers tend to assume that because the differences between traditional and modern forms of work were quite great the process of transition from one to the other would be extremely difficult. A not untypical description assumes that labor moves into the modern sector reluctantly, that it is forced into large enterprises by economic and social disabilities in the traditional environment. It is argued that workers tend to retain emotional and social attachments to the traditional sector and view their employment in the modern enterprise as purely temporary. The initial stage of labor relations is seen, therefore, as possessed of specific difficulties because of the still unsevered links with the countryside. This interpretation goes on to suggest that once modernization proceeds to the point that a sizable permanent proletariat appears in the modern sector, labor relations will increasingly assume the typical characteristics which exist in already industrialized countries. Much discussion of employer–employee and employer–trade union relations in newly developing countries tends to evaluate developments according to the extent to which they do or do not move in the direction of already established forms, forms typically Anglo-Saxon in character. There is, in other words, a tendency to assume a unilinear theory of labor relations development not unlike that suggested in Marx's comment in the preface to *Capital* that the "country that is more developed industrially only shows, to the less developed, the image of its own future."

In recent years evidence has been accumulating which suggests that the actual task of creating a disciplined labor force capable of providing for the needs of modern enterprise is not as difficult as the statement of the logical requirements would imply. Difficulties which do arise seem to flow more from the lack of complementary institutions in the society, from the character and pace of development, and from the wage and employment policies of employers rather than from the tradition-bound psychology or social structure of the work force. At the same time, current research suggests that the emerging pattern of labor relations is not likely to follow the example of already developed regions. The industrial relations systems of newly developing countries are being shaped by their contemporary economic and political circumstances more than by the experience and influence of developed countries.

**Labor supply.** It is frequently suggested that modern economic development is retarded by the difficulty of obtaining labor from the traditional sector. Unfortunately, much of the discussion fails to distinguish between the supply of raw, inexperienced labor and the supply of skilled workers. Unquestionably, a society developing new occupations is bound to be short of skills which have never before existed. Lacking adequate or appropriate educational facilities, a newly developing economy will inevitably find it hard to get a satisfactory supply of highly skilled labor. Wages for such labor tend to be high either because labor must be brought in from developed countries or because the competition for the limited supply of indigenous talent is great. This is a major reason why industry in newly developing regions tends to organize activity in such a way as to minimize skill requirements.

On the other hand, there is little evidence that the expansion of modern economic activity has been retarded by the difficulty of recruiting raw labor. In many traditional societies—for example, Japan, China, and India—where economic life was sophisticated and trade and urban life fairly highly developed, a crude but reasonably effective labor market already existed, and thus it was possible from the beginning to generate a labor supply for the new enterprises. In parts of Africa, where even rudimentary market institutions did not exist, the indigenous population had first to be forced into the market via the imposition of taxes which had to be paid in cash. Once this commitment to the commercial sector had been established, the supply of raw labor ceased being a problem. Most evidence we now have suggests that labor supply responds fairly flexibly to monetary incentives in the market place when there are consumer goods on which money wages can be spent. Employer complaints, when carefully examined, typically refer to shortages of skilled labor or to the failure to obtain workers at wage rates lower than the going market rate.

**Instability of the labor force.** Many observers, recognizing that a raw labor force is easily available to new enterprises, still believe that absenteeism and labor turnover in newly developing regions are quite high relative to the situation in developed countries. They suggest that this indicates that the work force is only partially committed to employment in the modern sector. This is an issue for which little unambiguous evidence is available. Absenteeism and turnover data are notoriously imprecise in newly developing regions and tend to exaggerate the phenomena. Impoverished backgrounds, low wages, and the generally inadequate health and housing standards are likely to produce a very high rate of labor instability from medical causes alone. But even when allowance has been made for illness, relatively high absenteeism and turnover rates may still exist. Where economic growth is rapid and new enterprises are multiplying, high turnover rates may only reflect the demand for experienced workers. Apart from this, recent research suggests that high labor turnover is not so much the expression of the worker's desire to return to a traditional way of life or his inability to adjust to modern employment requirements as it is a consequence of the way in which modern enterprises frequently function.

In newly developing regions the demand for the product of many enterprises tends to be quite unstable. Employers, using a very high proportion of unskilled labor, are not concerned with establishing a fixed, identifiable group of workers. Their only interest is that there be available to them an easily accessible pool of workers which can be drawn upon as need dictates. In other words, much of the labor requirement is quite casual. Under such circumstances the individual worker may be forced to sustain a link with the traditional sector wherever he can. Faced with only casual employment in the modern sector, he cannot afford to sever completely his connection with the limited bits of economic and social security he still possesses. It is this which produces the impression that labor has only a tenuous link with large enterprise.

This view is supported by correlations between industries in which employment tends to be unstable or casual and high rates of turnover and absenteeism. For example, in Indian enterprises where activity is reasonably constant and employment fluctuations limited—railways, the steel industry, and many commercial firms—absenteeism and turnover tend to be lower than in industries, such as coal mining and cotton textiles, where demand for labor has fluctuated sharply. In fact, government action which stabilized labor requirements in the Bombay cotton mills after 1947 seems to have been accompanied by marked falls in both turnover and absenteeism. However, even where employment is relatively stable, it may still be impractical for workers to sever their ties with the countryside because the typically desperate shortage of urban housing makes it difficult, if not impossible, for families to accompany them.

Where labor supply is easy and new recruits come into an environment about which they have few, if any, preconceptions, the employer is largely free, subject only to existing legal restraints, to establish the work regulations he deems necessary. The nature of the production processes and factor cost relationships will determine the general form of industrial discipline. In situations where capital per worker is relatively large and processes require considerable skill, regulation is likely to be quite precise and the amount and quality of supervision will be high. Supervisors may have to be foreign or, because they must be literate, will be drawn from higher social classes than those from which the labor force is itself drawn. In the more typical case, where the proportion of unskilled labor is very high, sophisticated and costly supervision is kept to a minimum. Much responsibility can be placed upon essentially illiterate, inexpensive foremen drawn from the same social strata as the work force. As a way of keeping administrative overhead to a minimum, it is not unusual to allow the foreman the effective authority to recruit and discharge workers as well as to supervise and discipline them. As a result, job tenure is even more insecure than it might otherwise be. There can be no effective provisions for leave or promotion, and the application of penalties for work-rule violations tends to be uncertain. The critical feature in such situations is not that regulation and discipline are harsh but that they are erratic and imprecise.

To the outside observer this type of work-force administration, so typical in newly developing regions, may seem irrational, and it frequently leads to charges of poor management. In fact, given the relative price of factors and the level of skills required, such organization makes good economic sense. But it does tend to generate attitudes and behavior patterns within the new work force which may have long-run effects on labor relations.

**Collective action.** Whatever the specific style of labor administration established in new enterprises, one notable fact is that collective action in the form of strikes manifests itself quite early. In many parts of the world strikes have been recorded within a few years after modern industry has been introduced. Many observers see strikes as symptoms of generalized protest by tradition-bound workers against the demands imposed by the modern sector. It would seem more probable, however, that generalized protest against the employment relationship would reveal itself in a flight from the system rather than by strikes within it. The notion that strikes are a protest against the system, a frequently stated but never tested proposition, carries with it the implication that strikes would be most frequent and extensive during the initial phases of development and would decline in number and scope as workers become habituated to modern requirements. The facts seem to indicate the reverse. Insofar as the society permits, strikes tend to become larger and more purposeful and disciplined as the labor force becomes effectively proletarianized.

The suddenness with which protest can manifest itself and the fierceness with which even modest changes are often resisted frequently lead observers to interpret these incidents as essentially irrational. What is ignored is the fact that in regions where underemployment is endemic any effort to modify initially established work relationships, however modest, tends to be seen as a threat to reduce the number of jobs available. Moreover, in the absence of organizational experience on the part of the workers and of familiarity with the formulation of demands, early protest will often take on an unpredictable, riotous character. Careful investigation seems to confirm the view that even the earliest strikes represent an objective commitment to the modern employment relationship in that they are attempts by the work force to share somehow in the decisions affecting it. The immediate causes tend to be the obvious ones—reductions in money wages, sharp rises in the cost-of-living, layoffs, or other changes in existing conditions of work.

As would be expected, the initial stoppages tend to affect a single department or firm. In the absence of formal organization, they also tend to be brief. But the strikes do seem to leave a residue of experience, a sense of capacity for wider collective action. Over time the occasional strike will take on multifirm characteristics, sometimes embracing an entire city or district. But even these incidents tend to be isolated, spontaneous expressions of immediate grievance. They do not arise out of any pre-existing formal or semiformal organization, nor do they necessarily establish the conditions for the development of permanent institutions for collective action.

*Trade union development.* The development of trade unions is a slow process for reasons inherent in the nature of newly emerging societies. The labor force is mainly unskilled, and employers can easily find substitutes for troublesome employees. If modern enterprise is growing rapidly, the work force is constantly being diluted with new recruits who have to develop the sense of common grievance and imbibe the tradition of common action. Where the work force is cosmopolitan, there are internal divisions of language, religion, and regional origin and tradition to be overcome. The traditional environment typically offers no experience with voluntary associations capable of coping with relationships of the modern sort. Moreover, workers usually lack the education that might make easier the task of developing appropriate formal organizations.

These features are not dissimilar to those which once tended to inhibit union development in the now industrialized countries. But workers in newly developing countries face at least one novel disability. Almost from the beginning the structure of enterprise generally requires the use of the industrial union form of organization.

During the early stage of development of the now developed countries, many of the then modern enterprises depended on the use of a relatively high proportion of skilled workers, craftsmen who found it relatively easy to create permanent unions. As large-scale industry based on greater proportions of semiskilled and unskilled labor developed, the craft unions were able to provide the experience and cadres of organizers on which to build industrial unions. Even so, the creation of unions of unskilled and semiskilled workers was not easy. Specific techniques of organization, union administration, tactics, and relations with employers still had to be worked out. The difficulty is illustrated by the fact that even in the United States and Great Britain successful industrial unions did not appear widely until about a century after craft organizations had made their appearance.

By contrast, in newly developing countries the modern sector from the beginning minimizes its use of skilled labor. The stress on the use of unskilled and semiskilled workers is encouraged by the tendencies of modern technology, by the relative costs of skilled and unskilled labor, and by specific advantages in international competition. As a consequence, there is no substantial basis for the development of craft unions. Worker organization logically must be of the industrial type. This simple fact imposes inordinate difficulties on the process of creating stable associations of workers. An industrial union must be larger and is faced by more sophisticated tasks than a craft organization. Its problems of administration as they affect the membership and relations with employers are far more complex. Yet the work force in these new regions, when compared with the early situation in the now developed countries, is far less well prepared to undertake the responsibilities involved. It has fewer potential leaders within its own ranks. Illiteracy is probably much more widespread. There is no indigenous craft union tradition on which to draw. Moreover, much of the skilled labor force that does exist is likely to be foreign. Such a group may have its own traditions of organization, but these are unlikely to be of use to the native work force. Foreign cadres are frequently in supervisory positions. Even where foreign workers are in laboring positions, they are not likely to find their positions and interests linked with those of the indigenous work force. More likely, the foreign group will be actively hostile to the development of a militant, organized native labor force.

**Political elements in labor unrest.** It is possible, of course, if the economic development proceeded and no other factors intervened, that over some very long period the work force might ultimately be able to generate permanent organizations by its own efforts. But in newly developing regions economic responses are not the only important ones. The politics of emergence are equally significant. Most underdeveloped areas have colonial backgrounds, and the struggle for independence is part of the context within which working-class unrest occurs.

Here the role of the "outsider"—typically middle-class professionals and intellectuals—is extremely significant in the development of labor organizations. Middle-class elements have certain obvious advantages when they become involved in this process. They are not employed in the sectors where they seek to organize workers and need not fear the threat of discharge. They can therefore take the risks of leadership. They are frequently well-educated and may have some ideas about the kind of organization that is needed. They typically come from higher social classes than the work

force and are less likely to be intimidated by employers.

There are some countries in which significant economic change begins before a nationalist movement gets under way. In these circumstances middle-class humanitarians may engage in welfare activities among the working class and may occasionally intervene to attempt to resolve problems between workers and their employers. Their efforts sometimes lead them to organize small trade unions, but for all the reasons already suggested these usually prove abortive, having virtually no effect on the industrial relations between workers and employers.

The major impulse which brings middle-class elements into contact with the modern work force in most newly developing regions is the nationalist struggle. Whatever else is at stake, a nationalist movement typically incorporates a protest against the excessively slow pace at which economic development proceeds. The unsatisfactory condition of the work force in the modern sector becomes identified with the colonial and underdeveloped status of the society. If employers are foreign, the problem is directly associated with the evils of imperialist exploitation. Middle-class nationalists quickly identify the effort to organize workers with the more general process of economic improvement, and many of them commit themselves to organizational activity.

The middle-class nationalist sees the issue in a broader context. The workers not only represent a substantial group, but they also tend to be concentrated in urban areas and are frequently engaged in critical economic activities. By virtue of location they seem relatively easy to mobilize; by virtue of function their withdrawal from work can have profound effects on the entire economy. Worker organization offers concentrated political power of great promise.

Middle-class leadership tends to give strikes a wider political meaning, using the incidents as educational devices to sharpen the nationalist struggle in the society. Wage workers, typically frustrated by their limited coercive power at the workplace, tend to respond to these broader appeals. However, the incorporation of worker protest into wider nationalist objectives tends to make it even more difficult to establish any direct collective bargaining relations between employers and employees. Nationalist issues blur the immediate workplace objectives of the employees. Demands tend to be formulated in such ways as to make compromise at the workshop level difficult to attain. Moreover, the incorporation of worker discontent into nationalist channels tends to limit leadership efforts to establish effective plant organization. Activity tends to be oriented toward the establishment of labor movements rather than toward the creation of trade unions narrowly conceived. In other words, middle-class leadership, emerging in the circumstances it does, sharpens labor protest without making it much more effective in any direct confrontation with individual employers.

Labor force restlessness and militance are sharpened if the nationalist movement is not unified but consists of groups with differing long-run sociopolitical objectives. These various groups see in the work force a political prize of great value and contend with one another for its loyalty. Each rivals the other in attempts to exploit the existing economic grievances, and each expands the demands which it encourages workers to make of their employers. Each seeks in this way to capture the political strength of the work force for use in shaping the economic and political character of the nationalist movement and, ultimately, the form of the forthcoming independent society.

Working-class protest in such a context tends to exhibit a profoundly disruptive character. To the existing government these developments inevitably seem to threaten the very fabric of society, particularly if among the contending groups Marxist elements are strong. Employers are unable to stem the tide of unrest. At the same time, because of the way in which developments have occurred, individual trade unions are too weak to impose effective collective bargaining relationships upon the employers. Faced by the failure of effective voluntary industrial relations systems to emerge, the state tends to intervene. The policies adopted will, of course, vary in different areas, depending on the character of the government and its specific objectives.

**State role in employer–employee relations.** Typically, governments are aware of the pattern of events in already developed societies. They are not only conscious of the fact that work-force discontent stems from the relatively weak bargaining position of labor in the employment relationship, but they also sense that such discontent cannot be suppressed entirely. The object of the state is to minimize unrest by providing some framework of formal relationships between employees and employers. If its ideological predisposition is hostile to the development of trade unions, its policy will seek to create a system of facilities—labor courts, wage tribunals, arbitration boards—which will serve to eliminate the need for an institution so

capable of being subverted to political ends. If the government favors the ultimate emergence of stable, responsible (that is, nonrevolutionary) unions and a system of voluntary collective bargaining, its program will still attempt to shape and limit the forms of working-class collective action and organization which are permitted or favored.

Whatever the specific form of its policy, the government has as a major objective the creation in the minds of the workers of a sense of loyalty to the state. Given the persistent weakness of the work force in direct relations with employers, the state is gradually forced to do more than merely open formal channels of protest as a means of reducing dissatisfaction and limiting the violence of its expression. The state finds it necessary to intervene substantively, to provide to the work force the wage–welfare conditions which in Western countries traditionally have been obtained through unions bargaining collectively with employers. To achieve these objectives, state administrative organs gradually develop which interpose themselves between workers and employers. Even where this is not the long-run intention, state intervention tends to inhibit the growth of trade unions because it offers more powerful alternatives. And even where trade unions are encouraged by state policy, they are unable to achieve an independent status; rather they become an essentially dependent feature of a state-dominated and state-defined system of industrial relations.

One striking characteristic of this development is that it does not tend to change very much after independence is achieved. The new government, inheriting a weak trade union structure and a thinly developed pattern of voluntary collective bargaining relationships, like its predecessor is faced by the need to hold the loyalty of the work force. If the new state is to gain working-class support it must seek to expand the apparent contributions it makes to worker well-being. It tends to intervene in increasingly elaborate ways in the relations between employers and employees. Whether the new government is totalitarian or democratic, the tendency is the same. A totalitarian government cannot afford the luxury of independent protest; and in a democratic system the party in power, seeking to remain in power, tends to make use of new and existing administrative devices to tie the unions and the labor movement to itself so as to guarantee its own maintenance in office. The same phenomenon also manifests itself in those countries where a wage working class of the modern sort appears only after independence. In these circumstances the governing group frequently sets out consciously to organize the work force on its own terms and within a framework of its own making so that it can control from the beginning the political consequences of economic conflict.

But it is not only the political significance of a modern work force that leads to government intervention in newly developing regions. At least one other major factor strengthens the state's effort to minimize the rough-and-tumble of independent collective bargaining. Almost invariably, the new state is committed to a program of economic development on a planned basis. The modern work force is located at strategic points in the national economy. In these circumstances the state feels unable to tolerate the luxury of sharp and extended conflicts between workers and employers. To permit these might prove disruptive to all hopes of rapid economic development. The state, therefore, intervenes to establish or extend a system of regulations which defines the process and content of industrial relations between employees and employers.

By way of summary the following conclusions can be suggested. In most newly developing regions trade unions are extremely weak and collective bargaining virtually nonexistent. For all the reasons suggested, the state intervenes in labor relations to channel and control working-class discontent before it gets out of hand. Where trade unions and a labor movement have not emerged before independence, the state will typically move to establish and direct them and their activities. Where working-class organizations have appeared at an earlier stage, the state will increasingly regulate their form and the content of relations with employers. In either case, the state will gradually create a system of rules and a structure of administrative bodies that define and to an increasing extent direct the permissible limits of behavior of workers and employers. The role of the state and its agencies will become so pervasive as to inhibit the growth of strong independent worker organizations and vital collective relations with employers.

This tendency is not a temporary one. It shapes the long-run character of all the labor relations institutions of a newly developing region. Consequently, we cannot envisage the ultimate emergence in the developing countries of private collective bargaining institutions of the sort familiar to the Anglo-Saxon world. What is more important is that we should not interpret this phenomenon as a distortion of some normal, unilinear evolutionary pattern. The problems generated by the emergence of a wage labor force are inevitable, but the form of the solution will vary in accord with historical circumstances. The Anglo-Saxon format of labor

relations emerged in a special political, economic, and technical environment. Newly developing regions are modernizing their economies and creating a proletariat within a quite novel economic and political setting. The system of labor and industrial relations that is emerging in these areas must, therefore, inevitably exhibit systematically different features of the sort described above.

MORRIS DAVID MORRIS

### BIBLIOGRAPHY

*The literature of any quality on trade unions, labor movements, and industrial relations in newly developing regions dates mainly from 1945. The amount of this literature is constantly increasing. Any attempt to provide detailed references would be quickly outdated. The best way to keep up with current facts and views is through the quite systematic bibliographies provided in the issues of the* International Labour Review *and the* Industrial and Labor Relations Review.

GALENSON, WALTER (editor) 1959 *Labor and Economic Development.* New York: Wiley.

GALENSON, WALTER (editor) 1962 *Labor in Developing Economies.* Berkeley: Univ. of California Press.

*Industrial and Labor Relations Review.* → Published since 1947.

*International Labour Review.* → Published since 1921.

KERR, CLARK et al. 1960 *Industrialism and Industrial Man: The Problems of Labor and Management in Economic Growth.* Cambridge, Mass.: Harvard Univ. Press. → A second edition was published in paperback in 1964 by Oxford University Press.

MORRIS, MORRIS DAVID 1965 *The Emergence of an Industrial Labor Force in India: A Study of the Bombay Cotton Mills, 1854–1947.* Berkeley and Los Angeles: Univ. of California Press.

ROBERTS, B. C. 1964 *Labour in the Tropical Territories of the Commonwealth.* Durham, N.C.: Duke Univ. Press.

# LABOR THEORY OF VALUE

*See* VALUE, LABOR THEORY OF.

# LABOR UNIONS

## I
### THEORIES OF THE LABOR MOVEMENT

There are three principal groups currently developing theories of unionism. The communist group, primarily located in the Soviet Union, is concerned with how unions can increase productivity in communist societies. To them unions are workers' morale agencies, and it seems irrelevant whether the state or the plant management (*in loco* employer) dominates the organization.

Most Western neoclassical economists who are concerned with unions focus on the effects that worker-controlled monopolies will have on factor prices, levels of employment, labor mobility, technological change, and profits. Hence they view unions as logical constructs, units intent on maximizing gains for all or only some of their members —much as a business firm (also a construct) is supposed to operate. They are not usually interested in exploring the forces that bring unions into being and keep them operating effectively.

The third group includes most of the well-known Western labor union theorists. They attempt to explain workers' historical behavior regarding wages, hours, working conditions, and job rights by answering all or most of four questions: (1) Why did unions come into existence? (2) How do unions choose their goals and tactics? (3) What explains varying individual worker attitudes toward unions? (4) What is the impact of national cultural and legal experience on worker organizations? In other words, these writers study the historical records of institutions.

Each of these three groups is discussed separately below—the third group first because chronologically it first developed the bulk of labor union theory.

### The Western historical tradition

Originally the central questions about unions were why and how socially inferior bargaining groups managed to redistribute wealth and gain recognition. Answers were first furnished by theologians and philosophers, historians and economists. Later, as the newer disciplines of psychology and sociology developed, they, too, influenced the analysis of unionism. All had in common an interest in the dynamic nature of workers' group identification and organization. I have discussed the relationship of the disciplines to the theories more fully elsewhere (M. Perlman 1958).

**The revolutionaries.**  In the western European tradition, interest in union theory stemmed originally from the study of Marx's law of historical materialism. From it was fashioned a theory of revolutionary unionism which, in its many forms, is based on a supposedly scientific understanding of the historical process. Technological advances change the relationships between the bourgeois or property-holding classes and the working or propertyless classes. Inevitably the bourgeoisie, motivated by profits, exploits the workers, and workers

frequently retaliate by forming unions. Thus, the proximate cause of class conflict is bourgeois exploitation of the workers, which in turn is caused by technological change.

What a specific union does in a given situation depends upon its leaders' appreciation of the historical process. Unions that further the revolutionary ends of the working class are considered to be acting wisely. Unions that accede to the demands of bourgeois employers or that temporize with their revolutionary purpose, perhaps because of misleadership, are thought to be useless and undeserving of historical sanction. Only the socialist theorist, who can comprehend the full historical consequences of a given act, can be trusted to judge what is good and bad. These theorists consider any union leader who tries to make peace with a bourgeois employer to be a "faker" or class traitor.

According to this philosophy, unionism is a useful device in the workers' class war against the bourgeoisie. But when a socialist society is achieved, the role of unionism is indistinct. Some Marxist writers believe that the workers' organizations should not materially change their personalities. Others, discussed below, believe that a whole new set of objectives is essential.

Two discordant elements of the revolutionary theory stand out: its teleological nature and its dependence upon "proper" understanding of the historical process. The former gives certainty and confidence in the future. The latter creates dissension among the theorists since any human action or program, regardless of the alleged motives involved, encourages speculations about the "real" consequences. Advocates of the revolutionary theory have therefore each tended to give his own interpretation of the historical meaning of any action. These writers can be divided into three general categories: the right wing, the left wing, and the anarcho–syndicalists (M. Perlman 1958, chapter 3).

The right-wing theorists embrace political gradualism, like Bernsteinian revisionism. They agree that unions should represent the class interest of all workers (including particularly the less skilled) and should keep a steady economic pressure on employers for improved benefits and for the peaceful nationalization of industry. They advocate industrial unionism on the economic front (unions organized by industries or by geographic areas) and a labor party embracing gradualism on the political front. Where unions have become craft-particularistic, right-wing theorists urge constant education or "boring from within" to reorient them to their true historical purpose. The best-known American theorists in this tradition were such American Federation of Labor (AFL) socialist–pragmatists as Max Hayes, Nahum I. Stone, Victor Berger, and Norman J. Ware. All agreed that in the American context, craft-particularistic unions were ideologically misled, but nevertheless historically legitimate, representatives of the working class.

The left-wing theorists saw unions sometimes as the "protecting shield" and sometimes as the "avenging sword" of the working class. To them the particularistic craft unions, which they believed all AFL constituent organizations to be, were traitors to the working class and to the *deus ex machina* of history. Despairing of changing the AFL unions, this group formed "dual unions." Among the American leaders in this tradition were Daniel De Leon and William Z. Foster; both advocated political action and urged the development of aggressive, socialist-dominated unions as the main revolutionary instrument in bourgeois society.

The third or anarcho–syndicalist subcategory is often confused with the left-wing revolutionaries because both groups urged violence in bourgeois societies. Although both opposed craft-particularistic unions, they differed in their interpretation of the teleological nature of Marxism and of historical causation. The anarcho–syndicalists, lacking faith in the inevitability of the historical process, urged sabotage, duplicity in dealing with employers and public officials, assassination, and physical violence to bring about the disorder which they believed essential for the development of true freedom. The best-known American theorists in this group were William Trautmann, Vincent St. John, and William D. Haywood.

The impact of such revolutionary theorizing has not been great in the United States. Many of the egalitarian and social welfare programs advocated by the revolutionaries, particularly the right wing, have become part of American public policy. However, these changes were not brought about by the realignment of class structure which the revolutionaries considered essential to the fruition of their plans.

**The historical empiricists.** Although the Marxians raised questions providing the most intriguing discussion, Sidney and Beatrice Webb used analytical methods that were the most widely admired. They went beyond the old Marxian question of why history should be dominated by worker organizations and asked how British workers had historically formed their organizations. The Webbs's theory involved a new social science method, combining the patient fact collection of the German historical school with cautious, bit-at-a-time analy-

sis. Their labor union theory was based on British labor history but goes beyond the recording of its facts to present generalizations. Since the Webbs were among the earliest British Fabians, it is not surprising to discover that their intellectual method incorporated political norms.

The Webbs noted that British unionism had, over time, developed several doctrines, each in response both to the workers' desire to form their own continuous associations for improving wages, hours, and working conditions and to the key institutional features of a particular time (1897). Initially, when unions were small, weak, and at the mercy of employers and unsympathetic judges, workers embraced the self-interested doctrine of vested interests. They used the "method of mutual insurance," implying mutual help within the workers' group according to the self-insurance principle. The group was kept small in order to enhance job opportunity, and just large enough to spread the risk.

Later, as unions became stronger, successful attempts were made at bargaining with employers. In these instances the doctrine of vested interest was replaced by a market-price oriented "doctrine of [equilibration of] supply and demand." The method of mutual insurance gave way to a newer "method of collective bargaining." This was a bilateral arrangement which postulated worker solidarity but which could produce the flexibility sought by workers intent on improving their collective lot. The great shortcoming of this type of unionism was its parochialism—it gave benefits to the strong, that is, to those needing help the least.

Ultimately, the Webbs believed, unions would turn to a third, broader theory, namely a "doctrine of the living wage," applying to all workers, not just to the strong among them (S. Webb 1918). This doctrine would be presented through the "method of legal enactment," which was national in scope and parliamentary in means.

The Webbs favored the third doctrine as well as the third method. Indeed, so strong was their endorsement of these that there is a danger of assuming that they deprecated the others. On the contrary, they implicitly noted the usefulness of both the other methods and at least the doctrine of supply and demand. Even in a socialist state there would be a need for workers in advanced and profitable industries to bargain bilaterally with employers so that new and higher standards could be set where economically possible.

The burden of the Webbs's normativism fell on their moral condemnation of what they considered to be an all-too-frequent union device, restriction of numbers—restricted entry into the trade and the union (S. Webb 1919). They condemned it as parochial, selfish, and inefficient. Rather, they endorsed another device, "the common rule," a minimum working standard.

It is hard to overemphasize the impact of the Webbs's work. It was soundly based on fact, where the earlier Marxian thinking was conjectural history at best. It advocated reasonable evolution where some Marxists suggested violent revolution. And most important, it did not present a teleological face, which practical men distrust.

The Webbs have had severe critics. Some have pointed out the influence of their inarticulated norms, namely a moral commitment to social efficiency (S. Perlman 1928); others have noted their anticapitalistic (anti-free-market) orientation (Cummings 1899); and some have even seen a coloring of history in their selection of episodes. Nevertheless, their monumental studies provided the groundwork for most of the later labor union theory. [*See* WEBB, SIDNEY AND BEATRICE.]

Although there were several earlier American theorists of the labor movement, the impact of the Webbs's work on John R. Commons and his subsequent reformulation of it mark the beginning of the most important American school. Using the Webbs's research techniques, Commons and his students at the University of Wisconsin fashioned a general Spiethoffian theory of the development of the labor movement. It is built in large part on extending the concept of private property to include job rights and on analysis of the effects of geographical expansion of the product market on factor-market (particularly wage) relationships.

Commons believed that unionism was a protective device for social and economic inferiors, who had to be protected from the impersonal rigorousness of the market. He took care to point out that this impersonality was caused by the growth of the market (leading to transactions between strangers) and by technological change. Commons did not believe in natural harmony; unlike the Webbs he had little hope for the development of social consensus on economic matters. Rather, he put his faith in the functioning of countervailing large groups, which he thought would be able to fashion acceptable modi vivendi with good faith and a modicum of luck. [*See the biography of* COMMONS.]

**Contemporary theorists.**    The best-known (and the most controversial) theory of labor unions was presented by Selig Perlman, who was Commons' student and collaborator and the first holder of the John R. Commons chair in economic research at the University of Wisconsin (where both Commons

and he did most of their academic work). Perlman, a Russian-Jewish *emigré*, had in his youth been a Social Democratic *Bundist* (a Jewish right-wing Marxian socialist). Commons' influence on his thinking led him to shed his earlier Marxian conclusions. In the Commons–Perlman approach, unions are considered to have an importance in the western European democratic social structure quite apart from their ability to raise wages and improve working conditions. Unionism is the technique by which workers band together to secure social and industrial rights. Having secured these rights, workers use unions to protect themselves from the effects of market competition, which through history has been intensified by the growth of markets (bringing once separate communities into direct economic competition) and changes in production techniques (resulting in competition among the workers in any one area). Thus unionism has both an offensive and a defensive characteristic, but invariably it was intended to promote the social interests of its membership rather than the needs of an abstract "working class." The Commons–Perlman approach to unionism devolved from a study of historical records showing how specific groups of workingmen sought to protect their jobs. These records were found in court trials for conspiracy and in the development of job customs or working rules in particular trades and industries.

According to Commons and Perlman, the older a union gets the more it tends to draw on its own historical experience. It tends to rely upon the "common will" as interpreted by union leaders. Consequently, unions are reluctant to follow the advice, however well intentioned, of outside sympathizers and experts. Unions generally attempt hegemony over only a limited job territory, having discovered by experience what limits are most effective. In Anglo-American countries, unions pursue policies intended to create property rights in job possession similar to those already guaranteed to ownership of real estate and chattels.

Although there are some differences between Commons' and Perlman's ideas, it is erroneous to think that the two men were ever in conflict. However, it must be realized that Commons, unlike Perlman, was not particularly interested in developing a general theory of unionism.

Perlman's theory drew heavily on the historical generalizations of Max Weber and Werner Sombart. From Sombart he took an appreciation of the role of psychology in explaining both the *Zeitgeist* and the individual's reactions to changes in economic opportunities.

Perlman took care to define the confines of

worker group loyalty because he did not believe that in the American context there was any "class" loyalty as such. Rather, the ambit of such loyalty was set by the manual workers' innate fear of factor-market competition for the job. Perlman's phrase "dynamic job-consciousness" sought to explain the changes made by technology and market expansion in a once tightly defined craft concept of job ownership. The "manual worker" (an ideal type in the Weberian tradition) was the key to Perlman's theory of unionism. These workers, he felt, were willing to trade a purported freedom of contract for a small share of the collective voice controlling job ownership because they had little faith in their ability to survive in the junglelike factor market in which they sold their services. Perlman emphasized that the diffusion of wealth, and unfavorable worker experience with industrial self-government, made American workers and labor movements reluctant to embrace abstract social experiments like socialism (S. Perlman 1928). Later in his life, after the Nazi holocaust, Perlman added that even mature labor movements appeared unable to resist highly nationalistic leaders; indeed, they did not always try. At no time was he sanguine about colonial labor movements' abilities to resist the appeals of nationalistic or socialistic reformers. [*See the biography of* PERLMAN.]

The traditional Marxians, the Webbs, Commons, and Perlman had much in common in their labor movement theories. Each tried to explain the development of the labor movements of western Europe, North America, and Australasia. Where Marx had first asked "why organization?", the Webbs added "how does organization work?" Commons and, particularly, Perlman reformulated the basic questions to "under what conditions will a labor movement develop, and what specific rational and historical factors shape its development?"

There have been several vigorous criticisms of the Wisconsin theory. Some have disliked its selection of the parochial, American ideal-type union, with its limited social objectives, arguing that Perlman "liked" or "approved" of that type of union's particularism (see Hardman 1950; Laski 1948, pp. 221–222; 1950, pp. 37–40; Sturmthal 1953; Gulick 1948, vol. 1, pp. 294–297, 300 ff.; Gulick & Bers 1953). Others have felt that the theory was applicable only to nonexpanding industries (Meyer & Conrad 1957) or to already industrialized and capitalistic societies (Kerr & Siegel 1955).

Criticism from the last point of view has resulted in several interesting discussions, most of which are not presented as formal theories. Two of these were written by John T. Dunlop. The first (1948)

summarized both the questions earlier theorists had discussed and what he thought were the shortcomings of their work. He argued that individual theorists had neglected some of the dynamic economic roles in the development of the labor movement played by changing technology, product-market and factor-market forces, public opinion, and the government. Subsequently Dunlop (1958) further clarified his dissatisfaction with labor movement theory. The key to this analysis is an interest in the process by which production and distribution decisions are made by firms within society and by society itself (cf. Moore 1960). He relegated the labor movement to a role somewhat different from the one that had become traditional. Unlike earlier writers who viewed the labor movement partly as a political and social force, Dunlop directed his attention exclusively to the processes of decision making in the allocation of labor. Consequently, unionism in his framework varies in importance among countries and requires a subtheory of labor movements. Where unions play an important industrial role (for example, in bipartite collective bargaining), their significance is great; where they play only a political role, their significance is less.

## Communist tradition

At the turn of the century, in response to public opinion, the tsarist government attempted to set up "legal unions," which anticipated both Italian fascist unions and American company unions. As substitutes for genuine unionism these organizations were not successful, and in 1905 the Soviet of the Workers Deputies of St. Petersburg was founded. In October of 1905, at the time of the granting of a constitution, the first Russian Trade Union Conference was held, made up of 26 Moscow unions and 10 from other localities. With the failure of the Russian revolution of 1905, the reactionary government reasserted its authority, and in 1907 the police claimed to have disbanded 107 unions and exiled or imprisoned their leaders.

In March 1917 the Petrograd soviet reappeared in the central role and, together with revolutionary soldiers, declared a strike. The following month 82 such local soviets were represented at the first Soviet Conference meeting in Petrograd. Two months later a Russian Trade Union Conference was held whose 220 delegates represented a total membership of nearly 1.5 million workers. Within the organization there was a strong Menshevik, or Social Democratic, opposition. Bolshevik leadership was far from assured of support from the renascent older trade unions. From this distrust of the older group emerged both the Leninist policy toward unions and, later, the Leninist theory of unions. Lenin made an important speech in January 1919. His views were later circulated in 1921 and appeared as "The Task of the Trade Unions." Lenin was concerned with the deterioration of factory equipment during World War I, which aggravated the country's previous backwardness. He sought to improve production facilities and wanted the unions to abandon all policies which directly or indirectly hindered production. In both his 1919 speech and his reformulated views, he endorsed Taylorism, or scientific management.

Taylorism as Lenin knew it gave the workers virtually no voice in the handling of industrial problems. Nonetheless, Lenin sought to provide a place for union activity in the general framework of a scientifically managed industrial system. Trade unions were to discipline the workers, on the one hand, and be a quasi-public watchdog over managerial efficiency, on the other. The union was to minimize production loss and eliminate discrimination against particular workers, rather than improve wages generally or even improve working conditions for the workers in a given plant or area.

After Lenin's death the government union system, which Lenin originally urged, was taken up by Leon Trotsky. Trotsky wanted the state to control and eventually absorb all unions. He was opposed by Michael Tomsky and the functional leaders of the trade unions. Up to the time of his dismissal as head of the trade union's executive committee in 1929, Tomsky held strongly that the unions should occupy an independent place in the development of industrial policy. A third or middle view, popular within the party itself, held that the union should be apparently independent but actually controlled by party cells within it.

With the gradual sidetracking of Trotsky following Lenin's death, the first view ceased to be an important issue. The second view, Tomsky's, obtained until the New Economic Policy (NEP) yielded to the first five-year plan. Thereafter the third, or party, plan became official.

Under the NEP there was a tripartite control arrangement with three supposedly equal parties: the plant manager, representatives of the local unions, and representatives of the party. The manager was usually chosen by the party, and the leaders of the local unions were chosen by popular acclamation—which in practice also meant by the party. This troika arrangement continued for some time. Yet it is clear that by 1930 the unions had ceased to count; plant managers were in fact in unchallenged charge of all plant activity, and the trade unions had lost their voice in policy determi-

nation. By World War II the unions themselves seemed to have become primarily interested in increasing productivity through the Stakhanovite and the Udarniki movements. They were also concerned with providing rest resorts for deserving workers and the processing of a few types of grievances against unpopular plant managers. The best-known theorists of Soviet unionism have been Lenin and A. Lozovskii, who became the party's semiofficial spokesman. [See the biographies of LENIN and TROTSKY.]

## The neoclassical approach

Although most neoclassical economists have concentrated on the economic effects of wages and of particular union policies, such as strikes and secondary boycotts, several have also written on union power to affect the rate of technological change within the firm and the right of licensure (entry to the trade) [see LICENSING, OCCUPATIONAL; see also Hicks 1932; Friedman 1962]. Until fairly recently the typical neoclassical analysis of unions concentrated upon the conditions under which a union would raise the wages of its membership at the expense of employers or other workers (Simons 1944; Machlup 1952). Now, however, attention has turned to the various alternative goals which unions can maximize. These include wage rates, wage payments, and employment levels as possible goals of the membership as a whole or of a dominant (even if minor) fraction of the membership. Moreover, these models admit a different selection of goals by a given union at different stages of the business cycle and during different phases of a long-term technological development. Different assumptions are also made about the price elasticity of demand for the product, and there has been recognition of the importance of treating each firm within an industry differently for tactical reasons. Finally, the impact of tax provisions, among other factors, leads to different types of wage payments —as in the case of pensions and nontaxable services such as health benefits [see WAGES, article on FRINGE BENEFITS; see also Dunlop 1944; Cartter 1959; Pen 1950; and Rees 1962].

The recent emphasis on statistical measurement has increased our knowledge of the effects of unionization on wage rates [see LABOR UNIONS, article on INFLUENCE ON WAGES]. Some economists have held that the gains made by one group of workers have been offset by a rise in prices or by a decline in the earnings or employment of others (Friedman 1962). Other writers, not necessarily rejecting that finding, have emphasized the "possible" result; one "guesses" that the "average effects of all American unions on the wages of their members in recent years will lie somewhere between 10 and 15%" (Rees 1962, p. 79).

One of the best summaries of the neoclassical position concludes simply that the direct effect of unions on the economy is detrimental but that the total social effect of unions (going beyond considerations of prices, wages, and the allocation of resources) turns the conclusion on its head (Rees 1962, pp. 194–195). This judgment, however, merely reflects the dichotomy within the field of Western labor union theory. One group of theorists approaches the topic from the institutional and historical position, while the other approaches it from the standpoint of economic theory.

MARK PERLMAN

### BIBLIOGRAPHY

ALEXANDER, ROBERT J. 1962 *Labor Relations in Argentina, Brazil, and Chile.* New York: McGraw-Hill.

BAUDER, RUSSELL S. 1943 Three Interpretations of the American Trade Union Movement. *Social Forces* 22:215–224.

CARTTER, ALLAN M. 1959 *Theory of Wages and Employment.* Homewood, Ill.: Irwin.

COMMONS, JOHN R. (1899–1913) 1913 *Labor and Administration.* New York: Macmillan. → Contains essays and speeches previously published in various publications.

COMMONS, JOHN R. 1919 *Industrial Goodwill.* New York: McGraw-Hill.

CROCE, BENEDETTO (1900) 1922 *Historical Materialism and the Economics of Karl Marx.* London: Allen & Unwin; New York: Macmillan. → First published as *Materialismo storico ed economica marxistica.*

CUMMINGS, E. A. 1899 A Collectivist Philosophy of Trade Unionism. *Quarterly Journal of Economics* 13:151–186.

[DRIDZO, SOLOMON A.] (1934) 1942 *Marx and the Trade Unions,* by A. Lozovskii [pseud.]. New York: International Publishers. → First published as *Karl Marks i profsoiuzy.*

DUNLOP, JOHN T. (1944) 1950 *Wage Determination Under Trade Unions.* New York: Kelley.

DUNLOP, JOHN T. 1948 The Development of Labor Organization: A Theoretical Framework. Pages 163–193 in Richard A. Lester and Joseph Shister (editors), *Insights Into Labor Issues.* New York: Macmillan.

DUNLOP, JOHN T. (1949) 1953 *Collective Bargaining: Principles and Cases.* Rev. ed. Homewood, Ill.: Irwin.

DUNLOP, JOHN T. 1958 *Industrial Relations Systems.* New York: Holt.

FRIEDMAN, MILTON 1962 *Capitalism and Freedom.* Univ. of Chicago Press.

GULICK, CHARLES A. 1948 *Austria From Hapsburg to Hitler.* 2 vols. Berkeley: Univ. of Calif. Press. → Volume 1: *Labor's Workshop of Democracy.* Volume 2: *Fascism's Subversion of Democracy.*

GULICK, CHARLES A.; and BERS, MELVIN K. 1953 Insight and Illusion in Perlman's *Theory of the Labor Movement. Industrial and Labor Relations Review* 6:510–531.

HARDMAN, J. B. S. (1950) 1951 From "Job-consciousness" to Power Accumulation. Pages 146–157 in Industrial Relations Research Association, *Proceedings of Third Annual Meeting.* Chicago: The Association.

HICKS, JOHN R. (1932) 1964 *The Theory of Wages.* New York: St. Martins.

KERR, CLARK; and SIEGEL, ABRAHAM 1955 The Structuring of the Labor Force in Industrial Society: New Dimensions and New Questions. *Industrial and Labor Relations Review* 8:151–168.

KERR, CLARK et al. 1960 *Industrialism and Industrial Man: The Problems of Labor and Management in Economic Growth.* Cambridge, Mass.: Harvard Univ. Press. → A second edition was published in paperback in 1964 by the Oxford University Press.

LASKI, HAROLD J. 1948 *The American Democracy: A Commentary and an Interpretation.* New York: Viking.

LASKI, HAROLD J. 1950 *Trade Unions in the New Society.* London: Allen & Unwin.

LENIN, VLADIMIR I. (1902) 1961 What Is to Be Done? Volume 5, pages 347–529 in Vladimir I. Lenin, *Collected Works.* 4th ed. Moscow: Foreign Languages Publishing House. → First published as *Chto delat'?*.

LENIN, VLADIMIR I. (1919) 1921 Scientific Management and Dictatorship of the Proletariat. Pages 177–199 in John R. Commons (editor), *Trade Unionism and Labor Problems: Second Series.* Boston and New York: Ginn. → First published in Russian.

LENIN, VLADIMIR I. (1921) 1945 The Task of the Trade Unions. Volume 23, pages 503–518 in Vladimir I. Lenin, *Collected Works.* New York: International Publishers. → First published in Russian.

MACHLUP, FRITZ 1952 *The Political Economy of Monopoly: Business, Labor and Government Policies.* Baltimore: Johns Hopkins Press.

MEYER, JOHN R.; and CONRAD, ALFRED H. 1957 Economic Theory, Statistical Inference and Economic History. *Journal of Economic History* 17:524–544.

MOORE, WILBERT E. 1960 Notes for a General Theory of Labor Organization. *Industrial and Labor Relations Review* 13:387–397.

PEN, JAN (1950) 1959 *The Wage Rate Under Collective Bargaining.* Cambridge, Mass.: Harvard Univ. Press. → First published as *De loonvorming in de moderne volkshuishouding.*

PERLMAN, MARK 1958 *Labor Union Theories in America: Background and Development.* Evanston, Ill.: Row, Peterson.

PERLMAN, MARK 1960 Labor Movement Theories: Past, Present, and Future. *Industrial and Labor Relations Review* 13:338–348.

PERLMAN, SELIG (1922) 1950 *A History of Trade Unionism in the United States.* New York: Kelley.

PERLMAN, SELIG (1928) 1949 *The Theory of the Labor Movement.* New York: Kelley.

REDER, MELVIN W. 1960 Job Scarcity and the Nature of Union Power. *Industrial and Labor Relations Review* 13:349–362.

REES, ALBERT 1962 *The Economics of Trade Unions.* Univ. of Chicago Press.

SIMONS, HENRY (1944) 1948 Some Reflections on Syndicalism. Pages 121–159 in Henry Simons, *Economic Policy for a Free Society.* Univ. of Chicago Press. → First published in Volume 52, No. 1 of the *Journal of Political Economy.*

STURMTHAL, ADOLF 1953 *Unity and Diversity in European Labor: An Introduction to Contemporary Labor Movements.* Glencoe, Ill.: Free Press.

TAFT, PHILIP 1952 Theories of the Labor Movement. Pages 1–38 in Industrial Relations Research Association, *Interpreting the Labor Movement*. Madison, Wis.: The Association.

Webb, Sidney 1918 *The Works Manager To-day: An Address Prepared for a Series of Private Gatherings of Works Managers*. London: Longmans.

Webb, Sidney 1919 *National Finance and a Levy on Capital: What the Labour Party Intends*. London: Fabian Society.

Webb, Sidney 1920 *The Root of Labour Unrest: An Address to Employers and Managers*. London: Fabian Society.

Webb, Sidney; and Webb, Beatrice (1897) 1920 *Industrial Democracy*. New ed. London and New York: Longmans.

**II**

**LABOR MOVEMENTS AND COLLECTIVE BARGAINING IN EUROPE**

Trade unionism is a child of industrialization; therefore it is not surprising that the country that pioneered in industrial development, Great Britain, was also among the first to develop modern trade unions. No attempt will be made here to retrace the history of unionism in Great Britain or elsewhere. However, some general considerations regarding the development of unionism are appropriate.

When trade unions first arose in the Western world they were regarded everywhere as criminal organizations; even if their existence was tolerated most of their activities were unlawful. The difficult stage of early industrialization was, therefore, passed by most Western nations without the intervention of effective unions. The British Combination Acts of 1800, the Loi Le Chapelier of 1791 in France, and the fairly general prohibition of unions until late in the nineteenth century in the countries that later formed Germany are examples of this proscription.

## Union–political party relations

The growth of unions, since this first stage, has followed widely different courses in different parts of the world. On the Continent, unionism typically developed as part of a wider labor movement, with a political party of the workers usually taking the lead. Frequently the party organized the unions and provided them with leadership. In view of the low educational level of the workers, the extremely long hours of work, and the low incomes on the Continent at the time when unions came into being, it is doubtful whether labor organizations could have been formed at the time without the active participation of political leaders who were, for the most part, intellectuals. Moreover, the effective defense of the workers' interests at the time encompassed far more than the specialized activities of unions. Throughout the Continent, workers

were denied equality of status as citizens, in education, and in the life of the community in general. To meet the demand of the workers for political, social, and cultural equality, as well as to make the unions effective instruments for the attainment of the economic objectives of their members, a wider labor movement was required, of which the unions formed a part. The political organization was most commonly the elite of the movement, and the unions accepted party guidance. It seemed obvious that only a profound transformation of the social and political system would permit an improvement of the worker's standard of living and the attainment of his full status as a citizen and a human being. This transformation had to be brought about primarily by the party. Moreover, the long-run situation on the labor market made collective bargaining an effective device for skilled workers only. Underemployment in agriculture was constantly being created, or at least was a threat, because of technological advances; and the actual or potential weight of this supply of unskilled labor greatly impaired the bargaining power of unskilled groups. This fact, too, tended to make political action appear relatively more promising than collective bargaining.

Political control of the unions led in many countries to politically divided labor movements, since different political parties established competitive unions. Until World War II the predominant current was socialist; Christian (mostly Roman Catholic), nationalist, democratic, and at times communist organizations represented the main minority groups. In Scandinavia, however, the socialist blue-collar unions remained almost without competition. French syndicalism, primarily representing skilled workers, rejected political control of the unions; indeed, the syndicalists regarded any political activity as futile. But after the decline of syndicalism, the Communist party assumed the leadership of the strongest trade union federation, the Confédération Générale du Travail (CGT).

Starting under political guidance, the unions gradually acquired more status within the labor movement as industrialization progressed. Education was provided for leaders arising in increasing numbers from the working class. Union membership rose and with it union funds and prestige. While retaining their basic political philosophy, the unions claimed and obtained equality of status with the party. The Mannheim agreement of 1906 in Germany is one example of this shift in relative weight. In Great Britain, the evolution proceeded from a different starting point. Unions of skilled workers, rejecting social reform ideas and concentrating on bread and butter issues, arose after the failure of the Chartist reform movement. These "business unions" dominated the movement until attempts at organizing unskilled workers were successful in the last two decades of the century. This introduced socialist—although non-Marxian—ideas into the labor movement. A major court decision, the Taff Vale case, which endangered the effective operations of the unions, greatly increased the unions' support of the organization of the Labour party. This party was thus essentially a creation of the unions, and for a long time it remained primarily their political instrument—the political branch of the movement. These differences in the origin of unions and party have lost most of their former significance. Different systems of union–party relations remain. In Great Britain and some parts of Scandinavia, unions are collectively affiliated with the Labour party or the Social Democratic party of their country. Union members pay a "political levy" along with their union dues, unless, as they may do in Britain, they "contract out," i.e., state in writing their refusal to do so. In other countries union leaders are at the same time party leaders; in a formal or informal way, the union federation is represented on the party executive and vice versa. At the other extreme is the tradition of the French "Charter of Amiens"—nowadays often honored in the breach—which, following the syndicalist ideas, requires complete separation of unions and parties.

### International labor organizations

The problem of union–party relations has also affected the life of the international organizations of labor. The early international socialist congresses were at the same time international trade union gatherings. Separate international union organizations arose first under the name of international trade secretariats. These were associations of unions of the same craft or industry. The typographical unions were the first to establish their international association in 1889, followed by the miners and others, so that by the turn of the century almost thirty of them were operating. The national trade union centers—federations of unions of different crafts or industries in the same country—held their first independent international gathering in Copenhagen in 1901. They established a small international secretariat, whose administration was entrusted to the German trade unions, then the leading labor movement of the world. The activities, however, were modest and purely technical as the unions continued to accept in policy matters the leadership of the socialist parties and

of their international. This aroused the protest first of the syndicalists in the French CGT and later of the American Federation of Labor, which joined the secretariat after an exploratory visit by Samuel Gompers in 1909. Under their combined pressure, the international secretariat was renamed the International Federation of Trade Unions (IFTU) in 1913, and its activities were gradually expanded. This development was interrupted by World War I. When the IFTU was reconstituted in Amsterdam in 1919, the AFL withdrew, primarily because of the "revolutionary principle" to which the organization, in Gompers' view, was now committed. Instead, the AFL turned increasingly toward collaboration with Latin American unions. Shortly before World War II, however, the AFL rejoined the IFTU, whose activity, soon afterwards, was paralyzed by the advance of Hitlerism. The reorganization of the international labor movement into the World Federation of Trade Unions (WFTU) after the war brought the Russians and the CIO into the movement, while the AFL opposed the WFTU. Sharp conflicts between communists and anticommunists led to the breakup of the WFTU. The immediate issue was the attitude to be taken toward the Marshall Plan. The noncommunist unions, including both the AFL and the CIO, formed the International Confederation of Free Trade Unions (ICFTU) in 1949, with headquarters in Brussels. The WFTU has continued to operate, primarily as an international body of the communist-dominated organizations.

Unions of socialist persuasion were, and continue to be, the predominant current in the international labor movement, but they are by no means without competition. Until the 1880s, business unionism set the tone in Great Britain while anarchosyndicalists won out over Marxists in France and Spain and formed an influential group in Italy. In Germany, France, Belgium, and other countries with strong Roman Catholic populations, Christian trade unions arose, often under the inspiration of the papal encyclical *Rerum novarum*. As a result, divided and competitive trade unions arose in several countries of the Continent. Communist unions came and went after 1919, following the complicated zigzag of the party line, which at times ordered the communists to conquer socialist unions by "boring from within" and at other times to defeat them by setting up communist unions in competition with them. In some countries, such as Germany and Gaullist France, nationalist movements set up their own unions, in general with only modest success except at times among the white-collar workers.

## Plant organizations and workers' councils

British unions, from an early stage, operated in the plant or close to the plant. Being craft unions, they were greatly concerned with "working rules," which often were determined by mutual agreement at the local or plant level. Still more important in bringing the union into the plant was the necessity for regulating piecework rates, which rarely can be done in a satisfactory way outside the plant. The handling of grievances arising out of the piece rate system and, later, out of the collective agreement as a whole, required a union organization in the plant. Many, although by no means all, British unions perform such functions in the plant, even though their formal organization and their constitutions do not always reflect this orientation.

Entry into the plant was, of course, the result of a long battle against hostile laws and employers. The repeal of the Combination Acts in 1824–1825 had less impact upon union activities than the enactment of labor laws in 1871 (amended in 1876) and 1875. By 1910, as a government report of that year indicated, collective bargaining still concerned only a minority of "industrial workers," but a substantial part of the bargaining that did occur proceeded on the plant level. When World War I greatly enlarged the area of collective bargaining and caused a shift in emphasis to national agreements, union activity in the plant was already established.

Quite different was the evolution in those countries of the Continent in which competitive unions arose. Compared with England, industrial development in most of these countries was either delayed or slower; and unionism and collective bargaining were less advanced until the revolutionary movement following World War I gave the labor movements in many countries the power to impose union recognition and collective bargaining. Thus for a long period, unions existed without being able to enter the plant itself. The employers' resistance to union activity within the plant was strengthened by political–religious divisions of the unions. Union operations in the establishment, it was said, would carry ideological disputes into the plant and interfere with its operation.

These differences between the British and the Continental evolution of the movement are to some extent reflected in the organizational structure of the unions. There are, of course, great variations among the unions of different crafts and different industries, as well as among those of different countries. But a frequent pattern on the Continent is represented by the union whose lowest administrative level is geographic, combining union members in several plants or firms. Even where, as in France, a lower level organization has been added informally to the local *syndicat*, this group, the so-called section, will usually still cover several plants. The communist CGT has been working to make the *syndicat* coincide with the membership in one plant, but so far it has met with only limited success. In Germany, some unions, particularly the metalworkers union (I.G. Metall), are engaged in setting up union stewards in the plants to work with the geographically based local (Ortsverwaltung). British unions, on the other hand, sometimes have the same organizational pattern as American unions and are officially represented at the workplace, although many unions also have geographic branches at their base.

In the absence of well-developed plant-union groups in most countries on the Continent, plant organizations of a different kind have arisen to fill the void. There is a need for bargaining within the plant, in order to interpret the collective agreement, to make it fit the particular conditions of the plant, to supplement it where necessary, and, especially, to handle individual grievances. The organizations that meet these needs go under different names in different countries. Their German designation, translated as "workers' council," will serve here as a general term for all of them. They show considerable variations as to their exact functions, election systems, relationships to unions, etc. Some are designed to enable the workers to participate in managerial functions. Characteristically, most of them perform tasks in the plant that in the United States are basic union activities. The council members are elected by all workers, whether union members or not. The councils are consequently not an organic part of the union itself and derive their existence and authority from legislation rather than collective agreements. The industrial relations function that is of most immediate relevance to the individual workers is thus in the hands of a body that does not form part of the union. At times, in some countries, union–council relations have been competitive rather than complementary. In Britain, shop steward movements, particularly after World War I, threatened for a while to turn into rival labor movements.

## Union structure

There are few other organizational features that European labor organizations have in common. They vary greatly in their degree of centralization. In most Scandinavian countries, the union federation has a high degree of control over its affiliated unions. In Great Britain, the Trades Union Congress (TUC) has little power under the statutes but considerable moral stature; collective bargaining, however, is fully in the hands of the affiliated unions. The German Union Federation (DGB), organized by Hans Böckler in 1949, has lost a good deal of its influence in favor of its affiliates. In France, the national union has only limited functions. The centers of gravity of the movement are, on the one hand, the (local) *syndicats* and, on the other hand, the union federations—CGT, the Christian CFTC, the socialist Force Ouvrière (CGT–FO), and the white-collar Confédération Générale des Cadres (CGC). Significantly, it is the *syndicats*, not the national unions, that are represented at the federation congresses.

In contrast to the United States, the issue of craft versus industrial unions rarely has led to serious internal cleavages. In most countries, both types exist within the same federation. In Germany, where the unions were rebuilt afresh after the Hitler era, a relatively neat organizational layout was established: 16 industrial unions divide the job territory among themselves. One of them, the Metalworkers Union, with close to two million members, represents almost one-third of the entire DGB membership. At the other extreme, Great Britain shows a complex pattern of overlapping organizations ranging in size from a few hundred to more than a million members. Amalgamations have tended to simplify the system somewhat, but in the main it continues to be unplanned. Two great general unions, the Transport and General Workers Union and the National Union of General and Municipal Workers, representing together more than a quarter of the total TUC membership, include among their members large numbers of unskilled workers in various industries. The existence of industrial federations of unions, comparable to some of the departments in the AFL–CIO, is one device by which the untidy pattern has been rendered more workable. Within the trade union movement in Italy, the existence of associations of sharecroppers (*mezzadri*) and farmers on different lease arrangements adds a confusing feature to the otherwise predominantly industrial organization scheme.

Even where the industrial union is the basic pattern, as in West Germany, it has been impossible to apply the principle without qualification to the white-collar employees. In many European countries, e.g., Sweden, Austria, and France, a considerable number of white-collar workers are unionized, including government employees. In Germany, the organized white-collar workers are distributed over the industrial unions, a special white-collar federation (DAG), and a separate organization of civil servants. While the DAG has relatively friendly relations with the DGB which is predominantly a manual workers' organization, the highly effective civil servants' union maintains its independence in line with the social distance that in Germany traditionally separates the civil servant from the public, and especially from the manual worker. The Swedish federation of white-collar unions (TCO) has friendly relations with the general trade union federation (LO) but is politically neutral, while LO maintains intimate contacts with the Social Democratic party. In France, however, the civil servants form the strongest single bloc within the CGT–FO. A separate organization, the CGC, exists for higher white-collar employees and professional workers outside the government.

Practically everywhere government employees are free to organize and to engage in some forms of collective bargaining. Most of them—in some countries even the police—are legally free to engage in strikes. In Britain, the laws enacted after World War II providing for the nationalization of the coal mines, the railroads, and the electricity, gas, and other industries require the governing boards of these industries to engage in collective bargaining with the appropriate unions. Strike restrictions imposed during World War II have been removed.

### The unions' role in management

Nationalization of industry has given rise to prolonged debates about the role of the unions in management. In Great Britain, in spite of the guild socialist tradition of advocating the handing over of industrial management to the unions, the movement came ultimately to the conclusion that union representatives could not serve as such on the management boards without running the risk of conflicting loyalties. The post-World War II nationalization laws thus provide that the management be composed of experts, including industrial relations experts. Trade unionists have been regularly appointed as such experts, but upon appointment they have had to resign their union offices. The French nationalization measures followed a scheme proposed by the Austrian socialist Otto Bauer, who in turn was inspired by the writings of the British guild socialist G. D. H. Cole. According to Bauer, nationalized industries were to be administered by tripartite boards consisting of equal numbers of representatives of the government, of the employees, and of the consumers. This was to ensure labor's participation in the management of the enterprise, while avoiding the danger that labor would take advantage of monopolistic situations to exploit the public. Most observers agree that neither the British nor the French scheme has given the employees the sense that they are effectively participating in managerial decision making. German codetermination, limited to coal and steel, gives the employees themselves and the union the right to be represented on the supervisory boards of the corporations, together with an equal number of representatives of the stockholders and a jointly elected chairman. In addition, the labor director, one of the three managers of the company, must be appointed with the approval of the union. While this scheme was being discussed, extreme fears were expressed that it would destroy the effectiveness of company management and/or of the union. Events so far have done little to justify these fears. Nor has codetermination had any visible impact on productivity or the degree of the employees' involvement in the enterprise. Other devices whose purpose is to ensure some measure of participation by workers in management are the workers' councils, particularly in Germany and France, and the participation of shop stewards and union officials in consultative bodies in Great Britain. While the record of the French and German councils in the administration of plant welfare agencies is praiseworthy, their participation in consultation or decisions on technical and general business matters has so far only rarely been effective.

In the Yugoslav system of workers' self-government, the councils are to act as managers, although the plant director himself is primarily responsible to the public authorities of the area and only partly responsible to the workers' council. Under the general political and economic conditions of the country, the council system, which has aroused a good deal of interest, has only limited possibilities of development. When the general administration of a country is of an authoritarian nature, full self-government in the plant, which might create many problems, particularly in countries undergoing rapid industrialization processes, would appear to be impossible to attain.

### Collective bargaining

Great Britain has been described as the motherland of collective bargaining; it has been traced back there to the end of the eighteenth century (Webb & Webb 1897). Shortly after the turn of the twentieth century it had become widely accepted in British industry. It has remained the predominant form of determining wages and working conditions, even though the introduction of a general legal obligation to engage in collective bargaining after the pattern of the Wagner Act in the United States has been rejected by the unions. An obligation to engage in collective bargaining exists only under the post-World War II statutes providing for the nationalization of certain industries.

On the Continent developments have been slower, in line perhaps with the less rapid progress of industrialization and prolonged legal restrictions upon the existence or the functioning of unions. Significant collective bargaining occurred in France only after World War I (syndicalist refusals to engage in collective bargaining may have contributed to the delay), and even then it was limited to a few years. In 1936, a new trend began during the socialist-led Popular Front regime. This was soon interrupted, however, by World War II. The present system is based upon legislation enacted in 1950. In Germany, the legal restrictions on unionism were reduced in the North German Confederation in 1867, but the antisocialist legislation under Bismarck did not allow collective bargaining to start on a larger scale until the 1890s. Unionism and collective bargaining flourished in the Weimar Republic and resumed after the fall of Hitler.

Yet, apart from England, collective bargaining has never achieved the importance in Europe that it has in the United States. In general, collective bargaining is relatively most important in the United States and Great Britain, of least significance in the newly industrializing nations, with the Continent somewhere in between. In most Continental countries, mixtures of collective bargaining and other methods of wage setting exist that make it difficult, if not impossible, to determine exactly where collective bargaining begins and other methods end. In many of the underdeveloped countries, governmental wage setting is customary, although not always enforceable. Two factors seem particularly relevant in explaining these differences in the importance of collective bargaining: (1) the tradition of regulating social relationships either by contract or by law and administrative action and (2) the long-run situation on the labor market. The first depends upon the continued impact of mercantilistic thinking or, alternatively, the breakthrough of economic liberalism. The second depends upon the long-run existence (or absence) of excess supplies of labor, mainly in the form of underemployment (primarily in agriculture, but also in small-scale crafts and trade).

The British wage councils are one example of such mixtures of bargaining and other forms of wage setting. These were set up, by special legislation, for industries in which inadequate collective bargaining machinery existed and also for some specifically designated industries (Agricultural Wage Act, 1948, 1949; the Road Haulage Act, 1938; and the Catering Wage Act, 1943). Although controlled by a minister in both composition and procedure, the councils operate in a way not very different from collective bargaining. In France, some of the nationalized industries are exempt from the obligations of collective bargaining; wages and working conditions in these industries are determined by a law, a *statut*. But the working out of the *statut* involves a process not dissimilar to collective bargaining. Moreover, French law provides for a government-appointed committee to recommend a minimum wage for all occupations. This process itself is not very different from collective bargaining, as the committee comprises labor and management representatives as well as others. In addition, changes in the minimum wage often exert a direct impact upon the rates set in collective bargaining, since the lowest rates set in many agreements are often close to the legal minimum.

A further complication in estimating the importance of collective bargaining in different countries arises from differences in the function of collective agreements. In many countries, in periods of full employment, effective wage rates exceed contract rates. This phenomenon—labeled "wages drift" in Sweden—must, however, be distinguished from the German system. In the German system, it is expected at all times that the contract rates are merely a minimum upon which will be based effective rates, which are arrived at sometimes in agreements between the workers' council and the management but more often in individual negotiations. The distance between effective and contract rates varies over time, but in periods of full employment it is significant enough to make union demands for changes in contract rates often appear irrelevant to a substantial portion of the union membership —the portion whose effective rates are above the level the union is aiming at. The labor organizations have tried to meet this problem, which threatens to devalue collective bargaining for the rank and file, by "bringing bargaining closer to the plant," i.e., concluding union-sponsored agreements for smaller areas and moving contract rates closer to effective rates. Occasionally they have included a so-called effective clause in their contract demands, which stipulates that any improvements granted in contract rates would also be added to effective rates above the contract level. But the absence of effective union organizations at the plant level in most European countries has proven a serious handicap for such developments.

**"Extension" of agreements.** In a number of countries, among them New Zealand, Australia, Germany, France, and the Netherlands, contracts can under certain circumstances be extended, usually by the government. Extension usually has two attributes: (1) the agreement is given the force of a law and (2) it is made applicable to plants and workers not represented at the bargaining table. The main purpose of extension is to protect the firms operating under the standards established by the agreement against the competition of firms not subject to them. Extension thus reduces the incentive to organize these firms; at the same time it makes essential a shaping of the agreement in such a way that it can be extended according to the prevailing rules. In Germany, for instance, and with a slight modification in the Netherlands, extension is possible only if the employers' association represents firms employing a majority of the employees in the industry or portion of the industry covered by the contract. No requirements for the coverage of the union are included in the law. Union concern for the extension of the agreement may restrain union wages policy, since excessive demands may induce marginal employers to leave the association, thus depriving it of the membership necessary for the extension of the agreement. In France, extension is limited to contracts concluded by the "most representative unions." In 1936, when the principle was first introduced into the legislation by the Popular Front government, this term may have been intended to refer to the union representing a majority of the employees in the bargaining unit. This interpretation would have given an effective bargaining monopoly to the then socialist-controlled CGT. Under political pressure this interpretation was abandoned, and the term "most representative union" now refers to all major unions.

The emphasis on the coverage of the employers' association rather than that of the union tends to reduce labor's interest in union security clauses of the type found in the United States. However, concern for union strength, financially and in terms of membership, operates in the opposite direction, particularly since the traditional incentive for union membership—class consciousness and a sense of class solidarity—has been waning in the postwar climate of prosperity and diminishing social and political discrimination against workers. European legislation frowns upon such institutions as the closed shop or the union shop. To be lawful, French agreements must contain clauses about the freedom of workers to join unions or not to join them. In the Netherlands, the law specifically exempts, from extension, provisions of a collective agreement "which aim at . . . coercing employers or workers into joining an employers' or workers' association . . . bringing about discrimination in treatment between organized and unorganized parties or persons. . . ." The close relationships between unions and certain political parties tend to make compulsory unionism appear a violation of freedom of conscience and thus to give moral support to the prohibition of union security clauses. However, the agency shop, which requires payment of a fee by the worker to the union to compensate it for representing a nonmember, appears to be legal in certain countries, for example, in Switzerland. Moreover, when unions aspire to union shop clauses, it is commonly understood that the worker can join any bona fide union rather than a specific union. This may go back to the sense of class solidarity, which, at least until recently, meant more to the rank and file than did interunion competition.

Extension tends to reinforce the fairly general emphasis in Europe and other industrial nations outside the United States on large area-wide agreements. One of the implications of this is that the basic agreement must be sufficiently general to be applicable to many different firms in a fairly large area, which is frequently the entire country, as in France and Great Britain, or large parts of it, as in Germany. As a result, the basic agreement is rather brief; essential clauses are worked out at lower levels. Negotiations in the plant, however, and at least portions of the grievance handling are often in the hands of a nonunion organization, namely the workers' council.

**Centralization of bargaining.** From the point of view of the degree of centralization of bargaining, the industrialized countries can be grouped into two categories. The Netherlands and Norway are examples of countries with highly centralized wage bargaining. Britain stands for the group characterized by competitive sectional bargaining. This classification relates to the role that the trade union federation plays in relation to the collective bargaining policies of its affiliates. Another possible classification refers to the degree of public control of the wage-setting process. Control may go hand in hand with centralization, since the latter facilitates the former, but logically the two must be kept apart; control is possible, although perhaps difficult to enforce, without centralized bargaining systems. Finally, the term "centralization" might refer to the territorial coverage of the agreement: whether it is national, regional, or local in scope or whether it is a firm or plant agreement. In this sense, most European agreements tend to be far more centralized than most agreements in the United States.

In the Netherlands, central control over bargaining has been in force since the end of the war. The key role in the process is played in fact, although not under the law, by the Labor Foundation. Officially this body merely provides advice on questions of general importance, but this advice has been so consistently accepted that it must be interpreted as almost decisive. In composition the foundation follows the general pattern of bipartite bodies: it consists of equal numbers of representatives of management and the unions. The union representatives come from the three main union federations, the socialistic NVV, the Roman Catholic KAB, and the Protestant CNV. This ranking corresponds to their numerical strength. The NVV has close to 500,000 members, the KAB 400,000, and the CNV more than 200,000. All three endeavor to organize workers in all industries. On the employers' side a similar division exists, except that the religious organizations are relatively far weaker. The combined coverage of the employers' organizations, expressed as a percentage of those eligible for membership, is double that of the unions.

Collective bargaining usually begins with discussions in the foundation, which lead to an expression of opinion as to mandatory or permissive changes in the existing agreements. These are then translated into more concrete terms by negotiations on lower levels. All agreements negotiated at the level of the firm or industry must be approved by the central authorities before they become legally valid. This decision is in fact in the hands of the Social and Economic Council, although the council merely advises the government, which has the legal authority to approve or reject agreements through a board of government mediators. The council, consisting of union, employer, and public representatives, seems to follow the recommendations of the foundation rather closely, and the minister in turn almost always accepts the council's advice. The two elements of centralized bargaining and government control of wage change are thus closely intertwined. The wage structure is regulated by way of centrally determined principles of job evaluation and regional differentials. Since 1962 this system has undergone considerable change; it has been decentralized and controls have been reduced. The main impetus for these changes has come from extreme labor shortages.

Centralization without, or at least with a far lesser degree of, government control than the earlier Dutch system is exemplified by Norway, Sweden, and Denmark. In all three countries union membership comprises about two-thirds or more of all employees. This, together with the small size of the countries, facilitates centralized wage bargaining. The Norwegian system started after World War II with compulsory arbitration of contract changes. This was later limited to cases where wage demands had not received the approval of the central labor federation. In 1952, the principle of compulsory arbitration was altogether abandoned. As a result, wage policy is set in negotiations between the trade union federation and the employers' association. However, the close relationship between the unions and the Labor party, which has been the government for most of the time, has provided for informal mutual coordination. In emergencies, such as the sharp price increases of 1958, the government has not hesitated to invoke compulsory arbitration procedures. The Swedish system, although similar in some respects to that in Norway, has been relying less on compulsory arbitration, which is used, if necessary, to settle disputes about the interpretation of agreements, and more on the internal discipline of employers' and union federations, whose position is buttressed by their control over substantial funds. Cooperation between the government—led by the Social Democrats—and the socialist-led unions provides a high degree of assurance that union wage policy and government policy run along fairly parallel lines.

A higher degree of decentralization in bargaining has gradually evolved in Germany. While union organization after the fall of the Third Reich began on the local and regional level, the center of gravity of the movement shifted rapidly toward the main trade union federation, the DGB, when it was set up in 1949. Part of the DGB's authority derived from the fact that whereas in the Weimar Republic the labor movement had been divided into competitive organizations along religious and political lines, the new unions were unified and at first exerted considerable public influence. Essentially this unity has been preserved in spite of the rise of a small Roman Catholic federation, whose main strength is concentrated in the Saar district, and the establishment of separate organizations, one for civil servants and another for part of the white-collar labor force. With the DGB acting as its official spokesman, the movement concentrated its efforts in the first phase of its life toward the attainment of changes in the structure of industrial management and the re-establishment of workers' representation at the plant level. The first was achieved for coal and steel by the system of codetermination, the second by the Works Constitution Law. The main provisions of this law relate to the establishment of workers' councils within the plants of private enterprise; later legislation extended this institution to public services. Although during the struggle for passage of these laws the federation took the lead, the later shift of emphasis to collective bargaining brought with it a transfer of power to the 16 industrial unions affiliated with the DGB, since the unions have full power in wage movements. The Metalworkers Union, in particular, has played a key part in bargaining developments. In spite of large membership figures in absolute terms, the DGB unions represent only about 35 per cent of the wage earners. The percentage is constantly declining, and union membership is frequently short-lived so that a considerable recruitment effort is necessary merely to maintain membership at a steady level.

Within the individual unions in Germany there is a high degree of centralization of authority. The full-time district officials, who were at first elected in some unions, are now usually appointed by the national executive committee of the union. This has particular significance since collective bargaining is carried on typically in the districts or for even larger areas and involves the top union officers. The plant organization of the unions, on the other hand, although eagerly promoted, is rather weak, as the workers' councils, which are elected by all workers, perform the union functions at the plant level.

German employers' associations—about which relatively little detail is known—are strong and have great discipline. The associations are combined in one central confederation, the BDA. Combativeness, after a long period of social peace devoted to the reconstruction of the country, is growing on both sides. The weapon of the lockout has been employed on a large scale, although it met with only modest success during a metalworkers' strike in early 1963.

Although agreements are most commonly concluded for large areas, there are few really nationwide agreements. The basic contract is of limited scope, as far as subject matter is concerned, partly because the well-developed social security system and supplementary legislation regulate many fringe issues and partly because only principles are settled in this master contract and the details are regulated in agreements with less geographic coverage. Not infrequently special contracts with differing geographic application settle different subject matters. In particular, plant agreements worked out with the assistance of the workers' council frequently supplement and improve, from the workers' point of view, the terms of the master contract. Many companies offer voluntary fringe benefits beyond those set by law or by contract. The administration of these voluntary benefits and the supervision of the observation of contracts and laws form one of the main activities of the workers' council. As the rates set in master contracts or other large-area agreements are usually quite modest in order to facilitate extension of the contracts, great emphasis is placed upon the improvements that plant or personal agreements can bring.

While there may be a consistent wage policy on a national scale on the part of the well-organized and disciplined employers, unions set their policy primarily within the limits of the individual industrial union. Attempts at a national wage policy —for example, a proposal that the government appoint a body of experts to review wage demands —have been without result. The government, however, has intervened rather frequently in wage negotiations by pleas for wage restraints.

British collective bargaining is far more decentralized. Union organization and bargaining systems have grown up over the decades without plan. Written and unwritten agreements and law and custom regulate industrial relations in an almost chaotic fashion. The central organizations on both sides—the Trades Union Congress (TUC) and the British Employers' Confederation (BEC)—have only limited power.

The TUC combines pure craft, amalgamated craft, industrial, and general unions ranging from a few hundred members to more than a million. Some unions are not affiliated with the TUC, some because of legal inhibitions and a few out of choice. With close to ten million members, the movement represents less than half the wage earners. A certain amount of order is established for bargaining purposes by the creation of federations of unions in related industries, as for instance those in shipbuilding or the National Federation of Building Trade Operatives. A slow process of amalgamation of smaller unions has been under way for many years, encouraged by TUC resolutions. The haphazard character of the organizations, the relatively weak position of the TUC, and the tradition of union autonomy in bargaining have pre-

vented the movement so far from playing a part in formulating a national wage policy. Yet the idea is gaining ground that such a policy may be required and that the unions should accept their responsibilities within the framework necessary to formulate and implement it.

The experience of the Labour government that came into office in 1945 does not facilitate the task of the partisans of a national wage policy. "Voluntary wage restraint" was inaugurated in 1948 without union participation, and union support was lukewarm from the beginning. Yet in order to support the Labour government, the union drive for higher wages slowed down noticeably for some two years. Contract rates continued to rise, but distinctly less rapidly than prior to the "wage pause." Under the impact of full employment, however, effective rates increased more rapidly than contract rates. The British unions thus suffered the same experience that the Swedish unions suffered under similar circumstances during the same period. The resulting tension within the movement led the unions in both countries to abandon the policy of voluntary restraint. A new experiment in a government-sponsored "incomes policy" has been under way in Britain since 1961. A balance of payments crisis in 1966 caused the government to establish a temporary wage freeze. A Prices and Incomes Board has been set up whose functions are not quite clear. The role that unions are to play under full employment, particularly in the systems of democratic planning that some countries in Europe are endeavoring to develop, is still uncertain.

The most immediate channel through which the government can exert influence upon wages is its control of the nationalized enterprises. Collective bargaining in many of these industries is subject to government instructions to the managing boards, and the impact of the wage bargains in nationalized industries is considerable since these industries are of great importance in the total economy of Great Britain, France, and several other European countries. Various forms of arbitration are potential levers for the implementation of a wage policy, as arbitration about the terms of a new contract, contrary to U.S. custom, is not infrequent in British industry. This may occur through an existing agreement or, as is more frequently the case, through the Industrial Court, which was established by the Industrial Courts Act of 1919. In fact, however, arbitrators have been more concerned with settling conflicts rapidly than with implementing any particular policy. No long-run solution has yet been found for the problem of fitting free collective bargaining into full employment economies.

## Unionism and prosperity

Most observers agree that the prolonged boom in western and central Europe since the early 1950s has been accompanied by substantial changes in the spirit and operations of the unions. Full employment, indeed a labor shortage, rapidly rising real wages, and the continuing decline of social discrimination against workers have led to a transformation of European society. One aspect of this has been a distinct decrease of class consciousness among the workers and considerable modifications of the meaning of the traditional socialist allegiance of the majority of the workers. This has been one factor weakening union–party relations. Another has been the transformation of the structure of the labor force, particularly the growing share of white-collar and professional employees. As a result, union membership has been stagnating and the social democratic and labor parties have tended to change from class parties into people's parties by de-emphasizing their working-class character.

Within the unions these developments have sharpened the need for stronger representation in the plant and for a shift of the center of gravity of collective bargaining away from union headquarters. At the same time, however, newly developing efforts toward some form of democratic planning extending into the area of personal incomes accentuate the necessity of centralized union leadership that is capable of implementing income policies arrived at by the planning process. The outcome of these contradictory tendencies is uncertain. Some relationship may exist between the trend toward planning and the decreasing use of the strike weapon in western Europe. However, the latter phenomenon also has been observed in countries rejecting the use of planning.

The decline of class consciousness threatens to remove the strongest pillar upon which European unionism has rested in the past. Effectiveness in the performance of the practical tasks of unionism is increasingly the appeal that the labor organizations are holding out to the younger generation. This, however, involves a transformation of spirit, structure, and emphasis, which long-established organizations are often reluctant to undergo.

ADOLF STURMTHAL

### BIBLIOGRAPHY

BRY, GERHARD 1960 Wages in Germany, 1871–1945. Princeton Univ. Press.

CLEGG, HUGH A. 1960 A New Approach to Industrial Democracy. Oxford: Blackwell.

CLEGG, HUGH A.; FOX, ALAN; and THOMPSON, A. F. 1964 A History of British Trade Unions Since 1889. Vol. 1. Oxford: Clarendon.

COLE, G. D. H. (1925–1927) 1948 A Short History of the British Working-class Movement: 1789–1947. Rev. ed. New York: Macmillan; London: Allen & Unwin.

EDELMAN, J. MURRAY; and FLEMING, ROBBEN W. 1965 The Politics of Wage–Price Decisions: A Four-country Analysis. Urbana: Univ. of Illinois Press.

EHRMANN, HENRY W. 1957 Organized Business in France. Princeton Univ. Press.

FLANDERS, ALLAN 1964 The Fawley Productivity Agreements: A Case Study of Management and Collective Bargaining. London: Faber & Faber.

FLANDERS, ALLAN; and CLEGG, HUGH A. (editors) 1954 The System of Industrial Relations in Great Britain: Its History, Law and Institutions. Oxford: Blackwell.

GALENSON, WALTER 1949 Labor in Norway. Cambridge, Mass.: Harvard Univ. Press.

GALENSON, WALTER (editor) 1952a Comparative Labor Movements. Englewood Cliffs, N.J.: Prentice-Hall.

GALENSON, WALTER 1952b The Danish System of Labor Relations: A Study in Industrial Peace. Cambridge, Mass.: Harvard Univ. Press.

HOROWITZ, DANIEL L. 1963 The Italian Labor Movement. Cambridge, Mass.: Harvard Univ. Press.

JOHNSTON, T. L. 1962 Collective Bargaining in Sweden: A Study of the Labour Market and Its Institutions. Cambridge, Mass.: Harvard Univ. Press.

KERR, CLARK et al. (1960) 1964 Industrialism and Industrial Man: The Problems of Labor and Management in Economic Growth. 2d ed. New York: Oxford Univ. Press.

KNOELLINGER, CARL E. 1960 Labor in Finland. Cambridge, Mass.: Harvard Univ. Press.

LORWIN, LEWIS L. 1953 The International Labor Movement: History, Policies, Outlook. New York: Harper.

LORWIN, VAL R. 1954 The French Labor Movement. Cambridge, Mass.: Harvard Univ. Press.

McCARTHY, WILLIAM E. J. 1964 The Closed Shop in Britain. Berkeley and Los Angeles: Univ. of California Press.

MEYERS, FREDERIC H. 1961 European Coal Mining Unions: Structure and Function. Monograph Series, No. 7. Los Angeles: Univ. of California, Institute of Industrial Relations.

PERLMAN, SELIG (1928) 1949 The Theory of the Labor Movement. New York: Kelley.

REID, GRAHAM L.; and ROBERTSON, DONALD J. (editors) 1965 Fringe Benefits, Labour Costs and Social Security. London: Allen & Unwin.

ROBERTS, BENJAMIN C. 1956 Trade Union Government and Administration in Great Britain. Cambridge, Mass.: Harvard Univ. Press.

ROSS, ARTHUR M.; and HARTMAN, PAUL T. 1960 Changing Patterns of Industrial Conflict. New York: Wiley.

STURMTHAL, ADOLF (1943) 1951 The Tragedy of European Labor: 1918–1939. New York: Columbia Univ. Press.

STURMTHAL, ADOLF (editor) 1957 Contemporary Collective Bargaining in Seven Countries. Cornell International Industrial and Labor Relations Reports, No. 4. Ithaca, N.Y.: Cornell Univ., Institute of International Industrial and Labor Relations.

STURMTHAL, ADOLF 1958 The Labor Movement Abroad. Pages 174–205 in Neil W. Chamberlain et al. (edi-

tors), *A Decade of Industrial Relations Research,
1946–1956.* New York: Harper.

STURMTHAL, ADOLF 1964 *Workers Councils: A Study of
Workplace Organization on Both Sides of the Iron
Curtain.* Cambridge, Mass.: Harvard Univ. Press.

STURMTHAL, ADOLF (editor) 1966 *White Collar Trade
Unions: Contemporary Developments in Industrialized Societies.* Urbana: Univ. of Illinois Press.

TURNER, HERBERT A. 1962 *Trade Union Growth; Structure and Policy: A Comparative Study of the Cotton
Unions in England.* Univ. of Toronto Press.

WEBB, SIDNEY; and WEBB, BEATRICE (1897) 1920 *Industrial Democracy.* New ed. London and New York:
Longmans.

## III

### THE STRUCTURE OF UNIONS IN THE UNITED STATES

The structure of labor unions is the result of a
variety of influences. Industrial processes, the size
and form of the employing unit, the skills, character, and ethnic and national origin of the work
force, as well as the time at which the union was
first founded, all exercise some influence upon the
structure and functions of labor organizations.
While one might reduce all unions to a few primary
types, many variants have been developed in an
effort to adjust the activities of the organizations
to the needs of specific groups.

**The local.** The basic unit of structure and government of labor organizations is the local union.
The local takes a number of forms, though all have
some characteristics in common. It may be made
up of workers of a single craft—bricklayers,
plumbers; of employees of an industry—automobile or steel workers; or of a number of occupational groups—but not all those employed in an
industry. The International Typographical Union
allows only one local to function in a community.
Thus Big Six, the New York local, includes in its
ranks the more than eleven thousand union printers
in New York City. The basic working conditions
and problems in the industry are sufficiently uniform so that labor–management issues can be
handled by one local. Of course, the size of the
business unit and conditions of employment in the
newspaper, book, and job branches are different,
but these variations may not be significant for collective bargaining or contract administration.

The majority of unions, even those which were
originally craft organizations, usually allow more
than one local to function in a given community.
This practice, however, does not automatically give
any group within the organization the right to set
up new local units. The basis for multiple local
unions is not always clear, especially in organizations established in the early years of the century
or before. In some early unions, locals were established on the basis of language. Thus, Swedish or
German carpenters, Italian or Puerto Rican dress-
makers, and German- or Yiddish-speaking printers
might establish local unions which were chartered
to allow non-English-speaking groups to conduct
union affairs efficiently.

Multiple local unions were also established because the union included more than one type of
worker. For example, there are separate local
unions of plumbers and steamfitters; linemen and
journeyman electricians; garment cutters and operators; carpenters and workers manufacturing doors,
trim, and window frames; coal- and milk-wagon
drivers; and garage mechanics and machinists.
From the beginning it may have been believed that
special problems could be better handled if members were segregated on the basis of skill or occupation. Another basis for union organization is
residence of members. Here again, the purpose of
establishing more than one local in a community
is to facilitate union business.

The rise of unionism in manufacturing created
new grounds for multiple local organizations. For
example, unions operating in the steel, automobile,
and electrical manufacturing industries also recruit workers from a variety of other related industries. Under such conditions local unions may be
based upon the employer unit or even a division
or department of a single establishment. No common rule for deciding the number of local unions
exists, although internationals may seek to prevent
the existence of two locals in a particular area. It is
not always easy to eliminate locals which have
shrunk in size or which might be merged with
another without loss of efficiency. Loyalty to a local
union or pride of leadership may be obstacles to
mergers. National officers sometimes seek to combine two or more locals to eliminate political opponents, but opposition to mergers arises more
generally because of loyalty to the old unit.

The local union transacts its business at periodic
meetings and chooses officers to manage its affairs.
If the number of members is small, the business
of the union will be conducted by unpaid staff
members who receive nominal payments and wages
for time lost on union business. Locals are governed by their constitutions and bylaws, and if they
are affiliated with a national or international union,
their rules and policies must conform to the general constitution and bylaws.

The authority and the importance of local unions
vary. In some organizations, the local union has
almost complete discretion in the negotiation of the
terms of employment. There may, at the same
time, be some general objectives or standards which

the locals are obligated to incorporate in their agreements; for example, the 5-day week or the 35-hour week. The power of the local in collective bargaining is influenced by the type of industry and market in which it operates, and especially by whether the employing firms cater to a local, regional, or national market. Because their product is not transferable, unions in the building construction industry have usually exercised a great deal of autonomy in collective bargaining and in the management of their own affairs. On the other hand, unions that bargain with firms or groups of firms operating in national product markets are likely to limit more severely the discretion of their local unions in the bargaining area. The national unions in coal mining, men's clothing, glass, automobile, steel, and pottery manufacture are among those that exercise a more direct influence over the bargaining of their locals than do unions in the service trades and in building construction.

Locals of every union play important roles in carrying out the purposes of the organization, in collecting dues and assessments, in handling grievances, and in protecting the rights and prerogatives of members. Unless a local is a purely administrative unit, as in the seagoing unions, the local can manage much of its business without interference from higher union authorities. On many issues, however, the local union must conform to rules and standards developed by the national or international organization. The local is formally a creature of the international union, and in many instances locals have arisen from the efforts of organizers employed by the international union.

As a rule, the local holds periodic business meetings at which expenditures are approved, appeals for financial or other kinds of assistance are made, and general issues are discussed under the heading "good and welfare." Attention has often been called to the low attendance at local union meetings, the lack of interest shown in union affairs by large numbers of members, and the ability of minorities to determine policy. The question is whether low attendance is a recent development or a problem that faced unionists in earlier generations. A certain answer cannot be given, but evidence of an indirect kind does exist. The fines levied for non-attendance and the rewards given for being present indicate that union meetings were not normally overcrowded in the past, for reasons that are not difficult to perceive. The emphasis upon attendance at local meetings springs from an implicit view that unions are general organizations for discussing social and economic policies. Few members regard the union from that point of view. The pri-

mary function of the union, from the point of view of the member, is to deal with the terms of employment. Attendance at local meetings will therefore be greater as contract-renewal time approaches, or when serious difficulties arise in the administration of the contract. Normally, however, the business of the union is conducted by a few activists— stewards, local officers, and those deeply concerned with union policy.

To argue that poor attendance at meetings indicates the absence of democracy is to give that term a curious definition. Democracy is a system of government that provides citizens with an opportunity to influence policy directly or through elected officers. There are countries that compel voting in elections, but the United States does not. The reasons for low attendance are complex. The greater dispersion of members makes the gathering of large numbers more difficult than in the past. Members may find that to attend a union meeting they will have to eat out, reach home late, and miss their customary radio or television entertainment. Although failure to attend meetings may reflect inertia and lack of interest, it might also show satisfaction with the performance of the union.

Under present conditions it is not difficult for large numbers of workers in most industries to withdraw from a union if they are dissatisfied with its policies. While decertification requires effort and even courage, workers intent upon ridding themselves of a particular labor organization can usually succeed, providing they can muster a majority. Low attendance at union meetings is accompanied by willingness to accept the decisions of the organization, and this is the test of loyalty to the union.

On the whole, trade unions are among the most democratic institutions in the United States, even though some local unions and larger bodies have been guilty of oppression and undemocratic practices. The typical rather than the extreme instances must be held in view when making judgments. Investigations of election complaints under the Landrum–Griffin Act have revealed few violations of the members' rights. Of the more than 52,000 local unions which held elections between September 14, 1959, and March 31, 1963, investigation disclosed violations in 380, but in only 207 instances might the results have been affected. In a number of these instances it is doubtful whether a court of law would overturn the election were it to public office.

**Intermediate bodies.** The existence of a number of local unions in a community has led to the development of such intermediate bodies as the joint or district board or council, a delegate body from a number of local unions of the same organization. These organizations exercise a considerable, and in some unions a predominant, influence over policy. In others, major power is retained by the locals. In the International Ladies Garment Workers Union, the joint board has the primary role in negotiating and administering contracts. The district, as it is called in the International Association of Machinists, is an important delegate body engaging in organization, negotiations, and assistance to local unions, but the locals retain considerable autonomy. District councils are established in a number of the building trades whenever more than a given number of local unions operate in a particular area. In some of these unions the district councils supervise the activities of the business agents and initially consider appeals from members. The teamsters' union requires that locals in a particular area join the district council, but the power these bodies exercise is not uniform throughout the union. In some areas, the district council is powerful in collective bargaining and in its influence upon the affiliated locals; in others, its influence is only nominal. A district council may cover a particular community or stretch over a large area, as do the district councils of some of the building trades. These councils may negotiate and administer contracts with employers.

The need for rapid and decentralized decisions has compelled national unions to develop regional forms of organization. Regional heads may be appointed, or they may be vice-presidents or members of the executive board elected on a regional basis. In some unions the officer is chosen by the delegates or members from the district he represents, and in others he is elected by the entire delegate body at a convention or by the general membership in a referendum.

The United Mine Workers of America was organized on a district basis from its beginning. Some districts were established prior to the national union. District organizations became small-scale replicas of the national union, with a president, vice-president, and executive board chosen by the district membership. At one time, the districts in the United Mine Workers were much more powerful administratively and politically than they are now. Most national leaders served apprenticeships in district offices, although John Mitchell and John L. Lewis, the greatest and most creative leaders, did not occupy significant offices on that level. The districts exercised sufficient autonomy so that they could refuse to accept the interstate agreements with the operators if they believed their interests were not well served. During the 1920s the United

Mine Workers of America faced a serious internal crisis that was generated in part by the decline in economic importance of the older, northern districts. The districts' loss of membership and power led in a number of instances to their being placed in provisional status, with their officers appointed by the international president. West Virginia and Kentucky, which were newly organized in the early 1930s, were also placed under provisional rule, so that the districts became mere administrative units under the control of the international office. This development was influenced not only by the shift of the locus of power within the union from the older organized districts of Indiana, Illinois, Ohio, and Pennsylvania to the newer, southern regions but also by economic shifts which required a single national policy and subordination of regional leaders to the needs of the national organization.

Even when the regional organization is not formally established in the same way as in the mine workers' union, it may perform important organizational and administrative functions, especially when the regional office is headed by an international officer. Usually the regional director or vice-president will direct a number of organizers, who may also handle issues that cannot be settled through direct negotiation at the plant level. The regional head is ultimately responsible for developments within his region, and in some unions he rules initially on appeals for or against members involving internal union affairs or questions of collective bargaining affecting such issues as seniority and grievance processing. The regional head may be responsible for organizing work, act as a mediator between rival groups in locals, and participate in the more difficult or more important collective bargaining negotiations within the region. Regional directors often acquire an independent position within the union. They may have a considerable following among the locals, and they are among the chief molders of the organization's policy.

Unions on the railroads have established lodges at various terminal points, and the lodges on a particular carrier are members of a system federation. Local lodge chairmen perform the same functions as business agents or staff members in other unions, and general chairmen might be regarded as regional representatives.

A number of unions have established state conferences of local unions. These may be formally organized as in the bricklayers' union, or they may be informal meetings of local representatives to discuss common problems. A variety of structural forms have developed as a result of the breakdown of the old American Federation of Labor principle of exclusive jurisdiction. Under this rule, a union claimed the right to organize all workers within its jurisdiction, and other affiliates were obliged to avoid infringement upon its jurisdiction by refraining from organizing such workers. This principle could not be effectively applied in manufacturing industries, especially in those that used mass-production methods. Moreover, when the AFL ceased to be the only federation, the principle could not be enforced. As a result, unions have been organizing a greater variety of workers than previously, and new types of units have been devised to allow special groups to work out their problems.

Unions may set up conferences or divisions for particular industries or occupations within their jurisdiction. The Textile Workers' Union of America has a dyers' division because the problems and pay scales of dyers are different from those of other textile workers. Longshoremen may allow warehousemen who belong to the same union to have a separate unit. The automobile workers' union has established a skilled trades department to handle problems of training, bargaining, apprenticeship, and other matters affecting skilled workers. The union's primary activities are in an industry made up of firms with many establishments. A variety of departments—General Motors, Ford, Chrysler, aircraft, foundry, die casting, and many more—have been set up to coordinate activities. The heads of departments are appointed by the president of the union with the consent of the executive board.

The teamsters' union has developed two types of intermediate units. The geographical conference, the Western Conference of Teamsters, was initiated by David Beck. This was, at first, an informal grouping of teamster locals from 11 western states and British Columbia. The principal reason given for the formation of this body was the need to coordinate bargaining with employers who operated over a wide geographical area. Geographical conferences have now been established over the entire United States and Canada. In addition, conferences of locals in particular industries have been set up on a regional and national level. Meetings are held periodically at which bargaining and organizing methods are discussed.

The Associated Actors and Artists of America is a federation of eight unions in the entertainment industry, although the component organizations appear as divisions of the federation. The Actors' Equity Association, American Federation of Television and Radio Artists, and the Screen Actors Guild contain about 70 per cent of the total membership. The Seafarers International Union of North America is an all-inclusive organization of unlicensed personnel on the East and Gulf coasts, but it has three nominal departments on the Pacific coast antedating the formation of the SIU— the Sailors' Union of the Pacific, the Marine Cooks and Stewards Union, and the Pacific Coast Marine Firemen, Oilers and Watertenders Union.

District 50 of the United Mine Workers of America presents another exception. Originally established by the parent organization to recruit workers in nonmining occupations, it functioned for a long time as a district of the miners' union. It has, however, organized several hundred thousand workers in utilities, manufacturing, and construction and now functions as a sort of English-type general union.

**National and international unions.** For many purposes the international or national union is the most important unit of structure and government. It is autonomous, and it establishes its own rules for managing its own affairs and for collective bargaining. Normally, international unions claim that their geographical jurisdiction extends over the United States and Canada. A number of the unions formed prior to World War I began as national unions and changed their title when they expanded into Canada. Not all international unions function in every state, province, and region of the two countries, nor are the unions spread uniformly over them. The spatial dispersion of membership is determined by the location of the employing units whose workers the union recruits, by the responses of workers it seeks to organize, and by the resistance it encounters from employers.

Officers of the international unions are elected by the delegates to the convention or by the membership in a referendum. It has been noted that the tenure of international officers is long, regardless of the structure of the union, the kinds of workers recruited, and even the political coloration of the union. Contests for higher union office are unusual. Heads of unions, like their counterparts in other kinds of organizations, become well known. Unless there is serious division within the official hierarchy or widespread dissatisfaction with performance or policy, incumbents of national office tend to be re-elected repeatedly. In contests for office, incumbents have several inherent advantages. They perform tasks that bring them into direct contact with the membership, their reports appear in the official press, and they may handle collective bargaining and grievance negotiations for large groups within the union. Because the functions of union officers are likely to be more administrative than political, an argument can be made for long tenure. Contests for office at this level have recently increased, and it appears that this change reflects the influence of the Landrum–Griffin Act.

Local unions and district councils hold their charters from the international unions, and the jurisdiction, rights, and duties of the locals are defined in the international union's constitution. The international union has the right under defined conditions to investigate the policies and conduct of its subordinate units, and if evidence of malfeasance, incompetence, or dishonesty is found, it may impose a receivership or trusteeship upon the local.

*Trusteeships.* Trusteeships are regulated by the Landrum–Griffin Act. They must be reported to the United States Department of Labor, and the reasons for their imposition must be given. They can continue for only 18 months and can be renewed only upon a show of necessity and with the permission of the secretary of labor. The need for occasional intervention in local affairs is generally recognized, but the possibility of abuse of this power is obvious. Evidence of dishonesty, failure to carry out organizational tasks or conform to union rules, and factional rivalries that make it difficult for the union to function or administer its contracts fairly and effectively may warrant the intervention of the international union. The rigor with which trusteeships are applied is not uniform. In some instances a trusteeship may simply mean the appointment of a representative of the international to supervise or to oversee the local's activities. In other cases it can mean the displacement of some or all of the local officers and the transfer of their functions to an appointed representative.

*Appellate tribunals.* International unions also serve as appellate tribunals to which members can appeal penalties imposed by subordinate units or make complaints against local officers or policies. Unions as a rule permit appeal to more than one tribunal; in some a member dissatisfied with the verdict can appeal successively to the district council, regional vice-president, the international president, and finally the convention. Some unions limit the number of appeals on certain questions and allow appeals on other issues to go to the convention at the request of the appellant. As of 1965, the requirement of charges being presented in writing and a trial being allowed was written into law. However, in the past, unions generally required charges to be made in writing and laid down trial procedures and methods of appeal. In many unions the membership of the local ultimately determines, through a vote, the guilt or innocence of a defendant and assesses the penalty. Some writers have argued that this is unfair because members are interested parties. It might be noted that this method does not always work to the disadvantage of the defendant. There have been more than a few cases in which members rejected overwhelming evidence against a popular defendant and refused to impose a penalty. Moreover, many penalties are reduced or set aside on appeal. Most of the charges made against members are for violation of union rules that govern conduct on the job. Charges do not customarily involve internal political questions. However, the latter are likely to result in charges of denial of rights.

*Other international functions.* The most important direct activity of the international union is the organization of the workers in its jurisdiction. The size of the organizing staff, the amounts expended for such purposes, and the significance of such activities differ among organizations. Several of the international industrial unions maintain large numbers of organizers and other staff people who perform functions similar to those of local business agents in other unions. In these cases, the central organization manages more of the local's business than, for example, in the printing and building trades unions, where organizing activity by the international is likely to be largely in the form of monetary or staff aid to locals.

The international union sometimes administers benefit programs. The older unions, largely although not exclusively in the skilled trades, were organized before governmental systems of social security were in operation. These unions were formed to carry on both protective and beneficial activities. The latter include mortuary, sickness, pension, and unemployment benefits, which may be paid under specified conditions.

In the seagoing unions the international union is the only significant unit. Locals are mainly administrative centers to collect dues and to handle grievances and other problems. The shore delegates for the various ports are elected by a general membership referendum or by conventions.

**Finances.** The income of the locals is derived mainly from dues, initiation and readmission fees, and assessments, although the last are not a significant source in most unions. Dues tend to be higher in the unions of skilled workers who earn high wages. It is those organizations which provide the more extensive welfare benefits, and dues must be high enough to finance them. As a rule, international unions tend to discourage the levying of assessments by their locals. Because these contributions are imposed irregularly they are likely to arouse dissatisfaction and opposition among members. Consequently, in many organizations the local must demonstrate serious need before such a levy will be approved by the national officers. The Landrum–Griffin Act provides that increases of local dues or levying of assessments can be made only by a majority vote through a secret ballot of members in good standing at a general or special meeting.

Like dues, initiation and readmission fees tend to be higher among the unions of skilled than of semiskilled and unskilled workers. Some unions base their dues and initiation fees upon skill and upon the benefit rights particular members enjoy. Dues are usually a specified amount per month or quarter, but a few organizations charge a percentage of income earned at the trade or calling. International unions may require that all locals levy uniform dues and initiation fees, others allow a range of charges, a third group places a floor under these payments, and a fourth places a ceiling upon them.

International unions are mainly financed by a tax of a given amount per member per month. The size of the per capita tax also depends upon the kind of workers the union recruits, their skills, and the benefits the union provides. Per capita taxes tend to be higher in the skilled trades unions in building, printing, and entertainment. The tax may be divided into separate portions for carrying on various activities or placed in a general fund. For example, many unions allocate a set amount to a journal or publication fund. Another part may be placed in the mortuary, pension, or health and welfare fund, and a third into a general fund for administrative expenditures. Organizing costs may be drawn from a general or a special fund. Many unions maintain separate funds for the payment of strike benefits and allocate some part of the per capita payment for this purpose. Assessments are another source of income, although there is a tendency to avoid such levies. The conditions under which international assessments can be imposed are frequently defined in union constitutions; in a number of organizations they require the approval of the membership. Some unions also require locals to remit part of their initiation and readmission fees. Interest from securities and rents from property are also sources of income for international unions.

**Officers and salaries.**  International officers are chosen either by the delegates at the conventions or by the membership in a referendum. The head of the union is usually the president, who as the chief executive officer is in charge of organizing and acts in general as a supervisor of the affairs of the locals under his jurisdiction. He ordinarily has authority to appoint organizers and much of the staff at headquarters. He is likely to be the most powerful person in the union, but in some unions the executive board may have more influence on final decisions. Unions also elect a secretary and a treasurer or combine the two offices into a secretary–treasurer.

Below the president, secretary, and treasurer in rank are the vice-presidents and members of the executive board; in some unions the vice-presidents constitute the executive boards. These bodies hold considerable power in many unions. They can review most decisions made by the officers stationed at headquarters, and they must approve a wide variety of decisions. To some extent their power depends upon the caliber of the persons serving. Vice-presidents and executive board members are selected by the entire union or by districts and serve for specific terms.

Salaries of union officers can be divided into several levels. The highest are the salaries of the presidents, secretaries, and treasurers. Next in line are vice-presidents and executive board members; staff men may be included in the latter group or occupy a position of their own. The lowest group are the local officers, although in some unions the heads of large locals may be paid salaries equal to those of organizers or even international vice-presidents. In a few organizations the leaders of large locals also serve as executive board members or vice-presidents of the international union and may receive extra compensation for these services. As a rule the business agents and other full-time officers in local unions of skilled trades will receive salaries somewhat in excess of the wages received by the members. In addition to salaries, union officers receive expenses. Organizers and other international officers are allowed either a specified amount for daily expenses and travel expenditures or are paid for expenses incurred.

**The AFL–CIO.**  The American Federation of Labor–Congress of Industrial Organizations is made up (as of 1965) of 137 national and international unions. About another fifty international unions remain unaffiliated. There are, in addition, several small federations of unaffiliated unions and a large number of independent single-plant unions. Some of the national unions outside of federation have withdrawn because of policy differences, as did the United Mine Workers of America; some were expelled by the AFL on charges of corruption, as were the teamsters' and bakery and confectionery workers' international unions; some were ousted by the CIO on charges of communist domination, as were the United Electrical, Radio and Machine Workers of America and a number of others.

The AFL–CIO is engaged in organizing, or in assisting its affiliates to organize, and carries on educational campaigns on behalf of the labor movement. It seeks to settle jurisdictional differences among its affiliates, and it aids those occupying the same or contiguous jurisdictions to merge, an activity in which it has had only modest success. It is engaged in two types of political activity. First, it supports before Congress legislation it regards as benefiting the population, irrespective of whether it affects the organized or the unorganized. Its legislative committee examines every bill introduced in the Congress to determine its effect upon labor. This committee carries out the instructions of conventions or the directives of the executive council. Second, through the Committee on Political Education, the AFL–CIO makes known the voting records of congressmen, aids in registering voters, and endorses and aids those candidates it holds worthy of support. It publishes bulletins and leaflets and seeks to rally union members and friends in support of its endorsements.

The supreme governing body of the AFL–CIO is the biennial or special convention. The officers are a president and a secretary-treasurer, who are the executive officers, and 27 vice-presidents, each of whom must be a member of an affiliated organization and be chosen by the convention. The president, as the chief executive officer of the organization, supervises its affairs and presides at all conventions and at meetings of the executive council and the general board. He has the power to interpret the constitution, but he can be overruled by the council. The secretary-treasurer is in charge of monies and property. The executive council is the governing body between conventions, and it carries out the directives and decisions of conventions. In addition, an executive committee of the president, secretary-treasurer, and six vice-presidents consults with and advises the president on policy matters. A general board is made up of members of the executive council and a principal officer of each of the affiliated national or international unions and of each trade and industrial department. It meets at least once a year and decides questions submitted to it by the executive council.

A department of organization is prescribed by the constitution. In addition, the constitution calls for the appointment by the president of 14 stand-

ing committees to carry out the tasks of the federation and the directives of the convention. These committees deal with legislation, civil rights, political education, ethical practices, international affairs, education, social security, community services, economic policy, housing, research, public relations, safety and occupational health, and veterans' affairs.

A large staff carries out the work of the federation. The organizing department maintains 23 regional offices, each headed by a regional director. The organizing staff of the federation can be of considerable importance in a given area or situation. Generally, however, it serves as an aid or auxiliary to the activities of affiliated unions. The social security division assembles information on various aspects of welfare legislation and prepares memoranda for the officers and releases for the press. The research department analyzes economic data, prepares briefs and testimony, and issues a monthly economic bulletin. The publications division issues a weekly newspaper, a monthly magazine, and other printed materials.

*Central bodies.* Central bodies are directly affiliated with the AFL–CIO on a city, state, or regional basis. These are composed exclusively of locals of national and international unions and organizing committees affiliated with the federation. In addition, a number of local unions and organizing committees are directly chartered by the federation. Whenever a sufficiently large group of locals in a particular trade or industry is affiliated with the federation, it may at the decision of the executive council be formed into a national council, but it remains directly affiliated with the federation. Finally, groups of local unions may be authorized to combine into autonomous national and international unions. Groups of directly affiliated local unions may request the executive council to authorize such combinations. The federation performs all the services and exercises the same authority toward directly affiliated locals as national and international unions do in the case of their locals.

The AFL–CIO is supported by a per capita tax levied upon all affiliates and upon directly chartered local unions. Revenue may also be derived from assessments authorized by a convention, and the executive council can call for the payment of limited assessments.

*Trade and industrial departments.* The need to devise a method of cooperation among unions operating in contiguous trades was early recognized. Local trades councils in the building and metal trades were formed in the 1880s. These organizations sought to develop cooperation among the separate trades employed in the same industry. The AFL recognized the building trades councils and allowed these bodies to affiliate with it. The AFL, however, feared that formal cooperation by a group of international unions might lead to the emergence of a competing power in the trade union world. After several unofficial efforts, the AFL recognized the need for formal cooperation and established departments in a number of industries in 1908. The building and construction trades department charters trades councils and seeks to devise general policies that will promote the unions and the construction industry. It has developed, after many trials, a fairly successful method of handling jurisdictional disputes among its members, who have been drawn closer together by the desire to present a common front against the industrial unions in the work assignment disputes. The functions of the metal trades department are similar to those of other trades departments, except that it has not faced many internal disputes. It charters trades councils in the metal-working industries that sometimes negotiate common contracts with employers. The union label and service trades department conducts campaigns for the use of union-made products and the patronage of service establishments which display the union insignia.

The railway employees department is made up of six international unions whose members maintain and service railroad equipment. These unions bargain jointly with the carriers. The maritime trades department seeks to enroll unions whose members are employed in seagoing services, or in serving vessels, or in handling cargo. Similarly, the food trades department is made up of unions in the food processing and distributing industries. The industrial union department is made up of a wide variety of unions, and it functions more like a general federation than a department. It has sought to develop common organizing drives and unified negotiations with employers—coalition bargaining —in firms where a number of unions hold bargaining rights. It also carries on educational, research, and lobbying activities.

The Government Employees' Council was formed in 1945 so that unions of government employees would be able to prepare common programs for legislative and administrative action. The Railway Labor Executives' Association is made up of the chief executive officers of the railway unions, all but two of which are affiliated with the AFL–CIO. Most of the railway unions have virtually all of their members in the railroad industry, but eight have members outside of that industry and several have the majority of their members outside. The association, formed in 1926, functions as a policy-making body on legislation and other issues of interest to railroad workers. It is not a federation of unions.

PHILIP TAFT

#### BIBLIOGRAPHY

BARBASH, JACK 1961 *Labor's Grass Roots.* New York: Harper.

CHAMBERLAIN, NEIL W. 1965 *The Labor Sector: An Introduction to Labor in the American Economy.* New York: McGraw-Hill.

COMMONS, JOHN ROGERS et al. 1918–1935 *History of Labour in the United States.* 4 vols. New York: Macmillan.

GALENSON, WALTER 1960 *The CIO Challenge to the AFL: A History of the American Labor Movement, 1935–1941.* Cambridge, Mass.: Harvard Univ. Press.

GITLOW, ABRAHAM L. (1957) 1963 *Labor and Industrial Society.* Rev. ed. Homewood, Ill.: Irwin. → First published as *Labor Economics and Industrial Relations.*

HOXIE, ROBERT (1917) 1936 *Trade Unionism in the U.S.* 2d ed. New York: Appleton.

LEISERSON, WILLIAM M. 1959 *American Trade Union Democracy.* New York: Columbia Univ. Press.

MIERNYK, WILLIAM H. 1965 *The Economics of Labor and Collective Bargaining.* Boston: Heath.

NATIONAL INDUSTRIAL CONFERENCE BOARD 1956 *Sourcebook of Union Government, Structure and Procedures.* New York: The Board.

SAPOSS, DAVID J. 1926 *Left Wing Unionism.* New York: International Publishers.

SLICHTER, SUMNER H.; HEALY, JAMES J.; and LIVERNASH, E. ROBERT 1960 *The Impact of Collective Bargaining on Management.* Washington: Brookings Institution.

TAFT, PHILIP 1954 *The Structure and Government of Labor Unions.* Cambridge, Mass.: Harvard Univ. Press.

TAFT, PHILIP 1964 *Organized Labor in American History.* New York: Harper.

ULMAN, LLOYD 1955 *The Rise of the National Union: The Development and Significance of Its Structure, Governing Institutions, and Economic Policies.* Cambridge, Mass.: Harvard Univ. Press.

## IV

### INFLUENCE ON WAGES

The main questions to which this article is addressed are empirical ones: (1) To what extent have labor unions affected the relative wages of different groups of labor in the United States? (2) What factors account for the observed differences in effects of unions? (3) How variable were the relative wage effects from one date to another during the period 1929–1958? (4) What regularities appear in the variations of the effects over time?

**Absolute and relative wages.** Throughout this article, the term *wages* covers the earnings of self-employed persons as well as the compensation of wage and salary workers. The latter includes all remuneration for time worked at either straight-time or premium rates and for time not worked (vacation, holiday, sick leave, call-in pay, and other paid leave) and employer contributions to public and private unemployment, pension, health, and other employee welfare funds. A worker's absolute money wage per hour—for short, his *money* wage —is the sum in dollars of all of the pecuniary rewards to him per hour of his labor services. His *real* wage is the same sum expressed in dollars of fixed purchasing power.

The *general wage level*, which may be expressed in either money or real units, is the average (mean) wage per hour of all workers in the U.S. labor force.

The *relative* wage of a group of workers is the ratio of the average (mean) wage of all workers in the group to the average wage of all workers in the labor force, i.e., to the general wage level. Relative wages are indicators of the percentage differences in wages among groups of workers. For example, if the relative wage of one group is 1.5 and that of a second group is 0.75, the average wage of the first group is 50 per cent greater than the average wage of all workers and 100 per cent greater than the average wage of the second group, and the average wage of the second group is 25 per cent below the average wage of all workers.

It is impossible for the wage of every worker to exceed (or, alternatively, to be below) the average wage of all workers. Indeed, the average relative wage of all workers is always exactly equal to unity. Therefore, if the relative wages of some workers exceed unity, the relative wages of some other workers must be less than unity.

This article deals only with the effects of labor unions on relative wages. Unionism affects the relative wages of different groups only if it causes the absolute wages of the groups to change by percentage amounts that differ among the groups. Furthermore, if unionism raises the relative wages of some groups, it thereby lowers the relative wages of some other groups. For example, if nonunion workers outnumber union workers in the labor force in a three to one ratio, a 9 per cent increase in the average relative wage of union workers implies a 3 per cent decline in the average relative wage of nonunion workers.

On the other hand, that unionism has increased the average wage of union workers by, say, 12 per cent relative to the average wage of nonunion workers does not imply that unionism has raised the average *absolute* money or real wage of union

workers by 12 per cent rather than some different percentages. *The effects of unionism on the general level of either money or real wages cannot be deduced from knowledge only of the relative wage impact of unionism.*

**Methods of estimation.** The average relative wage of a group of labor in the presence of the unionism existing at a particular date can be observed directly. What the corresponding average would have been in the absence of unionism, however, can be estimated only uncertainly from observable data. Two different types of approaches have been used to estimate the relative wage effects of unionism:

The *indirect* approach estimates the effect of unionism on the relative wage of a group of labor from estimates of the effects of unionism on other economic magnitudes pertaining to the group, such as its relative employment, its relative quit rate, and the excess supply (queuing) of labor to the group. Evidence that such nonwage effects are not zero often can be taken as evidence that unionism has affected the relative wage of the group. It is usually difficult, however, to estimate the size of the implied relative wage effect from evidence on the nonwage effects.

In the *direct*, or *wage comparison*, approach the relative wage effects are estimated from comparisons of the wages or changes in wages of two or more groups of labor differing in their degree of unionization. The relative wage effect estimates presented later in this article are based almost entirely on studies that have used this approach.

Four types of wage comparisons may be distinguished in these studies:

Variant 1 compares the average wage of a given, usually more or less highly unionized, group at a particular date with the average wage at the same date of a bench mark group. The latter group commonly is a nonunion group considered highly comparable to the given group. In a few studies, however, the bench mark group approximates all labor in the economy. The difference in average wage between the two groups is adjusted to eliminate the effects of factors other than unionism, and the adjusted difference is attributed to unionism. This procedure yields an estimate of the effect of unionism on the average wage of the given group relative to the average wage of the bench mark group at the particular date.

Variant 2 treats simultaneously three or more groups differing in degree of unionization. This variant adjusts the average wages of the covered groups for the effects of factors other than unionism and correlates the adjusted average wages with the degree of unionization of the groups. Commonly the adjustment and the correlation take place simultaneously in a multivariate analysis of wages, degree of unionization, and other variables. Variant 2 estimates the effect of unionism on the average wage of union workers in the covered groups, relative to the average wage of the covered nonunion workers. The resulting estimate may be biased, however, even when the adjustment of the wage data for the effects of factors other than unionism is perfect. In general, the algebraic size of the bias can be calculated only roughly.

Variant 3 compares the change from a base date to a given date in the average wage of a given group with the corresponding change for a bench mark group and adjusts the difference between the two wage changes for effects of factors other than unionism. The effect estimated by this procedure is the change from the base date to the given date in the effect of unionism on the average wage of the given group relative to the average wage of the bench mark group.

Variant 4 correlates the adjusted changes from a base date to a given date in the average wages of several groups of labor with the degree of unionization of the groups at the given date. This variant estimates the change between the two dates in the effect of unionism on the average wage of covered union labor relative to the average wage of covered nonunion labor. This estimate, like that from Variant 2, may be biased.

The central problem in all of the wage comparison procedures is adjusting the wage data for the effects of variables, other than unionism, that may be correlated with the effects of unionism. The data and procedures that have been used to make such adjustments are too detailed and too specialized to the individual studies to be summarized briefly. It should be said, however, that in general the adjustments have not been so refined as to leave little margin for error in the estimates of the relative wage effects of unions. For this reason the estimates given below should be regarded as quite tentative.

**Recent research in the United States.** Although unionism in the United States is well over a century old, it was not until the end of World War II that union members comprised as much as 25 per cent of the U.S. labor force. A decade earlier union membership was about 8 per cent of the labor force, which was only slightly higher than the corresponding percentage in 1905. Since 1945 unionization in the U.S. labor force has remained around 25 per cent, rising by a small amount from 1945 to 1953 and then declining to a level in 1960 almost the same as that in 1945.

It is not surprising, therefore, that almost all of the empirical research on the relative wage impact of unionism in the United States was done after 1945. Two other factors help to explain the concentration of the research in the recent period. First, the supply of wage and other data required for research in this area also expanded greatly during the 1930s and 1940s. Second, command of the techniques of statistical economics was uncommon among economists until after 1945.

The empirical findings summarized below are based on evidence presented in 21 of the recent studies of unionism and wage differentials in the United States (see Lewis 1963, chapters 3–4, for reviews of these studies). Since a considerable part of the recent research has been reported only in unpublished papers and doctoral dissertations, the summary undoubtedly is not exhaustive.

Nine of the studies cover large segments of the U.S. labor force and use the Variant 2 or Variant 4 wage comparison procedures to estimate the relative wage effect of unionism. Thus the summary numbers that emerge from these global studies all tend to be estimates either of the effect of unionism on the average wage of all union workers, relative to the average wage of all nonunion workers at a particular date—in short, the average union/nonunion relative wage effect—or of the change in this effect between two dates. These studies provide little or no information on the dispersion of the relative wage effects among different groups of union workers.

The other 12 studies deal with relatively small parts of the U.S. labor force as follows: production workers in basic steel manufacturing (Rees 1951); hotel employees in large cities (Scherer 1956); production workers in rubber tire manufacturing (Sobel 1954); skilled craftsmen and, separately, common labor in building construction in large cities (Sobotka 1953); production workers in bituminous coal mining (Greenslade 1952); employees in selected establishments, localities, and occupations, separately, by industry, in the manufacturing of paints and varnishes, wooden furniture, footwear, cotton textiles, hosiery, automotive parts, and women's dresses (Maher 1956); barbers in large cities (reported in Lewis 1963, chapter 3); production workers in the manufacturing of men's and boys' suits and coats (Rayack 1958); commercial airline pilots (Sobotka et al. 1958); street railway and bus motormen (Lurie 1961); seamen in east coast ocean transportation (Rapping 1961); and physicians (Friedman & Kuznets 1945; Lewis 1963, chapter 3).

These detailed studies provide a check on the estimates of the average union/nonunion relative wage effect drawn from the global studies. More importantly, it is only from such studies that the dispersion in the relative wage effects of unionism among detailed industries and occupations can be gauged.

**Variation of influence over time.**    The clearest finding emerging from the 21 studies is that the size of the effect of unionism on the average union/nonunion relative wage in the United States has varied greatly and in a systematic fashion over time. The largest effect apparently occurred about 1932, during the rapid downturn of the depression. In 1932 the average union/nonunion relative wage effect may have been 25 per cent or even larger. In the recovery period from 1933 to the outbreak of World War II the effect dropped sharply to a level that was probably between 10 and 20 per cent in 1939.

The decline in the effect continued through World War II and into the period of rapid inflation that followed the war. At the trough, which occurred in the period 1945–1948, the effect of unionism on the average union/nonunion relative wage was approximately zero. (There is some evidence that the union/nonunion relative wage effect also was near zero at the peak of the inflation following World War I.)

The very low relative wage effect observed during 1945–1948 did not persist, however, in the following ten years. By 1957–1958 the effect of unionism on the average wage of union labor relative to the average wage of nonunion labor had risen to about 10 to 15 per cent. It should be noted in this connection that the rate of inflation of the U.S. general price level during 1949–1958 was only about a third as large as that during 1939–1948.

In the late 1950s the extent of unionization of the U.S. labor force was approximately 25 per cent. Therefore, about one-fourth—or three to four percentage points of the 10 to 15 per cent effect of unionism on the average union/nonunion relative wage estimated for 1957–1958—consists of a decline in the average wage of nonunion workers relative to the average wage of all workers. The remainder, 7 to 11 per cent, is the estimated effect of unionism on the average wage of union workers relative to the average wage of all workers.

*Role of money wage rigidity.*    That the effects of unionism on the relative wages of union workers tended to be greatest during periods of rapid deflation of the general price level and lowest during times of unexpectedly rapid inflation was observed and commented upon by the authors of several of the unionism wage studies. Albert Rees, Milton Friedman, Walter A. Morton, and numerous other economists have attributed the apparent negative

correlation between the rate of inflation and the union/nonunion relative wage effect of unionism to wage rigidities introduced by collective bargaining: the union contract running for a period of a year or more, the reluctance of employers of union labor to agree to unusually large money wage increases during periods of unexpectedly great inflation lest the inflation not continue, and the similar opposition of unions to wage decreases during periods of declining prices.

One of the studies (Lewis 1963, chapter 6) has tried to measure the sensitivity of the average union/nonunion relative wage effect of unionism to variations in the rate of inflation and the rate of unemployment in the U.S. labor force during the period 1919–1958. The results of the study tend to confirm the large variability over time of the relative wage effect observed in other studies and suggest that the variability is more largely accounted for by negative correlation with the rate of inflation than by positive correlation with the rate of unemployment.

**Effects on the interindustrial relative wage structure.**    The effect of unionism on the average relative wage of the workers employed in a particular industry is a weighted average of corresponding relative wage effects for (*a*) the union labor and (*b*) the nonunion labor in the industry, where the relative weight for the union labor is the extent of unionization of the workers in the industry. For example, if the extent of unionization were 50 per cent and if unionism had raised the relative wage of the union workers in the industry by 20 per cent and lowered the relative wage of nonunion workers by 2 per cent, the effect of unionism on the average relative wage of the industry would be a plus 9 per cent. Therefore, the greater the dispersion among industries in the extent of their unionization and in the effects of unions on the relative wages of union workers and of nonunion workers, the greater will be the dispersion among industries in the effects of unionism on their average relative wages.

Since 1944 roughly three-fourths of the persons engaged in transportation and about half of those in mining, construction, manufacturing, communications, and electric and gas utilities have been covered by collective bargaining arrangements. However, within each of these industry divisions there is considerable dispersion in extent of unionization among detailed industries.

In contrast, the extent of unionization has been close to zero in agriculture, trade, finance and insurance, and government (excluding government enterprises). The same is true in general of the service industries except for hotels and eating and drinking places in large cities, the entertainment industries, and some of the personal service industries. About half of the labor force is employed in the agriculture, trade, finance and insurance, service, and government industry divisions.

Estimates of extent of unionization by industry, with considerable industry detail, are available for all of the major industry divisions in the United States. On the other hand, the 12 detailed "industry" studies of unionism and wages provide estimates of the relative wage effects of unionism for only a short list of industries. Nevertheless, the general character of the distribution of the relative wage effects among all U.S. industries can be gauged by combining the results of the 12 studies with the data on extent of unionization by industry. In the late 1950s the majority of workers probably were employed in industries whose average relative wages were raised or lowered by unionism by no more than 4 per cent. The data also indicate that the distribution was positively skewed with relative wage effects in some industries equal to or exceeding 20 per cent. It is unlikely, however, that the payroll of these industries was more than a very small fraction of the aggregate compensation of the whole labor force.

The industries in which the relative wage effects of unionism were the largest algebraically tended to be those with above average relative wages. Therefore, unionism has been a factor making the relative inequality of average wages among industries larger than it otherwise would be. In 1958 the coefficient of variation of average wages among industries was about 6 to 10 per cent larger than it would have been in the absence of any effects of unions on relative wages.

**Effects on relative wages by occupation.** Fragmentary data indicate that the dispersion of extent of unionization among occupations is probably at least as large as that among industries. Within industries characterized by industrial unionism—unionism of wage earners regardless of occupation—there is, of course, relatively little dispersion in extent of unionization among the wage earner occupations. On the other hand, in both these industries and others, white-collar (supervisory and other nonproduction) employees typically have not been organized by unions. In addition, in industries in which unionism follows craft (occupation) lines, such as printing and building construction, there are some substantial differences in extent of unionization among the wage earner occupations.

These differences in extent of unionization by occupation, together with the estimates of relative wage effects of unionism drawn from the studies that have dealt with occupations, suggest that the dispersion in relative wage effects of unionism among all occupations in the United States may be as large or larger than that among all industries. Furthermore, the interoccupational distribution of relative wage effects of unionism, like that for industries, probably is positively skewed, with a small fraction of the labor force employed in occupations in which the relative wage effects were larger than 20 per cent.

**Differing effects among union workers.** The 12 studies that dealt with fairly small groups of union workers indicate that the dispersion across union jurisdictions of the effects of unions on the relative wages of union workers probably was substantial except in the period near the end of World War II. For the period 1954–1957, for example, the estimates of these effects, drawn from the six studies that provided figures for this period, ranged from zero to about 50 per cent.

Unfortunately, although the 12 "industry" studies covered 18 different groups of workers, there is no single date at which numerical estimates are available for each of these groups. For example, for the period 1936–1939 there are estimates for seven groups: (1) bituminous coal miners (30%); (2) skilled building craftsmen (25%); (3) wage earners in men's clothing manufacturing (16%); (4) wage earners in rubber tire manufacturing (14%); (5) motormen in local transit (8%); (6) unskilled building labor (5%); (7) hotel employees (0%). For the later period, 1954–1957, there are estimates for six groups, only three of which are on the preceding list: (1) bituminous coal miners (50%); (2) commercial airline pilots (27%); (3) east coast seamen (20%); (4) barbers (19%); (5) motormen in local transit (12%); (6) wage earners in men's clothing manufacturing (0%). Furthermore, some of the differences among the studies in the estimates at these and other dates consist more largely, no doubt, of errors of estimation than of real differences in effects, and in some other instances estimation errors may have hidden real differences. For these reasons any ranking of the 18 groups according to the size of the relative wage effect at a particular date is subject to considerable uncertainty.

Nevertheless, it can hardly be doubted that there were some large differences in relative wage effects from one union jurisdiction to another in the latter part of the 1950s. What factors account for this dispersion? In the literature on labor unions, there is much evidence that the relative wage effect for the union workers in an industry will tend to be greater the larger the ratio of the output of union firms in the industry to the corresponding output of nonunion firms. The studies of unionism and wages also support the view that the relative wage effect will be larger, other things the same, the greater the rate of increase in the demand for labor in the industry.

That these two factors may fail to explain a substantial fraction of the dispersion among unions in relative wage effects for union workers is indicated by the fact that, except for 1945–1948, the largest effects estimated in the 12 studies consistently were those for bituminous coal miners. These miners, to be sure, have been relatively highly unionized; but so were many of the other groups covered in the studies. Furthermore, since World War II the relative demand for labor in bituminous coal mining has been declining.

Some observers of unionism in the United States have attributed the large relative wage effects for unionized coal miners in part to an unusual lack of concern by the United Mine Workers, the union representing most of the unionized coal miners, for the reduced employment of union miners resulting from high relative wage effects. It may be true that differences among unions in the extent of their concern for the employment of their members are important in explaining the differences in their relative wage effects. Until measures of such "taste" or "choice" differences among unions are developed, however, the quantitative significance of these differences for relative wages cannot be gauged.

Numerous other factors have been suggested by economists to explain the dispersion among unions in their effects on the relative wages of union workers: the ease of substituting other productive services for the services of union labor in production; the elasticity of supply of these other productive services to employers of union labor; the ratio of the cost of union labor to the cost of the other productive services; the degree of concentration of output ("degree of monopoly") among firms in unionized industries; the ease of entry of new firms into unionized industries; the extent to which union control of the supply of labor in its jurisdiction is facilitated by governmental licensing of occupations and trades; and other factors. For each of the enumerated factors it is relatively easy to find cases that apparently support its inclusion among the variables explaining interunion dispersion of relative wage effects.

However, the absence of data on several of these factors, the small number and likely selection biases in the sample of groups of union workers for which estimates of relative wage effects of unionism are

available, the differences among the estimates in the dates to which they pertain, the errors in the estimates, and the need to control for the effects of other factors while examining those of each particular factor impede, at present, evaluation of the relative importance of these factors or even the estimation of the *direction* of their effects. Such evaluation will require much additional research on the factors themselves and on the impact of unionism in industries and occupations for which relative wage effect estimates are unavailable for recent years.

H. Gregg Lewis

### BIBLIOGRAPHY

Friedman, Milton; and Kuznets, Simon 1945 *Income From Independent Professional Practice.* National Bureau of Economic Research, General Series, No. 45. New York: The Bureau.

Garbarino, Joseph W. 1950 A Theory of Interindustry Wage Structure Variation. *Quarterly Journal of Economics* 64:282–305.

Goldner, William 1958 Labor Market Factors and Skill Differentials in Wage Rates. Pages 207–216 in Industrial Relations Research Association, *Proceedings of the Tenth Annual Meeting.* New York: The Association.

Greenslade, Rush V. 1952 The Economic Effects of Collective Bargaining in Bituminous Coal Mining. Ph.D. dissertation, Univ. of Chicago.

Levinson, Harold M. 1951 Unionism, Wage Trends, and Income Distribution, 1914–1947. *Michigan Business Studies* 10, no. 4.

Levinson, Harold M. 1960 *Postwar Movement of Prices and Wages in Manufacturing Industries.* U.S. Congress, Joint Economic Committee, Study Paper No. 21. Washington: Government Printing Office.

Lewis, H. Gregg 1963 *Unionism and Relative Wages in the United States: An Empirical Inquiry.* Univ. of Chicago Press.

Lurie, Melvin 1961 The Effects of Unionization on Wages in the Transit Industry. *Journal of Political Economy* 69:558–572.

Maher, John E. 1956 Union, Nonunion Wage Differentials. *American Economic Review* 46, no. 3:336–352.

Princeton University, Industrial Relations Section 1960 *Wage Behavior in the Postwar Period: An Empirical Analysis.* Research Report Series, No. 100. Princeton Univ., Industrial Relations Section.

Rapping, Leonard A. 1961 The Impact of Federal Subsidies and Maritime Unionism on the Relative Earnings of Seamen. Ph.D. dissertation, Univ. of Chicago.

Rayack, Elton 1958 The Impact of Unionism on Wages in the Men's Clothing Industry: 1911–1956. Pages 674–688 in Industrial Relations Research Association, *Proceedings of the Spring Meeting.* New York: The Association.

Rees, Albert 1951 Postwar Wage Determination in the Basic Steel Industry. *American Economic Review* 41:389–404.

Rees, Albert 1962 *The Economics of Trade Unions.* Univ. of Chicago Press.

Ross, Arthur M.   1948   The Influence of Unionism Upon Earnings. *Quarterly Journal of Economics* 62:263–286.

Ross, Arthur M.; and Goldner, William   1950   Forces Affecting the Interindustry Wage Structure. *Quarterly Journal of Economics* 64:254–281.

Scherer, Joseph   1956   The Union Impact on Wages: The Case of the Year-round Hotel Industry. *Industrial and Labor Relations Review* 9:213–224.

Sobel, Irvin   1954   Collective Bargaining and Decentralization in the Rubber-tire Industry. *Journal of Political Economy* 62:12–25.

Sobotka, Stephen P.   1953   Union Influence on Wages: The Construction Industry. *Journal of Political Economy* 61:127–143.

Sobotka, Stephen P. et al.   1958   Analysis of Airline Pilot Earnings. Unpublished manuscript, Northwestern Univ., Transportation Center.

# LAISSEZ-FAIRE

The term "laissez-faire" has been used in the literature of economics and politics with such a wide variety of meanings that it is necessary to be somewhat arbitrary in defining what I shall take it to mean for the purpose of this article. Most of the explicit use of the term in the literature wears a negative aspect, being used by the writer not merely as a description but as a term of obloquy and even derision of the supposed views of others. This article however, deals with the positive substance of the concept of laissez-faire rather than with the etymological history of the term. For this purpose, I shall regard it as referring to a theory of the role of the state in economic life, but as something more than a theory—rather a maxim or doctrine, a principle of political theory that is *fundamental*, in the sense that particular questions of politics may be referred to it for judgment while it need not itself be referred to anything else.

The origin of the term has been ascribed to one Legendre, who, when the great Colbert asked a meeting of French businessmen what the state might do to assist them, pointedly replied, *"laissez-nous faire."* The French *économistes* (physiocrats) of the third quarter of the eighteenth century used the term as a maxim of policy and were inclined to speak of the economy in terms which seemed to imply a belief in the natural harmony of the economic system. Despite the strong liberalist character of their political views, their disposition to argue in a priori terms, and their conception of the economy as an *ordre naturel*, they did not in fact hold as a principle that the state should never interfere in economic matters, so they ought not to be characterized as espousing a laissez-faire doctrine.

**In England.**   Laissez-faire as a doctrinaire belief in the harmonious functioning (when let alone) of

an economy of self-seeking private agents is most commonly attributed to the English school of classical economists. The name of Adam Smith, founder of the school, is treated in much of the literature, scholarly as well as popular, as almost a synonym for laissez-faire. Viner's penetrating study (1927) of Smith shows that there is some ground for interpreting his first book, *The Theory of Moral Sentiments*, as representing a harmonistic conception of society but that this is not true of *The Wealth of Nations*. Viner's interpretation is supported by any moderately attentive and unprejudiced reading of *The Wealth of Nations* and is deepened by an appreciation of the nature of governmental economic intervention in Smith's time. *The Wealth of Nations* was a tract as much as a treatise, Smith being greatly concerned with attacking the chaotic mass of legislative and administrative restrictions that hampered economic activity in his day. If the phrase "laissez-faire" were construed to identify one who distrusts state intervention and believes that the world would be better off with less of it, Adam Smith, in the context of his own time, could properly be called an advocate of laissez-faire. But if it is a dogmatic principle that we are seeking to ascribe to him, we would be forced to depend for evidence on brief isolated passages from *The Wealth of Nations* that are clearly designed more for literary effect than for analytical service.

Robbins (1952) and others have shown that the writings and activities of the major classical economists after Ricardo also cannot be validly interpreted as evidencing doctrinaire laissez-faire. The classical economists did not attempt to present a harmonistic view of the unregulated economic world, and they did not advocate that the role of the state should be solely that of justice and defense. They supported state intervention in such concrete matters as sanitation, health, and conditions of factory employment. What misgivings they expressed regarding such proposals of state intervention in their time were based more on a concern for the maintenance of freedom of individual action than on any belief that the economic process would work best (normatively or technically) if left to work itself out without governmental intervention.

Doctrinaire laissez-faire views were, however, extensively expressed in Britain during the mid-nineteenth century by other, mainly popular, writers; and political economy was often claimed by them as scientific authority for a strict laissez-faire maxim. Harriet Martineau's didactic novels, *Illustrations of Political Economy*, and the weekly issues of the London *Economist* under James Wilson's editorship are outstanding examples of laissez-faire advocacy in this period (Gordon 1955). Thomas Hodgskin's writings are interesting in that he carried the laissez-faire dogma to the point of anarchism and, as a result, is classified by most historians as a socialist! The most elaborated and thoroughgoing philosophy of individualism of the nineteenth century is to be found in the writings of Herbert Spencer. He and Frédéric Bastiat in France should be cited as the prime sources of laissez-faire doctrine in the writings of the mid-nineteenth century that pretended to more than journalistic significance. Bastiat referred to what he conceived to be the analytic content of classical political economy, but Spencer, whose scholarly influence proved to be much greater and more enduring, drew little or not at all from this source. There is some evidence that laissez-faire beliefs were strongly held by some influential members of the British bureaucracy in the mid-century period, and that, through them, the doctrine exerted an important influence upon policy in particular cases. This is a matter of uncommon historical interest, but too little is known as yet about this aspect of British political life to judge how extensive or how important it was. Late in the century, in response to a growing current of political radicalism and trade union agitation, extreme individualist views were expressed by a group of writers mainly connected with the Liberty and Property Defence League (e.g., the Duke of Argyll, Donisthorpe, Mallock, and Mackay), but no intellectual movement of any depth or persistence resulted.

A large part of the identification of classical political economy with laissez-faire stems from the role played by Malthusian population theory and classical wage theory in the intense controversies of the 1830s over the poor law and the legal status of workmen's combinations. The "laws of political economy" were sternly invoked against labor unions and state welfare provisions. It was a small step for the working classes and others who felt keenly for their condition to conclude, first, that classical political economy preached laissez-faire and, second, that the whole business was only to be regarded as middle-class propaganda. From this period and this connection stem the most common use and identification of laissez-faire to be found in the literature down to the present day—that is, as a (rather scornful) label for the viewpoint of the bourgeois class, not really having to do with the limits of state intervention but with the question of who is to control, and in whose interest, the power structure of society.

The controversy over the corn laws in the 1840s also played an important role in the history of laissez-faire ideology. The leaders of the free-trade movement did not hold a general maxim of laissez-faire (Grampp 1960), although they often spoke in harmonist terms, which suggested a general laissez-faire belief, in their energetic attack on tariffs. The repeal of the corn laws in 1846 was followed by an extraordinary free-trade enthusiasm, amounting almost to the fervor of an evangelical faith. A good deal of the current belief that the Victorian age was actually one of laissez-faire results from a failure to distinguish between the general principle of laissez-faire and the much more limited scope of free international trade policy. England was a free-trade nation in the latter half of the century, but simultaneously with this development the state accepted more and more responsibilities (and opportunities) in the domestic economy. What is often called "the age of laissez-faire" was, in fact, the beginning of the modern welfare state (and even the planned economy). The political philosophy of liberalism, whose basic foundations were utilitarianism and humaneness (not, as is often supposed, fear of and opposition to state power), gradually evolved during the nineteenth century into its modern form, in which the state is regarded as a useful, indeed indispensable, instrument of human progress.

**In the United States.**   American economic and political thought of the early nineteenth century is sometimes characterized as laissez-faire, and, indeed, there is a strong general tradition of fear of governmental power in American life. The Jeffersonian conception of a severely limited government did not, however, become established, either in thought or in policy, in the first century of the republic. The economic writers who are sometimes represented to have held laissez-faire views (for example, John McVickar, Henry Vethake, Francis Wayland, and others) turn out, upon examination, to mark out a larger role for government in the economy than is consistent with a laissez-faire dogma. The presidential contest between Andrew Jackson and John Quincy Adams in 1828 was focused to a considerable degree on the issue of state economic intervention, but Jackson's victory did not in fact begin an era of laissez-faire in either the domestic or external economic policy of the United States.

It is not possible to describe any substantial period of United States economic policy as one of general laissez-faire, but there was a period in American intellectual history when a dogmatic school of laissez-faire thought was of some significance. This was during the last quarter of the nineteenth century and was associated with the great popularity in American intellectual and business circles of Herbert Spencer's ideas. Spencer's chief intellectual disciple in America was William Graham Sumner, who taught at Yale and energetically advanced a thoroughly doctrinaire faith in laissez-faire. Sumner and the social Darwinists (Hofstadter 1944) were for a time an important influence in American academic circles, but there is little evidence that their extreme individualist doctrine penetrated generally into American intellectual life. The doctrine was sometimes advanced by businessmen during the period of radical ferment, muckraking, and trade union agitation of the late years of the nineteenth and early years of the twentieth century, but this was too palpably self-serving to win widespread support. Generally, the phase of social Darwinism has been much exaggerated in American intellectual historiography.

Whatever laissez-faire leanings existed among the established American economists (and they were by and large too qualified to be considered doctrinaire) were opposed frontally in the 1880s by the younger economists led by R. T. Ely. The American Economic Association was founded by them explicitly as a vehicle for the expression of their views on the principle of the necessary positive role of the state.

There are certain elements of American history and political tradition that would seem to provide good conditions for the persistence and growth of an extreme individualist philosophy, but, in fact, such views have never had more than a peripheral, though recurring, manifestation in American political life and thought. A general antigovernment predilection is an important element of the contemporary school of American conservatism and of some popular political movements of the right. But, fundamentally, philosophical conservatism is based upon an organismic, not an atomistic–mechanistic, conception of society, and the writings of many of the modern American conservatives are more closely related to this (Burkeian) political tradition than to individualism and laissez-faire. More distinctly and fundamentally in the laissez-faire category are the writings of the contemporary Russian-born American novelist Ayn Rand. These are of interest because of their notable sales records and because they present the most extreme philosophy of individualism to be found in the whole literature of political thought, not excepting Herbert Spencer or the nineteenth-century philosophical anarchists.

Another branch of contemporary laissez-faire doctrine, of more technical interest but possibly less political importance than the currents of thought mentioned above, is a branch of academic economics. To appreciate this properly it is necessary to recognize that there is a sense in which the whole history of economic analysis since Adam Smith can be thought of as the investigation of the functioning of the "invisible hand." The welter of buying and selling that goes on in a division-of-labor economy is not a chaos. It is an orderly integrated system by which wants and productive efforts are meshed together, and the autonomous changes that occur in either are accommodated by a disciplined adjustment in the system of economic interdependencies. The full model of such a system was first clearly developed by Léon Walras' analysis of the economy as a general equilibrium system in his *Éléments d'économie politique pure* of 1874–1877. Alfred Marshall's *Principles of Economics*, appearing in 1890, presented a similar, though less explicit, picture, which has been very influential in the development of English-language economics in the twentieth century.

This neoclassical theory is a model of a competitive private enterprise economy without government, and therefore, in a positive (i.e., nonnormative) sense, it is a model of a system of laissez-faire. The construction of this theory, though it is one of great intellectual elegance, even beauty, did not, however, lead immediately to any significant development of laissez-faire ideology among economists. The trend of economic thought in the generation after Marshall was, in fact, more in the direction of the analysis of the needs and opportunities for state intervention.

An important current of thought, best represented by Henry C. Simons, was the development of a "positive program for laissez-faire"—an analysis of the institutional changes and governmental interventions required to permit and to induce the economy to operate like the competitive model and so achieve the optimum use of scarce economic resources. A more doctrinaire laissez-faire current in contemporary economics is represented by Ludwig von Mises and Milton Friedman. In the writings of these and associated economists, a political philosophy of extreme individualism, opposition to the governmental form (and certain other forms) of social coercion, and modern economic theory are joined in support of a laissez-faire maxim which, though much more sophisticated than earlier examples, is nonetheless quite doctrinaire in nature.

H. S. GORDON

[*Other relevant material may be found in the biographies of* BASTIAT; MARSHALL; SIMONS; SMITH, ADAM; SPENCER; SUMNER; VON MISES, LUDWIG.]

BIBLIOGRAPHY

BREBNER, J. BARTLET 1948 Laissez-faire and State Intervention in Nineteenth-century Britain. *Journal of Economic History* 8 (Supplement):59–73. → On the theme that the characterization of nineteenth-century Britain as laissez-faire is a myth. Criticism of Albert Venn Dicey's interpretation of the thought of the period.

COATES, WILLSON H. 1950 Benthamism, Laissez-faire, and Collectivism. *Journal of the History of Ideas* 11:357–363. → On the controversy concerning the relation between laissez-faire and utilitarianism.

FINE, SIDNEY 1956 *Laissez-faire and the General-welfare State: A Study of Conflict in American Thought, 1865–1901.* Ann Arbor: Univ. of Michigan Press; London: Cresset.

GORDON, H. SCOTT 1955 The London *Economist* and the High Tide of Laissez-faire. *Journal of Political Economy* 63:461–488. → A study of the early years of this famous periodical, during which it advanced a doctrinaire laissez-faire philosophy.

GRAMPP, WILLIAM D. 1960 *The Manchester School of Economics.* Stanford Univ. Press; London: Oxford Univ. Press. → A study of the political and economic theories of the businessmen who fought for the repeal of the British corn laws in the 1840s.

HENRICH, FREDERICK K. et al. 1943 Symposium on "The Development of American Laissez-faire." *Journal of Economic History* 3, no. 3:51–100.

HOFSTADTER, RICHARD 1944 *Social Darwinism in American Thought.* Philadelphia: Univ. of Pennsylvania Press.

KEYNES, JOHN M. 1926 *The End of Laissez-faire.* London: Woolf. → One of Keynes's great essays on current affairs. Reprinted in John M. Keynes, *Laissez-faire and Communism,* published by New Republic, New York, 1926.

MACGREGOR, DAVID H. 1949 *Economic Thought and Policy.* London, New York, Toronto: Oxford Univ. Press. → See especially Chapter 3.

MACPHERSON, C. BROUGH 1962 *The Political Theory of Possessive Individualism: Hobbes to Locke.* Oxford: Clarendon Press. → A new interpretation of seventeenth-century political theory which throws light on the relation between the political and economic philosophies of liberalism.

ROBBINS, LIONEL CHARLES 1952 *The Theory of Economic Policy in English Classical Political Economy.* London: Macmillan. → An extensive examination of the views of the classical economists on the proper role of the state in the economy.

VINER, JACOB (1927) 1958 *The Long View and the Short: Studies in Economic Theory and Policy.* Glencoe, Ill.: Free Press. → See especially "Adam Smith and Laissez-faire," pages 213–245.

VINER, JACOB 1960 The Intellectual History of Laissez-faire. *Journal of Law and Economics* 3:49–69. → A penetrating study of the historical background of the idea of laissez-faire broadly construed.

# LAMPRECHT, KARL

Karl Gotthard Lamprecht, German historian, was born in Jessen an der Schwarzen Elster in 1856, the son of the theologian and rector C. N. Lamprecht, and died in Leipzig in 1915. Lamprecht attended the classical Gymnasium in Wittenberg and then the celebrated Schulpforta school. He studied history, German, Latin, and Greek in the universities of Göttingen and Leipzig; after obtaining his doctorate in 1878, he went to Munich for postgraduate study. In 1879 he took the examination that qualified him for secondary-school teaching in the above-mentioned subjects. Then he spent a year as a private tutor in Cologne. There, certain benefactors provided him with the means of continuing his scholarly work; in 1880 he was able to qualify as an academic lecturer in history at the University of Bonn. There he remained until 1890, when he accepted a professorship at the University of Marburg (Lahn). In 1891 he accepted a similar appointment at Leipzig, where he taught until his death.

Lamprecht's work in the history of civilization was probably inspired by Wilhelm Scherer, a literary historian, and his work in economic history by Wilhelm Roscher, the earliest representative of the so-called historical school in political economy, under both of whom he studied. Lamprecht's early works deal with problems in the history of civilization and art. His studies led him to collect "libri picturati," illustrated medieval manuscripts. He continued such studies until 1882, when he concluded them with a monograph on the illumination of initials from the eighth to the thirteenth century. At this time he was also engaged in studies in economic history, research which was to produce his most enduring work, *Deutsches Wirtschaftsleben im Mittelalter* (1885–1886).

As early as 1882 Lamprecht, together with Felix Hettner, founded the *Westdeutsche Zeitschrift für Geschichte und Kunst* (note the inclusion of art in the title). He established in Leipzig in 1909 the Institute of Universal History and the History of Civilization, which likewise reflected his particular views. In 1910–1911, as the rector of the University of Leipzig, he advocated significant innovations in the field of cultural policy. Lamprecht gained wide recognition, receiving honorary doctorates from Columbia, Christiania, and St. Andrews. He was also a member of numerous academies and learned societies.

**Conception of universal history.** All Lamprecht's efforts early became concentrated on his *Deutsche Geschichte* (1891–1909), which established his importance for historiography. It was based on his conception of universal history, formulated when he was only 22, although he published it in explicit form only in the twelfth volume of his *Deutsche Geschichte*. Lamprecht, like others, did not share Ranke's optimism about the state of historical scholarship; he felt that it was generally declining and attributed this decline to excessive specialization, especially one-sided concentration upon political history. His vision was of a universal history that would deal with the interrelationships of events of every kind. But this task required an appropriate method.

Lamprecht developed a new method, drawing on positivist ideas and ordering behavior patterns in accordance with the theoretical principles of natural science. Under the influence of Wilhelm Wundt, he related this method to psychological concepts. He believed that historical epochs are characterized by collective psychological dispositions: the symbolic, the typical, the conventional, the individualistic, the subjectivistic, and the impressionistic.

Both Lamprecht's theory and his method gave rise to lively controversy and were bluntly rejected by almost all historians (K. Breysig being an exception), who found fault especially with the way he had applied his new ideas. For a time, Lamprecht did receive the approval of those French historians who had been influenced by Hippolyte Taine. Moreover, he was supported by anthropologists, historians of civilization, sociologists, and historically oriented economists, as well as by the adherents of a materialist conception of history, although he was far from sympathetic to their point of view. Lamprecht's scholarly work was not carried forward by others, one reason being that he was much too fair-minded to expect his students to accept his theses. The methodological dispute, often inappropriately treated as the antinomy between "individualistic" and "collectivistic" concepts, was prolonged and partly pointless, since under the impact of criticism Lamprecht himself modified his method in the course of writing the 12 volumes of his *Deutsche Geschichte*. The work thus turned out to be a respectable but premature and, in the end, unsuccessful venture that had no lasting influence. This does not mean that the endeavor may not some day be repeated with the use of more appropriate methods and with an extensive array of detailed studies in all areas. The perspective of universal history is still an objective of historiography.

FRIEDRICH LÜTGE

[*For the historical context of Lamprecht's work, see the biographies of* RANKE; ROSCHER; WUNDT. *For discussion of a parallel development of historiographical ideas, see the biography of* ROBINSON.]

### WORKS BY LAMPRECHT

1882    *Initial-ornamentik des VIII. bis XIII. Jahrhunderts.* Leipzig: Dürr.

1885–1886    *Deutsches Wirtschaftsleben im Mittelalter: Untersuchungen über die Entwicklung der materiellen Kultur des platten Landes auf Grund der Quellen, zunächst des Mosellandes.* 3 vols. in 4. Leipzig: Dürr.

1891–1909    *Deutsche Geschichte.* 14 vols. in 19. Berlin: Gärtner.

1905    *Moderne Geschichtswissenschaft: Fünf Vorträge.* Freiburg im Breisgau: Heyfelder.

1908    *Europäische Expansion.* Volume 6, pages 597–625 in Julius A. G. Pflugk-Harttung (editor), *Weltgeschichte.* Berlin: Ullstein.

1909    *Zur universalgeschichtlichen Methodenbildung.* Sächsische Gesellschaft der Wissenschaften, Leipzig, Philologisch-historische Klasse, Abhandlungen, Vol. 27, No. 2. Leipzig: Teubner.

1912    *Einführung in das historische Denken.* Leipzig: Voigtländer.

1912–1913    *Deutsche Geschichte der jüngsten Vergangenheit und Gegenwart.* 2 vols. Berlin: Weidmann.

### SUPPLEMENTARY BIBLIOGRAPHY

ARENS, FRANZ 1926 Karl Lamprecht. *Preussische Jahrbücher* 203:306–328.

BELOW, GEORG A. H. VON (1916) 1924 *Die deutsche Geschichtschreibung von den Befreiungskriegen bis zu unseren Tagen.* 2d ed. Munich and Berlin: Oldenbourg. → See especially pages 95 ff.

HÜBSCHMANN, S. 1929 Karl Lamprecht. *Mitteldeutsche Lebensbilder* 4:405–415.

KÖTZSCHKE, RUDOLF 1915 Verzeichnis der Schriften Karl Lamprechts. Sächsische Gesellschaft der Wissenschaften, Leipzig, Philologisch-historische Klasse, *Berichte über die Verhandlungen* 67:105–119.

KÖTZSCHKE, RUDOLF; and TILLE, ARMIN 1915 *Karl Lamprecht.* Gotha: Perthes.

[MEINECKE, FRIEDRICH] 1915 Karl Lamprecht [Obituary Notice], by M. *Historische Zeitschrift* 114:696–698.

SCHÖNEBAUM, HERBERT 1951 Vom Werden der *Deutschen Geschichte* Karl Lamprechts. *Deutsche Vierteljahrsschrift für Literaturwissenschaft und Geistesgeschichte* 25:94–111.

SCHÖNEBAUM, HERBERT 1956 Karl Lamprechts hochschulpädagogische Bestrebungen. *Zeitschrift für Pädagogik* 2:1–16.

SEIFERT, FRIEDRICH 1925 *Der Streit um Karl Lamprechts Geschichtsphilosophie.* Augsburg: Filser.

SPIESS, EMIL J. 1921 *Die Geschichtsphilosophie von Karl Lamprecht.* Erlangen: Junge.

WAGNER, FRITZ 1951 *Geschichtswissenschaft.* Freiburg im Breisgau: Alber.

# LAND

I. ECONOMIC ASPECTS                *Marion Clawson*
II. CLASSIFICATION                *L. Dudley Stamp*

## I

### ECONOMIC ASPECTS

Land is everywhere that man is; most men get their living from the land, directly or indirectly. Even those who live by or from the sea need a shore base or terminus. However, man is not ordinarily everywhere that there is land; a few deserts and the polar regions are too inhospitable to support men.

We use the word "land" to include all the characteristics and qualities of the earth, of what is popularly known as land; we do not limit it to soil, and our concern is not merely with agriculture.

Land may take many physical forms: plains, swamps, hills, mountains, or valleys; it may have many kinds of vegetation, such as forest, prairie, or tundra; and it may have one of many kinds of climate, from hot to cold, from humid to dry. It may also vary in numerous other ways. Space would not permit even a modest listing of the numerous kinds of land, in the physical sense; and our concern is more with its economic and social aspects. Land is useful to man in many ways: as a source of food, for wood for many purposes, for hunting, as a place to play, as a place to live, as a place to work. The uses of land are as many and varied as the whole range of human culture (U.S. Department of Agriculture 1958; Davis 1960; Food and Agriculture Organization 1961; Stamp 1948; Best & Coppock 1962).

As with any broadly inclusive idea, especially one which has popular as well as professional use, "land" obviously means many different things to different people. We could try to define it precisely, but this would be largely useless. Once an idea has escaped from any original, confined meaning into a broadly ranging, nearly universal usage, it is impossible to recapture and redefine it. Barlowe (1958) shows that the word has at least seven major meanings: (1) it is space, or room and surface, upon which life takes place; (2) it is nature, or natural environment, including access to sunlight, rainfall, wind, and other climatic conditions and including soil and natural vegetation; (3) it is a factor of production in economic processes, comparable to labor and capital; (4) it is a consumption good, especially when used as a site for dwellings, parks—and other essentially consumption processes; (5) it is a situation, or a location, with respect to markets, geographic features, other resources, and other countries; (6) it is property, with legal connotations as to rights of ownership of individuals and rights and responsibilities of ownership and sovereignty of governments; and (7) it is capital, in a realistic, economic sense, as will be discussed below. Ely and Wehrwein (1940) use a less detailed classification or definition of land, but they describe it as nature, space, and property, thus including many of the ideas expressed by Barlowe.

In this article we shall consider land in a num-ber of meanings, without attempting to define each precisely or, within the space available, necessarily treating each completely.

**Role in different societies.**    Partly because "land" means so many different things, but also because societies and cultures differ greatly in different parts of the world, land plays many different roles. Almost everywhere it is a productive economic factor in agriculture, forestry, grazing, mining, and even in fishing. In a later section, we shall explore its role in this respect somewhat further. Land is indeed basic to life for any considerable group of people, and its value cannot be overstated. But at this point we wish only to stress that its usefulness for production is not its only role.

Land has often been a major foundation for social prestige. Various societies have existed where social position was closely related to landownership, especially to landownership of a hereditary kind. The people who mattered owned land, and the people who owned land mattered; others were in an inferior position. This was largely true in England two or more centuries ago and to some extent still later. To some degree, it is true in most Latin American countries today. Where land plays or played this role, it was probably true at an earlier date that land was the basis of economic security and wealth, but the social prestige of land has often remained after its economic rationale has vanished.

Land has also often been the basis of political power. In the simplest relationship, this was because the franchise was extended only to landowners. But the same societies that gave high social position to landownership were likely also to give large political power to it. In colonial Virginia, it was the landed proprietors who governed the colony. Again, in many Latin American countries today, or at least until a few decades ago, political power rested heavily with the larger landowners. In modern United States, rural areas still have much more political power than do urban areas in proportion to their respective populations; while this is no longer directly tied to ownership of land, it largely arose from it.

Because land has been, and to a degree still is, owned for purposes other than to produce income, it is logical that goals other than maximization of income, especially of money income, should be uppermost in the minds of some landowners. It is frequently stated that much land is held in Latin America by owners who do not seek a maximum income from it. The argument goes that they are content with an income sufficient to meet their needs but that they own land for sentimental, historical, family, prestige, political, and other reasons. In some parts of Africa, ownership of cattle confers prestige, and land is valued in proportion to its ability to keep cattle alive, not in terms of income from it. Even within the United States, much land is held for consumption reasons, or as a hobby, or as a hedge against inflation, or for other reasons that are not connected with maximum current income.

Land is held under many different tenure situations around the world, reflecting in part the different reasons why it is owned but reflecting also different cultural histories (Conference on World Land Tenure . . . 1956; Ely & Wehrwein 1940; Renne 1947; Barlowe 1958; and many other land economists). Ownership, or exclusive control by an individual, subject only to certain rather general laws and public powers is not the only concept under which land is held and used in the world. Ownership is a Western idea, but even in the West there are many variations. In just such a limited matter as the relation between ownership of subsurface mineral rights and ownership of surface rights, there are great differences among the countries of Europe and of the Western Hemisphere. But the American Indians prior to the coming of the Europeans, many African peoples today, and other groups at various times and places have never had the same concept of individual ownership of land. With them, the group possesses the land, in a general sort of way, and individuals are assigned the use of specific tracts for limited periods of time, with periodic reassignment. Transfer of title, in the Western sense, is not practiced, and borrowing based on land for security is unknown and impossible. No small part of the clash between Western people and native groups in North America, Africa, and elsewhere has arisen out of these widely divergent concepts of social arrangements for the use of land.

In all societies, the group exercises some control over the use the individual makes of land, even when the individual "owns" it in the Western sense of the term. In the United States, for instance, much land is subject to zoning, which limits the uses that can be made of it. Even when the individual is subject to no such general control, he may be subject to suits from neighbors and others if they can prove that they have been damaged by his use of land. The power of government to take private land by use of its powers of eminent domain, the power to levy taxes on land to raise general revenue, and other general legal powers are widely recognized.

## Land as a factor of production

The traditional economic factors of production are labor, capital, and land. In this broad classification, land is defined to include all natural properties but to exclude invested capital. As we shall note below, the latter is unrealistic; some capital is so firmly blended with land that it is impossible to separate the two. The important fact to bear in mind is that no factor is productive alone; each requires some of the others in order to be productive. The proportion of the factors can vary and, thus, often their productivity. If one is scarce or expensive, it can be economized by using the others more liberally. An important field of economic theory is concerned with this matter of the proportions among productive factors and their effect upon output and upon the earnings and value of each factor. [See PRODUCTION; WAGES, *article on* THEORY.]

Land, if defined as the properties of nature without admixture of capital, has no reproduction cost because it is not capable of reproduction, and hence it has no supply cost or price. However, land, so defined, can and often does earn income when combined with other productive factors. If the others are paid at their reproduction costs or at their current prices—which over the long run tend to coincide—then the remaining surplus becomes rent. The definition, determination, and measurement of rent is a complex subject [see RENT].

Where rent exists, particularly where a monetary price is well known, it serves as a rationing device for land use. Only that use or those uses which can pay the rent can be undertaken. The most productive uses of land may have to bid the needed land away from somewhat less profitable uses. As in many aspects of economics, the next best alternative sets limits. However, something of the same result is sometimes achieved even when rent is fixed at artificially low levels. In modern Israel, for instance, land is publicly owned and rented on long leases to individual farmers or to groups of farmers at purely nominal prices. Rent is almost nonexistent in either a commercial or an economic sense. Yet land tends to be rationed among uses in more or less the same way a commercial rent would ration it because the farmer or the group must consider the earnings from land in alternative uses, since the total area allotted to him or to them is limited. Scarcity and alternative economic opportunities achieve the same result as would a more formally established rent.

The relation between inputs—of current production materials, such as fertilizer, and of labor and capital in various forms, into cropland or other land —and the resulting output is known as a production function. At a given stage in technological development, there is a more or less specific relationship between the inputs and the outputs. This does not preclude the use of additional inputs of fertilizer or any other productive factor, but says instead that the response will follow a known and defined path. The production function differs according to many factors, including climate and soil.

It also changes from time to time as new technology becomes known. The development of hybrid corn in the United States led to corn yields of about ten bushels more per acre, at the time an increase of about 25 per cent, with all other inputs remaining at their previous levels. Often, however, a new production function is not as simple; it takes the form of the use of additional or different inputs than formerly. As a result of modern soil science, for instance, the role of certain chemical elements, especially of the trace elements, has been discovered. The addition of chemicals previously lacking may change the production function drastically, with completely new input–output relationships.

Modern science and technology have resulted in a vast array of new production functions, which have in large measure transformed the productivity and use of land. Much land not previously usable by man for agriculture, forestry, grazing, or recreation, for example, is today usable for one or more of these things because new technology has enabled man to overcome earlier critical deficiencies.

In total, science and technology have diminished the economic importance of land without at the same time rendering land unessential. More fertilizer can substitute for additional land, for instance, at least within quite wide limits. In an earlier time, man was heavily dependent upon the native fertility and other natural qualities of land, and the only way to increase total output was to increase area of land under use—whatever the kind of use. Today, on the contrary, especially in the advanced countries, other productive inputs can lead to greater output and thus, in effect, substitute for more land. Agriculture in North America and in western Europe is being transformed by modern science and technology, with output increasing from the same or a smaller area of land at such a rapid rate as to create agricultural surpluses. The same thing is technically possible in other parts of the world but has not yet occurred, in part because the technology has not been adequately developed but primarily because the social

and economic organization to apply the necessary technology is lacking.

Although the relative role of land in productive processes has declined, land is still an indispensable part of the total productive process and is likely to remain so. One unalterable characteristic of land is that it receives energy from the sun; and as yet in our total society and economy, we have found no other method of capturing this energy as economical as that provided by land through agriculture, forestry, and grazing.

**Natural properties and improvements.** Adam Smith, Ricardo, and other early economists made much of the permanent and indestructible properties of land, but we now realize that their attitude was largely an unconscious reflection of the historical period and geography in which they lived. England is a humid country with a gentle rainfall, rounded hills, and natural grass and forest vegetation. Soil erosion has never been a serious problem there, as it has been in much of the rest of the world. At the end of the eighteenth century, man lacked the means to greatly damage such a landscape and lacked the knowledge to greatly improve the soils through use of artificial fertilizers. He was largely dependent upon the natural soil. But today we realize that man can often greatly damage the soil and the land where he lives—by earth moving, by cultivation, by fire, and in many other ways. Sometimes he can greatly improve the land, as by irrigation, drainage, protection against floods, and incorporation of needed plant foods. Land, as man finds it, is no longer so indestructible or unchangeable (International Symposium . . . 1956).

Man can place improvements *on* land by erecting buildings, constructing roads and fences, planting and improving forests, and so on. Before the improvements are actually made, the money they will cost is capital which might be used elsewhere. But once the improvement is constructed, it can ordinarily be used only jointly with the land; it is likely to have little salvage value apart from the land, if in fact it can be separated at all. For a long period of time, often for decades, these improvements are to all intents and purposes land itself.

Man can also make improvements *in* land. The construction of drains, either surface or underground, the provision of irrigation water, and similar improvements may greatly affect the productivity of agricultural land. Pipelines for water or sewage, underground cables for telephone and power, and similar improvements affect the value of the land for other purposes. These improvements in land are like those on land, in that they are identified with the land, but they are often less obvious and may be overlooked.

Improvements can actually be made *to* land. The whole microbiology of a soil can be changed by fertilizers, lime, irrigation, and other amendments. The tilth or structure of the soil particles can also be modified. Leveling or other earth movement may affect soil moisture relations greatly and may alter the susceptibility of the land to erosion. Plantings of trees, grasses, and shrubs may establish wholly new plant communities. All these improvements to land may last for long periods of time, with only modest upkeep or none at all.

In each of the foregoing ways, man can improve land, or at least land including closely incorporated capital. He can also damage or unfavorably alter it in many ways. He can accelerate its erosion for example, through unwise cropping, overgrazing, improper forest cutting, and use of fire. He can impair the natural drainage of the land, leading to waterlogging and lowered soil productivity. He can seriously and permanently alter its original ecological structure. But he cannot modify some aspects of land—its location on the face of the earth, its basic geology, or its climate—to a significant degree.

With so many important ways of modifying land, either for better or for worse, we conclude that relatively few of the characteristics of land are as indestructible as once was thought to be the case. Moreover, the distinction between land and capital is not as clear as it once seemed to be. Modern land often embodies substantial amounts of capital. Although the capital is relatively fixed in form and not easily separable from the land, it does have to be maintained in many cases and does have a different origin from the land itself.

**Location as a factor in land value and use.** Location affects land value and use in a number of ways. The physical characteristics of land, often associated with location, affect land value and use. Climate and other relatively unchangeable characteristics of land limit or modify use and, hence, its value. Soil differences are often highly correlated with local locational differences—the valley plain as against the hills, for instance. These and other microlocational differences are most significant within a locality where external influences are relatively constant.

On a larger scale, markets for the outputs of land are basic to the use and value of land. In the case of agriculture, the influence of distance from market has been noticed since the days of von Thünen (see Barlowe 1958 for a modern restate-

ment). The cost of reaching a market may be so great that the agricultural commodity has little or no value at the farm where it is produced. But the time required to reach the market may be as important as the cost. Perishables such as fruits, vegetables, and whole milk tend to be produced relatively close to their final market. With modern transport technology, including refrigeration in transit, "relatively close" may still stretch to hundreds of miles, and other factors may outweigh the time and distance which once would have been determinative. Very bulky and heavy commodities must also be produced close to market. In a former day when draft horses and mules were used within cities, the hay to feed them had to be raised moderately close to the cities concerned.

Only agricultural commodities that are relatively valuable in relation to weight or are nonperishable (or both) can withstand long shipments to market, especially under conditions of relatively primitive transport. Wool, for instance, which meets both criteria well, has for many centuries been transported relatively long distances. Variations in transport or other conditions may greatly affect the localization of production—a navigable river or a single highway or railroad will often result in a long finger of localized production of the kind found close to cities. Nearness to the transport artery substitutes for nearness to the city.

But the same factor of location also affects industrial and commercial uses of land. A factory or a trading center requires access to supplies of raw materials or goods and, above all, access to customers. It is likewise important for outdoor recreational use of land. People want playgrounds for their children within half a mile or less of where they live, but they will go 25 to 50 miles for an all-day outing at an attractive place and will drive hundreds or even thousands of miles on an annual vacation.

Cost, speed, comfort, and safety of transportation are highly important for every land use. Where once food had to be consumed locally, today it can be shipped hundreds of miles or even further, if necessary. Where once people shopped only at stores to which they could walk, today in the United States the housewife typically drives to market and will go distances which to her mother or grandmother would have been prohibitive. Where once a 5-mile trip by horse and buggy to a park was an annual occasion, now a man may drive farther than that for a round of golf after the day's work. The size of a metropolitan complex is to some degree governed by the willingness of people to travel from its periphery to its core, and this in turn depends heavily upon the kind of transport facilities available (Wingo 1961).

Input factors of various kinds, such as agricultural machinery and fertilizer for farming, also affect the locational aspects of land use to some extent. To a large degree, however, such inputs come from the urban centers to which the agricultural products are shipped; hence, inputs may exert little effect in addition to that resulting from differences in markets.

Land values are affected by the same general factors which affect land use. When land is used for some particular purpose, say for wheat growing, the land closer to market absorbs the lower transport costs, and a rent and a land value arise out of such gain to the land. More commonly, the land closer to urban centers will be used for other purposes, including rural residences, and will have higher values for these purposes. Within the city, the land at the effective center commands a higher value because it provides access to a larger body of potential customers. These factors influence differences in rent. [See RENT; SPATIAL ECONOMICS.]

**Externalities in value and use.** Very little land in the world today has its use and value determined wholly by its internal values. The availability of markets, discussed above, is one form of externality which is often decisive in determining land use and value. In most cases the markets are the result of the activities of others than the landowner or user; he adapts to them but rarely makes them.

But there are externalities other than markets for products. In the case of residential use of land, the character of the neighborhood may be far more important than the nature of the house. If the general neighborhood is deteriorating, then the value of all houses tends to decline, no matter how well-maintained a particular house may be. On the other hand, if the character of the neighborhood remains high, then even a poorly maintained house may bring a fairly good price. The ability of the individual homeowner to affect this situation is severely limited. It is the action of other owners, in maintenance of their property, which has the greatest effect upon him and his property.

Externalities also affect use and value of commercial, recreational, and other land. The existence of rival shopping or recreational centers may affect the volume of use, and hence the value, of a particular spot more than can any circumstances confined to the specific area. The total level of economic activity within a reasonable use radius greatly affects each of these land uses and others. Many complex forces are often involved, of which differences in transport is one of the more obvious. But, whatever may be the particular constellation of outside forces, it seems fairly clear that externalities and interdependencies dominate land use and value today, especially in the advanced countries but to a considerable extent everywhere.

**Public lands**

All countries, not merely the communist ones, have some publicly owned land. For the United States, all forms of public landownership include about one-third of the total area. This is true even within cities, where streets, alleys, parks, and other public areas are frequently one-third of the total area. Road and street transport area, airfields, and sometimes even railroads are publicly owned in most countries. Private toll roads and bridges are not unknown but are not typical. Most countries have publicly owned park and recreation areas; some have a great many. While much outdoor recreation is on privately owned land, there are several advantages to public ownership. Most parks are far too costly for individual use and have far more capacity than a family needs. While it would be possible for private groups to own and manage parks, in practice it is often easier for some unit of government to own the necessary land and provide its management and to let it be used by relatively large numbers of citizens. Some countries have extensive publicly owned forests and grazing areas, but public ownership of agricultural land is less common outside of communist countries.

The history and management of federally owned lands in the United States has been studied and reported upon by many American writers (Carstensen 1963; Clawson 1951; Dana 1956; Peffer 1951; and various others). Other publicly owned lands in the United States have had less attention, and relatively few studies have been directed specifically toward public lands in most countries.

One basic matter in the disposal and management of public and private land is cadastral survey to establish and mark on the ground the boundaries of various tracts. Closely related to such a survey is the establishment and maintenance of accurate and reliable records of landownership. Either or both of these functions may be done entirely by government or partly by government and partly by private activity, but some measure of public action is almost always necessary. In the absence of accurate surveys and reliable land records, individual owners are not sure either of title to their land or of its boundaries, and this is likely to inhibit severely their improvement and use of the land. Likewise, government improvement and use of its land are handicapped by the absence of such records.

Accurate cadastral surveys, clearly marked on the ground, and dependable records of land title are notably lacking in most underdeveloped countries today and constitute one more serious obstacle to the economic development of such countries. Hill (1964), for instance, shows that the lack of a cadastral survey and deficiencies in land titles are serious obstacles to land reform and land development in Costa Rica. The same could be said for almost all Central and South American countries and for many Asian, African, and Middle Eastern countries as well. Until a land occupier knows exactly which land is his and can defend his claim against all comers, he will naturally not try to develop his land to the fullest.

The handling of presently public lands can be highly influential in the future economy and society of those less developed countries in nearly all parts of the world that still have relatively large areas of public land. On the one hand, it could be disposed of or leased to large operators, with one kind of use and society developing, or it could be disposed of or leased to smaller owner–occupiers, who would make a different kind of use of it. In such countries, land is often the base for the society and the economy, as noted above, and the role of the public lands is, therefore, extremely important.

MARION CLAWSON

### BIBLIOGRAPHY

BARLOWE, RALEIGH 1958 *Land Resource Economics: The Political Economy of Rural and Urban Land Use.* Englewood Cliffs, N.J.: Prentice-Hall.

BEST, ROBIN H.; and COPPOCK, J. T. 1962 *Changing Use of Land in Britain.* London: Faber & Faber.

CARSTENSEN, VERNON R. (editor) 1963 *The Public Lands: Studies in the History of the Public Domain.* Madison: Univ. of Wisconsin Press.

CLAWSON, MARION 1951 *Uncle Sam's Acres.* New York: Dodd.

CONFERENCE ON WORLD LAND TENURE PROBLEMS, UNIVERSITY OF WISCONSIN, *1951* 1956 *Land Tenure: Proceedings.* Edited by Kenneth H. Parsons, Raymond J. Penn, and Philip M. Raup. Madison: Univ. of Wisconsin Press.

DANA, SAMUEL T. 1956 *Forest and Range Policy: Its Development in the United States.* New York: McGraw-Hill.

DAVIS, ELIZABETH G. 1960 *Urbanization and Changing Land Uses: A Bibliography of Selected References, 1950–1958.* Washington: U.S. Department of Agriculture.

ELY, RICHARD T.; and WEHRWEIN, GEORGE S. (1940) 1964 *Land Economics.* Madison: Univ. of Wisconsin Press.

FOOD AND AGRICULTURE ORGANIZATION OF THE UNITED NATIONS 1961 *Land Utilization.* Rome: The Organization.

HIBBARD, BENJAMIN H. 1924 *A History of Public Land Policies.* New York: Macmillan.

HILL, GEORGE W. 1964 The Agrarian Reform in Costa Rica. *Land Economics* 11, no. 1:41–48.

INTERNATIONAL SYMPOSIUM ON MAN'S ROLE IN CHANGING THE FACE OF THE EARTH, PRINCETON, N.J., *1955* 1956 *Man's Role in Changing the Face of the Earth.* Edited by William L. Thomas, Jr. Univ. of Chicago Press.

ISE, JOHN 1920 *The United States Forest Policy.* New Haven: Yale Univ. Press.

PEFFER, E. LOUISE 1951 *The Closing of the Public Domain.* Stanford Univ. Press.

RENNE, ROLAND R. (1947) 1958 *Land Economics: Principles, Problems and Policies in Utilizing Land Resources.* Rev. ed. New York: Harper.

ROBBINS, ROY M. 1942 *Our Landed Heritage.* Princeton Univ. Press.

STAMP, L. DUDLEY (1948) 1962 *The Land of Britain: Its Use and Misuse.* 3d ed. London: Longmans.

U.S. BUREAU OF LAND MANAGEMENT 1962 *Public Lands Bibliography.* Washington: Government Printing Office.

U.S. DEPARTMENT OF AGRICULTURE 1958 *Yearbook of Agriculture: Land.* Washington: Government Printing Office.

WINGO, LOWDON JR. 1961 *Transportation and Urban Land.* Washington: Resources for the Future.

## II
### CLASSIFICATION

The pressure of growing populations on fixed land area has caused one country after another to face the necessity of surveying and classifying its land resources. There is an enormous range in the character and quality of land that influences its productive potential. In the older settled countries —in most of those of Europe, for example—the best agricultural lands have been known for centuries, indeed frequently for thousands of years. A map of present land use may thus reflect land potential with considerable accuracy. On the other hand, in the newer developing countries, present use may represent but an early stage in a process of trial and error, and the tendency is to attempt a direct assessment of land potential.

One of the several useful approaches to land classification is directed to the study and mapping of soil, itself the result of the interaction between soil-forming processes, especially climatic, and the bedrock material. Many pedologists insist, however, upon studying soils as soils and are not directly concerned with the relationships of soils to production. When a soil map has been produced, therefore, it is still necessary to carry out an assessment of the productive capacity of each type.

Especially in areas where natural or almost original vegetation prevails, an ecological survey will reflect the sum total of existing habitat conditions. Under these conditions, certain plants can commonly be used as "indicators." The development of this line of work owes much to the pioneer studies of the American botanist Frederick E. Clements (1905; 1916–1920). However, except where soil or the nature of the terrain renders it impossible, natural vegetation is conceived as developing steadily toward a "climax" dictated by climate, and the natural vegetation is described as a climatic-climax vegetation. By studying the major climatic factors of moisture supply (rainfall) and temperature it should be possible to predict both the natural vegetation and the potential range of crops. This is the basis of the phyto-climatological maps which have been constructed over large areas by the French botanist Henri Gaussen from the institute which he long directed at Toulouse. His maps of the arid lands and their margins, prepared as part of the UNESCO program, have been used to indicate or suggest potential land use.

There is little doubt that land potential is closely related to the details of land form and there is a link with geomorphological studies. Large areas in the northern and central parts of Australia have been studied and the land has been classified on this basis under the direction of C. S. Christian. Monica Cole (1960; 1961; 1963) has shown that the tropical grassland areas of southern Africa and Brazil would also seem to be capable of interpretation by similar methods.

Evolved by American workers, a widely used classification of land into eight productivity classes attempts to include all these factors. Though the classification is simple, it is obvious that the observer's subjective judgment must play a major part. Briefly, the classification is as follows:

(I) Few limitations; very good land from every standpoint.

(II) Moderate limitations or risks of damage; good land from all-round standpoint.

(III) Severe limitations; regular cultivation is possible if limitations are observed.

(IV) Very severe limitations; suited for occasional cultivation or for some kinds of limited cultivation.

(V) Not suited for cultivation because of wetness, stones, overflows (flooding); few limitations for grazing or forestry use.

(VI) Too steep, stony, arid, wet, etc., for cultivation; moderate limitations for grazing or forestry.

(VII) Very steep, rough, wet, etc.; severe limitations for grazing or forestry.

(VIII) Extremely rough, arid, swampy, etc.; not suited for cultivation or forestry; suited for wildlife, watersheds, or recreation.

It will be noted that this classification is directed primarily to *suitability for cultivation* and reflects the American attitude toward grazing land rather than the viewpoint of the European or New Zealand farmer, who often regards improved grazing land as most profitable.

Many countries have developed similar productivity classifications to suit their own local conditions. Thus in 1963 the British Directorate of Overseas Surveys published sheets of a 1:500,000 map of Bechuanaland, showing ten types of land: the first five types included land suitable for both cultivation and grazing; the next three, land suitable for grazing; one, land unsuitable for agriculture (some areas could be used as forest reserves); and finally, land presently cultivated. About this time the same authority published a map of part of the southern Cameroons that showed seven quite different categories. As another example a survey of Jordan divided the whole country into "range-types."

Consideration of the varied approaches to land classification led A. P. A. Vink to distinguish six categories of classification. He noted that classes of land could be expressed in terms of: (1) inherent characteristics (soil and relief), (2) inherent qualities (soil quality classification), (3) present use (soil use), (4) use capabilities (soil suitability), (5) recommended use, and (6) program effectuation (1963).

The American system would belong to category 5. However, the system of ten land classes used in Britain, though paying attention to present use, belongs rather to Vink's fourth category. It arose from the Land Utilisation Survey of Britain, established in 1930, which carried out a field-to-field survey over the whole of England, Wales, and Scotland using maps on the scale of 6 inches to one mile (1:10,560) and publishing maps on the scale of 1 inch to one mile (1:63,360).

The British survey mapped land use according to seven major categories: A, Arable or tilled land, with fallow and rotation grass; M, Meadowland and permanent grass, enclosed and improved; H, Heathland, moorland, commons, and rough hill pasture; F, Forest and woodland (several types distinguished); G, Gardens, allotments; O, Orchards; and W, Land agriculturally unproductive, buildings, yards, mines, and so on.

The maps reveal a remarkably complex pattern —the result over the centuries of the interaction of such physical factors as relief, soil, drainage, and climate, of historical, social, and economic factors, including landownership, size and character of holdings, agricultural fashions, and prices.

The land-use map so produced depicted the actual base from which any planning for the future must start, but it is obviously far from being a land classification map. To attempt the classification of land was a next step. In the first place the history of land use proved to be very instructive. Over much of Britain, when the 6-inch-scale maps were being prepared in the 1870s, the surveyors recorded in their notebooks the use of each individual field. Where this was done—it was discontinued for reasons of "economy"—it is possible, laboriously it is true, to reconstruct a land-use map of about 1870–1875. Earlier large-scale maps, also showing land use, had been made of all lands subject to the old medieval tithes and these yield land-use maps of the period about 1840–1845. In addition there are privately produced county maps from the eighteenth and early nineteenth centuries. From even earlier times there are isolated estate maps, and a broad picture can be reconstructed for some areas from the Domesday survey of A.D. 1086. When all this historical matter is put together, one remarkable fact emerges: the stability of the land-use pattern through the centuries. It was the Anglo-Saxon settlers—essentially agriculturalists—in the early centuries after the Roman withdrawal who identified and reclaimed the best lands, those with deep loamy water-holding soils. Despite all the economic vicissitudes, these intrinsically good lands have remained in arable cultivation right to this day, except where the ever rising tide of urban-industrial development has obliterated them. At the other extreme the light sandy, stony, and mountain lands were recognized as agriculturally intractable by the Anglo-Saxons. Today they are the moorlands and heathlands. In many cases determined efforts, including the expenditure of much capital, have been made to bring them into improved agricultural use, but nature has won. The major changes over the years have been on land of intermediate quality, land which it paid to cultivate only when agricultural prices were high. Thus land use, studied historically, was found in Britain to be an important guide to land potential. Combined with a detailed study of the terrain, of site and soil, a tentative classi-

**Table 1 — Classification of land in Great Britain**[a]

| | Per cent[b] |
|---|---|
| (I) Good quality lands | 38.7 |
| (1) First-class land capable of intensive cultivation, especially of foodstuffs for human consumption — mainly deep loams, naturally fertile | (4.2) |
| (2) Good general purpose farmland with a wide range of crops | (20.6) |
| (3) First-class land but with a high water table or liable to periodic flooding, hence largely in grass | (2.2) |
| (4) Good but heavy land often with a naturally high fertility but presenting problems in working | (11.7) |
| (II) Medium quality lands | 26.3 |
| (5) Medium quality light land | (4.8) |
| (6) Medium quality general purpose farmland, often very mixed | (21.5) |
| (III) Poor quality lands | 32.8 |
| (7) Poor quality heavy land—intractable clays needing drainage | (1.6) |
| (8) Mountain land and moorland | (29.3) |
| (9) Poor quality light land | (1.5) |
| (10) Poorest land | (0.4) |
| Residue—closely built over | 2.2 |
| | 100.0 |

a. 1938–1940.

b. The figures in each case indicate the percentage of the total surface of Great Britain in each category. What is striking is the very small proportion of first-class land—less than 2½ million acres.

*Source: Stamp (1948) 1962.*

fication of land into ten types was drawn up in 1938–1940 (see Table 1). In the course of the succeeding 30 years or more, no better has yet been devised, though a simplified version based on the same criteria but separating five categories only was brought into use by the Ministry of Agriculture in 1965–1966.

Before the outbreak of World War II, two major trends were worrying the British government. One was the marked growth of population and industry in two main areas—Greater London and Greater Birmingham—at the same time as there was serious unemployment in the older industrial areas. This led the government to set up the Royal Commission on the Geographical Location of the Industrial Population under the chairmanship of Sir Montague Barlow. In due course this commission recommended positive steps to secure a wider distribution of industry (Great Britain 1940).

The other trend was that of using the better types of agricultural land for housing and industry, with the result that over 50,000 acres a year were being lost from food production. The government set up the Committee on Land Utilisation in Rural Areas under the chairmanship of Lord Justice Scott to study the problem. The government eventually declared its intention to conserve the good agricultural lands and to direct development, wherever possible, to poorer lands. At the time there was no classification of land; hence the scheme of ten classes outlined above was developed. The Scott Committee on Land Utilisation in Rural Areas reported in 1942 (see Great Britain 1942). Its main recommendations were embodied in the Agriculture Act of 1947, the Town and Country Planning Act 1947, the National Parks and Access to the Countryside Act 1949, and later legislation. Britain thus became the first major country to accept compulsory land planning over the whole. The planning unit was normally the county: each was required to prepare a plan according to which future development could be sanctioned. The Agricultural Act gave tenant farmers great security of tenure; it gave farmers a guaranteed market and prices guaranteed in advance (subsidized) for principal products. A general planning directive was to avoid major housing or other urban development on good lands, to improve hill land, and to direct forestry to the poorest lands.

It would be quite wrong to suggest that the principle of conserving the better agricultural lands in food production is fully accepted. However good the quality of the land and however effectively farmed, it is scarcely possible for the value of the output per acre in foodstuffs to equal the value of the output from a factory on the same site. Similarly the capital or rental value of the land in agricultural production is far below its value or rental for "development" purposes. Consequently, under laissez-faire economics, little if any attention was or is paid to quality of land if it is required for industrial or other forms of development. The contradiction lies in the simple fact that man must be fed, but the area of really productive land is everywhere in the world restricted. Some poorer lands can be "upgraded" to a limited extent, but the capital cost is high. Further, if the amount of capital available for land improvement is restricted, there is a far greater return if the money is devoted to inherently good lands than if the expenditure is on basically poor land. On the other hand, the quality of land makes little if any difference when siting an industrial complex.

The nations of the world show very great contrasts in their land resources, and this obviously influences very strongly their attitude toward land planning and to the urgency of an inventory of their land resources. Taking the world as a whole, the total land surface represented about 11.5 acres per head of population in 1964. Of this total one-fifth is too cold—covered with ice or semipermanently frozen—to be capable of agricultural produc-tion; another fifth has inadequate moisture and no known available source of water; still a third fifth is too elevated, mountainous, or broken in relief; finally, one-tenth is soilless—bare rock surfaces. This leaves 30 per cent, approximately 3.5 acres of land per individual which has some soil, adequate moisture, and a range of temperature which put it into the general category of "potentially usable" in the sense of agricultural production. But it includes much land (the great tropical forests and grasslands) that with our present knowledge and techniques is very difficult to manage. Out of this per capita total of 3.5 acres, just over 1 acre is actually used—plowed or worked by hand and cropped. Equating the nonfood crops on these lands with a production of meat from natural grazing land we may say that, averaging all the varied world diets, standards of production, and levels of sustenance, it takes at the present time 1 acre to feed 1 person, or 1 hectare to 2.5 persons. This gives a world standard of comparison; Table 2 gives the corresponding figures for a number of countries. Some of the lessons to be learned are obvious. The United States and Canada are rich in land on whatever basis one chooses to take. They have not yet felt the pressure of population on land, which is so severe in most of the countries of Europe and many parts of Asia, notably Japan. India and Pakistan have an extreme shortage of cultivated land, since unlike Great Britain and Japan, their productivity per acre is low, and they lack the funds to import food.

Table 2 is purely a factual statement of acres per head of population. Obviously land is used far more intensively in some countries than others. Obviously, too, the potential of farmland is far higher in some areas than in others.

We can, of course, attempt to measure actual productivity, though even that is far from simple. A useful device for equating various crops is in

### Table 2 — Acreage per capita, 1964

|  | Total | Cultivable | Cultivated |
|---|---|---|---|
| World | 11.5 | 3.5 | 1.1 |
| United States | 11.5 | 6.0ᵃ | 3.5 |
| Canada | 125 | 20 | 4.0 |
| Australia | 180 | b | 5.0 |
| New Zealand | 28 | 17 | 1.1 |
| India | 2 | 1.0 | 0.9 |
| Pakistan | 3 | 1.0 | 0.7 |
| Great Britain | 1.1 | 0.6 | 0.55 |
| England and Wales | 0.8 | 0.6 | 0.55 |
| France | 3.3 | 2.0 | 1.8 |
| Japan | 1.1 | 0.2ᵃ | 0.15 |

a. Estimated.
b. Unknown.

Source: Updated from Stamp 1960.

terms of calories and I have suggested (Stamp 1960) that a useful unit is one million calories of farm production per annum. This I have called a Standard Nutrition Unit (SNU) because with 10 per cent loss in preparation, it represents 2,460 calories per day—a reasonable average intake for human health. On a largely rice and bean diet, intensive Japanese cultivation can produce 6 or 7 SNU per acre—in other words an acre intensively cultivated can be made to support 6 or 7 people. Good wheatland can produce 4 units, but a milk–meat–fruit diet requires 2 to 3 acres of average land to produce one unit.

But in using output of farm produce or similar units such as stock carried per unit area we are not measuring land potential, we are measuring land productivity combined with existing level of techniques and farming skill. Various systems of calculating "stock units" (sometimes "cow units" is the normal) have been devised, which differ in detail. One adult horse, cow, bull, or bullock may be considered as one unit, a young animal as one-half, a mature sheep as one-seventh, a lamb as one-fourteenth, a fat pig as one-tenth, and so on. As a measure of the "carrying capacity" of natural grazing we can then say it is, for example, 2 units per acre. This would imply a proper balance: not overgrazed to cause erosion nor undergrazed to allow development of coarse vegetation. Improvement can then be measured against increased capacity. Another approach to the measurement of the relative value of grazing land is in the production of meat per acre. This in turn can be converted into money values and so the output of beef or mutton by value can be compared with output of similar land under forest.

Can we think in terms of a Potential Production Unit? If one equates good average farmland in Britain with a potential productivity of one (1 PPU), there is at least some evidence to show that the best lands should have a ranking of 2 PPU and poor hill land of 0.1 PPU. If this general method of assessment can be perfected, its use in land planning is obvious. One thousand acres of the best land would have a productive potential of 2,000; one thousand acres of poor sandy land only 100. When a country has limited land resources, industrial and housing development should surely be on the low ranking land; the country thereby loses but little of its potential productivity in food.

Before linking land classification with land planning, however, it is necessary to pose the question: What basic needs of mankind must be satisfied by an adequate allocation of land? High priority must be given to the need of work, which translated into terms of land requirement means allocation of land for industry. Many industries—the extraction of coal, oil, minerals, and heavy industries based thereon—are fixed by the location of the raw materials; many others, such as shipbuilding and oil refining, require a certain juxtaposition of favorable physical factors. Only a limited number of industries are uninfluenced by land requirements and are thus capable of planned location. In a highly competitive world those countries, such as Japan and Britain, which depend for their very existence on manufacturing for export must give their industries the best possible chances of success by allowing industrial interests to choose the most favorable locations. Such choice may clash with other interests, especially recreational and agricultural. What is important is that there should be a full consideration of all interests.

A second basic need of mankind is for shelter. Perhaps more than in any other sphere in questions of town planning and especially the allocation of land for housing there is bitter controversy between high and low density, between the advantages of apartments and individual houses, the optimum size of towns, the journey to work, and many other problems. The world seems to be moving toward a compromise of type of dwelling with limits to development set by green belts and amenities preserved by an adequate open-space network. But there is by no means general agreement on desirable standards; just as one example, consider the demand by schools and colleges for an increase of land area relative to population numbers.

This last consideration is closely linked with a third need, that of land for recreation. One thinks of parks in towns, playing fields attached to schools and for the postschool population, but there are also the larger demands of land for state and national parks and for nature conservation. The national parks of the United States and Canada and many of the countries of Africa are at the same time conservation areas with vast land resources but few human inhabitants. When Britain established national parks under an act of 1949, the areas chosen were ones of great natural beauty but for the most part are occupied by farmers and, in fact, include numerous villages. The effect of designation as a national park in such cases is to make especially difficult further development and, especially, to prevent extensive and incongruous building.

A fourth need of mankind is for freedom of movement—land for airports and especially for roads. In the older crowded countries the existing road systems were never intended for the crush of modern automobile traffic, yet the close spacing of towns and villages and the intensive farming of the intervening land make the provision of new motor roads very difficult. Nevertheless, Hitler's drive for *Autobahnen* and Mussolini's for *autostrade* have been continued and extended to nearly all countries in the world. But the land-consuming road junctions common in America take up so much land that they must be introduced with great caution in the more crowded countries. The current demand for huge tracts for airports—runways of over two miles—may in the near future be obviated with the introduction of vertical take-off aircraft.

It is unfortunately true that a fifth need of land is for defense and training of the fighting services, and the demand is often very large.

All these are uses which eat into the open land, whose function should be primarily to produce foodstuffs and raw materials. It is here that there is the utmost need to integrate arable farming, pastoral husbandry, and forestry. Fortunately the conservation of nature makes its primary demands on intrinsically poor land of relatively little interest to the farmer, but for the maintenance of the balance of nature the need is to conserve and actively manage so as to maintain the character and the adequacy of the varied natural habitats demanded by plants and animals. This is the problem actively studied by the various conservation services now found in most countries.

In crowded countries the problem of land planning is urgent. This is certainly the case in Britain, and it is now appreciated as a social problem which cannot be settled by the free play of economic forces. Three principles are being generally observed. The first is the principle of optimal use—to find the optimum use of every parcel of land in the national interest. The second is the principle of multiple use—much hill land can serve as grazing land or can be afforested yet also serve as a watershed and, in many cases, for public recreation. It is only in a few cases of particularly rare species that nature conservation requires the exclusive use of land. A third principle is the total elimination of wasteland: all land should have some function in the national economy. Unfortunately it is usually cheaper to develop virgin land than to redevelop wasteland such as derelict industrial sites.

There is, however, in many countries a demand for over-all land planning, possibly based on a "land budget." Otherwise there is a natural human tendency for the specialist to make excessive demands for his own particular interests. For example, how much land can a crowded country afford for housing the people if thereby there is a serious loss in food-producing capacity? What should be the allocation for different forms of recreation? What control should be exercised over mining—especially if large areas are rendered derelict by it?

In the preceding paragraphs emphasis has been placed on current interest in land classification as a basis for national planning and the allocation of scarce land resources for the varied needs of a nation. It is tempting to use "productivity classes" for such purposes, but warnings come from archeologists, historians, and progressive agriculturists, who would emphasize the importance of changing technology. Most of the older countries afford examples. In England the pre-Roman, Celtic farmers sought the rolling uplands of the south where the land was naturally well drained, the light scrub relatively easily cleared, and the thin light soils could be worked in small square fields by hand. The heavily wooded valleys and lowlands were avoided. Then came the Anglo-Saxons who, with their ox-drawn plows, were able to cultivate long strips of land. It was they who found the rich loam soils of the valleys and undertook the forest clearance needed. Until late in the Middle Ages, the fens of eastern England remained a water-logged morass. Windmill drainage converted them to fine sheep pasture, then more efficient pumps made them the country's finest arable lands. Major changes are still taking place. The water table and former winter flooding in alluvial lowlands can now be controlled; the greatest contrast in the land-use maps of eastern Kent for 1932 and 1962 is in the conversion of grazing to arable on alluvial lands formerly flooded in winter. Today, the most prized arable fields of the Celt are among the lowest priced farmlands in those parts of the country where they are found. Another aspect of technological progress is in the simple provision of dressings with appropriate trace elements completely altering previously assessed "potential." This has been demonstrated in Australia. Over considerable parts of tropical Africa today settlements and cultivation avoid the river valleys because of the prevalence of river blindness transmitted by the fly *Simulium*. If the fly can be exterminated or a cure found then the whole land potential is changed. The same is true if effective measures for the control of the tsetse fly, carrying the nagana disease of cattle, can be developed. A comparable example is familiar from the "villages which have moved downhill" in New England—the earlier settlement on the "healthy" hilltops, the later development of the valley lands.

A vast amount of information with examples described by experts from all parts of the world will be found in the *History of Land Use in Arid Regions* (Stamp 1961). Not unexpectedly many aboriginal peoples have developed their own systems of land classification.

The Burmese peasant cultivators are familiar with a classification based on soil type, each with a distinctive name. One of the most elaborate of all is the land classification of parts of India used as a basis for village land allocation and taxation. It was taken over by the British administration in India, and it was one of the tasks of the land settlement officers to prepare maps. It often surprises present-day researchers to find these very detailed manuscript maps, going back to the 1870s perhaps, on the scale of 16 inches to one mile, in many local offices. They were of course used as a basis of taxation.

This is the prime reason for land classification in many countries. Every resident in Canada, taxed annually on the assessed capital value of his land, knows the difference it makes if his holding is classified as "improved" or "unimproved." Much land reverts to the state by becoming "tax delinquent." Examples of land classification for revenue purposes could be detailed from many countries. A survey of Denmark was undertaken about 1826 and is still in use. Owners of property in many lands are resentful of the fact that as soon as they make additions or improvements they are reassessed and taxed accordingly. The principle was long used in Denmark that taxation was on the basic character and quality of the land and not on the results of improvements—a great incentive to good farming. East Germany may be cited as an example of a country using an elaborate land classification with values theoretically from 0 to 100. The approach in the U.S.S.R. is naturally somewhat different, since the land is state-owned, but production targets are based on a land classification—with a strong emphasis on soil. The Russians dislike the approach from "natural" regions: anything "natural" is a challenge to the technologists to improve. So in setting targets of production the techniques available at the moment can be married with assessments of land potential. Land classification becomes part of the business of government.

Although land classification is linked primarily with economic output and taxable capacity as part of the technique of government, it can and should be used more widely. It is possible to measure what loss in food production will result if an area is declared a nature reserve or a recreational area. Thus a major planning decision affecting more than just the physical needs of man can be taken with the broader implications clearly in view. Land classification becomes then an essential requirement in every part of the world as population pressure on land increases.

L. DUDLEY STAMP

[*See also* AGRICULTURE; LANDSCAPE.]

BIBLIOGRAPHY

CLEMENTS, FREDERICK E. 1905 *Research Methods in Ecology.* Lincoln, Nebr.: University Pub. Co.

CLEMENTS, FREDERICK E. (1916–1920) 1928 *Plant Succession and Indicators: A Definitive Edition of* Plant Succession *and* Plant Indicators. New York: Wilson.

COLE, MONICA M. 1960 Cerrado, Caatinga and Pantanal: The Distribution and Origin of the Savanna Vegetation of Brazil. *Geographical Journal* 126:168–179.

COLE, MONICA M. 1961 *South Africa.* London: Methuen.

COLE, MONICA M. 1963 Vegetation and Geomorphology in Northern Rhodesia: An Aspect of the Distribution of the Savanna of Central Africa. *Geographical Journal* 129:290–305.

GREAT BRITAIN, COMMITTEE ON LAND UTILISATION IN RURAL AREAS 1942 *Report.* Papers by Command, Cmd. 6378. London: H.M. Stationery Office.

GREAT BRITAIN, ROYAL COMMISSION ON THE DISTRIBUTION OF THE INDUSTRIAL POPULATION 1940 *Report.* Papers by Command, Cmd. 6153. London: H.M. Stationery Office.

STAMP, L. DUDLEY (1948) 1962 *The Land of Britain: Its Use and Misuse.* 3d ed. London: Longmans.

STAMP, L. DUDLEY 1960 *Our Developing World.* London: Faber.

STAMP, L. DUDLEY (editor) 1961 *A History of Land Use in Arid Regions.* Arid Zone Research, No. 17. Paris: UNESCO. → In both English and French.

VINK, A. P. A. 1963 *Aspects de pédologie appliquée.* Neuchâtel (Switzerland): La Baconnière.

# LAND REFORM

*See under* LAND TENURE.

# LAND TENURE

I. INTRODUCTION      *Daniel P. Biebuyck*
II. AGRICULTURAL TENANCY      *John F. Timmons*
III. LAND REFORM      *Philip M. Raup*

## I
### INTRODUCTION

Under the general and confusing label "land tenure," we are concerned with the complex relationships that exist between categories of individuals and groups in reference to land, water, and their respective products. These relationships can be analyzed in terms of sets of rights and obligations held by these categories of people with regard to the acquisition, exploitation, preservation, and transfer of specific portions of terrain and products. Some of these rights and obligations are highly formal and have little practical bearing. Some are part of a well-established system of legal rules, while others have their foundations in *de facto* situations. Rarely do these rights, in practice, have an absolute or fully exclusive character. They are, in other words, subject to certain limitations and modalities that are contained in various principles of social organization, situational contexts, ethical principles, and rules of etiquette. Such factors as reciprocity, gift exchange, attitudes toward food and labor, prestige, and recognition contribute to give a special overtone to these rights and obligations.

**Patterns of landholding.** In order to gain a complete idea of the complicated issues involved, an abstract enumeration or a static view of rights and obligations cannot suffice. To show their content and scope, their practicality and bearing, and the range of entities and social personalities concerned, these rights and obligations must be viewed against a background of highly variable and varying activities and situations. These rights are held in reference to specific parcels of land that can simultaneously be the object of many activities: planting, harvesting, clearing, trapping, hunting, food collecting, building, passage, grazing, etc.; the particular situations and social context in which these activities are performed may differ according to occasion, person, purpose, and time period. These rights are not merely concerned with exploitation, disposal, or control of land, but include also the sharing of products, the levying of tribute, the inauguration of economic activities, the performance of rites, and the claim to settle disputes.

All peoples subdivide the land on which they live for particular purposes of exploitation and residence. This does not mean that *all* the land on which a given people live is actually subdivided or that there is only one way in which it is subdivided. In all societies there exists a set of minimal regulations that determine the nature of these subdivisions and the kind of groups or categories of individuals that are associated with them. The vast deserts and steppes inhabited by Arab, Persian, or central Asian nomads are not *res nullius*. These peoples have well-defined ideas about tribal, state, sacred, and personal lands. They have (and respect) fixed patterns of movement and seasonal migration over well-known routes, which are conceived in such a way as to provide each of the groups associated with them with a complete range of seasonal necessities. The point is not that these peoples may be more interested in the products than in the land that provides them, but rather that

there exist recognized zones of land control associated with defined human groups.

The principles of land tenure are correlated with various interlocking historical, ecological, demographic, technological, sociopolitical, religious, and psychological factors. The multiple ways in which these factors operate together or against each other render difficult any attempt to set up types of correlations. Generally, in the societies studied by anthropologists, everybody is entitled to obtain land for specific purposes of exploitation and residence. Individuals achieve this by a fairly simple method through membership and/or residence in local kinship groups, villages, bands, tribes, and less frequently, through more involved contractual relationships such as purchase, pledge, loan, lease, clientship, or service. Population density in these societies is, for the most part, low, and this enhances the possibilities for generalized access to land and resources. Landless individuals and groups are thus an exception; indeed, in many societies, land is the single most significant patrimony held by groups of people. This does not, of course, mean that everybody holds equal title to, or equal amounts of, land, nor does it imply that everybody secures these rights in the same manner, under the same conditions, or with the same implications. Even in societies where land is plentiful, marked competition for land and its resources may exist, which is often expressed in rigid demarcation of certain boundaries, highly individualized rights in regard to some types of exploitation, and concurrence of apparently multiple antagonistic principles of land tenure. Population concentrations within certain parts of an otherwise sparsely inhabited region, different qualities of soil and diverse seasonal necessities, local availability of specific animal or plant resources that are highly rated in the value or food systems, and the religious significance attached to select stretches of land account for this situation. The presence of oases or permanent water holes in desert country, forest galleries amidst poor savanna country, natural palm groves in forest or savanna, alluvial soil or rich marshland, the occurrence of seals' breathing holes, etc., provide ample scope for intensive exploitation and rigid delineation of rights in an otherwise flexible context.

There has been a tendency to correlate some patterns of landholding with the basic economic systems of food gathering, hunting, agriculture, and pastoralism. Most of these simplifications have proven to be of little value. The greater portion of known populations are at the same time involved in multiple and complementary forms of land exploitation. If not, they are embedded in a broader community in which highly different economic activities that definitely influence attitudes toward land are carried out by various populations (that is, the many instances of complex contacts between pastoral and agricultural societies or those between Pygmies and Bantu- and Sudanic-speaking populations). But more significantly, these basic economies can and must be broken down into a wide variety of activities, patterns, and technological components. There is no simple category of hunting rights; there are several methods of hunting (with bow and arrow, with dogs and nets and spears, with traps, etc.), a fact that may imply participation of highly diverse categories of people and multiple forms of interaction. There are many kinds of animals hunted, some scarce and some common, some royal or sacred and some not, some economically valuable and others not, some nomadic and others rather sedentary. Again these fea-ciples of land tenure. Furthermore, the purposes of the hunt vary greatly, some hunting parties having tures are not without profound effect on the prin-a magical character or being connected with seasonal ceremonies or initiations, others being linked merely to subsistence. Trapping rights, which are but one aspect of hunting, have to be analyzed in terms of types of traps, durability, degree of specialization, and nature of environmental alteration.

In different societies, individual rights in land, water, and their products are most commonly secured through membership in tribes, bands, local kinship groups, and villages; descent, residence, marriage and broader affinal relationships, friendships, and political allegiance are basic criteria in establishing this membership. Contractual relationships based on gift, sale (often conditional), lease, tenancy, and pledge are most certainly present in many societies but have often been incorrectly related to the broader social framework. It is clear that in the majority of societies, the bulk of land rights are secured through membership in local kinship groups, but again, for a number of evident reasons, there is no way of drawing simple correlations. The very principles on which these groups are built up—their internal structure, the character of their connections with other similar entities within the larger community, their degree of permanence, and the extent to which affinal and friendship relationships operate to shape residence patterns—leave ample room for a wide range of patterns of rights in land and products. The nature of land control exercised by political officeholders makes patterns all the more unpredictable. In politically centralized societies, kings or paramount chiefs may lay claim to all the land occupied by their subjects. This claim may be expressed by a continued manipulation of land, the giving and withdrawing of it being dictated by political necessities and whims; it may merely manifest itself in the levying of tribute on certain products, or in the right to settle disputes over land, or the right to resume and reallocate unoccupied land. The claim may be purely theoretical and overshadowed by the chief's duties to insure the fertility of land and everything living on it or by his obligation to see to it that everybody has sufficient land. In other politically centralized societies, chiefs and other subordinate political officeholders may have claims only to specific tracts of land or to vacant land; in still others, they have no claim whatsoever in land, or their rights simply are similar in scope to those held by any lineage head.

**Nature and function of landholding.**   The strictly structural and functional approach to the study of land tenure fails to account for a number of vital questions, the answers to which may be found in the ethnohistorical traditions of particular groups. Thus, in many cases, peculiar features of land tenure result from the history of migration or of settlement and occupation of a given territory, from subsequent contacts between groups of similar and dissimilar cultures, or from the internal history of segmentation, fission, and fusion in local kinship and political units. Furthermore, different elements of folk taxonomy and linguistic classification dealing with land, water, and products shed considerable light on the nature of rights and the entities with which they are associated in a specific social and geographical context.

In virtually all societies, various forms of communal, joint, familial, and individual rights in land and its resources are intricately interwoven with one another. In many cases either the individual or joint aspects of these rights and obligations are emphasized, or are at least most clearly manifest, but this does not automatically lead to the absence of the other aspects. Thus in pastoral tribes, where grazing rights are normally vested in larger entities such as the tribe itself, restrictive claims to certain pastures or wells are seasonally or permanently enhanced. In hunting and food-gathering societies, where control over defined tracts of land is associated with bands or local kinship groups, certain forms of exploitation on smaller portions of the general domain are restricted to segments of bands or to families and individuals. In simple agricultural societies, where general control of a given land tract is vested in a local kinship group or in a village, individualized rights in fields, agricultural products, trees, trapping sites, etc., do exist.

Many authors, apparently without full ethnographic validation, have tended to stress the imprecision and casualness of the rules relating to control over land. The rules are precise and well known, but they are multifaceted and flexible and can therefore be fully grasped only within the broadest possible framework of the above-mentioned interconnecting factors. We must realize that in any given society multiple systems may be simultaneously at work. The group controlling land for agricultural purposes is not necessarily the same as the group controlling it for hunting or trapping or food-gathering activities, which again allow for differences in degree and nature of control in terms of their many technological aspects. In addition, within a given society it is not necessarily true, as is so often implied in the literature, that the same type of group at the same level of segmentation is necessarily associated with a given land tract. Nor can we exclude for a precise understanding of rules of land tenure such less frequently mentioned features as virgin versus occupied and fallow land, geographical remoteness of parts of the estate, cyclic differences in quality and quantity of food supplies caused by variable amounts of rainfall, etc. To illustrate this point, among the Nyanga living in the east of the Congo Republic the resident members of local clans are in direct control of the virgin parts of a well-defined territory (where several forms of hunting and food gathering take place), whereas segments of these clans and extended families control specific, but not necessarily contiguous, tracts within it as trapping sites and fallow or cultivated land. Hunting and gathering rights are much less rigidly sanctioned for the most remote parts of the virgin tract than they are for the more accessible ones; in years of abundance, explicitly recognized by the Nyanga, great permissiveness is allowed with regard to the collecting of natural products and even the harvesting of cultivated ones. At all times, the pygmoid groups surviving in the country are permitted to take freely, but not overtly, certain species of cultivated bananas. All these and many other permissive types of behavior prevail in an otherwise rigid code of rules pertaining to land control.

The many tedious speculations as to whether or not ownership of land exists as a legal and philosophical concept are largely irrelevant, since they are culture-bound and fail to account for the originalities of non-Western thought systems. The question must be placed in a different perspective and can be solved only to the extent that we are willing to get rid of certain stereotypes, such as alienability or absoluteness, thought to be diagnostic elements of land ownership. A better grasp of linguistic concepts and folk classifications would greatly contribute to leading us out of this impasse. In some central African populations, all rights pertaining to land and its products are covered by one single concept, which in the minds of the people means as much as "to be with . . . ," and are therefore thought to be basically similar to each other in their legal implications. However, any given category of persons is always rigidly said "to be with" a well-defined entity, so that the scope of the rights, and the extent to which they bear, are fundamentally distinct. Thus women are said "to be with" crops, married men residing with their kinship group are said "to be with" gardens (or rather banana groves), extended families residing on land traditionally associated with the local clan of which their heads are members are said "to be with" *ndimo* (land under cultivation and fallow land, which is also the object of intensive gathering and trapping), etc. The bearing of every right is well circumscribed in a specific context, and the rights cannot be reversed. The connotations of "being with" are clear to these people; for the outsider they are understandable only in full reference to ties of kinship, marriage, residence, and friendship; to ideas about solidarity, reciprocity, and etiquette; and to concepts about incorporation of labor that prevail among these people.

Regarding the critical concept of land alienation, the transfer of certain rights is definitely a well-known phenomenon. However, in many instances, we are unclear as to the exact scope and content of the rights transferred. It is clear that in traditional subsistence economies alienation by outright sale of land is extremely rare. This is understandable since land is quite plentiful and the methods for using it securely are relatively simple and multifold; there also exists a series of alternatives for obtaining it. Furthermore, land is vitally linked with the perpetuation of groups of people and with their autonomy, solidarity, and cohesion. Most commonly the rights transferred bear on specific usages, are subject to many modalities (including reversibility), and operate within a well-defined social framework (for example, transfers are restricted to certain categories of persons, excluding nonincorporated strangers). Transfers are either an exception or occur only in cases of dire necessity. It is also true that very often portions of land are not transferable at all because of religious values connected with them or because of their high productivity. Alienation of land through direct conquest or gradual peaceful expansion has, of course, been a widespread occurrence. Here again, the conquerors have not necessarily occupied all the land or claimed full title to it, and there has been a marked tendency in many societies to consider, as is often expressed in various ritual arrangements, that the ultimate title to the land remains with the original settlers.

**Sociocultural change.** Under conditions of sociocultural and technological change, land tenure systems, which are so intimately bound to many facets of culture and environment, are due to undergo many modifications, but the outcome is unpredictable. Under the impact of new factors such as increase in population, development of more intensive agriculture, cash cropping, and money economy, the bulk of the rules of land-tenure systems may be nevertheless perpetuated. A variety of responses can result from this. Rights in land may become more exclusive, litigation about boundaries and the nature of titles may increase, landlessness and tenancy may develop, rights of political officeholders may emerge more strongly, groups of people may be compelled to emigrate, and so on. In this process the unity and cohesion of traditional land-controlling units may be disturbed or consolidated. Increased demand for land may lead to fragmentation of holdings, and new concepts of alienability may emerge, with the corresponding uneconomic implications of conflict situations. Often traditional systems, when exposed to a multiplicity of new factors, have proven to be slow in adjusting themselves to the new necessities and demands. It is then that various legislative measures have had to be taken with regard to consolidation, resettlement, reallocation, and redistribution of land and people. Likewise, conflicts of law have paved the way to greater complexity of the problems involved and to difficult social situations, which have sometimes found only uneasy solutions. The creation of secure individualized title, the correlated registration of titles, the organization of successoral systems, and the introduction of new attitudes toward land without a corresponding radical transformation of the social system have proven to be very complex, often producing problems insoluble in the traditional contexts. Entire populations, or sections of a population, have failed to recognize the validity of modern types of land transactions and land titles, and adjustments between widely divergent values and laws have been slow to come.

As far as problems of research are concerned, a theoretical, precise framework for dealing with land-tenure systems and a cross-culturally valid and applicable method of investigation are badly needed at all levels of descriptive and comparative analysis. It is particularly important that we get rid of some of the stereotypes about ownership and set up a well-founded system of terminology. Comprehensive anthropological descriptions that view single land-tenure systems in a multifaceted way are still very necessary. In this respect, an exhaustive analysis of the linguistic concepts and taxonomic categories that various peoples have devised in regard to their environment, their land, their water, and the products obtained from them could shed new light on our methods and concepts. The exact connotations of issues such as alienation and other types of transfer and the precise scope of various forms of permissiveness and exclusiveness would have to be more thoroughly investigated and clarified. The exploration of land tenure has all too often been a subsidiary interest, casually treated and camouflaged behind a number of classic categories for analysis. There must be a distinctive, and hopefully rewarding, way of looking at relationships between groups and categories of persons with land, water, and their products as a referent.

DANIEL P. BIEBUYCK

[*Other relevant material may be found in* AFRICAN SOCIETY; ASIAN SOCIETY, *article on* SOUTHEAST ASIA; LAND, *article on* CLASSIFICATION.]

## BIBLIOGRAPHY

CROCOMBE, RONALD G. 1964 *Land Tenure in the Cook Islands.* Melbourne: Oxford Univ. Press.

FOOD AND AGRICULTURE ORGANIZATION OF THE UNITED NATIONS 1955 *Bibliography on Land Tenure.* Rome: The Organization.

FOOD AND AGRICULTURE ORGANIZATION OF THE UNITED NATIONS 1959 *Bibliography on Land Tenure: Supplement.* Rome: The Organization.

GLUCKMAN, MAX 1959 The Technical Vocabulary of Barotse Jurisprudence. *American Anthropologist* New Series 61:743–759.

GOODENOUGH, WARD H. 1955 A Problem in Malayo–Polynesian Social Organization. *American Anthropologist* New Series 57:71–83. → See Volume 58, pages 170–176, for comments by Charles O. Frake and a reply by Goodenough.

HERSKOVITS, MELVILLE J. (1940) 1952 *Economic Anthropology: A Study in Comparative Economics.* 2d ed., rev. & enl. New York: Knopf. → First published as *The Economic Life of Primitive Peoples.*

HOEBEL, E. ADAMSON 1954 *The Law of Primitive Man: A Study in Comparative Legal Dynamics.* Cambridge, Mass.: Harvard Univ. Press.

HOWARD, ALAN 1963 Land, Activity Systems, and Decision-making Models in Rotuma. *Ethnology* 2:407–440.

INTERNATIONAL AFRICAN SEMINAR, SECOND, LEOPOLDVILLE, CONGO, *1960* 1963 *African Agrarian Systems: Studies Presented and Discussed.* Edited by Daniel Biebuyck. Published for the International African Institute. Oxford Univ. Press.

LIVERSAGE, VINCENT 1945 *Land Tenure in the Colonies.* Cambridge Univ. Press.

POSPISIL, LEOPOLD 1965 A Formal Analysis of Substantive Law: Kapauku Papuan Laws of Land Tenure. *American Anthropologist* New Series 67, no. 5, part 2: 186–214.

Sonius, H. W. J. (1962) 1963 *Introduction to Aspects of Customary Land Law in Africa as Compared With Some Indonesian Aspects.* Leiden (Netherlands): Universitaire Pers Leiden.

White, Charles M. N. 1958 Terminological Confusion in African Land Tenure. *Journal of African Administration* 10:124–130.

## II

### AGRICULTURAL TENANCY

Nearly three-fifths of the world's 3,100 million people derive their livelihood from agriculture. Of this estimated 1,860 million people within agriculture, most do not own the land on which they live and work. Instead many purchase rights of cultivation and occupancy from others. In return for hired rights in land, these people pay the landowners, or their intermediaries, a share of the produce, a fixed amount of produce, a fixed amount of money, personal services, or some combination of these payments. These people are tenants.

Throughout the world tenants and their families probably constitute as many as two-fifths of the population engaged in agriculture. Thus, as many as 700 to 800 million people over the globe work and live under conditions of agricultural tenancy.

Most tenants aspire to ownership of their lands. Therefore, tenancy may well be appraised in terms of how well it provides tenants with opportunities to gain experience, acquire capital, and make decisions in the process of acquiring landownership. On the other hand, many tenants are not likely to become owners in the foreseeable future. Hence, for them, tenancy must be appraised in terms of additional objectives, including increasing the productivity of their labor, capital, and land resources and improving their living conditions. These objectives are consistent with the pursuit of ownership and are equally appropriate for tenants who never become owners, either through choice or lack of opportunity.

**In the United States.**   Within the United States, about 20 per cent of the farmers are *full tenants,* who rent all the land they operate (U.S. Bureau of Census . . . 1963, pp. 1008–1013). An additional 23 per cent of the nation's farmers rent part and own part of the land they operate; they are termed *part owners.* The remaining 57 per cent of the nation's farmers hold ownership to all the land they operate and are designated *full owners.*

The proportion of farms in the United States operated by tenants in 1959 (20 per cent) was the lowest in 80 years. It represents a drop from 24 per cent in 1954 and from 42 per cent in 1930, the highest percentage on record.

Throughout the United States much variation exists in the prevalence of tenancy. The proportion of farms operated by tenants in 1959 varied from 6 per cent in the eastern states to 22 per cent in the north central and southern states to 12 per cent in the western states.

Nearly 50 per cent of all farms operated by tenants were in the southern states and 42 per cent were in the north central states. In the South, the tenant-operated farms were concentrated in the cotton- and tobacco-producing regions.

Six subclasses of tenants are identified in the United States (U.S. Bureau of Census . . . 1963, p. 1003). *Cash tenants* pay a fixed cash rent for the use and occupancy of their land. *Share-cash tenants* pay part of their rent in cash and part in a share of the crops and/or livestock and livestock products. *Crop-share tenants* pay a share of the crops only. *Livestock-share tenants* pay a share of the livestock and/or livestock products; their rent may or may not include a share of the crops. *Croppers* pay a share of the crops, a share of the livestock and livestock products, or both, but usually work under the close supervision of the landlord or his agent, who furnishes all the work animals or tractor power. Data for croppers are restricted to the 16 southern states where the cropper system developed following the Civil War. In other states, croppers are included with share-tenants. *Other and unspecified tenants* include those farmers who hire their land under various other arrangements.

Tenants in the United States are made up of 27 per cent crop-share, 18 per cent share-cash, 16 per cent croppers, 15 per cent cash, 12 per cent livestock-share, and 12 per cent other and unspecified (*ibid.,* p. 1010).

During the 1950s important changes took place among several classes of tenants in the United States. The proportion of tenant farms operated by croppers decreased from 24.0 to 16.4 per cent between 1950 and 1959. The proportion of tenant farms operated by livestock-share tenants increased from 8.0 to 11.7 per cent during the same period. The proportion of tenant farms operated by crop-share and by cash tenants remained fairly constant during this period.

Changes in proportions of farms operated by tenants in the United States are associated with the changing character of American agriculture (*ibid.,* p. 1016). Between 1950 and 1959, the number of farm operators dropped from 5.4 million to 3.7 million, a decrease of 1.7 million farm operators. In 1964, the number of farm operators was 3.2 million, a drop of 0.5 million from the 1959 figure (U.S. Bureau of Census . . . 1966, p. 2).

During the 1950–1959 period, tenant operators decreased from 1.4 million to 0.7 million, a drop of 0.7 million, or a 50 per cent decrease. By 1964, tenant operators had decreased to 0.5 million, a drop of 0.2 million more. Because of their younger age and lack of ownership of land, tenants are more mobile than owner operators and more readily shift to jobs outside agriculture. Also, associated with the increase of farm size from 215 acres per farm in 1950 to 303 acres in 1959 and to 352 acres in 1964, tenant-operated farms have been combined or have been added to owner-operated farms, thus reducing opportunities on farms for tenant operators.

The 0.5 million tenant operators in 1964 constitute the least number reported in a census since 1880, the first year tenant operators were counted in the United States (U.S. Bureau of Census . . . 1963). The 1964 count of tenant operators is 2.3 million less than the number of tenant operators reported in 1935, the year of peak tenant numbers.

**Variations throughout the world.**    Throughout the world wide variations exist in the prevalence of tenancy. In Scotland 77 per cent of the farmers are tenants, while in Denmark the percentage is as low as 5 (Food and Agriculture Organization . . . 1953a). In England and Wales the percentage is 65, while in West Germany it is 5. In the less-developed countries, similar variations exist. In Cambodia, the proportion of tenant farmers is around 5 per cent, while in India the percentage is 53 (Food and Agriculture Organization . . . 1955). Within other countries variations in the proportion of farms operated by tenants exist just as in the United States. For example, in the Philippines the proportion of tenancy varies from 2 per cent of all farmers in the mountain section of Luzon to over two-thirds of the farmers in central Luzon.

Tenancy fulfills the objectives of productivity, levels of living, and progress to ownership in varying degrees throughout the world. In Britain, tenant farmers possess security of occupancy, are productive, and share in living conditions equal to other groups. In other areas of the world, tenancy is associated with human exploitation, low productivity, lack of opportunity, and substandard living conditions. In some areas of Latin America, the tenancy system represents the continuation of a feudal structure wherein the tenants remain virtual serfs of the landlords and agricultural development is severely retarded (Food and Agriculture Organization . . . 1953b).

**Advantages and problems.**    Tenancy per se is neither good nor bad. The nature of tenancy structures is the key to its utility. Tenancy may serve well the needs of a progressive agriculture, as it is doing in Britain and in midwestern United States, or it may impede agricultural development, as it is doing in several Latin American and Asiatic countries. Tenancy can provide the means by which landowners and the landless may join their respective resources in a productive and complementary manner. The landowner, in addition to some management, furnishes his land and possibly capital; the tenant furnishes his labor, ability, and some operating capital. In the process the tenant gains experience, accumulates capital, and improves his living conditions; the landlord receives returns from his investment. Under tenancy the tenant may invest his limited capital in working stock rather than in fixed assets of land. Usually, working capital returns more than fixed capital in land for each unit of investment.

As a result of this combination of complementary resources, the productivity of farm operations is enhanced, creating a larger income to be distributed between the resource contributors, landlord and tenant. On the other hand, defects within tenancy structures may block the achievement of these objectives.

Uncertainty of expectations may arise, so that tenants do not possess assurance that they will reap the benefits from their efforts. The tenancy arrangement may discourage tenants from making investments in improvements necessary for a productive agriculture. The bargaining position between tenants and landlords may be such that all additional productivity of the tenants' efforts will flow to the landlord. Lack of operating capital or capital obtainable only at excessive cost may prevent the tenant from adopting improved production practices and from enjoying better living conditions.

The size of holdings may be so small, particularly under "minifundia" conditions, that the value productivity of the tenants' labor approaches zero. High fixed costs of rents may both preclude needed production investments and prevent improving the family's level of living. The tenant may not possess adequate legal protection to enforce the laws which have been developed to protect his interests in the farm and its income.

**Remedies.**    In developing remedies for the problems tenants face throughout the world, there are certain objectives that appear desirable. First, the tenant farmer must be provided with incentives to improve his economic and social position through increasing his productivity. Second, the tenant must be provided with sufficient certainty of expectations of receiving the returns from the investments which he must make to increase the productivity of his resources. In this sense his planning horizon must equal the optimum planning period for the investments. Third, the tenant must be provided motivations to save and to create capital as his productivity increases in order to provide seed capital for further increases in productivity. Fourth, the tenant must have access to sufficient land, capital resources, technological knowledge, and management aids to enable him to increase the productivity of resources under his control.

In achieving these objectives, an essential function of tenancy improvement is to provide a structural framework in which individual tenants and landowners can work together to improve their own financial and social positions and, at the same time, to improve the position of the nation in which they live. A second essential function of tenancy improvement is to provide a basis whereby productive resources of landlord and tenant can be combined to provide for the most economic allocation of combined resources and, in accordance with the productivities of each of the combined resources, for the equitable distribution of returns.

In addition to these two essential economic functions, there are social and political aims in the development of tenants. These are to enable the tenant and his family to improve their social, as well as economic, position and to participate in community activities and public affairs. In many less developed areas of the world, tenancy has been a major cause of social and political unrest (Jacoby 1949). Thus, improvements in tenancy conditions may be expected to facilitate the achievement of political stability, as well as social development and economic growth.

There exist three major alternatives for tenants to improve themselves. One approach is through policies which encourage ownership of their land. This approach has been followed successfully in Denmark, Japan, and the United States. Another approach is group tenures, wherein tenants join together and share in the resources and the productivities of their common resources. The *ejido* in Mexico, the proportional profit farm in Puerto Rico, the kibbutz in Israel, the cooperative in Poland, and the recognized Indian community in the sierra of South America are examples. The third approach consists of improvements within the tenancy structure (Timmons 1957). England, the Republic of China (Taiwan), and India are examples of nations which have emphasized improvements within tenancy structures.

*Improvement of structure.* Within this third approach of improving tenancy structures, coun-

tries have taken steps toward providing tenants with security of expectations for remaining on the farm and for developing their resources over relevant planning periods. Particular provisions used in these countries include (1) written lease provisions, (2) long-term leases, (3) minimum (in years) lease terms, (4) minimum periods for termination notices and automatic renewals, (5) heritability of leases, (6) restrictions on transfer of leased land, (7) permanent occupancy and use rights which cannot be violated by owners, and (8) compensation to the tenant for the unexhausted value of improvements made by him in case he leaves the farm before receiving full value of the improvements which he has made or in case the landlord wishes to operate the farm himself. In addition to these eight provisions, leasing arrangements have also been designed to provide compensation to the landlord for unnecessary waste and deterioration of his resources caused by the tenant. Within these provisions, adjustment in the kind and amount of rental payments in accordance with types of production and productivity of resource inputs available to the tenant and his landlord is necessary in order to bring forth a maximum net return for the combined resources.

Under the provision for compensation, which has been developed most highly under the provisions of the Agricultural Holdings Act of 1948 in England, the tenant has a statutory right to compensation for (1) long-term improvements (2) medium-term improvements, and (3) rights of occupancy. In computing compensations for improvements or deterioration, three methods of assessing values for improvements are used: compensation may be based upon (1) the original cost of the improvement, (2) the replacement cost of the improvement, and (3) the added return the improvement is expected to yield.

As pointed out earlier, tenants may pay landlords in a number of ways for the hire of land. Although most tenants pay a share of their product or a service payment as rent for their land, the cash rental or fixed price rental has a number of advantages in encouraging individual initiative and operation of the farm at a maximum level of production. The cash rental automatically satisfies two necessary conditions for maximizing the productivity of factors (Hurlburt 1954). The requirement that variable cost be shared in the same proportion as output is satisfied since the tenant is responsible for all variables under the cash rent arrangement and in turn receives the full value from additional output. The condition that the tenant pay the same share of the value of each product is also satisfied, since the cash rental may be considered a fixed cost for all products and charged in the same proportion to each (Benedictis & Timmons 1961). Under the cash rent form of lease, the tenant has maximum freedom to develop his management ability.

The cash rent system, however, does possess certain difficulties, in that the tenant is required to assume the costs of many risks and uncertainties, which under the share arrangement are shared with landlords. Also under the cash rent system, the tenant must have access to sufficient capital to operate the farm with no financial aid from the landowner.

Another direction of tenancy improvements includes the regulation of levels of rental payments. Inasmuch as the level of rents determines the landlord's as well as the tenant's income and the amount of capital available to the tenant for crop and livestock production, levels and rigidities of rental payments are important in tenancy improvement measures. Rental rates frequently exceed two-thirds of the production in the less developed countries. Measures taken to bring rental payments into line with productivity have included the establishment of rental ceilings such as the $37\frac{1}{2}$ per cent Rent Control Law in Taiwan; the setting of minimum levels of tenant income; and adjustments of rents to income changes resulting from productivity, cost, and price trends (Chryst & Timmons 1955).

In addition to rents as payments for land hire, there exists in numerous areas throughout the world the practice of extra rental payments in the form of usurious interest rates, excessive charges for processing and marketing services, and feudal dues and services to landlords. Improvements in these defects in rental structures have been instituted in a number of countries in the form of (1) abolition of feudal dues and services, (2) maximum processing and marketing charges, (3) maximum interest charges, and (4) access to public credit.

All these potential improvements in tenancy structures may come to naught unless they are implemented by legislation, administration, education, research, and judicial processes. The problem of implementation of tenancy improvements is serious and must receive adequate attention or the tenancy improvements contained in laws and government reports will never be extended into practices that benefit rural people and their communities.

JOHN F. TIMMONS

### BIBLIOGRAPHY

BENEDICTIS, MICHELE DE; and TIMMONS, JOHN F. 1961 Identification and Measurement of Inefficiencies in Leasing Systems. Iowa Agricultural Experiment Station, Ames, *Research Bulletin* 490:39–72.

CHRYST, WALTER E.; and TIMMONS, JOHN F. 1955 Adjusting Farm Rents to Changes in Prices, Costs and Production. Iowa Agricultural Experiment Station, Ames, *Special Report* 9:1–44.

FOOD AND AGRICULTURE ORGANIZATION OF THE UNITED NATIONS, AGRICULTURE DIVISION 1953a *Agricultural Development and Rural Reform in Denmark*, by F. Skrubbeltrang. FAO Agricultural Studies No. 22. Rome: FAO.

FOOD AND AGRICULTURE ORGANIZATION OF THE UNITED NATIONS 1953b *Report on the Latin American Seminar on Land Problems, Campinas, Brazil*. FAO–ETAP Report No. 205. Rome: FAO.

FOOD AND AGRICULTURE ORGANIZATION OF THE UNITED NATIONS 1955 *Report of the Center on Land Problems in Asia and the Far East, Bangkok, Thailand*. FAO–ETAP Report No. 393. Rome: FAO.

HURLBURT, VIRGIL L. 1954 Farm Rental Practices and Problems in the Midwest. Iowa Agricultural Experiment Station, Ames, *Research Bulletin* 416:78–120.

JACOBY, ERICH H. (1949) 1961 *Agrarian Unrest in Southeast Asia*. 2d ed., rev. and enl. New York: Asia Publishing House.

TIMMONS, JOHN F. 1957 *Improving Agricultural Tenancy: An FAO Land Tenure Study*. FAO Agricultural Studies, No. 35. Rome: FAO.

U.S. BUREAU OF THE CENSUS, CENSUS OF AGRICULTURE, *1959* 1963 *General Report*. Volume 2: Statistics by Subjects. Washington: Government Printing Office.

U.S. BUREAU OF THE CENSUS, CENSUS OF AGRICULTURE, *1964* 1966 *Preliminary Report of U.S. Summary*. AC64–P1. Washington: Government Printing Office.

### III
### LAND REFORM

In its simplest meaning, land reform has meant the breaking up of large holdings and redistribution of the land to peasants, cultivators, or landless workers. Documented reforms of this type took place in the sixth century B.C. in Greece and in the second century B.C. in Rome. Modern land reforms in this classic pattern characterized the revolution in Mexico after 1910, Egypt in 1952, and Bolivia in 1953. A common feature was dispossession of former landowning classes coupled with changes in size of farm operating units.

A related class of reforms has emphasized change in land tenure relationships without substantial change in size of operating units. This was the principal outcome of land reforms accompanying the French Revolution after 1789. Twentieth-century examples include the Japanese land reform of 1946; reforms in western India after independence, beginning with the Bombay Tenures Abolition Act of 1949; and land reform on Taiwan after 1949. Principal goals have been abolition of feudal tenures or servitudes and rent reduction or conversion of tenants into owners.

Land reform in this traditional pattern reflects a striving for political equity and social justice. While agricultural technology was dominated by custom and tradition, little thought was given to land reform as a device to promote technological advance or output increases. Marxian thought contributed to a major break with the classic tradition of land reform by combining a doctrinal stress on socialization or nationalization of land with emphasis on presumed economies that could be achieved through large-scale production.

A third class of land reforms has resulted, in which peasant yearning for land has been used as a political vehicle for the initial achievement of tenure reform, often accompanied by land redistribution. Subsequent reforms in farm operation have then created large managerial units, under a variety of forms of communal, cooperative, or collective tenure, or state ownership. The pattern for this trend was set by events in the Soviet Union between 1917 and 1931, repeated in a compressed time dimension in eastern Europe after 1944, in mainland China after 1949, and in Cuba, 1959–1963.

Confusion has been introduced by use of the term "agrarian reform." In countries with Latin-based languages, reference to agrarian reform carries a connotation that may or may not involve major land tenure changes. Some agrarian reform programs in Latin America, for example, have emphasized agricultural modernization, extension work, and land settlement.

In order to maintain integrity of relationships between means and ends, land reform is defined here as a basic change in land tenure arrangements —in relations among men with respect to land— together with supporting measures necessary to achieve its objectives. The nature of these objectives has undergone substantial change in the past century.

**Historical background.** Evolution of land reform in its modern meaning traces from the emancipation of serfs in imperial Russia in 1861 and of slaves in the United States in 1863—two disparate versions of land reform with a common emphasis on personal freedom, equity, and social justice.

Although widely different in setting, scale, and consequences, abolition of serfdom in Russia and of slavery in the United States dramatized the inadequacies of land tenure systems in which men, rather than land, were owned and in which labor was the major component of agricultural capital.

Over a century later, traces of tenure in men rather than in land still exist in portions of Asia, the Middle East, and Latin America. One dimension of the civil rights movement of the 1960s in the United States is the attempt to bring to an end any form of political dominance over men that is rooted in control of land or in restrictions on freedom of occupational choice.

This goal characterized many rural land reform movements of the nineteenth and early twentieth centuries, in particular, Irish struggles to abolish absentee ownership after 1870, the triumph of the Danish small holder movement in 1901, and the Stolypin reforms in Russia between 1906 and 1911. Political considerations were dominant, with a focus on creation of a middle class of small peasant proprietors.

Urban land reform movements, also a feature of the late nineteenth century, were greatly stimulated by publication of Henry George's *Progress and Poverty* in 1879. George argued for a "single tax" that would recapture any land value increases not justified by the labor and investment of the landowner or land user. Rapid urbanization accompanying early industrial growth made this a particularly appealing argument in emerging industrial centers. Land reform long had a predominantly urban connotation in Germany, for example, reflected in urban housing and homestead (small house and garden) proposals of the German Land Reform League, organized in 1898 under the leadership of Adolph Damaschke, an ardent disciple of Henry George.

Nineteenth-century views of land, including those of Karl Marx and Henry George, were dominated by a belief in the physical limits of land supply. Disappearance of frontiers of settlement, the limitations revealed by geographical explorations of hitherto unknown areas, and the first wave of population increase brought about by improvements in medical care and public health all fostered a belief in the inevitability of growing population pressure on a fixed resource base. Land policy prescriptions took the form of demands for land redistribution, in the name of equity. Alternatively, land nationalization was advanced as the only feasible method of securing equal access to land resources for all the people. Elements of both prescriptions characterized almost all of the twentieth-century land reforms that occurred prior to World War II.

The current era of land reforms was introduced on two fronts: by the Soviet Union after 1944 in eastern European states dominated by the Red

Army, and by the Japanese land reform of 1946, enacted under the tutelage of United States occupation forces. Further impetus to this trend was given by the breakup of colonial empires, most prominently by the British grant of independence to India and Pakistan in 1947, and by the conquest of the Chinese mainland by revolutionary communist forces in 1949. Between 1945 and 1950, some type of land reform was begun in countries that together account for slightly under half of the world's population.

During the 1950s the center of land reform activity shifted. Latin America emerged as an area in which land redistribution was most needed—and most vigorously debated. Since 1960, 14 Latin American states have enacted some type of land reform legislation.

**Impact of technological change.** After 1945 a major change occurred in economic thinking regarding land reform and was manifested in 1950 when the topic came before the General Assembly of the United Nations. In later discussions in 1951 before the Economic and Social Council and the Conference of the Food and Agriculture Organization, it was emphasized that the concept of land reform should be expanded to include more than the breaking up of large estates or the consolidation of small holdings. It was defined to include opportunity for land ownership, improved conditions of tenancy, agricultural credit at reasonable rates of interest, reform of exorbitant rents and taxes, and facilities for obtaining agricultural supplies and marketing agricultural products, with emphasis on cooperatives.

This shift in emphasis reflected the impact of the technological revolution in agriculture that began after 1910 with perfection of the internal combustion engine and the tractor. Contemporary advances in fertilizer production, seed varieties, and agricultural chemicals greatly expanded the range and potential of purchased inputs available to modern agriculture. Parallel advances in marketing, storage, and processing called for increasing attention to the demand side of the agricultural supply and demand equation. It was no longer sufficient to focus on production alone in promoting agricultural advances, or to regard only land and labor as the major agricultural inputs. In more advanced economies, access to purchased production requisites became as important as access to land. And access to markets was of growing importance in all economies, from the simplest to the most complex. Land reform limited to land tenure change alone was an obsolete concept.

A fundamental shift also occurred in attitudes toward fixity of land supply. Faster and cheaper transport brought more land within the reach of national and world markets. Fertilizers, chemicals, hybrid seeds, and better cultivation practices made infertile lands productive and augmented the output of fertile lands. Improved techniques of dam building, irrigation, drainage, and water management greatly increased intensities of land use.

As a result, motives that propel land reforms in the second half of the twentieth century go beyond those of equity and social justice. Output increase becomes a third goal. With growing commercialization and monetization in even the most primitive agrarian economies, social justice is increasingly measured in terms of patterns of income distribution. And the consequences of land reforms must be judged in terms of the extent to which they can expand internal markets. Output increases, more equitable income distribution, and internal market expansion emerge as the major tests of modern efforts at land reform.

**Potentials of land reform.** One criterion of land reform is the degree to which it can promote capital formation and investment. This can be judged in the private sector at the level of the farm firm, and in the public sector at the level of the rural community.

Much private capital in agriculture is the result of slow processes of accumulation. Examples include increases in number and quality of livestock; development of tree crops; improvements in buildings, fencing, or drainage or irrigation systems; and better soil management. On peasant-type or family-sized farms much of this investment is accomplished at the expense of what might otherwise have been leisure time.

Because of the dispersed and biological nature of agricultural production, it is difficult to concentrate it either in time or in space. Waiting—for crops to ripen, for trees to grow, or for animals to mature—is a major cost. On the best-organized farms there are time periods when labor must be present but cannot be fully employed. The incentive structure that can maximize capital formation is one that will promote productive use of this seasonally or cyclically underemployed labor.

One test of a land tenure system thus becomes whether it can provide incentives for productive use of the total rural labor supply. On big farms, estates, or plantations it has been difficult to devise labor-wage and supervisory systems to maximize accretionary processes of capital formation. Land reform that creates viable peasant or family-type farms may increase the likelihood that leisure time will be converted into capital at minimum cost.

In the public sector, it is an almost universal experience that land taxes can be collected more readily from many relatively small landowners than from a few large ones. If land taxes are spent locally on schools, roads, or welfare, the benefits are apparent to every taxpayer. Large landowners often succeed in tax evasion or in holding tax rates low. Land reform that promotes tax reform can thus provide a climate of civic responsibility in which local taxation can be used for public capital formation. If local infrastructures must be financed by the central government, costs may be higher and the quality of services lower, and taxpayers may lose a sense of identification with processes of government. Good rural school systems are as much a hallmark of sound land tenure structures as are productive farms.

Land tenure systems also affect rates of technological change. Older histories of agricultural advances were cast in a heroic mold, with a few great names associated with new discoveries, inventions, and innovations. After 1945, the rebirth of interest in processes of economic development led to a critical re-examination of this interpretation of history. Evidence from three sharply different economies—England (Mingay 1963), Colombia (Hagen 1962), and Japan (Sawada 1964)—points to the importance of innovation and experimentation by small farmers, tenants, and actual land users in general in early periods of agricultural development.

Contemporary data suggest that large-scale agricultural units in developing countries are best suited to application of known technology involving a comparatively small number of repetitive tasks per production cycle. The Soviet Union's experience with collective and state farms is paralleled by performance records of sugar and coffee plantations in Latin America and rubber production in Malaysia. Crops once classed as plantation crops are increasingly produced on peasant-type farms (Wickizer 1960). Large, centrally directed units apparently discourage flexibility. Scarce capital must be committed in large amounts, and innovation is inhibited by bureaucratic rigidity or political risk. Managers are often unwilling to accept the high costs of technological change. [See PLANTATIONS.]

The most rapid and lasting advances occur in agricultural systems characterized by a mixture of farms of different size and type. Farm units need to be large enough to permit risk taking and capital accumulation. But an agrarian structure composed of a relatively few large farms may introduce rigidity, reduce the opportunity to acquire experience in small doses, and increase the cost of mistakes.

This is one of the lessons to be learned from the British groundnut scheme in Tanganyika after 1945 and the Soviet virgin lands program after 1953. A major task of land reform is the creation of an agrarian structure that can maximize opportunities for innovation, experimentation, and selective retention of new technology.

**Problems of land reform.** A management gap typically results if former landlords or managers are replaced by new owners, who often lack managerial skill or experience. This was a major defect of the Bolivian land reform in 1953 and the Syrian and Iraqi land reforms of 1958. In Bolivia and Iraq agricultural output fell by over 50 per cent after the reforms. After independence Morocco, Algeria, and Tunisia encountered similar difficulties in replacing the managerial skills of departed or evicted French entrepreneurs. A notable feature of the Egyptian land reform of 1952 was the accompanying effort to deal with this management gap through creation of supervised cooperatives that could take over functions formerly performed by the landlords (Warriner 1962).

Removal of a former landowning or managerial class can result in equally serious problems of public management. Where land reform is a critical issue, it is not only ownership of land or men that is in question but also "ownership" of government. Realization of potential gains from land reform may call for a new generation of farm managers. It will almost surely require reform in the structure of local government.

Efforts in many countries to introduce communal, collective, or cooperative types of farm organization can be re-examined in this light. Large-scale collective-type farms may have their greatest value as proxy forms of local government rather than as efficient forms of farm production organization. The average collective farm in the Soviet Union in 1964 was approximately the size of the average rural township in the Midwest of the United States. The average state farm was the size of half a county in the United States.

In many functional respects, the Soviet farm is the minor civil division of local government. It has been responsible for road building, health, sanitation, and welfare within the farm area. Cumbersome inefficiency as a production organization may be partially offset by relative efficiency as a unit of local government.

Failure to fill the governmental vacuum left by destruction of rural political power structures centered on a few landowning families has been a weakness of many land reforms. It does little good to provide capital, fertilizers, or farm advisers to new landowners without corresponding attention to reconstruction of local government.

The management gap following land reform has a close parallel in the credit gap. In many traditional land tenure systems the landowner often provided production credit, thus opening the door to labor exploitation. A cycle of advances to cultivators, crop mortgages to insure repayment, usurious interest rates, and perpetual indebtedness has been distressingly frequent, especially in Asia (Jacoby 1961). If former landowner–creditors are dispossessed, one of the most pressing needs is for replacement credit.

Provision of credit is not enough, although it is essential. A more intractable problem has been to persuade new owners to use credit wisely and to regard it as a production tool rather than as a supplement to income. Attitudes toward debt in traditional rural societies have identified it with disaster, celebration, or moral degeneracy. One of the most significant functions governments can perform in the wake of land reform is to provide cultivators with credit under sufficient supervision to insure that they use it wisely.

The credit gap is compounded by defective land title and survey systems in most developing countries. Land reform legislation in Iran in 1960 set a maximum limit in hectares on the land any one owner could retain. A hasty effort was needed to redraft the legislation when it became apparent that necessary land survey records were lacking. The resultant law of 1962 provided that a landlord could retain only one village, without specifying size.

The attempt by Iraq in 1958 to pattern its land reform on the 1952 Egyptian model failed in part because Egypt had a system of cadastral survey records, and Iraq did not. Prompt execution of the relatively modest Pakistan land reform after 1959 was aided by good land title and survey records. Contributing to the success of land reform on Taiwan after 1949 were the Chinese tradition of careful attention to land records and meticulously complete land surveys compiled by the Japanese.

Latin America and the Philippines inherited defective land survey and title systems from the era of Spanish rule. Landowners, merchants, and religious leaders often discouraged systematic land surveys. It was thought easier to control serf-like labor, maintain trade hegemony of coastal cities, or promote orderly settlement if survey was done piecemeal. The result has been illegal squatter settlement, acute problems of latifundia and minifundia, disregard for law and order, and defective bases for tax assessment and credit extension.

Crash programs are under way in a number of Latin American countries to construct cadastral survey systems, preparatory to land reforms.

Much agonizing indecision has surrounded African fears that a too hasty provision of land titles might lead to repetition on a continental scale of past histories of individualization of title, mortgage debt, and foreclosure. Squatter settlement is growing, and monetization is leading to land speculation. Pressure for individualization of land titles increases. New African states south of the Sahara are relatively free of land tenure problems represented by large estates, absentee landlordism, and excessive concentration of land ownership. Emphasis in Africa falls heavily on development of land tenure systems, rather than on their reform.

Compensation to dispossessed landowners has generated acute problems of policy. If reform abolishes private ownership of land, the compensation question is an aspect of welfare policy, or social security. The Cuban land reform after 1963 expropriated private landholdings above stated limits but specified that owners who had tilled or managed their lands personally were to receive monthly payments of 100 to 200 pesos for ten years, depending on the amount of land owned.

Cash payment for large landholdings is beyond the financial capacity of most developing countries. Recent approaches to this problem were influenced by the Japanese experience after 1946, when inflation reduced compensation to nominal amounts. The subsequent Chinese land reform on Taiwan after 1953 compensated landowners 70 per cent in bonds pegged to official prices for rice or sweet potatoes and 30 per cent in shares of denationalized businesses. Philippine land reform legislation of 1963 provided for compensation in 25-year bonds, with the option of taking up to 30 per cent in Land Bank preferred stock, exchanging bonds for shares in corporations, and several other alternatives.

Valuation of land for purposes of compensation to old owners or sale to new owners has posed a dilemma. Past histories of labor exploitation can lead to land price levels far above any productivity values based on equitable labor returns. Payment of compensation at these unrealistic prices has appeared to be a reward for past exploitative practices. Denial of compensation, on the other hand, has cast doubt on the validity of new land titles and on security of property rights in general.

Land reform through tenant protection legislation has been attempted in parts of India and in the Philippines. Rent reductions or rent ceilings in the Chinese (Taiwan) and Egyptian reforms affected larger areas of private land than were directly concerned in land redistribution. Although a number of countries have tried tenancy reform as a substitute for more comprehensive attacks on land tenure problems, it has generally failed unless coupled with thoroughgoing efforts at land redistribution. Threat of loss of land has apparently been a necessary precondition for an attack on tenancy problems. Even this threat has been ineffective in densely populated countries, where demographic pressures make it out of the question to promise land to all the landless.

**Lessons of land reform.**   Where there are large populations of landless workers or subtenants, land reform may not be a sufficient tool for the solution of rural poverty problems. It may be impossible to give land to all claimants without creating farms that are too small. This realization has sometimes inhibited attempts at land reform. A distinction is needed between problems of defective incentive structures that can be attacked through land reform, and problems of endemic rural poverty that must be attacked with other tools.

Land reform has frequently left untouched problems of domestic petty landlordism. Upper limits on permissible holdings can create new structures of inequity. Small landholdings held by absentee landlords have been difficult to bring within the land reform framework, and bootleg tenancy appears. In Colombia, for example, existing land reform legislation leaves small absentee owners untouched (although the cost of absentee ownership has been increased through threat of expropriation at declared tax values), thus exerting indirect influence on land use intensity.

The economic consequences of land reform depend very much on whether or not market forces are to be allowed to operate in determining combinations of resources, choices of enterprises, and scale of operation. Can land be transferred? Will market prices influence allocation of land to different uses or influence shifts in size of firm? Are farmers bound to their lands by new bonds that restrict occupational choice?

Release of productive potential is one of the greatest promises of land reform. It is in this sense that experiences in Japan, Taiwan, and Egypt are most significant. Agricultural productivity was already high when these three countries undertook land reform between 1946 and 1952. Yet in Egypt the index of gross agricultural output (1935 = 100) rose from 106 in 1951–1952 to 135 in 1962. In Japan the agricultural productivity index (1934 = 100) rose from 106 in 1940 to 157 in 1964. In Taiwan the aggregate agricultural output index

rose from 100 in 1951 to 221 in 1964 (to 184, for crops only). Many factors contributed to these performance records, but there is general consensus that land reform was one of the most powerful driving forces.

PHILIP M. RAUP

[*See also* AGRICULTURE, *especially the articles on* CAPITAL, DEVELOPING COUNTRIES, *and* PRODUCTION; COMMUNISM, ECONOMIC ORGANIZATION OF, *article on* AGRICULTURE; CREDIT, *article on* AGRICULTURAL CREDIT.]

### BIBLIOGRAPHY

CONFERENCE ON WORLD LAND TENURE PROBLEMS, UNIVERSITY OF WISCONSIN, *1951* 1956 *Land Tenure: Proceedings.* Edited by K. H. Parsons, R. J. Penn, and P. M. Raup. Madison: Univ. of Wisconsin Press.
DORE, RONALD P. 1959 *Land Reform in Japan.* Oxford Univ. Press.
GEORGESCU-ROEGEN, NICHOLAS 1960 Economic Theory and Agrarian Economics. *Oxford Economic Papers* New Series 12:1–40.
HAGEN, EVERETT E. (1962) 1964 *On the Theory of Social Change: How Economic Growth Begins.* London: Tavistock.
INTERNATIONAL LABOR OFFICE 1965 *Agrarian Reform With Particular Reference to Employment and Social Aspects.* Report 6, Forty-ninth Session, International Labour Conference. Geneva: The Office.
JACOBY, ERICH H. 1961 *Agrarian Unrest in Southeast Asia.* 2d ed., rev. & enl. New York: Asia Publishing House. → The first edition was published in 1949.
MEADE, JAMES E. (1964) 1965 *Efficiency, Equality, and the Ownership of Property.* Cambridge, Mass.: Harvard Univ. Press.
MINGAY, G. E. 1963 *English Landed Society in the Eighteenth Century.* London: Routledge.
SAWADA, SHUIIRO 1964 [A Book Review of] Bruce F. Johnston, *Agricultural Development and Economic Transformation: A Comparative Study of the Japanese Experience. Rural Economic Problems* 1, no. 2:88–92.
TUMA, ELIAS H. 1965 *Twenty-six Centuries of Agrarian Reform: A Comparative Analysis.* Berkeley: Univ. of California Press.
UNITED NATIONS, ECONOMIC AND SOCIAL COUNCIL 1966 *Progress in Land Reform, Fourth Report.* New York: United Nations.
WARRINER, DOREEN 1962 *Land Reform and Development in the Middle East: A Study of Egypt, Syria, and Iraq.* 2d ed. Oxford Univ. Press. → The first edition was published in 1957.
WICKIZER, V. D. 1960 The Smallholder in Tropical Export Crop Production. Stanford University, Food Research Institute, *Food Research Institute Studies* 1:49–99.

# LANDSCAPE

In any discussion of the development of geography as a modern academic discipline, attention must be directed to the important concept of "landscape," for the identification, description, and interpretation of landscapes has long been a major geographic enterprise. Indeed, during the 1920s and 1930s several attempts were made to construct methodologies that made landscape study the essential, if not exclusive, task of geography (Passarge 1921–1930; Sauer 1925; Bryan 1933; Dickinson 1939). While geographers are no longer preoccupied with landscape to this extent, there remains substantial agreement that landscape study is one of the important themes of geographic research, most notably in the subfield of cultural geography (Wagner & Mikesell 1962). If a count were taken of technical terms used most frequently in geographic publications, the number of references to landscape would probably be exceeded only by those to area and region. Moreover, the same generalization can be made for the corresponding term in other languages, for example, *Landschaft* (German), *landskap* (Swedish), *landschap* (Dutch), *paysage* (French), *paesaggio* (Italian), and *paisaje* (Spanish).

## Historical development

The etymology of the common use of landscape is reasonably clear. In its Old English form (*landscipe*), the term was used in the Middle Ages to refer to a district owned by a particular lord or inhabited by a particular group of people. The modern forms of the word (landskip, landscape) date from the late sixteenth or early seventeenth century, when the influence of Dutch *landschap* painters encouraged a revival and redefinition of landscape to refer to representations of scenery, especially rural scenery, and then to scenery in general or a particular scene (James 1934; Jackson 1964).

The popular conception of landscape was well expressed by Philip Gilbert Hamerton, who wrote several books on landscape painting and landscape appreciation in the latter half of the nineteenth century. In a book entitled *Landscape* (1885), he wrote that the word could be used "in two senses— a general and a particular. In the general sense, the word 'landscape' without the article means the visible world, all that can be seen on the surface of the earth by a man who is himself upon the surface; and in the special sense, 'a landscape' means a piece of the earth's surface that can be seen at once; and it is always understood that this piece will have a certain artistic unity" (Hamerton [1885] 1890, p. 10).

This dual definition is reiterated in *Webster's New International Dictionary of the English Language*, where landscape is described as "a portion of land or territory which the eye can comprehend in a single view, including all the objects so seen, especially in its pictorial aspect." Moreover, both Hamerton and *Webster's* give the term a subjective connotation, for the reference is to area or scenery as viewed by a particular human observer. The dual popular meaning of landscape and its subjective overtones caused persistent difficulty when geographers spoke of the "objective reality" of landscape and tried to employ the term as a scientific concept.

## The influence of Sauer

The conception of geography as the scientific study of landscape is developed most completely in the American geographic literature in Carl Sauer's "The Morphology of Landscape" (1925), where the *Landschaft* studies of German geographers are reviewed and endorsed as an alternative to the philosophy then current in American geography. During the first quarter of the twentieth century American geographers moved away from their initial interest in physiography, and many redefined their concern as an attempt to trace causal relationships between elements of the natural environment and the activities or creations of man. To Sauer this development represented a denial of the proper task of the discipline, which was to establish a system embracing the "phenomenology of landscape." He argued that geography could not claim an independent status if it were preoccupied with a particular causal relationship and failed to claim a body of phenomena or "naively given section of reality" as its own. Just as the facts of history are time facts and their association gives rise to the concept of period, so the facts of geography could be regarded as place facts and their association could be expressed by the concept of landscape. According to this view, a landscape, defined as "an area made up of a distinct association of forms, both physical and cultural," has objective identity based on recognizable constitution, limits, and generic relation to other landscapes. Departing from the popular conception of the term, Sauer held that a landscape should not be regarded as an actual scene viewed by a particular observer but rather as a generalization derived from the observation of many individual scenes. Beginning with infinite diversity, the geographer should select salient and related features in order to establish the character of a landscape and place it in a system. Personal judgment in the selection of landscape content could be minimized by agreement on a logical, predetermined mode of inquiry. In other words, the underlying assumption of Sauer's argument was that the features thus studied would be characteristic and could be grouped into a pattern and that the landscape defined eventually by this inductive procedure could be described as belonging to a specific group in a general series. In addition, Sauer, following Krebs (1923), felt that landscapes should be studied genetically, that the structural units of a landscape should be placed in a developmental sequence, with the condition of the area prior to the introduction of man's activities as the datum line. The essential task of landscape study was thus to trace the development of a "natural landscape" into a "cultural landscape."

Sauer's statement had considerable influence in the development of American geographic thought, not only because it offered an alternative to "environmentalism" but also because he transmitted the ideas of several European geographers who were more advanced methodologically than their American counterparts at that time. However, the redefinition of geography as the study of landscape morphology proved to have serious practical and methodological difficulties, and Sauer repudiated many features of this initial programmatic statement in later publications (Sauer 1963). Perhaps the most serious weakness of his argument of 1925 was the assumption that geographers should begin their inquiry by reconstructing the prehuman or natural condition of an area. In a world nearly devoid of undisturbed natural landscapes (*Urlandschaften*), the difficulties entailed in such a task are forbidding, and geographers concerned primarily with the present visible landscape were understandably reluctant to begin their studies in antiquity. Moreover, the genetic–morphological method proved uncongenial to economic geographers whose studies tended to develop along generic and functional lines. Even in Broek's study of the Santa Clara Valley (1932), which is probably the most complete substantive application of Sauer's methodology, the datum line is not a reconstructed natural landscape but rather the "primitive" condition of the area when the first Europeans arrived. Similarly, studies of landscape development in Europe usually start not at the time of initial human occupation but rather at the period immediately preceding the great phase of forest clearing, draining of marshes, and reclamation of heathlands (Darby 1951). As geographers accumulated a comprehensive record of the effects of human activity on vegetation, soil, and surface features, they became increasingly wary of the concept of natural landscape (International Symposium

. . . 1956). The distinction most generally accepted today is between a "wild" or "primitive" landscape, in which features of the natural environment are altered but not eradicated or completely controlled, and "cultivated" or "artificial" landscapes (Aschmann 1959; Raup 1959; Nelson 1959).

## Geography as landscape science

The methodological objections raised against the definition of geography as landscape science centered on two issues, the vagueness of the term and certain philosophical difficulties (Broek 1938; Hartshorne 1939). Landscape had been employed by geographers to refer to the impression conveyed by an area, to the objects producing that impression, and to the area itself. In other words, the dual meaning of "scenery" and "area" was carried over from the popular use of the term "landscape." In German usage, *Landschaft* refers most commonly to a territorial unit and can usually be regarded as a synonym for "district," "area," or "region" (Bürger 1935; Lautensach 1938; Schmithüsen 1964; Wernli 1958). The ambiguity of *Landschaft* is enhanced by the fact that *Land* cannot be defined as the coincident areal expression of *Landschaft*, as in the case of the French terms *pays* and *paysage*, because a *Landschaft* is usually regarded as being smaller than a *Land*, as, for example, in the *Landschaften* of Rhineland or Siegerland. The German geographic literature also abounds in such expressions as *Kleinlandschaften* (small districts or tracts), *Grosslandschaften* (large areas or regions), *Landschaftsgruppe* (groups of functionally related or morphologically similar areas or regions), *Landschaftsgürtel* (extensive belts or zones), and in such specific terms as *Stadtlandschaften* (urbanized areas), *Agrarlandschaften* (rural areas), and *historische Landschaften* (areas in which functional or morphologic unity is enhanced by the long continuation of an integrative force). Each of these terms refers to a general class of *Landschaften*. However, in the case of such expressions as *Alpenlandschaft* reference is made not only to the general characteristics of mountainous areas but also to the European Alps as a specific delimited area. Moreover, *Landschaftskunde* may refer to the study of particular *Landschaften* or to the regional differentiation of the entire globe. It is not surprising, therefore, that a substantial part of the methodological literature of German geographers deals with the problem of defining *Landschaft* and *Landschaften* (Passarge 1921–1930; Waibel 1933; Bürger 1935; Lautensach 1938; 1953; Bobek & Schmithüsen 1949; Schmithüsen 1964), and that the attempts to translate these terms compounded the inherent ambiguity of "landscape."

## Current usage

In addition to the semantic problem, many geographers felt that it could not be maintained that the study and interpretation of landscape is the exclusive preserve of the geographer or that landscape, however defined, contains all that is geographical. By the 1940s, the notion that landscape study should be regarded as the essential task of geography was generally discarded in favor of the view that landscape features constitute merely one of several documents and points of reference in geographic research.

**Features studied.**   The landscape features studied most often by geographers are those that have to do with the occupation and utilization of land (Sauer 1925; Bryan 1933; Sorre 1961; Houston 1964). Such features include the form and arrangement of settlement (houses and other buildings); field patterns, roads, paths, and other communication lines; crops and the "wild" or "tame" vegetation associated with settlements; irrigation works; and surface modifications—in short, the patterns and imprints of culture. Tangible, visible objects thus constitute the essential raw material of landscape study. However, the perspective of the geographer is not that of an individual observer located at a particular point on the ground. The geographer's work entails map interpretation as well as direct observation, and he makes no distinction between foreground and background (Vallaux 1925). The landscape of the geographer is thus very different from that of the painter, poet, or novelist. By means of survey, sampling, or detailed inventory, he achieves the comprehensive but synthetic perspective of a helicopter pilot or balloonist armed with maps, photographs, and a pair of binoculars. Indeed, it has been suggested that the geographic definition of landscape might be framed with reference to air photographs, both vertical and oblique, in which case the corresponding German term would not be *Landschaft* but rather *Landschaftsbild* (Hartshorne 1959, p. 23).

However, landscape studies inevitably include consideration of cultural expressions that are invisible. If the rationale is to discover landscape features coincident with a culture area, then one may begin by delimiting the area according to linguistic or other nonmaterial phenomena. Moreover, without recourse to historical study there is no way to distinguish between what is ancient or recent, native or foreign. Culture history, accordingly, must enter strongly into any explanatory study of landscape (Wagner & Mikesell 1962, pp. 1–24; Sauer 1963). Again, a landscape may be regarded not as an end in itself but merely as empirical data that can be employed to document culture change (Hill 1964). Most geographers who employ landscape data or seek to explain entire landscapes have ceased to be preoccupied (if indeed they ever were) with what is visible or invisible, material or nonmaterial, for "there can be no finite limit placed upon the variety of data with which the regional cultural geographer must deal in his effort to depict the operation of man in his chosen landscape" (Spencer 1954, p. vii).

A good indication of the scope of recent research is provided by a symposium dealing with the development of the agrarian landscape in northwestern Europe (International Geographical Congress 1961). The subjects covered in this collection include (1) the prehistoric landscape and its connection with later development of settlement and field patterns, (2) medieval regulations of settlement and field patterns, (3) the influence of agrarian revolutions (e.g., the enclosure movement) on the landscape, and (4) recent changes in the agrarian landscape of industrialized and commercialized countries.

The virtues of an uninhibited approach to landscape study are perhaps most effectively illustrated by one early and three recent attempts to determine the effect of landscape tastes on landscape evolution (Gradmann 1924; Lowenthal & Prince 1964; 1965; Hard 1965). In greater or lesser degree, landscapes always embody irrational creation. Accordingly, the origin, persistence, or disappearance of the concrete features of a landscape may be explained most adequately not by their form or function but by the idealized images and visual prejudices of human groups or of individuals.

## Other uses of the concept

Finally, it must be noted that landscape is an important concept in several fields apart from geography. The origin of landscape as a painter's term has already been mentioned (Clark 1949). The reconstruction and interpretation of ancient landscapes is one of the essential tasks of archeology (Bradford 1957). Novelists, poets, and travel writers employ landscape description either as an end in itself or as a way to establish a mood or set a scene (Bart 1957; Durrell 1960). In addition, a large critical literature on local and regional landscapes has been produced by architects, city planners, and others concerned with problems of landscape design (Colvin 1948; Nairn 1965). These several conceptions have been presented since 1952 in the magazine *Landscape,* published by J. B.

Jackson of Santa Fe, New Mexico. Indeed, the diverse contributions to this magazine—from architects, ecologists, geographers, planners, and observers from many other backgrounds—provide an effective illustration of the continued value of landscape as an integrating concept in social science.

MARVIN W. MIKESELL

[*Directly related are the entries* AREA; ENVIRONMENT; ENVIRONMENTALISM; REGION. *Other relevant material may be found in* GEOGRAPHY; *and in the biography of* SAUER.]

### BIBLIOGRAPHY

ASCHMANN, HOMER 1959 The Evolution of a Wild Landscape and Its Persistence in Southern California. Association of American Geographers, *Annals* 49 (Supplement): 34–46.

BART, BENJAMIN F. 1957 *Flaubert's Landscape Descriptions.* Ann Arbor: Univ. of Michigan Press.

BOBEK, HANS; and SCHMITHÜSEN, J. 1949 Die Landschaft im logischen System der Geographie. *Erdkunde* 3:112–120.

BRADFORD, JOHN 1957 *Ancient Landscapes.* London: Bell.

BROEK, JAN O. M. 1932 *The Santa Clara Valley, California: A Study in Landscape Changes.* Utrecht (Netherlands): Oosthoek.

BROEK, JAN O. M. 1938 The Concept Landscape in Human Geography. Volume 2, section 3a, pages 103–109 in International Geographical Congress, Fifteenth, Amsterdam, 1938, *Comptes rendus.* Leiden (Netherlands): Brill.

BRYAN, PATRICK W. 1933 *Man's Adaptation of Nature: Studies of the Cultural Landscape.* Univ. of London Press.

BÜRGER, KURT 1935 Der Landschaftsbegriff: Ein Beitrag zur geographischen Erdraumauffassung. *Dresdener geographische Studien* 7:1–131.

CLARK, KENNETH M. 1949 *Landscape Into Art.* London: Murray.

COLVIN, BRENDA 1948 *Land and Landscape.* London: Murray.

DARBY, H. C. 1951 The Changing English Landscape. *Geographical Journal* 117:377–394.

DICKINSON, ROBERT E. 1939 Landscape and Society. *Scottish Geographical Magazine* 55:1–15.

DURRELL, LAWRENCE 1960 Landscape With Literary Figures. *New York Times Book Review* June 12: 1 only.

GRADMANN, ROBERT 1924 Das harmonische Landschaftsbild. Gesellschaft für Erdkunde zu Berlin, *Zeitschrift* [1924]:129–147.

HAMERTON, PHILIP (1885) 1890 *Landscape.* Boston: Roberts.

HARD, GERHARD 1965 Arkadien in Deutschland: Bemerkungen zu einem landschaftlichen Reiz. *Erde* 96, no. 1:21–41.

HARTSHORNE, RICHARD 1939 The Nature of Geography: A Critical Survey of Current Thought in the Light of the Past. Association of American Geographers, *Annals* 29:173–658.

HARTSHORNE, RICHARD 1959 *Perspective on the Nature of Geography.* Association of American Geographers, Monograph Series, No. 1. Chicago: Rand McNally.

HILL, A. DAVID 1964 *The Changing Landscape of a Mexican Municipio: Villa Las Rosas, Chiapas.* Univ. of Chicago, Department of Geography.

HOUSTON, JAMES M. 1964 *The Western Mediterranean World: An Introduction to Its Regional Landscapes.* London: Longmans.

INTERNATIONAL GEOGRAPHICAL CONGRESS, NINETEENTH, 1960, SYMPOSIUM ON THE MORPHOGENESIS OF THE AGRARIAN CULTURAL LANDSCAPE, VADSTENA (SWEDEN) 1961 Papers. Edited by Staffan Helmfrid. *Geografiska annaler* (Stockholm) 43, no. 1–2.

INTERNATIONAL SYMPOSIUM ON MAN'S ROLE IN CHANGING THE FACE OF THE EARTH, PRINCETON, N.J., 1955 1956 *Man's Role in Changing the Face of the Earth.* Edited by William L. Thomas et al. Univ. of Chicago Press.

JACKSON, J. B. 1964 The Meanings of Landscape. *Kulturgeografi* (Aarhus, Denmark) 88:47–51.

JAMES, PRESTON E. 1934 The Terminology of Regional Description. Association of American Geographers, *Annals* 24:78–86.

KREBS, NORBERT 1923 Natur- und Kulturlandschaft. Gesellschaft für Erdkunde zu Berlin, *Zeitschrift* [1923]:81–94.

LAUTENSACH, HERMANN 1938 Über die Erfassung und Abgrenzung von Landschaftsräumen. Volume 2, section 5, pages 12–26 in International Geographical Congress, Fifteenth, Amsterdam, 1938, *Comptes rendus.* Leiden (Netherlands): Brill.

LAUTENSACH, HERMANN 1953 Über die Begriffe Typus und Individuum in der geographischen Forschung. *Münchener geographische Hefte* 3:1–31.

LOWENTHAL, DAVID; and PRINCE, HUGH C. 1964 The English Landscape. *Geographical Review* 54:309–346.

LOWENTHAL, DAVID; and PRINCE, HUGH C. 1965 English Landscape Tastes. *Geographical Review* 55:186–222.

NAIRN, IAN 1965 *The American Landscape: A Critical View.* New York: Random House.

NELSON, HOWARD J. 1959 The Spread of an Artificial Landscape Over Southern California. Association of American Geographers, *Annals* 49 (Supplement): 80–99.

PASSARGE, SIEGFRIED 1919–1921 *Grundlagen der Landschaftskunde: Ein Lehrbuch und eine Anleitung zu landschaftskundlicher Forschung und Darstellung.* 3 vols. Hamburg (Germany): Friedrich.

PASSARGE, SIEGFRIED 1921–1930 *Vergleichende Landschaftskunde.* 5 vols. Berlin: Reimer.

PASSARGE, SIEGFRIED (1923) 1929 *Die Landschaftsgürtel der Erde: Natur und Kultur.* Breslau (then Germany): Hirt.

RAUP, H. R. 1959 Transformation of Southern California to a Cultivated Land. Association of American Geographers, *Annals* 49 (Supplement): 58–78.

SAUER, CARL O. (1925) 1963 The Morphology of Landscape. Pages 315–350 in Carl O. Sauer, *Land and Life: A Selection From the Writings of Carl Ortwin Sauer.* Berkeley: Univ. of California Press.

SAUER, CARL O. 1963 *Land and Life: A Selection From the Writings of Carl Ortwin Sauer.* Edited by John Leighly. Berkeley: Univ. of California Press.

SCHMITHÜSEN, JOSEF 1964 Was ist eine Landschaft? *Erdkundliches Wissen* 9:1–24.

SORRE, MAXIMILIEN 1961 *L'homme sur la terre.* Paris: Hachette.

SPENCER, JOSEPH E. 1954 *Asia, East by South: A Cultural Geography.* New York: Wiley.

VALLAUX, CAMILLE (1925) 1929 *Les sciences géographiques.* New ed. Paris: Alcan.

WAGNER, PHILIP L.; and MIKESELL, MARVIN W. (editors) 1962 *Readings in Cultural Geography.* Univ. of Chicago Press.

WAIBEL, LEO H. 1933 Was verstehen wir unter Landschaftskunde? *Geographischer Anzeiger* 34:197–207.

WERNLI, OTTO 1958 Die neuere Entwicklung des Landschaftsbegriffes. *Geographica helvetica* 13:1–59.

# LANG, ANDREW

Andrew Lang (1844–1912), British anthropologist and folklorist, was born in Selkirk, in that border country of Scotland whose turbulent past provided the substance for a corpus of evolving legend. It was a proper setting for Lang, whose lifelong interest lay in the past of man as it is revealed, often dimly, in myths and tales. He was born just at the time when folklore (the word was coined in 1846) began to be used as a tool for unraveling the past. His own work, both critical and synthetic, represents the first maturing of a scientific interest in the folk narrative as a means of discovering the nature of primeval man and the details of his unrecorded history. "The student of this lore," he wrote, "can look back and see the long trodden way behind him, the winding tracks through marsh and forest and ever burning sands" (quoted in Green 1946, p. 37).

Lang entered the University of St. Andrews in 1861 and four years later became a scholar at Oxford, where he was regarded as a brilliant and promising classicist. Even then what amounted almost to a mania for writing had manifested itself, and he left the university in 1874 to devote his full time and energy to popular writing. This suited not only his own particular talents but also the needs and interests of an expanding English intelligentsia, whose appetite for a literate and sophisticated journalism on subjects of science and scholarship was insatiable. Until his death in 1912, Lang made his living by writing—and he wrote incessantly. His bibliography includes 120 separate books (including pamphlets) and over 150 volumes in whose publication he was associated either as editor or as contributor. In addition, there are several hundred uncollected poems and over five thousand essays, articles, reviews, and miscellaneous letters scattered in periodicals and newspapers. Much that he wrote—in whichever of the several fields of his interest—was, of course, only topical and made no permanent impression upon the development of knowledge.

He did contribute, however, and with some significance, to the restructuring of notions concerning the nature of human society, its origins, and its evolution—a series of problems sharpened by the discovery of the antiquity of man and the publication of the Darwinian theory of evolution. These problems were central to a recently emerged anthropology that adopted the comparative method as a major analytical tool for their solution. This new approach applied the accumulating body of knowledge about the wide range of human behavior in the present to the reconstruction of man's past.

Where others used the data of kinship, religion, technology, physical appearance, or language, Lang used the myth and the folk narrative not only as keys to the relationships among prehistoric populations and to their migrations but also as a means for reconstructing the thought systems which provided the underlying rational order to the behavior of their communities. Myth, Lang maintained in something of a charter for the renovated study of folklore, is not simply a linguistic device but much more the reflection of a cultural system whose particular logical base the scientist must seek to reveal. "We propose," he noted, "to seek for a demonstrably actual condition of the human intellect, whereof myth would be the natural and inevitable fruit" (1887, vol. 1, p. 29). His contention that the myth is a "historical" document, useful for the revelation of a cultural or value system, became so generally accepted as an assumption in anthropology that his originality is often forgotten.

To describe that primal, savage state of human thought, Lang abstracted the common elements from myths as they occurred all over the world. In this way he arrived at his particular conception of totemism, which referred to such habits of mind as (1) an unwillingness to distinguish between animalism and rationality: man and animal belong to the same cognitive world; (2) a belief in sorcery and spiritualism; and (3) a lack of curiosity and an easy credulity as part of a general mental indolence. These habits of mind formed the essential elements of a primitive mentality, whose manifestations, preserved within the protective shell of myth and folk tale, have persisted into the present. With this basically new and revolutionary method for the reconstruction of earlier stages in the evolution of human behavior Lang divorced the study of folk literature from its philological origins and affiliations; he provided it with an anthropological perspective and thus expanded its scope far beyond the limits of Europe.

As in his equation of evolution with progress, Lang followed the prevailing views of his time in his acceptance of the concept of cultural stages as a framework for the evolution of human society.

However, his acquaintance with world-wide comparative data—particularly those relating to myth, ritual, and religion—led him to reject the overly simple systems of human evolution or the ethnocentric views concerning primitive mentality which still characterized much of the anthropological theory of the time. He was much more apt to criticize the theories of others than to construct his own. Thus, he demolished the idea of primitive promiscuity as a basic level of social organization by using the same linguistic materials adduced by its proponents, and in one of his earliest, and most significant, articles he used his extensive knowledge of comparative mythology to refute Max Müller's then popular thesis that all myth is the result of "a disease of language," an irrational gloss on an original Vedic explanatory system of nature. It was Lang's documented refutation of Müller's assumption of a universal rationality that formed the basis for his evolutionary concepts; the documentation was drawn from folklore. His recognition that a system of thought can be understood even if it is "rational" only in terms of its own premises, rather than in terms of those of a later and possibly more highly evolved stage, anticipated the approach of cultural relativism.

Equally trenchant, although less effective, were his criticisms of the conceptions of the evolution of religion that were based on Tylor's definition of animism as the basic element from which all "higher" and monotheistic religious conceptions had evolved. While accepting the importance of Tylor's animism for an understanding of the history of religion, Lang rejected the simple unilineal system to which it gave rise. He maintained that in addition to animistic belief there also occurred on the most simple social level the idea of some all-pervading spirit. Such a monotheism (which Wilhelm Schmidt was later to redefine as "the High God concept") was, in Lang's view, equally primitive, in an evolutionary sense, and may always have existed as a second basic means of religious expression.

Lang was very much the nineteenth-century anthropologist: although the rapid professionalization of the field made him and his writing outmoded, he captured and expressed the first enthusiasm of anthropology. To him and to his contemporaries, anthropology was, in his words, ". . . the science which studies man in the sum of all his works and thoughts, as evolved through the whole process of his development. This science . . . studies the development of law out of custom; the development of weapons from the stick or stone to the latest repeating rifle; the development

of society from the horde to the nation. It is the study which does not despise the most backward nor degraded tribe, nor neglect the most civilised, and it frequently finds in Australians or Nootkas the germ of ideas and institutions which Greeks or Romans brought to perfection, or retained, little altered from their early rudeness, in the midst of civilisation" (1887, vol. 1, pp. 27–28). No one in his time said it better.

JACOB W. GRUBER

[See also FOLKLORE; MYTH AND SYMBOL.]

### WORKS BY LANG

(1884) 1893 *Custom and Myth.* New ed. London: Longmans.
(1887) 1899 *Myth, Ritual and Religion.* New ed. 2 vols. London: Longmans.
(1897) 1899 *The Book of Dreams and Ghosts.* New ed. London: Longmans.
1901 *Magic and Religion.* London: Longmans.
1903 *Social Origins.* London: Longmans.
1905 *The Secret of the Totem.* London: Longmans.

### SUPPLEMENTARY BIBLIOGRAPHY

GREEN, ROGER L. 1946 *Andrew Lang: A Critical Biography With a Short-title Bibliography of the Works of Andrew Lang.* Leicester (England): Ward.

## LANGE, OSKAR

Oskar Lange's intellectual pursuits followed three lines: economic analysis, the propagation of Marxian socialist ideas, and didactic work. This diversity in his interests reflects the diversity of Lange's career, divided as it was between Poland and the United States and between academic and political activities.

Lange was born in Tomaszow, Poland, in 1904 and died in Warsaw in 1965. He attended the University of Poznan and later was connected with the University of Krakow, first as a student (obtaining an LL.M. in 1927 and an LL.D. in 1928) and then as a lecturer from 1931 to 1935. He also studied at the London School of Economics in 1929 and toured several American universities as a Rockefeller fellow in 1932.

In 1936 Lange went to the University of Michigan as a lecturer. He settled in the United States a year later, rose rapidly through the academic ranks, and was appointed to a professorship at the University of Chicago in 1943.

Lange's political career began during the closing years of World War II. His early interest in socialism—he had been a member of a socialist students' organization at Krakow and later worked with the educational committee of the Polish Socialist party

—was evident in several of his prewar Polish and English publications. However, Lange's active participation in politics was triggered by the conflicts that arose between the Polish government-in-exile and the Soviet-backed Union of Polish Patriots. Lange gave the latter his (initially very cautious) endorsement. Between 1943 and 1945 he intensified his political activities; in the latter year he resumed his Polish citizenship (he had become a United States citizen in 1943) and was appointed ambassador to the United States by the newly created left-wing Polish government. Lange was Poland's delegate to the United Nations from 1946 to 1949. In 1949 the Polish government's policy took a sharp turn toward Stalinist orthodoxy; Lange was recalled to Poland and relegated to insignificant jobs. By 1955/1956 his undogmatic socialism once again became acceptable, and he was appointed a member, and, for a period, deputy chairman of the Council of the Polish People's Republic —a position of high prestige, though of little real influence. He was also appointed deputy chairman and later chairman of the State Economic Council —a body designed to provide expert advice on ways and means of improving the Polish economy.

Upon his return to Poland in 1949, Lange resumed his academic work, interrupted by his four years of diplomatic service. Between 1952 and 1955 he was rector of the Central School of Planning and Statistics and from 1955 until his death in 1965 was a professor at the University of Warsaw.

**Economic analysis.** Lange's analytic work seems very remote from his political activities. During his most creative period (the late 1930s and early 1940s) he worked very much in the mainstream of economic thought. He was concerned with the logic of welfare economics (1942a), with interest theory (1936; 1937; 1938), and with the theoretical derivation of supply and demand elasticities (1942b). Above all, he dealt (very much in the Keynesian vein) with the imperfections of the free-enterprise system and with the shortcomings of neoclassical economics.

The distinguishing marks of Lange's approach are the ease with which he operated within a general equilibrium framework, his judicious use of mathematics, and—sometimes—his tendency to confuse theoretical models with empirical reality. Two of his major analytical works illustrate both his virtues and weaknesses.

In "Say's Law: A Restatement and Critique" (1942c) Lange showed that Say's law implies zero degree homogeneity of supply and demand functions for all commodities and first degree homogeneity of expectation functions. These relations hold in a barter economy, but in a money economy they leave money prices indeterminate. The division of price theory into two subsystems that determine, respectively, relative prices and the price level is logically inconsistent. Relative prices and the price level must be determined simultaneously: any theory applying to a monetary economy must start by rejecting Say's law.

In *Price Flexibility and Employment* (1944), Lange set out to examine systematically the effect of flexible factors of production on employment and economic stability. He showed that within a general equilibrium context a fall in the price of an underemployed factor leads to an increase in its employment if the monetary effect is positive, that is, if a proportional fall in all prices leads to a reduction in excess demand for cash balances sufficient to cause a substitution of goods for money. He examined the conditions under which the monetary effect is positive, in terms of the responsiveness of the monetary system to price changes and in terms of price expectations:

If price expectations are prevailingly of unit elasticity . . . [for the positive monetary effect to occur] the real quantity of money in the economy [must] increase as prices fall and decrease as prices rise. If price expectations are prevailingly inelastic, the real quantity of money must diminish less than the real demand for cash balances when prices fall and increase less than the latter when prices rise. The reverse must take place if price expectations are elastic.   ([1944] 1952, p. 23)

Even when the right combination of elasticity of expectation and responsiveness of the money system exists, the stabilizing effects of price flexibility are likely to be dulled by such factors as uncertainty, oligopoly, and destabilizing international repercussions.

Lange treated all the possible cases as if they were equally likely to occur. Since only relatively few of the cases result in stability, he concluded that "only under very special conditions does price flexibility result in the automatic maintenance or restoration of equilibrium of demand for factors of production" (*ibid.*, p. 83). Although he did qualify this conclusion by adding that these conditions were approximately realized from the 1840s until 1914, it is not clear how such an assertion can be made on the basis of pure analysis unchecked by empirical inquiries.

**Concern with Marxian socialism.** Late in the 1920s and early in the 1930s Lange began to write articles devoted to the propagation of Marxian socialist ideas (1929; 1931; 1934). The volume of such publications increased after he started to play an important role in the political life of postwar

Poland. At times his Marxist beliefs came into conflict with his economic analysis. In a 1956 article Lange ascribed the increasing well-being of workers in some capitalist countries to the influence of strong labor unions. "Where capitalism encounters a weak, disorganized mass of workers devoid of political rights, it becomes fully evident how it degrades and impoverishes the workers. Such is the case in Spain and in Latin America." A year later Lange stated that there is a "fundamental law" which determines the purpose of the use of means of production: "under capitalism it determines that production is done for private profit; under socialism . . . that production is done for the satisfaction of human wants" (1958a, pp. 26–27). These statements do not appear compatible with the thought of an analytical economist.

Yet Lange saw no irreconcilable conflict between socialist economies and analytical principles of efficiency or between Marxism and modern economics. On the contrary, he held that a socialist system can operate more rationally than a market economy. To convince free-enterprise critics of this he wrote an extended essay in 1936 entitled "On the Economic Theory of Socialism," in which he built a model of an economy with fully nationalized means of production. Earlier writers, notably Barone, had formulated efficiency conditions for a socialist system without indicating how the efficient position is to be reached. [*See the biography of* BARONE.] Lange formulated operational rules to be followed by managers of nationalized industry and by planners. The application of these rules results in a process of Walrasian *tâtonnement*, which leads to efficient allocation yet avoids the reliance on capitalist processes with their concomitant evils of monopoly distortions, unemployment, and social inequities.

Lange never looked upon his model of market socialism as a blueprint for a socialist state. His commitment to the Marxian doctrine of historical materialism precluded any a priori prescriptions for socioeconomic organizations. Historical materialism does not require, however, the acceptance of Marxian economics, which ignores "the whole development of economic theory since the time of Ricardo," and which relies on long discredited concepts, such as the labor theory of value (1935).

After many trial formulations, Lange undertook a synthesis of Marxism with modern economics in his *Political Economy* (1959; only the first volume of a planned three-volume work was published in its entirety in Lange's lifetime). The work was ambitiously conceived to provide a systematic treatment of the entire field of political economy in a manner consistent with Marxian premises. Starting with the definition of the scope of political economy ("political economy is concerned with the social laws of production and distribution") the reader is led through the materialistic interpretation of history as it applies to modes of production and social formation, to the problem of economic laws, the general methodology of political economy, the principles of economic rationality, and, finally, to technical aspects of economics.

**Significance of Lange's work in socialist countries.** To a non-Marxian reader, and especially to one brought up in the Anglo-Saxon unphilosophical tradition of economics, Lange's *Political Economy* is bewildering. Subtle distinctions between laws of political economy and economic laws, lengthy classifications of such laws, discussions of the place of praxiology in economics, not to mention the critique of "subjectivist" and "historical" schools of economics, seem pointless. Quotations from Marx do not bolster the plausibility or improve the clarity of the principle of diminishing marginal rate of substitution (1964). Claims that modern national income accounting and input–output techniques derive directly from Soviet material balancing seem dubious. To label welfare economics as a "petty and middle bourgeois critique of capitalist monopolies" seems silly.

For Marxian socialists, however, the appearance of Lange's *Political Economy* was an event of cardinal importance. Here is a work that accepts the basic Marxian premises and the Marxian approach and that also accepts modern economic tools. The "subjectivist" school is damned, as before, but the marginalist approach, once rejected as a worthless figment of subjectivist imagination, is accepted into the canon. The historical relativity of economic laws is reasserted, but it is also stated that "the technical and balance laws of production, the laws of human behavior, and the laws of interplay of human actions continue to operate objectively, independently of human will and consciousness. This cannot be changed by socialist, or any other mode of production" (1958a, p. 82). To be an economist (in the Western sense) no longer means, then, being a traitor to Marxism.

The purely technical works in which Lange tries to show the relevance of modern economic tools to socialist reality are not as problematic as *Political Economy*. It was Lange's belief that when there is no market mechanism in socialist countries, it is all the more important to strive consciously toward economic rationality. Rational planning requires consistency and optimization. The plans must result in an efficient growth pattern; their success is contingent upon a reverse flow of information, that is, on a feedback mechanism that informs the planners of the changes which result from the execution of the plans. Lange expressed these ideas in courses on growth and accumulation, econometrics, mathematical programming, and cybernetics; he also wrote a series of books based on these courses (1958b; 1961). As in *Political Economy*, there are numerous references to Marx: there is a short step from Marx's two-sector scheme of simple reproduction to the optimum path of accumulation. Yet such references in no way subtract from the treatment, which is clear, logical, and often extremely elegant.

Lange's own contributions to econometrics, programming, cybernetics, and growth theory are minor. Yet his works on these subjects may prove to be his most lasting monument: they introduced modern economics to the socialist world and helped educate a new generation of Polish economists and econometricians in the tradition of Western scientific inquiry.

STANISLAW WELLISZ

[*See also* ECONOMIC EQUILIBRIUM; ECONOMIC THOUGHT, *article on* SOCIALIST THOUGHT.]

### WORKS BY LANGE

1929   Wrastanie w socjalizm czy nowa faza kapitalizmu (Growth Into Socialism or a New Phase of Capitalism)? *Robotniczy przegląd gospodarczy* 3:69–74.

(1931) 1961   Rola państwa w kapitalizmie monopolistycznym (The Role of the State in Monopoly Capitalism). Pages 11–29 in Oscar Lange, *Pisma ekonomiczne i społeczne: 1930–1960*. Warsaw: Państwowe Wydawnictwo Naukowe. → First published in Volume 1 of the *Kwartalnik socjalistyczny*.

(1934) 1961   Z pracy: Droga do socjalistycznej gospodarki planowej (The Road to a Socialist Planned Economy). Pages 29–42 in Oscar Lange, *Pisma ekonomiczne i społeczne: 1930–1960*. Warsaw: Państwowe Wydawnictwo Naukowe. → First published in *Gospodarka-polytika-taktyka-organizacja socjalizmu* published by Płomienie.

1935   Marxian Economics and Modern Economic Theory. *Review of Economic Studies* 2:189–201.

1936   The Place of Interest in the Theory of Production. *Review of Economic Studies* 3:159–192. → See also Volume 4, page 82, "Correction."

1936–1937   On the Economic Theory of Socialism. Parts 1–2. *Review of Economic Studies* 4, no. 1:53–71; 4, no. 2:123–144. → A correction of Part 1 appeared in the February 1937 issue of the same journal, as "Mr. Lerner's Note on Socialist Economics." Subsequently the essay was reprinted with minor changes in Benjamin E. Lippincott (editor), *On the Economic Theory of Socialism*, published by the University of Minnesota Press.

1937   Professor Knight's Note on Interest Theory. *Review of Economic Studies* 4:231–235.

1938   The Rate of Interest and the Optimum Propensity to Consume. *Economica* New Series 5:12–32.

1942a   The Foundations of Welfare Economics. *Econometrica* 10:215–228.

1942b   Theoretical Derivation of Elasticities of Demand and Supply: The Direct Method. *Econometrica* 10:193–214.

1942c   Say's Law: A Restatement and Critique. Pages 49–68 in Chicago, University of, Department of Economics, *Studies in Mathematical Economics and Econometrics in Memory of Henry Schultz*. Edited by Oskar Lange, Francis McIntyre, and Theodore O. Yntema. Univ. of Chicago Press.

(1944) 1952   *Price Flexibility and Employment*. Cowles Commission Monographs, No. 8. Bloomington, Ind.: Principia.

(1956) 1961   John Strachey o współczesnym kapitalizmie (John Strachey on Contemporary Capitalism). Pages 25–29 in Oscar Lange, *Pisma ekonomiczne i społeczne: 1930–1960*. Warsaw: Państwowe Wydawnictwo Naukowe. → First published in No. 270 of *Życie Warszawy*. The translation of the extract in the text was provided by Stanislaw Wellisz.

1958a   *The Political Economy of Socialism: Two Lectures*. The Hague: Van Keulen. → Lectures delivered at the Institute for International Politics and Economics, Belgrade, November 18 and 19, 1957, and Institute of Social Studies, The Hague, June 6 and 9, 1958.

(1958b) 1963   *Introduction to Econometrics*. 2d ed., rev. & enl. New York: Macmillan. → First published as *Wstep do ekonometrii*.

(1959) 1963   *Political Economy*. Vol. 1. New York: Macmillan. → First published as *Ekonomia polityczna*.

(1961) 1965   *Teoria reprodukcji*. 2d ed. Warsaw: Państwowe Wydawnictwo Naukowe. → Contains summaries in English and Russian.

1964   Relacje ilściowe w produkcji (Quantitative Relations in Production). *Ekonomista* [1964], no. 4. → To be reprinted in the projected second volume of *Political Economy*.

*Economic Development, Planning, and International Cooperation*. New York: Monthly Review Press, 1963.

*Essays on Economic Planning*. Bombay: Asia Publishing House, 1963.

*Pisma ekonomiczne i społeczne: 1930–1960* (Economic and Social Essays: 1930–1960). Warsaw: Państwowe Wydawnictwo Naukowe, 1961. → Contains several of Lange's early articles and a comprehensive bibliography of his writings from 1925 to 1961.